A-Z LEEDS & BRADFORD

C000183486

CONT

Key to Map Pages	2-3
Large Scale Centres	4-7 & 164
Map Pages	8-163

REFERE

Motorway	**M62**
A Road	A61
B Road	B6153
Dual Carriageway	
One-way Street Traffic flow on A Roads is also indicated by a heavy line on the driver's left.	→
Road Under Construction Opening dates are correct at the time of publication.	
Proposed Road	
Restricted Access	
Pedestrianized Road	
Leeds City Centre Loop Junctions are shown on Large Scale Pages only	①
Track / Footpath	
Residential Walkway	
Railway Station Level Crossing Heritage Sta. Tunnel	
Built-up Area MANOR ST.	
Local Authority Boundary	
Posttown Boundary	
Postcode Boundary (within Posttown)	
Map Continuation **75** Large Scale Centres **4**	

Airport	✈
Car Park (selected)	P
Church or Chapel	†
Cycleway (selected)	⬲
Fire Station	■
Hospital	Ⓗ
House Numbers (A & B Roads only)	13 8
Information Centre	ℹ
National Grid Reference	435
Park & Ride	King Lane P+R
Police Station	▲
Post Office	★
Safety Camera with Speed Limit Fixed cameras and long term road works cameras. Symbols do not indicate camera direction.	㉚
Toilet: without facilities for the Disabled with facilities for the Disabled Disabled use only	▽ ▽ ▽
Viewpoint	⁕ ✳
Educational Establishment	▢
Hospital or Healthcare Building	▢
Industrial Building	▢
Leisure or Recreational Facility	▢
Place of Interest	▢
Public Building	▢
Shopping Centre or Market	▢
Other Selected Buildings	▢

SCALE

Map Pages 8-163 1:18,103

0	¼	½ Mile
0	250 500	750 Metres

3½ inches (8.89 cm) to 1 mile 5.52 cm to 1 km

Map Pages 4-7 & 164 1:9,051

0	⅛	¼ Mile
0	100 200	300 Metres

7 inches (17.78 cm) to 1 mile 11.05 cm to 1 km

Copyright of Geographers' A-Z Map Company Limited

Fairfield Road, Borough Green, Sevenoaks, Kent TN15 8PP
Telephone: 01732 781000 (Enquiries & Trade Sales)
01732 783422 (Retail Sales)
www.az.co.uk
Copyright © Geographers' A-Z Map Co. Ltd.
Edition 4 2013

Ordnance Survey® This product includes mapping data licensed from Ordnance Survey® with the permission of the Controller of Her Majesty's Stationery Office.
© Crown Copyright 2012. All rights reserved. Licence number 100017302
Safety camera information supplied by www.PocketGPSWorld.com
Speed Camera Location Database Copyright 2012 © PocketGPSWorld.com

KEY TO MAP PAGES

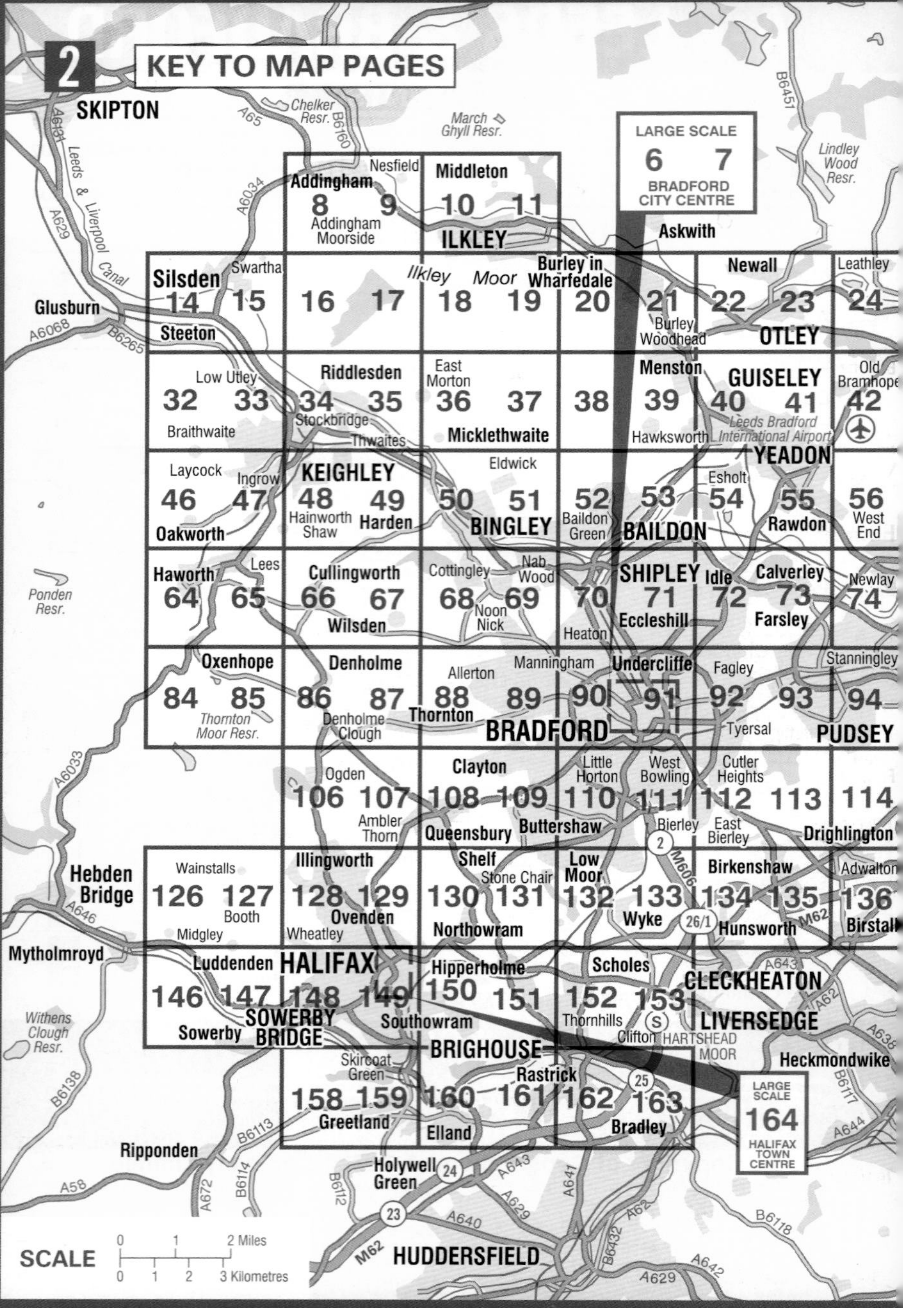

SKIPTON

Chelker Resr.

March Ghyll Resr.

Nesfield

LARGE SCALE
6 **7**
BRADFORD CITY CENTRE

Leeds & Liverpool Canal

Lindley Wood Resr.

Addingham
8 **9**
Addingham Moorside

Middleton
10 **11**
ILKLEY

Askwith

Silsden
14 **15**
Steeton

Swartha

Ilkley Moor
16 **17**

Burley in Wharfedale
18 **19** **20** **21**
Burley Woodhead

Newall
22 **23** **24**
OTLEY

Leathley

Glusburn

Low Utley
32 **33**
Braithwaite

Riddlesden
34 **35**
Stockbridge
Thwaites

East Morton
36 **37**
Micklethwaite

38

Menston
39
Hawksworth

GUISELEY
40 **41** **42**
Leeds Bradford International Airport
Old Bramhope

Laycock
46 **47**
Oakworth

Ingrow

KEIGHLEY
48 **49**
Hainworth Shaw Harden

50 **51**
BINGLEY

Eldwick

52 **53**
Baildon Green

YEADON
Esholt
54 **55** **56**
BAILDON Rawdon West End

Haworth
64 **65**
Lees

Cullingworth
66 **67**
Wilsden

Cottingley
68 **69**
Noon Nick

Nab Wood
70 **71**
Heaton

SHIPLEY Idle
Eccleshill

Calverley
72 **73** **74**
Farsley Newlay

Ponden Resr.

Oxenhope
84 **85**
Thornton Moor Resr.

Denholme
86 **87**
Denholme Clough

Allerton
88 **89**
Thornton

Manningham
90

Undercliffe
91
BRADFORD

Fagley
92 **93** **94**
Tyersal PUDSEY

Stanningley

Ogden
106 **107**
Ambler Thorn

Clayton
108 **109**
Queensbury Buttershaw

Little Horton
110 **111**
Bierley

West Bowling
East Bierley

Cutler Heights
112 **113** **114**
DRIGHLINGTON

Hebden Bridge

Wainstalls
126 **127**
Booth

Illingworth
128 **129**
Ovenden
Wheatley

Shelf
130 **131**
Stone Chair
Northowram

Low Moor
132 **133**
Wyke Hunsworth

Birkenshaw
134 **135** **136**
Adwalton Birstall

Mytholmroyd

Midgley

Luddenden HALIFAX
146 **147** **148** **149**
SOWERBY BRIDGE
Sowerby Southowram

Hipperholme
150 **151**
BRIGHOUSE

Scholes
152 **153**
Thornhills
Clifton HARTSHEAD MOOR

CLECKHEATON
LIVERSEDGE

Heckmondwike

LARGE SCALE
164
HALIFAX TOWN CENTRE

Withens Clough Resr.

Ripponden

Skircoat Green
158 **159**
Greetland

160 **161** **162** **163**
Rastrick
Elland Bradley

Holywell Green

HUDDERSFIELD

SCALE

0   1   2 Miles

0   1   2   3 Kilometres

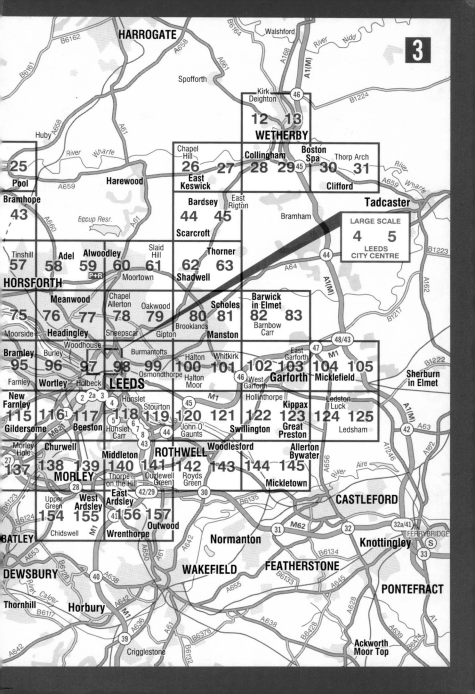

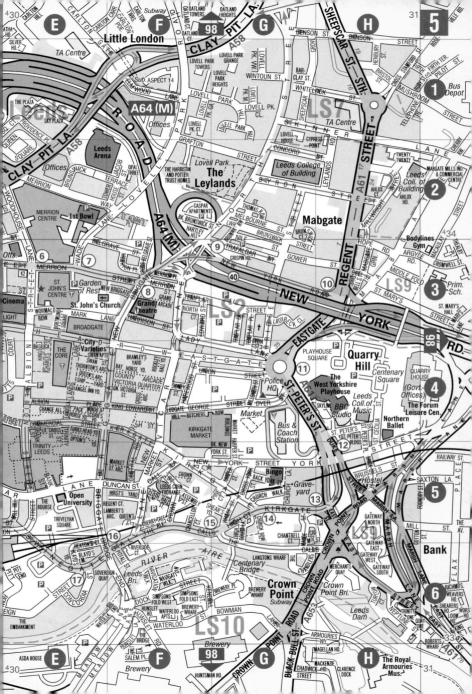

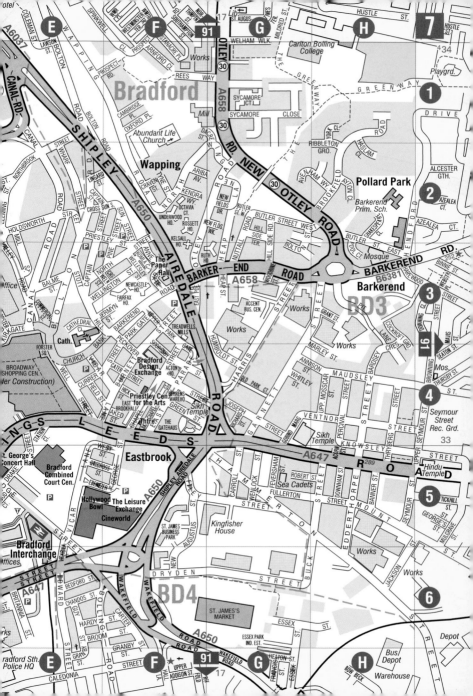

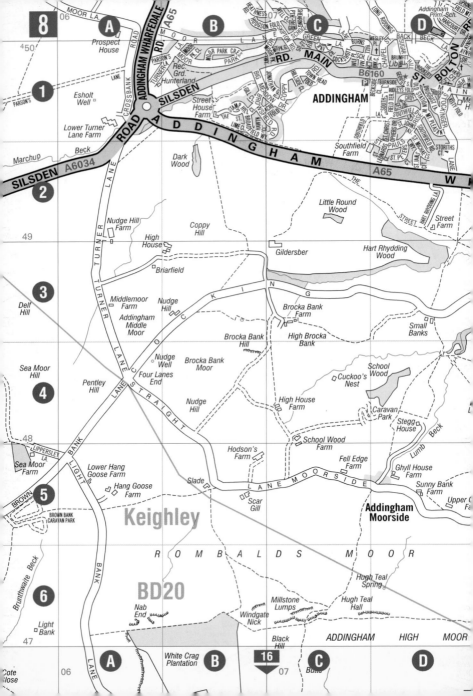

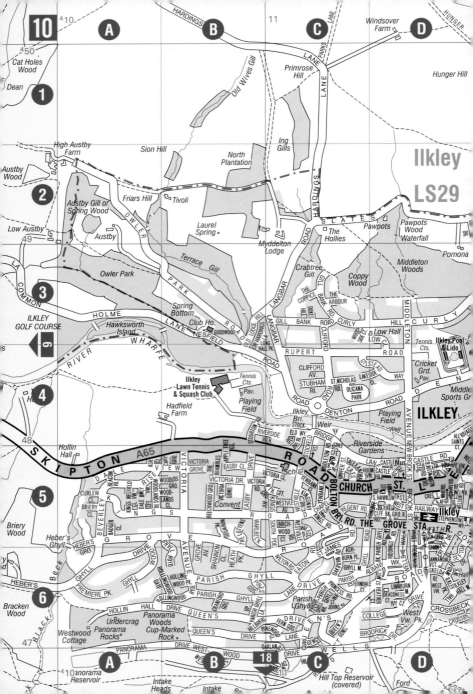

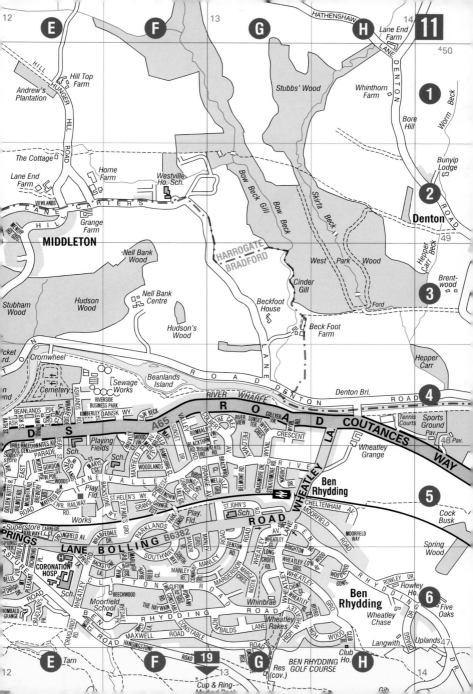

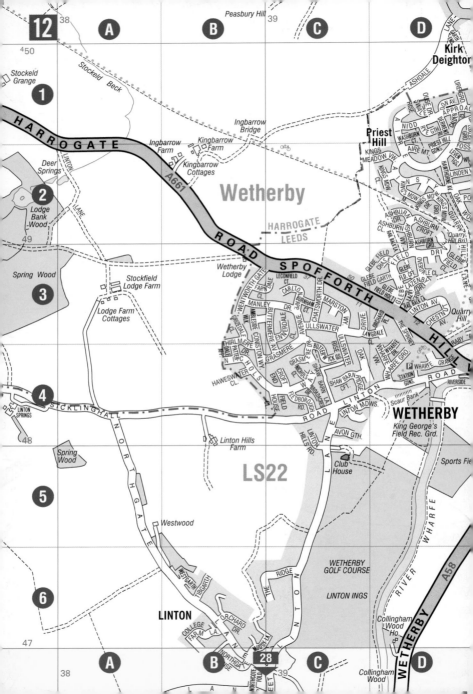

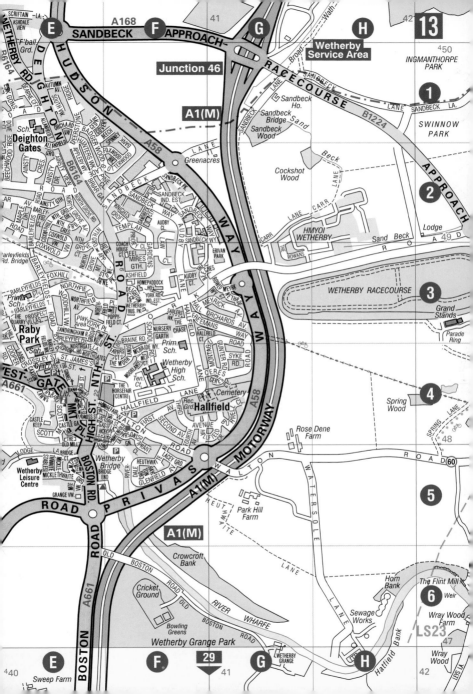

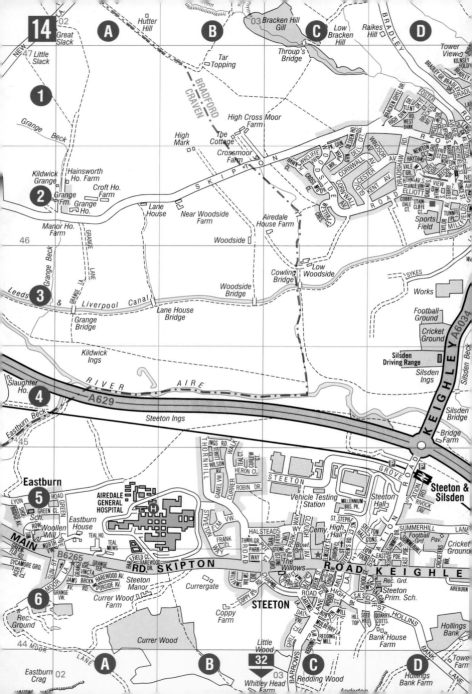

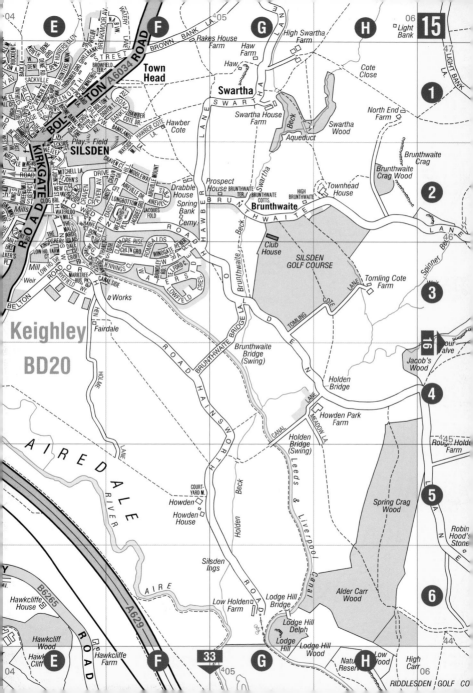

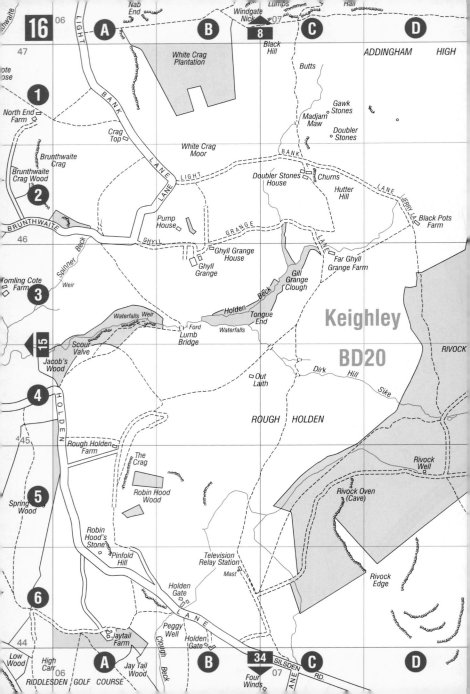

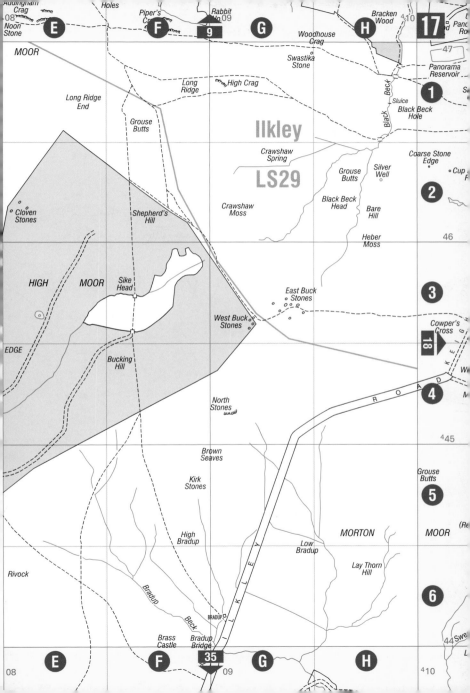

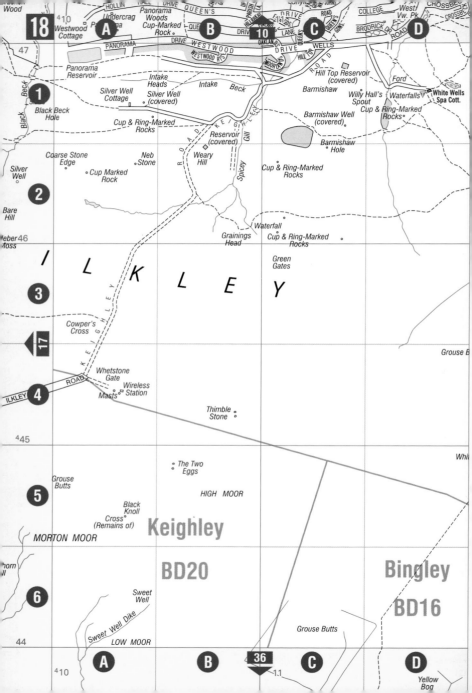

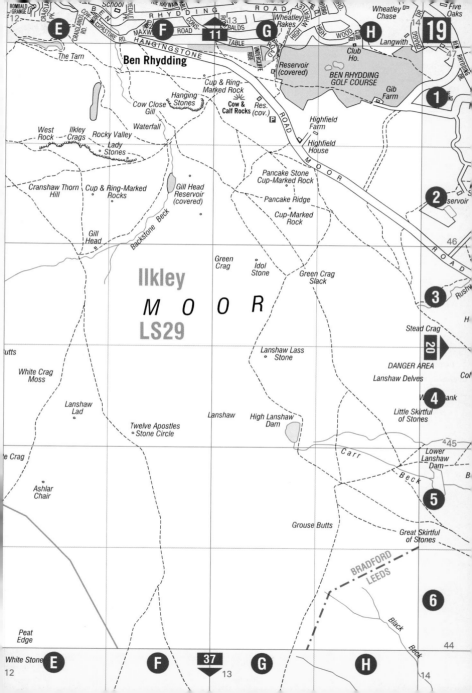

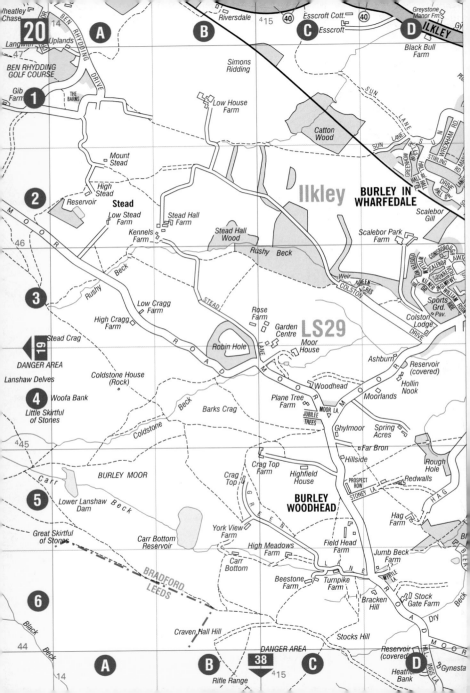

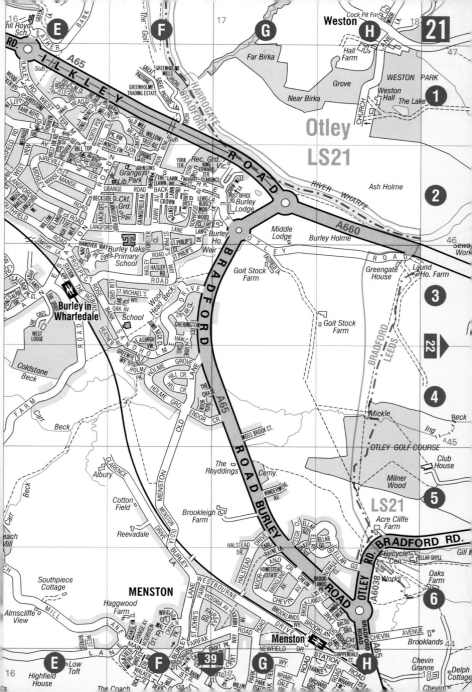

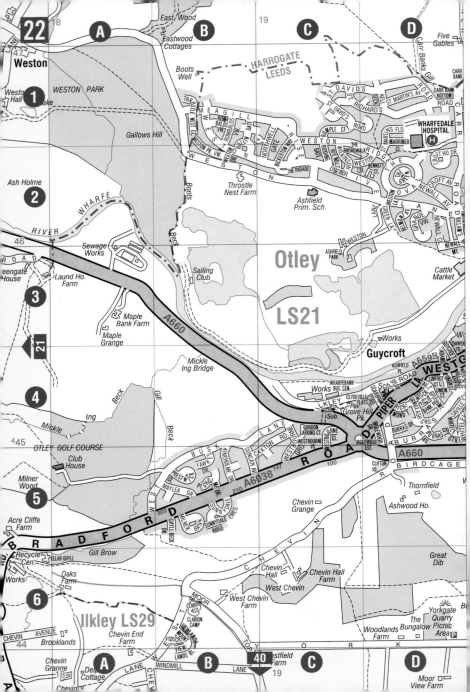

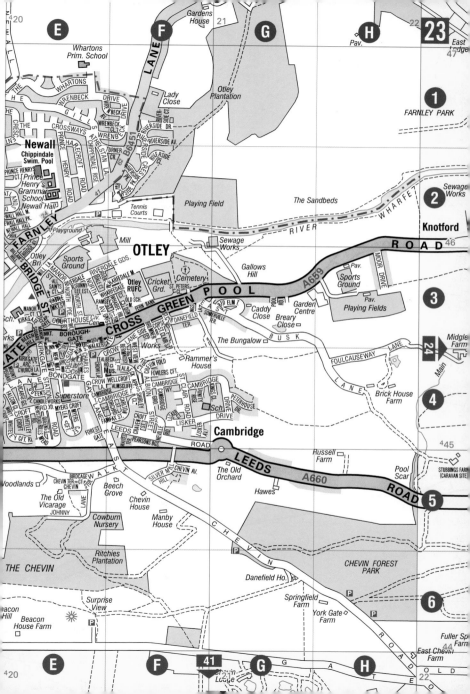

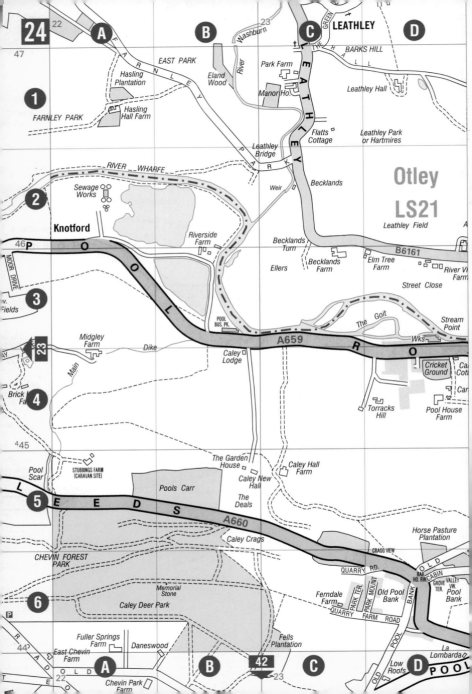

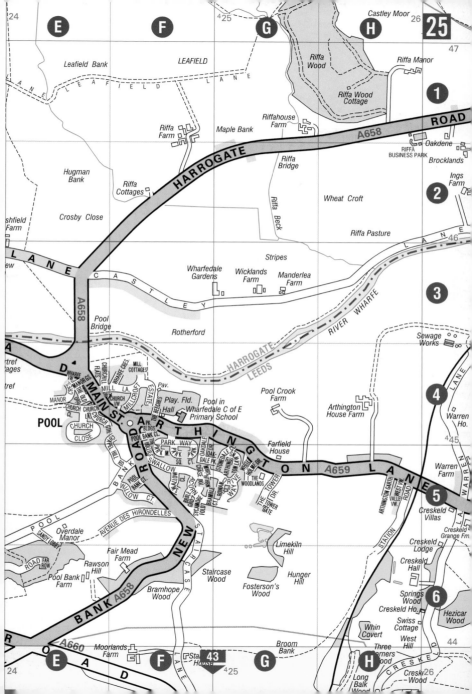

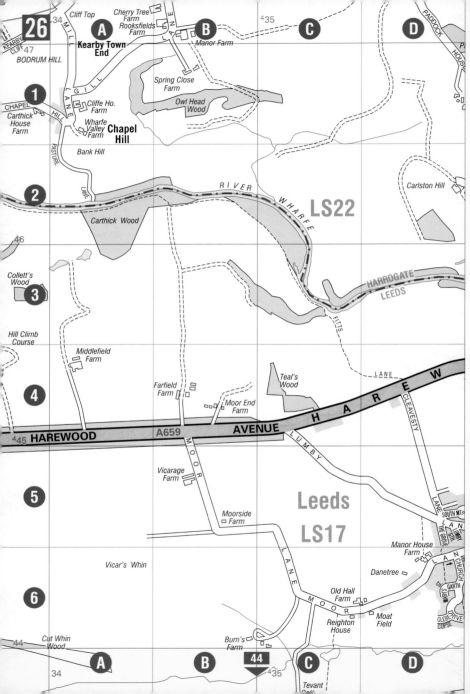

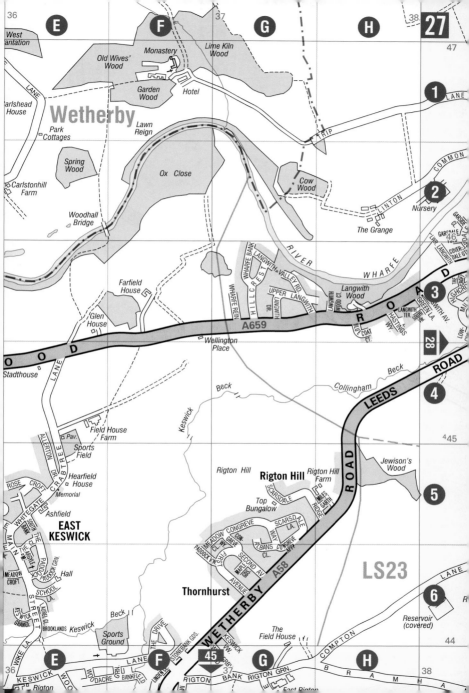

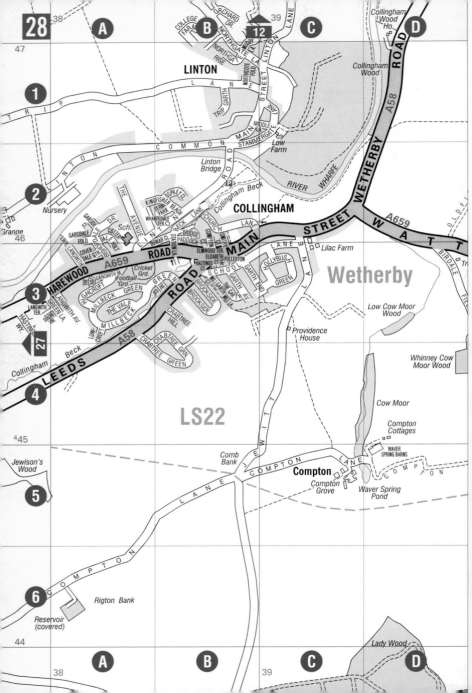

28

A   B   12   C   D

38   ORCHARD DR   39   Collingham Wood Ho.

COLLEGE FARM   NORTHGATE

NORTHGA   LINTON LANE

1   47

NORTHGA RISE

Collingham Wood

LINTON

NORTHCOTE FOLD   LINTON STREET   A58

T   R   I   P

L   A   N   E

TRIP   GARTH

MIDDLE LA   WETHERBY ROAD

COMMON   STAMMERGATE   Low Farm

2   Nursery   THE AVENUE   Linton Bridge   ROAD   Collingham Beck

NTON   Grange   46

KINGFISHER REACH   OSPREY CL   TERN   WHARFEDALE   BRIDGE   COLLINGHAM   RIVER WHARFE

GARSDALE   DR   ASPREY CL   PADDOCK   WER. CT   BECK LANE   CHURCH ST   A659   WATT

GARSDALE FOLD   DALE COTTAGES   LWR LANGWITH   DEWAR CL   BRIDGE   ELMWOOD TER   LANE   Lilac Farm   MAIN STREET   WETHERBY

COVER VALE GT   CRICKET Grd.   HASTINGS CT   ELIZABETH CT   FULLERTON   BIRDALE

3   HAREWOOD   A659   LANGWITH M.   Football Grd.   GREEN   SCHOOL   GARTH AV.   GARTH END   HOLLYBUSH   **Wetherby**   OLDFI

LANGWITH TER.   HIGHCROFT   THE   MILLBECK GREEN   McGARRY LA   GREEN   Low Cow Moor Wood

HASTINGS WY.   SOUTH LA   GREEN LA.   THE VALE   BROOKSIDE   ROAD

27   Collingham   MILLBECK   LOW CROFT   CRABTREE HILL   A58   Providence House

Beck   LEEDS   CRABTREE GRN   CRABTREE GREEN

4   45

LS22   COMB BANK   JEWITT LANE   COMPTON   LANE   Cow Moor   Compton Cottages

Jewison's Wood   WAVER SPRING BARNS

5   Comb Bank   **Compton**   Compton Grove   Waver Spring Pond   COMPTON

COMPTON LANE

6   Rigton Bank

Reservoir (covered)

44   Lady Wood

A   38   B   39   C   D

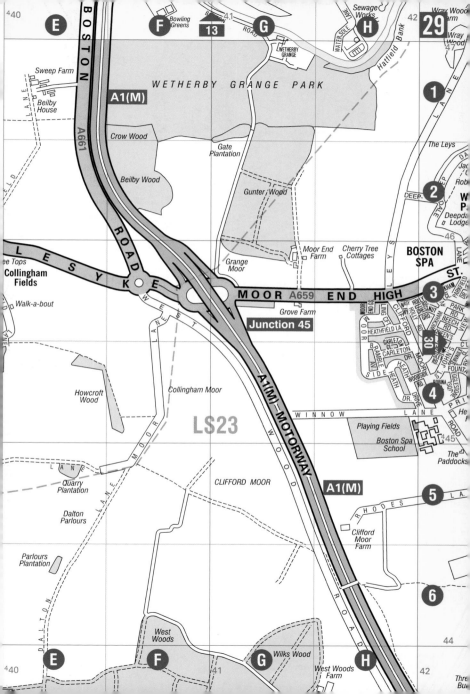

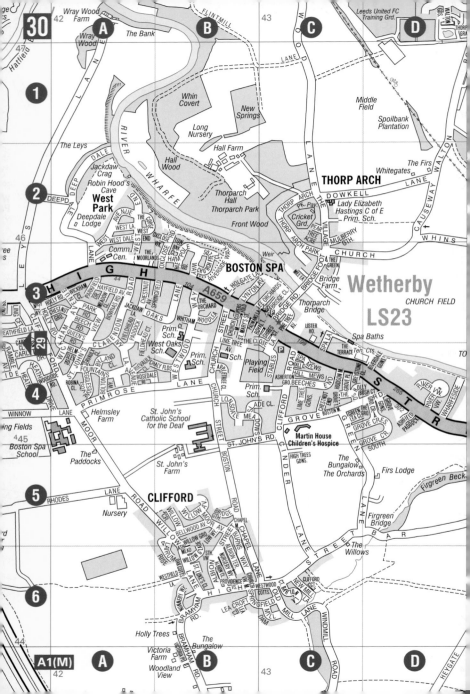

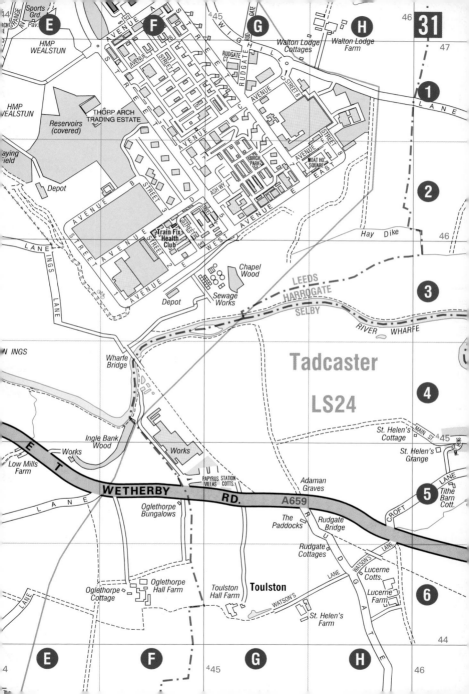

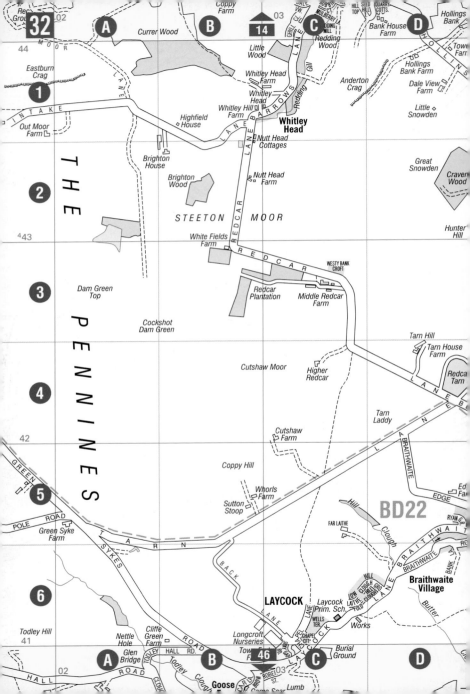

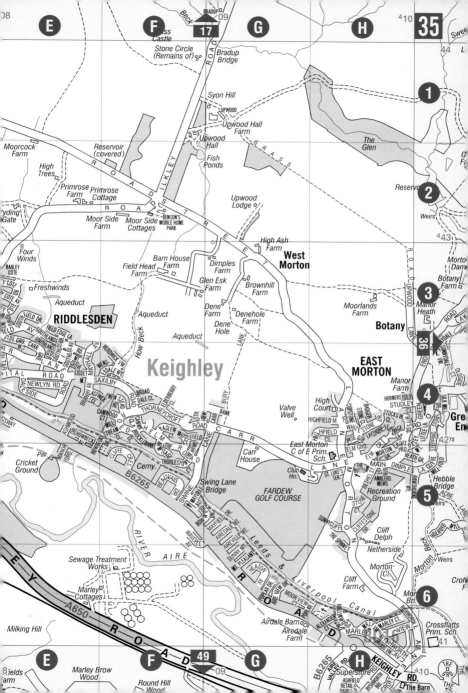

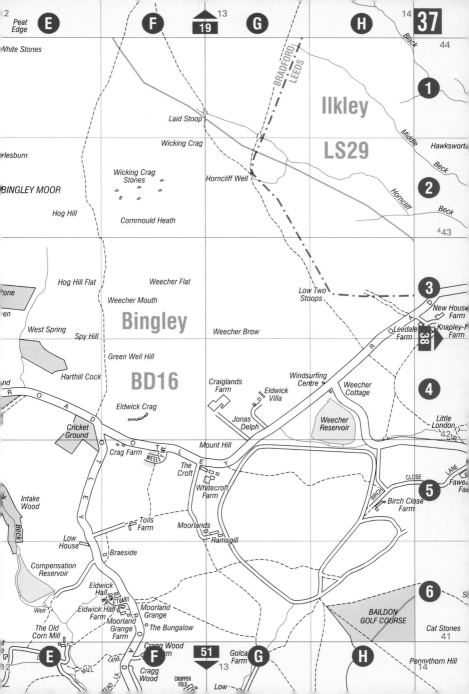

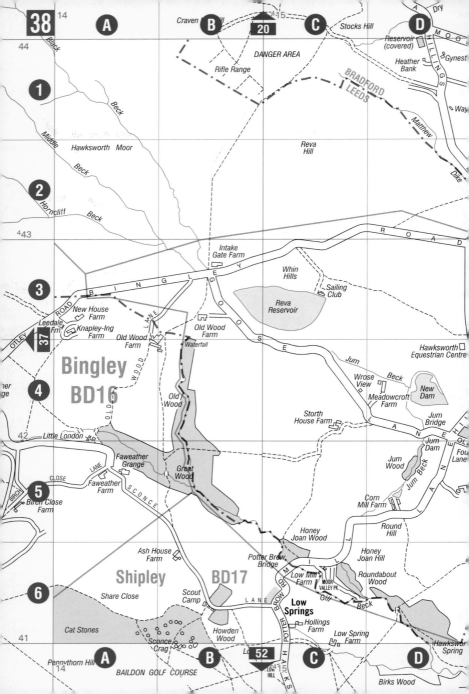

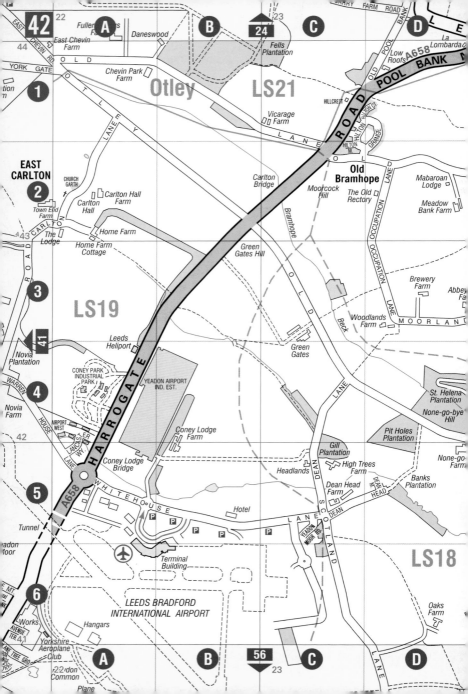

43

Bramhope map (LS16)

Top row grid labels: E · F · G · H · **43**

Left edge: W RD. · E · W DS · 24

- Moorlands Farm
- Staircase House
- STAIRCASE LANE
- 25
- Broom Bank
- Creskeld Ho.
- Swi.26 Cottage
- West Hill
- 44
- Three Corners Wood
- Long Balk Wood
- Creskeld Wood
- Crag Wood
- **1**
- Wood Top Farm
- Coates's Wood
- The Grange
- Hotel
- CRESKELD LY.
- Old Manor Farm
- HOLLAND MT.
- CHURCHGATE
- HALL RISE CLOSE
- HALL CL.
- HALL RISE
- RISE CRESKELD
- CRESKELD GTH.
- Creskeld Pk.
- CRESKELD DRIVE
- **West Breary**
- A660
- EASTGATE
- BREARY
- BREARY LANE
- **2**
- EAST
- The Brow
- LANE
- Pav. Rec. Grd.
- HIGH MOOR GRANGE
- MANOR PL.
- MANOR GNS.
- SILVER TREES
- PARKLANDS
- HARKLANDS WALK
- Bramhope Prim. Sch.
- WEST HALL CT.
- THE PDE.
- PIT CT.
- BREARY RISE
- TREDGOLD CRES.
- TREDGOLD
- TREDGOLD AVENUE
- WYNMORE
- WYNMORE DR.
- WYNMORE CRES.
- HIGH RIDGE WY.
- Spring Wood
- **3**
- 43
- Leeds
- Hill Top
- Bramhope Nurseries
- ROAD
- SCHOOL GRN.
- LONG MEADOWS
- MEADOW END
- NORTH MEAD
- SANDY WALK
- SOUTH MEAD
- SOUTHFIELD
- MEADOW GTH.
- THE POPLARS
- THE CEDARS
- THE ROWANS
- BIRCHES
- **BRAMHOPE**
- Cemetery
- Camp Plantation
- **LS16**
- Bramhope Grove
- THE SYCAMORES
- West Park Leeds RUFC
- **4**
- Bramhope Moor
- Moor Cottage
- CAMP ROAD
- Camp House Farm
- SYCAMORE CL.
- Sports Pitch
- 42
- Breary Marsh
- St. Helenas Caravan Park
- Tunnel
- Bramhope ROAD
- Bog Plantation
- Marsh Beck
- Marshes Plantation
- **5**
- Old Rushes Farm
- Beck Plantation
- Fish Pond Plantation
- **6**
- Wrinklewood
- Wrinkle Hill Wood
- LANE
- New Rushes Farm
- Fish Pond
- Crag House Farm
- Crag Hill
- COOKRIDGE ROAD
- Lane End Farm
- Pav.
- Sports Ground
- COOKRIDGE AV.
- CRAG HILL LANE
- PINFOLD LANE
- COOKRIDGE HALL GOLF COURSE
- 41
- Moselbeck
- Kings Lea
- 57
- Cricket Ground Pav.
- SOUTH 25 LA.
- Ridgeside
- HALL LA.
- Driving Range
- 26

Bottom row grid labels: 24 · E · F · 57 · G · H · 26

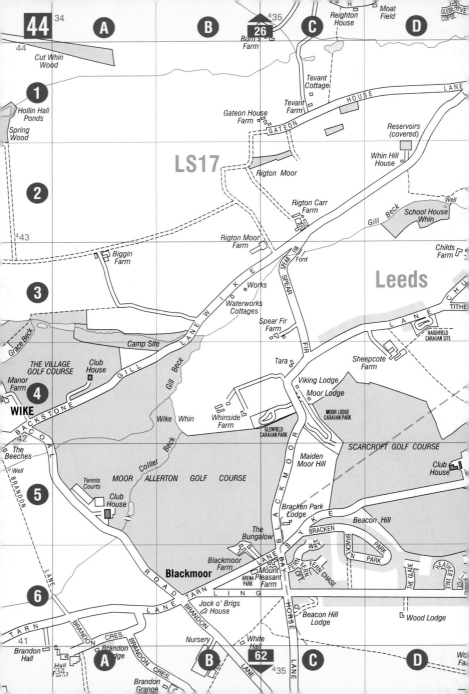

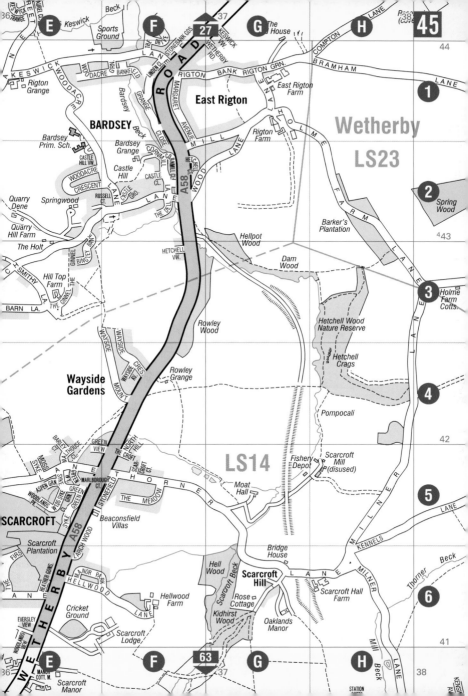

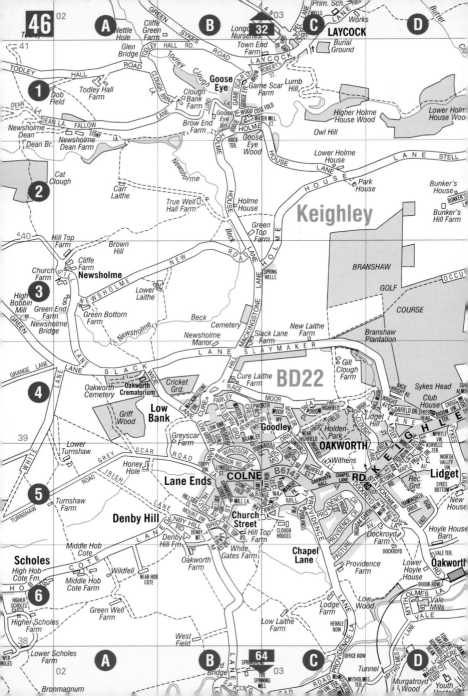

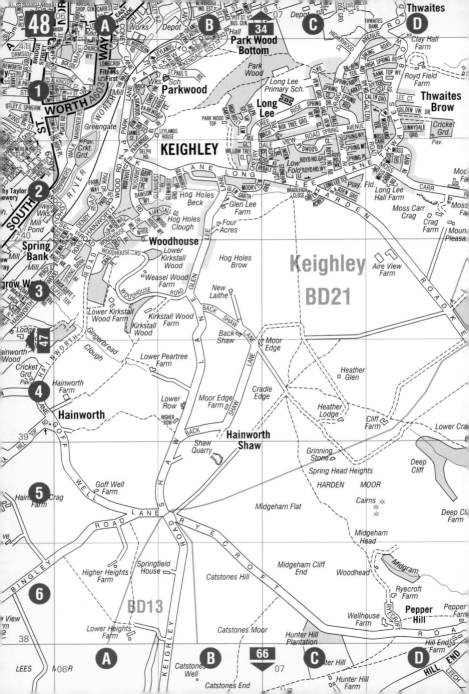

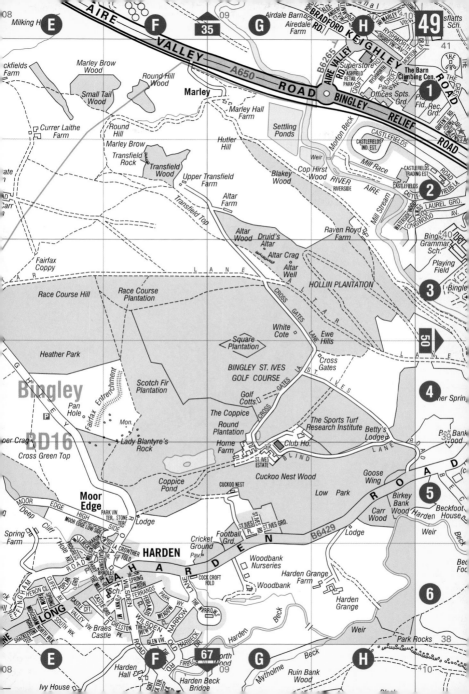

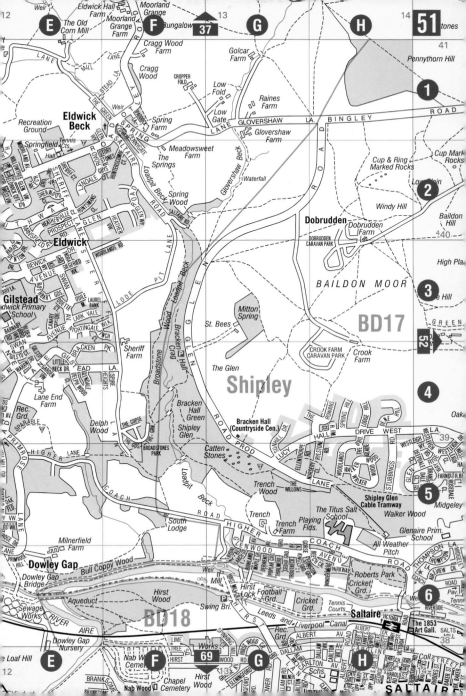

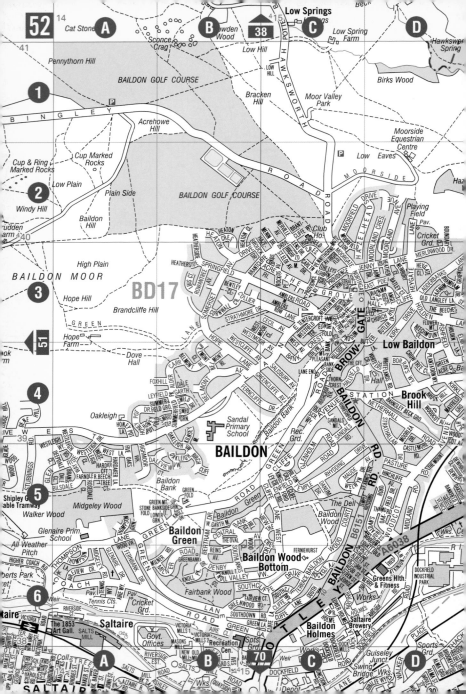

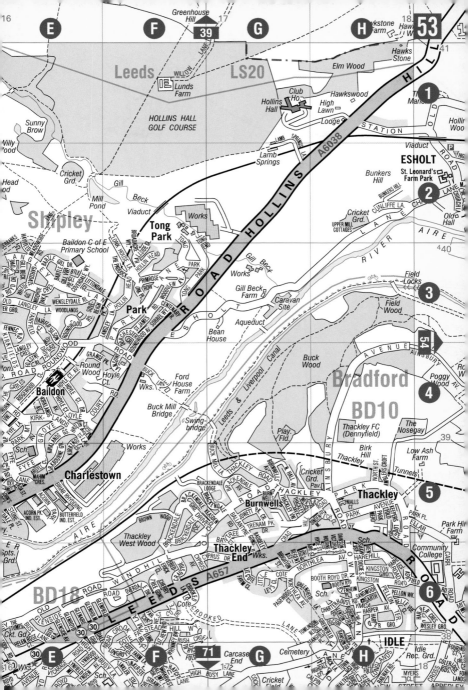

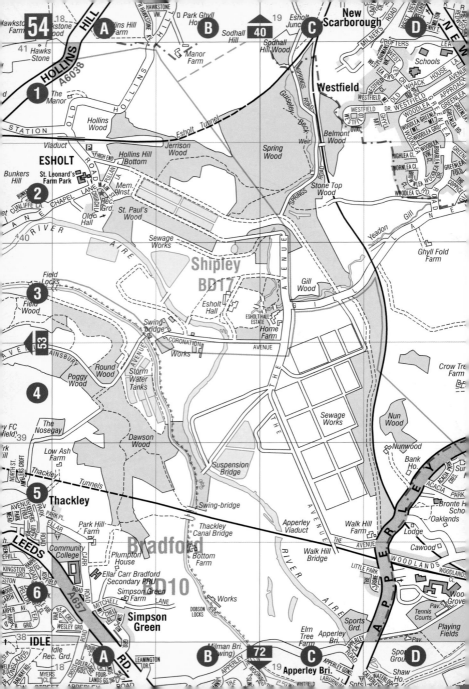

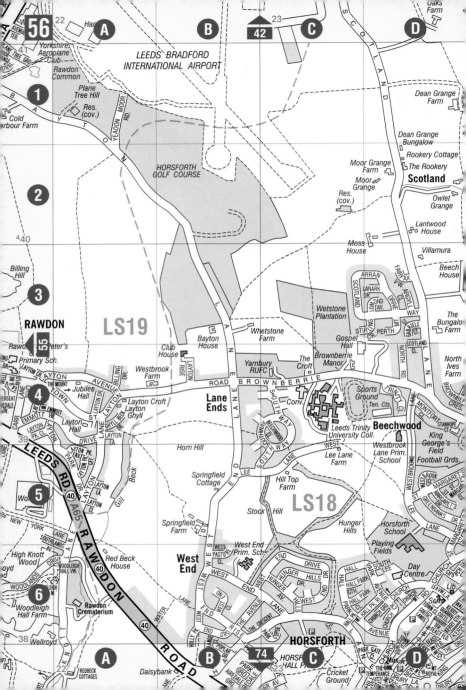

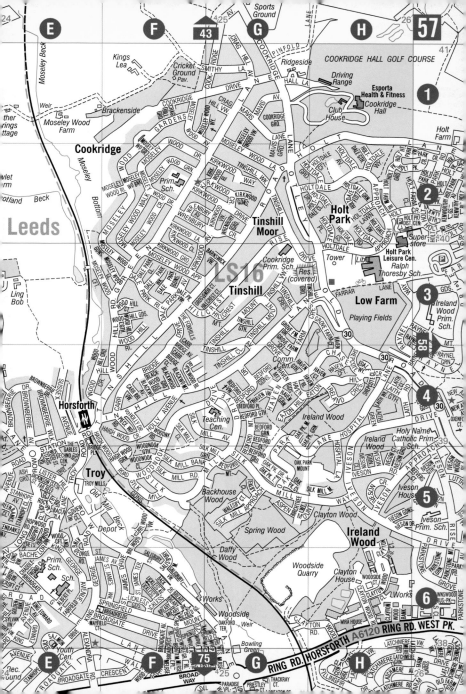

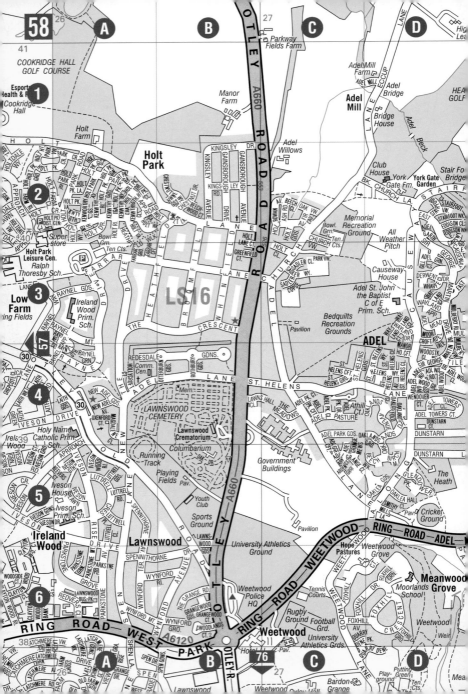

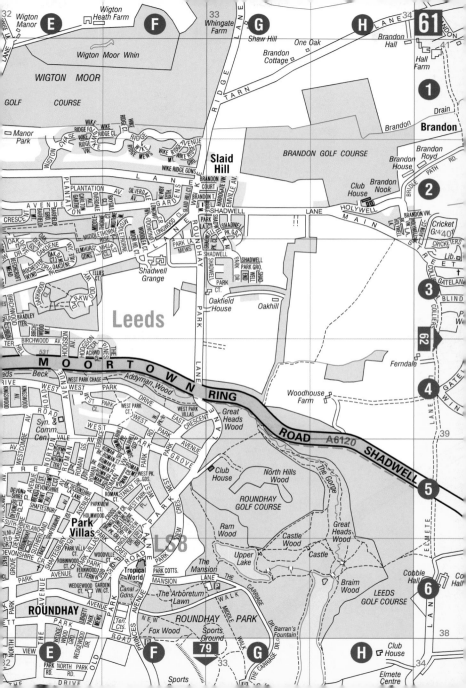

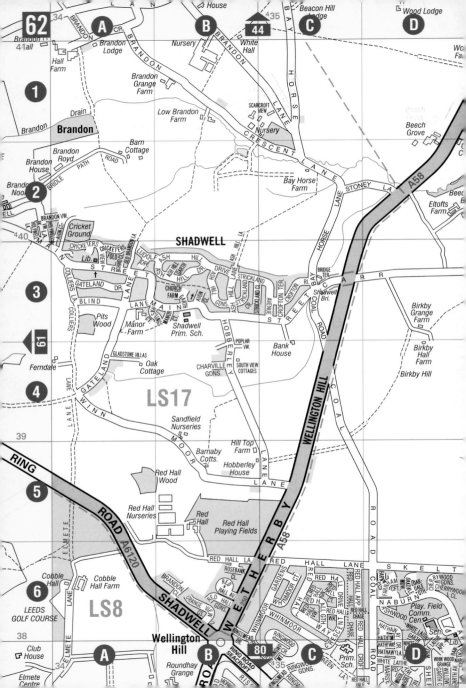

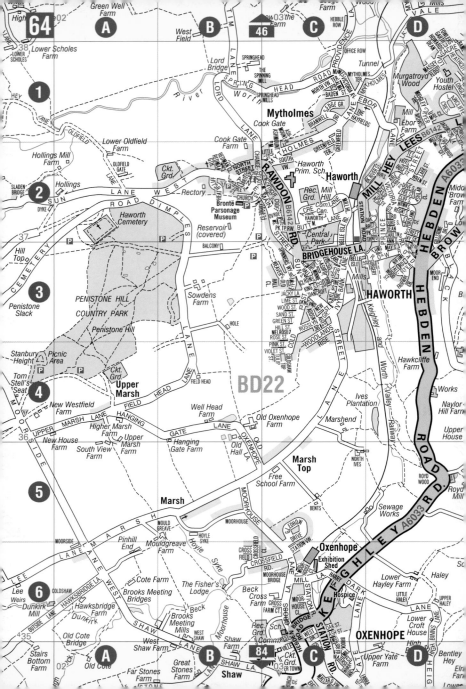

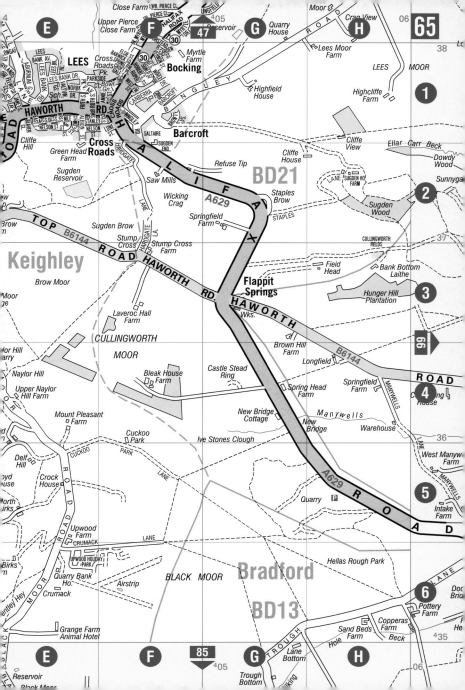

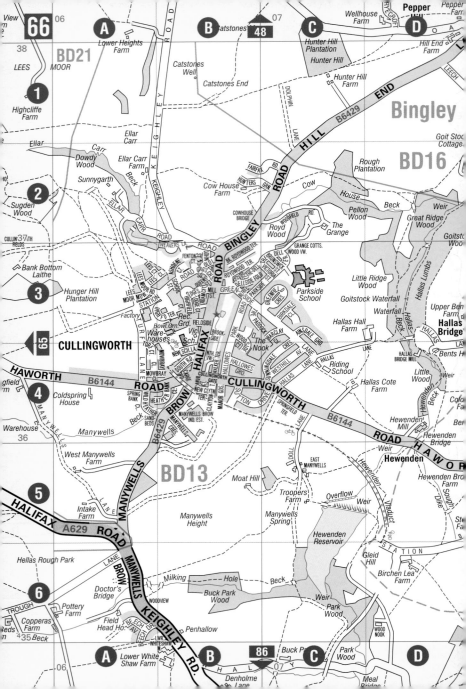

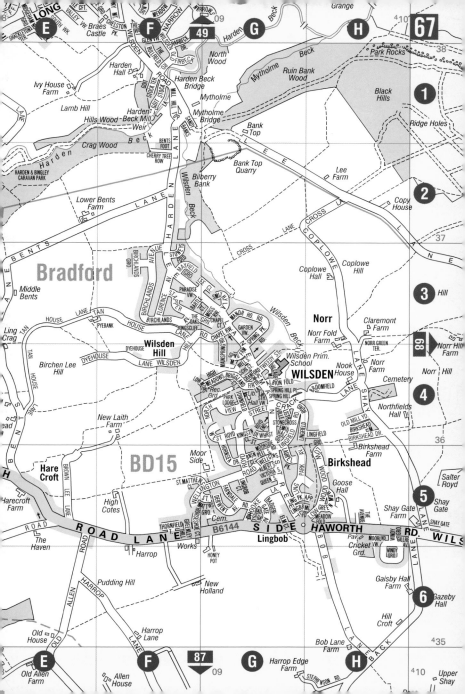

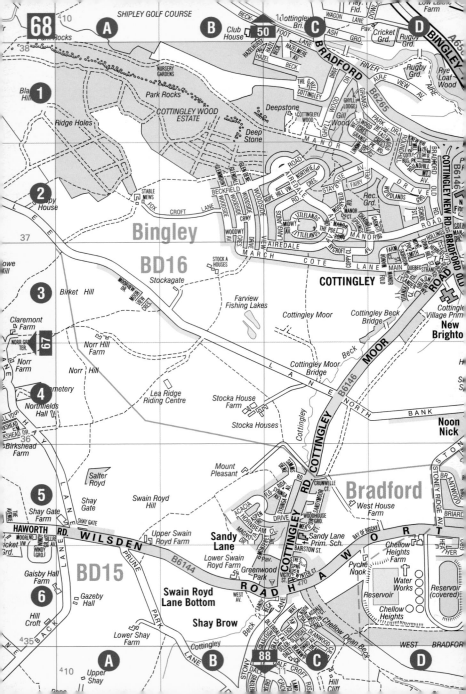

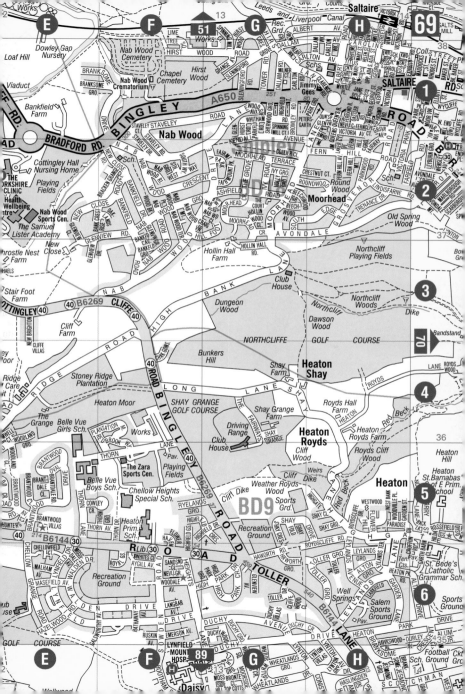

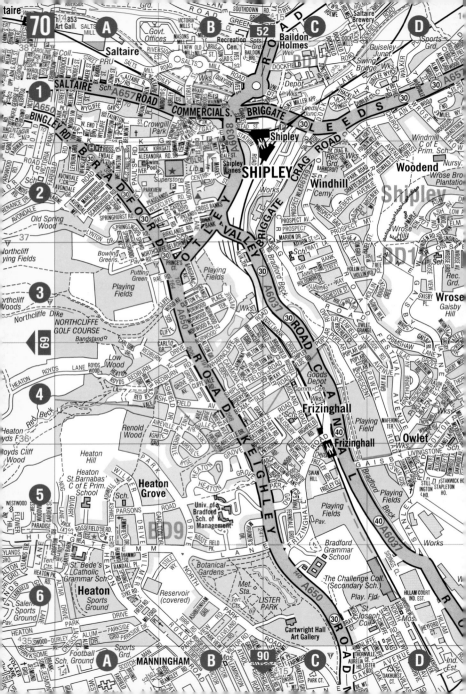

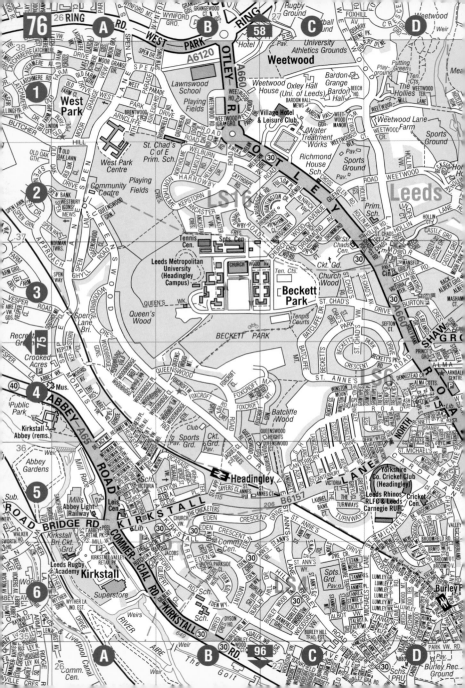

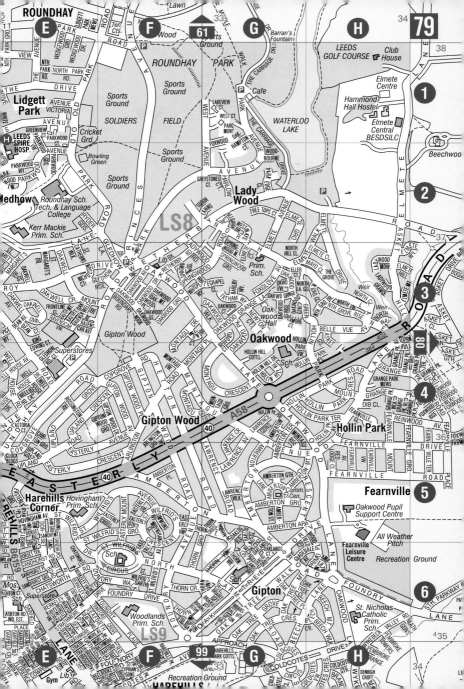

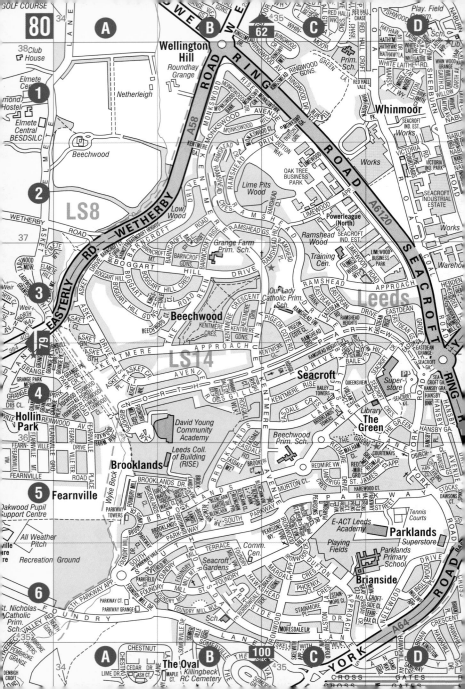

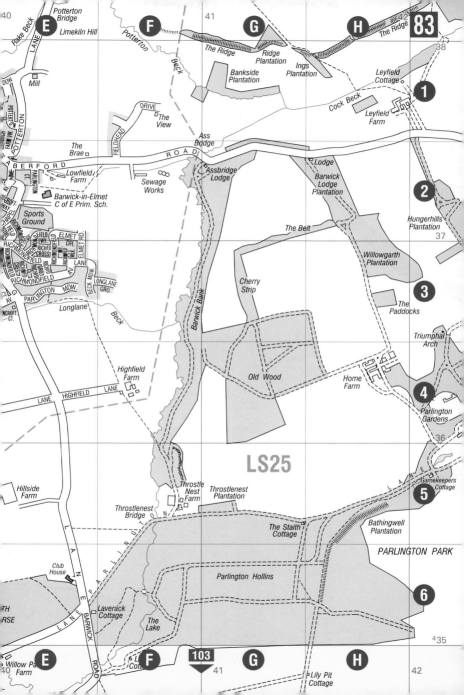

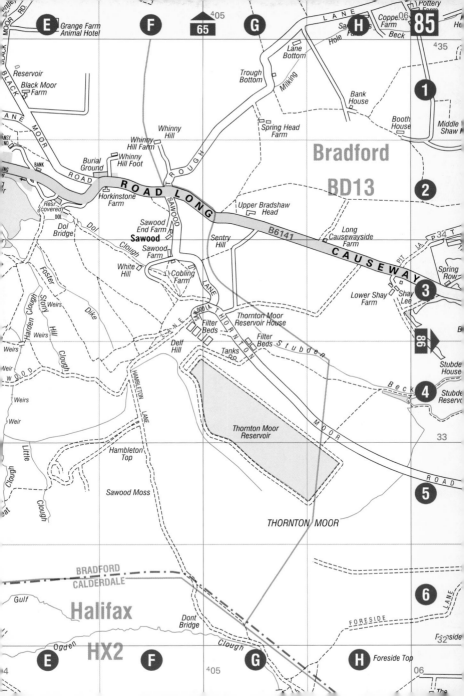

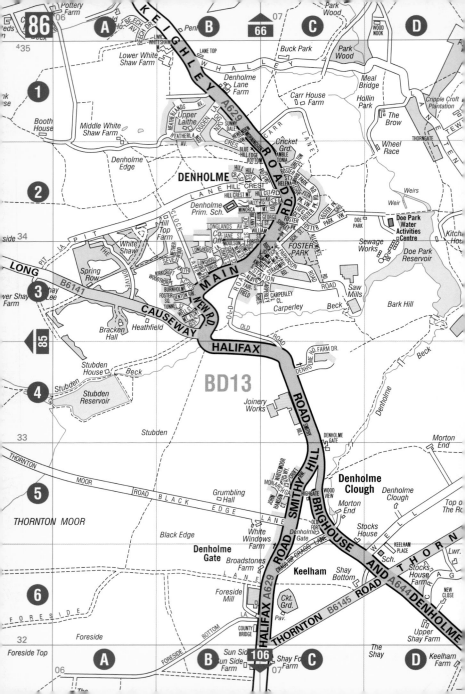

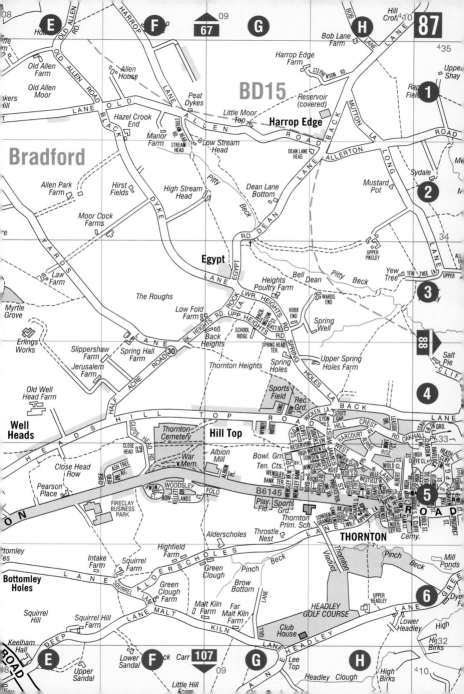

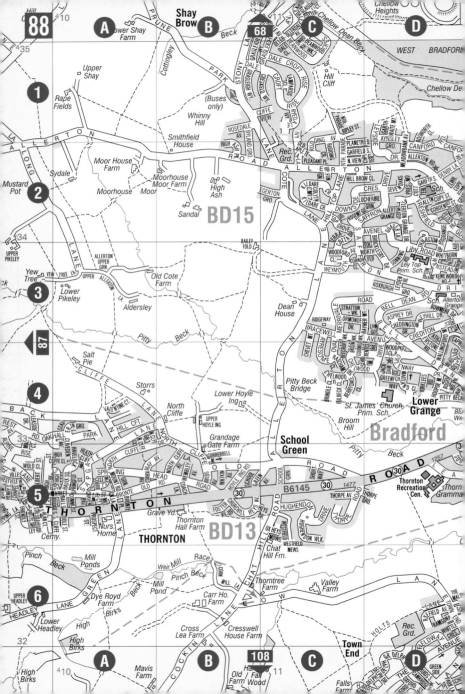

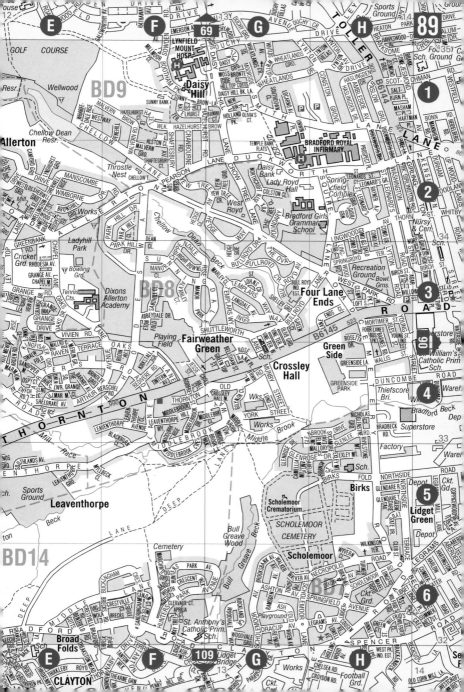

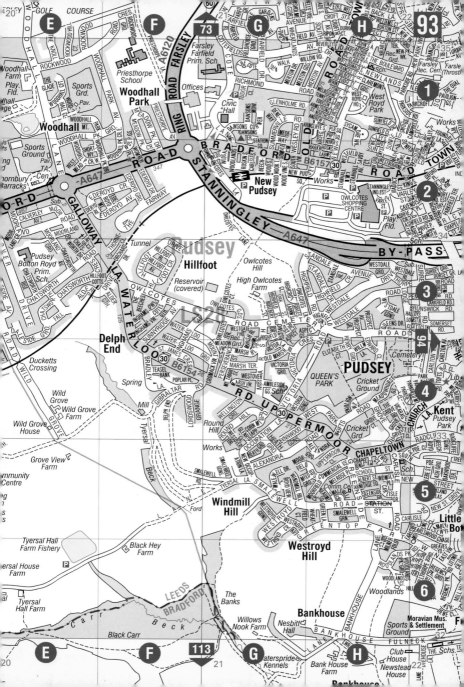

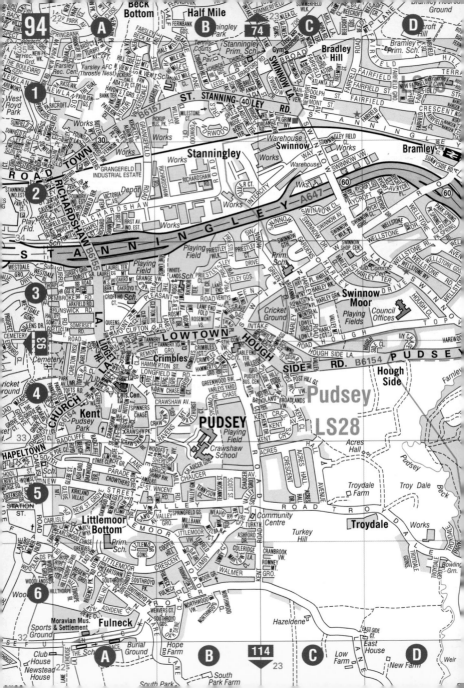

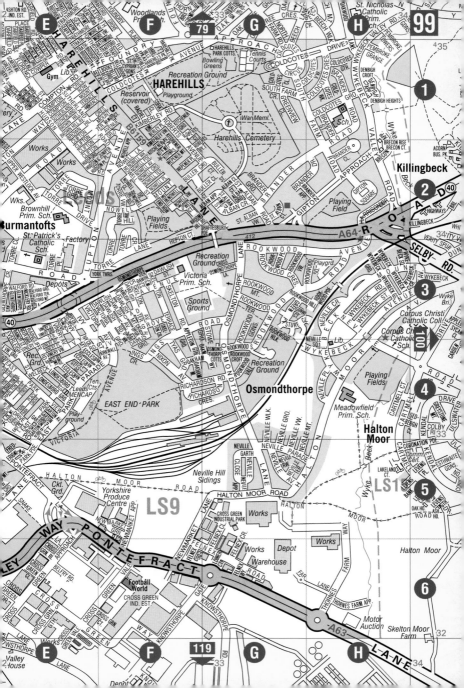

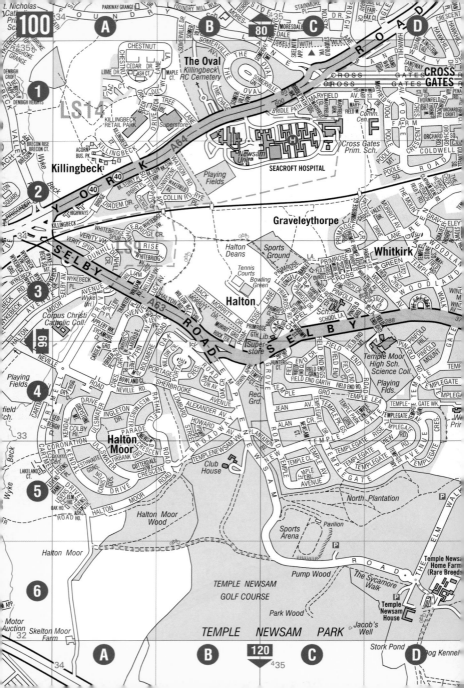

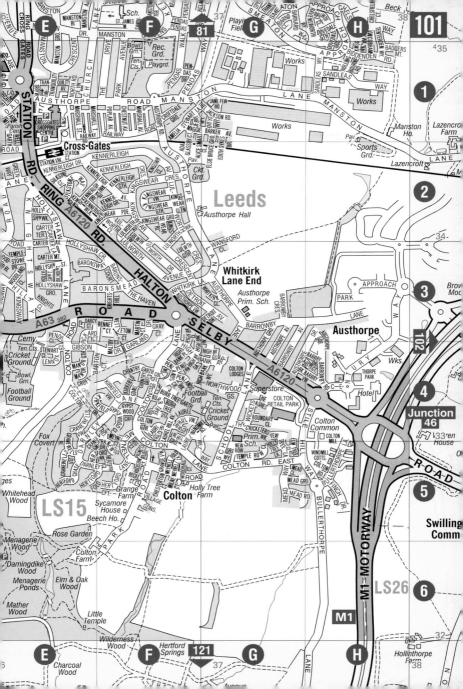

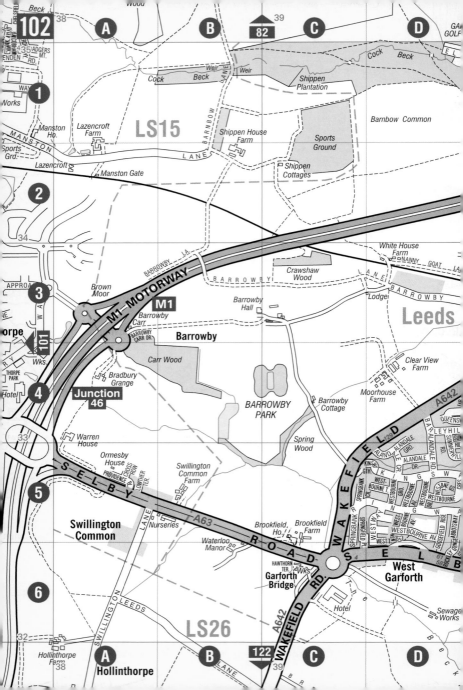

104 42

4 35

Park House Farm

A ABERFORD ROAD B1217 B 43 C D

Hookmoor Cottage

Junction 43 A1(M)

1

Junction 47

M1-MOTORWAY

Beech Plantation

Bracken-ridge House

ROAD

M1

A1(M) A1(M)-MOTORW

2

ABERFORD ROAD A642

A656

Ridge Road Farm

Roman Road

34

High se

EAST RISE
MULE RISE
WHI'S
WOODRIDGE TW.
EAST RIDGE
ASHLEY PK.
RIDG...

Sturton

Roman Ridge

LANDS
BRAEMAR
WINGATE
MUNCASTER RD.
GLAMIS CL.
DRIVE
GILLING
GRETA
PK.

Stand

Ash Plantation

Well House Farm

St. Helen's Well

Leeds

3

Garforth Town FC (Wheatley Park)

East Garforth

RIDGE

Dyke

103

SUNNINGDALE

BRAEMAR
STURTON
CHASE
GARFORTH WLK.
THE GRANGE
ATHLONE
GRANGE LANE

RO AD

WHITFIELD

4

Moat

Three Acre Plantation

Old Micklefield

CHURCH

AV
33

Sturton Grange Farm

Roman Road

LS25

ON LANE

ROMAN PL.
YEW LA. DRIVE
ELDER
GREEN

Stub Wood

Greenfthe Academy

AVENUE

5

Roman Ridge Bridge

Ridge Bridge Cottage

PHOENIX

PECKFIELD BUS. PK.

CLIFFE VILLAS
CLIFFE HOUSES
AERIAL VW.
CLIFFE BUNGS.
WARREN FARM COTTAGES

DRIVE

RIDGE A656

Warren Farm

6

FIELD CHASE
32

CLIFF TOP PK.
HOME EST.
rth

LANE

Peck

42 A B **124** 43 C D

PECKFIELD Peckfield WARREN HOUSE

E F G Ringhay Wood H 46

445 435

RANGER'S WALK

1

Near Fox Covert

Coburnhill Wood

Scott's Wood

SELBY LEEDS

The Marsh

Weet Wood

2

34

Longroyd Wood

Daniel Hartly's Wood

3

Huddleston Old Wood

HARTLEY WOOD COTTAGES

Hartly Wood

Gunner Hill

4

S h e e p

Sheep Dyke Road

DIKE

Grange Fm.

CHURCH CL.

Vic. NORTH DIKE

CHURCHVILLE NEW ROW CHAPEL CT.

Manor House Fm.

Micklefield C of E Prim. Sch.

MICKLEFIELD

33

Newthorpe Farm

LANE

THE VILLAGE BUNGS

GARDEN STATION VILLAGE

Football Ground

Ckt. Grd.

RAILWAY COTTS.

A1(M)

5

Micklefield

PROSPECT

RISE CT.

LANE THE FIELD

CRESCENT HONEYSUCKLE CL. SUNNYBANK WEST VW. NEW CL.

Brookfield House Newthorpe Barrack

Newthorpe Beck

New Micklefield

A1(M) — MOTORWAY

Highroyds Wood

6

Highfield

NORTH

Castle Hills

Newthorpe Quarry

Castle Plains

Micklefield Plantation

E

Peckfield Plantation

F efield tation

125

445

G HIGHFIELD H

LANE 32

46

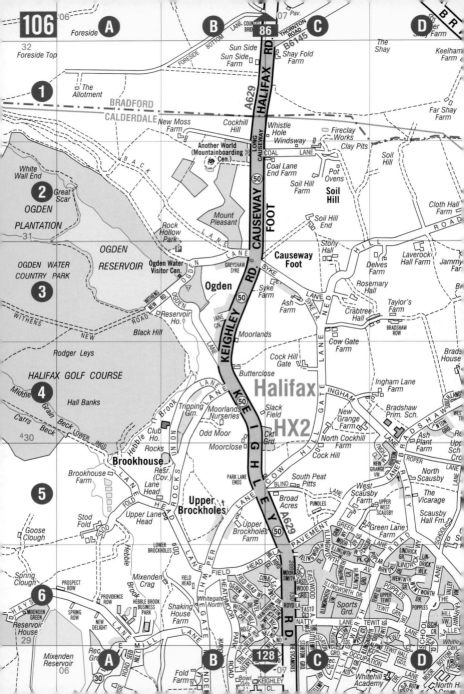

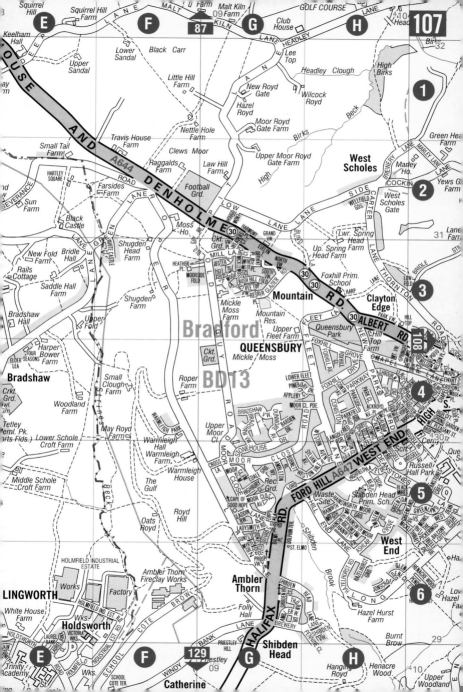

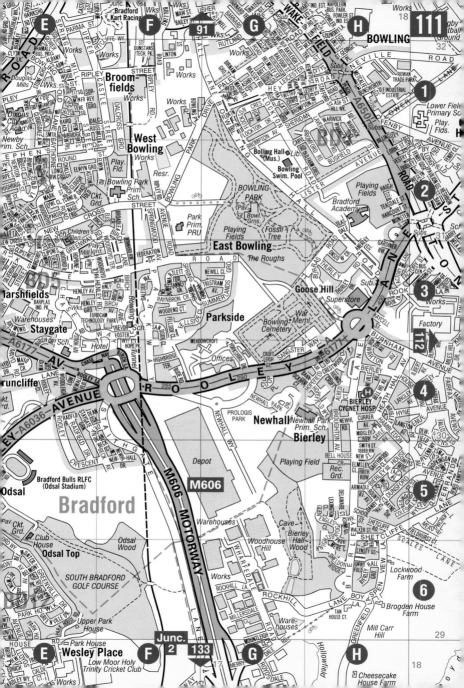

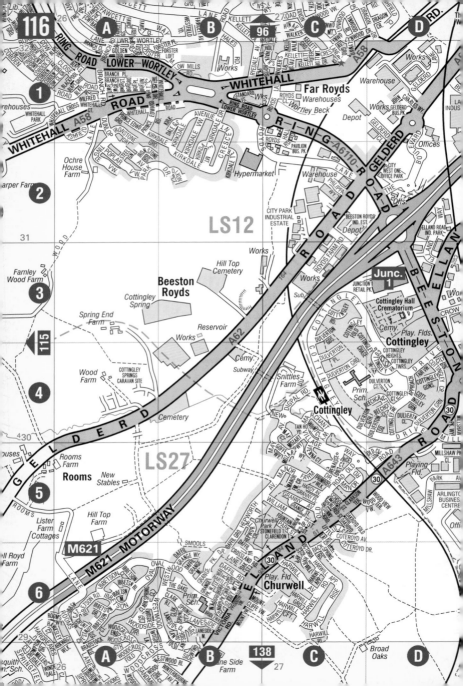

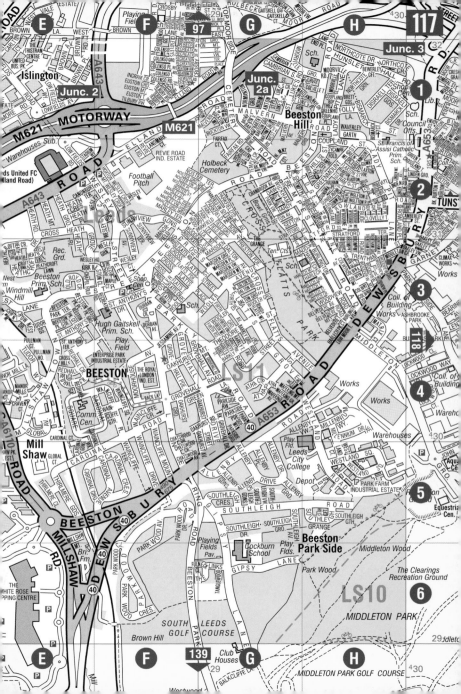

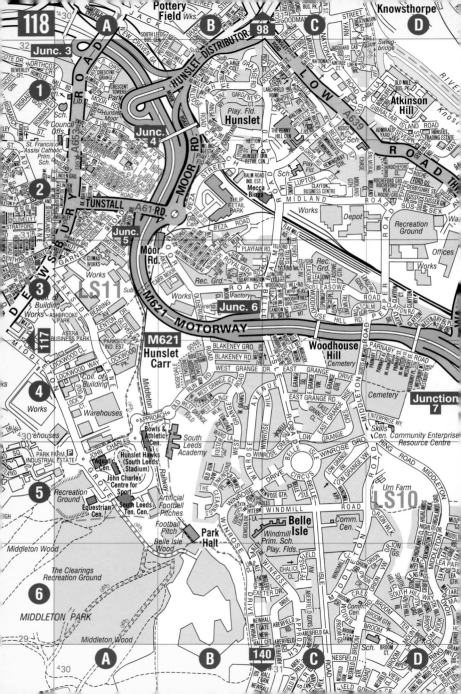

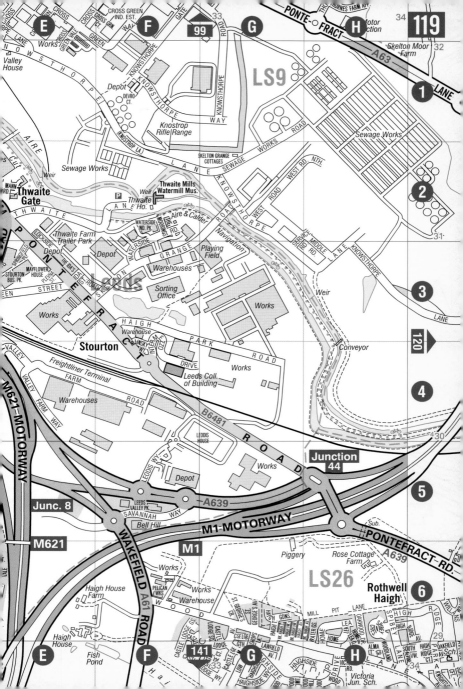

120

A · B · C · D

Map of Temple Newsam Park / Leeds (LS9) area, page 120

Labels visible:
- 120 (page number, top left)
- 34 Moor Auct...
- Moor Farm
- 32
- PONTEFRACT
- A63
- LANE
- Sewage Works
- 31
- Wyke Beck
- LS9
- Junction 45
- KNOWSTHORPE LANE
- Pump Ho.
- M1
- 119
- M1 MOTORWAY
- 430
- Junc. 44
- Sub.
- Cottage
- PONTEFRACT RD. A639 LEEDS
- Rothwell Haigh
- MILL PIT LANE
- Haigh Cottage Farm
- Haigh Farm
- John O'Gaunts Trading Estate
- Auction Mart
- Warehouses
- HIGH RIDGE
- OAKFIELD
- Victoria Jn. Sch.
- 34
- 29
- TEMPLE NEWSAM GOLF COURSE
- 435 Park Wood
- 100
- Bell Wood
- Spring Wood
- TEMPLE NEWSAM PARK
- Temple Newsam House
- Jacob's Well
- Stork Pond
- Dog Kennel
- Pegasus Wood
- Dunstan Hills
- Leeds
- PONTEFRACT LANE
- R I V E R
- Fishpond Lock
- The Goit
- Aire
- ROTHWELL COUNTRY PARK
- John O'Gaunts
- PICKPOCKET
- Recreation Ground
- Comm. Cen.
- Football Ground
- Cemy.
- 142
- 435
- 430
- DE LACIES CT
- PYMONT
- HOLMSLEY

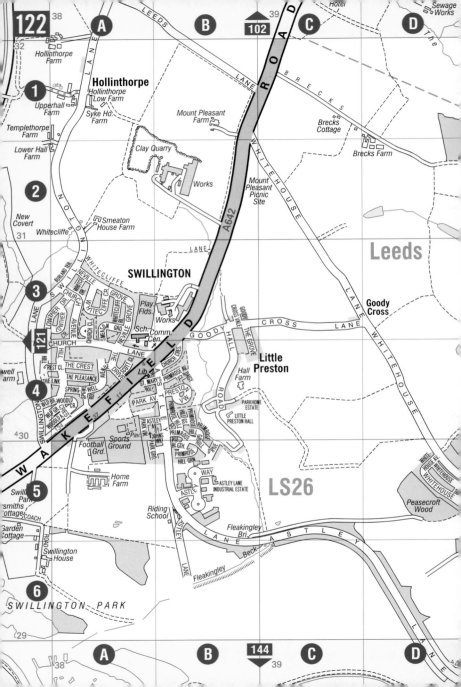

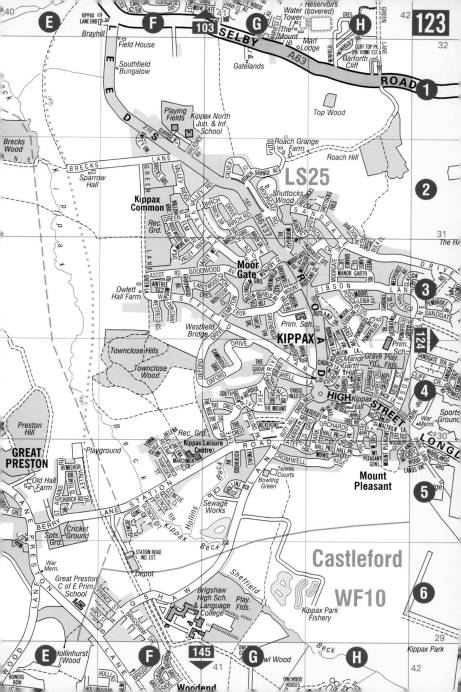

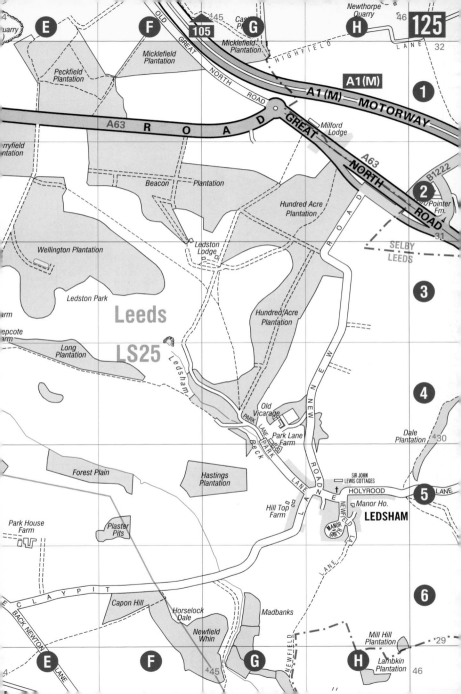

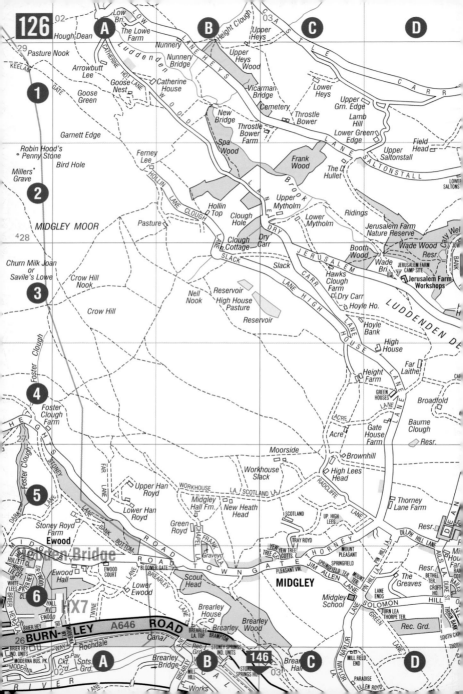

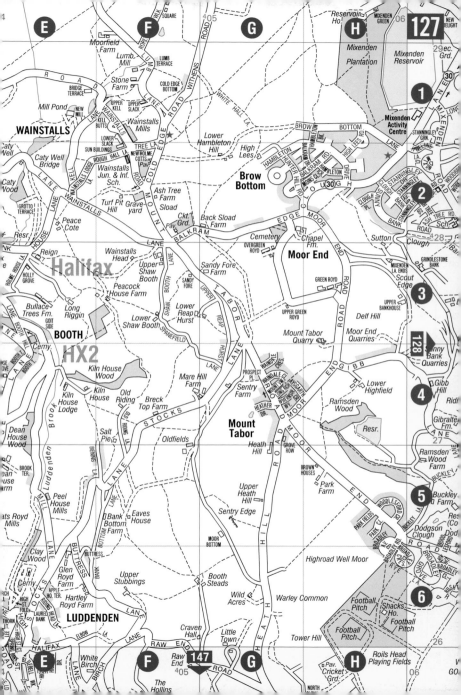

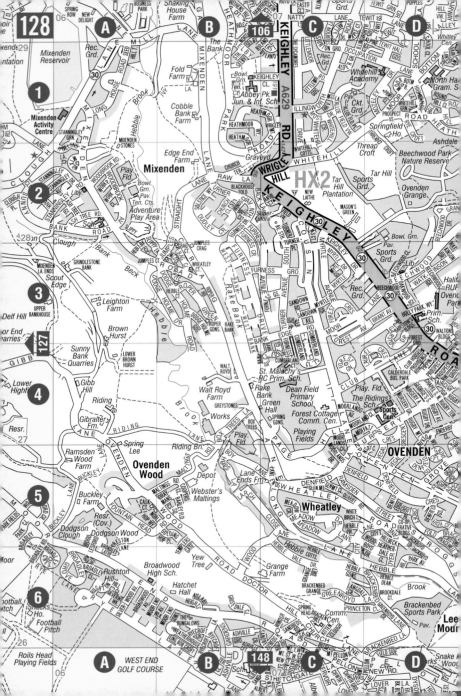

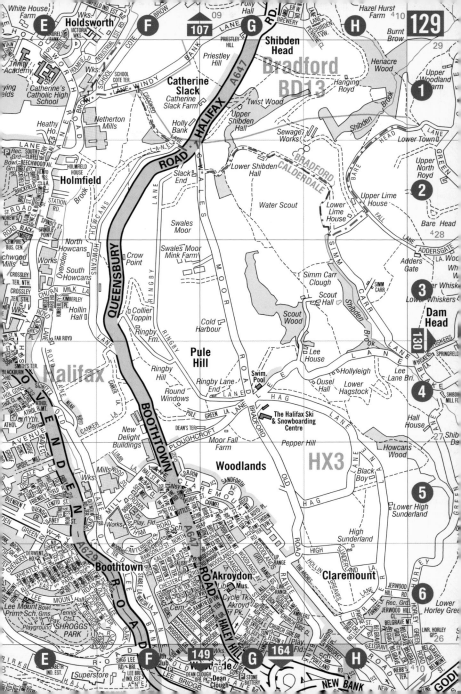

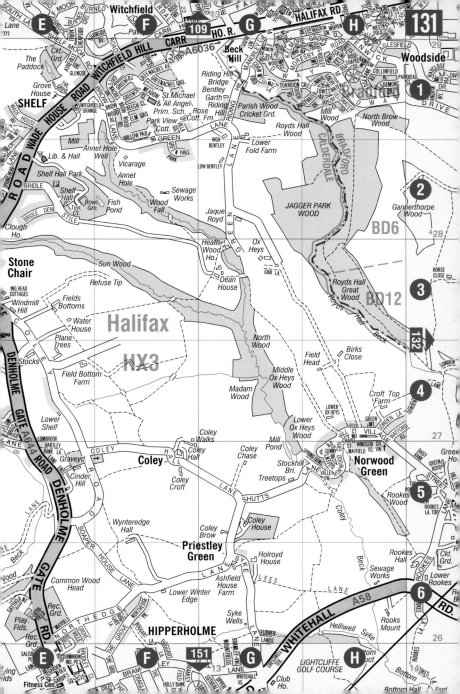

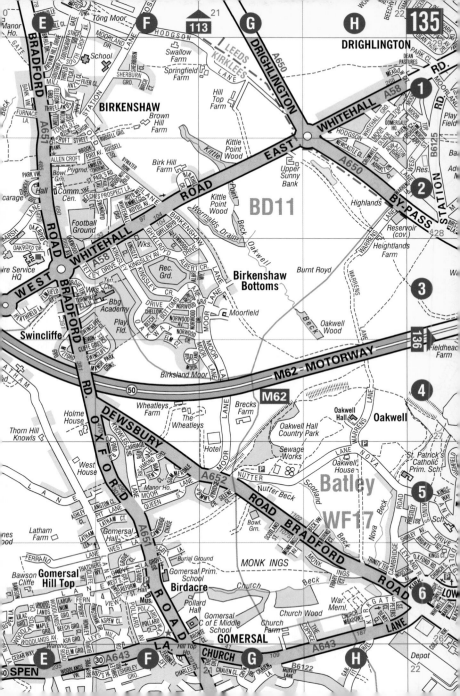

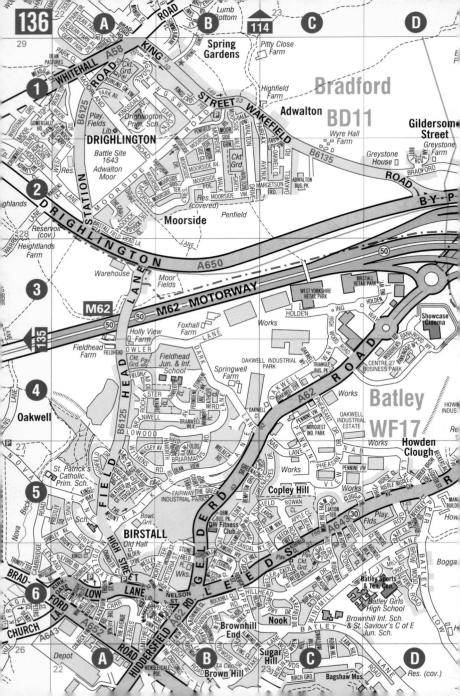

Leeds
LS27

Junction 27

MORLEY

Bruntcliffe

Morley
Hole

Birks

America
Moor

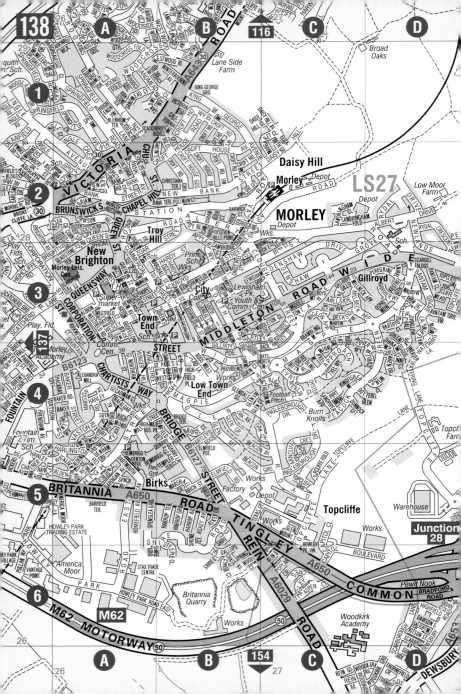

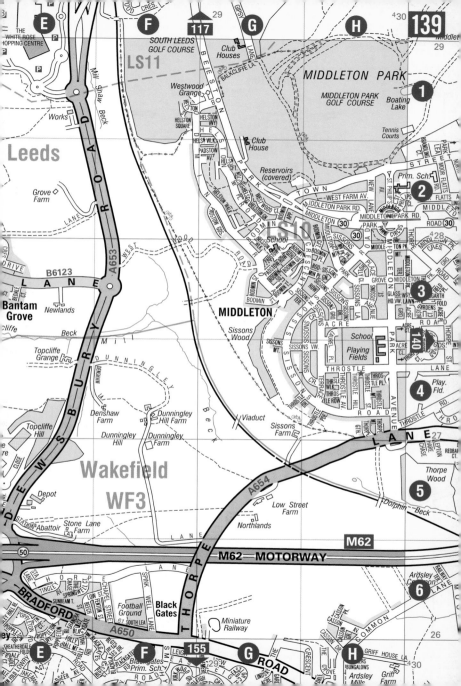

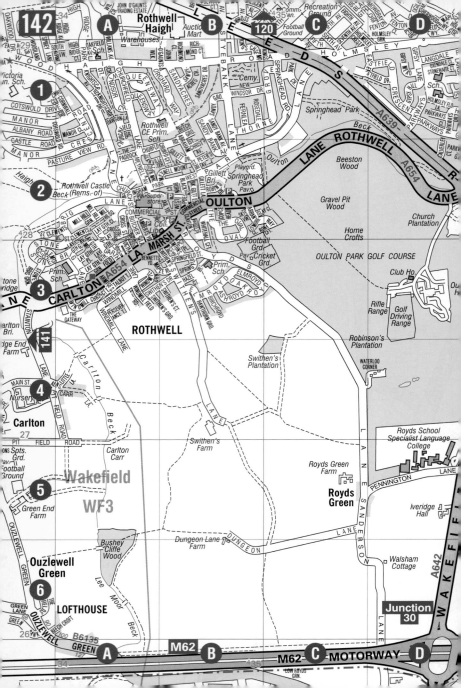

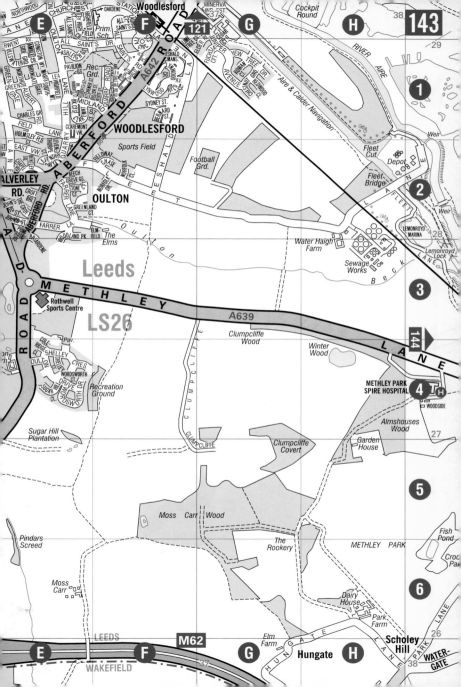

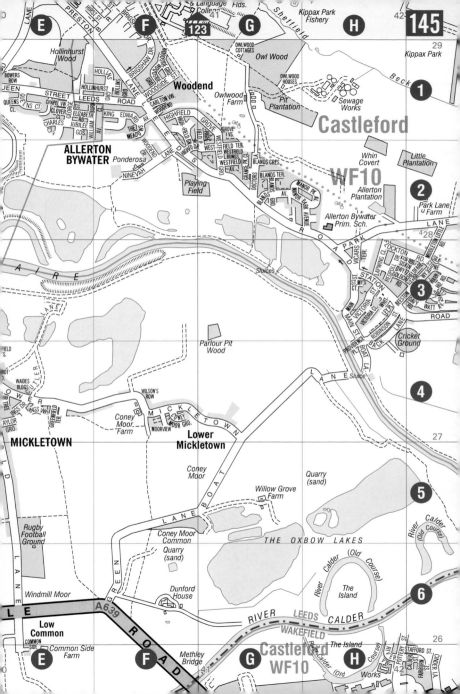

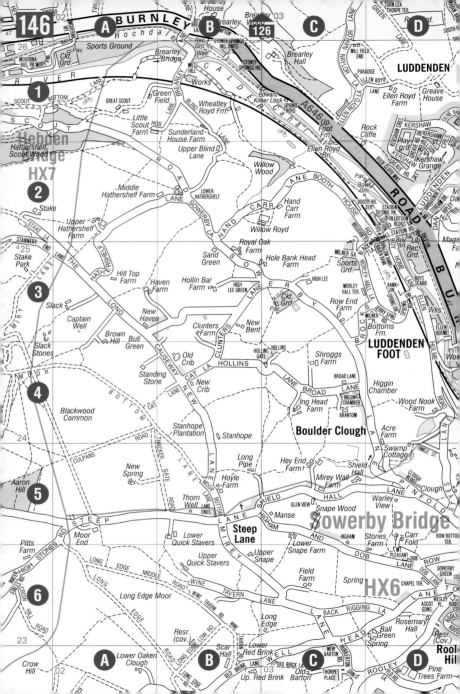

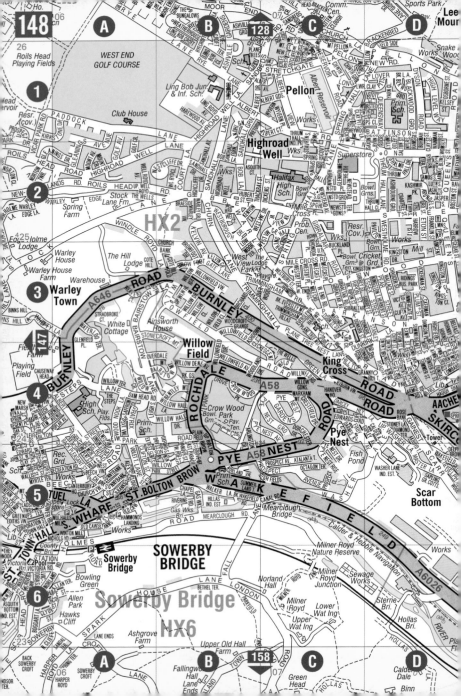

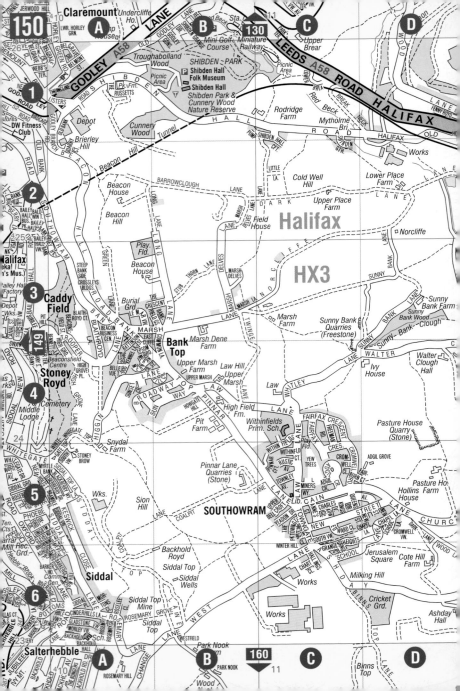

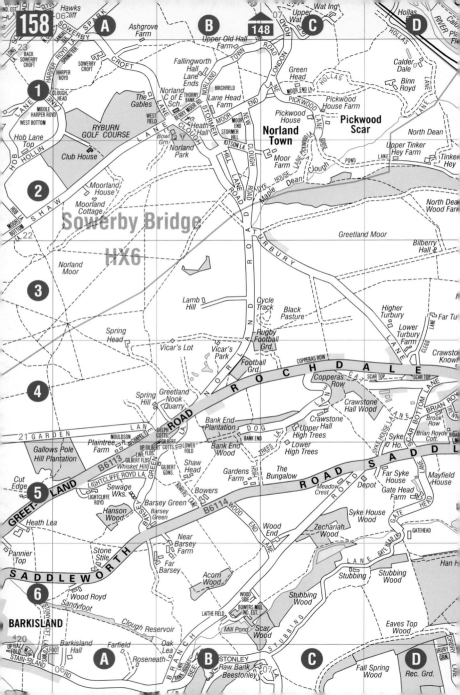

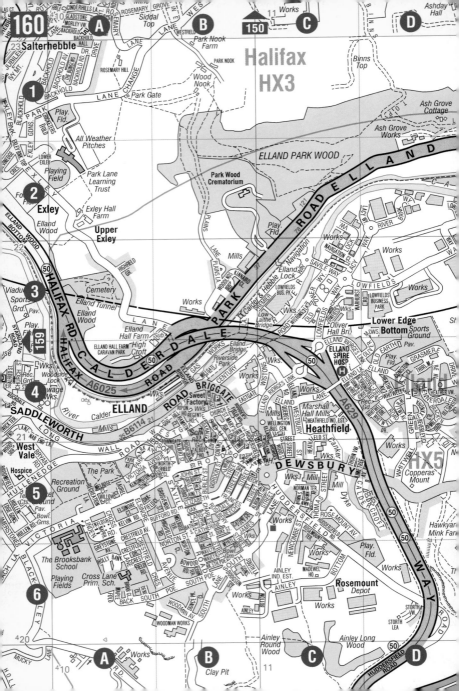

Halifax HX3

23 Salterhebble

A **B** **150** **C** **D**

1

2 Exley

3

159

4

SADDLEWORTH

West Vale

Hospice

5

6

A **B** Clay Pit **C** **D**

ELLAND PARK WOOD

Park Wood Crematorium

Upper Exley

Exley Hall Farm

Elland Wood

Cemetery

Elland Tunnel

Elland Wood

Elland Hall Farm

ELLAND

River Calder

B6114

Lower Edge Bottom

ELLAND SPIRE HOSP.

Heathfield

DEWSBURY

HX5

Copperas Mount

Rosemount Depot

HUDDERSFIELD ROAD

Ainley Round Wood

Ainley Long Wood

The Brooksbank School

Cross Lane Prim. Sch.

Playing Fields

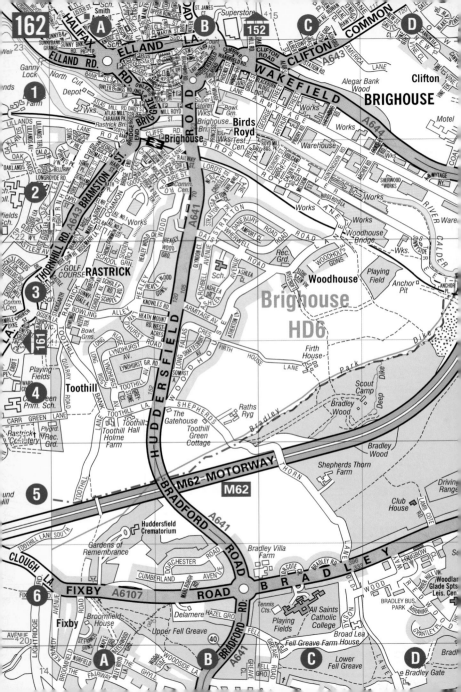

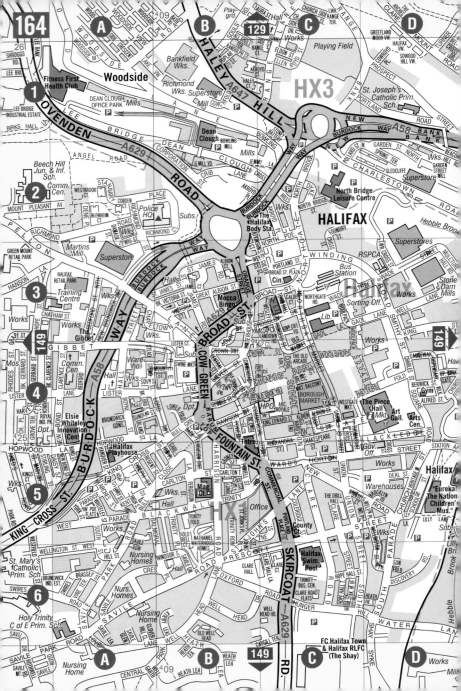

INDEX

Including Streets, Places & Areas, Industrial Estates,
Selected Flats & Walkways, Service Areas, Stations and Selected Places of Interest.

HOW TO USE THIS INDEX

1. Each street name is followed by its Postcode District, then by its Locality abbreviation(s) and then by its map reference;
   e.g. **Aachen Way** HX1: Hal . . . 4D **148** is in the HX1 Postcode District and the Halifax Locality and is to be found in
   square 4D on page **148**. The page number is shown in bold type.

2. A strict alphabetical order is followed in which Av., Rd., St., etc. (though abbreviated) are read in full and as part of the street name;
   e.g. **Ash Fold** appears after **Ashfield Way** but before **Ashford Dr.**

3. Streets and a selection of flats and walkways that cannot be shown on the mapping, appear in the index with the thoroughfare to
   which they are connected shown in brackets; e.g. **Abbeyfield Gro. Ho.** LS2: I'ly . . . .6D **10** (off Riddings Rd.)

4. Addresses that are in more than one part are referred to as not continuous.

5. Places and areas are shown in the index in BLUE TYPE and the map reference is to the actual map square in which the town centre or
   area is located and not to the place name shown on the map; e.g. **ADDINGHAM** 1D 8

6. An example of a selected place of interest is **Abbey House Mus.** 4H 75

7. An example of a station (Rail) . . . .4E 53, also included is **Park & Ride**.
   e.g. **King Lane (Park & Ride)** 4H 59

8. Service Areas are shown in the index in BOLD CAPITAL TYPE; e.g. **HARTSHEAD MOOR SERVICE AREA** 4G 153

9. Map references for entries that appear on large scale pages **4-7** & **164** are shown first, with small scale map references
   shown in brackets; e.g. **Barkerend Rd.** BD1: B'frd 3F **7** (4F **91**)

GENERAL ABBREVIATIONS

All. : Alley	**E.** : East	**Mt.** : Mount
App. : Approach	**Ent.** : Enterprise	**Mus.** : Museum
Arc. : Arcade	**Est.** : Estate	**Nth.** : North
Av. : Avenue	**Fld.** : Field	**No.** : Number
Bk. : Back	**Flds.** : Fields	**Pde.** : Parade
Blvd. : Boulevard	**Gdn.** : Garden	**Pk.** : Park
Bri. : Bridge	**Gdns.** : Gardens	**Pas.** : Passage
B'way. : Broadway	**Gth.** : Garth	**Pl.** : Place
Bldg. : Building	**Ga.** : Gate	**Prom.** : Promenade
Bldgs. : Buildings	**Gt.** : Great	**Res.** : Residential
Bungs. : Bungalows	**Grn.** : Green	**Ri.** : Rise
Bus. : Business	**Gro.** : Grove	**Rd.** : Road
C'way. : Causeway	**Hgts.** : Heights	**Shop.** : Shopping
Cen. : Centre	**Ho.** : House	**Sth.** : South
Chu. : Church	**Ho's.** : Houses	**Sq.** : Square
Circ. : Circle	**Ind.** : Industrial	**St.** : Street
Cir. : Circus	**Info.** : Information	**Ter.** : Terrace
Cl. : Close	**Junc.** : Junction	**Twr.** : Tower
Coll. : College	**La.** : Lane	**Trad.** : Trading
Comn. : Common	**Lit.** : Little	**Up.** : Upper
Cnr. : Corner	**Lwr.** : Lower	**Va.** : Vale
Cott. : Cottage	**Mnr.** : Manor	**Vw.** : View
Cotts. : Cottages	**Mans.** : Mansions	**Vs.** : Villas
Ct. : Court	**Mkt.** : Market	**Vis.** : Visitors
Cres. : Crescent	**Mdw.** : Meadow	**Wlk.** : Walk
Cft. : Croft	**Mdws.** : Meadows	**W.** : West
Dr. : Drive	**M.** : Mews	**Yd.** : Yard

LOCALITY ABBREVIATIONS

Aber : **Aberford**	B'ham : **Bramham**	Crag V : **Cragg Vale**
Add : **Addingham**	B'hpe : **Bramhope**	Cros R : **Cross Roads**
All : **Allerton**	Brigh : **Brighouse**	Cull : **Cullingworth**
All B : **Allerton Bywater**	Burl W : **Burley in Wharfedale**	Denh : **Denholme**
Arth : **Arthington**	Cal : **Calverley**	Den : **Denton**
Bail : **Baildon**	Carl : **Carlton**	Dew : **Dewsbury**
B Bri : **Bailiff Bridge**	Carr G : **Carr Gate**	Drig : **Drighlington**
Bard : **Bardsey**	C'frd : **Castleford**	E Ard : **East Ardsley**
Bark : **Barkisland**	Cast : **Castley**	E Bier : **East Bierley**
Bar E : **Barwick in Elmet**	Chur : **Churwell**	E Car : **East Carlton**
Bat : **Batley**	Clay : **Clayton**	E Kes : **East Keswick**
Bgly : **Bingley**	Cleck : **Cleckheaton**	E Mor : **East Morton**
Birk : **Birkenshaw**	Cliff : **Clifford**	East : **Eastburn**
Birs : **Birstall**	Clift : **Clifton**	Ell : **Elland**
B Spa : **Boston Spa**	Coll : **Collingham**	Esh : **Esholt**
B'frd : **Bradford**	Comp : **Compton**	F'ley : **Farnley**
Brad : **Bradshaw**	Cot : **Cottingley**	Fars : **Farsley**

Fix : **Fixby**
Gar : **Garforth**
Gil : **Gildersome**
Gom : **Gomersal**
Gt P : **Great Preston**
Gree : **Greetland**
Guis : **Guiseley**
Hal : **Halifax**
Har : **Harden**
Hare : **Harewood**
Hawk : **Hawksworth**
Haw : **Haworth**
Hip : **Hipperholme**
Holy : **Holywell Green**
H'fth : **Horsforth**
Hud : **Huddersfield**
Hun : **Hunsworth**
I'ly : **Ilkley**
Illing : **Illingworth**
Kear : **Kearby**
Keigh : **Keighley**
Kild : **Kildwick**
Kip : **Kippax**
K Dei : **Kirk Deighton**
Kirk : **Kirkhamgate**
Lay : **Laycock**
Leat : **Leathley**
Led : **Ledsham**
Leds : **Ledston**
Leeds : **Leeds**
Lin : **Linton**
Liv : **Liversedge**
Loft : **Lofthouse**
Low M : **Low Moor**
Lud : **Luddenden**
Lud M : **Luddenden Foot**

Men : **Menston**
Meth : **Methley**
M'fld : **Micklefield**
Midd : **Middleton**
Midg : **Midgley**
Mir : **Mirfield**
Mix : **Mixenden**
Morl : **Morley**
Mt T : **Mount Tabor**
Myth : **Mytholmroyd**
Nes : **Nesfield**
N Far : **New Farnley**
N Kym : **Newton Kyme**
Norl : **Norland**
North : **Northowram**
Nor G : **Norwood Green**
O'haw : **Oakenshaw**
Oak : **Oakworth**
Ogd : **Ogden**
Otley : **Otley**
Oul : **Oulton**
Out : **Outwood**
Oxen : **Oxenhope**
Pool : **Pool**
Pott : **Potterton**
Pud : **Pudsey**
Que : **Queensbury**
Ras : **Rastrick**
Raw : **Rawdon**
Rid : **Riddlesden**
Rob H : **Robin Hood**
Rothw : **Rothwell**
S'cft : **Scarcroft**
Scho : **Scholes**
Shad : **Shadwell**
She : **Shelf**

Ship : **Shipley**
Sick : **Sicklinghall**
Sils : **Silsden**
S Mil : **South Milford**
Sou : **Southowram**
Sow B : **Sowerby Bridge**
Stainl : **Stainland**
S'bury : **Stanbury**
S'ley : **Stanley**
Stan : **Stanningley**
Stee : **Steeton**
Swil : **Swillington**
Swil C : **Swillington Common**
Tad : **Tadcaster**
T'ner : **Thorner**
Thorn : **Thornton**
T Arch : **Thorpe Arch**
Thpe H : **Thorpe on the Hill**
Ting : **Tingley**
Tri : **Triangle**
Wads : **Wadsworth**
Wain : **Wainstalls**
Wake : **Wakefield**
W'ton : **Walton**
W Ard : **West Ardsley**
W Mor : **West Morton**
Weston : **Weston**
Weth : **Wetherby**
Wike : **Wike**
Wils : **Wilsden**
Wood : **Woodlesford**
Wren : **Wrenthorpe**
Wyke : **Wyke**
Yead : **Yeadon**

1st Bowl
Leeds 2E 5 (2A 98)
5 Rise Shop. Cen. BD16: Bgly 4B 50
1853 Art Gallery, The 6A 52

A

Aachen Way HX1: Hal 4D 148
Abaseen Cl. BD3: B'frd 4H 91
Abbey Av. LS5: Leeds 6H 75
Abbey Cl. LS29: Add 1E 9
    WF3: E Ard 6B 140
Abbey Ct. BD8: B'frd 2A 6
    LS18: H'fth 3D 74
Abbeydale Dr. BD8: B'frd 3F 89
Abbeydale Gdns. LS5: Leeds 3G 75
Abbeydale Gth. LS5: Leeds 3G 75
Abbeydale Gro. LS5: Leeds 3G 75
Abbeydale Mt. LS5: Leeds 3G 75
Abbeydale Oval LS5: Leeds 3G 75
Abbeydale Va. LS5: Leeds 3G 75
Abbeydale Way LS5: Leeds 3G 75
Abbeyfield Gro. Ho. LS29: I'ly 6D 10
    (off Riddings Rd.)
Abbey Gth. LS19: Yead 1F 55
    (off Well Hill)
Abbey Gorse LS5: Leeds 4A 76
Abbey House Mus. 4H 75
Abbey La. HX2: Hal 2F 147
Abbey Lea BD15: All 3E 89
Abbey Light Railway 5A 76
Abbey Mt. LS5: Leeds 6H 75
Abbey Rd. LS5: Leeds 3F 75
Abbey St. LS3: Leeds 3F 97
Abbey Ter. LS5: Leeds 6H 75
Abbey Vw. LS5: Leeds 4A 76
Abbey Wlk. HX3: Hal 5G 149
    LS5: Leeds 4H 75
Abbey Wlk. Sth. HX3: Hal 5H 149
Abbotside Ho. BD10: B'frd 3A 72

Abbots M. LS4: Leeds 1D 96
Abbots Pl. HD2: Hud 6F 163
Abbotsway LS25: Gar 5D 102
Abbots Wood BD9: B'frd 6A 70
    (off Firth Rd.)
Abbott Ct. LS12: Leeds 3D 96
Abbott Rd. LS12: Leeds 4D 96
Abbott's Ladies Home
    HX3: Hal 6G 149
Abbott's Ter. HX1: Hal 2E 149
    (off Leafland St.)
Abbott Vw. LS12: Leeds 3D 96
Abb Scott La. BD6: B'frd 1B 132
    BD12: Low M 1B 132
Abelia Mt. BD7: B'frd 5G 89
Abel St. BD12: Wyke 3C 132
Aberdeen BD22: Oxen 2B 84
Aberdeen Dr. LS12: Leeds 4A 96
Aberdeen Gro. LS12: Leeds 4A 96
Aberdeen Pl. BD7: B'frd 6A 90
Aberdeen Rd. LS12: Leeds 4A 96
    BD14: Clay 1F 109
Aberdeen Ter. BD7: B'frd 5A 90
Aberdeen Wlk. LS12: Leeds 4A 96
Aberfield Bank
    LS10: Leeds 1C 140
Aberfield Cl. LS10: Leeds 6C 118
Aberfield Crest LS10: Leeds 1C 140
Aberfield Dr. LS10: Leeds 1C 140
Aberfield Gdns.
    LS10: Leeds 6C 118
Aberfield Ga. LS10: Leeds 6C 118
Aberfield Mt. LS10: Leeds 1C 140
Aberfield Ri. LS10: Leeds 1C 140
Aberfield Ter. LS10: Leeds 6C 118
Aberfield Wlk.
    LS10: Leeds 1B 140
Aberford Rd. BD8: B'frd 2B 90
    LS15: Bar E 2E 83
    LS25: Aber, Gar 3F 103
    LS26: Oul, Wood 2E 143
Abingdon St. BD8: B'frd 2B 90
Abinger Cl. BD10: B'frd 3A 72
Abraham Hill LS26: Rothw 2B 142
Abram St. BD5: B'frd 1E 111

Acacia Dr. BD15: All 5B 68
    HX3: Hip 2A 152
Acacia Pk. Cres. BD10: B'frd 5D 54
Acacia Pk. Dr. BD10: B'frd 5D 54
Acacia Pk. Ter. BD10: B'frd 5E 55
Acaster Dr. BD12: Low M 1C 132
    LS25: Gar 5G 103
Accent Bus. Cen.
    BD1: B'frd 3G 7 (4G 91)
Accommodation Rd. LS9: Leeds 2C 98
Acer Cl. BD20: East 6A 14
Acer Way BD19: Scho 1F 153
Ackroyd Dr. BD13: Thorn 5H 87
Ackroyd Pl. BD13: Que 4H 107
Ackroyd Sq. BD13: Que 4D 108
    (off Highgate Rd.)
Ackroyd St. LS27: Morl 3B 138
Ackworth Av. LS19: Yead 1G 55
Ackworth Cres. LS19: Yead 1G 55
Ackworth Dr. LS19: Yead 1G 55
Ackworth St. BD5: B'frd 1E 111
Acomb Ter. BD12: Wyke 4C 132
Acorn Bus. Pk. LS14: Leeds 2A 100
Acorn Cl. BD6: B'frd 1G 131
Acorn Ct. LS14: Leeds 1E 81
Acorn Pk. BD17: Bail 5E 53
Acorn Pk. Ind. Est. BD17: Bail 5E 53
Acorn St. BD3: B'frd 5H 7 (5G 91)
    BD21: Keigh 2H 47
    HX1: Hal 2E 149
Acorn Way LS21: Pool 5F 25
Acre, The BD12: Wyke 2B 132
Acre Av. BD2: B'frd 4H 71
Acre Cir. LS10: Leeds 3A 140
Acre Cl. BD2: B'frd 4H 71
    LS10: Leeds 4H 139
Acre Ct. BD6: B'frd 4C 110
    LS10: Leeds 3A 140
Acre Cres. BD2: B'frd 4H 71
    LS10: Leeds 3A 140
Acre Dr. BD2: B'frd 4H 71
Acre Fold LS29: Add 1C 8
Acre Gro. BD2: B'frd 4H 71
    LS10: Leeds 3A 140
Acrehowe Ri. BD17: Bail 3E 53

Acre La. BD2: B'frd 5H **71**
(not continuous)
BD6: B'frd 4C **110**
BD16: Bgly 5A **36**
BD22: Haw 2C **64**
HX2: Midg 4C **126**
Acre Mt. LS10: Leeds 3A **140**
Acre Pl. *BD6: B'frd* *4C 110*
(off Acre La.)
LS10: Leeds 3A **140**
Acre Ri. BD17: Bail 3C **52**
Acre Rd. LS10: Leeds 3H **139**
Acres, The *LS17: Leeds* *2F 59*
(off The Avenue)
Acres Hall Av. LS28: Pud 5C **94**
Acres Hall Cres. LS28: Pud 5C **94**
Acres Hall Dr. LS28: Pud 5C **94**
Acre Sq. LS10: Leeds 3A **140**
Acres Rd. WF3: Loft 1G **157**
Acre St. BD21: Keigh 1H **47**
Acre St. LS10: Leeds 3B **140**
Acre Ter. LS10: Leeds 3B **140**
Acrewood Cl. LS17: Leeds 4E **61**
Acton Av. BD1: B'frd 4F **7**
Acton St. BD3: B'frd 4A **92**
Ada Glassby Ct. LS15: Leeds 2F **101**
Adam Cft. BD13: Cull 3B **66**
Adams Ct. HD6: Brigh 4G **151**
Adams Gro. LS15: Leeds 5G **81**
Adam St. BD6: B'frd 4B **110**
Adam's Wlk. LS6: Leeds 1F **97**
Ada's Pl. LS28: Stan 1A **94**
Ada St. BD3: Que 4H **107**
BD17: Bail 5E **53**
BD18: Ship 1H **69**
BD21: Keigh 6G **33**
HX3: Hal 6G **129**
Addenbrook Cl. BD10: B'frd 3A **72**
Addersgate La. HX3: North 3A **130**
ADDINGHAM 1D **8**
Addingham Gdns. LS12: Leeds 4A **96**
ADDINGHAM MOORSIDE 5D **8**
Addingham Wharfedale Rd.
LS29: Add 1A **8**
Addison Av. BD3: B'frd 2B **92**
Addison Ct. LS15: Leeds 5F **101**
Addison Dr. BD22: Haw 3C **64**
Addi St. BD4: B'frd 2A **112**
ADEL 4D **58**
Adelaide Ho. BD16: Bgly 5D **50**
Adelaide Ri. BD17: Bail 6C **52**
Adelaide St.
BD5: B'frd 6D **6** (6E **91**)
HX1: Hal 2D **148**
ADEL EAST MOOR 4E **59**
Adel Gth. LS16: Leeds 2D **58**
Adel Grange Cl. LS16: Leeds 5C **58**
Adel Grange Cft. LS16: Leeds 5C **58**
Adel Grange M. LS16: Leeds 5C **58**
(not continuous)
Adel Grn. LS16: Leeds 3D **58**
Adel La. LS16: Leeds 3C **58**
Adel Mead LS16: Leeds 3D **58**
ADEL MILL 1D **58**
Adel Mill LS16: Leeds 1C **58**
Adel Pk. Cl. LS16: Leeds 4C **58**
Adel Pk. Ct. LS16: Leeds 4C **58**
Adel Pk. Cft. LS16: Leeds 4C **58**
Adel Pk. Dr. LS16: Leeds 4C **58**
Adel Pk. Gdns. LS16: Leeds 4C **58**
Adel Pasture LS16: Leeds 4C **58**
Adel Towers Cl. LS16: Leeds 4D **58**
Adel Towers Ct. LS16: Leeds 4D **58**
Adel Vale LS16: Leeds 3D **58**
Adel Wood Cl. LS16: Leeds 4D **58**
Adel Wood Dr. LS16: Leeds 4D **58**
Adel Wood Gdns. LS16: Leeds 4D **58**
Adel Wood Gro. LS16: Leeds 4D **58**
Adel Wood Pl. LS16: Leeds 4D **58**
Adel Wood Rd. LS16: Leeds 4D **58**
Adgil Cres. HX3: Sou 5C **150**

Adgil Gro. HX3: Sou 5D **150**
Admiral St. LS11: Leeds 1A **118**
Admirals Yd. LS10: Leeds 1D **118**
Admiral Way BD21: Keigh 5A **34**
ADWALTON 1C **136**
Adwalton Bus. Pk.
BD11: Drig 2C **136**
Adwalton Cl. BD11: Drig 2H **135**
Adwalton Grn. BD11: Drig 2H **135**
Adwalton Gro. BD13: Que 4B **108**
Adwalton Moor Bus. Pk.
BD11: Birk 6F **113**
Adwick Pl. LS4: Leeds 1C **96**
Aerial Vw. LS25: M'fld 6D **104**
Agar St. BD8: B'frd 3H **89**
(not continuous)
Agar Ter. BD8: B'frd 3H **89**
Agincourt Dr. BD16: Bgly 4D **50**
Agnes St. BD20: Keigh 4A **34**
Ahlux Ct. LS2: Leeds 2H **5** (2B **98**)
Ahlux Ho. LS2: Leeds 2H **5** (2B **98**)
Ailsa Ho. *BD10: B'frd* *2A 72*
(off Fairhaven Grn.)
Ails La. HX2: Lud 6D **126**
Ainley Bottom HX5: Ell 6B **160**
Ainley Ind. Est. HX5: Ell 6C **160**
Ainley St. HX5: Ell 5B **160**
Ainsbury Av. BD10: B'frd 5H **53**
Ainsdale Gro. BD13: Cull 3C **66**
Ainsley Ct. LS14: Leeds 4G **81**
Ainsley M. LS14: Leeds 4G **81**
Ainsley Vw. LS14: Leeds 4G **81**
Ainsty Cres. LS22: Weth 2E **13**
Ainsty Dr. LS22: Weth 2E **13**
Ainsty Gth. LS22: Weth 2E **13**
Ainsty Rd. LS22: Weth 2D **12**
Ainsty Vw. LS22: Weth 2E **13**
Aintree Cl. LS25: Kip 3F **123**
Aintree Ct. LS10: Leeds 1C **118**
Airdale Ter. *LS13: Leeds* *4B 74*
(off Airedale Cft.)
Airebank BD16: Bgly 4B **50**
Aireborough Leisure Cen. 5C **40**
Aireburn Av. BD20: Stee 6D **14**
Aire Cl. BD17: Bail 6B **52**
Aire Ct. *BD20: Sils* *3E 15*
(off Calder Way)
LS10: Leeds 3A **140**
Airedale Av. BD16: Cot 2C **68**
Airedale Cliff LS13: Leeds 4E **75**
Airedale Coll. Mt. *BD3: B'frd* *2G 91*
(off Airedale Coll. Rd.)
Airedale Coll. Rd. BD3: B'frd 2G **91**
Airedale Coll. Ter.
BD3: B'frd 2G **91**
Airedale Ct. LS14: Leeds 4B **80**
Airedale Cres. BD3: B'frd 2G **91**
Airedale Cft. LS13: Leeds 4B **74**
Airedale Dr. HX3: She 2D **130**
LS18: H'fth 1B **74**
LS25: Gar 5H **103**
Airedale Gdns. LS13: Leeds 5B **74**
Airedale Gro. LS18: H'fth 1B **74**
LS26: Wood 1F **143**
Airedale Ho. LS11: Leeds 5D **74**
Airedale M. BD20: Sils 2E **15**
Airedale Mills BD16: Bgly 1A **50**
Airedale Mt. BD20: Rid 5G **35**
LS13: Leeds 4A **74**
Airedale Pl. BD17: Bail 5E **53**
Airedale Quay LS13: Leeds 5C **74**
Airedale Rd. BD3: B'frd 2F **91**
BD21: Keigh 5D **34**
LS26: Wood 1F **143**
Airedale Shop. Cen.
BD21: Keigh 6A **34**
Airedale St. BD2: B'frd 6H **71**
BD16: Bgly 4B **50**
BD21: Keigh 5C **34**
Airedale Ter. BD17: Bail 5D **52**
LS26: Wood 1F **143**
LS27: Morl *3B 138*
(off Gillroyd Pde.)

Airedale Vw. *LS13: Leeds* *4B 74*
(off Town St.)
LS19: Raw 4H **55**
LS26: Wood 1F **143**
Aire Gro. LS19: Yead 1G **55**
Aire Mt. LS22: Weth 2D **12**
Aire Pl. LS3: Leeds 2E **97**
Aire Quay LS10: Leeds 6D **98**
Aire Rd. LS22: Weth 1D **12**
Aireside Rd. BD17: Ship 6D **52**
Aire St. BD10: B'frd 6G **53**
BD16: Bgly 1A **50**
BD21: Keigh 5B **34**
BD22: Haw 2D **64**
HD6: Ras 2B **162**
LS1: Leeds 5C **4** (4H **97**)
Aire Valley Bus. Cen.
BD21: Keigh 5A **34**
Aire Valley Ct. BD16: Bgly 5B **50**
Aire Valley Marina LS4: Leeds 2B **96**
Aire Valley Pk. BD16: Bgly 6D **50**
Aire Valley Rd. BD16: Bgly 1H **49**
BD21: Keigh 5C **34**
LS9: Leeds 6D **98**
Aire Vw. Av. BD16: Cot 1D **68**
Aireview Cres. BD17: Bail 6A **52**
Aire Vw. Dr. BD20: Rid 6G **35**
Aire Vw. Gdns. LS5: Leeds 3H **75**
Aire Vw. Nth. BD18: Ship 1A **70**
Aire Vw. Ter. LS13: Leeds 5C **74**
Aireview Ter. BD21: Keigh 1C **48**
Aireville Av. BD9: B'frd 4A **70**
BD18: Ship 4B **70**
Aireville Cl. BD18: Ship 4B **70**
BD20: Keigh 3G **33**
Aireville Cres. BD9: B'frd 5B **70**
BD20: Sils 2F **15**
Aireville Dr. BD18: Ship 4B **70**
BD20: Sils 2F **15**
Aireville Grange BD18: Ship 4B **70**
Aireville Gro. BD18: Ship 4B **70**
BD20: Sils 2F **15**
Aireville Ri. BD9: B'frd 4B **70**
Aireville Rd. BD9: B'frd 4B **70**
Aireville St. BD20: Keigh 3G **33**
Aireville Ter. LS29: Burl W 2E **21**
Aire Way BD17: Bail 6A **52**
AIREWORTH 5C **34**
Aireworth Cl. BD21: Keigh 4C **34**
Aireworth Gro. BD21: Keigh 5C **34**
Aireworth Rd. BD21: Keigh 4C **34**
Aireworth St. BD21: Keigh 1H **47**
Airey St. BD21: Keigh 6G **33**
Airlie Av. LS8: Leeds 5D **78**
Airlie Pl. LS8: Leeds 5D **78**
Airport West LS19: Yead 4A **42**
Aislaby Hgts. HX2: Hal 6B **128**
Akam Rd. BD1: B'frd 3A **6** (4D **90**)
Aked's Rd. HX1: Hal 5A **164** (3F **149**)
Aked St. BD1: B'frd 4F **7** (4F **91**)
Akroyd Ct. HX3: Hal 1B **164**
AKROYDON 6G **129**
Akroyd Pl. HX1: Hal 2B **164** (1G **149**)
(not continuous)
Akroyd Ter. HX2: Hal 4D **148**
Alabama St. HX1: Hal 2D **148**
Alanby Dr. BD10: B'frd 2A **72**
Alan Ct. BD13: Thorn 5H **87**
Alan Cres. LS15: Leeds 4C **100**
Alandale Cres. LS25: Gar 5D **102**
Alandale Dr. LS25: Gar 5D **102**
Alandale Gro. LS25: Gar 5D **102**
Alandale Rd. HD2: Hud 5E **163**
LS25: Gar 5D **102**
Alaska Pl. LS7: Leeds 3C **78**
Albans Cl. LS17: Bard 6G **27**
Alban St. BD4: B'frd 1H **111**
Albany Ct. BD20: Keigh 5G **33**

Albany Rd. LS26: Rothw 1H **141**
Albany St. BD5: B'frd 1E **111**
  BD6: B'frd 4C **110**
  HX3: Hal 4H **149**
  LS12: Leeds 4A **96**
Albany Ter. HX3: Hal 4H **149**
  LS12: Leeds 4A **96**
Albany Vw. HX4: Holy 6F **159**
        (off Stainland Rd.)
Albany Wlk. LS29: I'ly 6D **10**
Alberta Av. LS7: Leeds 3C **78**
Albert Av. BD10: B'frd 1A **72**
  BD18: Ship 6G **51**
  HX2: Hal 1C **148**
Albert Bldgs. BD10: B'frd 3H **71**
  HX6: Sow B 5A **148**
        (off Albert Rd.)
Albert Ct. HX2: Hal 1C **148**
Albert Cres. BD11: Birk 3F **135**
  BD13: Que 4A **108**
Albert Dr. HX2: Hal 1B **148**
  LS27: Morl 2D **138**
Albert Edward St. BD13: Que ...4A **108**
Albert Gdns. HX2: Hal 1C **148**
Albert Gro. LS6: Leeds 3D **76**
Albert Mt. LS18: H'fth 1F **75**
        (off Broadgate La.)
Albert Pl. BD3: B'frd 3C **92**
  LS18: H'fth 6E **57**
  LS26: Meth 4B **144**
Albert Prom. HX3: Hal 5E **149**
Albert Rd. BD13: Que 3H **107**
  BD18: Ship 1H **69**
  HX2: Hal 1B **148**
  HX6: Sow B 4A **148**
  LS26: Oul 1E **143**
  LS27: Morl 2B **138**
Albert Simmons Way
  LS29: Burl W 2E **21**
Albert Sq. BD20: Sils 2E **15**
  LS19: Yead 6G **41**
Albert St. BD6: B'frd 5B **110**
  BD10: B'frd 3H **71**
  BD12: Wyke 5C **132**
  BD13: Que 4B **108**
  BD13: Thorn 5H **87**
  BD13: Wils 5G **67**
  BD17: Bail 6C **52**
  BD21: Keigh 6H **33**
  BD22: Cros R 1F **65**
        (off Bingley Rd.)
  HD6: Clift 1C **162**
  HX1: Hal 2F **149**
  HX5: Ell 5B **160**
  LS28: Pud 5H **93**
Albert Ter. BD12: O'haw 2F **133**
  BD12: Wyke 5D **132**
  BD18: Ship 6H **51**
  LS19: Yead 6G **41**
        (off Rockfield Ter.)
Albert Vw. HX2: Hal 1C **148**
Albert Wlk. BD18: Ship 1G **69**
Albert Way BD11: Birk 3F **135**
Albert Yd. BD21: Keigh 1A **48**
        (off Church St.)
Albion Av. LS12: Leeds 4D **96**
Albion Cl. LS23: Cliff 6B **30**
Albion Ct. BD1: B'frd 4D **6** (4E **91**)
  HX1: Hal 3B **164**
Albion Fold BD15: Wils 4G **67**
Albion Pk. LS12: Leeds 3E **97**
Albion Pl. BD13: Thorn 5G **87**
  HD6: Brigh 6A **152**
        (off Waterloo Rd.)
  LS1: Leeds 4E **5** (3A **98**)
  LS20: Guis 4C **40**
Albion Rd. BD10: B'frd 1H **71**
  LS28: Stan 1A **94**
Albion St. BD1: B'frd 4C **6** (4E **91**)
  BD6: B'frd 6G **109**
  BD13: Denh 3B **86**
  BD13: Que 4H **107**
  BD22: Cros R 1E **65**

Albion St. HD6: Brigh 6A **152**
  HX1: Hal 4C **164** (2G **149**)
        (not continuous)
  HX5: Ell 5C **160**
  LS1: Leeds 4E **5** (3A **98**)
        (not continuous)
  LS2: Leeds 4E **5** (3A **98**)
  LS21: Otley 4F **23**
  LS23: Cliff 6B **30**
  LS27: Morl 3A **138**
        (Corporation St.)
  LS27: Morl 3A **138**
        (Windsor Ct.)
  WF3: Carl 4H **141**
Albion Ter. LS23: Cliff 6B **30**
Albion Way LS12: Leeds 3E **97**
Albion Yd. BD1: B'frd 4D **6** (4E **91**)
Alcester Gth.
  BD3: B'frd 2H **7** (3H **91**)
Alcester Pl. LS8: Leeds 5D **78**
Alcester Rd. LS8: Leeds 5D **78**
Alcester Ter. LS8: Leeds 5D **78**
Alden Av. LS27: Morl 5A **138**
Alden Cl. LS27: Morl 5A **138**
Alden Ct. LS27: Morl 5A **138**
Alden Fold LS27: Morl 5A **138**
Alder Av. BD21: Keigh 2C **48**
Alder Carr BD17: Bail 4B **52**
Alder Dr. LS28: Pud 3E **93**
Alder Gth. LS28: Pud 3F **93**
Alder Gro. HX2: Illing 1C **128**
Alder Hill Av. LS6: Leeds 2G **77**
Alder Hill Cotts. LS6: Leeds 2F **77**
Alder Hill Gro. LS7: Leeds 2G **77**
Alderholt Dr. BD6: B'frd 1A **132**
Aldermanbury BD1: B'frd ..5C **6** (5E **91**)
Alderney Rd. WF12: Dew 6A **154**
Alders, The LS7: Leeds 2B **78**
Alderscholes Cl. BD13: Thorn 5H **87**
        (off Alderscholes La.)
Alderscholes La. BD13: Thorn 6F **87**
Aldersgate LS12: Leeds 4C **96**
        (off Wesley Rd.)
Alderson St. BD6: B'frd 6G **109**
Aldersyde WF17: Birs 6A **136**
Aldersyde Rd. LS20: Guis 5B **40**
Aldersyde Way LS20: Guis 5B **40**
Alderton Bank LS17: Leeds 5F **59**
Alderton Cres. LS17: Leeds 5F **59**
Alderton Hgts. LS17: Leeds 5F **59**
Alderton Mt. LS17: Leeds 5F **59**
Alderton Pl. LS17: Leeds 5F **59**
Alderton Ri. LS17: Leeds 5G **59**
Alegar St. HD6: Brigh 1C **162**
Alexander Av. LS15: Leeds 4B **100**
Alexander Ct. BD20: Rid 6H **35**
  LS1: Leeds 3D **4** (3H **97**)
Alexander Sq. BD14: Clay 1D **108**
Alexander St. BD6: B'frd 5B **110**
  LS1: Leeds 3D **4** (3H **97**)
Alexander Ter. HX1: Hal 2D **148**
Alexandra Av. WF17: Birs 6B **136**
Alexandra Cl. HX6: Sow B 5A **148**
Alexandra Cres. HX5: Ell 4D **160**
  LS29: I'ly 5C **10**
Alexandra Gro. LS6: Leeds 1E **97**
  LS28: Pud 5H **93**
Alexandra Mill LS27: Morl 4A **138**
Alexandra Pl. LS29: I'ly 5C **10**
        (off Alexandra Cres.)
Alexandra Rd. BD2: B'frd 4A **72**
  BD18: Ship 2A **70**
  LS6: Leeds 1E **97**
  LS18: H'fth 6E **57**
  LS28: Pud 5G **93**
Alexandra Sq. BD18: Ship 1H **69**
Alexandra St. BD7: B'frd 6C **90**
  BD13: Que 4H **107**
  HX1: Hal 5C **164** (2G **149**)
Alexandra Ter. BD2: B'frd 1A **92**
  LS19: Yead 6G **41**
        (not continuous)
Alford Ter. BD7: B'frd 4A **90**

Alfred St. HD6: Brigh 6B **152**
  HX1: Hal 2D **148**
  HX4: Gree 4H **159**
  LS27: Chur 5C **116**
Alfred St. E. HX1: Hal 4D **164** (2H **149**)
Alhambra Theatre & Studio
        ....5C **6** (5E **91**)
Alice Smart Cl. LS15: Leeds 2F **101**
Alice St. BD8: B'frd 1A **6** (3D **90**)
  BD19: Cleck 6B **134**
  BD21: Keigh 6A **34**
  BD22: Haw 3C **64**
Alkincote St. BD21: Keigh 1A **48**
All Alone BD10: B'frd 2G **71**
All Alone Rd. BD10: B'frd 2F **71**
Allanbridge Cl. BD10: B'frd 2A **72**
Allandale Av. BD6: B'frd 6A **110**
Allandale Rd. BD6: B'frd 6A **110**
Allenby Cres. LS11: Leeds 5G **117**
Allenby Dr. LS11: Leeds 5G **117**
Allenby Gdns. LS11: Leeds 5G **117**
Allenby Gro. LS11: Leeds 5G **117**
Allenby Pl. LS11: Leeds 5G **117**
Allenby Rd. LS11: Leeds 5G **117**
Allenby Vw. LS11: Leeds 4H **117**
Allen Cft. BD11: Birk 2E **135**
Allerby Grn. BD6: B'frd 6H **109**
ALLERTON 2D **88**
Allerton Av. LS17: Leeds 5B **60**
ALLERTON BYWATER 1F **145**
Allerton Cl. BD15: All 2D **88**
Allerton Ct. LS17: Leeds 4C **78**
        (off Allerton Gro.)
Allerton Cft. LS7: Leeds 4C **78**
        (off Harehills La.)
Allerton Dr. LS17: E Kes 4E **27**
Allerton Grange Av. LS17: Leeds ..6C **60**
Allerton Grange Cl. BD15: All 2D **88**
  LS17: Leeds 1A **78**
Allerton Grange Cres.
  LS17: Leeds 1B **78**
Allerton Grange Cft. LS8: Leeds ..1C **78**
Allerton Grange Dr. BD15: All 2D **88**
  LS17: Leeds 1B **78**
Allerton Grange Gdns.
  LS17: Leeds 1B **78**
Allerton Grange Ri. LS17: Leeds ..1A **78**
Allerton Grange Va. LS17: Leeds ..1B **78**
Allerton Grange Wlk. LS17: Leeds .1B **78**
Allerton Grange Way LS8: Leeds ..1B **78**
  LS17: Leeds 1B **78**
Allerton Gro. LS17: Leeds 5B **60**
Allerton Hall LS7: Leeds 2A **78**
Allerton Hill LS7: Leeds 2A **78**
Allerton La. BD13: Thorn 4C **88**
  BD15: All 4C **88**
Allerton M. LS17: Leeds 6B **60**
Allerton Pk. LS7: Leeds 2B **78**
Allerton Pl. HX1: Hal 2E **149**
  LS17: Leeds 5B **60**
Allerton Rd. BD8: B'frd 2E **89**
  BD15: All 2H **87**
        (Long La.)
  BD15: All 2D **88**
        (Meadowbank Av.)
Allerton St. LS4: Leeds 1D **96**
Allerton Ter. LS4: Leeds 1D **96**
Allerton Up. Grn. BD15: All 3A **88**
Alliance St. LS12: Leeds 4A **96**
Allinson St. LS12: Leeds 5E **97**
Allison La. BD2: B'frd 5D **70**
Alloe Fld. Pl. HX2: Illing 1C **128**
Alloe Fld. Vw. HX2: Illing 1C **128**
Allotments Rd. BD13: Denh 2C **86**
All Saints Av. LS9: Leeds 3D **98**
        (off Aysgarth Mt.)
All Saint's Circ. LS26: Wood 1F **143**
All Saints Cl. BD21: Keigh 6H **33**
  LS21: Otley 3E **23**
  LS29: I'ly 4D **10**

All Saint's Dr. LS26: Wood 1E 143
All Saints Hall BD5: B'frd 6C 90
All Saints St. BD7: B'frd 6B 90
  LS9: Leeds 3D 98
  LS26: Wood 6F 121
All Saints Ter. BD21: Keigh 6H 33
  LS9: Leeds *3D 98*
  (off Aysgarth Mt.)
All Saint's Vw. LS26: Wood 6E 121
All Souls' Rd.
  HX3: Hal 1B 164 (6G 129)
All Souls' St. HX3: Hal 6G 129
All Souls' Ter. HX3: Hal . .1B 164 (6G 129)
Alma Cl. LS28: Fars 6G 73
Alma Cotts. *BD13: Que* *5G 107*
  (off Moor Cft. La.)
  LS6: Leeds 4D 76
Alma Gro. BD18: Ship 1D 70
Alma Pl. BD3: B'frd 3B 92
  BD21: Keigh 2A 48
Alma Rd. LS6: Leeds 4D 76
Alma St. BD4: B'frd 6A 92
  (Buller St.)
  BD4: B'frd 1B 112
  (Inkerman St.)
  BD13: Que 4H 107
  BD18: Ship 1D 70
  BD21: Keigh 3A 48
  (not continuous)
  BD22: Haw 1C 64
  HX5: Ell *5C 160*
  (off South La.)
  LS9: Leeds 2D 98
  LS19: Yead 6G 41
  LS26: Wood 6E 121
Alma Ter. BD20: E Mor 4A 36
  BD21: Keigh 2A 48
  LS26: Rothw 1H 141
Alma Vs. LS26: Wood 6F 121
Almond Ct. HX3: North 3C 130
Almond St. BD3: B'frd 5A 92
Almond Way WF17: Bat 6B 136
Almscliffe Pl. BD2: B'frd 5B 72
Almscliffe Ter. LS21: Otley 4F 23
Alnwick Vw. LS16: Leeds 2C 76
Alpha St. BD21: Keigh 6B 34
Alpine Cl. HX2: Illing 6D 106
Alpine Ri. BD13: Thorn 4H 87
Alpine Ter. LS26: Rothw 1A 142
Alred Ct. BD4: B'frd 4H 111
Alston Cl. BD9: B'frd 2F 89
Alston La. LS14: Leeds 6C 80
Alston Retail Pk. BD21: Keigh 4B 34
Alston Rd. BD21: Keigh 4B 34
Altar Dr. BD9: B'frd 6A 70
  BD20: Rid 4E 35
Altar La. BD16: Bgly 3D 48
Altar Vw. BD20: Rid 3D 34
Altar Vs. BD21: Rid 4D 34
Althorpe Gro. BD10: B'frd 3G 71
Alton Cft. BD14: Clay 2C 108
Alton Gro. BD9: B'frd 6H 69
  BD18: Ship 4B 70
Alum Ct. BD9: B'frd 6A 70
Alum Dr. BD9: B'frd 6A 70
Alva Cl. LS20: Guis 3B 40
Alva Ct. LS20: Guis 3B 40
Alvanley Ct. BD8: B'frd 3F 89
Alva Ter. BD18: Ship 3F 89
ALWOODLEY 3A 60
Alwoodley Chase LS17: Leeds 2C 60
Alwoodley Ct. LS17: Leeds 2F 59
Alwoodley Ct. Gdns. LS17: Leeds . .1G 59
Alwoodley Gdns. LS17: Leeds 1G 59
ALWOODLEY GATES 1C 60
Alwoodley Gates LS17: Leeds 1C 60
Alwoodley Golf Course 1C 60
Alwoodley La. LS17: Leeds 1F 59
ALWOODLEY PARK 1G 59
Amberley Ct. *BD3: B'frd* *5A 92*
  (off Amberley St.)
Amberley Gdns. LS12: Leeds 5D 96
Amberley Rd. LS12: Leeds 5C 96

Amberley St. BD3: B'frd 4A 92
  (not continuous)
  LS12: Leeds 5C 96
Amberton App. LS8: Leeds 5G 79
Amberton Cl. LS8: Leeds 4G 79
Amberton Cres. LS8: Leeds 5G 79
Amberton Gdns. LS8: Leeds 5G 79
Amberton Gth. LS8: Leeds 5G 79
Amberton Gro. LS8: Leeds 5G 79
Amberton La. LS8: Leeds 5G 79
Amberton M. LS8: Leeds 6H 79
Amberton Mt. LS8: Leeds 5G 79
Amberton Pl. LS8: Leeds 5F 79
Amberton Rd. LS8: Leeds 5F 79
  LS9: Leeds 5F 79
Amberton St. LS8: Leeds 5G 79
Amberton Ter. LS8: Leeds 5G 79
Ambler Gro. HX2: Illing 1D 128
Amblers Bldgs. *LS28: Pud* *5A 94*
  (off Amblers Ct.)
Amblers Bungs. WF3: E Ard 1H 155
Amblers Ct. LS28: Pud 5A 94
Amblers Cft. BD10: B'frd 5H 53
Amblers M. BD17: Bail 3C 52
  BD20: E Mor 5H 35
Amblers Row BD17: Bail 3C 52
Amblers Ter. HX3: Hal 6G 129
Ambler St. BD8: B'frd 2C 90
  BD21: Keigh 6B 34
AMBLER THORN 6G 107
Amblerthorne BD11: Birk 2F 135
Ambler Way BD13: Que 6G 107
Ambleside Av. BD9: B'frd 1H 89
Ambleside Gdns. LS28: Pud 4G 93
Ambleside Gro. LS26: Wood 1E 143
Ambleside Wlk. LS22: Weth 3B 12
Amble Tonia BD17: Denh 2C 86
Ambleton Way BD13: Que 5G 107
Amelia Stewart La. LS15: Leeds 1F 101
Amelia St. BD18: Ship 6H 51
America La. HD6: Clift 1C 162
America Moor La. LS27: Morl 5A 138
Amisfield Rd. HX3: Hip 1F 151
Amos St. HX1: Hal 2D 148
Amport Cl. HD6: Ras 2B 162
Amspool Ct. WF3: Carl 4G 141
Amundsen Av. BD2: B'frd 4G 71
Amy Busfield Grn. LS29: Burl W 2E 21
Amyroyce Dr. BD18: Ship 2E 71
Amy St. BD16: Bgly 4C 50
  HX3: Hal 5E 129
Anaheim Dr. WF1: Out 4H 157
Ancaster Cres. LS16: Leeds 2B 76
Ancaster Rd. LS16: Leeds 2B 76
Ancaster Vw. LS16: Leeds 2B 76
Anchorage, The BD16: Bgly 3B 50
Anchor Ct. BD8: B'frd 2A 6
Anchor Pl. HD6: Brigh 3D 162
Anderson Av. LS8: Leeds 1C 98
Anderson Ho. *BD17: Bail* *6B 52*
  (off Fairview Ct.)
Anderson Mt. LS8: Leeds 1C 98
Anderson St. BD8: B'frd 2C 90
Anderton Fold HX3: North 5C 130
Andover Grn. BD4: B'frd 1C 112
Andrew Cl. HX3: Sou 5C 150
Andrew Cres. WF1: Out 4F 157
Andrew Ho. *LS28: Fars* *6H 73*
  (off Water La.)
Andrews Mnr. *LS19: Yead* *6F 41*
  (off Haworth La.)
Andrew Sq. LS28: Fars 6H 73
Andrew St. LS28: Fars 1H 93
Anerley St. BD4: B'frd 3H 111
Angel Cl. LS3: Leeds 2F 97
Angel Inn Yd. LS1: Leeds 4E 5
Angel Pl. BD16: Bgly 2C 50
Angel Rd. HX1: Hal 1H 149
  (Crossley Retail Pk.)
  HX1: Hal 2A 164 (1F 149)
  (Stannary Pl.)
Angel Row LS26: Rothw 2E 141
Angel St. BD17: Bail 3D 52

Angerton Way BD6: B'frd 1A 132
Angram Rd. BD20: Keigh 2G 33
Angus Av. BD12: Wyke 6C 132
Anlaby St. BD4: B'frd 6B 92
Annandale Ct. LS29: I'ly 6D 10
Annandale Vw. BD13: Que 3D 108
Anne Ga. BD1: B'frd 3F 7 (4F 91)
Anne's Ct. HX3: Sou 5C 150
Anne St. BD7: B'frd 2H 109
Annie St. BD18: Ship 3C 70
  BD21: Keigh 4A 34
  BD22: Cros R 1F 65
  HX6: Sow B 5H 147
  LS27: Morl 3B 138
  WF1: Out 5F 157
Anning Fold LS25: Gar 3H 103
Annison St. BD3: B'frd 4G 7 (4G 91)
Ann Pl. BD5: B'frd 6C 6 (6E 91)
Ann St. BD21: Keigh 1H 47
  BD22: Haw 2D 64
Another World (Mountainboarding Cen.)
  . . . . .2B 106
Anson Gro. BD7: B'frd 3H 109
Anstey Ho. LS3: Leeds 3A 4
Anstone Dr. BD5: B'frd 3C 110
Anthony La. BD16: Har 5F 49
Antler Complex LS27: Morl 3F 137
Anton Rd. LS29: Guis, Men 3A 40
Anvil Ct. *BD8: B'frd* *2B 90*
  (off Carlisle St.)
  BD13: Cull 4B 66
  HX2: Illing 2C 128
Anvil St. BD8: B'frd 2B 90
  (not continuous)
  HD6: Brigh 6A 152
Apex Bus. Cen. LS11: Leeds 6A 98
Apex Vw. LS11: Leeds 6H 97
Apex Way LS11: Leeds 6A 98
APPERLEY BRIDGE 1C 72
Apperley Gdns. BD10: B'frd 1C 72
Apperley La. BD10: B'frd, Yead 1C 72
  LS19: Raw, Yead 6D 54
Apperley Rd. BD10: B'frd 1A 72
  (not continuous)
Appleby Cl. BD13: Que 4G 107
Appleby La. LS25: Gar 4H 103
Appleby Pl. LS15: Leeds 3A 100
Appleby Wlk. LS15: Leeds 3A 100
Appleby Way LS22: Weth 2E 13
  LS27: Morl 2B 138
Apple Cl. WF17: Birs 5C 136
Applegarth BD14: Clay 2E 109
Applehaigh Cl. BD10: B'frd 2A 72
Apple Ho. Ter. HX2: Lud 6E 127
Appleshawn Cres. WF2: Wren 6D 156
Apple St. BD21: Keigh 4G 47
  BD22: Oxen 1C 84
Appleton Cl. BD12: O'haw 2F 133
  BD16: Bgly 2D 50
  LS9: Leeds 3D 98
Appleton Ct. *BD13: Thorn* *5H 87*
  (off John St.)
  LS9: Leeds 3D 98
Appleton Gro. LS9: Leeds 3F 99
Appleton Sq. LS9: Leeds 3D 98
Appleton Vs. LS9: Leeds 3D 98
Appleton Way LS9: Leeds 3D 98
Apple Tree Cl. WF3: E Ard 1A 156
Apple Tree Ct. WF3: E Ard 2A 156
Apple Tree Gdns. LS29: I'ly 5B 10
Apple Tree La. LS25: Kip 5H 123
Apple Tree M. LS25: Kip 4H 123
Apple Tree Wlk. LS25: Kip 4H 123
Appleyard Wing *HX1: Hal* *4F 149*
  (off Haworth Cl.)
Approach, The LS15: Scho 2H 81
April Gdns. BD13: Que 4A 108
Apricia Ct. BD14: Clay 6F 89
Apsley Cres. BD8: B'frd 2C 90
Apsley St. BD21: Keigh 2H 47
  BD22: Haw 2D 64
  BD22: Oak 4D 46

Apsley Ter. BD22: Oak 4D 46
(off Apsley St.)
Apsley Vs. BD8: B'frd 2D 90
Aragon Ct. LS7: Leeds 2G 77
Arbour, The LS29: I'ly 3C 10
Arcade, The LS29: I'ly 5D 10
(off Church St.)
Arcade Royale HX1: Hal 4C 164
Arcadia St. BD21: Keigh 2H 47
Archbell Av. HD6: Ras 3B 162
Archer Rd. HD6: Brigh 2D 162
Archery Pl. LS2: Leeds 1H 97
Archery Rd. LS2: Leeds 1H 97
Archery St. LS2: Leeds 1H 97
Archery Ter. LS2: Leeds 1H 97
Arches, The HX3: Hal 1D 164 (6G 129)
Arches St. HX1: Hal 5A 164 (3F 149)
Archibald St. BD7: B'frd 4C 90
Arctic Pde. BD7: B'frd 1A 110
Arctic St. BD20: Keigh 3H 33
BD22: Cros R 1E 65
Arden Ct. LS16: Leeds 5C 58
Arden Grange LS16: Leeds 5C 58
Arden Ho. HX1: Hal 4F 149
(off Arden Rd.)
Arden M. HX1: Hal 4F 149
Ardennes Cl. BD2: B'frd 5F 71
Arden Rd. BD8: B'frd 4E 89
HX1: Hal 3F 149
Ardsley Cl. BD4: B'frd 3D 112
(not continuous)
Ardsley Ct. WF3: E Ard 1C 156
Arena Pk. LS17: Leeds 6B 44
Argent Way BD4: B'frd 3D 112
Argie Av. LS4: Leeds 6B 76
Argie Gdns. LS4: Leeds 1C 96
Argie Rd. LS4: Leeds 1C 96
Argie Ter. LS4: Leeds 1C 96
Argyle M. LS17: E Kes 6E 27
Argyle Rd. LS9: Leeds 3H 5 (3B 98)
Argyle St. BD4: B'frd 2H 111
BD21: Keigh 6H 33
Argyll Cl. BD17: Bail 5E 53
LS18: H'fth 3D 56
Ariba Av. BD3: B'frd 2F 7 (3F 91)
Arkendale M. BD7: B'frd 2G 109
Arksey Pl. LS12: Leeds 3C 96
Arksey Ter. LS12: Leeds 3C 96
Arkwright Hall BD7: B'frd . . .4B 6 (4D 90)
Arkwright St. BD4: B'frd 5C 92
BD14: Clay 1D 108
Arkwright Wlk. LS27: Morl 1A 138
Arlesford Rd. BD4: B'frd 3C 112
Arley Gro. LS12: Leeds 3C 96
Arley Pl. LS12: Leeds 3C 96
Arley St. LS12: Leeds 3C 96
Arley Ter. LS12: Leeds 3C 96
Arlington Bus. Cen. LS11: Leeds 5D 116
Arlington Cres. HX2: Hal 4B 148
Arlington Gro. LS8: Leeds 4F 79
Arlington Rd. LS8: Leeds 5F 79
Armadale Av. BD4: B'frd 5H 111
Armgill La. BD2: B'frd 5D 70
Armidale Way BD2: B'frd 6F 71
Armitage, The BD20: E Mor 5F 35
Armitage Av. HD6: Ras 3B 162
Armitage Bldgs. WF12: Dew 3B 154
Armitage Ct. LS28: Pud 5H 93
(off Armitage Sq.)
Armitage Rd. BD12: O'haw 3F 133
HX1: Hal 4D 148
Armitage Sq. LS28: Pud 5H 93
Armitage St. LS26: Rothw 3A 142
ARMLEY 3D 96
Armley Ct. LS12: Leeds 3D 96
Armley Grange Av. LS12: Leeds 2H 95
Armley Grange Cres. LS12: Leeds . . .2H 95
Armley Grange Dr. LS12: Leeds 3H 95
Armley Grange Mt. LS12: Leeds 3H 95
Armley Grange Oval LS12: Leeds 2H 95
Armley Grange Ri. LS12: Leeds 3H 95
Armley Grange Vw. LS12: Leeds 3A 96
Armley Grange Wlk. LS12: Leeds 3A 96

Armley Gro. Pl. LS12: Leeds 4D 96
Armley Ho. LS14: Leeds 3A 80
(off Kingsdale Ct.)
Armley Leisure Cen. 4B 96
Armley Lodge Rd. LS12: Leeds 2C 96
Armley Mills Leeds Industrial Mus.
. . . . .2C 96
Armley Pk. Ct. LS12: Leeds 3C 96
(off Cecil Rd.)
Armley Pk. Rd. LS12: Leeds 2C 96
Armley Ridge Cl. LS12: Leeds 3A 96
Armley Ridge Rd. LS12: Leeds 6H 75
(not continuous)
Armley Ridge Ter. LS12: Leeds 2A 96
Armley Ridge Vw. LS12: Leeds 3C 96
(not continuous)
Armley Tennis Club 2A 96
Armouries Dr. LS10: Leeds 5B 98
Armouries Way
LS10: Leeds 6H 5 (4B 98)
Armstrong St. BD4: B'frd 5B 92
LS28: Fars 1H 93
Armytage Rd. HD6: Brigh 1C 162
Armytage Way HD6: Brigh 2D 162
Arncliffe Av. BD22: Keigh 1G 47
Arncliffe Cres. HD6: Ras 3G 161
LS27: Morl 5C 138
Arncliffe Gth. LS28: Stan 1H 93
Arncliffe Grange LS17: Leeds 5B 60
Arncliffe Gro. BD22: Keigh 2G 47
Arncliffe Path BD22: Keigh 1G 47
(off Arncliffe Av.)
Arncliffe Pl. BD22: Keigh 1G 47
(off Arncliffe Av.)
Arncliffe Rd. BD22: Keigh 2G 47
LS16: Leeds 1A 76
Arncliffe St. LS28: Stan 1H 93
Arncliffe Ter. BD7: B'frd 5B 90
Arndale Cen. LS6: Leeds 4D 76
Arndale Ho. BD1: B'frd 4D 6
Arndale Shop. Cen. BD18: Ship 2B 70
(off Market Sq.)
Arnford Cl. BD3: B'frd 1F 7 (3F 91)
Arnhem Cl. BD16: Bgly 4D 50
Arnold Pl. BD8: B'frd 3C 90
Arnold Royd HD6: Ras 4G 161
Arnold St. BD8: B'frd 2C 90
HX1: Hal 2E 149
HX6: Sow B 5H 147
Arnside Av. BD20: Rid 4C 34
Arnside Rd. BD5: B'frd 3E 111
Arran Cl. LS25: Gar 6F 103
Arran Dr. LS18: H'fth 3D 56
LS25: Gar 6F 103
Arran Way LS26: Rothw 2B 142
Arthington Av. LS10: Leeds 3B 118
Arthington Cl. WF3: W Ard 2D 154
Arthington Ct. LS10: Leeds 3B 118
Arthington Gth. LS21: Arth 5H 25
Arthington Gro. LS10: Leeds 3B 118
Arthington La. LS21: Arth, Pool 4F 25
Arthington Lawns LS21: Pool 5G 25
Arthington Pl. LS10: Leeds 3B 118
Arthington St. BD8: B'frd 3C 90
LS10: Leeds 3B 118
Arthington Ter. LS10: Leeds 3B 118
Arthington Vw. LS10: Leeds 3B 118
Arthur Av. BD8: B'frd 4E 89
ARTHURSDALE 1H 81
Arthursdale Cl. LS15: Scho 2H 81
Arthursdale Dr. LS15: Scho 2H 81
Arthursdale Grange LS15: Scho 2H 81
Arthur St. BD10: B'frd 3H 71
BD16: Bgly 3B 50
BD22: Oak 5C 46
HD6: Brigh 1C 162
LS28: Fars 1H 93
LS28: Stan 1A 94
Arthur Ter. LS28: Fars 1H 93
(off Arthur St.)
Artist St. LS12: Leeds 4F 97
Aruba LS12: Leeds 5A 4
Arum St. BD5: B'frd 2C 110

Arundel Cl. WF17: Bat 5D 136
Arundel St. HX1: Hal 2D 148
LS25: Gar 3H 103
LS28: Pud 4A 94
Arundel Ter. LS15: Leeds 1E 101
(off Tranquility Av.)
Arundel Wlk. WF17: Bat 6D 136
Ascot Av. BD7: B'frd 3G 109
Ascot Dr. BD7: B'frd 3G 109
Ascot Gdns. BD7: B'frd 3G 109
HX6: Sow B 6D 146
LS10: Leeds 4B 140
Ascot Gro. HD6: Ras 3G 161
Ascot Pde. BD7: B'frd 3G 109
Ascot Rd. LS25: Kip 3F 123
Ascot Ter. LS9: Leeds 4D 98
Asda Ho. LS11: Leeds 6E 5 (5A 98)
Ash Av. LS6: Leeds 4D 76
Ashbourne Av. BD2: B'frd 6F 71
Ashbourne Bank
BD2: B'frd 6F 71
Ashbourne Cl. BD2: B'frd 5F 71
Ashbourne Cres. BD2: B'frd 6F 71
BD13: Que 4H 107
LS25: Gar 6F 103
Ashbourne Dr. BD2: B'frd 6F 71
Ashbourne Gdns. BD2: B'frd 6F 71
Ashbourne Gth. BD2: B'frd 5G 71
Ashbourne Gro. BD2: B'frd 6F 71
HX1: Hal 2D 148
Ashbourne Haven
BD2: B'frd 6F 71
Ashbourne Mt. BD2: B'frd 6F 71
Ashbourne Oval BD2: B'frd 6F 71
Ashbourne Ri. BD2: B'frd 6F 71
Ashbourne Rd. BD2: B'frd 6F 71
BD21: Keigh 3G 47
Ashbourne Way BD2: B'frd 5F 71
Ashbrooke Pk. LS11: Leeds 3A 118
Ashburn Cl. LS22: Weth 2D 12
Ashburn Cft. LS22: Weth 2D 12
Ashburn Dr. LS22: Weth 2D 12
Ashburn Gro. BD17: Bail 3C 52
LS22: Weth 2D 12
Ashburnham Gro.
BD9: B'frd 6B 70
Ashburn Pl. LS29: I'ly 6C 10
Ashburn Way LS22: Weth 2D 12
Ashbury Chase WF1: Out 4E 157
Ashby Av. LS13: Leeds 1F 95
Ashby Cres. LS13: Leeds 2F 95
Ashby Mt. LS13: Leeds 1F 95
Ashby Sq. LS13: Leeds 1F 95
Ashby St. BD4: B'frd 1G 111
Ashby Ter. LS13: Leeds 1F 95
Ashby Vw. LS13: Leeds 1F 95
Ash Cl. HX3: Hip 1F 151
LS27: Gil 1F 137
LS29: I'ly 5A 10
Ash Ct. BD19: Scho 1F 153
LS14: Leeds 1A 100
Ash Cres. LS6: Leeds 4D 76
Ash Cft. BD6: B'frd 5A 110
Ashdale La. LS22: K Dei 1D 12
Ashdale Vw. LS22: K Dei 1E 13
Ashday La. HX3: Sou 6C 150
Ashdene LS12: N Far 2F 115
Ashdene Cl. LS28: Pud 6A 94
Ashdene Ct. BD13: Cull 3B 66
Ashdene Cres. LS28: Pud 6A 94
Ashdown Cl. BD6: B'frd 4B 110
HX2: Hal 3B 148
Ashdown Ct. BD18: Ship 2A 70
Ashdowne Pl. BD8: B'frd 2C 90
(off E. Squire La.)
Ashdown St. LS13: Leeds 2E 95
Asherton Gro. LS23: B Spa 4C 30
Ashfield BD4: B'frd 4B 112
LS12: N Far 1A 116
LS22: Weth 3F 13
Ashfield Av. BD9: B'frd 4B 70
BD18: Ship 4B 70
LS27: Morl 4H 137

Ashfield Cl. HX3: Hal 5D **128**
   LS12: N Far 1H **115**
   LS15: Leeds 5F **81**
   WF17: Birs 6C **136**
Ashfield Cotts. *BD16: Bgly* *5C 50*
   (off Healey Av.)
Ashfield Ct. BD16: Bgly 5C **50**
Ashfield Cres. BD16: Bgly 5C **50**
   LS28: Stan 2H **93**
Ashfield Dr. BD9: B'frd 4B **70**
   BD17: Bail 3D **52**
   HX3: Hal 5D **128**
   LS28: Stan 2A **94**
Ashfield Gro. BD9: B'frd 4A **70**
Ashfield Paddock LS23: B Spa 4D **30**
Ashfield Pk. LS6: Leeds 4E **77**
   LS21: Otley 3C **22**
Ashfield Pl. BD2: B'frd 1H **91**
   LS21: Otley 4D **22**
Ashfield Retail Pk. BD16: Bgly 1H **49**
Ashfield Rd. BD10: B'frd 6H **53**
   BD13: Thorn 5H **87**
   BD18: Ship 2G **69**
   HX4: Gree 4F **159**
   LS27: Morl 4H **137**
   LS28: Stan 2H **93**
   WF17: Birs 5B **136**
Ashfield St. *BD21: Keigh* *1H 47*
   (off Minnie St.)
Ashfield Ter. BD12: Wyke 3D **132**
   BD16: Bgly 5C **50**
   BD22: Haw 3C **64**
   HX4: Gree 3F **159**
   LS15: Leeds 5F **81**
   WF3: Thpe H 5D **140**
Ashfield Way LS12: N Far 1G **115**
Ash Fold BD7: B'frd 6G **89**
Ashford Dr. LS28: Pud 5B **94**
Ashford Grn. BD6: B'frd 4H **109**
Ash Gdns. LS6: Leeds 4D **76**
Ash Ghyll Gdns. BD16: Bgly 3B **50**
Ash Gro. BD11: Birk 1E **135**
   BD16: Bgly 6C **50**
   BD19: Cleck 3H **153**
   BD19: Gom 6E **135**
   BD21: Keigh 3G **47**
   HD6: Clift 6C **152**
   (not continuous)
   LS6: Leeds 6F **77**
   LS18: H'fth 5E **57**
   LS21: Otley 4D **22**
   LS28: Pud 5A **94**
   LS29: I'ly 4E **11**
Ashgrove BD2: B'frd 6A **72**
   BD7: B'frd 6A **6** (5D **90**)
   BD10: B'frd 2C **72**
   BD20: Stee 6D **14**
Ashgrove Av. HX3: Hal 6H **149**
Ashgrove Cres. LS25: Kip 2H **123**
Ashgrove Cft. LS25: Kip 3H **123**
Ashgrove M. LS13: Leeds 5B **74**
Ashgrove Mt. LS25: Kip 2G **123**
Ashgrove Pl. HX3: Hal 6A **150**
Ashgrove Rd. BD20: Keigh 3G **33**
Ash Gro. Ter. *HD6: Ras* *2A 162*
   (off Thomas St.)
Ash Hill Dr. LS17: Shad 3B **62**
Ash Hill Gdns. LS17: Shad 3B **62**
Ash Hill Gth. LS17: Shad 3B **62**
Ash Hill La. LS17: Shad 3B **62**
Ash Hill Wlk. BD4: B'frd 1H **111**
Ash Ho. LS15: Leeds 5A **100**
Ashington Cl. BD2: B'frd 5B **72**
Ashlands Rd. LS29: I'ly 4E **11**
Ash La. LS25: Gar 3G **103**
Ashlar Cl. BD22: Haw 2D **64**
Ashlar Gro. BD13: Que 6H **107**
Ashlea Av. HD6: Ras 3B **162**
Ashlea Cl. HD6: Ras 3B **162**
   LS25: Gar 6F **103**
Ashlea Ct. *LS13: Leeds* *5E 75*
   (off Ashlea Ga.)
Ashlea Dr. HD6: Ras 3B **162**

Ashlea Ga. LS13: Leeds 6E **75**
Ashlea Grn. LS13: Leeds 6E **75**
Ashleigh Gdns. LS26: Oul 1E **143**
Ashleigh Rd. LS16: Leeds 1A **76**
Ashleigh St. BD21: Keigh 5A **34**
   HX3: Hal 4E **129**
Ashley Av. LS9: Leeds 1E **99**
Ashley Cl. BD19: Gom 5E **135**
Ashley Ct. *LS16: Leeds* *6B 58*
   (off Otley Rd.)
Ashley Ind. Est. LS7: Leeds 6A **78**
Ashley La. BD17: Ship 1B **70**
Ashley Pk. M. LS25: Gar 2A **104**
Ashley Rd. BD12: Wyke 5C **132**
   BD16: Bgly 5C **50**
   LS9: Leeds 1D **98**
   LS12: Leeds 5B **96**
Ashley St. BD18: Ship 1B **70**
   HX1: Hal 2D **148**
Ashley Ter. LS9: Leeds 1E **99**
Ashmead LS23: Cliff 6B **30**
Ash Mews BD10: B'frd 2C **72**
Ashmore Gdns.
   BD4: B'frd 5H **111**
Ash Mt. BD7: B'frd 6B **90**
   BD21: Keigh 2G **47**
Ashmount BD14: Clay 1F **109**
Ashmount M. BD22: Haw 1C **64**
Ashmount Pl. BD22: Haw 1C **64**
Ash Rd. LS6: Leeds 5C **76**
   LS16: Leeds 2C **58**
Ashroyd LS26: Rothw 3B **142**
Ash St. BD22: Oxen 6C **64**
   LS29: I'ly 4E **11**
Ash Ter. BD16: Bgly 5B **50**
   LS6: Leeds 4D **76**
   LS25: Gar 3G **103**
Ashtofts Mt. LS20: Guis 4C **40**
Ashton Av. BD7: B'frd 6G **89**
   LS8: Leeds 6D **78**
Ashton Ct. LS8: Leeds 6E **79**
Ashton Cres. WF3: Carl 4H **141**
Ashton Gro. LS8: Leeds 1D **98**
Ashton Ho. *BD5: B'frd* *6E 91*
   (off Croscombe Wlk.)
Ashton Mt. LS8: Leeds 1D **98**
Ashton Pl. LS8: Leeds 1D **98**
Ashton Rd. LS8: Leeds 6E **79**
Ashton Rd. Ind. Est. LS8: Leeds ...6E **79**
Ashton St. BD1: B'frd 3A **6** (4D **90**)
   LS8: Leeds 6D **78**
Ashton Ter. LS8: Leeds 1D **98**
   WF3: Rob H 3F **141**
Ashton Vw. LS8: Leeds 1D **98**
Ashton Wlk. BD10: B'frd 2G **71**
Ash Tree App. LS14: Leeds 5F **81**
Ash Tree Av. BD13: Thorn 5F **87**
Ash Tree Cl. LS14: Leeds 4F **81**
Ash Tree Gdns. HX2: Mix 2A **128**
   LS14: Leeds 4F **81**
Ash Tree Gro. LS14: Leeds 4F **81**
Ashtree Gro. BD7: B'frd 3H **109**
   LS25: Kip 4H **123**
Ash Tree Pk. LS25: Kip 4H **123**
Ash Tree Rd. HX2: Mix 2A **128**
Ash Tree Vw. *LS14: Leeds* *4F 81*
   (off Stanks Gdns.)
Ash Tree Wlk. *LS14: Leeds* *4F 81*
   (off Ash Tree Gdns.)
   LS29: Burl W 2E **21**
Ash Vw. LS6: Leeds 4D **76**
   WF3: E Ard 2A **156**
Ash Vs. LS15: Leeds 5F **81**
Ashville Av. LS6: Leeds 6D **76**
Ashville Cft. HX2: Hal 1B **148**
Ashville Gdns. HX2: Hal 1B **148**
Ashville Gro. HX2: Hal 6B **128**
   LS6: Leeds 6D **76**
Ashville Rd. LS4: Leeds 6D **76**
   LS6: Leeds 6D **76**
Ashville St. HX3: Hal 6E **129**
Ashville Ter. BD22: Oak 5D **46**
   LS6: Leeds 6D **76**

Ashville Ter. *LS28: Fars* *1H 93*
   (off New St.)
Ashville Vw. LS6: Leeds 1E **97**
Ash Way LS23: T Arch 2G **31**
Ashwell La. BD9: B'frd 5A **70**
Ashwell Rd. BD8: B'frd 2B **90**
   BD9: B'frd 5A **70**
Ashwood LS14: Leeds 6D **62**
Ashwood Dr. BD20: Rid 4E **35**
   LS27: Gil 6D **114**
Ashwood Gdns. LS27: Gil 6D **114**
Ashwood Gro. LS27: Gil 6E **115**
Ashwood Pde. *LS27: Gil* *6D 114*
   (off Ashwood Gdns.)
Ashwood St. BD4: B'frd 4B **112**
Ashwood Ter. LS6: Leeds 5F **77**
Ashwood Vs. LS6: Leeds 5F **77**
Ashworth Pl. BD6: B'frd 4D **110**
Asket Av. LS14: Leeds 4A **80**
Asket Cl. LS14: Leeds 3A **80**
Asket Cres. LS14: Leeds 4A **80**
Asket Dr. LS14: Leeds 3A **80**
Asket Gdns. LS8: Leeds 3H **79**
Asket Gth. LS14: Leeds 4A **80**
Asket Grn. LS14: Leeds 3A **80**
Asket Hill LS8: Leeds 2H **79**
Asket Pl. LS14: Leeds 4A **80**
Asket Wlk. LS14: Leeds 4A **80**
Askey Av. LS27: Morl 5B **138**
Askey Cres. LS27: Morl 5B **138**
Askrigg Ct. LS29: Men 3H **39**
Askrigg Dr. BD2: B'frd 6H **71**
Aspect 14 LS7: Leeds 1F **5** (2A **98**)
Aspect Gdns. LS28: Pud 3G **93**
Aspect Ter. LS28: Pud 3G **93**
Aspen Cl. BD19: Gom 6F **135**
   BD21: Keigh 2C **48**
Aspen Ct. WF3: Ting 6C **138**
Aspen Grn. LS14: S'cft 5E **45**
Aspen Gro. HX3: North 3C **130**
Aspen Mt. LS16: Leeds 5G **57**
Aspen Ri. BD15: All 5B **68**
Aspinalls Fold HX5: Ell 5E **161**
Aspire Citygate BD5: B'frd 6E **91**
Asprey Dr. BD15: All 3D **88**
Asquith Av. LS27: Morl 1G **137**
Asquith Av. Bus. Pk. LS27: Gil 1G **137**
Asquith Bottom HX6: Sow B 6H **147**
Asquith Bldgs. *BD12: O'haw* *2F 133*
   (off Cleckheaton Rd.)
Asquith Cl. LS27: Morl 2H **137**
Asquith Ct. HX2: Hal 2B **148**
Asquith Dr. LS27: Morl 2H **137**
Asquith St. WF17: Birs 5D **136**
Asquith Ter. *HX6: Sow B* *6H 147*
   (off Scar Head Rd.)
Assembly St. LS2: Leeds 5F **5** (4A **98**)
Assisi Pl. LS10: Leeds 1C **118**
Asthall Cl. BD21: Keigh 6H **33**
Astley Av. LS26: Swil 4A **122**
Astley La. LS26: Swil 4B **122**
Astley La. Ind. Est. LS26: Swil 5B **122**
Astley Way LS26: Swil 5B **122**
Aston Av. LS13: Leeds 1F **95**
Aston Cres. LS13: Leeds 1G **95**
Aston Dr. LS13: Leeds 1G **95**
Aston Gro. LS13: Leeds 1G **95**
Aston Mt. LS13: Leeds 1G **95**
Aston Pl. LS13: Leeds 1G **95**
Aston Rd. BD5: B'frd 2E **111**
   LS13: Leeds 1F **95**
Aston St. LS13: Leeds 1F **95**
Aston Ter. LS13: Leeds 1G **95**
Aston Vw. LS13: Leeds 1F **95**
Astor Gro. LS13: Leeds 1C **94**
Astor Cl. LS8: Leeds 4E **79**
Astor St. LS13: Leeds 1C **94**
Astra Bus. Pk. LS11: Leeds 3A **118**
Astral Av. HX3: Hip 1F **151**
Astral Cl. HX3: Hip 1F **151**
Astral Vw. BD6: B'frd 3A **110**
Astura Ct. LS7: Leeds 4H **77**
Astwick Cl. BD20: E Mor 4E **35**

Atalanta Ter. HX2: Hal 5C **148**
Atha Cl. LS11: Leeds 4G **117**
Atha Cres. LS11: Leeds 4G **117**
Atha Ho. LS2: Leeds 1E **5**
Atha St. LS11: Leeds 4G **117**
Athelstan La. LS21: Otley 1E **23**
Athens LS20: Guis 4B **40**
Atherstone Rd. BD15: All 3D **88**
Atherton La. HD6: Ras 3B **162**
Athlone Gro. LS12: Leeds 4C **96**
Athlone Ri. LS25: Gar 4H **103**
Athlone St. LS12: Leeds 4C **96**
Athlone Ter. LS12: Leeds 4C **96**
Athol Cl. HX3: Hal 4E **129**
Athol Cres. HX3: Hal 4E **129**
Athol Gdns. HX3: Hal 4E **129**
Athol Grn. HX3: Hal 4E **129**
Athol Mt. HX3: Hal 4E **129**
Athol Rd. BD9: B'frd 1B **90**
   HX3: Hal 4E **129**
Athol St. BD21: Keigh 4C **34**
   HX3: Hal 4E **129**
ATKINSON HILL 1D **118**
Atkinson Quay LS10: Leeds 6C **98**
Atkinson's Ct.
   HX1: Hal 3B **164** (1G **149**)
Atkinson St. BD18: Ship 1B **70**
   LS10: Leeds 6C **98**
Atlanta St. LS13: Leeds 1C **94**
Atlantic Apartments LS1: Leeds 5C **4**
Atlas Mill Caravan Pk.
   HD6: Brigh 1A **162**
Atlas Mill Rd. HD6: Brigh 1A **162**
Atlas St. BD8: B'frd 2B **90**
Attlee Gro. WF1: Out 5G **157**
Auckland Rd. BD6: B'frd 4A **110**
Audby Cl. LS22: Weth 2F **13**
Audby Ct. LS22: Weth 3F **13**
Audby La. LS22: Weth 2F **13**
Aurelia Ho. BD8: B'frd 1C **90**
AUSTHORPE 3G **101**
Austhorpe Av. LS15: Leeds 4G **101**
Austhorpe Ct. LS15: Leeds 4H **101**
Austhorpe Dr. LS15: Leeds 4G **101**
Austhorpe Gdns. LS15: Leeds 3H **101**
Austhorpe Gro. LS15: Leeds 4G **101**
Austhorpe La. LS15: Leeds 2F **101**
Austhorpe Rd. LS15: Leeds 1E **101**
Austhorpe Vw. LS15: Leeds 3F **101**
Austin Av. HD6: Brigh 5H **151**
Austin St. BD21: Keigh 5B **34**
Authorpe Rd. LS6: Leeds 3F **77**
Autumn Av. LS6: Leeds 1E **97**
   LS22: Weth 1E **13**
Autumn Cres. LS18: H'fth 2F **75**
Autumn Gro. LS6: Leeds 1E **97**
Autumn Pl. LS6: Leeds 1E **97**
Autumn St. HX1: Hal 4D **148**
   LS6: Leeds 1E **97**
Autumn Ter. LS6: Leeds 1E **97**
Auty Sq. LS27: Morl 4B **138**
Avenel Rd. BD15: All 2D **88**
Avenel Ter. BD15: All 3D **88**
Avenham Way BD3: B'frd 2G **7** (3G **91**)
Avenue, The BD10: B'frd 4C **54**
   BD14: Clay 1C **108**
   BD15: Wils 5H **67**
   BD16: Cot 1D **68**
   BD17: Esh 4C **54**
   HX3: Hip 1F **151**
   LS8: Leeds 1E **79**
   LS9: Leeds 5H **5** (4C **98**)
   LS15: Leeds 6F **81**
   LS15: Leeds, Swil 3F **121**
         (not continuous)
   LS15: Scho 1H **81**
   LS17: Leeds 2F **59**
   LS18: H'fth 6B **56**
   LS22: Coll 2A **28**
   WF1: Out 5E **157**
   WF3: Ting 1G **155**
   WF17: Birs 6A **136**
         (not continuous)

Avenue A LS23: T Arch 1F **31**
Avenue B LS23: T Arch 1F **31**
         (Street 1)
   LS23: T Arch 1F **31**
         (Street 5)
Avenue C LS23: T Arch 2F **31**
Avenue Ct. LS17: Leeds 2F **59**
Avenue Cres. LS8: Leeds 5D **78**
Avenue D LS23: T Arch 3F **31**
Avenue Des Hirondelles
   LS21: Pool 5E **25**
Avenue E East LS23: T Arch 2G **31**
Avenue E West
   LS23: T Arch 3F **31**
Avenue F LS23: T Arch 2G **31**
Avenue Gdns. LS17: Leeds 2G **59**
Avenue Hill LS8: Leeds 5C **78**
Avenue Lawns LS17: Leeds 2F **59**
Avenue No. 1 HD6: Ras 2A **162**
Avenue No. 2 HD6: Ras 2A **162**
Avenue Rd. BD5: B'frd 2F **111**
Avenue St. BD4: B'frd 4B **112**
Avenue Ter. LS19: Yead 6H **41**
   LS21: Otley 4D **22**
Avenue Victoria LS8: Leeds 1E **79**
Avenue Wlk. LS2: Leeds 6G **77**
   LS6: Leeds 6G **77**
Averingcliffe Rd.
   BD10: B'frd 3B **72**
Avery Tulip Ct.
   BD12: Low M 1C **132**
         (off Edward Turner Cl.)
Aviary Gro. LS12: Leeds 3C **96**
Aviary Mt. LS12: Leeds 3C **96**
Aviary Pl. LS12: Leeds 3C **96**
Aviary Rd. LS12: Leeds 3C **96**
Aviary Row LS12: Leeds 3C **96**
Aviary St. LS12: Leeds 3C **96**
Aviary Ter. LS12: Leeds 3C **96**
Aviary Vw. LS12: Leeds 3C **96**
Avocet Cl. BD8: B'frd 4E **89**
Avocet Gth. LS10: Leeds 2B **140**
Avon Cl. LS17: Shad 3B **62**
Avon Ct. LS17: Shad 2A **62**
Avondale BD20: Keigh 5G **33**
Avondale Ct. LS17: Leeds 4B **60**
Avondale Cres. BD18: Ship 2A **70**
Avondale Dr. WF3: S'ley 4H **157**
Avondale Gro. BD18: Ship 2A **70**
Avondale Mt. BD18: Ship 2A **70**
Avondale Pl. HX3: Hal 5F **149**
Avondale Rd. BD18: Ship 2G **69**
Avondale St. LS13: Leeds 2E **95**
Avondale Vs. LS14: T'ner 4G **63**
Avon Dr. LS25: Gar 5F **103**
Avon Gth. LS22: Weth 4C **12**
Axeminster Dr. HD6: B Bri 2B **152**
Axis Ct. LS27: Gil 2G **137**
Aydonway HX3: She 6G **109**
Aygill Av. BD9: B'frd 6F **69**
Aylesbury St. BD21: Keigh 3G **47**
Aylesford Rd. LS15: Leeds 6H **81**
Aylesham Ind. Est.
   BD12: Low M 1D **132**
Aynholme Cl. LS29: Add 1D **8**
Aynholme Dr. LS29: Add 1D **8**
Aynsley Gro. BD15: All 1D **88**
Ayresome Av. LS8: Leeds 5E **61**
Ayresome Oval
   BD15: All 4C **88**
Ayresome Ter. LS8: Leeds 5D **60**
Ayreville Dr. HX3: She 1E **131**
Ayrton Cres. BD16: Bgly 4C **50**
Aysgarth Av. HX3: Hip 3A **152**
Aysgarth Cl. BD12: Wyke 5C **132**
   LS9: Leeds 4D **98**
Aysgarth Ct. LS29: Men 3H **39**
Aysgarth Cres. HX2: Mt T 4G **127**
Aysgarth Dr. LS9: Leeds 4D **98**
Aysgarth Fold LS10: Leeds 3A **140**
Aysgarth Pl. LS9: Leeds 4D **98**
Aysgarth Wlk. LS9: Leeds 4D **98**
Ayton Cl. BD3: B'frd 2H **7** (3G **91**)

Ayton Ho. BD4: B'frd 4D **112**
Azealea Ct. BD3: B'frd 2H **7** (3H **91**)
         (not continuous)

B

Bachelor La. LS18: H'fth 6E **57**
Bk. Ada St. BD21: Keigh 6G **33**
         (off Devonshire St. W.)
Bk. Aire St. HD6: Ras 2B **162**
         (off Victoria St.)
Bk. Aireview Ter. BD21: Keigh 1C **48**
Bk. Aireville St. BD20: Keigh 3G **33**
Bk. Airlie Av. LS8: Leeds 5D **78**
         (off Airlie Av.)
Bk. Airlie Pl. LS8: Leeds 5D **78**
         (off Airlie Pl.)
Bk. Albert Gro. LS6: Leeds 3D **76**
Bk. Albert Ter. LS6: Leeds 1E **97**
         (off Spring Gro. Ter.)
Bk. Alcester Pl. LS8: Leeds 5D **78**
         (off Alcester Pl.)
Bk. Alcester Rd. LS8: Leeds 5D **78**
         (off Alcester Rd.)
Bk. Alcester Ter. LS8: Leeds 5D **78**
         (off Hill Top Av.)
Bk. Allerton Ter. LS7: Leeds 2B **78**
Bk. Alma St. LS19: Yead 6G **41**
         (off Alma St.)
Bk. Ann St. BD13: Denh 2B **86**
Bk. Archery Pl. LS2: Leeds 1H **97**
         (off Archery Rd.)
Bk. Archery Rd. LS2: Leeds 1H **97**
         (off Archery Rd.)
Bk. Archery St. LS2: Leeds 1H **97**
         (off Archery Rd.)
Bk. Archery Ter. LS2: Leeds 1H **97**
         (off Archery Rd.)
Bk. Ash Gro. LS6: Leeds 6F **77**
         (not continuous)
Bk. Ashgrove W.
   BD7: B'frd 6A **6** (5D **90**)
Bk. Ashley Av. LS9: Leeds 1E **99**
         (off Ashley Rd.)
Bk. Ashley St. LS9: Leeds 1E **99**
         (off Ashley Rd.)
Bk. Ashville Av. LS6: Leeds 6E **77**
         (off Cardigan Rd.)
Bk. Ashville Gro. LS6: Leeds 6D **76**
         (off Cardigan Rd.)
Bk. Ashville Rd. LS6: Leeds 6D **76**
         (off Cardigan Rd.)
Bk. Ashville Ter. LS6: Leeds 6D **76**
         (off Cardigan Rd.)
Bk. Ashwood Ter. LS6: Leeds 5F **77**
Bk. Aston Pl. LS13: Leeds 1G **95**
         (off Aston Rd.)
Bk. Aston Rd. LS13: Leeds 1F **95**
Bk. Aston St. LS13: Leeds 1F **95**
         (off Aston Av.)
Bk. Aston Ter. LS13: Leeds 1G **95**
         (off Aston Av.)
Bk. Aston Vw. LS13: Leeds 1G **95**
         (off Aston Av.)
Bk. Athlone Av. LS12: Leeds 4C **96**
Bk. Athlone Gro. LS12: Leeds 4C **96**
         (off Athlone St.)
Bk. Athlone St. LS12: Leeds 4C **96**
         (off Athlone St.)
Bk. Atlanta St. LS13: Leeds 1C **94**
         (off Fairfield Av.)
Bk. Austhorpe Rd. LS15: Leeds 1E **101**
         (off Austhorpe Rd.)
Bk. Autumn Rd. LS6: Leeds 1E **97**
         (off Autumn Gro.)
Bk. Autumn Ter. LS6: Leeds 1E **97**
         (off Alexandra Rd.)
Bk. Aviary Rd. LS12: Leeds 3C **96**
         (off Aviary Gro.)
Bk. Aylesbury St. BD21: Keigh 3G **47**
         (off Oakfield Rd.)
Bk. Bailey's Pl. LS16: Leeds 3D **76**

Bk. Baker St. BD18: Ship 1A 70
Bk. Baldovan Ter. LS8: Leeds 5D 78
   (off Baldovan Ter.)
Bk. Balfour St. BD16: Bgly 5B 50
   BD21: Keigh 1H 47
Bk. Bank Ter. LS28: Stan 1A 94
Bk. Banstead St. LS8: Leeds 6D 78
   (off Harehills Rd.)
Bk. Barden Pl. LS12: Leeds 4A 96
   (off Conference St.)
Bk. Barkly Gro. LS11: Leeds 3G 117
   (off Theodore St.)
Bk. Barkly Pde. LS11: Leeds 4G 117
   (off Barkly Dr.)
Bk. Barkly Ter. LS11: Leeds 3G 117
   (off Barkly Dr.)
Bk. Barrowby Vw.
   LS15: Leeds 4G 101
Bk. Bath Rd. LS13: Leeds 1E 95
   (off Cross Bath Rd.)
Bk. Beamsley Gro. LS6: Leeds 1E 97
   (off Harold Gro.)
Bk. Beamsley Mt. LS6: Leeds 1E 97
   (off Royal Pk. Rd.)
Bk. Beamsley Ter. LS6: Leeds 1E 97
   (off Royal Pk. Rd.)
Bk. Beck La. LS29: Add 1D 8
Bk. Beech St. BD16: Bgly 5B 50
Bk. Beechwood Gro. LS4: Leeds 6D 76
Bk. Beechwood Rd. LS4: Leeds 6D 76
   (off Beechwood Pl.)
Bk. Bellbrooke Gro. LS9: Leeds 1F 99
   (off Bellbrooke St.)
Bk. Bellbrooke Pl. LS9: Leeds 1F 99
   (off Bellbrooke St.)
Bk. Bellbrooke Ter. LS9: Leeds 1F 99
   (off Coldcotes Av.)
Bk. Belvedere Av. LS11: Leeds 3H 117
   (off Harlech Av.)
Bk. Bentley Av. LS6: Leeds 3F 77
   (off Bentley Mt.)
Bk. Bentley Gro. LS6: Leeds 3F 77
   (off Bentley Mt.)
Bk. Berkeley Av. LS8: Leeds 6E 79
   (off Berkeley Rd.)
Bk. Berkeley Ter. LS8: Leeds 6E 79
   (off Berkeley Rd.)
Bk. Blackwood Gro. HX1: Hal 1D 148
Bk. Blenheim Av. LS2: Leeds 1H 97
Bk. Blenheim Mt. BD8: B'frd 1C 90
Bk. Blenheim Ter. LS2: Leeds 1H 97
Bk. Blythe Av. BD8: B'frd 3A 90
Bk. Boundary Ter. LS6: Leeds 2E 97
   (off Woodsley Rd.)
Bk. Bower Rd. HX5: Ell 4C 160
Bk. Branch Pl. LS12: Leeds 1A 116
   (off Branch Rd.)
Bk. Breary Av. LS18: H'fth 6F 57
Bk. Breary Ter. LS18: H'fth 6F 57
   (off Breary Av.)
Back Briggate BD20: Sils 1E 15
Bk. Broad La. LS13: Leeds 5F 75
Bk. Broomfield Cres. LS6: Leeds 5D 76
Bk. Broomfield Pl. LS6: Leeds 6D 76
   (off Newport Rd.)
Bk. Broomfield Rd. BD21: Keigh 6H 33
   LS6: Leeds 6D 76
   (off Newport Rd.)
Bk. Broomfield St. BD21: Keigh 6H 33
Bk. Broughton Av. LS9: Leeds 1E 99
   (off Foundry App.)
Bk. Broughton Ter. LS9: Leeds 1E 99
   (off Foundry App.)
Bk. Brudenell Gro. LS6: Leeds 6E 77
   (off Royal Pk. Rd.)
Bk. Brudenell Mt. LS6: Leeds 6E 77
   (off Royal Pk. Rd.)
Bk. Brudenell Rd. LS6: Leeds 6E 77
   (off Thornville Rd.)
Bk. Brunswick St.
   LS2: Leeds 2F 5 (2A 98)
Bk. Burchett Gro. LS6: Leeds 5G 77
   (off Hartley Av.)

Bk. Burchett Pl. LS6: Leeds 5G 77
   (off Hartley Av.)
Bk. Burley Hill LS4: Leeds 1C 96
Bk. Burley Lodge Rd. LS6: Leeds 1E 97
   (off Chiswick St.)
Bk. Burley Lodge Ter. LS4: Leeds 2E 97
   (off Woodsley Rd.)
Bk. Burley St. LS3: Leeds 3A 4
Bk. Burlington Pl. LS11: Leeds 3H 117
   (off Tempest Rd.)
Bk. Burlington Rd. LS11: Leeds 3H 117
   (off Harlech Av.)
Bk. Burton Cres. LS6: Leeds 3D 76
Bk. Burton Ter. LS11: Leeds 2A 118
Bk. Buxton St. BD21: Keigh 6B 34
   (off Chatsworth St.)
Bk. Byrl St. BD21: Keigh 4A 34
   (off Hard Ings Rd.)
Bk. Caister St. BD21: Keigh 3H 47
   (off Oakfield Rd.)
Bk. Caledonia Rd. BD21: Keigh 5B 34
   (off Hard Ings Rd.)
Bk. Camberley St. LS11: Leeds 2H 117
   (off Camberley St.)
Bk. Carberry Pl. LS6: Leeds 1E 97
   (off Carberry Rd.)
Bk. Carberry Rd. LS6: Leeds 1E 97
   (off Chiswick St.)
Bk. Carberry Ter. LS6: Leeds 1E 97
   (off Carberry Rd.)
Bk. Carter Mt. LS15: Leeds 3E 101
   (off Carter La.)
Bk. Carter Ter. LS15: Leeds 2E 101
   (off Carter La.)
Bk. Cartmel Rd. BD21: Keigh 6G 33
   (off Devonshire St. W.)
Bk. Castle St. BD21: Keigh 5H 33
Bk. Cavendish Rd. BD10: B'frd 2H 71
Bk. Cavendish St. BD21: Keigh 6A 34
Bk. Cavendish Ter. HX1: Hal 2E 149
Bk. Chapel La. LS6: Leeds 5D 76
   (off Broomfield Rd.)
Bk. Chapel St. BD1: B'frd 4F 7 (4F 91)
Bk. Charles St. HD6: Brigh 6A 152
   (off Waterloo Rd.)
Bk. Charlton Rd. LS9: Leeds 4E 99
Bk. Chatsworth Rd. LS8: Leeds 6E 79
   (off Harehills La.)
Bk. Chestnut Av. LS15: Leeds 1F 101
   (off Railway Rd.)
Bk. Chiswick Ter. LS6: Leeds 1E 97
   (off Carberry Rd.)
Bk. Christ Chu. Vw. LS12: Leeds 3B 96
   (off Stanningley Rd.)
Bk. Church La. LS5: Leeds 5A 76
   (off Hesketh Rd.)
   LS16: Leeds 2D 58
Bk. Claremont Av. LS3: Leeds 2A 4
Bk. Claremont Gro. LS3: Leeds 2A 4
Bk. Claremont St. LS26: Oul 1E 143
Bk. Claremont Ter. LS3: Leeds 2A 4
Bk. Claremount Ter. HX3: Hal 5G 129
Bk. Clarence Rd. LS18: H'fth 2D 74
Bk. Clarence St.
   HX1: Hal 4A 164 (2F 149)
   LS13: Leeds 2E 95
Bk. Clarendon Pl. HX1: Hal 2E 149
Bk. Clarkson Vw. LS6: Leeds 5G 77
   (off Quarry St.)
Bk. Cliffe Ter. BD21: Keigh 3A 48
Bk. Cliff Mt. LS6: Leeds 5G 77
   (off Cliff Mt. Ter.)
Bk. Clifton Ter. LS9: Leeds 1F 99
   (off Clifton Av.)
Bk. Clipston Av. LS6: Leeds 3F 77
   (off Clipston Av.)
Bk. Clock Vw. St. BD20: Keigh 3H 33
   (off Royd St.)
Back Cl. Lea HD6: Ras 2A 162
   (off Close Lea)
Back Clough HX3: North 5C 130
Bk. Clovelly Pl. LS11: Leeds 2H 117
   (off Rowland Rd.)

Bk. Colenso Mt. LS11: Leeds 1F 117
   (off Cleveleys Av.)
Bk. Colenso Rd. BD21: Keigh 4C 34
   (off Cornwall Rd.)
   LS11: Leeds 1F 117
   (off Cleveleys Av.)
Bk. Colton Rd. LS12: Leeds 4C 96
Bk. Colwyn Vw. LS11: Leeds 3H 117
   (off Colwyn Av.)
Bk. Commercial St. HX1: Hal 4B 164
Bk. Compton St. BD21: Keigh 5B 34
   (off Compton St.)
Bk. Conway St. LS8: Leeds 6D 78
   (off Harehills Rd.)
Bk. Cowper Gro. LS8: Leeds 6E 79
   (off Ashley Rd.)
Bk. Cowper St. LS7: Leeds 6C 78
   (off Cross Cowper St.)
Bk. Craggwood Rd. LS18: H'fth 2E 75
Bk. Crag Rd. BD18: Ship 2C 70
Bk. Cranbrook Av. LS11: Leeds 2G 117
   (off Wickham St.)
Bk. Cranbrook Ter. LS11: Leeds 2G 117
   (off Hird St.)
Bk. Crescent, The LS6: Leeds 6G 77
   (off Woodhouse La.)
Back Cft. Ho. La. BD20: Keigh 3G 33
Bk. Cromer Av. BD21: Keigh 2H 47
   (off Foster Rd.)
Bk. Cromer Gro. BD21: Keigh 3H 47
   (off Foster Rd.)
Bk. Cromer Ter.
   LS2: Leeds 1B 4 (1G 97)
Bk. Cromwell Ter. HX1: Hal 2F 149
Bk. Cross Flatts Av. LS11: Leeds 3G 117
   (off Theodore St.)
Bk. Cross Flatts Cres.
   LS11: Leeds 3F 117
   (off Wooler St.)
Bk. Cross Flatts Gro.
   LS11: Leeds 3G 117
   (off Wooler Dr.)
Bk. Cross Flatts Mt. LS11: Leeds 3G 117
   (off Wooler Gro.)
Bk. Cross Flatts Pl. LS11: Leeds 3F 117
   (off Wooler St.)
Bk. Cross Flatts Row
   LS11: Leeds 3F 117
   (off Wooler St.)
Bk. Cross Grn. La. LS9: Leeds 5D 98
   (off Cross Grn. La.)
   LS9: Leeds 5D 98
   (off Cross Grn. Rd.)
Bk. Cross La. HX5: Ell 5A 160
   (off Cross La.)
Bk. Cunliffe Rd. LS29: I'ly 5D 10
Bk. Dale St. BD18: Ship 2B 70
   (off Dale St.)
Bk. Dalton Gro. LS11: Leeds 3G 117
   (off Cross Flatts Av.)
Bk. Dalton Rd. LS11: Leeds 3G 117
Bk. Dawlish Av. LS9: Leeds 3F 99
   (off Ivy Av.)
Bk. Dawlish Mt. LS9: Leeds 3F 99
   (off Ivy Av.)
Bk. Dawlish Rd. LS9: Leeds 3F 99
   (off Dawlish Cres.)
Bk. De Lacy Mt. LS5: Leeds 4A 76
   (off Morris La.)
Bk. Delph Mt. LS6: Leeds 5G 77
   (off Delph La.)
Bk. Dent St. LS9: Leeds 4D 98
   (off Kippax Mt.)
Bk. Devonshire La. LS8: Leeds 5E 61
Bk. Dewsbury Dr. LS11: Leeds 3A 118
   (off Dewsbury Rd.)
Bk. Dorset Mt. LS8: Leeds 5E 79
   (off Dorset St.)
Bk. Dorset Rd. LS8: Leeds 5E 79
   (off Dorset Av.)
Bk. Dorset Ter. LS8: Leeds 6E 79
   (off Harehills La.)
Bk. Dudley Hill Rd. BD2: B'frd 1H 91

Bk. East Pk. Rd. *LS9: Leeds* 4E **99**
    (off Garton Rd.)
Bk. Eaton St. *BD21: Keigh* 3G **47**
    (off Oakfield Rd.)
Bk. Ecclesburn Gro. *LS9: Leeds* 4F **99**
    (off Ivy St.)
Bk. Ecclesburn St. *LS9: Leeds* 4E **99**
    (off Park Pde.)
Bk. Edensor Rd. *BD21: Keigh* 6G **33**
    (off Devonshire St.)
Bk. Edinburgh Rd. *LS12: Leeds* 3A **96**
    (off Moorfield Rd.)
Bk. Elford Pl. *LS8: Leeds* 6D **78**
    (off Roundhay Rd., not continuous)
Bk. Elizabeth St. *BD5: B'frd* 6E **91**
Bk. Ellers Gro. *LS8: Leeds* 5D **78**
    (off Ellers Gro.)
Bk. Ellers Rd. *LS8: Leeds* 5D **78**
    (off Ellers Rd.)
Bk. Elmfield Ter. *HX1: Hal* 4F **149**
Bk. Elsworth St. *LS12: Leeds* 4D **96**
Bk. Emily St. *BD21: Keigh* 5A **34**
    (off Lawkholme La.)
Bk. Eric St. *BD21: Keigh* 5A **34**
    (off Lawkholme La.)
    LS13: Leeds 4E **75**
Bk. Eshald Pl. *LS26: Wood* 1F **143**
Bk. Esmond Ter. *LS12: Leeds* 4C **96**
Bk. Estcourt Av. *LS6: Leeds* 4C **76**
    (off Canterbury Dr.)
Bk. Estcourt Ter. *LS6: Leeds* 5C **76**
    (off Canterbury Dr.)
Bk. Eversley Mt. *HX2: Hal* 3C **148**
Bk. Fairford Pl. *LS11: Leeds* 2A **118**
Bk. Featherbank Ter. *LS18: H'fth* 2D **74**
Bk. Ferguson St.
    HX1: Hal 4B **164** (3G **149**)
Back Fld. *BD13: Thorn* 5A **88**
    (off Market St.)
Bk. Florist St. *BD21: Keigh* 4C **34**
    (off Athol St.)
Back Fold *BD14: Clay* 6D **88**
Bk. Foster Rd. *BD21: Keigh* 3H **47**
    (off Oakfield Rd.)
Bk. Garton Rd. *LS9: Leeds* 4E **99**
    (off East Pk. Rd.)
Bk. Garton Ter. *LS9: Leeds* 4E **99**
    (off East Pk. Pde.)
Bk. Gathorne St. *LS7: Leeds* 6C **78**
    (off Gathorne St.)
Bk. Gerrard St.
    HX1: Hal 4A **164** (2F **149**)
Bk. Giles St. Nth. *BD5: B'frd* 6D **90**
Bk. Giles St. Sth. *BD5: B'frd* 6D **90**
Bk. Gillett La. *LS26: Rothw* 2B **142**
Bk. Girlington Rd. *BD8: B'frd* 2H **89**
    (not continuous)
Bk. Gladstone Rd. *HX1: Hal* 2F **149**
Bk. Gladstone St. *BD16: Bgly* 5B **50**
Bk. Glebe Ter. *LS16: Leeds* 3D **76**
    (off Weetwood La.)
Bk. Glen Ter. *HX1: Hal* 4F **149**
Bk. Glenthorpe Ter. *LS9: Leeds* 3E **99**
    (off Walford St.)
Bk. Glossop St. *LS6: Leeds* 5H **77**
    (off Elm St.)
Bk. Gooder La. *HD6: Ras* 2B **162**
Bk. Gordon Ter. *LS6: Leeds* 3F **77**
    (off Gordon Vw.)
Bk. Graham Gro. *LS4: Leeds* 6D **76**
Bk. Granby Gro. *LS6: Leeds* 5D **76**
    (off Granby Rd.)
Bk. Grange Av. *LS7: Leeds* 5B **78**
    (off Grange Av.)
Bk. Grange Cres. *LS7: Leeds* 5C **78**
    (off Hamilton Ter.)
Bk. Grange Ter. *LS7: Leeds* 5B **78**
    (off Nassau Pl.)
Bk. Grange Vw. *LS7: Leeds* 5C **78**
    (off Nassau Pl.)
Bk. Grant St. *BD21: Keigh* 6G **33**
Bk. Grassington Ter. *BD21: Keigh* 5A **34**
    (off Plover St.)

Bk. Gt. Russell St. *BD7: B'frd* 4C **90**
Bk. Greaves St. *BD5: B'frd* 2D **110**
    (off Greaves St.)
Back Grn. *LS27: Chur* 6C **116**
Bk. Greenhow Wlk. *LS4: Leeds* 1D **96**
    (off Greenhow Wlk.)
Bk. Greenmount Ter.
    LS11: Leeds 2H **117**
    (off Greenmount La.)
Bk. Grosvenor Ter. *HX1: Hal* 2E **149**
    LS6: Leeds 5F **77**
    (off Cliff La.)
Bk. Grouse St. *BD21: Keigh* 5B **34**
    (off Parson St.)
Bk. Grove Gdns. *LS6: Leeds* 3E **77**
    (off Grove Av.)
Bk. Grovehall Av. *LS11: Leeds* 4G **117**
Bk. Grovehall Dr. *LS11: Leeds* 4G **117**
Bk. Grove Rd. *LS29: I'ly* 5D **10**
Bk. Haigh Av. *LS26: Rothw* 6H **119**
Bk. Haigh St. *LS26: Rothw* 6G **119**
Bk. Haigh Vw. *LS26: Rothw* 6G **119**
Bk. Halliday Gro. *LS12: Leeds* 3A **96**
Bk. Halliday Pl. *LS12: Leeds* 3A **96**
Bk. Hamilton Av. *LS7: Leeds* 5C **78**
    (off Nassau Pl.)
Bk. Hamilton Vw. *LS7: Leeds* 5C **78**
    (off Hamilton Ter.)
Bk. Hanson La. *HX1: Hal* 1C **148**
    (off Hanson La., not continuous)
Bk. Harehills Av. *LS8: Leeds* 5C **78**
    (off Nassau Pl.)
Bk. Harehills Pk. Vw. *LS9: Leeds* 1F **99**
    (off Foundry App.)
Bk. Harehills Pl. *LS8: Leeds* 6D **78**
    (off Harehills Pl.)
Bk. Harehills Rd. *LS8: Leeds* 6D **78**
    (off Harehills Pl.)
Bk. Hares Av. *LS8: Leeds* 5D **78**
    (off Hares Av.)
Bk. Hares Mt. *LS8: Leeds* 5C **78**
    (off Hares Rd.)
Bk. Hares Ter. *LS8: Leeds* 5D **78**
    (off Hares Ter.)
Bk. Hares Vw. *LS8: Leeds* 5D **78**
    (off Hares Rd.)
Bk. Harold Gro. *LS6: Leeds* 1E **97**
    (off Cardigan Rd.)
Bk. Hartley Av. *LS6: Leeds* 5H **77**
    (off Burchett Ter.)
Bk. Hartley Gro. *LS6: Leeds* 5G **77**
    (off Glossop Vw.)
Bk. Hartley St. *LS27: Morl* 4C **138**
Bk. Hawksworth Gro. *LS5: Leeds* 3F **75**
Bk. Headingley Av. *LS6: Leeds* 4C **76**
    (off Canterbury Dr.)
Bk. Headingley Mt. *LS6: Leeds* 4C **76**
    (off Canterbury Dr.)
Bk. Heathfield Ter. *LS6: Leeds* 3D **76**
    (off Heathfield Ter.)
Bk. Heddon St. *LS6: Leeds* 3E **77**
    (off Brookfield Rd.)
Bk. Heights Rd. *BD13: Thorn* 3F **87**
Bk. Hessle Av. *LS6: Leeds* 6E **77**
    (off Walmsley Rd.)
Bk. Hessle Mt. *LS6: Leeds* 6E **77**
    (off Brundenell Rd.)
Bk. Hessle Ter. *LS6: Leeds* 6E **77**
    (off Walmsley Rd.)
Bk. Hessle Vw. *LS6: Leeds* 6E **77**
    (off Welton Rd.)
Bk. Highbury Ter. *LS6: Leeds* 3E **77**
    (off Highbury Mt.)
Bk. Highfield Rd. *LS13: Leeds* 1F **95**
    (off Aston Mt.)
Bk. High St. *BD13: Thorn* 5H **87**
    LS19: Yead 6E **41**
Bk. Highthorne Gro. *LS12: Leeds* 3A **96**
    (off Highthorne St.)
Bk. Highthorne St. *LS12: Leeds* 3A **96**
    (off Armley Ridge Rd.)
Bk. Hillcrest Av. *LS7: Leeds* 5C **78**
    (off Grange Av.)

Bk. Hillcrest Vw. *LS7: Leeds* 5C **78**
    (off Hillcrest Pl.)
Bk. Hilltop Av. *LS8: Leeds* 5D **78**
    (off Shepherd's La.)
Bk. Hill Top Mt. *LS8: Leeds* 5D **78**
    (off Hill Top Mt.)
Bk. Hilton Pl. *LS8: Leeds* 5D **78**
    (off Hilton Pl.)
Bk. Hilton Rd. *LS8: Leeds* 5D **78**
    (off Avenue Cres.)
Bk. Hird St. *BD21: Keigh* 1H **47**
Backhold *HX3: Hal* 6A **150**
Backhold Av. *HX3: Hal* 1A **160**
Backhold Dr. *HX3: Hal* 1H **159**
Backhold Hall *HX3: Hal* 6A **150**
Backhold La. *HX3: Hal* 1H **159**
Backhold Rd. *HX3: Hal* 1A **160**
Bk. Hollyshaw Ter. *LS15: Leeds* 3E **101**
Bk. Holywell La. *LS17: Shad* 2H **61**
Bk. Hope Hall Ter.
    HX1: Hal 6C **164** (3G **149**)
Bk. Hovingham Gro. *LS8: Leeds* 5E **79**
    (off Sandhurst Mt.)
Bk. Hovingham Mt. *LS8: Leeds* 5E **79**
    (off Dorset Av.)
Bk. Hovingham Ter. *LS8: Leeds* 5E **79**
    (off Dorset Av.)
Bk. Hyde Gro. *BD21: Keigh* 5B **34**
    (off Kirby St.)
Bk. Hyde Ter. *LS2: Leeds* 1A **4** (2G **97**)
Bk. Ibbetson Pl. *LS1: Leeds* 1C **4**
Bk. Ingledew Cres. *LS8: Leeds* 5F **61**
Bk. Irwell St. *BD4: B'frd* 6G **91**
Bk. Ivy Av. *LS9: Leeds* 4F **99**
    (off Ivy Av.)
Bk. Ivy Gro. *LS9: Leeds* 4F **99**
    (off Victoria Av.)
Bk. Ivy Mt. *LS9: Leeds* 3E **99**
    (off Ivy Vw.)
Bk. Ivy St. *LS9: Leeds* 3E **99**
    (off Ivy Av.)
Bk. John St. *BD13: Thorn* 5H **87**
Bk. Karnac Rd. *LS8: Leeds* 5D **78**
    (off Nice St.)
Bk. Kelso Rd. *LS2: Leeds* 1A **4** (1F **97**)
Bk. Kendal La. *LS3: Leeds* 2A **4**
Bk. Kennerleigh Wlk.
    LS15: Leeds 2E **101**
    (off Kingswear Pde.)
Bk. Kensington St. *BD8: B'frd* 2A **90**
    (off Thorn St.)
Bk. Kensington Ter. *LS6: Leeds* 6F **77**
Bk. Kings Av. *LS6: Leeds* 1E **97**
    (off Alexandra Rd.)
Bk. Kirby St. *BD21: Keigh* 5B **34**
    (off Caledonian Rd.)
Back Kirkgate *BD18: Ship* 2A **70**
Bk. Kitson St. *LS9: Leeds* 4D **98**
    (off Kippax Mt.)
Bk. Knowle Mt. *LS4: Leeds* 6D **76**
    (off Stanmore Hill)
Bk. Laisteridge La.
    BD7: B'frd 6A **6** (5C **90**)
Bk. Lake St. *LS10: Leeds* 3B **118**
Bk. Lambton Gro. *LS8: Leeds* 5D **78**
    (off Lambton Gro.)
Bk. Landseer Av. *LS13: Leeds* 6G **75**
    (off Victoria Pk. Av.)
Bk. Landseer Gro. *LS13: Leeds* 6G **75**
    (off Victoria Pk. Av.)
Bk. Landseer Ter. *LS13: Leeds* 6G **75**
    (off Victoria Pk. Av.)
Back La. *BD9: B'frd* 5A **70**
    BD10: B'frd 1H **71**
    BD11: Drig 6B **114**
    BD13: Que 3D **108**
    BD13: Thorn 4H **87**
    BD14: Clay 1E **109**
    BD15: All 1H **87**
    BD20: E Mor 4H **35**
    BD20: Sils 1E **15**
    BD22: Lay 6B **32**
    HX2: Illing 2B **128**

Back La. HX2: Ogd 2A **106**
LS11: Leeds 4F **117**
LS12: N Far 3E **115**
LS13: Leeds 2F **95**
LS18: H'fth 1D **74**
LS19: Yead 1E **55**
LS20: Guis 4A **40**
LS25: Kip 4H **123**
LS28: Fars 6H **73**
LS29: Burl W 2F **21**
WF3: Loft 6G **141**
WF10: All B 4H **145**
Bk. Langdale Gdns. LS6: Leeds 5C **76**
(off Canterbury Dr.)
Bk. Langdale Ter. LS6: Leeds 5C **76**
(off Canterbury Dr.)
Bk. Laurel Mt. LS7: Leeds 4B **78**
Back Leeming BD22: Oxen 2D **84**
Bk. Lime St. BD21: Keigh 4H **47**
(off Hainworth Wood Rd.)
Bk. Linden Gro. LS11: Leeds 2A **118**
(off Linden Gro.)
Bk. Lindum Ter. BD8: B'frd 1C **90**
(off Oak La.)
Bk. Lodge La. LS11: Leeds 3H **117**
(off Stratford Ter.)
Bk. Lombard St. LS19: Raw 3E **55**
Bk. Longroyd Ter. LS11: Leeds 2A **118**
(off Burton Av.)
Bk. Lord St. HX1: Hal 4A **164** (2F **149**)
Bk. Low La. LS18: H'fth 6F **57**
(off Bk. Breary Av.)
Bk. Lucas St. LS6: Leeds 5G **77**
(off Delph La.)
Bk. Lunan Pl. LS8: Leeds 5D **78**
(off Lunan Pl.)
Bk. Lunan Ter. LS8: Leeds 5D **78**
(off Lunan Ter.)
Bk. Lyons St. BD13: Que 4B **108**
Bk. Lytton St. HX3: Hal 6G **129**
Bk. Mafeking Av. LS11: Leeds 4G **117**
(off Dewsbury Rd.)
Bk. Mafeking Mt. LS11: Leeds 4G **117**
Bk. Malt St. BD22: Keigh 3G **47**
(off Bracken Rd.)
Bk. Mannville Rd. BD21: Keigh 1G **47**
(off Malsis Rd.)
Bk. Manor Dr. LS6: Leeds 5E **77**
(off Manor Av.)
Bk. Manor Gro. LS7: Leeds 3B **78**
(off St Martin's Dr.)
Bk. Manor St. BD2: B'frd 6H **71**
Bk. Market St. BD6: B'frd 4C **110**
Bk. Markham St. LS8: Leeds 5D **78**
(off Markham Av.)
Bk. Marshall Av. LS15: Leeds 1F **101**
(off Railway Rd.)
Bk. Marshall St. LS15: Leeds 1E **101**
(off Austhorpe Rd.)
Bk. Marshall Ter. LS15: Leeds 1E **101**
(off Railway Rd.)
Bk. Mary St. WF3: E Ard 1C **156**
Bk. Masham St. LS12: Leeds 4D **96**
(off Bk. Middle Cross St.)
Bk. Maud Av. LS11: Leeds 3H **117**
(off Maud Pl.)
Bk. Mayville Av. LS6: Leeds 6E **77**
(off Mayville Rd.)
Bk. Mayville Pl. LS6: Leeds 6E **77**
(off Cardigan La.)
Bk. Mayville St. LS6: Leeds 6E **77**
(off Mayville St.)
Bk. Mayville Ter. LS6: Leeds 6E **77**
(off Mayville Rd.)
Bk. Meadow Vw. LS6: Leeds 6E **77**
(off Brundenell Rd.)
Bk. Methley Dr. LS7: Leeds 3B **78**
Bk. Mexborough Av. LS7: Leeds 5B **78**
(off Savile Av.)
Bk. Mexborough Dr. LS7: Leeds 5B **78**
(off Savile Av.)
Bk. Mexborough Gro. LS7: Leeds 5B **78**
(off Savile Av.)

Bk. Mexborough St. LS7: Leeds 5B **78**
(off Savile Av.)
Bk. Meynell Av. LS26: Rothw 2A **142**
Bk. Middle Cross St.
LS12: Leeds 4D **96**
Bk. Middleton Rd. LS29: I'ly 5C **10**
Bk. Middleton Vw. LS11: Leeds 2G **117**
Bk. Midland Rd. LS6: Leeds 6F **77**
(off Hyde Pk. Ter.)
Bk. Milan Av. LS8: Leeds 6D **78**
(off Milan Rd.)
Bk. Milan Rd. LS8: Leeds 6D **78**
(off Harehills Rd.)
Bk. Milan St. LS8: Leeds 6E **79**
(off Harehills La.)
Bk. Mill Hey BD22: Haw 2D **64**
(off Mill Hey)
Bk. Milton Ter. HX1: Hal 2F **149**
Bk. Minnie St. BD22: Haw 3C **64**
(off Minnie St.)
Bk. Mitchell Ter. BD16: Bgly 5B **50**
Bk. Mitford Rd. LS12: Leeds 4D **96**
Bk. Model Rd. LS12: Leeds 4D **96**
Bk. Model St. LS12: Leeds 4D **96**
Bk. Model Vw. LS12: Leeds 4D **96**
(off Bentley Mt.)
Bk. Monk Bri. Dr. LS6: Leeds 3F **77**
Bk. Monk Bri. St. LS6: Leeds 3F **77**
(off Monk Bri. St.)
Bk. Montpelier Ter. LS6: Leeds 5G **77**
(off Cliff Rd.)
Bk. Moorfield St. HX1: Hal 4E **149**
Bk. Moorfield Ter. LS12: Leeds 3A **96**
Bk. Moorland Ter. LS2: Leeds 1G **97**
Bk. Morning St. BD21: Keigh 3H **47**
(off Hainworth Wood Rd.)
Bk. Morritt Dr. LS15: Leeds 3B **100**
Bk. Mount Pleasant LS10: Leeds 2A **140**
Bk. Mount Royd BD8: B'frd 1C **90**
Bk. Mount Vw. LS6: Leeds 5F **77**
(off Regent Pk. Av.)
Bk. Muff St. BD4: B'frd 6H **91**
Bk. Myrtle Av. BD16: Bgly 5B **50**
Bk. Myrtle Ter. BD22: Cros R 6F **47**
Bk. Nansen St. LS13: Leeds 1C **94**
(off Fairfield Av.)
Bk. Napier Rd. BD3: B'frd 4B **92**
Bk. Nelson Rd. LS29: I'ly 5D **10**
Bk. Newport Gdns. LS6: Leeds 6D **76**
(off Newport Rd.)
Bk. Newport Mt. LS6: Leeds 6D **76**
(off Newport Rd.)
Bk. Newport Pl. LS6: Leeds 6D **76**
(off Newport Rd.)
Bk. New St. BD12: O'haw 2H **133**
(off Mill Carr Hill St.)
Bk. Newton Gro. LS7: Leeds 5B **78**
Bk. Newton La. WF10: Led, Leds 5B **124**
Bk. New York St.
LS2: Leeds 5G **5** (4B **98**)
Bk. Nice Vw. LS8: Leeds 5D **78**
(off Nice Vw.)
Bk. Norman Mt. LS5: Leeds 5A **76**
(off Morris La.)
Bk. Norman Pl. LS8: Leeds 5E **61**
(off Norton Rd.)
Bk. Norman Ter. LS8: Leeds 5E **61**
(off Norton Rd.)
Bk. Northbrook St. LS7: Leeds 2B **78**
(off Northbrook St.)
Bk. Northfield Pl. BD8: B'frd 2C **90**
(off Carlisle Rd.)
Bk. North Pk. Av. LS8: Leeds 1D **78**
Bk. North St. BD12: O'haw 3G **133**
Bk. Norwood Gro. LS6: Leeds 6E **77**
(off Norwood Rd.)
Bk. Norwood Pl. LS6: Leeds 6E **77**
(off Norwood Rd.)
Bk. Norwood Rd. LS6: Leeds 6E **77**
(off Norwood Vw.)
Bk. Norwood Ter. LS6: Leeds 6E **77**
Bk. Nowell Cres. LS9: Leeds 2F **99**
(off Harehills La.)

Bk. Nowell Mt. LS9: Leeds 2F **99**
(off Harehills La.)
Bk. Nowell Pl. LS9: Leeds 2F **99**
(off Harehills La.)
Bk. Nowell Ter. LS9: Leeds 2F **99**
(off Harehills La.)
Bk. Nunington St. LS12: Leeds 3D **96**
(off Armley Pk. Rd.)
Bk. Nunington Vw. LS12: Leeds 2C **96**
(off Nunnington Vw.)
Bk. Nunroyd Rd. LS17: Leeds 6B **60**
(off Nunroyd Ter.)
Bk. Oak Av. BD16: Bgly 6B **50**
Bk. Oakfield Ter. LS6: Leeds 3E **77**
(off Brookfield Rd.)
Bk. Oakley St. WF3: Thpe H 6C **140**
Bk. Oakley Ter. LS11: Leeds 3A **118**
(off Garnet Rd.)
Bk. Oak Rd. LS7: Leeds 4B **78**
(off St Mary's Rd.)
Bk. Oakwood Av. LS8: Leeds 3F **79**
(off Oakwood Av.)
Bk. Oakwood Dr. LS8: Leeds 3F **79**
(off Oakwood Boundary Rd.)
Back of the Mill BD16: Har 6E **49**
Bk. Osmondthorpe La.
LS9: Leeds 3G **99**
(off Cross Osmondthorpe La.)
Bk. Otterburn St. BD21: Keigh 5A **34**
(off Ashleigh St.)
Bk. Outwood La. LS18: H'fth 2E **75**
Bk. Overdale Ter. LS15: Leeds 3C **100**
(off Cross St.)
Bk. Oxford Pl. LS1: Leeds 3C **4**
Bk. Oxford St. WF3: E Ard 1C **156**
Bk. Paget St. BD21: Keigh 6G **33**
(off Devonshire St.)
Bk. Parish Ghyll Rd. LS29: I'ly 6D **10**
Bk. Park Cres. LS8: Leeds 5F **61**
Bk. Parkfield Pl. LS11: Leeds 2G **117**
(off Parkfield Row)
Bk. Parkfield Rd. LS11: Leeds 2G **117**
(off Parkfield Row)
Bk. Park Ter. HX1: Hal 3E **149**
Bk. Park Vw. LS11: Leeds 2G **117**
(off Dawson Rd.)
Bk. Park Vw. Av. LS4: Leeds 6D **76**
Bk. Parkville Rd. LS13: Leeds 6E **75**
Bk. Parnaby Av. LS10: Leeds 4D **118**
(off Parnaby Rd.)
Bk. Parnaby Rd. LS10: Leeds 4D **118**
Bk. Parnaby Ter. LS10: Leeds 4D **118**
(off Parnaby Rd.)
Bk. Pasture Gro. LS7: Leeds 2B **78**
(off Hillside Rd.)
Bk. Pasture Rd. LS8: Leeds 5D **78**
(off Ellers Rd.)
Bk. Pawson St. WF3: E Ard 1C **156**
Bk. Pelham Rd. BD2: B'frd 6H **71**
(off Pelham Rd.)
Bk. Pleasant St. HX6: Sow B 5A **148**
Bk. Pollard La. LS13: Leeds 4E **75**
Bk. Poplar Av. LS15: Leeds 1F **101**
(off Railway Rd.)
Bk. Potternewton La. LS7: Leeds 3A **78**
Bk. Potters St. LS7: Leeds 3B **78**
(off St Martin's Dr.)
Bk. Prospect Pl. BD21: Keigh 1H **47**
Bk. Prospect Ter. LS9: Leeds 4D **98**
Bk. Providence Av. LS6: Leeds 5G **77**
(off Delph La.)
Bk. Quarry Mt. Ter. LS6: Leeds 5G **77**
(off Providence Rd.)
Bk. Queen St. HX4: Gree 5G **159**
Bk. Raglan Rd. LS2: Leeds 6G **77**
(off Raglan Rd.)
Bk. Ravenscar Av. LS8: Leeds 3E **79**
(off Ravenscar Wlk.)
Bk. Raynville Mt. LS13: Leeds 6G **75**
(off Victoria Pk. Av.)
Bk. Regent Pk. Ter. LS6: Leeds 5F **77**
(off Regent Pk. Av.)
Bk. Regent Ter. LS6: Leeds 1F **97**

Bk. Reginald Mt. *LS7: Leeds* 5B **78**
(off Hall La.)
Bk. Reginald Pl. *LS7: Leeds* 5B **78**
(off Reginald Row)
Bk. Reginald St. *LS7: Leeds* 5B **78**
(off Reginald St.)
Bk. Rhodes St. *HX1: Hal* 2F **149**
Bk. Ribble St. *BD21: Keigh* 5D **34**
(off Airedale Rd.)
Bk. Ripley St. *BD20: Rid* 4D **34**
(off Canal Rd.)
Bk. Ripon St. *HX1: Hal* 3C **148**
Bk. Ripon Ter. *HX3: Hal* 6F **129**
Bk. River St. *BD22: Haw* 2D **64**
Back Rd. *BD3: B'frd* 2G **91**
BD12: Wyke 3C **132**
Bk. Roberts St. *LS26: Wood* 1E **143**
Bk. Rochester Ter. *LS6: Leeds* 5D **76**
(off Broomfield Rd.)
Bk. Rokeby Gdns. *LS6: Leeds* 4C **76**
(off Ash Rd.)
Bk. Roman Av. *LS8: Leeds* 5E **61**
Bk. Roman Pl. *LS8: Leeds* 5F **61**
Bk. Roman St. *LS8: Leeds* 5F **61**
Bk. Rose Av. *LS18: H'fth* 2D **74**
(off Rose St.)
Bk. Rosebank Cres. *LS3: Leeds* 1F **97**
Bk. Rosemont Wlk. *LS13: Leeds* 1E **95**
(off Rosemont St.)
Bk. Rossall Rd. *LS8: Leeds* 5F **79**
(off Nice St.)
Bk. Rossington Rd. *LS8: Leeds* 5C **78**
(off Rossington Gro.)
Bk. Roundhay Cres. *LS8: Leeds* 4D **78**
(off Cross Roundhay Av.)
Bk. Roundhay Gro. *LS8: Leeds* 4D **78**
(off Cross Roundhay Av., not continuous)
Bk. Roundhay Pl. *LS8: Leeds* 4D **78**
(off Harehills La.)
Bk. Roundhay Vw. *LS8: Leeds* 4D **78**
(off Cross Roundhay Av.)
Back Row *LS11: Leeds* 5H **97**
Bk. Rowland Ter. *LS11: Leeds* 2A **118**
(off Rowland Pl.)
Bk. Rowsley St. *BD21: Keigh* 6B **34**
(off Chatsworth St.)
Bk. Roydwood Ter. *BD13: Cull* 3B **66**
Bk. Rupert St. *BD21: Keigh* 5A **34**
(off Lawkholme La.)
Bk. Russell St. *BD5: B'frd* 6B **6** (6D **90**)
Bk. Ruthven Vw. *LS8: Leeds* 6E **79**
(off Strathmore Ter.)
Bk. Rydal St. *BD21: Keigh* 1G **47**
Bk. Rylstone St. *BD21: Keigh* 5C **34**
(off Harehills La.)
Back St Alban Cres. *LS9: Leeds* 2G **99**
(off Vinery Av.)
Back St Elmo Gro. *LS9: Leeds* 3E **99**
(off Vinery Av.)
Back St Ives Mt. *LS12: Leeds* 3A **96**
Back St Luke's Cres. *LS11: Leeds* . . .1G **117**
(off St Luke's Cres.)
Back St Mary's Rd. *LS7: Leeds* 4B **78**
Back St Mary's Rd. W. *BD9: B'frd* 1C **90**
Back St Paul's Rd. *BD18: Ship* 2A **70**
Bk. Salisbury Gro. *LS12: Leeds* 3C **96**
(off Armley Lodge Rd.)
Bk. Salisbury Ter. *HX3: Hal* 6F **129**
LS12: Leeds 3C **96**
(off Armley Lodge Rd.)
Bk. Salisbury Vw. *LS12: Leeds* 3C **96**
(off Armley Lodge Rd.)
Bk. Saltaire Rd. *BD18: Ship* 1A **70**
Bk. Saltaire Rd. Nth. *BD18: Ship* 1A **70**
Bk. Sandhurst Gro. *LS8: Leeds* 6E **79**
(off Harehills La.)

Bk. Sandhurst Pl. *LS8: Leeds* 6E **79**
(off Harehills La.)
Bk. Sandhurst Rd. *LS8: Leeds* 6E **79**
(off Harehills La.)
Bk. Savile Pde. *HX1: Hal* 4F **149**
Bk. Savile Pl. *LS7: Leeds* 6B **78**
(off Savile Av.)
Bk. Savile Rd. *LS7: Leeds* 6B **78**
(off Savile Av.)
Bk. School St. *LS27: Morl* 3B **138**
(off South St.)
Bk. School Vw. *LS6: Leeds* 6E **77**
(off Welton Rd.)
Bk. Seaforth Av. *LS9: Leeds* 1F **99**
(off Foundry App.)
Bk. Seaforth Pl. *LS9: Leeds* 6E **79**
(off Strathmore Ter.)
Bk. Seaforth Ter. *LS9: Leeds* 6E **79**
(off Strathmore Ter.)
Bk. Sefton Av. *LS11: Leeds* 2G **117**
(off Wickham St.)
Bk. Sefton Ter. *LS11: Leeds* 2G **117**
(off Wickham St.)
Bk. Shaftesbury Av. *LS8: Leeds* 6E **61**
Bk. Shaw La. *BD21: Keigh* 3B **48**
Bk. Shepherd's Pl. *LS8: Leeds* 5D **78**
(off Shepherd's Pl.)
Bk. Sholebroke Av. *LS7: Leeds* 4B **78**
(off Hall La.)
Bk. Sholebroke Pl. *LS7: Leeds* 5B **78**
(off Hall La.)
Bk. Sholebroke Vw. *LS7: Leeds* 5B **78**
(off Hall La.)
Bk. Sidlaw Ter. *LS8: Leeds* 5D **78**
(off Markham Av.)
Bk. Simpson St. *BD21: Keigh* 6G **33**
(off Edensor Rd.)
Bk. Sladen St. *BD21: Keigh* 6G **33**
Bk. Smith Row *BD5: B'frd* 2C **110**
Bk. South End Gro. *LS13: Leeds* 1G **95**
(off South End Av.)
Bk. Southfield Sq. *BD8: B'frd* 2C **90**
(off Laburnum Pl.)
Bk. South Pde. *HX5: Ell* 6A **160**
(not continuous)
Bk. Sowerby Cft. *HX6: Sow B* 6H **147**
Bk. Spencer Mt. *LS7: Leeds* 5C **78**
(off Gathorne St.)
Bk. Springfield Mt. *LS12: Leeds* 3A **96**
Bk. Springfield Pl. *BD1: B'frd* 1B **6**
Bk. Springfield Rd. *HX5: Ell* 4C **160**
Bk. Spring Gro. Wlk. *LS6: Leeds* 1E **97**
(off Harold Ter.)
Bk. Stanley St. *LS9: Leeds* 1D **98**
(off Ashley Rd.)
Bk. Stanmore Pl. *LS4: Leeds* 6C **76**
(off St Michael's La.)
Bk. Stanmore St. *LS4: Leeds* 6C **76**
(off St Michael's La.)
Bk. Stonegate Rd. *LS6: Leeds* 2F **77**
Backstone Gill La. *LS17: Wike* 4A **44**
Bk. Stone Hall Rd. *BD2: B'frd* 5H **71**
Backstone La. *LS29: I'ly* 6E **11**
Backstone Way *LS29: I'ly* 5F **11**
Bk. Storey Pl. *LS14: Leeds* 2A **100**
Bk. Stratford Av. *LS11: Leeds* 2G **117**
(off Wickham St.)
Bk. Stratford St. *LS11: Leeds* 2H **117**
(off Rowland Pl.)
Bk. Stratford Ter. *LS11: Leeds* 2H **117**
(off Bude Rd.)
Bk. Strathmore Dr. *LS9: Leeds* 6E **79**
(off Seaforth Dr.)
Back Sunnydene *LS14: Leeds* 2B **100**
Bk. Sutton App. *LS14: Leeds* 2A **100**
Bk. Swinton St. *HX1: Hal* 3D **148**
Bk. Sycamore Av. *BD16: Bgly* 5B **50**
Bk. Tamworth St. *BD4: B'frd* 5C **92**
Bk. Tempest Rd. *LS11: Leeds* 2G **117**
(off Sefton Ter.)
Bk. Temple Vw. *LS11: Leeds* 2G **117**
Bk. Thornhill St. *LS28: Cal* 3F **73**
Bk. Thornville Row *LS6: Leeds* 6E **77**
(off Thornville St.)

Bk. Tower Gro. *LS12: Leeds* 3A **96**
Bk. Trafford Av. *LS9: Leeds* 1F **99**
(off Foundry App.)
Bk. Trentham Pl. *LS11: Leeds* 3H **117**
(off Trentham St.)
Bk. Trinity Ter. *BD5: B'frd* 6D **90**
Bk. Unity St. Nth. *BD16: Bgly* 5B **50**
Bk. Unity St. Sth. *BD16: Bgly* 5B **50**
Bk. Vicars Rd. *LS8: Leeds* 5D **78**
(off Shepherd's La.)
Bk. Victoria Av. *LS9: Leeds* 3E **99**
(off Dawlish Cres.)
Bk. Victoria Gro. *LS9: Leeds* 3F **99**
(off Dawlish Cres.)
Bk. Victoria St.
HX1: Hal 3B **164** (2G **149**)
Bk. Victor Ter. *HX1: Hal* 1D **148**
Bk. Violet Ter. *HX6: Sow B* 5A **148**
(off Park Rd.)
Bk. Wakefield Rd. *HX6: Sow B* 5B **148**
Bk. Walmsley Rd. *LS6: Leeds* 6E **77**
(off Mayville Rd.)
Bk. Walnut St. *BD21: Keigh* 3H **47**
(off Hainworth Wood Rd.)
Bk. Waverley Rd. *HX5: Ell* 6B **160**
Bk. Welburn Av. *LS16: Leeds* 2B **76**
Bk. Welton Av. *LS6: Leeds* 6E **77**
(off Welton Rd.)
Bk. Welton Gro. *LS6: Leeds* 6E **77**
(off Welton Rd.)
Bk. Welton Mt. *LS6: Leeds* 6E **77**
(off Welton Rd.)
Bk. Welton Pl. *LS6: Leeds* 6E **77**
(off Welton Rd.)
Bk. Wesley Rd. *LS12: Leeds* 4C **96**
Bk. Westbury St. *LS10: Leeds* 4D **118**
Bk. Westfield Rd. *LS3: Leeds* 2F **97**
(off Westfield Cres.)
Bk. Westlock Av. *LS9: Leeds* 2E **99**
(off Burton Way)
Bk. Westmorland Mt. *LS13: Leeds* . . .5F **75**
Bk. Weston Rd. *LS29: I'ly* 5D **10**
Bk. West St. *HX6: Sow B* 6H **147**
Bk. Wetherby Gro. *LS4: Leeds* 1C **96**
(off Argie Av.)
Bk. Wetherby Rd. *LS8: Leeds* 3F **79**
(off Wetherby Rd.)
Bk. Wheat St. *BD22: Keigh* 3G **47**
(off Bracken Rd.)
Bk. Wickham St. *LS11: Leeds* 2G **117**
(off Hardy St.)
Bk. William Av. *LS15: Leeds* 3A **100**
(off Selby Rd.)
Bk. William St. *HD6: Ras* 2A **162**
(off William St.)
Bk. Wilton Gro. *LS6: Leeds* 3E **77**
(off Monk Bri. Rd.)
Bk. Winfield Gro. *LS2: Leeds* 1H **97**
(off Devon Rd.)
Bk. Winston Gdns. *LS6: Leeds* 4C **76**
(off Ash Rd.)
Bk. Winterburn St. *BD21: Keigh* 5A **34**
(off Ashleigh St.)
Bk. Wolseley Ter. *HX1: Hal* 2D **148**
Bk. Woodbine Ter. *LS6: Leeds* 3E **77**
Bk. Woodland Pk. Rd. *LS6: Leeds* . . .4E **77**
(off Coniston Av.)
Bk. Woodstock St. *LS2: Leeds* 1H **97**
(off Bk. Blenheim Ter.)
Bk. Wright Av. *BD22: Oak* 4D **46**
Bk. York Pl. *LS1: Leeds* 5B **4** (4G **97**)
(not continuous)
Bk. York St. *LS2: Leeds* 5G **5** (4B **98**)
Bacon St. *LS20: Guis* 5D **40**
Baddeley Gdns. *BD10: B'frd* 5G **53**
Baden St. *BD22: Haw* 1C **64**
Baden Ter. *LS13: Leeds* 3E **95**
(off Pudsey Rd.)
Badger Cl. *LS29: I'ly* 5A **10**
Badger Ga. *BD15: Wils* 5G **67**
Badgergate Av. *BD15: Wils* 5G **67**
Badger Hill *HD6: Ras* 5G **161**
Badger La. *HX3: Hip* 2D **150**

Badgers Drift BD20: Keigh 3H **33**
Badgers Mt. LS15: Leeds 1H **101**
Badgerstone Cl. BD20: E Mor 4H **35**
Badgers Way BD2: B'frd 5E **71**
Badger Wood Glade LS22: Weth 1E **13**
Badminton Dr. LS10: Leeds 4B **140**
Badminton Vw. LS10: Leeds 4B **140**
Badsworth Ct. BD14: Clay 6F **89**
BAGBY FIELDS 6H **77**
BAGHILL 3D **154**
Baghill Grn. WF3: W Ard 3D **154**
Baghill Rd. WF3: W Ard 2D **154**
BAGLEY 5A **74**
Bagley La. LS13: Fars, Leeds 5A **74**
LS28: Fars 5H **73**
Bagnall Ter. BD6: B'frd 4B **110**
Bagshaw Mus. 6C **136**
BAILDON 4C **52**
Baildon Av. LS25: Kip 2H **123**
Baildon Bri. BD17: Ship 1B **70**
Baildon Chase LS14: Leeds 2E **81**
Baildon Cl. LS14: Leeds 3E **81**
Baildon Dr. LS14: Leeds 3E **81**
Baildon Golf Course 2C **52**
BAILDON GREEN 5B **52**
Baildon Grn. LS14: Leeds 3E **81**
BAILDON HOLMES 6C **52**
Baildon Holmes BD17: Bail 6C **52**
Baildon Mills BD17: Bail *3C 52*
(off Providence Row)
Baildon Path LS14: Leeds 3E **81**
Baildon Pl. LS14: Leeds 3E **81**
Baildon Recreation Cen. 6B **52**
Baildon Rd. BD17: Bail 4C **52**
LS14: Leeds 2E **81**
Baildon Station (Rail) 4E **53**
Baildon Wlk. LS14: Leeds 2E **81**
BAILDON WOOD BOTTOM 6C **52**
Baildon Wood Ct. BD17: Bail 6C **52**
Bailes Rd. LS7: Leeds 4G **77**
Bailey Fold BD15: All 2B **88**
Bailey Hall Bank HX3: Hal 2H **149**
Bailey Hall Bus. Pk. HX3: Hal 2H **149**
Bailey Hall Rd. HX3: Hal 3H **149**
Bailey Hall Vw. HX3: Hal 2H **149**
Bailey Hills Rd. BD16: Bgly 3A **50**
Bailey's Cl. LS14: Leeds 3C **80**
Baileys Cft. BD20: Keigh 3H **33**
Bailey's Hill LS14: Leeds 4C **80**
Bailey's La. LS14: Leeds 4C **80**
Bailey's Lawn LS14: Leeds 4C **80**
Bailey St. BD4: B'frd 6F **91**
Bailey Towers LS14: Leeds 4C **80**
Bailey Wells Av. BD5: B'frd 2C **110**
BAILIFF BRIDGE 2B **152**
Bainbrigge Rd. LS6: Leeds 5D **76**
Baines St. HX1: Hal 1E **149**
LS26: Rothw 2A **142**
Baird St. BD5: B'frd 1E **111**
Bairstow Ct. HX6: Sow B 3A **148**
Bairstow La. HX2: Hal 3B **148**
HX6: Sow B 3A **148**
Bairstow Mt. HX6: Sow B 4B **148**
Bairstow St. BD15: All 6C **68**
Baker Cres. LS27: Morl 4A **138**
Baker Fold HX1: Hal *2E 149*
(off Crossley Gdns.)
Baker La. WF3: S'ley 3H **157**
Baker Rd. LS27: Morl 4A **138**
Bakers Cotts. LS28: Pud *4A 94*
(off Park Vw.)
Baker St. BD2: B'frd 1H **91**
BD18: Ship 1A **70**
LS27: Morl 4A **138**
Baker St. Nth. HX2: Hal 2E **129**
Bakes St. BD7: B'frd 1A **110**
Balbec Av. LS6: Leeds 4E **77**
Balbec St. LS6: Leeds 4E **77**
Balcony BD22: Haw 3B **64**
Balcony Cotts. BD13: Que 5A **108**
Balcony Ter. BD22: Cros R *1F 65*
(off Halifax Rd.)

Baldovan Mt. LS8: Leeds 5D **78**
Baldovan Pl. LS8: Leeds 5D **78**
Baldovan Ter. LS8: Leeds 5D **78**
Baldwin La. BD13: Que 3C **108**
BD14: Clay 3C **108**
Baldwin Ter. HX3: Hal 2H **149**
Baldwin Wing HX1: Hal *4G 149*
(off Emily Way)
Bale Dr. BD10: B'frd 1F **71**
Balfour St. BD4: B'frd 1G **111**
BD16: Bgly 5B **50**
BD21: Keigh 1H **47**
Balkcliffe La. LS10: Leeds 1G **139**
Balk La. BD7: B'frd 1B **110**
Balkram Dr. HX2: Mix 2H **127**
Balkram Edge HX2: Mt T 2F **127**
Balkram Rd. HX2: Mix 2H **127**
Ballantyne Rd. BD10: B'frd 5G **53**
Ball St. BD13: Thorn 3A **88**
Balme La. BD12: Wyke 4D **132**
Balme Rd. BD19: Cleck 6B **134**
Balme St. BD1: B'frd 3E **7** (4F **91**)
BD2: Wyke 4C **132**
Balmoral Chase
LS10: Leeds 2D **118**
Balmoral Ct. WF3: W Ard 2F **155**
Balmoral Dr. LS26: Meth 4C **144**
Balmoral Ho. LS17: Leeds 2B **60**
Balmoral Pl. BD13: Que 5G **107**
HX1: Hal 5A **164** (3G **149**)
Balmoral Ter. LS6: Leeds 3E **77**
Balmoral Way LS19: Yead 1H **55**
Balm Pl. LS11: Leeds 6G **97**
Balm Rd. LS10: Leeds 3C **118**
Balm Rd. Ind. Est.
LS10: Leeds 2B **118**
Balm Wlk. LS11: Leeds 6F **97**
Bamburgh Cl. LS15: Leeds 6G **81**
Bamburgh Rd. LS15: Leeds 6G **81**
Bamford Ho. BD4: B'frd *4C 112*
(off Tong St.)
Bamlett Brow BD22: Haw 1D **64**
Bancroft St. BD22: Cros R *1F 65*
(off Halifax Rd.)
Bangor Gro. LS12: Leeds 1A **116**
Bangor Pl. LS12: Leeds 1A **116**
Bangor St. LS12: Leeds 1A **116**
Bangor Ter. LS12: Leeds 1A **116**
Bangor Vw. LS12: Leeds 1A **116**
BANK 5H **5** (4C **98**)
Bank BD22: Oxen 2E **85**
Bank, The BD10: B'frd 4A **72**
Bank Av. LS18: H'fth 1D **74**
LS27: Morl 2A **138**
Bank Bottom HX3: Hal 2H **149**
HX7: Myth 5A **126**
Bank Bottom La. HX2: Lud 6F **127**
Bank Cl. BD10: B'frd 4A **72**
Bank Crest BD17: Bail 4C **52**
Bank Crest Ri. BD18: Ship 2E **69**
Bank Dr. BD6: B'frd 4D **110**
Bank Edge Gdns.
HX2: Illing 4C **128**
Bank Edge Rd. HX2: Illing 3C **128**
Bank End HX4: Gree 4B **158**
Banker St. LS4: Leeds 2D **96**
Bankfield LS17: Bard 1F **45**
Bankfield Av. BD18: Ship 2F **69**
Bankfield Ct. WF2: Wren 6D **156**
Bankfield Dr. BD18: Ship 2F **69**
BD22: Keigh 6E **33**
WF2: Wren 6D **156**
Bankfield Gdns. HX3: Sou 3B **150**
LS4: Leeds 1C **96**
Bankfield Grange HX4: Gree 4G **159**
Bankfield Gro. BD18: Ship 3F **69**
LS4: Leeds 6C **76**
Bankfield Mt. BD22: Keigh 6E **33**
Bankfield Mus. 6G **129**
Bankfield Rd. BD18: Ship 2F **69**
BD22: Keigh 5E **33**
LS4: Leeds 1C **96**
Bankfield St. BD22: Keigh 5E **33**

Bankfield Ter. BD17: Bail 5D **52**
HX6: Sow B 4G **147**
LS4: Leeds 1C **96**
LS28: Stan 5F **73**
(off Richardshaw Rd.)
Bankfield Vw. HX3: Hal 6F **129**
Bankfield Wlk. BD22: Keigh 5E **33**
Bankfield Yd. HX3: Hal 6F **129**
(off Boothtown Rd.)
BANK FOOT 4C **110**
Bank Gdns. LS18: H'fth 1D **74**
Bank Gdns. Cl. HX2: Illing 4C **128**
Bankholme Ct. BD4: B'frd 3D **112**
BANKHOUSE 6H **93**
Bank Ho. LS27: Morl *3A 138*
(off Queen St.)
Bankhouse LS28: Pud 6H **93**
BANKHOUSE BOTTOM 1H **113**
Bank Ho. Cl. LS27: Morl 2A **138**
Bankhouse Ct. LS28: Pud 6H **93**
Bank Ho. La. HX2: Lud, Wain 3D **126**
Bankhouse La. HX3: Hal 1H **159**
LS28: Pud 6H **93**
Bank Ho. Ter. HX3: Hal 1H **159**
Banklands BD20: Sils 1E **15**
Banklands Av. BD20: Sils 1F **15**
Banklands La. BD20: Sils 1F **15**
Bank La. BD22: Keigh 6D **32**
BD22: Oak 5B **46**
Bank Pde. LS21: Otley 4D **22**
Bank Rd. HX6: Sow B 6H **147**
Banks, The HX6: Sow B 4G **147**
Banks End HX5: Ell 5E **161**
Banks End Rd. HX5: Ell 5E **161**
Banksfield Av. LS19: Yead 5F **41**
Banksfield Cl. LS19: Yead 5F **41**
Banksfield Cres. LS19: Yead 5F **41**
Banksfield Gro. LS19: Yead 5F **41**
Banksfield Mt. LS19: Yead 5F **41**
Banksfield Ri. LS19: Yead 5F **41**
Banksfield Ter. LS19: Yead 6F **41**
Bankside BD17: Bail 4C **52**
Bank Side St. LS8: Leeds 6D **78**
(not continuous)
Bankside Ter. BD17: Bail 5B **52**
Banks La. BD20: Rid 1C **34**
Bank Sq. LS27: Morl 2A **138**
Bank St. BD1: B'frd 4D **6** (4E **91**)
(not continuous)
BD6: B'frd 4C **110**
BD18: Ship 2B **70**
BD19: Cleck 2H **153**
BD21: Keigh *6A 34*
(within Airedale Shop. Cen.)
BD22: Haw *2C 64*
(off Main St.)
HD6: Brigh 1A **162**
LS1: Leeds 4E **5**
(Commercial St.)
LS1: Leeds 5E **5** (4A **98**)
(Trinity Leeds)
LS22: Weth 4E **13**
LS27: Morl 2A **138**
Bank Ter. HX2: Lud *1E 147*
(off High St.)
LS27: Morl 2B **138**
LS28: Stan 1A **94**
BANK TOP
BD10 .4A **72**
HX3 . . . . .4B **150**
HX4: Gree 3G **159**
Bank Top HX3: Sou 3A **150**
Bank Top Dr. BD20: Rid 3D **34**
Bank Top Way BD21: Keigh 1D **48**
Bank Vw. BD11: Birk 1E **135**
BD17: Bail 5B **52**
BD22: Oak 5B **46**
(off Low Bank La.)
HX2: Lud M 3D **146**
LS7: Leeds 2H **77**
Bank Vw. Ho. BD17: Bail *5C 52*
(off Bank Vw.)
Bank Wlk. BD17: Bail 4C **52**

Bankwell Fold BD6: B'frd 4D 110
Bankwood Way WF17: Birs 3D 136
Bannerman St. BD12: O'haw 2G 133
Banner St. BD3: B'frd 5H 7 (5G 91)
Bannockburn Ct. BD5: B'frd 4H 111
Banstead St. E. LS8: Leeds 6D 78
Banstead St. W. LS8: Leeds 6D 78
Banstead Ter. E. LS8: Leeds 6D 78
Banstead Ter. W. LS8: Leeds 6D 78
Bantam Cl. LS27: Morl 3D 138
BANTAM GROVE 3D 138
Bantam Gro. La. LS27: Morl 3D 138
Bantam Gro. Vw. LS27: Morl 3D 138
Bantree Ct. BD10: B'frd 5G 53
Baptist Fold BD13: Que 4A 108
Baptist Pl. BD1: B'frd 3B 6 (4D 90)
Baptist Way LS28: Stan 1C 94
Barberry Av. BD3: B'frd 3C 92
Barber St. HD6: Brigh 6B 152
Barclay Cl. BD13: Cull 3C 66
Barclay St. LS7: Leeds 1G 5
BARCROFT .1F 65
Barcroft BD22: Cros R 1F 65
Barcroft Gro. LS19: Yead 1E 55
Barden Av. BD6: B'frd 4F 109
Barden Cl. LS12: Leeds 4A 96
Barden Dr. BD16: Bgly 3E 51
Barden Grn. LS12: Leeds 4A 96
Barden Gro. LS12: Leeds 4A 96
Barden Mt. LS12: Leeds 4A 96
Barden Pl. LS12: Leeds 4A 96
Barden St. BD8: B'frd 2B 90
Barden Ter. LS12: Leeds 4A 96
Bardon Hall Gdns. LS16: Leeds 1C 76
Bardon Hall M. LS16: Leeds 1C 76
BARDSEY 2F 45
Bardsey Cres. BD3: B'frd 4H 7 (4G 91)
Bardsey Ho. BD4: B'frd 6B 92
(off Parsonage Rd.)
Bare Head La. HX3: North 2H 129
Barfield Av. LS19: Yead 1E 55
Barfield Cres. LS17: Leeds 2D 60
Barfield Dr. LS19: Yead 1E 55
Barfield Gro. LS17: Leeds 2E 61
Barfield Mt. LS17: Leeds 2E 61
Barfield Rd. HX3: Hip 2E 151
Barfield Ter. LS27: Morl 5A 138
Bargess Ter. LS25: Kip 4H 123
Bargrange Av. BD18: Ship 3B 70
Barham Ter. BD10: B'frd 5B 72
Bar Ho. La. BD20: Keigh 2F 33
Bar Ho. Row LS21: Pool 6D 24
Baring Av. BD3: B'frd 3B 92
Barker Cl. HX3: Hal 6A 150
BARKEREND 3H 7 (4H 91)
Barkerend Rd. BD1: B'frd 3F 7 (4F 91)
BD3: B'frd 3F 7 (4G 91)
Barker Hill LS12: Gil 4D 114
Barker Ho. HX3: Hal 6H 149
Barker Pl. LS13: Leeds 2F 95
Barkers Well Fold LS12: N Far 2F 115
Barkers Well Gth. LS12: N Far 2G 115
Barkers Well Ga. LS12: N Far 2G 115
Barkers Well Lawn LS12: N Far 2G 115
BARKISLAND 6A 158
Bark La. LS29: Add 1E 9
Barkly Av. LS11: Leeds 4G 117
Barkly Dr. LS11: Leeds 4G 117
Barkly Gro. LS11: Leeds 3G 117
Barkly Pde. LS11: Leeds 4G 117
Barkly Pl. LS11: Leeds 4G 117
Barkly Rd. LS11: Leeds 3F 117
Barkly St. LS11: Leeds 4G 117
Barkly Ter. LS11: Leeds 4G 117
Barkston Wlk. BD15: All 4C 88
Bar La. BD20: Rid 4D 34
LS18: H'fth 1A 74
LS23: Cliff 5D 30
LS25: Gar 4G 103
Barlby Way LS8: Leeds 3G 79
Barleycorn Yd. LS17: Leeds 4B 96
Barley Cote BD20: Rid 3E 35
Barley Cote Av. BD20: Rid 3D 34

Barley Cote Gro. BD20: Rid 3E 35
Barley Cote Rd. BD20: Rid 3E 35
Barley Fld. Ct. LS15: Leeds 3C 100
Barley Flds. Cl. LS22: Weth 5E 103
Barleyfields Cl. LS22: Weth 2E 13
Barleyfields Ct. LS22: Weth 3E 13
Barleyfields La. LS22: Weth 3E 13
Barley Fld. Sq. HX2: Hal 5B 128
Barleyfields Rd. LS22: Weth 2E 13
(not continuous)
Barleyfields Ter. LS22: Weth 3E 13
Barleyfields Wlk. LS22: Weth 4E 13
Barleyhill Cres. LS25: Gar 5E 103
Barleyhill La. LS25: Gar 4E 103
Barleyhill Rd. LS25: Gar 4D 102
Barley M. WF3: Rob H 4F 141
Barlow Rd. BD21: Keigh 5H 33
Barlow St. BD3: B'frd 4H 91
Barmby Pl. BD2: B'frd 2H 91
Barmby Rd. BD2: B'frd 2H 91
Barmby St. BD12: Wyke 3D 132
Bar Mt. LS25: Gar 4G 103
Barmouth Ter. BD3: B'frd 2F 91
Barnaby Rd. BD16: Bgly 3E 51
Barnard Cl. LS15: Leeds 6G 81
Barnard Rd. BD4: B'frd 6G 91
Barnard Ter. BD4: B'frd 6G 91
Barnard Way LS15: Leeds 6G 81
BARNBOW CARR 4C 82
Barnbow La. LS15: Leeds 5B 82
Barnbrough St. LS4: Leeds 1C 96
Barnby Av. BD8: B'frd 4E 89
Barn Climbing & Activity Centre, The
. . . . .1H 49
Barn Cl. LS29: Men 1F 39
Barncroft BD18: Ship 2C 70
Barncroft Cl. LS14: Leeds 2B 80
Barncroft Ct. LS14: Leeds 3A 80
Barncroft Dr. LS14: Leeds 2B 80
Barncroft Gdns. LS14: Leeds 3B 80
Barncroft Grange LS14: Leeds 3A 80
Barncroft Hgts. LS14: Leeds 2A 80
Barncroft Mt. LS14: Leeds 3A 80
Barncroft Ri. LS14: Leeds 3B 80
Barncroft Rd. LS14: Leeds 3B 80
Barncroft Towers LS14: Leeds 3A 80
Barnes Av. WF1: Wake 6E 157
Barnes Rd. BD8: B'frd 3H 89
Barnet Gro. LS27: Morl 5A 138
Barnet Rd. LS12: Leeds 4D 96
Barns, The LS29: I'ly 1A 20
Barnsdale Rd. LS26: Meth 6D 144
WF10: All B 6B 124
Barnsley Beck Gro. BD17: Bail 4D 52
Barnstaple Way BD4: B'frd 3B 112
Barn St. BD22: Oxen 1C 84
Barnswick Vw. LS16: Leeds 3G 57
Baron Cl. LS11: Leeds 1G 117
Baronscourt LS15: Leeds 3F 101
Baronsmead LS15: Leeds 3E 101
Baronsway LS15: Leeds 3E 101
Barplas Ind. Pk. BD5: B'frd 3E 111
Barrack Rd. LS7: Leeds 6B 78
Barrack St. LS7: Leeds 1B 98
Barraclough Bldgs. BD10: B'frd 2C 72
Barraclough Sq. BD12: Wyke 3C 132
Barraclough St. BD12: Low M 1B 132
Barran Ct. LS8: Leeds 6D 78
Barran St. BD16: Bgly 4C 50
Barras Gth. Ind. Est. LS12: Leeds 5B 96
Barras Gth. Pl. LS12: Leeds 5B 96
Barras Gth. Rd. LS12: Leeds 5B 96
Barras Pl. LS12: Leeds 5B 96
Barras St. LS12: Leeds 5B 96
Barras Ter. LS12: Leeds 5B 96
Barrett St. BD20: Sils 2D 14
Barrington Cl. HX3: Sou 5C 150
Barrington Pde. BD19: Gom 6E 135
BARROWBY 3B 102
Barrowby Av. LS15: Leeds 4G 101
Barrowby Carr Dr. LS25: Gar 3A 102

Barrowby Cl. LS29: Men 1H 39
Barrowby Cres. LS15: Leeds 3G 101
Barrowby Dr. LS15: Leeds 4H 101
Barrowby La. LS15: Leeds 3G 101
LS25: Gar 3D 102
LS25: Gar, Leeds 3A 102
Barrowby Rd. LS15: Leeds 4H 101
Barrowby Vw. LS25: Gar 3E 103
Barrowclough La. HX3: Sou 2B 150
Barrows La. BD20: Stee 1B 32
Barr Ter. BD8: B'frd 3H 89
(off Washington St.)
Barry St. BD1: B'frd 4C 6 (4E 91)
Barsey Grn. La. HX4: Bark 3A 158
Barthorpe Av. LS17: Leeds 1H 77
Barthorpe Cl. BD4: B'frd 3D 112
Barthorpe Cres. LS17: Leeds 1A 78
Bartle Cl. BD7: B'frd 2H 109
Bartle Ct. BD15: Wils 3F 67
Bartle Fold BD7: B'frd 1A 110
Bartle Gill Dr. BD17: Bail 3E 53
Bartle Gill Ri. BD17: Bail 3E 53
Bartle Gill Vw. BD17: Bail 3E 53
Bartle Gro. BD7: B'frd 2H 109
Bartle La. BD7: B'frd 2H 109
Bartle Pl. BD7: B'frd 2H 109
Bartle Sq. BD7: B'frd 1A 110
Barton Ct. LS15: Leeds 4E 101
Barton Gro. LS11: Leeds 1G 117
Barton Hill LS11: Leeds 1G 117
Barton Mt. LS11: Leeds 1G 117
Barton Pl. LS11: Leeds 1G 117
Barton Rd. LS11: Leeds 1G 117
Barton St. BD5: B'frd 2B 110
HD6: Brigh 6A 152
(off Manley St.)
Barton Ter. LS11: Leeds 1G 117
Barton Vw. LS11: Leeds 1G 117
Barum Top HX1: Hal 4B 164 (2G 149)
Barwick Ct. LS27: Morl 2B 138
Barwick Grn. BD6: B'frd 4G 109
BARWICK IN ELMET 2D 82
Barwick Rd. LS15: Leeds 6D 80
LS25: Bar E, Gar 3E 103
Barwick Sq. BD22: Cros R 1F 65
Basilica LS1: Leeds 4E 5
Basil St. BD5: B'frd 2B 110
Baslow Gro. BD9: B'frd 1H 89
Batcliffe Dr. LS6: Leeds 3C 76
Batcliffe Mt. LS6: Leeds 4C 76
Bateman Fold BD12: O'haw 2H 133
(off Mill Carr Hill St.)
Bateman St. BD8: B'frd 2D 90
Bates Av. HX6: Sow B 6F 147
Bateson St. BD10: B'frd 2C 72
Bath Cl. LS13: Leeds 1E 95
Bath Gro. LS13: Leeds 1E 95
Bath La. LS13: Leeds 2E 95
Bath Pl. HD6: Ras 2A 162
HX3: Hal 1B 164 (6F 129)
Bath Rd. HX3: Hal 5G 149
LS11: Leeds 5G 97
LS13: Leeds 2E 95
Bath St. BD21: Keigh 6H 33
HX1: Hal 5D 164 (3H 149)
HX5: Ell 5B 160
LS29: I'ly 4E 11
Batley Cl. BD17: Bail 3D 52
Batley Rd. WF2: Kirk 4D 154
WF3: W Ard 3D 154
Batley Sports & Tennis Cen. 6D 136
Batley St. HX3: Hal 6E 129
Batter La. LS19: Raw 3G 55
Battinson Rd. HX1: Hal 1D 148
Battinson St. HX3: Sou 4A 150
Battlefield Vw. BD11: Birk 6F 113
Battye St. BD4: B'frd 5A 92
Bavaria Pl. BD8: B'frd 2B 90
BAWN 6H 95
Bawn App. LS12: Leeds 6G 95
Bawn Av. LS12: Leeds 5G 95
Bawn Chase LS12: Leeds 5G 95
Bawn Dr. LS12: Leeds 5G 95

Bawn Gdns.—Beech Tree Av.

Bawn Gdns. LS12: Leeds 5G **95**
Bawn La. LS12: Leeds 5G **95**
Bawn Path *LS12: Leeds* *5H* ***95***
(off Bawn Av.)
Bawn Va. *LS12: Leeds* *5G* ***95***
(off Bawn Gdns.)
Bawn Wlk. *LS12: Leeds* *5H* ***95***
(off Bawn Gdns.)
Bawson Ct. BD19: Gom 6E **135**
Baxandall St. BD5: B'frd 2D **110**
Baxendale Dr. LS13: Leeds 3D **74**
Baxter La. HX3: North 4C **130**
Bay Horse Ct. *LS21: Otley* *3E* ***23***
(off Clapgate)
Bay Horse La. LS14: S'cft 6C **44**
LS17: Leeds, S'cft 6C **44**
Bay Horse Yd. LS1: Leeds 4F **5**
LS28: Fars 6H **73**
Bayne Dr. BD4: B'frd 5H **111**
Bay of Biscay BD15: All 5C **68**
Bayonne *LS20: Guis* *4B* ***40***
(off Silver Cross Way)
Bayswater Cres. LS8: Leeds 6D **78**
Bayswater Gro. BD2: B'frd 1B **92**
LS8: Leeds 6D **78**
Bayswater Mt. LS8: Leeds 6D **78**
Bayswater Pl. LS8: Leeds 6D **78**
Bayswater Rd. LS8: Leeds 6C **78**
Bayswater Row LS8: Leeds 6D **78**
Bayswater Ter. HX3: Hal 6G **149**
LS8: Leeds 6D **78**
Bayswater Vw. LS8: Leeds 6D **78**
Bayton La. LS18: H'fth 1H **55**
LS19: H'fth, Yead 1H **55**
Beacon Av. LS27: Morl 5B **138**
Beacon Brow BD6: B'frd 3F **109**
Beacon Bus. Cen. HX3: Hal 3A **150**
Beacon Cl. BD16: Bgly 4D **50**
Beacon Gro. BD6: B'frd 4H **109**
LS27: Morl 5B **138**
Beacon Hill Rd.
HX3: Hal 2D **164** (1H **149**)
Beacon Pl. BD6: B'frd 4G **109**
Beacon Ri. LS29: I'ly 5A **10**
Beacon Rd. BD6: B'frd 3F **109**
Beaconsfield Ct. LS25: Gar 3F **103**
Beaconsfield Rd. BD14: Clay 1E **109**
Beaconsfield St. HX3: Hal 3A **150**
Beacon St. BD6: B'frd 4A **110**
BD7: B'frd 3G **109**
LS29: Add .1E **9**
Beacon Vw. *LS27: Morl* *5B* ***138***
(off Tingley Comn.)
Beamsley Cl. LS29: Men 2G **39**
Beamsley Ct. LS29: Men 3G **39**
Beamsley Cft. LS29: Men 3G **39**
Beamsley Gro. BD16: Bgly 4D **50**
LS6: Leeds 1E **97**
Beamsley Ho. *BD18: Ship* *4B* ***70***
(off Bradford Rd.)
Beamsley Mt. LS6: Leeds 1E **97**
Beamsley Pl. LS6: Leeds 1E **97**
Beamsley Rd. BD9: B'frd 1B **90**
BD18: Ship 4B **70**
Beamsley Ter. LS6: Leeds 1E **97**
Beamsley Vw. LS29: I'ly 5A **10**
Beamsley Wlk. BD9: B'frd 1A **90**
LS29: Men 2G **39**
Beanland Ct. *BD18: Ship* *4B* ***70***
(off Aireville Av.)
Beanland Gdns. BD6: B'frd 5H **109**
Beanlands Pde. LS29: I'ly 4E **11**
Bean St. HX5: Ell 5E **161**
Bearing Av. LS11: Leeds 3A **118**
Bear Pit Gdns. *LS6: Leeds* *6D* ***76***
(off Chapel La.)
Beatrice St. BD19: Cleck 6B **134**
BD20: Keigh 4A **34**
BD22: Oxen 1C **84**
Beaufort Gro. BD2: B'frd 6G **71**
Beaumont Av. LS8: Leeds 5E **61**
Beaumont Rd. BD8: B'frd 2B **90**
Beaumont Sq. LS28: Pud 5H **93**
Beauvais Dr. BD20: Rid 5F **35**
Beaver Cl. BD22: Cros R 1E **65**
BECK BOTTOM **6A 156**
Beck Bottom LS28: Cal 3C **72**
LS28: Fars 5A **74**
WF2: Kirk 6A **156**
Beckbury Cl. LS28: Fars 1H **93**
Beckbury St. LS28: Fars 1H **93**
Beckenham Pl. HX1: Hal 1C **148**
Beckers Av. WF17: Birs 5D **136**
Becket La. WF3: Loft 5F **141**
Beckett Ct. LS15: Leeds 5F **101**
BECKETT PARK **3D 76**
Becketts, The *LS6: Leeds* *3F* ***77***
(off Monk Bri. Rd.)
Beckett's Pk. Cres.
LS6: Leeds 4C **76**
Beckett's Pk. Dr. LS6: Leeds 4C **76**
Beckett's Pk. Rd. LS6: Leeds 4D **76**
Beckett St. LS9: Leeds 2C **98**
Beckfield Cl. HD6: B Bri 3B **152**
Beckfield Rd. BD16: Cot 2B **68**
Beckfoot La. BD16: Bgly, Cot 5A **50**
BECK HILL **1G 131**
Beck Hill BD6: B'frd 6G **109**
Beckhill App. LS7: Leeds 3G **77**
Beckhill Av. LS7: Leeds 3G **77**
Beckhill Chase LS7: Leeds 3G **77**
Beckhill Cl. LS7: Leeds 3G **77**
Beckhill Dr. LS7: Leeds 2G **77**
Beckhill Fold LS7: Leeds 2G **77**
Beckhill Gdns. LS7: Leeds 3G **77**
Beckhill Gth. LS7: Leeds 3G **77**
Beckhill Ga. LS7: Leeds 3G **77**
Beckhill Grn. LS7: Leeds 3G **77**
Beckhill Gro. LS7: Leeds 3G **77**
Beckhill Lawn LS7: Leeds 3G **77**
Beckhill Pl. LS7: Leeds 2G **77**
Beckhill Row LS7: Leeds 2G **77**
Beckhill Va. LS7: Leeds 2G **77**
(not continuous)
Beckhill Vw. LS7: Leeds 3G **77**
Beckhill Wlk. LS7: Leeds 2G **77**
Beck Ho's. *BD16: Bgly* *3C* ***50***
(off Gawthorpe La.)
Beck La. BD16: Bgly 2B **50**
LS22: Coll 2B **28**
Beck Mdw. LS15: Bar E 3E **83**
Beck Rd. BD16: Bgly 5A **36**
LS8: Leeds 5D **78**
Beck Side BD21: Keigh 1A **48**
Beckside BD1: B'frd 1E **91**
HX3: She 6F **109**
Beckside Cl. LS29: Add 1D **8**
LS29: Burl W 2E **21**
Beckside Ct. BD20: Sils 2E **15**
Beckside Gdns.
LS16: Leeds 2D **76**
Beckside La. BD7: B'frd 1A **110**
Beckside Rd. BD7: B'frd 6A **90**
Beckside Vw. LS27: Morl 3C **138**
Becks Rd. BD21: Keigh 1G **47**
Beck St. BD21: Keigh 1H **47**
Beck Vw. WF17: Birs 5H **135**
Beck Way WF3: E Ard 1D **156**
Beckwith Dr. BD10: B'frd 4B **72**
Bedale WF3: W Ard 1D **154**
Bedale Av. HD6: Ras 3G **161**
Bedale Ct. LS27: Morl 3E **139**
Bedale Dr. BD6: B'frd 4G **109**
Bede's Cl. BD13: Thorn 5H **87**
Bedford Chambers
LS1: Leeds 4D **4**
Bedford Cl. LS16: Leeds 4G **57**
Bedford Ct. LS8: Leeds 3G **79**
Bedford Dr. LS16: Leeds 4G **57**
Bedford Fld. LS6: Leeds 5G **77**
Bedford Gdns. LS16: Leeds 4G **57**
Bedford Gth. LS16: Leeds 4G **57**
Bedford Grn. LS16: Leeds 4G **57**
Bedford Gro. LS16: Leeds 5G **57**
Bedford Mt. LS16: Leeds 5G **57**
(not continuous)
Bedford Pl. LS16: Leeds 4G **57**
LS20: Guis *5C* ***40***
(off Otley Rd.)
LS21: Otley 3G **23**
Bedford Row LS10: Leeds 1B **118**
Bedford St. BD4: B'frd 6E **7** (5F **91**)
BD21: Keigh 6H **33**
HX1: Hal 4A **164** (2F **149**)
HX5: Ell .5B **160**
LS1: Leeds 4D **4** (3H **97**)
Bedford St. Nth.
HX1: Hal 3A **164** (2F **149**)
Bedford Vw. LS16: Leeds 4G **57**
Bedivere Rd. BD8: B'frd 4F **89**
Beech Av. BD13: Denh 6A **66**
HX6: Sow B 4H **147**
LS12: Leeds 3C **96**
LS18: H'fth 2E **75**
BEECHCLIFFE **4H 33**
Beech Cl. BD10: B'frd 5H **53**
HX3: She .1F **131**
LS16: Leeds 2C **58**
LS29: Men 5G **21**
Beech Ct. *BD17: Bail* *6B* ***52***
(off Southcliffe Dr.)
LS14: Leeds 1A **100**
Beech Cres. BD3: B'frd 2H **91**
BD17: Bail 6H **51**
LS9: Leeds 6H **79**
Beech Cft. WF3: Loft 6A **142**
Beechcroft Cl. LS11: Leeds 4D **116**
Beechcroft Mead LS17: Leeds 3E **61**
Beechcroft Vw. LS11: Leeds 4D **116**
Beech Dr. BD13: Denh 6A **66**
LS12: Leeds 3C **96**
LS14: Leeds 1A **100**
LS18: H'fth 2D **74**
Beecher St. BD21: Keigh 5C **34**
HX3: Hal .5F **129**
Beeches, The BD11: Birk 2E **135**
BD17: Bail 3D **52**
LS20: Guis 3C **40**
LS21: Pool 4F **25**
LS22: Weth 3F **13**
LS28: Pud 3F **93**
Beeches End LS23: B Spa 4C **30**
Beeches Rd. BD21: Keigh 5C **34**
Beechfield LS12: N Far 2F **115**
Beech Gro. BD3: B'frd 2H **91**
BD14: Clay 6E **89**
BD16: Bgly 2E **51**
BD19: Gom 6E **135**
BD20: Sils 2D **14**
HX3: Hip 2A **152**
LS6: Leeds 3D **76**
LS26: Rothw 1B **142**
LS27: Morl 4H **137**
LS29: Men 2G **39**
Beech Gro. Av. LS25: Gar 5E **103**
Beech Gro. Gdns. LS26: Oul 2E **143**
Beech Gro. Ter. LS2: Leeds 1G **97**
LS25: Gar 5E **103**
Beech Hill LS21: Otley 3E **23**
Beech Ho. LS16: Leeds 1C **76**
Beech La. LS9: Leeds 6G **79**
Beech Lees LS28: Fars 5G **73**
Beech Mt. LS9: Leeds 6H **79**
Beechmount Cl. BD17: Bail 3D **52**
Beech Rd. BD6: B'frd 6C **110**
HX6: Sow B 5A **148**
LS23: B Spa 3A **30**
Beechroyd LS28: Pud 5A **94**
Beechroyd Ter. BD16: Bgly 5B **50**
Beech Spinney LS22: Weth 1F **13**
Beech Sq. BD14: Clay 1E **109**
Beech St. BD16: Bgly 5B **50**
BD20: Stee 6C **14**
BD21: Keigh 5C **34**
HX1: Hal 1F **149**
HX5: Ell .5B **160**
WF3: Ting 6E **139**
Beech Ter. BD3: B'frd 3H **91**
Beech Tree Av. LS5: Leeds 6H **75**

A-Z Leeds & Bradford 179

Beechtree Ct. BD17: Bail 5A 52
Beech Vw. HX6: Sow B 4H 147
Beech Vs. HX6: Sow B 5A 148
Beech Wlk. BD11: Birk 3F 135
   LS9: Leeds 6H 79
   LS16: Leeds 5D 58
Beech Way WF17: Birs 5C 136
BEECHWOOD
   HX6 . . . . .6F 147
   LS14 . . . . .3B 80
   LS18 . . . . .4D 56
Beechwood LS26: Wood 6E 121
   LS29: I'ly 6F 11
Beechwood Av. BD6: B'frd 3A 110
   BD11: Drig 6H 113
   BD18: Ship 2G 69
   BD20: Rid 4D 34
   HX2: Hal 2E 129
   HX3: She 2D 130
   HX6: Sow B 6F 147
   LS4: Leeds 6D 76
Beechwood Cen. LS26: Wood 6E 121
               (off Beechwood)
Beechwood Cl. HX2: Hal 3D 128
   LS17: Shad 3A 62
   LS18: H'fth 4C 56
Beechwood Ct. LS4: Leeds 6D 76
          (off Beechwood Gro.)
   LS14: Leeds 3A 80
   LS16: Leeds 2B 58
Beechwood Cres. HX6: Sow B 6F 147
   LS4: Leeds 6D 76
Beechwood Dr. BD6: B'frd 3B 110
   HX2: Hal 2D 128
   HX6: Sow B 6F 147
Beechwood Gro. BD6: B'frd 3B 110
   BD11: Drig 6H 113
   BD18: Ship 2G 69
   HD2: Fix 6A 162
   HX2: Hal 3D 128
   LS4: Leeds 6D 76
   LS29: I'ly 5B 10
Beechwood Mt. LS4: Leeds 6D 76
Beechwood Ri. HD6: B'frd 3B 152
Beechwood Park Nature Reserve
                        .2D 128
Beechwood Pl. LS4: Leeds 6D 76
Beechwood Ri. LS22: Weth 2E 13
Beechwood Rd. BD6: B'frd 3A 110
   HX2: Hal 3D 128
   LS4: Leeds 6D 76
Beechwood Row LS4: Leeds 6D 76
Beechwood St. LS4: Leeds 6D 76
   LS28: Stan 2G 93
Beechwood Ter. LS4: Leeds 6D 76
Beechwood Vw. LS4: Leeds 6D 76
Beechwood Vs. HX2: Hal 3D 128
Beechwood Wlk. LS4: Leeds 6D 76
Beecroft Cl. LS13: Leeds 6C 74
Beecroft Cres. LS13: Leeds 6C 74
Beecroft Gdns. LS13: Leeds 6C 74
Beecroft Mt. LS13: Leeds 6C 74
Beecroft St. BD21: Keigh 6B 34
   LS5: Leeds 6A 76
Beecroft Wlk. BD15: All 4C 88
Beehive St. BD6: B'frd 6H 109
Beehive Yd. BD6: B'frd 6H 109
BEESTON 4F 117
BEESTON HILL 1G 117
Beestonley La.
   HX4: Bark, Holy, Stainl 6B 158
Beeston Pk. Cft. LS11: Leeds 3E 117
Beeston Pk. Gth. LS11: Leeds 3E 117
Beeston Pk. Gro. LS11: Leeds 3E 117
Beeston Pk. Pl. LS11: Leeds 3E 117
BEESTON PARK SIDE 5G 117
Beeston Pk. Ter. LS11: Leeds 3E 117
Beeston Rd. LS11: Leeds 3F 117
BEESTON ROYDS 3B 116
Beeston Royds Ind. Est.
   LS12: Leeds 2C 116
Beeston Way WF10: All B 3H 145
Beevers Cotts. LS25: Gar 3E 103

Beevers Ct. LS16: Leeds 5A 58
BEGGARINGTON HILL 3D 154
Behrens Warehouse BD1: B'frd 4F 7
Bela Av. BD4: B'frd 3A 112
Belcross Dr. HX3: Hal . . .1D 164 (6H 129)
BELDON HILL 3G 109
Beldon La. BD7: B'frd 4H 109
Beldon Pk. Av. BD7: B'frd 3H 109
Beldon Pk. Cl. BD7: B'frd 3H 109
Beldon Rd. BD7: B'frd 2A 110
Belfast St. HX1: Hal 3D 148
Belford Cl. BD4: B'frd 2B 112
Belford Ct. LS6: Leeds 6E 59
Belfry, The LS19: Yead 1G 55
Belfry Ct. WF1: Out 4G 157
Belfry Rd. LS9: Leeds 6E 99
Belgrave Av. HX3: Hal 1H 149
Belgrave Cl. HX3: Hal 1H 149
Belgrave Ct. HD6: Ras 4G 161
Belgrave Cres. HX3: Hal 1H 149
Belgrave Dr. HX3: Hal 1A 150
Belgrave Gdns. HX3: Hal 6H 129
Belgrave Gro. HX3: Hal 6H 129
Belgrave M. LS19: Raw 3E 55
Belgrave Mt. HX3: Hal 6H 129
Belgrave Pk. HX3: Hal 6H 129
Belgrave Rd. BD16: Bgly 3C 50
   BD21: Keigh 5H 33
Belgrave St. HX6: Sow B 5H 147
   LS2: Leeds 3E 5 (3A 98)
Belgravia Bldgs. LS8: Leeds 2G 79
Belinda St. LS10: Leeds 1C 118
Bell Bank Vw. BD16: Bgly 3A 50
Bellbrooke Av. LS9: Leeds 1F 99
Bellbrooke Gro. LS9: Leeds 1F 99
Bellbrooke Pl. LS9: Leeds 1F 99
Bellbrooke St. LS9: Leeds 1E 99
Bell Dean Rd. BD8: B'frd 3D 88
   BD15: All 3D 88
BELLE ISLE 5C 118
Belle Isle BD22: Haw 3C 64
Belle Isle Cir. LS10: Leeds 5C 118
Belle Isle Cl. LS10: Leeds 5C 118
Belle Isle Pde. LS10: Leeds 4C 118
Belle Isle Rd. BD22: Haw 2C 64
   LS10: Leeds 3C 118
Bellerby Brow BD6: B'frd 4F 109
Belle Vw. Ter. LS23: Cliff 6B 30
                  (off Albion Ter.)
Belle Vue BD2: B'frd 4A 72
   BD8: B'frd 2D 90
   BD13: Que 6A 108
   LS29: I'ly 6E 11
Belle Vue Av. LS8: Leeds 3H 79
   LS15: Scho 2H 81
Belle Vue Cl. BD10: B'frd 6H 53
Belle Vue Ct. LS3: Leeds 2F 97
               (off Consort Ter.)
Belle Vue Cres. HX3: She 2D 130
Belle Vue Dr. LS28: Fars 6G 73
Belle Vue Est. LS15: Scho 3H 81
Belle Vue Ri. HX3: She 2D 130
Belle Vue Rd. HX3: She 2D 130
   LS3: Leeds 3A 4 (2F 97)
   LS15: Scho 3H 81
Belle Vue Ter. BD21: Keigh 1B 48
               (off Feather St.)
   HX2: Lud M 2C 146
   HX3: Sou 4A 150
   LS20: Guis 5C 40
   LS27: Gil 1F 137
Bell Gro. LS13: Leeds 6E 75
Bell Hall Mt. HX1: Hal 4E 149
Bell Hall Ter. HX1: Hal 4E 149
Bell Hall Vw. HX1: Hal 4F 149
Bell Ho. Av. BD4: B'frd 4H 111
Bell Ho. Cres. BD4: B'frd 5H 111
Bell La. LS13: Leeds 6E 75
Bellmount Cl. LS13: Leeds 6F 75
Bellmount Gdns. LS13: Leeds 5E 75
Bellmount Grn. LS13: Leeds 6F 75
Bellmount Pl. LS13: Leeds 5E 75

Bellmount Vw. LS13: Leeds 6F 75
Belloe St. BD5: B'frd 1D 110
Bell Rd. LS13: Leeds 6E 75
Bell Row HD6: Ras 2A 162
Bellshaw St. BD8: B'frd 4G 89
Bell St. BD12: Wyke 3C 132
   HX3: Hal 6H 129
   LS9: Leeds 3H 5 (3B 98)
Bellwood Av. LS23: Cliff 5B 30
Belmont Av. BD12: Low M 6E 111
   BD17: Bail 4B 52
   LS21: Otley 2D 22
Belmont Cl. BD17: Bail 4B 52
Belmont Cres. BD12: Low M 6E 111
   BD18: Ship 1A 70
Belmont Gdns. BD12: Low M 6D 110
Belmont Gro. BD6: B'frd 6D 110
   LS2: Leeds 2B 4 (2G 97)
   LS19: Raw 2G 55
Belmont Pl. HX1: Hal 3E 149
Belmont Ri. BD12: Low M 6E 111
   BD17: Bail 4B 52
Belmont Rd. LS29: I'ly 5G 11
Belmont St. BD2: B'frd 4A 72
   HX3: Hal 1A 150
   HX6: Sow B 5A 148
Belmont Ter. BD18: Ship 1A 70
   HX2: Lud M 4E 147
   WF3: Thpe H 5D 140
Belton Cl. BD7: B'frd 2A 110
Belton Rd. BD20: Sils 3E 15
Belvedere Av. LS11: Leeds 3H 117
   LS17: Leeds 3B 60
Belvedere Ct. LS7: Leeds 4C 78
             (off Harehills La.)
   LS17: Leeds 3C 60
   WF1: Out 4G 157
Belvedere Gdns. LS17: Leeds 3C 60
Belvedere Gro. LS17: Leeds 3B 60
Belvedere Mt. LS11: Leeds 3H 117
Belvedere Rd. LS17: Leeds 3B 60
Belvedere St. BD8: B'frd 2B 90
Belvedere Ter. BD8: B'frd 3B 90
   LS11: Leeds 3H 117
Belvedere Vw. LS17: Leeds 3C 60
Belvoir Gdns. HX3: Hal 6G 149
Bempton Cl. BD7: B'frd 1B 110
Bempton Gro. WF17: Birs 5B 136
Bempton Pl. BD7: B'frd 1B 110
Benbow Av. BD10: B'frd 4C 72
Benn Av. BD7: B'frd 1H 109
Benn Cres. BD7: B'frd 1H 109
Bennet Ct. LS15: Leeds 3F 101
Bennett Ct. LS21: Otley 2D 22
Bennett Rd. LS6: Leeds 4D 76
Bennett St. HX3: Hal 3A 150
Bennetts Yd. LS26: Rothw 3A 142
Benn Gdns. BD14: Clay 2D 108
Benns La. HX2: Lud 5E 127
BEN RHYDDING 5G 11
Ben Rhydding Dr.
   LS29: I'ly . . . . .5G 11 & 1A 20
Ben Rhydding Golf Course 1H 19
Ben Rhydding Rd. LS29: I'ly 6E 11
Ben Rhydding Station (Rail) 5G 11
Benson Cl. BD2: B'frd 4D 70
Benson Gdns. LS12: Leeds 5B 96
Benson's Mobile Home Pk.
   BD20: Rid 2F 35
Benson St. LS7: Leeds 1G 5 (1B 98)
Bentcliffe Av. LS17: Leeds 5B 60
Bentcliffe Cl. LS17: Leeds 6C 60
Bentcliffe Ct. LS17: Leeds 6C 60
Bentcliffe Dr. LS17: Leeds 5C 60
Bentcliffe Gdns. LS17: Leeds 6C 60
Bentcliffe Gro. LS17: Leeds 6C 60
Bentcliffe La. LS17: Leeds 6B 60
Bentcliffe Mt. LS17: Leeds 6C 60
Bentcliff Wlk. BD15: All 4D 88
Bentfield Cotts. BD14: Clay 6E 89
Bentfield Ter. BD14: Clay 6E 89
             (off Bentfield Cotts.)
Bent Lea HD2: Hud 5F 163

Bentley Av. HX3: Hip 2A **152**
Bentley Cl. BD17: Bail 3B **52**
Bentley Ct. LS7: Leeds 3F **77**
  LS26: Wood 6E **121**
Bentley Gdns. LS7: Leeds 3F **77**
Bentley Gro. LS6: Leeds 3F **77**
Bentley La. LS6: Leeds 3F **77**
  LS7: Leeds 3F **77**
Bentley M. LS6: Leeds 3F **77**
Bentley Mt. HX6: Sow B 4B **148**
  LS6: Leeds 3F **77**
Bentley Pde. LS6: Leeds 3F **77**
Bentley Royd Cl. HX6: Sow B 6G **147**
Bentley Sq. LS26: Oul 2E **143**
Bentley St. BD12: Wyke 4D **132**
Benton Pk. Av. LS19: Raw 2G **55**
Benton Pk. Cres. LS19: Raw 2G **55**
Benton Pk. Dr. LS19: Raw 2G **55**
Benton Pk. Rd. LS19: Raw 2G **55**
Bents BD22: Oxen 5C **64**
Bents Foot BD16: Har 1F **67**
Bents La. BD15: Wils 5E **67**
Benyon Pk. Way LS12: Leeds 1D **116**
Beresford Rd. BD6: B'frd 6B **110**
Beresford St. BD12: O'haw 2G **133**
Beringa LS12: Leeds 5A 4 (4G **97**)
Berkeley Av. LS8: Leeds 6E **79**
Berkeley Cl. BD2: B'frd 6H **71**
Berkeley Ct. LS2: Leeds 1A 4 (2F **97**)
  LS8: Leeds 6E **79**
  (off Chatsworth Rd.)
Berkeley Cres. LS8: Leeds 6E **79**
Berkeley Gro. LS8: Leeds 6E **79**
Berkeley Ho. *BD4: B'frd* 2C **112**
  (off Stirling Cres.)
Berkeley Mt. LS8: Leeds 6E **79**
Berkeley Rd. LS8: Leeds 6E **79**
Berkeley St. LS8: Leeds 6E **79**
Berkeley Ter. LS8: Leeds 6E **79**
Berkeley Vw. LS8: Leeds 6E **79**
Berking Av. LS9: Leeds 3D **98**
Berking Row LS9: Leeds 3D **98**
Bermondsey M. LS21: Otley 4F **23**
Bermondsey St. LS21: Otley 4F **23**
Bernard St. LS26: Wood 1F **143**
Berrington Way BD22: Oak 4B **46**
Berrydale Cl. BD15: All 4C **88**
Berry Dr. BD17: Bail 6D **52**
Berry La. BD21: Keigh 2H **47**
  HX1: Hal 2H **149**
  LS26: Gt P 5E **123**
Berry Moor Rd. HX6: Norl 1B **158**
Berry's Bldgs. *HX2: Hal* 3D **128**
  (off Bairstow's Bldgs.)
Berry St. BD21: Keigh 6B **34**
Bertha St. LS28: Fars 1H **93**
Bertie St. BD4: B'frd 2A **112**
Bertram Dr. BD17: Bail 6B **52**
Bertram Rd. BD8: B'frd 1C **90**
Bertrand St. LS11: Leeds 6G **97**
Berwick St. HX1: Hal 4D **164** (2H **149**)
Bescaby Gro. BD17: Bail 3E **53**
Bescot Way BD18: Ship 4E **71**
Besha Av. BD12: Low M 1D **132**
Besha Gro. BD12: Low M 1D **132**
Bessbrook St. LS10: Leeds 2B **118**
Bessingham Gdns. BD6: B'frd 5H **109**
Best La. BD22: Oxen 1C **84**
Beswick Cl. BD3: B'frd 4B **92**
Bethel Rd. BD18: Ship 1D **70**
Bethel St. BD20: E Mor 5H **35**
  HD6: Brigh 1B **162**
  HX3: Hal 5E **129**
Bethel Ter. HX2: Lud 6D **126**
  HX6: Sow B 6B **148**
Beulah Gro. LS6: Leeds 6H **77**
Beulah Mt. LS6: Leeds 6H **77**
Beulah Pl. HX2: Lud M 4E **147**
Beulah St. LS6: Leeds 6H **77**
Beulah Ter. *LS6: Leeds* 6H **77**
  (off Beulah Gro.)
  LS15: Leeds 1E **101**
  (off Austhorpe Rd.)

Beulah Vw. LS6: Leeds 6H **77**
Bevan Ct. BD7: B'frd 2H **109**
Beverley Av. BD12: Wyke 5D **132**
  LS11: Leeds 2H **117**
Beverley Cl. HX5: Ell 4D **160**
Beverley Ct. LS17: Leeds 5B **60**
  LS28: Fars 1H **93**
Beverley Dr. BD12: Wyke 5D **132**
Beverley Gdns. WF17: Bat 5D **136**
Beverley Pl. HX3: Hal 6F **129**
Beverley Ri. LS29: I'ly 5A **10**
Beverley Sq. LS11: Leeds 2H **117**
Beverley St. BD4: B'frd 6B **92**
Beverley Ter. HX3: Hal 6F **129**
  (not continuous)
  LS11: Leeds 2H **117**
Beverley Wlk. LS25: Gar 5F **103**
Bevin Cl. WF1: Out 4G **157**
Bevin Cres. WF1: Out 4G **157**
Bewerley Cres. BD6: B'frd 1A **132**
Bewerley Cft. LS11: Leeds 1H **117**
Bewick Cl. BD6: B'frd 3D **108**
Bewick Dr. BD16: Bgly 3E **51**
Bewick Gro. LS10: Leeds 6D **118**
Bexley Av. LS8: Leeds 1D **98**
Bexley Gro. LS8: Leeds 1D **98**
Bexley Mt. LS8: Leeds 1D **98**
Bexley Pl. LS8: Leeds 1D **98**
Bexley Rd. LS8: Leeds 1D **98**
Bexley Ter. LS8: Leeds 1D **98**
Bexley Vw. LS8: Leeds 1D **98**
Beza Ct. LS10: Leeds 3B **118**
Beza Rd. LS10: Leeds 2B **118**
Beza St. LS10: Leeds 2B **118**
Bickerdike Pl. *WF10: All B* 3H **145**
  (off Victoria St.)
Bickerdike Ter. LS25: Kip 4G **123**
Bickerdyke Bldgs. *LS26: Meth* 4D **144**
  (off Main St.)
Bickerton Way LS21: Otley 2C **22**
Biddenden Rd. LS15: Leeds 1H **101**
Bidder Dr. WF3: E Ard 6A **140**
Bideford Av. LS8: Leeds 4D **60**
Bideford Mt. BD4: B'frd 2C **112**
BIERLEY 4H **111**
Bierley Hall Gro. BD4: B'frd 6H **111**
Bierley Ho. Av. BD4: B'frd 4H **111**
Bierley La. BD4: B'frd 6H **111**
Bierley Vw. BD4: B'frd 4A **112**
Big Mdw. Dr. LS29: Add 1B **8**
Bilberry Cl. BD14: Clay 2E **109**
Bilberry Ri. BD22: Haw 3D **64**
Billam's Hill LS21: Otley 2D **22**
Billey La. LS12: Leeds 6G **95**
  (not continuous)
Billingbauk Ct. LS13: Leeds 2F **95**
Billingbauk Dr. LS13: Leeds 2F **95**
Billing Ct. LS19: Raw 4H **55**
Billing Dr. LS19: Raw 4A **56**
Billingsley Ter. BD4: B'frd 1H **111**
Billington Cl. LS13: Leeds 3D **74**
Billing Vw. BD10: Leeds 2A **72**
  LS19: Raw 4H **55**
Billingwood Dr. LS19: Raw 4H **55**
Bilsdale Grange BD6: B'frd 5H **109**
Bilsdale Way BD17: Bail 5A **52**
Bilton Pl. BD8: B'frd 3C **90**
Bingham Pl. WF3: Loft 4E **157**
BINGLEY 4B **50**
Bingley Arts Centre & Little Theatre
  . . . . .4B **50**
Bingley Bank LS17: Bard 3E **45**
Bingley Five-Rise Locks 3B **50**
Bingley Pool 4B **50**
Bingley Relief Rd. BD16: Bgly, Cot . .1H **49**
Bingley Rd. BD9: B'frd 4F **69**
  BD13: Cull 3B **66**
  BD17: Bail 1H **51**
  BD18: Ship 1F **69**
  BD21: Haw, Keigh 1F **65**
  BD22: Cros R 1F **65**
  LS20: Hawk 3A **38**
  LS29: Men 2E **39**

Bingley St Ives Golf Course 5G **49**
Bingley Station (Rail) 4B **50**
Bingley St. BD8: B'frd 4A **90**
  BD21: Keigh 6A **34**
  LS3: Leeds 4A 4 (3F **97**)
Binks Fold BD12: Wyke 5D **132**
Binks St. WF1: Out 5G **157**
Binnie St. BD3: B'frd 3H 7 (4H **91**)
Binns Fold *BD15: Wils* 4G **67**
  (off Main Rd.)
Binns Hill HX2: Hal 3H **147**
Binns La. HX2: Hal 3H **147**
Binns La. BD7: B'frd 6H **89**
Binns St. BD16: Bgly 4C **50**
Binns Top La. HX3: Sou 6C **150**
  HX5: Ell 6C **150**
Binswell Fold BD17: Bail 3C **52**
Bircham Cl. BD16: Bgly 2E **51**
Birch Av. BD5: B'frd 3F **111**
  LS15: Leeds 3C **100**
Birch Cliff BD17: Bail 5B **52**
Birch Cl. BD5: B'frd 3F **111**
  HD6: Clift 6C **152**
Birch Cl. La. BD16: Bgly 5H **37**
Birch Ct. BD11: Birk 1F **135**
  LS27: Morl 5B **138**
Birch Cres. LS15: Leeds 3C **100**
Birchdale BD16: Bgly 1B **50**
Birch Dr. LS25: Kip 2G **123**
Birches, The LS16: B'hpe 3H **43**
  LS20: Guis 3C **40**
Birchfield HX6: Norl 1B **158**
Birchfield Av. LS27: Gil 1E **137**
Birchfields Av. LS14: Leeds 1E **81**
Birchfields Cl. LS14: Leeds 2E **81**
Birchfields Ct. LS14: Leeds 1E **81**
Birchfields Cres. LS14: Leeds 2E **81**
Birchfields Gth. LS14: Leeds 2E **81**
Birchfields Ri. LS14: Leeds 2E **81**
Birch Gro. BD5: B'frd 4E **111**
  BD21: Keigh 3H **47**
  LS25: Kip 3G **123**
  WF17: Bat 6C **136**
Birch Hill Ri. LS18: H'fth 1G **75**
Birch Ho. LS7: Leeds 2B **78**
Birchlands Av. BD15: Wils 3F **67**
Birchlands Gro. BD15: Wils 3F **67**
Birch La. BD5: B'frd 2E **111**
  (not continuous)
  HX2: Lud 1E **147**
Birch M. LS16: Leeds 5D **58**
Birch Pk. LS23: T Arch 2G **31**
Birch Rd. LS25: Kip 2G **123**
Birchroyd LS26: Rothw 3B **142**
Birch St. BD8: B'frd 3H **89**
  (not continuous)
  LS27: Morl 5B **138**
Birch Tree Gdns. BD21: Keigh 1C **48**
Birchtree Way LS16: Leeds 5G **57**
Birch Way BD5: B'frd 3F **111**
Birchwood *HD6: Brigh* 6H **151**
  (off Elmwood Dr.)
Birchwood Av. BD20: Keigh 3H **33**
  LS17: Leeds 4E **61**
  WF17: Birs 5B **136**
Birchwood Ct. LS29: I'ly 5C **10**
Birchwood Dr. BD20: Keigh 3G **33**
Birchwood Gdns. BD10: B'frd 2A **72**
Birchwood Hill LS17: Leeds 3E **61**
Birchwood Mt. LS17: Leeds 3E **61**
Birchwood Rd. BD20: Keigh 3G **33**
BIRDACRE 6F **135**
Birdale Fld. La. LS22: Coll 3D **28**
Birdcage HX3: Hal 1H **149**
Birdcage Ct. LS21: Otley 5E **23**
Birdcage Hill HX3: Hal 6E **149**
Birdcage La. HX3: Hal 6E **149**
Birdcage Wlk. LS21: Otley 5D **22**
Bird Holme La. HX3: Hip 6D **130**
BIRDS ROYD 2B **162**
Birds Royd La. HD6: Brigh 2B **162**
Birdswell Av. HD6: Clift 6D **152**
Birdwalk, The BD6: B'frd 3E **109**

Birfed Cres.—Body Mania Fitness

Birfed Cres. LS4: Leeds 6B **76**
Birkby Brow Cres. WF17: Birs 5D **136**
Birkby Haven BD6: B'frd 5G **109**
Birkby La. BD19: Scho 2B **152**
HD6: B Bri 2B **152**
Birkby St. BD12: Wyke 3D **132**
Birkdale Cl. BD13: Cull 3C **66**
LS17: Leeds 3H **59**
Birkdale Ct. BD20: Keigh 2G **33**
Birkdale Dr. LS17: Leeds 3G **59**
Birkdale Grn. LS17: Leeds 3H **59**
Birkdale Gro. HX2: Illing 6D **106**
LS17: Leeds 3G **59**
Birkdale Mt. LS17: Leeds 3H **59**
Birkdale Pl. LS17: Leeds 3G **59**
Birkdale Ri. LS17: Leeds 3G **59**
Birkdale Wlk. LS17: Leeds 3G **59**
Birkdale Way LS17: Leeds 3H **59**
BIRKENSHAW 2E **135**
BIRKENSHAW BOTTOMS 3G **135**
Birkenshaw La. BD11: Birk 2F **135**
Birk Hey Cl. HD6: B Bri 3B **152**
Birkhill Cres. BD11: Birk 2F **135**
BIRKHOUSE 3C **152**
Birkhouse La. HD6: B Bri 3C **152**
Birkhouse Rd. HD6: B Bri 2C **152**
Birklands Rd. BD18: Ship 2B **70**
Birklands Ter. BD18: Ship 2B **70**
Birk La. LS27: Morl 3G **137**
Birk Lea St. BD5: B'frd 1F **111**
BIRKS
BD7 .5H **89**
LS27 .5B **138**
Birks Av. BD7: B'frd 6H **89**
Birks Fold BD7: B'frd 5H **89**
Birks Hall La. HX1: Hal . . .1A **164** (1E **149**)
Birkshall La. BD4: B'frd 5H **91**
Birks Hall St. HX1: Hal 1E **149**
Birks Hall Ter. HX1: Hal 1E **149**
BIRKSHEAD 5H **67**
Birkshead Dr. BD15: Wils 4H **67**
Birkshead M. BD15: Wils 4H **67**
Birksland Ind. Est. BD4: B'frd 6H **91**
Birksland Moor BD11: Birk 4F **135**
Birksland St. BD3: B'frd 6H **91**
BD4: B'frd 6H **91**
Birkwith Cl. LS14: Leeds 1D **80**
Birnam Gro. BD4: B'frd 1G **111**
Birr Rd. BD9: B'frd 6B **70**
BIRSTALL 6A **136**
Birstall La. BD11: Drig 2A **136**
Birstall Retail Pk. WF17: Birs 3C **136**
Bishopdale Ct. HX1: Hal 4F **149**
Bishopdale Dr. LS22: Coll 3A **28**
Bishopdale Holme BD6: B'frd 5G **109**
Bishopgate St.
LS1: Leeds 5D **4** (4H **97**)
Bishop St. BD9: B'frd 6B **70**
Bishops Way LS14: Leeds 4A **80**
Bishop Way WF3: Ting 1F **155**
Bismarck Ct. LS11: Leeds 1H **117**
Bismarck Dr. LS11: Leeds 1H **117**
Bismarck St. LS11: Leeds 1H **117**
Bittern Ct. BD6: B'frd 3E **109**
Bittern Ri. LS27: Morl 4C **138**
Blackberry Way BD14: Clay 2D **108**
HX3: Hal 5A **150**
Blackbird Gdns. BD8: B'frd 4D **88**
Black Brook Ct. HD6: Brigh 5H **151**
Black Brook Way HX4: Gree 5G **159**
Black Bull St. LS10: Leeds . . .6G **5** (5B **98**)
Blackburn Bldgs. HD6: Brigh 1C **162**
Blackburn Cl. BD8: B'frd 4F **89**
HX3: Hal 4D **128**
Blackburn Ct. LS26: Rothw 2B **142**
Blackburn Ho. HX3: Hal 4E **129**
Blackburn Rd. HD6: Brigh 5H **151**
WF17: Birs 6A **136**
Black Dyke La. BD13: Thorn 1F **87**
Black Edge La. BD13: Denh 5B **86**
Blackett St. LS28: Cal 2F **73**
Blackgate M. WF3: Ting 6E **139**
BLACK GATES 6F **139**
Blackgates Ct. WF3: Ting 1F **155**
Blackgates Cres. WF3: Ting 1F **155**
Blackgates Dr. WF3: Ting 1F **155**
Blackgates Fold WF3: Ting 1F **155**
Blackgates Ri. WF3: Ting 1F **155**
BLACK HILL 5F **33**
Black Hill La. BD20: Keigh 4D **32**
Blackhouse Fold HX2: Illing 2B **128**
Blackledge HX1: Hal 4D **164** (2H **149**)
Blackley Rd. HX5: Ell 6H **159**
Blackman La. LS2: Leeds 1D **4** (1H **97**)
LS7: Leeds 1H **97**
Blackmires BD13: Que 5H **107**
HX2: Hal 2E **129**
BLACK MOOR 3G **59**
BLACKMOOR 6B **44**
Blackmoor Ct. LS17: Leeds 2F **59**
Blackmoor La. LS17: Bard, S'cft 5C **44**
Black Moor Rd. BD22: Oxen 1E **85**
LS17: Leeds 4F **59**
Black Moor Top BD22: Haw, Oxen . . .3D **64**
Blackpool Gro. LS12: Leeds 1A **116**
Blackpool Pl. LS12: Leeds 1A **116**
Blackpool St. LS12: Leeds 1A **116**
Blackpool Ter. LS12: Leeds 1A **116**
Blackpool Vw. LS12: Leeds 1A **116**
Blackshaw Beck La. BD13: Que 6C **108**
Blackshaw Dr. BD6: B'frd 5F **109**
Black Shepherd's La. *LS7: Leeds 5C 78*
(off Shepherd's Gro.)
Blacksmith Fold BD7: B'frd 1A **110**
Blacksmith M. WF3: Rob H 4F **141**
Blackstone Av. BD12: Wyke 5C **132**
Black Swan Ginnell HX1: Hal 4B **164**
Black Swan Pas. HX1: Hal 4B **164**
Blackthorn Cl. HX3: North 3C **130**
Blackthorn Ct. LS10: Leeds 5B **118**
Blackthorn Rd. LS29: I'ly 4F **11**
Blackwall HX1: Hal 5B **164** (3G **149**)
Blackwall La. HX6: Sow B 4G **147**
Blackwall Ri. HX6: Sow B 4G **147**
Blackwood Av. LS16: Leeds 4F **57**
Blackwood Gdns. LS16: Leeds 4F **57**
Blackwood Gro. HX1: Hal 1D **148**
LS16: Leeds 4F **57**
Blackwood Hall La. HX2: Lud M . . .3C **146**
Blackwood Mt. LS16: Leeds 4F **57**
Blackwood Ri. LS16: Leeds 4F **57**
Blairsville Gdns. LS13: Leeds 5D **74**
Blairsville Gro. LS13: Leeds 5E **75**
Blaithroyd Ct. HX3: Hal 3A **150**
Blaithroyd La. HX3: Hal 3A **150**
Blake Cres. LS20: Guis 5D **40**
Blake Gro. LS7: Leeds 3B **78**
Blake Hill HX3: North 4A **130**
Blakehill Av. BD2: B'frd 1A **92**
Blake Hill End HX3: North 2B **130**
Blakehill Ter. BD2: B'frd 1A **92**
Blakelaw Dr. HD6: Clift 6D **152**
Blake Law La. HD6: Clift 1F **163**
Blakeney Gro. LS10: Leeds 4B **118**
Blakeney Rd. LS10: Leeds 4B **118**
Blamires Pl. BD7: B'frd 2H **109**
Blamires St. BD7: B'frd 2H **109**
Blanche St. BD4: B'frd 5B **92**
Blandford Gdns. LS2: Leeds 1H **97**
Blandford Gro. *LS2: Leeds 1H 97*
(off Bk. Blenheim Ter.)
Blands Av. WF10: All B 2G **145**
Blands Cotts. *LS25: Kip 4H 123*
(off Ashtree Gro.)
Blands Cres. WF10: All B 2G **145**
Blands Gro. WF10: All B 2G **145**
Blands Ter. WF10: All B 2G **145**
Bland St. HX1: Hal 4A **164** (2F **149**)
Blantyre Ct. BD13: Cull 3B **66**
Blayds Gth. LS26: Wood 6C **120**
Blayd's M. LS1: Leeds 6E **5** (4A **98**)
Blayds St. LS9: Leeds 4D **98**
Blayd's Yd. LS1: Leeds 6E **5** (4A **98**)
Bleach Mill La. LS29: Men 6D **20**
Blencarn Cl. LS14: Leeds 5B **80**
Blencarn Gth. LS14: Leeds 5B **80**
Blencarn Lawn LS14: Leeds 5B **80**
Blencarn Path LS14: Leeds 5B **80**
Blencarn Rd. LS14: Leeds 5B **80**
Blencarn Vw. LS14: Leeds 5B **80**
Blencarn Wlk. LS14: Leeds 5B **80**
Blenheim Av. LS2: Leeds 1H **97**
Blenheim Ct. HX1: Hal 2A **164**
LS2: Leeds 1H 97
(off Blackman La.)
Blenheim Cres. *LS2: Leeds 1H 97*
(off Blenheim Av.)
Blenheim Gro. LS2: Leeds 1H **97**
Blenheim Mt. BD8: B'frd 1C **90**
Blenheim Pl. BD10: B'frd 6H **53**
Blenheim Rd. BD8: B'frd 2C **90**
Blenheim Sq. LS2: Leeds 1H **97**
Blenheim St. BD21: Keigh 2H **47**
Blenheim Ter. *LS2: Leeds 1H 97*
(off Bk. Blenheim Ter.)
LS27: Morl 1A **138**
Blenheim Vw. LS2: Leeds 1H **97**
Blenheim Wlk. LS2: Leeds 1H **97**
Blenkinsop Ct. *LS27: Morl 5B 138*
(off Britannia Rd.)
Blenkinsop Dr. LS10: Leeds 3C **140**
Blenkinsop Way LS10: Leeds 3C **140**
Blind La. BD11: Drig 6B **114**
BD13: Que 2G **107**
BD16: Har 5G **49**
HX2: Lud M 1B **146**
HX2: Ogd 5C **106**
LS17: Shad 3A **62**
WF3: E Ard 4G **155**
Bloomer Ga. HX7: Myth 6A **126**
Bloomfield Sq. *LS21: Otley 4E 23*
(off Gay La.)
Blossom Ct. LS19: Yead 1F **55**
Blossoms, The LS26: Meth 4D **144**
Blucher St. BD4: B'frd 6B **92**
Bluebell Av. LS25: Gar 6G **103**
Bluebell Cl. BD15: All 3D **88**
BD18: Ship 4D **70**
Bluebell Ct. LS14: Leeds 1C **80**
WF17: Birs 5A **136**
Bluebell Rd. WF3: E Ard 1C **156**
Bluebell Wlk. HX2: Lud 1E **147**
Bluebird Wlk. BD16: Bgly 3E **51**
Bluecoat Ct. LS22: Coll 3H **27**
Blue Hill BD13: Denh 2B **86**
Blue Hill Cres. LS12: Leeds 5A **96**
Blue Hill Grange LS12: Leeds 6A **96**
Blue Hill Gro. LS12: Leeds 5A **96**
Blue Hill La. LS12: Leeds 5A **96**
Blundell St. LS1: Leeds 2C **4** (2H **97**)
Blythe Av. BD8: B'frd 3A **90**
Blythe St. BD7: B'frd 4A **6** (4D **90**)
Boar La. LS1: Leeds 5E **5** (4A **98**)
Boat La. LS26: Meth 5G **145**
WF10: All B 4H **145**
Bobbin Cl. HD6: B Bri 2C **152**
Bobbin Mill Cl. *BD20: Stee 6C 14*
(off Bobbin Mill Ct.)
Bobbin Mill Ct. BD20: Stee 6C **14**
Bob La. BD15: All, Wils 5H **67**
HX2: Hal 2B **148**
BOCKING .1F **65**
Bodiham Hill LS25: Gar 3H **103**
Bodley Ter. LS4: Leeds 2D **96**
Bodmin App. LS10: Leeds 2G **139**
Bodmin Av. BD18: Ship 2F **71**
Bodmin Cres. LS10: Leeds 2G **139**
Bodmin Cft. LS10: Leeds 2H **139**
Bodmin Gdns. LS10: Leeds 3G **139**
Bodmin Gth. LS10: Leeds 3G **139**
Bodmin Pl. LS10: Leeds 3H **139**
(not continuous)
Bodmin Rd. LS10: Leeds 1F **139**
Bodmin Sq. LS10: Leeds 3G **139**
Bodmin St. LS10: Leeds 3G **139**
Bodmin Ter. LS10: Leeds 3G **139**
Bodylines Gym 2H **5**
Body Mania Fitness *2A 142*
(off Marsh St.)

182 A-Z Leeds & Bradford

Bodytech 2B 140
(within Middleton District Cen.)
Boggart Hill LS14: Leeds 3A 80
Boggart Hill Cres. LS14: Leeds 3A 80
Boggart Hill Dr. LS14: Leeds 3A 80
Boggart Hill Gdns. LS14: Leeds 3A 80
Boggart Hill Rd. LS14: Leeds 3A 80
Boggart La. HX3: Hip 6F 131
(not continuous)
HX6: Sow B 6H 147
Boggart Wood Vw. BD15: All 4D 88
BOG GREEN 6H 163
Bog Grn. La. HD5: Hud 6H 163
Bog La. LS15: Leeds, Scho 4A 82
BOGTHORN 3F 47
Boland Ct. BD22: Oak 4E 47
Boldmere Rd. LS15: Leeds 4A 100
Boldron Holt BD6: B'frd 5H 109
Boldshay St. BD3: B'frd 3H 91
Bold St. BD8: B'frd 2C 90
Bolehill Pk. HD6: Brigh 3G 151
Bolingbroke Ct. BD5: B'frd 6E 91
(off Elsdon Gro.)
Bolingbroke St. BD5: B'frd 3D 110
Bolland Bldgs. BD12: Low M 2F 133
Bolland St. BD12: Low M 2E 133
Bolling Hall (Museum) 2G 111
Bolling Rd. BD4: B'frd 6E 7 (6F 91)
LS29: I'ly 6F 11
Bolsover Cl. LS25: Gar 4H 103
Boltby La. BD6: B'frd 5G 109
BOLTON 6F 71
Bolton Bri. Ct. LS29: I'ly 5C 10
(off Bolton Bri. Rd.)
Bolton Bri. Rd. LS29: I'ly 5C 10
Bolton Brow HX6: Sow B 5A 148
Bolton Ct. BD2: B'frd 1G 91
Bolton Cres. BD2: B'frd 5H 71
Bolton Dr. BD2: B'frd 4H 71
Bolton Grange LS19: Yead 1G 55
Bolton Gro. BD2: B'frd 5H 71
Bolton Hall Rd. BD2: B'frd 4D 70
(not continuous)
Bolton La. BD2: B'frd 1D 90
BOLTON OUTLANES 5G 71
Bolton Rd. BD1: B'frd 3E 7 (4F 91)
(not continuous)
BD2: B'frd 6F 71
BD3: B'frd 1E 7 (1F 91)
BD20: Sils 1E 15
LS19: Yead 1G 55
LS29: Add 1D 8
Bolton St. BD3: B'frd 3G 7 (4G 91)
BD12: Low M 1C 132
(not continuous)
Bolton Ter. BD20: Sils 1E 15
Bolton Way LS23: B Spa 4A 30
BOLTON WOODS 5E 71
Bolus Cl. WF1: Out 5G 157
Bolus La. WF1: Out 5F 157
Bonaire LS12: Leeds 5A 4 (4F 97)
Bond Ct. LS1: Leeds 4D 4
Bondgate LS21: Otley 4E 23
Bond St. HD6: Brigh 6A 152
HX1: Hal 4A 164
LS1: Leeds 4D 4 (3H 97)
WF17: Birs 6A 136
Bonegate Av. HD6: Brigh 6B 152
Bonegate Ct. HD6: Brigh 6B 152
(off Old La.)
Bonegate Rd. HD6: Brigh 6A 152
Bonham Ct. LS27: Morl 4A 138
(off Queen St.)
Bonn Rd. BD9: B'frd 1A 90
Bonwick Mall BD6: B'frd 6G 109
Boocock St. LS28: Stan 2A 94
(off Varley St.)
Bookbinders, The LS2: Leeds 5G 5
(off Bk. York St.)
BOOTH 3E 127
Bootham Pk. BD9: B'frd 1F 89
Booth Hill HX2: Lud 3E 127
Booth Ho. Rd. HX2: Lud M 2C 146

Booth Ho. Ter. HX2: Lud M 2C 146
Boothman Wlk. BD21: Keigh 2G 47
Booth Royd BD10: B'frd 6H 53
Booth Royd Dr. BD10: B'frd 6H 53
Boothroyd Dr. LS6: Leeds 4F 77
Boothroyd La. HD6: Ras 3F 161
Booth's Bldgs. HD6: B Bri 2B 152
(off Field Top)
Booth St. BD10: B'frd 2H 71
BD13: Que 4H 107
BD18: Ship 2D 70
BD19: Cleck 6B 134
LS29: Burl W 1E 21
Booth's Yd. LS28: Pud 3A 94
BOOTHTOWN 6E 129
Boothtown Rd. HX3: Hal 4F 129
Boroughgate LS21: Otley 3E 23
Borough Mkt. HX1: Hal 4C 164
Borrin's Way BD17: Bail 4D 52
Borrough Av. LS8: Leeds 1C 78
Borrough Vw. LS8: Leeds 1C 78
Borrowdale Cl. LS12: Leeds 1H 95
Borrowdale Cl. LS29: Men 3H 39
Borrowdale Cres. LS12: Leeds 1H 95
Borrowdale Cft. LS19: Yead 6F 41
Borrowdale Ter. LS14: Leeds 6B 80
Boston Av. LS5: Leeds 6H 75
Boston M. LS23: B Spa 4C 30
Boston Rd. LS22: Coll, Weth 5E 13
LS23: Cliff 5B 30
BOSTON SPA 3C 30
Boston St. HX1: Hal 2D 148
HX6: Sow B 6G 147
Boston Towers LS9: Leeds 2C 98
(off Lindsey Gdns.)
Boston Wlk. BD6: B'frd 5H 109
Bosworth Cl. BD15: All 1D 88
BOTANY 3A 36
Botany Av. BD2: B'frd 5F 71
Botany Dr. BD20: E Mor 3A 36
BOTTOMLEY HOLES 6E 87
Bottomley St. BD5: B'frd 1D 110
BD6: B'frd 6H 109
HD6: Brigh 5B 152
Bottoms HX3: Hal 6H 149
Bottoms La. BD11: Birk 3F 135
BOULDER CLOUGH 5D 146
Boulevard, The LS10: Leeds 5B 98
LS12: Leeds 2D 116
LS28: Fars 1H 93
Boulevard Ri. LS10: Leeds 3C 140
Boundary, The BD8: B'frd 2G 89
Boundary Cl. BD17: Bail 2D 52
LS15: Leeds 4G 101
Boundary Farm Rd. LS17: Leeds 4G 59
Boundary Pl. BD2: B'frd 1H 91
(off Baker St.)
Boundary St. LS7: Leeds 1C 98
Bourbon Cl. BD6: B'frd 5B 110
Bourne St. BD10: B'frd 6H 53
Bourse, The LS1: Leeds 5E 5
Bouverie Ct. LS9: Leeds 5C 98
Bowater Ct. BD4: B'frd 3D 112
Bow Beck BD4: B'frd 6H 7 (6G 91)
Bowbridge Rd. BD5: B'frd 1E 111
Bowcliffe Rd. LS10: Leeds 1D 118
Bower Grn. BD3: B'frd 4A 92
Bower Rd. LS15: Leeds 6G 81
Bowers La. HX4: Bark 5B 158
Bowers Mill Ind. Est. HX4: Bark 6B 158
Bowers Row LS26: Wood 1E 145
Bowes Cl. BD7: B'frd 6C 6
Bowes Nook BD6: B'frd 6G 109
Bowfell Cl. LS14: Leeds 5C 80
Bow Grn. BD14: Clay 1G 109
Bowland Av. BD17: Bail 6G 51
(not continuous)
Bowland St. LS15: Leeds 4A 100
Bowland St. BD1: B'frd 1A 6 (3D 90)
Bowler Cl. BD12: Low M 1C 132
BOWLING 1H 111

Bowling All. HD6: Ras 3A 162
Bowling All. Ter. HD6: Ras 3A 162
Bowling Bk. La. BD4: B'frd 6G 91
Bowling Cl. HD6: Brigh 6H 151
Bowling Ct. Ind. Est. BD4: B'frd 6A 92
Bowling Dyke HX1: Hal 2C 164 (1G 149)
HX3: Hal 1C 164 (1G 149)
Bowling Grn. Fold BD12: Wyke 4C 132
Bowling Grn. Ter. LS11: Leeds 6H 97
Bowling Grn. Vw. BD11: Drig 1A 136
Bowling Hall Rd. BD4: B'frd 1G 111
Bowling Mill HX1: Hal 2B 164 (1G 149)
Bowling Old La. BD5: B'frd 1E 111
(Albany St.)
BD5: B'frd 3D 110
(Manchester Rd.)
Bowling Pk. Cl. BD4: B'frd 1F 111
Bowling Pk. Dr. BD4: B'frd 2F 111
Bowling Swimming Pool 2G 111
Bowl Shaw La. HX3: North 1B 130
Bowman Av. BD6: B'frd 6B 110
Bowman Gro. HX1: Hal 2E 149
Bowman La. LS10: Leeds 6G 5 (4B 98)
Bowman Pl. HX1: Hal 2E 149
Bowman Rd. BD6: B'frd 6B 110
Bowman St. HX1: Hal 2E 149
Bowmere Dr. BD15: All 3D 88
Bownas Rd. LS23: B Spa 3A 30
Bowness Av. BD10: B'frd 5B 72
Bowood Av. LS7: Leeds 2G 77
Bowood Cres. LS7: Leeds 2G 77
Bowood Gro. LS7: Leeds 2G 77
Bowood HX5: Ell 6B 160
Bow St. BD21: Keigh 6A 34
LS9: Leeds 4C 98
Bowwood Dr. BD20: Rid 5F 35
Boxall Rd. HX5: Ell 4B 160
Box Tree Cl. BD8: B'frd 2G 89
Box Tree Gro. BD21: Keigh 1C 48
Box Trees HX2: Mix 4B 128
Box Trees La. HX2: Mix 4B 128
Boyd Av. BD3: B'frd 2C 92
Boy Home La. HX2: Lud M 3D 146
Boy La. BD4: B'frd 6H 111
HX3: Hal 5B 128
Boyle, The LS15: Bar E 1D 82
Boyne St. HX1: Hal 4A 164 (2F 149)
Boynton St. BD5: B'frd 2D 110
(not continuous)
Boynton Ter. BD5: B'frd 2E 111
Boys La. HX3: Hal 4H 149
Boys Scarr HX2: Lud M 3D 146
Bracewell Av. BD15: All 3C 88
Bracewell Bank HX3: Hal 5E 129
Bracewell Dr. HX3: Hal 5D 128
Bracewell Gro. HX3: Hal 6E 129
Bracewell Mt. HX3: Hal 5D 128
(off Bracewell Dr.)
Bracewell St. BD21: Keigh 6C 34
Bracken Av. HD6: Brigh 4A 152
BRACKEN BANK 4F 47
Bracken Bank Av. BD22: Keigh 5F 47
Bracken Bank Cres.
BD22: Keigh 4F 47
Bracken Bank Gro. BD22: Keigh 4F 47
Bracken Bank Wlk. BD22: Keigh 5F 47
Bracken Bank Way BD22: Keigh 4F 47
Brackenbeck Rd. BD7: B'frd 1H 109
Brackenbed Grange HX2: Hal 6C 128
Brackenbed La. HX2: Hal 6D 128
(not continuous)
Brackenbed Ter. HX2: Hal 6D 128
(off Brackenbed La.)
Bracken Cl. HD6: Brigh 4A 152
Bracken Ct. LS12: Leeds 6E 97
LS17: Leeds 6A 60
Brackendale BD10: B'frd 5F 53
Brackendale Av. BD10: B'frd 5G 53
Brackendale Dr. BD10: B'frd 5F 53
Brackendale Gro. BD10: B'frd 5F 53
Brackendale Lodge BD10: B'frd 5F 53
Brackendale Pde. BD10: B'frd 5F 53

Bracken Edge—Branksome Gro.

Bracken Edge BD10: B'frd ... 2A **72**
LS8: Leeds ... 4D **78**
Bracken Ghyll Dr. BD20: Sils ... 1D **14**
Bracken Grange Ct. BD18: Ship ... 2F **69**
Bracken Grn. WF3: E Ard ... 1C **156**
Bracken Hall (Countryside Cen.) ... 4G **51**
Brackenhall Ct. BD7: B'frd ... 1H **109**
Bracken Hill HX2: Hal ... 6C **128**
LS17: Leeds ... 6A **60**
Brackenhill Dr. BD7: B'frd ... 2H **109**
Brackenhill M. BD7: B'frd ... 1H **109**
Brackenholme Royd
BD6: B'frd ... 5G **109**
Brackenhurst Dr. LS17: Leeds ... 5A **60**
Brackenhurst Pl. LS17: Leeds ... 5A **60**
Bracken Mt. BD20: Sils ... 1D **14**
Bracken Pk. BD16: Bgly ... 4E **51**
(Gilstead La.)
BD16: Bgly ... 2D **50**
(Moor Cft.)
LS14: S'cft ... 5C **44**
Bracken Rd. BD20: East ... 6A **14**
BD22: Keigh ... 3G **47**
HD6: Brigh ... 4A **152**
Brackens La. HX3: She ... 6D **108**
Bracken St. BD21: Keigh ... 3H **47**
Bracken Way HX5: Ell ... 4D **160**
Brackenwood Cl. LS8: Leeds ... 2C **78**
LS29: I'ly ... 5G **11**
Brackenwood Ct. WF1: Out ... 4H **157**
Brackenwood Dr. LS8: Leeds ... 1C **78**
Brackenwood Grn. LS8: Leeds ... 1C **78**
Brackenwood Rd. WF1: Out ... 4H **157**
Bradbeck Rd. BD7: B'frd ... 4H **89**
Bradburn Rd. WF3: Rob H ... 4E **141**
Bradfield Cl. HD2: Hud ... 6E **163**
BRADFORD ... 3C **6** (4E **91**)
Bradford 1 Gallery ... 5C **6** (5E **91**)
Bradford & Heckmondwick Rd.
BD4: E Bier ... 5D **112**
Bradford & Wakefield Rd.
BD4: B'frd ... 6G **113**
Bradford Bulls RLFC ... 5E **111**
Bradford Bus. Pk. BD1: B'frd ... 2E **91**
Bradford Cathedral Church of St Peter
... 3E **7** (4F **91**)
Bradford Chamber Bus. Pk.
BD4: B'frd ... 5B **92**
Bradford City AFC ... 2E **91**
Bradford City Farm ... 3B **90**
Bradford City Hall ... 5D **6** (5E **91**)
Bradford Design Exchange ... 4F **7**
Bradford Forster Square Station (Rail)
... 3D **6** (4E **91**)
Bradford Golf Course ... 6G **39**
Bradford Ice Arena ... 6C **6** (5E **91**)
Bradford Industrial Mus. ... 6B **72**
Bradford Interchange Station (Rail)
... 5E **7** (5F **91**)
Bradford Kart Racing ... 6F **91**
Bradford La. BD3: B'frd ... 4B **92**
BRADFORD MOOR ... 3A **92**
Bradford Moor Golf Course ... 2A **92**
Bradford Old Rd. BD16: Cot ... 2D **68**
(not continuous)
HX3: Hal ... 4G **129**
Bradford Park Avenue FC ... 6B **110**
Bradford Playhouse and Film Theatre
... 4F **7**
Bradford Rd. BD3: B'frd ... 2D **92**
BD4: E Bier ... 5D **112**
BD10: B'frd ... 4G **71**
BD11: Birk ... 3E **135**
BD11: Drig ... 2D **136**
(Buttercup Way)
BD11: Drig ... 6H **113**
(Woodview)
BD12: O'haw ... 3G **133**
BD14: Clay ... 6E **89**
BD16: Bgly, Cot ... 5C **50**
BD18: Ship ... 2A **70**
BD19: Cleck ... 5A **134**
BD19: Gom ... 3E **135**
Bradford Rd. BD20: Rid ... 4C **34**
BD21: Keigh, Rid ... 6B **34**
HD2: Fix, Hud ... 5B **162**
HD6: B Bri, Brigh ... 1B **152**
HX3: North ... 4C **130**
(Oaklands Av.)
HX3: North ... 6C **130**
(Park Vw. Av.)
LS20: Guis ... 1H **39**
LS21: Otley ... 5H **21**
LS27: Gil ... 2D **136**
LS28: Pud, Stan ... 2G **93**
LS29: Burl W ... 3G **21**
LS29: Men ... 6H **21**
WF1: Wake ... 5C **156**
WF2: Carr G, Wren ... 4C **156**
(not continuous)
WF3: E Ard, Ting ... 6D **138**
WF17: Bat, Birs ... 5G **135**
Bradford St. BD21: Keigh ... 5A **34**
Bradlaugh Rd. BD6: B'frd ... 4B **110**
Bradlaugh Ter. BD6: B'frd ... 4C **110**
Bradleigh Cl. BD21: Keigh ... 2C **48**
BRADLEY ... 6F **163**
Bradley Av. BD20: Sils ... 1D **14**
Bradley Bus. Pk. HD2: Hud ... 6D **162**
Bradley Colliery La. HD2: Hud ... 6F **163**
Bradley Ct. HX4: Gree ... 5F **159**
Bradley Dr. BD20: Sils ... 1D **14**
Bradley Grange Gdns. HD2: Hud ... 5F **163**
Bradley Gro. BD20: Sils ... 1D **14**
BRADLEY HILL ... 6C **74**
Bradley Hill Vw. *LS28: Stan ... 1C **94***
(off Swinnow La.)
Bradley Junc. Ind. Est.
HD2: Hud ... 6G **163**
Bradley La. HX4: Gree ... 5F **159**
LS28: Pud ... 4F **93**
Bradley Pk. Golf Course ... 5D **162**
Bradley Quarry Cl. HD2: Hud ... 5G **163**
Bradley Quarry Nature Reserve ... 5G **163**
Bradley Ri. BD20: Sils ... 1D **14**
Bradley Rd. BD20: Sils ... 1D **14**
HD2: Hud ... 6C **162**
Bradley Sq. BD16: Har ... 6F **49**
Bradley St. BD9: B'frd ... 5C **70**
BD16: Bgly ... 3B **50**
Bradley Ter. LS17: Leeds ... 3E **61**
Bradley Vw. HX4: Holy ... 6E **159**
BRADSHAW ... 4D **106**
Bradshaw La. HX2: Brad ... 5D **106**
Bradshaw Row HX2: Brad ... 3D **106**
Bradshaw Vw. BD13: Que ... 4G **107**
*HX2: Illing ... 6C **106***
(off W. Scausby Pk.)
Bradstock Gdns. LS27: Morl ... 1A **138**
Bradup BD20: Rid ... 6G **17**
Brae Av. BD2: B'frd ... 6F **71**
Braemar Dr. LS25: Gar ... 3H **103**
Braeside HX2: Hal ... 2B **148**
Brafferton Arbor BD6: B'frd ... 5G **109**
Braine Cft. BD6: B'frd ... 6H **109**
Braine Rd. LS22: Weth ... 3F **13**
BRAITHWAITE ... 5E **33**
Braithwaite Av. BD22: Keigh ... 5E **33**
Braithwaite Cres. BD22: Keigh ... 6F **33**
Braithwaite Dr. BD22: Keigh ... 6F **33**
Braithwaite Edge Rd.
BD22: Keigh ... 5D **32**
Braithwaite Gro. BD22: Keigh ... 6F **33**
Braithwaite Rd. BD22: Keigh ... 6D **32**
Braithwaite Row LS10: Leeds ... 3C **118**
Braithwaite St. LS11: Leeds ... 5F **97**
BRAITHWAITE VILLAGE ... 6D **32**
Braithwaite Wlk. BD22: Keigh ... 6F **33**
Braithwaite Way BD22: Keigh ... 6F **33**
Bramall Bus. Pk. BD5: B'frd ... 1E **111**
Bramall Ho. *BD3: B'frd ... 3D **92***
(off Chapman Rd.)
Bramble Av. LS23: B Spa ... 4H **29**
Bramble Cl. BD14: Clay ... 2E **109**
BD22: Haw ... 3D **64**
HX3: Hal ... 5A **150**
Bramble Ct. LS21: Pool ... 5F **25**
WF1: Out ... 4E **157**
Bramble Gro. HX5: Ell ... 4D **160**
LS21: Pool ... 5F **25**
Bramble M. LS17: Leeds ... 2G **61**
Brambles, The LS29: I'ly ... 5B **10**
Brambleside BD13: Denh ... 2C **86**
Bramble Sq. WF3: E Ard ... 1D **156**
Bramble Wlk. WF17: Bat ... 6B **136**
Brambling Dr. BD6: B'frd ... 3E **109**
Brambling M. LS27: Morl ... 3C **138**
Bramham Dr. BD17: Bail ... 3D **52**
Bramham La. LS23: B'ham ... 1H **45**
Bramham Pk. Ct. LS10: Leeds ... 4B **140**
Bramham Rd. BD16: Bgly ... 3C **50**
LS23: Cliff ... 6B **30**
Bramham's Yd. LS25: Kip ... 4H **123**
BRAMHOPE ... 2G **43**
Bramleigh Dr. LS27: Morl ... 1A **138**
Bramleigh Gro. LS27: Morl ... 1A **138**
BRAMLEY ... 6F **75**
Bramley Baths (Swimming Pool) ... 6D **74**
Bramley Cen. LS13: Leeds ... 6F **75**
Bramley Cl. BD22: Oak ... 4B **46**
Bramley Cres. WF1: Out ... 5F **157**
Bramley Fold HX3: Hip ... 1F **151**
Bramley Gdns. LS14: Leeds ... 6E **63**
Bramley La. HX3: Hip ... 1E **151**
Bramley Station (Rail) ... 2D **94**
Bramley St. BD5: B'frd ... 6E **91**
(not continuous)
Bramley's Yd. LS1: Leeds ... 4F **5**
Bramley Vw. HX3: Hip ... 1G **151**
Brampton HX2: Lud M ... 6B **126**
Bramstan Av. LS13: Leeds ... 6C **74**
Bramstan Cl. LS13: Leeds ... 6C **74**
Bramstan Gdns. LS13: Leeds ... 6C **74**
Bramston Gdns. HD6: Ras ... 3A **162**
Bramston St. HD6: Ras ... 2A **162**
Bramwell Way HX1: Hal ... 4F **149**
Branby Av. BD20: E Mor ... 4E **35**
Brancepeth Pl. LS12: Leeds ... 4E **97**
Branch Cl. LS12: Leeds ... 1A **116**
Branch End LS27: Gil ... 6F **115**
Branch Pl. LS12: Leeds ... 1A **116**
Branch Rd. BD19: Scho ... 6F **133**
HX4: Bark, Gree ... 6B **158**
LS12: Leeds ... 1A **116**
(Branch Pl.)
LS12: Leeds ... 3C **96**
(Stocks Hill)
Branch St. LS12: Leeds ... 1A **116**
Brander App. LS9: Leeds ... 2H **99**
Brander Cl. BD10: B'frd ... 3H **71**
LS9: Leeds ... 2H **99**
Brander Dr. LS9: Leeds ... 2G **99**
Brander Gro. LS9: Leeds ... 2G **99**
Brander Rd. LS9: Leeds ... 1H **99**
Brander St. LS9: Leeds ... 1H **99**
Brandfort St. BD7: B'frd ... 6A **90**
Brandling Ct. LS10: Leeds ... 2A **140**
BRANDON ... 2A **62**
Brandon Cl. LS17: Leeds ... 6B **62**
Brandon Ct. LS17: Leeds ... 2G **61**
WF1: Out ... 5F **157**
Brandon Cres. LS17: Leeds ... 6A **44**
Brandon Golf Course ... 2H **61**
Brandon Ho. *BD4: B'frd ... 3C **112***
(off Fontmell Cl.)
Brandon La. LS17: Leeds ... 6B **44**
LS17: Wike ... 5A **44**
Brandon Rd. LS3: Leeds ... 3A **4** (3G **97**)
Brandon St. LS12: Leeds ... 4F **97**
Brandon Ter. LS17: Leeds ... 2F **61**
Brandon Vw. LS17: Shad ... 2H **61**
Brandon Way LS7: Leeds ... 4B **78**
Brandon Way Cres. LS7: Leeds ... 4C **78**
BRANDY CARR ... 5B **156**
Brandy Carr Rd. WF2: Kirk, Wren ... 6H **155**
Branksome Ct. BD9: B'frd ... 1H **89**
Branksome Cres. BD9: B'frd ... 6H **69**
Branksome Dr. BD18: Ship ... 1E **69**
Branksome Gro. BD18: Ship ... 1E **69**

184 A-Z Leeds & Bradford

Branksome Pl. LS6: Leeds 1E 97
Branksome St. LS6: Leeds 1E 97
(off Queen's Rd.)
Branksome Ter. LS6: Leeds 1E 97
(off Queen's Rd.)
Bransby Cl. LS28: Fars 1A 94
Bransby Ct. LS28: Fars 1A 94
Bransby Ri. LS28: Fars 6A 74
Bransdale Av. LS20: Guis 5C 40
Bransdale Cl. BD17: Bail 5A 52
    LS20: Guis 5C 40
Bransdale Clough BD6: B'frd 4G 109
Bransdale Gdns. LS20: Guis 5C 40
Bransdale Gth. LS20: Guis 5C 40
Branshaw Dr. BD22: Keigh 2E 47
Branshaw Golf Course 4D 46
Branshaw Gro. BD22: Keigh 2E 47
Branshaw Mt. BD22: Keigh 2E 47
Bran St. BD21: Keigh 3H 47
Brant Av. HX2: Illing 3D 128
Brant Bank La. LS29: Nes 3H 9
Brantcliffe Dr. BD17: Bail 3B 52
Brantcliffe Way BD17: Bail 2C 52
Brantdale Cl. BD9: B'frd 5E 69
Brantdale Rd. BD9: B'frd 5E 69
Brantford St. LS7: Leeds 3B 78
Brantom HX2: Lud M 4C 146
Brantwood Av. BD9: B'frd 5E 69
Brantwood Cl. BD9: B'frd 5E 69
Brantwood Cres. BD9: B'frd 5D 68
Brantwood Dr. BD9: B'frd 5E 69
Brantwood Gro. BD9: B'frd 5E 69
Brantwood Oval BD9: B'frd 5E 69
Brantwood Rd. BD9: B'frd 5D 68
Brantwood Vs. BD9: B'frd 5E 69
Branwell Av. LS20: Guis 4B 40
    WF17: Birs 4A 136
Branwell Cl. LS20: Guis 4B 40
Branwell Ct. BD9: B'frd 1G 89
Branwell Dr. BD22: Haw 1C 64
Branwell Lodge BD7: B'frd 2A 110
Branwell Rd. LS20: Guis 4B 40
Branwell Wlk. WF17: Birs 4B 136
Branxholme Ind. Est. HD6: B Bri 2B 162
Brassey Rd. BD4: B'frd 1G 111
Brassey St. HX1: Hal 6A 164 (3F 149)
Brassey Ter. BD4: B'frd 1G 111
Brathay Gdns. LS14: Leeds 6C 80
Braunstone Ct. LS29: Men 1F 39
Braybrook Ct. BD8: B'frd 6C 70
Bray Cl. BD3: B'frd 3F 109
Brayshaw Dr. BD7: B'frd 3F 109
Brayshaw Fold BD12: Low M 1E 133
Brayshaw Rd. WF3: E Ard 3A 156
Brayton App. LS14: Leeds 4E 81
Brayton Cl. LS14: Leeds 4E 81
Brayton Gth. LS14: Leeds 4E 81
Brayton Grange LS14: Leeds 4F 81
Brayton Grn. LS14: Leeds 4F 81
(not continuous)
Brayton Gro. LS14: Leeds 4F 81
Brayton Pl. LS14: Leeds 4F 81
Brayton Sq. LS14: Leeds 4F 81
Brayton Ter. LS14: Leeds 4E 81
Brayton Wlk. LS14: Leeds 4E 81
Breakmoor Av. BD20: Sils 1E 15
Break Neck HX3: Hip 1C 150
Breaks Fold BD12: Wyke 5D 132
Breaks Rd. BD12: Low M 1E 133
Bream Av. BD19: Cleck 2H 153
Brearcliffe Cl. BD6: B'frd 5B 110
Brearcliffe Dr. BD6: B'frd 6A 110
Brearcliffe Gro. BD6: B'frd 6A 110
Brearcliffe Rd. BD6: B'frd 6B 110
Brearcliffe St. BD6: B'frd 6A 110
Brearley La. Lud M 6A 126
Brearley La. Top HX2: Lud M 6B 126
Brearton St. BD1: B'frd 1C 6 (3E 91)
Breary Av. LS18: H'fth 6F 57
(not continuous)
Breary Cl. LS16: B'hpe 2G 43
Breary La. LS16: B'hpe 2G 43
Breary La. E. LS16: B'hpe 2H 43

Breary Ri. LS16: B'hpe 2G 43
Breary Ter. LS18: H'fth 6F 57
Breary Wlk. LS18: H'fth 6F 57
Breck Lea HX6: Sow B 6G 147
Brecks BD14: Clay 6F 89
Brecks Gdns. LS25: Kip 2F 123
Brecks La. LS25: Kip 2E 123
    LS26: Swil 1C 122
Brecks Rd. BD14: Clay 6F 89
Breck Willows HX6: Sow B 6F 147
Brecon App. LS9: Leeds 2H 99
Brecon Cl. BD10: B'frd 2H 71
Brecon Ct. LS9: Leeds 2H 99
Brecon Ri. LS9: Leeds 2H 99
Bredon Av. BD18: Ship 2F 71
Breighton Adown BD6: B'frd 5F 109
Bremit Wlk. BD6: B'frd 5B 110
Bremner St. LS21: Otley 3F 23
Brendon Cl. BD4: B'frd 2B 112
Brendon Wlk. BD4: B'frd 3B 112
(not continuous)
Brentford Rd. BD12: Low M 6C 110
Brentwood Ct. LS16: Leeds 1A 76
Brentwood Gdns. BD6: B'frd 5D 110
Brentwood Gro. LS12: Leeds 4C 96
Brentwood St. LS12: Leeds 4C 96
Brentwood Ter. LS12: Leeds 4C 96
Brett Gdns. LS11: Leeds 1H 117
Bretton Cl. BD6: B'frd 5H 109
Brewery La. BD13: Que 6G 107
(Ambler Way)
    BD13: Que 2H 107
(Carter La.)
Brewery Pl. LS10: Leeds 6G 5
Brewery Rd. BD21: Keigh 4G 47
    LS29: I'ly 5E 11
Brewery St. BD21: Keigh 6B 34
    HX3: Hal 5G 129
Brewery Wharf
    LS10: Leeds 6G 5 (4B 98)
(Bowman La.)
    LS10: Leeds 6F 5
(Waterloo St.)
Brexdale Av. LS25: Kip 2F 123
Brian Cres. LS15: Leeds 6D 80
Brian Pl. LS15: Leeds 6D 80
Brian Royd La. HX4: Gree 4D 158
Brian Royd Mills HX4: Gree 4D 158
Brian Vw. LS15: Leeds 6E 81
Briar Cl. HX5: Ell 6A 160
    LS28: Fars 1H 93
Briardale Rd. BD9: B'frd 5D 68
Briardene LS26: Oul 3E 143
Briarfield Av. BD10: B'frd 2G 71
Briarfield Cl. BD10: B'frd 2G 71
    LS29: I'ly 6F 11
Briarfield Gdns. BD18: Ship 3B 70
Briarfield Gro. BD10: B'frd 2G 71
Briarfield Rd. BD18: Ship 4C 70
Briar Ga. LS22: Weth 2E 13
Briarlea Cl. LS19: Yead 2D 54
Briarmains Rd. WF17: Birs 5B 136
Briar Rhydding BD17: Bail 5E 53
Briarsdale Ct. LS8: Leeds 6G 79
Briarsdale Gth. LS8: Leeds 6G 79
Briarsdale Hgts. LS9: Leeds 6G 79
Briarsdale M. LS8: Leeds 6F 79
Briar Wood BD18: Ship 2E 71
Briarwood Av. BD6: B'frd 4B 110
    BD20: Rid 4D 34
Briarwood Cres.
    BD6: B'frd 4B 110
Briarwood Dr. BD6: B'frd 4B 110
Briarwood Gro. BD6: B'frd 3B 110
Brick & Tile Ter. HD6: Ras 2A 162
Brickfield Gro. HX2: Hal 2E 129
Brickfield La. HX2: Hal 2E 129
Brickfield Ter. HX2: Hal 2E 129
Brick Mill Rd. LS28: Pud 5B 94

Brick Row BD12: Wyke 4C 132
    HX3: Hal 3H 149
(off Siddal La.)
Brick St. BD19: Cleck 2H 153
    BD21: Keigh 1A 48
    LS9: Leeds 5H 5 (4B 98)
Brick Ter. HD6: Ras 2B 162
Bridge, The LS10: Leeds 6F 5
Bridge Av. LS21: Otley 3E 23
Bridge Cl. LS23: B Spa 3C 30
Bridge Ct. HD6: B Bri 2B 152
    LS11: Leeds 6G 97
    LS22: Weth 5E 13
    LS27: Morl 4B 138
Bridge End HD6: Ras 2A 162
    LS1: Leeds 5E 5 (4A 98)
    LS11: Leeds 6F 5
    LS22: Weth 5F 13
Bridge Fold LS5: Leeds 5H 75
Bridge Foot LS23: T Arch 3C 30
Bridge Gth. LS23: Cliff 5B 30
Bridgegate Fold BD10: B'frd 4B 72
Bridgegate Way BD10: B'frd 3B 72
Bridgehouse La. BD22: Haw 3C 64
Bridge La. HX3: She 1C 130
    LS29: I'ly 4C 10
Bridge Paddock LS22: Coll 2B 28
Bridge Pl. LS18: H'fth 5E 57
Bridge Rd. BD20: Sils 1E 15
    HD5: Hud 6G 163
    HD6: Brigh 1A 162
    LS5: Leeds 5H 75
    LS11: Leeds 6G 97
    LS13: Leeds 4A 74
    LS23: B Spa 3C 30
Bridge St. BD1: B'frd 5D 6 (5E 91)
    BD13: Thorn 5A 88
    BD20: Sils 1E 15
    BD21: Keigh 1H 47
    BD22: Oak 5B 46
    HX6: Sow B 6H 147
    LS2: Leeds 4G 5 (3B 98)
    LS21: Otley 3E 23
    LS27: Morl 4B 138
Bridge Ter. HX2: Wain 1E 127
    LS17: Shad 3C 62
    LS27: Morl 4B 138
Bridge Vw. LS13: Leeds 4A 74
Bridgewater Ct. LS6: Leeds 3F 77
Bridgewater Pl.
    LS11: Leeds 6D 4 (5H 97)
Bridgeway BD4: B'frd 3B 112
Bridgewater Rd. LS9: Leeds 6D 98
Bridge Wood Cl. LS18: H'fth 6F 57
Bridge Wood Vw. LS18: H'fth 5F 57
Bridgland Av. LS29: Men 6G 21
Bridgwater Rd. BD9: B'frd 1A 90
Bridle Dene HX3: She 2E 131
Bridle Path Rd. LS17: Leeds 2H 61
Bridle Path Wlk. LS15: Leeds 1C 100
Bridle Stile HX3: She 2E 131
Bridle Stile La. BD13: Que 3A 108
Bridleway LS27: Chur 6B 116
Brierdene BD20: Sils 1E 15
Brier Hey HX7: Myth 6A 126
Brier Hey Cl. HX7: Myth 6A 126
Brier Hey Ind. Units HX7: Myth 6A 126
Brier Hey La. HX7: Myth 6A 126
Brier Hill Cl. BD19: Cleck 3G 153
Brier Hill Vw. HD2: Hud 6D 162
Brierlands Cl. LS25: Gar 3H 103
Brierlands Fold LS25: Gar 3H 103
Brier La. HD6: Brigh 1F 161
Brierley Cl. BD18: Ship 3C 70
Brier St. BD21: Keigh 3H 47
    HX3: Hal 5G 129
Briery Cl. LS29: I'ly 5A 10
Briery Fld. BD18: Ship 4B 70
Briggate BD17: Ship 1B 70
    BD18: Ship 2B 70
    BD20: Sils 1E 15
    HD6: Brigh 1A 162
(not continuous)

Briggate HX5: Ell 4B 160
   LS1: Leeds 5E 5 (4A 98)
   LS29: Nes 1G 9
Brigg Gdns. BD22: Keigh 6F 33
Briggland Ct. BD15: Wils 4G 67
Briggs Av. BD6: B'frd 4A 110
Briggs Bldgs. LS27: Morl 3B 138
           (off Melbourne St.)
Briggs Gro. BD6: B'frd 4A 110
Briggs Pl. BD6: B'frd 4A 110
Briggs St. BD13: Que 4H 107
Briggs Vs. BD13: Que 4A 108
            (off Briggs St.)
BRIGHOUSE 6A 152
Brighouse & Denholme Gate Rd.
   HX3: North, She 3D 130
   HX3: She 1C 130
Brighouse & Denholme Rd.
   BD13: Denh, Que, Thorn 5C 86
Brighouse Rd. BD12: Low M 2D 132
   BD13: Que 4B 108
   HX3: Hip 2E 109
   HX3: She 4B 108
Brighouse Station (Rail) 2B 162
Brighouse Swimming Pool & Fitness Cen.
              . . . . .6B 152
Brighouse Wood La. HD6: Brigh . .6H 151
Brighouse Wood Row
   HD6: Brigh 6H 151
Brighton Av. LS27: Morl 2H 137
Brighton Cliff LS13: Leeds 1E 95
Brighton Gro. HX1: Hal 1E 149
            (off Pellon La.)
   LS13: Leeds 2F 95
Brighton Rd. LS29: I'ly 6G 11
Brighton St. BD10: B'frd 6G 53
   BD17: Ship 1B 70
   HX3: Hal 6E 129
Brighton Ter. BD19: Scho 1F 153
Bright St. BD4: B'frd 3A 112
   BD13: Que 4B 108
   BD14: Clay 1D 108
   BD15: All 2D 88
   BD22: Haw 2D 64
   HX6: Sow B 4H 147
   LS27: Morl 3H 137
   LS28: Stan 1B 94
   WF3: E Ard 1B 156
Brignall Cft. LS9: Leeds 2D 98
Brignall Gth. LS9: Leeds 2D 98
Brignall Way LS9: Leeds 2D 98
Brigshaw Dr. WF10: All B 6F 123
Brigshaw La. LS25: Kip 6F 123
   WF10: All B 6F 123
Brindle Cl. BD15: All 4C 88
Brindley Gro. BD8: B'frd 4E 89
Brindley Rd. BD20: Sils 3F 15
Brindley Way WF2: Carr G 5D 156
Brinsmead Ct. LS26: Rothw 6B 120
Brisbane Av. BD2: B'frd 6E 71
Briscoe La. HX4: Gree 4F 159
Bristol Av. BD20: Rid 5F 35
            (off Ford Rd.)
Bristol St. HX3: Hal 6H 149
   LS7: Leeds 1H 5 (2B 98)
Britannia Bldgs. LS27: Morl 5H 137
         (off Britannia Rd.)
Britannia Cl. LS28: Stan 1B 94
Britannia Ct. LS13: Leeds 3C 94
Britannia Ho. LS1: Leeds 4C 4
Britannia M. LS28: Pud 3C 94
Britannia Rd. LS27: Morl 5H 137
Britannia Sq. LS27: Morl 5H 137
Britannia St. BD5: B'frd 6E 7 (5F 91)
   BD16: Bgly 4C 50
   LS1: Leeds 5C 4 (4H 97)
   LS28: Stan 1B 94
Britannia Wharf BD16: Bgly 4C 50
Broadacres HD6: B Bri 2B 152
Broadacres Dr. LS22: Weth 4C 12
Broadacre Way BD17: Bail 2F 53
BROAD CARR 6G 159
Broad Carr La. HX4: Holy 6G 159

Broad Carr Ter. HX4: Holy 6H 159
Broadcasting Pl. LS2: Leeds 1D 4
Broadcroft Chase WF3: Ting 2E 155
Broadcroft Dr. WF3: Ting 2E 155
Broadcroft Gro. WF3: Ting 1E 155
Broadcroft Way WF3: Ting 1E 155
Broad Dale Cl. BD20: E Mor 4F 35
Broadfield Cl. BD4: B'frd 4C 112
Broadfields LS11: H'fth 6F 57
Broadfield Way LS29: Add 1B 8
BROAD FOLDS 1E 109
Broadgate LS2: Leeds 3E 5 (3A 98)
Broadgate Av. LS18: H'fth 1F 75
Broadgate Ct. LS18: H'fth 1F 75
Broadgate Cres. LS18: H'fth 1E 75
Broadgate Dr. LS18: H'fth 6F 57
Broadgate Ho. BD1: B'frd 3D 6
Broadgate La. LS18: H'fth 6E 57
Broadgate M. LS18: H'fth 1F 75
Broadgate Ri. LS18: H'fth 1F 75
Broadgate Wlk. LS18: H'fth 1E 75
Broad Ings Way HX3: She 2D 130
Broadlands BD20: Keigh 5F 33
Broadlands Av. LS28: Pud 4B 94
Broadlands Ct. LS28: Pud 4B 94
Broadlands Gdns. LS28: Pud 4C 94
Broadlands Pl. LS28: Pud 4B 94
Broadlands St. BD4: B'frd 1B 112
Broadlands Vw. LS28: Pud 4C 94
Broadland Way WF3: Loft 1G 157
Broad La. BD4: B'frd 6B 92
   HX2: Lud M 4C 146
         (not continuous)
   LS5: Leeds 5E 75
   LS13: Leeds 5E 75
   LS28: Leeds 1C 94
Broad La. Cl. LS13: Leeds 5G 75
Broadlea Av. LS13: Leeds 5G 75
Broadlea Cl. LS13: Leeds 5G 75
Broadlea Cres. BD5: B'frd 2F 111
   LS13: Leeds 5G 75
Broadlea Gdns. LS13: Leeds 5G 75
Broadlea Gro. LS13: Leeds 5G 75
Broadlea Hill LS13: Leeds 5H 75
Broadlea Mt. LS13: Leeds 6H 75
Broadlea Oval LS13: Leeds 5G 75
Broadlea Pl. LS13: Leeds 6G 75
Broadlea Rd. LS13: Leeds 5G 75
Broadlea St. LS13: Leeds 5G 75
Broadlea Ter. LS13: Leeds 5G 75
Broadlea Vw. LS13: Leeds 5F 75
Bradley Av. HX2: Hal 5H 127
Bradley Cl. HX2: Hal 6A 128
Bradley Cres. HX2: Hal 6H 127
Bradley Gro. HX2: Hal 6A 128
Bradley Lathe HX2: Hal 6A 128
Bradley Rd. HX2: Hal 6H 127
Broadmeadows WF1: Out 4G 157
Broad Oak HX3: Hip 3F 151
Broad Oak La. HX3: Hip 3F 151
Broad Oak Pl. HX3: Hip 3F 151
Broad Oak St. HX3: Hip 3F 151
Broad Oak Ter. HX3: Hip 3F 151
Broadstones Pk. BD16: Bgly 5F 51
Broadstone Way BD4: B'frd 4C 112
Broad St. BD1: B'frd 3D 6 (4E 91)
   HX1: Hal 4B 164 (2G 149)
   LS28: Fars 6G 73
Broad St. Plaza HX1: Hal 3C 164
Broad Tree Rd. HX3: Hal 5E 129
Broad Wlk. LS2: Leeds 6G 77
Broadwalk, The LS21: Otley 2C 22
Broadway BD1: B'frd 4D 6 (4E 91)
   BD16: Bgly 4C 50
   HX3: Sou 4A 150
   HX6: Sow B 6E 147
   LS5: Leeds 2G 75
   LS15: Leeds 5B 100
   LS18: H'fth 3A 74
   LS20: Guis 5A 40
Broadway Av. BD5: B'frd 3D 110
   LS6: Leeds 1E 97

Broadway Cl. BD5: B'frd 3D 110
Broadway Ct. HX6: Sow B 6E 147
Broadway Dr. LS18: H'fth 1D 74
Broadway Shop. Cen.
   BD1: B'frd 4E 7 (4F 91)
Broadwell Dr. BD18: Ship 3E 71
Broadwood Av. HX2: Hal 6A 128
Brocklebank Cl. BD20: E Mor 4F 35
Brocklesby Dr. BD15: All 3D 88
Brocklyn Yd. HX1: Hal 5D 164
Brocks HX2: Lud M 4C 146
Brockwell Gdns. HX6: Sow B 6G 147
Brockwell Ga. HX6: Sow B 6G 147
Brockwell La. HX6: Sow B 6F 147
          (not continuous)
   HX6: Tri 6F 147
Brodley Cl. HX3: Hip 1E 151
Brodrick Ct. LS6: Leeds 4D 76
Brodrick Dr. LS29: I'ly 6C 10
Brodwell Grange LS18: H'fth 1G 75
Brogans Yd. LS21: Otley 4F 23
        (off Cambridge St.)
Broken Way BD5: B'frd 3D 110
        (off Delamere St.)
Bromet Pl. BD2: B'frd 5H 71
Bromford Rd. BD4: B'frd 1H 111
Bromley Gro. BD22: Keigh 2E 47
Bromley Rd. BD16: Bgly 3B 50
   BD18: Ship 1G 69
Brompton Av. BD4: B'frd 2G 111
Brompton Gro. LS11: Leeds 3H 117
Brompton Mt. LS11: Leeds 3H 117
Brompton Rd. BD4: B'frd 1G 111
Brompton Row LS11: Leeds 3H 117
Brompton Ter. BD4: B'frd 1G 111
   LS11: Leeds 3H 117
Brompton Vw. LS11: Leeds 3H 117
Bronshill Gro. BD15: All 2E 89
Bronte Caravan Pk. BD22: Cros R . . .6F 47
Bronte Cl. BD9: B'frd 1G 89
   BD19: Gom 6F 135
   WF3: E Ard 6B 140
Bronte Dr. BD22: Oak 4E 47
Bronte Ho. LS7: Leeds 6A 78
Bronte Old Rd. BD13: Thorn 5A 88
Bronte Pl. BD13: Thorn 5A 88
Bronte Rd. WF17: Birs 6A 136
Bronte St. BD21: Keigh 5B 34
   BD22: Haw 2B 64
Bronte Vs. BD22: Cros R 1F 65
Brontë Parsonage Mus. 2B 64
Brookdale Ct. HX2: Hal 6D 128
Brooke Grn. HX3: Hip 1E 151
Brookelea HX3: Hip 2G 151
Brooke St. HD6: Ras 2A 162
Brookeville HX3: Hip 2F 151
        (off Brighouse Rd.)
Brookeville Av. HX3: Hip 2E 151
Brook Farm Ct. HX3: She 6F 109
        (off Cooper La.)
Brookfield Av. BD18: Ship 1D 70
   BD19: Cleck 6B 134
   LS8: Leeds 5D 78
   LS13: Leeds 3H 73
Brookfield Ct. LS13: Leeds 3H 73
Brookfield Gdns. LS13: Leeds 4H 73
Brookfield Pl. LS6: Leeds 3E 77
         (not continuous)
Brookfield Rd. BD3: B'frd 2H 7 (3G 91)
   BD18: Ship 1D 70
   LS6: Leeds 3E 77
Brookfields Av. BD12: Wyke 6E 133
Brookfields Rd. BD12: Wyke 6E 133
Brookfield St. LS10: Leeds 6B 98
Brookfield Ter. BD19: Cleck 6B 134
   LS6: Leeds 3E 77
        (off Brookfield Rd.)
   LS10: Leeds 6B 98
Brookfield Vw. BD19: Cleck 6C 134
BROOKFOOT 6H 151
Brookfoot Av. BD11: Birk 2E 135
Brookfoot Bus. Pk. HD6: Brigh 6H 151
Brookfoot Ind. Est. HD6: Brigh 1H 161

Brookfoot La. HD6: Brigh 6H **151**
HX3: Sou 6F **151**
Brookfoot Old La. HD6: Brigh 6H **151**
Brook Grain Hill HD6: Ras 3A **162**
BROOK HILL 4D 52
Brook Hill BD17: Bail 4D **52**
Brookhill Av. LS17: Leeds 3C **60**
Brookhill Cl. LS17: Leeds 3C **60**
Brookhill Cres. LS17: Leeds 3C **60**
Brookhill Dr. LS17: Leeds 3C **60**
Brookhill Gro. LS17: Leeds 3C **60**
BROOKHOUSE 5A **106**
Brookhouse Gdns. BD10: B'frd 1D **72**
BROOKLANDS 5B **80**
Brooklands HD2: Hud 6F **163**
HX3: Hip 2F **151**
LS17: E Kes 6E **27**
Brooklands Av. BD13: Thorn 5B **88**
LS14: Leeds 5B **80**
Brooklands Cl. LS14: Leeds 5A **80**
LS29: Men 6H **21**
Brooklands Ct. LS14: Leeds 5B **80**
Brooklands Cres. LS14: Leeds 5A **80**
LS19: Yead 1F **55**
Brooklands Dr. LS14: Leeds 5A **80**
LS19: Yead 1F **55**
Brooklands Gth. LS14: Leeds 5B **80**
Brooklands Gro. LS29: Men 6H **21**
Brooklands La. LS14: Leeds 5B **80**
LS29: Men 6G **21**
Brooklands Pk. LS29: Men 6H **21**
Brooklands Towers LS14: Leeds . . .4C **80**
Brooklands Vw. LS14: Leeds 5B **80**
(not continuous)
Brooklands Wlk. LS29: Men 6H **21**
Brooklands Way LS29: Men 6G **21**
Brook La. BD14: Clay 2C **108**
Brookleigh LS28: Cal 3F **73**
Brooklyn Av. LS12: Leeds 4C **96**
Brooklyn Ct. BD19: Cleck 6B **134**
Brooklyn Dr. BD19: Cleck 6B **134**
Brooklyn Grange BD19: Cleck 6C **134**
Brooklyn Pl. LS12: Leeds 4C **96**
Brooklyn Rd. BD19: Cleck 6B **134**
Brooklyn St. BD20: Keigh 2G **33**
LS12: Leeds 4C **96**
Brooklyn Ter. HD6: Brigh 4G **151**
LS12: Leeds 4C **96**
Brook Row BD22: Oak 6D **46**
Brookroyd Av. HD6: B Bri 3B **152**
Brookroyd La. WF17: Bat 6B **136**
Brooksbank Av. BD7: B'frd 6G **89**
Brooksbank Dr. LS15: Leeds 3C **100**
Brooksbank Gdns. HX5: Ell 5B **160**
Brookside BD13: Cull 3B **66**
LS17: Leeds 2C **60**
LS22: Coll 3B **28**
Brookside Fold BD22: Oxen 1C **84**
Brooks Ter. BD13: Que 3D **108**
BD21: Keigh 2H **47**
HX2: Lud 6E **127**
(off High St.)
HX5: Ell 5C **160**
LS29: I'ly 5D **10**
Brooks Yd. HD2: Hud 5G **163**
Brook Ter. HX2: Lud 5E **127**
Brookwater Cl. HX3: Hal 6H **149**
Brookwater Dr. BD18: Ship 3E **71**
Brookwoods Ind. Est. HX4: Holy . . .6F **159**
Broom Cl. LS10: Leeds 6D **118**
Broom Ct. LS10: Leeds 1D **140**
Broom Cres. LS10: Leeds 6C **118**
Broomcroft BD14: Clay 1D **108**
Broom Cross LS10: Leeds 6C **118**
Broome Av. BD2: B'frd 6E **71**
Broomfield BD14: Clay 2C **108**
BD15: Wils 4H **67**
BD19: Cleck 3H **153**
(off West End Dr.)
HX5: Ell 5H **159**
LS16: Leeds 3B **58**
Broomfield Av. HX3: Hal 6F **149**

Broomfield Cres. LS6: Leeds 5D **76**
Broomfield Pl. BD14: Clay 2C **108**
BD21: Keigh 6H **33**
LS6: Leeds 6D **76**
Broomfield Rd. BD21: Keigh 6H **33**
HD2: Fix 6A **162**
LS6: Leeds 5D **76**
BROOMFIELDS 6E **91**
Broomfield St. BD13: Que 4A **108**
BD21: Keigh 6H **33**
LS6: Leeds 6D **76**
Broomfield Ter. BD19: Cleck 3H **153**
LS6: Leeds 6D **76**
Broomfield Vw. LS6: Leeds 6D **76**
Broom Gdns. LS10: Leeds 6C **118**
Broom Gth. LS10: Leeds 6D **118**
Broom Gro. LS10: Leeds 1D **140**
Broomhead Cl. HX2: Illing 2B **128**
Broomhill BD21: Keigh 6D **34**
Broomhill Av. BD21: Keigh 2G **47**
LS17: Leeds 5B **60**
Broomhill Cres. LS17: Leeds 5B **60**
Broomhill Dr. BD21: Keigh 2G **47**
LS17: Leeds 6A **60**
(not continuous)
Broomhill Gro. BD21: Keigh 2G **47**
Broomhill Mt. BD21: Keigh 2G **47**
Broom Hill Rd. LS9: Leeds 2F **99**
Broomhill St. BD21: Keigh 3G **47**
Broomhill Wlk. BD21: Keigh 2G **47**
Broomhill Way BD21: Keigh 2G **47**
Broom Lawn LS10: Leeds 6C **118**
Broom Mills Rd. LS28: Fars 6A **74**
Broom Mt. LS10: Leeds 1D **140**
Broom Nook LS10: Leeds 6D **118**
Broom Pl. LS10: Leeds 6D **118**
Broom Rd. LS10: Leeds 1C **140**
Broom St. BD4: B'frd 6E **7**
BD19: Cleck 3H **153**
BD21: Keigh 1A **48**
Broom Ter. BD22: Oak 4D **46**
LS10: Leeds 6D **118**
Broom Vw. LS10: Leeds 6D **118**
Broom Wlk. LS10: Leeds 1D **140**
Broster Av. BD22: Keigh 6F **33**
Brougham Rd. HX3: Hal 6G **129**
Brougham St. HX3: Hal 6G **129**
Brougham Ter. HX3: Hal 5G **129**
Broughton Av. BD4: B'frd 4H **111**
LS9: Leeds 1E **99**
Broughton Ho. BD4: B'frd 4D **112**
Broughton Ter. LS9: Leeds 1E **99**
LS28: Stan 3A **94**
Brow, The *BD17: Bail* 4C **52**
(off Bank Wlk.)
BROW BOTTOM 2G **127**
Brow Bottom La. HX2: Mix 1G **127**
Browcliff BD20: Sils 1E **15**
Brow Cotts. HD6: Brigh 4F **151**
Browfield Ter. BD20: Sils 1E **15**
Browfield Vw. BD22: Keigh 2E **47**
Browfoot BD18: Ship 1D **70**
Browfoot Dr. HX2: Hal 3B **148**
Brow Foot Ga. HX2: Hal 3B **148**
(off Brow Foot Ga. La.)
Brow Foot Ga. La. HX2: Hal 3B **148**
Browgate BD17: Bail 4C **52**
Brow La. BD14: Clay 2A **108**
HX3: Hal 1E **129**
HX3: North 3A **130**
HX3: She 1F **131**
Brow Mills Ind. Est. HX3: Hip 3F **151**
Brown Av. LS11: Leeds 1E **117**
Brown Bank Caravan Pk.
BD20: Sils 5A **8**
Brown Bank La. BD20: Sils . . .1F **15** & 5A **8**
Brownberrie Av. LS18: H'fth 4E **57**
Brownberrie Cres. LS18: H'fth 4D **56**
Brownberrie Dr. LS18: H'fth 4E **57**
(not continuous)
Brownberrie Gdns. LS18: H'fth 4D **56**
Brownberrie La. LS18: H'fth 4B **56**
Brownberrie Wlk. LS18: H'fth 4E **57**

Brownberry Gro. HX3: She 6F **109**
BROWN HILL 6B **136**
Brown Hill Av. LS9: Leeds 1E **99**
Brownhill Cl. BD11: Birk 6E **113**
WF17: Bat 6B **136**
Brown Hill Cres. LS9: Leeds 1E **99**
Brown Hill Dr. BD11: Birk 6E **113**
BROWNHILL END 6B **136**
Brownhill Gth. WF17: Bat 6B **136**
Brownhill Rd. WF17: Bat 6B **136**
Brown Hill Ter. LS9: Leeds 1E **99**
Brown Ho's. HX2: M T 5H **127**
Browning Av. HX3: Hal 6H **149**
Browning St. BD3: B'frd 4H **7** (4H **91**)
Brown La. E. LS11: Leeds 6F **97**
Brown La. W. LS11: Leeds 6E **97**
LS12: Leeds 6E **97**
Brownlea Cl. LS19: Yead 2D **54**
Brown Lee La. BD15: Wils 5E **67**
Brown Pl. LS11: Leeds 1E **117**
Brown Rd. LS11: Leeds 1E **117**
BROWN ROYD 3B **90**
Brownroyd Fold BD5: B'frd 3B **110**
BROWNROYD HILL 3C **110**
Brownroyd Hill Rd. BD6: B'frd 4B **110**
Brownroyd St. BD7: B'frd 5B **90**
BD8: B'frd 3B **90**
Brownroyd Wlk. BD6: B'frd 3B **110**
Brown Springs BD22: Oak 3E **47**
Brown Springs La. BD22: Oak 3E **47**
Brown St. BD22: Keigh 5B **34**
Brown Wood BD10: B'frd 5F **53**
Brow Rd. BD22: Haw 3D **64**
Browsfield Rd. LS29: Add 1B **8**
Browsholme St. BD21: Keigh 1A **48**
Brow St. BD21: Keigh 1B **48**
Brow Top BD14: Clay 3C **108**
Brow Top Rd. BD22: Cros R 3D **64**
Brow Wood Cres. BD2: B'frd 6E **71**
Brow Wood Ri. HX3: She 1F **131**
Brow Wood Rd. HX3: She 1F **131**
WF17: Bat 6D **136**
Brow Wood Ter. BD6: B'frd 6H **109**
Bruce Gdns. LS12: Leeds 4E **97**
Bruce Lawn LS12: Leeds 4E **97**
Bruce St. HX1: Hal 4D **148**
Brudenell Av. LS6: Leeds 6F **77**
Brudenell Gro. LS6: Leeds 6F **77**
Brudenell Mt. LS6: Leeds 6E **77**
Brudenell Rd. LS6: Leeds 6E **77**
Brudenell St. LS6: Leeds 6F **77**
Brudenell Vw. LS6: Leeds 6F **77**
Brumfitt Hill LS29: Add 1D **8**
Brunel Cl. BD9: B'frd 1A **90**
WF2: Carr G 5D **156**
Brunel Ct. BD3: B'frd 1G **91**
HX3: Hal 5F **129**
(off Mill La.)
Brunel Gdns. *BD5: B'frd* 2C **110**
(off Ida St.)
Brunel Rd. WF2: Carr G 4D **156**
Brunswick Arc. *BD21: Keigh* 6A **34**
(within Airedale Shop. Cen.)
Brunswick Ct. LS2: Leeds 2G **5** (2B **98**)
Brunswick Gdns.
HX1: Hal 4A **164** (2F **149**)
LS25: Gar 4F **103**
Brunswick Ho. BD16: Bgly 5D **50**
Brunswick Ind. Est.
HX1: Hal 6A **164** (3F **149**)
LS27: Morl 3B **138**
Brunswick Pl. BD10: B'frd 2B **72**
LS27: Morl 3B **138**
Brunswick Rd. BD10: B'frd 2B **72**
LS28: Pud 2A **138**
Brunswick Row LS2: Leeds . . .2G **5** (2B **98**)
Brunswick St. BD13: Cull 3C **66**
BD13: Que 4B **108**
BD16: Bgly 4D **50**
LS27: Morl 2A **138**
Brunswick Ter. BD12: Low M 6C **110**
LS2: Leeds 2E **5** (2A **98**)
LS27: Morl 3D **138**
BRUNTCLIFFE 3F **137**

Bruntcliffe Av. LS27: Morl 3G 137
Bruntcliffe Cl. LS27: Morl 3H 137
Bruntcliffe Dr. LS27: Morl 3H 137
Bruntcliffe La. LS27: Morl 3H 137
Bruntcliffe Rd. LS27: Morl 3F 137
Bruntcliffe Way LS27: Morl 3G 137
BRUNTHWAITE 2G 15
Brunthwaite Bri. La. BD20: Sils 4F 15
Brunthwaite Cotts. BD20: Sils 2G 15
Brunthwaite La. BD20: Sils 2G 15
Brunthwaite Ter. BD20: Sils 2G 15
Brussels Ct. HX1: Hal 5C 164
Brussels St. LS9: Leeds ...5H 5 (4B 98)
Bryan Rd. HX5: Ell 5H 159
Bryanstone Rd. BD4: B'frd 6B 92
Bryan St. HD6: Ras 2A 162
  LS28: Fars 5H 73
Bryan St. Nth. LS28: Fars 5H 73
Bryden Cl. HD6: Brigh 4H 151
Bryngate LS26: Oul 1E 143
Bryony Ct. LS10: Leeds 2D 140
Bubwith Gro. HX2: Hal 3C 148
  (off Bk. Eversley Mt.)
Buchan Towers BD5: B'frd 6C 6
Buckden Ct. BD20: Sils 1E 15
  LS29: Men 2H 39
  (off Jackson Wlk.)
Buckfast Ct. BD10: B'frd 2H 71
Buckingham Av. LS6: Leeds 5E 77
Buckingham Cres. BD14: Clay 6F 89
Buckingham Dr. LS6: Leeds 5E 77
Buckingham Gro. LS6: Leeds 5E 77
Buckingham Ho. LS6: Leeds 5E 77
Buckingham Mt. LS6: Leeds 6E 77
Buckingham Rd. LS6: Leeds 6E 77
Buckland Pl. HX1: Hal 3C 148
Buckland Rd. BD8: B'frd 3H 89
Buck La. BD17: Bail 4F 53
Buckle La. LS29: Men 2H 39
Buckley Av. LS11: Leeds 2H 117
Buckley La. HX2: Hal 5A 128
Buck Mill La. BD10: B'frd 5G 53
Buckstone Av. LS17: Leeds 3F 59
Buckstone Cl. LS17: Leeds 3G 59
Buckstone Cres. LS17: Leeds 3G 59
Buckstone Dr. LS17: Leeds 3F 59
  LS19: Raw 4E 55
  (not continuous)
Buckstone Gdns. LS17: Leeds 3G 59
Buckstone Gth. BD20: E Mor 4H 35
Buckstone Grn. LS17: Leeds 3F 59
Buckstone Mt. LS17: Leeds 3F 59
Buckstone Gro. LS17: Leeds 3F 59
Buckstone Oval LS17: Leeds 3F 59
Buckstone Ri. LS17: Leeds 3F 59
Buckstone Rd. LS17: Leeds 3F 59
Buckstone Vw. LS17: Leeds 3F 59
Buckstone Way LS17: Leeds 3F 59
Buck St. BD3: B'frd 6G 7 (5G 91)
  BD13: Denh 3C 86
Buckthorne Cl. WF3: E Ard 1B 156
Buckthorne Dr. WF3: E Ard 1B 156
Buckthorne Dr. WF3: E Ard 1B 156
Buckthorne Fold WF3: E Ard 1B 156
Buckton Cl. LS11: Leeds 1G 117
Buckton Mt. LS11: Leeds 1G 117
Buckton Vw. LS11: Leeds 1G 117
Bude Rd. BD5: B'frd 4F 111
  LS11: Leeds 2H 117
Bula Cl. LS25: Kip 3H 123
Bull Cl. La. HX1: Hal ...5A 164 (3F 149)
Buller Cl. LS9: Leeds 2G 99
Buller Ct. LS9: Leeds 2G 99
Buller Gro. LS9: Leeds 2F 99
Buller St. BD4: B'frd 6A 92
  LS26: Wood 1F 143
Bullerthorpe La. LS15: Leeds ...5H 101
  LS26: Swil 5G 121
Bullfield, The BD16: Har 1F 67
Bull Grn. HX1: Hal 4B 164 (2G 149)
Bull Hill BD22: Oxen 2C 84
Bullough La. LS26: Rothw 6B 120
Bullroyd Av. BD8: B'frd 3G 89

Bullroyd Cres. BD8: B'frd 3G 89
Bullroyd Dr. BD8: B'frd 3G 89
Bull Royd Ind. Est. BD8: B'frd 3G 89
Bullroyd La. BD8: B'frd 3G 89
Bungalow, The BD5: B'frd 1E 111
Bungalows, The HX2: Hal 6B 128
  HX3: Hal 1A 160
  (Backhold Av.)
  HX3: Hal 5D 128
  (High Cft.)
  HX6: Sow B 5G 147
  LS15: Leeds 6F 81
  (off Church La.)
  LS25: Kip 3B 124
  LS25: M'fld 5E 105
Bunkers BD22: Haw 3C 64
  (off Bridgehouse La.)
Bunkers Hill BD17: Esh 2H 53
Bunker's Hill La. BD22: Keigh 2D 46
Bunney Grn. HX3: North 3B 130
Bunting Dr. BD6: B'frd 3D 108
Burberry Cl. BD4: B'frd 5A 112
Burchett Gro. LS6: Leeds 5G 77
Burchett Pl. LS6: Leeds 5G 77
Burchett Ter. LS6: Leeds 5H 77
Burdale Pl. BD7: B'frd 5B 90
Burdett Ter. LS4: Leeds 1C 96
Burdock Way HX1: Hal 5A 164 (3F 149)
Burghley M. LS10: Leeds 4B 140
Burghley Wlk. BD18: Ship 3E 71
Burland Ter. LS26: Swil 3A 122
Burleigh St. HX1: Hal 4D 148
BURLEY 1D 96
Burley Cl. BD20: Stee 6C 14
Burley Grange Rd. LS4: Leeds 1C 96
Burley Hill Cres. LS4: Leeds 6B 76
Burley Hill Dr. LS4: Leeds 6B 76
Burley Hill Trad. Est. LS4: Leeds ...6C 76
BURLEY IN WHARFEDALE 2F 21
Burley in Wharfedale Station (Rail)
  ......3E 21
Burley La. LS18: H'fth 1D 74
  LS29: Men 6F 21
Burley Lodge Pl.
  LS6: Leeds 2E 97
  (off Burley Lodge Rd.)
Burley Lodge Rd. LS6: Leeds 1E 97
Burley Lodge St. LS6: Leeds 2E 97
Burley Lodge Ter. LS6: Leeds 1E 97
Burley M. BD20: Stee 6C 14
Burley Park Station (Rail) 6D 76
Burley Pl. LS4: Leeds 2D 96
Burley Rd. LS3: Leeds 1E 97
  LS4: Leeds 6C 76
  LS29: Men 5G 21
Burley St. BD2: B'frd 5D 70
  HX5: Ell 5B 160
  LS3: Leeds 3A 4 (3A 97)
Burley Wood Ct. LS4: Leeds 6B 76
Burley Wood Cres.
  LS4: Leeds 6B 76
BURLEY WOODHEAD 5C 20
Burley Wood La. LS4: Leeds 6C 76
Burley Wood Mt. LS4: Leeds 6B 76
Burley Wood Vw. LS4: Leeds 6C 76
Burlington Av. BD3: B'frd 2C 92
Burlington Pl. LS11: Leeds 3H 117
Burlington Rd. LS11: Leeds 3H 117
Burlington St. BD8: B'frd 2D 90
  HX1: Hal 2D 148
Burmah St. HX1: Hal 2D 148
BURMANTOFTS 2D 98
Burmantofts St. LS9: Leeds 3C 98
Burn Cl. LS26: Wood 1E 145
Burned Gro. HX3: She 6E 109
Burned Rd. HX3: She 6E 109
Burneston Gdns. BD6: B'frd 5G 109
Burnett Av. BD5: B'frd 2D 110
Burnett Pl. BD5: B'frd 2D 110
Burnett Ri. BD13: Que 5G 107
Burnett St. BD1: B'frd 4F 7 (4F 91)
Burnham Av. BD4: B'frd 3H 111
Burnham Ct. LS22: Weth 3C 12

Burnham Rd. LS25: Gar 6F 103
Burnham Wlk. BD4: B'frd 4A 112
Burnholme BD13: Denh 3B 86
Burniston Cl. BD15: Wils 5G 67
Burnley Hill HX3: North 3C 130
Burnley Hill Ter. HX3: She 3D 130
Burnley Rd. HX2: Hal 3B 148
  HX2: Lud M 3D 146
  HX6: Sow B 3D 146
  HX7: Myth 6A 126
Burnleys Ct. LS26: Meth 6D 144
Burnleys Dr. LS26: Meth 6D 144
Burnley's Mill Rd. BD19: Gom 6D 144
Burnleys Vw. LS26: Meth 6D 144
Burnleyville BD19: Gom 6F 135
Burnsall Ct. LS12: Leeds 3B 96
Burnsall Cft. LS12: Leeds 3B 96
Burnsall Gdns. LS12: Leeds 3B 96
Burnsall Grange LS12: Leeds 3B 96
  (off Theaker La.)
Burnsall M. BD20: Sils 1D 14
Burnsall Rd. BD3: B'frd 4H 91
  (not continuous)
  HD6: Ras 3G 161
Burns Ct. WF17: Birs 5H 135
Burnsdale BD15: All 6C 68
Burnshaw M. LS10: Leeds 4A 140
Burns Hill LS29: Add 1C 8
Burnside LS29: Add 1D 8
Burnside Av. HX3: She 6F 109
Burnside Cl. WF17: Bat 6C 136
Burns St. HX3: Hal 3D 128
Burnstall Cl. LS29: Men 2H 39
Burnstall Cres. LS29: Men 3G 39
Burns Way LS23: Cliff 5B 30
Burnt Side Rd.
  LS12: N Far 3E 115
BURNWELLS 5G 53
Burnwells BD10: B'frd 5G 53
Burnwells Av. BD10: B'frd 5G 53
Burrage St. BD16: Bgly 4B 50
Burras Av. LS21: Otley 4D 22
Burras Dr. LS21: Otley 4D 22
Burras La. LS21: Otley 4D 22
Burras Rd. BD4: B'frd 3H 111
Burrell Cl. LS22: Weth 4G 13
Burrow St.
  BD5: B'frd 6C 6 (5E 91)
Burr Tree Dr. LS15: Leeds 4F 101
Burr Tree Gth. LS15: Leeds 4F 101
Burr Tree Va. LS15: Leeds 4F 101
Burrwood Ter. HX4: Holy 6F 159
Burrwood Way HX4: Holy 6F 159
Burton Av. LS11: Leeds 2A 118
Burton Cres. LS6: Leeds 3D 76
Burton Ho. LS17: Leeds 3D 60
Burton M. LS17: Leeds 2B 60
Burton Rd. LS11: Leeds 2A 118
Burton Row LS11: Leeds 1A 118
Burton St. BD4: B'frd 1G 111
  BD20: Keigh 3H 33
  HX2: Hal 2E 129
  LS11: Leeds 1A 118
  LS28: Fars 6H 73
Burton Ter. LS11: Leeds 2A 118
Burton Way LS9: Leeds 2E 99
Bury La. BD20: E Mor 4G 35
Busely Ct. LS27: Morl 2H 137
Busfield St. BD16: Bgly 4B 50
Busfield St. BD4: B'frd 2H 111
Bush Hill Fold BD13: Que 3G 107
BUSLINGTHORPE 5A 78
Buslingthorpe Grn.
  LS7: Leeds 6A 78
Buslingthorpe La. LS7: Leeds 5A 78
Buslingthorpe Va. LS7: Leeds 5A 78
Bussey Ct. LS6: Leeds 6G 77
Busy La. BD18: Ship 6E 53
Butcher Hill LS5: Leeds 1G 75
  LS16: Leeds 1G 75
  LS18: H'fth 1G 75
Butcher La. LS26: Rothw 2A 142
Butchers Row LS2: Leeds 4F 5

Butcher St. LS11: Leeds 5H 97
Bute Av. HD6: Brigh 4A 152
Bute St. BD2: B'frd 5D 70
Butler La. BD17: Bail 3D 52
(not continuous)
Butler's Fold BD16: Bgly 6B 36
Butler St. E. BD3: B'frd 2H 7 (3G 91)
Butler St. W. BD3: B'frd 2G 7 (3G 91)
Butlers Vw. HX3: Hal 5F 129
(off Crown Rd.)
Butterbowl Dr. LS12: Leeds 6G 95
Butterbowl Gdns.
LS12: Leeds 6H 95
Butterbowl Gth. LS12: Leeds 6G 95
Butterbowl Gro. LS12: Leeds 6G 95
Butterbowl Lawn
LS12: Leeds 6G 95
Butterbowl Mt. LS12: Leeds 6H 95
Butterbowl Rd. LS12: Leeds 6H 95
Buttercup La. WF3: E Ard 6C 140
Buttercup Way BD11: Drig 2D 136
Butterfield Homes BD16: Cot 3D 68
(off Cottingley Moor Rd.)
Butterfield Ind. Est. BD17: Bail 5E 53
Butterfield's Bldgs.
LS27: Morl 2H 137
Butterfield St. LS9: Leeds 4D 98
Butterley St. LS10: Leeds 6A 98
Buttermead Cl. BD6: B'frd 6A 110
Buttermere Av. LS22: Weth 3C 12
Buttermere Rd. BD2: B'frd 6G 71
BUTTERSHAW 5G 109
Buttershaw Dr. BD6: B'frd 5G 109
Buttershaw La. BD6: B'frd 6B 110
WF15: Liv 4H 153
Butterwick Gdns. LS22: Weth 4C 12
Butt Hill LS25: Kip 4G 123
Buttholme Ga. BD6: B'frd 5H 109
Butt La. BD10: B'frd 1H 71
BD22: Haw 2C 64
LS12: Leeds 5F 95
LS13: Leeds 4G 95
Button Hill LS7: Leeds 5B 78
Buttress HX2: Lud 6E 127
Buttress La. HX2: Lud 6E 127
Butt Row LS12: Leeds 5G 95
Butts, The BD20: E Mor 5H 35
Butts Ct. LS1: Leeds 4E 5 (3A 98)
Butts Gth. LS14: T'ner 2H 63
Butts Gth. Ct. LS14: T'ner 2H 63
Butts Gth. Farm LS14: T'ner 2H 63
Butts Gth. Vw. LS14: T'ner 2H 63
Butts Gth. Wlk. LS14: T'ner 2H 63
Butts Grn. La. HX2: Hal 2F 147
Butts Grn. Rd. HX2: Lud M 2E 147
Butts Hill BD19: Gom 6F 135
Butts La. BD20: Guis 4C 40
Butts Mt. LS12: Leeds 4D 96
Butts Ter. LS20: Guis 4C 40
Buxton Av. BD9: B'frd 4C 70
Buxton La. BD9: B'frd 5C 70
Buxton St. BD9: B'frd 1B 90
BD21: Keigh 6B 34
HX3: Hal 6E 129
Buxton Way HX3: Hal 4D 128
Byeway LS20: Guis 4A 40
Byland HX2: Illing 6C 106
Byland Cl. LS23: B Spa 4A 30
Byland Gro. BD15: All 1B 88
Bylands Av. BD20: Rid 3C 34
Byre Way BD22: Keigh 2E 47
Byrl St. BD21: Keigh 4B 34
Byron Av. HX6: Sow B 4H 147
Byron Halls BD3: B'frd 3H 91
Byron Ho. LS29: I'ly 5F 11
Byron M. BD16: Bgly 2C 50
Byron St. BD3: B'frd 3H 91
HX1: Hal 2D 148
HX6: Sow B 4H 147
LS2: Leeds 2G 5 (2B 98)
Byron Studios BD3: B'frd 3H 91
(off Barkerend Rd.)

Byron Ter. HX6: Sow B 4H 147
(off Byron St.)
Bywater Row BD11: Birk 2F 135

C

CABBAGE HILL 5A 96
Cabbage Hill LS12: Leeds 5B 96
Cabin Rd. LS21: Pool 6D 24
Cable Pl. LS10: Leeds 1C 118
CACKLESHAW 5E 47
Cad Beeston LS11: Leeds 2G 117
Cad Beeston M.
LS11: Leeds 2G 117
CADDY FIELD 3A 150
Caddy Fld. St. HX3: Hal 3H 149
(off Jubliee St.)
Cadman Cl. LS27: Morl 4A 138
Cadney Cft. HX1: Hal 5B 164
Caernarvon Av. LS25: Gar 4H 103
Caernarvon Cl. LS15: Leeds 4D 98
Cain Cl. LS5: Leeds 4D 98
(not continuous)
Cain La. HX3: Sou 5C 150
Cairn Av. LS20: Guis 3A 40
Cairn Cl. BD20: Keigh 3G 33
Cairn Gth. LS20: Guis 3A 40
Cairns Cl. BD2: B'frd 6F 71
Cairn Vw. LS29: I'ly 4F 11
(off Hauxley Ct.)
Caister Cl. WF17: Birs 5C 136
Caister Gro. BD21: Keigh 3H 47
(off Oakfield Rd.)
Caister St. BD21: Keigh 3H 47
Caister Way BD21: Keigh 3H 47
Caistor Gth. BD10: B'frd 3A 72
(off Rowantree Dr.)
Calde Ct. BD12: Low M 1E 133
Caldene Av. BD12: Low M 1E 133
Calder Av. HX2: Hal 4D 148
CALDER BANKS 4C 108
Calder Banks BD13: Que 4C 108
Calder Cl. HX4: Gree 4H 159
(off Calder St.)
LS22: Weth 1D 12
Calder Ct. HX1: Hal 3C 164
Caldercroft HX5: Ell 5C 160
Calderdale Bus. Pk. HX2: Hal 4D 128
Calderdale Way HX5: Ell 4A 160
Calder Ho. HX5: Ell 4B 160
(off St Mary's Ga.)
Calderstone Av. BD6: B'frd 1H 131
Calder St. HD6: Brigh 2C 162
HX4: Gree 4H 159
WF10: C'frd 6H 145
Calder Trad. Est. HD5: Hud 5G 163
HD6: B Bri 2H 161
Calder Vw. HD6: Ras 2H 161
Calder Vw. Ct. HX3: She 1C 130
Calder Way BD20: Sils 3E 15
Calderwood Cl. BD7: B'frd, Ship . . .4E 71
Caledonia Rd. BD21: Keigh 5B 34
Caledonia St. BD4: B'frd 6E 7 (6E 91)
BD5: B'frd 6E 7 (6E 91)
Calgary Cres. WF3: W Ard 2F 155
Calgary Pl. LS7: Leeds 3B 78
California M. LS27: Morl 1B 138
California St. LS27: Morl 1B 138
Call La. LS1: Leeds 6F 5 (4A 98)
Calls, The LS2: Leeds 5F 5 (4A 98)
Calpin Cl. BD10: B'frd 1H 71
Calton Gro. BD21: Keigh 1D 48
Calton Rd. BD21: Keigh 1D 48
Calton St. BD21: Keigh 2H 47
(not continuous)
Calver Av. BD21: Keigh 5F 33
Calver Gro. BD21: Keigh 5G 33
CALVERLEY .2E 73
Calverley Av. BD3: B'frd 3B 92
LS13: Leeds 6D 74
CALVERLEY BRIDGE 3A 74

Calverley Ct. LS13: Leeds 6D 74
LS26: Oul 2D 142
Calverley Cutting BD10: B'frd 1D 72
LS28: Cal 1D 72
Calverley Dr. LS13: Leeds 6D 74
Calverley Gdns. LS13: Leeds 5C 74
Calverley Gth. LS13: Leeds 6D 74
Calverley Golf Course 6E 73
Calverley Gro. LS13: Leeds 6D 74
Calverley La. LS13: Leeds 5B 74
LS18: H'fth 2A 74
LS28: Cal, Fars 3G 73
(not continuous)
Calverley Moor Av. LS28: Pud 2E 93
Calverley Rd. LS26: Oul 2E 143
Calverley St. LS1: Leeds 2C 4 (2H 97)
Calverley Ter. LS13: Leeds 6D 74
Calver Rd. BD21: Keigh 6G 33
Calversyke St. BD21: Keigh 6G 33
Calvert Cl. LS25: Kip 2G 123
Camargue Fold BD2: B'frd 5F 71
Camberley Cl. LS28: Pud 5A 94
Camberley Mt. BD4: B'frd 1C 112
Camberley St. LS11: Leeds 2A 118
Camberley Way LS28: Pud 5A 94
Camborne Way BD22: Keigh 2E 47
Cambrian Bar BD12: Low M 1B 132
Cambrian St. LS11: Leeds 1G 117
Cambrian Ter. LS11: Leeds 1G 117
CAMBRIDGE 4F 23
Cambridge Chase BD19: Gom 5F 135
Cambridge Cl. LS27: Morl 2B 138
Cambridge Ct. LS27: Morl 3B 138
Cambridge Dr. LS13: Leeds 6D 74
LS21: Otley 4F 23
Cambridge Gdns. LS13: Leeds 6D 74
Cambridge Gro. LS21: Otley 4F 23
LS25: Kip 4G 123
Cambridge Pl. BD3: B'frd 1F 7 (3H 91)
BD13: Que 4A 108
Cambridge Rd. LS6: Leeds 6H 77
WF17: Birs 6H 135
Cambridge St. BD7: B'frd 1B 110
BD13: Que 4B 108
BD14: Clay 1D 108
LS20: Guis 4C 40
LS21: Otley 4E 23
Cambridge Ter. LS21: Otley 4E 23
Cambridge Way LS21: Otley 4F 23
Camden St. HX6: Sow B 6H 147
Camden Ter. BD8: B'frd 2D 90
Camellia Ct. BD18: Ship 4D 70
Camellia Mt. BD7: B'frd 5G 89
Cameron Av. BD12: Wyke 6B 132
Cameron Gro. BD2: B'frd 6H 71
Cameronian Ct. BD21: Keigh 6A 34
Camerton Grn. BD5: B'frd 3F 111
Cam La. HD6: Clift 5D 152
Camm St. HD6: Brigh 6B 152
Camomile Ct. BD13: Thorn 5F 87
Campbell St. BD13: Que 4B 108
BD21: Keigh 6A 34
LS28: Stan 1H 93
CAMP FIELD 5H 97
Camp Rd. LS16: B'hpe 4F 43
Camp Sq. LS14: T'ner 2H 63
CAMP TOWN 3H 59
Campus Rd. BD7: B'frd 4A 6 (5C 90)
Camwood Ct. BD20: E Mor 6F 35
Canada Cres. LS19: Raw 3G 55
Canada Dr. LS19: Raw 2G 55
Canada Rd. LS19: Raw 2G 55
Canada Ter. LS19: Raw 3G 55
Canalbank Vw. LS13: Leeds 4B 74
Canal Ct. WF3: Loft 3H 157
Canal Gdns. 6F 61
Canal La. BD20: Sils 4G 15
WF3: Loft, S'ley 3G 157
Canal Pl. LS12: Leeds 4F 97
Canal Rd. BD1: B'frd 4C 70
BD2: B'frd 1D 6 (4C 70)
BD16: Bgly 1A 50
BD20: Rid 4C 34

Canal Rd. HX6: Sow B 5C 148
  LS12: Leeds 3C 96
  LS13: Leeds 3A 74
Canal Side BD20: Sils 3E 15
Canal St. HD6: Brigh 1B 162
  HX3: Hal 3H 149
  LS12: Leeds 4E 97
Canal Vw. HX6: Sow B 5G 147
Canal Wharf LS5: Leeds 6H 75
  LS11: Leeds 6C 4 (4H 97)
Canary Dr. BD16: Bgly 3E 51
Canary St. BD19: Cleck 6B 134
Canberra Cl. BD22: Cros R 1F 65
Canberra Dr. BD22: Cros R 1F 65
Candle Ho. LS1: Leeds 6C 4
Candleworks Yd. LS21: Otley 4E 23
Canford Dr. BD15: All 2D 88
Canford Gro. BD15: All 2E 89
Canford Rd. BD15: All 2D 88
Canker La. HX3: Hal 4E 129
Cannon Hall Cl. HD6: Clift 6D 152
Cannon Hall Dr. HD6: Clift 1D 162
Cannon Mill La. BD7: B'frd 1A 110
Cannon St. BD16: Bgly 5C 50
  HX1: Hal 4D 148
Cannon Wlk. LS2: Leeds 1G 97
Canonbury Ter. LS11: Leeds 2E 117
Canon Pinnington M. BD16: Cot 2C 68
                   (off Littlelands)
Canter, The LS10: Leeds 4B 140
Canterbury Av. BD5: B'frd 2C 110
Canterbury Cres. HX3: Hal 6F 129
Canterbury Dr. LS6: Leeds 5C 76
Canterbury Ho. HX6: Sow B 5A 148
Canterbury Rd. LS6: Leeds 5C 76
Canwick Cl. BD20: E Mor 4F 35
Cape Ind. Est. LS28: Fars 6A 74
Capel Ct. LS28: Cal 3F 73
Capel St. HD6: Ras 2A 162
  LS28: Cal 3F 73
Cape of Good Hope BD13: Que 5G 107
Cape St. BD1: B'frd 1D 6 (3E 91)
Capitol Blvd. LS27: Morl 6C 138
Capitol Cl. LS27: Morl 5C 138
Capitol Pde. LS6: Leeds 2F 77
Captain St. BD1: B'frd 2E 7 (4F 91)
Caraway Cl. LS6: Leeds 6F 59
Caraway Dr. LS6: Leeds 6F 59
Caraway M. LS6: Leeds 6F 59
Carberry Pl. LS6: Leeds 1E 97
Carberry Rd. LS6: Leeds 1E 97
Carberry Ter. LS6: Leeds 1E 97
                   (off Carberry Rd.)
Cardan Dr. LS29: I'ly 5G 11
Carden Av. LS15: Leeds 4A 100
Carden Gro. LS15: Leeds 4A 100
Carden Rd. BD4: B'frd 6C 92
Cardigan Av. LS27: Morl 5A 138
Cardigan Ct. LS6: Leeds 5E 77
Cardigan Flds. Rd. LS4: Leeds ...2C 96
Cardigan La. LS4: Leeds 1D 96
                   (not continuous)
  LS6: Leeds 6E 77
Cardigan Rd. LS6: Leeds 5D 76
Cardigan Ter. WF3: E Ard 1C 156
Cardigan Trad. Est. LS4: Leeds ..2D 96
Cardinal Av. LS11: Leeds 5F 117
Cardinal Ct. LS11: Leeds 4E 117
Cardinal Cres. LS11: Leeds 5F 117
Cardinal Gdns. LS11: Leeds 5E 117
Cardinal Gro. LS11: Leeds 5E 117
Cardinal Rd. LS11: Leeds 5E 117
Cardinal Sq. LS11: Leeds 4F 117
Cardinal Wlk. LS11: Leeds 4E 117
Carisbrooke Cres. BD6: B'frd 5B 110
Carisbrooke La. LS25: Gar 3H 103
Carisbrooke Rd. LS16: Leeds 2B 76
Cark Rd. BD21: Keigh 5A 34
Carlby Gro. BD22: Keigh 1G 47
                   (off Carlby St.)
Carlby St. BD22: Keigh 1G 47
Carleton Cl. LS23: B Spa 3H 29

Carleton Dr. LS23: B Spa 4H 29
Carleton St. BD20: Keigh 4H 33
Carling Cl. BD7: B'frd 2H 109
Carlisle Av. LS19: Yead 1G 55
Carlisle Bus. Cen. BD8: B'frd 2C 90
                   (off Carlisle Rd.)
Carlisle Dr. LS28: Pud 5H 93
Carlisle Gro. LS28: Pud 5H 93
Carlisle Pl. BD8: B'frd 2C 90
Carlisle Rd. BD8: B'frd 2B 90
  LS10: Leeds 5B 98
  LS28: Pud 5H 93
Carlisle St. BD8: B'frd 2C 90
  BD21: Keigh 6B 34
  HX2: Hal 1C 148
  LS28: Stan 2G 93
Carlisle Ter. BD8: B'frd 2C 90
Carlrayne La. LS29: Men 6G 21
CARLTON 4H 141
Carlton App. LS22: Weth 3C 12
Carlton Av. BD18: Ship 1G 69
  LS28: Pud 4A 94
Carlton Carr LS7: Leeds 1E 5 (1A 98)
Carlton Cl. LS7: Leeds 1A 98
                   (off Carlton Ri.)
Carlton Cft. LS7: Leeds 1A 98
                   (off Carlton Gdns.)
Carlton Dr. BD9: B'frd 5B 70
  BD17: Bail 3C 52
  BD18: Ship 4A 70
  LS20: Guis 3D 40
  LS25: Gar 6F 103
Carlton Gdns. LS7: Leeds 1A 98
Carlton Gth. LS7: Leeds 1A 98
  LS17: Leeds 2E 61
Carlton Ga. LS7: Leeds 1E 5 (1A 98)
Carlton Grange LS19: Yead 6G 41
Carlton Gro. BD5: B'frd 2D 110
  BD18: Ship 4B 70
  HX5: Ell 4D 160
  LS7: Leeds 1A 98
Carlton Hill LS2: Leeds 1E 5 (1A 98)
Carlton Ho. Ter. HX1: Hal 4E 149
Carlton La. LS19: E Car 3D 40
  LS20: Guis 3D 40
  LS26: Rothw 3H 141
  WF3: Loft 6G 141
Carlton M. LS20: Guis 4D 40
Carlton Mill HX6: Sow B 5A 148
                   (off Old Cawsey)
Carlton Moor M. LS10: Leeds 2D 140
Carlton Mt. LS19: Yead 5G 41
Carlton Pde. LS7: Leeds 1F 5 (1A 98)
Carlton Pl. HX1: Hal 5B 164 (3G 149)
  LS7: Leeds 1A 98
Carlton Ri. LS7: Leeds 1A 98
  LS28: Pud 4A 94
Carlton Row LS12: Leeds 4A 96
Carlton St. BD7: B'frd 5A 6 (5D 90)
  BD22: Haw 2D 64
  HX1: Hal 5B 164 (3G 149)
  LS21: Otley 4F 23
Carlton Ter. HX1: Hal 5B 164 (3G 149)
  LS19: Yead 6G 41
  LS28: Pud 3A 94
Carlton Towers LS7: Leeds ..1F 5 (1A 98)
Carlton Trad. Est. LS12: Leeds ...3D 96
Carlton Vw. LS7: Leeds 1A 98
  WF10: All B 1F 145
Carlton Wlk. BD18: Ship 1H 69
  LS7: Leeds 1A 98
Carmel Rd. HX3: Hal 5G 129
Carmona Av. BD18: Ship 4B 70
Carmona Gdns. BD18: Ship 4B 70
Carnaby Rd. BD7: B'frd 3G 109
Carnation St. BD3: B'frd 5A 92
Carnegie Cl. LS29: I'ly 5E 11
Carnegie Dr. BD18: Ship 2C 70
Carnegie Landing BD18: Ship 2C 70
                   (off Carr La.)

Carnegie Regional Indoor Tennis Cen.
                   ....3B 76
Carnoustie Gro. BD16: Cot 2D 68
Caroline St. BD18: Ship 1H 69
Carperley Cres. BD13: Denh 3C 86
Carr Bank BD20: E Mor 4G 35
  LS21: Otley 1D 22
Carr Bank Bottom LS21: Otley 1D 22
Carr Bottom Av. BD5: B'frd 3B 110
Carr Bottom Fold BD5: B'frd 4C 110
Carr Bottom Gro. BD5: B'frd 3B 110
Carr Bottom Rd. BD5: B'frd 3B 110
  BD10: B'frd 2C 72
Carr Bri. Av. LS16: Leeds 4F 57
Carr Bri. Cl. LS16: Leeds 4F 57
Carr Bri. Dr. LS16: Leeds 4F 57
Carr Bri. Vw. LS16: Leeds 4F 57
Carr Cl. LS19: Raw 4H 55
CARR CROFTS 4B 96
Carr Crofts LS12: Leeds 4B 96
Carr Crofts Dr. LS12: Leeds 4B 96
Carr Fld. Dr. HX2: Lud 1E 147
Carrfield Dr. LS15: Bar E 2D 82
Carrfield La. LS15: Bar E 2C 82
Carrfield Rd. LS15: Bar E 2D 82
CARR GATE 4C 156
Carr Gate Cres. WF2: Carr G 4B 156
Carr Gate Dr. WF2: Carr G 4B 156
Carr Gate Mt. WF2: Carr G 4B 156
Carr Grn. Av. HD6: Ras 5H 161
Carr Grn. Cl. HD6: Ras 5H 161
Carr Grn. Dr. HD6: Ras 5H 161
Carr Grn. La. HD6: Ras 4H 161
Carr Gro. BD20: Rid 4E 35
Carr Hall Rd. BD12: Wyke 4C 132
Carr Hill Av. LS28: Cal 3E 73
Carr Hill Dr. LS28: Cal 3E 73
Carr Hill Gro. LS28: Cal 3E 73
Carr Hill Nook LS28: Cal 3E 73
Carr Hill Ri. LS28: Cal 3E 73
Carr Hill Rd. LS28: Cal 3E 73
Carrholm Cres. LS7: Leeds 2H 77
Carrholm Dr. LS7: Leeds 2H 77
Carrholme Ct. HX1: Hal 4D 148
                   (off Dundas St.)
Carrholm Grn. BD6: B'frd 1B 132
Carrholm Gro. LS7: Leeds 2H 77
Carrholm Mt. LS7: Leeds 2H 77
Carrholm Rd. LS7: Leeds 2H 77
Carrholm Vw. LS7: Leeds 2H 77
Carr Ho. HX2: Lud 4D 126
CARR HOUSE GATE 3C 132
Carr Ho. Ga. BD12: Wyke 3C 132
Carr Ho. Gro. BD12: Wyke 3C 132
Carr Ho. La. BD12: Wyke 2B 132
                   (not continuous)
  HX3: She 6F 109
Carr Ho. Mt. BD12: Wyke 3C 132
Carr Ho. Rd. HX3: She 1F 131
Carriage Dr. BD19: Gom 5F 135
Carriage Drive, The HX4: Gree ...3G 159
  LS8: Leeds 6G 61
Carriage Fold BD13: Cull 4B 66
Carriageworks Theatre, The
                   ....3D 4 (3H 97)
Carrick Dr. BD3: B'frd 3D 92
Carricks Cl. BD12: Low M 1E 133
Carrier St. HX1: Hal 4C 164 (2G 149)
Carrington St. BD3: B'frd 4A 92
                   (not continuous)
Carrington Ter. LS20: Guis 5B 40
Carr La. BD12: Low M 3D 132
  BD13: Denh 1C 86
  BD16: Bgly 5A 36
  BD18: Ship 1C 70
  BD20: E Mor 4G 35
  BD20: Rid 4E 35
  LS14: T'ner 3C 62
  LS19: Raw 4H 55
  LS22: Weth 2G 13
  WF3: Carl 4A 142
Carr Mnr. Av. LS17: Leeds 1H 77
Carr Mnr. Cres. LS17: Leeds 6H 59

Carr Mnr. Cft. LS17: Leeds 2H 77
Carr Mnr. Dr. LS17: Leeds 1H 77
Carr Mnr. Gdns. LS17: Leeds 1H 77
Carr Mnr. Grth. LS17: Leeds 6H 59
Carr Mnr. Gro. LS17: Leeds 1H 77
Carr Mnr. Mt. LS17: Leeds 1H 77
Carr Mnr. Pde. LS17: Leeds 1H 77
Carr Mnr. Pl. LS17: Leeds 1H 77
Carr Mnr. Rd. LS17: Leeds 2H 77
Carr Mnr. Vw. LS17: Leeds 6H 59
Carr Mnr. Wlk. LS17: Leeds 2H 77
Carr Mills LS7: Leeds 5H 77
Carr Moor Side LS11: Leeds 2A 118
Carr Moor St. LS10: Leeds 2A 118
Carroll St. BD3: B'frd 5G 7 (5G 91)
Carr Rd. BD12: Wyke 4C 132
  LS28: Cal 2D 72
Carr Row BD12: Wyke 4C 132
Carr St. BD5: B'frd 3D 110
  BD21: Keigh 6A 34
  HD6: Brigh 5A 152
  WF17: Birs 6A 136
Carr Ter. HX2: Lud 1D 146
Carr Vw. HX2: Lud 1D 146
Carr Wood Cl. LS28: Cal 3E 73
Carr Wood Gdns. LS28: Cal 3E 73
Carr Wood Way LS28: Cal 2E 73
Carter Av. LS15: Leeds 3E 101
Carter La. BD13: Que 2H 107
  LS15: Leeds 2E 101
Carter Mt. LS15: Leeds 3E 101
Carter's La. LS29: I'ly, Midd 2E 11
Carter St. BD4: B'frd 6F 7 (5F 91)
Carter Ter. LS15: Leeds 2E 101
Cart Ga. BD6: B'frd 4D 110
Cartier Ho. LS10: Leeds 5B 98
Cartmel La. BD20: Stee 6C 14
Cartmell Ct. LS15: Leeds 4H 99
Cartmell Dr. LS15: Leeds 4H 99
Cartmel Rd. BD21: Keigh 5G 33
Carton Ct. BD5: B'frd 2E 111
  (off New Cross St.)
Caryl Rd. BD4: B'frd 2G 111
Cashmere St. BD21: Keigh 6G 33
Cask Ct. HX2: Hal 5A 128
Caspar Apartments LS2: Leeds 2F 5
Casson Av. WF3: E Ard 6H 139
Casson Dr. WF3: E Ard 6H 139
Casson Fold HX3: North 5C 130
Casson Gro. WF3: E Ard 6H 139
Castle Av. HD6: Ras 3H 161
Castle Carr Rd. HX2: Midg, Wain . . .1C 126
Castle Cl. LS17: Bard 2F 45
  WF17: Birs 6C 136
Castle Cft. BD16: Har 6E 49
Castlefields BD16: Bgly 2H 49
  LS26: Rothw 2F 141
Castlefields Cres. HD6: Ras 3H 161
Castlefields Dr. HD6: Ras 3H 161
Castlefields Golf Course 3A 162
Castlefields Ind. Est. BD16: Bgly 2H 49
Castlefields La. BD16: Bgly 2H 49
  HD6: Ras 3H 161
Castlefields Rd. BD16: Bgly 1H 49
  HD6: Ras 3H 161
Castlefields Trad. Est. BD16: Bgly . .2H 49
Castle Gate LS22: Weth 4E 13
  LS29: I'ly 5D 10
Castlegate Dr. BD10: B'frd 3A 72
Castlegate Ho. HX5: Ell 4B 160
  (off Huddersfield Rd.)
Castle Grange LS19: Yead 1H 55
Castle Gro. BD16: Har 6E 49
  LS17: Bard 2F 45
Castle Gro. Av. LS6: Leeds 2D 76
Castle Gro. Dr. LS6: Leeds 3D 76
Castle Head Cl. WF3: Loft 1G 157
Castle Head La. WF3: Loft 2D 156
  WF3: Thpe H 1D 156
Castle Hill BD22: Keigh 1G 47
  HD6: Ras 3H 161
  LS29: I'ly 5D 10

Castle Hill Vw. LS17: Bard 2E 45
Castle Ings Cl. LS12: N Far 2F 115
Castle Ings Dr. LS12: N Far 2F 115
Castle Ings Gdns. LS12: N Far 2F 115
Castle Keep LS22: Weth 4E 13
Castle Lodge Av. LS26: Rothw 6F 119
Castle Lodge Ct. LS26: Rothw 1G 141
Castle Lodge Gdns.
  LS26: Rothw 1F 141
Castle Lodge Gth. LS26: Rothw 6G 119
Castle Lodge M. LS26: Rothw 1G 141
Castle Lodge Sq.
  LS26: Rothw 6G 119
Castle Lodge Way
  LS26: Rothw 1F 141
Castle M. BD18: Ship 2B 70
Castlemore Rd. BD17: Bail 5D 52
Castle Pl. HD6: Ras 3A 162
Castlerigg Grn. BD6: B'frd 1H 131
Castle Rd. BD18: Ship 2B 70
  BD21: Keigh 5H 33
  LS26: Rothw 2H 141
  LS29: I'ly 5D 10
  (not continuous)
Castle St. BD5: B'frd 6E 91
  LS1: Leeds 4B 4 (3G 97)
Castle Ter. HD6: Ras 3H 161
Castleton Cl. LS12: Leeds 4F 97
Castleton Rd. LS12: Leeds 3E 97
Castle Vw. LS12: Leeds 6H 59
Castlewood Cl. LS18: H'fth 1F 75
Castle Yd. LS29: I'ly 5D 10
Castley La. LS21: Cast, Leat 3F 25
Catalina LS12: Leeds 6A 4 (4G 97)
Cater St. BD1: B'frd 4F 7 (4F 91)
  (not continuous)
Cathcart St. HX3: Hal 6F 129
  LS6: Leeds 6G 77
Cathedral Cl. BD1: B'frd 3E 7 (4F 91)
Catherine Cres. HX5: Ell 5B 160
Catherine Gro. LS11: Leeds 2H 117
Catherine Ho. La. HX2: Midg 1A 126
CATHERINE SLACK 1F 129
Catherine Slack HD6: Brigh 3H 151
Catherine St. BD21: Keigh 2H 47
  (not continuous)
  HD6: Brigh 6A 152
  HX5: Ell 5B 160
Cat La. HX2: Lud M 4A 146
  HX4: Gree 4C 158
Catstones Wood BD18: Ship 2E 71
Cattle Mkt. St. LS21: Otley 3E 23
Cauldwell Gdns. BD5: B'frd 1E 111
Causeway HX1: Hal 4D 164 (2H 149)
CAUSEWAY FOOT 3C 106
Causeway Foot HX2: Ogd 2B 106
Causeway Head HX6: Sow B 4H 147
Cautley Rd. LS9: Leeds 5D 98
Cavalier App. LS9: Leeds 5D 98
Cavalier Cl. LS9: Leeds 5D 98
Cavalier Ct. LS9: Leeds 5D 98
Cavalier Dr. BD10: B'frd 1C 72
Cavalier Gdns. LS9: Leeds 5D 98
Cavalier Ga. LS9: Leeds 5D 98
Cavalier Grn. LS9: Leeds 5D 98
CAVALIER HILL 4C 98
Cavalier M. LS9: Leeds 5D 98
Cavalier Vw. LS9: Leeds 5D 98
Cave Hill HX3: North 3B 130
Cave La. WF3: E Ard 1B 156
Cavendish App. BD11: Drig 1A 136
Cavendish Ct. BD10: B'frd 4A 72
  (off Park Rd.)
  BD1: Drig 1A 136
  (off Cavendish App.)
  BD21: Keigh 6A 34
Cavendish Dr. BD16: Bgly 3D 50
  LS20: Guis 5B 40
Cavendish Gro. LS20: Guis 5B 40
Cavendish M. BD11: Drig 1A 136
  LS17: Leeds 3B 60
Cavendish Pl. LS28: Stan 2H 93
Cavendish Ri. LS28: Pud 4C 94

Cavendish Rd. BD2: B'frd 4A 72
  BD10: B'frd 2H 71
  (Buckfast Ct.)
  BD10: B'frd 4A 72
  (Park Rd.)
  LS2: Leeds 1C 4 (1H 97)
  LS20: Guis 5B 40
Cavendish Sq. LS28: Stan 2A 94
Cavendish St. BD21: Keigh 6A 34
  HX1: Hal 2E 149
  LS3: Leeds 3A 4 (3F 97)
  LS19: Yead 6G 41
  LS28: Pud 4C 94
Cavendish Ter. HX1: Hal 2E 149
  (not continuous)
Cawcliffe Dr. HD6: Brigh 4A 152
Cawcliffe Rd. HD6: Brigh 5A 152
Cawood Haven BD6: B'frd 5G 109
Caxton Rd. LS21: Otley 5C 22
Caxton St. LS22: Weth 4E 13
Caygill Ter. HX1: Hal 6B 164 (4G 149)
Caythorpe Rd. LS16: Leeds 2B 76
Caythorpe Wlk. BD10: B'frd 4A 72
Cecil Av. BD7: B'frd 1B 110
  BD17: Bail 3C 52
  HX3: Hip 1G 151
Cecil Gro. LS12: Leeds 3C 96
Cecil Mt. LS12: Leeds 3C 96
Cecil Rd. LS12: Leeds 3C 96
Cecil St. BD22: Cros R 1F 65
  LS12: Leeds 3C 96
Cedar Av. LS12: Leeds 4C 96
Cedar Cl. BD4: B'frd 5A 112
  LS12: Leeds 4C 96
Cedar Ct. LS17: Leeds 5B 60
  (off Harrogate Rd.)
  LS26: Wood 6G 121
Cedar Covert LS22: Weth 1E 13
Cedar Dr. BD12: Wyke 3E 133
  LS14: Leeds 1A 100
Cedar Gro. BD17: Bail 6G 51
  HD6: B Bri 3B 152
  HX4: Gree 4F 159
Cedar Mt. LS12: Leeds 4B 96
Cedar Pl. LS12: Leeds 4B 96
Cedar Ridge LS25: Gar 2H 103
Cedar Rd. LS12: Leeds 4B 96
Cedars, The LS16: B'hpe 3H 43
Cedar St. BD16: Bgly 2A 50
  BD21: Keigh 3H 47
  HX1: Hal 3D 148
  LS12: Leeds 4B 96
Cedar Ter. LS12: Leeds 4B 96
Cedar Way BD19: Gom 6E 135
Cemetery La. BD20: Keigh 3H 33
  HX6: Sow B 5G 147
  WF3: Carl 6G 141
Cemetery Rd. BD6: B'frd 6B 110
  BD7: B'frd 3H 89
  BD8: B'frd 3H 89
  BD12: Low M 6B 110
  BD16: Bgly 3A 50
  BD22: Haw 3A 64
  LS11: Leeds 1G 117
  LS19: E Car, Yead 6G 41
  LS28: Pud 3G 93
Centaur Ho. LS1: Leeds 3B 4 (3G 97)
Centenary Rd. BD17: Bail 3F 53
Centenary Sq. BD1: B'frd 5D 6 (5E 91)
Central Av. BD5: B'frd 1C 110
  BD17: Bail 5B 52
  BD18: Ship 2B 70
  BD22: Keigh 4F 47
  WF15: Liv 4H 153
Central Dr. BD22: Keigh 4F 47
Central Pk.
  HX1: Hal 6A 164 (4F 149)
  LS11: Leeds 5H 97
Central Pl. BD14: Clay 1D 108
  (off Clayton La.)
Central Rd. LS1: Leeds 5F 5 (4A 98)

Central St. HX1: Hal 4B **164** (2G **149**)
LS1: Leeds 4C **4** (3H **97**)
Central Village Leeds
LS1: Leeds 1C **4**
Centre 27 Bus. Pk. WF17: Birs . . .4D **136**
Centre St. BD5: B'frd 2C **110**
Centurion Way BD19: Cleck 5A **134**
Century Pl. BD8: B'frd 2C **90**
Century Rd. HX5: Ell 4B **160**
Century St. BD21: Keigh 3A **48**
(off Percy St.)
Century Way LS15: Leeds 4H **101**
Ceres Ct. LS22: Weth 4G **13**
Ceres Rd. LS22: Weth 4G **13**
Chaddlewood Cl. LS18: H'fth 6E **57**
Chadwell Springs BD16: Cot 2C **68**
Chadwick St. LS10: Leeds 6G **5** (5B **98**)
Chadwick St. Sth. LS10: Leeds 5B **98**
Chaffinch Rd. BD8: B'frd 4E **89**
Chain Bar Rd. BD19: Cleck 6A **134**
Chain St. BD1: B'frd 3B **6** (4D **90**)
Chak Gdns. BD9: B'frd 4F **69**
Chalfont Rd. LS16: Leeds 1B **76**
Chalice Cl. LS10: Leeds 6C **118**
Challenge Way BD4: B'frd 1B **112**
WF17: Bat 5A **154**
Challis Gro. BD5: B'frd 2E **111**
Chalner Av. LS27: Morl 5H **137**
Chalner Cl. LS27: Morl 5H **137**
Chaly Flds. LS23: B Spa 4B **30**
Chancellor Ct. LS2: Leeds . . .5F **5** (4A **98**)
Chancellor St. LS6: Leeds 6H **77**
Chancel Sq. LS6: Leeds 6F **59**
Chancery Ter. HX3: Hal 1G **159**
Chandler Cl. WF17: Birs 6A **136**
Chandlers, The LS2: Leeds 6G **5**
Chandlers Cl. WF1: Out 4F **157**
Chandlers Wharf LS13: Leeds 3A **74**
Chandos Av. LS8: Leeds 1C **78**
Chandos Fold LS8: Leeds 2C **78**
Chandos Gdns. LS8: Leeds 1C **78**
Chandos Gth. LS8: Leeds 1C **78**
Chandos Grn. LS8: Leeds 1C **78**
Chandos M. LS8: Leeds 1C **78**
Chandos Pl. LS8: Leeds 1D **78**
Chandos St. BD4: B'frd 6E **7** (5F **91**)
BD21: Keigh 2H **47**
(not continuous)
Chandos Ter. LS8: Leeds 1D **78**
Chandos Wlk. LS8: Leeds 1C **78**
Change All. LS1: Leeds 4E **5**
Changegate BD22: Haw 2B **64**
Changegate Ct. BD22: Haw 2B **64**
Change La. HX3: Hal 1A **160**
Channing Way BD1: B'frd 5D **6** (5E **91**)
Chantrell Ct. LS2: Leeds 5G **5** (4B **98**)
Chantry Cl. LS29: I'ly 6D **10**
Chantry Ct. LS27: Morl 2B **138**
Chantry Cft. LS15: Leeds 4F **101**
Chantry Dr. LS29: I'ly 6D **10**
Chantry Gth. LS15: Leeds 4F **101**
Chapel, The LS26: Oul 2E **143**
(off Calverley La.)
CHAPEL ALLERTON 3H **77**
Chapel Allerton Lawn Tennis,
Squash & Gym 2A **78**
Chapel Cl. BD22: Cros R 1E **65**
(off East Ter.)
HX3: She 1F **131**
HX4: Holy 6F **159**
LS25: Gar 4E **103**
Chapel Ct. BD13: Que 3D **108**
(off Chapel La.)
BD15: Wils 3G **67**
HD6: Brigh 1B **162**
(off Park St.)
LS15: Leeds 3C **100**
LS25: M'fld 4E **105**
Chapel Cft. BD22: Lay 6C **32**
HD6: Ras 4H **161**
Chapel Fold BD6: B'frd 4B **110**
BD12: Wyke 1C **152**
HX3: She 1F **131**

Chapel Fold LS6: Leeds 6D **76**
LS11: Leeds 3E **117**
LS12: Leeds 4C **96**
(off Wesley Rd.)
LS15: Leeds 3C **100**
LS28: Pud 6C **73**
(off Littlemoor Rd.)
CHAPEL GREEN 2D **110**
Chapel Grn. LS28: Pud 5H **93**
Chapel Gro. BD16: Bgly 2A **50**
CHAPEL HILL 1A **26**
Chapel Hill LS10: Leeds 2B **140**
LS19: Yead 6F **41**
LS22: Kear 1A **26**
LS27: Morl 2A **138**
Chapel Hill Rd. LS21: Pool 4F **25**
Chapel Ho. LS29: I'ly 6D **10**
(off Wells Prom.)
Chapel Ho. Apartments HX2: Hal . .4D **128**
(off Club La.)
Chapel Ho. Bldgs. BD12: Low M . . .1E **133**
(off Chapel Ho. Rd.)
Chapel Ho. Rd. BD12: Low M 6D **110**
CHAPEL LANE 6C **46**
Chapel La. BD13: Que 4H **107**
(Foxhill Gro.)
BD13: Que 3D **108**
(Stocks La.)
BD15: All 3E **89**
BD16: Bgly 4B **50**
BD17: Esh 2A **54**
BD21: Keigh 6H **33**
BD22: Lay 6C **32**
BD22: Oak 5C **46**
HX2: Midg 5B **126**
HX2: Hal 6H **149**
HX3: Sou 5C **150**
HX6: Sow B 5B **148**
LS6: Leeds 5D **76**
(not continuous)
LS12: Leeds 4C **96**
LS12: N Far 6F **95**
LS15: Bar E 2E **83**
LS19: Yead 6F **41**
LS23: Cliff 5B **30**
LS25: Gar 4E **103**
LS25: Kip 4H **123**
LS29: I'ly 5C **10**
WF17: Birs 6A **136**
Chapel Lofts LS27: Morl 3B **138**
(off Commercial St.)
Chapel M. BD15: All 3E **89**
LS23: Cliff 5B **30**
Chapel Pl. LS6: Leeds 4D **76**
Chapel Rd. BD12: Low M 1D **132**
(not continuous)
BD16: Bgly 2A **50**
BD20: Stee 6C **14**
LS15: Leeds 4B **78**
Chapel Row BD15: Wils 3G **67**
LS21: Pool 4F **25**
(off Main St.)
Chapel Sq. LS6: Leeds 4D **76**
(off Chapel St.)
Chapel St. BD1: B'frd 4F **7** (4F **91**)
BD2: B'frd 5B **72**
BD5: B'frd 1D **110**
BD6: B'frd 4C **110**
BD13: Denh 3B **86**
BD13: Que 4A **108**
BD13: Thorn 5H **87**
BD16: Bgly 2A **50**
BD20: Sils 1E **15**
HD6: Brigh 4G **151**
HX2: Hal 1C **148**
HX3: Nor G 4H **131**
HX4: Holy 6F **159**
LS6: Leeds 4D **76**
LS13: Leeds 4A **74**
LS15: Leeds 3C **100**
LS19: Raw 3F **55**
LS28: Cal 2F **73**
LS28: Stan 2A **94**

Chapel St. LS29: Add 1D **8**
WF3: Carl 4H **141**
WF3: E Ard 2A **156**
WF3: Ting 6F **139**
Chapel St. Nth. HX3: Hal 4D **128**
Chapel Ter. BD13: Thorn 5H **87**
BD15: All 2D **88**
HX4: Bark 4A **158**
HX6: Sow B 6D **146**
LS6: Leeds 4D **76**
(off Chapel St.)
CHAPELTOWN 3A **164** (2G **149**)
Chapeltown HX1: Hal 3A **164** (2G **149**)
LS28: Pud 5H **93**
Chapeltown Bus. Cen. LS7: Leeds . . .5B **78**
(off Chapeltown Rd.)
Chapeltown Rd. LS7: Leeds 6B **78**
Chapel Vw. LS26: Wood 1E **145**
LS27: Gil 5E **115**
Chapel Wlk. BD2: B'frd 5B **72**
Chapel Yd. LS15: Leeds 5F **101**
(off Meynell Rd.)
LS26: Oul 2E **143**
Chapman Rd. BD3: B'frd 3D **92**
Chapman St. BD4: B'frd 5B **92**
Charles Apartments LS3: Leeds 3A **4**
Charles Av. BD3: B'frd 4B **92**
HX3: Sou 5C **150**
LS9: Leeds 5D **98**
WF1: Out 4F **157**
Charles Ct. BD22: Oxen 1C **84**
(off Station Rd.)
LS26: Wood 1E **145**
Charles Gdns. LS11: Leeds 6G **97**
Charles Gro. LS26: Oul 1E **143**
Charles Morris Hall BD5: B'frd 6C **90**
LS2: Leeds 1A **4** (2G **97**)
Charles St. BD1: B'frd 4D **6** (4E **91**)
BD13: Que 4H **107**
BD16: Bgly 4B **50**
BD17: Ship 1B **70**
BD19: Gom 6F **135**
HD6: Brigh 6A **152**
HX1: Hal 4D **164** (2H **149**)
HX5: Ell 5B **160**
HX6: Sow B 5H **147**
LS18: H'fth 1D **74**
LS21: Otley 4E **23**
LS27: Morl 3B **138**
LS28: Fars 6H **73**
CHARLESTOWN 5E **53**
Charlestown Rd.
HX3: Hal 2D **164** (1H **149**)
Charlesworth Gro. HX2: Hal 1C **148**
Charlesworth Ter. HX2: Hal 1C **148**
Charlotte Cl. HX1: Hal 4G **149**
WF17: Birs 4B **136**
Charlotte Ct. BD7: B'frd 2A **110**
BD22: Haw 1D **64**
Charlotte Gro. LS15: Leeds 3D **100**
Charlton Cl. BD2: B'frd 5H **71**
Charlton Ct. HX2: Hal 1C **148**
(off Reservoir Rd.)
Charlton Gro. BD20: Sils 3F **15**
LS9: Leeds 4E **99**
Charlton Pl. LS9: Leeds 4E **99**
Charlton Rd. LS9: Leeds 4E **99**
Charlton St. LS9: Leeds 4E **99**
Charnley Dr. LS7: Leeds 3C **78**
Charnock St. HX1: Hal 4G **149**
Charnwood Cl. BD2: B'frd 1A **92**
Charnwood Gro. BD2: B'frd 1A **92**
Charnwood Rd. BD2: B'frd 1A **92**
Chart Cl. LS25: Gar 4E **103**
Charterhouse Rd. BD10: B'frd 6H **53**
Charteris Rd. BD8: B'frd 4E **89**
Chartist's Ct. LS27: Morl 4A **138**
(off Gt. Northern St.)
Chartists Way LS27: Morl 4A **138**
Chartwell Ct. LS17: Leeds 2F **61**
(off Shadwell La.)
Chartwell Dr. BD6: B'frd 4G **109**
Charville Gdns. LS17: Shad 4B **62**

Chase, The BD20: Keigh 5F 33
  LS19: Raw 3E 55
  LS22: Weth 3F 13
  LS25: Gar 4H 103
  LS29: Burl W 4F 21
  WF3: Ting 6E 139
Chase Av. LS27: Morl 6B 138
Chase Ct. LS27: Morl 6B 138
Chase Way BD5: B'frd 3E 111
Chassum Gro. BD9: B'frd 1A 90
Chatham St. BD3: B'frd 2F 91
  HX1: Hal 3A 164 (2F 91)
  HX6: Sow B 4H 147
Chat Hill Rd. BD13: Thorn 6B 88
Chatswood Av. LS11: Leeds 5F 117
Chatswood Cres. LS11: Leeds 5F 117
Chatswood Dr. LS11: Leeds 4F 117
Chatsworth Av. LS28: Pud 3E 93
Chatsworth Cl. LS8: Leeds 6E 79
Chatsworth. BD8: B'frd 3A 90
  (off Girlington Rd.)
Chatsworth Cres. LS28: Pud 3E 93
Chatsworth Dr. LS22: Weth 3C 12
  LS28: Pud 3E 93
Chatsworth Fall LS28: Pud 3E 93
Chatsworth Ind. Est. LS12: Leeds . . .5D 96
Chatsworth M. LS27: Morl 4C 138
Chatsworth Pl. BD7: B'frd 1B 90
Chatsworth Ri. LS28: Pud 3E 93
Chatsworth Rd. LS8: Leeds 6E 79
  LS28: Pud 3E 93
Chatsworth St. BD21: Keigh 6B 34
Chatts Wood Fold BD12: O'haw . . .2H 133
Chaucer Av. LS28: Pud 5B 94
Chaucer Gdns. LS28: Pud 5B 94
Chaucer Gro. LS28: Pud 5B 94
Chaucer St. HX1: Hal 3D 148
Cheapside BD1: B'frd 3D 6 (4E 91)
  HX1: Hal 4C 164 (2G 149)
  HX3: She 1E 131
  LS27: Morl 2A 138
  (off Chapel Hill)
Cheddington Gro. BD15: All 3D 88
Chelker Cl. BD6: B'frd 3F 109
Chellowfield Ct. BD9: B'frd 6E 69
Chellow Gdns. BD15: All 1C 88
  (off Deanwood Cres.)
Chellow Grange Rd.
  BD9: B'frd 6E 69
Chellow La. BD9: B'frd 1E 89
Chellow St. BD5: B'frd 3D 110
Chellow Ter. BD9: B'frd 2F 89
  BD11: Birk 3F 135
Chelmsford Rd. BD3: B'frd 3A 92
  (not continuous)
Chelmsford Ter. BD3: B'frd 4A 92
Chelsea Cl. LS12: Leeds 5C 96
Chelsea Mans. HX3: North 5C 130
Chelsea Rd. BD7: B'frd 1H 109
Chelsea St. BD21: Keigh 1H 47
Chelsea Vw. HX3: North 6C 130
Chelsfield Ct. LS15: Leeds 6H 81
Chelsfield Way LS15: Leeds 6H 81
Chelston Pk. BD16: Har 6F 49
Cheltenham Av. LS29: I'ly 5H 11
Cheltenham Ct. HX3: Hal 5H 149
Cheltenham Gdns.
  HX3: Hal 5H 149
Cheltenham Pl. HX3: Hal 5H 149
Cheltenham Rd. BD2: B'frd 4F 71
Cheltenham St. LS12: Leeds 5D 96
Chelwood Av. LS8: Leeds 4D 60
Chelwood Cres. LS8: Leeds 5D 60
Chelwood Dr. BD15: All 4C 88
  LS8: Leeds 4D 60
Chelwood Gro. LS8: Leeds 4D 60
Chelwood Mt. LS8: Leeds 4D 60
Chelwood Pl. LS8: Leeds 4C 60
Chenies Cl. LS14: Leeds 2A 100
Chepstow Cl. LS25: Gar 4H 103
Chepstow Dr. LS10: Leeds 4B 140
Cherington Ct. LS29: Burl W 3F 21
Cheriton Dr. BD13: Que 4B 108

Cherry Ct. HX1: Hal 1E 149
  (off Crossley Gdns.)
  LS6: Leeds 3F 77
  LS9: Leeds 2C 98
  (off Cherry Row)
  LS19: Yead 1F 55
Cherry Flds. BD2: B'frd 5E 71
Cherry Gro. LS6: Leeds 4F 77
  LS29: I'ly 5B 10
Cherry Lea Ct. LS19: Raw 2F 55
Cherry Pl. LS9: Leeds 2C 98
Cherry Ri. LS14: Leeds 1E 81
Cherry Row LS9: Leeds 2H 5 (2C 98)
Cherry St. BD21: Keigh 5C 34
  BD22: Haw 1E 65
Cherry Tree Av. BD10: B'frd 2B 72
Cherry Tree Cres. LS28: Fars 6H 73
Cherry Tree Dr. HX4: Gree 4F 159
  LS28: Fars 6H 73
Cherry Tree Gdns. BD10: B'frd 6F 53
Cherry Tree Ri. BD21: Keigh 2B 48
Cherry Tree Row BD16: Har 2F 67
Cherry Tree Wlk. LS2: Leeds 5F 5
  WF3: E Ard 2A 156
Cherrywood Cl. LS14: Leeds 6D 62
Cherrywood Gdns. LS14: Leeds 6D 62
Chervana Ct. BD4: B'frd 1C 112
Cherwell Cft. LS25: Gar 6H 103
Cherwell Dr. BD6: B'frd 6A 110
Chesham St. BD21: Keigh 6B 34
Chesney Av. LS10: Leeds 1B 118
Chester Cl. HX3: Hal 6F 129
Chester Ct. HX3: Hal 6F 129
Chester Gro. HX3: Hal 6F 129
Chester Pl. HX3: Hal 6F 129
Chester Rd. HX3: Hal 6F 129
Chester St. BD5: B'frd 5B 6 (5E 91)
  BD7: B'frd 6C 6 (5D 90)
  HX3: Hal 6F 129
  HX6: Sow B 5H 147
  LS12: Leeds 3C 96
Chester Ter. HX3: Hal 6F 129
Chesterton Ct. LS15: Leeds 5F 101
Chestnut Av. LS6: Leeds 6E 77
  LS15: Leeds 1F 101
  LS22: Weth 3D 12
  LS23: B Spa 3A 30
Chestnut Cl. BD22: Keigh 1F 47
  HX4: Gree 3F 159
  LS29: I'ly 6G 11
Chestnut Ct. BD18: Ship 2H 69
Chestnut Dr. LS16: Leeds 2B 58
Chestnut End LS23: B Spa 4C 30
Chestnut Gdns. LS12: Leeds 5C 96
  LS27: Chur 6A 116
Chestnut Gro. BD2: B'frd 5D 70
  LS6: Leeds 6E 77
  LS23: B Spa 3A 30
  LS26: Wood 1G 143
  LS28: Cal 3F 73
Chestnut La. LS14: Leeds 1A 100
Chestnut Pl. LS6: Leeds 6E 77
Chestnut Ri. LS12: Leeds 5B 96
Chestnut St. HX1: Hal 3D 148
  LS6: Leeds 6E 77
Chestnut Vw. LS27: Chur 6A 116
Chestnut Way LS16: Leeds 2B 58
Chevet Mt. BD15: All 4C 88
Chevin Av. LS21: Otley 5F 23
  LS29: Men 6H 21
  (Bradford Rd.)
  LS29: Men 6G 21
  (Bridgland Av.)
Chevin Ct. LS21: Otley 3E 23
  (off Courthouse St.)
Chevinedge Cres. HX3: Hal 2H 159
Chevin End LS29: Guis, Men 2H 39
Chevin End Rd. LS20: Guis 2B 40
Chevin Fold LS21: Otley 4F 23
Chevington Ct. LS19: Raw 4E 55
Chevin Ho. LS29: Men 2H 39
  (off High Royds Dr.)

Chevins Cl. WF17: Bat 6B 136
Chevin Side LS21: Otley 5E 23
Chevin Ter. LS21: Otley 5E 23
Chevin Vw. LS21: Pool 4E 25
  (off Main St.)
Cheviot Ct. LS25: Gar 6F 103
Cheviot Ga. BD12: Low M 1B 132
Cheyne Wlk. BD22: Keigh 1G 47
Chichester St. LS12: Leeds 3C 96
CHIDSWELL 6A 154
Chidswell Gdns. WF12: Dew 6B 154
Chidswell La. WF12: Dew 6B 154
Childs La. BD18: Ship 3E 71
Chiltern Cl. LS25: Gar 6F 103
Chiltern Ct. LS13: Leeds 4A 74
  LS25: Gar 6F 103
Chilver Dr. BD4: B'frd 3E 113
Chippendale Ct. LS29: Men 1H 39
Chippendale Ri. BD8: B'frd 3F 89
  LS21: Otley 2E 23
Chippindale Swimming Pool 2E 23
Chirton Gro. LS8: Leeds 4E 79
Chislehurst Pl. BD5: B'frd 2C 110
Chiswick St. LS6: Leeds 1E 97
Chiswick Ter. LS6: Leeds 1E 97
  (off Carberry Rd.)
Chorley La. LS2: Leeds 2B 4 (2G 97)
  LS3: Leeds 3B 4 (3G 97)
Chrisharben Ct. BD14: Clay 1E 109
  (off Henry St.)
Chrisharben Pk. BD14: Clay 1E 109
Chrismoor BD10: B'frd 2G 71
Christ Chu. Av. LS12: Leeds 3B 96
Christ Chu. Mt. LS12: Leeds 3B 96
Christ Chu. Pde. LS12: Leeds 3B 96
Christ Chu. Pl. LS12: Leeds 3B 96
Christ Chu. Rd. LS12: Leeds 3B 96
Christ Chu. Ter. LS12: Leeds 3B 96
Christ Chu. Vw. LS12: Leeds 3B 96
Christiana Ter. LS27: Morl 2B 138
Christopher Cl. BD20: Sils 2E 15
Christopher Rd. LS6: Leeds 6H 77
Christopher St. BD5: B'frd 2C 110
Christopher Ter. BD5: B'frd 2C 110
Church App. LS25: Gar 4F 103
Church Av. LS6: Leeds 2F 77
  LS18: H'fth 6D 56
  LS26: Swil 3A 122
  LS27: Gil 5E 115
Church Bank BD1: B'frd 4E 7 (4F 91)
  HX2: Hal 3B 148
  HX6: Sow B 5A 148
Church C'way. LS23: T Arch 3C 30
Church Cl. BD20: Stee 6C 14
  BD22: Oak 5B 46
  (off Commercial St.)
  HX1: Hal 4A 164
  HX2: Illing 2B 128
  HX6: Sow B 6E 147
  LS14: Leeds 5D 80
  (not continuous)
  LS21: Pool 4E 25
  LS25: M'fld 3E 105
  LS26: Swil 3A 122
Church Ct. BD7: B'frd 6H 89
  BD20: Rid 3D 34
  LS19: Yead 1F 55
  LS27: Morl 2A 138
Church Cres. LS17: Leeds 4A 60
  LS18: H'fth 6D 56
  LS19: Yead 1E 55
  LS26: Swil 4B 122
Church Cft. LS29: Men 1F 39
  WF3: Loft 1G 157
Church Dr. LS17: E Kes 6D 26
Church Farm HD6: Clift 1E 163
  LS14: T'ner 1H 63
Church Farm Cl. WF3: Loft 1G 157
Church Farm Gth. LS17: Shad 3B 62
Church Farm Vw. LS15: Bar E 2E 83
Churchfield Cft. LS26: Rothw 2B 142
Churchfield Gro. LS26: Rothw 1A 142
Churchfield La. LS26: Rothw 1A 142

Churchfield Rd. LS26: Rothw 2A **142**
Churchfields BD2: B'frd 1B **92**
Churchfields Cl. LS23: B Spa 3B **30**
Churchfields Rd. HD6: Brigh 6A **152**
Church Gdns. LS17: Leeds 4B **60**
   LS25: Gar 4F **103**
   LS27: Gil 6E **115**
CHURCH GARFORTH 5F **103**
Church Gth. LS19: E Car 2A **42**
   LS21: Pool 4E **25**
Church Ga. LS18: H'fth 6D **56**
Churchgate LS16: B'hpe 2F **43**
   LS27: Gil 6E **115**
Church Grn. BD8: B'frd 2C **90**
                    (off Church St.)
   HX2: Hal 6C **128**
Church Gro. LS6: Leeds 2E **77**
   LS18: H'fth 6D **56**
Church Hill BD17: Bail 3D **52**
   HX2: Lud 6E **127**
   LS14: T'ner 1H **63**
   LS16: B'hpe 2F **43**
Church Hill Gdns. LS28: Stan 1B **94**
Church Hill Grn. LS28: Stan 1B **94**
Church Hill Mt. LS28: Stan 1B **94**
Church Ho. HX5: Ell 4B **160**
                  (off St Mary's Ga.)
Churchill Flats LS21: Pool 4E **25**
Churchill Gdns. LS2: Leeds 1H **97**
            (off Bk. Blenheim Ter.)
Churchill Ho. BD4: B'frd 1C **112**
                  (off Tyersal La.)
Churchill Rd. BD13: Thorn 5B **88**
Church La. BD6: B'frd 5B **110**
   BD17: Esh 2A **54**
   BD19: Gom 6G **135**
   HD6: Brigh 6A **152**
                  (not continuous)
   HX2: Hal 6C **128**
   HX3: Sou 5D **150**
   HX4: Holy, Stainl 6E **159**
                  (not continuous)
   HX5: Ell 4F **161**
   LS2: Leeds 5G **5** (4B **98**)
   LS6: Leeds 2F **77**
   LS7: Leeds 3B **78**
   LS15: Leeds 1E **101**
   LS16: Leeds 3C **58**
   LS17: Bard 3D **44**
   LS18: H'fth 6D **56**
   LS21: Otley 4E **23**
   LS21: Pool 4E **25**
   LS21: Weston 1H **21**
   LS22: Coll 2B **28**
   LS25: Gar 4F **103**
   LS25: Kip 4H **123**
   LS25: M'fld 4C **104**
   LS26: Meth 5B **144**
   LS26: Swil 4H **121**
   LS28: Pud 4A **94**
   WF1: Out 4F **157**
   WF3: E Ard 2A **156**
   WF3: W Ard 2D **154**
   WF15: Liv 6H **153**
   WF17: Birs 6G **135**
Church La. Av. WF1: Out 4F **157**
Church La. Nth. LS25: Kip 4H **123**
Church Mdws. WF17: Birs 6H **135**
Church Mt. LS18: H'fth 6D **56**
Church Paddocks HD6: Clift 1A **162**
Church Pl. HX1: Hal 4A **164** (2F **149**)
   LS25: Gar 4F **103**
Church Rd. BD6: B'frd 5B **110**
   LS9: Leeds 4C **98**
             (off Cross Catherine St.)
   LS12: Leeds 4C **96**
   LS18: H'fth 1D **74**
   LS26: Gt P 5E **123**
   WF17: Bat 6B **136**

Church Row LS2: Leeds 5G **5** (4B **98**)
Church Side LS26: Meth 5B **144**
Church Side Cl.
   HX3: Hal 1C **164** (6G **129**)
Church Side Dr.
   HX3: Hal 1C **164** (6G **129**)
Churchside Vs. LS26: Meth 5C **144**
Church Sq. LS25: Gar 4F **103**
Church Stile Farm HX6: Sow B 6E **147**
CHURCH STREET 5B **46**
Church St. BD6: B'frd 6G **109**
   BD8: B'frd 2B **90**
   BD13: Cull 3B **66**
   BD16: Bgly 5C **50**
   BD18: Ship 1D **70**
   BD21: Keigh 6B **34**
                  (Bradford Rd.)
   BD21: Keigh 1H **47**
                  (Bridge St.)
   BD22: Haw 2B **64**
   BD22: Oxen 1C **84**
   HD6: Ras 3H **161**
   HX1: Hal 4D **164** (2H **149**)
                  (Alfred St. E.)
   HX1: Hal 5D **164** (3H **149**)
                  (Lily La.)
   HX4: Gree 4H **159**
   HX5: Ell 4B **160**
   LS5: Leeds 5A **76**
   LS10: Leeds 1B **118**
   LS19: Yead 1E **55**
   LS20: Guis 4C **40**
   LS22: Weth 4E **13**
   LS23: B Spa, Cliff 4B **30**
   LS26: Rothw 2A **142**
   LS26: Wood 6E **121**
   LS27: Gil 6E **115**
   LS27: Morl 2A **138**
   LS29: Add 1E **9**
   LS29: I'ly 5C **10**
   WF17: Birs 6A **136**
Church Ter. HX2: Illing 2B **128**
   HX6: Sow B 6E **147**
Church Vw. BD19: Cleck 1H **153**
   HX3: Nor G 5H **131**
   HX6: Sow B 5A **148**
   LS5: Leeds 5B **76**
   LS14: T'ner 1H **63**
   LS16: Leeds 2C **58**
   LS21: Pool 4F **25**
   LS25: Kip 3B **124**
   LS29: Men 1F **39**
Church Vw. M. LS23: Cliff 6B **30**
Churchville LS25: M'fld 4E **105**
Churchville Av. LS25: M'fld 4D **104**
Churchville Dr. LS25: M'fld 4E **105**
Churchville Ter. LS25: M'fld 4E **105**
Church Wlk. HX3: North 5C **130**
   LS2: Leeds 5G **5** (4B **98**)
   LS27: Morl 2A **138**
Church Way BD21: Keigh 1A **48**
   LS16: Leeds 3C **76**
Church Wood Av. LS6: Leeds 3B **76**
   LS16: Leeds 3C **76**
Church Wood Mt. LS16: Leeds 2C **76**
Church Wood Rd. LS16: Leeds 3C **76**
Churn Dr. BD6: B'frd 5G **109**
Churn La. HX2: Hal 2B **148**
Churn Milk La. HX3: Hal 3E **129**
CHURWELL 5C **116**
Cinderhills La. HX3: Hal 6A **150**
Cinder La. LS23: Cliff 5C **30**
   WF10: C'frd 6H **145**
Cineworld Cinema
   Bradford 5F **7** (5F **91**)
CITY 3B **138**
City Bloc Indoor Climbing Wall 6B **98**
City Gla. LS3: Leeds 3F **97**
City Golf Course 2C **96**
City La. HX3: Hal 6C **128**
City Link Ind. Pk. BD4: B'frd 5C **92**
City Mills LS27: Morl 3B **138**
                      (off Peel St.)
City Pk. Ind. Est. LS12: Leeds 2C **116**

City Rd. BD1: B'frd 3C **90**
   BD8: B'frd 2A **6** (3C **90**)
City Sports 4H **91**
                 (in Greystone Mill)
City Sq. LS1: Leeds 5D **4** (4H **97**)
City Ter. HX3: Hal 6C **128**
City Varieties Music Hall 4E **5** (3A **98**)
City Vw. LS11: Leeds 3F **117**
                 (off Kirk Beston Rd.)
City Wlk. LS11: Leeds 5H **97**
Cityway Ind. Est. BD4: B'frd 6H **91**
City West One Office Pk.
   LS12: Leeds 2D **116**
Clapgate LS21: Otley 3E **23**
Clapgate La. LS10: Leeds 2D **140**
Clapham Dene Rd.
   LS15: Leeds 2D **100**
Clapham St. BD13: Denh 3C **86**
Clapton Av. HX1: Hal 3E **149**
Clapton Gro. HX1: Hal 3E **149**
Clapton Mt. HX1: Hal 3E **149**
                  (off Clapton Av.)
Clara Dr. LS28: Cal 2D **72**
Clara Rd. BD2: B'frd 4F **71**
Clara St. HD6: Ras 2A **162**
   LS28: Fars 1H **93**
Clare Ct. HX1: Hal 6C **164**
Clare Cres. BD12: Wyke 5C **132**
Clare Hall HX1: Hal 6C **164**
Clare Hall La. HX1: Hal . .6C **164** (3G **149**)
Claremont BD7: B'frd 6A **6** (5D **90**)
   BD12: Wyke 5C **132**
   LS28: Pud 4B **94**
Claremont Av. BD18: Ship 3E **71**
   LS3: Leeds 2A **4** (2G **97**)
Claremont Ct. LS6: Leeds 3E **77**
Claremont Cres. BD18: Ship 3E **71**
   LS6: Leeds 4F **77**
Claremont Dr. LS6: Leeds 3E **77**
Claremont Gdns. BD16: Bgly 3C **50**
   LS28: Fars 1H **93**
Claremont Gro. BD18: Ship 3E **71**
   LS3: Leeds 2A **4** (2G **97**)
   LS28: Pud 4A **94**
Claremont Pl. LS12: Leeds 4A **96**
Claremont Rd. BD18: Ship 3E **71**
   LS6: Leeds 3E **77**
Claremont St. HX5: Ell 5C **160**
   HX6: Sow B 4A **148**
   LS12: Leeds 4A **96**
   LS26: Oul 1E **143**
Claremont Ter. BD5: B'frd 6B **6** (5D **90**)
   LS12: Leeds 4A **96**
Claremont Vw. LS3: Leeds . . .2A **4** (2G **97**)
   LS26: Oul 1E **143**
Claremont Vs. BD5: B'frd 6B **6**
   HX6: Sow B 5A **148**
                  (off Victoria Av.)
   LS2: Leeds 2B **4**
                (off Clarendon Rd.)
CLAREMOUNT 1H **149**
Claremount LS6: Leeds 3E **77**
Claremount Ho. HX3: Hal 1H **149**
                (off Claremount Rd.)
Claremount Rd.
   HX3: Hal 1D **164** (5F **129**)
Claremount Ter. HX3: Hal 5G **129**
Clarence Dock
   LS10: Leeds 6H **5** (5B **98**)
Clarence Dr. LS18: H'fth 2D **74**
   LS29: Men 5F **21**
Clarence Gdns. LS18: H'fth 2D **74**
Clarence Gro. LS18: H'fth 2D **74**
Clarence Ho. LS10: Leeds 5B **98**
Clarence M. LS18: H'fth 2D **74**
Clarence Pl. LS29: Burl W 2F **21**
Clarence Rd. BD18: Ship 1H **69**
   LS10: Leeds 5C **98**
   LS18: H'fth 2D **74**
Clarence St. HX1: Hal 4A **164** (2F **149**)
   LS13: Leeds 2E **95**
Clarence Ter. LS28: Pud 3A **94**
Clarendon Ct. BD8: B'frd 1A **6** (2D **90**)

Clarendon Pl. BD13: Que 5G **107**
  HX1: Hal 2E **149**
  LS2: Leeds 1G **97**
Clarendon Rd. BD16: Bgly 3D **50**
  LS2: Leeds 1A 4 (1G **97**)
  LS23: B Spa 4A **30**
Clarendon St. BD21: Keigh 2H **47**
  BD22: Haw 3C **64**
Clarendon Ter. LS27: Chur 5C **116**
  LS28: Pud 5A **94**
Clarendon Way
  LS2: Leeds 2B 4 (2G **97**)
Clare Rd. BD12: Wyke 5C **132**
  HX1: Hal 5C **164** (3G **149**)
Clare Rd. Flats
  HX1: Hal 6C **164** (3G **149**)
Clare Royd HX3: Hip 2A **152**
Clare St. HX1: Hal 5C **164** (3G **149**)
Clarges St. BD5: B'frd 2C **110**
Clarion Camp LS29: Men 6B **22**
Clarion Fld. LS29: Men 6B **22**
Clark Av. LS9: Leeds 4D **98**
Clark Cres. LS9: Leeds 4D **98**
Clarke Rd. WF3: W Ard 4E **155**
Clarke St. LS28: Cal 3F **73**
Clark Gro. LS9: Leeds 5D **98**
Clark La. LS9: Leeds 4D **98**
  (not continuous)
Clark Mt. LS9: Leeds 4D **98**
Clark Rd. LS9: Leeds 5D **98**
Clark Row LS9: Leeds 5D **98**
Clarkson Ter. LS27: Chur 5C **116**
Clarkson Vw. LS6: Leeds 5G **77**
Clark Spring Cl. LS27: Morl 6A **116**
Clark Spring Ct. LS27: Morl 6B **116**
Clark Spring Ri. LS27: Morl 6B **116**
Clark Ter. LS9: Leeds 4D **98**
Clark Vw. LS9: Leeds 5D **98**
Clay Brow BD22: Haw 1C **64**
  (off North Vw. Ter.)
Clayfield Dr. BD7: B'frd 3A **110**
Clay Hill Dr. BD12: Wyke 4D **132**
  (not continuous)
Clay Ho. La. HX4: Gree 4G **159**
Claymore Ri. BD20: Sils 3F **15**
Clay Pit La. LS2: Leeds 2E 5 (2A **98**)
  LS7: Leeds 1F 5 (2A **98**)
Claypit La. LS14: T'ner 2H **63**
  LS25: Led 6E **125**
  WF10: Leeds 6E **125**
Clay Pits La. HX1: Hal 1C **148**
Clay Royd La. HX3: Sou 4E **151**
Clay St. HX1: Hal 2D **148**
  HX6: Sow B 5A **148**
  (Bk. Pleasant St.)
  HX6: Sow B 5H **147**
  (John St. W.)
CLAYTON 1D **108**
Clayton Av. LS25: Kip 3H **123**
Clayton Bus. Cen. LS10: Leeds 2C **118**
Clayton Cl. LS10: Leeds 3D **118**
Clayton Ct. LS10: Leeds 3D **118**
  LS16: Leeds 1H **75**
Clayton Dr. LS10: Leeds 3D **118**
CLAYTON EDGE 3H **107**
Clayton Grange LS19: Leeds 1H **75**
Clayton Gro. LS19: Yead 6F **41**
CLAYTON HEIGHTS 4D **108**
Clayton La. BD5: B'frd 1E **111**
  BD14: Clay 2D **108**
Clayton Ri. BD20: Keigh 5G **33**
  WF1: Out 4F **157**
Clayton Rd. BD7: B'frd 1G **109**
  LS10: Leeds 3D **118**
Claytons Cl. LS26: Meth 4B **144**
Clayton St. LS26: Rothw 2B **142**
Clayton Ter. BD13: Cull 4B **66**
Clayton Way LS10: Leeds 3D **118**
Clayton Wood Bank LS16: Leeds . . .6H **57**
Clayton Wood Cl. LS16: Leeds 6H **57**
Clayton Wood Ct. LS16: Leeds 6H **57**
Clayton Wood Ri. LS16: Leeds 6H **57**

Clayton Wood Rd.
  LS16: Leeds 6G **57**
Clearings, The LS10: Leeds 5B **118**
Cleasby Rd. LS29: Men 2G **39**
Cleavesty La. LS17: E Kes 4D **26**
Cleckheaton & District Golf Course
   . . . . .5H **133**
Cleckheaton Rd. BD6: B'frd 1D **132**
  BD12: Low M, O'haw 1D **132**
Cleeve Hill LS19: Raw 3F **55**
Clegg La. HX4: Gree 4D **158**
Clegg St. BD12: Wyke 4C **132**
Clement Ct. HX1: Hal 2E **149**
Clement St. BD8: B'frd 3H **89**
  HX6: Sow B 5H **147**
Clement Ter. LS26: Rothw 3A **142**
Clervaux Ct. BD14: Clay 6F **89**
Clevedon Ho. BD8: B'frd 2C **90**
  (off Trenton Dr.)
Clevedon Pl. HX3: Hal 5E **129**
Cleveland Av. HX3: Hal 5H **149**
Cleveland Rd. BD9: B'frd 6B **70**
Cleveland Ter. BD16: Bgly 4C **50**
  (off Elizabeth St.)
Cleveleys Av. HX6: Sow B 4H **147**
  (off Edward St.)
  LS11: Leeds 1F **117**
Cleveleys Ct. LS11: Leeds 1F **117**
  (off Cleveleys Av.)
Cleveleys Gdns. HX6: Sow B 4H **147**
Cleveleys Mt. LS11: Leeds 1F **117**
Cleveleys Rd. LS11: Leeds 1F **117**
Cleveleys St. LS11: Leeds 1F **117**
  (off Cleveleys Rd.)
Cleveleys Ter. LS11: Leeds 1F **117**
Clifby HX2: Hal 1B **148**
Cliff Ct. LS6: Leeds 5G **77**
Cliff Cres. HX2: Hal 4C **148**
  LS25: Kip 4A **124**
Cliffdale Rd. LS7: Leeds 5H **77**
Cliffdale Rd. Light Ind. Est.
  LS7: Leeds 5H **77**
Cliffe HX2: Hal 3H **147**
Cliffe Av. BD6: Har 6E **49**
  BD17: Bail 5C **52**
  HX3: Hip 2A **152**
Cliffe Bungs. LS25: M'fld 6D **104**
Cliffe Castle (Museum) 4H **33**
Cliffe Ct. LS19: Yead 6G **41**
  (off High St.)
Cliffe Cres. BD20: Rid 5F **35**
Cliffe Dr. LS19: Raw 4E **55**
Cliffe Gdns. BD18: Ship 3B **70**
Cliffe Ho. Av. LS25: Gar 6G **103**
Cliffe Ho's. LS25: M'fld 6D **104**
Cliffe La. BD13: Thorn 4A **88**
  BD17: Bail 6C **52**
  BD19: Cleck, Gom 6C **134**
  LS19: Raw 5G **55**
Cliffe La. Sth. BD17: Bail 6C **52**
Cliffe La. W. BD17: Bail 5C **52**
Cliffe Mill Fold BD20: E Mor 5A **36**
Cliffe Mt. BD19: Gom 6E **135**
Cliffe Pk. Chase LS12: Leeds 5A **96**
Cliffe Pk. Cl. LS12: Leeds 5A **96**
Cliffe Pk. Cres. LS12: Leeds 5A **96**
Cliffe Pk. Dr. LS12: Leeds 5A **96**
Cliffe Pk. Mt. LS12: Leeds 5A **96**
Cliffe Pk. Ri. LS12: Leeds 5A **96**
Cliffe Pk. Way LS27: Morl 4F **137**
Cliffe Rd. BD3: B'frd 1F **91**
  BD21: Keigh 3H **47**
  HD6: Ras 1A **162**
Cliffestone Dr. BD20: E Mor 5H **35**
Cliffe St. BD13: Thorn 4G **87**
  BD21: Keigh 5H **33**
Cliffe Ter. BD8: B'frd 2D **90**
  BD13: Denh 3C **86**
  (off Station Rd.)
  BD17: Bail 6C **52**
  BD21: Keigh 3A **48**
  HX3: Hal 1G **159**
  HX6: Sow B 4G **147**

Cliffe Ter. LS22: Weth 4E **13**
  (off Greenfold La.)
  LS25: M'fld 5F **105**
  WF3: Rob H 4E **141**
Cliffe Va. Rd. BD18: Ship 4B **70**
Cliffe Vw. BD15: All 1C **88**
  LS27: Morl 4F **137**
Cliffe Vs. BD16: Cot 4E **69**
  LS25: M'fld 5D **104**
Cliffe Wood Av. BD18: Ship 3B **70**
Cliffe Wood Cl. BD9: B'frd 6G **69**
Cliff Gdns. HX2: Hal 4C **148**
Cliff Hill La. HX2: Hal 3H **147**
Cliff Hollins La. BD4: E Bier 3H **133**
  BD12: O'haw 3H **133**
Cliff La. LS6: Leeds 5F **77**
Cliff Mt. LS6: Leeds 5G **77**
Cliff Mt. Ter. LS6: Leeds 5G **77**
CLIFFORD 6B **30**
Clifford Av. LS29: I'ly 4C **10**
Clifford Cl. BD2: B'frd 4E **71**
Clifford Ct. LS23: Cliff 6C **30**
Clifford Dr. LS29: Men 2H **39**
Clifford Moor Rd.
  LS23: B Spa, Cliff 3H **29**
Clifford Pl. LS27: Chur 6B **116**
Clifford Rd. BD17: Bail 5C **52**
  LS23: B Spa 4C **30**
  LS29: I'ly 3C **10**
Clifford St. BD5: B'frd 6D 6 (6E **91**)
  BD20: Sils 1D **14**
Clifford Way LS25: Kip 1F **123**
Cliff Rd. LS6: Leeds 5G **77**
Cliff Rd. Gdns. LS6: Leeds 5G **77**
Cliff Side Gdns. LS6: Leeds 5G **77**
Cliff St. BD22: Haw 2D **64**
Cliff Ter. LS6: Leeds 5G **77**
  LS25: Gar 1H **123**
Cliff Top Pk. (Park Home Est.)
   . . . . .1D **162**
CLIFTON 1D **162**
Clifton Av. HX1: Hal 3D **148**
  LS9: Leeds 2E **99**
Clifton Comn. HD6: Brigh 1C **162**
Clifton Ct. LS28: Pud 3A **94**
  (off Clifton Rd.)
Clifton Dr. LS28: Pud 3A **94**
Clifton Gro. LS9: Leeds 2E **99**
Clifton Hill LS28: Pud 3A **94**
Clifton M. LS28: Pud 3A **94**
Clifton Mt. LS9: Leeds 1E **99**
Clifton Pl. BD18: Ship 3B **70**
  LS28: Pud 3B **94**
Clifton Rd. HD6: Brigh 1B **162**
  (not continuous)
  HX3: Hal 5G **149**
  LS28: Pud 3A **94**
  LS29: I'ly 6E **11**
Clifton Side HD2: Hud 5F **163**
Clifton St. BD8: B'frd 2D **90**
  BD13: Que 4A **108**
  BD22: Keigh 1G **47**
  HX3: Hal 6E **129**
  HX6: Sow B 5A **148**
Clifton Ter. LS9: Leeds 2E **99**
  LS29: I'ly 5D **10**
  (off Lwr. Wellington Rd.)
CLIFTON VILLAS 2D **90**
Clifton Vs. BD8: B'frd 2D **90**
  LS21: Otley 5D **22**
  LS29: I'ly 6F **11**
Climax Works LS11: Leeds 3A **118**
Clipston Av. LS6: Leeds 3F **77**
Clipston Mt. LS6: Leeds 3F **77**
Clipstone St. BD5: B'frd 3E **111**
Clipstone Ter. LS6: Leeds 3F **77**
Clipston St. LS6: Leeds 3F **77**
Cliveden Av. BD13: Thorn 4A **88**
Clive Mt. Ho. LS5: Leeds 6H **75**
  (off Broad La.)
Clive Pl. BD7: B'frd 6B **90**
Clive Ter. BD7: B'frd 6B **90**
Cloberry St. LS2: Leeds 1A 4 (1G **97**)
Clock Bldgs. LS8: Leeds 5E **79**

Clock La. BD13: Denh 2B 86
Clock Vw. St. BD20: Keigh 3H 33
Clog Bri. BD20: Sils 2E 15
Clog Sole Rd. HD6: Brigh 5H 151
Cloisters, The HX1: Hal 4E 149
(off Constitutional St.)
Close, The BD2: B'frd 3F 71
LS9: Leeds 4C 98
LS14: T'ner 1H 63
LS15: Bar E 3D 82
LS17: E Kes 6E 27
LS17: Leeds 2G 59
LS20: Guis 5A 40
LS22: Coll 3B 28
LS23: B Spa 3B 30
LS25: Kip 4G 123
WF3: E Ard 2B 156
Close Head BD13: Thorn 5F 87
Close Head Dr. BD13: Thorn 5F 87
Close Head Rd. BD13: Thorn 4F 87
Close Lea HD6: Ras 2H 161
Close Lea Av. HD6: Ras 2H 161
Close Lea Dr. HD6: Ras 2H 161
Close Lea Way HD6: Ras 2H 161
Closes Pl. HD6: Ras 2A 162
(off Closes Rd.)
Closes Rd. HD6: Ras 2H 161
Cloth Hall St. LS1: Leeds . . .5F 5 (4A 98)
Cloudsdale Av. BD5: B'frd 1E 111
Clough Av. BD20: Stee 5C 14
Clough Bank HX2: Mix 2H 127
Clough Bank La. BD22: Oak 1A 46
Clough Bldgs. HX6: Sow B 5D 146
Clough Ct. BD13: Denh 5C 86
Clough Dr. WF17: Birs 5C 136
Clough Fold BD21: Keigh 4G 47
Clough Ga. BD22: Oak 5D 46
(off Clough La.)
Clough Head HX6: Norl 1A 158
Clough Ho's. BD22: Oak 5C 46
Clough La. BD22: Oak 4C 46
HD2: Fix 5G 161
HD6: B Bri, Clift 3C 152
HD6: Ras 5G 161
HX2: Midg 2B 126
HX2: Mix 2H 127
Clough Pl. HX2: Mix 2H 127
Clough Rd. HX6: Norl 1B 158
Clough St. BD5: B'frd 2E 111
LS27: Morl 3B 138
Clough Ter. HX6: Sow B 5A 148
Clovelly Av. LS11: Leeds 2H 117
Clovelly Gro. LS11: Leeds 2H 117
Clovelly Pl. LS11: Leeds 2H 117
Clovelly Row LS11: Leeds 2H 117
Clovelly Ter. LS11: Leeds 2H 117
Clover Ct. LS26: Wood 1E 145
Clover Ct. LS28: Cal 3E 73
Clover Cres. LS28: Cal 2E 73
Cloverdale HX3: She 6F 109
Clover Hill Cl. HX1: Hal 6A 164 (3F 149)
Clover Hill Rd. HX1: Hal 4F 149
Clover Hill Ter. HX1: Hal 4F 149
Clover Hill Vw. HX1: Hal 4F 149
(off Clover Hill Rd.)
Clover Hill Wlk. HX1: Hal 4F 149
Clover Ri. BD21: Keigh 6C 34
Clover St. BD5: B'frd 2B 110
Cloverville App. BD6: B'frd 6C 110
Club Energy 3E 23
Clubhouse, The HX4: Gree 4H 159
(off Rochdale Rd.)
Club Ho's. HX2: Hal 4D 128
Club La. HX2: Hal 4C 128
LS13: Leeds 4A 74
Club Row BD15: Wils 4G 67
(off Main St.)
LS7: Leeds 2A 78
LS19: Yead 6G 41
Club St. BD7: B'frd 6H 89
Clumpcliffe LS26: Meth 4F 143
Clunters La. HX2: Lud M 4B 146
Clyde App. LS12: Leeds 5E 97

Clyde Chase LS12: Leeds 5E 97
(off Clyde App.)
Clyde Ct. LS12: Leeds 5E 97
(off Copley St.)
Clyde Gdns. LS12: Leeds 5E 97
Clyde Grange LS12: Leeds 5E 97
(off Clyde Vw.)
Clydesdale Dr. BD6: B'frd 6H 109
Clyde St. BD16: Bgly 4B 50
HX6: Sow B 6H 147
Clydeville Flats LS21: Otley 4C 22
Clyde Vw. LS12: Leeds 5E 97
Clyde Wlk. LS12: Leeds 5E 97
Coachfold HX3: Hal 1B 164 (1G 149)
Coach Ho. Cl. BD7: B'frd 2H 109
Coach Ho. Ct. LS22: Weth 3F 13
Coach La. BD13: Thorn 5B 88
Coach Rd. BD17: Bail 6A 52
HD6: Brigh 4H 151
HX3: Hip 2G 151
LS12: N Far 2G 115
LS20: Guis 6B 40
LS26: Swil 5H 121
WF1: Out 4G 157
Coach Row BD3: B'frd 3A 92
Coal Hill Dr. LS13: Leeds 5B 74
Coal Hill Fold LS13: Leeds 5B 74
Coal Hill Gdns. LS13: Leeds 5B 74
Coal Hill Ga. LS13: Leeds 5B 74
Coal Hill Grn. LS13: Leeds 5B 74
Coal Hill La. LS13: Leeds 5A 74
LS28: Fars 5A 74
Coal La. HX2: Ogd 2C 106
Coal Pit La. HD6: Brigh 2D 162
Coalpit La. HX3: Hal, Sou 5A 150
Coal Rd. LS14: Leeds 4C 62
LS17: Leeds 3C 62
LS17: Wike 4A 44
Coates St. BD5: B'frd 2D 110
Coates Ter. BD5: B'frd 1D 110
Cobblestone Dr. HX2: Illing 6C 106
Cobbydale Ct. BD20: Sils 2D 14
Cobden Av. LS12: Leeds 1H 115
Cobden Ct. HX1: Hal 2A 164
Cobden Gro. LS12: Leeds 1H 115
Cobden M. LS27: Morl 2A 138
Cobden Pl. LS12: Leeds 1H 115
Cobden Rd. LS12: Leeds 1H 115
Cobden St. BD10: B'frd 2H 71
BD13: Que 4B 108
BD14: Clay 1D 108
BD15: All 2D 88
HX6: Sow B 6G 147
(off Sowerby New Rd.)
LS12: Leeds 1H 115
LS27: Morl 2A 138
Cobden Ter. HX3: Hip 1E 151
HX5: Ell 6B 160
LS12: Leeds 1H 115
Cock Ct. LS29: Add 4A 8
Cockin La. BD14: Clay 2H 107
Cockroft Gro. BD3: B'frd 3H 7 (4G 91)
Cockshott Cl. LS12: Leeds 2H 95
Cockshott Dr. LS12: Leeds 2H 95
Cockshott Hill LS28: Fars 6H 73
Cockshott La. BD10: B'frd 1G 71
LS12: Leeds 2H 95
(not continuous)
Cockshott Pl. LS29: Add 1C 8
Colbeck Row WF17: Birs 6A 136
Colbert Av. LS29: I'ly 4F 11
Colby Ri. LS15: Leeds 4A 100
Coldbeck Dr. BD6: B'frd 5G 109

Coldcotes Av. LS9: Leeds 1F 99
Coldcotes Cir. LS9: Leeds 1G 99
Coldcotes Cl. LS9: Leeds 1G 99
Coldcotes Cres. LS9: Leeds 1H 99
Coldcotes Dr. LS9: Leeds 1G 99
Coldcotes Gth. LS9: Leeds 1H 99
Coldcotes Gro. LS9: Leeds 1H 99
Coldcotes Vw. LS9: Leeds 1H 99
Coldcotes Wlk. LS9: Leeds 1H 99
Cold Edge Bottom HX2: Wain 1F 127
Cold Edge Rd. HX2: Wain 2F 127
(Mt. Tabor Rd.)
HX2: Wain 6C 84
(Nab Water La.)
Coldshaw BD22: Oxen 6A 64
Coldshaw Top BD22: Haw 4C 64
Cold St. BD22: Haw 4C 64
Coldwell Rd. LS15: Leeds 2D 100
Coldwell Sq. LS15: Leeds 2D 100
Coleman St. BD3: B'frd 1E 7 (2F 91)
LS12: Leeds 5F 97
Colenso Gdns. LS11: Leeds 1F 117
Colenso Gro. BD21: Keigh 4C 34
(off Aireworth Cl.)
LS11: Leeds 1F 117
Colenso Mt. LS11: Leeds 1F 117
Colenso Pl. LS11: Leeds 1F 117
Colenso Rd. LS11: Leeds 1F 117
Colenso Ter. LS11: Leeds 1F 117
Colenso Wlk. BD21: Keigh 4C 34
(off Cornwall Cl.)
Colenso Way BD21: Keigh 4C 34
(off Cornwall Rd.)
Coleridge Cl. LS26: Oul 4E 143
Coleridge Cres. WF2: Wren 6D 156
Coleridge Gdns. BD10: B'frd 1A 72
Coleridge La. LS28: Pud 6B 94
Coleridge St. HX1: Hal 5C 164 (3G 149)
Coleshill Way BD4: B'frd 5H 111
Coles Way BD20: Rid 3B 34
COLEY 5F 131
Coley Hall La. HX3: Nor G 5F 131
Coley Rd. HX3: North 3E 131
Coley Vw. HX3: Hip 1F 151
HX3: North 4C 130
Collbrook Av. BD6: B'frd 5C 110
College Ct. LS27: Gil 1F 137
College Dr. LS29: I'ly 6D 10
College Farm La. LS22: Lin 6B 12
College Gdns. BD16: Bgly 2C 50
College Lawns LS12: Leeds 3H 95
College Rd. BD16: Bgly 1C 50
LS27: Gil 1F 137
College St. WF17: Birs 6A 136
College Ter. HX1: Hal 4E 149
(off Skircoat Moor Rd.)
College Vw. LS12: Leeds 4H 95
College Wlk. BD21: Keigh 6A 34
(within Airedale Shop. Cen.)
Collier Cl. BD18: Ship 2G 69
Colliers La. BD17: Bail 3B 52
Colliers La. LS17: Shad 3A 62
Colliery App. WF3: Loft 3F 157
Collindale Cl. BD10: B'frd 3C 72
Collinfield Ri. BD6: B'frd 1H 131
COLLINGHAM 3B 28
Collingham Av. BD6: B'frd 5G 109
Collingham Dr. LS25: Gar 5F 103
COLLINGHAM FIELDS 3D 28
Collingwood Ct. BD5: B'frd 2E 111
(off Ladywell Cl.)
Collin Moor La. HX4: Gree 3G 159
Collin Rd. LS14: Leeds 2B 100
Collins Cl. BD22: Haw 1E 65
Collinson St. BD19: Cleck 6B 134
Collins St. BD4: B'frd 1H 111
BD7: B'frd 2A 110
COLL PLACE 6D 110
Coll Pl. BD6: B'frd 5D 110
Collyer Vw. LS29: I'ly 4G 11
Colmore Gro. LS12: Leeds 6D 96
Colmore Rd. LS12: Leeds 6D 96
Colmore St. LS12: Leeds 5D 96

Colne Rd. BD22: Oak 5B 46
Colonial Bldg. BD1: B'frd 4B 6
Colour Experience 4B 6 (4D 90)
Colston Cl. BD8: B'frd 2G 89
Colston Dr. LS29: Burl W 3C 20
COLTON .5F 101
Colton Ct. LS15: Leeds 4F 101
Colton Cft. LS15: Leeds 4F 101
Colton Gth. LS15: Leeds 4F 101
Colton La. LS15: Leeds 4F 101
Colton Lodges LS15: Leeds 4G 101
Colton Mill LS15: Leeds 4H 101
Colton Retail Pk.
    LS15: Leeds 4G 101
Colton Rd. LS12: Leeds 4C 96
    LS15: Leeds 4E 101
Colton Rd. E. LS15: Leeds 5G 101
Colton St. LS12: Leeds 4C 96
Columbus St. HX3: Hal 6E 129
Colville Ter. LS11: Leeds 1H 117
    WF3: Thpe H 6C 140
Colwyn Av. LS11: Leeds 3H 117
Colwyn Mt. LS11: Leeds 3H 117
Colwyn Pl. LS11: Leeds 3H 117
Colwyn Rd. LS11: Leeds 3H 117
Colwyn Ter. LS11: Leeds 3H 117
Colwyn Vw. LS11: Leeds 3H 117
Colyton Mt. BD15: All 2C 88
Combined Court Cen.
    Bradford 5E 7 (5F 91)
    Leeds 3C 4 (3H 97)
Commerce Ct. BD4: B'frd 1B 112
Commerce St. BD1: B'frd 3D 6 (4E 91)
Commercial Bldgs. BD12: O'haw . .3H 133
Commercial Rd. LS5: Leeds 5A 76
Commercial St. BD1: B'frd 3E 7
    BD13: Denh 3B 86
    BD13: Que 4H 107
    BD13: Thorn 5A 88
    BD18: Ship 1B 70
    BD22: Oak 5B 46
    HD6: Brigh 1A 162
    HX1: Hal 4B 164 (2G 149)
                        (not continuous)
    LS1: Leeds 4E 5 (3A 98)
    LS26: Rothw 2A 142
    LS27: Morl 3A 138
Commercial Vs. LS28: Pud 5H 93
Commercial Way LS28: Pud 3B 94
Commondale Way BD4: B'frd 1G 133
Common End HD6: B Bri 3C 152
Common Holme La. LS29: Nes 3H 9
Common La. HX3: Sou 4B 150
    WF3: E Ard 1H 155
Common Rd. BD12: Low M 1B 132
    HX5: Ell 5E 161
Common Rd. Ind. Est.
    BD12: Low M 1D 132
Common Side LS26: Meth 6E 145
Common Ter. HD6: Ras 2A 162
Como Av. BD8: B'frd 2H 89
Como Dr. BD8: B'frd 3H 89
Como Gdns. BD8: B'frd 2H 89
Como Gro. BD8: B'frd 2H 89
Compeigne Av. BD21: Rid 4D 34
COMPTON 5C 28
Compton Av. LS9: Leeds 1E 99
Compton Ct. LS22: Coll 2B 28
Compton Cres. LS9: Leeds 1E 99
Compton La. LS22: Comp 5C 28
                        (not continuous)
    LS23: B'ham 1H 45
Compton Pl. LS9: Leeds 1E 99
Compton Rd. LS9: Leeds 1E 99
Compton Row LS9: Leeds 1E 99
Compton St. BD4: B'frd 3A 112
    BD21: Keigh 5B 34
Compton Ter. LS9: Leeds 1E 99
Compton Vw. LS9: Leeds 1E 99
Concept LS7: Leeds 2A 78
Concept Pl. LS3: Leeds 2F 97
Concordia St. LS1: Leeds . . .6E 5 (4A 98)
Concord St. LS2: Leeds 2G 5 (2B 98)

Concourse Ho. LS11: Leeds 5F 117
                    (off Dewsbury Rd.)
Concrete St. HX3: Hal 6E 129
Condor St. HX3: Hal 3E 109
Conduit St. BD8: B'frd 2C 90
Coney La. BD21: Keigh 6A 34
    HX2: Hal 1E 129
Coney Moor Gro. LS26: Meth 4F 145
Coney Pk. Ind. Pk. LS19: Yead 4A 42
Conference Pl. LS12: Leeds 4A 96
Conference Rd. LS12: Leeds 4A 96
Conference Ter. LS12: Leeds 4A 96
Congress Mt. LS12: Leeds 4A 96
Congress St. LS12: Leeds 4A 96
Congreve App. LS17: Bard 6G 27
Congreve Way LS17: Bard 5G 27
Conisborough Cl. LS29: Burl W 3D 20
Conisborough La. LS25: Gar 4H 103
Coniston Av. BD13: Que 4H 107
    LS6: Leeds 4E 77
Coniston Cl. BD13: Que 4H 107
    HX5: Ell 4D 160
Coniston Ct. WF3: Loft 3F 157
Coniston Gdns. LS15: Leeds 5A 100
Coniston Gro. BD9: B'frd 1H 89
    BD17: Bail 6G 51
Coniston Ho. HX5: Ell 4B 160
                    (off St Mary's Ga.)
Coniston Rd. BD7: B'frd 2G 109
    LS26: Wood 6E 121
Coniston Way LS22: Weth 3B 12
    LS26: Wood 1E 143
Connaught Fold HD2: Hud 6E 163
Connaught Rd. LS29: I'ly 6F 11
Consort St. LS3: Leeds 2F 97
Consort Ter. LS3: Leeds 2F 97
Consort Vw. LS3: Leeds 2F 97
Consort Wlk. LS3: Leeds 2F 97
                        (not continuous)
Constable Gro. WF3: S'ley 3H 157
Constable Rd. LS29: I'ly 6F 11
    WF3: Ting 1E 155
Constance Gdns. LS7: Leeds 1H 97
Constance St. BD18: Ship 1H 69
Constance Way LS7: Leeds 1H 97
Constitutional St. HX1: Hal 4E 149
Conway Av. LS8: Leeds 6D 78
Conway Dr. LS8: Leeds 6D 78
Conway Gro. LS8: Leeds 6D 78
Conway Mt. LS8: Leeds 6D 78
Conway Pl. LS8: Leeds 6D 78
Conway Rd. LS8: Leeds 6D 78
Conway St. BD4: B'frd 6F 91
    HX1: Hal 3E 149
    LS8: Leeds 6D 78
    LS28: Stan 2H 93
Conway Ter. LS8: Leeds 6D 78
Conway Vw. LS8: Leeds 6D 78
Cooke St. BD21: Keigh 6A 34
Cook La. BD21: Keigh 6A 34
COOKRIDGE 2F 57
Cookridge Av. LS16: Leeds 1G 57
Cookridge Dr. LS16: Leeds 1F 57
Cookridge Gro. LS16: Leeds 1G 57
Cookridge Hall Golf Course 1H 57
Cookridge La. LS16: Leeds 5F 43
Cookridge St. LS1: Leeds 3D 4 (3H 97)
    LS2: Leeds 2D 4 (3H 97)
                        (not continuous)
Cookson St. HD6: Brigh 6H 151
Coombe Hill BD13: Que 3D 108
Co-operation St. LS12: Leeds 1A 116
Co-operative Bldgs. HD6: B Bri 2B 152
Co-operative Bldgs. HX3: Hal 5D 128
Co-operative Rd. LS27: Morl 5H 137
Co-operative St. BD21: Keigh 4G 47
    LS27: Chur 5C 116
    LS27: Morl 2A 138
    WF3: Loft 6G 141
Co-operative Yd. BD19: Cleck 6B 134
                    (off Heaton Rd.)
Cooper Bri. Rd. WF14: Mir 5H 163
Cooper Cl. BD16: Bgly 2C 50

Cooperfields HX2: Lud M 3E 147
Cooper Gro. HX3: She 6F 109
Cooper Hill LS28: Pud 6B 94
Cooper La. BD6: B'frd 3F 109
    HX3: She 3F 109
Cooper Rd. LS22: Weth 4E 13
Coopers Cl. HX2: Hal 5B 128
Coopers Fold LS23: B Spa 3B 30
Coop Pl. BD5: B'frd 4G 111
Copeland St. BD4: B'frd 6B 92
Copgrove Cl. BD4: B'frd 2C 112
Copgrove Ct. BD4: B'frd 2C 112
Copgrove Rd. BD4: B'frd 2C 112
    LS8: Leeds 5E 79
COPLEY 1F 159
Copley Av. HX2: Hal 4D 148
Copley Circ. HX3: Hal 2E 159
Copley Cl. HX3: Hal 2F 159
Copley Dr. HX3: Hal 1E 159
Copley Glen HX3: Hal 1F 159
Copley Gro. HX3: Hal 1F 159
Copley Hall St. HX3: Hal 2F 159
Copley Hall Ter. HX3: Hal 1F 159
COPLEY HILL 5C 136
Copley Hill LS12: Leeds 5E 97
    WF17: Birs 6B 136
Copley Hill Trad. Est. LS12: Leeds . .6E 97
Copley Hill Way LS12: Leeds 6E 97
Copley La. HX3: Hal 2E 159
    WF3: Rob H 3F 141
Copley Mill Ho. HX3: Hal 1E 159
                    (off St Stephen's St.)
Copley Mt. HX3: Hal 1F 159
Copley St. BD5: B'frd 2B 110
    LS12: Leeds 5E 97
Copley Ter. HX3: Hal 1F 159
Copley Vw. HX3: Hal 1F 159
Copley Wood Ter. HX3: Hal 1F 159
Copley Yd. LS12: Leeds 5E 97
Coplowe La. BD15: Wils 2H 67
Copperas Row HX4: Gree 4C 158
Copperfield Av. LS9: Leeds 5D 98
Copperfield Cres. LS9: Leeds 5D 98
Copperfield Dr. LS9: Leeds 5D 98
Copperfield Gro. LS9: Leeds 5D 98
Copperfield Mt. LS9: Leeds 5E 99
Copperfield Pl. LS9: Leeds 5D 98
Copperfield Row LS9: Leeds 5D 98
Copperfield Ter. LS9: Leeds 5D 98
Copperfield Vw. LS9: Leeds 5D 98
Copperfield Wlk. LS9: Leeds 5D 98
Coppice, The BD19: Gom 6H 135
    HX1: Hal 4F 149
    LS15: Bar E 3D 82
    LS19: Yead 2D 54
    LS29: I'ly 3C 10
Coppice Grange LS19: Yead 5F 41
Coppice Head LS26: Rothw 2B 142
Coppice Vw. BD10: B'frd 1G 71
Coppice Way LS8: Leeds 3E 79
Coppice Wood Av. LS19: Yead 5E 41
    LS20: Guis, Yead 5E 41
Coppicewood Av. BD7: B'frd 5A 90
Coppice Wood Cl. LS20: Guis 4E 41
Coppice Wood Cres. LS19: Yead . . .5E 41
Coppice Wood Gro. LS20: Guis 5E 41
Coppicewood Gro. BD7: B'frd 5A 90
Coppice Wood Ri. LS19: Yead 5E 41
Coppies, The BD12: Wyke 3B 132
Copplestone Wlk. BD4: B'frd 3C 112
Coppy Cl. BD16: Cot 3C 68
Coppy La. LS13: Leeds 5E 75
Coppy Rd. BD20: Stee 6B 14
    LS29: Add 1C 8
Coppy Row BD22: Oak 5B 46
Coppy Wood Dr. LS29: I'ly 2D 10
Copse, The BD16: Bgly 4F 51
    BD19: Scho 2F 153
    HD6: Brigh 5H 151
    LS23: B Spa 2A 30
    LS29: Burl W 3E 21
    WF3: E Ard 2H 155
Copthorne Gdns. HD2: Hud 6F 163

Copthorne Sq. HD2: Hud 6F 163
Copt Royd Gro. LS19: Yead 6E 41
Copy Nook HX4: Gree 4E 159
Copy St. BD15: All 2D 88
Coral Windows Stadium 2E 91
Corban St. BD4: B'frd 2A 112
Cordingley Cl. BD4: B'frd 4C 112
Cordingley St. BD4: B'frd 4C 112
Core Shop. Centre, The
    LS1: Leeds 4E 5 (3A 98)
Corfe Cl. WF17: Bat 5D 136
Coriander Cl. BD15: All 3C 88
Corner Ho. Shops LS17: Leeds 5B 60
Cornerstones Cl. LS29: Add 1E 9
Corn Mkt. HX1: Hal 4C 164 (2G 149)
Cornmill App. LS28: Pud 4G 93
Cornmill Cl. LS17: Bard 2F 45
Corn Mill Ct. LS13: Leeds 3F 95
Corn Mill Fold BD6: B'frd 1G 131
    LS14: Clay 6B 88
    LS29: Burl W 2G 21
Cornmill La. LS17: Bard 2F 45
Cornmill Vw. LS18: H'fth 1G 75
Cornstone Fold LS12: Leeds 4E 95
Corn St. BD21: Keigh 3G 47
Cornus Gdns. LS10: Leeds 5B 118
Cornwall Av. BD20: Sils 2C 14
Cornwall Cl. LS26: Rothw 1H 141
Cornwall Cres. BD17: Bail 3B 52
    HD6: B Bri 3B 152
    LS26: Rothw 1H 141
Cornwall Ho. HX5: Ell 5B 160
                                        (off Crown St.)
Cornwall Pl. BD8: B'frd 1B 6 (2D 90)
Cornwall Rd. BD8: B'frd 1B 6 (2D 90)
    BD16: Bgly 5D 50
    BD21: Keigh 4C 34
Cornwall Ter. BD8: B'frd 1B 6 (2D 90)
Coronation Av. BD17: Esh 3B 54
    LS25: Kip 4A 124
Coronation Bungs. LS25: Kip 4A 124
Coronation Bus. Cen.
    BD21: Keigh 4B 34
Coronation Mt. BD22: Keigh 6F 33
Coronation Pde. LS15: Leeds 5A 100
                                        (not continuous)
Coronation Rd. HX3: Hal 5G 149
Coronation St. BD12: O'haw 3G 133
    HX4: Gree 3G 159
    HX5: Ell 5B 160
    WF3: Carl 4H 141
Coronation Ter. WF17: Birs 6B 136
Coronation Wlk. BD22: Keigh 5F 33
Coronation Way BD22: Keigh 6E 33
Corporal La. BD13: North 1A 130
    HX3: North 1A 130
Corporation St. BD2: B'frd 6A 72
    HX1: Hal 2B 164 (1G 149)
    HX6: Sow B 5H 147
    LS27: Morl 2H 137
Corrance Rd. BD12: Wyke 6D 132
Corrie Fold BD13: Thorn 5A 88
                                        (off Corrie St.)
Corrie St. BD13: Thorn 5A 88
Corsair Av. BD10: B'frd 3A 72
Cote, The LS28: Fars 1G 93
Cote Farm La. BD10: B'frd 6F 53
Cotefields Av. LS28: Fars 6G 73
Cote Hill HX2: Hal 3A 148
Cote Hill Fold HX2: Hal 3B 148
Cote La. BD15: All 2C 88
    HD6: Ras 6G 161
    LS28: Fars, Stan 1G 93
Coteroyd Av. LS27: Chur 5C 116
Coteroyd Dr. LS27: Chur 6C 116
Cotewall Rd. BD5: B'frd 2D 110
Cotswold Av. BD18: Ship 2E 71
Cotswold Dr. LS25: Gar 6F 103
    LS26: Rothw 1H 141
Cotswold Rd. LS26: Rothw 1A 142
Cottage Grn. BD8: B'frd 3H 89
                                    (off Lane Ends Cl.)

Cottage Rd. BD10: B'frd 2B 72
    LS6: Leeds 3D 76
Cottage Road Cinema 3D 76
Cottam Av. BD7: B'frd 5B 90
Cottam Ter. BD7: B'frd 5B 90
Cotterdale BD15: All 6C 68
    LS29: Men 2H 39
                                    (off Clifford Dr.)
Cotterdale Holt LS22: Coll 2A 28
Cotterdale Vw. LS15: Leeds 5A 100
COTTINGLEY
    BD16 .3D 68
    LS11 .4D 116
Cottingley App. LS11: Leeds 4D 116
Cottingley Bus. Pk. BD16: Cot 2D 68
Cottingley Chase LS11: Leeds 4C 116
Cottingley Cliffe Rd. BD16: Cot 3E 69
Cottingley Ct. LS11: Leeds 4D 116
Cottingley Cres. LS11: Leeds 4D 116
Cottingley Dr. BD16: Cot 1C 68
    LS11: Leeds 3C 116
Cottingley Fold LS11: Leeds 3C 116
Cottingley Gdns. LS11: Leeds 4D 116
Cottingley Grn. LS11: Leeds 4D 116
Cottingley Gro. LS11: Leeds 4D 116
Cottingley Hall Crematorium
    LS11: Leeds 3D 116
Cottingley Hgts. LS11: Leeds 4D 116
Cottingley Mnr. Pk. BD16: Cot 2D 68
Cottingley Moor Rd. BD16: Cot 5C 68
Cottingley New Rd. BD16: Cot 2D 68
Cottingley Rd. BD15: All 6C 68
    LS11: Leeds 3C 116
Cottingley Springs Caravan Site
    LS27: Leeds 4A 116
Cottingley Station (Rail) 4C 116
Cottingley Ter. BD8: B'frd 2D 90
Cottingley Towers LS11: Leeds 4D 116
Cottingley Va. LS11: Leeds 4D 116
Cottingley Wood BD16: Cot 1C 68
Cotton St. LS9: Leeds 5H 5 (4C 98)
Couford Gro. HD2: Hud 6F 163
Cougar Park 4B 34
Coulsdon Ho. BD8: B'frd 2D 90
                                    (off Green La.)
Coultas St. LS29: Men 1H 39
County Arc. LS1: Leeds 4F 5 (3A 98)
County Bri. BD13: Denh 6B 86
County Court
    Halifax 5C 164
Coupland Pl. LS11: Leeds 1H 117
Coupland Rd. LS11: Leeds 1H 117
    LS25: Gar 4E 103
Coupland St. LS11: Leeds 2H 117
Court, The BD18: Ship 2G 69
    LS17: Leeds 2F 59
Court Barton La. LS23: Cliff 6C 30
Courtenay Cl. BD3: B'frd 4C 92
Courtenays LS14: Leeds 5D 80
Courthouse St. LS21: Otley 3E 23
Court La. HX2: Hal 2B 148
Courtney Ho. BD8: B'frd 2D 90
                                    (off Trenton Dr.)
Courts Leet BD12: Wyke 3C 132
Court Yard, The BD17: Bail 3D 52
                                    (off East Pde.)
Courtyard, The BD7: B'frd 3G 109
    LS10: Leeds 1B 118
    LS12: Leeds 2H 95
    WF17: Birs 5B 136
Courtyard M. BD20: Sils 5F 15
Courtyards, The LS14: Leeds 2D 80
Cousen Av. BD7: B'frd 6H 89
Cousen Pl. BD7: B'frd 1B 110
Cousen Rd. BD7: B'frd 1B 110
Cousin La. HX2: Illing 2C 128
Coutances Way LS29: I'ly 4H 11
Coventry St. BD4: B'frd 1H 111
    HX2: Hal 2C 148
Coverdale Cl. LS12: Leeds 1H 95
Coverdale Gth. LS22: Coll 3A 28
Coverdale Way BD17: Bail 3E 53
Cover Dr. BD6: B'frd 5A 110

Coverley Gth. LS19: Yead 6D 40
Coverley Ri. LS19: Yead 6D 40
Covet, The BD10: B'frd 1B 72
Cow & Calf Rocks 1G 19
Cow Cl. Cotts. BD12: Wyke 5F 133
Cow Cl. Gro. LS12: Leeds 1A 116
Cow Cl. La. BD12: Wyke 5E 133
Cow Cl. Rd. LS12: Leeds 1H 115
Cowdray Dr. BD19: Scho 1F 153
Cowgill St. BD8: B'frd 2C 90
Cow Grn. HX1: Hal 4B 164 (2G 149)
Cow Hill Ga. La. HX2: Ogd 5C 106
Cowhouse Bri. BD13: Cull 2B 66
Cow La. HX3: Hal 1G 159
    HX3: Sou 5F 151
Cowley Cres. BD9: B'frd 5E 69
Cowley Rd. LS13: Leeds 4B 74
Cowling La. HX3: North 1B 130
Cowpasture Rd. LS29: I'ly 5D 10
Cowper Av. LS9: Leeds 1E 99
Cowper Cres. LS9: Leeds 1E 99
Cowper Gro. LS8: Leeds 6E 79
Cowper Mt. LS9: Leeds 1E 99
Cowper Rd. LS9: Leeds 1E 99
Cowper St. LS7: Leeds 5B 78
Cowper Ter. LS9: Leeds 1E 99
Cowroyd Pl. HX3: Hal 1D 164 (6H 129)
Coxwall Hill LS22: Weth 2E 13
Coxwold Vw. LS22: Weth 2E 13
Coxwold Wlk. BD15: All 4C 88
Crab La. LS12: Leeds 3C 96
Crabtree Grn. LS22: Coll 3A 28
Crabtree Hill LS22: Coll 3B 28
Crabtree La. LS17: E Kes 5E 27
Crabtree Pl. BD7: B'frd 1B 110
Crabtree St. BD7: B'frd 1A 110
    HX1: Hal 2D 148
Crabtree Way WF3: W Ard 1F 155
Crack La. BD15: Wils 4G 67
Cracoe Rd. BD3: B'frd 5H 91
Crag Cl. HX2: Mix 3B 128
Crag Ct. HX2: Mix 3B 128
Cragg Av. LS18: H'fth 1D 74
Cragg Dr. LS29: I'ly 6H 11
Cragg Hill LS18: H'fth 1E 75
Cragg La. BD7: B'frd 2A 110
    BD13: Denh 6C 86
    BD13: Thorn 6D 86
Cragg Rd. LS18: H'fth 1E 75
Cragg St. BD7: B'frd 2A 110
Cragg Ter. BD7: B'frd 2A 110
    LS18: H'fth 1D 74
                                        (not continuous)
    LS19: Raw 5F 55
Cragg Top BD13: Denh 6C 86
Cragg Vw. BD20: Sils 1E 15
    LS21: Pool 6D 24
    LS29: Add 1D 8
                                    (off Bolton Rd.)
Craggwell Ter. LS18: H'fth 2E 75
                                    (off Wood La.)
Craggwood Cl. LS18: H'fth 2E 75
Cragg Wood Dr. LS19: Raw 5E 55
Craggwood Rd. LS18: H'fth 2E 75
Craggwood Ter. LS18: H'fth 2E 75
                                    (off Craggwood Rd.)
Crag Hill Av. LS16: Leeds 6G 43
Crag Hill Rd. BD10: B'frd 5G 53
Crag Hill Vw. LS16: Leeds 1G 57
Crag La. HX2: Mix 3B 128
    LS17: Leeds 2E 59
Crag Pl. BD21: Keigh 3A 48
Crag Rd. BD18: Ship 2C 70
Cragside BD10: B'frd 6F 53
Cragside Cl. LS5: Leeds 2G 75
Cragside Cres. LS5: Leeds 2G 75
Cragside Gdns. LS5: Leeds 2G 75
Cragside Gro. LS5: Leeds 3F 75
Cragside Mt. LS5: Leeds 2G 75
Cragside Pl. LS5: Leeds 2G 75
Cragside Wlk. LS5: Leeds 3F 75
Crag Vw. BD10: B'frd 3A 72
Craiglands HX3: Hip 1F 151

Craiglands Pk. LS29: I'ly 6E 11
Craiglands Rd. LS29: I'ly 6E 11
Craiglea Dr. BD12: Wyke 5D 132
Craigmore Ct. BD4: B'frd 3D 112
Craigmore Dr. LS29: I'ly 5G 11
Craig Vw. BD18: Ship 2F 69
Crake Dr. BD6: B'frd 4E 109
Cranbourne Rd. BD9: B'frd 1F 89
Cranbrook Av. BD6: B'frd 5C 110
LS11: Leeds 2G 117
Cranbrook Pl. BD5: B'frd 2E 111
Cranbrook St. BD5: B'frd 2E 111
BD14: Clay 1D 108
Cranbrook Vw. LS28: Pud 6C 94
Cranehouse Gdns. LS29: I'ly 6B 10
Cranford Pl. BD15: Wils 4G 67
Cranleigh Mt. BD21: Keigh 2G 47
Cranmer Bank LS17: Leeds 4G 59
Cranmer Cl. LS17: Leeds 4G 59
Cranmer Gdns. LS17: Leeds 4G 59
Cranmer Ri. LS17: Leeds 3G 59
Cranmer Rd. BD3: B'frd 2F 91
LS17: Leeds 4G 59
(not continuous)
Cranmore Cres. LS10: Leeds 2D 140
Cranmore Dr. LS10: Leeds 2D 140
Cranmore Gdns. LS10: Leeds 2C 140
Cranmore Gth. LS10: Leeds 2C 140
Cranmore Grn. LS10: Leeds 2C 140
Cranmore Gro. LS10: Leeds 2C 140
Cranmore La. LS10: Leeds 2D 140
Cranmore Ri. LS10: Leeds 2D 140
Cranmore Rd. LS10: Leeds 2C 140
Craven Av. BD13: Thorn 5A 88
BD20: Sils 2E 15
Craven Cl. BD19: Gom 6G 135
Craven Ct. BD8: B'frd 3H 89
(off Lane Ends Cl.)
BD20: Sils 2F 15
HX1: Hal 2E 149
LS11: Leeds 4E 117
Craven Cres. LS29: Add 1C 8
Craven Dr. BD19: Gom 6G 135
BD20: Sils 2E 15
Craven Edge HX1: Hal 3E 149
Craven Ent. Cen. HX1: Hal 3E 149
(off Hopwood La.)
Craven Gro. BD20: Sils 2F 15
Craven La. BD19: Gom 6G 135
Craven Mt. HX1: Hal 3E 149
(off Lister La.)
Craven Pk. LS29: Men 6F 21
Craven Pl. HX1: Hal 3E 149
(off Hopwood La.)
Craven Rd. BD21: Keigh 5C 34
LS6: Leeds 6H 77
Craven St. BD3: B'frd 2F 7 (3F 91)
LS21: Otley 4F 23
Craven Ter. BD2: B'frd 6A 72
HX1: Hal 3E 149
LS21: Otley 4F 23
(off Fairfax St.)
Crawford Av. BD6: B'frd 5C 110
Crawford Cl. BD6: B'frd 5C 110
Crawford St. BD4: B'frd 1G 111
Crawshaw Av. LS28: Pud 4B 94
Crawshaw Cl. LS28: Pud 4A 94
Crawshaw Gdns. LS28: Pud 4B 94
Crawshaw Hill LS28: Pud 4A 94
Crawshaw Pk. LS28: Pud 4A 94
Crawshaw Ri. LS28: Pud 5A 94
Crawshaw Rd. LS28: Pud 4A 94
Crediton Av. BD15: All 3D 88
Crediton Ct. BD15: All 3D 88
Crescent, The BD6: B'frd 5G 109
BD11: Birk 6E 113
BD16: Bgly 1A 50
BD17: Bail 5C 52

Crescent, The HD6: Brigh 6B 152
HX3: Hip 1F 151
HX3: Sou 3B 150
LS6: Leeds 6G 77
(off Woodhouse La.)
LS13: Leeds 6E 75
LS15: Leeds 3D 100
LS16: Leeds 3A 58
LS17: Leeds 1F 59
LS18: H'fth 6B 56
LS20: Guis 5A 40
LS21: Otley 1E 23
LS25: Gar 3G 103
LS25: Kip 4G 123
LS25: M'fld 5E 105
LS28: Pud 3B 94
LS29: Burl W 3E 21
LS29: I'ly 4G 11
LS29: Men 1H 39
WF3: Ting 1G 155
Crescent Av. LS26: Rothw 6B 120
Crescent Bungs.
WF3: Thpe H 5B 140
Crescent Ct. LS17: Leeds 1F 59
Crescent Gdns. LS17: Leeds 3B 60
Crescent Grange LS11: Leeds 1A 118
Crescent Ter. LS29: I'ly 5D 10
Crescent Towers
LS11: Leeds 1A 118
Crescent Vw. BD22: Keigh 4G 47
LS17: Leeds 1F 59
Crescent Wlk. BD14: Clay 6F 89
Creskeld Cres. LS16: B'hpe 2H 43
Creskeld Dr. LS16: B'hpe 1G 43
Creskeld Gdns. LS16: B'hpe 2G 43
Creskeld Gth. LS16: B'hpe 2H 43
Creskeld La.
LS16: Arth, B'hpe 1H 43
LS21: Arth 1H 43
Creskeld Pk. LS16: B'hpe 2H 43
Creskeld Vw. LS16: B'hpe 2G 43
Creskeld Way BD15: All 1C 88
Cressingham Vs. BD13: Cull 4B 66
(off Cullingworth La.)
Cresswell Mt. BD7: B'frd 3G 109
Cresswell Pl. BD7: B'frd 3G 109
Cresswell Ter. BD7: B'frd 3G 109
HX3: Hip 1G 151
Crest, The HD2: Hud 5E 163
Crest Av. BD12: Wyke 6C 132
Crestfield Av. HX5: Ell 5A 160
Crestfield Cres. HX5: Ell 6A 160
Crestfield Dr. HX2: Hal 4C 148
HX5: Ell 6A 160
Crestfield Rd. HX5: Ell 6A 160
Crest Pl. HD6: Brigh 4G 151
(off Halifax Rd.)
Crest Vw. HD6: Brigh 4G 151
Crestville Cl. BD14: Clay 6F 89
Crestville Rd. BD14: Clay 6E 89
Crestville Ter. BD14: Clay 6F 89
Crestwood Cl. BD5: B'frd 4H 111
Crib La. HX1: Hal 2B 164 (1G 149)
Cricketers, The LS5: Leeds 5B 76
Cricketers App. WF2: Wren 6C 156
Cricketers Cl. LS25: Gar 4G 103
Cricketers Fold HX3: Hal 1H 159
LS17: Shad 3A 62
Cricketers Grn. LS19: Yead 1G 55
Cricketers Ter. LS12: Leeds 4C 96
Cricketers Vw. LS17: Shad 3A 62
Cricketers Wlk. BD20: Stee 6D 14
LS15: Leeds 4G 101
Cricklegate LS15: Leeds 3D 100
Crimble Cl. HX3: Hip 2G 151
CRIMBLES 4B 94
Crimbles Ct. LS28: Pud 4B 94
Crimbles Pl. LS28: Pud 4B 94
Crimbles Rd. LS28: Pud 4B 94
Crimbles Ter. LS28: Pud 4B 94
Crimple Grn. LS25: Gar 5H 103

Crimshaw La. BD18: Ship 3D 70
Cripplegate HX1: Hal 2H 149
Cripple Syke LS18: H'fth 5E 57
Crispin Ho. LS22: Leeds 3G 5
Croft, The BD11: Drig 2A 136
BD12: O'haw 3F 133
BD17: Bail 4C 52
BD21: Keigh 6D 34
LS14: S'cft 5F 45
LS15: Leeds 2D 100
LS22: Coll 3A 28
LS26: Oul 2E 143
WF3: W Ard 4D 154
Croft Av. BD16: Bgly 1H 49
LS21: Otley 2D 22
LS28: Fars 6H 73
WF3: E Ard 2B 156
Croft Bank BD11: Birk 2E 135
Croft Bri. LS26: Oul 2E 143
Croft Cl. LS29: Men 1F 39
Croft Cotts. LS12: N Far 2G 115
Croft Ct. HD6: Ras 5G 161
LS18: H'fth 6E 57
LS29: Men 1G 39
Croftdale Gro. LS15: Leeds 1F 101
Croft Dr. LS29: Men 1G 39
Croft End LS22: Weth 4C 12
Crofters Grn. BD10: B'frd 1G 71
Crofters Lea LS19: Yead 1D 54
Croft Fld. BD20: Sils 3E 15
Croft Fold HX3: Hal 5D 128
Croft Foulds Ct. LS25: Gar 4F 103
Croft Head LS20: Guis 4C 40
Croft Ho. HX2: Lud 6D 126
HX5: Ell 4B 160
(off St Mary's Ga.)
Croft Ho. Av. LS27: Morl 2B 138
Croft Ho. Cl. BD6: B'frd 5B 110
LS27: Morl 1B 138
Croft Ho. Ct. LS28: Pud 3A 94
Croft Ho. Dr. LS21: Otley 2D 22
LS27: Morl 2B 138
Croft Ho. Fold LS29: Add 1E 9
Croft Ho. Gdns. LS27: Morl 2B 138
Croft Ho. Gro. LS27: Morl 2B 138
Croft Ho. La. BD20: Keigh 3G 33
LS27: Morl 2B 138
Croft Ho. M. LS27: Morl 2B 138
Croft Ho. Mt. LS27: Morl 1B 138
Croft Ho. Ri. LS27: Morl 1B 138
Croft Ho. Rd. BD6: B'frd 5B 110
LS27: Morl 2B 138
Croft Ho. Vw. LS27: Morl 2B 138
Croft Ho. Wlk. LS27: Morl 1B 138
Croft Ho. Way LS27: Morl 1B 138
Croftlands BD10: B'frd 1G 71
Croft La. LS24: N Kym 5H 31
Crofton Ct. BD9: B'frd 5H 69
(off Crofton Rd.)
Crofton Ri. LS17: Shad 3C 62
Crofton Rd. BD9: B'frd 6A 70
Crofton Ter. LS17: Shad 3C 62
Croft Pk. LS29: Men 1F 39
Croft Pl. BD6: B'frd 4H 109
BD22: Cros R 1F 65
HD6: Brigh 5B 152
Croft Ri. HX3: Hal 5D 128
LS29: Men 1G 39
Croft Rd. BD16: Bgly 1H 49
BD20: E Mor 4H 35
Croft Row BD13: Denh 5C 86
Croft's Ct. LS1: Leeds 4D 4 (3H 97)
Croftside Cl. LS14: Leeds 6D 62
Croft St. BD5: B'frd 6D 6 (5E 91)
(not continuous)
BD6: B'frd 4C 110
BD10: B'frd 1A 72
BD11: Birk 2E 135
(not continuous)
BD18: Ship 2B 70
BD20: Stee 6C 14
BD21: Keigh 1H 47

Croft St. BD22: Haw 2C 64
HD6: Brigh 1A 162
HX6: Sow B 5A 148
LS21: Otley 4F 23
LS28: Fars 6H 73
Croft Ter. BD22: Oak 5D 46
(off Dockroyd La.)
LS12: N Far 2G 115
Croft Way LS20: Men 1G 39
Croftway LS15: Bar E 2E 83
Cromack Vw. LS28: Pud 4G 93
Cromer Av. BD21: Keigh 2H 47
(off Foster Rd.)
Cromer Gro. BD21: Keigh 2H 47
Cromer Pl. LS2: Leeds 1G 97
(not continuous)
Cromer Rd. BD21: Keigh 2H 47
LS2: Leeds 1A 4 (1G 97)
Cromer St. BD21: Keigh 2H 47
HX1: Hal 4D 148
LS2: Leeds 1A 4 (1G 97)
Cromer Ter. LS2: Leeds 1A 4 (2G 97)
Crompton Dr. LS27: Morl 1H 137
Cromwell Bottom Dr.
HD6: Brigh 2E 161
Cromwell Bottom Nature Reserve
. . . . .2F 161
Cromwell Cl. HX3: Sou 5C 150
Cromwell Ct. BD9: B'frd 4E 69
BD11: Drig 2H 123
Cromwell Hgts. LS9: Leeds 2C 98
(off Thealby Lawn)
Cromwell M. LS9: Leeds 2C 98
Cromwell Mt. LS9: Leeds 2C 98
LS10: Leeds 5B 118
Cromwell Ri. LS25: Kip 5G 123
Cromwell Rd. HX3: Sou 5C 150
Cromwells Mt. HX2: Hal 2H 147
Cromwell St. LS9: Leeds . .3H 5 (3C 98)
Cromwell Ter. HX1: Hal 2F 149
(not continuous)
Cromwell Vw. HX3: Sou 5D 150
Cromwell Wood La. HD6: Brigh . . .1F 161
Crooked La. BD10: B'frd 6F 53
HX3: Hal 1F 129
Crooke La. BD15: Wils 5G 67
Crook Farm Caravan Pk.
BD17: Bail 4H 51
Crooklands LS20: Guis 4C 40
(off Kelcliffe La.)
Cropper Fold BD16: Bgly 1F 51
Cropper Ga. LS1: Leeds 4A 4 (3G 97)
Cropredy Cl. BD13: Que 4B 108
Crosby Av. LS11: Leeds 1F 117
Crosby Pl. LS11: Leeds 6G 97
Crosby Rd. LS11: Leeds 1F 117
Crosby St. BD21: Keigh 5H 33
LS11: Leeds 6F 97
Crosby Ter. LS11: Leeds 6G 97
Crosby Vw. LS11: Leeds 6G 97
Croscombe Wlk. BD5: B'frd . . .6C 6 (6E 91)
Crosley Ho. BD16: Bgly 5C 50
Crosley Vw. BD16: Bgly 5D 50
Crosley Wood Rd. BD16: Bgly 5D 50
Cross, The LS15: Bar E 2D 82
LS16: B'hpe 2F 49
Cross Albert Pl. LS12: Leeds 5D 96
Cross Arc. LS1: Leeds 4F 5
Cross Aston Gro. LS13: Leeds 1G 95
Cross Av. LS26: Rothw 6B 120
Cross Aysgarth Mt. LS9: Leeds 3D 98
Crossbank Rd. LS29: Add 1A 8
Cross Bath Rd. LS13: Leeds 1E 95
Crossbeck Cl. LS29: I'ly 6D 10
Crossbeck Rd. LS29: I'ly 6D 10
Cross Belgrave St.
LS2: Leeds 3F 5 (3A 98)
Cross Bellbrooke Av. LS9: Leeds 1F 99
(off Bellbrooke Av.)
Cross Bell St. LS9: Leeds 3H 5
Cross Bentley La. LS6: Leeds 3F 77

Cross Burley Lodge Rd.
LS6: Leeds 1E 97
(off Broadway Av.)
Cross Cardigan Ter. LS4: Leeds 2C 96
Cross Catherine St. LS9: Leeds 4C 98
Cross Chancellor St. LS6: Leeds . . .6H 77
Cross Chapel St. LS6: Leeds 4D 76
Cross Chestnut Gro. LS6: Leeds 6E 77
(off Chestnut Gro.)
Cross Cliff Rd. LS6: Leeds 5F 77
Cross Conway Mt. LS8: Leeds 6D 78
Cross Cowper St. LS7: Leeds 6B 78
Crossdale Av. BD6: B'frd 5G 109
Cross Easy Rd. LS9: Leeds 5D 98
Cross Elford St. LS8: Leeds 6D 78
(off Elford Gro.)
Cross Emily St. BD21: Keigh 5A 34
Cross End Fold LS29: Add 1E 9
Cross Farm Ct. BD22: Oxen 6C 64
Crossfield Cl. BD22: Oxen 6B 64
Crossfield Rd. BD22: Oxen 6B 64
Crossfields Cl. HX4: Gree 4F 159
Crossfield St. LS2: Leeds 6G 77
CROSSFLATTS 1A 50
Cross Flatts Av. LS11: Leeds 3G 117
Cross Flatts Cres. LS11: Leeds 3F 117
Cross Flatts Dr. LS11: Leeds 2F 117
Cross Flatts Gro. LS11: Leeds 3F 117
Cross Flatts Mt. LS11: Leeds 3G 117
Cross Flatts Pde. LS11: Leeds 3F 117
Cross Flatts Pl. LS11: Leeds 3F 117
Cross Flatts Rd. LS11: Leeds 3F 117
Cross Flatts Row LS11: Leeds 3F 117
Crossflatts Station (Rail) 2A 50
Cross Flatts St. LS11: Leeds 3F 117
Cross Flatts Ter. LS11: Leeds 3F 117
Cross Francis St. LS7: Leeds 6B 78
Crossgate LS21: Otley 4E 23
CROSS GATES 1E 101
Cross Gates Av. LS15: Leeds 6E 81
LS15: Leeds 6D 80
Cross Gates La. BD16: Har 3G 49
Cross Gates Rd. LS15: Leeds 1C 100
(not continuous)
Crossgates Shop. Cen.
LS15: Leeds 1E 101
Cross Gates Station (Rail) 2E 101
Cross Glen Rd. LS16: Leeds 2C 76
Cross Granby Ter. LS6: Leeds 4D 76
Cross Grange Av. LS7: Leeds 6C 78
Cross Grasmere St. LS12: Leeds . . .4D 96
CROSS GREEN 6E 99
Cross Grn. BD4: B'frd 1C 112
LS21: Otley 3F 23
Cross Grn. App. LS9: Leeds 6E 99
Cross Grn. Av. LS9: Leeds 5D 98
Cross Grn. Cl. LS9: Leeds 6E 99
Cross Grn. Ct. LS9: Leeds 6F 99
Cross Grn. Cres. LS9: Leeds 5D 98
Cross Grn. Dr. LS9: Leeds 6E 99
Cross Grn. Gth. LS9: Leeds 6E 99
Cross Grn. Gro. LS9: Leeds 5D 98
Cross Grn. Ind. Est. LS9: Leeds 6F 99
Cross Grn. Ind. Pk. LS9: Leeds 5G 99
Cross Grn. La. LS9: Leeds 5C 98
LS15: Leeds 3C 100
Cross Grn. Ri. LS9: Leeds 6E 99
Cross Grn. Rd. LS9: Leeds 5D 98
Cross Grn. Row LS6: Leeds 2E 77
Cross Grn. Va. LS9: Leeds 1E 119
Cross Grn. Way LS9: Leeds 6E 99
Cross Greenwood Mt. LS6: Leeds . . .2E 77
Cross Hartley Av. LS6: Leeds 5G 77
(off Lucas Pl.)
Cross Heath Gro. LS11: Leeds 2E 117
Cross Henley Rd. LS13: Leeds 1E 95
CROSS HILL 4G 159
Cross Hill HX4: Gree 4G 159
LS11: Leeds 4E 117
Cross Hill La. WF15: Liv 2H 163
Cross Hills HX1: Hal 2C 164 (1G 149)
LS25: Kip 4G 123

Cross Hills Ct. LS25: Kip 4G 123
Cross Hills Dr. LS25: Kip 4G 123
Cross Hills Gdns. LS25: Kip 4G 123
Crosshills HX3: She 4G 159
Cross Hilton Gro. LS8: Leeds 5D 78
Cross Ho. Ct. BD12: O'haw 3G 133
Cross Ingledew Cres.
LS8: Leeds 5F 61
Cross Ingram Rd. LS11: Leeds 6F 97
Crossings, The WF17: Bat 6B 136
Cross Kelso Rd.
LS2: Leeds 1A 4 (2F 97)
Crossland Ct. BD12: Wyke 3C 132
(off Carr Ho. La.)
LS11: Leeds 5G 97
Crossland Rd. LS27: Chur 6B 116
Crossland Ter. LS11: Leeds 2A 118
Cross La. BD7: B'frd 1B 110
(Cousen Rd.)
BD7: B'frd 2A 110
(Low Grange)
BD11: Birk 6F 113
BD13: Que 5G 107
BD15: Wils 3G 67
BD16: Bgly 3B 50
BD22: Oxen 6C 64
HD6: Clift 2E 163
HX3: She 1C 130
(Brighouse & Denholme Gate Rd.)
HX3: She 3D 130
(West St.)
HX5: Ell 5A 160
LS12: Leeds 4B 96
(Privilege St.)
LS12: Leeds 6G 95
(Stonebridge La.)
LS20: Guis 1D 40
Cross Lea Farm Rd. LS5: Leeds 2H 75
Cross Leeds St. BD21: Keigh 6H 33
Crossley Bri. BD22: Oxen 2D 84
Crossley Cl. HX1: Hal 2E 149
(off Crossley Gdns.)
Crossley Gdns. HX1: Hal 2E 149
(Bowman Ter.)
HX1: Hal 1E 149
(Halifax Ind. Cen.)
CROSSLEY HALL 4G 89
Crossley Hall M. BD8: B'frd 4G 89
Crossley Hall St. BD8: B'frd 4F 89
Crossley Hill HX3: Hal 6H 149
Crossley Hill La. HX3: Hal 6H 149
(off Westbourne Rd.)
Crossley Ho. HX1: Hal 3C 164
(off Town Hall St. E.)
Crossley Retail Pk. HX1: Hal 1F 149
Crossleys Bldgs. HX3: Hal 3A 150
Crossley St. BD7: B'frd 6B 90
BD13: Que 4B 108
HD6: Ras 2B 162
HX1: Hal 3B 164 (2G 149)
LS22: Weth 4E 13
Crossley Ter. Nth. HX3: Hal 3E 129
Crossley Ter. Sth. HX3: Hal 3E 129
Crossley Wing HX1: Hal 4F 149
(off Haworth Cl.)
Cross Lidgett Pl. LS8: Leeds 1D 78
Cross Lister St. BD21: Keigh 1G 47
(off Lister St.)
Cross Louis St. LS7: Leeds 6B 78
Cross Maude St. LS2: Leeds 5G 5
Cross Mitford Rd. LS12: Leeds 4D 96
Cross Moor Cl. BD20: Sils 2C 14
Cross Myrtle St. LS11: Leeds 6A 98
Cross Osmondthorpe La.
LS9: Leeds 3G 99
Cross Pk. St. LS15: Leeds 3C 100
Cross Peel St. LS27: Morl 3B 138
Cross Pl. HD6: Brigh 5B 152
(off Cross St.)
Cross Platts HX3: Sou 5E 151
Cross Quarry St. LS6: Leeds 5G 77
Cross Regent Pk. Av. LS6: Leeds . . .5F 77
(off Regent Pk. Av.)

Cross Reginald Mt. LS7: Leeds 5B 78
Cross River St. BD21: Keigh 4C 34
(off Dale St.)
Cross Rd. BD8: B'frd 2B 90
BD10: B'frd 1A 72
BD12: O'haw 2F 133
LS18: H'fth 1C 74
CROSS ROADS 1E 65
Cross Roads BD22: Cros R 1F 65
HX3: She 3D 130
Cross Roseville Rd. LS8: Leeds 6C 78
(off Bayswater Rd.)
Cross Rosse St. BD18: Ship 1B 70
Cross Roundhay Av.
LS8: Leeds 4D 78
Cross Row LS15: Swil C 5A 102
Cross Rydal St. BD21: Keigh 1G 47
Cross St Michaels La.
LS6: Leeds 5D 76
Cross Speedwell St. LS6: Leeds 6H 77
Cross Stamford St.
LS7: Leeds 1H 5 (2B 98)
Cross St. BD6: B'frd 6H 109
BD12: O'haw 3G 133
BD14: Clay 1E 109
HD6: Brigh 5A 152
HX1: Hal 5D 164 (3H 149)
(Blackledge)
HX1: Hal 3C 164 (2G 149)
(Winding Rd.)
HX4: Gree 4H 159
LS15: Leeds 3C 100
LS22: Weth 4E 13
LS26: Rothw 2A 142
WF3: E Ard 1C 156
Cross St. W. HX2: Hal 1C 148
Cross Sun St. BD1: B'frd 2E 7 (3F 91)
Cross Ter. LS26: Rothw 2A 142
Cross Valley Dr. LS15: Leeds 2D 100
Cross Vw. BD22: Oak 4D 46
Crossway BD16: Cot 2B 68
Crossways, The LS21: Otley 1E 23
Cross Wellington St. BD1: B'frd 3F 7
Cross Westfield Rd. LS3: Leeds 2F 97
(off Westfield Rd.)
Cross Wingham St. LS7: Leeds 1B 98
Cross Woodstock St. LS2: Leeds 1H 97
(off Blenheim Wlk.)
Cross Woodview St.
LS11: Leeds 3H 117
(off Woodview St.)
Cross York St. LS2: Leeds 5G 5 (4B 98)
Crowgill Rd. BD18: Ship 1B 70
Crow Hill Rd. HX7: Crag V 6A 146
Crowhurst Gdns. HD6: Brigh 3H 151
Crow La. LS21: Otley 4E 23
Crow La. M. LS21: Otley 4E 23
(off Crow La.)
Crown Ct. LS2: Leeds 5F 5 (4A 98)
Crown Dr. BD12: Wyke 3C 132
CROW NEST 4C 50
Crow Nest Cotts. HX3: Hip 2G 151
Crow Nest Dr. LS11: Leeds 3E 117
Crow Nest La. LS11: Leeds 3D 116
Crownest La. BD16: Bgly 3C 50
Crow Nest M. LS11: Leeds 3E 117
Crow Nest Park Golf Course 3H 151
Crownest Rd. BD16: Bgly 4C 50
CROWN POINT 6G 5 (4B 98)
Crown Point Retail Pk.
LS10: Leeds 5A 98
Crown Point Rd.
LS2: Leeds 6G 5 (4B 98)
LS9: Leeds 6G 5 (4B 98)
LS10: Leeds 6G 5 (5A 98)
Crown Rd. HX3: Hal 5F 129
Crown St. BD1: B'frd 4C 90
BD12: Wyke 3C 132
HD6: Brigh 6A 152
HX1: Hal 4B 164 (2G 149)
HX5: Ell 4B 160
LS2: Leeds 5F 5 (4A 98)
LS29: Burl W 2F 21

Crown St. Bldg. LS2: Leeds 5F 5
(off Crown St.)
Crowther Av. LS28: Stan 3D 72
Crowther Fold BD16: Har 6F 49
Crowther Pl. LS6: Leeds 6H 77
Crowthers St. BD12: Wyke 3C 132
Crowthers St. BD10: B'frd 2B 72
Crowthers Yd. LS28: Pud 5A 94
Crow Tree Cl. BD17: Bail 4D 52
Crow Tree La. BD8: B'frd 2G 89
Crowtrees Cl. LS19: Raw 3G 55
Crowtrees Cres. HD6: Ras 3H 161
Crowtrees La. HD6: Ras 4H 161
Crowtrees Pde. HD6: Ras 4H 161
(off Crowtrees La.)
Crow Trees Pk. LS19: Raw 3F 55
Crowtrees Pk. HD6: Ras 4H 161
Crow Wood Pk. HX2: Hal 4B 148
Croydon Rd. BD7: B'frd 1H 109
Croydon St. BD13: Que 4A 108
LS11: Leeds 5F 97
Crozier Ho. LS10: Leeds 5B 98
Crumack La. BD22: Oxen 6E 65
Crunwelle Ct. BD15: All 5C 68
Cryer Mdws. BD22: Haw 1D 64
Crystal Ct. HX1: Hal 2E 149
(off Lister's Ct.)
Crystal Ter. BD4: B'frd 2A 112
Cuckoo Nest BD7: B'frd 4C 90
BD16: Har 5G 49
Cuckoo Nest Ind. Est.
BD7: B'frd 4C 90
Cuckoo Pk. La. BD22: Oxen 5E 65
Cudbear St. LS10: Leeds 5B 98
CULLINGWORTH 3B 66
Cullingworth Flds. BD21: Keigh 2H 65
Cullingworth Ga. BD13: Cull 4B 66
Cullingworth Rd. BD13: Cull 4B 66
Culpans Rd. HX2: Lud M 5A 146
Culver Ct. HX1: Hal 3C 164 (2G 149)
Culvert BD12: Wyke 1B 152
Cumberland Av. HD2: Fix 6A 162
Cumberland Cl. HX2: Illing 3C 128
Cumberland Ct. HX2: Illing 4C 128
LS6: Leeds 6D 76
Cumberland Rd. BD7: B'frd 6A 90
LS6: Leeds 5F 77
Cunliffe La. BD17: Esh 2H 53
Cunliffe Rd. BD8: B'frd 1C 90
LS29: I'ly 5D 10
Cunliffe Ter. BD8: B'frd 1D 90
Cunliffe Vs. BD8: B'frd 6D 70
Cunningham Ct. WF3: Rob H 3E 141
Cupstone Cl. BD20: E Mor 4H 35
Cure Hill BD22: Oak 4B 46
Curlew Cl. LS29: I'ly 5A 10
Curlew Ct. BD20: Stee 5B 14
Curlew Ri. LS27: Morl 4D 138
Curlew St. BD5: B'frd 2C 110
Curly Hill LS29: I'ly 3C 10
Currer Av. BD4: B'frd 4H 111
Currerbell M. BD13: Thorn 5B 88
Currer St. BD1: B'frd 4E 7 (4F 91)
BD12: O'haw 3G 133
Currer Wlk. BD20: Stee 5B 14
Curtis Ct. BD13: Cull 3B 66
(off Halifax Rd.)
Curzon Rd. BD3: B'frd 4H 91
(not continuous)
Curzon St. HD2: Hud 5G 163
Cusworth Cl. HX1: Hal 1D 148
Cuthberts Cl. BD13: Que 5H 107
Cut La. HX3: North 2B 130
CUTLER HEIGHTS 2A 112
Cutler Hgts. La. BD4: B'frd 2A 112
Cutler La. LS26: Meth 4E 145
Cutler Pl. BD4: B'frd 1B 112
Cypress Cl. HX3: She 6G 109
Cypress Point LS7: Leeds 1G 5
Cypress Av. BD10: B'frd 6F 53
Cyprus Dr. BD10: B'frd 6G 53
Cyprus Gro. LS25: Gar 4E 103
Cyprus Rd. LS25: Gar 4E 103

Cyprus Ter. LS25: Gar 4E 103
Czar St. LS11: Leeds 6G 97

D

Dacre St. BD3: B'frd 1G 7 (3F 91)
Daffels Wood Cl. BD4: B'frd 5H 111
Daffil Av. LS27: Chur 6B 116
Daffil Grange M. LS27: Morl 6B 116
Daffil Grange Way LS27: Morl 6B 116
Daffil Gro. LS27: Chur 6B 116
Daffil Rd. LS27: Chur 6B 116
Daffodil Ct. BD15: All 3D 88
Daily Ct. BD5: B'frd 2B 110
Daisy Bank HX1: Hal 4F 149
HX3: Nor G 5A 132
Daisy Cl. WF17: Birs 5A 136
Daisy Cft. BD20: Sils 2F 15
Daisyfield Grange LS13: Leeds 2F 95
(off Rossefield App.)
Daisyfield Rd. LS13: Leeds 1F 95
DAISY HILL
BD9 . . . . .1G 89
LS27 .2C 138
Daisy Hill BD12: Wyke 4C 132
BD20: Sils 2F 15
LS27: Morl 2C 138
Daisy Hill Av. LS27: Morl 1C 138
Daisy Hill Bk. La. BD9: B'frd 1G 89
LS27: Morl 1B 138
Daisy Hill Cl. HX2: Lud M 2D 146
LS27: Morl 1B 138
Daisy Hill Gro. BD9: B'frd 1G 89
Daisy Hill La. BD9: B'frd 1G 89
Daisy La. WF3: E Ard 1D 156
Daisy Lea HX6: Sow B 5F 147
Daisy Mt. HX6: Sow B 4G 147
Daisy Pl. BD18: Ship 1H 69
(off Saltaire Rd.)
Daisy Rd. HD6: Ras 2B 162
Daisy Row LS13: Leeds 2F 95
Daisy St. BD7: B'frd 2A 110
BD22: Haw 1E 65
HD6: Brigh 1A 162
HX1: Hal 5A 164 (3F 149)
Daisy Va. M. WF3: Thpe H 6C 140
Daisy Va. Ter. WF3: Thpe H 6C 140
Dalby Av. BD3: B'frd 2A 92
Dalby St. BD3: B'frd 3A 92
Dalby Way LS10: Leeds 3C 140
Dalcross Gro. BD5: B'frd 1F 111
Dalcross St. BD5: B'frd 1E 111
Dale Cl. LS20: Guis 5H 39
Dale Cres. BD20: Stee 6C 14
Dale Cft. LS25: Gar 3E 103
LS29: I'ly 5A 10
Dale Cft. Ri. BD15: All 1B 88
Dale Gth. BD17: Bail 4B 52
Dale Gro. BD10: B'frd 6E 53
Dale Pk. Av. LS16: Leeds 3F 57
Dale Pk. Cl. LS16: Leeds 3F 57
Dale Pk. Gdns. LS16: Leeds 3F 57
Dale Pk. Ri. LS16: Leeds 3F 57
Dale Pk. Vw. LS16: Leeds 3F 57
Dale Pk. Wlk. LS16: Leeds 3F 57
Dale Rd. BD11: Drig 4C 114
Dales Dr. LS20: Guis 5H 39
Daleside Av. LS28: Pud 3E 93
Daleside Cl. LS28: Pud 2D 92
Daleside Gro. BD12: O'haw 3F 133
LS28: Pud 3E 93
Dale Side Ho. BD8: B'frd 1D 90
Daleside Rd. BD18: Ship 6E 53
BD20: Rid 4E 35
LS28: Pud 2D 92
Daleside Wlk. BD5: B'frd 3F 111
Daleson Cl. HX3: North 4C 130
Dale St. BD1: B'frd 3D 6 (4E 91)
BD18: Ship 2B 70
BD21: Keigh 4C 34
HX6: Sow B 5H 147
Dale St. Nth. HX3: Hal 6H 129

Dales Way—Delph Hill

Dales Way LS20: Guis 5H **39**
Dalesway BD16: Bgly 2D **50**
Dale Ter. *HX6: Sow B 5H 147*
(off Greenups Ter.)
Dale Vw. BD11: Drig 1B **136**
BD20: Sils 1E **15**
BD20: Stee 6C **14**
HX2: Lud M 2D **146**
LS29: I'ly 5A **10**
Dale Vw. Cl. BD21: Keigh 1C **48**
Daleview Ct. BD17: Bail 5A **52**
Dale Vw. Gro. BD21: Keigh 1C **48**
Dale Vw. Rd. BD21: Keigh 2C **48**
Dale Vw. Way BD21: Keigh 1C **48**
Dale Vs. LS18: H'fth 2F **75**
Dallam Av. BD18: Ship 1G **69**
Dallam Gro. BD18: Ship 6G **51**
Dallam Rd. BD18: Ship 1G **69**
Dallam Wlk. BD18: Ship 1H **69**
Dalton Av. LS11: Leeds 3G **117**
Dalton Bank Rd. HD5: Hud 6H **163**
Dalton Gro. LS11: Leeds 3G **117**
Dalton La. BD21: Keigh 6B **34**
LS23: B'ham 6E **29**
Dalton Mills Bus. Complex
BD21: Keigh 6B **34**
Dalton Rd. BD21: Keigh 6C **34**
LS11: Leeds 3G **117**
Dalton St. HX6: Sow B 4H **147**
Dalton Ter. BD8: B'frd 3B **90**
BD21: Keigh 5C 34
(off Sussex St.)
Damask St. HX1: Hal 2A **164** (1F **149**)
Damems BD22: Keigh 5F **47**
Damems La. BD22: Keigh 5F **47**
Damems Rd. BD21: Keigh 5G **47**
Damems Station
Keighley & Worth Valley Railway
. . . . 5G 47
DAM HEAD **4A 130**
Dam Head Rd. HX6: Sow B 4A **148**
Dam La. LS19: Yead 6G **41**
Damon Av. BD10: B'frd 5C **72**
Damside BD21: Keigh 1H **47**
Damson Cl. HX6: Sow B 6H **147**
Damson Ct. BD14: Clay 2E **109**
Damson Pl. HX1: Hal 3D **148**
Danby Av. BD4: B'frd 5H **111**
Danby Ct. WF3: Rob H 3E **141**
Danby Wlk. LS9: Leeds 4D **98**
Dancroft BD22: Haw 3C **64**
Danebury Rd. HD6: Ras 2B **162**
Danecourt Rd. BD4: B'frd 2C **112**
Danefield Ter. LS21: Otley 3F **23**
Dane Hill Dr. BD4: B'frd 1C **112**
Danella Cres. WF2: Wren 6D **156**
Daniel Cl. BD21: Keigh 4G **47**
Daniel Ct. BD4: B'frd 3D **112**
Daniel St. BD3: B'frd 4B **92**
Dan La. BD6: B'frd 4E **109**
(not continuous)
Danny La. HX2: Lud M 2D **146**
Dansk Way LS29: I'ly 4F **11**
Danum Dr. BD17: Bail 5C **52**
Danum Ter. HX3: North 4C **130**
Darcey Hey La. HX2: Hal 4C **148**
Darcy Ct. LS15: Leeds 3E **101**
Darfield Av. LS8: Leeds 6E **79**
Darfield Cres. LS8: Leeds 6E **79**
Darfield Gro. LS8: Leeds 6D **78**
Darfield Pl. LS8: Leeds 6E **79**
Darfield Rd. LS8: Leeds 6E **79**
Darfield St. BD1: B'frd 2B **6** (3D **90**)
LS8: Leeds 6E **79**
Darfield Vs. *LS8: Leeds 1E 99*
(off Darfield Cres.)
Dark La. BD22: Oxen 6C **64**
HX2: Hal 3H **147**
HX3: Hip 2C **150**
HX3: Sou 5D **150**
HX7: Myth 5A **126**
LS15: Bar E 1D **82**
WF17: Birs 4B **136**
Dark Neville St. LS1: Leeds 6D **4**
Darkwood Cl. LS17: Leeds 3E **61**
Darkwood Way LS17: Leeds 3E **61**
Darley Av. LS10: Leeds 6B **118**
Darley Mall BD1: B'frd 4D **6**
Darley St. BD1: B'frd 3C **6** (4E **91**)
(not continuous)
BD20: Keigh 4H **33**
Darnay La. BD5: B'frd 2E **111**
Darnes Av. HX2: Hal 4C **148**
Darnley La. LS15: Leeds 5E **101**
Darnley Rd. LS16: Leeds 2B **76**
Darren St. BD4: B'frd 5C **92**
Dartmouth Av. LS27: Morl 5A **138**
Dartmouth M. LS27: Morl 4H **137**
Dartmouth Ter. BD8: B'frd 1C **90**
Dartmouth Way LS11: Leeds 3A **118**
Darwin St. BD5: B'frd 2C **110**
David Lloyd Leisure
Leeds **5H 59**
David St. LS11: Leeds 5H **97**
Davies Av. LS8: Leeds 1D **78**
Davy Rd. WF10: All B 3H **145**
Dawlish Av. LS9: Leeds 3F **99**
Dawlish Cres. LS9: Leeds 3F **99**
Dawlish Gro. LS9: Leeds 4F **99**
Dawlish Mt. LS9: Leeds 3F **99**
Dawlish Pl. LS9: Leeds 3F **99**
Dawlish Rd. LS9: Leeds 3F **99**
Dawlish Row LS9: Leeds 3F **99**
Dawlish St. LS9: Leeds 3F **99**
Dawlish Ter. LS9: Leeds 3F **99**
Dawlish Wlk. LS9: Leeds 3F **99**
Dawnay Rd. BD5: B'frd 2B **110**
Dawslack *BD20: Keigh 2G 33*
(off Parker's La.)
Dawson Av. BD6: B'frd 5C **110**
Dawson Hill LS27: Morl 2A **138**
Dawson La. BD4: B'frd 4A **112**
(Dawson Mt.)
BD4: B'frd 3A **114**
(Keeper La.)
LS26: Rothw 1A **142**
Dawson Mt. BD4: B'frd 4A **112**
Dawson Pl. BD4: B'frd 4B **112**
BD21: Keigh 2A **48**
Dawson Rd. BD21: Keigh 2A **48**
LS11: Leeds 2G **117**
Dawsons Cnr. LS28: Stan 1G **93**
Dawsons Ct. LS14: Leeds 5D **80**
Dawsons Mdw. LS28: Stan 1G **93**
Dawsons Ter. LS28: Stan 1G **93**
Dawson St. BD4: B'frd 3A **112**
BD10: B'frd 5H **53**
LS28: Stan 2H **93**
WF3: Ting 6D **138**
Dawsons Yd. LS21: Otley 4D **22**
Dawson Ter. BD4: B'frd 4B **112**
Dawson Way BD21: Keigh 2A **48**
Deacon Cl. BD2: B'frd 1B **92**
Deaconess Ct. LS29: I'ly 6D **10**
Dealburn Rd. BD12: Low M 2E **133**
Deal St. BD21: Keigh 5C **34**
HX1: Hal 5D **164** (3H **149**)
Dean Av. LS8: Leeds 3E **79**
Dean Beck Av. BD6: B'frd 4E **111**
Dean Beck Ct. BD6: B'frd 4F **111**
Dean Cl. BD8: B'frd 2F **89**
WF2: Wren 6D **156**
Dean Clough . . . . **1B 164 (1G 149)**
Dean Clough HX3: Hal 2B **164** (1G **149**)
Dean Clough Galleries *1B 164*
(in Dean Clough)
Dean Clough Office Pk.
HX3: Hal 1A **164** (1F **149**)
Dean Ct. HX3: Hal 1E **159**
LS8: Leeds 3E **79**
Dean End HX4: Gree 3G **159**
Deanery Gdns. BD10: B'frd 4A **72**
Deanfield Av. LS27: Morl 1H **137**
Dean Hall Cl. LS27: Morl 3H **137**
Dean Head LS18: H'fth 5C **42**
Dean Ho. La. HX2: Lud 5D **126**
Deanhurst Gdns. LS27: Gil 1F **137**
Deanhurst Ind. Cen.
LS27: Gil 1F **137**
Dean La. BD13: Thorn 2G **87**
BD22: Oak 1A **46**
HX6: Sow B 6E **147**
LS18: H'fth, Yead 5C **42**
LS20: Hawk 5F **39**
Dean La. Head BD13: Thorn 2G **87**
Dean M. LS18: H'fth 5D **42**
Dean Pk. Av. BD11: Drig 6A **114**
Dean Pk. Dr. BD11: Drig 6A **114**
Dean Pastures BD11: Drig 1A **136**
Dean Rd. BD6: B'frd 5D **110**
Deans Laithe BD21: Keigh 6B **34**
Dean's Ter. HX3: Hal 4F **129**
Deanstones Cres.
BD13: Que 5A **108**
Deanstones La. BD13: Que 5H **107**
Dean St. BD22: Haw 2D **64**
HX4: Gree 5G **159**
HX5: Ell 5B **160**
LS29: I'ly 4E **11**
Deansway LS27: Morl 1H **137**
Deanswood Cl. LS17: Leeds 4G **59**
Deanswood Dr. LS17: Leeds 4F **59**
Deanswood Gdns. LS17: Leeds 4F **59**
Deanswood Gth. LS17: Leeds 4G **59**
Deanswood Grn. LS17: Leeds 4F **59**
Deanswood Hill LS17: Leeds 4F **59**
Deanswood Pl. LS17: Leeds 4G **59**
Deanswood Ri. LS17: Leeds 4G **59**
Deanswood Vw. LS17: Leeds 4G **59**
Dean Vw. WF17: Birs 5B **136**
Deanwood Av. BD15: All 1C **88**
Deanwood Cres. BD15: All 6C **68**
Dean Wood Vw. HX3: Hal 1G **159**
Deanwood Wlk. BD15: All 1C **88**
Dearden St. HX6: Sow B 4H **147**
Dearne Cft. LS22: Weth 1E **13**
Dee Ct. BD22: Oak 5C **46**
Deep Dale LS23: B Spa 2A **30**
Deepdale Cl. BD17: Bail 5A **52**
Deepdale La. LS23: B Spa 2H **29**
Deep La. BD13: Thorn 1E **107**
BD14: Clay 6E **89**
HD6: Clift 1E **163**
HX2: Lud M 2F **147**
Deerstone Ridge LS22: Weth 1E **13**
Defarge Ct. BD5: B'frd 2E **111**
Deighton Cl. LS22: Weth 3F **13**
DEIGHTON GATES **1E 13**
Deighton Rd. LS22: Weth 1E **13**
Deighton Vw. LS6: Leeds 6E **59**
De Lacies Ct. LS26: Wood 6C **120**
De Lacies Rd. LS26: Wood 6C **120**
De Lacy Av. BD4: B'frd 5H **111**
De Lacy Mt. LS5: Leeds 5A **76**
Delamere St. BD5: B'frd 3D **110**
Delauney Cl. BD6: B'frd 5H **109**
Delaware Ct. BD4: B'frd 5H **111**
Delf Cl. HX3: She 6G **109**
Delf Hill HD6: Ras 4G **161**
Delf Pl. HD6: Ras 4G **161**
Delius Av. BD10: B'frd 4C **72**
Dell, The BD13: Cull 3B **66**
LS17: Bard 2F **45**
Dell Cft. BD20: Sils 2C **14**
Dellside Fold BD13: Cull 3B **66**
Dellside Gdns. BD13: Cull 3B **66**
Delph Brow HX3: Hal 5D **148**
Delph Cotts. HX4: Bark 4B **158**
Delph Ct. LS6: Leeds 5G **77**
Delph Cres. BD14: Clay 1D **108**
Delph Cft. Vw.
BD21: Keigh 1B **48**
Delph Dr. BD14: Clay 1D **108**
DELPH END **4G 93**
Delph End LS28: Pud 4F **93**
Delph Gro. BD14: Clay 1D **108**
DELPH HILL
BD12 . . . . **2C 132**
HX3 . . . . **5E 149**

Delph Hill BD17: Bail 3C **52**
HX2: Hal 5E **149**
LS28: Pud 3A **94**
(off Clifton Hill)
Delph Hill Fold HX2: Hal 5D **148**
Delph Hill La. HX2: Lud 5D **126**
Delph Hill Rd. HX2: Hal 5D **148**
Delph Hill Ter. HX2: Hal 5D **148**
(off Delph Hill Rd.)
Delph Ho. BD21: Keigh 2A **48**
Delph La. LS6: Leeds 5G **77**
Delph Mt. LS6: Leeds 5G **77**
Delph St. HX1: Hal 5A **164** (3F **149**)
Delph Ter. BD14: Clay 1D **108**
HX4: Bark 4B **158**
(off Barsey Grn. La.)
Delph Vw. LS6: Leeds 5G **77**
Delph Wood Cl. BD16: Bgly 4E **51**
Delver Fold BD2: B'frd 1H **91**
(off Idle Rd.)
Delverne Gro. BD2: B'frd 6A **72**
Denbigh App. LS9: Leeds 1H **99**
Denbigh Cft. LS9: Leeds 1H **99**
Denbigh Hgts. LS9: Leeds 1H **99**
Denbrook Av. BD4: B'frd 4D **112**
Denbrook Cl. BD4: B'frd 4D **112**
Denbrook Cres. BD4: B'frd 5D **112**
Denbrook Wlk. BD4: B'frd 4D **112**
Denbrook Way BD4: B'frd 4D **112**
Denbury Mt. BD4: B'frd 3C **112**
Denby Cl. WF17: Birs 6H **135**
Denby Ct. BD22: Oak 5B **46**
Denby Dr. BD17: Bail 6B **52**
DENBY HILL .5A **46**
Denby Hill Rd. BD22: Oak 5B **46**
Denby Ho. BD4: B'frd 4D **112**
BD17: Bail 6C **52**
(off Denby Dr.)
Denby La. BD15: All 2D **88**
Denby Mt. BD22: Oak 5B **46**
BD22: Oxen 1C **84**
Denby Pl. HX6: Sow B 4H **147**
Denby Rd. BD21: Keigh 2A **48**
Denby St. BD8: B'frd 3C **90**
Dence Grn. BD4: B'frd 6C **92**
Dence Pl. LS15: Leeds 3A **100**
Dendrum Cl. BD22: Oak 4C **46**
Dene Bank BD16: Bgly 1C **50**
Dene Cl. HX5: Ell 6A **160**
Dene Cres. BD7: B'frd 1G **109**
Dene Gro. BD20: Sils 1E **15**
Dene Hill BD17: Bail 4H **51**
Denehill BD9: B'frd 1F **89**
Dene Ho. Ct. LS2: Leeds 1H **97**
Dene Mt. BD15: All 2E **89**
Dene Pl. HX1: Hal 2A **164** (1F **149**)
Dene Rd. BD6: B'frd 4F **109**
Deneside Mt. BD5: B'frd 3D **110**
Deneside Ter. BD5: B'frd 3D **110**
Denesway LS25: Gar 6G **103**
Dene Vw. HX2: Lud M 1D **146**
Deneway LS28: Stan 1G **93**
Denfield Av. HX3: Hal 5C **128**
Denfield Cres. HX3: Hal 5D **128**
Denfield Edge HX3: Hal 5D **128**
Denfield Gdns. HX3: Hal 5D **128**
Denfield La. HX3: Hal 5C **128**
Denfield Sq. HX3: Hal 5D **128**
Denham Av. LS27: Morl 5A **138**
Denham St. HD6: Ras 2A **162**
DENHOLME 2C **86**
DENHOLME CLOUGH 5C **86**
DENHOLME GATE 6B **86**
Denholme Ga. BD13: Denh 4C **86**
Denholme Ga. Rd.
HX3: Hip, North 5E **131**
Denholme Ho. Farm Dr.
BD13: Denh 4C **86**
Denholme Rd. BD22: Oxen 1D **84**
Denison Hall LS3: Leeds 2A 4 (2G **97**)
Denison Rd. LS3: Leeds 3A 4 (3G **97**)
Denison St. LS19: Yead 6F **41**
Dennil Cres. LS15: Leeds 5F **81**

Dennil Rd. LS15: Leeds 6F **81**
Dennis Bellamy Hall
BD5: B'frd 6C **90**
Dennison Fold BD4: B'frd 6C **92**
Dennison Hill LS21: Otley 3F **23**
Dennistead Cres.
LS6: Leeds 4D **76**
Denshaw Dr. LS27: Morl 3C **138**
Denshaw Gro. LS27: Morl 3C **138**
Denshaw La. WF3: Ting 4F **139**
DENTON 2H **11**
Denton Av. LS8: Leeds 1D **78**
Denton Dr. BD16: Bgly 3E **51**
Denton Gro. LS8: Leeds 1D **78**
Denton Ho. LS14: Leeds 3A **80**
(off Kingsdale Ct.)
Denton Rd. LS29: Den 1H **11**
LS29: I'ly 5G **11**
(Margerison Rd.)
LS29: I'ly 4C **10**
(Olicana Pk.)
Denton Row BD13: Denh 3B **86**
LS12: Leeds 5A **96**
Denton Ter. LS27: Morl 5A **138**
Dent St. LS9: Leeds 4D **98**
Derald Ho. HX1: Hal 5A **164**
(off Kings Cross St.)
Derby Pl. BD3: B'frd 4B **92**
LS19: Raw 3F **55**
(off North St.)
Derby Rd. BD3: B'frd 4C **92**
LS19: Raw 3F **55**
Derbyshire St. LS10: Leeds 2D **118**
Derby St. BD7: B'frd 1B **110**
BD13: Que 4H **107**
BD14: Clay 1D **108**
HX6: Sow B 4B **148**
Derby Ter. BD10: B'frd 1C **72**
Derry Hill LS29: Men 2F **39**
Derry Hill Gdns. LS29: Men 1F **39**
Derry La. LS29: Men 1F **39**
Derwent Av. BD15: Wils 5G **67**
BD17: Bail 6G **51**
(not continuous)
LS25: Gar 5F **103**
LS26: Wood 1E **143**
Derwent Cl. BD20: Sils 3E **15**
Derwent Dr. LS16: Leeds 3D **58**
Derwent Ho. HX3: Hal 6E **129**
Derwent Pl. BD13: Que 3G **107**
LS11: Leeds 5G **97**
Derwent Ri. LS22: Weth 1D **12**
Derwent Rd. BD2: B'frd 6G **71**
BD21: Keigh 5D **34**
Derwentwater Gro.
LS6: Leeds 4D **76**
Derwentwater Ter. LS6: Leeds 4D **76**
Detroit Av. LS15: Leeds 3F **101**
Detroit Dr. LS15: Leeds 3G **101**
Devon Cl. LS2: Leeds 1H **97**
Devon Rd. LS2: Leeds 1H **97**
Devonshire Av. LS8: Leeds 6E **61**
Devonshire Cl. LS8: Leeds 5E **61**
(not continuous)
Devonshire Cres. LS8: Leeds 6E **61**
Devonshire Gdns. LS2: Leeds 6H **77**
Devonshire La. LS8: Leeds 5E **61**
Devonshire Pl. LS19: Yead 6F **41**
Devonshire St. BD21: Keigh 6G **33**
Devonshire St. W.
BD21: Keigh 6G **33**
Devonshire Ter. BD9: B'frd 1C **90**
Devon St. HX1: Hal 3D **148**
Devon Way HD6: B Bri 3B **152**
Devro Ct. LS9: Leeds 1F **119**
Dewar Cl. LS22: Coll 2B **28**
Dewberry Cl. BD7: B'frd 2G **109**
Dewfield Cl. BD4: B'frd 4A **112**
Dewhirst Pl. BD4: B'frd 6B **92**
Dewhirst Rd. BD17: Bail 5D **52**
HD6: Brigh 5A **152**
Dewhurst St. BD15: Wils 4G **67**

Dewsbury Rd. BD19: Gom 4F **135**
HD6: Ras 5C **160**
HX5: Ell 5C **160**
LS11: Leeds 5A **98**
(Meadow La.)
LS11: Leeds 6F **117**
(Park Wood Cl.)
LS27: Leeds, Morl 5E **139**
WF3: Ting 1D **154**
(not continuous)
WF12: Dew, E Ard 3B **154**
WF17: Birs 4F **135**
Diadem Dr. LS14: Leeds 2A **100**
Dial St. LS9: Leeds 5D **98**
Diamond St. BD22: Keigh 3G **47**
HX1: Hal 1E **149**
Diamond Ter. HX1: Hal 1E **149**
HX2: Hal 1E **149**
Dibb La. LS19: Yead 6D **40**
Dib Cl. LS8: Leeds 4H **79**
Dib La. LS8: Leeds 4H **79**
Dickens St. BD5: B'frd 2E **111**
HX2: Hal 2C **148**
Dickinson St. LS18: H'fth 5E **57**
Dick La. BD3: B'frd 4C **92**
BD4: B'frd 1B **112**
Dick's Gth. Rd. LS29: Men 1F **39**
Digby Rd. LS29: Men 1G **39**
Digley Av. BD6: B'frd 3E **109**
Digpal Rd. LS27: Chur 4C **116**
Dimples La. BD20: E Mor 5H **35**
BD22: Haw 2B **64**
Dinsdale Bldgs. LS19: Yead 1E **55**
DIRK HILL 6C **90**
Dirkhill Rd. BD7: B'frd 6C **90**
Dirkhill St. BD7: B'frd 6B **90**
Discovery Rd. HX1: Hal . . .6D **164** (3H **149**)
Dispensary Wlk.
HX1: Hal 4D **164** (2H **149**)
Disraeli Gdns. LS11: Leeds 1H **117**
Disraeli Ter. LS11: Leeds 1H **117**
Dixon Av. BD7: B'frd 6H **89**
Dixon Cl. BD20: Stee 6C **14**
HX4: Gree 3F **159**
Dixon Ct. LS12: N Far 2B **116**
Dixon La. LS12: Leeds 6C **96**
Dixon La. Rd. LS12: Leeds 6C **96**
Dob HX6: Sow B 6D **146**
Dobb Kiln La. BD16: Bgly 6C **52**
Dob La. HX6: Sow B 6D **146**
DOBRUDDEN 2H **51**
Dobrudden Caravan Pk.
BD17: Bail 2H **51**
Dobson Av. LS11: Leeds 2A **118**
Dobson Gro. LS11: Leeds 2A **118**
Dobson Locks BD10: B'frd 6B **54**
Dobson Pl. LS11: Leeds 2A **118**
Dobsons Row WF3: Carl 5H **141**
Dobsons Wharf BD20: Sils 3E **15**
Dobson Ter. LS11: Leeds 2A **118**
Dobson Vw. LS11: Leeds 2A **118**
Dockfield Ind. Pk. BD17: Ship 6D **52**
Dockfield Pl. BD17: Ship 1C **70**
Dockfield Rd. BD17: Ship 6C **52**
Dockfield Ter. BD17: Ship 6C **52**
Dock La. BD17: Ship 6C **52**
BD18: Ship 1C **70**
Dock Mills BD17: Ship 6C **52**
Dockroyd BD22: Oak 6D **46**
Dockroyd La. BD22: Oak 5D **46**
Dock St. LS10: Leeds 6F 5 (4A **98**)
Doctor Hill BD10: B'frd 2H **71**
(Evesham Gro.)
BD10: B'frd 3G **71**
(The Stray)
HX2: Hal 6B **128**
Doctor La. BD10: B'frd 6H **53**
Doctors La. WF10: All B 2G **145**
Dodge Holme La. HX2: Mix 3B **128**
Dodge Holme Ct. HX2: Mix 3B **128**
(off Dodge Holme Cl.)
Dodge Holme Dr. HX2: Mix 3A **128**
Dodge Holme Gdns. HX2: Mix 3B **128**

Dodge Holme Rd. HX2: Mix 3B 128
Dodgson Av. LS7: Leeds 6C 78
Dodgson St. HX5: Ell 6B 160
Doe Pk. BD13: Denh 2C 86
Doe Park Water Activities Cen. 2D 86
Dog Kennel La. HX3: Sou 4A 150
Dog La. HX4: Gree 4B 158
Dol BD22: Oxen 2E 85
Doles La. HD6: Clift 5E 153
Dole St. BD13: Thorn 5A 88
Dolfin Pl. HD2: Hud 6F 163
Doll La. BD13: Cull 5C 66
Dolly La. LS9: Leeds 2C 98
Dolly La. Bus. Cen. LS9: Leeds 1C 98
Dolphin Ct. LS9: Leeds 4C 98
LS13: Leeds 2D 94
Dolphin La. BD16: Har 1C 66
WF3: Thpe H 6C 140
(not continuous)
Dolphin Rd. LS10: Leeds 2C 140
Dolphin St. LS9: Leeds 4C 98
Dolphin Ter. BD13: Que 5G 107
Dombey St. HX1: Hal 2E 149
Domestic Pl. LS12: Leeds 6F 97
Domestic St. LS11: Leeds 5F 97
Dominion Av. LS7: Leeds 3B 78
Dominion Cl. LS7: Leeds 3B 78
Dominion Ind. Pk. HX3: Hip 1E 151
Donald Aldred Dr. LS29: Burl W 3E 21
Donald Av. BD6: B'frd 5C 110
Donald St. LS28: Fars 1H 93
Don Av. LS22: Weth 1D 12
Doncaster St. HX3: Hal 6H 149
Don Ct. BD20: Sils 2E 15
Donisthorpe St. BD5: B'frd 2D 110
LS10: Leeds 6C 98
Don St. BD21: Keigh 5H 33
Dorchester Ct. BD4: B'frd 2C 112
Dorchester Cres. BD4: B'frd 2C 112
BD17: Bail 3F 53
Dorchester Dr. HX2: Hal 4C 148
LS19: Yead 1H 55
Dorchester Rd. HD2: Fix 6B 162
Dorian Cl. BD10: B'frd 3B 72
Dorothy St. BD21: Keigh 4G 47
Dorset Av. LS8: Leeds 5E 79
Dorset Gro. LS28: Stan 3A 94
Dorset Mt. LS8: Leeds 6E 79
Dorset Rd. LS8: Leeds 5E 79
Dorset St. BD5: B'frd 2C 110
LS8: Leeds 5E 79
Dorset Ter. LS8: Leeds 6E 79
Dortmund Sq. LS2: Leeds 3E 5
Dotterel Glen LS27: Morl 4C 138
Douglas Av. WF17: Bat 3A 154
Douglas Cres. BD18: Ship 3D 70
Douglas Dr. BD4: B'frd 1A 112
Douglas Rd. BD4: B'frd 1A 112
Douglas St. BD22: Cros R 1E 65
HX3: Hal 5F 129
Douglas Towers BD5: B'frd 6C 6
Dove Cl. LS22: Weth 1E 13
Dovedale Cl. HX3: She 1D 130
Dovedale Gdns. LS15: Leeds 1H 101
Dovedale Gth. LS15: Leeds 6H 81
Dover St. BD3: B'frd 2F 91
LS25: Gar 4H 103
Dovesdale Gro. BD5: B'frd 3C 110
Dovesdale Rd. BD5: B'frd 3D 110
Dove St. BD18: Ship 1H 69
BD22: Haw 2D 64
Dowkell La. LS23: T Arch 2C 30
Dowker St. HX1: Hal 4D 148
DOWLEY GAP 6E 51
Dowley Gap La. BD16: Bgly 6D 50
Downham St. BD3: B'frd 5H 7 (5G 91)
Downing Cl. BD3: B'frd 3H 7 (4H 91)
Downside Cres. BD15: All 2C 88
DPM Ind. Est. BD4: B'frd 1B 112
Dracup Av. BD7: B'frd 6G 89
Dracup Rd. BD7: B'frd 2H 109
Dradishaw Rd. BD20: Sils 2D 14

Dragon Ct. LS12: Leeds 5F 97
Dragon Cres. LS12: Leeds 6D 96
Dragon Dr. LS12: Leeds 6C 96
Dragon Rd. LS12: Leeds 6D 96
Drake Fold BD12: Wyke 4C 132
Drake Hill La. BD16: Bgly 5C 36
Drake La. BD11: Drig 2A 136
Drakes Ind. Est. HX3: Hal 3E 129
Drake St. BD1: B'frd 5E 7 (5F 91)
BD21: Keigh 5A 34
Draughton Gro. BD5: B'frd 3D 110
Draughton St. BD5: B'frd 4D 110
Draycott Wlk. BD4: B'frd 3C 112
Draymans Ct. HX4: Hal 5B 128
Drayton Mnr. Yd. LS11: Leeds 1A 118
(off Moor Cres.)
Drewry Rd. BD21: Keigh 6H 33
Drewton Rd. BD1: B'frd 3B 6 (4D 90)
Driftholme Rd. BD11: Drig 6B 114
DRIGHLINGTON 1A 136
Drighlington By-Pass BD11: Drig . . .6G 113
LS27: Gil 6G 113
Drill Hall, The HX1: Hal 5C 164
Drill Hall Bus. Cen. LS29: I'ly 5E 11
Drill Pde. BD8: B'frd 2D 90
Drill St. BD21: Keigh 6A 34
BD22: Haw 3C 64
Drive, The BD10: B'frd 3B 72
BD13: Denh 3A 86
BD16: Bgly 1A 50
HX3: Hip 1F 151
LS8: Leeds 1D 78
LS9: Leeds 4C 98
LS15: Leeds 1F 101
LS16: Leeds 4A 58
LS17: Bard 1F 45
LS17: Leeds 1F 59
LS25: Kip 4G 123
LS26: Swil 4A 122
LS29: Burl W 3E 21
Driver Pl. LS12: Leeds 5E 97
Driver St. LS12: Leeds 5F 97
Driver Ter. BD20: Sils 1E 15
LS12: Leeds 5E 97
Drove Rd. Ho. BD5: B'frd 2E 111
(off Bowling Old La.)
Drovers Way BD2: B'frd 5E 71
DRUB 5C 134
Drub La. BD19: Cleck 5C 134
Druggist St. LS29: Add 1D 8
Druids St. BD14: Clay 1D 108
Druids Vw. BD16: Bgly 6H 35
Drummond Av. LS16: Leeds 3C 76
Drummond Ct. LS16: Leeds 3C 76
Drummond Rd. BD8: B'frd 2C 90
LS16: Leeds 2C 76
Drummond Trad. Est.
BD8: B'frd 1A 6 (3D 90)
Drury Av. LS18: H'fth 1D 74
Drury Cl. LS18: H'fth 1D 74
Drury La. HX4: Stainl 6D 158
LS18: H'fth 1D 74
(not continuous)
Dry Carr La. HX2: Midg 2C 126
Dryclough Cl. HX3: Hal 6G 149
Dryclough La. HX3: Hal 6G 149
Dryden St. BD1: B'frd 6F 7 (5F 91)
BD16: Bgly 4B 50
Dubb La. BD16: Bgly 4B 50
Duchy Av. BD9: B'frd 6G 69
Duchy Cres. BD9: B'frd 6G 69
Duchy Dr. BD9: B'frd 1G 89
Duchy Gro. BD9: B'frd 6G 69
Duchy Vs. BD9: B'frd 6G 69
Duchywood BD9: B'frd 6G 69
Ducie St. BD10: B'frd 6H 53
Duckett Gro. LS28: Pud 3D 92
Duckett La. BD1: B'frd 3C 6 (4E 91)
Ducking Pond Cl. BD22: Haw 3C 64
Duckworth Gro. BD9: B'frd 1H 89
Duckworth La. BD9: B'frd 2G 89
Duckworth Ter. BD9: B'frd 1H 89
Dudley Av. WF17: Birs 5C 136

Dudley Cres. HX2: Illing 2B 128
Dudley Gro. BD4: B'frd 6C 92
DUDLEY HILL 3A 112
Dudley Hill Bus. Cen. BD4: B'frd . . .3A 112
Dudley Hill Rd. BD2: B'frd 6H 71
Dudley St. BD4: B'frd 6C 92
(Dennison Fold)
BD4: B'frd 2A 112
(School St.)
BD4: B'frd 2H 111
(Vestry St.)
Dudwell Av. HX3: Hal 1H 159
Dudwell Gro. HX3: Hal 1G 159
Dudwell La. HX3: Hal 1G 159
Dufton App. LS14: Leeds 6C 80
Duich Rd. BD6: B'frd 1G 131
Duinen St. BD5: B'frd 6F 91
Duke of Wellington Regimental Mus.
. . . . .6G 129
(within Bankfield Mus.)
Dukes Hill LS29: I'ly 3C 10
Duke St. BD1: B'frd 3D 6 (4E 91)
BD20: Keigh 4A 34
BD22: Haw 2D 64
HX2: Lud 6D 126
HX5: Ell .5B 160
LS9: Leeds 5H 5 (4B 98)
Dulverton Cl. LS11: Leeds 4D 116
Dulverton Ct. LS11: Leeds 4D 116
Dulverton Gdns. LS11: Leeds 3C 116
Dulverton Gth. LS11: Leeds 4C 116
Dulverton Grn. LS11: Leeds 4D 116
Dulverton Gro. BD4: B'frd 2B 112
LS11: Leeds 4C 116
Dulverton Pl. LS11: Leeds 4D 116
Dulverton Sq. LS11: Leeds 4D 116
Dunbar Ct. LS26: Meth 4C 144
Dunbar Cft. BD13: Que 4B 108
Duncan Av. LS21: Otley 5B 22
Duncan St. BD5: B'frd 6E 91
LS1: Leeds 5F 5 (4A 98)
Dunce Pk. Cl. HX5: Ell 6B 160
Duncombe Rd. BD8: B'frd 4H 89
Duncombe St. BD8: B'frd 4A 90
LS1: Leeds 3A 4 (3G 97)
Duncombe Way BD8: B'frd 4A 90
Dundas St. BD21: Keigh 1B 48
HX1: Hal 4D 148
Dungeon La. LS26: Oul 5B 142
Dunhill Cres. LS9: Leeds 3A 100
Dunhill Ri. LS9: Leeds 3A 100
Dunkhill Cft. BD10: B'frd 2H 71
DUNKIRK 2A 130
Dunkirk Cres. HX1: Hal 3C 148
Dunkirk Gdns. HX1: Hal 4C 148
Dunkirk Hill LS12: Leeds 2D 96
Dunkirk La. HX1: Hal 4C 148
Dunkirk Ri. BD20: Rid 3C 34
Dunkirk St. HX1: Hal 3C 148
Dunkirk Ter. HX1: Hal 3D 148
Dunlin Cl. LS27: Morl 4D 138
Dunlin Ct. LS10: Leeds 2B 140
Dunlin Cft. LS10: Leeds 2B 140
Dunlin Dr. LS10: Leeds 2B 140
Dunlin Fold LS10: Leeds 2B 140
Dunlin Way BD8: B'frd 4E 89
Dunlop Av. LS12: N Far 1A 116
Dunmore Av. BD13: Que 4G 107
Dunn Cl. WF2: Wren 6D 156
Dunningley La. WF3: Ting 4F 139
Dunnington Wlk. BD6: B'frd 1A 132
Dunnock Av. BD6: B'frd 4D 108
Dunnock Cft. LS27: Morl 4C 138
Dunrobin Av. LS25: Gar 3H 103
Dunsford Av. BD4: B'frd 5H 111
Dunstarn Ct. LS16: Leeds 4D 58
Dunstarn Dr. LS16: Leeds 4D 58
Dunstarn Gdns. LS16: Leeds 4E 59
Dunstarn La. LS16: Leeds 5D 58
Durban Av. LS11: Leeds 3F 117
Durban Cres. LS11: Leeds 3F 117
Durham Ct. LS28: Fars 6H 73
Durham Rd. BD8: B'frd 2A 90

Durham St. HX2: Hal 1C 148
Durham Ter. BD8: B'frd 2A 90
Durkheim Ct. BD3: B'frd 4A 92
(off Amberley St.)
Durley Av. BD9: B'frd 6A 70
Durling Dr. BD18: Ship 2E 71
Durlston Gro. BD12: Wyke 3D 132
Durlston Ter. BD12: Wyke 3D 132
Durrance St. BD22: Keigh 1F 47
Durrant Cl. LS22: Weth 4F 13
Dutton Grn. LS14: Leeds 1C 80
Dutton Way LS14: Leeds 2C 80
Duxbury Ri. LS7: Leeds 1H 97
DW Fitness Club
   Birstall 5B 136
   Halifax 1H 149
Dyehouse BD15: Wils 4F 67
Dyehouse Dr. BD9: Cleck 5A 134
Dyehouse Fold BD12: O'haw 2G 133
Dye Ho. La. HX6: Norl 2C 158
Dyehouse La. BD15: Wils 4E 67
   HD6: Brigh 2B 162
   LS28: Pud 1A 114
(not continuous)
Dyehouse Rd. BD12: O'haw 2F 133
Dyer La. HX3: Hal 6D 128
Dyers Ct. LS6: Leeds 5F 77
Dyer St. LS2: Leeds 4G 5 (3B 98)
Dyke BD22: Haw 2A 64
Dyke Nook BD22: Oxen 2A 84
Dyneley Grange LS16: B'hpe 2G 43
Dyson Ho. HX3: Hal 6B 76
Dyson Pl. HX3: Hal 6H 149
Dyson St. BD1: B'frd 3A 6 (4D 90)
   BD9: B'frd 5A 70
   HD6: Brigh 6A 152
Dyson Wood Way HD2: Hud 6C 162

E

Eaglescliffe HX6: Sow B 5A 148
(off Beech Rd.)
Eaglesfield Dr. BD6: B'frd 1H 131
Eagle St. BD21: Keigh 6H 33
   BD22: Haw 2D 64
Earlsmere Dr. LS27: Morl 2H 137
Earl St. BD21: Keigh 5H 33
   BD22: Haw 3C 64
Earlswood BD12: Wyke 4D 132
Earlswood Av. LS8: Leeds 5D 60
Earlswood Chase LS28: Pud 5A 94
Earlswood Cres. LS25: Kip 3F 123
Earlswood Mead LS28: Pud 5H 93
Earl Ter. HX3: Hal 5E 129
Easby Cl. LS29: I'ly 5B 10
Easby Dr. LS29: I'ly 5B 10
Easby Rd. BD7: B'frd 6A 6 (6D 90)
Easdale Cl. LS14: Leeds 4B 80
Easdale Cres. LS14: Leeds 4C 80
Easdale Mt. LS14: Leeds 5B 80
Easdale Rd. LS14: Leeds 5B 80
Easington Av. BD6: B'frd 5G 109
EAST ARDSLEY 2A 156
East Av. BD21: Keigh 5A 34
(not continuous)
EAST BIERLEY 6D 112
East Bierley Golf Course 6C 112
Eastbourne Rd. BD9: B'frd 4B 70
EAST BOWLING 3G 111
EASTBROOK 5F 7 (5F 91)
East Brookhall BD1: B'frd 4F 7
EASTBURN 6A 14
Eastbury Av. BD6: B'frd 4F 109
E. Busk La. LS21: Otley 3G 23
East Byland HX2: Illing 1C 128
EAST CARLTON 2H 41
East Causeway LS16: Leeds 2D 58
E. Causeway Cl. LS16: Leeds 2D 58
E. Causeway Cres. LS16: Leeds 3D 58
E. Causeway Va. LS16: Leeds 3E 59
E. Chevin Rd. LS21: Otley 5F 23

East Cliffe HX3: Sou 3A 150
East Cft. LS28: Fars 6H 73
(off Water La.)
East Cft. BD12: Wyke 5D 132
East Cft. M. BD12: Wyke 5D 132
(off Garden Fld.)
Eastdean Bank LS14: Leeds 3C 80
Eastdean Dr. LS14: Leeds 3C 80
Eastdean Gdns. LS14: Leeds 3D 80
Eastdean Ga. LS14: Leeds 4D 80
Eastdean Grange
   LS14: Leeds 4D 80
Eastdean Gro. LS14: Leeds 3D 80
Eastdean Ri. LS14: Leeds 3C 80
Eastdean Rd. LS14: Leeds 3C 80
East Dene BD20: Sils 1E 15
Easterly Av. LS8: Leeds 5E 79
Easterly Cl. LS8: Leeds 6F 79
Easterly Cres. LS8: Leeds 5E 79
Easterly Cross LS8: Leeds 5F 79
Easterly Gth. LS8: Leeds 5F 79
Easterly Gro. LS8: Leeds 5E 79
Easterly Mt. LS8: Leeds 5F 79
Easterly Rd. LS8: Leeds 5E 79
Easterly Sq. LS8: Leeds 5F 79
Easterly Vw. LS8: Leeds 5F 79
Eastfield BD13: Denh 3B 86
Eastfield Cres. LS26: Wood 1D 142
Eastfield Dr. LS26: Wood 1D 142
Eastfield Gdns. BD4: B'frd 2C 112
Eastfield La. LS29: Burl W 3G 21
East Fld. St. LS9: Leeds 4C 98
East Fountains HX2: Illing 4B 106
(off Field Head La.)
EAST GARFORTH 3H 103
East Garforth Station (Rail) 4G 103
Eastgate HX5: Ell 4B 160
   LS2: Leeds 4F 5 (3A 98)
   LS16: B'hpe 2F 43
Eastgate Cl. LS16: B'hpe 2F 43
E. Grange Cl. LS10: Leeds 4C 118
E. Grange Dr. LS10: Leeds 4C 118
E. Grange Gth. LS10: Leeds 4C 118
E. Grange Ri. LS10: Leeds 4C 118
E. Grange Rd. LS10: Leeds 4C 118
E. Grange Sq. LS10: Leeds 4C 118
E. Grange Vw. LS10: Leeds 4C 118
Easthorpe Ct. BD4: B'frd 5B 72
EAST KESWICK 6E 27
East King St. LS9: Leeds 6H 5 (4C 98)
Eastland Wlk. LS13: Leeds 2G 95
Eastleigh Dr. WF3: Ting 1G 155
Eastleigh Dr. WF3: Ting 1F 155
Eastleigh Gro. BD5: B'frd 2D 110
Eastleigh M. WF3: Ting 1G 155
East Manywells BD13: Cull 5C 66
EAST MOOR 3D 58
East Moor Av. LS8: Leeds 6D 60
East Moor Cl. LS8: Leeds 6D 60
East Moor Cres. LS8: Leeds 5D 60
East Moor Dr. LS8: Leeds 6E 61
Eastmoor Ho. BD4: B'frd 3D 112
East Moor La. LS16: Leeds 3D 58
East Moor Rd. LS8: Leeds 5D 60
EAST MORTON 5H 35
East Mt. HD6: Brigh 6A 152
East Mt. Pl. HD6: Brigh 6A 152
East Pde. BD1: B'frd 4F 7 (4F 91)
(not continuous)
   BD17: Bail 3D 52
   BD20: Stee 6D 14
   BD21: Keigh 6A 34
   HX6: Sow B 5B 148
   LS1: Leeds 4D 4 (3H 97)
   LS29: I'ly 5E 11
   LS29: Men 1G 39
East Pk. Dr. LS9: Leeds 4D 98
East Pk. Gro. LS9: Leeds 4E 99
East Pk. Mt. LS9: Leeds 4E 99
East Pk. Pde. LS9: Leeds 4E 99
East Pk. Pl. LS9: Leeds 4E 99
East Pk. Rd. HX3: Hal 6E 129
   LS9: Leeds 4D 98

East Pk. St. LS9: Leeds 4E 99
   LS27: Morl 4H 137
East Pk. Ter. LS9: Leeds 4E 99
East Pk. Vw. LS9: Leeds 4E 99
East Riddlesden Hall 4D 34
E. Ridge Vw. LS25: Gar 2A 104
EAST RIGTON 1F 45
East Rd. BD12: Low M 1E 133
East Royd BD22: Oak 5D 46
   HX3: Hip 6E 131
(off Northedge La.)
E. Side Cl. LS28: Pud 6D 94
E. Squire La. BD8: B'frd 2C 90
East St. HD6: Ras 2A 162
   HX3: Hip 2A 152
   LS2: Leeds 5H 5 (4B 98)
   LS9: Leeds 6H 5 (4B 98)
East Ter. BD22: Cros R 1E 65
East Vw. BD12: O'haw 2F 133
   BD13: Que 3E 109
   BD13: Thorn 3G 87
   BD19: Cleck 3G 153
   BD20: Sils 2E 15
   HX3: Hip 2A 152
   HX5: Ell 5E 161
   HX6: Sow B 4A 148
   LS15: Leeds 1E 101
   LS19: Yead 1G 55
   LS25: Kip 3H 123
   LS25: M'fld 6F 105
   LS26: Oul 2E 143
   LS27: Gil 2E 137
   LS28: Pud 6A 94
East Vw. Cotts. LS28: Pud 3B 94
(off Priestley Gdns.)
East Vw. Rd. LS19: Yead 1G 55
East Vw. Ter. BD12: Wyke 3E 133
   LS21: Otley 4F 23
(off Carlton St.)
EASTWOOD 5B 34
Eastwood Av. HX2: Illing 6C 106
   HX6: Sow B 6F 147
Eastwood Cl. HX2: Illing 6C 106
Eastwood Cl. HX3: Hal 5E 149
Eastwood Cres. BD16: Cot 1D 68
   LS14: Leeds 5F 81
Eastwood Dr. LS14: Leeds 4F 81
Eastwood Gdns. LS14: Leeds 5E 81
Eastwood Gth. LS14: Leeds 5F 81
Eastwood Gro. HX2: Illing 6C 106
   LS25: Gar 6G 103
Eastwood La. LS14: Leeds 5F 81
Eastwood Nook LS14: Leeds 5F 81
Eastwood's Farm HX2: Illing 6C 106
(off Keighley Rd.)
Eastwood St. BD4: B'frd 6F 91
   HD6: Brigh 6B 152
   HX3: Hal 5E 129
Easy Rd. LS9: Leeds 5D 98
Eaton Hill LS16: Leeds 4G 57
Eaton M. LS16: Leeds 2A 140
Eaton Rd. LS29: I'ly 6C 10
Eaton Sq. LS10: Leeds 3A 140
Eaton St. BD21: Keigh 3G 47
Ebberston Gro. LS6: Leeds 6F 77
Ebberston Pl. LS6: Leeds 6F 77
Ebberston Ter. LS6: Leeds 6F 77
Ebenezer Ho. LS27: Morl 3A 138
(off Fountain St.)
Ebenezer Pl. BD7: B'frd 1A 110
Ebenezer St. BD1: B'frd 5E 7 (5F 91)
   LS28: Fars 6H 73
   WF3: Rob H 4F 141
Ebony Vw. BD22: Keigh 3G 47
Ebor Ct. BD21: Keigh 1H 47
(off Aireworth St.)
Ebor La. BD22: Haw 1C 64
Ebor Mt. LS6: Leeds 1F 97
   LS25: Kip 3G 123
Ebor Pl. LS6: Leeds 1F 97
Ebor St. LS6: Leeds 1F 97
Ebor Ter. LS10: Leeds 3C 118
(off Woodhouse Hill Rd.)

Ebridge Ct. BD16: Bgly 4C **50**
(off Edward St.)
Ecclesburn Av. LS9: Leeds 4E **99**
Ecclesburn Rd. LS9: Leeds 4E **99**
Ecclesburn St. LS9: Leeds 4E **99**
Ecclesburn Ter. LS9: Leeds 4E **99**
Eccles Ct. BD2: B'frd 5H **71**
ECCLESHILL 4A **72**
Eccleshill Swimming Pool 3B **72**
Eccup La. LS16: Leeds 1D **58**
Echo Central LS9: Leeds 5C **98**
Echo Central Two LS9: Leeds 5C **98**
(off Cross Grn. La.)
Edale Gro. BD13: Que 5G **107**
Edale Way LS16: Leeds 4H **57**
Edderthorpe St.
BD3: B'frd 5H **7** (5G **91**)
Eddison Cl. LS16: Leeds 2D **58**
Eddison St. LS28: Fars 1H **93**
Eddison Wlk. LS16: Leeds 2D **58**
Eden Cl. BD12: Wyke 4D **132**
Eden Cres. LS4: Leeds 5B **76**
Eden Dr. LS4: Leeds 6B **76**
Eden Gdns. LS4: Leeds 6B **76**
Eden Gro. LS4: Leeds 6B **76**
Eden Mt. LS4: Leeds 6B **76**
Eden Rd. LS4: Leeds 6B **76**
Edensor Rd. BD21: Keigh 6G **33**
Eden Wlk. LS4: Leeds 6B **76**
Eden Way LS4: Leeds 6B **76**
Ederoyd Av. LS28: Stan 2F **93**
Ederoyd Cres. LS28: Stan 2F **93**
Ederoyd Dr. LS28: Stan 2F **93**
Ederoyd Gro. LS28: Stan 2F **93**
Ederoyd Mt. LS28: Stan 2F **93**
Ederoyd Ri. LS28: Stan 2E **93**
Edgar St. BD14: Clay 1F **109**
Edgbaston Cl. LS16: Leeds 1G **59**
Edgbaston Wlk. LS17: Leeds 1G **59**
Edgebank Av. BD6: B'frd 1H **131**
Edge Bottom BD13: Denh 2B **86**
Edgecumbe Ho. HX1: Hal 4G **149**
(off Bramwell Way)
Edge End BD13: Denh 2C **86**
(off Pleasant Views)
Edge End Gdns. B'frd 6G **109**
Edge End Rd. BD6: B'frd 5G **109**
Edgefield Gro. HX3: Hal 6E **149**
Edgehill Cl. BD13: Que 4B **108**
Edgeholme La. HX2: Hal 2H **147**
Edgemoor Cl. BD4: B'frd 5C **112**
HX3: Hal 5F **149**
Edge Nook BD6: B'frd 4A **110**
(off Windmill Hill)
Edgerton Rd. LS16: Leeds 1B **76**
Edgware Av. LS8: Leeds 1D **98**
Edgware Gro. LS8: Leeds 1D **98**
Edgware Mt. LS8: Leeds 1D **98**
Edgware Pl. LS8: Leeds 1D **98**
Edgware Row LS8: Leeds 1D **98**
Edgware St. LS8: Leeds 1D **98**
Edgware Ter. LS8: Leeds 1D **98**
Edgware Vw. LS8: Leeds 1D **98**
Edinburgh Av. LS12: Leeds 3A **96**
Edinburgh Gro. LS12: Leeds 3A **96**
Edinburgh Pl. LS12: Leeds 3A **96**
LS25: Gar 4H **103**
Edinburgh Rd. LS12: Leeds 3A **96**
Edinburgh Ter. LS12: Leeds 3A **96**
Edison Gdns. LS20: Guis 3B **40**
(off Netherfield Rd.)
Edison Ho. LS20: Guis 4B **40**
Edison Way LS20: Guis 3B **40**
Ediths Vw. LS6: Sow B 5H **147**
Edith Syke Dr. LS15: Leeds 2G **101**
Edlington Cl. BD4: B'frd 2C **112**
Edmonton Pl. LS7: Leeds 3B **78**
Edmund St. BD5: B'frd 6B **6** (5D **90**)
Edrich Cl. BD12: Low M 1E **133**
Edroyd Pl. LS28: Fars 6H **73**
Edroyd St. LS28: Fars 6H **73**
Edson Cl. BD6: B'frd 5G **109**
Education Rd. LS7: Leeds 6A **78**

Edward Cl. HX3: Sou 5C **150**
LS28: Pud 4H **93**
Edward Ct. WF2: Carr G 4C **156**
Edward Dr. WF1: Out 4F **157**
Edwards Rd. HX2: Hal 4C **148**
Edward St. BD4: B'frd 6E **7** (5F **91**)
(Bedford St.)
BD4: B'frd 4C **111**
(Lister St.)
BD16: Bgly 4C **50**
BD18: Ship 6H **51**
HD6: Brigh 6A **152**
HD6: Clift 1C **162**
HX6: Sow B 5H **147**
LS2: Leeds 3F **5** (3A **98**)
Edward Turner Cl. BD12: Low M 1C **132**
Edwin Av. LS20: Guis 4B **40**
Edwin Rd. LS6: Leeds 1E **97**
Eelholme Vw. St. BD20: Keigh 3H **33**
Eel Mires St. LS22: Weth 3F **13**
Effingham Rd. BD16: Har 6E **49**
Egerton Gro. BD15: All 2C **88**
Egerton St. HX6: Sow B 5H **147**
Egerton Ter. LS19: Raw 4H **55**
(off Town St.)
Eggleston Dr. BD4: B'frd 3D **112**
Egglestone Sq. LS23: B Spa 4A **30**
Eggleston St. LS13: Leeds 4B **74**
Egham Grn. BD10: B'frd 2H **71**
(off Booth St.)
Egremont Cres. BD6: B'frd 1H **131**
Egremont St. HX6: Sow B 6G **147**
Egremont Ter. HX6: Sow B 6G **147**
(off Sowerby New Rd.)
EGYPT .3G **87**
Egypt Rd. BD13: Thorn 3G **87**
Eider Cl. BD6: B'frd 4E **109**
Eighth Av. LS12: Leeds 5D **96**
LS26: Rothw 6C **120**
WF15: Liv 4H **153**
Eightlands Av. LS13: Leeds 1F **95**
Eightlands La. LS13: Leeds 1F **95**
Ekota Pl. LS8: Leeds 5D **78**
Elam Grange BD20: Rid 3A **34**
Elam Wood Rd. BD20: Rid 2B **34**
Eland Ho. HX5: Ell 4B **160**
(off Westgate)
Elba LS12: Leeds 5A **4** (4F **97**)
Elbow La. BD2: B'frd 1H **91**
HX2: Lud 6E **127**
Elder Bank BD13: Cull 3B **66**
(off Keighley Rd.)
Elderberry Cl. BD20: E Mor 4F **35**
Elderberry Dr. HX3: Hal 5A **150**
Elder Cl. WF17: Birs 5B **136**
Elder Cft. LS13: Leeds 2E **95**
Elder Gth. LS25: Gar 5H **103**
Elder La. HD2: Hud 6G **163**
Elder Lea HX2: Brad 4E **107**
Elder Mt. LS13: Leeds 2E **95**
Elder Pl. LS13: Leeds 2E **95**
Elder Ri. LS26: Wood 1G **143**
Elder Rd. HD2: Hud 6F **163**
LS13: Leeds 2E **95**
Elder St. BD10: B'frd 2C **72**
BD20: Keigh 3G **33**
LS13: Leeds 2E **95**
Elderwood Gdns. BD10: B'frd 4C **72**
Eldon Ct. LS2: Leeds 1H **97**
Eldon Mt. LS20: Guis 4C **40**
Eldon Pl. BD1: B'frd 2B **6** (4D **90**)
BD4: B'frd 1B **112**
Eldon St. HX3: Hal 1C **164** (6G **129**)
Eldon Ter. BD1: B'frd 2B **6** (3D **90**)
LS2: Leeds 1H **97**
(off Eldon Ct.)
Eldroth Mt. HX1: Hal 4E **149**
Eldroth Rd. HX1: Hal 4E **149**
ELDWICK 3D **50**
ELDWICK BECK 2E **51**
Eldwick Beck BD16: Bgly 1F **51**
Eldwick Cft. BD16: Bgly 2E **51**

Eleanor Dr. LS28: Cal 2D **72**
Eleanor St. HD6: Ras 2A **162**
Eleventh Av. WF15: Liv 4H **153**
Elford Gro. LS8: Leeds 6D **78**
Elford Pl. E. LS8: Leeds 6D **78**
Elford Pl. W. LS8: Leeds 6D **78**
Elford Rd. LS8: Leeds 6D **78**
Elgar Wlk. WF3: S'ley 4H **157**
Elia St. BD21: Keigh 5B **34**
Eliot Gro. LS20: Guis 5D **40**
Eli St. BD5: B'frd 2F **111**
Elizabethan Manor House
Art Gallery & Museum 5D **10**
Elizabeth Av. BD12: Wyke 3D **132**
Elizabeth Cl. BD12: Wyke 3D **132**
Elizabeth Ct. LS22: Coll 3B **28**
LS28: Pud 4H **93**
Elizabeth Cres. BD12: Wyke 3D **132**
Elizabeth Dr. BD12: Wyke 3D **132**
Elizabeth Gro. LS27: Morl 1C **138**
Elizabeth Ho. HX2: Illing 4C **128**
(off Furness Pl.)
Elizabeth Ind. Est. HX3: Hal 1E **149**
Elizabeth Pl. LS14: Leeds 4C **80**
Elizabeth Rd. LS26: Wood 1E **145**
Elizabeth St. BD5: B'frd 6E **91**
BD12: Wyke 3C **132**
BD16: Bgly 4C **50**
BD21: Keigh 6C **34**
BD22: Oak 5D **46**
HX4: Gree 4H **159**
HX5: Ell 5B **160**
LS6: Leeds 6E **77**
ELLAND 5B **160**
Elland Bri. HX5: Ell 4B **160**
Elland Golf Course 6H **159**
Elland Hall Farm Caravan Pk.
HX5: Ell 4A **160**
Elland Ho. LS14: Leeds 3A **80**
(off Kingsdale Ct.)
Elland La. HD6: Brigh 1A **162**
HX5: Ell 4C **160**
(not continuous)
ELLAND LOWER EDGE 4F **161**
Elland Riorges Link HX5: Ell 4C **160**
Elland Road 2E **117**
Elland Rd. HD6: Brigh 2C **160**
HX5: Ell 4C **160**
HX5: Ell, Hal 2C **160**
LS11: Leeds 3D **116**
(Crow Nest La.)
LS11: Leeds 6B **116**
(Daffil Rd.)
LS11: Leeds 1F **117**
(Tilbury Rd.)
LS27: Chur 6B **116**
Elland Rd. Ind. Pk. LS11: Leeds . . .2D **116**
Elland Ter. LS11: Leeds 6H **97**
ELLAND UPPER EDGE 5E **161**
Elland Way LS11: Leeds 3D **116**
Elland Wood Bottom HX3: Hal 2H **159**
BD13: Cull 2A **66**
Ellar Carr Rd. BD10: B'frd 5A **54**
Ellar Gdns. LS29: Men 5G **21**
Ellar Ghyll LS21: Otley 6A **22**
Ellen Holme HX2: Lud M 3D **146**
Ellen Holme Rd. HX2: Lud M 3D **146**
Ellen Royd La.
HX2: Lud M, Midg 1C **146**
Ellen Royd St. HX2: Lud M . . .1C **164** (1G **149**)
Ellen St. BD16: Bgly 4C **50**
Ellenthorpe Rd. BD17: Bail 5G **51**
Ellerburn Dr. BD6: B'frd 5G **109**
Ellerby La. LS9: Leeds 5C **98**
Ellerby Rd. LS9: Leeds 4C **98**
Eller Ct. LS8: Leeds 3G **79**
Ellers Gro. LS8: Leeds 5D **78**
Ellerslie Hall LS2: Leeds 1G **97**
(off Lyddon Ter.)
Ellers Rd. LS8: Leeds 5D **78**

Ellerton St. BD3: B'frd 4A 92
Ellicott Ct. LS29: Men 1G 39
Ellies Ct. LS17: Leeds 3E 61
Ellingham Ct. BD13: Thorn 5A 88
(off Havelock Sq.)
Ellinthorpe St. BD4: B'frd 6H 91
Elliot Ct. BD13: Que 4H 107
LS13: Leeds 5C 74
Elliott St. BD18: Ship 1A 70
BD20: Sils 2D 14
Ellis Ct. HX3: Nor G 4H 131
Ellis Fold LS12: Leeds 4B 96
Ellis La. LS25: Gar 1D 102
Ellison Fold BD17: Bail 3C 52
Ellison Gro. BD11: Birk 1E 135
Ellison St. HX3: Hal 6E 129
Ellis St. BD5: B'frd 2D 110
Ellis Ter. LS6: Leeds 3D 76
(off Glebe Ter.)
Ellistones Gdns. HX4: Gree 4E 159
Ellistones La. HX4: Gree 5E 159
Ellistones Pl. HX4: Gree 5E 159
Elton Gro. BD6: B'frd 4A 110
Ellwood Cl. LS7: Leeds 2F 77
Elm Av. HX6: Sow B 4H 147
LS25: Kip 2F 123
Elm Ct. BD11: Birk 3F 135
BD15: Wils 5G 67
Elm Cres. BD20: E Mor 5H 35
Elm Cft. LS14: Leeds 1E 81
Elmet Dr. LS15: Bar E 2E 83
Elmete Av. LS8: Leeds 2G 79
LS15: Scho 3H 81
Elmete Cl. LS8: Leeds 3H 79
Elmete Ct. LS8: Leeds 3G 79
Elmete Cft. LS15: Scho 3H 81
Elmete Dr. LS8: Leeds 2H 79
Elmete Grange LS29: Men 1G 39
Elmete Gro. LS8: Leeds 2G 79
Elmete Hill LS8: Leeds 3H 79
Elmete La. LS8: Leeds 2H 79
LS17: Shad 6A 62
Elmete Mt. LS8: Leeds 3H 79
Elmete Wlk. LS8: Leeds 3G 79
Elmete Way LS8: Leeds 3H 79
Elmet Rd. LS15: Bar E 3E 83
Elmet Way LS14: Leeds 5E 81
Elmfield BD17: Bail 3D 52
LS26: Oul 2F 143
Elmfield Bus. Pk. LS25: Gar 3G 103
Elmfield Ct. BD11: Birk 3E 135
LS13: Leeds 2F 95
LS27: Morl 4B 138
Elmfield Dr. BD6: B'frd 5C 110
Elmfield Gro. LS12: Leeds 5D 96
Elmfield Pde. LS27: Morl 5B 138
Elmfield Pl. LS12: Leeds 5D 96
Elmfield Rd. LS12: Leeds 5D 96
LS27: Morl 5B 138
Elmfield Ter. HX1: Hal 4F 149
Elmfield Way LS13: Leeds 2F 95
Elm Gdns. HX3: Hal 4G 149
Elm Gro. BD18: Ship 2E 71
BD19: Gom 6E 135
BD20: E Mor 5H 35
BD20: Sils 2D 14
BD21: Keigh 3G 47
HX3: She 1F 131
LS29: Burl W 3F 21
Elm Ho. LS7: Leeds 2C 78
(off Allerton Pk.)
LS15: Leeds 5A 100
Elmhurst Cl. LS17: Leeds 3E 61
Elmhurst Gdns. LS17: Leeds 3E 61
Elm Pl. HX1: Hal 2D 148
HX6: Sow B 4H 147
Elm Rd. BD18: Ship 2D 70
Elmroyd LS26: Rothw 3B 142
Elms, The LS7: Leeds 3B 78
LS13: Leeds 2G 95
LS20: Guis 4C 40
Elms Ct. HX2: Illing 2C 128
Elmsley St. BD20: Stee 6C 14

Elm St. BD22: Oxen 6C 64
LS6: Leeds 5H 77
Elm Ter. HD6: Brigh 4B 152
LS21: Otley 3G 23
Elmton Cl. LS10: Leeds 6B 118
Elm Tree Av. BD6: B'frd 5C 110
Elm Tree Cl. BD6: B'frd 5D 110
BD21: Keigh 1B 48
LS15: Leeds 5G 101
LS28: Pud 5A 94
Elm Tree Gdns. BD6: B'frd 4C 110
Elmtree La. LS10: Leeds 1B 118
Elm Vw. BD20: Stee 5B 14
HX3: Hal 5G 149
(off Skircoat Grn. Rd.)
Elm Walk, The LS15: Leeds 6D 100
Elm Way WF17: Birs 5C 136
Elmwood Av. LS15: Bar E 2D 82
Elmwood Chase LS15: Bar E 2D 82
Elmwood Ct. LS15: Bar E 2D 82
Elmwood Dr. BD22: Keigh 3F 47
HD6: Brigh 6H 151
Elmwood La. LS2: Leeds 1F 5 (2A 98)
LS15: Bar E 2D 82
Elmwood Pl. BD2: B'frd 2A 92
(off Fagley Rd.)
Elmwood Rd. BD22: Keigh 4F 47
Elmwood St. HD6: Brigh 5B 152
HX1: Hal 4E 149
Elmwood Ter. BD22: Keigh 3F 47
LS22: Coll 3B 28
Elsdon Gro. BD5: B'frd 6E 91
Elsham Ter. LS4: Leeds 1C 96
Elsie Bruce Gro. LS15: Leeds 2G 101
Elsie St. BD20: Keigh 3H 33
BD22: Cros R 1F 65
Elsie Whiteley Innovation Cen. 4A 164
Elsinore Av. HX5: Ell 5A 160
Elsinore Ct. HX5: Ell 5A 160
Elston Dr. BD20: Rid 5F 35
(off Ford Rd.)
Elstone Vw. WF1: Out 5E 157
Elsworth Av. BD3: B'frd 2B 92
Elsworth Ho. LS5: Leeds 5H 75
Elsworth St. LS12: Leeds 4D 96
Eltham Av. LS6: Leeds 6H 77
Eltham Cl. LS6: Leeds 6H 77
Eltham Ct. LS6: Leeds 6H 77
Eltham Dr. LS6: Leeds 6H 77
Eltham Gdns. LS6: Leeds 6H 77
Eltham Gro. BD6: B'frd 5A 110
Eltham Ri. LS6: Leeds 6H 77
Elvaston Rd. LS27: Morl 4A 138
Elvey Cl. BD2: B'frd 5B 72
Elwell Cl. HX3: She 6F 109
Elwell St. WF3: Thpe H 6C 140
Elwyn Gro. BD5: B'frd 2E 111
Elwyn Rd. BD5: B'frd 2F 111
Ely St. HX4: Gree 5H 159
LS12: Leeds 3C 96
Embankment, The
LS1: Leeds 6E 5 (4A 98)
LS4: Leeds 1D 96
Emblem Ct. BD13: Que 5H 107
Embleton Rd. LS26: Meth 6C 144
Emerald St. BD22: Keigh 3G 47
Emerson Av. BD9: B'frd 6F 69
Emily Ct. BD7: B'frd 2B 110
(off Oakwell Cl.)
Emily Hall Gdns. BD15: Wils 4G 67
Emily St. BD21: Keigh 5A 34
BD22: Haw 2D 64
(off Victoria Rd.)
Emily Way HX1: Hal 4G 149
Emley Vw. LS25: Kip 2F 123
Emmanuel Trad. Est. LS12: Leeds 5G 97
Emmeline Cl. BD10: B'frd 1H 71
Emmet Cl. BD11: Birk 2F 135
Emmfield Dr. BD9: B'frd 5A 70
Emm La. BD9: B'frd 6A 70
Emmott Dr. LS19: Raw 4H 55
Emmott Farm Fold BD22: Haw 3C 64
Emmott Vw. LS19: Raw 4H 55

Empire Bus. Cen. HX2: Hal 3E 129
Empire Ct. HD6: B Bri 2B 152
Empsall Row HD6: Brigh 6B 152
(off Bonegate Rd.)
Emscote Av. HX1: Hal 4E 149
Emscote Gdns. HX1: Hal 4E 149
Emscote Gro. HX1: Hal 4E 149
Emscote Pl. HX1: Hal 4E 149
Emscote St. Sth. HX1: Hal 4E 149
Emsley Cl. BD4: B'frd 5H 111
Emsley Pl. LS10: Leeds 6C 98
Emsley's Farm Shop Vis. Cen. 2E 55
Emville Av. LS17: Leeds 2G 61
Endecliff M. LS6: Leeds 5F 77
Enderby Cl. HX3: Hal 4D 128
Enderley Rd. BD13: Thorn 5H 87
Endor Cres. LS29: Burl W 4F 21
Endor Gro. LS29: Burl W 4F 21
Endsleigh Pl. BD14: Clay 1D 108
Enfield LS19: Yead 1F 55
Enfield Av. LS7: Leeds 1C 98
Enfield Dr. BD6: B'frd 4A 110
Enfield Pde. BD6: B'frd 4A 110
Enfield Rd. BD17: Bail 5C 52
Enfield St. BD21: Keigh 6H 33
LS7: Leeds 1B 98
Enfield Ter. LS7: Leeds 1C 98
Enfield Wlk. BD6: B'frd 4A 110
Engine Fields Nature Reserve 1E 55
Englefield Cl. BD4: B'frd 3C 112
Englefield Cres. BD4: B'frd 3C 112
Ennerdale Cl. LS22: Weth 3C 12
Ennerdale Dr. BD2: B'frd 6H 71
HX5: Ell 4D 160
Ennerdale Rd. BD2: B'frd 6G 71
LS12: N Far 3F 115
Ennerdale Way LS12: N Far 2F 115
Enterprise 5 Lane Ends
BD10: B'frd 3H 71
Enterprise Ct. BD4: B'frd 4A 112
LS25: M'fld 5E 105
Enterprise Park Ind. Est.
LS11: Leeds 4F 117
Enterprise Way BD10: B'frd 3H 71
LS10: Leeds 4D 118
Envoy St. LS11: Leeds 1A 118
Epsom Gro. HX3: Sou 4A 150
Epsom Rd. LS25: Kip 3F 123
Epworth Pl. BD22: Oak 4B 46
LS6: Leeds 1C 118
Equity Chambers BD1: B'frd 3D 6
Eric St. BD21: Keigh 5A 34
LS13: Leeds 4E 75
Erivan Pk. LS22: Weth 3G 13
Escroft Cl. BD12: Wyke 6D 132
Escroft Ct. LS29: Men 2H 39
(off Clifford Dr.)
Eshald La. LS26: Wood 2F 143
Eshald Mans. LS26: Wood 1F 143
Eshald Pl. LS26: Wood 1F 143
ESHOLT 2A 54
Esholt Av. LS20: Guis 6B 40
Esholt Hall Est. BD17: Esh 3B 54
Esholt La. BD17: Bail, B'frd 3F 53
Eshton Av. BD12: O'haw 2F 133
Eskdale Av. HX3: She 2D 130
Eskdale Cl. LS20: Guis 5C 40
Eskdale Cft. LS20: Guis 5C 40
Eskdale Gro. LS25: Gar 5G 103
Eskdale Ri. BD15: All 3D 88
Esk Gdns. LS22: Weth 1E 13
Eskine Pde. BD6: B'frd 1H 131
Esmond St. BD7: B'frd 2H 109
LS12: Leeds 4C 96
Esmond Ter. LS12: Leeds 4C 96
Esporta Health & Fitness
Cookridge 1H 57
Essex Pk. Ind. Est.
BD4: B'frd 6G 7 (5G 91)
Essex St. BD4: B'frd 6G 7 (5G 91)
HX1: Hal 3D 148
Estcourt Av. LS6: Leeds 4C 76
Estcourt Gro. BD7: B'frd 6A 90

Estcourt Rd. BD7: B'frd	6A 90
Estcourt Ter. LS6: Leeds	4C 76
Esthwaite Gdns. LS15: Leeds	5A 100
Ethel Jackson Rd.	
LS15: Leeds	1G 101
Ethel St. BD20: Keigh	4H 33
Etna St. BD7: B'frd	2H 109
Eton Ct. LS7: Leeds	2C 78
Eton Fold BD8: B'frd	3F 89
Eton St. HX1: Hal	2D 164
Eureka! The National Children's Mus.	
	5D 164 (3H 149)
Eurocam Technology Pk.	
BD5: B'frd	3E 111
Euroway Trad. Est. BD4: B'frd	1G 133
Euston Gro. LS11: Leeds	1F 117
Euston Mt. LS11: Leeds	1F 117
Euston Ter. LS11: Leeds	1F 117
Evanston Av. LS4: Leeds	2C 96
Evans Towers BD5: B'frd	6E 91
(off Tennhill Gro.)	
Evelyn Av. BD3: B'frd	3C 92
Evelyn Pl. LS12: Leeds	5C 96
Evelyn Ter. BD13: Que	3G 107
Evens Ter. BD5: B'frd	3E 111
Everest Av. BD18: Ship	2E 71
Evergreen Wlk. BD16: Bgly	2A 50
(off Canal Rd.)	
Everleigh St. LS9: Leeds	3E 99
Eversley Dr. BD4: B'frd	1C 112
Eversley Mt. HX2: Hal	3C 148
(off Bk. Eversley Mt.)	
Eversley Pl. HX2: Hal	3C 148
Eversley Vw. LS14: S'cft	6E 45
Evesham Gro. BD10: B'frd	2H 71
Ewart Pl. BD7: B'frd	2A 110
Ewart St. BD7: B'frd	2A 110
BD13: Que	4A 108
EWOOD	6A 126
Ewood Ct. HX7: Myth	6A 126
Ewood Dr. HX7: Myth	6A 126
Ewood Hall Av. HX7: Myth	6A 126
Exchange St. BD19: Cleck	6B 134
HX4: Gree	5H 159
Exe St. BD5: B'frd	2C 110
Exeter Dr. LS10: Leeds	6B 118
Exeter St. HX3: Hal	6H 149
HX6: Sow B	4A 148
Exhibition BD18: Ship	1H 69
EXLEY	2H 159
Exley Av. BD21: Keigh	3G 47
Exley Bank HX3: Hal	1H 159
Exley Bank Top HX3: Hal	2H 159
Exley Cres. BD21: Keigh	2G 47
(not continuous)	
Exley Dr. BD21: Keigh	2G 47
Exley Gdns. HX3: Hal	2H 159
Exley Gro. BD21: Keigh	2G 47
EXLEY HEAD	2F 47
Exley Head Vw. BD22: Keigh	5E 33
Exley La. HX3: Hal	2H 159
HX5: Ell, Hal	2H 159
Exley Mt. BD7: B'frd	5H 89
BD21: Keigh	2G 47
Exley Rd. BD21: Keigh	2G 47
Exley St. BD22: Keigh	1G 47
Exley Way BD21: Keigh	3G 47
Exmoor St. HX1: Hal	3D 148
Exmouth Pl. BD3: B'frd	2F 91
Eyres Av. LS12: Leeds	3C 96
Eyres Gro. LS12: Leeds	3C 96
(off Eyres Ter.)	
Eyres Mill Side LS12: Leeds	3B 96
Eyres St. LS12: Leeds	3C 96
(off Eyres Ter.)	
Eyres Ter. LS12: Leeds	3C 96
Eyrie App. LS27: Morl	4C 138

F

Factory La. BD4: B'frd	3H 111
Factory St. BD4: B'frd	3H 111

FAGLEY	1B 92
Fagley Cres. BD2: B'frd	1A 92
Fagley Cft. BD2: B'frd	1B 92
Fagley Dr. BD2: B'frd	1A 92
Fagley La. BD2: B'frd	5B 72
Fagley Pl. BD2: B'frd	2A 92
Fagley Rd. BD2: B'frd	2A 92
Fagley Ter. BD2: B'frd	2A 92
Fairbairn Fold BD4: B'frd	5C 92
Fair Bank BD18: Ship	3C 70
Fairbank Pl. BD18: Ship	3C 70
(off Fair Bank)	
Fairbank Rd. BD8: B'frd	2A 90
Fairbanks HX6: Sow B	5A 148
Fairbank Ter. BD8: B'frd	2A 90
Fairburn Ct. HX3: Sou	5C 150
Fairburn Dr. LS25: Gar	4G 103
Fairburn Gdns. BD2: B'frd	5A 72
Fairburn Ho. LS18: H'fth	2D 74
(off Regent Cres.)	
Fairburn St. WF10: C'frd	6H 145
Fairclough Gro. HX3: Hal	4D 128
Fairfax Av. BD4: B'frd	4A 112
BD11: Drig	1C 136
LS29: Men	6G 21
Fairfax Cl. LS14: Leeds	6D 80
Fairfax Ct. LS11: Leeds	2G 117
Fairfax Cres. BD4: B'frd	4A 112
HX3: Sou	4C 150
Fairfax Flats LS21: Otley	4F 23
(off Fairfax St.)	
Fairfax Gdns. LS29: Men	6G 21
Fairfax Gro. LS19: Yead	6D 40
Fairfax Ho. BD1: B'frd	3F 7
Fairfax Rd. BD13: Cull	2B 66
BD16: Bgly	2B 50
LS11: Leeds	2G 117
LS29: Men	6F 21
Fairfax St. BD4: B'frd	6F 91
BD20: Sils	2D 14
BD22: Haw	2D 64
LS21: Otley	4F 23
Fairfax Vw. BD4: E Bier	6D 112
LS18: H'fth	3D 56
Fairfield BD13: Denh	3B 86
LS18: H'fth	6E 57
Fairfield Av. LS13: Leeds	1C 94
LS28: Pud	3A 94
WF3: W Ard	2D 154
Fairfield Cl. LS13: Leeds	1D 94
LS26: Rothw	3F 141
Fairfield Cl. BD17: Bail	3E 53
LS17: Leeds	2C 60
Fairfield Cres. LS13: Leeds	1C 94
Fairfield Dr. BD17: Bail	3E 53
LS26: Rothw	3F 141
Fairfield Gdns. LS26: Rothw	3F 141
Fairfield Gro. LS13: Leeds	1D 94
LS26: Rothw	3F 141
Fairfield Hill LS13: Leeds	1D 94
Fairfield La. LS13: Leeds	1D 94
LS26: Rothw	3F 141
Fairfield M. LS13: Leeds	1D 94
Fairfield Mt. LS13: Leeds	1D 94
Fairfield Rd. BD8: B'frd	2B 90
BD12: Wyke	4D 132
LS13: Leeds	1C 94
Fairfield Sq. LS13: Leeds	1D 94
Fairfield St. BD4: B'frd	4B 112
LS13: Leeds	1C 94
(not continuous)	
Fairfield Ter. LS13: Leeds	1D 94
Fairford Av. LS11: Leeds	2A 118
Fairford Cl. BD7: B'frd	6H 71
Fairford Mt. LS6: Leeds	6E 59
Fairford Ter. LS11: Leeds	2A 118
Fairhaven Grn. BD10: B'frd	2A 72
Fair Isle Ct. BD21: Keigh	6A 34
(off Alice St.)	
Fairlands Cl. HX2: Illing	1D 128
Fairleigh Cres. WF3: Ting	1F 155
Fairleigh Rd. WF3: Ting	1F 155
Fairless Av. HX3: Hip	2A 152

Fairmount BD9: B'frd	1C 90
BD21: Keigh	1D 48
(off Fairmount Ter.)	
Fairmount Pk. BD18: Ship	2G 69
(not continuous)	
Fairmount Ter. BD21: Keigh	1D 48
Fair Rd. BD6: B'frd	4B 110
Fair Vw. LS11: Leeds	4D 116
Fairview BD12: O'haw	3G 133
Fairview BD17: Bail	6B 52
Fairview Ter. HX3: Hal	6E 129
Fairway BD7: B'frd	4H 109
BD10: B'frd	6E 55
BD18: Ship	2H 69
LS20: Guis	4H 39
Fairway, The HD2: Fix	6A 162
HX2: Illing	6D 106
LS17: Leeds	1H 59
LS28: Stan	2F 93
Fairway Av. BD7: B'frd	4H 109
Fairway Cl. BD7: B'frd	4H 109
LS20: Guis	5A 40
Fairway Cres. BD22: Haw	3D 64
Fairway Dr. BD7: B'frd	3H 109
Fairway Gro. BD7: B'frd	3H 109
Fairway Ind. Pk. WF17: Birs	5B 136
Fairways, The BD9: B'frd	4G 69
BD20: Keigh	2G 33
Fairway Wlk. BD7: B'frd	3H 109
FAIRWEATHER GREEN	4F 89
Fairweather M. BD8: B'frd	4G 89
Fairwood Gro. BD10: B'frd	6C 72
Fairy Dell BD16: Cot	2C 68
Falcon Cliffe BD20: Stee	6D 14
Falcon Cl. LS21: Otley	4E 23
Falcon M. BD8: B'frd	3E 89
LS27: Morl	4C 138
Falcon Rd. BD16: Bgly	2B 50
Falcon St. BD7: B'frd	6B 90
HX3: Hal	6H 149
Falkland Ct. BD16: Bgly	4C 50
LS17: Leeds	6A 60
Falkland Cres. LS17: Leeds	6A 60
Falkland Gdns. LS17: Leeds	6B 60
Falkland Gro. LS17: Leeds	6A 60
Falkland Mt. LS17: Leeds	6A 60
Falkland Ri. LS17: Leeds	6A 60
Falkland Rd. BD10: B'frd	5C 72
LS17: Leeds	6A 60
FALL, THE	1B 156
Fall Brow Cl. BD14: Clay	2C 108
Fall La. HX3: North	2H 129
HX6: Sow B	6B 148
WF3: E Ard	1B 156
Fallow Cft. HD2: Hud	6F 163
Fallowfield Cl. BD4: B'frd	5A 112
Fallowfield Dr. BD4: B'frd	4A 112
Fallowfield Gdns. BD4: B'frd	4A 112
Fallow La. BD22: Oak	1A 46
Fall Pk. Ct. LS13: Leeds	4F 75
Fallswood Gro. LS13: Leeds	5F 75
Fallwood Marina LS13: Leeds	4D 74
Fallwood St. BD22: Haw	3D 64
Falmers Cotts. LS6: Leeds	5F 77
(off Cliff La.)	
Falmouth Av. BD3: B'frd	2F 91
Falsgrave Av. BD2: B'frd	1B 92
Faltis Sq. BD10: B'frd	3A 72
Fanny St. BD18: Ship	6H 51
BD21: Keigh	1H 47
Faraday LS20: Guis	3B 40
(off Netherfield Rd.)	
Farcliffe Pl. BD8: B'frd	2B 90
Farcliffe Rd. BD8: B'frd	2B 90
Farcliffe Ter. BD8: B'frd	2B 90
Far Cft. Ter. LS12: Leeds	5D 96
Far Crook BD10: B'frd	6F 53
Fardene St. BD20: Sils	1D 14
Fardew Ct. BD16: Bgly	3B 50
Fardew Golf Course	5G 35
Farfield Av. BD6: B'frd	6G 109
LS28: Fars	6G 73
Farfield Ct. LS25: Gar	4D 102

Farfield Cres. BD6: B'frd 6H 109
Farfield Dr. LS28: Fars 1G 93
Farfield Gro. BD6: B'frd 6H 109
  LS28: Fars 6G 73
Farfield Ri. HD6: B Bri 3B 152
  LS28: Fars 6G 73
Farfield Rd. BD6: B'frd 6A 110
  BD17: Bail 5D 52
  BD18: Ship 2H 69
Farfield St. BD9: B'frd 1A 90
  BD19: Cleck 6B 134
Farfield Ter. BD9: B'frd 1A 90
FAR FOLD 3B 96
FAR HEADINGLEY 3F 77
Far Highfield BD22: Oak 4C 46
Far Highfield Cl. BD10: B'frd 2G 71
Farhills BD6: B'frd 4H 109
Far Laithe BD22: Lay 5C 32
Far La. HX2: Midg 5A 126
  LS9: Leeds 6G 99
Farlea Dr. BD2: B'frd 6A 72
Farleton Dr. BD2: B'frd 6B 72
Farley Cres. BD22: Oak 4B 46
Far Low Bank BD22: Oak 4B 46
                 (off Keilburn Gro.)
Farm Ct. LS15: Leeds 1D 100
Far Mead Cft. LS29: Burl W 1E 21
Farm Hill Cl. BD10: B'frd 4H 71
Farm Hill Cres. LS7: Leeds 4G 77
Farm Hill M. LS27: Morl 2G 137
Farm Hill Nth. LS7: Leeds 3G 77
Farm Hill Ri. LS7: Leeds 4G 77
Farm Hill Rd. BD10: B'frd 3H 71
  LS27: Morl 1H 137
Farm Hill Sth. LS7: Leeds 4G 77
Farm Hill Way LS7: Leeds 4G 77
Farm Mt. LS15: Leeds 1E 101
Far Moss LS17: Leeds 2G 59
Farm Rd. LS15: Leeds 1D 100
Farmstead Rd. BD10: B'frd 3A 72
Farndale App. LS14: Leeds 4E 81
Farndale Cl. LS14: Leeds 4E 81
  LS22: Weth 3B 12
Farndale Ct. LS25: Gar 6F 103
Farndale Gdns. LS14: Leeds 3E 81
Farndale Gth. LS14: Leeds 3E 81
Farndale Pl. LS14: Leeds 3E 81
Farndale Rd. BD15: Wils 5G 67
  BD17: Bail 5A 52
Farndale Sq. LS14: Leeds 4E 81
Farndale Ter. LS14: Leeds 4E 81
Farndale Vw. LS14: Leeds 3E 81
                 (off Stanks Dr.)
Farnham Cl. BD17: Bail 3D 52
  LS14: Leeds 6D 62
  LS16: Leeds 2C 76
Farnham Cft. LS14: Leeds 6D 62
Farnham Rd. BD7: B'frd 6B 90
FARNLEY 6G 95
Farnley Cl. LS29: Men 1H 39
Farnley Cres. LS12: Leeds 5G 95
Farnley Ho. LS14: Leeds 3A 80
              (off Kingsdale Ct.)
Farnley La. LS21: Otley 2E 23
Farnley Pk. LS21: F'ley, Leat 1A 24
Farnley Rd. LS29: Men 1G 39
Farnley Vw. BD11: Drig 2C 136
Faroe LS12: Leeds 6A 4 (4G 97)
Farrar Bldgs. BD12: Wyke 4C 132
                (off Brick Row)
Farrar Cl. HX5: Ell 4D 160
Farrar Ct. LS13: Leeds 6E 75
Farrar Cft. LS16: Leeds 3A 58
Farrar Gro. LS16: Leeds 3A 58
Farrar La. LS16: Leeds 3H 57
               (not continuous)
Farrar Mill La. HX3: Hal 5H 149
Farra St. BD22: Oxen 1C 84
Far Reef Cl. LS18: H'fth 5E 57
Farrer La. LS26: Oul 2E 143
Farriers Ct. BD11: Drig 1A 136
  LS22: Weth 4F 13

Farriers Cft. BD2: B'frd 5F 71
Farrier Way WF3: Rob H 4F 141
Farringdon Cl. BD4: B'frd 1B 112
Farringdon Dr. BD4: B'frd 2C 112
Farringdon Gro. BD6: B'frd 6A 110
Farringdon Sq. BD4: B'frd 1C 112
Far Row LS21: Pool 6E 25
Farrow Bank LS12: Leeds 4G 95
Farrow Grn. LS12: Leeds 4H 95
Farrow Hill LS12: Leeds 4H 95
Farrow Rd. LS12: Leeds 4G 95
Farrow Va. LS12: Leeds 4G 95
Far Royd HX3: Hal 3E 129
Farr Royd LS29: Burl W 1E 21
Farside Grn. BD5: B'frd 2C 110
FARSLEY 6H 73
FARSLEY BECK BOTTOM 6A 74
Farsley Beck M. LS13: Leeds 6A 74
Fartown LS28: Pud 5H 93
Fartown Cl. LS28: Pud 6A 94
Far Vw. HX2: Illing 1C 128
Farway BD4: B'frd 1C 112
Far Well Fold LS19: Raw 4H 55
Far Well Rd. LS19: Raw 4H 55
Fascination Pl. BD13: Que 3G 107
                (off Mill La.)
Faulkland Ho. BD8: B'frd 2C 90
             (off Green La.)
Faversham Wlk. BD4: B'frd 1C 112
Fawcett Av. LS12: Leeds 6B 96
Fawcett Bank LS12: Leeds 6A 96
Fawcett Cl. LS12: Leeds 6A 96
Fawcett Dr. LS12: Leeds 6A 96
Fawcett Gdns. LS12: Leeds 6A 96
Fawcett La. LS12: Leeds 6A 96
Fawcett Pl. BD4: B'frd 5A 112
  LS12: Leeds 6A 96
Fawcett Rd. LS12: Leeds 6A 96
Fawcett Va. LS12: Leeds 6A 96
Fawcett Vw. LS12: Leeds 6A 96
              (off Fawcett Va.)
Fawcett Way LS12: Leeds 6A 96
Fawdon Dr. LS14: Leeds 4F 81
Fawdon Pl. LS14: Leeds 4G 81
Fawkes Dr. LS21: Otley 5B 22
Faxfleet St. BD5: B'frd 4D 110
Faye Gdns. BD4: B'frd 4B 112
FC Halifax Town 6C 164 (3G 149)
Fearnley Cl. BD12: Leeds 4D 96
Fearnley Cft. BD19: Gom 6F 135
Fearnley Mill Dr. HD5: Hud 5G 163
Fearnley Pl. LS12: Leeds 4D 96
Fearnsides St. BD8: B'frd 3B 90
Fearnsides Ter. BD8: B'frd 3B 90
FEARN'S ISLAND 5C 98
FEARNVILLE .5H 79
Fearnville Av. LS8: Leeds 5H 79
Fearnville Cl. LS8: Leeds 4H 79
Fearnville Dr. BD4: B'frd 6B 92
  LS8: Leeds 5H 79
Fearnville Gro. LS8: Leeds 4H 79
Fearnville Leisure Cen. 6H 79
Fearnville Mt. LS8: Leeds 4H 79
Fearnville Pl. LS8: Leeds 4A 80
Fearnville Ter. LS8: Leeds 4A 80
Fearnville Vw. LS8: Leeds 5H 79
Feast Fld. LS18: H'fth 6D 56
Feather Bank BD22: Keigh 3G 47
Feather Bank Ct. LS18: H'fth 2D 74
Featherbank Av. LS18: H'fth 2D 74
Featherbank Ct. LS18: H'fth 2D 74
           (off Featherbank La.)
Featherbank Gro. LS18: H'fth 1D 74
Featherbank La. LS18: H'fth 1D 74
Featherbank Mt. LS18: H'fth 1D 74
Featherbank Ter. LS18: H'fth 2D 74
Featherbank Wlk. LS18: H'fth 2D 74
Featherbed Cl. HX4: Gree 5H 159
Featherbed La. HX4: Gree 5H 159
Feather Rd. BD3: B'frd 4H 91
Feather St. BD21: Keigh 1B 48
Federation St. BD5: B'frd 3F 111

Felbrigg Av. BD22: Keigh 1F 47
Felcourt Dr. BD4: B'frd 3C 112
Felcourt Fold BD4: B'frd 3C 112
Fell Cres. BD22: Keigh 2E 47
Fell Greave Rd. HD2: Hud 6B 162
Fell Gro. BD22: Keigh 1F 47
  HD2: Hud 6C 162
Fell La. BD22: Keigh 2E 47
Fellside Cl. BD5: B'frd 3F 111
Fellwood Av. BD22: Haw 1E 65
Fellwood Cl. BD22: Haw 1E 65
Felnex Cl. LS9: Leeds 6G 99
Felnex Cres. LS9: Leeds 6G 99
Felnex Rd. LS9: Leeds 6F 99
Felnex Sq. LS9: Leeds 6F 99
Felnex Way LS9: Leeds 6G 99
Fenby Av. BD4: B'frd 1H 111
             (not continuous)
Fenby Cl. BD4: B'frd 2A 112
             (not continuous)
Fenby Gdns. BD4: B'frd 2A 112
Fenby Gro. BD4: B'frd 2A 112
Fencote Cres. BD2: B'frd 6B 72
Fender Rd. BD6: B'frd 4H 109
Fennec Rd. BD17: Bail 3E 53
Fennel Ct. LS26: Meth 4C 144
Fenny Royd HX3: Hip 1D 150
Fenton Av. LS26: Wood 6D 120
Fenton Cl. LS26: Wood 6D 120
Fenton Ct. BD13: Cull 3B 66
Fenton Fold BD12: O'haw 3F 133
Fenton Ga. LS10: Leeds 3C 140
Fenton Pl. LS10: Leeds 3C 140
Fenton Rd. HX1: Hal 4D 148
Fentonsgate WF3: Loft 6G 141
Fenton St. LS1: Leeds 1D 4 (2H 97)
  LS29: Burl W 2F 21
  WF3: Ting 6F 139
Fenwick Dr. BD6: B'frd 6H 109
Ferguson St. HX1: Hal 5B 164 (3G 149)
Fern Bank HX6: Sow B 6H 147
  LS21: Otley 3F 23
Fernbank Av. BD16: Bgly 4C 50
  BD22: Oak 3F 47
  LS13: Leeds 6B 74
Fernbank Cl. LS13: Leeds 6B 74
Fernbank Dr. BD16: Bgly 4C 50
  BD17: Bail 6A 52
  LS13: Leeds 6B 74
Fernbank Gdns. LS13: Leeds 6B 74
Fernbank Pl. LS13: Leeds 6B 74
Fernbank Rd. BD3: B'frd 2H 91
  LS13: Leeds 6B 74
Fernbank St. BD16: Bgly 4C 50
Fernbank Ter. BD16: Bgly 4C 50
  LS19: Yead 6E 41
               (off Park La.)
Fernbank Wlk. LS13: Leeds 6B 74
Fern Chase LS14: S'cft 6C 44
FERNCLIFFE .4E 51
Ferncliffe Cl. BD18: Ship 1H 69
Ferncliffe Dr. BD17: Bail 4B 52
  BD20: Keigh 3F 33
Ferncliffe Rd. BD16: Bgly 4B 50
  BD18: Ship 1H 69
  LS13: Leeds 1E 95
Ferncliffe Ter. LS13: Leeds 1D 94
Fern Cft. BD20: Keigh 3G 33
Fern Cft. LS14: S'cft 6C 44
  LS29: I'ly .6C 156
Ferncroft WF15: Liv 5H 153
Ferndale BD14: Clay 2C 108
Ferndale Av. BD14: Clay 2C 108
Ferndale Ct. LS29: I'ly 6C 10
Ferndale Gro. BD9: B'frd 5C 70
Ferndene BD16: Bgly 4D 50
Ferndene Av. WF17: Birs 4B 136
Ferndene Wlk. WF17: Birs 4B 136
Ferndown Grn. BD5: B'frd 2D 110
Fernfield Ter. HX3: Hal 5G 129
Fern Gdns. LS29: I'ly 6C 10
Fern Gro. LS5: Leeds 5A 76
              (off Tordoff Pl.)

Fernhill BD16: Bgly 2C 50
Fern Hill Av. BD18: Ship 2H 69
Fern Hill Gro. BD18: Ship 2H 69
Fern Hill Mt. BD18: Ship 2H 69
Fern Hill Rd. BD18: Ship 2H 69
Ferniehurst BD17: Bail 6C 52
Fern Lea *BD13: Que* *4B 108*
                                (off Sandbeds)
Fernlea LS26: Rothw 1B 142
Fern Lea St. HX6: Sow B 4H 147
Fern Lea Vw. LS28: Stan 1A 94
Fernley Gdns. BD12: Wyke 3C 132
Fern Pl. *BD18: Ship* *1H 69*
                                (off Saltaire Rd.)
Fern Ri. HX5: Ell 4D 160
Fern St. BD4: B'frd 2B 112
   BD21: Keigh 5A 34
   BD22: Haw *3C 64*
                                (off Sun St.)
   HX3: Hal 5F 129
Fern Ter. BD8: B'frd 1C 90
   BD20: Rid *4D 34*
                                (off Carr La.)
   LS28: Stan 1A 94
Fern Vw. BD19: Gom 6E 135
Fern Way LS14: S'cft 6C 44
Fernwood LS8: Leeds 6E 61
Fernwood Ct. LS8: Leeds 6E 61
Ferrand Av. BD4: B'frd 5A 112
Ferrand La. BD16: Bgly 4B 50
   BD19: Gom 6E 135
Ferrand Rd. BD18: Ship 1H 69
Ferrands Cl. BD16: Har 6F 49
Ferrands Pk. Way BD16: Har 6F 49
Ferrand St. BD16: Bgly 4C 50
Ferriby Cl. BD2: B'frd 6B 72
Ferriby Towers *LS9: Leeds* *2C 98*
                                (off Granville St.)
Festival Av. BD18: Ship 4D 70
Feversham Grange HX3: Hal 6F 149
Feversham St. BD3: B'frd 5G 7 (5G 91)
Fewston Av. BD6: B'frd 3E 109
   LS9: Leeds 5D 98
                                (not continuous)
Fewston Ct. LS9: Leeds 5D 98
Fiddlers Mill *BD16: Bgly* *1A 50*
                                (off Wood St.)
Fidler Cl. LS25: Gar 4E 103
Fidler La. LS25: Gar 4E 103
Fidler Ter. LS25: Gar 4E 103
Field Cl. HX3: Hal 6D 128
Field Ct. BD13: Thorn 5A 88
Fieldedge La. BD20: Rid 3E 35
Field End LS15: Leeds 4C 100
Field End Cl. LS15: Leeds 4C 100
Field End Ct. LS15: Leeds 4C 100
Field End Cres. LS15: Leeds 4C 100
Field End Gdns. LS15: Leeds 4C 100
Field End Gth. LS15: Leeds 4C 100
Field End Grn. LS15: Leeds 4C 100
Field End Gro. LS15: Leeds 3D 100
Field End Mt. LS15: Leeds 4C 100
Field End Rd. LS15: Leeds 4C 100
Fieldfare Dr. BD6: B'frd 4D 108
   WF10: All B 3H 145
Fieldfares, The *BD20: Sils* *2E 15*
                                (off The Mallards)
Fieldgate Rd. BD10: B'frd 2B 72
Field Head BD22: Oxen 4B 64
   HX2: Ogd 6B 106
Fieldhead WF17: Birs 4A 136
Fieldhead Bus. Cen. *BD7: B'frd* *4C 90*
                                (off Gt. Russell Ct.)
Fieldhead Ct. LS23: B Spa 4A 30
Fieldhead Cres. WF17: Birs 4A 136
Fieldhead Dr. LS15: Bar E 2F 83
   LS20: Guis 5A 40
Fieldhead Gdns. WF12: Dew 6B 154
Fieldhead Gro. LS20: Guis 5A 40
Field Head La. BD11: Drig 2A 136
   BD22: Oxen 4A 64
   HX2: Illing 6B 106
   WF17: Birs 5A 136

Fieldhead Paddock LS23: B Spa . . .3A 30
Field Head Pde. WF17: Birs 5B 136
Fieldhead Rd. LS20: Guis 5A 40
Fieldhead St. BD7: B'frd 5B 90
Field Head Way HX2: Illing 6B 106
Field Ho. Cl. LS22: Weth 4C 12
Fieldhouse Cl. LS17: Leeds 5A 60
Field Ho. Cotts. *HX1: Hal* *4E 149*
                                (off Haugh Shaw Rd.)
Fieldhouse Ct. BD14: Clay 2E 109
Fieldhouse Dr. LS17: Leeds 5A 60
Fieldhouse Gro. LS28: Fars 1G 93
Fieldhouse Lawn LS17: Leeds 5A 60
Fieldhouse St. BD3: B'frd 4B 92
Fieldhouse Wlk. LS17: Leeds 5A 60
                                (not continuous)
Field Hurst LS29: Scho 2F 153
Fieldhurst Ct. BD4: B'frd 5A 112
Fielding Cl. LS27: Morl 2H 137
Fielding Ga. LS12: Leeds 3D 96
Fielding Ga. M. LS12: Leeds 3D 96
Fielding Way LS27: Morl 2H 137
FIELD LANE 3G 161
Field La. HD6: Ras 3H 161
Fieldmoor Lodge LS28: Pud 5A 94
Field Pk. Grange LS27: Gil 1F 137
Fields, The WF3: Loft 6H 141
Field Side HX1: Hal 1D 148
Fieldside BD13: Cull 3B 66
Fieldside Cl. BD4: B'frd 3D 112
Fields Rd. BD12: Low M 2E 133
Field St. BD1: B'frd 4E 7 (4F 91)
Field Ter. LS15: Leeds 3C 100
                                (Cross St.)
   LS15: Leeds 2D 100
                                (Hermon Rd.)
Field Top HD6: B Bri 2B 152
Field Top Rd. HD6: Ras 3H 161
Field Vw. HX2: Illing 2C 128
   HX3: Hal 5D 128
   LS25: M'fld 5E 105
Fieldway BD14: Clay 6D 88
   LS29: I'ly 4G 11
Fieldway Av. LS13: Leeds 5C 74
Fieldway Chase LS26: Oul 2F 143
Fieldway Cl. LS13: Leeds 5C 74
Fieldway Ri. LS13: Leeds 5C 74
Fife St. BD22: Haw 2D 64
Fifth Av. BD3: B'frd 2A 92
   LS26: Rothw 6C 120
Fifth Av. E. WF15: Liv 4H 153
Fifth Av. W. WF15: Liv 5H 153
Fifth St. BD12: Low M 1D 132
Filey St. BD1: B'frd 5F 7 (5F 91)
Fillingfir Dr. LS16: Leeds 1H 75
Fillingfir Rd. LS16: Leeds 1H 75
Fillingfir Wlk. LS16: Leeds 1H 75
Finch Cl. BD16: Bgly 3E 51
Finch Dr. LS15: Leeds 5H 101
Finchley St. BD5: B'frd 2D 110
Finchley Way LS27: Morl 4A 138
Finch St. BD5: B'frd 1D 110
Findon Ter. BD10: B'frd 5C 72
Fink Hill LS18: H'fth 1C 74
Finkil St. HD6: Brigh 4G 151
Finkin La. WF3: S'ley 6H 157
Finkle Cl. LS27: Gil 1E 137
Finkle La. LS27: Gil 1E 137
Finkle St. HX6: Sow B 5D 146
Finsbury Dr. BD2: B'frd 3F 71
Finsbury Rd.
   LS1: Leeds 1C 4 (2H 97)
Fir Av. LS16: Leeds 2C 58
Firbank Grn. BD2: B'frd 6B 72
Firbank Gro. LS15: Leeds 5A 100
Firbeck BD16: Har 1F 67
Fireclay Bus. Pk. BD13: Thorn 5F 87
Firethorn Cl. BD8: B'frd 3A 90
Firs, The LS14: S'cft 6E 45
First Av. BD3: B'frd 2A 92
   BD21: Keigh 1H 47
   HX3: Hal 5F 149
   LS12: Leeds 4D 96

First Av. LS17: Bard 6G 27
   LS19: Raw 2G 55
   LS22: Weth 4F 13
   LS26: Rothw 6B 120
   LS28: Stan 2A 94
   WF15: Liv 4H 153
First Av. Ind. Est. LS28: Stan 2A 94
Fir St. BD21: Keigh 3H 47
   BD22: Haw 3C 64
First St. BD12: Low M 1E 133
Firth Av. HD6: Brigh 6A 152
   LS11: Leeds 3G 117
Firth Carr BD18: Ship 4B 70
Firthfields LS25: Gar 4G 103
Firth Gro. LS11: Leeds 3G 117
Firth Ho. La. HD6: Ras 4B 162
Firth La. BD15: Wils 4G 67
Firth Mt. LS11: Leeds 3G 117
Firth Rd. BD9: B'frd 6A 70
   LS11: Leeds 3G 117
Firth Row BD4: B'frd 5H 111
Firths Ter. *HX3: Hal* *5D 128*
                                (off Wheatley Rd.)
Firth St. BD13: Thorn 5H 87
   HD6: Ras 2B 162
   LS9: Leeds 1H 5 (2C 98)
Firth Ter. LS9: Leeds 1H 5 (2C 98)
Firth Vw. LS11: Leeds 3G 117
Fir Tree App. LS17: Leeds 3H 59
Firtree Av. LS25: Gar 5H 103
Fir Tree Cl. LS17: Leeds 3A 60
Fir Tree Gdns. BD10: B'frd 3B 72
   LS17: Leeds 3H 59
Fir Tree Grn. LS17: Leeds 3A 60
Fir Tree Gro. LS17: Leeds 4A 60
Fir Tree La. LS17: Leeds 4B 60
Fir Tree Ri. LS17: Leeds 4A 60
Fir Tree Va. LS17: Leeds 4A 60
Fir Tree Vw. LS26: Meth 4E 145
Fish St. LS1: Leeds 4F 5 (3A 98)
Fitness Fast *5B 160*
                                (off Burley St.)
Fitness First
   Halifax 1A 164 (1A 14)
   Keighley 1A 48
   Leeds 2C 96
Fitness First for Women
   Bradford .4C 6
Fitness Studio, The *1B 162*
                                (off Park Row)
Fitts La. LS17: E Kes 3C 26
Fitzgerald St. BD5: B'frd 6D 90
Fitzroy Dr. LS8: Leeds 3E 79
Fitzroy Rd. BD3: B'frd 4H 91
                                (not continuous)
Fitzwilliam St. BD4: B'frd 6F 91
FIVE LANE ENDS 3H 71
Five Oaks BD17: Bail 5A 52
Five Ri. BD16: Bgly 2B 50
FIXBY 6A 162
Fixby Av. HX2: Hal 4C 148
Fixby Fold HX5: Ell 5E 161
Fixby Rd. HD2: Fix 6H 161
                                (not continuous)
Flagship Sq. WF12: Dew 6A 154
FLAPPIT SPRINGS 3G 65
Flasby Av. *BD20: Rid* *5F 35*
                                (off Ford Rd.)
Flasby St. BD21: Keigh 5A 34
Flat Nook BD16: Bgly 4D 50
Flats, The LS19: Yead 1G 55
Flats La. LS15: Bar E 3D 82
Flawith Dr. BD2: B'frd 1B 92
Flaxen Cl. BD6: B'frd 4D 110
Flaxman Rd. BD2: B'frd 5A 72
Flax Mill Rd. LS10: Leeds 2C 118
Flax Pl. LS9: Leeds 6H 5 (4C 98)
Flaxton Cl. LS11: Leeds 2H 117
Flaxton Ct. BD4: B'frd 5B 92
Flaxton Gdns. LS11: Leeds 2H 117
Flaxton Grn. BD2: B'frd 1B 92
Flaxton Pl. BD7: B'frd 5B 90
Flaxton St. LS11: Leeds 2H 117

Flaxton Vw. LS11: Leeds 2H 117
Fledborough Rd. LS22: Weth 4C 12
Fleece St. BD6: B'frd 6H 109
   BD21: Keigh 6A 34
Fleet La. BD13: Que 3H 107
   LS26: Meth 3A 144
   LS26: Oul 2F 143
Fleet Thro' Rd. LS18: H'fth 3D 74
Fletcher Av. BD20: Sils 1E 15
Fletcher Cres. HD6: Ras 5G 161
Fletcher La. BD2: B'frd 5D 70
Fletcher Rd. BD6: B'frd 4B 110
Fletton Ter. BD2: B'frd 1H 91
Flexbury Av. LS27: Morl 4A 138
Flintmill La. LS23: T Arch 1B 30
Flinton Gro. BD2: B'frd 6B 72
Flockton Av. BD4: B'frd 1G 111
Flockton Cl. BD4: B'frd 1G 111
Flockton Cres. BD4: B'frd 1G 111
Flockton Dr. BD4: B'frd 1G 111
Flockton Gro. BD4: B'frd 1G 111
Flockton Rd. BD4: B'frd 1G 111
   WF10: All B 3H 145
Flockton Ter. BD4: B'frd 1G 111
Floral Av. LS7: Leeds 3A 78
Florence Av. BD15: Wils 3F 67
   LS9: Leeds 1E 99
Florence Gro. LS9: Leeds 1E 99
Florence Mt. LS9: Leeds 1E 99
Florence Pl. LS9: Leeds 1E 99
Florence St. BD3: B'frd 5A 92
   HX1: Hal 2E 149
   LS9: Leeds 1E 99
Florence Ter. *LS27: Morl* *3B 138*
          (off Gillroyd Pde.)
Florida Rd. BD15: All 5C 68
Florist St. BD21: Keigh 4C 34
Flossmore Way LS27: Gil 6E 115
Flower Acre HX5: Ell 5B 160
Flower Bank BD2: B'frd 5F 71
   HX6: Sow B 6F 147
Flower Chase LS20: Guis 4D 40
Flower Cl. LS19: Yead 6E 41
Flower Ct. BD2: B'frd 1A 92
   LS18: H'fth 2D 74
Flower Cft. BD21: Keigh 2F 47
Flower Gth. BD10: B'frd 3B 72
   LS18: H'fth *1D 74*
          (off Stanhope Dr.)
Flower Haven BD9: B'frd 5F 69
Flower Hill BD9: B'frd 5H 69
Flowerlands HX3: Hip 6G 131
Flower Mt. BD17: Bail 3D 52
   LS19: Yead *6G 41*
          (off Alexandra Ter.)
Flowerpot La. BD13: Que 5G 107
Floyd St. BD5: B'frd 2B 110
Focus Way LS19: Raw 2F 55
Fold, The *BD22: Haw* *2B 64*
          (off West La.)
   LS15: Leeds 5G 81
Foldings Av. BD19: Scho 1F 153
Foldings Cl. BD19: Scho 1E 153
Foldings Ct. BD19: Scho 1E 153
Foldings Gro. BD19: Scho 1E 153
Foldings Pde. BD19: Scho 1E 153
Foldings Rd. BD19: Scho 1E 153
Folkestone St. BD3: B'frd 4H 91
          (not continuous)
Folkton Holme BD2: B'frd 1B 92
Folly Hall Av. BD6: B'frd 5B 110
Folly Hall Cl. BD6: B'frd 5B 110
Folly Hall Gardens, The
   BD6: B'frd 5B 110
Folly Hall Mt. WF3: Ting 1E 155
Folly Hall Rd. BD6: B'frd 5B 110
   WF3: Ting 1E 155
Folly Hall Wlk. BD6: B'frd 5B 110
Folly La. LS11: Leeds 1H 117
Folly Vw. Rd. BD22: Haw 3D 64
Fontmell Cl. BD4: B'frd 3C 112
Football LS19: Yead 6G 41
Football World 6F 99

Forber Gro. BD4: B'frd 6C 92
Forber Pl. LS15: Leeds 4A 100
Forbes Ho. *BD4: B'frd* *2C 112*
          (off Stirling Cres.)
Ford BD13: Que 5G 107
Ford Hill BD13: Que 5G 107
Ford St. BD21: Keigh 4C 34
Fore La. HX6: Sow B 6G 147
Fore La. Av. HX6: Sow B 6F 147
Foreside Bottom La. BD13: Denh . . .1B 106
Foreside La. BD13: Denh 6H 85
Forest Av. HX2: Illing 3C 128
Forest Bank LS27: Gil 6E 115
Forest Cres. HX2: Illing 3C 128
Forestdale Way BD18: Ship 3E 71
Forester Ct. BD13: Denh 3B 86
Forest Ga. LS21: Otley 4E 23
Forest Grn. HX2: Hal 4C 128
Forest Gro. HX2: Hal 3D 128
Forest Ridge WF3: E Ard 6A 140
Forest Yd. LS10: Leeds 3C 140
Forge La. LS12: Leeds 3D 96
Forge Row LS12: N Far 2F 115
Forge Vw. BD20: Stee 6C 14
Forman's Dr. WF3: Rob H 4E 141
Forrester Ct. WF3: Rob H 4F 141
Forrest Ter. *LS21: Otley* *4D 22*
          (off Piper La.)
Forrest Vs. *LS21: Otley* *4D 22*
          (off Piper La.)
Forster Cl. LS29: Burl W 2F 21
Forster Dr. BD1: B'frd 3E 7 (4F 91)
Forster Loft LS12: Leeds 1B 116
Forster M. LS12: Leeds 1A 116
Forster Pl. LS12: Leeds 1A 116
Forster Sq. BD1: B'frd 4E 7 (4F 91)
Forster Sq. Retail Pk.
   BD1: B'frd 2D 6 (3E 91)
   LS10: Leeds 6C 98
Forsythia Av. WF3: E Ard 1A 156
Forth Ct. LS11: Leeds 5G 97
Forum Leisure Centre, The
   Leeds 4H 5 (3B 98)
Foss Av. LS22: Weth 2D 12
Fosse Way LS25: Gar 5H 103
Foster Av. BD13: Thorn 5B 88
   BD20: Sils 1D 14
Foster Cl. LS27: Morl 2A 138
Foster Cres. LS27: Morl 2A 138
Foster Gdns. BD22: Keigh 6F 33
Foster Pk. BD13: Denh 2C 86
Foster Pk. Gro. BD13: Denh 2C 86
Foster Pk. Rd. BD13: Denh 2C 86
Foster Pk. Vw. BD13: Denh 2C 86
          (not continuous)
Foster Rd. BD21: Keigh 3H 47
Foster St. HX1: Hal 4C 164
Foster Sq. BD13: Denh 3B 86
   LS10: Leeds 5B 118
Foster St. BD13: Que 4A 108
   LS27: Morl 2A 138
Foster Ter. LS13: Leeds 6F 75
Foston Cl. BD2: B'frd 1C 92
Foston La. BD2: B'frd 1B 92
Foulcauseway La. LS21: Otley 4H 23
Foulds Ter. BD16: Bgly 3C 50
Foundry App. LS9: Leeds 1F 99
Foundry Av. LS8: Leeds 6F 79
   LS9: Leeds 6F 79
Foundry Dr. LS9: Leeds 6F 79
Foundry Hill BD16: Bgly 4B 50
Foundry Ind. Est. LS28: Stan 2A 94
Foundry La. BD4: B'frd 6H 91
   LS9: Leeds 6H 79
   LS14: Leeds 6H 79
   LS28: Stan 1A 94
Foundry Mill Cres. LS14: Leeds 6B 80
Foundry Mill Dr. LS14: Leeds 6A 80
          (not continuous)
Foundry Mill Gdns. LS14: Leeds 4A 80
Foundry Mill Mt. LS14: Leeds 6B 80
Foundry Mill St. LS14: Leeds 6A 80
Foundry Mill Ter. LS14: Leeds 6B 80

Foundry Mill Vw. LS14: Leeds 6B 80
Foundry Mill Wlk. LS14: Leeds 6B 80
Foundry Pl. LS9: Leeds 6F 79
Foundry Rd. LS28: Stan 2A 94
Foundry Sq. *LS11: Leeds* *5H 97*
          (off Foundry St.)
Foundry St. HD6: Brigh 2C 162
   HX1: Hal 2C 164 (1G 149)
   HX6: Sow B 6H 147
   LS9: Leeds 5H 5 (4C 98)
   LS11: Leeds 5H 97
Foundry St. Nth. HX3: Hal 4D 128
Foundry Wlk. LS8: Leeds 6E 79
Fountain Ct. LS27: Morl 3G 137
Fountain Hall *LS27: Morl* *5H 137*
          (off Fountain St.)
Fountain Head Rd. HX2: Hal 5A 128
Fountain M. *BD13: Que* *4A 108*
          (off Fountain St.)
Fountains Av. LS23: B Spa 4A 30
Fountain St. BD1: B'frd 3C 6 (4E 91)
   BD12: Low M 1C 132
   BD13: Que 4A 108
   BD13: Thorn 5H 87
   HX1: Hal 5B 164 (2G 149)
   LS1: Leeds 3B 4 (3G 97)
   LS27: Chur 5C 116
   LS27: Morl 5H 137
Fountain Ter. BD12: Wyke 4D 132
Fountain Vs. *BD22: Oxen* *6C 64*
          (off Old Manse Cft.)
Fountain Way BD18: Ship 2C 70
FOURLANDS 1A 72
Fourlands Ct. BD10: B'frd 1A 72
Fourlands Cres. BD10: B'frd 1A 72
Fourlands Dr. BD10: B'frd 1A 72
Fourlands Gdns. BD10: B'frd 1A 72
Fourlands Gro. BD10: B'frd 1A 72
Fourlands Rd. BD10: B'frd 1A 72
FOUR LANE ENDS 3H 89
Four Lanes Bus. Pk. BD8: B'frd 3H 89
Four Seasons HX2: Brad 4E 107
Fourteenth Av. LS12: Leeds 5D 96
Fourth Av. BD3: B'frd 2A 92
   BD21: Keigh 1G 47
   LS22: Weth 4F 13
   LS26: Rothw 6C 120
   WF15: Liv 4H 153
Fourth St. BD12: Low M 1E 133
Fowlers Ct. LS21: Otley 4F 23
Fowlers Cft. LS21: Otley 4F 23
Fowlers Gth. BD22: Haw 6D 46
Fowler's Pl. LS28: Stan 1A 94
Fowler St. BD4: B'frd 6H 91
Fowler St. Ind. Est. BD4: B'frd 6H 91
Fox Cl. HX4: Gree 4H 159
Foxcroft Cl. BD13: Que 6G 107
   LS6: Leeds 4B 76
Foxcroft Dr. HD6: Ras 3G 161
Foxcroft Gth. LS6: Leeds 4B 76
Foxcroft Grn. LS6: Leeds 4B 76
Fox Croft La. BD16: Cot 2A 68
Foxcroft Mt. LS6: Leeds 4B 76
Foxcroft Rd. LS6: Leeds 4B 76
Foxcroft Wlk. LS6: Leeds 4B 76
Foxcroft Way LS6: Leeds 4B 76
Foxglove Av. LS8: Leeds 3G 79
Foxglove Rd. WF17: Birs 5A 136
Foxhill BD17: Bail 4B 52
   LS22: Weth 3E 13
Foxhill Av. BD13: Que 4H 107
   LS16: Leeds 6C 58
Foxhill Cl. BD13: Que 4H 107
Foxhill Ct. LS16: Leeds 6C 58
Foxhill Cres. LS16: Leeds 6D 58
Foxhill Dr. BD13: Que 4H 107
   LS16: Leeds 6C 58
Foxhill Grn. LS16: Leeds 6D 58
Foxhill Gro. BD13: Que 4H 107
   LS16: Leeds 6D 58
Foxhills, The LS16: Leeds 3F 57
Foxholes Cres. LS28: Cal 3F 73
Foxholes La. LS28: Cal 3F 73

Foxstone Ri. BD17: Bail 4E **53**
Fox St. BD16: Bgly 4B **50**
  BD19: Cleck 2H **153**
Foxton Gdns. LS27: Morl 4H **137**
Fox Way LS10: Leeds 6C **98**
Foxwood LS8: Leeds 1G **79**
Foxwood Av. LS8: Leeds 4A **80**
Foxwood Cl. LS8: Leeds 4A **80**
Foxwood Farm Way
  LS8: Leeds 4A **80**
Foxwood Gro. LS8: Leeds 4A **80**
Foxwood Ho. BD4: B'frd 6B **92**
                   (off Westbury St.)
Foxwood Ri. LS8: Leeds 4A **80**
Foxwood Wlk. LS8: Leeds 4A **80**
  LS22: Weth 2F **13**
Fraisthorpe Mead BD2: B'frd 1B **92**
Frances St. BD21: Keigh 5G **33**
  HD6: Brigh 6A **152**
  HX5: Ell 5B **160**
  LS28: Fars 1H **93**
Francis Cl. BD12: Wyke 5C **132**
  HX1: Hal 2E **149**
Francis Ct. LS7: Leeds 6B **78**
                    (off Francis St.)
Francis Gro. LS11: Leeds 2H **117**
Francis Ho. BD2: B'frd 1H **91**
                   (off Hatfield Rd.)
Francis Sq. BD13: Cull 3B **66**
                 (off George's Sq.)
Francis St. BD4: B'frd 6G **7** (6G **91**)
  HX1: Hal 2E **149**
  LS7: Leeds 6B **78**
Frankland Gro. LS7: Leeds 6C **78**
Frankland Pl. LS7: Leeds 6C **78**
                 (not continuous)
Frank La. HX2: Midg 5B **126**
Franklin St. HX1: Hal 2D **148**
Frank Parkinson Ct. LS20: Guis . . .4C **40**
                  (off W. Villa Rd.)
Frank Parkinson Homes
          LS20: Guis 4C **40**
                   (off Lands La.)
Frank Pl. BD7: B'frd 1B **110**
Frank St. BD7: B'frd 1B **110**
  HX1: Hal 3E **149**
Fraser Av. LS18: H'fth 1B **74**
Fraser Rd. LS28: Cal 3D **72**
Fraser St. BD8: B'frd 3C **90**
  LS9: Leeds 2D **98**
Freakfield La. WF15: Liv 1H **163**
Fred Atkinson Way BD17: Bail 6D **52**
Frederick Av. LS9: Leeds 5E **99**
Frederick Cl. BD10: B'frd 6F **53**
Frederick St. BD21: Keigh 6B **34**
  LS28: Fars 6G **73**
Fred's Pl. BD4: B'frd 2A **112**
Fred St. BD21: Keigh 1H **47**
Freeman Ct. HD6: B Bri 2B **152**
                 (off Axminster Dr.)
Freeman Rd. HX3: Sou 4C **150**
Freemans Way LS22: Weth 3F **13**
Freemantle Pl. LS15: Leeds 4A **100**
Freemont St. LS13: Leeds 1C **94**
Free School La. HX1: Hal 4E **149**
  HX3: Hal 4E **149**
Freestone M. LS12: Leeds 4E **95**
Fremantle Gro. BD4: B'frd 6C **92**
Frensham Av. LS27: Morl 4H **137**
Frensham Dr. BD7: B'frd 2F **109**
Frensham Gro. BD7: B'frd 2F **109**
Frensham Way BD7: B'frd 2F **109**
Freshfield Gdns. BD15: All 2D **88**
Friar Cl. BD3: B'frd 3A **72**
Friar Pl. HD2: Hud 6F **163**
Friars Ind. Est. BD10: B'frd 2H **71**
Friary Ct. WF17: Birs 6H **135**
FRIENDLY 4H **147**
Friendly Av. HX6: Sow B 4G **147**
Friendly Fold HX3: Hal 5E **129**
Friendly Fold Ho. HX3: Hal 5E **129**
                 (off Lentifield St.)
Friendly Fold Rd. HX3: Hal 5E **129**

Friendly St. BD13: Thorn 5H **87**
  HX3: Hal 5E **129**
Frimley Dr. BD5: B'frd 3C **110**
Frith St. BD22: Cros R 1E **65**
FRIZINGHALL 5B **70**
Frizinghall Rd. BD9: B'frd 5C **70**
Frizinghall Station (Rail) 5C **70**
Frizley Gdns. BD9: B'frd 5C **70**
Frodingham Vs. BD2: B'frd 1B **92**
Frogmoor Av. BD12: O'haw 2F **133**
Frogmore Ter. BD12: O'haw 2F **133**
Frontline Cl. LS8: Leeds 3E **79**
Front Row LS11: Leeds 5H **97**
                 (not continuous)
Front St. LS11: Leeds 5H **97**
Front Vw. HX3: She 2E **131**
Fruit St. BD21: Keigh 5C **34**
Fuchsia Cft. LS26: Wood 1G **143**
Fulbeck Cl. BD15: All 4C **88**
Fulford Wlk. BD2: B'frd 1B **92**
Fulham Pl. LS11: Leeds 2H **117**
Fulham Sq. LS11: Leeds 2H **117**
                  (off Fulham St.)
Fulham St. LS11: Leeds 2H **117**
Fullers Ho. LS9: Leeds 6H **5**
                   (off East St.)
Fullerton Cl. BD3: B'frd 5G **7** (5G **91**)
Fullerton Ter. LS22: Coll 3B **28**
Fulmar Cl. LS10: Leeds 2B **140**
Fulmar M. BD8: B'frd 4E **89**
FULNECK 6A **94**
Fulneck LS28: Pud 1H **113**
Fulneck Cl. LS11: Leeds 6G **117**
Fulneck Ct. LS28: Pud 6B **94**
Fulneck Golf Course 1H **113**
Fulneck M. LS28: Pud 6B **94**
Fulton Pl. LS16: Leeds 2C **76**
Fulton St. BD1: B'frd 4C **6** (4D **90**)
Furnace Gro. BD12: O'haw 2F **133**
Furnace Inn St. BD4: B'frd 6B **92**
Furnace La. BD11: Birk 1E **135**
Furnace Rd. BD12: O'haw 2F **133**
                 (not continuous)
Furness Av. HX2: Illing 2B **128**
Furness Cres. HX2: Illing 2B **128**
Furness Dr. HX2: Illing 2B **128**
Furness Gdns. HX2: Illing 3C **128**
Furness Gro. HX2: Illing 3B **128**
Furness Pl. HX2: Illing 4C **128**
Fusden La. BD19: Gom 6E **135**
Fusion Point LS25: Gar 3G **103**
Future Bodies Gym 2A **138**
                   (off Bank Av.)
Future Flds. BD6: B'frd 4G **109**
Futures Way BD4: B'frd 6F **91**
Fyfe Cres. BD17: Bail 5E **53**
Fyfe Gro. BD17: Bail 5E **53**
Fyfe La. BD17: Bail 5E **53**

G

Gable End Ter. LS28: Pud 4B **94**
Gables, The BD17: Bail 4E **53**
  BD21: Keigh 6G **33**
                 (off W. Leeds St.)
  LS17: Leeds 3E **61**
  LS18: H'fth 4E **57**
Gabriel Ct. LS10: Leeds 1B **118**
              (off Hunslet Grn. Way)
Gadwall Dr. WF10: All B 3H **145**
Gainest HX2: Hal 4D **148**
Gainford Dr. LS25: Gar 5F **103**
Gain La. BD2: B'frd 2B **92**
  BD3: B'frd 2B **92**
Gainsborough Av. LS16: Leeds 2B **92**
Gainsborough Cl. BD3: B'frd 1G **91**
Gainsborough Dr. LS16: Leeds 1G **91**
Gainsborough Flds. LS12: N Far . . .2G **115**
                  (off Coach Rd.)
Gainsborough Pl. LS12: N Far 2G **115**
                  (off Coach Rd.)
Gainsborough Way WF3: S'ley 4H **157**

GAISBY 4D **70**
Gaisby La. BD2: B'frd, Ship 5D **70**
  BD18: Ship 3D **70**
Gaisby Mt. BD18: Ship 4D **70**
Gaisby Pl. BD18: Ship 3D **70**
Gaisby Ri. BD18: Ship 3D **70**
Gaitskell Ct. LS11: Leeds 6G **97**
Gaitskell Grange
          LS11: Leeds 6G **97**
Gaitskell Wlk. LS11: Leeds 6G **97**
Gala Bingo
  Bradford 4C **112**
  Leeds 5H **95**
Gala Casino
  Leeds 4A **4** (3F **97**)
Galefield Grn. BD6: B'frd 1H **131**
Gale St. BD21: Keigh 5A **34**
  BD22: Cros R 1F **65**
Gallagher Leisure Pk.
          BD3: B'frd 3D **92**
Gallery 339 . . . . .6G **149**
Gallops, The LS27: Morl 6B **138**
Galloway Cl. LS28: Pud 3E **93**
Galloway La. LS28: Pud 2E **93**
Galloway Rd. BD10: B'frd 2B **72**
Galsworthy Av. BD9: B'frd 6E **69**
GAMBLE HILL 3F **95**
Gamble Hill LS13: Leeds 3F **95**
Gamble Hill Chase LS13: Leeds . . .3F **95**
Gamble Hill Cl. LS13: Leeds 3F **95**
Gamble Hill Cft. LS13: Leeds 3F **95**
                (off Gamble Hill Vw.)
Gamble Hill Cross LS13: Leeds 3F **95**
                (off Gamble Hill Lawn)
Gamble Hill Dr. LS13: Leeds 3F **95**
Gamble Hill Fold LS13: Leeds 3F **95**
                (off Gamble Hill Lawn)
Gamble Hill Grange LS13: Leeds . . .3F **95**
                 (off Gamble Hill Dr.)
Gamble Hill Grn. LS13: Leeds 3F **95**
Gamble Hill Lawn LS13: Leeds 3F **95**
Gamble Hill Path LS13: Leeds 3F **95**
                (off Gamble Hill Grn.)
Gamble Hill Pl. LS13: Leeds 3F **95**
Gamble Hill Ri. LS13: Leeds 3F **95**
Gamble Hill Va. LS13: Leeds 3F **95**
Gamble Hill Vw. LS13: Leeds 3F **95**
Gamble Hill Wlk. LS13: Leeds 3F **95**
                 (off Gamble Hill Ri.)
Gamble La. LS12: Leeds 5E **95**
Gambles Hill LS28: Fars 6H **73**
Gamel Vw. BD20: Stee 5B **14**
Game Scar La. BD22: Lay, Oak . . .1B **46**
Gang, The LS12: Leeds 4C **96**
                  (off Town St.)
Ganners Cl. LS13: Leeds 5E **75**
Ganners Gth. LS13: Leeds 5E **75**
Ganners Grn. LS13: Leeds 5E **75**
Ganners Gro. LS13: Leeds 5F **75**
Ganners Hill LS13: Leeds 5F **75**
Ganners La. LS13: Leeds 5E **75**
Ganners Mt. LS13: Leeds 5E **75**
Ganners Ri. LS13: Leeds 5F **75**
Ganners Rd. LS13: Leeds 5E **75**
Ganners Wlk. LS13: Leeds 5F **75**
Ganners Way LS13: Leeds 5E **75**
Gannerthorpe Cl.
          BD12: Wyke 4C **132**
Ganny Rd. HD6: Brigh 1B **162**
Ganton Cl. LS6: Leeds 5H **77**
Gant Pl. BD2: B'frd 6F **71**
Gaol La. HX1: Hal 3C **164** (2G **149**)
                 (not continuous)
Garden Cl. BD12: Wyke 3C **132**
Gardeners Ct. LS10: Leeds 1B **118**
Garden Fld. BD12: Wyke 4C **132**
Garden Fold HX3: Hip 1E **151**
Garden Ho. Cl. LS26: Meth 4D **144**
Garden Ho. La. WF3: Ting 1G **155**
Gardenhurst LS6: Leeds 5E **77**
Garden La. BD9: B'frd 6H **69**
  HX4: Bark 4A **158**
Garden Rd. HD6: Brigh 5H **151**

Gardens, The—Gillroyd Ri.

Gardens, The BD16: Bgly 4F **51**
HX1: Hal 4G **149**
LS10: Leeds 3A **140**
LS27: Morl 5H **137**
LS28: Fars 6G **73**
Garden St. BD9: B'frd 5H **69**
BD22: Cros R 1F **65**
Garden St. Mill HX3: Hal 2D **164**
Garden St. Nth.
HX3: Hal 2D **164** (1H **149**)
Garden Ter. BD9: B'frd 6A **70**
Garden Vw. BD15: Wils 3G **67**
BD16: Bgly 4E **51**
Garden Vw. Ct. LS8: Leeds 6F **61**
Garden Village LS25: M'fld 5E **105**
Gardiner Row BD4: B'frd 3H **111**
Gardiners Sq. HX3: Hip 1E **151**
Garfield Av. BD8: B'frd 1B **90**
Garfield Pl. *BD15: All 2C 88*
(off North Vw.)
Garfield St. BD15: All 2C **88**
HX3: Hal 6E **129**
Garfit Hill BD19: Gom 6H **135**
WF17: Gom 6H **135**
GARFORTH 4E **103**
Garforth Av. BD20: Stee 5C **14**
GARFORTH BRIDGE 6C **102**
Garforth Golf Course 6E **83**
Garforth Rd. BD21: Keigh 5C **34**
Garforth Squash & Leisure Cen.
. . . . .5G **103**
Garforth Station (Rail) 4F **103**
Garforth St. BD15: All 2D **88**
Gargrave App. LS9: Leeds 3D **98**
Gargrave Cl. HD6: Ras 3F **161**
Gargrave Ct. LS9: Leeds 2D **98**
Gargrave Pl. LS9: Leeds 2D **98**
Garibaldi St. BD3: B'frd 4C **92**
(not continuous)
Garland Dr. LS15: Leeds 4F **101**
Garlick St. HD6: Ras 5G **161**
Garmont M. LS7: Leeds 3B **78**
Garmont Rd. LS7: Leeds 3B **78**
Garnet Av. LS11: Leeds 2A **118**
Garnet Cres. LS11: Leeds 2A **118**
Garnet Gro. LS11: Leeds 2A **118**
Garnet Pde. LS11: Leeds 2A **118**
Garnet Pl. LS11: Leeds 2A **118**
Garnet Rd. LS11: Leeds 3A **118**
Garnet Ter. LS11: Leeds 2A **118**
Garnett St. BD3: B'frd 4G **7** (4G **91**)
LS21: Otley 3E **23**
Garnet Vw. LS11: Leeds 2A **118**
Garrowby Ho. *BD10: B'frd 1H 71*
(off Thorp Gth.)
Garsdale Av. BD10: B'frd 2A **72**
Garsdale Cres. BD17: Bail 3E **53**
Garsdale Fold LS22: Coll 2A **28**
Garside Dr. HX2: Hal 3D **128**
Garth, The LS9: Leeds 4C **98**
LS22: Coll 3B **28**
LS25: Gar 4G **103**
Garth Av. LS17: Leeds 6H **59**
LS22: Coll 3B **28**
Garth Barn Cl. BD9: B'frd 6A **70**
Garth Dr. LS17: Leeds 6H **59**
Garth End LS22: Coll 3B **28**
LS22: K Dei 1D **12**
Garth Fold BD10: B'frd 1H **71**
Garth Gro. LS29: Men 1G **39**
Garthland Way BD4: B'frd 2A **112**
Garth Rd. LS17: Leeds 6H **59**
Garth St. BD21: Keigh 6H **33**
Garthwaite Mt. BD15: All 1D **88**
Garth Wlk. LS17: Leeds 6H **59**
Garthwood Cl. BD4: B'frd 5H **111**
Garton Av. LS9: Leeds 4E **99**
Garton Dr. BD10: B'frd 4B **72**
Garton Gro. LS9: Leeds 4E **99**
Garton Rd. LS9: Leeds 4E **99**
Garton Ter. LS9: Leeds 4E **99**
Garton Vw. LS9: Leeds 4E **99**
Garvey Vw. BD5: B'frd 1E **111**
Garwick Ter. HX4: Gree 4H **159**
Gascoigne Av. LS15: Bar E 3D **82**
Gascoigne Ct. LS15: Bar E 3E **83**
Gascoigne Rd. LS15: Bar E 3D **82**
WF3: Thpe H 6C **140**
Gascoigne Vw. LS15: Bar E 3D **82**
Gashouse La. LS22: Weth 4F **13**
Gas Ho. Yd. BD12: O'haw 2E **133**
Gas St. BD22: Haw 2D **64**
Gas Works La. HX5: Ell 4B **160**
Gas Works Rd. BD21: Keigh 5D **34**
(not continuous)
HX6: Sow B 5B **148**
Gatefield Mt. BD6: B'frd 1B **132**
Gatehaus, The
BD1: B'frd 4F **7** (4F **91**)
Gatehead HX4: Gree 5D **158**
Gate Head La. HX4: Gree 6D **158**
Gate Ho. Ct. LS26: Wood 6G **121**
Gateland Dr. LS17: Shad 3A **62**
Gateland La. LS17: Shad 4A **62**
Gatenby Cl. BD6: B'frd 4G **109**
Gateon Ho. La. LS17: E Kes 1C **44**
Gatesway BD16: Har 6E **49**
Gateway, The LS26: Rothw 3A **142**
Gate Way Dr. LS19: Yead 6E **41**
Gateway E. LS9: Leeds 5H **5**
Gateway Nth. LS9: Leeds 5H **5**
Gateways WF1: Out 4G **157**
Gateways, The BD12: Low M 2C **132**
Gateway Sth. LS9: Leeds 6H **5**
Gateway W. LS9: Leeds 6H **5**
Gathorne Cl. LS8: Leeds 6C **78**
Gathorne St. BD7: B'frd 1B **110**
HD6: Brigh 6B **152**
LS8: Leeds 6C **78**
(not continuous)
Gathorne Ter. LS8: Leeds 6C **78**
(not continuous)
Gaukroger La. HX1: Hal 4H **149**
Gaunts Pl. LS28: Fars 6A **74**
Gavin Cl. BD3: B'frd 4C **92**
Gawcliffe Rd. BD18: Ship 3C **70**
Gawthorpe BD16: Bgly 2C **50**
Gawthorpe Av. BD16: Bgly 2C **50**
Gawthorpe Dr. BD16: Bgly 2C **50**
Gawthorpe La. BD16: Bgly 3C **50**
Gay La. LS21: Otley 4E **23**
Gayle Cl. BD12: Wyke 5C **132**
Gaynor St. BD1: B'frd 3A **6** (4D **90**)
Gaythorne Rd. BD2: B'frd 6A **72**
BD5: B'frd 2E **111**
Gaythorne Ter. BD14: Clay 1E **109**
HX3: Hip 6E **131**
Geelong Cl. BD2: B'frd 6F **71**
Gelderd Bus. Pk. LS12: Leeds 1D **116**
Gelderd Cl. LS12: Leeds 1D **116**
Gelderd La. LS12: Leeds 1D **116**
Gelderd Pl. LS12: Leeds 5E **97**
Gelderd Rd. LS12: Gil, Leeds 2E **137**
LS12: Leeds 2D **116**
LS27: Gil 2E **137**
WF17: Birs 6B **136**
Gelderd Trad. Est.
LS12: Leeds 6E **97**
Gelder Rd. LS12: Leeds 4B **96**
Gemini Bus. Pk. LS7: Leeds 6B **78**
Genista Dr. LS10: Leeds 5B **118**
George Mann Rd. LS10: Leeds 2E **119**
George Mann Way
LS10: Leeds 2D **118**
George Sq. HX1: Hal 4B **164** (2G **149**)
George's Sq. BD13: Cull 3B **66**
BD21: Keigh 1H **47**
George's St. HX3: Hal 4D **128**
George St. BD1: B'frd 5F **7** (5F **91**)
BD13: Denh 2C **86**
BD13: Thorn 5H **87**
BD17: Bail 6C **52**
BD18: Ship 1H **69**
HD6: Brigh 1C **162**
HD6: Ras 2A **162**
HX1: Hal 4B **164** (2G **149**)
George St. HX3: Hip 2F **151**
HX4: Gree 4H **159**
HX5: Ell 5B **160**
HX6: Sow B 6H **147**
LS2: Leeds 4F **5** (3A **98**)
LS19: Raw 3F **55**
LS26: Wood 1E **145**
LS29: Add 1D **8**
WF1: Out 4F **157**
Georgian Sq. LS13: Leeds 4A **74**
Geraldton Av. BD2: B'frd 6E **71**
Gerard Av. LS27: Morl 3H **137**
Gerard Ho. *BD10: B'frd 2A 72*
(off Fairhaven Grn.)
Germaine Ter. LS14: T'ner 4G **63**
Gernhill Av. HD2: Fix 6H **161**
Gerrard St. HX1: Hal 4A **164** (2F **149**)
Ghyll, The BD16: Cot 1C **68**
HD2: Fix 6A **162**
Ghyllbank BD20: Sils 1E **15**
Ghyll Beck Dr. LS19: Raw 4A **56**
LS21: Otley 5B **22**
Ghyll Cl. BD20: Stee 6C **14**
Ghyll Dr. BD22: Haw 3C **64**
Ghyll Grange La. BD20: Sils 2A **16**
Ghyll Lodge BD16: Cot 1C **68**
Ghyll M. LS29: I'ly 6C **10**
Ghyll Mt. LS19: Yead 1D **54**
Ghyll Rd. LS6: Leeds 3A **76**
Ghyll Royd LS20: Guis 6C **40**
(not continuous)
LS29: I'ly 5B **10**
Ghyllroyd LS19: Yead 2E **55**
Ghyllroyd Av. BD11: Birk 2F **135**
Ghyllroyd Dr. BD11: Birk 2F **135**
Ghyll Wood LS29: I'ly 6A **10**
Ghyll Wood Dr. BD16: Cot 1C **68**
Gibbet, The 3A **164**
Gibbet St. HX1: Hal 4A **164** (2E **149**)
HX2: Hal 2B **148**
Gibb La. HX2: Mt T 4H **127**
Gibraltar HX1: Hal 3C **148**
Gibraltar Av. HX1: Hal 3C **148**
Gibraltar Island Rd. LS10: Leeds . . .1D **118**
Gibraltar Rd. HX1: Hal 2C **148**
LS28: Pud 4F **93**
Gibson Dr. LS15: Leeds 4E **101**
Gibson La. LS25: Kip 3H **123**
Gibson St. BD3: B'frd 5H **91**
Gilbert Chase LS5: Leeds 6A **76**
Gilbert Cl. LS5: Leeds 6B **76**
Gilbert Cotts. HX4: Bark 4B **158**
Gilbert Gdns. HX4: Bark 5B **158**
Gilbert Mt. LS5: Leeds 6B **76**
Gilbert St. LS28: Fars 1H **93**
GILDERSOME 6E **115**
Gildersome Cross LS27: Gil 1E **137**
Gildersome La. LS12: Gil, N Far . . .5D **114**
LS27: Gil 5D **114**
Gildersome Spur LS27: Gil 2F **137**
GILDERSOME STREET 2D **136**
Giles Hill La. HX3: She 6C **108**
Giles St. BD5: B'frd 6D **90**
BD6: B'frd 4A **110**
Giles' Wlk. BD16: Bgly 5E **51**
Gill Bank Rd. LS29: I'ly 3C **10**
Gill Beck Cl. BD17: Bail 3E **53**
Gill Cl. LS29: Add 1B **8**
Gillett Dr. LS26: Rothw 2B **142**
Gillett La. LS26: Rothw 2B **142**
Gilling Av. LS25: Gar 3H **103**
Gillingham Grn. BD4: B'frd 2C **112**
Gill La. BD13: Thorn 6G **87**
BD22: Oak 3A **46**
LS19: Yead 3C **54**
LS22: Kear 1A **26**
LS29: Nes 2G **9**
Gillrene Av. BD15: Wils 5H **67**
GILLROYD 3C **138**
Gillroyd Mt. LS27: Morl 3C **138**
Gillroyd Pde. LS27: Morl 4B **138**
Gillroyd Pl. LS27: Morl 3B **138**
Gillroyd Ri. BD7: B'frd 4B **90**

Gillroyd Ter.—Gloucester Ct.

Gillroyd Ter. LS27: Morl 3C **138**
Gills, The LS21: Otley 1E **23**
LS27: Morl 3C **138**
Gill's Ct. HX1: Hal 4C **164** (2G **149**)
Gillstead Ho. *LS14: Leeds 3B **80***
(off Kingsdale Ct.)
Gillstone Dr. BD22: Cros R 2D **64**
Gilmour St. HX3: Hal 6F **129**
Gilpin Pl. LS12: Leeds 5D **96**
Gilpin St. BD3: B'frd 3H **91**
LS12: Leeds 5D **96**
Gilpin Ter. LS12: Leeds 5D **96**
Gilpin Vw. LS12: Leeds 5D **96**
GILSTEAD .3E **51**
Gilstead Ct. BD16: Bgly 4E **51**
Gilstead Dr. BD16: Bgly 4E **51**
Gilstead La. BD16: Bgly 4D **50**
Gilstead Way LS29: I'ly 4C **10**
Gilwell Ct. WF3: Thpe H 5D **140**
Gilynda Cl. BD8: B'frd 4G **89**
Ginnel, The LS17: Bard 3E **45**
LS22: Weth 4E **13**
Gipsy Hill LS26: Wood 1D **142**
Gipsy La. LS11: Leeds 5G **117**
LS26: Wood 1D **142**
Gipsy Mead LS26: Wood 1D **142**
Gipsy St. BD3: B'frd 3C **92**
GIPTON 6F **79**
Gipton App. LS9: Leeds 2G **99**
Gipton Av. LS7: Leeds 6C **78**
Gipton Ga. E. LS9: Leeds 6G **79**
Gipton Ga. W. LS9: Leeds 6F **79**
Gipton Lodge *LS8: Leeds 5E **79***
(off Copgrove Rd.)
Gipton Sq. LS9: Leeds 2H **99**
Gipton St. LS8: Leeds 6C **78**
GIPTON WOOD 4F **79**
Gipton Wood Av. LS8: Leeds 4F **79**
Gipton Wood Cres. LS8: Leeds 4F **79**
Gipton Wood Gro. LS8: Leeds 4F **79**
Gipton Wood Pl. LS8: Leeds 4F **79**
Gipton Wood Rd. LS8: Leeds 4F **79**
GIRLINGTON 2A **90**
Girlington Ind. Cen. *BD8: B'frd 3A **90***
(off Girlington Rd.)
Girlington Rd. BD8: B'frd 2H **89**
Gisbourne Rd. HD2: Hud 6E **163**
Gisburn St. BD21: Keigh 5H **33**
Glade, The BD17: Bail 5H **51**
LS14: S'cft 6D **44**
LS28: Stan 1E **93**
Gladedale Av. LS8: Leeds 6G **79**
Glade Wlk. LS10: Leeds 3D **140**
Gladstone Ct. *LS28: Stan 1B **94***
(off Gladstone Ter.)
Gladstone Cres. LS19: Raw 2F **55**
Gladstone Ho. *BD4: B'frd 1C **112***
(off Tyersal La.)
Gladstone Pl. BD13: Denh 3B **86**
*BD22: Oak 5D **46***
(off Keighley Rd.)
Gladstone Rd. HX1: Hal 2E **149**
LS19: Raw 3F **55**
Gladstone St. BD3: B'frd 5A **92**
BD13: Que 4B **108**
BD15: All 2D **88**
BD16: Bgly 5B **50**
BD21: Keigh 1H **47**
LS28: Fars 6H **73**
Gladstone Ter. LS27: Morl 3A **138**
LS28: Stan 1B **94**
Gladstone Vw. HX3: Hal 6A **150**
Gladstone Vs. LS17: Shad 4A **62**
Glaisdale Cl. BD20: Sils 2E **15**
Glaisdale Ct. BD15: All 6C **68**
Glaisdale Gro. HX3: Hip 2F **151**
Glamis Cl. LS25: Gar 3H **103**
Glanville Ter. LS26: Rothw 2A **142**
Glasshouse St. LS10: Leeds 6B **98**
Glasshouse Vw. LS10: Leeds 3H **139**
Glastonbury Ct. BD4: B'frd 1B **112**
Glazier Rd. BD13: Que 3G **107**
Gleanings Av. HX2: Hal 2A **148**
Gleanings Dr. HX2: Hal 2H **147**
Glebe Av. LS5: Leeds 5B **76**
Glebe Ct. LS26: Rothw 2E **141**
Glebe Field Chase LS22: Weth 3D **12**
Glebe Field Cl. LS22: Weth 3D **12**
Glebe Field Cft. LS22: Weth 3D **12**
Glebe Field Dr. LS22: Weth 3D **12**
Glebe Field Gth. LS22: Weth 3C **12**
Glebe Field Holt LS22: Weth 3D **12**
Glebe Fold BD20: Rid 3D **34**
Glebe Gdns. HX1: Hal 4E **149**
Glebelands Cl. LS25: Gar 5F **103**
Glebelands Dr. LS6: Leeds 3D **76**
Glebe Mt. LS28: Pud 5A **94**
Glebe Pl. LS5: Leeds 5B **76**
Glebe St. LS28: Pud 5A **94**
Glebe Ter. LS16: Leeds 2D **76**
Gledcliffe HX3: Hal 2D **164**
Gleddings Cl. HX3: Hal 6E **149**
Gledhill Rd. BD3: B'frd 5H **91**
Gledhills Yd. *HX1: Hal 4D **148***
(off Haugh Shaw Rd. W.)
GLEDHOW .2D **78**
Gledhow Av. LS8: Leeds 1D **78**
Gledhow Ct. LS7: Leeds 2C **78**
Gledhow Dr. BD22: Oxen 5C **64**
Gledhow Grange Vw. LS8: Leeds 2D **78**
Gledhow Grange Wlk. LS8: Leeds . . .2D **78**
Gledhow La. LS7: Leeds 2B **78**
LS8: Leeds 2C **78**
Gledhow La. End LS7: Leeds 2B **78**
Gledhow Mt. LS8: Leeds 1C **98**
Gledhow Pk. Av. LS7: Leeds 3C **78**
Gledhow Pk. Cres. LS7: Leeds 3C **78**
Gledhow Pk. Dr. LS7: Leeds 3B **78**
Gledhow Pk. Gro. LS7: Leeds 3C **78**
Gledhow Pk. Rd. LS7: Leeds 3C **78**
Gledhow Pk. Vw. LS7: Leeds 3C **78**
Gledhow Pl. LS8: Leeds 1C **98**
Gledhow Ri. LS8: Leeds 3F **79**
Gledhow Rd. LS8: Leeds 1C **98**
Gledhow Ter. LS8: Leeds 1C **98**
Gledhow Towers LS8: Leeds 2C **78**
Gledhow Valley Rd. LS7: Leeds 1B **78**
LS8: Leeds 1B **78**
LS17: Leeds 1A **78**
Gledhow Wood Av. LS8: Leeds 2D **78**
Gledhow Wood Cl. LS8: Leeds 2D **78**
Gledhow Wood Ct. LS8: Leeds 4E **79**
Gledhow Wood Gro. LS8: Leeds 2D **78**
Gledhow Wood Rd. LS8: Leeds 2D **78**
Glenaire BD18: Ship 6E **53**
Glenaire Dr. BD17: Bail 6A **52**
Glenbrook Dr. BD7: B'frd 4G **89**
Glencoe HX3: She 1E **131**
Glencoe Cl. LS25: Kip 5F **123**
Glencoe Cft. LS25: Kip 5F **123**
Glencoe Gdns. LS25: Kip 5F **123**
Glencoe Ter. LS25: Kip 5F **123**
Glencoe Vw. LS9: Leeds 5D **98**
Glen Ct. LS27: Morl 4B **138**
Glendale BD16: Bgly 4E **51**
BD16: Cot 2B **68**
Glendale Av. LS25: Gar 5F **103**
Glendale Cl. BD6: B'frd 6A **110**
Glendale Dr. BD6: B'frd 6A **110**
Glendale Gdns. LS27: Morl 4B **138**
Glendare Av. BD7: B'frd 5H **89**
Glendare Rd. BD7: B'frd 5H **89**
Glendare Ter. BD7: B'frd 5H **89**
Glen Dene BD16: Cot 2B **68**
LS29: Men 1H **39**
Glen Dene Cl. BD13: Que 6H **107**
Glendower Pk. LS16: Leeds 5D **58**
Gleneagles Cl. BD4: B'frd 5H **111**
Gleneagles Rd. LS17: Leeds 3H **59**
Glenfield BD18: Ship 6E **53**
HX4: Gree 4F **159**
Glenfield Av. BD6: B'frd 5D **110**
LS22: Weth 5F **13**
Glenfield Caravan Pk. LS17: Bard . . .4C **44**
Glenfield Mt. BD6: B'frd 5D **110**
Glenfield Pl. HX6: Sow B 3A **148**
Glen Garth BD21: Keigh 2B **48**
Glen Gro. LS27: Morl 4B **138**
Glenholm BD18: Ship 6E **53**
Glenholme Heath HX1: Hal 2C **148**
Glenholme Pk. BD14: Clay 2E **109**
Glenholme Rd. BD8: B'frd 2B **90**
LS28: Fars 1G **93**
Glenholm Rd. BD17: Bail 5C **52**
Glenhurst BD4: B'frd 4B **112**
Glenhurst Av. BD21: Keigh 2A **48**
Glenhurst Dr. BD21: Keigh 2B **48**
Glenhurst Gro. BD21: Keigh 2B **48**
Glenhurst Rd. BD18: Ship 1G **69**
Glen Lea HX6: Sow B 4H **147**
Glenlea Cl. LS28: Stan 6C **74**
Glenlea Gdns. LS28: Stan 6C **74**
Glen Lee La. BD21: Keigh 3B **48**
Glenlee Rd. BD7: B'frd 4H **89**
Glenlow Rd. WF12: Dew 6A **154**
Glenlyon Av. BD20: Keigh 4G **33**
Glenlyon Dr. BD20: Keigh 4G **33**
Glenmere Mt. LS19: Yead 6H **41**
Glenmore Cl. BD2: B'frd 2A **92**
Glenmore Ct. LS16: B'hpe 2G **43**
Glen Mt. HX3: Hal 5C **128**
LS27: Morl 4B **138**
LS29: Men 2H **39**
Glenmount BD16: Cot 2B **68**
Glen Mt. Cl. HX3: Hal 5C **128**
Glenmount Ter. LS27: Morl 5C **138**
Glen Ri. BD17: Bail 5H **51**
Glen Rd. BD16: Bgly 2E **51**
BD17: Bail 3F **51**
LS16: Leeds 2C **76**
LS27: Morl 4B **138**
Glenrose Dr. BD7: B'frd 5G **89**
Glenroyd BD18: Ship 6E **53**
Glenroyd Av. BD6: B'frd 5D **110**
Glenroyd Cl. LS28: Pud 4G **93**
Glensdale Gro. LS9: Leeds 4D **98**
Glensdale Mt. LS9: Leeds 4D **98**
Glensdale Rd. LS9: Leeds 4D **98**
Glensdale St. LS9: Leeds 4D **98**
Glensdale Ter. LS9: Leeds 4D **98**
Glenside Av. BD18: Ship 6E **53**
Glenside Rd. BD18: Ship 6E **53**
Glenstone Gro. BD7: B'frd 4H **89**
Glen Ter. HX1: Hal 4F **149**
*HX3: Hip 2E **151***
(off Waverley Cres.)
Glenthorpe Av. LS9: Leeds 3E **99**
Glenthorpe Cres. LS9: Leeds 3E **99**
Glenthorpe Ter. LS9: Leeds 3E **99**
Glenton Sq. BD9: B'frd 1B **90**
Glen Vw. BD16: Har 6F **49**
HX1: Hal 4F **149**
HX6: Sow B 5C **146**
LS27: Morl 4B **138**
Glenview Av. BD9: B'frd 6G **69**
Glenview Cl. BD18: Ship 2E **69**
Glenview Dr. BD18: Ship 3E **69**
Glenview Gro. BD18: Ship 2F **69**
Glen Vw. Rd. BD16: Bgly 2E **51**
Glenview Rd. BD18: Ship 3E **69**
Glenview Ter. BD18: Ship 1H **69**
Glen Way BD16: Bgly 2F **51**
(Heather Vw.)
BD16: Bgly 1E **51**
(The Green)
Glenwood Av. BD17: Bail 6G **51**
Global Av. LS11: Leeds 4E **117**
Global Ct. LS11: Leeds 5E **117**
Globe Fold BD8: B'frd 3C **90**
Globe Rd. LS11: Leeds 6A **4** (4G **97**)
Glossop Gro. *LS6: Leeds 5H **77***
(off Glossop Vw.)
Glossop Mt. LS6: Leeds 5H **77**
Glossop St. LS6: Leeds 5H **77**
Glossop Vw. LS6: Leeds 5H **77**
Gloucester Av. BD3: B'frd 2B **92**
BD20: Sils 2C **14**
Gloucester Ct. LS12: Leeds 4E **97**
WF2: Wren 6D **156**

Gloucester Rd. BD16: Bgly 5D 50
Gloucester Ter. LS12: Leeds 3E 97
Glover Ct. BD5: B'frd 1E 111
Glovershaw La. BD16: Bgly 1G 51
Glover Way LS11: Leeds 3A 118
Glydegate BD5: B'frd 5C 6 (5E 91)
Glyndon Ct. HD6: Ras 3B 162
Glynn Ter. BD8: B'frd 3B 90
G Mill Yd. HX3: Hal 2B 164
Goals Soccer Cen.
  Leeds 2C 96
Gobind Marg BD3: B'frd 4G 7 (4G 91)
Godfrey Rd. HX3: Hal 1G 159
Godfrey St. BD8: B'frd 4F 89
Godley Branch Rd. HX3: Hal 1A 150
Godley Gdns. HX3: Hal 6B 130
Godley La. HX3: Hal 1A 150
Godley Rd. HX3: Hal 1H 149
Godwin Pl. HD2: Hud 6F 163
Godwin St. BD1: B'frd 4C 6 (4E 91)
Goffee Way LS27: Chur 5C 116
Goff Well La. BD21: Keigh 4A 48
Gog Hill HX5: Ell 4B 160
Goit Side BD1: B'frd 4A 6 (4D 90)
                        (not continuous)
  HX2: Lud 3E 127
Goit Stock La. BD16: Har 1F 67
Goit Stock Ter. BD16: Har 1F 67
Goldcrest Av. BD8: B'frd 4D 88
Goldcrest Rd. WF10: All B 3H 145
Golden Bank LS18: H'fth 6E 57
Golden Butts Rd. LS29: I'ly 5E 11
Golden Elders WF2: Kirk 6G 155
Golden Ter. LS12: Leeds 1A 116
Golden Vw. Dr. BD21: Keigh 1D 48
Goldfields Av. HX4: Gree 3F 159
Goldfields Cl. HX4: Gree 3F 159
Goldfields Vw. HX4: Gree 3F 159
Goldfields Way HX4: Gree 3F 159
Golding Hop Cl. HX2: Hal 5B 128
Goldsmith Dr. WF3: Rob H 4F 141
Golf Av. HX2: Hal 2A 148
Golf Cres. HX2: Hal 2A 148
Golf La. LS27: Morl 6G 137
GOMERSAL 6F 135
GOMERSAL HILL TOP 6F 135
Gomersall Ho. BD11: Drig 1H 135
Gondal Ct. BD5: B'frd 2C 110
Goodcomb Pl. LS25: M'fld 2A 124
Gooder La. HD6: Ras 2A 162
Gooder St. HD6: Brigh 1A 162
Goodfellow Cl. BD16: Cot 3D 68
GOODLEY 4C 46
Goodman St. LS10: Leeds 6C 98
Goodrick La. LS17: Leeds 1H 59
Goodwin Ho. BD13: Que 4A 108
                    (off Minstrel Dr.)
Goodwin Rd. LS12: Leeds 5C 96
Goodwood LS10: Leeds 4B 140
  LS29: Nes 3B 10
Goodwood Av. LS25: Kip 3F 123
GOODY CROSS 3C 122
Goody Cross La. LS26: Swil 3B 122
Goody Cross Va. LS26: Swil 3B 122
Goose Cote La. BD22: Oak 4E 47
Goose Cote Way BD22: Oak 4E 47
Goosedale Ct. BD4: B'frd 4E 113
GOOSE EYE 1B 46
Goose Eye BD22: Oak 1B 46
Goose Eye Brow BD22: Oak 1B 46
Goosefield Ri. LS25: Gar 6D 102
Goose Grn. BD22: Oxen 1C 84
GOOSE HILL 3H 111
Goose La. LS20: Hawk 3B 38
Goose Pond La. HX4: Gree 2C 158
  HX6: Norl 2C 158
Gordon Dr. LS6: Leeds 3E 77
Gordon Larking Ct. LS21: Otley ..4C 22
Gordon Pl. LS6: Leeds 3F 77
Gordon St. BD5: B'frd 6H 33
  BD14: Clay 1D 108
  BD21: Keigh 6H 33
  BD22: Cros R 1E 65

Gordon St. HX3: Hal 5F 129
  HX5: Ell 5B 160
  HX6: Sow B 6G 147
  LS29: I'ly 5E 11
  WF3: E Ard 1C 156
Gordon Ter. BD10: B'frd 6H 53
  LS6: Leeds 3F 77
Gordon Vw. LS6: Leeds 3F 77
Gorse Av. BD17: Bail 6G 51
Gorse Lea LS10: Leeds 5B 118
Gothic St. BD13: Que 4A 108
Gotts Pk. Av. LS12: Leeds 2H 95
Gotts Pk. Cres. LS12: Leeds 2H 95
Gotts Park Golf Course 2A 96
Gotts Pk. Vw. LS12: Leeds 1H 95
Gotts Rd. LS12: Leeds 5A 4 (4F 97)
Gotts Ter. BD20: Keigh 3G 33
Gott St. BD22: Cros R 1F 65
Goulbourne St.
  BD21: Keigh 1H 47
Gower St. BD5: B'frd 1E 111
  LS2: Leeds 3G 5 (3B 98)
Gracechurch St.
  BD8: B'frd 2A 6 (3D 90)
Grace St. BD21: Keigh 6B 34
  LS1: Leeds 4B 4 (3G 97)
Gracey La. BD6: B'frd 4H 109
Grady Cl. BD10: B'frd 3H 71
Grafton Cl. BD17: Bail 3D 52
Grafton Pl. HX3: Hal 4E 129
Grafton Rd. BD21: Keigh 2G 47
Grafton St. BD5: B'frd 6E 91
  BD21: Keigh 2H 47
  LS7: Leeds 2F 5 (2A 98)
Grafton Vs. LS15: Leeds 5F 81
Graham Av. LS4: Leeds 6D 76
Graham Gro. LS4: Leeds 6D 76
Graham Ho. LS5: Leeds 6H 75
                      (off Broad La.)
Graham Mt. LS4: Leeds 6D 76
Graham St. BD9: B'frd 1A 90
  LS4: Leeds 6D 76
Graham Ter. LS4: Leeds 6D 76
Graham Vw. LS4: Leeds 6D 76
Graham Wlk. LS27: Gil 6F 115
Graingers Way
  LS12: Leeds 6A 4 (4F 97)
Grampian Cl. BD5: B'frd 3B 110
Grammar School Pl.
  HD6: Ras 3H 161
                 (off Thornhill Rd.)
Grammar School St.
  BD1: B'frd 2C 6 (3E 91)
Granary Ct. BD2: B'frd 4A 72
Granary Wharf
  LS1: Leeds 6D 4 (4H 97)
Granby Av. LS6: Leeds 4D 76
Granby Cl. LS6: Leeds 5D 76
Granby Dr. BD20: Rid 4D 34
Granby Gro. LS6: Leeds 5D 76
Granby La. BD20: Rid 4D 34
Granby Mt. LS6: Leeds 4D 76
Granby Pl. LS6: Leeds 4D 76
Granby Rd. LS6: Leeds 5D 76
Granby St. BD4: B'frd 6E 7 (6F 91)
                        (not continuous)
  BD13: Que 4A 108
  LS6: Leeds 4D 76
Granby Ter. LS6: Leeds 4D 76
Granby Vw. LS6: Leeds 4D 76
Grandage Ter. BD8: B'frd 3B 90
Grand Arc. LS1: Leeds 3F 5
Grandsmere Pl. HX3: Hal 5F 149
Grandstand Rd.
  WF2: Carr G 4C 156
  WF3: Loft 4C 156
Grand Theatre & Opera House
  ....3F 5 (3A 98)
Grand Vw. BD13: Que 2G 107
  HX3: Hal 6E 129
                   (off Ovenden Av.)
  HX6: Sow B 6H 147
                   (off Lwr. Clyde St.)

Grange, The HX3: Hal 6F 149
  LS6: Leeds 4E 77
  LS11: Leeds 3G 117
  LS12: Leeds 2H 95
  LS13: Leeds 2E 95
  LS25: Gar 4H 103
  WF3: Carl 4H 141
Grange Av. BD3: B'frd 3D 92
  BD4: E Bier 5E 113
  BD15: All 3E 89
  BD18: Ship 1G 69
  HX2: Hal 2D 128
  LS7: Leeds 5C 78
  LS19: Yead 1G 55
  LS23: T Arch 1E 31
  LS25: Gar 4F 103
  LS29: I'ly 5F 11
  LS29: Men 6F 21
Grange Bank HX3: She 1E 131
Grange Bldgs. LS27: Morl 5C 138
                   (off Hodgson St.)
Grange Cl. LS10: Leeds 1B 118
  LS17: Bard 1F 45
  LS18: H'fth 1B 74
  LS29: I'ly 5F 11
Grange Cotts. BD13: Cull 3C 66
Grange Ct. BD16: Cot 2C 68
  HX3: Sou 6C 150
  LS6: Leeds 4F 77
  LS15: Scho 3H 81
  LS17: Leeds 2A 60
  LS26: Wood 6E 121
Grange Cres. BD20: Rid 4C 34
  LS7: Leeds 5C 78
  LS19: Yead 1G 55
Grange Cft. LS17: Leeds 2A 60
Grange Dr. BD15: All 3E 89
  LS18: H'fth 1B 74
Grange Est. LS29: I'ly 5F 11
Grange Farm Cl. LS29: Men 6F 21
Grangefield Av. LS29: Burl W 2F 21
Grangefield Ct. LS25: Gar 4F 103
Grangefield Ind. Est.
  LS28: Stan 2A 94
Grangefield Rd. LS28: Stan 1A 94
                      (not continuous)
Grange Flds. Mt. LS10: Leeds ...1D 118
Grange Flds. Rd.
  LS10: Leeds 1D 140
Grange Flds. Way
  LS10: Leeds 1D 140
Grange Fold BD15: All 3D 88
Grange Gro. BD3: B'frd 3D 92
  BD20: Rid 4C 34
Grange Hgts. HX3: Sou 6C 150
Grange Holt LS17: Leeds 2A 60
Grange La. BD20: Kild 2A 14
  BD22: Oak 4A 46
  HD6: Clift 1E 163
  LS25: Kip 3H 123
Grange Mt. LS19: Yead 1G 55
Grange Pk. BD17: Bail 4E 53
  HX3: Hal 6F 149
Grange Pk. Av. LS8: Leeds 4H 79
Grange Pk. Cl. LS8: Leeds 4H 79
  LS27: Morl 6B 116
  WF10: All B 2G 145
Grange Pk. Ct. LS27: Morl 6B 116
                  (off Grange Pk. Dr.)
Grange Pk. Cres. LS8: Leeds 4H 79
  LS27: Morl 6B 116
Grange Pk. Dr. BD16: Cot 1C 68
  LS27: Morl 6B 116
Grange Pk. Gro. LS8: Leeds 4H 79
Grange Pk. M. LS8: Leeds 4H 79
  LS27: Morl 6B 116
Grange Pk. Pl. LS8: Leeds 4H 79
Grange Pk. Ri. LS8: Leeds 4H 79
Grange Pk. Rd. BD16: Cot 1C 68
  LS8: Leeds 4H 79
Grange Pk. Ter. LS8: Leeds 4A 80
Grange Pk. Wlk. LS8: Leeds 4H 79
Grange Pk. Way
  LS27: Morl 6B 116

Grange Rd. BD15: All 3E **89**
  BD16: Bgly 3D **50**
  BD20: East 6A **14**
  BD20: Rid 4C **34**
  LS10: Leeds 1B **118**
  LS19: Yead 1G **55**
  LS29: Burl W 2F **21**
  WF12: Dew 6A **154**
  WF17: Bat 5A **154**
    (not continuous)
Grange Road, The LS16: Leeds . .6B **58**
Grange St. BD21: Keigh 5A **34**
  HX3: Hal 6E **129**
  LS27: Chur 5C **116**
Grange Ter. BD15: All 3E **89**
  BD18: Ship 3B **70**
  BD20: East 6A **14**
  LS7: Leeds 5B **78**
  LS19: Yead 1G 55
    (off Grange Rd.)
  LS27: Morl 6B **116**
  LS28: Pud 3A **94**
Grange Vw. BD3: B'frd 3D **92**
  BD20: East 6A **14**
  LS7: Leeds 5C **78**
  LS15: Leeds 5F **101**
  LS21: Otley 2D **22**
  LS22: Weth 5E **13**
  LS28: Pud 3A **94**
Grange Vw. Gdns. LS17: Leeds . .6B **62**
Grangeway BD15: All 3E **89**
Grangewood Ct. LS16: Leeds 6B **58**
  WF1: Out 4H **157**
Grangewood Gdns. LS16: Leeds . .6B **58**
Granhamthorpe LS13: Leeds 1E **95**
Granny Av. LS27: Chur 5C **116**
Granny Hall Gro. HD6: Brigh 5H **151**
Granny Hall La. HD6: Brigh 5H **151**
Granny Hall Pk. HD6: Brigh 5H **151**
Granny Hill Ter. HX1: Hal 4D **148**
Granny La. LS12: Leeds 6A **96**
Granny Pl. LS27: Chur 5C **116**
Grant Av. LS7: Leeds 1C **98**
Grantham Pl. BD7: B'frd 5F **129**
  HX3: Hal 5F **129**
Grantham Rd. BD7: B'frd . . .6A **6** (6C **90**)
  HX3: Hal 5F **129**
Grantham Ter. BD7: B'frd . . .6A **6** (6C **90**)
Grantham Towers *LS9: Leeds 2C 98*
    (off Lindsey Gdns.)
Grantley Pl. HD2: Hud 6D **162**
Granton Rd. LS7: Leeds 4B **78**
Granton St. BD3: B'frd 4A **92**
Grant St. BD3: B'frd 3H **7** (4G **90**)
  BD21: Keigh 6G **33**
  BD22: Oxen 1C **84**
Granville Ct. *LS21: Otley 4D 22*
    (off Granville Mt.)
Granville Mt. LS21: Otley 4D **22**
Granville Pl. BD15: All 2D **88**
  LS21: Otley 4D **22**
Granville Rd. BD9: B'frd 4B **70**
  BD18: Ship 4B **70**
  LS9: Leeds 2C **98**
Granville St. BD14: Clay 6E **89**
  BD21: Keigh 6H 33
    (off Enfield St.)
  HX5: Ell 5B **160**
  LS28: Pud 3G **93**
  LS28: Stan 1B **94**
Granville Ter. BD16: Bgly 4C **50**
  BD18: Ship 4B **70**
  LS19: Yead 6G **41**
  LS20: Guis 3D **40**
  LS21: Otley 4D **22**
Grape St. BD15: All 2E **89**
  BD21: Keigh 5C **34**
  HX1: Hal 3A **164** (2F **149**)
  LS10: Leeds 6B **98**
Grasleigh Av. BD15: All 1C **88**
Grasleigh Way BD15: All 1B **88**
Grasmere Av. LS22: Weth 4C **12**
Grasmere Cl. LS12: Leeds 5D **96**

Grasmere Ct. LS12: Leeds 4D **96**
Grasmere Dr. HX5: Ell 4D **160**
  LS22: Weth 4C **12**
Grasmere Pl. HX3: Hal 3E **129**
Grasmere Rd. BD2: B'frd 6G **71**
  BD12: Wyke 6E **133**
  LS12: Leeds 5D **96**
Grass Rd. BD20: E Mor, W Mor . . .2G **35**
Gratrix La. HX6: Sow B 4A **148**
Grattan Rd. BD1: B'frd . .4A **6** (4D **90**)
GRAVELEYTHORPE 3C **100**
Graveleythorpe Ri. LS15: Leeds . .2D **100**
Graveleythorpe Rd. LS15: Leeds . .2D **100**
Gray Av. BD18: Ship 4D **70**
Gray Ct. LS15: Leeds 3F **101**
Grayrigg Cl. LS15: Leeds 4A **100**
Grayshon Dr. BD6: B'frd 4C **110**
Grayshon St. BD11: Drig 2B **136**
Grayson Crest LS4: Leeds 6B **76**
Grayson Hgts. LS4: Leeds 6B **76**
Grayswood Cres. BD4: B'frd 2B **112**
Grayswood Dr. BD4: B'frd 1B **112**
Gt. Albion St. HX1: Hal . .3B **164** (2G **149**)
Gt. Cross St. BD1: B'frd 5E **7** (5F **91**)
Gt. Edge Rd. HX2: Hal 2F **147**
Greater Elland Historical Society
  . . . . .4B **160**
    (off Northgate)
Gt. George St. LS1: Leeds . .3C **4** (3H **97**)
  LS2: Leeds 3C **4** (3H **97**)
GREAT HORTON 1A **110**
Gt. Horton Rd. BD7: B'frd . .6A **6** (3F **109**)
Gt. Northern Rd. BD21: Keigh 1A **48**
Gt. Northern St. LS27: Morl 4A **138**
Great Nth. Rd. LS25: S Mil 1G **125**
Great Pasture LS29: Burl W 1F **21**
Gt. Pasture La. LS29: Burl W 1F **21**
GREAT PRESTON 5E **123**
Gt. Russell Ct. BD7: B'frd 4C **90**
Gt. Russell St. BD7: B'frd 4B **90**
Great Scout HX2: Lud M 1A **146**
Gt. Wilson St. LS11: Leeds 5H **97**
Greave Cl. HD2: Hud 6B **162**
Greave Ho. Dr. HX2: Lud M 2D **146**
Greave Ho. Flds. HX2: Lud M 1E **147**
Greave Ho. Pk. HX2: Lud M 2D **146**
Greaves St. BD5: B'frd 2D **110**
Greaves Yd. LS28: Pud 6A **94**
Grebe Cl. BD6: B'frd 4E **109**
Greek St. LS1: Leeds 4D **4** (3H **97**)
GREEN, THE
  LS14 . . . . .5D **80**
  LS28 . . . . .5H **73**
Green, The BD4: E Bier 6D **112**
  BD7: B'frd 5A **6** (5D **90**)
  BD10: B'frd 1H **71**
  BD16: Bgly 1C **50**
    (College Rd.)
  BD16: Bgly 1E **51**
    (Stead La.)
  BD16: Bgly 4F **51**
    (The Gardens)
  BD16: Bgly 6A **36**
    (Victoria St.)
  HD2: Hud 6D **162**
  LS14: Leeds 5C **80**
    (not continuous)
  LS17: Leeds 5C **60**
  LS18: H'fth 1D **74**
  LS19: Yead 6G 41
    (off Town St.)
  LS20: Guis 5C **40**
  LS21: Leat 1C **24**
  LS21: Otley 2D **22**
  LS23: T Arch 3C **30**
  LS25: Gar 5G **103**
  LS25: Kip 4G **123**
  LS27: Gil 6F **115**
  LS28: Fars 5H **73**
  LS29: Add 1C **8**
  WF2: Wren 6D **156**
  WF17: Birs 5B **136**
Greenacre Av. BD12: Wyke 5D **132**

Green Acre Cl. BD17: Bail 4D **52**
Greenacre Cl. BD12: Wyke 5D **132**
Greenacre Ct. LS25: Gar 4G **103**
Greenacre Dr. BD12: Wyke 5D **132**
Greenacre Pk. LS19: Raw 2F **55**
Greenacre Pk. Av. LS19: Raw 2F **55**
Greenacre Pk. M. LS19: Raw 2G **55**
Greenacre Pk. Ri. LS19: Raw 2F **55**
Green Acres BD21: Keigh 2C **48**
  LS29: Burl W 3D **20**
Greenacres HX3: She 1F **131**
Greenacres Av. HX3: She 1F **131**
Greenacres Dr. BD20: Keigh 4G **33**
  HX3: She 1F **131**
  WF17: Birs 5B **136**
Greenacres Gro. HX3: She 1F **131**
Greenacre Way BD12: Wyke 5D **132**
Greenaire Pl. BD1: B'frd . . .4B **6** (4D **90**)
Green Av. BD20: Sils 1D **14**
  LS25: Kip 2F **123**
Green Bank WF3: Loft 6H **141**
Greenbank BD17: Bail 6B **52**
Greenbank Rd. BD15: All 3E **89**
Greenbanks Av. LS18: H'fth 5E **57**
Greenbanks Cl. LS18: H'fth 5E **57**
Greenbanks Dr. LS18: H'fth 5D **56**
GREENBOTTOM 5C **40**
Green Chase LS6: Leeds 2E **77**
Greencliffe Av. BD17: Bail 4C **52**
Green Cl. BD8: B'frd 3G **89**
  BD20: East 5A **14**
  LS6: Leeds 2F **77**
Green Ct. BD7: B'frd 6H **89**
  BD19: Scho 1F **153**
  LS15: Scho 2H **81**
  LS17: Leeds 5B **60**
Green Cres. LS6: Leeds 2E **77**
Greencroft Av. HX3: North 4D **130**
Greencroft Cl. BD10: B'frd 2G **71**
Greencroft M. LS20: Guis 4C **40**
Greendown Cl. LS29: I'ly 5F **11**
Green Dragon Yd. LS1: Leeds 4D **4**
GREEN END 4A **36**
Green End Rd. BD14: Clay 1D **108**
  HD6: Ras 2A **162**
Green End Rd. BD6: B'frd 5B **110**
  BD20: E Mor 4A **36**
Greenfell Cl. BD22: Haw 2C **64**
Greenfield BD22: Haw 2C **64**
Greenfield Av. BD18: Ship 3C **70**
  HX3: Hip 2A **152**
  LS20: Guis 6H **39**
  LS25: Kip 3G **123**
  LS27: Gil 6D **114**
Greenfield Cl. HX3: North 4C **130**
  LS25: Kip 3G **123**
  LS29: Burl W 4F **21**
Greenfield Ct. BD7: B'frd 1H **109**
  BD22: Keigh 6G **33**
  LS16: Leeds 3B **58**
Greenfield Cres. BD13: Cull 3C **66**
Greenfield Dr. BD19: Scho 1F **153**
  LS27: Gil 6D **114**
Greenfield Gdns. BD20: East 5A **14**
Greenfield Gth. LS25: Kip 3G **123**
Greenfield La. BD4: B'frd 1H **133**
  BD7: B'frd 1H **109**
  BD10: B'frd 6G **53**
  LS20: Guis 6G **39**
Greenfield Pl. BD8: B'frd 2C **90**
  HX3: Hip 2A **152**
Greenfield Ri. LS25: Kip 3G **123**
Greenfield Rd. LS9: Leeds 4C **98**
Greenfields HX6: Sow B 6E **147**
Greenfields Way LS29: Burl W 4F **21**
Greenfield Ter. BD22: Haw 2C **64**
  LS26: Meth 4E **145**
Greenfield Va. LS25: Kip 3G **123**
Greenfield Vw. LS25: Kip 3G **123**
Greenfinch Way BD15: All 4D **89**
Green Fold *BD2: B'frd 1H 91*
    (off Idle Rd.)
  BD17: Bail 5B **52**

Greenfold La. LS22: Weth 4F 13
Greengate BD20: Sils 1D 14
  LS26: Oul 1E 143
Greengate Rd. BD21: Keigh 1A 48
GREENGATES 2C 72
Greengates Av. BD12: Wyke 6C 132
Green Hall Pk. HX3: She 2F 131
Green Head Av. BD20: Keigh . . .3G 33
Green Head Dr. BD20: Keigh . . .3G 33
Green Head La. BD20: Keigh . . .3G 33
Greenhead La. HD6: Ras 5G 161
Green Head Rd. BD20: Keigh 3G 33
Greenhead Rd. LS16: Leeds 1B 76
Green Hill HX2: Hal 3H 147
Green Hill Chase
  LS12: Leeds 5B 96
Green Hill Cl. LS12: Leeds 2H 95
Green Hill Cres. LS12: Leeds 5B 96
Green Hill Cft. LS12: Leeds 5B 96
Green Hill Dr. LS13: Leeds 2G 95
Greenhill Dr. BD16: Bgly 6A 36
Green Hill Gdns. LS12: Leeds 5B 96
Green Hill Holt LS12: Leeds 5B 96
Green Hill La. LS12: Leeds 6A 96
Greenhill La. BD3: B'frd 4A 92
  BD16: Bgly 1B 50
Green Hill Mt. LS13: Leeds 2G 95
Green Hill Pk. HX3: She 5F 109
Green Hill Pl. LS13: Leeds 2G 95
Green Hill Rd. LS12: Leeds 2H 95
  LS13: Leeds 2G 95
Greenhills LS19: Raw 4G 55
Greenhill St. BD3: B'frd 4A 92
Green Hill Way LS13: Leeds 2G 95
Greenholme Cl. LS29: Burl W 1F 21
Greenholme Ct. BD4: B'frd 3D 112
  HX4: Gree 4G 159
Greenholme Mills LS29: Burl W 1F 21
Greenholme Trad. Est.
  LS29: Burl W 1F 21
Greenhouse LS11: Leeds 1H 117
             (off Beeston Rd.)
Greenhouse, The LS11: Leeds 1H 117
Green Houses HX2: Midg 4D 126
Greenhow Cl. LS4: Leeds 1D 96
Greenhow Gdns. LS4: Leeds 1D 96
Greenhow Pk. LS29: Burl W 2D 20
Greenhow Rd. LS4: Leeds 1D 96
Greenhow Wlk. LS4: Leeds 1D 96
Greenland Av. BD13: Que 5A 108
Greenland Ct. LS26: Oul 2E 143
Greenland Vs. BD13: Que 5A 108
Green La. BD2: B'frd 6B 72
  BD7: B'frd 6A 90
  BD8: B'frd 1A 6 (2C 90)
  BD10: B'frd 1A 72
              (Apperley Rd.)
  BD10: B'frd 2G 71
             (Sandhill Fold)
  BD12: O'haw 3F 133
  BD12: Wyke 5B 132
  BD13: Que 1A 130
             (Corporal La.)
  BD13: Que 3F 107
           (White Castle Ct.)
  BD13: Thorn 5A 88
  BD17: Bail 6A 52
      (Milner Rd., not continuous)
  BD17: Bail 3A 52
           (Somerset Av.)
  BD19: Hun 5B 134
  BD20: East 5A 14
  BD22: Oak 3A 46
              (Gill La.)
  BD22: Oak 5D 46
           (Keighley Rd.)
  BD22: Oxen 3D 84
  HD6: Brigh 4G 151
  HD6: Clift 6F 153
  HX2: Hal 4C 148
  HX2: Illing 5C 106
  HX2: Lud 6D 126
  HX3: North 2A 130

Green La. HX3: She 6F 109
             (Cloverdale)
  HX3: She 1F 131
        (Willow Pk. Dr.)
  HX3: Sou 3A 150
  HX4: Gree 5G 159
  LS11: Leeds 4F 117
  LS12: Leeds 5E 97
  LS12: N Far 6E 95
  LS14: Leeds 1C 80
  LS15: Leeds 2D 100
  LS16: Leeds 3F 57
  LS18: H'fth 2D 74
  LS19: Yead 2F 55
  LS21: Otley 2D 22
  LS22: Coll 3A 28
  LS23: B Spa 4C 30
  LS25: Gar 4G 103
          (Greenacre Ct.)
  LS25: Gar 5H 103
        (Ribblesdale Av.)
  LS25: Kip 2F 123
  LS26: Meth 6F 145
  LS28: Pud 5H 93
  LS29: Add 1C 8
  LS29: Burl W 1E 21
           (Leather Bank)
  LS29: Burl W 5B 20
            (Moor Rd.)
  WF3: Loft 6G 141
  WF15: Liv 6G 153
Green La. Vs. LS25: Gar 4G 103
Green Lea LS26: Oul 1D 142
Greenlea Av. LS19: Yead 1D 54
Green Lea Cl. LS23: B Spa 4C 30
Greenlea Cl. LS19: Yead 2D 54
Greenlea Fold LS19: Yead 2D 54
Greenlea Mt. LS19: Yead 1D 54
Greenlea Rd. LS19: Yead 1D 54
Greenley Hill BD15: Wils 5F 67
Green Mdw. BD15: Wils 5H 67
Greenmoor Av. LS12: Leeds 4F 95
  WF3: Loft 6G 141
Greenmoor Cl. WF3: Loft 6G 141
Greenmoor Ct. WF3: Carl, Loft 6G 141
Greenmoor Cres. WF3: Loft 6H 141
Green Mt. BD4: B'frd 1B 112
  BD17: Bail 5A 52
  HX3: Nor G 4H 131
Greenmount LS11: Leeds 2H 117
          (off Fulham St.)
Greenmount La. LS11: Leeds 2H 117
Greenmount Pl. LS11: Leeds 2H 117
Green Mt. Retail Pk.
  HX1: Hal 3A 164 (2F 149)
Greenmount St. LS11: Leeds 2H 117
Greenmount Ter. LS11: Leeds 2H 117
Greenock Pl. LS12: Leeds 3A 96
Greenock St. LS12: Leeds 3A 96
Greenock Ter. LS12: Leeds 3A 96
Green Pk. LS17: Leeds 5C 60
Green Pk. Av. HX3: Hal 1G 159
Green Pk. Dr. HX3: Hal 1G 159
Green Pk. Ga. HX3: Hal 1G 159
Green Pk. Rd. HX3: Hal 1G 159
Green Pk. St. HX3: Hal 6H 149
Green Pasture Cl. LS9: Leeds 3G 99
Green Pl. BD2: B'frd 1H 91
Green Rd. BD17: Bail 5A 52
  LS6: Leeds 1E 77
Green Row BD10: B'frd 3H 71
  LS6: Leeds 2E 77
  LS26: Meth 6D 144
Green Row Fold LS26: Meth 6D 144
Green Royd HX2: Mt T 3H 127
  HX3: Nor G 4H 131
  HX4: Gree 5G 159
          (not continuous)
Greenroyd Av. BD19: Hun 5B 134
  HX3: Hal 6F 149
Greenroyd Cl. HX3: Hal 1F 159

Greenroyd Cres. HX2: Hal 6D 128
Greenroyd La. HX2: Hal 6C 128
Greenroyd Ter. HX3: Hal 1G 159
Greenshank M. LS27: Morl 3D 138
Greenshaw Ct. LS20: Guis 4B 40
         (off Branwell Av.)
Greenshaw Ter. LS20: Guis 4B 40
Greens Health & Fitness
  Shipley .6D 52
GREEN SIDE 4H 89
Greenside BD12: O'haw 3G 133
  BD14: Clay 1D 108
  LS19: Yead 2E 55
           (off Warm La.)
  LS28: Pud 5H 93
Greenside Av. LS12: Leeds 6B 96
Greenside Cl. LS12: Leeds 6C 96
Greenside Ct. LS27: Gil 6F 115
Greenside Dr. LS12: Leeds 6C 96
Greenside Gro. LS28: Pud 5H 93
Greenside La. BD8: B'frd 4H 89
  BD13: Cull 3B 66
Greenside Pk. BD8: B'frd 4H 89
Greenside Rd. LS12: Leeds 6C 96
Greenside Ter. LS12: Leeds 6B 96
Greenside Wlk. LS12: Leeds 6B 96
Green Sq. LS25: Kip 4G 123
Green's Sq. HX2: Hal 1C 148
Green's Ter. BD12: O'haw 3F 133
Green St. BD1: B'frd 4F 7 (4F 91)
  BD12: O'haw 2H 133
  BD22: Haw 3C 64
  BD22: Oxen 1C 84
Greensway LS25: Gar 4E 103
Green Sykes Rd. BD22: Oak 5A 32
Green Ter. BD2: B'frd 1H 91
             (off Idle Rd.)
  LS11: Leeds 2A 118
  LS20: Guis 5C 40
Green Ter. Sq. HX1: Hal 4E 149
Greenthorpe Ct. LS13: Leeds 4G 95
Greenthorpe Hill LS13: Leeds 4G 95
Greenthorpe Mt. LS13: Leeds 3G 95
Greenthorpe Rd. LS13: Leeds 4G 95
Greenthorpe St. LS13: Leeds 4G 95
Greenthorpe Wlk. LS13: Leeds 3G 95
Greenthwaite Cl. BD20: Keigh 4G 33
Greenton Av. BD19: Scho 6E 133
Greenton Cres. BD13: Que 5H 107
Green Top LS12: Leeds 6B 96
Greentop LS28: Pud 5H 93
Green Top Gdns. LS12: Leeds 6B 96
Green Top St. BD8: B'frd 4G 89
Greentrees BD6: B'frd 1B 132
Greenups Mill HX6: Sow B 3A 148
         (off Old Cawsey)
Greenups Ter. HX6: Sow B 5H 147
Green Vw. LS7: Leeds 2E 77
  LS14: S'cft 5E 45
Greenview Cl. LS9: Leeds 1G 99
Greenview Ct. LS8: Leeds 1E 79
Greenville Av. LS12: Leeds 6B 96
Greenville Dr. BD12: Low M 6E 111
Greenville Gdns. LS12: Leeds 6B 96
Green Way HX2: Illing 5C 106
  LS14: S'cft 5E 45
Greenway LS15: Leeds 2E 101
  LS20: Guis 6A 40
Greenway, The
  BD3: B'frd 1G 7 (3G 91)
Greenway Cl. LS15: Leeds 2E 101
Greenway Dr. BD15: All 4D 88
Greenway Rd. BD5: B'frd 3E 111
Greenwell Ct. LS9: Leeds 3G 99
Greenwood Av. BD2: B'frd 4G 71
Greenwood Ct. BD1: B'frd 5D 6 (5E 91)
  LS6: Leeds 1E 77
Greenwood Dr. BD2: B'frd 5G 71
Greenwood Fold BD4: B'frd 6H 111
Greenwood Mt. BD2: B'frd 5G 71
  LS6: Leeds 2E 77
Greenwood Pk. LS6: Leeds 2E 77

Greenwood Rd. BD17: Bail 6B **52**
  WF3: Ting 1F **155**
Greenwood Row LS28: Pud 4B **94**
Greenwood's Ter. HX3: Hal 6D **128**
GREETLAND 4F **159**
Greetland Moor Vw.
  HX3: Hal 1D **164**
Greetland Rd. HX4: Bark 5A **158**
Gregory Ct. BD14: Clay 1E **109**
Gregory Cres. BD7: B'frd 3G **109**
Grenfell Dr. BD3: B'frd 3B **92**
Grenfell Rd. BD3: B'frd 3B **92**
Grenfell Ter. BD3: B'frd 3B **92**
Grennshaw M. LS20: Guis 4B **40**
    (off Branwell Av.)
Gresham Av. BD2: B'frd 5F **71**
Gresley Ho. LS18: H'fth 4E **57**
    (off Sussex Av.)
Gresley Rd. BD21: Keigh 6A **34**
Grey Cl. WF1: Out 6F **157**
Grey Ct. WF1: Out 6F **157**
Greycourt Cl. BD10: B'frd 3G **71**
  HX1: Hal 3E **149**
Greycourt Ho. HX1: Hal 3E **149**
    (off Greycourt Cl.)
Greyfriar Wlk. BD7: B'frd 2G **109**
Greyhound Dr. BD7: B'frd 5B **90**
Grey Scar Ct. BD22: Oak 5B **46**
    (off Grey Scar Rd.)
Grey Scar Rd. BD22: Oak 5A **46**
Greyshaw Syke HX2: Ogd 3B **106**
Greyshiels Av. LS6: Leeds 5C **76**
Greyshiels Cl. LS6: Leeds 5C **76**
Greystone Av. HX5: Ell 6A **160**
Greystone Cl. LS23: B Spa 4C **30**
  LS29: Burl W 1E **21**
Greystone Cres. BD10: B'frd 3A **72**
Greystone Mill BD3: B'frd 4H **91**
Greystone Mt. LS15: Leeds 4A **100**
Greystones HX2: Mix 4B **128**
Greystones Ct. LS8: Leeds 2G **79**
  LS17: Leeds 3A **60**
Greystones Dr. BD22: Keigh 5F **47**
Greystones Mt. BD22: Keigh 5F **47**
Greystones Ri. BD22: Keigh 4F **47**
Greystones Rd. HX2: Lud M 2E **147**
Grey St. WF1: Out 6F **157**
Griffe Dr. BD12: Wyke 6C **132**
Griffe Gdns. BD22: Oak 4B **46**
Griffe Head Cres.
  BD12: Wyke 5C **132**
Griffe Head Rd. BD12: Wyke 5C **132**
Griffe Rd. BD12: Wyke 5C **132**
Griffe Ter. BD12: Wyke 6C **132**
Griffe Vw. BD22: Oak 4B **46**
Griff Ho. La. WF3: E Ard 1H **155**
Grimthorpe Av. LS6: Leeds 4C **76**
Grimthorpe Pl. LS6: Leeds 4D **76**
Grimthorpe St. LS6: Leeds 4C **76**
Grimthorpe Ter. LS6: Leeds 4D **76**
Grindlestone Bank HX2: Mt T 3A **128**
Grisedale Cl. BD7: B'frd 2H **109**
  HX2: Hal 6B **128**
Gritstone Cl. LS29: Burl W 1E **21**
Grizedale Cl. LS22: Weth 3B **12**
Grosmont Pl. LS13: Leeds 6E **75**
Grosmont Rd. LS13: Leeds 1E **95**
Grosmont Ter. LS13: Leeds 6E **75**
Grosvenor Av. BD18: Ship 1H **69**
Grosvenor Ct. LS16: Leeds 3F **57**
Grosvenor Hill LS7: Leeds 1A **98**
Grosvenor M. LS19: Raw 3E **55**
Grosvenor Mt. LS6: Leeds 5F **77**
Grosvenor Pk. LS7: Leeds 2A **78**
Grosvenor Pk. Gdns.
  LS6: Leeds 5F **77**
Grosvenor Pl. HX2: Lud M 2D **146**
Grosvenor Rd. BD8: B'frd 2D **90**
  BD18: Ship 2H **69**
  LS6: Leeds 5F **77**
Grosvenor St. BD8: B'frd 2D **90**
  HX5: Ell 5B **160**

Grosvenor Ter. BD8: B'frd 2D **90**
  HX1: Hal 2E **149**
    (off West Hill St.)
  HX1: Hal 2H **149**
    (Stansfield Cl.)
  LS6: Leeds 5F **77**
  LS21: Otley 3F **23**
    (off Cross Grn.)
  LS22: Weth 3E **13**
Grotto Ter. HX2: Wain 2E **127**
Grouse Moor La. BD13: Que 3G **107**
Grouse St. BD21: Keigh 5B **34**
Grove, The BD10: B'frd 2B **72**
    (Galloway Rd.)
  BD10: B'frd 2H **71**
    (Woodbine Ter.)
  BD13: Que 4H **107**
    (off New Pk. Rd.)
  BD16: Bgly 1A **50**
  BD17: Bail 3C **52**
  BD18: Ship 2G **69**
  HX3: Hip 1F **151**
  HX3: She 1E **131**
  LS8: Leeds 3H **79**
  LS17: E Kes 5D **26**
  LS17: Leeds 2F **59**
  LS18: H'fth 1D **74**
  LS19: Yead 1F **55**
  LS23: B Spa 4D **30**
  LS25: Kip 4G **123**
  LS26: Swil 3B **122**
  LS27: Gil 6F **115**
  LS28: Pud 4H **93**
  LS29: I'ly 5C **10**
  WF3: E Ard 1H **155**
Grove Av. BD18: Ship 4B **70**
  HX3: Hal 5D **128**
  LS6: Leeds 3E **77**
  LS28: Pud 4H **93**
  LS29: I'ly 6B **10**
Grove Cl. BD2: B'frd 5G **71**
  BD19: Gom 6F **135**
Grove Cotts. HD6: Brigh 1G **161**
Grove Ct. HX3: Hal 4E **129**
  LS6: Leeds 3E **77**
  LS28: Pud 4H **93**
Grove Cres. HX2: Lud M 2D **146**
  LS23: B Spa 4D **30**
Grove Cres. Sth. LS23: B Spa 4D **30**
Grove Cft. HX3: Hal 5D **128**
Grove Dr. HX3: Hal 5D **128**
Grove Edge HX3: Hal 5D **128**
Grove Farm Cl. LS16: Leeds 3H **57**
Grove Farm Cres. LS16: Leeds 4G **57**
Grove Farm Cft. LS16: Leeds 3G **57**
Grove Farm Dr. LS16: Leeds 3G **57**
Grove Gdns. HX3: Hal 5E **129**
  LS6: Leeds 3E **77**
  LS23: B Spa 4D **30**
Grovehall Av. LS11: Leeds 4F **117**
Grovehall Dr. LS11: Leeds 4F **117**
Grovehall Pde. LS11: Leeds 4F **117**
Grovehall Rd. LS11: Leeds 4F **117**
Grove Ho. LS7: Leeds 5C **78**
    (off Woodland Gro.)
Grove Ho. Ct. LS8: Leeds 3H **79**
    (off Nth. Grove Cl.)
Grove Ho. Cres. BD2: B'frd 5G **71**
Grove Ho. Dr. BD2: B'frd 6G **71**
Grove Ho. Rd. BD2: B'frd 5G **71**
Grovelands BD2: B'frd 5G **71**
Grove La. BD19: Gom 6F **135**
  LS6: Leeds 3D **76**
Grove Mill Cl. LS21: Otley 4C **22**
Grove Mill Dr. BD21: Keigh 4G **47**
Grove Mill La. HX3: Hal 5E **129**
Grove Pk. HX3: Hal 4D **128**
  LS6: Leeds 4F **77**
Grove Pl. LS23: B Spa 4C **30**
Grove Promenade, The
  LS29: I'ly 5D **10**
    (off West St.)
Grove Ri. LS17: Leeds 2F **59**

Grove Rd. BD16: Bgly 5B **50**
  BD18: Ship 4B **70**
  HX5: Ell 4C **160**
  LS6: Leeds 4E **77**
  LS10: Leeds 2C **118**
  LS15: Leeds 4C **100**
  LS18: H'fth 1D **74**
  LS23: B Spa 4C **30**
  LS28: Pud 4H **93**
  LS29: I'ly 5A **10**
  LS29: Men 1G **39**
Grove Row HX2: Mt T 4G **127**
Grove Royd HX3: Hal 5E **129**
Grove Sq. BD19: Gom 6F **135**
  HX3: Hal 5D **128**
Grove St. HD6: Brigh 1B **162**
  HX2: Hal 4D **128**
  HX6: Sow B 5B **148**
  LS1: Leeds 4A **4**
  LS28: Stan 1A **94**
Grove St. Sth. HX1: Hal 2D **148**
Grove Ter. BD7: B'frd 5B **6** (5D **90**)
  BD11: Birk 3E **135**
  HD6: Brigh 1G **161**
  LS21: Pool 6D **24**
  LS23: B Spa 4C **30**
  LS28: Pud 4H **93**
Grove Vs. WF10: All B 1G **145**
Groveville HX3: Hip 6E **131**
Groveway BD2: B'frd 5G **71**
Grovewood LS6: Leeds 3D **76**
Grunberg Pl. LS6: Leeds 4D **76**
Grunberg St. LS6: Leeds 4D **76**
GUARD HOUSE 6E **33**
Guard Ho. Av. BD22: Keigh 6G **33**
Guard Ho. Dr. BD22: Keigh 6G **33**
Guard Ho. Gro. BD22: Keigh 6F **33**
Guard Ho. Rd. BD22: Keigh 6G **33**
Guardian Ct. LS29: I'ly 5D **10**
    (off Wells Prom.)
Guardian M. LS12: Leeds 6C **96**
    (off Lynwood Gth.)
Guernsey Rd. WF12: Dew 6A **154**
Guide Post Farm HX2: Illing 6C **106**
    (off Keighley Rd.)
Guild Way HX2: Hal 2H **147**
Guillemot App. LS27: Morl 4D **138**
GUISELEY 4C **40**
Guiseley Dr. LS29: Men 3H **39**
Guiseley Retail Pk. LS20: Guis 5C **40**
Guiseley Station (Rail) 4B **40**
Guiseley Theatre 5C **40**
Gunter Rd. LS22: Weth 4G **13**
Gurbax Ct. BD3: B'frd 4C **92**
Gurney Cl. BD5: B'frd 2D **110**
GUYCROFT .4D **22**
Guycroft LS21: Otley 4D **22**
Guys Cft. BD16: Bgly 2F **51**
Guy St. BD4: B'frd 6E **7**
Gwynne Av. BD3: B'frd 2C **92**
Gym Health & Fitness Club, The . . .1E **99**
Gypsy Wood Cl. LS15: Leeds 4F **101**
Gypsy Wood Crest LS15: Leeds 4F **101**

H

Hadassah St. HX3: Hal 5H **149**
Haddon Av. HX3: Hal 6G **149**
  LS4: Leeds 1C **96**
Haddon Pl. LS4: Leeds 1C **96**
Haddon Rd. LS4: Leeds 1D **96**
Hadleigh Ct. LS17: Leeds 5B **60**
Hadley's Ct. LS27: Gil 1F **137**
    (off Gelderd Rd.)
Hag Farm Rd. LS29: Burl W 5D **20**
Hag La. HX3: Hal 4G **129**
Haigh Av. LS26: Rothw 6G **119**
Haigh Beck Vw. BD10: B'frd 2A **72**
Haigh Cnr. BD10: B'frd 2B **72**
Haighfield Caravan Site
  LS17: Bard 3D **44**
HAIGH FOLD 6A **72**

Haigh Fold BD2: B'frd 6A 72
Haigh Gdns. LS26: Rothw 6G 119
Haigh Hall BD10: B'frd 2B 72
Haigh Hall Rd. BD10: B'frd 2B 72
Haigh La. HX3: Hal 5H 149
HAIGH MOOR 3E 155
Haigh Moor Av. WF3: W Ard 3E 155
Haigh Moor Cres. WF3: W Ard 3E 155
Haigh Moor Rd. WF3: W Ard 4E 155
Haigh Moor Vw. WF3: W Ard 3E 155
Haigh Pk. Rd. LS10: Leeds 3F 119
Haigh Rd. LS26: Rothw 1A 142
Haighside LS26: Rothw 1G 141
Haighside Cl. LS26: Rothw 1G 141
Haighside Dr. LS26: Rothw 1G 141
Haighside Way LS26: Rothw 1G 141
Haigh St. BD4: B'frd 2H 111
    HD6: Brigh 6A 152
    HX1: Hal 1D 148
    HX4: Gree 4F 159
Haigh Ter. LS26: Rothw 6G 119
Haigh Vw. LS26: Rothw 6G 119
Haigh Wood Cres. LS16: Leeds 4F 57
Haigh Wood Grn. LS16: Leeds 5F 57
Haigh Wood Rd. LS16: Leeds 4E 57
Haincliffe Pl. BD21: Keigh 3H 47
Haincliffe Rd. BD21: Keigh 3H 47
Haines Pk. LS7: Leeds 1C 98
Hainsworth Ct. LS28: Fars 6H 73
                        (off Ebenezer St.)
Hainsworth Moor Cres.
    BD13: Que 5H 107
Hainsworth Moor Dr. BD13: Que . .5H 107
Hainsworth Moor Gth.
    BD13: Que 5H 107
Hainsworth Moor Gro.
    BD13: Que 5H 107
Hainsworth Moor Vw. BD13: Que . .5H 107
Hainsworth Rd. BD20: Sils 2E 15
                        (not continuous)
Hainsworth Sq. LS28: Fars 6H 73
Hainsworth St. BD20: Sils 2E 15
                        (off Howden Rd.)
    LS12: Leeds 5E 97
    LS26: Rothw 3A 142
HAINWORTH 4H 47
Hainworth Crag Rd. BD21: Keigh . . .5G 47
Hainworth La. BD21: Keigh 3H 47
Hainworth Rd. BD21: Keigh 4H 47
HAINWORTH SHAW 4B 48
Hainworth Wood Rd. BD21: Keigh . .4H 47
Hainworth Wood Rd. Nth.
    BD21: Keigh 2A 48
Halcyon Hill LS7: Leeds 1A 78
Halcyon Way BD5: B'frd 2C 110
Hales Rd. LS12: Leeds 6B 96
Halesworth Cres. BD4: B'frd 2C 112
Haley Ct. HX3: Hal 1B 164
Haley Hill HX3: Hal 1B 164 (6G 129)
Haley's Yd. LS13: Leeds 6E 75
Half Acre Rd. BD13: Thorn 4F 87
Half Ho. La. HD6: Brigh 4F 151
HALF MILE 6B 74
Half Mile LS13: Leeds 1B 94
Half Mile Cl. LS28: Stan 1B 94
Half Mile Ct. LS28: Stan 1B 94
Half Mile Gdns. LS13: Leeds 1B 94
Half Mile Grn. LS28: Stan 1B 94
Half Mile La. LS13: Leeds 6B 74
    LS28: Fars 6B 74
Half St. BD21: Keigh 5H 33
HALIFAX 4C 164 (2G 149)
Halifax Antiques Cen. HX1: Hal 2D 148
                        (off Queen's Rd.)
Halifax Body Station, The 2C 164
Halifax Bradley Hall Golf Course . . .6E 159
Halifax Golf Course 4A 106
Halifax Ind. Cen. HX1: Hal 1E 149
Halifax La. HX2: Lud 1E 147
Halifax Old Rd. HX3: Hip 1D 150
Halifax Playhouse 5A 164 (3F 149)
Halifax Retail Pk.
    HX1: Hal 3A 164 (2F 149)

Halifax RLFC 6C 164 (4G 149)
Halifax Rd. BD6: B'frd 6G 109
    BD13: Cull 4B 66
    BD13: Denh 1B 106
                        (Foreside Bottom La.)
    BD13: Denh 1B 106
                        (Old Rd.)
    BD13: Que 1G 129
    BD19: Cleck, Scho 2E 153
    BD21: Cros R, Keigh 1F 65
    BD21: Keigh 4H 47
    BD22: Cros R 6F 47
    HD6: Brigh 3F 151
    HX3: Hip 3F 151
                        (Broad Oak La.)
    HX3: Hip 1D 150
                        (Halifax Old Rd.)
    HX3: North, She 4D 130
    HX5: Ell, Hal 3A 160
    WF15: Liv 2E 153
Halifax Ski & Snowboarding Centre, The
    . . . . .4G 129
Halifax Station (Rail) 5D 164 (3H 149)
Halifax Swimming Pool
    . . . . .6C 164 (3G 149)
Halifax Vw. HX3: Hal 1D 164
Halifax Vis. Cen. 2H 149
                        (within The Piece Hall)
Hall, The LS7: Leeds 2A 78
Hallamfield LS20: Guis 5C 40
Hallam St. LS20: Guis 5B 40
HALLAS BRIDGE 3D 66
Hallas Bri. Mill BD13: Cull 4D 66
Hallas La. BD13: Cull 4C 66
                        (not continuous)
Hall Av. BD2: B'frd 4B 72
Hallbank Cl. BD5: B'frd 4D 110
Hall Bank Dr. BD16: Bgly 3C 50
Hallbank Dr. BD5: B'frd 4D 110
Hallcliffe BD17: Bail 3D 52
Hall Cl. HX3: North 4C 130
    LS16: B'hpe 1G 43
    LS23: B Spa 4C 30
    LS29: Burl W 2D 20
Hall Ct. LS7: Leeds 5B 78
Hall Cft. BD20: Sils 1E 15
Hallcroft BD16: Bgly 2B 50
Hallcroft Dr. LS29: Add 2F 9
Hall Dr. LS16: B'hpe 1F 43
    LS29: Burl W 2D 20
Hall Farm M. LS25: M'fld 3E 105
Hall Farm Pk. LS25: M'fld 3D 104
HALLFIELD 4F 13
Hallfield Av. LS25: M'fld 4D 104
Hallfield Ct. LS22: Weth 3F 13
Hallfield Cres. LS22: Weth 4F 13
Hallfield Dr. BD1: B'frd 4C 52
Hallfield Dr. LS22: Weth 3F 13
Hallfield Pl. BD1: B'frd 1C 6 (3E 91)
Hallfield Rd. BD1: B'frd 2B 6 (3D 90)
Hallfield St. BD1: B'frd 2C 6 (3E 91)
Hallfield Ter. LS25: M'fld 4D 104
Hallgate BD1: B'frd 2C 6 (3E 91)
Hall Gro. LS6: Leeds 1F 97
Halliday Av. LS12: Leeds 3A 96
Halliday Ct. BD3: B'frd 3D 92
    LS25: Gar 4E 103
Halliday Dr. LS12: Leeds 3A 96
Halliday Gro. LS12: Leeds 3A 96
Halliday Mt. LS12: Leeds 3A 96
Halliday Pl. LS12: Leeds 3A 96
Halliday Rd. LS12: Leeds 3A 96
    LS25: Gar 4E 103
Halliday St. LS28: Pud 3A 94
Hall Ings BD1: B'frd 5D 6 (5E 91)
    HX3: Sou 6F 151
Hall La. BD4: B'frd 6F 7 (6F 91)
    BD18: Ship 1C 70
    HX3: North 3B 130
    LS7: Leeds 4B 78
    LS12: Leeds 4C 96
    LS12: N Far 5E 95
    LS16: Leeds 1G 57

Hall La. LS18: H'fth 1B 74
    LS21: Leat 1C 24
    WF10: Leds 6D 124
Hall Mews LS23: B Spa 4C 30
Hall Orchards Av. LS22: Weth 3F 13
Hallowes Gro. BD13: Cull 4B 66
Hallowes Pk. Rd. BD13: Cull 4B 66
Hallows, The BD20: Keigh 5G 33
Hallows Rd. BD21: Keigh 4C 34
Hall Park Av. LS18: H'fth 6C 56
Hall Park Cl. LS18: H'fth 6C 56
Hall Park Ct. LS25: Kip 4H 123
Hall Park Cft. LS25: Kip 5H 123
Hall Park Gth. LS18: H'fth 6C 56
Hall Park Mdws. LS25: Kip 5H 123
Hall Park Mt. LS18: H'fth 6C 56
Hall Park Orchards LS25: Kip 5H 123
Hall Park Ri. LS18: H'fth 6C 56
    LS25: Kip 4H 123
Hall Pl. LS9: Leeds 4D 98
Hall Ri. LS16: B'hpe 2G 43
    LS29: Burl W 2D 20
Hall Rise Cl. LS16: B'hpe 2G 43
Hall Rise Cft. LS16: B'hpe 2G 43
Hall Rd. BD2: B'frd 4A 72
    LS12: Leeds 4C 96
    LS26: Swil 4B 122
Hall Royd BD18: Ship 2B 70
Hallside Cl. BD17: Bail 3F 53
Hall Sq. LS28: Cal 2F 73
Hall Stone Ct. HX3: She 2E 131
Hall St. BD6: B'frd 4C 110
    BD22: Haw 3C 64
    BD22: Oak 5D 46
                        (off Clough La.)
    HD6: Brigh 1B 162
    HX1: Hal 4A 164 (2F 149)
Hall St. Nth. HX3: Hal 5F 129
Hall Ter. BD2: B'frd 4A 72
    BD21: Rid 4D 34
Hallwood Grn. BD10: B'frd 4C 72
Halstead Dr. LS29: Men 6G 21
Halstead Pl. BD7: B'frd 2B 110
Halsteads Way BD20: Stee 5B 14
HALTON 3B 100
Halton Dr. LS15: Leeds 3C 100
Halton Hill LS15: Leeds 3B 100
HALTON MOOR 4A 100
Halton Moor Av. LS9: Leeds 5H 99
Halton Moor Rd. LS9: Leeds 5E 99
                        (not continuous)
    LS15: Leeds 5A 100
Halton Pl. BD5: B'frd 2B 110
Hambledon Av. BD4: B'frd 4H 111
Hambleton Bank HX2: Mix 1H 127
Hambleton Cres. HX2: Mix 2H 127
Hambleton Dr. HX2: Mix 2G 127
Hambleton La. BD22: Oxen 4F 85
Hamilton Av. LS7: Leeds 5C 78
Hamilton Gdns. LS7: Leeds 6B 78
Hamilton Pl. LS7: Leeds 6C 78
Hamilton St. BD1: B'frd 1B 6
Hamilton Ter. LS7: Leeds 6C 78
    LS21: Otley 3F 23
                        (off North Av.)
Hamilton Vw. LS7: Leeds 5C 78
Hammerstone Leach La. HX5: Ell . . .6H 159
Hammerstones Rd. HX5: Ell 5H 159
Hammerton Cl. HX5: Ell 4B 160
Hammerton Dr. LS25: Gar 6G 103
Hammerton Gro. LS28: Pud 4B 94
Hammerton St. BD3: B'frd 5G 7 (5G 91)
    LS28: Pud 4A 94
Hammond Cres. BD11: Drig 6H 113
Hammond Pl. BD9: B'frd 6A 70
Hammonds Landing HX6: Sow B . . .5A 148
Hammond Sq. BD9: B'frd 6A 70
Hammond St. HX1: Hal 3D 148
Hamm Strasse BD1: B'frd 2D 6 (3E 91)
Hampden Pl. BD5: B'frd 1D 110
    HX1: Hal 2F 149
Hampden St. BD5: B'frd 1D 110
Hampole Rd. LS23: B Spa 3B 30

Hampole Way—Harris St.

Hampole Way LS23: B Spa 3B **30**
Hampshire Cl. LS29: I'ly 5F **11**
Hampton Ct. *LS29: I'ly 5C **10***
(off Grove Rd.)
Hampton Cres. *LS9: Leeds 4D **98***
(off Long La. Cl.)
Hampton Pl. BD10: B'frd 1H **71**
LS9: Leeds 4D **98**
Hampton St. HX1: Hal 4D **148**
Hampton Ter. LS9: Leeds 4D **98**
Hamworth Dr. BD22: Oak 5D **46**
Hanbury Gdns. LS25: Gar 3F **103**
Hand Carr La. HX2: Lud M 2B **146**
Handel St. BD7: B'frd 4C **90**
Hanging Ga. La. BD22: Oxen 4A **64**
Hangingstone Rd. LS29: I'ly 6F **11**
Hanging Wood Way BD19: Cleck 5A **134**
Hangram St. HD6: Brigh 1B **162**
Hanley Rd. LS27: Morl 4A **138**
Hannah Ct. BD12: Wyke 4C **132**
Hanover Av. LS3: Leeds 2A **4** (3G **97**)
Hanover Cl. BD8: B'frd 2A **90**
Hanover Ct. LS27: Morl 2B **138**
Hanover Gdns. BD5: B'frd 6D **90**
LS29: Burl W 3E **21**
Hanover Ho. *BD1: B'frd 4F **7***
(off Chapel St.)
HX2: Hal 4C **148**
*LS19: Yead 6G **41***
(off Harper La.)
Hanover La. LS3: Leeds 3B **4** (3G **97**)
Hanover Mt. LS3: Leeds 2A **4** (2G **97**)
Hanover Pl. LS25: Kip 4H **123**
Hanover Sq. BD1: B'frd 1B **6** (3D **90**)
BD12: Wyke 4C **132**
LS3: Leeds 2A **4** (2G **97**)
Hanover St. BD21: Keigh 6A **34**
HX1: Hal 5A **164** (3F **149**)
HX6: Sow B 5B **148**
Hanover Wlk. LS3: Leeds 3B **4** (3G **97**)
Hanover Way LS3: Leeds 3A **4** (3G **97**)
LS29: Burl W 3E **21**
Hansby Av. LS14: Leeds 4D **80**
Hansby Bank LS14: Leeds 4D **80**
Hansby Cl. LS14: Leeds 5D **80**
Hansby Dr. LS14: Leeds 4D **80**
Hansby Gdns. LS14: Leeds 5D **80**
Hansby Ga. LS14: Leeds 4D **80**
Hansby Grange LS14: Leeds 4D **80**
Hansby Pl. LS14: Leeds 5D **80**
Hanson Ct. BD12: Wyke 5C **132**
Hanson Fold BD12: Wyke 4C **132**
Hanson La. HX1: Hal 3A **164** (2C **148**)
Hanson Mt. BD12: Wyke 5C **132**
Hanson Pl. BD12: Wyke 4C **132**
Hanson Rd. HD6: Ras 3G **161**
Hanworth Rd. BD12: Low M 1D **132**
Hapsburg Ct. *BD5: B'frd 6E **91***
(off Elsdon Gro.)
Harbeck Dr. BD16: Har 6F **49**
Harborough Grn. BD10: B'frd 1C **72**
Harbour Cres. BD6: B'frd 5A **110**
Harbour Pk. BD6: B'frd 5H **109**
Harbour Rd. BD6: B'frd 5H **109**
Harclo Rd. BD21: Keigh 5C **34**
Harcourt Av. BD13: Thorn 4H **87**
Harcourt Dr. LS27: Morl 2H **137**
LS29: Add 1D **8**
Harcourt Pl. LS1: Leeds 4A **4** (3F **97**)
Harcourt St. BD4: B'frd 2H **111**
Hardaker Cft. BD17: Bail 5A **52**
Hardaker La. BD17: Bail 5A **52**
Hardaker St. BD8: B'frd 2A **6** (3D **90**)
HARDEN 6F **49**
Harden & Bingley Caravan Pk.
BD16: Har 2E **67**
Harden Brow La. BD16: Har 5E **49**
Harden Gro. BD10: B'frd 6C **72**
BD21: Keigh 2C **48**
Harden La. BD15: Wils 2F **67**
BD16: Har 2F **67**
Harden Rd. BD16: Bgly, Har 6F **49**
BD21: Keigh 2C **48**
Hardgate La. BD21: Cros R 2F **65**
Hardhill Ho's. *BD16: Har 6F **49***
(off Wilsden Rd.)
Hardings La. LS29: I'ly 3B **10**
LS29: Midd 1B **10**
Hard Ings Rd. BD21: Keigh 4A **34**
Hardknot Cl. BD7: B'frd 2G **109**
Hardnaze BD22: Oxen 2A **84**
Hard Nese La. BD22: Oxen 2A **84**
Hardrow Grn. LS12: Leeds 6D **96**
Hardrow Gro. LS12: Leeds 6D **96**
Hardrow Rd. LS12: Leeds 6C **96**
Hardrow Ter. LS12: Leeds 6D **96**
Hardwick Cl. HX1: Hal 2C **148**
Hardwick Cft. LS7: Leeds 3B **78**
Hardwick St. BD21: Keigh 1G **47**
Hardy Av. BD6: B'frd 5C **110**
LS27: Chur 5C **116**
Hardy Ct. LS27: Morl 3B **138**
Hardy Gro. LS11: Leeds 2G **117**
Hardy Pl. HD6: Brigh 4G **151**
Hardy St. BD4: B'frd 6E **7**
BD6: B'frd 4C **110**
HD6: Brigh 6B **152**
LS11: Leeds 2G **117**
LS27: Morl 3B **138**
Hardy Ter. *BD6: B'frd 4C **110***
(off Hardy St.)
LS11: Leeds 2H **117**
Hardy Vw. LS11: Leeds 2G **117**
HARE CROFT 5E **67**
Harecroft Rd. LS21: Otley 2E **23**
Hare Farm Av. LS12: Leeds 4F **95**
Hare Farm Cl. LS12: Leeds 3F **95**
Harefield Cl. BD20: East 6A **14**
Harefield Dr. WF17: Bat 6C **136**
Harefield E. LS15: Leeds 4A **100**
Harefield W. LS15: Leeds 4A **100**
Harehill Cl. BD10: B'frd 6H **53**
Harehill Rd. BD10: B'frd 6H **53**
HAREHILLS 1F **99**
Harehills Av. LS7: Leeds 5C **78**
LS8: Leeds 5C **78**
HAREHILLS CORNER 5D **78**
Harehills La. LS7: Leeds 4C **78**
LS8: Leeds 5E **79**
LS9: Leeds 5E **79**
Harehills Pk. Av. LS9: Leeds 1F **99**
Harehills Pk. Cotts.
LS9: Leeds 1G **99**
Harehills Pk. Rd. LS9: Leeds 1F **99**
Harehills Pk. Ter. LS9: Leeds 1F **99**
Harehills Pk. Vw.
LS9: Leeds 1F **99**
Harehills Pl. LS8: Leeds 6D **78**
Harehills Rd. LS8: Leeds 5D **78**
Hare La. LS28: Pud 6A **94**
Hare Pk. Av. WF15: Liv 5H **153**
Hare Pk. Cl. WF15: Liv 5H **153**
Hare Pk. La. WF15: Liv 6H **153**
Hare Pk. Mt. LS12: Leeds 4E **95**
Hares Av. LS8: Leeds 5D **78**
Hares Mt. LS8: Leeds 5C **78**
Hares Rd. LS8: Leeds 5C **78**
Hares Ter. LS8: Leeds 5D **78**
Hare St. HX1: Hal 2E **149**
Hares Vw. LS8: Leeds 5D **78**
Harewood Av.
BD20: East 6A **14**
HX2: Hal 1B **148**
LS17: Bard, Hare 4A **26**
Harewood Ct. LS14: Leeds 5C **80**
LS17: Leeds 6B **60**
Harewood Cres. BD22: Oak 4E **47**
Harewood Dr. BD20: East 6A **14**
Harewood Pl. HX2: Hal 3C **148**
Harewood Ri. BD22: Oak 4F **47**
Harewood Rd. BD22: Oak 5E **47**
LS17: E Kes 4C **26**
LS22: Coll 4C **26**
Harewood St. BD3: B'frd 3H **7** (4H **91**)
(not continuous)
LS2: Leeds 4F **5** (3A **98**)
Harewood Way LS13: Leeds 3D **94**
Hargrave Cres. LS29: Men 1F **39**
Hargreaves Av. WF3: S'ley 4H **157**
Hargreaves Cl. LS27: Morl 6H **115**
Hargreaves St. LS26: Rothw 2B **142**
Harker Rd. BD12: Low M 6C **110**
Harker Ter. LS28: Stan 2H **93**
Harland Cl. BD2: B'frd 1E **91**
Harland Sq. *LS2: Leeds 6G **77***
(off Moorfield St.)
Harlech Av. LS11: Leeds 3H **117**
Harlech Cres. LS11: Leeds 3H **117**
Harlech Gro. LS11: Leeds 3H **117**
Harlech Mt. LS11: Leeds 3H **117**
Harlech Pk. Ct. LS11: Leeds 3H **117**
Harlech Rd. LS11: Leeds 3H **117**
Harlech St. LS11: Leeds 3H **117**
Harlech Ter. LS11: Leeds 3H **117**
Harlech Way LS25: Gar 4H **103**
Harley Cl. LS13: Leeds 3C **94**
Harley Ct. LS13: Leeds 3C **94**
Harley Dr. LS13: Leeds 3C **94**
Harley Gdns. LS13: Leeds 3C **94**
Harley Grn. LS13: Leeds 3C **94**
Harley Pl. *HD6: Ras 2A **162***
(off Harley St.)
Harley Ri. LS13: Leeds 3C **94**
Harley Rd. LS13: Leeds 3C **94**
Harley St. HD6: Ras 2A **162**
Harley Ter. LS13: Leeds 3C **94**
Harley Vw. LS13: Leeds 3C **94**
Harley Wlk. LS13: Leeds 3C **94**
Harlington Ct. LS27: Morl 5A **138**
Harlington Rd. LS27: Morl 5A **138**
Harlow Ct. LS8: Leeds 2G **79**
Harlow Rd. BD7: B'frd 6A **90**
Harmon Cl. BD4: B'frd 5A **112**
Harmony Pl. BD13: Que 2G **107**
Harold Av. LS6: Leeds 1E **97**
Harold Ct. BD12: Low M 2C **132**
Harold Gdns. LS27: Morl 3C **138**
Harold Gro. LS6: Leeds 1E **97**
Harold Mt. LS6: Leeds 1E **97**
Harold Pl. BD18: Ship 1H **69**
LS6: Leeds 1E **97**
Harold Rd. LS6: Leeds 1E **97**
Harold Sq. LS6: Leeds 1E **97**
Harold St. BD16: Bgly 3A **50**
LS6: Leeds 1E **97**
Harold Ter. LS6: Leeds 1E **97**
Harold Vw. LS6: Leeds 1E **97**
Harold Wlk. LS6: Leeds 1E **97**
Harper Av. BD10: B'frd 6H **53**
Harper Cres. BD10: B'frd 6A **54**
Harper Ga. BD4: B'frd 1D **112**
Harper Gro. BD10: B'frd 6H **53**
Harper La. LS19: Yead 1F **55**
Harper Rock *LS19: Yead 1F **55***
(off Harper La.)
Harper Royd HX6: Sow B 1A **158**
Harper Royd La. HX6: Sow B 6H **147**
Harper St. LS2: Leeds 5G **5** (4B **98**)
Harper Ter. *LS19: Yead 1F **55***
(off Harper La.)
Harp La. BD13: Que 3H **107**
Harrier Cl. BD8: B'frd 4D **88**
Harrier Way LS27: Morl 3D **138**
Harriet St. BD8: B'frd 3B **90**
HD6: Brigh 5A **152**
LS7: Leeds 6B **78**
Harris Ct. BD7: B'frd 2A **110**
Harrison and Potter Trust Homes, The
LS2: Leeds 2F **5**
Harrison Cres. LS9: Leeds 2H **99**
Harrison Potter Trust Almshouses
*LS2: Leeds 6G **77***
(off Raglan Rd.)
Harrison Rd. HX1: Hal 5B **164** (3G **149**)
Harrison's Av. LS28: Stan 1B **94**
Harrison St. BD16: Bgly 5C **50**
LS1: Leeds 3F **5** (3A **98**)
Harris St. BD1: B'frd 4G **7** (4G **91**)
BD16: Bgly 5C **50**

Harrogate Av. BD3: B'frd 1G 91
Harrogate Pde. LS17: Leeds 5B 60
Harrogate Pl. BD3: B'frd 1G 91
Harrogate Rd. BD2: B'frd 1H 91
   BD10: B'frd 5B 72
   LS7: Leeds 1A 78
   LS16: B'hpe 5A 42
   LS17: Leeds 1A 78
   LS17: Leeds, Wike 4B 60
   LS19: B'hpe, Yead 5A 42
   LS19: Raw, Yead 3F 55
      (not continuous)
   LS21: Cast, Leat 2F 25
   LS22: Weth 1A 12
Harrogate St. BD3: B'frd 1G 91
Harrogate Ter. BD3: B'frd 1G 91
Harrogate Vw. LS17: Leeds 2G 61
Harrop Av. LS27: Morl 5B 138
HARROP EDGE 1G 87
Harrop Gro. LS27: Morl 5B 138
Harrop La. BD15: Wils 6E 67
Harrop Ter. LS27: Morl 5B 138
Harrowby Cres. LS16: Leeds 2B 76
Harrowby Rd. LS16: Leeds 2B 76
Harrows, The BD20: E Mor 5F 35
Harrow St. HX1: Hal 2D 148
Harry La. BD14: Clay 1D 108
   BD22: Oxen 6C 64
Harry St. BD4: B'frd 2A 112
Harthill LS27: Gil 6F 115
Harthill Av. LS27: Gil 6F 115
Harthill Cl. LS27: Gil 6F 115
Harthill La. LS27: Gil 6F 115
Harthill Paddock LS27: Gil 6F 115
Harthill Pde. *LS27: Gil* *6F 115*
      (off Town St.)
Harthill Ri. LS27: Gil 6F 115
Hartington St. BD21: Keigh 5A 34
Hartington Ter. BD7: B'frd 6A 90
Hartland Rd. BD4: B'frd 1C 112
Hartley Av. LS6: Leeds 5G 77
Hartley Bank La. HX3: North 5E 131
Hartley Bus. Pk. BD4: B'frd 5B 92
Hartley Cres. LS6: Leeds 5G 77
Hartley Gdns. LS6: Leeds 5H 77
Hartley Gro. LS6: Leeds 5G 77
Hartley Hill LS2: Leeds . . .2F 5 (2A 98)
Hartley Pl. LS27: Morl 4B 138
Hartley's Bldgs. LS27: Morl 4B 138
Hartley Sq. BD13: Que 2E 107
Hartley's Sq. BD20: E Mor 4H 35
Hartley St. BD4: B'frd 6G 91
   HX1: Hal 1E 149
   LS27: Chur 6B 116
   LS27: Morl 3B 138
Hartley's Yd. LS12: Leeds 4B 96
Hartley Wood Cotts.
   LS25: M'fld 3G 105
Hartlington Ct. BD17: Bail 4E 53
Hartman Pl. BD9: B'frd 1H 89
Hart Rhydding La. LS29: Add 2D 8
Hartshead Ct. WF15: Liv 5H 153
Hartshead Hall La. WF15: Liv 3H 163
Hartshead La. WF15: Liv 1H 163
HARTSHEAD MOOR SERVICE AREA
   . . . . .4G 153
HARTSHEAD MOOR SIDE 3G 153
HARTSHEAD MOOR TOP 3F 153
Hart St. BD7: B'frd 1A 110
Hartwell Rd. LS6: Leeds 1E 97
Harvest Cl. LS25: Gar 6G 103
Harvest Ct. HX1: Hal 4A 164 (2F 149)
Harvest Cft. LS29: Burl W 2D 20
Harvest Mt. BD10: B'frd 1F 71
Harwill App. LS27: Chur 6C 116
Harwill Av. LS27: Chur 6C 116
Harwill Cft. LS27: Chur 6C 116
Harwill Gro. LS27: Chur 6C 116
Harwill Ri. LS27: Chur 6C 116
Harwill Rd. LS27: Chur 6C 116
Harwin Cl. HX3: North 4C 130
Haslam Cl. BD3: B'frd 2H 7 (3G 91)
Haslam Gro. BD18: Ship 3E 71

Haslemere Cl. BD4: B'frd 2B 112
Haslewood Cl. LS9: Leeds 3C 98
Haslewood Ct. LS9: Leeds 3D 98
Haslewood Dene LS9: Leeds 3D 98
Haslewood Dr. LS9: Leeds 3C 98
Haslewood Gdns. LS9: Leeds 3D 98
Haslewood Grn. LS9: Leeds 3D 98
Haslewood M. LS9: Leeds 3D 98
Haslewood Pl. LS9: Leeds 3D 98
Haslewood Sq. LS9: Leeds 3D 98
Haslewood Vw. LS9: Leeds 3D 98
Hasley Rd. LS29: Burl W 3F 21
Haslingden Dr. BD9: B'frd 1H 89
Hastings Av. BD5: B'frd 3D 110
Hastings Ct. LS17: Shad 3A 62
   LS22: Coll 3B 28
Hastings Pl. BD5: B'frd 2D 110
Hastings St. BD5: B'frd 3D 110
Hastings Ter. BD5: B'frd 3D 110
Hastings Way HX1: Hal 4F 149
   LS22: Coll 3H 27
Hatcham Cl. BD15: All 4C 88
Hatchet La. BD12: O'haw 3G 133
Hatfield Rd. BD2: B'frd 1H 91
Hathaway Av. BD9: B'frd 6F 69
Hathaway Dr. LS14: Leeds 6D 62
Hathaway La. LS14: Leeds 1D 80
Hathaway M. LS14: Leeds 6D 62
Hathaway Wlk. LS14: Leeds 1D 80
Hathenshaw La. LS29: Den 1H 11
Hathershelf La. HX2: Lud M 3A 146
Hatters Fold HX1: Hal 4D 164 (2H 149)
      (not continuous)
Hatton Cl. BD6: B'frd 5D 110
Haugh End La. HX6: Sow B 6G 147
Haugh Shaw Cft. HX1: Hal 4E 149
Haugh Shaw Rd. HX1: Hal 4E 149
Haugh Shaw Rd. W. HX1: Hal 4D 148
Hauxley Ct. LS29: I'ly 4F 11
Hauxwell Dr. LS19: Yead 1F 55
Havelock Sq. BD13: Thorn 5A 88
Havelock St. BD7: B'frd 1H 109
   BD13: Thorn 5A 88
Haven, The BD10: B'frd 3A 72
   LS15: Leeds 3F 101
Haven Chase LS16: Leeds 4G 57
Haven Cl. HX3: North 4C 130
   LS16: Leeds 3H 57
Haven Ct. LS16: Leeds 4H 57
Haven Cft. LS16: Leeds 4H 57
Haven Gdns. LS16: Leeds 4H 57
Haven Gth. LS16: Leeds 4G 57
Haven Grn. LS16: Leeds 4G 57
Haven Mt. LS16: Leeds 4G 57
Haven Ri. LS16: Leeds 4G 57
Haven Vw. LS16: Leeds 4G 57
Havercroft LS12: Leeds 6G 95
Havercroft Gdns. LS12: Leeds 6G 95
Haw Av. LS19: Yead 5G 41
Hawber Cote Dr. BD20: Sils 1F 15
Hawber Cote La. BD20: Sils 1F 15
Hawber La. BD20: Sils 2F 15
Hawes Av. BD5: B'frd 3C 110
Hawes Cres. BD5: B'frd 3C 110
      (not continuous)
Hawes Dr. BD5: B'frd 3C 110
Hawes Gro. BD5: B'frd 3C 110
Hawes Mt. BD5: B'frd 3C 110
Hawes Rd. BD5: B'frd 3C 110
Hawes Ter. BD5: B'frd 3C 110
Haweswater Cl. LS22: Weth 4B 12
Hawkcliffe Vw. BD20: Sils 2C 14
Hawke Way BD12: Low M 1E 133
Hawkhill Av. LS15: Leeds 1D 100
   LS20: Guis 5B 40
Hawkhill Dr. LS15: Leeds 6D 80
Hawkhill Gdns. LS15: Leeds 6D 80
Hawkhills LS7: Leeds 2C 78
Hawkhurst Rd. LS12: Leeds 5C 96
Hawkins Dr. LS7: Leeds 1A 98
Hawksbridge La. BD22: Oxen 6A 64
Hawkshead Cl. BD5: B'frd 6E 91
Hawkshead Cres. LS14: Leeds 6B 80

Hawkshead Dr. BD5: B'frd 6E 91
Hawkshead Wlk. BD5: B'frd 6E 91
Hawkshead Way *BD5: B'frd* *6E 91*
      (off Hawkshead Dr.)
Hawksley Ct. LS27: Morl 6H 115
Hawk's Nest Gdns. E.
   LS17: Leeds 3B 60
Hawk's Nest Gdns. Sth.
   LS17: Leeds 3B 60
Hawk's Nest Gdns. W.
   LS17: Leeds 3B 60
Hawk's Nest Ri. LS17: Leeds 3B 60
Hawkstone Av. LS20: Guis 6A 40
Hawkstone Dr. BD20: Keigh 4G 33
Hawkstone Vw. LS20: Guis 6A 40
Hawk St. *BD21: Keigh* *5B 34*
      (off Parson St.)
Hawkswood Av. BD9: B'frd 6H 69
   LS5: Leeds 2G 75
Hawkswood Cres. LS5: Leeds 2G 75
Hawkswood Gro. LS5: Leeds 2G 75
Hawkswood Mt. LS5: Leeds 2G 75
Hawkswood Pl. LS5: Leeds 2G 75
Hawkswood St. LS5: Leeds 3H 75
Hawkswood Ter. LS5: Leeds 3H 75
Hawkswood Vw. LS5: Leeds 2G 75
HAWKSWORTH
   LS5 . . . . .3G 75
   LS20 .5F 39
Hawksworth Av. LS20: Guis 6B 40
Hawksworth Cl. LS29: Men 2G 39
Hawksworth Commercial Pk.
   LS13: Leeds 2E 95
Hawksworth Dr. LS20: Guis 6B 40
   LS29: Men 1F 39
Hawksworth Gro. LS5: Leeds 3F 75
Hawksworth La. LS20: Guis 5F 39
Hawksworth Rd. BD17: Bail 1C 52
   LS18: H'fth 2F 75
Hawksworth St. LS29: I'ly 5D 10
Haw La. LS19: Yead 6F 41
Hawley Cl. LS27: Morl 5H 137
Hawley Ter. BD10: B'frd 5C 72
Hawley Way LS27: Morl 5H 137
HAWORTH 2C 64
Haworth Cl. HX1: Hal 4F 149
Haworth Dr. *LS19: Yead* *6F 41*
      (off Chapel La.)
Haworth Gro. BD9: B'frd 6G 69
Haworth La. LS19: Yead 6F 41
Haworth M. BD22: Haw 2C 64
Haworth Rd. BD9: B'frd 6G 69
   BD13: Cull 3G 65
   BD15: All 6C 68
   BD15: Wils 5H 67
      (Bob La.)
   BD15: Wils 5D 66
      (Cullingworth Rd.)
   BD21: Keigh 3F 65
   BD22: Cros R 1E 65
   WF17: Birs 5B 136
Haworth Station
   Keighley & Worth Valley Railway
   . . . . .2C 64
Hawthorn Av. LS19: Yead 6F 41
   LS21: Pool 5F 25
Hawthorn Cl. HD6: Clift 6C 152
   LS29: Add 1B 8
Hawthorn Cres. BD17: Bail 4D 52
   LS7: Leeds 2B 78
   LS19: Yead 6F 41
Hawthorn Cft. WF3: Loft 6G 141
Hawthorn Dr. BD10: B'frd 2A 72
   LS13: Leeds 3H 73
   LS19: Yead 5G 41
Hawthorne Av. BD3: B'frd 3C 92
   BD18: Ship 4D 70
   LS22: Weth 2D 12
Hawthorne Cl. LS27: Gil 6F 115
   WF2: Kirk 6H 155
Hawthorne Dr. LS27: Gil 6G 115
Hawthorne Gdns. LS16: Leeds 2B 58
Hawthorne Gro. LS29: Burl W 3F 21

Hawthorne Mills LS12: Leeds 1A 116
(off Cobden Rd.)
Hawthorne Ri. LS14: Leeds 1E 81
Hawthorne St. BD20: Sils 2D 14
Hawthorne Vw. LS27: Gil 6G 115
Hawthorne Way BD20: E Mor 5A 36
Hawthorn Gro. LS13: Leeds 4H 73
LS26: Rothw 3B 142
Hawthorn La. BD19: Cleck 6A 134
LS7: Leeds 2B 78
Hawthorn M. LS14: Leeds 1D 80
Hawthorn Mt. LS7: Leeds 2B 78
Hawthorn Pk. LS14: Leeds 1C 80
Hawthorn Pl. LS7: Leeds 2B 78
LS19: Yead 6F 41
Hawthorn Va. LS7: Leeds 2B 78
Hawthorn Vw. BD17: Bail 4D 52
LS7: Leeds 2B 78
Hawthorn Way BD2: Illing 6B 106
Haw Vw. LS19: Yead 5G 41
Haycliffe Av. BD7: B'frd 3A 110
Haycliffe Dr. BD7: B'frd 3H 109
Haycliffe Gro. BD7: B'frd 3A 110
HAYCLIFFE HILL 3B 110
Haycliffe Hill Rd. BD5: B'frd 3B 110
Haycliffe La. BD5: B'frd 3A 110
BD6: B'frd 3A 110
Haycliffe Mill Fold
BD7: B'frd 3A 110
Haycliffe Rd. BD5: B'frd 2B 110
Haycliffe Ter. BD5: B'frd 2B 110
Hayclose Mead BD6: B'frd 1A 132
Hay Cft. BD10: B'frd 1F 71
Hayden St. BD3: B'frd 5H 91
Haydn Av. WF3: S'ley 3H 157
Haydn Cl. LS27: Morl 3A 138
Haydn Ct. LS27: Morl 3A 138
Haydn Pl. BD13: Que 4A 108
Haydn's Ter. LS28: Stan 1A 94
Hayfield Av. LS23: B Spa 3A 30
Hayfield Cl. BD17: Bail 2E 53
Hayfields, The BD22: Haw 1C 64
Hayfields Cl. BD22: Keigh 2E 47
Hayfield Ter. LS12: Leeds 5C 96
Hayhills Rd. BD20: Sils 1E 15
Hayleigh Av. LS13: Leeds 6E 75
Hayleigh Mt. LS13: Leeds 6E 75
Hayleigh St. LS13: Leeds 6E 75
Hayleigh Ter. LS13: Leeds 1E 95
Haynes St. BD21: Keigh 1B 48
Hays La. HX2: Mix 6A 106
Haythorns Av. BD20: Sils 2D 14
Haythorns Mt. BD20: Sils 2D 14
Hayton Dr. LS22: Weth 5F 13
Haywain, The LS29: I'ly 6F 11
Hazebrouck Dr. BD17: Bail 3B 52
Hazel Av. LS14: Leeds 1E 81
Hazel Beck BD16: Cot 1B 68
Hazel Cl. BD11: Birk 1E 135
Hazel Ct. HX2: Illing 4C 128
(off Cumberland Cl.)
LS26: Rothw 3B 142
Hazel Cft. BD18: Ship 3C 70
Hazelcroft BD2: B'frd 5B 72
Hazeldene BD13: Que 5H 107
Hazel Dr. HX2: Illing 6B 106
Hazel Gro. HD2: Fix 6B 162
HX3: Hip 2A 150
Hazelheads BD17: Bail 3C 52
Hazelhurst Av. BD16: Cot 1B 68
Hazelhurst Brow BD9: B'frd 1F 89
Hazelhurst Ct. BD3: B'frd 4A 92
BD9: B'frd 1F 89
LS28: Pud 4B 94
Hazelhurst Gro. BD13: Que 6H 107

Hazelhurst Rd. BD9: B'frd 1F 89
BD13: Que 6H 107
Hazelhurst Ter. BD9: B'frd 1F 89
Hazel La. WF3: E Ard 1D 156
Hazelmere Av. BD16: Cot 1C 68
Hazel M. LS25: Gar 4G 103
Hazel Mt. BD18: Ship 2C 70
Hazel Ri. LS26: Meth 6C 144
Hazelton Cl. BD18: Ship 3E 71
Hazel Wlk. BD9: B'frd 1F 89
Hazelwood Av. BD20: Rid 4D 34
LS25: Gar 6G 103
Hazelwood Ct. HX1: Hal 4G 149
WF1: Out 4H 157
Hazelwood Rd. BD9: B'frd 6E 69
WF1: Out 4H 157
HEADINGLEY 4D 76
Headingley 5D 76
Headingley Av. LS6: Leeds 4C 76
Headingley Ct. LS6: Leeds 5F 77
Headingley Cres. LS6: Leeds 5D 76
Headingley Golf Course 2D 58
HEADINGLEY HILL 5E 77
Headingley Ho. BD3: B'frd 3D 92
(off Chapman Rd.)
Headingley La. LS6: Leeds 5E 77
Headingley Mt. LS6: Leeds 4C 76
Headingley Office Pk. LS6: Leeds 5F 77
Headingley Ri. LS6: Leeds 6F 77
(off Welton Rd.)
Headingley Station (Rail) 5B 76
Headingley Ter. LS6: Leeds 5F 77
Headingley Vw. LS6: Leeds 5D 76
Headland Ct. LS25: Gar 3E 103
(off Aberford Rd.)
Headland Gro. BD6: B'frd 4H 109
Headley Golf Course 6G 87
Headley La. BD13: Thorn 1C 107
Headrow, The LS1: Leeds 3D 4 (3H 97)
Headrow Ct. BD13: Thorn 5H 87
(off Thornton Rd.)
Headway Bus. Cen. BD4: B'frd 3A 112
Healey Av. BD16: Bgly 5C 50
Healey Ct. WF3: W Ard 2H 155
Healey Cft. La. WF3: E Ard 2H 155
Healey La. BD16: Bgly 5C 50
Healey Wood Bottom HD6: Ras 2B 162
(off Gooder La.)
Healey Wood Cres. HD6: Ras 3A 162
Healey Wood Gdns. HD6: Ras 3A 162
Healey Wood Gro. HD6: Ras 3B 162
Healey Wood Rd. HD6: Ras 3A 162
Heap La. BD3: B'frd 3G 7 (4G 91)
(not continuous)
Heap St. BD3: B'frd 3G 7 (4G 91)
HX3: Hal 5G 129
Heath Av. HX3: Hal 5F 149
Heathcliffe Cl. WF17: Birs 4B 136
Heathcliffe Ct. LS27: Morl 3F 137
(off Bruntcliffe Rd.)
Heathcliffe M. BD22: Haw 2C 64
Heathcliff M. BD13: Thorn 5A 88
Heathcote Av. LS14: T'ner 2H 63
Heathcote Ri. BD22: Haw 1D 64
Heath Cres. HX1: Hal 4G 149
LS11: Leeds 2E 117
Heathcroft Bank LS11: Leeds 3E 117
Heathcroft Cres. LS11: Leeds 3E 117
Heathcroft Dr. LS11: Leeds 3E 117
Heathcroft Lawn LS11: Leeds 3E 117
Heathcroft Ri. LS11: Leeds 3E 117
Heathcroft Va. LS11: Leeds 3E 117
Heath Dr. LS23: B Spa 4H 29
Heather Bank HX2: Hal 4D 148
(off Darcey Hey La.)
Heather Bank Av. BD22: Haw 3F 47
Heather Bank Cl. BD13: Cull 4A 66
Heather Cl. WF1: Out 4H 157
Heather Ct. BD16: Bgly 2C 50
LS29: I'ly 6D 10
WF1: Out 4H 157
WF17: Birs 5A 136

Heathercroft LS7: Leeds 3C 78
Heatherdale Cl. HX3: Hal 6D 128
Heatherdale Ct. WF3: Ting 1E 155
Heatherdale Dr. WF3: Ting 1E 155
Heatherdale Fold WF3: Ting 1E 155
Heatherdale Rd.
WF3: Ting 1D 154
Heather Dr. HX2: Mt T 4G 127
Heather Gdns. LS13: Leeds 3G 95
LS14: S'cft 6E 45
Heather Gro. BD9: B'frd 6D 68
BD21: Keigh 5F 33
LS13: Leeds 2G 95
Heatherlands Av.
BD13: Denh 1B 86
Heather Pl. BD13: Que 3F 107
Heather Ri. LS29: Burl W 3E 21
Heather Rd. BD17: Bail 3D 52
Heatherside BD17: Bail 2B 52
Heatherstones HX3: Hal 5F 149
Heather Va. LS14: S'cft 6D 44
Heather Vw. BD16: Bgly 2F 51
HX5: Ell 4D 160
Heatherville Cl.
BD16: Bgly 2E 51
HEATHFIELD 4C 160
Heathfield LS16: Leeds 3A 58
Heathfield Av. HX5: Ell 4D 160
Heathfield Cl. BD16: Bgly 3C 50
WF3: W Ard 2F 155
Heathfield Gro. BD7: B'frd 1G 109
HX3: Hal 5G 149
(off Heath Rd.)
Heathfield Ind. Est. HX5: Ell 4C 160
Heathfield La. BD11: Birk 3E 135
LS23: B Spa 3H 29
Heathfield Pl. HX3: Hal 5G 149
Heathfield St. HX5: Ell 5C 160
Heathfield Ter. HX3: Hal 5G 149
LS6: Leeds 3D 76
Heathfield Wlk. LS16: Leeds 2A 58
Heath Gdns. HX3: Hal 5G 149
Heath Gro. BD20: E Mor 5H 35
LS11: Leeds 2E 117
LS28: Pud 5G 93
Heath Hall HX1: Hal 4G 149
Heath Hill Rd. HX2: Hal, Mt T 1G 147
Heath La. HX3: Hal 5G 149
Heath Lea HX1: Hal 6B 164 (4G 149)
Heathmoor Cl. BD10: B'frd 1G 71
HX2: Illing 1B 128
Heathmoor Mt. HX2: Illing 1B 128
Heathmoor Pk. Rd. HX2: Illing 6B 106
Heathmoor Way HX2: Illing 1B 128
Heath Mt. HX1: Hal 4F 149
LS11: Leeds 2E 117
Heath Mt. Rd. HD6: Ras 3A 162
Heathness Rd. LS29: Add 1B 8
Heath Pk. LS29: I'ly 6B 10
Heath Pk. Av. HX1: Hal 4G 149
Heath Pl. LS11: Leeds 2E 117
Heath Ri. LS11: Leeds 3E 117
Heath Rd. BD3: B'frd 2H 91
HX1: Hal 5G 149
HX3: Hal 5G 149
LS11: Leeds 2E 117
Heath Royd HX3: Hal 5G 149
Heath St. BD3: B'frd 4A 92
BD16: Bgly 4C 50
HX3: Hal 5F 149
Heath Ter. BD3: B'frd 4H 91
Heath Vw. HX1: Hal 6C 164
Heath Vw. St. HX1: Hal . . .6C 164 (3H 149)
(not continuous)
Heath Vs. HX3: Hal 5G 149
Heathy Av. HX2: Hal 2E 129
Heathy La. HX2: Hal 1D 128
HEATON 6A 70
Heaton Av. BD20: Rid 6G 35
LS12: Leeds 6C 96
Heaton Cl. BD16: Bgly 3D 50
BD17: Bail 2B 52

Heaton Ct. BD16: Bgly 5B **50**
          (off Bk. Unity St. Nth.)
  LS14: Leeds 3B **80**
          (off Kingsdale Ct.)
Heaton Cres. BD16: Bgly 3D **50**
  BD17: Bail 2B **52**
Heaton Dr. BD16: Bgly 3D **50**
  BD17: Bail 2B **52**
HEATON GROVE 5B **70**
Heaton Gro. BD9: B'frd 5B **70**
  BD18: Ship 2C **70**
Heaton Hill BD6: B'frd 6G **109**
Heaton Lodge WF17: Birs 5A **136**
Heaton Pk. Dr. BD9: B'frd 6H **69**
Heaton Pk. Rd. BD9: B'frd 6H **69**
Heaton Rd. BD8: B'frd 6A **70**
  BD9: B'frd 6A **70**
Heaton Royd BD16: Bgly 4D **50**
          (off Fernbank Dr.)
HEATON ROYDS 4H **69**
Heaton Royds La.
  BD9: B'frd, Ship 4H **69**
  BD18: Ship 4A **70**
Heaton's Ct. LS1: Leeds 6E **5** (4A **98**)
HEATON SHAY 4G **69**
Heaton St. BD4: B'frd 6G **7** (6G **91**)
  BD19: Cleck 6B **134**
  HD6: Brigh 1A **162**
Heatons Yd. HD6: Ras 2B **162**
Hebble Brook Bus. Pk.
  HX2: Mix 6A **106**
Hebble Brook Cl. HX2: Mix 3A **128**
Hebble Cotts. HX2: Hal 6C **128**
Hebble Ct. HX2: Mix 3B **128**
Hebble Dean HX2: Hal 6D **128**
Hebble Gdns. HX2: Hal 6C **128**
Hebble La. HX3: Hal 6D **128**
Hebble Row BD22: Haw 6C **46**
Hebble Va. Dr. HX2: Hal 5C **128**
Hebble Vw. HX3: Hal 6A **150**
          (Cinderhills La.)
  HX3: Hal 5C **128**
          (Meadow Dr.)
Hebb Vw. BD6: B'frd 3G **109**
Hebden App. LS14: Leeds 3D **80**
Hebden Bri. Rd. BD22: Oxen 3A **84**
Hebden Chase LS14: Leeds 3D **80**
Hebden Cl. LS14: Leeds 3D **80**
Hebden Grn. LS14: Leeds 3D **80**
Hebden Path LS14: Leeds 3D **80**
Hebden Pl. LS14: Leeds 3D **80**
Hebden Rd. BD22: Haw, Oxen 3D **64**
Hebden Wlk. LS14: Leeds 3D **80**
Heber's Ghyll Dr. LS29: I'ly 6H **9**
Heber's Gro. LS29: I'ly 5A **10**
Heber St. BD21: Keigh 1H **47**
Hector Cl. BD6: B'frd 4C **110**
Heddon Cl. BD5: B'frd 6E **91**
Heddon Gro. BD5: B'frd 6E **91**
Heddon Pl. LS6: Leeds 3E **77**
Heddon St. LS6: Leeds 3E **77**
Heddon Wlk. BD5: B'frd 6E **91**
          (off Hawkshead Dr.)
Hedge Cl. BD8: B'frd 2F **89**
Hedge Nook BD12: Wyke 3C **132**
Hedge Side BD8: B'frd 3G **89**
Hedge Top La. HX3: North 5D **130**
Hedge Way BD8: B'frd 2G **89**
Hedley Chase LS12: Leeds 4E **97**
Hedley Cres. WF1: Wake 6F **157**
Hedley Gdns. LS12: Leeds 4E **97**
Hedley Grn. LS12: Leeds 4E **97**
Heidelberg Rd. BD9: B'frd 1A **90**
Height Grn. HX6: Sow B 5H **147**
Height La. BD22: Oxen 1D **84**
Heights Bank LS12: Leeds 4H **95**
Heights Cl. LS12: Leeds 4G **95**
Heights Ct. WF15: Liv 4H **153**
Heights Dr. LS12: Leeds 3G **95**
Heights East, The LS12: Leeds . . .4H **95**
Heights Gth. LS12: Leeds 4G **95**
Heights Grn. LS12: Leeds 4H **95**

Heights La. BD9: B'frd 6F **69**
  BD16: Bgly 4B **36**
  LS12: Leeds 4H **95**
Heights Pde. LS12: Leeds 4G **95**
Heights Rd. HX2: Midg 4A **126**
  HX7: Myth, Wads 4A **126**
Heights Wlk. LS12: Leeds 4H **95**
Heights Way LS12: Leeds 4G **95**
Heights West, The LS12: Leeds . . .4G **95**
Helena Cl. LS25: Kip 4F **123**
Helena Pl. LS25: Kip 5F **123**
Helena St. LS25: Kip 5F **123**
Helena Way BD4: B'frd 5A **112**
Helen Rose Ct. BD8: Ship 6E **53**
Helen St. BD18: Ship 1H **69**
Helen Ter. HD6: Brigh 6H **151**
Helios 47 LS25: Gar 3H **103**
Hellewell St. BD6: B'frd 6H **109**
Hellwood La. LS14: S'cft 6E **45**
Helmsley Ct. LS10: Leeds 3A **140**
Helmsley Dr. LS16: Leeds 2B **76**
Helmsley Rd. LS16: Leeds 2B **76**
  LS23: B Spa 4A **30**
Helmsley St. BD4: B'frd 1G **111**
Helston Cft. LS10: Leeds 2G **139**
Helston Gth. LS10: Leeds 2G **139**
Helston Grn. LS10: Leeds 2G **139**
Helston Pl. LS10: Leeds 2G **139**
Helston Rd. LS10: Leeds 1G **139**
Helston Sq. LS10: Leeds 1F **139**
Helston St. LS10: Leeds 1F **139**
Helston Wlk. LS10: Leeds 2G **139**
          (not continuous)
Helston Way LS10: Leeds 1G **139**
Hembrigg Gdns. LS27: Morl 5A **138**
Hembrigg Ter. LS27: Morl 5A **138**
Hemingway Cl. LS10: Leeds 1C **118**
Hemingway Gth. LS10: Leeds 2C **118**
Hemingway Grn. LS10: Leeds 2C **118**
Hemingway Rd. BD10: B'frd 1B **72**
Hemishor Dr. LS26: Gt P 5E **123**
Hemsby Gro. BD21: Keigh 3H **47**
          (off Hemsby St.)
Hemsby St. BD21: Keigh 3H **47**
Henacre Wood Ct. BD13: Que 6A **108**
Henage St. BD13: Que 4H **107**
Henbury St. LS7: Leeds 1H **5** (2B **98**)
Henconner Av. LS7: Leeds 3A **78**
Henconner Cres. LS7: Leeds 3A **78**
Henconner Dr. LS7: Leeds 3A **78**
Henconner Gdns. LS7: Leeds 3A **78**
Henconner Gth. LS7: Leeds 3A **78**
Henconner Gro. LS7: Leeds 3A **78**
Henconner La. LS7: Leeds 3A **78**
  LS13: Leeds 2G **95**
Henconner Rd. LS7: Leeds 3A **78**
Henderson Pl. BD6: B'frd 4C **110**
Hendford Dr. BD3: B'frd 3H **7** (3G **91**)
Hen Holme La. BD20: Sils 3E **15**
Henley Av. BD5: B'frd 3E **111**
  LS13: Leeds 1E **95**
  LS19: Raw 4H **55**
Henley Cl. LS19: Raw 4H **55**
Henley Cres. LS13: Leeds 1E **95**
  LS19: Raw 4H **55**
Henley Dr. LS19: Raw 4G **55**
Henley Gro. BD5: B'frd 3E **111**
  LS13: Leeds 1E **95**
Henley Hill LS19: Raw 4G **55**
Henley Mt. LS19: Raw 4H **55**
Henley Pl. LS13: Leeds 1E **95**
Henley Rd. BD5: B'frd 3F **111**
  LS13: Leeds 1E **95**
Henley St. LS13: Leeds 1E **95**
Henley Ter. LS13: Leeds 1E **95**
Henley Vw. LS13: Leeds 1E **95**
  LS19: Raw 4G **55**
Henley Vs. LS19: Raw 4G **55**
          (off Well La.)
Henna Cl. BD7: B'frd 3G **109**
Henry Av. LS12: Leeds 6C **96**
Henry Gro. LS28: Pud 4H **93**

Henry Moore Foundation Studio, The
  . . . . .1B **164**
          (in Dean Clough)
Henry Moore Institute 3D **4**
Henry Pl. LS27: Morl 3A **138**
Henry Price Bldgs. LS2: Leeds . . .1G **97**
Henry St. BD13: Thorn 5H **87**
  BD14: Clay 1E **109**
  BD21: Keigh 6A **34**
  HD6: Brigh 5A **152**
  HX1: Hal 5A **164** (3F **149**)
Henry Ter. LS19: Yead 6D **40**
HENSHAW 1E **55**
Henshaw Av. LS19: Yead 1F **55**
Henshaw Cres. LS19: Yead 1F **55**
Henshaw La. LS19: Yead 2E **55**
Henshaw M. LS19: Yead 2F **55**
Henshaw Oval LS19: Yead 1F **55**
Hepton Ct. LS9: Leeds 3F **99**
Hepworth Av. LS27: Chur 5B **116**
Hepworth Cres. LS27: Chur 5B **116**
Herbalist St. LS12: Leeds 5E **97**
Herbert Pl. BD3: B'frd 3C **92**
Herbert St. BD5: B'frd 1D **110**
  BD14: Clay 2E **109**
  BD16: Bgly 4C **50**
  BD16: Cot 3D **68**
  BD18: Ship 6H **51**
  HX1: Hal 3D **148**
Herdwick Vw. BD20: Rid 4F **35**
Hereford St. LS12: Leeds 3C **96**
Hereford Way BD4: B'frd 1G **111**
Heritage M. HX1: Hal 5D **164**
Heritage Pk. BD16: Bgly 1C **50**
Heritage Way BD22: Oak 5B **46**
HERMIT HOLE 5G **47**
Hermit St. BD22: Keigh 5G **47**
Hermon Av. HX1: Hal 3E **149**
Hermon Gro. HX1: Hal 3E **149**
Hermon Rd. LS15: Leeds 2D **100**
Hermon St. LS15: Leeds 2D **100**
Heron Cl. BD13: Que 3G **107**
  BD16: Har 6E **49**
  BD20: Stee 5B **14**
  LS17: Leeds 3D **60**
Heron Ct. LS27: Morl 3D **138**
Heron Gro. LS17: Leeds 3D **60**
Herries Ct. LS29: Men 1H **39**
          (off Leathley Rd.)
Herschel Rd. BD8: B'frd 4F **89**
Hertford Chase LS15: Leeds 5E **101**
Hertford Cl. LS15: Leeds 5F **101**
Hertford Cft. LS15: Leeds 5F **101**
Hertford Fold LS15: Leeds 5E **101**
Hertford Lawn LS15: Leeds 5E **101**
Heshbon St. BD4: B'frd 2A **112**
Hesketh Av. LS5: Leeds 4A **76**
  WF3: Ting 1D **154**
Hesketh La. WF3: Ting, W Ard . . .1D **154**
Hesketh Mt. LS5: Leeds 4A **76**
Hesketh Pl. HX3: Hip 2A **152**
  LS5: Leeds 4A **76**
Hesketh Rd. LS5: Leeds 4A **76**
Hesketh Ter. LS5: Leeds 5A **76**
Hessle Av. LS6: Leeds 6E **77**
Hessle Mt. LS6: Leeds 6E **77**
Hessle Pl. LS6: Leeds 6E **77**
Hessle Rd. LS6: Leeds 6E **77**
Hessle St. LS6: Leeds 6E **77**
Hessle Ter. LS6: Leeds 6E **77**
Hessle Vw. LS6: Leeds 6E **77**
Hessle Wlk. LS6: Leeds 6E **77**
Hetchell Ct. LS17: Bard 2F **45**
Hetchell Vw. LS17: Bard 3F **45**
Hetchell Wood Nature Reserve . . .3H **45**
Hetton Cl. LS10: Leeds 2B **118**
Hetton Dr. BD3: B'frd 5B **92**
Hetton Rd. LS8: Leeds 4F **79**
Heuthwaite Av. LS22: Weth 5F **13**
Heuthwaite La. LS22: Weth 5G **13**
Hew Clews BD7: B'frd 2G **109**
HEWENDEN 5D **66**
Hewenden Vw. BD13: Denh 1B **86**

Hew Royd. BD10: B'frd 1F **71**
HEY BECK 4C **154**
Heybeck La. WF12: Dew 4C **154**
Heybeck Wlk. BD4: B'frd 3D **112**
Heydon Cl. LS6: Leeds 6F **59**
Heyford Ct. BD2: B'frd 6D **70**
Heygate Cl. BD17: Bail 3D **52**
Heygate La. BD17: Bail 3D **52**
    LS23: B'ham 6D **30**
Hey La. BD22: S'bury 1A **64**
Heys Av. BD13: Thorn 5B **88**
Heys Cres. BD13: Thorn 5C **88**
Heysham Dr. BD4: B'frd 2C **112**
Heys Ho. HX2: Hal 1C **148**
    (off Cross tS. W.)
Heys La. HX2: Wain 1B **126**
Hey St. BD7: B'frd 4A **6** (4D **90**)
    HD6: Brigh 5B **152**
Heywood Cl. HX3: North 5C **130**
Heywood Ct. HX3: North 5C **130**
Heywood M. HX1: Hal 1C **148**
Hicks La. LS26: Meth 4D **144**
Hick St. BD1: B'frd 4F **7** (4F **91**)
Hi Energy Dance, Health & Fitness Cen.
    . . . . .6H **33**
    (off Russell St.)
Higgin Chamber HX2: Lud M 4C **146**
Higgin La. HX3: Sou 4A **150**
Higham HX6: Sow B 5C **146**
Higham and Dob La.
    HX6: Sow B 5C **146**
Higham Way LS25: Gar 3F **103**
High Ash BD18: Ship 2E **71**
High Ash Av. LS17: Leeds 2C **60**
High Ash Cres. LS17: Leeds 2C **60**
High Ash Dr. LS17: Leeds 2C **60**
High Ash Mt. LS17: Leeds 2C **60**
High Ash Pk. BD15: All 2B **88**
High Bank App. LS15: Leeds 4F **101**
High Bank Cl. HX5: Ell 4E **161**
    LS15: Leeds 4F **101**
    LS29: Add 1D **8**
High Bank Gdns. LS15: Leeds 4G **101**
High Bank Ga. LS15: Leeds 4F **101**
High Bank La. BD18: Ship 3F **69**
High Bank Pl. LS15: Leeds 4F **101**
High Banks Cl. BD20: Rid 3D **34**
High Bank St. *LS28: Fars* 6H **73**
    (off Low Bank St.)
High Bank Vw. LS15: Leeds 4F **101**
High Bank Way LS15: Leeds 4F **101**
High Bentley HX3: She 2G **131**
High Binns La. BD22: Oxen 1D **84**
Highbridge Ter. BD5: B'frd 4F **111**
High Brook Fall WF3: Loft 3G **157**
High Brunthwaite BD20: Sils 2G **15**
Highbury Cl. BD13: Que 5G **107**
    LS6: Leeds 3E **77**
Highbury La. LS6: Leeds 3E **77**
Highbury Mt. LS6: Leeds 3E **77**
Highbury Pl. LS6: Leeds 3E **77**
    LS13: Leeds 3C **94**
Highbury Rd. LS6: Leeds 3E **77**
Highbury St. LS6: Leeds 3E **77**
Highbury Ter. LS6: Leeds 3E **77**
High Busy La. BD10: B'frd 1F **71**
    BD18: Ship 1E **71**
High Cliffe *LS4: Leeds* 6C **76**
    (off St Michael's La.)
High Cliffe Ct. BD13: Thorn 5A **88**
Highcliffe Ct. HX3: She 2D **130**
    LS22: Weth 4F **13**
Highcliffe Dr. HX2: Hal 2B **148**
Highcliffe Ind. Est.
    LS27: Morl 2G **137**
Highcliffe Rd. LS27: Morl 3H **137**
High Cliffe Ter. LS22: Weth 4E **13**
High Cl. LS19: Raw 4F **55**
    LS20: Guis 5H **39**
High Cote BD20: Rid 3B **34**
High Ct. LS2: Leeds 5G **5** (4B **98**)
High Ct. La.
    LS2: Leeds 5G **5** (4B **98**)

High Cft. BD13: Que 4A **108**
    HX3: Hal 5D **128**
    LS29: Add 1D **8**
Highcroft Cl. LS28: Pud 3G **93**
Highcroft Cl. LS28: Pud 3G **93**
Highcroft Gdns. BD21: Keigh 1D **48**
High Cross La. BD13: Que 6B **108**
    HX3: She 6B **108**
Highdale Cft. BD10: B'frd 1H **71**
High End BD17: Esh 2A **54**
Higher Brockwell
    HX6: Sow B 6F **147**
Higher Coach Rd.
    BD16: Bail, Bgly 5E **51**
    BD17: Bail 5G **51**
Higher Downs BD8: B'frd 3F **89**
Higher Grange Rd. LS28: Pud 3A **94**
Higher Intake Rd. BD2: B'frd 1A **92**
Higher Row BD21: Keigh 4B **48**
Higher Scholes BD22: Oak 6A **46**
Higher School St. BD18: Ship 1H **69**
Higher Springhead BD22: Oak 4E **47**
Higherwood Cl. BD21: Keigh 6C **34**
Highfell Ri. BD22: Keigh 2E **47**
High Fernley Ct. BD12: Wyke 3C **132**
High Fernley Rd. BD12: Wyke 4A **132**
    (not continuous)
HIGHFIELD 6G **33**
Highfield BD4: B'frd 4B **112**
    HX3: She 2D **130**
    LS23: B Spa 3C **30**
    (off Bridge Rd.)
    WF3: Ting 6D **138**
Highfield Av. BD10: B'frd 2G **71**
    HD6: B Bri 1B **152**
    HX3: She 6F **109**
    HX4: Gree 4F **159**
    LS12: Leeds 5C **96**
Highfield Cl. BD20: E Mor 4H **35**
    LS12: Leeds 6D **96**
    LS27: Gil 6G **115**
Highfield Ct. BD13: Cull 3B **66**
    BD22: Oak 5C **46**
    LS12: Leeds 6C **96**
    (off Highfield Av.)
Highfield Cres. BD9: B'frd 5F **69**
    BD17: Bail 3C **52**
    LS12: Leeds 5D **96**
    LS26: Wood 6E **121**
    LS28: Pud 3H **93**
    WF10: All B 2F **145**
    (off Highfield Dr.)
Highfield Dr. BD9: B'frd 5F **69**
    HX2: Lud 1E **147**
    LS19: Raw 4G **55**
    LS25: Gar 6F **103**
    LS27: Gil 6F **115**
    WF10: All B 2F **145**
    WF17: Birs 5A **136**
Highfield Gdns. BD9: B'frd 6F **69**
    LS12: Leeds 5C **96**
    LS27: Gil 6F **115**
Highfield Gth. LS12: Leeds 6D **96**
Highfield Grn. LS28: Pud 3H **93**
    WF10: All B 1F **145**
Highfield Gro. BD10: B'frd 3G **71**
    HX5: Ell 3A **160**
    WF10: All B 1F **145**
High Fld. La. BD22: Oak 4C **46**
Highfield La. BD20: Sils 1E **15**
    BD21: Keigh 5G **33**
    BD22: Oak 5C **46**
    LS15: Bar E 4D **82**
    LS25: S Mil 1G **125**
    LS26: Wood 6E **121**
Highfield M. BD17: Bail 3C **52**
    BD20: E Mor 4H **35**
    LS25: Gar 6F **103**
Highfield Mt. LS26: Oul 1E **143**
Highfield Pl. *BD8: B'frd* 2C **90**
    (off Church St.)
    HX1: Hal 3D **148**
    (not continuous)

Highfield Pl. HX6: Sow B 6E **147**
    (off Towngate)
    LS25: Gar 4E **103**
    LS27: Morl 4B **138**
    WF10: All B 1G **145**
Highfield Rd. BD2: B'frd 3G **71**
    BD9: B'frd 4C **70**
    BD10: B'frd 3G **71**
    BD19: Cleck 2H **153**
    BD21: Keigh 6G **33**
    HD6: Ras 3G **161**
    HX2: Lud 1E **147**
    HX5: Ell 5B **160**
    LS13: Leeds 1F **95**
    LS28: Pud 3G **93**
High Flds. HX6: Sow B 5C **148**
Highfield St. BD21: Keigh 6H **33**
    LS13: Leeds 1F **95**
    LS28: Pud 3G **93**
Highfield Ter. BD13: Cull 3B **66**
    BD13: Que 5H **107**
    BD16: Bgly 4C **50**
    BD18: Ship 1G **69**
    HX1: Hal 3D **148**
    (off Highfield Pl.)
    LS19: Raw 4G **55**
    LS28: Pud 3G **93**
Highfield Vw. *LS12: Leeds* 6D **96**
    (off Hardrow Grn.)
    LS27: Gil 6G **115**
High Fold BD16: Bgly 5A **36**
    BD17: Bail 3C **52**
    BD20: E Mor 4H **35**
    (off Stocks Hill Cl.)
    BD22: Keigh 2F **47**
Highfold LS19: Yead 2E **55**
High Fold La. BD20: Keigh 3G **33**
Highgate BD9: B'frd 5H **69**
    BD13: Denh 5C **86**
Highgate Cl. BD13: Que 3E **109**
Highgate Gdns. *HX2: Hal* 1C **148**
    (off Reservoir Rd.)
Highgate Gro. BD13: Que 3E **109**
Highgate Mill Fold BD13: Que 3E **109**
Highgate Mills BD13: Que 3E **109**
Highgate Rd. BD13: Que 4C **108**
High Grn. Dr. BD20: Sils 1D **14**
High Gro. La. HX3: Hal 4A **150**
High Gro. Pl. HX3: Hal 4A **150**
High Holly Gth. BD21: Keigh 1B **48**
High Ho. Av. BD2: B'frd 5G **71**
High Ho. La. HX2: Midg 3C **126**
High Ho. Rd. BD2: B'frd 5G **71**
Highland HX3: North 3B **130**
Highlands LS17: Leeds 2C **60**
    LS29: Burl W 3E **21**
Highlands Cl. BD7: B'frd 2G **109**
    LS10: Leeds 5D **118**
Highlands Dr. LS10: Leeds 5D **118**
Highlands Gro. BD7: B'frd 2G **109**
    LS10: Leeds 5D **118**
Highlands La. HX2: Illing 1D **128**
Highlands Pk. HX2: Illing 1D **128**
Highlands Wlk. LS10: Leeds 5D **118**
Highland Ville HX3: Hip 1F **151**
High La. HX2: Hal 1H **147**
Highlea Cl. LS19: Yead 2D **54**
High Lee HX2: Lud M 3C **146**
High Lee Grn. HX2: Lud M 3B **146**
High Lees Rd. HX2: Wain 2H **127**
High Level Way HX1: Hal 1D **148**
Highley Hall Cft. HD6: Clift 6D **152**
Highley Pk. HD6: Clift 1E **163**
High Mdw. BD20: Keigh 4F **33**
High Mdws. BD15: Wils 5B **70**
    HX4: Gree 4G **159**
High Mill Bus. Pk. LS27: Morl 4A **138**
High Moor Av. LS17: Leeds 5C **60**
High Moor Cl. LS17: Leeds 4C **60**
High Moor Cl. LS17: Leeds 5C **60**
High Moor Cres. LS17: Leeds 4C **60**

Highmoor Cres. HD6: Clift 6D 152
High Moor Dr. LS17: Leeds 4C 60
High Moor Grange LS16: B'hpe 2F 43
High Moor Gro. LS17: Leeds 4C 60
Highmoor La. BD19: Cleck 4G 153
    HD6: Clift 6D 152
                         (not continuous)
Highmoor Wlk. BD17: Bail 5A 52
Highoak Gth. BD22: Oak 5C 46
High Pk. Cres. BD9: B'frd 6G 69
High Pk. Dr. BD9: B'frd 6G 69
High Pk. Gro. BD9: B'frd 6G 69
High Pastures BD22: Keigh 2E 47
High Peal Ct. BD13: Que 4H 107
High Poplars BD2: B'frd 5F 71
High Ridge LS26: Rothw 6H 119
High Ridge Ct. LS26: Rothw 1A 142
High Ridge Pk. LS26: Rothw 6H 119
High Ridge Way LS16: B'hpe 3H 43
HIGHROAD WELL 2B 148
Highroad Well HX2: Hal 2B 148
Highroad Well Ct. HX2: Hal 2B 148
Highroad Well Grn. HX2: Hal 2A 148
Highroad Well La. HX2: Hal 2B 148
High Royd HX6: Sow B 4F 147
High Royds Dr. LS29: Men 2G 39
High Shann Farm BD20: Keigh 4G 33
High Spring Gdns. La.
    BD20: Keigh 4G 33
High Spring Rd. BD21: Keigh 1D 48
High Stones Rd. HX7: Crag V 6A 146
High St. BD6: B'frd 4B 110
    BD10: B'frd 1H 71
    BD13: Que 4A 108
    BD13: Thorn 5H 87
    BD20: Stee 6C 14
    BD21: Keigh 6H 33
    HD6: Brigh 6A 152
    HX1: Hal 5A 164 (3F 149)
                          (not continuous)
    HX2: Lud 6E 127
    HX4: Gree 5H 159
    LS19: Yead 6F 41
    LS22: Weth 4E 13
    LS23: B Spa 3H 29
    LS23: Cliff 6B 30
    LS25: Kip 4H 123
    LS27: Morl 5A 138
    LS28: Fars 6H 73
    WF17: Bat 6A 154
    WF17: Birs 6A 136
High St. Ct. HX2: Lud 6E 127
High St. Fold HX2: Lud 6E 127
High St. Pl. BD10: B'frd 1H 71
    BD13: Que 4A 108
                          (off High St.)
High Sunderland La. HX3: Hal 6H 129
Highthorne Av. BD3: B'frd 2A 92
Highthorne Ct. LS17: Leeds 3D 60
Highthorne Dr. LS17: Leeds 3D 60
Highthorne Gro. LS12: Leeds 3A 96
    LS17: Leeds 3E 61
Highthorne Mt. LS17: Leeds 3D 60
Highthorne St. LS12: Leeds 3A 96
Highthorne Vw. LS12: Leeds 3A 96
HIGHTOWN HEIGHTS 4H 153
High Trees Gdns. LS23: Cliff 5C 30
High Trees La. HX4: Gree 5B 158
HIGH UTLEY 4G 33
Highway LS20: Guis 4H 39
Highways LS14: Leeds 2A 100
High Wheatley LS29: I'ly 6G 11
High Wicken Cl. BD13: Thorn 5G 87
High Wood LS29: I'ly 6H 11
Highwood Av. LS17: Leeds 4A 60
High Wood Cl. LS6: Leeds 4E 77
Highwood Cres. LS17: Leeds 4A 60
Highwood Gro. LS17: Leeds 5A 60
High Wood Head BD20: Rid 1B 34
High Woodlands WF3: E Ard 2A 156
High Wood Rd. WF17: Birs 3C 136
Hilda St. BD9: B'frd 5A 70
Hillam Ct. Ind. Est. BD2: B'frd 6D 70
Hillam Rd. BD2: B'frd 6D 70

Hillam St. BD5: B'frd 2B 110
Hillary Pl. LS2: Leeds 1C 4 (1H 97)
Hillary Rd. BD18: Ship 2E 71
Hillas Ct. HX3: Hal 6H 149
Hillas Ind. Est. HX6: Sow B 5B 148
Hillbeck HX3: Hal 5D 128
Hillbrook Ri. LS29: I'ly 6B 10
Hill Brow Cl. BD15: All 2C 88
Hill Cl. BD17: Bail 5B 52
Hill Clough Dr. BD22: Lay 6D 32
Hill Clough Gro. BD22: Lay 6C 32
Hillcote Dr. BD5: B'frd 1E 111
Hill Ct. Av. LS13: Leeds 5E 75
Hillcourt Cft. LS13: Leeds 5E 75
Hill Ct. Dr. LS13: Leeds 5E 75
Hill Ct. Fold LS13: Leeds 5E 75
Hill Ct. Gro. LS13: Leeds 5E 75
Hill Ct. Vw. LS13: Leeds 5D 74
Hill Cres. HX3: Sou 4B 150
    LS19: Raw 2G 55
    LS29: Burl W 4F 21
    WF17: Birs 5C 136
Hill Crest HX6: Sow B 4H 147
    LS26: Swil 4A 122
Hillcrest LS16: B'hpe 1C 42
    LS22: Coll 3G 27
    LS27: Gil 5D 114
Hill Crest Av. BD13: Que 2B 86
    HX6: Sow B 4H 147
                        (off Dearden St.)
Hillcrest Av. BD13: Que 5B 108
    BD20: Sils 1E 15
    LS7: Leeds 6C 78
Hill Crest Cl. HX6: Sow B 4H 147
    LS26: Swil 4H 121
Hillcrest Ct. LS16: Leeds 3G 57
Hill Crest Dr. BD13: Denh 2B 86
Hillcrest Dr. BD13: Que 5B 108
Hill Crest Mt. BD13: Denh 2B 86
Hillcrest Mt. BD19: Scho 2F 153
    LS16: Leeds 3G 57
Hillcrest Pl. LS7: Leeds 5C 78
Hillcrest Ri. LS16: Leeds 3F 57
Hill Crest Rd. BD13: Denh 2B 86
    BD13: Thorn 4H 87
Hillcrest Rd. BD13: Que 5B 108
Hill Crest Vw. BD13: Denh 2B 86
Hillcrest Vw. LS7: Leeds 5C 78
Hill Cft. BD13: Thorn 4A 88
HILL END 3G 95
Hill End Cres. LS12: Leeds 3H 95
Hill End Cft. BD7: B'frd 2G 109
Hill End Gro. BD7: B'frd 2G 109
Hill End La. BD13: Que 5H 107
    BD16: Har 1C 66
Hill End Rd. LS12: Leeds 3H 95
Hillesley Rd. WF12: Dew 6A 154
HILLFOOT 3F 93
Hillfoot BD18: Ship 2G 69
Hillfoot Av. LS28: Pud 3F 93
Hillfoot Cotts. LS28: Pud 3E 93
Hillfoot Cres. LS28: Pud 3F 93
Hillfoot Dr. LS28: Pud 3F 93
Hillfoot Ri. LS28: Pud 3F 93
HILL GREEN 3A 114
Hill Grn. Ct. BD4: B'frd 3A 114
Hillhead Dr. WF17: Bat 6B 136
Hill Ho. Edge La. BD22: Oxen 2B 84
Hill Ho. La. BD22: Oxen 2C 84
Hillidge Rd. LS10: Leeds 1B 118
Hillidge Sq. LS10: Leeds 1B 118
Hillingdon Ri. LS17: Leeds 1G 59
Hillings La. LS20: Hawk, Men 4D 38
    LS29: Men 1D 38
Hill Lands BD12: Wyke 2C 132
Hill Pk. Av. HX3: Hal 6D 128
Hill Rise Av. LS13: Leeds 5E 75
Hill Rise Gro. LS13: Leeds 5E 75
Hill Royd Cl. HX2: Illing 6C 106
Hillside LS25: Gar 5G 103

Hillside Av. BD22: Oak 5B 46
    HX2: Lud M 2D 146
    LS20: Guis 2B 40
Hillside Bldgs. LS11: Leeds 2G 117
                       (off Beeston Rd.)
Hillside Cl. LS29: Add 1C 8
Hillside Ct. LS7: Leeds 2C 78
    LS29: Men 1F 39
Hillside Gro. BD22: Oak 5B 46
    LS28: Pud 4B 94
Hill Side Mt. LS28: Stan 1A 94
Hillside Mt. LS28: Pud 4C 94
Hillside Ri. LS20: Guis 2B 40
Hill Side Rd. BD3: B'frd 3G 7 (4G 91)
Hillside Rd. BD16: Bgly 3B 50
    BD18: Ship 3C 70
    LS7: Leeds 2C 78
Hill Side Ter. BD3: B'frd 2G 7 (3G 91)
Hillside Ter. BD17: Bail 4C 52
Hillside Vw. HX6: Sow B 5G 147
    LS28: Pud 4C 94
Hillside Works Ind. Est.
    BD19: Hun 5B 134
Hill St. BD4: B'frd 6H 91
    BD6: B'frd 4A 110
    BD22: Haw 3C 64
    HX1: Hal 6A 164 (3F 149)
    LS9: Leeds 2C 98
    LS11: Leeds 2H 117
Hillthorpe Ct. LS10: Leeds 4A 140
Hillthorpe Ri. LS28: Pud 6A 94
Hillthorpe Rd. LS28: Pud 6A 94
Hillthorpe Sq. LS28: Pud 6A 94
Hillthorpe St. LS28: Pud 6A 94
Hillthorpe Ter. LS28: Pud 6A 94
HILL TOP
    BD13 .4G 87
    LS6 . . . . .1E 77
    LS12 . . . . .3H 95
Hill Top BD13: Que 3A 108
    BD16: Cot 3E 69
    BD20: Stee 6C 14
    HX2: Hal 4C 148
    HX6: Sow B 4G 147
    LS29: Burl W 2E 21
    LS29: I'ly 1C 18
Hill Top Av. LS8: Leeds 5D 78
Hill Top Cl. LS12: Leeds 3H 95
    WF3: W Ard 3E 155
Hill Top Cotts. BD9: B'frd 1G 89
Hill Top Ct. WF3: W Ard 3E 155
Hill Top Fold
    BD12: Low M 1D 132
                       (off Low Moor St.)
Hill Top Gdns. WF3: W Ard 3E 155
Hill Top Grn. WF3: W Ard 3D 154
Hill Top Gro. BD15: All 2C 88
    WF3: W Ard 3E 155
Hill Top La. BD15: All 2C 88
    BD16: Bgly 5B 36
    WF3: W Ard 4D 154
Hill Top Mt. LS8: Leeds 5D 78
Hill Top Pl. LS6: Leeds 1F 97
    LS8: Leeds 5D 78
Hill Top Rd. BD13: Thorn 4F 87
    BD21: Keigh 6G 47
    BD22: Oak 5B 46
    LS6: Leeds 1F 97
    LS12: Leeds 3H 95
Hill Top St. LS6: Leeds 1F 97
Hill Top Vw. WF3: W Ard 3D 154
Hilltop Vs. WF3: W Ard 3D 154
Hill Top Wlk. BD22: Keigh 6F 33
Hill Top Way BD22: Keigh 6F 33
Hill Vw. HX2: Illing 6D 106
Hill Vw. Av. LS7: Leeds 2B 78
Hill Vw. Gdns. HX3: North 6C 130
Hill Vw. Mt. LS7: Leeds 2B 78
Hill Vw. Pl. LS7: Leeds 2B 78
Hillview Ri. BD4: B'frd 1C 112
Hill Vw. Ter. LS7: Leeds 2B 78
Hillway LS20: Guis 6A 40

Hillworth Ho.—Hollywell La.

Hillworth Ho. *BD21: Keigh* *1H* ***47***
(off Oakworth Rd.)
Hillworth Village BD21: Keigh 1H **47**
Hilton Av. BD18: Ship 4B **70**
Hilton Ct. LS16: B'hpe 1C **42**
Hilton Cres. BD17: Bail 5C **52**
Hilton Dr. BD18: Ship 4B **70**
Hilton Grange LS16: B'hpe 1C **42**
Hilton Gro. BD7: B'frd 5A **90**
BD18: Ship 4B **70**
LS8: Leeds 4D **78**
Hilton M. LS16: B'hpe 2C **42**
Hilton Pl. LS8: Leeds 5D **78**
Hilton Rd. BD7: B'frd 5A **90**
BD18: Ship 4B **70**
LS8: Leeds 5D **78**
Hilton St. LS8: Leeds 5D **78**
Hilton Ter. LS8: Leeds 5D **78**
Hinchcliffe St. BD3: B'frd 3H **91**
Hinchliffe Av. BD17: Bail 5D **52**
Hindle Pl. LS27: Chur 6B **116**
Hindley Wlk. BD7: B'frd 3F **109**
Hind St. BD8: B'frd 2A **6** (3C **90**)
BD12: Wyke 5C **132**
Hinsley Ct. LS6: Leeds 4E **77**
Hions Cl. HD6: Ras 3A **162**
HIPPERHOLME 1F **151**
Hipswell St. BD3: B'frd 3A **92**
Hird Av. BD6: B'frd 5C **110**
Hird Rd. BD12: Low M 1D **132**
Hird St. BD17: Ship 1B **70**
BD21: Keigh 2H **47**
LS11: Leeds 2G **117**
Hirst Fold *BD12: Wyke* *4C* ***132***
(off Town Ga.)
Hirst La. BD18: Ship 6G **51**
Hirst Lodge Ct. BD2: B'frd 4F **71**
Hirst Mill Cres. BD18: Ship 6G **51**
Hirst St. WF10: All B 6E **123**
Hirst's Yd. LS1: Leeds 5F **5**
Hirst Wood Cres. BD18: Ship 1G **69**
Hirst Wood Rd. BD18: Ship 1F **69**
Hive St. BD22: Keigh 1G **47**
HMP Leeds LS12: Leeds 4D **96**
HMP Wealstun LS23: T Arch 1E **31**
HMYOI Wetherby LS22: Weth 2G **13**
Hobb End BD13: Thorn 3G **87**
Hobberley La. LS17: Leeds, Shad 3B **62**
Hob Cote La. BD22: Oak 6A **46**
Hob La. HX2: Lud M 1A **146**
HX6: Norl 2A **158**
Hobson Fold *BD12: Wyke* *5D* ***132***
(off Wyke La.)
Hockney Rd. BD8: B'frd 3B **90**
Hockney Rd. Ind. Est. BD8: B'frd 3B **90**
Hodgson Av. BD3: B'frd 3B **92**
LS17: Leeds 4E **61**
Hodgson Cres. LS17: Leeds 4E **61**
Hodgson Fold BD2: B'frd 5F **71**
LS29: Add 1B **8**
Hodgson La. BD11: Birk 6F **113**
BD11: Drig 1H **135**
Hodgson Pl. LS27: Chur 6B **116**
Hodgson St. LS27: Morl 6C **138**
Hodgson Yd. *BD2: B'frd* *4A* ***72***
(off Sovereign Ct.)
HOLBECK 6G **97**
Holbeck La. LS11: Leeds 5F **97**
Holbeck Moor Rd. LS11: Leeds 6G **97**
Holbeck Towers LS11: Leeds 6G **97**
Holborn App. LS6: Leeds 6G **77**
Holborn Central *LS6: Leeds* *6G* ***77***
(off Rampart Rd.)
Holborn Ct. BD12: Low M 1C **132**
LS6: Leeds 6H **77**
Holborn Gdns. LS6: Leeds 6G **77**
Holborn Grn. LS6: Leeds 6G **77**
Holborn Gro. LS6: Leeds 6G **77**
Holborn St. LS6: Leeds 6H **77**
Holborn Ter. LS6: Leeds 6H **77**
Holborn Towers LS6: Leeds 6H **77**
Holborn Vw. LS6: Leeds 6G **77**
Holborn Wlk. LS6: Leeds 6G **77**
Holby Bus. Pk. HX6: Sow B 6H **147**
Holden Ing Way WF17: Birs 3C **136**
Holden La. BD17: Bail 3D **52**
(not continuous)
BD20: Sils 3G **15**
BD22: Oxen 2A **84**
Holden Rd. BD6: B'frd 4B **110**
Holdforth Cl. LS12: Leeds 4E **97**
Holdforth Gdns. LS12: Leeds 4E **97**
Holdforth Grn. LS12: Leeds 4E **97**
Holdforth Pl. LS12: Leeds 4E **97**
HOLDSWORTH 1E **129**
Holdsworth Bldgs. *BD2: B'frd* *5B* ***72***
(off Elvey Cl.)
BD12: Wyke *3C* ***132***
(off Huddersfield Rd.)
Holdsworth Pl. LS12: Leeds 4B **96**
Holdsworth Rd. HX2: Hal 6E **107**
HX3: Hal 6E **107**
Holdsworth Sq. BD2: B'frd 5B **72**
Holdsworth St. BD1: B'frd 2E **7** (3F **91**)
BD18: Ship 3C **70**
Holdsworth Ter. HX1: Hal 4H **149**
Holdsworth Yd. *BD1: B'frd* *4B* ***6***
(off Thornton Rd.)
Hole BD22: Haw 3B **64**
Holgate La. LS23: B Spa 3B **30**
Holker St. BD8: B'frd 3B **90**
BD21: Keigh 5A **34**
Holland Mt. LS16: B'hpe 2F **43**
Holland Pk. BD9: B'frd 1G **89**
Holland Rd. LS25: Kip 3A **124**
Holland St. BD4: B'frd 5C **92**
Hollas La. HX6: Norl 1C **158**
(not continuous)
Hollerton La. WF3: W Ard 1F **155**
Hollies, The LS12: Leeds 4C **96**
LS21: Pool 5F **25**
Hollin Cl. La. BD2: B'frd 6E **71**
Hollin Ct. BD18: Ship 3C **70**
LS16: Leeds 2D **76**
Hollin Cres. LS16: Leeds 2D **76**
Hollin Dr. LS16: Leeds 2E **77**
Hollin Gdns. LS16: Leeds 2C **76**
Hollin Ga. LS21: Otley 1B **22**
Hollingbourne Rd. LS15: Leeds 1H **101**
Hollin Greaves La. HX3: Hal 6H **129**
Hollings, The LS26: Meth 4B **144**
Hollings Gro. HX6: Sow B 4G **147**
Hollings Rd. BD8: B'frd 2B **90**
Hollings Sq. BD8: B'frd 3B **90**
Hollings St. BD8: B'frd 3B **90**
BD16: Cot 2D **68**
Hollings Ter. BD8: B'frd 3B **90**
Hollingwell Hill BD14: Clay 2A **108**
Hollingwood Av. BD7: B'frd 1H **109**
Hollingwood Dr. BD7: B'frd 1G **109**
Hollingwood Ga. LS29: I'ly 6B **10**
Hollingwood La. BD7: B'frd 2F **109**
Hollingwood Mt. BD7: B'frd 1G **109**
Hollingwood Pk. LS29: I'ly 6B **10**
Hollingwood Ri. LS29: I'ly 6B **10**
Hollin Hall Dr. LS29: I'ly 6A **10**
Hollin Hall Rd. BD18: Ship 3G **69**
Hollin Head BD17: Bail 3F **53**
Hollin Hill Av. LS8: Leeds 4G **79**
Hollin Hill Cotts. LS8: Leeds 4G **79**
Hollin Hill Dr. LS8: Leeds 4G **79**
Hollinhurst WF10: All B 1E **145**
Hollin La. BD18: Ship 3D **70**
HX2: Midg 2A **126**
HX6: Norl 2A **158**
LS16: Leeds 2D **76**
Hollin M. LS16: Leeds 2D **76**
Hollin Mt. LS16: Leeds 2C **76**
HOLLIN PARK 4H **79**
Hollin Pk. Av. LS8: Leeds 4H **79**
Hollin Pk. Ct. LS28: Cal 3E **73**
Hollin Pk. Cres. LS8: Leeds 4H **79**
Hollin Pk. Dr. LS28: Cal 3E **73**
Hollin Pk. Mt. LS8: Leeds 3H **79**
Hollin Pk. Pde. LS8: Leeds 4G **79**
Hollin Pk. Pl. LS8: Leeds 4G **79**
Hollin Pk. Rd. LS8: Leeds 4G **79**
LS28: Cal 3E **73**
Hollin Pk. Ter. LS8: Leeds 4G **79**
Hollin Pk. Vw. LS8: Leeds 4G **79**
Hollin Ri. BD18: Ship 3C **70**
Hollin Rd. BD18: Ship 3C **70**
LS16: Leeds 2D **76**
Hollins HX2: Lud M 4C **146**
Hollins, The HX6: Sow B 5H **147**
Hollins Bank HX6: Sow B 5H **147**
Hollins Bank La. BD20: Stee 6D **14**
Hollins Beck Cl. LS25: Kip 5G **123**
Hollins Cl. BD20: Keigh 3F **33**
Hollins Ga. HX2: Lud M 4B **146**
Hollins Gro. WF10: All B 1F **145**
Hollins Hall Golf Course 1G **53**
Hollins Hey Rd. HX4: Holy 6H **159**
Hollins Hill BD17: Bail 2G **53**
LS20: Guis 2G **53**
Hollins La. BD20: Keigh 2F **33**
HX2: Lud M 4B **146**
HX2: Mix 2A **128**
HX6: Sow B 4G **147**
Hollins Mill La.
HX6: Sow B 5G **147**
Hollins Pk. LS25: Kip 4G **123**
Hollin Ter. BD18: Ship 3C **70**
HOLLINTHORPE 1A **122**
Hollin Vw. LS16: Leeds 2D **76**
Hollin Wood Cl. BD18: Ship 2G **69**
Hollinwood Vw. BD16: Bgly 6H **35**
Hollis Pl. LS3: Leeds 2F **97**
Hollowfield Cft.
BD12: O'haw 2H **133**
Holly Av. LS16: Leeds 4F **57**
Holly Bank HX5: Ell 6A **160**
LS6: Leeds 3D **76**
LS20: Guis 4B **40**
LS25: Gar 5H **103**
Holly Bank Ct. HX3: Hip 1F **151**
Holly Bank Dr. HX3: Hip 1F **151**
Hollybank Gdns. BD7: B'frd 2G **109**
Hollybank Gro. BD7: B'frd 2G **109**
Holly Bank Ho. *HD6: Ras* *3H* ***161***
(off Holly Bank Pk.)
Holly Bank Pk. HD6: Ras 3H **161**
Holly Bank Rd. HD6: Ras 3G **161**
Hollybank Rd. BD7: B'frd 2G **109**
Holly Bush Ct. LS23: B Spa 4C **30**
Hollybush Grn. LS22: Coll 3C **28**
Holly Cl. LS10: Leeds 3H **139**
Holly Ct. LS20: Guis 5B **40**
WF1: Out 4G **157**
WF3: W Ard 3E **155**
Holly Cres. WF3: E Ard 1D **156**
Hollycroft Ct. LS16: Leeds 4A **58**
Holly Dr. LS16: Leeds 4F **57**
Holly Gro. HX1: Hal 3E **149**
HX2: Lud 3E **127**
Holly Hall La. BD12: Low M 2C **132**
Hollyhock Cl. HX6: Sow B 6H **147**
Holly Mt. *HX3: Hal* *4A* ***150***
(off High Gro. La.)
Hollynsmill HX4: Gree 4H **159**
Hollyns Ter. HX4: Gree 4H **159**
Holly Pk. LS18: H'fth 6B **56**
Holly Pk. Dr. BD7: B'frd 1G **109**
Holly Pk. Gro. BD7: B'frd 1G **109**
Holly Pk. Mills LS28: Cal 3E **73**
Holly Pk. Way HX2: Hal 3D **128**
Holly Rd. LS23: B Spa 3H **29**
Holly Royd HX3: Sou 5E **151**
Hollyshaw Cres. LS15: Leeds 3E **101**
Hollyshaw Gro. LS15: Leeds 3E **101**
Hollyshaw La. LS15: Leeds 2E **101**
Hollyshaw St. LS15: Leeds 3E **101**
Hollyshaw Ter. LS15: Leeds 3E **101**
Hollyshaw Wlk. LS15: Leeds 2E **101**
Holly St. BD6: B'frd 3F **109**
Holly Tree La. LS15: Leeds 5G **101**
Holly Way LS14: Leeds 1A **100**
Hollywell Gro. LS12: Leeds 3B **96**
Hollywell La. LS12: Leeds 4B **96**

Hollywood Bowl
  Bradford 5E 7 (5F 91)
  Leeds 2D 96
Holman Av. LS25: Gar 6F 103
Holme Bank BD4: B'frd 1D 112
Holme Bank Bd. BD4: B'frd 3D 112
Holmecarr Ct. BD16: Bgly 3C 50
Holme Dr. HX2: Hal 3H 147
Holme Farm Ct. LS12: N Far 2F 115
Holme Farm La. LS17: Bard, Coll . . .1G 45
  LS23: B'ham 1G 45
Holmefield Vw. BD4: B'frd 1D 112
Holme Gro. LS29: Burl W 4F 21
Holme Ho. La. BD22: Oak 1B 46
  HX2: Lud 3E 127
Holme Ings LS29: Add 2G 9
Holme La. BD4: B'frd 2D 112
Holmelea Cft. LS6: Leeds 2E 77
               (off Church Gro.)
Holme Mill La. BD22: Keigh 1F 47
Holme Pk. LS29: Burl W 4F 21
Holme Rd. HX2: Hal 3H 147
Holmes Rd. HX6: Sow B 5A 148
Holmes St. BD1: B'frd 2A 6 (3D 90)
  LS11: Leeds 5A 98
Holme's Ter. HX2: Hal 1C 148
Holme St. BD5: B'frd 1D 110
  BD22: Oxen 1C 84
  HX3: Hip 2A 152
HOLME TOP 1D 110
Holme Top La. BD5: B'frd 1D 110
Holme Top St. BD5: B'frd 1D 110
Holme Vw. LS29: I'ly 5C 10
HOLME VILLAGE 2D 112
HOLME WOOD 2B 112
Holme Wood BD22: Keigh 1G 47
Holme Wood Rd. BD4: B'frd 2B 112
  BD22: Keigh 1F 47
HOLMFIELD 2E 129
Holmfield BD22: Oxen 2C 84
Holmfield Cotts. LS26: Meth 4E 145
Holmfield Ct. BD1: B'frd 4B 6
Holmfield Dr. LS8: Leeds 6E 61
Holmfield Gdns. HX2: Hal 2E 129
Holmfield Ho. HX3: Hal 2E 129
Holmfield Ind. Est. HX2: Hal 6E 107
Holmfield Ind. Est. Rd. HX2: Hal . . .6E 107
Holmfield St. BD1: B'frd 4B 6 (4D 90)
Holmsley Crest LS26: Wood 6C 120
Holmsley Fld. Ct. LS26: Oul 1E 143
Holmsley Fld. La. LS26: Oul 1D 142
Holmsley Gth. LS26: Wood 6D 120
Holmsley Grn. LS26: Wood 6D 120
Holmsley La. LS26: Wood 1C 142
Holmsley Wlk. LS26: Oul 1D 142
Holmwood LS8: Leeds 5E 61
Holmwood Av. LS6: Leeds 1E 77
Holmwood Cl. LS6: Leeds 1F 77
Holmwood Cres. LS6: Leeds 1F 77
Holmwood Dr. LS6: Leeds 1E 77
Holmwood Gro. LS6: Leeds 1F 77
Holmwood Mt. LS6: Leeds 1F 77
Holmwood Vw. LS6: Leeds 1E 77
Holroyd Hill BD6: B'frd 4C 110
Holroyd Mill La. BD16: Bgly 5A 36
Holroyd St. LS7: Leeds 1B 98
Holsworthy Rd. BD4: B'frd 3C 112
Holt, The BD18: Ship 1C 70
Holt Av. LS16: Leeds 2C 58
Holtby Gro. HX3: Hip 2A 152
Holt Cl. LS16: Leeds 3C 58
Holt Cres. LS16: Leeds 2H 57
Holtdale App. LS16: Leeds 2G 57
Holtdale Av. LS16: Leeds 2H 57
Holtdale Cl. LS16: Leeds 2H 57
Holtdale Cft. LS16: Leeds 2H 57
Holtdale Dr. LS16: Leeds 2H 57
Holtdale Fold LS16: Leeds 2H 57
Holtdale Gdns. LS16: Leeds 2H 57
Holtdale Gth. LS16: Leeds 2H 57
Holtdale Grn. LS16: Leeds 2H 57
Holtdale Gro. LS16: Leeds 2G 57
Holtdale Lawn LS16: Leeds 2H 57

Holtdale Pl. LS16: Leeds 2H 57
Holtdale Rd. LS16: Leeds 2H 57
Holtdale Vw. LS16: Leeds 2H 57
Holtdale Way LS16: Leeds 2H 57
Holt Dr. LS16: Leeds 2A 58
Holt Farm Cl. LS16: Leeds 2H 57
Holt Farm Ri. LS16: Leeds 2H 57
Holt Gdns. BD10: B'frd 1G 71
  LS16: Leeds 2C 58
Holt Gth. LS16: Leeds 2A 58
Holt Ga. LS16: Leeds 2A 58
Holt Grn. LS16: Leeds 2A 58
Holt La. LS16: Leeds 2G 57
Holt La. Ct. LS16: Leeds 3B 58
HOLT PARK 2H 57
Holt Pk. App. LS16: Leeds 2A 58
Holt Pk. Av. LS16: Leeds 2A 58
Holt Pk. Cl. LS16: Leeds 2A 58
Holt Pk. Cres. LS16: Leeds 2H 57
Holt Pk. District Cen. LS16: Leeds . . .2H 57
Holt Pk. Dr. LS16: Leeds 2A 58
Holt Pk. Gdns. LS16: Leeds 2A 58
Holt Pk. Ga. LS16: Leeds 2A 58
Holt Pk. Grange LS16: Leeds 2A 58
Holt Pk. Grn. LS16: Leeds 2A 58
Holt Pk. Gro. LS16: Leeds 2H 57
Holt Pk. La. LS16: Leeds 2A 58
Holt Park Leisure Cen. 3H 57
Holt Pk. Ri. LS16: Leeds 2A 58
Holt Pk. Rd. LS16: Leeds 2A 58
Holt Pk. Va. LS16: Leeds 2A 58
Holt Pk. Vw. LS16: Leeds 2H 57
Holt Pk. Way LS16: Leeds 2A 58
Holt Ri. LS16: Leeds 2A 58
Holt Rd. LS16: Leeds 2A 58
Holts La. BD14: Clay 6D 88
Holts Ter. HX3: Hal 5H 149
Holt Va. LS16: Leeds 2A 58
Holt Wlk. LS16: Leeds 2A 58
Holt Way LS16: Leeds 2A 58
Holybrook Av. BD10: B'frd 3B 72
HOLY CROFT 1H 47
Holycroft St. BD21: Keigh 1H 47
Holyoake Av. BD16: Bgly 6B 50
Holyrood La. LS25: Led 5H 125
Holywell Ash La. BD8: B'frd 2D 90
HOLYWELL GREEN 6F 159
Holywell La. LS17: Shad 2H 61
Holywell Vw. LS17: Shad 2H 61
Home Farm Cl. BD6: B'frd 4F 109
Home Farm Dr. LS29: Men 2F 39
Home Farm M. LS29: Men 2G 39
Homefield Av. LS27: Morl 5A 138
Home Lea LS26: Rothw 6H 119
Home Lea Dr. LS26: Rothw 6H 119
Homepaddock Ho. LS22: Weth 3F 13
Homestead Est. LS29: Men 6G 21
Home Vw. Ter. BD8: B'frd 2B 90
Honey Pot BD15: Wils 6G 67
Honey Pot Dr. BD17: Bail 4A 52
Honey Pot Fold BD17: Bail 4A 52
Honey Pot La. BD17: Bail 4A 52
Honey Pot Vw. BD22: Oxen 1C 84
               (off Station Rd.)
Honeysuckle Cl. LS25: M'fld 6F 105
Hoods, The HD6: Ras 4H 161
Hoopoe M. BD15: All 4D 88
Hopbine Av. BD5: B'frd 3E 111
Hopbine Rd. BD5: B'frd 3E 111
Hope Av. BD5: B'frd 3C 110
  BD18: Ship 1D 70
Hopefield Chase LS26: Rothw 3F 141
Hopefield Cl. LS26: Rothw 3F 141
Hopefield Ct. LS26: Rothw 3F 141
  WF3: E Ard 2A 156
Hopefield Cres. LS26: Rothw 3F 141
Hopefield Dr. LS26: Rothw 3F 141
Hopefield Gdns. LS26: Rothw 3F 141
Hopefield Grn. LS26: Rothw 3F 141
Hopefield Gro. LS26: Rothw 3F 141
Hopefield M. LS26: Rothw 3F 141
Hopefield Pl. LS26: Rothw 3F 141
Hopefield Vw. LS26: Rothw 3F 141

Hopefield Wlk. LS26: Rothw 3F 141
Hopefield Way BD5: B'frd 4H 111
  LS26: Rothw 3F 141
Hope Hall St. HX1: Hal 6C 164 (3G 149)
Hope Hall Ter. HX1: Hal 6C 164
Hope Hill Vw. BD16: Cot 2C 68
Hope La. BD17: Bail 3B 52
Hope Pk. BD5: B'frd 4F 111
Hope Pastures 5C 58
Hope Pl. BD21: Keigh 2A 48
Hope Rd. LS9: Leeds 3H 5 (3B 98)
Hopes Farm Mt. LS10: Leeds 6D 118
Hopes Farm Rd. LS10: Leeds 6D 118
Hopes Farm Vw. LS10: Leeds 6D 118
Hope St. HX1: Hal 3A 164 (2F 149)
  HX3: She 3D 130
  HX6: Sow B 6H 147
  LS27: Morl 3A 138
Hope Vw. BD18: Ship 2D 70
Hopewell Pl. LS6: Leeds 1E 97
Hopewell Ter. LS18: H'fth 3F 75
  LS25: Kip 4H 123
Hopewell Vw. LS10: Leeds 2B 140
Hopkinson Bldgs. HX3: Hal 4D 128
          (off Foundry St. Nth.)
Hopkinson Dr. BD4: B'frd 5A 112
Hopkinson St. HX3: Hal 4D 128
Hopkin St. BD4: B'frd 4C 112
Hops La. HX3: Hal 5B 128
Hopton Av. BD4: B'frd 4H 111
Hopton Ct. LS12: Leeds 4B 96
             (off Hopton M.)
Hopton M. LS12: Leeds 4B 96
Hopwood Bank LS18: H'fth 5E 57
Hopwood Cl. LS18: H'fth 5E 57
Hopwood La. HX1: Hal 5A 164 (3C 148)
            (not continuous)
Hopwood Rd. LS18: H'fth 5E 57
Horace Waller VC Pde.
  WF12: Dew 6A 154
Horley Grn. La. HX3: Hal 6A 130
Horley Grn. Rd. HX3: Hal 6A 130
Hornbeam Cl. BD15: All 5B 68
Hornbeam Ct. LS20: Guis 4B 40
Hornbeam Gro. HX3: North 3B 130
Hornbeam Way LS14: Leeds 1E 81
Hornby St. HX1: Hal 3D 148
Hornby Ter. HX1: Hal 3D 148
Horner's Bldgs. HX2: Hal 2E 129
             (off Shay La.)
Horners Fold BD20: E Mor 4H 35
Horne St. HX1: Hal 2F 149
Hornsea Dr. BD15: Wils 5G 67
Horse Cl. BD12: Wyke 3A 132
Horsefair LS22: Weth 4F 13
Horsefair Centre, The LS22: Weth . . .4F 13
Horseshoe Ct. BD15: Wils 5F 67
Horsfall Stadium 6B 110
Horsfall St. HX1: Hal 4E 149
  LS27: Morl 1H 137
Horsforde Vw. LS13: Leeds 3D 74
HORSFORTH 1D 74
Horsforth Golf Course 4B 56
Horsforth New Rd.
  LS13: Leeds 3A 74
Horsforth Station (Rail) 4E 57
Horsforth Village Mus. 1D 74
Horsham Ct. BD22: Keigh 2E 47
Horsham Rd. BD4: B'frd 3C 112
Horsley Fold HD6: Clift 1E 163
Horsley St. BD6: B'frd 4C 110
Horsman St. BD4: B'frd 4C 112
HORTON BANK 2F 109
HORTON BANK BOTTOM 3A 110
Horton Bank Country Pk. 2F 109
HORTON BANK TOP 3F 109
Horton Cl. LS13: Leeds 5B 74
Horton Gth. LS13: Leeds 5B 74
Horton Grange Rd.
  BD7: B'frd 5B 90
Horton Hall Cl. BD5: B'frd 6D 90
Horton Ho. BD3: B'frd 3D 92
            (off Chapman Rd.)

Horton Ind. Est. BD7: B'frd 2H **109**
Horton Pk. Av. BD5: B'frd 6B **90**
   BD7: B'frd 6B **90**
Horton Pl. HX2: Brad 5D **106**
Horton Ri. LS13: Leeds 5B **74**
Horton St. HX1: Hal 5C **164** (3G **149**)
Horton Ter. HX3: Hip 1D **150**
Hospital La. LS16: Leeds 4H **57**
Hospital Rd. BD20: Rid 4D **34**
Hothfield St. BD20: Sils 2D **14**
Hough HX3: North 6B **130**
Hough Cl. LS13: Leeds 3D **94**
HOUGH END 3E **95**
Hough End Av. LS13: Leeds 2F **95**
Hough End Cl. LS13: Leeds 2F **95**
Hough End Ct. LS13: Leeds 2F **95**
Hough End Cres. LS13: Leeds 2E **95**
Hough End Gdns. LS13: Leeds 2F **95**
Hough End Gth. LS13: Leeds 2E **95**
Hough End La. LS13: Leeds 2E **95**
Hough Gro. LS13: Leeds 1E **95**
Houghley Av. LS12: Leeds 1H **95**
Houghley Cl. LS13: Leeds 1G **95**
Houghley Cres. LS12: Leeds 1H **95**
Houghley La. LS12: Leeds 1G **95**
   LS13: Leeds 1G **95**
Houghley Rd. LS12: Leeds 1H **95**
Houghley Sq. LS12: Leeds 1H **95**
HOUGH SIDE 4D **94**
Hough Side Cl. Pud 4D **94**
Hough Side La. LS28: Pud 4C **94**
Hough Side Rd. LS28: Pud 4B **94**
Hough Ter. LS13: Leeds 1E **95**
Houghton Pl. BD1: B'frd 2B **6** (3D **90**)
Houghton St. HD6: Brigh 6B **152**
Houghton Towers HX6: Sow B 5H **147**
Hough Top LS13: Leeds 4C **94**
Hough Tree Rd. LS13: Leeds 3E **95**
Hough Tree Ter. LS13: Leeds 3E **95**
Hougomont BD13: Que 2G **107**
Hoults La. HX4: Gree 3F **159**
HOVE EDGE .4H **151**
Hovingham Av. LS8: Leeds 5E **79**
Hovingham Gro. LS8: Leeds 5E **79**
Hovingham Mt. LS8: Leeds 5E **79**
Hovingham Ter. LS8: Leeds 5E **79**
Howard Av. LS15: Leeds 4B **100**
Howard Ct. LS15: Leeds 4B **100**
Howards Dean BD22: Haw 1D **64**
Howard St. BD5: B'frd 6B **6** (5D **90**)
   HX1: Hal .1E **149**
Howarth Av. BD2: B'frd 4G **71**
Howarth Cres. BD2: B'frd 4G **71**
Howbeck Av. BD20: Rid 4E **35**
Howbeck Dr. BD20: Rid 5E **35**
Howcans La. HX3: Hal 2E **129**
Howden Av. BD20: Keigh 3G **33**
Howdenbrook HX3: She 6G **109**
Howden Cl. BD4: B'frd 4D **112**
HOWDEN CLOUGH 5D **136**
Howden Clough Ind. Est.
   WF17: Birs 4D **136**
Howden Clough Rd. LS27: Morl 4E **137**
Howden Gdns. LS6: Leeds 1E **97**
Howden Pl. LS6: Leeds 1E **97**
Howden Rd. BD20: Sils 2E **15**
HOWDEN ROUGH 1H **33**
Howden Way LS27: Morl 3F **137**
Howes La. HX3: North 4B **130**
Howgate BD10: B'frd 1A **72**
Howgate Hill HX3: Sou 4B **150**
Howgill Grn. BD6: B'frd 1A **132**
Howley Cl. BD19: Gom 6E **135**
Howley Pk. Bus. Village
   LS27: Morl 6H **137**
Howley Pk. Cl. LS27: Morl 5H **137**
Howley Pk. Rd. LS27: Morl 5H **137**
Howley Pk. Rd. E. LS27: Morl 6H **137**
Howley Pk. Ter. LS27: Morl 5H **137**
Howley Pk. Trad. Est.
   LS27: Morl 5H **137**
Howley Pk. Vw. LS27: Morl 5C **138**

Howson Cl. LS20: Guis 4D **40**
Hoxton Mt. LS11: Leeds 2F **117**
Hoxton St. BD8: B'frd 3A **90**
Hoyle Cl. Av. BD17: Bail 4E **53**
Hoyle Ct. Dr. BD17: Bail 4E **53**
Hoyle Ct. Rd. BD17: Bail 4E **53**
Hoyle Fold BD22: Keigh 2F **47**
Hoyle Ing Rd. BD13: Thorn 5B **88**
Hoyle Syke BD22: Oxen 5B **64**
Hubberton Grn. Rd. HX6: Sow B 6C **146**
Hubert St. BD3: B'frd 5H **91**
   HX2: Hal 2B **148**
Huddersfield Crematorium
   HD2: Fix .5A **162**
Huddersfield Rd. BD5: B'frd 1C **132**
   BD6: B'frd 1C **132**
   BD12: Low M, Wyke 6B **132**
   (not continuous)
   HD6: Brigh, Ras 4B **162**
   HX3: Hal .4G **149**
   (not continuous)
   HX5: Ell 6D **160**
   WF17: Birs 6A **136**
Hud Hill HX3: She 3D **130**
Hudson, The BD7: Wyke 4C **132**
Hudson Av. BD7: B'frd 1B **110**
Hudson Ct. BD7: B'frd 2B **110**
   LS22: Weth 4E **13**
Hudson Cres. BD7: B'frd 2B **110**
Hudson Gdns. BD7: B'frd 1B **110**
Hudson Ga. BD12: Wyke 4C **132**
Hudson Gro. LS9: Leeds 2E **99**
Hudson M. LS23: B Spa 4C **30**
Hudson Pl. LS9: Leeds 2E **99**
Hudson Rd. LS9: Leeds 1E **99**
Hudson's Ter. LS19: Yead 6G **41**
Hudson St. BD3: B'frd 4B **92**
   LS9: Leeds 2E **99**
   LS28: Fars 2H **93**
Hudson Vw. BD12: Wyke 4B **132**
Hudson Way LS22: Weth 1E **13**
Hudswell Rd. LS10: Leeds 1B **118**
Huggan Row *LS28: Pud* *4B* ***94***
   (off Hammerton Gro.)
Hughenden Vw. LS27: Morl 1A **138**
Hughendon Dr. BD13: Thorn 5C **88**
Hughendon Wlk. BD13: Thorn 5C **88**
Hugill St. BD13: Thorn 5H **87**
Hulbert St. BD16: Bgly 5C **50**
Hullenedge Gdns. HX5: Ell 5H **159**
Hullenedge La. HX4: Gree 5G **159**
   HX5: Ell 5G **159**
Hullenedge Rd. HX5: Ell 5H **159**
Hullen Rd. HX5: Ell 5H **159**
Hullett Cl. HX7: Myth 6A **126**
Hullett Dr. HX7: Myth 6A **126**
Hull St. LS27: Morl 3B **138**
Hulme St. *HX6: Sow B* *6H* ***147***
   (off Syke La.)
Humboldt St. BD1: B'frd 3G **7** (4G **91**)
HUNGATE 6G **143**
Hungate La. LS26: Meth 6G **143**
HUNGER HILL 5B **108**
Hunger Hill HX1: Hal 6C **164** (3G **149**)
   LS27: Morl 4A **138**
   LS29: Midd 1D **10**
Hunger Hill Rd. LS29: Midd 1E **11**
Hunger Hills Av. LS18: H'fth 6C **56**
Hunger Hills Dr. LS18: H'fth 6C **56**
HUNSLET 1B **118**
Hunslet Bus. Pk. LS10: Leeds 6C **98**
HUNSLET CARR 4B **118**
Hunslet Distributor LS10: Leeds 1B **118**
Hunslet Grn. Retail Cen.
   LS10: Leeds 2B **118**
Hunslet Grn. Way LS10: Leeds 1B **118**
Hunslet Hall Rd. LS11: Leeds 1H **117**
Hunslet Hawks 5A **118**
Hunslet Ho. LS10: Leeds 6F **5**
Hunslet La. LS10: Leeds 6F **5**
   (Crown Point Rd.)
   LS10: Leeds 6F **5** (5A **98**)
   (Salem Pl.)

Hunslet Rd. LS10: Leeds 5B **98**
   (Sheaf St., not continuous)
   LS10: Leeds 6F **5** (4A **98**)
   (Waterloo St.)
Hunslet Trad. Est. LS10: Leeds 1D **118**
HUNSWORTH 5B **134**
Hunsworth La. BD4: E Bier 3B **134**
   BD19: Cleck, Hun 6B **134**
   (not continuous)
Hunter Hill Rd. HX2: Mix 2G **127**
Hunterscombe Ct. BD16: Bgly 2F **51**
Hunters Ct. BD9: B'frd 5E **69**
   LS15: Leeds 4C **100**
Hunters Glen BD20: Sils 1E **15**
Hunters Grn. BD13: Cull 2B **66**
Hunters Mdw. BD20: Sils 1E **15**
Hunters Pk. Av. BD14: Clay 6F **89**
Hunters Wlk. LS22: Weth 1E **13**
Hunters Way LS15: Leeds 4C **100**
Huntingdon Av. HD2: Hud 6F **163**
Huntingdon Rd. HD6: Brigh 2C **162**
Huntington Cres. LS16: Leeds 2C **76**
Huntock Pl. HD6: Brigh 4H **151**
Huntsman Ho.
   LS10: Leeds 6F **5** (5A **98**)
Huntsmans Cl. BD16: Bgly 2E **51**
   BD20: Keigh 5G **33**
Hunt Yd. BD7: B'frd 1A **110**
Hurstville Av. BD4: E Bier 1D **134**
Husler Gro. LS7: Leeds 6B **78**
Husler Pl. LS7: Leeds 6B **78**
Hustlergate BD1: B'frd 4D **6** (4E **91**)
Hustler's Row LS6: Leeds 1D **78**
Hustler St. BD3: B'frd 1H **7** (2G **91**)
   (not continuous)
Hutchinson La. HD6: Brigh 1B **162**
Hutchinson Pl. LS5: Leeds 6A **76**
Hutson St. BD5: B'frd 1D **110**
Hutton Cl. BD3: B'frd 3D **92**
Hutton Rd. BD5: B'frd 3C **110**
Hutton Ter. BD2: B'frd 4B **72**
   LS28: Pud 4A **94**
Huxley Mt. BD2: B'frd 4A **72**
Hydale Cl. BD21: Keigh 2C **48**
Hydale Cl. BD12: Low M 1C **132**
Hyde Gro. *BD21: Keigh* *5B* ***34***
   (off Kirby St.)
HYDE PARK .6E **77**
Hyde Pk. HX1: Hal 3E **149**
Hyde Pk. Cl. LS6: Leeds 1F **97**
Hyde Pk. Cnr. LS6: Leeds 6F **77**
Hyde Pk. Pl. LS6: Leeds 6F **77**
Hyde Pk. Rd. HX1: Hal 4E **149**
   LS6: Leeds 1F **97**
Hyde Pk. St. HX1: Hal 4E **149**
Hyde Pk. Ter. LS6: Leeds 6F **77**
Hyde Pk. Vs. *LS6: Leeds* 6F **77**
   (off Bk. Kensington Ter.)
Hyde Pl. LS2: Leeds 2A **4** (2G **97**)
Hyde St. BD10: B'frd 6H **53**
   LS2: Leeds 2A **4** (2G **97**)
Hyde Ter. LS2: Leeds 1A **4** (2G **97**)
Hyde Way WF3: Thpe H 5D **140**
Hydro Cl. LS29: I'ly 6H **11**
Hyne Av. BD4: B'frd 4H **111**

I

Ibbetson Cl. LS27: Chur 6A **116**
Ibbetson Ct. LS27: Chur 6A **116**
Ibbetson Cft. LS27: Chur 6A **116**
Ibbetson Dr. LS27: Chur 6A **116**
Ibbetson M. LS27: Chur 6A **116**
Ibbetson Oval LS27: Chur 6A **116**
Ibbetson Ri. LS27: Chur 6A **116**
Ibbetson Rd. LS27: Chur 6A **116**
Ida's, The LS10: Leeds 3E **119**
Ida St. BD5: B'frd 2C **110**
   LS10: Leeds 3E **119**
Iddesleigh St. BD4: B'frd 5A **92**
IDLE 1H **71**
Idlecroft Rd. BD10: B'frd 1H **71**

IDLE MOOR 2F 71
Idle Rd. BD2: B'frd 4G 71
Idlethorp Way BD10: B'frd 2A 72
Ilbert Av. BD4: B'frd 4A 112
Ilford St. LS27: Morl 3B 138
ILKLEY 5D 10
Ilkley Golf Course 3B 10
Ilkley Hall M. LS29: I'ly 6D 10
Ilkley Hall Pk. LS29: I'ly 6D 10
Ilkley Lawn Tennis & Squash Club
. . . . .4B 10
Ilkley Playhouse 5D 10
(off Weston Rd.)
Ilkley Pool & Lido 3D 10
Ilkley Rd. BD20: Rid 3D 34
LS21: Otley 4C 22
LS29: Add 2F 9
LS29: Burl W 1D 20
Ilkley Station (Rail) 5D 10
Ilkley Toy Mus. 5D 10
(off Whitton Cft. Rd.)
ILLINGWORTH 1C 128
Illingworth Av. HX2: Illing 5C 106
Illingworth Bldgs.
BD12: O'haw 3F 133
(off Illingworth Rd.)
Illingworth Cl. BD21: Keigh 4G 47
HX2: Illing 6C 106
LS19: Yead 2G 55
Illingworth Cres. HX2: Illing 6C 106
Illingworth Dr. HX2: Illing 6C 106
Illingworth Gdns. HX2: Illing 1C 128
Illingworth Gro. HX2: Illing 6C 106
Illingworth Rd. BD12: O'haw 3F 133
HX2: Illing 1C 128
Illingworth Way HX2: Illing 6C 106
IMAX Cinema
Bradford 6C 6
Imex Bus. Cen. BD19: Cleck 6B 134
(off Balme Rd.)
Imperial Av. WF2: Wren 6D 156
Imperial Cl. HD6: B Bri 2B 152
Imperial Ter. LS12: Leeds 3B 96
(off Theaker La.)
Incline, The HX3: Hal 1A 150
Independent St. BD5: B'frd 2C 110
Indigoblu LS10: Leeds 5A 98
(off Crown Point Rd.)
Indoor Bowls & Athletic Cen. 4A 118
Industrial Av. WF17: Birs 6H 135
Industrial Pl. HX1: Hal 5C 164
Industrial Rd. HX6: Sow B 5G 147
Industrial St. BD16: Bgly 4B 50
BD19: Scho 1F 153
BD22: Keigh 1G 47
HD6: Brigh 6B 152
LS9: Leeds 2D 98
Industrial Ter. HX1: Hal 4F 149
Infirmary St. BD1: B'frd 3B 6 (3D 90)
(not continuous)
LS1: Leeds 4D 4 (3H 97)
Ingester St. BD22: Haw 2B 64
(off West La.)
Ing Fld. BD12: O'haw 3G 133
Ingham Cl. HX2: Brad 5D 106
Ingham La. HX2: Brad 4C 106
Inghams Av. LS28: Pud 4F 93
Inghams Ct. HX3: Hal 6E 129
Inghams Ter. LS28: Pud 3F 93
Inghams Vw. LS28: Pud 3F 93
Ing Head Cotts. HX3: She 3E 131
Ing Head Gdns. HX3: She 3D 130
Ing Head Ter. HX3: She 3D 130
(not continuous)
Ingle Av. LS27: Morl 1H 137
Ingleborough Cl. BD4: B'frd 2C 112
Ingleborough Dr. LS27: Morl 4C 138
(not continuous)
Ingleby Pl. BD7: B'frd 5A 90
Ingleby Rd. BD7: B'frd 3A 90
BD8: B'frd 3A 90
Ingleby St. BD8: B'frd 4A 90
Ingleby Way LS10: Leeds 6C 118

Ingle Ct. LS27: Morl 2H 137
(Earlsmere Dr.)
LS27: Morl 1H 137
(Springfield Av.)
Ingle Cres. LS27: Morl 1A 138
Ingledew Ct. LS17: Leeds 3B 60
Ingledew Cres. LS8: Leeds 5F 61
Ingledew Dr. LS8: Leeds 6F 61
Ingle Gro. LS27: Morl 2H 137
Ingle La. LS29: Men 2H 39
Ingle Row LS7: Leeds 3B 78
Ingleton Cl. LS11: Leeds 2H 117
Ingleton Dr. LS15: Leeds 4A 100
Ingleton Gro. LS11: Leeds 2H 117
Ingleton Pl. LS11: Leeds 2H 117
Ingleton St. LS11: Leeds 2H 117
Inglewood App. LS14: Leeds 6D 80
Inglewood Cl. HX3: Hip 1F 151
Inglewood Dr. LS14: Leeds 6D 80
LS21: Otley 4D 22
Inglewood Est. LS21: Otley 4D 22
Inglewood Pl. LS14: Leeds 6D 80
Inglewood Ter. LS6: Leeds 5G 77
(off Delph La.)
INGROW 4G 47
Ingrow Bri. BD21: Keigh 3H 47
Ingrow La. BD21: Keigh 3G 47
BD22: Keigh 3F 47
Ingrow Railway Cen. 3H 47
Ingrow West Station
Keighley & Worth Valley Railway
. . . . .3H 47
Ings, The HX3: Hip 3A 152
Ings Av. LS20: Guis 3B 40
Ings Ct. LS20: Guis 3A 40
Ings Cres. LS9: Leeds 4F 99
LS20: Guis 4A 40
Ings Cft. HX3: She 1E 131
Ings Dr. LS26: Meth 4E 145
Ings La. LS20: Guis 4A 40
LS21: Otley 3F 23
LS23: T Arch 3E 31
Ings Rd. BD20: Stee 4B 14
LS9: Leeds 4F 99
Ing St. BD3: B'frd 4B 92
Ings Vw. LS26: Meth 4E 145
Ings Way BD8: B'frd 3G 89
BD20: Sils 2E 15
Ingwood Pde. HX4: Gree 5G 159
Inkerman St. BD2: B'frd 5B 72
Inkersley Rd. BD1: B'frd 1C 6 (2E 91)
Inmoor Rd. BD11: Birk 6F 113
Inner Ring Rd. LS1: Leeds 2B 4 (2G 97)
LS2: Leeds 2B 4 (2G 97)
Innings, The BD10: B'frd 1G 71
Institute Rd. BD2: B'frd 4A 72
INTAKE 5C 74
Intake Bd. LS25: Kip 1E 47
Intake, The LS25: Kip 4H 123
(off Roger Fold)
Intake Gro. BD2: B'frd 1A 92
Intake La. BD20: Stee 1A 32
BD22: Oxen 3A 84
LS10: Leeds 4A 140
LS13: Leeds 6B 74
LS14: T'ner 4F 63
LS19: Raw 4H 55
LS28: Stan 6B 74
WF17: Bat 6B 136
Intake Mt. LS10: Leeds 3A 140

Intake Rd. BD2: B'frd 1A 92
LS28: Pud 3B 94
Intake Sq. LS10: Leeds 3A 140
Intake Ter. BD2: B'frd 2A 92
Intake Vw. LS10: Leeds 3A 140
LS13: Leeds 6C 74
Intercity Way LS13: Leeds 2B 94
Intermezzo Dr. LS10: Leeds 4F 119
International Ho. BD5: B'frd 6C 90
Invargarry Cl. LS25: Gar 3H 103
Inverness Rd. LS25: Gar 4H 103
Invertrees Av. LS19: Raw 3G 55
Iona Pl. HX3: Hal 5G 129
Iona St. HX3: Hal 5G 129
Iqbal Ct. BD3: B'frd 5B 92
Ireland Cres. LS16: Leeds 4H 57
Ireland St. BD16: Bgly 4A 50
Ireland Ter. BD16: Bgly 4A 50
IRELAND WOOD 5H 57
Ireton St. BD7: B'frd 5B 90
Irish La. BD22: Oak 5A 46
Iron Row LS29: Burl W 2F 21
(Back La.)
LS29: Burl W 1F 21
(Gt. Pasture La.)
Ironstone Dr. LS12: N Far 1A 116
Ironstone Gdns. LS12: N Far 2A 116
Ironwood App. LS14: Leeds 6C 80
Ironwood Cres. LS14: Leeds 6C 80
Ironwood Vw. LS14: Leeds 5C 80
Irving St. HX1: Hal 4D 148
Irving Ter. BD14: Clay 2E 109
Irwell St. BD4: B'frd 6G 91
Irwin App. LS15: Leeds 4B 100
Irwin St. LS28: Fars 1H 93
(not continuous)
Isaac St. BD8: B'frd 3B 90
Isabella Rd. LS25: Gar 3G 103
Islay Cl. LS26: Rothw 2B 142
Isle La. BD22: Oxen 4C 84
Isles St. BD8: B'frd 3H 89
ISLINGTON 1D 116
Ivanhoe Rd. BD7: B'frd 6B 90
Ivegate BD1: B'frd 4D 6 (4E 91)
LS19: Yead 6F 41
Ive Ho. La. HX2: Lud 1E 147
Iveson App. LS16: Leeds 5H 57
Iveson Cl. LS16: Leeds 5H 57
Iveson Ct. LS16: Leeds 5H 57
Iveson Cres. LS16: Leeds 5H 57
Iveson Gdns. LS16: Leeds 5H 57
Iveson Gth. LS16: Leeds 5A 58
Iveson Grn. LS16: Leeds 5H 57
Iveson Gro. LS16: Leeds 5H 57
Iveson Lawn LS16: Leeds 5A 58
Iveson Ri. LS16: Leeds 5A 58
Iveson Rd. LS16: Leeds 5H 57
Iveson Wood Ri. LS16: Leeds 5A 58
Ives St. BD17: Ship 1B 70
(not continuous)
Ivey Way BD18: Ship 2A 70
Ivies, The LS28: Pud 4A 94
(off Lidget Hill)
Ivory St. LS10: Leeds 6A 98
Ivy Av. LS9: Leeds 3E 99
Ivy Bank BD12: Wyke 3C 132
LS19: Yead 6E 41
Ivy Bank Ct. BD17: Bail 5D 52
(off Dewhirst Cl.)
Ivy Bank La. BD22: Haw 3C 64
Ivy Chase LS28: Pud 3D 94
Ivy Cotts. HX1: Hal 4E 149
(off Ivy St.)
Ivy Ct. LS7: Leeds 3B 78
LS29: I'ly 6D 10
Ivy Cres. HX3: Hip 2G 151
LS9: Leeds 3E 99
Ivy Gdns. LS13: Leeds 5F 75
Ivy Gth. LS7: Leeds 3B 78
Ivy Gro. BD18: Ship 2G 69
LS9: Leeds 4F 99
Ivy Ho. Rd. BD5: B'frd 4E 111

Ivy La. BD15: All 1C 88
    HX2: Mix 1B 128
    LS23: B Spa 4A 30
Ivy Mt. HX3: Hal 1H 159
    LS9: Leeds 3E 99
Ivy Pl. BD2: B'frd 5H 71
    LS13: Leeds 5F 75
Ivy Rd. BD18: Ship 2G 69
    BD21: Keigh 1C 48
    LS9: Leeds 4E 99
Ivy St. BD21: Keigh 5H 33
    HD6: Brigh 6H 151
    HX1: Hal 4E 149
    LS9: Leeds 3E 99
Ivy St. Sth. BD21: Keigh 3H 47
    HX1: Hal 4E 149
Ivy Ter. BD8: B'frd 6B 110
    BD21: Keigh 1D 48
    HD6: Brigh 6H 151
               (off Ivy St.)
    HX1: Hal *4E 149*
               (off Ivy St.)
    HX3: Hip 2G 151
Ivy Vw. LS9: Leeds 3E 99
Ivywood Ct. BD7: B'frd 2G 109

J

Jacana Way BD6: B'frd 4E 109
Jackdaw Cl. BD15: All 4D 88
Jackdaw La. LS23: B Spa 3A 30
Jackie Smart Ct. LS7: Leeds 6C 78
Jackie Smart Rd. BD5: B'frd 1E 111
Jack La. LS10: Leeds 6A 98
               (Parkfield St.)
    LS10: Leeds 1C 118
               (Whitfield Sq.)
    LS11: Leeds 6H 97
               (Nineveh Rd.)
    LS11: Leeds 6A 98
               (Parkfield St.)
Jackman Dr. LS18: H'fth 1F 75
Jackroyd HX3: Hal 5D 128
Jackson Av. LS8: Leeds 2D 78
Jackson Hill BD13: Que 6B 108
            (not continuous)
Jackson Rd. LS7: Leeds 6A 78
Jackson St.
    BD3: B'frd 6H 7 (5G 91)
Jackson Wlk. LS29: Men 2H 39
Jacky La. BD22: Haw 3C 64
Jacobs Cl. LS5: Leeds 6B 76
Jacobs Cft. BD14: Clay 1D 108
Jacobs La. BD22: Haw 1D 64
Jacob St. BD5: B'frd 1D 110
    LS2: Leeds 2F 5 (2A 98)
Jacobs Well
    BD1: B'frd 5D 6 (5E 91)
Jacquard Ct. HD6: B Bri 2C 152
Jacquard Sq. LS10: Leeds 1C 118
Jacques Fold BD20: Sils 2F 15
Jacques Gro. BD20: Sils 2F 15
Jail Yd. LS26: Rothw 2B 142
Jail Yd. Pde. *LS26: Rothw* *2B 142*
               (off Jail Yd.)
Jakeman Cl. WF3: Ting 1E 155
Jakeman Ct. WF3: Ting 1E 155
Jakeman Cft. WF3: Ting 1E 155
Jakeman Dr. WF3: Ting 1E 155
Jakeman Fold WF3: Ting 1E 155
James Av. BD20: East 6A 14
    LS8: Leeds 1D 78
James Baillie Pk.
    LS6: Leeds 4F 77
James Cl. LS25: Gar 4H 103
James Ct. *LS22: Coll* *3B 28*
            (off Station La.)
    LS27: Morl 2C 138
James Ga. BD1: B'frd 3C 6 (4E 91)
James St. BD1: B'frd 3C 6 (4E 91)
    BD11: Birk 1E 135
    BD13: Thorn 5H 87

James St. BD15: All 2E 89
    BD22: Oak 5B 46
    HD6: Brigh 5A 152
    HX5: Ell 5B 160
    LS19: Raw 3F 55
James St. E. BD21: Keigh 1A 48
James St. Mkt. BD1: B'frd 3C 6
Jamie Ct. BD10: B'frd 3B 72
Jane Few Ho. LS15: Leeds 1G 101
Jane Grn. HX2: Ogd 3B 106
Jane Hills *BD17: Ship* *1A 70*
            (off Riverside Est.)
Jane St. BD13: Denh 2B 86
    BD18: Ship 1H 69
    BD22: Haw *2D 64*
               (off Park La.)
Janesway LS25: Kip 3F 123
Janet St. BD22: Haw 1E 65
Japonica Way BD3: B'frd 2A 92
Jaques Cl. LS6: Leeds 5B 76
Jardine Rd. BD16: Bgly 4C 50
Jardine St. BD16: Bgly 4C 50
Jarratt St. BD8: B'frd 2B 90
Jarratt St. E. BD8: B'frd 2B 90
Jarrom Cl. BD4: B'frd 1B 112
Jarvis Sq. WF3: Rob H 4E 141
Jarvis Wlk. WF3: Rob H 4E 141
Jasmine Gdns. HX1: Hal 3D 148
Jasmin Ter. BD8: B'frd 3C 90
Jason Ter. WF17: Birs 5C 136
Jasper St. BD10: B'frd 1H 71
    HX1: Hal 2D 148
Javelin Cl. BD10: B'frd 3H 71
JAW HILL 6G 155
Jay Ho. La. HD6: Clift 4C 152
Jay St. BD22: Haw 2D 64
Jean Av. LS15: Leeds 4C 100
Jemmy La. HX3: Hal 2B 164
Jenkinson Cl. LS11: Leeds 6G 97
Jenkinson Lawn LS11: Leeds 6G 97
Jenkinsons Pl. LS10: Leeds 5B 118
Jennetts Cres. LS21: Otley 4D 22
Jennie Blackamore Way
    LS15: Leeds 1F 101
Jennings Cl. BD20: Sils 3F 15
Jennings Pl. BD7: B'frd 1A 110
Jennings St. BD7: B'frd 1A 110
Jenny La. BD17: Bail 3D 52
Jepson La. HX5: Ell 5B 160
Jer Gro. BD7: B'frd 3G 109
Jer La. BD7: B'frd 3G 109
Jermyn St. BD1: B'frd 3F 7 (4F 91)
Jerry Clay La. WF2: Kirk, Wren . .6A 156
Jerry La. BD20: Sils 2D 16
    HX6: Sow B 6G 147
Jerry Spring Rd. HX2: Lud M 3D 146
Jersey Cl. WF12: Dew 6A 154
Jerusalem Farm Camp Site
    HX2: Midg 3D 126
Jerusalem Farm Nature Reserve
    . . . . .2D 126
Jerusalem Farm Workshops 3D 126
Jerusalem La. HX2: Lud, Midg . . .3C 126
Jervaulx Cl. LS23: B Spa 4A 30
Jervaulx Cres. BD8: B'frd 1A 6 (3C 90)
Jerwood Hill Cl. HX3: Hal 6H 129
Jerwood Hill Rd. HX3: Hal 6H 129
Jesmond Av. BD9: B'frd 1H 89
Jesmond Gro. BD9: B'frd 1H 89
Jesmond Sq. LS28: Fars 6A 74
Jessamine Av. LS11: Leeds 4F 117
Jesse St. BD5: B'frd 6E 91
    BD8: B'frd 4F 89
Jessop Row LS12: Leeds 4A 96
Jester Pl. BD13: Que 3G 107
Jewitt La. LS22: Coll 5B 28
Jew La. BD22: Oxen 1C 84
Jilley Royd La. HD2: Fix 6A 162
Jill Kilner Dr. LS29: Burl W 3D 20
Jim Allen La. HX2: Midg 6C 126
Jim Laker Pl. BD18: Ship 2H 69
Jimmy Gees 1G 69
Jinnah Ct. BD8: B'frd 1A 6 (3D 90)

Jinny Moor La. LS26: Swil 5G 121
Joba Av. BD3: B'frd 4H 91
Joffre Mt. *LS19: Yead* *1G 55*
            (off Springwell Cl.)
John Charles App.
    LS11: Leeds 5A 118
John Charles Centre for Sport . .5A 118
John Charles Way LS12: Leeds . .1D 116
John Escritt Rd. BD16: Bgly 5C 50
John Gilmour Way
    LS29: Burl W 3D 20
John Hanson Cl. BD13: Denh 5C 86
John Naylor La. HX2: Lud M 4E 147
John Nelson Cl. WF17: Bat 6B 136
Johnny La. LS21: Otley 5E 23
JOHN O'GAUNTS 6B 120
John O'Gaunts Trad. Est.
    LS26: Rothw 6A 120
John O'Gaunts Wlk.
    LS26: Rothw 1B 142
John Ormsby VC Way
    WF12: Dew 6A 154
Johns Av. WF3: Loft 3G 157
John Smeaton Leisure Cen. 6G 81
Johnson St. BD3: B'frd 4B 92
    BD16: Bgly 3B 50
Johnsons Yd. LS29: Burl W 2F 21
Johnson Ter. LS27: Morl 3B 138
Johnston St. LS6: Leeds 6H 77
John St. BD1: B'frd 3C 6 (4E 91)
    BD4: B'frd 4C 112
    BD13: Cull 3B 66
    BD13: Denh 2B 86
    BD13: Thorn 5H 87
    BD14: Clay 1E 109
    BD17: Bail 6C 52
    BD18: Ship 1A 70
    BD22: Oak 5D 46
    HD6: Brigh 6A 152
    HX1: Hal 4B 164 (2G 149)
    HX4: Gree 4G 159
    HX5: Ell 5B 160
    LS6: Leeds 6E 77
    LS19: Raw 3F 55
    WF17: Birs 6A 136
John St. W. HX6: Sow B 5H 147
John William St.
    BD19: Cleck 6B 134
    HX5: Ell 5B 160
Jonathan Gth. LS29: Add 1C 8
Jonscroft BD13: Que 6H 107
Jordan Rd. LS28: Stan 1C 94
Jordan Way BD2: B'frd 1A 92
Joseph Av. HX3: North 5C 130
Joseph Crossley's Almshouses
    HX1: Hal 3F 149
Joseph Dobson's Sweet Factory . .4B 160
Joseph Stones Ho. *LS2: Leeds* *4H 5*
            (off St Cecilia St.)
Joseph St. BD3: B'frd 4G 7 (4G 91)
    BD4: B'frd 4C 112
    LS10: Leeds 1C 118
Joseph's Well LS3: Leeds 3B 4
Joseph Wright Ct. *BD10: B'frd* *6G 53*
            (off Brighton St.)
Jowett Pk. Cres. BD10: B'frd 5G 53
Jowett St. BD1: B'frd 3A 6 (4C 90)
Jowett Ter. LS27: Morl 5A 138
Jowler HX2: Lud 3D 126
Jowler La. WF1: Out 5G 157
Jubilee Av. WF1: Out 5G 157
Jubilee Ct. BD18: Ship 1C 70
    LS27: Morl *3B 138*
            (off Marshall St.)
Jubilee Cres. BD11: Drig 6C 114
    WF1: Out 5G 157
Jubilee Cft. BD11: Drig 6B 114
Jubilee Dr. BD21: Keigh 2G 47
Jubilee Gdns. LS26: Wood 1E 145
Jubilee Ho. *HX6: Sow B* *6H 147*
            (off West St.)
Jubilee Mt. HD6: Ras 1H 161
Jubilee Pl. LS27: Morl 3B 138
Jubilee Rd. HX3: Hal 1H 159

Jubilee St. BD1: B'frd 1B 6 (2D 90)
HX3: Hal 3H 149
LS27: Morl 3B 138
Jubilee St. Nth. HX3: B'frd 4E 129
Jubilee Ter. HX3: Hal 3H 149
(off Jubilee St.)
LS27: Morl 3B 138
Jubilee Trees LS29: Burl W 4C 20
Jubilee Way BD18: Ship 1D 70
Jude Ct. LS13: Leeds 6G 75
Julian Dr. BD13: Que 3E 109
Jumb Beck Cl. LS29: Burl W 3F 21
Jumble Dyke HD6: Ras 3H 161
Jumbles Cl. WF3: Loft 6G 141
Jumbles La. WF3: Loft 6G 141
Jumples HX2: Mix 3B 128
Jumples Cl. HX2: Mix 3B 128
Jumples Ct. HX2: Mix 3A 128
Jumples Crag HX2: Mix 3B 128
Junction 1 Retail Pk.
LS11: Leeds 3C 116
Junction Rd. BD17: Ship 1C 70
Junction Row BD2: B'frd 5H 71
Junction St. LS10: Leeds 5A 98
Junction Ter. BD2: B'frd 5H 71
(off Bolton Rd.)
June St. BD21: Keigh 5A 34
Juniper Av. LS26: Wood 6G 121
Juniper Cl. BD8: B'frd 3B 90
Juniper Ct. HX3: North 3C 130
Juniper Pl. LS9: Leeds 2F 99
Junxion, The LS5: Leeds 5B 76
(off Station App.)
Jupiter Cres. BD2: B'frd 3G 71

K

Karam Cl. BD3: B'frd 4A 92
Karnac Rd. LS8: Leeds 5D 78
Kashmir Pk. HX1: Hal 2D 148
Katherine St. BD18: Ship 1H 69
Kaycell St. BD4: B'frd 3H 111
Kay Cl. LS27: Morl 6H 115
Kaye Hill BD13: Cull 3B 66
(off Old La.)
Kay St. BD18: Ship 4C 70
Kearby Cliff LS27: Kear 1A 26
KEARBY TOWN END 1A 26
Kearsley Ter. LS10: Leeds 3C 118
Keasden Cl. BD10: B'frd 5G 53
Keats Gro. WF3: S'ley 3H 157
Keats Ho. LS29: I'ly 5G 11
Keble Gth. LS25: Kip 3A 124
Kedleston Rd. LS8: Leeds 5D 60
Keeble Ho. BD2: B'frd 1B 92
(off St Clare's Av.)
Keelam Ga. HX7: Wads 1A 126
Keeldar Cl. BD7: B'frd 2B 110
KEELHAM 6C 86
Keelham Dr. LS19: Raw 3G 55
Keelham La. BD20: Keigh 3G 33
Keelham Pl. BD13: Denh 6D 86
Keel Moorings LS13: Leeds 4B 74
Keeper La. BD4: B'frd 2H 113
Keepers Fold BD10: B'frd 5H 53
Keeton St. LS9: Leeds 3D 98
KEIGHLEY 6A 34
Keighley & Worth Valley Railway
Damems Station 5G 47
Haworth Station 2C 64
Ingrow West Station 3H 47
Oakworth Station 6D 46
Oxenhope Station 6C 64
Keighley & Worth Valley Railway
Exhibition Shed 6C 64
Keighley Cl. HX2: Illing 1B 128
Keighley Cougars RLFC 4B 34
Keighley Dr. HX2: Illing 2C 128
Keighley Golf Course 1H 33
Keighley Ind. Pk. BD21: Keigh 4A 34
Keighley Leisure Cen. 5B 34
Keighley Pl. LS28: Stan 1A 94

Keighley Playhouse 6H 33
Keighley Retail Pk. BD21: Keigh 4A 34
Keighley Rd. BD8: B'frd 5B 70
BD9: B'frd 5B 70
BD13: Cull 2A 66
BD13: Denh 6A 66
BD16: Bgly 1H 49
BD16: Har 3D 48
BD20: Sils 4D 14
BD20: Stee 6D 14
BD21: Har 3D 48
BD22: Oak 5D 46
BD22: Oxen 6C 64
HX2: Hal, Illing 2C 128
HX2: Illing, Ogd 4B 106
(not continuous)
HX3: Hal 2C 128
LS29: I'ly 4A 18
Keighley Station (Rail) 6B 34
Keilder Cres. BD6: B'frd 3E 109
Kelburn Gro. BD22: Oak 4B 46
KELCLIFFE 3B 40
Kelcliffe Av. LS20: Guis 4C 40
Kelcliffe Gro. LS20: Guis 4C 40
Kelcliffe La. LS20: Guis 3B 40
(not continuous)
Keldholme Cl. LS13: Leeds 4A 74
Keldholme Rd. LS13: Leeds 4A 74
Keldregate HD2: Hud 6E 163
Kell Beck LS21: Otley 1D 22
Kell Butts HX2: Wain 1F 127
Kellett Av. LS12: Leeds 1C 116
Kellett Bldgs. BD12: Low M 2D 132
Kellett Cres. LS12: Leeds 1C 116
Kellett Dr. BD13: Thorn 5F 87
LS12: Leeds 1C 116
Kellett Gro. LS12: Leeds 1C 116
Kellett La. LS12: Leeds 6B 96
Kellett Mt. LS12: Leeds 1C 116
Kellett Pl. LS12: Leeds 1C 116
Kellett Rd. LS12: Leeds 6B 96
Kellett Ter. LS12: Leeds 1C 116
Kellett Wlk. LS12: Leeds 1C 116
Kell La. HX2: Wain 2E 127
HX3: North 4B 130
Kelloe St. BD19: Cleck 6B 134
Kellymoor Wlk. BD10: B'frd 2F 71
Kelmore Gro. BD6: B'frd 1G 131
Kelmscott Av. LS15: Leeds 6F 81
Kelmscott Cres. LS15: Leeds 6F 81
Kelmscott Gdns. LS15: Leeds 6F 81
Kelmscott Gth. LS15: Leeds 5G 81
Kelmscott Grn. LS15: Leeds 6F 81
Kelmscott Gro. LS15: Leeds 6F 81
Kelmscott La. LS15: Leeds 6F 81
Kelsall Av. LS6: Leeds 1E 97
Kelsall Gro. LS6: Leeds 1E 97
Kelsall Ho. BD3: B'frd 2F 7
Kelsall Pl. LS6: Leeds 1E 97
Kelsall Rd. LS6: Leeds 1E 97
Kelsall Ter. LS6: Leeds 1E 97
Kelseys Ct. HX2: Hal 1C 148
(off Stretchgate La.)
Kelsey St. HX1: Hal 1D 148
Kelso Ct. LS3: Leeds 2F 97
Kelso Gdns. LS2: Leeds 1A 4 (2F 97)
Kelso Hgts. LS3: Leeds 1F 97
Kelso Ho. BD4: B'frd 2C 112
(off Stirling Cres.)
Kelso Pl. LS2: Leeds 1F 97
Kelso Rd. LS2: Leeds 1A 4 (1F 97)
Kelso St. LS2: Leeds 1A 4 (2F 97)
Kelvin Av. HX2: Hal 2B 148
Kelvin Cres. HX2: Hal 3B 148
Kelvin Ho. BD4: B'frd 2D 112
Kelvin Rd. HX5: Ell 5A 160
Kelvin Way BD2: B'frd 1A 92
Kempton Rd. LS25: Kip 3G 123
Kemsing Wlk. LS15: Leeds 1H 101
Kendal Bank LS3: Leeds 2A 4 (2F 97)
Kendal Carr LS3: Leeds 2A 4 (2F 97)
Kendal Cl. LS3: Leeds 2A 4 (2F 97)

Kendal Dr. LS15: Leeds 4A 100
Kendal Gro. LS3: Leeds 2A 4 (2G 97)
Kendal La. LS3: Leeds 2A 4 (2F 97)
Kendall Av. BD18: Ship 2G 69
Kendal Mellor Ct. BD21: Keigh 6H 33
Kendal Ri. LS3: Leeds 2A 4
Kendal Rd. LS3: Leeds 2A 4 (2G 97)
Kendal St. BD21: Keigh 1B 48
Kendal Wlk. LS3: Leeds 2A 4
Kendell St. LS10: Leeds 6F 5 (4A 98)
Kendra Way BD3: B'frd 2F 7 (3F 91)
Kenilworth Av. LS27: Gil 1F 137
Kenilworth Dr. HX3: Hip 3A 152
Kenilworth Gdns. LS27: Gil 6F 115
Kenilworth Ho. BD15: All 3D 88
Kenilworth Rd. LS12: Leeds 6C 96
Kenilworth St. BD4: B'frd 1H 111
Kenley Av. BD6: B'frd 3A 110
Kenley Mt. BD6: B'frd 3A 110
Kenley Pde. BD6: B'frd 3H 109
BD7: B'frd 3H 109
Kenmore Av. BD19: Cleck 6A 134
Kenmore Cl. BD19: Cleck 6A 134
Kenmore Cres. BD6: B'frd 3A 110
BD19: Cleck 1H 153
Kenmore Dr. BD6: B'frd 3A 110
Kenmore Gro. BD6: B'frd 3A 110
Kenmore Rd. BD6: B'frd 3A 110
BD19: Cleck 6A 134
WF2: Carr G 5D 156
Kenmore Wlk. BD6: B'frd 3A 110
Kennedy Av. HD2: Fix 6A 162
Kennedy Cl. WF12: Dew 6A 154
Kennedy Ho. BD21: Keigh 3H 47
(off Hainworth La.)
Kennels La. LS14: Coll, S'cft 5H 45
Kennerleigh Av. LS15: Leeds 2E 101
Kennerleigh Cres. LS15: Leeds 2F 101
Kennerleigh Dr. LS15: Leeds 2E 101
Kennerleigh Gth. LS15: Leeds 2F 101
Kennerleigh Glen LS15: Leeds 2E 101
Kennerleigh Gro. LS15: Leeds 2F 101
Kennerleigh Ri. LS15: Leeds 2F 101
Kennerleigh Wlk. BD4: B'frd 3D 112
(off Wenborough La.)
LS15: Leeds 2E 101
Kenneth St. LS11: Leeds 6F 97
Kennet La. LS25: Gar 5G 103
Kennion St. BD5: B'frd 6D 90
Kensington Cl. HX3: Hal 5E 149
Kensington Ct. LS6: Leeds 6F 77
LS10: Leeds 5D 118
Kensington Fold WF3: W Ard 2E 155
Kensington Gdns. HX5: Ell 5A 160
LS10: Leeds 6D 118
Kensington Rd. HX3: Hal 5E 149
Kensington St. BD8: B'frd 2A 90
BD21: Keigh 1H 47
Kensington Ter. LS6: Leeds 6F 77
LS25: Gar 4E 103
(off Salem Pl.)
Kensington Way LS10: Leeds 6D 118
Kenstone Cres. BD10: B'frd 2G 71
Ken Syke Cotts. WF3: W Ard 2D 154
KENT 4A 94
Kent Av. BD20: Sils 2D 14
LS28: Pud 4C 94
Kent Cl. LS28: Pud 4C 94
Kent Cres. LS28: Pud 4B 94
Kent Dr. LS28: Pud 4C 94
Kentmere App. LS14: Leeds 4A 80
Kentmere Av. BD12: Wyke 6E 133
LS14: Leeds 2B 80
LS25: Gar 5H 103
Kentmere Cl. LS14: Leeds 4C 80
Kentmere Cres. LS14: Leeds 3B 80
Kentmere Gdns.
LS14: Leeds 3B 80
Kentmere Ga. LS14: Leeds 2B 80
Kentmere Grn. LS14: Leeds 3B 80
Kentmere Ri. LS14: Leeds 4C 80
Kent M. BD16: Bgly 5D 50

Kenton Way—Kingswear Ri.

Kenton Way BD4: B'frd 1B **112**
Kent Rd. BD16: Bgly 5D **50**
LS28: Pud 4B **94**
Kent St. BD1: B'frd 5D **6** (5E **91**)
HX1: Hal 5A **164** (3F **149**)
Kenwood M. LS18: H'fth 1F **75**
Kenworthy Cl. LS16: Leeds 2A **58**
Kenworthy Gdns. LS16: Leeds 2A **58**
Kenworthy Gth. LS16: Leeds 2A **58**
Kenworthy Ga. LS16: Leeds 2A **58**
Kenworthy Ri. LS16: Leeds 2A **58**
Kenworthy Va. LS16: Leeds 2A **58**
Kenya Mt. BD21: Keigh 5F **33**
Kenyon La. HX2: Hal 2B **148**
Kepler Gro. LS8: Leeds 1C **98**
Kepler Mt. LS8: Leeds 1C **98**
Kepler Ter. LS8: Leeds 1C **98**
Keplestone M. LS17: Leeds 1C **60**
Kepstorn Cl. LS5: Leeds 4A **76**
Kepstorn Ri. LS5: Leeds 4A **76**
Kepstorn Rd. LS16: Leeds 2B **76**
Kerry Ct. *LS18: H'fth 6D **56***
(off Kerry Gth.)
Kerry Gth. LS18: H'fth 6D **56**
Kerry Hill LS18: H'fth 1D **74**
(not continuous)
Kerry St. LS18: H'fth 6D **56**
Kerry Vw. LS18: H'fth 6E **57**
Kershaw Ct. HX2: Lud M 1D **146**
Kershaw Cres. HX2: Lud M 2D **146**
Kershaw Dr. HX2: Lud M 1D **146**
Kershaw St. BD3: B'frd 4B **92**
Kesteven Cl. BD4: B'frd 3D **112**
Kesteven Ct. BD4: B'frd 3D **112**
Kesteven Rd. BD4: B'frd 3C **112**
Kestrel Cl. BD6: B'frd 4E **109**
LS17: Leeds 3D **60**
Kestrel Dr. BD2: B'frd 5G **71**
Kestrel Gth. LS27: Morl 3D **138**
Kestrel Gro. LS17: Leeds 3D **60**
Kestrel Mt. BD2: B'frd 5G **71**
Kestrel Vw. BD19: Cleck 6B **134**
Keswick Cl. HX3: Hal 5A **150**
Keswick Grange LS17: E Kes 6E **27**
Keswick La. LS17: Bard 1E **45**
Keswick St. BD4: B'frd 6B **92**
Keswick Vw. LS17: Bard 6G **27**
Kettlewell Dr. BD5: B'frd 2B **110**
Keys Ct. *LS11: Leeds 5H **97***
(off Saw Mill St.)
Khalaq Ct. BD3: B'frd 3H **91**
Khus Wlk. BD21: Keigh 3A **48**
Kidacre St. LS10: Leeds 5A **98**
Kielder Dr. LS10: Leeds 3C **140**
Kielder Way LS26: Wood 6D **120**
Kilburn Rd. LS12: Leeds 4C **96**
Kildare Cres. BD15: All 2C **88**
Kildare Ter. LS12: Leeds 5E **97**
KILLINGBECK 2A **100**
Killingbeck Bri. LS14: Leeds 2A **100**
Killingbeck Ct. LS14: Leeds 1A **100**
Killingbeck Dr. LS14: Leeds 2A **100**
Killingbeck Retail Pk.
LS14: Leeds 1A **100**
Killinghall Av. BD2: B'frd 2H **91**
Killinghall Dr. BD2: B'frd 2H **91**
Killinghall Gro. BD2: B'frd 2H **91**
Killinghall Rd. BD2: B'frd 1A **92**
BD3: B'frd 1A **92**
Kiln Bank BD20: Rid 3C **34**
Kilner Ho. *BD2: B'frd 1B **92***
(off St Clare's Av.)
Kilner Rd. BD6: B'frd 4A **110**
(not continuous)
Kilners Cft. LS29: Add 1D **8**
Kiln Fold HD6: Clift 6D **152**
Kilns, The WF1: Wake 6D **156**
Kilnsea Mt. BD4: B'frd 2C **112**
Kilnsey Fold BD20: Sils 1D **14**
Kilnsey M. BD17: Bail 4B **52**
Kilnsey Rd. BD3: B'frd 5H **91**
Kilroyd Av. BD19: Hun 5B **134**
Kilroyd Dr. BD19: Hun 5C **134**
Kimberley Pl. HX3: Hal 3E **129**
LS9: Leeds 1F **99**
Kimberley Rd. LS9: Leeds 1F **99**
Kimberley St. BD3: B'frd 5A **92**
BD4: B'frd 5A **92**
HD6: Brigh 6B **152**
HX3: Hal 3E **129**
LS29: I'ly 4E **11**
Kimberley Vw. LS9: Leeds 2F **99**
Kinara Cl. BD21: Keigh 5C **34**
Kinder Cl. BD13: Thorn 5H **87**
Kineholme Dr. LS21: Otley 5B **22**
King Alfred's Dr. LS6: Leeds 6G **59**
King Alfred's Grn. LS6: Leeds 6G **59**
King Alfred's Wlk. LS6: Leeds 6G **59**
King Alfred's Way LS6: Leeds 6G **59**
King Charles St.
LS1: Leeds 4E **5** (3A **98**)
King Charles Wlk. *LS1: Leeds 4E **5***
(within The Core Shop. Cen.)
Kingcliff BD15: Wils 3F **67**
King Cl. LS17: Leeds 3G **59**
KING CROSS 4C **148**
King Cross Rd. HX1: Hal 4D **148**
King Cross St. HX1: Hal . . .5A **164** (3F **149**)
(not continuous)
King Dr. LS17: Leeds 3F **59**
King Edward Av. LS18: H'fth 1D **74**
WF10: All B 1F **145**
King Edward Cres. LS18: H'fth 6E **57**
King Edward Rd. BD13: Thorn 5H **87**
King Edward St.
HX1: Hal 4C **164** (2G **149**)
LS1: Leeds 4F **5** (3A **98**)
King Edward Ter. BD13: Thorn 5H **87**
LS29: Burl W 2F **21**
King Edwins Ct. LS8: Leeds 4E **79**
Kingfield LS20: Guis 3D **40**
Kingfisher Cl. LS17: Leeds 3D **60**
Kingfisher Ct. BD6: B'frd 4E **109**
*BD21: Keigh 6A **34***
(off East Pde.)
Kingfisher Gro. BD8: B'frd 4E **89**
Kingfisher M. LS27: Morl 4C **138**
Kingfisher Reach LS22: Coll 2A **28**
Kingfishers, The BD20: Sils 3E **15**
Kingfisher Way LS17: Leeds 3D **60**
King George Av. LS7: Leeds 2B **78**
LS18: H'fth 6E **57**
LS27: Morl 1B **138**
King George Cft. LS27: Morl 2B **138**
King George Gdns. LS7: Leeds 2B **78**
King George Gro. LS27: Morl 1B **138**
King George Rd. LS18: H'fth 6E **57**
King George St. WF1: Out 6F **157**
King Ho. *LS29: I'ly 5C **10***
(off Kings Rd.)
King La. LS17: Leeds 1E **59**
King Lane (Park & Ride) 4H **59**
Kings App. LS13: Leeds 1G **95**
Kings Av. LS6: Leeds 1E **97**
LS29: I'ly 5C **10**
Kingsbury Pl. HX1: Hal 2D **148**
Kings Chase LS26: Rothw 1B **142**
Kings Cl. LS21: Otley 4G **23**
LS29: I'ly 5A **10**
Kings Ct. BD16: Bgly 4B **50**
HX1: Hal 5A **164** (3F **149**)
LS17: Leeds 6A **60**
WF17: Birs 6A **136**
Kings Cft. BD11: Drig 1B **136**
LS25: Gar 5D **102**
King's Cft. Gdns. LS17: Leeds 6B **60**
Kingsdale Av. BD2: B'frd 6G **71**
BD11: Drig 1A **136**
LS29: Men 2G **39**
Kingsdale Cl. LS29: Men 2H **39**
Kingsdale Ct. LS14: Leeds 3A **80**
(not continuous)
Kingsdale Cres. BD2: B'frd 6G **71**
Kingsdale Dr. BD2: B'frd 6G **71**
LS29: Men 2H **39**
Kingsdale Gdns. BD11: Drig 1A **136**
Kingsdale Gro. BD2: B'frd 6F **71**
King's Dr. BD2: B'frd 3F **71**
WF17: Birs 5A **136**
Kingsfield LS26: Rothw 2F **141**
King's Ga. BD1: B'frd 2E **91**
Kings Gro. BD16: Bgly 3D **50**
BD17: Bail 6G **51**
Kings Lea HX3: Hal 1F **159**
Kingsley Av. BD2: B'frd 6E **71**
BD11: Birk 3F **135**
HX6: Sow B 6F **147**
LS16: Leeds 2B **58**
WF1: Out 4F **157**
Kingsley Cl. BD11: Birk 3F **135**
WF1: Out 4F **157**
Kingsley Cres. BD11: Birk 3F **135**
BD17: Bail 5C **52**
Kingsley Dr. BD11: Birk 3F **135**
LS16: Leeds 2B **58**
Kingsley Gth. WF1: Out 4F **157**
Kingsley Pl. HX1: Hal 3D **148**
Kingsley Rd. LS16: Leeds 2B **58**
Kingsmark Freeway BD12: O'haw . . .2F **133**
Kings Mead LS26: Rothw 1C **142**
Kingsmead LS14: Leeds 1C **80**
Kingsmead Dr. LS14: Leeds 6B **62**
Kings Mdw. Cl. LS22: Weth 2D **12**
Kings Mdw. Dr. LS22: Weth 2D **12**
Kings Mdw. Gro. LS22: Weth 2D **12**
Kings Mdw. M. LS22: Weth 2D **12**
Kings Mdw. Vw. LS22: Weth 2D **12**
Kingsmill Cl. LS27: Morl 2H **137**
King's Mt. LS17: Leeds 1A **78**
Kings Pk. WF17: Birs 5A **136**
Kings Pl. LS6: Leeds 5D **76**
Kings Rd. BD1: B'frd 1E **91**
BD2: B'frd 6E **71**
BD16: Bgly 1A **50**
LS6: Leeds 1E **97**
LS29: I'ly 5A **10**
Kingston Cl. BD15: Wils 4G **67**
HX1: Hal 3D **148**
Kingston Ct. HX1: Hal 3D **148**
Kingston Dr. HX1: Hal 3D **148**
Kingston Gdns. LS15: Leeds 1D **100**
Kingston Gro. BD10: B'frd 6H **53**
Kingston Rd. BD10: B'frd 6H **53**
Kingston St. HX1: Hal 3D **148**
Kingston Ter. HX1: Hal 3D **148**
LS2: Leeds 1H **97**
King St. BD2: B'frd 4A **72**
BD11: Drig 1A **136**
BD20: Sils 2E **15**
BD21: Keigh 1H **47**
BD22: Haw 3C **64**
HD6: Brigh 1B **162**
HX1: Hal 3D **164** (2H **149**)
*HX5: Ell 5C **160***
(off Brook St.)
HX6: Sow B 6E **147**
LS1: Leeds 5C **4** (4H **97**)
LS19: Raw 3E **55**
LS19: Yead 6G **41**
LS27: Morl 4A **138**
LS28: Stan 2H **93**
Kings Vw. HX3: Sou 5C **150**
Kingsway BD2: B'frd 2F **71**
BD11: Drig 1A **136**
BD16: Bgly 4C **50**
BD20: Rid 4E **35**
LS15: Leeds 3E **101**
LS25: Gar 5D **102**
WF17: Birs 5A **136**
Kingsway Ct. LS17: Leeds 6B **60**
Kingsway Dr. LS29: I'ly 5C **10**
Kingsway Gth. LS25: Gar 5D **102**
Kingswear Cl. LS15: Leeds 2F **101**
Kingswear Cres. LS15: Leeds 2F **101**
Kingswear Gth. LS15: Leeds 2F **101**
Kingswear Glen LS15: Leeds 2F **101**
Kingswear Gro. LS15: Leeds 2F **101**
Kingswear Pde. LS15: Leeds 2F **101**
Kingswear Ri. LS15: Leeds 2F **101**

Kingswear Vw. LS15: Leeds 2F **101**
Kingswell Av. WF1: Out 5G **157**
Kingswood Av. LS8: Leeds 4E **61**
Kingswood Cres. LS8: Leeds 4D **60**
Kingswood Dr. LS8: Leeds 4D **60**
Kingswood Gdns. LS8: Leeds 4D **60**
Kingswood Gro. LS8: Leeds 4E **61**
Kingswood Pl. BD7: B'frd 1A **110**
Kingswood Rd. LS12: Leeds 5C **96**
Kingswood St. BD7: B'frd 1A **110**
Kingswood Ter. BD7: B'frd 1A **110**
Kinnaird Cl. HX5: Ell 3B **160**
Kipling Cl. BD10: B'frd 2B **72**
KIPPAX 3G **123**
KIPPAX COMMON 2F **123**
Kippax La. End LS25: Gar 6E **103**
Kippax Leisure Cen. 5F **123**
Kippax Mt. LS9: Leeds 4D **98**
Kippax Park Fishery 6H **123**
Kippax Pl. LS9: Leeds 4D **98**
Kipping La. BD13: Thorn 5H **87**
Kipping Pl. BD13: Thorn 5H **87**
Kirby Leas HX1: Hal 6B **164** (3G **149**)
Kirby St. BD21: Keigh 5B **34**
Kirk Beston Cl. LS11: Leeds 3E **117**
Kirkbourne Gro. BD17: Bail 5E **53**
Kirkburn Pl. BD7: B'frd 5B **90**
Kirkby Av. LS25: Gar 6G **103**
Kirkby Gth. LS14: T'ner 1H **63**
Kirkcroft BD13: Denh 3B **86**
Kirkdale Av. LS12: Leeds 1B **116**
Kirkdale Cres. LS12: Leeds 2B **116**
Kirkdale Dr. LS12: Leeds 1B **116**
Kirkdale Gdns. LS12: Leeds 1B **116**
Kirkdale Gro. LS12: N Far 1A **116**
Kirkdale Mt. LS12: Leeds 2B **116**
Kirkdale Ter. LS12: Leeds 2B **116**
Kirkdale Vw. LS12: Leeds 2B **116**
Kirkdale Way BD4: B'frd 4D **112**
KIRK DEIGHTON 1D **12**
Kirk Dr. BD17: Bail 3D **52**
Kirkfield Dr. LS15: Leeds 4F **101**
Kirkfield Gdns. LS15: Leeds 4F **101**
Kirkfield La. LS14: T'ner 2H **63**
Kirkfields BD17: Bail 3E **53**
Kirkfields Ind. Cen.
    LS19: Yead 6E **41**
Kirkfield Vw. LS15: Leeds 4F **101**
Kirk Ga. BD11: Birk 6D **112**
Kirkgate BD1: B'frd 4C **6** (4E **91**)
    (not continuous)
    BD18: Ship 1A **70**
    BD20: Sils 2E **15**
    LS1: Leeds 4F **5** (3A **98**)
    (not continuous)
    LS2: Leeds 5G **5** (4A **98**)
    LS21: Otley 3E **23**
    (not continuous)
    WF17: Bat 6A **154**
    WF17: Birs 6H **135**
Kirkgate Arc. LS21: Otley 4E **23**
Kirkgate Cen. BD1: B'frd 4C **6** (4E **91**)
Kirkgate Mall BD1: B'frd 4D **6**
Kirkgate Mkt. LS2: Leeds 4F **5** (3A **98**)
Kirkgate Sq. BD1: B'frd 4D **6**
Kirkham Av. WF2: Kirk 6H **155**
KIRKHAMGATE 6H **155**
Kirkham Rd. BD7: B'frd 5B **90**
Kirkham St. LS13: Leeds 4B **74**
Kirkhills LS14: T'ner 2H **63**
Kirklands LS14: T'ner 2H **63**
Kirklands Av. BD13: Thorn 5A **88**
    BD17: Bail 4E **53**
Kirklands Cl. BD17: Bail 5E **53**
    LS19: Yead 6E **41**
    LS29: Men 1G **39**
Kirklands Gdns. BD17: Bail 5E **53**
Kirklands La. BD17: Bail 4E **53**
Kirklands Rd. BD17: Bail 4D **52**
Kirkland Vs. LS28: Pud 5A **94**
Kirk La. HX3: Hip 1E **151**
    LS19: Yead 6D **40**

Kirklees Cl. LS28: Fars 5H **73**
Kirklees Cft. LS28: Fars 5H **73**
Kirklees Dr. LS28: Fars 5H **73**
Kirklees Gth. LS28: Fars 5H **73**
Kirklees Ri. LS28: Fars 5H **73**
Kirklees Rd. BD15: All 4D **88**
Kirkley Av. BD12: Wyke 6C **132**
Kirkness St. LS27: Morl 3A **138**
KIRKSTALL 5A **76**
Kirkstall Abbey (remains) 4H **75**
Kirkstall Av. LS5: Leeds 6H **75**
Kirkstall Brewery LS5: Leeds 5H **75**
    (off Broad La.)
Kirkstall Gdns. BD21: Keigh 2A **48**
Kirkstall Hill BD8: B'frd 4F **89**
Kirkstall Hill LS4: Leeds 5B **76**
    LS5: Leeds 5B **76**
Kirkstall Ind. Pk. LS4: Leeds 2D **96**
Kirkstall La. LS5: Leeds 5A **76**
    LS6: Leeds 5A **76**
Kirkstall Leisure Cen. 5A **76**
Kirkstall Mt. LS5: Leeds 6H **75**
Kirkstall Rd. LS3: Leeds 3F **97**
    LS4: Leeds 6B **76**
Kirkstall Valley Nature Reserve 1A **96**
Kirkstall Valley Retail Pk.
    LS5: Leeds 6A **76**
Kirkstone Dr. HX2: Hal 1H **147**
Kirkstone Hall BD7: B'frd . . .5A **6** (5C **90**)
Kirkstone Ter. LS27: Morl 1A **138**
Kirkwall Av. LS9: Leeds 4F **99**
Kirkwall Dr. BD4: B'frd 2C **112**
Kirkwood Av. LS16: Leeds 2F **57**
Kirkwood Cl. LS16: Leeds 2F **57**
Kirkwood Cres. LS16: Leeds 2G **57**
Kirkwood Dr. LS16: Leeds 2F **57**
Kirkwood Gdns. LS16: Leeds 2G **57**
Kirkwood Gro. LS16: Leeds 3F **57**
    WF3: Ting 1F **155**
Kirkwood La. LS16: Leeds 2F **57**
Kirkwood Ri. LS16: Leeds 2G **57**
Kirkwood Vw. LS16: Leeds 2G **57**
Kirkwood Way LS16: Leeds 2G **57**
Kismet Cl. HX1: Hal 2E **149**
Kismet Gdns. BD3: B'frd 3A **92**
Kitchener Av. LS9: Leeds 2F **99**
Kitchener Gro. LS9: Leeds 1F **99**
Kitchener Mt. LS9: Leeds 2F **99**
Kitchener Pl. LS9: Leeds 2F **99**
Kitchener St. BD12: O'haw 2G **133**
    LS9: Leeds 2F **99**
    LS26: Wood 1E **143**
Kitchenman Ter. HX1: Hal 4G **149**
    (off Charlotte Cl.)
Kite M. BD8: B'frd 4E **89**
Kitson Cl. LS12: Leeds 5C **96**
Kitson Gdns. LS12: Leeds 5C **96**
Kitson La. HX6: Norl 2B **158**
Kitson Rd. LS10: Leeds 6B **98**
Kitson St. BD18: Ship 3C **70**
    LS9: Leeds 4D **98**
    WF3: Ting 6D **138**
Kitten Clough HX2: Hal 6C **128**
Kitty Fold LS29: Add 1D **8**
Kit Wood Cl. BD4: B'frd 3D **112**
Klick Fitness
    Bradford 1C **110**
Kliffen Pl. HX3: Hal 5H **149**
Knavesmire LS26: Rothw 2F **141**
    (not continuous)
Knightsbridge Ct. HD6: Brigh 6A **152**
Knightsbridge Wlk. BD4: B'frd 6H **111**
Knights Cl. LS15: Leeds 3E **101**
Knights Cft. LS22: Weth 2F **13**
Knightscroft Av. LS26: Rothw 1A **142**
Knightscroft Dr. LS26: Rothw 1A **142**
Knight's Fold BD7: B'frd 1A **110**
Knightshill LS15: Leeds 3F **101**
Knight St. HX1: Hal 4D **148**
Knights Way BD16: Bgly 3E **51**
Knightsway LS15: Leeds 2E **101**
    LS25: Gar 6D **102**
    WF3: Loft 5F **141**

Knightsway Ct. BD3: B'frd 2D **92**
Knoll, The LS28: Cal 1E **93**
Knoll Gdns. BD17: Bail 6B **52**
Knoll Pk. WF3: E Ard 2B **156**
Knoll Pk. Dr. BD17: Bail 6B **52**
Knoll Ter. BD17: Bail 6B **52**
Knoll Vw. BD17: Bail 5B **52**
    LS28: Fars 5A **74**
Knoll Wood Pk. LS18: H'fth 1F **75**
Knostrop La. LS9: Leeds 1F **119**
Knostrop Quay LS10: Leeds 1C **118**
KNOTFORD 2A **24**
Knott La. LS19: Raw 1H **73**
Knowle Av. LS4: Leeds 6D **76**
Knowle Cl. BD21: Keigh 4G **47**
Knowle Gro. LS4: Leeds 6D **76**
Knowle La. BD12: Wyke 5D **132**
Knowle Mt. LS4: Leeds 6D **76**
KNOWLE PARK 2G **47**
Knowle Pl. LS4: Leeds 6D **76**
Knowle Rd. LS4: Leeds 6D **76**
Knowles Av. BD4: B'frd 3B **112**
Knowles La. BD4: B'frd 3A **112**
    BD19: Gom 4F **135**
Knowle Spring Rd. BD21: Keigh 3H **47**
    (Foster Rd.)
    BD21: Keigh 2H **47**
    (Up. Calton St.)
Knowles Rd. HD6: Ras 3A **162**
Knowles St. BD4: B'frd 3A **112**
    BD13: Denh 3B **86**
Knowles Vw. BD4: B'frd 3B **112**
Knowle Ter. LS4: Leeds 1C **96**
Knowle Top Dr. HX3: Hip 1G **151**
Knowle Top Rd. HX3: Hip 1G **151**
Knowsley St.
    BD3: B'frd 4H **7** (4G **91**)
KNOWSTHORPE 6C **98**
Knowsthorpe Cres.
    LS9: Leeds 6D **98**
Knowsthorpe Ga. LS9: Leeds 1F **119**
Knowsthorpe La. LS9: Leeds 6D **98**
Knowsthorpe Rd. LS9: Leeds 6G **99**
Knowsthorpe Way LS9: Leeds 1F **119**
Knox St. LS13: Leeds 4H **73**
Knutsford Gro. BD4: B'frd 3C **112**
Komla Cl. BD1: B'frd 3F **7**
Kyffin Av. LS15: Leeds 4A **100**
Kyffin Pl. BD4: B'frd 6C **92**

L

Laburnum Cl. WF3: E Ard 2A **156**
Laburnum Dr. BD17: Bail 3D **52**
Laburnum Gro. BD19: Gom 6E **135**
    BD22: Cros R 1E **65**
    HX3: Hip 3A **152**
Laburnum Pl. BD8: B'frd 2C **90**
    BD10: B'frd 1C **72**
Laburnum Rd. BD18: Ship 4D **70**
Laburnum St. BD8: B'frd 2C **90**
    LS28: Fars 2H **93**
    LS28: Pud 3G **93**
Laburnum Ter. HX3: Nor G 5A **132**
    (off Rookes La.)
Laceby Cl. BD10: B'frd 1A **72**
Lacey Gro. LS22: Weth 5F **13**
Lacey M. BD4: B'frd 3A **112**
Lacy Way HX5: Ell 2D **160**
Ladbroke Gro. BD4: B'frd 4C **112**
Ladderbanks La. BD17: Bail 3D **52**
    (not continuous)
Ladstone Towers
    HX6: Sow B 5H **147**
Ladybeck Cl. LS2: Leeds 3G **5** (3B **98**)
Ladyfield BD13: Thorn 5H **87**
Lady La. BD16: Bgly 1C **50**
    LS2: Leeds 3F **5** (3A **98**)
Lady Pk. Av. BD16: Bgly 1C **50**
Lady Pk. Ct. LS17: Leeds 3D **60**
Lady Pit Ct. LS11: Leeds 1H **117**
    (off Lady Pit La.)

Lady Pit La.—Lapage Ter.

Lady Pit La. LS11: Leeds 1H **117**
(not continuous)
Ladyroyd Dr. BD4: E Bier 1C **134**
Ladysmith Rd. BD13: Que 5G **107**
Ladywell Cl. BD5: B'frd 2E **111**
Ladywell La. WF15: Liv 6H **153**
LADY WOOD 2G **79**
Ladywood Grange
LS8: Leeds 3H **79**
Ladywood Mead LS8: Leeds 3H **79**
Ladywood Rd. LS8: Leeds 3F **79**
Ladywood Ter. HX1: Hal 1E **149**
LA Fitness
Yeadon 6F **41**
Lairum Ri. LS23: Cliff 6B **30**
LAISTERDYKE 5B **92**
Laisterdyke BD4: B'frd 5B **92**
Laisteridge La. BD5: B'frd 5C **90**
BD7: B'frd 6A **6** (5C **90**)
Laith Cl. LS16: Leeds 4H **57**
Laithe Cl. BD20: Sils 1D **14**
Laithe Fld. HX4: Bark 6B **158**
Laithe Gro. BD6: B'frd 3A **110**
Laithe Hall Av. BD19: Cleck 6A **134**
Laithe Rd. BD6: B'frd 4B **110**
Laith Gdns. LS16: Leeds 4A **58**
Laith Gth. LS16: Leeds 4H **57**
Laith Grn. LS16: Leeds 4H **57**
Laith Rd. LS16: Leeds 4H **57**
Laith Wlk. LS16: Leeds 4H **57**
Lakeland Ct. LS15: Leeds 5H **99**
Lakeland Cres. LS17: Leeds 1G **59**
Lakeland Dr. LS17: Leeds 1H **59**
Lake Row BD4: B'frd 6H **91**
Lakeside BD20: E Mor 3A **36**
Lakeside Chase LS19: Raw 3G **55**
Lakeside Cl. LS29: I'ly 4C **10**
Lakeside Ct. LS10: Leeds 3B **118**
Lakeside Gdns. LS19: Raw 3G **55**
Lakeside Ind. Est.
LS12: Leeds 4G **95**
Lakeside Rd. LS12: Leeds 5G **95**
Lakeside Ter. LS19: Raw 3G **55**
Lakeside Vw. LS19: Raw 3G **55**
Lakeside Wlk. *LS19: Raw 3G **55***
(off Lakeside Ter.)
Lake St. BD4: B'frd 6H **91**
BD21: Keigh 4C **34**
*LS10: Leeds 3B **118***
(off Norwich Av.)
Lake Ter. LS10: Leeds 3B **118**
Lake Vw. HX3: Hal 1A **164** (1G **149**)
Lakeview Ct. LS8: Leeds 1G **79**
La Liga Soccer Cen. 3D **92**
Lamb Cote Rd. HD2: Hud 5D **162**
Lambert Av. LS8: Leeds 3D **78**
Lambert Cl. HX4: Gree 4H **159**
Lambert Dr. LS8: Leeds 3D **78**
Lambert Pl. *BD2: B'frd 1H **91***
(off Thirlmere Gdns.)
Lambert's Arc. LS1: Leeds 5F **5**
Lambert St. HX4: Gree 4H **159**
Lamberts Yd. LS26: Rothw 2A **142**
Lambert Ter. LS18: H'fth 1C **74**
(Parkside)
LS18: H'fth 6G **57**
(Springfield Cl.)
Lambourne Av. BD10: B'frd 4B **72**
Lambrigg Cres. LS14: Leeds 5C **80**
Lamb Springs La. BD17: Bail 1G **53**
Lambton Gro. LS8: Leeds 5D **78**
Lambton Pl. LS8: Leeds 5D **78**
Lambton St. LS8: Leeds 5D **78**
Lambton Ter. LS8: Leeds 5D **78**
Lambton Vw. LS8: Leeds 5D **78**
Lammas Ct. LS14: S'cft 6D **44**
Lampards Cl. BD15: All 1C **88**
Lanark Dr. LS18: H'fth 3D **56**
Lancaster Ct. *BD21: Keigh 2H **47***
(off Victoria Rd.)
Lancaster Pl. *LS26: Rothw 3B **142***
(off Royds La.)
Lancaster Way LS19: Yead 5A **42**
Lancastre Av. LS5: Leeds 6H **75**
(not continuous)
Lancastre Gro. LS5: Leeds 6H **75**
Lancefield Ho. WF1: Out 4F **157**
Lancet Ri. WF3: Rob H 4E **141**
Landemere Syke HX3: North 3C **130**
Landmark Ct. LS11: Leeds 2F **117**
Landmark Ho. BD1: B'frd 4D **6**
Landor St. BD21: Keigh 5B **34**
Landown Ho. HX1: Hal 3C **164**
Landscove Av. BD4: B'frd 3C **112**
Landseer Av. LS13: Leeds 6G **75**
WF3: Ting 1E **155**
Landseer Cl. LS13: Leeds 6F **75**
Landseer Cres. LS13: Leeds 6G **75**
Landseer Dr. LS13: Leeds 6F **75**
Landseer Gdns. LS13: Leeds 6F **75**
Landseer Grn. LS13: Leeds 6F **75**
Landseer Gro. LS13: Leeds 6G **75**
Landseer Mt. LS13: Leeds 6G **75**
Landseer Ri. LS13: Leeds 6F **75**
Landseer Rd. LS13: Leeds 6F **75**
Landseer Ter. LS13: Leeds 6G **75**
Landseer Vw. LS13: Leeds 6G **75**
Landseer Wlk. *LS13: Leeds 6F **75***
(off Landseer Way)
Landseer Way LS13: Leeds 6F **75**
Lands Head La. HX3: North 3B **130**
Landsholme Ct. BD4: B'frd 3D **112**
Lands La. BD10: B'frd 4A **72**
LS1: Leeds 4E **5** (3A **98**)
LS20: Guis 4C **40**
Landsmoor Gro. BD16: Bgly 2D **50**
Land St. LS28: Fars 6H **73**
Lane, The LS9: Leeds 4C **98**
LS17: Leeds 2F **59**
Lane Ct. *HD6: Brigh 6B **152***
(off Old La.)
LANE END 2D **108**
Lane End BD13: Thorn 5H **87**
*BD14: Clay 2E **109***
(off Station Rd.)
*BD16: Har 6F **49***
(off Harden Rd.)
BD17: Bail 4C **52**
LS28: Pud 3B **94**
(not continuous)
Lane End Ct. LS17: Leeds 2F **59**
Lane End Cft. LS17: Leeds 2F **59**
Lane End Fold LS28: Pud 3B **94**
Lane End Mt. LS28: Pud 3B **94**
Lane End Pl. LS11: Leeds 6H **97**
LANE ENDS
BD22 5B **46**
LS18 4B **56**
Lane Ends HX2: Hal 2G **147**
HX2: Lud 6D **126**
HX3: Hal 5C **128**
HX3: North 5E **131**
HX6: Sow B 5B **146**
(Mirey La.)
HX6: Sow B 6A **148**
(Spark Ho. La.)
Lane Ends Cl. BD8: B'frd 3H **89**
Lane Ends Grn. HX3: Hip 1D **150**
Lane Ends Ter. HX3: Hip 1E **151**
Lane Fox Ct. *LS19: Yead 1F **55***
(off Harper La.)
LANE HEAD 6H **151**
Lane Head La. HX2: Ogd 5A **106**
Lane Ho. Gro. HX2: Lud M 1E **147**
Lanes, The LS28: Pud 3B **94**
Lane Side BD12: Wyke 3B **132**
BD13: Que 2G **107**
BD15: Wils 5F **67**
LS12: Pud 1D **114**
Laneside LS27: Chur 6B **116**
Laneside Cl. LS27: Morl 6B **116**
Laneside Fold LS27: Morl 6B **116**
Laneside Gdns. LS27: Morl 6B **116**
Laneside M. LS27: Chur 6B **116**
Laneside Ter. *LS27: Chur 6B **116***
(off Elland Rd.)
Lane Top BD13: Denh 1B **86**
Langbar App. LS14: Leeds 3F **81**
Langbar Av. BD9: B'frd 6F **69**
Langbar Cl. LS14: Leeds 3F **81**
Langbar Gdns. LS14: Leeds 4F **81**
Langbar Gth. LS14: Leeds 3F **81**
Langbar Grn. LS14: Leeds 3F **81**
Langbar Gro. LS14: Leeds 4F **81**
Langbar Pl. LS14: Leeds 3F **81**
Langbar Rd. LS14: Leeds 4F **81**
LS29: I'ly 3C **10**
Langbar Sq. LS14: Leeds 4F **81**
Langbar Vw. LS14: Leeds 3F **81**
Langdale Av. BD8: B'frd 3G **89**
BD12: Wyke 6E **133**
LS6: Leeds 4C **76**
WF1: Out 4H **157**
Langdale Cl. LS22: Weth 3C **12**
Langdale Ct. BD16: Bgly 3C **50**
Langdale Cres. HX2: Hal 6C **128**
Langdale Dr. BD13: Que 4H **107**
Langdale Gdns. LS6: Leeds 5C **76**
Langdale Rd. BD10: B'frd 5C **72**
LS26: Wood 1D **142**
Langdales HX6: Sow B 5G **147**
Langdale St. HX5: Ell 5B **160**
Langdale Ter. LS6: Leeds 5C **76**
Langford Cl. LS29: Burl W 2E **21**
Langford Ct. LS29: Burl W 2D **20**
Langford La. LS29: Burl W 2E **21**
Langford M. LS29: Burl W 2E **21**
Langford Ride LS29: Burl W 2F **21**
Langford Rd. LS29: Burl W 2E **21**
Langlands Rd. BD16: Cot 2C **68**
Lang La. BD2: B'frd 4D **70**
Langlea Ter. HX3: Hip 1E **151**
LANGLEY 1F **157**
Langley Av. BD4: B'frd 4H **111**
BD16: Bgly 3C **50**
LS13: Leeds 5C **74**
Langley Cl. LS13: Leeds 5C **74**
Langley Cres. BD17: Bail 4E **53**
LS13: Leeds 5D **74**
Langley Gth. LS13: Leeds 5C **74**
Langley Gro. BD16: Bgly 3C **50**
Langley La. BD17: Bail 3E **53**
Langley Mt. LS13: Leeds 5D **74**
Langley Pl. LS13: Leeds 5C **74**
Langley Rd. BD16: Bgly 3C **50**
LS13: Leeds 5C **74**
Langley Ter. LS13: Leeds 5C **74**
Langport Cl. BD13: Que 4B **108**
Langsett Cft. HD2: Hud 6E **163**
Langthorne Ct. LS27: Morl 5C **138**
Langton Av. BD4: B'frd 4H **111**
Langton Cl. BD19: Gom 5F **135**
Langton Grn. LS12: Leeds 6C **96**
Langton St. HX6: Sow B 4H **147**
Langtons Wharf LS2: Leeds 6G **5**
Langwith Av. LS22: Coll 3A **28**
Langwith Ct. HX1: Hal 4F **149**
Langwith Dr. LS22: Coll 3G **27**
Langwith M. LS22: Coll 3A **28**
Langwith Ter. LS22: Coll 3H **27**
Langwith Valley Rd. LS22: Coll 3G **27**
(not continuous)
Langwith Wood Ct. LS22: Coll 3H **27**
Lansdale Ct. BD4: B'frd 3D **112**
Lansdowne Cl. BD17: Bail 4F **53**
Lansdowne Ho. *BD8: B'frd 2C **90***
(off Trenton Dr.)
Lansdowne Pl.
BD5: B'frd 6B **6** (5D **90**)
Lansdowne St. LS12: Leeds 5C **96**
Lanshaw Cl. LS10: Leeds 1C **140**
Lanshaw Cres. LS10: Leeds 2C **140**
Lanshaw Pl. LS10: Leeds 1C **140**
Lanshaw Rd. LS10: Leeds 1C **140**
Lanshaw Ter. LS10: Leeds 1C **140**
Lanshaw Vw. LS10: Leeds 1C **140**
Lanshaw Wlk. LS10: Leeds 1C **140**
Lapage St. BD3: B'frd 4A **92**
Lapage Ter. BD3: B'frd 5A **92**

Lapwing Cl. BD8: B'frd 4D 88
  WF10: All B 3H 145
Larch Cl. BD22: Oak 5D 46
  HX2: Hal 5B 128
  WF17: Birs 5C 136
Larch Cft. LS29: Burl W 2E 21
Larch Dr. BD6: B'frd 6C 110
Larches, The LS14: Leeds 5E 81
Larchfield Home LS10: Leeds . . .1C 118
Larchfield Rd. LS10: Leeds 6C 98
Larch Gro. BD16: Bgly 2C 50
  BD17: Bail 6G 51
Larch Hill BD6: B'frd 6D 110
Larch Hill Cres. BD6: B'frd 5D 110
Larch La. LS25: Gar 5H 103
Larchmont BD14: Clay 1E 109
Larch St. BD21: Keigh 3H 47
Larch Wood LS14: S'cft 6E 45
Larchwood LS19: Raw 5G 55
LARKFIELD 3G 55
Larkfield BD9: B'frd 6H 69
  BD20: Rid 1C 34
Larkfield Av. LS19: Raw 3G 55
Larkfield Ct. HD6: Brigh 6A 152
Larkfield Cres. LS19: Raw 3G 55
Larkfield Dr. LS19: Raw 3G 55
Larkfield Mt. LS19: Raw 3G 55
Larkfield Rd. LS19: Raw 3G 55
  LS28: Pud 3A 94
Larkfield Ter. BD21: Keigh 1C 48
  BD22: Oak 5D 46
     (off Keighley Rd.)
Lark Hill WF17: Bat 6C 136
Lark Hill Av. BD19: Cleck 3H 153
Lark Hill Cl. BD19: Cleck 3H 153
Larkhill Cl. LS8: Leeds 1C 78
Lark Hill Dr. BD19: Cleck 3H 153
Larkhill Grn. LS8: Leeds 6C 60
Larkhill Rd. LS8: Leeds 6C 60
Larkhill Vw. LS8: Leeds 1C 78
Larkhill Wlk. LS8: Leeds 6C 60
Larkhill Way LS8: Leeds 6C 60
Lark St. BD16: Bgly 4B 50
  BD21: Keigh 6H 33
  BD22: Haw 2D 64
  BD22: Oak 5D 46
Lark Vale BD16: Bgly 3E 51
Larwood Cl. BD10: B'frd 5C 72
Larwood Dr. BD10: B'frd 5C 72
La Salle LS10: Leeds 5B 98
Lascelles Mt. *LS8: Leeds* 6D 78
    (off Lascelles Rd. E.)
Lascelles Pl. LS8: Leeds 6D 78
Lascelles Rd. E. LS8: Leeds 6D 78
Lascelles Rd. W. LS8: Leeds 6D 78
Lascelles St. LS8: Leeds 6D 78
Lascelles Ter. LS8: Leeds 6D 78
Lascelles Vw. LS8: Leeds 6D 78
Lastingham Grn. BD6: B'frd 4G 109
Lastingham Rd. LS13: Leeds 4B 74
Latchmere Av. LS16: Leeds 1H 75
Latchmere Cl. LS16: Leeds 1A 76
Latchmere Crest LS16: Leeds 1H 75
Latchmere Cross LS16: Leeds 1H 75
Latchmere Dr. LS16: Leeds 1H 75
Latchmere Gdns. LS16: Leeds 6A 58
Latchmere Grn. LS16: Leeds 1H 75
Latchmere Rd. LS16: Leeds 1H 75
Latchmere Vw. LS16: Leeds 1H 75
    (not continuous)
Latchmere Wlk. LS16: Leeds 6A 58
Latchmore Ind. Est. LS12: Leeds . .1D 116
Latchmore Pl. LS12: Leeds 1E 117
Latham Ct. BD19: Gom 5F 135
Latham La. BD19: Gom 4E 135
Latham Lea BD19: Gom 5E 135
Latimer Cl. LS20: Guis 3B 40
Latimer Way LS20: Guis 3B 40
Launceston Dr. BD4: B'frd 3C 112
Laura St. HD6: Ras 3B 162
  HX3: Hal 1C 164 (6G 129)
Laureates, The *LS20: Guis* 5C 40
    (off Shakespeare Rd.)

Laurel Bank BD12: Wyke 1C 152
  BD16: Bgly 3E 51
  HX2: Hal 6E 107
  HX2: Lud 6E 127
  LS15: Leeds 5F 81
Laurel Bank Cl. HX2: Hal 1E 129
Laurel Bank Ct. LS6: Leeds 5C 76
Laurel Cl. HX3: She 6E 109
  HX5: Ell 5A 160
  LS17: E Kes 6E 27
Laurel Cres. BD21: Keigh 5H 33
  HX2: Hal 4D 128
Laurel Fold LS12: Leeds 4C 96
Laurel Gro. BD16: Bgly 2A 50
  BD20: Sils 2D 14
  BD21: Keigh 5H 33
  LS12: Leeds 4C 96
Laurel Hill Av. LS15: Leeds 5F 101
Laurel Hill Cft. LS15: Leeds 4F 101
Laurel Hill Gdns. LS15: Leeds 4F 101
Laurel Hill Gro. LS15: Leeds 4F 101
Laurel Hill Vw. LS15: Leeds 4F 101
Laurel Hill Way LS15: Leeds 5F 101
Laurel Mt. HX1: Hal 4E 149
  HX6: Sow B 4H 147
     (off Bright St.)
  LS7: Leeds 4B 78
  LS28: Stan 3A 94
Laurel Pk. BD15: Wils 5G 67
Laurel Pl. LS10: Leeds 3H 139
  LS12: Leeds 4C 96
Laurels, The BD16: Bgly 4D 50
  LS8: Leeds 3D 78
  LS10: Leeds 4B 140
Laurel St. BD3: B'frd 5A 92
  HX1: Hal 4E 149
  LS12: Leeds 4C 96
Laurel Ter. LS12: Leeds 4C 96
  LS15: Leeds 5F 81
    (off Stanks La. Sth.)
  LS28: Stan 3A 94
Laurence Ct. LS26: Wood 6F 121
Lauren Dr. *BD22: Keigh* 3G 47
    (off Wirefield Rd.)
Lavell M. BD2: B'frd 6A 72
Lavender Cl. BD18: Ship 4D 70
Lavender Hill BD10: B'frd 4A 72
Lavender Wlk. LS9: Leeds 4D 98
Laverack Fld. BD12: Wyke 4C 132
Laverock Cres. HD6: Brigh 4H 151
Laverock La. HD6: Brigh 4H 151
Laverock Pl. HD6: Brigh 4H 151
    (off Laverock La.)
Laverton Rd. BD4: B'frd 1H 111
Lavinia Ter. BD14: Clay 1F 109
Lawcliffe Cres. BD22: Haw 1D 64
Law Cl. LS22: Weth 2F 13
Lawfield Av. LS26: Rothw 1G 141
Lawkholme Cres. BD21: Keigh 6A 34
Lawkholme La. BD21: Keigh 6A 34
Law La. HX3: Sow 4B 150
Lawler Cl. *HX3: Hal* 4D 128
    (off Rugby Gdns.)
Lawn, The LS29: Burl W 2F 21
Lawn Av. LS29: Burl W 2F 21
Lawn Rd. LS29: Burl W 2F 21
LAWNS .3C 156
Lawns WF2: Carr G 3C 156
Lawns, The HX3: Hal 6F 149
  LS29: I'ly 5C 10
    (off Church St.)
Lawns Av. LS12: N Far 2F 115
Lawns Cl. LS12: N Far 2F 115
  WF2: Carr G 4C 156
Lawns Cres. LS12: N Far 2F 115
Lawns Cft. LS12: N Far 2F 115
Lawns Dene LS12: N Far 2F 115
Lawns Dr. LS12: N Far 2F 115
Lawns Grn. LS12: N Far 2F 115
Lawns Hall Cl. LS16: Leeds 4B 58
Lawns La. LS10: Leeds 2C 118
  LS12: N Far 1F 115
  WF2: Carr G 4C 156

Lawns Mt. LS12: N Far 2F 115
Lawns Sq. LS12: N Far 2F 115
Lawns Ter. LS12: N Far 2F 115
  WF3: E Ard 2B 156
LAWNSWOOD 5A 58
Lawnswood Bus. Pk.
  LS16: Leeds 6A 58
Lawnswood Crematorium
  LS16: Leeds 4B 58
Lawnswood Gdns. LS16: Leeds 5B 58
Lawnswood Rd. BD21: Keigh 2G 47
Lawn Wlk. LS29: Burl W 2F 21
Lawrence Av. LS8: Leeds 5G 79
Lawrence Ct. LS28: Pud 5H 93
Lawrence Cres. LS8: Leeds 5G 79
Lawrence Dr. BD7: B'frd 3G 109
Lawrence Gdns. LS8: Leeds 4G 79
Lawrence Rd. HX3: Hal 6F 149
  LS8: Leeds 5G 79
Lawrence St. HX3: Hal 6E 129
Lawrence Wlk. LS8: Leeds 5G 79
Lawson Ct. LS28: Fars 6A 74
Lawson Rd. HD6: Brigh 1B 162
Lawson St. BD3: B'frd 1E 7 (3F 91)
  LS12: Leeds 4B 96
Lawson Wood Ct. LS6: Leeds 6F 59
Lawson Wood Dr. LS6: Leeds 6F 59
Law St. BD4: B'frd 3A 112
  BD19: Cleck 6B 134
LAYCOCK 6C 32
Laycock La. BD22: Lay 1C 46
Laycock Pl. LS7: Leeds 6B 78
Lay Garth LS26: Rothw 3A 142
Lay Gth. Cl. LS26: Rothw 2A 142
Lay Gth. Ct. LS26: Rothw 3A 142
Lay Gth. Fold LS26: Rothw 3A 142
Lay Gth. Gdns. LS26: Rothw 3A 142
Lay Gth. Grn. LS26: Rothw 3A 142
Lay Gth. Mead
  LS26: Rothw 3A 142
Lay Gth. Pl. LS26: Rothw 3A 142
Lay Gth. Sq. LS26: Rothw 2A 142
Laythorp Ter. BD20: E Mor 4H 35
Layton Av. LS19: Raw 4H 55
Layton Cl. LS19: Raw 5A 56
Layton Cres. LS19: Raw 4H 55
Layton Dr. LS19: Raw 4A 56
Layton La. LS19: Raw 5A 56
Layton Mt. LS19: Raw 4H 55
Layton Pk. Av. LS19: Raw 5A 56
Layton Pk. Cl. LS19: Raw 4H 55
Layton Pk. Cft. LS19: Raw 5A 56
Layton Pk. Dr. LS19: Raw 4H 55
Layton Ri. LS18: H'fth 4B 56
Layton Rd. LS18: H'fth 4A 56
  LS19: Raw 4A 56
Lazenby Dr. LS22: Weth 3D 12
Lazenby Fold LS22: Weth 3D 12
Lea, The LS25: Gar 6F 103
Lea Av. HX3: Hal 6G 149
Leabank Av. LS25: Gar 6G 103
Leach Cres. BD20: Rid 3C 34
Leach Ri. BD20: Rid 3C 34
Leach Rd. BD20: Rid 3B 34
Leach Way BD20: Rid 3C 34
Lea Cl. HD6: Brigh 5A 152
Lea Ct. BD7: B'frd 3G 109
Lea Cft. LS21: Otley 4E 23
  LS23: Cliff 6B 30
Leadenhall St. HX1: Hal 4D 148
Leadwell La. LS26: Rothw 4F 141
  WF3: Rob H 4F 141
Lea Farm Cres. LS5: Leeds 3H 75
Lea Farm Dr. LS5: Leeds 2H 75
Lea Farm Gro. LS5: Leeds 3H 75
Lea Farm Mt. LS5: Leeds 2H 75
Lea Farm Pl. LS5: Leeds 3H 75
Lea Farm Rd. LS5: Leeds 2G 75
Lea Farm Row LS5: Leeds 3H 75
Lea Farm Wlk. LS5: Leeds 2H 75
Leafield Av. BD2: B'frd 5A 72
Leafield Cl. LS17: Leeds 5H 59
Leafield Cres. BD2: B'frd 5H 71

Leafield Dr. BD2: B'frd 5A 72
  LS17: Leeds 5H 59
  LS28: Pud 6B 94
Leafield Grange LS17: Leeds 5H 59
Leafield Gro. BD2: B'frd 6A 72
Leafield La. LS21: Leat 1E 25
Leafield Pl. LS19: Yead 6D 40
Leafield Ter. BD2: B'frd 6A 72
Leafield Towers LS17: Leeds 5H 59
Leafield Vs. LS19: Yead 6D 40
                 (off Leafield Pl.)
Leafield Way BD2: B'frd 6A 72
Leafland St. HX1: Hal 2E 149
Leaf St. BD22: Haw 1E 65
Leafsway BD6: B'frd 1H 131
Leah Pl. LS12: Leeds 5F 97
Leah Row LS12: Leeds 5F 97
Lea Mill Pk. Cl. LS19: Yead 6E 41
Lea Mill Pk. Dr. LS19: Yead 6E 41
Leamington Dr. BD10: B'frd 1A 72
Leamington Rd. LS2: I'ly 4E 11
Leamington St. BD9: B'frd 1B 90
Leamington Ter. LS29: I'ly 4E 11
Leamside Wlk. BD4: B'frd 3C 112
Lea Pk. Cl. LS10: Leeds 6D 118
Lea Pk. Cft. LS10: Leeds 6E 119
Lea Pk. Dr. LS10: Leeds 6D 118
Lea Pk. Gdns. LS10: Leeds 6D 118
Lea Pk. Gth. LS10: Leeds 6D 118
Lea Pk. Gro. LS10: Leeds 6D 118
Lea Pk. Va. LS10: Leeds 6E 119
Leaside Dr. BD13: Thorn 4H 87
Leasowe Av. LS10: Leeds 3C 118
Leasowe Cl. LS10: Leeds 3C 118
Leasowe Ct. LS10: Leeds 3C 118
             (off Springfield Pl.)
Leasowe Gdns. LS10: Leeds 3D 118
Leasowe Gth. LS10: Leeds 3C 118
Leasowe Rd. LS10: Leeds 3C 118
Lea Ter. LS17: Leeds 6A 60
Leather Bank LS29: Burl W 1E 21
LEATHLEY 1C 24
Leathley Av. LS29: Men 2H 39
Leathley Cl. LS29: Men 1H 39
Leathley Cres. LS29: Men 1H 39
Leathley La. LS21: Leat, Otley 1C 24
  LS29: Men 1H 39
Leathley Rd. LS10: Leeds 6A 98
  LS29: Men 1H 39
Leavens, The BD10: B'frd 1B 72
LEAVENTHORPE 5E 89
Leaventhorpe Av. BD8: B'frd 4E 89
Leaventhorpe Cl. BD8: B'frd 4F 89
Leaventhorpe Gro. BD13: Thorn 5E 89
Leaventhorpe La. BD8: B'frd 5D 88
  BD13: Thorn 5D 88
Leaventhorpe Way BD8: B'frd 4F 89
Lea Vw. LS18: H'fth 6D 56
Leavington Cl. BD6: B'frd 1B 132
Leconfield Ct. LS22: Weth 3C 12
Leconfield Ho. BD10: B'frd 2A 72
  LS29: I'ly 5D 10
             (off Springs La.)
Ledbury Av. LS10: Leeds 3D 140
Ledbury Cl. LS10: Leeds 3D 140
Ledbury Cft. LS10: Leeds 3D 140
Ledbury Dr. LS10: Leeds 3D 140
Ledbury Grn. LS10: Leeds 3D 140
Ledbury Gro. LS10: Leeds 3C 140
Ledbury Pl. BD4: B'frd 1H 111
Ledgard Way LS12: Leeds 3C 96
Ledger La. WF1: Out 4F 157
  WF3: Loft 6G 141
Ledger Pl. WF1: Out 5F 157
LEDSHAM 5H 125
Ledston Av. LS25: Gar 6G 103
LEDSTON LUCK 3B 124
Ledston Luck Cotts. LS25: Kip 3C 124
Ledston Luck Ent. Pk. LS25: Kip 3B 124
Ledston Luck Vs. LS25: Kip 3B 124
Ledston Mill La. WF10: Leeds 6C 124
Lee Bank HX3: Hal 1A 164 (6F 129)
Lee Bri. HX3: Hal 1A 164 (1F 149)
Lee Bri. Ind. Est.
  HX3: Hal 1A 164 (1F 149)
Leech La. BD16: Har 1D 66
Lee Cl. BD15: Wils 3G 67
Lee Ct. BD21: Keigh 1D 48
LEEDS 4E 5 (3A 98)
Leeds 27 Ind. Est. LS27: Morl 2G 137
Leeds and Bradford Rd.
  LS5: Leeds 4E 75
  LS13: Leeds 4E 75
  LS28: Stan 1B 94
Leeds Aquatic Cen. 5A 118
Leeds Arena 2E 5 (2A 98)
LEEDS BRADFORD
  INTERNATIONAL AIRPORT 6A 42
Leeds Bus. Centre, The
  LS27: Morl 2G 137
Leeds Carnegie RUFC
  Headingley Carnegie Stadium
                       . . . .5D 76
Leeds City Art Gallery 3D 4 (3H 97)
Leeds City Mus. 2D 4 (2H 97)
Leeds City Office Pk. LS11: Leeds . . .5A 98
Leeds Corn Exchange LS2: Leeds . . .5F 5
Leeds Golf Course 1H 79
Leeds La. LS26: Swil 6A 102
Leeds Metropolitan University
  City Campus 1D 4 (1H 97)
  Headingley Campus 3B 76
  Leslie Silver Building
                . . . .1D 4 (2H 97)
Leeds Metropolitan University Sports Cen.
                      . . . .3B 76
Leeds Museum Discovery Cen. 5C 98
Leeds Old Rd. BD3: B'frd 3B 92
Leeds Rhinos RLFC 5D 76
Leeds Rd. BD1: B'frd 4E 7 (4F 91)
              (not continuous)
  BD2: B'frd 5H 71
  BD3: B'frd 4E 7 (4F 91)
  BD10: B'frd 1C 70
  BD18: B'frd, Ship 1C 70
  HD2: Hud 6G 163
  HD5: Hud 6G 163
  HX3: Hal 6B 130
  HX3: Hip 1F 151
  LS15: Bar E, Scho 5G 81
  LS16: B'hpe 5G 23
  LS19: Raw 3F 55
  LS20: Guis 5C 40
  LS21: Otley, Pool 4F 23
              (not continuous)
  LS22: Coll 4H 27
  LS22: Coll, Weth 2D 28
  LS25: Gar, Kip 1F 123
  LS26: Meth 4A 144
  LS26: Oul, Rothw 6B 120
  LS29: I'ly 5D 10
  WF1: Out, Wake 5F 157
  WF3: Loft, Rob H 3F 141
  WF10: All B 1E 145
  WF12: Dew 6A 154
  WF14: Liv, Mir 4H 163
  WF17: Bat, Birs 6B 136
Leeds Rugby Academy 6A 76
Leeds Sailing & Activity Cen. 6A 76
Leeds Station (Rail) 6D 4 (4H 97)
Leeds St. BD21: Keigh 6H 33
Leeds United FC 2E 117
Leeds University Business School
                      . . . .1F 97
Leeds University Medical Cen. . . .1H 97
             (off Blenheim Wlk.)
Leeds Valley Pk. LS10: Leeds 5F 119
Leeds Wall, The 6E 97
Lee Edge LS10: Leeds 3B 140
Lee Fair Ct. WF3: W Ard 3D 154
Lee La. BD15: Wils 3F 67
  BD16: Cot 2G 67
  BD22: Oxen 6A 64
  HX3: Hal 4G 129
Lee La. E. LS18: H'fth 5D 56
Lee La. W. LS18: H'fth 5B 56

LEEMING 2D 84
Leemingbeck Cl. BD22: Oxen 6C 64
                 (off West Dr.)
Leeming St. BD1: B'frd 2E 7 (3F 91)
LEE MOUNT 6E 129
Lee Mt. Gdns. HX3: Hal 6E 129
Lee Mt. Rd. HX3: Hal 6E 129
Lee Orchards LS23: B Spa 3C 30
LEES 1E 65
Lees Bank Av. BD22: Cros R 1E 65
Lees Bank Dr. BD22: Cros R 1E 65
Lees Bank Hill BD22: Cros R 1E 65
Lees Bank Rd. BD22: Cros R 1E 65
Lees Bldgs. HX3: Hip 1E 151
Lees Cl. BD13: Cull 3A 66
Lees Ct. BD13: Cull 2D 64
  HX3: Hip 6G 131
  LS28: Fars 5H 73
Lees Moor 1H 65
Lees Moor Mdw. BD13: Cull 3A 66
Lees Moor Rd. BD13: Cull 3A 66
Lee St. BD13: Que 5H 107
  HD6: Brigh 5A 152
Leesworth Ct. BD22: Cros R 1E 65
             (off Haworth Rd.)
Lee Ter. BD12: O'haw 2F 133
Legrams Av. BD7: B'frd 6H 89
Legrams La. BD7: B'frd 6A 90
Legrams Mill La. BD7: B'frd 5A 90
Legrams St. BD7: B'frd 4B 90
Legrams Ter. BD7: B'frd 4C 90
Leicester Cl. LS7: Leeds 1H 97
Leicester Cres. LS29: I'ly 5D 10
Leicester Gro. LS7: Leeds 1H 97
Leicester Pl. LS2: Leeds 1H 97
  LS7: Leeds 1H 97
Leicester St. BD4: B'frd 1G 111
Leicester Ter. HX3: Hal 5F 149
Leigh Av. WF3: Ting 1G 155
Leigh Rd. WF3: Ting 1G 155
Leigh St. HX6: Sow B 4A 148
Leighton Pl. LS1: Leeds 3C 4
Leighton St. LS1: Leeds 3B 4 (3H 97)
Leigh Vw. WF3: Ting 1F 155
Leisure Exchange, The 5F 7
Leith Ho. BD4: B'frd 2C 112
             (off Stirling Cres.)
Leith St. BD21: Keigh 5H 33
Le Mar Vw. HX3: Sou 3A 150
Lemington Av. HX1: Hal 3E 149
Lemonroyd Marina LS26: Oul 2A 144
Lemon St. BD5: B'frd 2C 110
  HX1: Hal 2D 148
Leng Dr. BD3: B'frd 4D 92
Lenham Cl. LS27: Morl 5A 138
Lenhurst Av. LS12: Leeds 6H 75
Lennie St. BD21: Keigh 1H 47
Lennon Dr. BD8: B'frd 3B 90
Lennox Gdns. LS15: Leeds 4E 101
Lennox Rd. LS4: Leeds 2D 96
Lens Dr. BD17: Bail 3C 52
Lentilfield St. HX3: Hal 5E 129
Lentilfield Ter. HX3: Hal 5E 129
Lenton Dr. LS11: Leeds 3A 118
Lenton Vs. BD10: B'frd 6H 53
Leodis Cl. LS11: Leeds 5H 97
Leodis Ho. LS10: Leeds 4G 119
Leodis Residences LS6: Leeds 6H 77
Leodis Way LS10: Leeds 5F 119
Leonard's Pl. BD16: Bgly 5C 50
Leonard St. BD12: Wyke 4D 132
  BD16: Bgly 5C 50
Leonore Cft. HX3: North 5C 130
Leopold Gdns. LS7: Leeds 6C 78
Leopold Gro. LS7: Leeds 6B 78
Leopold St. LS7: Leeds 6B 78
Lepton Hare Chase LS10: Leeds 5A 140
Lepton Pl. LS27: Gil 6F 115
Leslie Av. LS19: Yead 5G 41
Leslie Ter. LS6: Leeds 6G 77
Lesmere Gro. BD7: B'frd 3H 109
Lessarna Ct. BD4: B'frd 6A 92
Leven Gdns. LS22: Weth 2D 12

Levens Bank LS15: Leeds 5H 99
Levens Cl. LS15: Leeds 5A 100
Levens Gth. LS15: Leeds 5A 100
Levens Pl. LS15: Leeds 5A 100
Leventhorpe Ct. LS26: Oul 2E 143
Leventhorpe Way LS26: Oul 2E 143
Leveret Way WF17: Bat 6D 136
Lever St. BD6: B'frd 4A 110
Levisham Cl. BD10: B'frd 4B 72
Levita Gro. BD4: B'frd 1B 112
Levita Pl. BD4: B'frd 6C 92
   LS15: Leeds 3A 100
Lewis Bldgs. LS29: Burl W 2F 21
Lewis Cl. BD13: Que 4H 107
Lewisham Ct. LS27: Morl 3B 138
Lewisham Gro. LS27: Morl 3B 138
Lewisham St. LS27: Morl 4G 137
Lexington Cl. BD4: B'frd 5H 111
Leyburn Av. HX3: Hip 1G 151
Leyburne St. BD8: B'frd 2C 90
Leyburn Gro. BD16: Bgly 3C 50
   BD18: Ship 2A 70
Leyden Ri. BD15: All 3D 88
Leyfield BD17: Bail 4A 52
Ley Fleaks Rd. BD10: B'frd 2H 71
   (not continuous)
Leyland Cft. HD2: Hud 5E 163
Leyland Rd. WF17: Birs 6H 135
LEYLANDS, THE 2F 5
Leylands Av. BD9: B'frd 6H 69
Leylands Gro. BD9: B'frd 6H 69
Leylands Ho. BD21: Keigh 1B 48
Leylands La. BD9: B'frd 6H 69
   BD21: Keigh 1B 48
Leylands Rd. LS2: Leeds 2H 5 (2B 98)
Leylands Ter. BD9: B'frd 6H 69
Ley La. LS12: Leeds 3D 96
Leys Cl. BD10: B'frd 6G 53
Leysholme Cres. LS12: Leeds 5A 96
Leysholme Dr. LS12: Leeds 6B 96
Leysholme Ter. LS12: Leeds 5B 96
Leysholme Vw. LS12: Leeds 5B 96
Leyside Dr. BD15: All 1D 88
Leys La. LS23: B Spa 3H 29
Leyton Cres. BD10: B'frd 2H 71
Leyton Dr. BD10: B'frd 2H 71
Leyton Gro. BD10: B'frd 2H 71
Leyton Ter. BD10: B'frd 2H 71
Ley Top La. BD15: All 3E 89
Leywell Ter. LS12: Leeds 3A 96
Libbey St. BD8: B'frd 2C 90
Liberty Pk. LS1: Leeds 4A 4
Liberty Vw. LS27: Morl 2A 138
   (off Chapel Hill)
Lichen Cl. BD17: B'frd 2A 110
Lichfield Mt. BD2: B'frd 5E 71
Lickless Av. LS18: H'fth 6F 57
Lickless Dr. LS18: H'fth 6F 57
Lickless Gdns. LS18: H'fth 6F 57
Lickless Ter. LS18: H'fth 6F 57
LIDGET .5D 46
Lidget Av. BD7: B'frd 6H 89
LIDGET GREEN 5A 90
Lidget Hill LS28: Pud 4A 94
Lidget Pl. BD7: B'frd 6H 89
LIDGETT 5E 103
Lidgett Av. LS8: Leeds 2D 78
Lidgett Ct. LS8: Leeds 1D 78
   LS25: Gar 5E 103
Lidgett Cres. LS8: Leeds 1D 78
Lidget Ter. BD7: B'frd 6H 89
   BD14: Clay 1F 109
Lidgett Gro. LS8: Leeds 2D 78
Lidgett Hill LS8: Leeds 2D 78
Lidgett La. LS8: Leeds 2D 78
   LS17: Leeds 6B 60
   LS25: Gar 6E 103
Lidgett Mt. LS8: Leeds 6D 60
LIDGETT PARK 1E 79
Lidgett Pk. Av. LS8: Leeds 6D 60
Lidgett Pk. Ct. LS8: Leeds 6D 60

Lidgett Pk. Gdns. LS8: Leeds 1D 78
Lidgett Pk. Gro. LS8: Leeds 1D 78
Lidgett Pk. M. LS8: Leeds 6E 61
Lidgett Pk. Rd. LS8: Leeds 6D 60
   (not continuous)
Lidgett Pk. Vw. LS8: Leeds 6D 60
Lidgett Pl. LS8: Leeds 1D 78
Lidgett Sq. WF10: All B 3H 145
Lidgett Towers LS8: Leeds 6C 60
Lidgett Wlk. LS8: Leeds 2D 78
   (not continuous)
Lifton Pl. LS2: Leeds 1G 97
Light, The LS2: Leeds 3D 4 (3H 97)
Light Bank La. BD20: Sils 5A 8
LIGHTCLIFFE 1G 151
Lightcliffe Golf Course 1G 151
Lightcliffe Rd. HD6: Brigh 4A 152
Lightcliffe Royd HX4: Bark 5A 158
Lightcliffe Royd La.
   HX4: Bark 5A 158
Lighthouse Fold WF3: Loft 1G 157
   (off The Poplars)
Lightowler Cl. HX1: Hal 2E 149
Lightowler Rd. HX1: Hal 2E 149
Lightowler St. BD6: B'frd 4C 110
Lightridge Rd. HD2: Fix 6H 161
Lilac Cl. HD6: Clift 6C 152
   LS29: Add 1E 9
Lilac Ct. LS14: Leeds 1A 100
Lilac Gro. BD4: B'frd 5B 92
   BD18: Ship 4D 70
   BD19: Gom 6E 135
Lilacs, The LS20: Guis 4C 40
Lilac St. HX3: Hal 6E 129
Lilian St. BD4: B'frd 2A 112
Lillands Av. HD6: Ras 1H 161
Lillands La. HD6: Ras 1H 161
Lillands Ter. HD6: Ras 1H 161
Lilly La. HX1: Hal 5D 164 (3H 149)
   (not continuous)
   HX3: Hal 5D 164 (3H 149)
Lilly St. HX6: Sow B 6H 147
Lily Cft. BD8: B'frd 1B 90
Lilycroft Pl. BD8: B'frd 1B 90
Lilycroft Rd. BD9: B'frd 2A 90
Lilycroft Wlk. BD9: B'frd 1A 90
   (not continuous)
Lily St. BD8: B'frd 1B 90
Lilythorne Av. BD10: B'frd 1A 72
Lime Cl. BD20: Keigh 4G 33
   LS29: Add 1B 8
Lime Ct. BD16: Bgly 1A 50
   (off Aire St.)
Lime Dr. LS14: Leeds 1A 100
Limefield Mills BD16: Bgly 1A 50
   (off Wood St.)
Lime Gro. LS7: Leeds 3B 78
   LS19: Yead 3E 55
Limes Av. HX3: Hal 5G 149
Lime St. BD7: B'frd 1A 110
   BD16: Bgly 4B 50
   BD21: Keigh 6H 33
   BD22: Haw 3C 64
Lime Tree Av. HX5: Ell 5C 160
   LS17: Leeds 5C 60
   LS23: B Spa 3B 30
Lime Tree Cl. LS26: Wood 1F 143
Lime Tree Ct. HX6: Sow B 5H 147
Lime Tree Cres. LS25: Kip 4A 124
Limetree Gro. BD11: Birk 6E 113
Lime Tree Sq. BD18: Ship 6F 51
Lime Va. Way BD6: B'frd 4G 109
Limewood App. LS14: Leeds 2C 80
Limewood Bus. Pk. LS14: Leeds 3D 80
Limewood Ct. LS14: Leeds 2C 80
Limewood Rd. LS14: Leeds 3C 80
Limewood Way LS14: Leeds 3D 80
Lincoln Cl. BD8: B'frd 2C 90
Lincoln Cl. LS28: Fars 1H 93
   (off South Dr.)
Lincoln Grn. Ct. LS9: Leeds 2C 98
Lincoln Grn. Rd. LS9: Leeds 2C 98

Lincoln Rd. BD8: B'frd 3C 90
   LS9: Leeds 2C 98
Lincoln St. BD15: All 3E 89
Lincoln Towers LS9: Leeds 2C 98
   (off Lincoln Rd.)
Lincoln Wlk. LS25: Kip 3A 124
Lincoln Way HX3: Hal 6F 129
Lincombe Bank LS8: Leeds 1C 78
Lincombe Dr. LS8: Leeds 1C 78
Lincombe Mt. LS8: Leeds 1C 78
Lincombe Ri. LS8: Leeds 1C 78
Lincroft Cres. LS13: Leeds 5F 75
Lincs Wold WF15: Liv 5H 153
Lindale Cl. LS10: Leeds 6B 118
Lindale Gth. WF2: Kirk 6A 156
Lindale La. WF2: Kirk, Wren 6A 156
Linden Av. BD3: B'frd 3C 92
   LS11: Leeds 2H 117
Linden Cl. HD6: Clift 6C 152
   LS17: Bard 1F 45
Linden Ct. LS16: Leeds 2D 76
   LS26: Rothw 3F 141
Linden Gdns. LS11: Leeds 2A 118
Linden Gro. LS11: Leeds 2A 118
Linden Mt. LS11: Leeds 2H 117
Linden Pl. LS11: Leeds 2A 118
Linden Ri. BD21: Keigh 2C 48
Linden Rd. HX3: Hal 5G 149
   HX5: Ell 5A 160
   LS11: Leeds 2H 117
Linden St. LS11: Leeds 2H 117
Linden Ter. HX3: Hip 2E 151
   (off Barfield Rd.)
   LS11: Leeds 2A 118
Linden Way LS22: Weth 2D 12
Lindholme Gdns. BD15: All 3D 88
Lindisfarne Rd. BD18: Ship 2H 69
Lindley Dr. BD7: B'frd 3H 109
Lindley Rd. BD5: B'frd 2D 110
Lindon St. BD22: Haw 3C 64
Lindrick Cl. HX2: Illing 6D 106
Lindrick Wlk. HX2: Illing 6D 106
Lindrick Way HX2: Illing 6D 106
Lindsay Acre WF3: Ting 1G 155
Lindsay Rd. LS25: Gar 5F 103
Lindsey Ct. LS9: Leeds 2C 98
Lindsey Gdns. LS9: Leeds 2C 98
Lindsey Mt. LS9: Leeds 2C 98
   (off Lindsey Rd.)
Lindsey Rd. LS9: Leeds 2C 98
LINDWELL 3H 159
Lindwell Av. HX4: Gree 4G 159
Lindwell Gro. HX4: Gree 4G 159
Lindwell Pl. HX4: Gree 4G 159
   (off Dean End)
Linen Wlk. LS10: Leeds 1C 118
Linfield LS6: Leeds 4E 77
Linfoot Ct. LS21: Otley 4D 22
Lingard St. BD1: B'frd 2E 7 (3F 91)
LINGBOB .5G 67
Ling Bob HX2: Hal 1B 148
Ling Bob Cl. HX2: Hal 1B 148
Lingbob Ct. BD15: Wils 5G 67
Ling Bob Cft. HX2: Hal 6B 128
Lingbob Mill Fold BD15: Wils 5G 67
Ling Ct. LS29: Men 1F 39
Ling Cft. LS23: B Spa 3H 29
Lingcroft Grn. BD5: B'frd 3G 111
   (off Newill Cl.)
Lingdale Rd. BD6: B'frd 1A 132
Lingfield App. LS17: Leeds 4H 59
Lingfield Bank LS17: Leeds 4H 59
Lingfield Cl. LS17: Leeds 4A 60
Lingfield Cres. BD13: Que 3E 109
   LS17: Leeds 4A 60
Lingfield Dr. BD22: Cros R 6G 47
   LS17: Leeds 4A 60
Lingfield Gdns. LS17: Leeds 4H 59
Lingfield Gth. LS17: Leeds 4A 60
Lingfield Ga. LS17: Leeds 4A 60
Lingfield Grn. LS17: Leeds 4A 60
Lingfield Gro. BD15: Wils 4H 67
   LS17: Leeds 4A 60

Lingfield Hill LS17: Leeds 3H 59
Lingfield Mt. LS17: Leeds 4A 60
Lingfield Rd. BD15: Wils 4G 67
    LS17: Leeds 4H 59
Lingfield Ter. BD13: Que 3E 109
Lingfield Vw. LS17: Leeds 4H 59
Lingfield Wlk. LS17: Leeds 4H 59
Lingmell Cres. BD4: B'frd 3D 112
                 (off Simon Cl.)
Ling Pk. App. BD15: Wils 5G 67
Ling Pk. Av. BD15: Wils 5G 67
Ling Royd Av. HX2: Hal 1B 148
Lingwell App. LS10: Leeds 3A 140
Lingwell Av. LS10: Leeds 2A 140
Lingwell Chase WF3: Loft 3G 157
Lingwell Ct. LS10: Leeds 3A 140
    WF3: Loft 3E 157
Lingwell Cres. LS10: Leeds 2A 140
Lingwell Gdns. LS10: Leeds 3A 140
LINGWELL GATE 2E 157
Lingwell Ga. Cres. WF1: Out 4F 157
Lingwell Ga. Dr. WF1: Out 4E 157
Lingwell Gate La. WF1: Out 2D 156
    WF3: Loft, Thpe H 5D 140
Lingwell Grn. LS10: Leeds 3A 140
Lingwell Gro. LS10: Leeds 3A 140
Lingwell M. LS10: Leeds 3A 140
LINGWELL NOOK 1D 156
Lingwell Nook Ct. WF3: Loft 3G 157
Lingwell Nook Crest WF3: Loft . . .3G 157
          (off Lingwell Nook La.)
Lingwell Nook La. WF3: Loft 1E 157
            (Castle Head La.)
    WF3: Loft 3F 157
              (Ridings La.)
Lingwell Pk. Ct. LS10: Leeds 2A 140
Lingwell Rd. LS10: Leeds 2A 140
Lingwell Vw. LS10: Leeds 3A 140
Lingwell Wlk. LS10: Leeds 3A 140
Lingwood Av. BD8: B'frd 2H 89
Lingwood Rd. BD8: B'frd 3H 89
Lingwood Ter. BD8: B'frd 3H 89
Link, The LS26: Swil 4A 122
Links, The LS11: Leeds 6G 117
Links Av. BD3: Hun 6B 134
Links Way BD11: Drig 6B 114
Linkway BD16: Cot 2C 68
Linnburn M. LS29: I'ly 6D 10
Linnet Cl. BD8: B'frd 3E 89
Linnet Ct. LS27: Morl 4D 138
Linnet St. BD21: Keigh 5A 34
Linnhe Av. BD6: B'frd 1H 131
LINTON 1B 28
Linton Av. BD20: Sils 1E 15
    LS17: Leeds 3D 60
    LS22: Weth 3D 12
Linton Cl. LS17: Leeds 3C 60
Linton Comn. LS22: Lin 2H 27
Linton Cres. LS17: Leeds 3D 60
Linton Cft. LS16: Leeds 6H 49
Linton Dr. LS17: Leeds 3C 60
Linton Gro. HD6: Ras 3G 161
    LS17: Leeds 3C 60
Linton Hills Rd. LS22: Weth 4C 12
Linton La. LS22: Lin, Weth 1C 28
    LS22: Weth 1A 12
Linton Mdws. LS22: Weth 4C 12
Linton Ri. LS17: Leeds 3C 60
Linton Rd. LS17: Leeds 3C 60
    LS22: Coll 2A 28
    LS22: Weth 4C 12
Linton Springs LS22: Weth 4A 12
Linton St. BD4: B'frd 1F 111
    BD22: Keigh 2F 47
           (off Oakbank Gro.)
Linton Vw. LS17: Leeds 2C 60
Lion Ct. LS29: Burl W 2F 21
Lippersley La. BD20: Sils 5A 8
         (not continuous)
Lisbon Sq. LS1: Leeds 4A 4
Lisbon St. LS1: Leeds 4B 4 (3G 97)

Lisker Av. LS21: Otley 4F 23
Lisker Ct. LS21: Otley 4F 23
Lisker Dr. LS21: Otley 4F 23
Lismore Cl. LS26: Rothw 2B 142
Lismore Rd. BD20: Keigh 5H 33
Lisset M. BD20: Rid 4E 35
Lister Av. BD4: B'frd 2H 111
Lister Ct. HX1: Hal 4B 164
    LS29: I'ly 5C 10
            (off Church St.)
Lister Gdns. BD8: B'frd 1D 90
Lister Hill LS18: H'fth 5E 57
LISTER HILLS 4C 90
Listerhills Ind. Est.
    BD1: B'frd 4A 6 (4D 90)
Listerhills Rd. BD7: B'frd . . .4A 6 (5C 90)
Listerhills Science Pk. BD7: B'frd . . .4C 90
Lister Ho. LS23: B Spa 3C 30
Lister La. BD2: B'frd 1F 91
    HX1: Hal 4A 164 (3E 149)
           (not continuous)
Lister's Ct. HX1: Hal 2E 149
Listers Rd. HX3: Hal 1A 150
Lister St. BD4: B'frd 3A 112
             (Bela Av.)
    BD4: B'frd 4C 112
            (Edward St.)
    BD21: Keigh 1G 47
    HD6: Brigh 6A 152
    LS29: I'ly 5C 10
Lister Vw. BD8: B'frd 2C 90
Lister Ville BD15: Wils 4G 67
Lister Wlk. LS27: Morl 1H 137
Lit. Baines St. HX1: Hal 2E 149
Littlebeck Dr. BD16: Bgly 4E 51
Little Bradley HX4: Gree 5G 159
Lit. Church La. LS26: Meth 5C 144
Little Cote BD10: B'frd 6G 53
Lit. Cote Farm Cl. BD10: B'frd 6G 53
Lit. Cross St. BD5: B'frd 3E 111
    LS1: Leeds 4E 5
Littlefield Wlk. BD6: B'frd 5B 110
Lit. Fountain St. LS27: Morl 4A 138
Little Haley BD22: Oxen 6D 64
Lit. Hew Royd BD10: B'frd 6F 53
LITTLE HORTON 1C 110
LITTLE HORTON GREEN 6D 90
Lit. Horton Grn. BD5: B'frd 6D 90
Lit. Horton La. BD5: B'frd 2C 110
            (Canterbury Av.)
    BD5: B'frd 6B 6 (6D 90)
      (Melbourne Pl., not continuous)
Lit. King St. LS1: Leeds 5C 4 (4H 97)
Littlelands BD16: Cot 2C 68
Little La. BD9: B'frd 1H 89
    BD20: E Mor 4A 36
    HX3: Hal 2C 150
    LS27: Chur 5C 116
    LS27: Morl 3A 138
    LS29: I'ly 5D 10
    WF3: Carl 4A 142
Lit. Lane Ct. LS27: Chur 5C 116
LITTLE LONDON
    LS7 . . . . .1F 5 (1A 98)
    LS19 . . . . .3E 55
Little London HX3: North 3B 130
LITTLE MOOR 4C 108
Little Moor BD13: Que 4C 108
LITTLEMOOR BOTTOM 6A 94
Littlemoor Ct. LS28: Pud 5A 94
Littlemoor Cres. LS28: Pud 6A 94
Littlemoor Cres. Sth. LS28: Pud 6A 94
Littlemoor Gdns. HX2: Illing 1C 128
    LS28: Pud 6A 94
Littlemoor La. LS14: T'ner 2H 63
Lit. Moor Pl. LS12: Leeds 4B 96
Littlemoor Rd. HX2: Illing 6C 106
    LS28: Pud 5A 94
Littlemoor Vw. LS28: Pud 5A 94
Lit. Neville St. LS1: Leeds 6D 4 (4H 97)
Little Park BD10: B'frd 6C 54
LITTLE PRESTON 4B 122
Lit. Preston Hall LS26: Swil 4B 122

Lit. Queen St. LS1: Leeds 5B 4 (4G 97)
Little St. BD22: Haw 2C 64
Littleway LS17: Leeds 6A 60
Littlewood Cl. BD19: Cleck 6C 110
Littlewood Dr. BD19: Cleck 5B 134
LITTLE WOODHOUSE 1A 4 (2G 97)
Lit. Woodhouse HD6: Ras 1A 162
Lit. Woodhouse St.
    LS2: Leeds 2B 4 (2G 97)
Litton Ct. LS29: Men 2H 39
Littondale Cl. BD17: Bail 3E 53
Litton Rd. BD22: Keigh 1G 47
Litton Way LS14: Leeds 1D 80
Liverpool Row HX2: Hal 3H 147
            (off Stock La.)
Liversedge Row BD7: B'frd 2A 110
         (off Perseverance La.)
Livingstone Cl. BD2: B'frd 3F 71
Livingstone Rd. BD2: B'frd 4F 71
            (Cheltenham Rd.)
    BD2: B'frd 5D 70
            (Gaisby La.)
Livingstone St. HX3: Hal 6E 129
Livingstone St. Nth. HX2: Hal 2E 129
Livingston Ho. BD10: B'frd 3A 72
Livinia Gro. LS7: Leeds 1A 98
Lloyds Dr. BD12: Low M 1E 133
Locarno Av. BD9: B'frd 1G 89
Locherbie Grn. BD15: All 2D 88
Lochy Rd. BD6: B'frd 1H 131
Locks, The BD16: Bgly 3B 50
Lockside Rd. LS10: Leeds 2E 119
Locksley Rd. HD6: Brigh 2D 162
Locks St. HX3: Hal 3H 149
Lock Vw. BD16: Bgly 3A 50
    HX5: Ell 3C 160
Lockwood Cl. LS11: Leeds 4A 118
Lockwood Ct. LS11: Leeds 4A 118
Lockwood Pk. LS11: Leeds 4A 118
Lockwood St. BD6: B'frd 4C 110
    BD12: Low M 2E 133
    BD18: Ship 1H 69
Lockwood Way LS11: Leeds 4A 118
Lode Pit La. BD16: Bgly 3F 51
Lodge Av. HX5: Ell 4E 161
Lodge Cl. HX2: Lud M 3D 146
           (off Boy Home La.)
Lodge Ct. BD13: Cull 3B 66
Lodge Dr. HX5: Ell 4E 161
Lodge Ga. BD13: Denh 2C 86
Lodge Ga. Cl. BD13: Denh 2C 86
Lodge Hill BD17: Bail 4H 51
    LS29: Add 1D 8
             (off Main St.)
Lodge Hill Cl. LS12: N Far 2G 115
Lodge Hill Wlk. LS12: N Far 2G 115
Lodge La. LS11: Leeds 2H 117
    LS22: Weth 5E 13
Lodge Pl. HX5: Ell 4E 161
Lodge Rd. BD10: B'frd 5H 53
    LS28: Pud 3H 93
Lodge Row LS15: Leeds 1E 101
         (off Tranquility Av.)
Lodge St. BD13: Cull 3B 66
    BD22: Haw 2C 64
    LS2: Leeds 1C 4 (1H 97)
           (not continuous)
Lodge Ter. LS11: Leeds 3H 117
Lodore Av. BD2: B'frd 6G 71
Lodore Pl. BD2: B'frd 6H 71
Lodore Rd. BD2: B'frd 6G 71
LOFTHOUSE 6G 141
Lofthouse Farm Fold WF3: Loft . . .2G 157
LOFTHOUSE GATE 3F 157
Lofthouse Hill Golf Course 2G 157
Lofthouse Pl. LS2: Leeds 1H 97
Loft St. BD8: B'frd 3H 89
Lo Grove WF1: Out 5F 157
Loiner Ct. LS9: Leeds 6G 99
Lombard St. HX1: Hal 4D 148
    LS15: Leeds 4B 100
    LS19: Raw 3E 55

Lomond Av. LS18: H'fth 3D 56
Londesboro Gro.
LS9: Leeds 4E 99
Londesboro Ter. LS9: Leeds 4E 99
London La. LS19: Raw 3E 55
London Rd. HX2: Norl 6B 148
London Sq. LS19: Raw 3E 55
London St. LS19: Raw 3E 55
Longacre La. BD22: Haw 1D 64
Longacres BD22: Haw 1E 65
Longbottom Av. BD20: Sils 2F 15
  HX6: Sow B 6E 147
Longbottom Ter. HX3: Hal 5H 149
Longbow Av. LS26: Meth 4C 144
Longbow Cl. HD2: Wyke 6D 162
Long Causeway BD13: Denh 2F 85
  BD22: Denh 2F 85
  HX2: Ogd 2B 106
  LS9: Leeds 6D 98
  LS16: Leeds 5D 58
Long Causeway, The
  HX2: Lud M 3A 146
Long Cl. BD12: Wyke 3B 132
Long Cl. La. LS9: Leeds 4D 98
Longcroft LS11: Leeds 1A 48
Longcroft Link BD1: B'frd 3B 6 (4D 90)
Longcroft Pl. BD1: B'frd 3B 6 (4D 90)
Longcroft Rd. LS29: I'ly 6G 11
Longdike Ct. LS25: Kip 4H 123
Longdike La. LS25: Kip 5A 124
Long Edge Low Rd.
  HX6: Sow B 6B 146
Long Edge Middle Rd.
  HX6: Sow B 6A 146
Long Edge Rd. HX6: Sow B 6A 146
Long Fallas Cres. HD6: Ras 4B 162
Longfield Av. HX3: North 6C 130
  LS28: Pud 4B 94
Longfield Ct. LS28: Pud 4B 94
Longfield Ct. BD4: B'frd 2A 112
  LS13: Leeds 4B 74
  LS15: Leeds 3C 100
Longfield Gth. LS13: Leeds 4B 74
Longfield Gro. LS28: Pud 4B 94
Longfield Mt. LS28: Pud 4B 94
Longfield Rd. BD5: B'frd 4A 94
Longfield Ter. HX3: North 6C 130
  (off Bradford Rd.)
  LS28: Pud 4A 94
Longfield Vw. LS28: Fars 6H 73
  (off Croft St.)
Longford Ter. BD7: B'frd 6H 89
Long Hall Pk. LS29: I'ly 3B 10
Long Heys HX4: Gree 5G 159
Longhouse Dr. BD13: Denh 3B 86
Longhouse La. BD13: Denh 3B 86
Long Ho. Rd. HX2: Mix 1A 128
Longlands BD10: B'frd 1H 71
Longlands Av. BD13: Denh 2B 86
Longlands Dr. BD22: Haw 1D 64
Longlands St.
  BD1: B'frd 3B 6 (4D 90)
  (Baptist Pl.)
  BD1: B'frd 3B 6 (4D 90)
  (Providence St.)
Long La. BD9: B'frd 4F 69
  BD13: Que 6H 107
  BD15: All 2H 87
  BD16: Har 6E 49
  HX2: Hal 5C 128
  HX3: Hal 5C 128
  HX3: Sou 2B 150
  HX6: Sow B . . . . . . .6H 147 & 1A 158
  LS15: Bar E 2E 83
  LS25: Bar E 2E 83
LONG LEE 1C 48
Long Lee La. BD21: Keigh 2B 48
Long Lee Ter. BD21: Keigh 2C 48
Longley's Yd. LS10: Leeds 3C 118
Long Lover La. HX1: Hal 1C 148
  HX2: Hal 1C 148
Long Meadow Ct. LS25: Gar 6G 103
Long Meadow Ga. LS25: Gar 6F 103

Long Meadows BD2: B'frd 5E 71
  LS16: B'hpe 3G 43
  LS25: Gar 6F 103
  LS29: Burl W 1E 21
Long Preston Chase BD10: B'frd 2B 72
Long Reach HX2: Mt T 4G 127
Long Riddings LS29: Add 1D 8
Long Ridge HD6: Ras 4A 162
Long Row BD12: Low M 2D 132
  BD13: Thorn 4G 87
  LS18: H'fth 6E 57
  (not continuous)
Long Row Ct. BD5: B'frd 2E 111
Long Royd BD17: Bail 1F 71
Longroyd Av. LS11: Leeds 2A 118
Long Royd Cl. BD17: Bail 3D 52
Longroyd Cres. LS11: Leeds 2A 118
Longroyd Cres. Nth.
  LS11: Leeds 2A 118
Long Royd Dr. BD17: Bail 3E 53
Longroyde Cl. HD6: Ras 3H 161
Longroyde Gro. HD6: Ras 3H 161
Longroyd Gro. LS11: Leeds 2A 118
Longroyd Pl. LS11: Leeds 2A 118
Longroyd St. Nth. LS11: Leeds 2A 118
Longroyd Ter. LS11: Leeds 2A 118
Longroyd Vw. LS11: Leeds 2A 118
Longside Hall BD7: B'frd 5C 90
Longside La. BD7: B'frd 5A 6 (5C 90)
Long St. BD4: B'frd 6H 91
Long Thorpe La.
  WF3: Loft, Thpe H 6D 140
Long Wall HX5: Ell 4H 159
Longwood Av. BD16: Bgly 2H 49
Longwood Cl. HX3: Hal 1F 149
  LS17: Leeds 2F 61
  WF3: Ting 1D 154
Longwood Ct. WF3: Ting 1E 155
Longwood Cres. LS17: Leeds 2F 61
Longwood Fold WF3: Ting 1E 155
Longwood Gth. WF3: Ting 1E 155
Longwood Rd. WF3: Ting 1D 154
Longwood Vw. WF3: Ting 1E 155
Longwood Vw. BD16: Bgly 2A 50
Longwood Way LS17: Leeds 2F 61
Lonk Ho. La. BD17: Bail 2F 53
Lonsdale Cl. LS10: Leeds 4B 118
Lonsdale Mdws. LS23: B Spa 4B 30
Lonsdale Ri. WF3: W Ard 1E 155
Lonsdale St. BD3: B'frd 3H 91
Loom Ho. LS9: Leeds 6H 5
Lord La. BD22: Haw 1B 64
Lord's Bldgs. LS27: Morl 5A 138
Lordsfield Pl. BD4: B'frd 4B 112
Lord's La. HD6: Ras 2B 162
Lord St. BD21: Keigh 6A 34
  BD22: Haw 2D 64
  HX1: Hal 4B 164 (2G 149)
  HX6: Sow B 4A 148
  LS12: Leeds 5F 97
Lord Ter. LS12: Leeds 5F 97
Lordswood Grange LS28: Pud 4F 93
Loris St. BD4: B'frd 4B 112
Lorne St. BD4: B'frd 2H 111
  BD21: Keigh 5C 34
  BD22: Cros R 1F 65
  (off Bingley Rd.)
Lorry Bank LS7: Leeds 5A 78
Lotherton Bus. Pk. LS25: Gar 3F 103
  (not continuous)
Lotherton Way LS25: Gar 3F 103
Lot St. BD22: Haw 2D 64
Loughrigg St. BD5: B'frd 2E 111
Louisa St. BD10: B'frd 1H 71
Louis Av. BD5: B'frd 1C 110
Louis Ct. LS7: Leeds 6B 78
Louis Gro. LS7: Leeds 6C 78
Louis Ho. LS27: Morl 2B 138
  (off Pullman Ct.)
Louis Le Prince Ct. LS8: Leeds 6D 78
  (off Bayswater Rd.)

Louis St. LS7: Leeds 6B 78
Lounge Apartments LS6: Leeds 4D 76
  (off North La.)
Lovatt Fold BD17: Bail 6D 52
Love La. HX1: Hal 6A 164 (4F 149)
  LS26: Rothw 2A 142
Lovell Ho. LS7: Leeds 1G 5
Lovell Pk. Cl. LS7: Leeds . . .1G 5 (2B 98)
Lovell Pk. Ct. LS7: Leeds . . .1F 5 (2B 98)
Lovell Pk. Ga. LS7: Leeds . . .1F 5 (2A 98)
Lovell Pk. Grange LS7: Leeds 1G 5
Lovell Pk. Hgts. LS7: Leeds 1G 5
Lovell Pk. Hill LS7: Leeds . . .1F 5 (2A 98)
Lovell Pk. M. LS7: Leeds 1G 5 (2B 98)
Lovell Pk. Rd. LS2: Leeds . . .2F 5 (2A 98)
  LS7: Leeds 2F 5 (2A 98)
Lovell Pk. Towers LS7: Leeds 1F 5
Lovell Pk. Vw. LS7: Leeds . . .1G 5 (2B 98)
Low Ash Av. BD18: Ship 2D 70
Low Ash Cres. BD18: Ship 2D 70
Low Ash Dr. BD18: Ship 2D 70
Low Ash Gro. BD18: Ship 2D 70
Low Ash Rd. BD18: Ship 2E 71
LOW BAILDON 3C 52
LOW BANK 4B 46
Low Bank Dr. BD22: Oak 4B 46
Low Bank La. BD22: Oak 4B 46
LOW BANKS 3D 34
Low Banks BD20: Rid 4D 34
Low Bank St. LS28: Fars 6H 73
Low Beck LS29: I'ly 4F 11
Low Bentley HX3: She 2G 131
Low Cl. BD16: Bgly 5D 50
  LS29: I'ly 3D 10
Low Cl. St. LS2: Leeds 6G 77
LOW COMMON 6E 145
Lowcroft LS22: Coll 3A 28
Low Cft. Ct. LS16: B'hpe 2G 43
Lowell Av. BD7: B'frd 6H 89
Lowell Gro. LS13: Leeds 3C 94
Lowell Pl. LS13: Leeds 3C 94
Lower Ainley HX2: Illing 1D 128
  (off Whitehill Rd.)
Lower Ashgrove
  BD5: B'frd 6B 6 (5D 90)
Lower Bankhouse LS28: Pud 1H 113
Lwr. Bank Ho's. HX4: Holy 6B 158
Lwr. Basinghall St.
  LS1: Leeds 4D 4 (3H 97)
Lower Bentley Royd HX6: Sow B 5G 147
Lwr. Bracken Bank BD22: Keigh 3G 47
  (off Diamond St.)
Lower Brea HX3: Hal 1C 150
Lower Brockholes HX2: Ogd 6B 106
Lwr. Brockwell La. HX6: Tri 6F 147
Lwr. Brown Hurst HX2: Mt T 4A 128
Lwr. Brunswick St.
  LS2: Leeds 2G 5 (2B 98)
Lwr. Clay Pits HX1: Hal 1C 148
Lwr. Clifton St. HX6: Sow B 5A 148
Lwr. Clyde St. HX6: Sow B 6H 147
Lwr. Constable Fold LS29: I'ly 6F 11
  (off Lwr. Constable Rd.)
Lwr. Constable Rd. LS29: I'ly 6F 11
Lwr. Copy BD15: All 2D 88
Lwr. Cross St. HX1: Hal . . .3D 164 (2H 149)
Lwr. Crow Nest Dr. HX3: Hip 2B 152
LOWER EDGE BOTTOM 4D 160
Lwr. Edge Rd. HD6: Ras 4D 160
  HX5: Brigh, Ell 4D 160
Lower Ellistones HX4: Gree 4E 159
  (off Saddleworth Rd.)
Lower Exley HX3: Hal 2H 159
LOWER FAGLEY 6C 72
Lwr. Finkil St. HD6: Brigh 4G 151
Lower Fleet BD13: Que 4G 107
Lower Fold HD6: Ras 5H 161
  HX1: Hal 4B 164
  HX4: Bark 5B 158
Lower Gaukrodger HX6: Sow B 6F 147
Lwr. George St. BD6: B'frd 4B 110
Lwr. Gilbert Flds. HX4: Bark 5A 158
Lwr. Globe St. BD8: B'frd 3C 90

LOWER GRANGE 4D 88
Lower Grange HD2: Hud 5E 163
Lwr. Grange Cl. BD8: B'frd 4E 89
Lwr. Grattan Rd.
  BD1: B'frd 4A 6 (4D 90)
Lower Grn. BD17: Bail 5B 52
Lower Grn. Av. BD19: Scho 1F 153
Lower Hathershelf
  HX2: Lud M 2B 146
Lower Hazelhurst BD13: Que 6A 108
Lower Hgts. Rd. BD13: Thorn 3G 87
Lower Hollins HX6: Sow B 5H 147
Lower Holme BD17: Bail 6C 52
Lwr. Horley Grn. HX3: Hal 6A 130
Lower Ho. Cl. BD10: B'frd 6F 53
Lower Ings HX2: Ogd 4A 106
Lwr. Kipping La. BD13: Thorn 5H 87
Lower Kirkgate BD1: B'frd 4D 6 (4E 91)
  HX1: Hal 2H 149
Lower La. BD4: B'frd 1H 111
  BD4: E Bier 2B 134
Lower Langwith LS22: Coll 3A 28
Lwr. Lark Hill BD19: Cleck 2H 153
LOWER MICKLETOWN 4F 145
Lower Mickletown
  LS26: Meth 4E 145
Lower Newlands HD6: Ras 2B 162
Lwr. Ox Heys HX3: Nor G 4H 131
Lwr. Park Grn. BD20: Sils 2C 14
Lwr. Pierce Cl. BD22: Cros R 6F 47
Lwr. Quarry Rd. HD2: Hud 4F 163
  HD5: Hud 4F 163
Lwr. Railway Rd. LS29: I'ly 5E 11
Lower Range Rd. HX3: Hal 6G 129
Lwr. Range Ter. HX3: Hal 1C 164
Lwr. Rayleigh St. BD4: B'frd 1G 111
Lwr. Rushton Rd. BD3: B'frd 4C 92
Lower Saltonstall HX2: Wain 2D 126
Lower Sandhills LS14: T'ner 4G 63
Lower Scholes BD22: Oak 1A 64
Lwr. School St.
  BD12: Low M 1C 132
  BD18: Ship 1H 69
Lwr. Skircoat Grn. HX3: Hal 1G 159
               (off Cow La.)
Lower Slack HX2: Wain 1F 127
Lower Springhead BD22: Oak 4E 47
Lwr. Tofts Rd. LS28: Pud 4A 94
LOWER TOWN 1D 84
Lowertown BD22: Oxen 1C 84
Lwr. Town Mills BD22: Oxen 1C 84
          (off Lower Town)
Lwr. Town St. LS13: Leeds 6F 75
Lower Wellgate HX4: Gree 4G 159
Lwr. Wellington Rd. LS29: I'ly 5E 11
Lwr. Westfield Rd. BD9: B'frd 2A 90
Lwr. Whiteshaw M.
  BD13: Denh 6B 66
LOWER WOODLANDS 2H 133
LOWER WORTLEY 6C 96
Lwr. Wortley Rd.
  LS12: Leeds 6A 96
LOWER WYKE 1C 152
Lwr. Wyke Grn. BD12: Wyke 1B 152
Lwr. Wyke La. BD12: Wyke 1B 152
Loweswater Av. BD6: B'frd 1H 131
LOW FARM 3H 57
Low Farm LS26: Gt P 5E 123
Low Fell Cl. BD22: Keigh 1E 47
Lowfield Cl. BD12: Low M 2E 133
Lowfield Cres. BD20: Sils 3F 15
Lowfields Av. LS12: Leeds 1E 117
Lowfields Bus. Pk. HX5: Ell 3D 160
         (not continuous)
Lowfields Cl. HX5: Ell 3C 160
Lowfields Rd. LS11: Leeds 2E 117
  LS12: Leeds 1E 117
         (not continuous)
Low Flds. Way LS12: Leeds 1E 117
Lowfields Way HX5: Ell 3C 160
LOW FOLD
  LS12 . . . . .5G 95
  LS18 . . . . .1C 74

Low Fold BD2: B'frd 6F 71
  BD13: Que 3A 108
  BD17: Bail 3C 52
         (off Moorgate)
  BD19: Scho 1F 153
  BD20: Stee 6C 14
  LS9: Leeds 5C 98
  LS18: H'fth 2C 74
  LS19: Raw 3F 55
Low Grange Cres. LS10: Leeds . . .4C 118
Low Grange Vw. LS10: Leeds 5C 118
LOW GREEN 4G 55
Low Green BD7: B'frd 2A 110
  LS19: Raw 4G 55
Low Grn. Ter. BD7: B'frd 2B 110
Low Hall Cl. LS29: Men 1G 39
Low Hall Pl. LS11: Leeds 5G 97
Low Hall Rd. LS18: H'fth 1A 74
  LS29: Men 1H 39
Low Hill BD17: Bail 1C 52
Low Ho. Dr. BD20: Sils 3E 15
Low Ho. Farm Ct. BD20: Sils 3E 15
Low Laithe Fold BD22: Lay 6C 32
Low Laithes HX6: Sow B 6G 147
Low La. BD13: Que 2G 107
  BD14: Clay 6B 88
  HD6: B Bri 3C 152
  HX2: Wain 1A 126
  LS18: H'fth 5E 57
  WF17: Birs 6A 136
Low Mill LS29: Add 2G 9
Low Mill La. BD21: Keigh 6B 34
  LS29: Add 1F 9
Low Mills Rd. LS12: Leeds 1B 116
LOW MILL VILLAGE 2F 9
LOW MOOR 1C 132
Low Moor Bus. Pk.
  BD12: Low M 1C 132
LOW MOOR SIDE 3E 115
Low Moor Side LS12: N Far 2F 115
Low Moorside Cl. LS12: N Far . . .2G 115
Low Moorside Ct. LS12: N Far . . .2G 115
Low Moor Side La. LS12: N Far . . .3E 115
Low Moor St. BD12: Low M 1D 132
Low Moor Ter. HX2: Hal 3B 148
  LS11: Leeds 3H 117
Low Newall Fold BD5: B'frd 4E 111
Lowood La. WF17: Birs 4A 136
Low Rd. LS10: Leeds 1C 118
Low Royds Grn. LS26: Oul 6C 142
Lowry Rd. WF3: Ting 1D 154
Lowry Vw. BD21: Keigh 1A 48
Low Shops La. LS26: Rothw 1G 141
Low Spring Rd. BD21: Keigh 1C 48
LOW SPRINGS 6C 38
Low St. BD21: Keigh 6A 34
         (not continuous)
  WF3: Ting 6F 139
Lowther Av. LS25: Gar 5E 103
Lowther Cres. LS26: Swil 3A 122
Lowther Dr. LS25: Gar 5E 103
  LS26: Swil 3H 121
Lowther Gro. LS25: Gar 5E 103
Lowther Rd. LS25: Gar 5E 103
Lowther St. BD2: B'frd 1H 91
  LS8: Leeds 6D 78
Lowther Ter. LS15: Swil C 5A 102
Lowtown LS28: Pud 3B 94
LOW TOWN END 4B 138
LOW UTLEY 3G 33
Low Way LS23: Cliff 5B 30
Low Well St. BD5: B'frd 2D 110
Low Whitehouse Row
  LS10: Leeds 6B 98
Low Wood BD15: Wils 5H 67
Low Wood Ct. BD20: Keigh 2H 33
Low Wood Head BD20: Rid 2B 34
Low Wood Ri. LS29: I'ly 6H 11
Loxley St. BD7: B'frd 1B 92
Loxley Gro. LS22: Weth 1D 13
Lucas Cl. LS6: Leeds 6A 78
Lucas Pl. LS6: Leeds 5G 77
Lucas St. LS6: Leeds 5G 77

Lucy Av. LS15: Leeds 3A 100
Lucy Hall Dr. BD17: Bail 5G 51
Lucy Hall Farm Cl. BD17: Bail 4H 51
Lucy St. HX3: Hal 1H 149
LUDDENDEN 6E 127
LUDDENDEN FOOT 2D 146
Luddenden La. HX2: Lud M 2D 146
Luddendon Pl. BD13: Que 3G 107
            (off Mill La.)
Ludgate Hill LS2: Leeds 4F 5 (3A 98)
Ludlam St. BD5: B'frd 6E 91
         (not continuous)
Ludlow Av. LS25: Gar 4H 103
Ludolf Dr. LS17: Shad 3A 62
Luis Ct. BD17: Bail 3B 52
Luke Rd. BD5: B'frd 1C 110
Lulworth Av. LS15: Leeds 2F 101
Lulworth Cl. LS15: Leeds 2F 101
Lulworth Cres. LS15: Leeds 2F 101
Lulworth Dr. LS15: Leeds 3F 101
Lulworth Gth. LS15: Leeds 3F 101
Lulworth Gro. BD4: B'frd 3B 112
         (not continuous)
Lulworth Vw. LS15: Leeds 2F 101
Lulworth Wlk. LS15: Leeds 2F 101
Lumb Bottom BD11: Drig 6B 114
Lumb Gill La. LS29: Add 3F 9
Lumb Hall Way BD11: Drig 6B 114
Lumb La. BD8: B'frd 1A 6 (2C 90)
  HX2: Wain 1F 127
  HX3: Hal 5F 129
Lumb La. Mills BD8: B'frd . . .1A 6 (3D 90)
Lumbrook HX3: North 4E 131
Lumbrook Cl. HX3: North 4E 131
Lumb Ter. HX2: Wain 1F 127
Lumby Cl. LS28: Pud 6B 94
Lumby Gth. LS17: E Kes 5D 26
Lumby La. LS17: E Kes 4C 26
  LS28: Pud 6B 94
Lumby St. BD10: B'frd 1H 71
Lumley Av. LS4: Leeds 6D 76
Lumley Gro. LS4: Leeds 6D 76
Lumley Mt. LS4: Leeds 6D 76
Lumley Pl. LS4: Leeds 6D 76
Lumley Rd. LS4: Leeds 6D 76
Lumley St. LS4: Leeds 6D 76
Lumley Ter. LS4: Leeds 6D 76
Lumley Vw. LS4: Leeds 6D 76
Lumley Wlk. LS4: Leeds 6D 76
Lunan Pl. LS8: Leeds 5D 78
Lunan Ter. LS8: Leeds 5D 78
Lund La. BD22: Oak 1B 46
Lund St. BD8: B'frd 4G 89
  BD16: Bgly 4C 50
  BD21: Keigh 5A 34
Lundy Ct. BD5: B'frd 2E 111
Lune St. BD22: Cros R 1F 65
Lupton Av. LS9: Leeds 3E 99
Lupton Flats LS6: Leeds 4D 76
Lupton's Bldgs. LS12: Leeds 4B 96
Lupton St. BD8: B'frd 2E 91
  LS10: Leeds 2C 118
Lustre St. BD21: Keigh 6G 33
Luther St. LS13: Leeds 4A 74
Luther Way BD2: B'frd 6F 71
Luton St. BD21: Keigh 6H 33
  HX1: Hal 2D 148
Luttrell Cl. LS16: Leeds 5A 58
Luttrell Cres. LS16: Leeds 5A 58
Luttrell Gdns. LS16: Leeds 5A 58
Luttrell Pl. LS16: Leeds 5A 58
Luttrell Rd. LS16: Leeds 5A 58
Lutyens, The LS29: I'ly 5B 10
Luxor Av. LS8: Leeds 5D 78
Luxor Rd. LS8: Leeds 5D 78
Luxor St. LS8: Leeds 5D 78
Luxor Vw. LS8: Leeds 5D 78
Lydbrook Pk. HX3: Hal 1E 159
Lydgate Hall LS21: Leeds 1B 4 (1G 97)
Lyddon Ter. LS2: Leeds 1A 4 (1G 97)
LYDGATE 2G 151
Lydgate HX3: North 4C 130
  LS9: Leeds 2D 98

Lydgate Dr. BD7: B'frd 5H 89
Lydgate Pk. HX3: Hip 2G 151
Lydgate Pl. LS28: Cal 2E 73
Lydgate St. LS28: Cal 2E 73
Lydget Ct. BD20: Keigh 4G 33
Lydia Hill HD6: Ras 2A 162
(off East St.)
Lydia St. LS2: Leeds 4G 5
Lyme Chase LS14: Leeds 1B 100
Lymington Dr. BD4: B'frd 1C 112
Lynch Av. BD7: B'frd 2H 109
Lyncroft BD2: B'frd 5F 71
Lyndale LS25: Kip 5G 123
Lyndale Dr. BD18: Ship 2F 71
WF2: Wren 6C 156
Lyndale Rd. BD16: Bgly 2E 51
Lyndean Gdns. BD10: B'frd 2G 71
Lynden Av. BD18: Ship 1E 71
Lynden Ct. BD6: B'frd 6A 110
Lyndhurst BD16: Bgly 3B 50
(off Hall Bank Dr.)
Lyndhurst Av. HD6: Ras 4A 162
Lyndhurst Cl. LS15: Scho 2H 81
Lyndhurst Cres. LS15: Scho 2H 81
Lyndhurst Gro. BD15: All 2E 89
Lyndhurst Rd.
HD6: Ras 4A 162
Lyndhurst Rd. HD6: Ras 3A 162
LS15: Scho 3H 81
Lyndhurst Vw. LS15: Scho 3H 81
Lyndon Av. LS25: Gar 4E 103
Lyndon Ter. BD16: Bgly 4C 50
Lyndsey Cl. BD22: Oak 5B 46
Lyndum Gro. LS25: Kip 3G 123
Lynfield Dr. BD9: B'frd 6E 69
WF15: Liv 4H 153
Lynfield Mt. BD18: Ship 1E 71
Lynmoor Ct. BD10: B'frd 2F 71
Lynnfield Gdns. LS15: Scho 3H 81
Lynnwood Gdns. LS28: Pud 4G 93
Lynsey Gdns. BD4: B'frd 6H 111
Lynthorne Rd. BD9: B'frd 5C 70
Lynton Av. BD9: B'frd 1H 89
LS23: B Spa 3B 30
WF3: Thpe H 5C 140
Lynton Dr. BD9: B'frd 1G 89
BD18: Ship 2A 70
BD20: Rid 4D 34
Lynton Gro. BD9: B'frd 1H 89
HX2: Brad 4D 106
Lynton Vs. BD9: B'frd 1H 89
Lynwood Av. BD18: Ship 1E 71
LS12: Leeds 6C 96
LS26: Wood 1F 143
Lynwood Cl. BD11: Birk 3F 135
Lynwood Cres. HX1: Hal 4D 148
LS12: Leeds 6C 96
LS26: Wood 1F 143
Lynwood Gth. LS12: Leeds 6C 96
Lynwood Gro. LS12: Leeds 1C 116
Lynwood M. BD4: B'frd 3D 112
Lynwood Mt. LS12: Leeds 6C 96
Lynwood Ri. LS12: Leeds 6C 96
Lynwood Vw. LS12: Leeds 6C 96
Lyon Rd. BD20: East 5A 14
Lyons St. BD13: Que 4B 108
Lyon St. BD13: Thorn 4H 87
Lysander Way BD16: Cot 3D 68
Lytham Dr. BD13: Que 3D 108
Lytham Gro. LS12: Leeds 1A 116
Lytham Pl. LS12: Leeds 1A 116
Lytham St. HX1: Hal 2D 148
Lytton Rd. BD8: B'frd 3H 89
Lytton St. HX3: Hal 6G 129
(off Ada St.)
LS10: Leeds 2B 118

M

M1 Ind. Est. LS10: Leeds 2B 118
Mabel Royd BD7: B'frd 6H 89

MABGATE 2G 5 (2B 98)
Mabgate LS9: Leeds 3H 5 (3B 98)
Mabgate Grn. LS9: Leeds 3H 5 (3B 98)
Mabgate Mills Industrial &
Commercial Cen.
LS9: Leeds 2H 5 (2C 98)
Macaulay St. LS9: Leeds 3H 5 (2C 98)
McBride Way LS22: Weth 4F 13
McBurney Cl. HX3: Hal 5F 129
McClintock Ho. LS10: Leeds 5B 98
(off The Boulevard)
McClure Ho. LS10: Leeds 5B 98
(off The Boulevard)
Mc Crea Wing HX1: Hal 4G 149
(off Emily Way)
Mackenzie Ho. LS10: Leeds 6H 5
Mackingstone Dr. BD22: Oak 4B 46
Mackingstone La. BD22: Oak 3B 46
Mackintosh Memorial Homes, The
HX3: Hal 5E 149
(off Albert Prom.)
McLaren Flds. LS13: Leeds 1F 95
McMahon Dr. BD13: Que 3E 109
McMillan Gdns. BD6: B'frd 6D 110
Macturk Gro. BD8: B'frd 2A 90
Maddocks St. BD18: Ship 1A 70
Madeline Joy Apartments
LS6: Leeds 5D 76
(off Broomfield Cres.)
Madewel Ho. HX5: Ell 6C 160
Madison Av. BD4: B'frd 4C 112
Madni Cl. HX1: Hal 2F 149
Mafeking Av. LS11: Leeds 4G 117
Mafeking Gro. LS11: Leeds 4G 117
Mafeking Mt. LS11: Leeds 4G 117
Mafeking Ter. BD18: Ship 4D 70
Magdalene Cl. LS16: Leeds 4A 58
Magdalin Dr. LS28: Stan 1C 94
Magellan Ho. LS10: Leeds 6H 5 (5B 98)
Maggie Barker Av. LS15: Leeds 1F 101
Magistrates' Court
Bradford & Keighley 5C 6 (5E 91)
Halifax 5B 164 (3G 149)
Leeds 3C 4 (3H 97)
Magnolia Dr. BD15: All 5B 68
Magpie Cl. BD6: B'frd 4E 109
Magpie La. LS27: Morl 4B 138
Mahim Cres. BD17: Bail 5E 53
Maidstone St. BD3: B'frd 4A 92
Maidwell Way BD6: B'frd 1A 132
Mail Cl. LS15: Leeds 6G 81
Main Rd. BD13: Denh 3B 86
BD20: E Mor 5H 35
BD20: East 5A 14
Mainspring Rd. BD15: Wils 4G 67
Main St. BD12: Low M 1E 133
BD12: Wyke 3C 132
BD15: Wils 4G 67
BD16: Bgly 4B 50
BD16: Cot 3D 68
BD17: Esh 2A 54
BD22: Haw 2C 64
LS14: T'ner 3H 63
LS15: Bar E 2D 82
LS15: Scho 3H 81
LS17: E Kes 6E 27
LS17: Shad 2H 61
LS20: Hawk 5E 39
LS21: Pool 4E 25
LS22: Coll 3B 28
LS22: Lin 1B 28
LS24: N Kym 5E 31
LS25: Gar 4E 103
LS26: Meth 4D 144
LS29: Add 1C 8
LS29: Burl W 1E 21
LS29: Men 6F 21
WF3: Carl 4H 141
WF3: E Ard 2B 156
WF10: All B 3H 145
Maister Pl. BD22: Oak 4B 46
Maitland Cl. BD15: All 4D 88
Maitland Pl. LS11: Leeds 1G 117

Maize St. BD21: Keigh 3G 47
Majestic Way BD22: Keigh 3G 47
(off Wirefield Rd.)
Malden Rd. LS6: Leeds 6F 59
Malham Av. BD9: B'frd 6E 69
HD6: Ras 3G 161
Malham Cl. LS14: Leeds 5C 80
Malham Ct. BD20: Sils 3E 15
(off Ings Way)
Malham Ho. LS29: Men 2G 39
Malham Rd. HD6: Ras 4G 161
Malin Rd. WF12: Dew 6A 154
Mallard Cl. BD10: B'frd 4A 72
LS10: Leeds 6D 118
Mallard Ct. BD8: B'frd 4E 89
Mallard M. BD10: B'frd 4A 72
Mallards, The BD20: Sils 2E 15
Mallard Vw. BD22: Oxen 1C 84
Mallard Way LS27: Morl 3D 138
Mall La. LS20: Guis 2F 41
LS21: Otley 2F 41
Mallory Cl. BD7: B'frd 5H 89
Malmesbury Cl. BD4: B'frd 4C 112
LS12: Leeds 5C 96
Malmesbury Gro. LS12: Leeds 5C 96
Malmesbury Pl. LS12: Leeds 5C 96
Malmesbury Ter.
LS12: Leeds 5C 96
Malsis Cres. BD21: Keigh 1G 47
Malsis Rd. BD21: Keigh 1G 47
Maltby Cl. LS15: Leeds 4F 101
Malthouse Cl. LS14: S'cft 5E 45
Malting Cl. WF3: Rob H 4F 141
Malting Ri. WF3: Rob H 4F 141
Maltings, The BD14: Clay 6D 88
BD20: Sils 1E 15
LS6: Leeds 1E 97
(off Spring Gro. Wlk.)
WF3: Rob H 4F 141
Maltings Ct. LS11: Leeds 1A 118
(off Maltings Rd.)
Maltings Rd. HX2: Hal 5B 128
LS11: Leeds 2A 118
Malt Kiln BD14: Clay 1D 108
(off Gordon St.)
Malt Kiln La. BD13: Thorn 6F 87
Maltkiln La. LS25: Kip 4H 123
Malton St. HX3: Hal 5G 129
HX6: Sow B 4H 147
Malt Shovel Yd. BD10: B'frd 1H 71
(off Town La.)
Malt St. BD22: Keigh 3G 47
Malvern Brow BD9: B'frd 1F 89
Malvern Cres. BD20: Rid 2C 34
Malvern Gro. BD9: B'frd 2F 89
LS11: Leeds 1G 117
Malvern Ri. LS11: Leeds 1G 117
Malvern Rd. BD9: B'frd 2F 89
LS11: Leeds 1G 117
Malvern St. LS11: Leeds 1G 117
Malvern Vw. LS11: Leeds 1G 117
Manchester Rd.
BD5: B'frd 6D 6 (3D 110)
Manchester Sq. LS21: Otley 3E 23
Mandale Gro. BD6: B'frd 5F 109
Mandale Rd. BD6: B'frd 5F 109
Mandarin Way LS10: Leeds 6D 118
Mandela Cl. LS7: Leeds 4B 78
Mandela Ho. LS7: Leeds 6B 78
Manderston Chase
LS12: Leeds 1H 95
Mandeville Cres. BD6: B'frd 5H 109
Manitoba Pl. LS7: Leeds 3C 78
Manley Ct. LS25: Gar 6F 103
Manley Dr. LS22: Weth 3B 12
Manley Gro. LS29: I'ly 5F 11
Manley Ri. LS29: I'ly 6F 11
Manley Rd. LS29: I'ly 6F 11
Manley St. HD6: Brigh 6A 152
Manley St. Pl. HD6: Brigh 6B 152
(off Bonegate Rd.)
Mannheim Rd. BD9: B'frd 1A 90
MANNINGHAM 1B 90

Manningham La.
BD1: B'frd 1B **6** (1C **90**)
BD8: B'frd 1B **6** (1C **90**)
Manningham La. Pk.
BD1: B'frd 2B **6** (3D **90**)
Manningham Sports Cen. 2B **90**
Mann's Bldgs. WF17: Bat 5D **136**
Mann's Ct. BD1: B'frd 4D **6**
Mannville Gro. BD22: Keigh 1G **47**
Mannville Pl. BD22: Keigh 1G **47**
Mannville Rd. BD22: Keigh 2G **47**
Mannville St. BD22: Keigh 1G **47**
Mannville Ter.
BD7: B'frd 5B **6** (5D **90**)
Mannville Wlk. BD22: Keigh 1G **47**
(off Mannville Pl.)
Mannville Way BD22: Keigh 1G **47**
Manor, The LS8: Leeds 3G **79**
(off Ladywood Rd.)
Manor Av. LS6: Leeds 5E **77**
Mnr. Barn Stables LS21: Otley ...3E **23**
(off Kirkgate)
Manor Cl. BD8: B'frd 3F **89**
BD11: B'frd 6A **114**
HX3: Hpe 5F **149**
LS16: B'hpe 2F **43**
LS19: Yead 6F **41**
LS26: Rothw 1A **142**
Manor Cott. M. LS14: S'cft 1E **63**
Manor Ct. BD16: Cot 2C **68**
BD19: Scho 2F **153**
LS11: Leeds 4E **117**
LS17: Shad 3B **62**
LS21: Otley 3E **23**
Manor Cres. LS21: Pool 4E **25**
LS26: Rothw 1H **141**
Manor Cft. LS15: Leeds 4E **101**
Manor Dr. BD16: Cot 1C **68**
HX3: Hal 5F **149**
LS6: Leeds 6E **77**
(not continuous)
Mnr. Farm Cl. BD16: Cot 3D **68**
LS10: Leeds 1B **140**
Mnr. Farm Ct. BD4: E Bier 6C **112**
LS20: Guis 4C **40**
Mnr. Farm Cres. LS27: Chur ...5C **116**
Mnr. Farm Dr. LS10: Leeds ...1A **140**
LS27: Chur 5C **116**
WF17: Bat 3A **154**
Mnr. Farm Gdns.
LS10: Leeds 1A **140**
Mnr. Farm Grn. LS10: Leeds ...1A **140**
Mnr. Farm Gro. LS10: Leeds ...1A **140**
Mnr. Farm Ri. LS10: Leeds 1B **140**
Mnr. Farm Rd. LS10: Leeds 1A **140**
Mnr. Farm Wlk. LS10: Leeds ...1B **140**
Mnr. Farm Way LS10: Leeds ...2A **140**
Manorfield LS11: Leeds 2F **117**
Manorfields LS20: Hawk 5F **39**
Manor Fold BD16: Cot 3D **68**
LS18: H'fth 1C **74**
Manor Gdns. BD13: Cull 4B **66**
LS14: T'ner 1H **63**
LS21: Pool 4E **25**
WF12: Dew 6A **154**
Manor Gth. LS15: Leeds 4E **101**
LS25: Led 5H **125**
Manor Gth. Rd. LS25: Kip 3H **123**
Manor Gates LS16: B'hpe 2F **43**
Manor Golf Course, The 6A **114**
Manor Gro. BD20: Rid 5E **35**
LS7: Leeds 3B **78**
Manor Heath Park & Jungle Experience
...............................5F **149**
Mnr. Heath Rd. HX3: Hal 5F **149**
Manor Ho. LS21: Otley 3E **23**
(off Kirkgate)
Manor Ho. Cft. LS16: Leeds 4D **58**
Manor Ho. La. LS11: Leeds 1D **60**
Manor Ho. Rd. BD15: Wils 3G **67**
Manor Ho's. BD22: Oak 5C **46**
(off Colne La.)
Manor Ho. St. LS28: Pud 4A **94**

Manor La. BD18: Ship 2B **70**
(not continuous)
LS26: Oul 2E **143**
(off Aberford Rd.)
Manorley La. BD6: B'frd 1G **131**
Mnr. Mill La. LS11: Leeds 4E **117**
Manor Mills LS11: Leeds 4E **117**
(Manor Ct.)
LS11: Leeds 5H **97**
(Manor Rd.)
Manor Pk. BD8: B'frd 3F **89**
BD22: Oak 5C **46**
LS14: S'cft 6E **45**
WF12: Dew 6B **154**
(Chidswell La.)
WF12: Dew 6B **154**
(Windsor Rd.)
Manor Pk. Av. WF10: All B 2G **145**
Manor Pk. Gdns. BD19: Gom 4F **135**
Manor Ri. LS29: I'ly 5F **11**
Manor Rd. BD16: Cot 2C **68**
BD20: Keigh 3G **33**
LS11: Leeds 5H **97**
LS12: Leeds 6C **96**
LS18: H'fth 1C **74**
LS26: Rothw 1H **141**
LS27: Chur 5C **116**
WF17: Bat 4A **154**
Manor Row BD1: B'frd 2C **6** (3E **91**)
BD12: Low M 6C **110**
Manor Royd HX3: Hal 5G **149**
Manor Sq. LS19: Yead 6F **41**
LS21: Otley 3E **23**
Manor St. BD2: B'frd 6H **71**
BD19: Scho 3F **153**
LS7: Leeds 1B **98**
LS21: Otley 3E **23**
Manor St. Ind. Est. LS7: Leeds ...1C **98**
(not continuous)
Manor Ter. BD2: B'frd 6H **71**
LS6: Leeds 5E **77**
LS19: Yead 6F **41**
LS25: Kip 4H **123**
(off Roger Fold)
Manor Vw. BD20: East 6A **14**
(off Moor La.)
LS6: Leeds 5E **77**
LS28: Pud 4A **94**
Manscombe Rd. BD15: All 2E **89**
Manse Cres. LS29: Burl W 2E **21**
Mansel M. BD4: B'frd 4C **112**
Manse Rd. LS29: Burl W 2E **21**
Manse St. BD3: B'frd 4A **92**
Mansfield Av. BD16: Bgly 2E **51**
Mansfield Pl. LS6: Leeds 3D **76**
Mansfield Rd. BD8: B'frd 1C **90**
LS29: Burl W 2D **20**
Mansion Ga. LS7: Leeds 3C **78**
Mansion Ga. Dr. LS7: Leeds 3C **78**
Mansion Ga. M. LS7: Leeds 3C **78**
Mansion Ga. Sq. LS7: Leeds 3C **78**
Mansion La. HX3: Hal 5G **149**
LS8: Leeds 6F **61**
MANSTON 6F **81**
Manston App. LS15: Leeds 6E **81**
Manston Av. LS15: Leeds 6E **81**
Manston Cres. LS15: Leeds 6E **81**
Manston Dr. LS15: Leeds 6E **81**
Manston Gdns. LS15: Leeds 6F **81**
Manston Gro. LS15: Leeds 1E **101**
Manston La. LS15: Leeds 1F **101**
Manston Ri. LS15: Leeds 6E **81**
Manston Ter. LS15: Leeds 6F **81**
Manston Way LS15: Leeds 6E **81**
Mantra Ho. Bus. Cen.
BD21: Keigh 1H **47**
(off South St.)
Manywells Brow BD13: Cull 5A **66**
(not continuous)
Manywells Brow Ind. Est.
BD13: Cull 4B **66**
Manywells Cres. BD13: Cull 4B **66**
Manywells La. BD13: Cull 4H **65**

Maple Av. BD3: B'frd 3C **92**
BD22: Oak 5D **46**
Maple Ct. BD16: Bgly 5B **50**
(off Ash Ter.)
HX2: Illing 6C **106**
LS11: Leeds 3F **117**
LS14: Leeds 1B **100**
LS26: Wood 6D **120**
Maple Cft. LS12: N Far 6F **95**
LS17: Leeds 4C **60**
Maple Dr. LS12: N Far 6F **95**
LS22: Weth 2E **13**
Maple Fold HX5: Ell 6A **160**
LS12: N Far 6F **95**
Maple Gdns. LS17: Bard 6G **27**
Maple Gro. BD17: Bail 6G **51**
BD19: Gom 6E **135**
BD20: Keigh 4G **33**
HD2: Fix 6A **162**
LS12: N Far 6G **95**
Maple Ho. LS26: Rothw 3A **142**
Maple St. HX1: Hal 4D **148**
Maple Ter. LS19: Yead 6D **40**
Maple Way LS14: Leeds 1E **81**
Marbridge Ct.
BD6: B'frd 3B **110**
Marchant Way LS27: Chur 4C **116**
Marchbank Rd. BD3: B'frd 3A **92**
March Cote La. BD16: Cot 3B **68**
Marchmont Cres. LS25: Kip 5F **123**
Marchwood Gro.
BD14: Clay 6F **89**
Marcia Cl. BD10: B'frd 3A **72**
Mardale Cres. LS14: Leeds 6C **80**
Margaret Av. LS17: Bard 1F **45**
Margaret Cl. LS27: Morl 2C **138**
Margaret St. BD21: Keigh 5G **33**
HX1: Hal 2F **149**
WF1: Out 5E **157**
Margate LS26: Oul 1E **143**
Margate Rd. BD4: B'frd 1G **111**
Margate St. HX6: Sow B 6G **147**
Margerison Cres. LS29: I'ly 6G **11**
Margerison Rd. LS29: I'ly 6G **11**
Margetson Rd. BD11: Drig 2C **136**
Margram Bus. Cen. HX1: Hal 1F **149**
(off Horne St.)
Marian Gro. LS11: Leeds 2H **117**
Marian Rd. LS6: Leeds 6H **77**
Marian Ter. LS6: Leeds 6H **77**
Maria St. LS29: Burl W 1E **21**
Marina Cres. LS27: Morl 4H **137**
Marina Gdns. HX6: Sow B 5B **148**
(off Park Rd.)
Marion Dr. BD18: Ship 2C **70**
Marion St. BD7: B'frd 4C **90**
BD16: Bgly 4C **50**
HD6: Brigh 5A **152**
Mark Cl. BD10: B'frd 1A **72**
Market Arc. HX1: Hal 4C **164**
Market Balcony HX1: Hal 4C **164**
Market Bldgs.
LS2: Leeds 4G **5** (3B **98**)
Market Bus. Centre, The
HX1: Hal 2D **148**
Market Ct. BD13: Thorn 5A **88**
Market Hall LS27: Morl 3A **138**
(off Hope St.)
Market Pl. BD21: Keigh 6A **34**
LS21: Otley 3E **23**
LS22: Weth 4E **13**
LS28: Pud 4A **94**
Market Sq. BD18: Ship 2B **70**
LS27: Morl 3B **138**
(off Hope St.)
Market Stall HX1: Hal 4C **164**
(off Market St.)
Market St. BD1: B'frd 4D **6** (4E **91**)
BD6: B'frd 4C **110**
BD13: Thorn 5A **88**
BD16: Bgly 4B **50**
BD18: Ship 2B **70**
BD20: Stee 6D **14**

Market St. BD21: Keigh 1A 48
  HD6: Brigh 1B 162
     (not continuous)
  HX1: Hal 4C 164 (2G 149)
  LS21: Otley 4E 23
  WF17: Birs 4F 127
Market St. Arc. LS1: Leeds ..5F 5 (4A 98)
Markfield Av. BD12: Low M 2C 132
Markfield Cl. BD12: Low M 2C 132
Markfield Cres. BD12: Low M ...2C 132
Markfield Dr. BD12: Low M 2C 132
Markham Av. LS8: Leeds 5D 78
  LS19: Raw 2G 55
Markham Cres. LS19: Raw 2G 55
Markham Cft. LS19: Raw 2G 55
Markham Mkt. HX2: Hal 4C 148
Markington M. LS10: Leeds 4A 140
Markington Pl. LS10: Leeds 4A 140
Mark La. LS2: Leeds 3E 5 (3A 98)
Mark St. BD5: B'frd 2E 111
Marland Rd. BD21: Keigh 5C 34
Marlborough Av. HX3: Hal 5F 149
Marlborough Cotts. LS29: Men ...1H 39
     (off Leathley La.)
Marlborough Ct. LS14: S'cft 5E 45
  LS29: Men 1H 39
Marlborough Gdns. LS2: Leeds ...1H 97
     (off Bk. Blenheim Ter.)
Marlborough Grange LS1: Leeds ...3A 4
Marlborough Gro. LS2: Leeds 1H 97
     (off Bk. Blenheim Ter.)
  LS29: I'ly 6F 11
Marlborough Ho. HX5: Ell 4B 160
     (off St Mary's Ga.)
Marlborough Rd. BD8: B'frd 3G 89
  BD10: B'frd 1A 72
  BD18: Ship 2A 70
  HD2: Fix 6B 162
Marlborough Sq. LS29: I'ly 6F 11
Marlborough St. BD21: Keigh 5B 34
  LS1: Leeds 4A 4 (3G 97)
Marlborough Towers
  LS1: Leeds 3A 4 (3G 97)
Marlborough Vs. LS29: Men 1H 39
Marldon Rd. HX3: North 6C 130
MARLEY 1F 49
Marley Activities & Coaching Cen.
  ....5D 34
Marley Cl. BD8: B'frd 3G 89
Marley Ct. BD16: Bgly 6H 35
Marley Gro. LS11: Leeds 2F 117
Marley La. BD14: Clay 2A 108
Marley Pl. LS11: Leeds 2F 117
Marley Rd. BD21: Keigh 5D 34
Marley St. BD3: B'frd 4H 7 (4G 91)
  BD21: Keigh 1H 47
  LS11: Leeds 2F 117
Marley Ter. LS11: Leeds 2F 117
Marley Vw. BD16: Bgly 6H 35
  LS11: Leeds 2F 117
Marlo Rd. WF12: Dew 6A 154
Marlott Rd. BD18: Ship 1D 70
Marlowe Cl. LS28: Pud 6B 94
Marlowe Ct. LS20: Guis 4B 40
     (off Holly Bank)
  LS25: Gar 4F 103
Marmion Av. BD8: B'frd 4E 89
Marne Av. BD14: Clay 2E 109
Marne Ct. BD14: Clay 2E 109
Marne Cres. BD10: B'frd 2H 71
Marquis Av. BD12: O'haw 2H 133
Marriner Cl. LS21: Otley 1D 22
Marriner Rd. BD21: Keigh 1A 48
Marriner's Dr. BD9: B'frd 5B 70
Marriner's Wlk. BD21: Keigh ...2A 48
Marrtree Bus. Pk. BD20: Sils ...3E 15
Marsden Av. LS11: Leeds 3G 117
Marsden Cl. LS28: Fars 6H 73
     (off Water La.)
Marsden Gro. LS11: Leeds 3G 117
Marsden Memorial Homes
  LS28: Fars 1H 93
     (off Newlands)

Marsden Mt. LS11: Leeds 3G 117
Marsden Pl. LS11: Leeds 3G 117
Marsden St. LS12: Leeds 5H 95
Marsden Vw. LS11: Leeds 3G 117
Marsett Way LS14: Leeds 1D 80
MARSH 5B 64
Marsh LS28: Pud 4G 93
Marsh, The BD4: E Bier 6D 112
Marshall Av. LS15: Leeds 1F 101
Marshall Cl. LS27: Morl 3A 138
     (off Marshall St.)
Marshall Ct. LS11: Leeds 5G 97
  LS19: Yead 6F 41
Marshall Cres. LS27: Morl 5B 138
Marshall Mills LS11: Leeds 5G 97
Marshall St. BD20: Keigh 4H 33
  LS11: Leeds 5H 97
  LS15: Leeds 1E 101
  LS19: Yead 6F 41
  LS27: Morl 3A 138
Marshall Ter. LS15: Leeds 1E 101
Marsh Ct. LS28: Pud 4G 93
Marsh Delves HX3: Sou 3B 150
Marsh Delves La. HX3: Sou 3B 150
Marshfield Pl. BD5: B'frd 2D 110
MARSHFIELDS 3D 110
Marshfield St. BD5: B'frd 2D 110
Marsh Gro. BD5: B'frd 2C 110
     (not continuous)
Marsh La. BD11: Birk 2E 135
  BD22: Oxen 5A 64
  HX3: Sou 3A 150
  LS9: Leeds 5H 5 (4B 98)
     (not continuous)
Marsh Ri. LS28: Pud 4G 93
Marsh St. BD5: B'frd 2D 110
  LS6: Leeds 6G 77
  LS26: Rothw 3A 142
Marsh Ter. LS28: Pud 4G 93
MARSH TOP 5C 64
Marsh Va. LS6: Leeds 6G 77
Marsh Vw. LS28: Pud 4G 93
Marshway HX1: Hal 1E 149
Marsland Ct. BD19: Hun 5B 134
Marsland Pl. BD3: B'frd 4B 92
Marston Av. LS27: Morl 4A 138
Marston Cl. BD13: Que 4B 108
Marston Mt. LS9: Leeds 2C 98
     (off Lincoln Rd.)
Marston Way LS22: Weth 3C 12
Marten Rd. BD5: B'frd 2C 110
Martin Cl. LS27: Morl 3C 138
Martin Ct. BD6: B'frd 4E 109
  LS15: Leeds 3F 101
Martindale Cl. BD2: B'frd 6B 72
Martindale Dr. LS13: Leeds 2G 95
Martingale Dr. LS10: Leeds 4A 140
Martingale Fold LS15: Bar E 2D 82
Martin Grn. La. HX4: Gree 4E 159
     (not continuous)
Martin St. HD6: Brigh 6B 152
  WF17: Birs 4A 136
Martin Ter. LS4: Leeds 1C 96
Martlett Dr. BD5: B'frd 3F 111
Marton Ct. BD3: B'frd 4B 92
Marton Hgts. HX6: Sow B 5G 147
Marwood Rd. LS13: Leeds 4G 95
Maryfield Av. LS15: Leeds 1C 100
Maryfield Cl. LS15: Leeds 1C 100
Maryfield Ct. LS15: Leeds 1D 100
Maryfield Cres. LS15: Leeds ...1D 100
Maryfield Gdns. LS15: Leeds ...1C 100
Maryfield Grn. LS15: Leeds 1C 100
Maryfield M. LS15: Leeds 1C 100
Maryfield Va. LS15: Leeds 1C 100
Mary Seacole Ct. LS15: Leeds ...6D 90
Mary Seacole Ct. BD5: B'frd 6E 91
     (off Park La.)
Mary St. BD4: B'frd 6A 92
  BD12: Wyke 3C 132
  BD13: Denh 2B 86
  BD13: Thorn 5H 87
  BD18: Ship 1H 69

Mary St. BD22: Oxen 1C 84
  HD6: Brigh 5A 152
  LS28: Fars 5A 74
  WF3: E Ard 1C 156
Mary St. Caravan Site BD4: B'frd ..6A 92
Mary Sunley Ho. LS8: Leeds 6D 78
     (off Banstead St. W.)
Mary's Way HX6: Sow B 6G 147
Maryville Av. HD6: Brigh 4G 151
Masefield Av. BD9: B'frd 6E 69
Masefield St. LS20: Guis 5D 40
Masham Ct. LS6: Leeds 3D 76
Masham Gro. LS12: Leeds 4D 96
Masham Pl. BD9: B'frd 1H 89
Masham St. LS12: Leeds 4D 96
Masino Ter. BD7: B'frd 1A 110
     (off Paternoster La.)
Masonic St. HX1: Hal 3C 148
Mason's Grn. HX2: Illing 2C 128
Masons Mill BD17: Ship 6B 52
Mason Sq. HX2: Hal 4D 128
     (off Keighley Rd.)
Massey Flds. BD22: Haw 1D 64
Master La. HX2: Hal 5D 148
Matlock St. HX3: Hal 6E 129
Matrix Ct. LS11: Leeds 3H 117
Matthew Cl. BD20: Rid 4C 34
Matty La. LS26: Rothw 3F 141
Maude Av. LS11: Leeds 3H 117
Maude Cres. HX6: Sow B 6E 147
Maude St. HX3: Hal 3E 129
  HX4: Gree 4H 159
  LS2: Leeds 5G 5 (4B 98)
Maud Pl. LS11: Leeds 3H 117
Maudsley St. BD3: B'frd ..4H 7 (4G 91)
Maud St. BD3: B'frd 5H 91
Maufe Way LS29: I'ly 6D 10
Maurice Av. HD6: Brigh 5H 151
Mavis Av. LS16: Leeds 1G 57
Mavis Gro. LS16: Leeds 2G 57
Mavis La. LS16: Leeds 1G 57
Mavis St. BD3: B'frd 3H 7 (4H 91)
Mawcroft Cl. LS19: Yead 2E 55
Mawcroft Grange Dr.
  LS19: Yead 2E 55
Mawcroft M. LS19: Yead 2F 55
Mawson Ct. BD1: B'frd 4C 6
Mawson St. BD18: Ship 1H 69
Maw St. BD4: B'frd 6F 91
Maxwell Rd. BD6: B'frd 5H 109
  LS29: I'ly 6F 11
May Av. BD13: Thorn 5A 88
  LS27: Chur 5C 116
Maybrook Ind. Pk.
  LS12: Leeds 3E 97
May Ct. LS27: Chur 4C 116
Mayfair BD5: B'frd 1D 110
Mayfair Way BD4: B'frd 6B 92
Mayfield HX3: Hip 6E 131
  HX3: Nor G 5H 131
Mayfield Av. BD12: Wyke 4C 132
  HD6: B Bri 1B 152
  HX1: Hal 3E 149
  LS29: I'ly 5F 11
Mayfield Cl. LS29: I'ly 5F 11
Mayfield Ct. LS18: H'fth 6E 57
Mayfield Dr. BD20: Rid 5G 35
  HX1: Hal 3E 149
Mayfield Gdns. HX1: Hal 3E 149
  HX6: Sow B 5B 148
     (off Park Rd.)
  LS29: I'ly 4F 11
Mayfield Gro. BD15: Wils 3F 67
  BD17: Bail 4D 52
  HD6: B Bri 1B 152
  HX1: Hal 3E 149
Mayfield Mt. HX1: Hal 3E 149
Mayfield Pl. BD12: Wyke 4C 132
Mayfield Ri. BD12: Wyke 4D 132
Mayfield Rd. BD20: Keigh 5H 33
  LS15: Leeds 3D 100
  LS29: I'ly 5E 11

Mayfield St. HX1: Hal 4E 149
Mayfield St. BD12: Wyke 4D 132
  BD14: Clay 2E 109
  HX1: Hal 2D 148
Mayfield Ter. Sth. HX1: Hal 4E 149
  (off Kings Cross Rd.)
Mayfield Vw. BD12: Wyke 4D 132
Mayflower Ho. LS10: Leeds 3E 119
Mayhall Av. BD20: Rid 4E 35
Maylea Dr. LS21: Otley 5B 22
Mayo Av. BD5: B'frd 3D 110
Mayo Cl. LS8: Leeds 3H 79
Mayo Cres. BD5: B'frd 4E 111
Mayo Dr. BD5: B'frd 4E 111
Mayo Gro. BD5: B'frd 4E 111
Mayo Rd. BD5: B'frd 4E 111
Maypole M. LS15: Bar E 1D 82
Mayroyde HX3: Hip 2F 151
Mayster Gro. HD6: Ras 4G 161
Mayster Rd. HD6: Ras 4H 161
May St. BD19: Cleck 6B 134
  BD21: Keigh 5A 34
  BD22: Haw 3D 64
May Ter. LS9: Leeds 5D 98
Maythorne Cl. BD4: B'frd 3D 112
Maythorne Cres.
  BD14: Clay 1F 109
Maythorne Dr. BD14: Clay 1G 109
May Tree Cl. BD14: Clay 6F 89
Mayville Av. BD20: Rid 5F 35
  LS6: Leeds 6E 77
Mayville Pl. LS6: Leeds 6E 77
Mayville Rd. LS6: Leeds 6E 77
Mayville St. LS6: Leeds 6E 77
Mayville Ter. LS6: Leeds 6E 77
Mazebrook Av. BD19: Cleck 5C 134
Mazebrook Cres. BD19: Cleck 5C 134
Mead Cl. LS15: Leeds 5G 101
Meade, The LS25: Gar 4F 103
Mead Gro. LS15: Leeds 5G 101
Meadow, The LS14: S'cft 5F 45
Meadowbank Av. BD15: All 2D 88
Meadowbrook Ct. LS27: Morl 4G 137
Meadow Cl. BD16: Har 6F 49
  HX3: She 1F 131
  LS17: Bard 5G 27
  LS23: B Spa 3A 30
  WF1: Out 4H 157
  WF17: Bat 6C 136
Meadow Ct. BD15: All 5C 68
  HD6: Clift 1E 163
Meadow Cres. HX3: Hal 5C 128
Meadow Cft. BD11: Drig 1H 135
  BD22: Keigh 1E 47
  HD2: Hud 6F 163
  HX4: Bark 6A 158
  LS11: Leeds 6H 97
  LS17: E Kes 6E 27
  LS29: Men 2G 39
  WF1: Out 4G 157
Meadowcroft BD5: B'frd 4F 111
Meadowcroft Cl. BD10: B'frd 1F 71
  WF1: Out 4H 157
Meadowcroft Ct. WF1: Out 4H 157
Meadowcroft M. LS9: Leeds 4C 98
Meadowcroft Ri. BD4: B'frd 5A 112
Meadowcroft Rd. WF1: Out 4H 157
Meadow Dr. HX3: Hal 5C 128
Meadow End LS16: B'hpe 3G 43
Meadow Fold BD15: Wils 5H 67
Meadow Gth. LS16: B'hpe 4H 43
  WF1: Out 4G 157
Meadowgate Cft. WF3: Loft 5F 141
Meadowgate Dr. WF3: Loft 5F 141
Meadowgate Va. WF3: Loft 6F 141
Meadowhurst Gdns.
  LS28: Pud 4H 93
Meadowlands BD19: Scho 6E 133
Meadow La. BD20: Sils 4H 15
  HX3: Hal 5C 128
  LS11: Leeds 6E 5 (5A 98)
Meadow Pk. Cres. LS28: Stan 1F 93
Meadow Pk. Dr. LS28: Stan 1F 93

Meadow Rd. BD10: B'frd 1C 72
  LS11: Leeds 6H 97
  LS25: Gar 4G 103
Meadows, The BD6: B'frd 4C 110
  HX6: Lud M 4G 147
  LS16: Leeds 4C 58
  WF10: All B 1F 145
Meadow Side Rd. WF3: E Ard 6C 140
Meadowside Rd. BD17: Bail 3E 53
Meadow Va. WF1: Out 4G 157
Meadow Valley LS17: Leeds 2H 59
Meadow Vw. BD12: Wyke 6C 132
  BD22: Oak 5D 46
  LS6: Leeds 6E 77
  LS15: Bar E 1E 83
  LS28: Pud 4G 93
Meadow Wlk. HX3: Hal 5C 128
  (off Meadow Dr.)
  LS7: Leeds 3C 78
Meadow Way LS17: Leeds 2G 59
  WF3: W Ard 2D 154
Mead Rd. LS15: Leeds 5G 101
Mead Vw. BD4: B'frd 2C 112
Mead Way LS15: Leeds 5G 101
Meadway BD6: B'frd 1G 131
Meagill Ri. LS21: Otley 1B 22
MEANWOOD 2F 77
Meanwood Cl. LS7: Leeds 5H 77
MEANWOOD GROVE 6E 59
Meanwood Gro. LS6: Leeds 6E 59
Meanwood Rd. LS6: Leeds 3F 77
  LS7: Leeds 3F 77
Meanwood Towers LS6: Leeds 1G 77
Meanwood Valley Cl. LS7: Leeds . . .3F 77
Meanwood Valley Dr. LS7: Leeds . . .3F 77
Meanwood Valley Grn. LS7: Leeds . .3F 77
Meanwood Valley Gro. LS7: Leeds . .3F 77
Meanwood Valley Mt. LS7: Leeds . . .3F 77
Meanwood Valley Urban Farm 4H 77
Meanwood Valley Wlk.
  LS7: Leeds 3F 77
Mearclough Rd. HX6: Sow B 5B 148
Mecca Bingo
  Bradford 6C 6
  Halifax 3B 164
  Leeds, Balm Rd. 2B 118
  Leeds, Cross Gates Rd. 1E 101
  Leeds, New York St. 5G 5
Medway LS28: Stan 1G 93
Medhurst Av. LS25: Kip 3H 123
Medley La. HX3: North 3B 130
Medway BD13: Que 5B 108
Medway Av. LS25: Gar 6G 103
Meggison Gro. BD5: B'frd 1C 110
Megna Way BD5: B'frd 1E 111
Melba Rd. BD5: B'frd 2B 110
Melbourne Av. WF2: Wren 6D 156
Melbourne Gro. BD3: B'frd 3C 92
  LS13: Leeds 1E 95
Melbourne Ho. BD5: B'frd 6B 6
Melbourne M. WF2: Wren 5C 156
Melbourne Mills LS27: Morl 3B 138
  (off Melbourne St.)
Melbourne Mill Yd. LS27: Morl 3B 138
  (off Middleton Rd.)
Melbourne Pl. BD5: B'frd 6B 6 (6D 90)
Melbourne St. BD18: Ship 1A 70
  HX3: Hal 1H 149
  LS2: Leeds 2G 5 (2B 98)
  LS13: Leeds 1E 95
  LS27: Morl 3B 138
  LS28: Fars 1H 93
Melbourne Ter. BD5: B'frd 6C 6 (6E 91)
Melcombe Wlk. BD4: B'frd 1C 112
Meldon Way BD6: B'frd 4E 109
Melford St. BD4: B'frd 3A 112
Melilot Cl. BD16: Bgly 5D 50
Mellor St. HX1: Hal 4E 149
Mellor Ter. HX1: Hal 4E 149
Melrose BD22: Haw 3C 64
Melrose Ct. HX5: Ell 5A 160
Melrose Dr. LS29: Burl W 1E 21
Melrose Gro. LS18: H'fth 1G 75

Melrose Pl. LS18: H'fth 1F 75
  LS28: Pud 5H 93
Melrose St. BD7: B'frd 1A 110
  HX3: Hal 6E 129
Melrose Ter. HX5: Ell 5B 160
  LS18: H'fth 1F 75
Melrose Vs. LS18: H'fth 1F 75
  (off Melrose Ter.)
Melrose Wlk. LS18: H'fth 1F 75
Melton Av. LS10: Leeds 3D 140
Melton Cl. LS10: Leeds 3D 140
Melton Gth. LS10: Leeds 3D 140
Melton M. BD22: Haw 1D 64
Melton Ter. BD10: B'frd 5C 72
Melville Cl. LS6: Leeds 6H 77
Melville Gdns. LS6: Leeds 5H 77
Melville Gro. LS29: I'ly 5G 11
Melville Ho. BD7: B'frd 4C 90
  (off Preston St.)
Melville Pl. LS6: Leeds 5H 77
Melville Rd. LS6: Leeds 6H 77
Melville St. BD7: B'frd 4C 90
Memorial Cotts. LS12: N Far 2F 115
  (off Lawn La.)
Memorial Dr. LS6: Leeds 2F 77
Mendip Cl. LS25: Gar 6F 103
Mendip Ho. Gdns. LS29: I'ly 2E 11
Mendip Way BD12: Low M 1B 132
Menin Dr. BD17: Bail 2C 52
MENSTON 1F 39
Menston Dr. LS29: Men 2G 39
Menstone St. BD8: B'frd 2A 6 (3C 90)
Menston Hall LS29: Men 1H 39
Menston Ho. LS29: Men 2G 39
  (off High Royds Dr.)
Menston Old La. LS29: Burl W 5F 21
Menston Station (Rail) 6G 21
Merchants Ct. BD4: B'frd 6G 91
  BD16: Bgly 5C 50
Merchants Ho. LS2: Leeds 2G 5
  (off North St.)
Merchants Quay
  LS9: Leeds 6H 5 (4B 98)
Mercia Way LS15: Leeds 6G 81
Mercury Row LS21: Otley 4E 23
Meriden Av. LS25: Gar 6F 103
Merlin Cl. LS27: Morl 4C 138
Merlin Ct. BD21: Keigh 2H 47
  WF17: Bat 6C 136
Merlin Gro. BD8: B'frd 4E 89
Merlinwood Dr. BD17: Bail 3D 52
Merlyn-Rees Av. LS27: Morl 3A 138
Merrall Cl. BD22: Haw 1D 64
Merrion Cen. LS2: Leeds 2E 5 (2A 98)
Merrion Cres. HX3: Sou 4A 150
Merrion Pl. LS1: Leeds 3F 5 (3A 98)
  (not continuous)
  LS2: Leeds 3A 98
Merrion St. HX3: Sou 4A 150
  LS1: Leeds 3F 5 (3A 98)
  LS2: Leeds 3E 5 (3A 98)
  (not continuous)
Merrion Way LS2: Leeds 2E 5 (2A 98)
Merrivale Rd. BD15: All 3C 88
Merriville LS18: H'fth 2F 75
Merrydale Rd. BD4: B'frd 1G 133
Merton Av. LS28: Fars 1H 93
Merton Cl. LS25: Kip 3A 124
Merton Dr. LS28: Fars 1G 93
Merton Fold BD5: B'frd 1E 111
Merton Gdns. LS28: Fars 1G 93
Merton Rd. BD7: B'frd 6A 6 (6D 90)
Merville Av. BD17: Bail 2C 52
Metcalfe St. BD4: B'frd 1H 111
METHLEY .5C 144
Methley Dr. LS7: Leeds 3A 78
Methley Gro. LS7: Leeds 3A 78
METHLEY JUNCTION 6D 144
Methley La. LS7: Leeds 3B 78
  LS26: Oul 3E 143
Methley Mt. LS7: Leeds 3B 78
Methley Pl. LS7: Leeds 3A 78
Methley Ter. LS7: Leeds 3B 78

Methley Vw. LS7: Leeds 3B 78
Methuen Oval BD12: Wyke 6C 132
Mexborough Av. LS7: Leeds 5B 78
Mexborough Ct. LS14: T'ner 2H 63
Mexborough Dr. LS7: Leeds 5B 78
Mexborough Gro.
   LS7: Leeds 5B 78
Mexborough Ho. HX5: Ell 4B 160
   (off Westgate)
Mexborough Pl. LS7: Leeds 6B 78
Mexborough Rd. BD2: B'frd 4D 70
   LS7: Leeds 6B 78
Mexborough St. LS7: Leeds 5B 78
Meynell App. LS11: Leeds 6G 97
Meynell Av. LS26: Rothw 2A 142
Meynell Ct. LS15: Leeds 4F 101
Meynell Fold LS15: Leeds 5F 101
Meynell Hgts. LS11: Leeds 6G 97
Meynell La. LS15: Leeds 5F 101
Meynell Mt. LS26: Rothw 2B 142
Meynell Rd. LS15: Leeds 4F 101
Meynell Sq. LS11: Leeds 6G 97
Meynell Wlk. LS11: Leeds 6G 97
Meyrick Av. LS22: Weth 3G 13
Miall St. HX1: Hal 1E 149
Michael Av. WF3: S'ley 4H 157
Mickledore Ridge BD7: B'frd 2G 109
MICKLEFIELD 4E 105
Micklefield Ct. LS19: Raw 3F 55
Micklefield La. LS19: Raw 3E 55
Micklefield Rd. LS19: Raw 3F 55
Micklefield Station (Rail) 5E 105
Micklemoss Dr. BD13: Que 3G 107
MICKLETHWAITE 6A 36
Micklethwaite Dr. BD13: Que 5H 107
Micklethwaite Gro. LS22: Weth 5E 13
Micklethwaite La. BD16: Bgly 1A 50
Micklethwaite M. LS22: Weth 5E 13
Micklethwaite Stables LS22: Weth . .5E 13
Micklethwaite Steps LS22: Weth . . .5E 13
Micklethwaite Vw. LS22: Weth 5E 13
MICKLETOWN 4D 144
Mickletown Rd. LS26: Meth 4D 144
Mickley St. LS12: Leeds 4D 96
Middlebrook Cl. BD8: B'frd 4F 89
Middlebrook Cres. BD8: B'frd 5F 89
Middlebrook Dr. BD8: B'frd 4F 89
Middlebrook Hill BD8: B'frd 4F 89
Middlebrook Ri. BD8: B'frd 4F 89
Middlebrook Vw. BD8: B'frd 4G 89
Middlebrook Wlk. BD8: B'frd 4G 89
Middlebrook Way BD8: B'frd 5F 89
Middlecroft Cl. LS10: Leeds 5D 118
Middlecroft Rd. LS10: Leeds 5D 118
Middle Cross St. LS12: Leeds 4D 96
   (not continuous)
Middle Dean St. HX4: Gree 5G 159
Middle Ellistones HX4: Gree 4E 159
   (off Saddleworth Rd.)
Middlefield Ct. BD20: E Mor 4F 35
Middle Fold LS9: Leeds 3H 5 (3B 98)
Middlegate BD4: B'frd 5H 111
Middleham Ct. BD4: B'frd 2C 112
Middleham Moor LS10: Leeds 4B 140
Middle Harper Royd HX6: Norl 1A 158
Middle La. BD14: Clay 6E 89
   LS22: Lin 1B 28
Middlemoor LS14: Leeds 1D 80
Middle Rd. LS9: Leeds 3H 119
Middle St. BD1: B'frd 3D 6 (4E 91)
Middlethorne Cl. LS17: Leeds 2F 61
Middlethorne Ct. LS17: Leeds 2E 61
Middlethorne M. LS17: Leeds 2F 61
Middlethorne Ri. LS17: Leeds 2E 61
MIDDLETON
   LS10 . . . . .2H 139
   LS29 . . . . .2E 11
Middleton Av. LS9: Leeds 2D 98
   LS26: Rothw 2E 141
   LS29: I'ly 3D 10
Middleton Cl. LS27: Morl 3C 138
Middleton Cres. LS11: Leeds 3H 117

Middleton District Cen.
   LS10: Leeds 2B 140
Middleton Gro. LS11: Leeds 4H 117
Middleton La. LS27: Morl 3C 138
Middleton La. LS26: Rothw 2E 141
   (not continuous)
   WF3: Thpe H 4B 140
Middleton Leisure Cen. 2A 140
Middleton Lit. Rd. WF10: All B 3H 145
Middleton Pk. Av. LS10: Leeds . . .3H 139
Middleton Pk. Cir. LS10: Leeds . . .2H 139
Middleton Pk. Ct. LS10: Leeds . . .3H 139
Middleton Pk. Cres. LS10: Leeds . .3A 140
Middleton Park Equestrian Cen. . . .5A 118
Middleton Park Golf Course 2G 139
Middleton Pk. Grn. LS10: Leeds . .2H 139
Middleton Pk. Gro. LS10: Leeds . .2H 139
Middleton Pk. Mt. LS10: Leeds . . .2H 139
Middleton Pk. Rd. LS10: Leeds . . .2H 139
Middleton Pk. Ter. LS10: Leeds . . .3A 140
Middleton Railway
   Moor Road Station 2B 118
   Park Halt Station 5B 118
Middleton Rd. LS10: Leeds 6C 118
   LS27: Morl 3B 138
   LS29: I'ly 5C 10
Middleton St. BD8: B'frd 2B 90
Middleton Ter. LS27: Morl 3C 138
Middleton Way LS10: Leeds 1D 140
Middle Wlk. LS8: Leeds 6G 61
Middle Way BD21: Keigh 6C 34
Middleway BD20: Sils 2F 15
Midge Hall Cl. LS29: Burl W 2E 21
Midgeham Gro. BD16: Har 6E 49
Midgeley Rd. BD17: Bail 6A 52
MIDGLEY 6C 126
Midgley Dr. BD22: Haw 1D 64
Midgley Gdns. LS6: Leeds 6G 77
Midgley Pl. LS6: Leeds 6H 77
Midgley Rd. HX7: Myth 5A 126
   LS29: Burl W 2E 21
Midgley Row BD4: B'frd 4H 111
Midgley Ter. LS6: Leeds 6H 77
Midland Cl. LS10: Leeds 2D 118
Midland Gth. LS10: Leeds 2C 118
Midland Hall BD17: Bail 4B 50
Midland Ho. LS26: Wood 1F 143
   (off Midland St.)
Midland Pas. LS6: Leeds 6F 77
Midland Pl. LS11: Leeds 5G 97
Midland Rd. BD1: B'frd 1D 90
   BD8: B'frd 1C 6 (1D 90)
   BD9: B'frd 4C 70
   BD17: Bail 5D 52
   LS6: Leeds 6F 77
   LS10: Leeds 2C 118
Midland St. LS26: Oul 1E 143
Midland Ter. BD2: B'frd 6D 70
   BD21: Keigh 5A 34
Mid Point BD3: B'frd 3D 92
Mid Point Bus. Pk. BD3: B'frd 3D 92
Midway Av. BD16: Cot 2C 68
Milan Rd. LS8: Leeds 6D 78
Milan St. LS8: Leeds 6E 79
Milan St. BD3: B'frd 1G 7 (2G 91)
Mile Cross Gdns. HX1: Hal 3C 148
Mile Cross Pl. HX1: Hal 3C 148
Mile Cross Rd. HX1: Hal 3C 148
Mile Cross Ter. HX1: Hal 3C 148
Miles Gth. LS17: Bard 5H 27
MILES HILL 3H 77
Miles Hill Av. LS7: Leeds 3H 77
Miles Hill Cres. BD4: B'frd 4A 112
   LS7: Leeds 3H 77
Miles Hill Dr. BD4: B'frd 4A 112
Miles Hill Gro. LS7: Leeds 3H 77
Miles Hill Mt. LS7: Leeds 2G 77
Miles Hill Pl. LS7: Leeds 2H 77
Miles Hill Rd. LS7: Leeds 3H 77
Miles Hill Sq. LS7: Leeds 3H 77
Miles Hill St. LS7: Leeds 3H 77
Miles Hill Ter. LS7: Leeds 3H 77
Miles Hill Vw. LS7: Leeds 3H 77

Milestone Ct. LS28: Stan 1B 94
Mile Thorn St. HX1: Hal 2D 148
Milford Gro. BD19: Gom 4E 135
Milford Pl. BD9: B'frd 6A 70
   LS4: Leeds 2D 96
Millbank LS19: Yead 5F 41
Millbank Ct. LS28: Pud 5B 94
Millbank Fold LS28: Pud 5B 94
Mill Banks BD20: Sils 2E 15
Millbank Vw. LS28: Pud 5B 94
Millbeck App. LS27: Morl 3C 138
Mill Beck Cl. LS28: Fars 5A 74
Millbeck Cl. BD8: B'frd 5E 89
Millbeck Dr. BD16: Har 5E 49
Millbeck Grn. LS22: Coll 3A 28
Mill Carr Hill Rd. BD4: B'frd 3H 133
   BD12: O'haw 3H 133
Mill Cotts. LS21: Pool 4F 25
Mill Ct. BD22: Oxen 1C 84
Mill Cft. LS27: Gil 6F 115
Mill Dale Rd. BD11: Drig 1B 136
   (off Moorside Va.)
Mill Dam LS23: Cliff 6C 30
Millennium Bus. Pk. BD20: Stee . . .5C 14
Millennium Ct. LS28: Pud 3B 94
   (off Lowtown)
Millennium Dr. LS11: Leeds 4H 117
Millennium Sq.
   LS2: Leeds 2D 4 (2H 97)
Millennium Way LS11: Leeds 4H 117
Miller Cl. BD2: B'frd 4D 70
Miller Ct. HD6: B Bri 3B 152
   (off Axminster Dr.)
Millergate BD1: B'frd 4C 6 (4E 91)
Millers Cft. WF17: Bat 6D 136
Millers Dale LS27: Morl 1H 137
Millersdale Cl. BD4: B'frd 6G 111
Mill Fld. Ct. BD20: Sils 2E 15
Mill Fld. End HX2: Midg 1C 146
Mill Fld. Rd. BD16: Cot 2D 68
Millfields BD20: Sils 2D 14
Mill Fold LS27: Gil 6F 115
   LS29: Add 2G 9
Mill Garth LS27: Gil 6F 115
   LS22: Coll 3B 28
Millgarth St. LS2: Leeds 4G 5 (3B 98)
Millgate BD16: Bgly 4B 50
   HX5: Ell 4B 160
MILL GREEN 4D 80
Mill Grn. LS12: Leeds 5F 97
Mill Grn. Cl. LS14: Leeds 4E 81
Mill Grn. Gdns. LS14: Leeds 4E 81
Mill Grn. Gth. LS14: Leeds 4E 81
Mill Grn. Pl. LS14: Leeds 4E 81
Mill Grn. Rd. LS14: Leeds 4E 81
Mill Grn. Vw. LS14: Leeds 4E 81
Mill Ho. HD6: Brigh 5H 151
Millhaven M. BD8: B'frd 2D 90
   (off Holywell Ash La.)
Mill Hey BD22: Haw 2D 64
Mill Hill BD22: Haw 2C 64
   HX2: Lud M 1B 146
   LS1: Leeds 5E 5 (4A 98)
   LS26: Rothw 2A 142
   LS28: Pud 6A 94
Mill Hill Grn. LS26: Rothw 2A 142
Mill Hill La. HD6: Brigh 5G 151
   (Springvale Works)
   HD6: Brigh 2F 163
   (Wakefield Rd.)
Mill Hill Sq. LS26: Rothw 2A 142
Mill Hill Top BD16: Har 1F 67
Mill Ho. Ri. BD5: B'frd 4H 111
Milligan Av. BD2: B'frd 4F 71
Milligan Ct. BD16: Har 6E 49
Mill La. BD4: B'frd 6E 91
   (Manchester Rd.)
   BD4: B'frd 2B 114
   (Tong La.)

Mill La. BD5: B'frd 6E **91**
   BD6: B'frd 1G **131**
   BD11: Birk 1E **135**
   BD13: Que 3G **107**
   BD16: Bgly 1E **51**
   BD19: Cleck, Hun 5B **134**
   BD20: Stee 6C **14**
   BD22: Oak 5B **46**
         (Commercial St.)
   BD22: Oak 5C **46**
         (Providence La.)
   BD22: Oxen 6C **64**
   HD5: Hud 6H **163**
   HD6: Brigh 1B **162**
   HX2: Lud 5E **127**
   HX2: Mix 6A **106**
   HX3: Hal 5F **129**
   LS13: Leeds 6C **74**
   LS17: Bard 1G **45**
   LS20: Hawk 6C **38**
   LS21: Otley 3E **23**
   LS21: Pool 4E **25**
   LS22: Coll 3B **28**
   LS22: Kear 1A **26**
   LS23: T Arch 3C **30**
   LS26: Meth 4C **144**
   LS27: Gil 6F **115**
   WF3: E Ard 1B **156**
   WF17: Birs 5D **136**
Millmoor Cl. BD9: B'frd 1F **89**
Mill Pit La. LS26: Rothw 6H **119**
Mill Pond Cl. LS6: Leeds 3E **77**
Millpond Gdns. LS12: Leeds 3B **96**
        (off Eyres Mill Side)
Mill Pond Gro. LS6: Leeds 3E **77**
Mill Pond La. LS6: Leeds 2E **77**
Mill Pond Sq. LS6: Leeds 2E **77**
Mill Race La. BD4: B'frd 5B **92**
Mill Row BD20: East 5A **14**
Mill Royd St. HD6: Brigh 1B **162**
MILL SHAW 4E **117**
Millshaw LS11: Leeds 4D **116**
Millshaw Mt. LS11: Leeds 5E **117**
Millshaw Pk. Av. LS11: Leeds 5D **116**
Millshaw Pk. Cl. LS11: Leeds 5D **116**
Millshaw Pk. Dr. LS11: Leeds 4D **116**
Millshaw Pk. La. LS11: Leeds 5D **116**
Millshaw Pk. Trad. Est.
   LS11: Leeds 5E **117**
Millshaw Pk. Way LS11: Leeds 4D **116**
Millshaw Rd. LS11: Leeds 6E **117**
Millside Wlk. LS27: Morl 3C **138**
Millside Way HX3: Hal 6H **149**
Millstream Cl. BD20: E Mor 4F **35**
Mill Stream Dr. HX2: Lud M 2D **146**
Mill St. BD1: B'frd 2E **7** (3F **91**)
   BD6: B'frd 4A **110**
   BD13: Cull 3B **66**
   HX3: Hal 2E **159**
   LS9: Leeds 5H **5** (4C **98**)
   LS27: Morl 4A **138**
Mill Vw. BD18: Ship 1A **70**
   LS29: Burl W 1E **21**
Mill West HX6: Sow B 6H **147**
         (off West St.)
Millwright St. LS2: Leeds . . .2H **5** (2B **98**)
Milne Ct. LS15: Scho 5F **101**
Milner Bank LS21: Otley 5B **22**
Milner Cl. HX4: Gree 4G **159**
Milner Ct. BD18: Ship 1G **69**
Milner Fold LS28: Pud 6H **93**
Milner Gdns. LS9: Leeds 5D **98**
Milner Ga. HX2: Lud M 3C **146**
Milner Ing BD12: Wyke 3C **132**
Milner La. HX4: Gree 4G **159**
   LS14: S'cft, T'ner 5H **45**
   WF3: Rob H 4E **141**
Milner Pl. HX2: Lud M 3D **146**
Milner Rd. BD17: Bail 6A **52**
Milner Royd La. HX6: Norl 6C **148**
Milner Royd Nature Reserve 5C **148**
Milner's Rd. LS19: Yead 6D **40**
Milner St. HX1: Hal 2F **149**

Milnes Ct. BD6: B'frd 5A **110**
Milnes St. LS12: Leeds 5E **97**
Milroyd Cres. WF17: Birs 5C **136**
Milton Av. HX6: Sow B 4H **147**
Milton Dr. LS15: Scho 2H **81**
Milton Pl. HX1: Hal 2F **149**
   HX6: Sow B 4H **147**
         (off Milton St.)
Milton St. BD7: B'frd 4C **90**
   BD13: Denh 3C **86**
   HX6: Sow B 4H **147**
Milton Ter. HX1: Hal 2F **149**
         (not continuous)
   LS5: Leeds 5A **76**
   LS19: Yead 6D **40**
Miners M. LS25: M'fld 5E **105**
         (off Pit La.)
Miners Way HX3: Sou 5C **150**
Minerva Ind. Est. LS26: Wood 6G **121**
Minnie St. BD21: Keigh 1H **47**
   BD22: Haw 3C **64**
Minor and Scurr's Yd. LS1: Leeds 4E **5**
Minorca Mt. BD13: Denh 2B **86**
Minstead Av. HX5: Ell 4F **161**
Minster Cl. HX4: Gree 4F **159**
Minster Dr. BD4: B'frd 6B **92**
Minstrel Dr. BD13: Que 4A **108**
Mint St. BD2: B'frd 1H **91**
Miramar HD2: Hud 6D **162**
Mires Beck Cl. BD8: Ship 1E **71**
Mirey La. HX6: Sow B 5B **146**
Mirfield Av. BD2: B'frd 4G **71**
Mirycarr La. LS14: Leeds, T'ner . . .5G **63**
Miry La. HX7: Crag V 3A **146**
   LS19: Yead 6F **41**
   WF15: Liv 5H **153**
         (not continuous)
Mission La. HD6: Brigh 2C **162**
Mistal, The BD10: B'frd 1F **71**
Mistral Cl. BD12: Wyke 5C **132**
Mistral Gro. WF15: Liv 4H **153**
Mistress La. LS12: Leeds 3C **96**
Mitcham Dr. BD9: B'frd 1A **90**
Mitchell Cl. BD10: B'frd 6A **54**
Mitchell La. BD10: B'frd 6A **54**
   BD20: Sils 2E **15**
Mitchell Sq. BD5: B'frd 1E **111**
   BD20: Sils 2E **15**
         (off Elliot St.)
Mitchell St. BD21: Keigh 5B **34**
   HD6: Brigh 6A **152**
   HX6: Sow B 5A **148**
Mitchell Ter. BD16: Bgly 5B **50**
Mitford Pl. LS12: Leeds 4D **96**
Mitford Rd. LS12: Leeds 4D **96**
Mitford Ter. LS12: Leeds 4D **96**
Mitford Vw. LS12: Leeds 4D **96**
Mitre Ct. BD4: B'frd 2B **112**
Mitton St. BD5: B'frd 2C **110**
   BD16: Cot 3D **68**
MIXENDEN 2A **128**
Mixenden Activity Cen. 1H **127**
Mixenden Cl. HX2: Mix 2A **128**
Mixenden Ct. HX2: Mix 3B **128**
         (off Jumples Cl.)
Mixenden Grn. HX2: Mix 6A **106**
Mixenden La. HX2: Mix 1B **128**
Mixenden La. Ends HX2: Mt T . . .3H **127**
Mixenden Rd. HX2: Mix 1A **128**
Mixenden Stones HX2: Mix 1A **128**
Moat Cres. BD10: B'frd 1A **72**
Moat End LS14: T'ner 2H **63**
Moat Hill WF17: Birs 5B **136**
Moat Hill Farm Dr. WF17: Birs 5C **136**
Moat Ho. Sq. LS23: T Arch 2H **31**
Modder Av. LS12: Leeds 4B **96**
Modder Pl. LS12: Leeds 4B **96**
Model Av. LS12: Leeds 4D **96**
Model Rd. LS12: Leeds 4D **96**
Model Ter. LS12: Leeds 4D **96**
Moderna Bus. Pk. HX7: Myth 1A **146**
Moderna Way HX7: Myth 6A **126**
Moffat Cl. BD6: B'frd 6H **109**

Moffatt Cl. HX3: Hal 4C **128**
Moins Cl. HX2: Mix 2H **127**
Monarch Ga. BD13: Denh 5C **86**
Mond Av. BD3: B'frd 2B **92**
Monk Barn Cl. BD16: Bgly 3C **50**
Monk Bri. Av. LS6: Leeds 3F **77**
Monk Bri. Dr. LS6: Leeds 3F **77**
Monk Bri. Gro. LS6: Leeds 3E **77**
Monk Bri. Mt. LS6: Leeds 3F **77**
Monk Bri. Pl. LS6: Leeds 3E **77**
Monk Bri. Rd. LS6: Leeds 3E **77**
Monk Bri. St. LS6: Leeds 3F **77**
Monk Bri. Ter. LS6: Leeds 3E **77**
Monk Ings WF17: Birs 6H **135**
Monk Ings Av. WF17: Birs 6G **135**
Monkmans Wharf BD20: Sils 2E **15**
Monk St. BD7: B'frd 4A **6** (4C **90**)
Monkswood LS5: Leeds 3H **75**
Monkswood Av. LS14: Leeds 1B **80**
Monkswood Bank LS14: Leeds 1B **80**
Monkswood Cl. LS14: Leeds 1B **80**
Monkswood Dr. LS14: Leeds 1B **80**
Monkswood Ga. LS14: Leeds 1C **80**
Monkswood Grn. LS14: Leeds 1B **80**
Monkswood Hill LS14: Leeds 1B **80**
Monkswood Ho. LS5: Leeds 5H **75**
Monkswood Ri. LS14: Leeds 1B **80**
Monkswood Wlk. LS14: Leeds 1C **80**
Monkwood Rd. WF1: Out 4F **157**
Monson Av. LS28: Cal 3F **73**
Montagu Av. LS8: Leeds 4F **79**
Montagu Cl. LS8: Leeds 3F **79**
Montagu Cres. LS8: Leeds 4G **79**
Montagu Dr. LS8: Leeds 3F **79**
Montague LS12: Leeds 5A **4**
Montague Ct. LS12: Leeds 4A **96**
Montague Cres. LS25: Gar 3G **103**
Montague Pl. LS25: Gar 4G **103**
Montague St. BD5: B'frd 2C **110**
   HX6: Sow B 6G **147**
Montagu Gdns. LS8: Leeds 4F **79**
Montagu Gro. LS8: Leeds 4G **79**
Montagu Pl. LS8: Leeds 4F **79**
Montagu Ri. LS8: Leeds 4G **79**
Montagu Rd. LS22: Weth 4G **13**
Montagu Vw. LS8: Leeds 4F **79**
Montcalm Cres. LS10: Leeds 3C **118**
Monterey Dr. BD15: All 6B **68**
Montfort Cl. LS18: H'fth 4D **56**
Montgomery Av. LS16: Leeds 2C **76**
Montgomery Ho. BD8: B'frd 2C **90**
         (off Trenton Dr.)
Mont Gro. BD5: B'frd 2C **110**
         (off Montague St.)
Montpelier Ter. LS6: Leeds 5G **77**
Montreal Av. LS7: Leeds 3B **78**
Montreal Ter. LS13: Leeds 3C **94**
Montrose Pl. BD13: Que 3G **107**
Montrose St. BD2: B'frd 5D **70**
Montserrat Rd. BD4: B'frd 4D **112**
Moody St. BD4: B'frd 6F **91**
Moon Cl. WF17: Birs 6B **136**
MOOR ALLERTON 4A **60**
Moor Allerton Av. LS17: Leeds 5C **60**
Moor Allerton Cen. LS17: Leeds . . .5H **59**
Moor Allerton Cres. LS17: Leeds . . .5C **60**
Moor Allerton Dr. LS17: Leeds 5C **60**
Moor Allerton Gdns. LS17: Leeds . .5B **60**
Moor Allerton Golf Course 5A **44**
Moor Allerton Hall LS8: Leeds 6D **60**
Moor Allerton Way LS17: Leeds . . .5C **60**
Moor Av. LS15: Leeds 4B **100**
   LS23: Cliff 5B **30**
Moor Bank BD4: B'frd 6E **113**
Moorbank Cl. LS6: Leeds 4E **77**
MOORBOTTOM 2H **153**
Moor Bottom HX2: Mt T 5G **127**
Moorbottom BD19: Cleck 2H **153**
Moor Bottom La. BD21: Keigh 5H **47**
   HX2: Lud M 5B **146**
   HX4: Gree 2E **159**
   HX6: Norl 2A **158**
   HX7: Crag V 4A **146**

Moorbottom La.—Moorside Av.

Moorbottom La. BD16: Bgly 4C **50**
Moor Bottom Rd. HX2: Illing 1D **128**
Moor Cl. LS10: Leeds 3B **118**
Moor Cl. Av. BD13: Que 5G **107**
Moor Cl. Farm M. BD13: Que 5G **107**
Moor Cl. La. BD13: Que 5G **107**
Moor Cl. Pde. BD13: Que 4G **107**
Moor Cl. Rd. BD13: Que 5G **107**
Moor Cres. LS11: Leeds 1A **118**
Moor Cres. Chase LS11: Leeds 1A **118**
Moor Cft. BD16: Bgly 2D **50**
LS16: Leeds 3D **58**
Moorcroft Av. BD3: B'frd 2B **92**
BD22: Oak 4E **47**
Moorcroft Dr. BD4: B'frd 4D **112**
Moorcroft Rd. BD4: B'frd 4D **112**
Moorcroft Ter. BD4: B'frd 4D **112**
Moor Dr. BD22: Oak 4C **46**
LS6: Leeds 3E **77**
LS21: Otley 3H **23**
LS28: Pud 6B **94**
Moore Av. BD6: B'frd 2H **109**
BD7: B'frd 2H **109**
MOOR EDGE **5E 49**
Moor Edge High Side BD16: Har 5E **49**
Moor Edge Low Side BD16: Har 5E **49**
Moorehouse Gro. LS9: Leeds 2C **98**
MOOR END
BD2 **3G 71**
HX2 **3H 127**
LS12 **4A 96**
MOOREND **6B 134**
Moor End BD22: Oxen 3D **64**
HX6: Norl 1B **158**
LS23: B Spa 3G **29**
Moor End Av. HX2: Hal 6A **128**
Moor End Gdns. HX2: Hal 6B **128**
LS23: B Spa 3H **29**
Moor End La. HX6: Norl 1B **158**
(not continuous)
Moor End Rd. HX2: Hal, Mt T 2H **127**
Moor End Vw. HX2: Hal 1C **148**
Moore St. BD21: Keigh 1A **48**
Moore Vw. BD7: B'frd 2H **109**
Moor Farm Gdns. LS7: Leeds 2A **78**
Moorfield LS27: Gil 6E **115**
Moorfield Av. BD3: B'frd 2B **92**
BD19: Scho 2E **153**
LS12: Leeds 3A **96**
LS29: Men 1F **39**
Moorfield Bus. Pk. LS19: Yead 1H **55**
Moorfield Cl. LS19: Yead 1H **55**
Moorfield Ct. LS19: Yead 1H **55**
Moorfield Cres. LS12: Leeds 3A **96**
LS19: Yead 1G **55**
LS28: Pud 5H **93**
Moorfield Cft. LS19: Yead 1H **55**
Moorfield Dr. BD17: Bail 2C **52**
BD22: Oak 4D **46**
LS19: Yead 1H **55**
Moorfield Gdns. LS28: Pud 5G **93**
Moorfield Gro. LS12: Leeds 3A **96**
LS28: Pud 5G **93**
Moorfield Ind. Est. LS19: Yead 6H **41**
Moorfield Pl. BD10: B'frd 1H **71**
(not continuous)
Moorfield Rd. BD16: Cot 2C **68**
LS12: Leeds 3A **96**
LS19: Yead 1H **55**
LS29: I'ly 5H **11**
Moorfields LS13: Leeds 6E **75**
LS17: Leeds 5B **60**
Moorfield St. HX1: Hal 4E **149**
LS2: Leeds 6G **77**
LS12: Leeds 3A **96**
Moorfield Ter. LS19: Yead 6G **41**
Moorfield Way BD19: Scho 2E **153**
LS29: I'ly 5H **11**
Moor Flatts Av. LS10: Leeds 2A **140**
Moor Flatts Rd. LS10: Leeds 2A **140**
MOOR GARFORTH **3F 103**
Moorgarth Av. BD3: B'frd 2B **92**
MOOR GATE **3G 123**
Moorgate BD17: Bail 3C **52**
Moorgate Av. BD3: B'frd 2B **92**
LS25: Kip 2G **123**
Moorgate Cl. LS25: Kip 3G **123**
Moorgate Dr. LS25: Kip 3H **123**
Moorgate Ri. LS25: Kip 3G **123**
Moorgate Rd. LS25: Kip 2G **123**
Moorgate St. HX1: Hal 4D **148**
Moor Grange LS19: Yead 1H **55**
Moor Grange Ct. LS16: Leeds 1H **75**
Moor Grange Dr. LS16: Leeds 1A **76**
Moor Grange Ri. LS16: Leeds 1A **76**
Moor Grange Vw.
LS16: Leeds 1A **76**
Moorgreen Fold BD10: B'frd 2G **71**
Moor Gro. HX3: She 6E **109**
LS28: Pud 6B **94**
Moor Haven LS17: Leeds 4G **59**
Moorhaven Ct. LS17: Leeds 4G **59**
MOOR HEAD **5E 115**
MOORHEAD **2G 69**
Moorhead Cres. BD18: Ship 2G **69**
Moorhead La. BD18: Ship 2G **69**
Moorhead Ter. BD18: Ship 2G **69**
Moorhead Vs. LS27: Gil 4D **114**
Moor Hey La. HD2: Fix 6E **161**
Moorhouse BD22: Oxen 5B **64**
Moorhouse Av. BD2: B'frd 4G **71**
LS11: Leeds 4F **117**
Moorhouse Bri. BD22: Oxen 6C **64**
Moorhouse Cl. BD22: Oxen 6C **64**
Moor Ho. Ct. LS17: Leeds 3F **61**
Moorhouse Ct. BD22: Oxen 6C **64**
Moorhouse Dr. BD11: Birk 6D **112**
Moorhouse La. BD11: Birk 6E **113**
BD22: Oxen 5B **64**
Moorhouse Ter. HX3: Hal 6F **129**
Moorings, The BD10: B'frd 1B **72**
LS10: Leeds 2F **119**
LS17: Leeds 2C **60**
Moor Knoll Cl. WF3: E Ard 1B **156**
Moor Knoll Dr. WF3: E Ard 1A **156**
Moor Knoll Gdns. WF3: E Ard 6A **140**
Moor Knoll La. WF3: E Ard 6A **140**
Moorland Av. BD16: Bgly 2E **51**
BD17: Bail 3D **52**
LS6: Leeds 1F **97**
LS20: Guis 4C **40**
LS27: Gil 5D **114**
Moorland Cl. HX2: Illing 4C **128**
LS17: Leeds 6B **60**
LS27: Gil 5E **115**
Moorland Cres. BD17: Bail 3D **52**
LS17: Leeds 6A **60**
LS20: Guis 3C **40**
LS27: Gil 5D **114**
LS28: Pud 3E **93**
LS29: Men 3A **40**
(Bradford Rd.)
LS29: Men 6G **21**
(Chevin Av.)
Moorland Dr. BD11: Birk 6F **113**
LS17: Leeds 6A **60**
LS20: Guis 3C **40**
LS28: Pud 2E **93**
Moorland Gdns. LS17: Leeds 6B **60**
Moorland Gth. LS17: Leeds 6A **60**
Moorland Gro. LS17: Leeds 5A **60**
LS28: Pud 2E **93**
Moorland Ings LS17: Leeds 6A **60**
Moorland Leys LS17: Leeds 6A **60**
Moorland Mills BD19: Cleck 6B **134**
Moorland Mt. BD19: Cleck 3H **153**
Moorland Pl. BD12: Low M 2E **133**
Moorland Ri. LS17: Leeds 6A **60**
Moorland Rd. BD11: Drig 1A **136**
LS6: Leeds 1F **97**
LS16: B'hpe 3D **42**
LS28: Pud 2E **93**
Moorlands LS29: I'ly 1C **18**
Moorlands, The LS17: Leeds 3C **60**
LS22: Weth 4F **13**
LS23: B Spa 3A **30**
Moorlands Av. BD3: B'frd 2B **92**
BD11: Birk 6E **113**
BD22: Oak 3F **47**
HX2: Illing 4C **128**
LS19: Yead 1H **55**
Moorlands Bus. Cen.
BD19: Cleck *6B* ***134***
(off Balme Rd.)
Moorlands Ct. HX4: Gree 3F **159**
LS22: Weth 4F **13**
Moorlands Cres. HX2: Illing 4C **128**
Moorlands Dr. HX3: Illing 5C **128**
LS19: Yead 1H **55**
Moorlands Pl. HX1: Hal 4F **149**
Moorlands Rd. BD11: Birk 6E **113**
HX4: Gree 3F **159**
Moorlands Vw. HX1: Hal 4F **149**
LS22: Weth 4F **13**
Moorland Ter. BD21: Keigh 1D **48**
LS25: Gar 5E **103**
Moorland Vw. BD12: Low M 2E **133**
BD15: Wils 5H **67**
HX6: Sow B 6F **147**
LS13: Leeds 5D **74**
LS17: Leeds 5A **60**
Moorland Wlk. LS17: Leeds 5A **60**
Moor La. BD11: Birk 3G **135**
BD19: Gom 5F **135**
BD20: East 6A **14**
HX2: Illing 3C **128**
LS17: E Kes 5B **26**
LS20: Guis 2C **40**
LS21: Weston 1H **21**
LS22: Coll 5F **29**
LS29: Add 1A **8**
(not continuous)
LS29: Burl W 4C **20**
LS29: Men 6D **20**
Moorlea Dr. BD17: Bail 4D **52**
Moorleigh Cl. LS25: Kip 3H **123**
Moorleigh Dr. LS25: Kip 3H **123**
Moor Lodge Caravan Pk.
LS17: Bard 4C **44**
Moor Pk. Av. LS6: Leeds 3D **76**
Moor Pk. Cl. BD3: B'frd 3A **92**
LS29: Add 1B **8**
Moor Pk. Cres. LS29: Add 1B **8**
Moor Pk. Dr. BD3: B'frd 3B **92**
LS6: Leeds 3D **76**
LS29: Add 1B **8**
Moor Pk. Gro. LS29: Add 1C **8**
Moor Pk. Mt. LS6: Leeds 3D **76**
Moor Pk. Rd. BD3: B'frd 3A **92**
Moor Pk. Vs. LS6: Leeds 3E **77**
Moor Pk. Way LS29: Add 1C **8**
Moor Rd. LS6: Leeds 3D **76**
LS10: Leeds 1B **118**
LS11: Leeds 1A **118**
LS16: B'hpe 2F **43**
LS29: Burl W, I'ly 2G **19**
WF3: S'ley 3H **157**
Moor Road Station
Middleton Railway **2B 118**
Moor Royd HX3: Hal 5E **149**
Moors Centre, The *LS29: I'ly* *5D* ***10***
(off Cunliffe Rd.)
MOOR SIDE
BD2 **1H 91**
BD12 **2C 132**
MOORSIDE
BD11 **2B 136**
LS13 **5E 75**
Moor Side LS23: B Spa 3H **29**
Moorside BD9: B'frd 1G **89**
BD17: Bail 2C **52**
BD19: Cleck 3G **153**
(not continuous)
BD22: Oxen 5A **64**
Moorside App. BD11: Drig 2B **136**
Moorside Av. BD2: B'frd 1A **92**
BD11: Birk 6E **113**
BD11: Drig 2B **136**
BD20: East 6A **14**

A-Z Leeds & Bradford 247

Moorside Cl. BD2: B'frd 6A **72**
   BD11: Drig 2B **136**
Moorside Ct. LS29: I'ly 6E **11**
Moorside Cres. BD11: Drig 2A **136**
Moorside Cft. BD2: B'frd 1A **92**
Moorside Dr. BD11: Drig 2B **136**
   LS13: Leeds 5E **75**
Moorside Fold BD13: Que 3F **107**
Moorside Gdns. BD2: B'frd 6A **72**
   BD11: Drig 2B **136**
   HX3: Hal 3D **128**
Moorside Grn. BD11: Drig 1B **136**
Moorside La. BD3: B'frd 4B **92**
   BD22: Haw, Oxen 4A **64**
   LS29: Add 5C **8**
Moorside Maltings LS11: Leeds . . .1A **118**
Moorside Mdws. BD2: B'frd 1B **92**
Moorside M. BD2: B'frd 6A **72**
Moorside Mt. BD11: Drig 2A **136**
Moorside Paddock BD19: Cleck . .3H **153**
Moorside Pde. BD11: Drig 2B **136**
Moorside Pl. BD3: B'frd 4B **92**
Moorside Ri. BD19: Cleck 2H **153**
Moorside Rd. BD2: B'frd 5A **72**
   BD3: B'frd 4B 92
   (off Moorside La.)
   BD11: Drig 2A **136**
   BD15: Wils 5G **67**
Moorside St. BD12: Low M 1B **132**
   LS13: Leeds 5E **75**
Moorside Ter. BD2: B'frd 1B **92**
   BD11: Drig 2B **136**
   LS13: Leeds 5E **75**
Moorside Va. BD11: Drig 1B **136**
Moorside Vw. BD11: Drig 2B **136**
Moorside Wlk. BD11: Drig 1B **136**
Moor Smith Copse HX2: Illing . . .6C **106**
Moor Stone Pl. HX3: She 2E **131**
Moor St. BD13: Que 4A **108**
   BD22: Haw 4D **46**
Moor Ter. *BD2: B'frd 2A 92*
   (off Higher Intake Rd.)
Moorthorpe Av. BD3: B'frd 2B **92**
MOOR TOP
   BD6 .1B **132**
   LS12 .4B **96**
Moor Top BD11: Drig 1H **135**
   (not continuous)
   LS12: N Far 3E **115**
   LS20: Guis 6B **22**
   LS21: Men 6B **22**
Moor Top Gdns. HX2: Illing 5C **106**
Moor Top Rd. BD12: Low M 1B **132**
   HX2: Hal 1H **147**
MOORTOWN 4B **60**
Moortown Cnr. LS17: Leeds 5B **60**
Moortown Golf Course 2B **60**
Moor Valley Pk. LS20: Hawk 6C **38**
Moor Vw. BD4: B'frd 6E **113**
   LS6: Leeds 6F 77
   (off Hyde Pk. Rd.)
   LS11: Leeds 6G **97**
   LS12: Leeds 4B **96**
   LS19: Yead 6H **41**
Moorview LS26: Meth 4F **145**
Moor Vw. Av. BD18: Ship 1A **70**
Moor Vw. Ct. BD20: Rid 6G **35**
Moorview Cft. *BD10: B'frd 6G 53*
   (off Northlea Av.)
Moor Vw. Cres. BD16: Cot 3A **68**
Moorview Cft. LS29: Men 6F **21**
Moorview Dr. BD16: Cot 3A **68**
   BD18: Ship 2F **71**
Moorview Gro. BD21: Keigh 2B **48**
Moorville Av. BD3: B'frd 2B **92**
Moorville Cl. LS11: Leeds 1H **117**
Moorville Ct. LS11: Leeds 1H **117**
Moorville Dr. BD11: Birk 6E **113**
Moorville Gro. LS11: Leeds 1G **117**
Moorville Rd. LS11: Leeds 1H **117**
Moor Way BD2: Oak 4C **46**
Moorway LS20: Guis 4H **39**
Moorwell Pl. BD2: B'frd 5A **72**

Moravia Bank *LS28: Pud 6A 94*
   (off Fartown)
Moravian Museum & Settlement . . .6A **94**
Moravian Pl. BD5: B'frd 1D **110**
Moravian Ter. *HX3: Hip 2F 151*
   (off Victoria Rd.)
Moresby Rd. BD6: B'frd 1G **131**
Moresdale La. LS14: Leeds 6B **80**
MORLEY 3A **138**
Morley Av. BD3: B'frd 2B **92**
Morley Bottoms LS27: Morl 2A **138**
MORLEY CARR 2D **132**
Morley Carr Rd.
   BD12: Low M 2D **132**
Morley Hall La. HX2: Lud M 3C **146**
Morley Hall Ter. HX2: Lud M 3C **146**
MORLEY HOLE 2H **137**
Morley Leisure Cen. 3A **138**
Morley Mkt. *LS27: Morl 3A 138*
   (off Hope St.)
Morley Station (Rail) 2C **138**
Morley St. BD7: B'frd 6B **6** (5D **90**)
Morley Vw. HX3: Hal 6A **150**
Morningside BD8: B'frd 2B **90**
   BD13: Denh 1B **86**
Morning St. BD21: Keigh 3H **47**
Mornington Rd. BD16: Bgly 4C **50**
   LS29: I'ly 5E **11**
Mornington St. BD21: Keigh 5H **33**
Mornington Vs. BD8: B'frd 2D **90**
Morpeth Pl. LS9: Leeds 4C **98**
Morpeth St. BD7: B'frd 4C **90**
   BD13: Que 4A **108**
Morrell Cl. BD4: B'frd 2B **112**
Morrell Cres. WF2: Wren 6D **156**
Morris Av. LS5: Leeds 4A **76**
Morris Gro. LS5: Leeds 5A **76**
Morris La. LS5: Leeds 4A **76**
Morris Mt. LS5: Leeds 5A **76**
Morris Pl. LS27: Morl 2H **137**
Morris Vw. LS5: Leeds 5A **76**
Morritt Av. LS15: Leeds 2D **100**
Morritt Dr. LS15: Leeds 3B **100**
Morritt Gro. LS15: Leeds 3B **100**
Mortec Pk. LS15: Leeds 2G **81**
Mortimer Av. BD3: B'frd 2B **92**
Mortimer Cl. LS25: Gar 4E **103**
Mortimer Row BD3: B'frd 4B **92**
Mortimer St. BD8: B'frd 3H **89**
Morton Gro. BD20: E Mor 5H **35**
Morton La. BD16: Bgly 1H **49**
   BD20: E Mor 5H **35**
Morton Rd. BD4: B'frd 6B **92**
Mortons Cl. HX3: Hal 6A **150**
Morton Ter. LS20: Guis 4B **40**
Morwick Gro. LS15: Scho 3H **81**
Morwick Ter. LS14: Leeds 1G **81**
Moseley Pl. LS6: Leeds 6H **77**
Moseley Wood App. LS16: Leeds . .3F **57**
Moseley Wood Av. LS16: Leeds . . .1F **57**
Moseley Wood Bank LS16: Leeds . .2F **57**
Moseley Wood Cl. LS16: Leeds . . .3F **57**
Moseley Wood Cres. LS16: Leeds . .2F **57**
Moseley Wood Cft. LS16: Leeds . . .3E **57**
Moseley Wood Dr. LS16: Leeds . . .2F **57**
Moseley Wood Gdns. LS16: Leeds . .2F **57**
Moseley Wood Grn. LS16: Leeds . . .2F **57**
Moseley Wood La. LS16: Leeds . . .2G **57**
Moseley Wood Ri. LS16: Leeds . . .2F **57**
Moseley Wood Vw. LS16: Leeds . . .1G **57**
Moseley Wood Wlk. LS16: Leeds . .2F **57**
Moseley Wood Way LS16: Leeds . . .1F **57**
Moser Av. BD2: B'frd 4G **71**
Moser Cres. BD2: B'frd 4G **71**
Mosley Ho. *BD4: B'frd 6B 92*
   (off Parsonage Rd.)
Moss Bri. Rd. LS13: Leeds 4B **74**
Moss Brook Cl. LS29: Burl W 4G **21**
Moss Carr Av. BD21: Keigh 2D **48**
Moss Carr Gro. BD21: Keigh 2D **48**
Moss Carr Rd. BD21: Keigh 2D **48**
Moss Carr Ter. BD21: Keigh 1D **48**

Mossdale Av. BD9: B'frd 6E **69**
Moss Dr. HX2: Illing 1C **128**
Moss Gdns. LS17: Leeds 2G **59**
Moss La. HX2: Illing 1C **128**
Moss Lea LS27: Chur 6B **116**
Moss Ri. LS17: Leeds 2G **59**
Moss Row BD15: Wils 3G **67**
Moss Side BD9: B'frd 1G **89**
Moss St. BD13: Thorn 4G **87**
   BD22: Cros R 1E **65**
Moss Syke LS14: S'cft 5E **45**
Mosstree Cl. BD13: Que 3G **107**
Moss Valley LS17: Leeds 2G **59**
Mossy Bank Cl. BD13: Que 3A **108**
Mostyn Gro. BD6: B'frd 5A **110**
Mostyn Mt. HX3: Hal 4E **129**
Motley La. LS20: Guis 3C **40**
Motley Row *LS20: Guis 3C 40*
   (off Motley La.)
Mould Greave BD22: Oxen 5B **64**
Mouldson Pl. HX4: Bark 4A **158**
Moule Ri. LS25: Gar 2H **103**
Moulson Cl. BD6: B'frd 4B **110**
Moulson St. BD5: B'frd 2E **111**
Moulson Ter. BD13: Denh 3B **86**
Mount, The BD17: Bail 5D **52**
   LS15: Bar E 3D **82**
   LS15: Leeds 2D **100**
   LS17: Leeds 1H **59**
   LS19: Raw 4H **55**
   LS25: Kip 4G **123**
   LS26: Rothw 6B **120**
   LS27: Chur 6B 116
   (off Elland Rd.)
   WF17: Birs 5A **136**
MOUNTAIN 3G **107**
Mountain Vw. BD18: Ship 3D **70**
   HX2: Illing 1E **129**
Mount Av. BD2: B'frd 4H **71**
   HX2: Hal 2A **148**
   WF2: Wren 6D **156**
Mountbatten Av. WF1: Out 4G **157**
Mountbatten Ct. BD5: B'frd 3E **111**
Mountbatten Cres. WF1: Out 4G **157**
Mountbatten Gro. WF1: Out 5H **157**
Mountcliffe Vw. LS27: Chur 6B **116**
Mount Cres. BD19: Cleck 6B **134**
   HX2: Hal 2A **148**
Mount Dr. LS17: Leeds 1H **59**
Mountfields HX3: Hip 1G **151**
   LS2: Leeds 1A **4**
Mount Gdns. BD19: Cleck 6B **134**
   LS17: Leeds 1H **59**
Mount Gro. BD2: B'frd 4H **71**
Mount La. HD6: Ras 4G **161**
Mountleigh Cl. BD4: B'frd 1G **133**
Mt. Pellon Rd. Hal 1C **148**
Mt. Pellon Rd. HX2: Hal 1C **148**
Mt. Pisgah LS21: Otley 4E **23**
Mt. Pisgah Ter. *LS21: Otley 4E 23*
   (off Well Hill)
Mount Pl. BD18: Ship 1A **70**
MOUNT PLEASANT 4H **123**
Mt. Pleasant BD6: B'frd 6G **109**
   BD9: B'frd 1C **90**
   BD13: Denh 3B **86**
   BD17: Bail 4C **52**
   BD20: Rid 6G **35**
   HD6: Ras 4G **161**
   HX2: Midg 6C **126**
   HX3: Sou 5C 150
   (off Cain La.)
   HX6: Sow B 6D **146**
   LS10: Leeds 2A **140**
   LS13: Leeds 5D **74**
   LS18: H'fth 1F 75
   (off Broadgate La.)
   LS20: Guis 3C **40**
   LS25: Kip 5H **123**
   LS28: Stan 2H 93
   (off Westbourne Pl.)
   LS29: Add 1D **8**
   LS29: I'ly 6E **11**

Mt. Pleasant Av.
 HX1: Hal 2A 164 (1F 149)
 LS8: Leeds 4D 78
Mt. Pleasant Cl. LS28: Pud 3A 94
Mt. Pleasant Gdns. LS8: Leeds 4D 78
 (off Sycamore Av.)
 LS25: Kip 5H 123
Mt. Pleasant Hgts. LS28: Pud 3A 94
 (off Mt. Pleasant Rd.)
Mt. Pleasant Rd. LS28: Pud 3A 94
Mt. Pleasant St. BD13: Que 4A 108
 LS28: Pud 3B 94
Mt. Preston St2: Leeds 1A 4
Mt. Preston St.
 LS2: Leeds 1A 4 (2G 97)
Mount Ri. LS17: Leeds 1H 59
Mount Rd. BD2: B'frd 4A 72
 BD6: B'frd 4A 110
Mount Royal LS18: H'fth 1D 74
Mount Royd BD8: B'frd 1D 90
Mount St. BD2: B'frd 4H 71
 BD3: B'frd 5H 7 (5G 91)
 BD4: B'frd 5H 91
 BD19: Cleck 6B 134
 BD21: Keigh 6H 33
 HX1: Hal 4B 164 (2G 149)
 HX6: Sow B 5H 147
Mount St. W. HX2: Hal 1C 148
MOUNT TABOR 4G 127
Mt. Tabor Rd. HX2: Mt T 2F 127
Mt. Tabor St. LS28: Pud 4G 93
Mount Ter. BD2: B'frd 4H 71
 HX2: Hal 1C 148
 HX2: Midg 6C 126
 HX6: Sow B 5H 147
Mt. Vernon Rd. LS19: Raw 3G 55
Mount Vw. BD13: Que 4H 107
 BD16: Bgly 4D 50
 BD22: Oak 5B 46
 HX2: Mt T 4G 127
 LS27: Chur 6B 116
Mount Vw. Ct. BD19: Cleck 1H 153
Mowat Ct. WF15: Liv 4H 153
Mowbray Chase LS26: Wood 6D 120
Mowbray Cl. BD13: Cull 4A 66
Mowbray Ct. LS14: Leeds 6C 80
Mowbray Cres. LS14: Leeds 6C 80
Moxon Gro. WF1: Wake 6F 157
Moxon St. WF1: Out 5G 157
Moxon Way WF1: Out 5G 157
Moynihan Cl. LS8: Leeds 5F 79
Mozart Way LS27: Chur 5C 116
Mozeley Dr. HX2: Illing 1D 128
Mucky La. HX4: Holy 6H 159
Muddy La. LS22: Lin 6B 12
Muffit La. BD19: Gom 6G 135
Muff St. BD4: B'frd 6H 91
Muff Ter. BD6: B'frd 4A 110
Muir Ct. LS6: Leeds 5D 76
 (off Sagar Pl.)
Muirhead Ct. BD4: B'frd 3C 112
Muirhead Dr. BD4: B'frd 3C 112
Muirhead Fold BD4: B'frd 3C 112
Muirlands. THD2: Hud 6E 163
Mulberry Av. LS16: Leeds 3D 58
Mulberry Chase LS21: Pool 5F 25
Mulberry Gdns. LS26: Meth 5B 144
Mulberry Gth. LS16: Leeds 4E 59
 LS23: T Arch 2C 30
Mulberry La. BD20: Stee 6C 14
Mulberry Ri. LS16: Leeds 3D 58
Mulberry St. BD21: Keigh 5B 34
 LS28: Pud 4A 94
Mulberry Vw. LS16: Leeds 4D 58
Mulberry Way HX3: North 3C 130
Mulcture Hall Rd.
 HX1: Hal 3D 164 (2H 149)
Mulgrave St. BD3: B'frd 5H 7 (5H 91)
Mulhalls Mill HX6: Sow B 5A 148
Mullins Ct. LS9: Leeds 4D 98
Mumford St. BD5: B'frd 2E 111
Munby St. BD8: B'frd 4G 89
Muncaster Rd. LS25: Gar 3H 103

Munster St. BD4: B'frd 2H 111
Munton Cl. BD4: B'frd 1G 131
Murdoch St. BD21: Keigh 5D 34
Murdstone Cl. BD5: B'frd 2E 111
Murgatroyd St. BD5: B'frd 3E 111
 (not continuous)
 BD18: Ship 1B 70
Murray Av. LS10: Leeds 3C 140
Murray Ct. LS18: H'fth 1G 75
Murray Dr. LS10: Leeds 3C 140
Murray St. BD5: B'frd 2C 110
Murray Vw. LS10: Leeds 3C 140
Murray Way LS10: Leeds 3C 140
Murton Cl. LS14: Leeds 5C 80
Murton Gro. BD20: Stee 6D 14
 (off East Pde.)
Museum Ct. BD2: B'frd 1A 92
Museum St. LS9: Leeds 2D 98
Musgrave Bank LS13: Leeds 1G 95
Musgrave Bldgs. LS28: Pud 3B 94
Musgrave Ct. BD2: Pud 4A 94
Musgrave Dr. BD2: B'frd 1A 92
Musgrave Gro. BD2: B'frd 1A 92
Musgrave Mt. BD2: B'frd 1A 92
 LS13: Leeds 1G 95
Musgrave Ri. LS13: Leeds 1G 95
Musgrave Rd. BD2: B'frd 1A 92
Musgrave St. WF17: Birs 6A 136
Musgrave Vw. LS13: Leeds 1G 95
Musgrove Ho. LS5: Leeds 5H 75
 (off Broad La.)
Mushroom St. LS9: Leeds 1H 5 (2B 98)
Musselburgh St. BD7: B'frd 4C 90
Mutton Fold HX3: North 5C 130
 (off Towngate)
Mutton La. BD15: All 1H 87
Myers Av. BD2: B'frd 5G 71
Myers Cl. BD10: B'frd 1H 71
Myers Cft. LS21: Otley 4E 23
Myers Dr. BD13: Leeds 3D 74
Myers La. BD2: B'frd 5G 71
Myrtle Av. BD16: Bgly 5H 49
 HX2: Illing 3C 128
Myrtle Bank HX3: Hal 5H 149
Myrtle Ct. BD16: Bgly 5B 50
Myrtle Dr. BD22: Cros R 6F 47
 HX2: Illing 3C 128
Myrtle Gdns. HX2: Illing 3C 128
Myrtle Gro. BD13: Que 6G 107
 BD16: Bgly 5B 50
 HX2: Illing 3C 128
Myrtle La. LS29: Burl W 6D 20
Myrtle Pl. BD16: Bgly 4B 50
 BD18: Ship 1H 69
 HX2: Illing 3C 128
Myrtle Rd. HX5: Ell 6B 160
Myrtle St. BD3: B'frd 5A 92
 BD16: Bgly 4C 50
Myrtle Ter. BD22: Cros R 6F 47
 HX6: Sow B 5H 147
Myrtle Vw. BD22: Oak 4D 46
Myrtle Wlk. BD16: Bgly 4B 50
 (off Main St.)
MYTHOLMES 1C 64
Mytholmes La. BD22: Haw 1C 64
Mytholmes La. BD22: Haw, Oak . . .2C 64
Mytholmes Ter. BD22: Haw 1C 64

N

NAB END 3E 109
Nab End BD12: Wyke 5D 132
Nab End Rd. HX4: Gree 4H 159
Nab La. BD18: Ship 2F 69
 WF17: Birs 5C 136
 (not continuous)
Naburn App. LS14: Leeds 6D 62
Naburn Chase LS14: Leeds 2E 81
Naburn Cl. LS14: Leeds 2E 81
Naburn Ct. LS14: Leeds 1D 80
Naburn Dr. LS14: Leeds 2D 80
Naburn Fold LS14: Leeds 2E 81

Naburn Gdns. LS14: Leeds 2D 80
Naburn Grn. LS14: Leeds 2D 80
Naburn Pl. LS14: Leeds 1D 80
Naburn Rd. LS14: Leeds 2D 80
Naburn Vw. LS14: Leeds 2E 81
Naburn Wlk. LS14: Leeds 2D 80
Nab Vw. BD20: Sils 1F 15
Nab Water La. BD22: Oxen 5B 84
NAB WOOD 2F 69
Nab Wood Bank BD18: Ship 2F 69
Nab Wood Cl. BD18: Ship 2G 69
Nab Wood Crematorium
 BD18: Ship 1F 69
Nab Wood Cres. BD18: Ship 2F 69
Nab Wood Dr. BD18: Ship 3F 69
Nab Wood Gdns. BD18: Ship 2G 69
Nab Wood Gro. BD18: Ship 2F 69
Nab Wood Mt. BD18: Ship 2F 69
Nab Wood Pl. BD18: Ship 2F 69
Nab Wood Ri. BD18: Ship 2F 69
Nab Wood Rd. BD18: Ship 3F 69
Nab Wood School Sports Cen. 2E 69
Nab Wood Ter. BD18: Ship 2F 69
Naden Cl. BD6: B'frd 3E 109
Nags La. LS22: Weth 4F 13
Nancroft Cres. LS12: Leeds 4C 96
Nancroft Mt. LS12: Leeds 4C 96
Nancroft Ter. LS12: Leeds 4C 96
Nann Hall Glade BD19: Cleck 6C 134
Nanny Goat La. LS25: Gar 3D 102
Nansen Av. LS13: Leeds 1D 94
Nansen Gro. LS13: Leeds 1D 94
Nansen Mt. LS13: Leeds 1D 94
Nansen Pl. LS13: Leeds 1D 94
Nansen St. LS13: Leeds 1C 94
Nansen Ter. LS13: Leeds 1D 94
Nansen Vw. LS13: Leeds 1D 94
Napier Rd. BD3: B'frd 4B 92
 HX5: Ell 5A 160
Napier St. BD3: B'frd 4B 92
 BD13: Que 4B 108
 BD21: Keigh 1B 48
Napier Ter. BD3: B'frd 4B 92
Naples St. BD8: B'frd 2B 90
Napoleon Bus. Pk.
 BD4: B'frd 6H 91
Nares St. BD21: Keigh 6H 33
 BD22: Cros R 1E 65
Narrowboat Wharf
 LS13: Leeds 4B 74
Narrow La. BD16: Har 6F 49
Narrows, The BD16: Har 6F 49
Naseby Gdns. LS9: Leeds 3C 98
Naseby Gth. LS9: Leeds 2C 98
Naseby Grange LS9: Leeds 3C 98
 (off Naseby Gdns.)
Naseby Ho. BD4: B'frd 4D 112
Naseby Pl. LS9: Leeds 3C 98
Naseby Ri. BD13: Que 4B 108
Naseby Ter. LS9: Leeds 3C 98
Naseby Vw. LS9: Leeds 3C 98
Naseby Wlk. LS9: Leeds 3C 98
Nashville Rd. BD22: Keigh 1G 47
Nashville St. BD22: Keigh 1G 47
Nashville Ter. BD22: Keigh 1G 47
 (off Salisbury Rd.)
Nassau Pl. LS7: Leeds 6C 78
Nateby Ri. WF3: Carl 4H 141
Nathaniel Waterhouse Homes
 HX1: Hal 5B 164
National Media Mus. 5C 6 (5E 91)
National Pk. LS10: Leeds 1C 118
National Rd. LS10: Leeds 6C 98
Natty Flds. Cl. HX2: Illing 6C 106
Natty La. HX2: Illing 6C 106
Nature Way BD6: B'frd 6G 109
Navigation Cl. HX5: Ell 3C 160
Navigation Ct. LS13: Leeds 3A 74
Navigation Dr. BD10: B'frd 1C 72
Navigation Rd. HX3: Hal 3H 149
Navigation Wlk.
 LS10: Leeds 6F 5 (4A 98)
Naylor Gth. LS6: Leeds 4F 77

Naylor La. HX2: Midg 1C 146
Naylor Pl. LS11: Leeds 1H 117
Naylor's Bldgs. BD19: Scho 1F 153
(off Tabbs La.)
Naylor St. HX1: Hal 2D 148
Neal St. BD5: B'frd 6C 6 (5E 91)
Nearcliffe Rd. BD9: B'frd 1A 90
Near Crook BD10: B'frd 6F 53
Near Highfield BD22: Oak 4C 46
Near Hob Cote BD22: Oak 6A 46
Near Peat La. BD22: Oxen 4A 84
Near Royd HX3: Hal 4E 129
Neath Gdns. LS9: Leeds 6H 79
Necropolis Rd. BD7: B'frd 6H 89
Ned Hill Rd. HX2: Ogd 3C 106
Ned La. BD4: B'frd 1C 112
Needless Inn La. LS26: Wood 6E 121
Nelson Ct. LS26: Meth 4D 144
LS27: Morl 5H 137
LS29: I'ly 5D 10
(off Nelson Rd.)
Nelson Cft. LS25: Gar 5D 102
Nelson Pl. BD13: Que 4A 108
HX6: Sow B 5B 148
LS27: Morl 2A 138
(off Croft Ho. Rd.)
Nelson Rd. LS29: I'ly 5D 10
Nelson St. BD1: B'frd 6D 6 (5E 91)
BD5: B'frd 6D 6 (5E 91)
BD13: Que 4A 108
BD15: All 2E 89
BD22: Cros R 1E 65
(Albion St.)
BD22: Cros R 1E 65
(East Ter.)
HX6: Sow B 5A 148
LS21: Otley 4E 23
WF17: Birs 6B 136
Nene St. BD5: B'frd 1C 110
Nepshaw La. LS27: Gil 3F 137
LS27: Morl 2H 137
Nepshaw La. Nth. LS27: Morl 2G 137
Nepshaw La. Sth. LS27: Gil 2G 137
Neptune St. LS9: Leeds 6H 5 (4B 98)
NESFIELD 2G 9
Nesfield Cl. LS10: Leeds 1D 140
Nesfield Cres. LS10: Leeds 1D 140
Nesfield Gdns. LS10: Leeds 1C 140
Nesfield Gth. LS10: Leeds 1C 140
Nesfield Grn. LS10: Leeds 1C 140
Nesfield La. LS29: Nes 1G 9
Nesfield Rd. LS10: Leeds 1C 140
LS29: I'ly, Nes 3B 10
Nesfield St. BD1: B'frd 1B 6 (3E 91)
Nesfield Vw. LS10: Leeds 1C 140
LS29: I'ly 5A 10
Nesfield Wlk. LS10: Leeds 1C 140
Nessfield Dr. BD22: Keigh 2F 47
Nessfield Gro. BD22: Keigh 2F 47
Nessfield Rd. BD22: Keigh 2F 47
Netherby St. BD3: B'frd 4H 91
Nethercliffe Cres. LS20: Guis 3B 40
Nethercliffe Rd. LS20: Guis 3B 40
Netherdale Ct. LS22: Weth 3G 13
Netherfield Cl. LS19: Yead 6F 41
Netherfield Ct. LS20: Guis 4B 40
(off Netherfield Rd.)
Netherfield Dr. LS20: Guis 3B 40
Netherfield Ri. LS20: Guis 4B 40
Netherfield Rd. LS20: Guis 3B 40
Netherfield Ter. LS19: Yead 6F 41
LS20: Guis 4B 40
(off Netherfield Rd.)
Netherhall Pk. BD17: Bail 4D 52
(off Netherhall Rd.)
Netherhall Rd. BD17: Bail 4D 52
Netherlands Av. BD6: B'frd 6C 110
BD12: Low M 6C 110
Netherlands Sq. BD12: Low M 6D 110
Nethermoor Vw. BD16: Bgly 4C 50
Nether St. LS28: Fars 6H 73
NETHERTOWN 6C 114
Netherwood BD13: Denh 3B 86

NETHER YEADON 3F 55
Nettle Gro. HX3: North 6C 130
Nettleton Cl. BD4: B'frd 3A 114
Nettleton Ct. LS15: Leeds 3F 101
Neville App. LS9: Leeds 5G 99
Neville Av. BD4: B'frd 4H 111
LS9: Leeds 5G 99
Neville Cl. LS9: Leeds 5G 99
Neville Ct. BD18: Ship 1H 69
Neville Cres. LS9: Leeds 3H 99
Neville Gth. LS9: Leeds 5G 99
Neville Gro. LS9: Leeds 5G 99
LS26: Swil 3A 122
Neville Mt. LS9: Leeds 5G 99
Neville Pde. LS9: Leeds 5G 99
Neville Pl. LS9: Leeds 4H 99
Neville Rd. BD4: B'frd 1H 111
LS9: Leeds 3H 99
LS15: Leeds 4A 100
LS21: Otley 4F 23
Neville Row LS9: Leeds 5G 99
Neville Sq. LS9: Leeds 4H 99
Neville St. BD21: Keigh 5B 34
LS1: Leeds 6D 4 (5H 97)
LS11: Leeds 6D 4 (5H 97)
Neville Ter. LS9: Leeds 5G 99
Neville Vw. LS9: Leeds 5G 99
Neville Wlk. LS9: Leeds 4G 99
Nevill Gro. BD9: B'frd 6F 69
New Adel Av. LS16: Leeds 4A 58
New Adel Gdns. LS16: Leeds 4A 58
New Adel La. LS16: Leeds 5A 58
NEWALL 2D 22
Newall Av. LS21: Otley 2D 22
Newall Carr Rd. LS21: Clift, Otley . . .1E 23
Newall Cl. LS21: Otley 2D 22
(not continuous)
LS29: Men 6H 21
Newall Hall M. LS21: Otley 2E 23
Newall Hall Pk. LS21: Otley 2E 23
Newall Mt. LS21: Otley 3D 22
Newall St. BD5: B'frd 1D 110
Newark Rd. BD16: Bgly 2B 50
Newark St. BD4: B'frd 6H 91
Newark Va. WF3: Rob H 4E 141
NEW BLACKPOOL 1A 116
New Bond St. HX1: Hal 4A 164 (2F 149)
Newbridge Ind. Est. BD21: Keigh . . .6B 34
New Briggate LS1: Leeds 3F 5 (3A 98)
LS2: Leeds 3F 5 (3A 98)
NEW BRIGHTON
BD16 . . . . .3E 69
LS27 . . . . .3A 138
New Brighton BD12: O'haw 2G 133
(off Dyehouse Rd.)
BD16: Cot 3E 69
New Brook St. LS29: I'ly 5D 10
New Brunswick St.
HX1: Hal 4A 164 (2F 149)
Newburn Rd. BD7: B'frd 6B 90
Newbury Cl. BD17: Bail 3D 52
Newbury Rd. HD6: Ras 4H 161
Newby Cl. LS29: Men 2H 39
Newby Ct. LS29: Men 2H 39
Newby Gth. LS17: Leeds 2F 61
Newby Ho. BD2: B'frd 1H 91
(off Mint St.)
Newby St. BD5: B'frd 1E 111
Newcastle Cl. BD11: Drig 2H 135
Newcastle Ho. BD3: B'frd 4H 91
New Centaur Ho.
LS11: Leeds 6D 4 (4H 97)
New Clayton Ter. BD13: Cull 4B 66
New Cl. BD13: Thorn 6D 86
New Cl. Av. BD20: Sils 2E 15
New Cl. Mill Fold BD20: Sils 2E 15

New Cl. Rd. BD18: Ship 2E 69
New Clough Rd. HX6: Norl 1B 158
Newcombe St. HX5: Ell 6C 160
New Cote Cotts. LS28: Fars 6A 74
New Craven Ga. LS11: Leeds 6A 98
New Cres. LS18: H'fth 1D 74
New Cft. LS18: H'fth 1D 74
New Cross St. BD5: B'frd 3E 111
(not continuous)
BD12: O'haw 2H 133
New Delight HX2: Mix 6A 106
Newell Sq. LS28: Pud 5H 93
(off Smalewell Rd.)
New England Rd. BD21: Keigh 2A 48
New Fairfield St. LS13: Leeds 1D 94
New Farmers Hill LS26: Wood 6F 121
NEW FARNLEY 2F 115
Newfield Chase LS25: Gar 6H 103
Newfield Cres. LS25: Gar 1H 123
Newfield Dr. LS25: Gar 1H 123
LS29: Men 1G 39
Newfield La. LS25: Led 5H 125
New Fields Dr. BD3: B'frd . .2G 7 (3G 91)
New Fields Wlk. BD3: B'frd . .2G 7 (3G 91)
New Fold BD6: B'frd 6G 109
New Forest Way LS10: Leeds 3C 140
Newforth Gro. BD5: B'frd 2C 110
New Grange Vw. HX2: Brad 5D 106
NEWHALL 4G 111
Newhall Bank LS10: Leeds 2B 140
Newhall Chase LS10: Leeds 1B 140
Newhall Cl. LS10: Leeds 1B 140
Newhall Cres. LS10: Leeds 1B 140
Newhall Cft. LS10: Leeds 6C 118
Newhall Dr. BD6: B'frd 5F 111
Newhall Gdns. LS10: Leeds 2B 140
Newhall Gth. LS10: Leeds 1B 140
Newhall Ga. LS10: Leeds 6B 118
Newhall Grn. LS10: Leeds 1C 140
Newhall Mt. BD6: B'frd 5F 111
LS10: Leeds 2B 140
Newhall Pk. Dr. BD5: B'frd 4G 111
Newhall Rd. BD4: B'frd 4H 111
LS10: Leeds 6B 118
Newhall Wlk. LS10: Leeds 1C 140
Newhall Way BD5: B'frd 4G 111
New Hey Rd. BD4: B'frd 1G 111
HD2: Hud 6E 161
HD6: Ras 6E 161
New Hold LS25: Gar 3G 103
Newhold Ind. Est. LS25: Gar 3G 103
New Holme HX3: Hip 2E 151
New Holme Cotts.
HX2: Wain 2F 127
New Holme Rd. BD22: Haw 3D 64
New Ho. La. BD13: Que 5D 108
Newill Cl. BD5: B'frd 3G 111
New Inn Ct. LS21: Otley 4E 23
New Inn St. LS12: Leeds 4A 96
New John St. BD1: B'frd 4C 6 (4D 90)
New Kirkgate BD18: Ship 1B 70
New Laithe HX2: Illing 2C 128
New Laithe Rd. BD6: B'frd 4A 110
Newlaithes Gdns.
LS18: H'fth 2D 74
Newlaithes Gth. LS18: H'fth 3C 74
Newlaithes Rd. LS18: H'fth 3C 74
Newlands LS28: Fars 1H 93
Newlands Av. BD3: B'frd 2B 92
HX3: North 3C 130
HX6: Sow B 6E 147
LS19: Yead 5E 41
Newlands Cl. HD6: Ras 2B 162
Newlands Cres. HX3: North 4C 130
LS27: Morl 3D 138
Newlands Dr. BD16: Bgly 1A 50
HX3: North 4C 130
LS27: Morl 2D 138
WF3: S'ley 4H 157
Newlands Ga. HX2: Hal 2G 147
Newlands Gro. HX3: North 4C 130
Newlands Pl. BD3: B'frd 2H 91

Newlands Ri.—Nook Grn.

Newlands Ri. LS19: Yead 6E **41**
Newlands Rd. HX2: Hal 2G **147**
Newlands Vw. HX3: North 4D **130**
Newlands Way BD10: B'frd 4B **72**
New La. BD3: B'frd 5B **92**
BD4: B'frd 5B **92**
(Armstrong St.)
BD4: B'frd 3F **113**
(Raikes La.)
BD11: Drig 5C **114**
BD19: Cleck 3G **153**
BD20: Kild, Sils 1A **14**
HX2: Lud M 4B **146**
HX3: Hal 6E **149**
(Birdcage La.)
HX3: Hal 5H **149**
(Whitegate)
LS10: Leeds 2H **139**
LS11: Leeds 5H **97**
LS27: Gil 5C **114**
WF3: E Ard 1H **155**
(not continuous)
NEWLAY **3D 74**
Newlay Bridle Path LS18: H'fth 2D **74**
Newlay Cl. BD10: B'frd 2C **72**
Newlay Gro. LS18: H'fth 3D **74**
Newlay La. LS13: Leeds 5E **75**
LS18: H'fth 2D **74**
Newlay La. Pl. LS13: Leeds 5E **75**
Newlay Mt. LS18: H'fth 3D **74**
Newlay Wood Av. LS18: H'fth 2E **75**
Newlay Wood Cl. LS18: H'fth 2E **75**
Newlay Wood Cres. LS18: H'fth 2E **75**
Newlay Wood Dr. LS18: H'fth 2E **75**
Newlay Wood Fold LS18: H'fth 2D **74**
Newlay Wood Gdns. LS18: H'fth 2E **75**
Newlay Wood Ri. LS18: H'fth 2E **75**
Newlay Wood Rd. LS18: H'fth 2D **74**
New Leeds LS13: Leeds 4D **74**
New Line BD10: B'frd 2B **72**
Newlyn Rd. BD20: Rid 4E **35**
Newman St. BD4: B'frd 3H **111**
New Market LS21: Otley 4E **23**
Newmarket App. LS9: Leeds 6F **99**
Newmarket Grn. LS9: Leeds 5F **99**
Newmarket La. LS9: Leeds 6F **99**
New Mkt. Pl. BD1: B'frd 4D **6**
New Market St.
LS1: Leeds 5F **5** (4A **98**)
New Marsh HX6: Sow B 4H **147**
NEW MICKLEFIELD **6E 105**
New Mill BD17: Ship 1B **70**
HX2: Wain 1E **127**
New Mill La. LS23: Cliff 6C **30**
New Moon Apartments
LS6: Leeds 4E **77**
New Occupation La. LS28: Pud 5G **93**
New Otley Rd. BD3: B'frd 2G **7** (3G **91**)
New Park Av. LS28: Fars 6A **74**
New Park Cl. LS28: Fars 6A **74**
New Park Cft. LS28: Fars 6A **74**
New Park Gro. LS28: Fars 6H **73**
New Park Pl. LS28: Fars 6A **74**
New Park Rd. BD13: Que 3H **107**
New Park St. LS27: Morl 4H **137**
New Park Va. LS28: Fars 6A **74**
New Park Vw. LS28: Fars 1A **94**
New Park Wlk. LS28: Fars 1H **93**
New Park Way LS28: Fars 6A **74**
New Pepper Rd. LS10: Leeds 2D **118**
New Popplewell La.
BD19: Scho 1F **153**
Newport Av. LS13: Leeds 1C **94**
Newport Cres. LS6: Leeds 6D **76**
Newport Gdns. LS6: Leeds 6D **76**
Newport Mt. LS6: Leeds 6D **76**
Newport Pl. BD8: B'frd 2C **90**
Newport Rd. BD8: B'frd 2C **90**
LS6: Leeds 6D **76**
Newport Vw. LS6: Leeds 5D **76**
New Princess St. LS11: Leeds 6H **97**
New Pudsey Sq. LS28: Stan 2G **93**
New Pudsey Station (Rail) **2G 93**
New Rd. BD13: Denh 3B **86**
BD20: Sils 2D **14**
HX1: Hal 5C **164** (3G **149**)
HX2: Lud 6D **126**
HX4: Gree 4E **159**
LS19: Yead 6D **40**
LS25: Led 4H **125**
WF3: Carl 4H **141**
New Rd. East BD19: Scho 1F **153**
NEW ROAD SIDE **3D 132**
New Rd. Side LS18: H'fth 1C **74**
LS19: Raw 2F **55**
New Rd. Sq. HD6: Ras 5G **161**
New Row BD9: B'frd 1G **89**
BD12: Wyke 5D **132**
BD16: Cot 1D **68**
LS15: Leeds 5G **101**
LS25: M'fld 4E **105**
LS28: Cal 6D **72**
Newroyd Rd. BD5: B'frd 3E **111**
Newsam Ct. LS15: Leeds 4C **100**
Newsam Dr. LS15: Leeds 4A **100**
NEWSAM GREEN **3F 121**
Newsam Grn. Rd. LS26: Wood 3F **121**
NEW SCARBOROUGH
LS13 . . . .**2F 95**
LS19 . . . .**6D 40**
New Scarbro' Rd. LS13: Leeds 1F **95**
New School La. BD13: Cull 4B **66**
NEWSHOLME **3A 46**
Newsholme New Rd. BD22: Oak 3A **46**
New Station St.
LS1: Leeds 5D **4** (4H **97**)
Newstead Av. HX1: Hal 2C **148**
WF1: Out 4E **157**
Newstead Gdns. HX1: Hal 2C **148**
Newstead Gro. HX1: Hal 2C **148**
Newstead Heath HX1: Hal 2C **148**
Newstead Pl. HX1: Hal 2C **148**
New Stead Ri. BD20: E Mor 4F **35**
Newstead Rd. LS21: Otley 4E **23**
Newstead Ter. HX1: Hal 2C **148**
New St. BD4: B'frd 5H **111**
BD10: B'frd 1H **71**
BD12: O'haw 2H **133**
BD13: Denh 3B **86**
BD16: Bgly 6A **36**
BD22: Haw 3C **64**
BD22: Oak 5D **46**
HD6: B Bri 2B **152**
HD6: Clift 6D **152**
HX2: Hal 1C **148**
HX3: Sou 5C **150**
LS18: H'fth 1D **74**
LS25: Kip 4H **123**
LS28: Fars 6H **73**
LS28: Pud 5H **93**
New St. Cl. LS28: Pud 5A **94**
New St. Gdns. LS28: Pud 5A **94**
New St. Gro. LS28: Pud 5A **94**
New Sturton La. LS25: Gar 3H **103**
New Temple Ga. LS15: Leeds 5C **100**
NEW TOFTSHAW **5B 112**
New Toftshaw BD4: B'frd 5B **112**
Newton Cl. BD20: Sils 2D **14**
LS26: Rothw 3F **141**
Newton Ct. LS8: Leeds 3G **79**
LS26: Rothw 3F **141**
WF1: Out 5F **157**
Newton Dr. WF1: Out 6G **157**
Newton Gth. LS7: Leeds 4C **78**
Newton Gro. LS7: Leeds 5C **78**
NEWTON HILL **6F 157**
Newton Hill Rd. LS7: Leeds 4B **78**
Newton La. WF1: Out 5F **157**
Newton Lodge Cl. LS7: Leeds 4A **78**
Newton Lodge Dr. LS7: Leeds 4A **78**
Newton Pde. LS7: Leeds 4B **78**
Newton Pk. HD6: Brigh 3H **151**
Newton Pk. Ct. LS7: Leeds 4C **78**
Newton Pk. Dr. LS7: Leeds 4C **78**
Newton Pk. Vw. LS7: Leeds 5C **78**
Newton Pl. BD5: B'frd 1D **110**
Newton Rd. LS7: Leeds 5B **78**
Newton Sq. LS12: N Far 2F **115**
Newton St. BD5: B'frd 1E **111**
(Ripley St.)
BD5: B'frd 2E **111**
(St Stephen's Ter.)
HX6: Sow B 5H **147**
Newton Ter. HX6: Sow B 6H **147**
LS7: Leeds 3A **78**
Newton Vw. LS7: Leeds 4B **78**
Newton Vs. LS7: Leeds 3A **78**
Newton Wlk. LS7: Leeds 5C **78**
Newton Way BD17: Bail 3C **52**
NEW TOWN
BD22 . . . .**1G 47**
LS9 . . . .**1C 98**
LS29 . . . .**1D 8**
New Town *HX3: Hal* *6G 129*
(off Boothtown Rd.)
New Town Cl. BD21: Keigh 6H **33**
New Town Ct. BD21: Keigh 6H **33**
New Village M. *LS27: Chur* *5C 116*
(off New Village Way)
New Village Way LS27: Chur 4C **116**
New Wlk. LS8: Leeds 6F **61**
New Way LS20: Guis 4H **39**
New Windsor Dr. LS26: Rothw 1B **142**
New Works Rd. BD12: Low M 2C **132**
NEW WORTLEY **4E 97**
New York Cotts. LS19: Raw 5H **55**
New York La. LS19: Raw 5H **55**
New York Rd. LS2: Leeds 3G **5** (3B **98**)
(not continuous)
LS9: Leeds 3G **5** (3B **98**)
New York St. LS2: Leeds 5F **5** (4B **98**)
Nialls Ct. BD10: B'frd 5H **53**
Nice Av. LS8: Leeds 5D **78**
Nice St. LS8: Leeds 5E **79**
Nice Vw. LS8: Leeds 5D **78**
Nicholas Cl. BD7: B'frd 4H **89**
Nichols Cl. LS22: Weth 4C **12**
Nicholson Cl. BD16: Bgly 1C **50**
Nicholson Ct. LS8: Leeds 3E **79**
Nichols Way LS22: Weth 4B **12**
Nichols Yd. HX6: Sow B 5A **148**
Nickleby Rd. LS9: Leeds 3E **99**
Nicola Ct. BD5: B'frd 1D **110**
Nicolsons Pl. BD20: Sils 2E **15**
Nidd App. LS22: Weth 1D **12**
Nidd Ct. BD20: Sils 2E **15**
Nidderdale Cl. LS25: Gar 6H **103**
Nidderdale Wlk. BD17: Bail 3E **53**
Nidd St. BD3: B'frd 5H **91**
Nightingale St. *BD21: Keigh* *5A 34*
(off Parson St.)
Nightingale Wlk. BD16: Bgly 3E **51**
Nijinsky Way LS10: Leeds 4F **119**
Nile Cres. BD22: Keigh 1F **47**
Nile Rd. LS29: I'ly 5D **10**
Nile St. BD22: Cros R 1E **65**
BD22: Keigh 1F **47**
LS2: Leeds 2G **5** (2B **98**)
Nina Rd. BD7: B'frd 2H **109**
Ninelands La. LS25: Gar 6G **103**
Ninelands Spur LS25: Gar 5G **103**
Ninelands Vw. LS25: Gar 4G **103**
Ninevah La. WF10: All B 2F **145**
Nineveh Gdns. LS11: Leeds 6G **97**
Nineveh Pde. LS11: Leeds 6G **97**
Nineveh Rd. LS11: Leeds 6G **97**
Ninth Av. WF15: Liv 4H **153**
Nippet La. LS9: Leeds 3C **98**
Nixon Av. LS9: Leeds 4F **99**
Noble Hop Way HX2: Hal 5A **128**
Noble Rd. WF1: Out 6F **157**
Noble St. BD7: B'frd 6B **90**
Nog La. BD9: B'frd 5A **70**
NOOK **6C 136**
Nook, The HX6: Sow B 6H **147**
LS17: Leeds 2B **60**
WF3: W Ard 3E **155**
Nook Gdns. LS15: Scho 1H **81**
Nook Grn. WF3: W Ard 2F **155**

Nooking WF2: Kirk 6H 155
Nooking, The WF2: Kirk 6H 155
Nook Rd. LS15: Scho 1H 81
Nooks, The LS27: Gil 6F 115
Nook Vw. WF3: W Ard 3E 155
NOON NICK 5E 69
Nora Pl. LS13: Leeds 6C 74
Nora Rd. LS13: Leeds 6C 74
Nora Ter. LS13: Leeds 6C 74
Norbreck Dr. BD22: Cros R 1E 65
Norbury Rd. BD10: B'frd 4C 72
Norcliffe La. HX3: Hip, Sou 3C 150
Norcroft Brow BD7: B'frd 5A 6 (5D 90)
Norcroft Ind. Est.
    BD7: B'frd 4A 6 (4C 90)
Norcroft St. BD7: B'frd 3A 6 (4C 90)
Nordale Cl. LS29: I'ly 4E 11
Norfield HD2: Fix 6A 162
Norfolk Cl. LS7: Leeds 2B 78
    LS26: Oul 2F 143
Norfolk Dr. LS26: Oul 2F 143
Norfolk Gdns. BD1: B'frd 5D 6 (5E 91)
    LS7: Leeds 2B 78
Norfolk Grn. LS7: Leeds 2B 78
Norfolk Mt. LS7: Leeds 2B 78
Norfolk Pl. HX1: Hal 3E 149
    LS7: Leeds 2B 78
Norfolk St. BD16: Bgly 4C 50
Norfolk Ter. LS7: Leeds 2B 78
Norfolk Vw. LS7: Leeds 2B 78
Norfolk Wlk. LS7: Leeds 2B 78
Norgarth Cl. WF17: Bat 4A 154
Norham Gro. BD12: Wyke 5D 132
Norland Rd. HX4: Gree 4B 158
    HX6: Sow B 6H 147
Norland St. BD7: B'frd 2H 109
NORLAND TOWN 1B 158
Norland Town Rd. HX6: Norl 1B 158
Norland Vw. HX2: Hal 5E 149
        (off Delph Hill Rd.)
    HX6: Sow B 5B 148
Norman Av. BD2: B'frd 4H 71
    HX5: Ell 5C 160
    LS5: Leeds 5A 76
Norman Cres. BD2: B'frd 4H 71
Norman Gro. BD2: B'frd 4H 71
    HX5: Ell 5C 160
Norman La. BD2: B'frd 4H 71
Norman Mt. BD2: B'frd 4H 71
    LS5: Leeds 5A 76
Norman Pl. LS8: Leeds 5E 61
Norman Row LS5: Leeds 5A 76
Norman St. BD16: Bgly 4C 50
    BD22: Haw 2D 64
    HX1: Hal 4D 148
    HX5: Ell 5C 160
    LS5: Leeds 5A 76
Norman Ter. BD2: B'frd 4H 71
    HX5: Ell 5C 160
    LS8: Leeds 5E 61
Normanton Golf Course 6H 157
Normanton Gro. LS11: Leeds 1G 117
Normanton Pl. LS11: Leeds 1G 117
Norman Towers LS16: Leeds 3A 76
Norman Vw. LS5: Leeds 5A 76
Normington Ho. LS13: Leeds 4A 74
Norquest Ind. Pk. WF17: Birs 4C 136
NORR 3H 67
Norr Grn. Ter. BD15: Wils 3H 67
Norset Ho. HX3: Hal 5F 129
        (off West Vw.)
Nortech Cl. LS7: Leeds 1B 98
Northallerton Rd. BD3: B'frd 2F 91
Northampton St.
    BD3: B'frd 1F 7 (2F 91)
North Av. BD8: B'frd 6D 70
    LS21: Otley 3E 23
Nth. Bank Rd. BD16: Cot 4C 68
Nth. Beck Ho. BD21: Keigh 1H 47
        (off Aireworth St.)
North Bri. HX1: Hal 2C 164 (1G 149)
North Bridge Leisure Cen.
    . . . . .2C 164 (1G 149)

North Bri. St.
    HX1: Hal 2C 164 (1G 149)
Nth. Broadgate La. LS18: H'fth 6E 57
Northbrook Cft. LS7: Leeds 2B 78
        (off Hill Vw. Mt.)
Northbrook Pl. LS7: Leeds 2B 78
Northbrook St. BD1: B'frd 2E 7 (3F 91)
    BD3: B'frd 2E 7 (3F 91)
    LS7: Leeds 2B 78
North Byland HX2: Illing 6C 106
North Cliffe HX6: Sow B 6H 147
Nth. Cliffe Av. BD13: Thorn 5B 88
Nth. Cliffe Cl. BD13: Thorn 4A 88
Nth. Cliffe Dr. BD13: Thorn 5A 88
Northcliffe Golf Course 3G 69
Nth. Cliffe Gro. BD13: Thorn 4A 88
Nth. Cliffe La. BD13: Thorn 5B 88
Northcliffe Rd. BD18: Ship 3A 70
North Cli. LS8: Leeds 3H 79
Nth. Clough Head HX2: Hal 1H 147
Northcote Cres. LS11: Leeds 1H 117
Northcote Dr. LS11: Leeds 1H 117
Northcote Fold LS22: Lin 1B 28
Northcote Grn. LS11: Leeds 1H 117
Northcote Rd. BD2: B'frd 1H 91
Northcote St. LS28: Fars 1H 93
North Ct. LS2: Leeds 3F 5 (3A 98)
Nth. Cft. Gro. LS29: I'ly 5C 10
Northcroft Ri. BD8: B'frd 2G 89
North Cut HD6: Brigh 1H 161
Northdale Av. BD5: B'frd 3C 110
Northdale Cres. BD5: B'frd 3C 110
Northdale Mt. BD5: B'frd 3C 110
Northdale Rd. BD9: B'frd 4B 70
Nth. Dean Av. BD22: Keigh 6E 33
Nth. Dean Bus. Pk. HX4: Gree 2G 159
Nth. Dean Rd. BD22: Keigh 6E 33
    HX4: Gree 2E 159
Nth. Dene Rd. BD20: Sils 1E 15
North Dr. LS16: B'hpe 3H 43
Northedge HX3: Hip 6E 131
        (off Denholme Ga. Rd.)
Northedge La. HX3: Hip 6E 131
Northedge Mdw. BD10: B'frd 3H 71
Northedge Pk. HX3: Hip 6F 131
Northern Ballet 4H 5
Northern Cl. BD7: B'frd 3H 109
Northern St. LS1: Leeds 5B 4 (4G 97)
Northern St. Apartments
    LS1: Leeds 5C 4
Nth. Farm Rd. LS8: Leeds 6F 79
    LS9: Leeds 6F 79
Northfield Av. LS22: Weth 3E 13
    LS26: Rothw 3G 141
Northfield Cl. HX5: Ell 5B 160
Northfield Cres. BD16: Cot 2C 68
Northfield Gdns. BD6: B'frd 4C 110
Northfield Gro. BD6: B'frd 4C 110
Northfield M. LS22: Weth 3E 13
Northfield Pl. BD8: B'frd 2C 90
    LS22: Weth 3E 13
    LS26: Rothw 3F 141
Northfield Rd. BD6: B'frd 4B 110
Northfield Ter. BD13: Que 4C 108
North Fold BD10: B'frd 1H 71
Northgate BD1: B'frd 3C 6 (4E 91)
    BD17: Bail 3D 52
    HX1: Hal 3C 164 (2G 149)
    HX5: Ell 4B 160
    LS26: Oul 1E 143
Northgate Ho. HX1: Hal 3C 164
    LS22: Weth 4E 13
Northgate La. LS22: Coll, Weth 4A 12
Northgate Ri. LS22: Lin 1B 28
Northgates LS22: Weth 4E 13
Nth. Grange M. LS6: Leeds 5F 77
Nth. Grange Mt. LS6: Leeds 5F 77
Nth. Grange Rd. LS6: Leeds 5E 77
North Gro. App. LS22: Weth 2E 13
North Gro. Av. LS22: Weth 2E 13
North Gro. Cl. LS8: Leeds 3H 79
North Gro. Ct. LS22: Weth 3E 13
North Gro. Cres. LS22: Weth 2E 13

North Gro. Dr. LS8: Leeds 3H 79
    LS22: Weth 2E 13
North Gro. Mt. LS22: Weth 3E 13
North Gro. Ri. LS8: Leeds 3H 79
North Gro. Rd. LS22: Weth 2E 13
North Gro. Way LS22: Weth 3E 13
North Hall Av. BD10: B'frd 5G 53
North Hill LS14: S'cft 5F 45
North Hill Cl. LS8: Leeds 3G 79
North Hill Cl. LS8: Leeds 4F 77
North Hill Rd. LS6: Leeds 5F 77
Nth. Holme St. BD1: B'frd 2D 6 (3E 91)
Nth. Ives BD22: Oxen 5C 64
Nth. John St. BD13: Que 4A 108
North La. LS6: Leeds 4D 76
    LS8: Leeds 2G 79
    LS26: Oul, Wood 1E 143
North La. Gdns. LS8: Leeds 3G 79
North Lea HX6: Sow B 5H 147
        (off Tuel La.)
Northlea Av. BD10: B'frd 6G 53
Nth. Lingwell Rd. LS10: Leeds 2A 140
North Lodge BD13: Denh 2C 86
        (off Foster Pk.)
North Mead LS16: B'hpe 3H 43
Northolme Av. LS16: Leeds 2B 76
Northolme Cres. LS16: Leeds 2B 76
NORTHOWRAM 4C 130
Northowram Grn. HX3: North 4C 130
North Pde. BD1: B'frd 3C 6 (4E 91)
    BD15: All 1C 88
    HX1: Hal 3C 164 (2G 149)
    LS16: Leeds 1A 76
    LS21: Otley 3E 23
    LS27: Morl 4B 138
        (off Gillroyd Pde.)
    LS29: Burl W 1E 21
    LS29: I'ly 5E 11
North Pk. HX1: Hal 3F 149
North Pk. Av. LS8: Leeds 1D 78
North Pk. Gro. LS8: Leeds 1E 79
North Pk. Pde. LS8: Leeds 6D 60
North Pk. Rd. BD9: B'frd 6B 70
    LS8: Leeds 1E 79
        (not continuous)
North Pk. Ter. BD9: B'frd 1C 90
North Parkway LS14: Leeds 4A 80
Nth. Queen St. BD21: Keigh 6A 34
North Rd. BD6: B'frd 4B 110
    LS15: Leeds 1E 101
    LS18: H'fth 4D 56
Northrop Cl. BD8: B'frd 2H 89
Northrops Yd. LS28: Pud 4A 94
North Royd HX3: Hip 6E 131
North Selby HX2: Illing 6B 106
Northside Av. BD7: B'frd 5A 90
Northside Bus. Pk. LS7: Leeds 1B 98
Northside Retail Pk.
    LS7: Leeds 2F 77
Northside Rd. BD7: B'frd 5H 89
Northside Ter. BD7: B'frd 5H 89
North St. BD1: B'frd 3F 7 (4F 91)
    BD10: B'frd 5H 53
    BD12: O'haw 3G 133
    BD20: Sils 1E 15
    BD21: Keigh 6A 34
    BD22: Haw 2B 64
    HX4: Gree 4H 159
    HX4: Holy 6F 159
    LS2: Leeds 2G 5 (2B 98)
    LS7: Leeds 2G 5 (1B 98)
    LS19: Raw 3F 55
    LS21: Otley 3E 23
    LS22: Weth 4E 13
    LS28: Stan 3A 94
    LS29: Add 1E 9
North Ter. BD16: Bgly 5C 50
        (off Leonard St.)
    LS15: Leeds 1E 101
        (off Tranquility Av.)
    LS19: Yead 6F 41
    WF17: Birs 6B 136
Nth. Vale Ct. HD6: B Bri 2B 152

North Vw.—Oakhurst St.

North Vw. BD13: Cull 4B **66**
BD13: Que 3G **107**
BD15: All 2C **88**
BD15: Wils 4G **67**
BD20: East 5A **14**
HX3: Hip 1E **151**
HX4: Holy 6F **159**
LS8: Leeds 3H **79**
*LS26: Rothw 2B **142***
(off Royds La.)
LS29: Burl W 2F **21**
LS29: Men 1G **39**
North Vw. Ct. *LS28: Stan 1A **94***
(off North Vw. St.)
North Vw. Rd. BD3: B'frd 1F **91**
BD4: B'frd 6E **113**
North Vw. St. BD20: Keigh 4H **33**
LS28: Stan 1A **94**
North Vw. Ter. *BD20: E Mor 5H **35***
(off Main Rd.)
BD22: Haw 1C **64**
LS28: Stan 1A **94**
North Wlk. BD16: Har 6E **49**
North Way LS8: Leeds 3H **79**
Northwell Ga. LS21: Otley 2C **22**
Northwest Bus. Pk. LS6: Leeds 6H **77**
North West Rd. LS6: Leeds 6H **77**
North Wing BD3: B'frd 2F **7** (3F **91**)
Northwood Cl. LS26: Wood 6E **121**
LS28: Pud 6B **94**
Northwood Cres. BD10: B'frd 2A **72**
Northwood Falls LS26: Wood 6E **121**
Northwood Gdns. LS15: Leeds 4G **101**
Northwood Grn. *LS28: Pud 6B **94***
(off Roker La.)
Northwood Mt. LS28: Pud 6B **94**
Northwood Pk. LS26: Wood 6E **121**
Northwood Vw. LS28: Pud 6B **94**
Norton Cl. HX2: Hal 2H **147**
HX5: Ell 6B **160**
Norton Dr. HX2: Hal 2H **147**
Norton Rd. LS8: Leeds 5E **61**
Norton St. BD20: Sils 2D **14**
HX5: Ell 5B **160**
NORTON TOWER 2H **147**
Norton Twr. HX2: Hal 2H **147**
Norton Way LS27: Morl 1A **138**
Norville Ter. *LS6: Leeds 5E **77***
(off Headingley La.)
Norwich Av. LS10: Leeds 3B **118**
Norwood Av. BD11: Birk 3F **135**
BD18: Ship 3B **70**
LS29: Burl W 2F **21**
LS29: Men 2G **39**
Norwood Cl. LS29: Burl W 2F **21**
LS29: Men 2G **39**
Norwood Ct. LS29: Men 3G **39**
Norwood Cres. BD11: Birk 3F **135**
LS28: Stan 1B **94**
Norwood Cft. LS28: Stan 1B **94**
Norwood Dr. BD11: Birk 3F **135**
WF17: Bat 6B **136**
NORWOOD GREEN 5H **131**
Norwood Grn. Hill HX3: Nor G 5H **131**
Norwood Gro. BD11: Birk 3F **135**
LS6: Leeds 6E **77**
Norwood Mt. LS6: Leeds 6E **77**
Norwood Pk. LS29: I'ly 5B **10**
Norwood Pl. BD18: Ship 3B **70**
LS6: Leeds 6E **77**
Norwood Rd. BD18: Ship 3B **70**
LS6: Leeds 6E **77**
Norwood St. BD5: B'frd 3D **110**
BD18: Ship 3B **70**
Norwood Ter. BD18: Ship 3B **70**
HX3: Nor G 5A **132**
LS6: Leeds 6E **77**
LS29: Burl W 2F **21**
Norwood Vw. LS6: Leeds 6E **77**
Nostell Cl. BD8: B'frd 1A **6** (3D **90**)
Noster Gro. LS11: Leeds 2F **117**
Noster Hill LS11: Leeds 2F **117**
Noster Pl. LS11: Leeds 2F **117**
Noster Rd. LS11: Leeds 2F **117**
Noster St. LS11: Leeds 2F **117**
Noster Ter. LS11: Leeds 2F **117**
Noster Vw. LS11: Leeds 2F **117**
Nottingham Cl. WF3: Rob H 4E **141**
Nottingham St. BD3: B'frd 4C **92**
Nova La. WF17: Birs 5H **135**
Nowell App. LS9: Leeds 2F **99**
Nowell Av. LS9: Leeds 2F **99**
Nowell Cl. LS9: Leeds 2F **99**
Nowell Ct. LS9: Leeds 2F **99**
Nowell Cres. LS9: Leeds 2F **99**
Nowell End Row LS9: Leeds 2F **99**
Nowell Gdns. LS9: Leeds 2F **99**
Nowell Gro. LS9: Leeds 2F **99**
Nowell La. LS9: Leeds 2F **99**
Nowell Mt. LS9: Leeds 2F **99**
Nowell Pde. LS9: Leeds 2F **99**
Nowell Pl. LS9: Leeds 2F **99**
Nowell St. LS9: Leeds 2F **99**
Nowell Ter. LS9: Leeds 2F **99**
Nowell Vw. LS9: Leeds 2F **99**
Nowell Wlk. LS9: Leeds 2F **99**
Nuffield Health Club
Cottingley 2D **68**
Guiseley 4A **40**
Nunburnholme Wlk.
BD10: B'frd 3A **72**
Nunlea Royd HX3: Hip 3A **152**
Nunnery La. HD6: Ras 4F **161**
Nunnery Way LS23: Cliff 6B **30**
Nunnington Av. LS12: Leeds 3C **96**
Nunnington St. LS12: Leeds 3C **96**
Nunnington Ter. LS12: Leeds 3C **96**
Nunnington Vw. LS12: Leeds 2C **96**
Nunroyd Av. LS17: Leeds 6B **60**
LS20: Guis 5D **40**
Nunroyd Gro. LS17: Leeds 6B **60**
Nunroyd Ho. *BD4: B'frd 5B **92***
(off Sticker La.)
Nunroyd Lawn LS17: Leeds 6B **60**
Nunroyd Rd. LS17: Leeds 6B **60**
Nunroyd St. LS17: Leeds 6B **60**
Nunroyd Ter. LS17: Leeds 6B **60**
Nunthorpe Rd. LS13: Leeds 4B **74**
Nurser La. BD5: B'frd 1C **110**
Nurser Pl. BD5: B'frd 1C **110**
Nursery Av. HX3: Hal 4D **128**
Nursery Cl. BD17: Bail 5H **51**
BD20: Keigh 2G **33**
HX3: Hal 5D **128**
LS17: Leeds 3A **60**
LS25: Kip 3G **123**
Nursery Gdns. BD16: Cot 1B **68**
Nursery Gth. LS22: Weth 3F **13**
Nursery Gro. HX3: Hal 4D **128**
LS17: Leeds 3G **59**
Nursery La. HX3: Hal 4C **128**
LS17: Leeds 3G **59**
LS29: Add 1E **9**
Nursery Mt. LS10: Leeds 4C **118**
Nursery Mt. Rd. LS10: Leeds 3C **118**
Nursery Rd. BD7: B'frd 3H **109**
BD14: Clay 1D **108**
LS20: Guis 2B **40**
Nursery Way LS23: B Spa 3H **29**
LS23: Cliff 6B **30**
Nussey Av. WF17: Birs 5A **136**
Nuthatch M. BD6: B'frd 4E **109**
Nuttall Rd. BD3: B'frd 3G **7** (4G **91**)
Nutter La. WF17: Birs 5G **135**
Nutting Gro. Ter. LS12: Leeds 6G **95**
Nutwood Wlk. BD6: B'frd 1G **131**

O

Oak Av. BD8: B'frd 1C **90**
BD16: Bgly 6B **50**
HX6: Sow B 4H **147**
LS25: Gar 4F **103**
LS27: Morl 4B **138**
LS29: Burl W 3F **21**
Oak Bank BD16: Bgly 5C **50**
BD18: Ship 4D **70**
Oakbank Av. BD22: Keigh 2F **47**
Oak Bank B'way. BD22: Oak 3F **47**
Oak Bank Ct. BD22: Oak 3F **47**
Oak Bank Cres. BD22: Oak 3F **47**
Oakbank Dr. BD22: Keigh 2F **47**
Oakbank Gro. BD22: Keigh 2F **47**
Oak Bank La. BD22: Oak 3F **47**
Oak Bank Mt. BD22: Oak 3F **47**
Oakburn Rd. LS29: I'ly 6C **10**
Oak Cl. LS29: Burl W 3F **21**
Oak Cotts. LS23: Cliff 6B **30**
Oak Cres. LS15: Leeds 4B **100**
LS25: Gar 4F **103**
Oakdale BD16: Bgly 2C **50**
Oakdale Av. BD6: B'frd 4B **110**
BD18: Ship 3D **70**
Oakdale Cl. BD10: B'frd 6C **72**
HX3: Hal 5E **129**
WF3: Loft 3F **157**
Oakdale Cres. BD6: B'frd 4B **110**
Oakdale Dr. BD10: B'frd 6C **72**
BD18: Ship 3E **71**
LS21: Pool 5F **25**
Oakdale Gth. LS14: Leeds 6D **62**
Oakdale Gro. BD18: Ship 3E **71**
Oakdale Mdw. LS14: Leeds 6D **62**
Oakdale Pk. LS21: Pool 5F **25**
Oakdale Rd. BD18: Ship 3E **71**
Oakdale Ter. BD6: B'frd 4B **110**
Oakdene LS26: Wood 6F **121**
Oakdene Cl. LS28: Pud 6B **94**
Oakdene Ct. LS17: Leeds 3E **61**
Oakdene Dr. LS17: Leeds 3E **61**
Oakdene Gdns.
LS17: Leeds 3E **61**
Oakdene Mt. BD14: Clay 2C **108**
Oakdene Va. LS17: Leeds 3E **61**
Oakdene Way LS17: Leeds 3E **61**
Oak Dr. LS10: Leeds 3B **140**
LS16: Leeds 5B **58**
LS25: Gar 4F **103**
OAKENSHAW 2F **133**
Oakenshaw Ct. BD12: Wyke 5C **132**
Oakenshaw La. BD12: O'haw 5G **133**
BD19: Cleck 5G **133**
Oakfield LS6: Leeds 5E **77**
Oakfield Av. BD16: Bgly 5E **51**
LS26: Rothw 1A **142**
Oakfield Cl. HX5: Ell 5A **160**
LS25: Gar 5F **103**
LS29: Men 5G **21**
Oakfield Dr. BD17: Bail 5D **52**
Oakfield Gro. BD9: B'frd 1C **90**
Oakfield Rd. BD21: Keigh 3G **47**
Oakfield Ter. BD18: Ship 2D **70**
*LS18: H'fth 1G **75***
(off Woodville St.)
Oakford Ter. LS18: H'fth 6G **57**
Oak Gro. BD20: Rid 3D **34**
BD21: Keigh 4G **47**
LS14: Leeds 5E **81**
LS25: Gar 4G **103**
LS27: Morl 4B **138**
Oakhall Pk. BD13: Thorn 4H **87**
Oakham Gth. LS9: Leeds 4G **99**
Oakham M. LS9: Leeds 4F **99**
Oakhampton Ct. LS8: Leeds 1G **79**
Oakham Wlk. BD4: B'frd 1G **111**
Oakham Way LS9: Leeds 4F **99**
Oak Hill Rd. HD6: Brigh 6B **152**
Oak Ho. LS5: Leeds 5H **75**
*LS7: Leeds 2B **78***
(off Allerton Pk.)
LS15: Leeds 5A **100**
Oakhurst LS6: Leeds 5E **77**
Oakhurst Av. LS11: Leeds 4G **117**
Oakhurst Ct. BD8: B'frd 1D **90**
Oakhurst Gro. LS11: Leeds 4F **117**
Oakhurst Mt. LS11: Leeds 4F **117**
Oakhurst Rd. LS11: Leeds 4F **117**
Oakhurst St. LS11: Leeds 4G **117**

A-Z Leeds & Bradford 253

Oaklands BD10: B'frd 1G 71
    BD18: Ship 2F 69
    HD6: Ras 2H 161
    LS29: I'ly 6C 10
    WF3: Rob H 4E 141
Oaklands Av. HX3: North 4D 130
    LS13: Leeds 4A 74
    LS16: Leeds 4D 58
Oaklands Cl. LS8: Leeds 5G 79
    LS16: Leeds 4D 58
Oaklands Ct. LS8: Leeds 6G 79
Oaklands Cres. LS8: Leeds 6G 79
    LS16: Leeds 5D 58
Oaklands Dr. LS8: Leeds 6G 79
    LS16: Leeds 5D 58
Oaklands Fold LS8: Leeds 5G 79
    LS16: Leeds 4D 58
Oaklands Gro. LS8: Leeds 6G 79
    LS13: Leeds 4A 74
    LS16: Leeds 4D 58
Oaklands Pl. LS8: Leeds 6G 79
Oaklands Rd. LS13: Leeds 4A 74
Oaklands St. LS8: Leeds 6G 79
Oakland St. BD20: Sils 2D 14
Oak La. BD9: B'frd 1B 90
    HX1: Hal 2E 149
Oaklea Gdns. LS16: Leeds 5D 58
Oaklea Hall Cl.
    LS16: Leeds 5D 58
Oaklea Rd. LS15: Scho 3H 81
Oakleigh Av. BD14: Clay 2D 108
                                (not continuous)
    HX3: Hal 6G 149
Oakleigh Cl. BD14: Clay 1D 108
Oakleigh Gdns. BD14: Clay 2D 108
Oakleigh Gro. BD14: Clay 2D 108
                                (not continuous)
Oakleigh M. BD22: Oak 5C 46
Oakleigh Rd. BD14: Clay 2D 108
Oakleigh Ter. BD14: Clay 1D 108
Oakleigh Vw. WF3: Thpe H 4B 52
Oakley Gro. LS11: Leeds 2A 118
Oakley St. WF3: Thpe H 6C 140
Oakley Ter. LS11: Leeds 3A 118
Oakley Vw. LS11: Leeds 3A 118
Oak Mt. BD8: B'frd 1D 90
    HX3: Hip 1G 151
Oak Pk. Cl. LS16: Leeds 5G 57
Oak Pk. Dr. LS16: Leeds 5G 57
Oak Pk. Grn. LS16: Leeds 4G 57
Oak Pk. La. LS16: Leeds 5G 57
Oak Pk. M. LS16: Leeds 4G 57
Oak Pk. Mt. LS16: Leeds 5G 57
Oak Pk. Ter. LS16: Leeds 5G 57
Oak Pl. BD17: Bail 3F 53
    HX1: Hal 2E 149
    HX6: Sow B 4H 147
Oak Ridge LS22: Weth 4C 12
Oakridge Av. LS29: Men 1H 39
Oakridge Ct. BD16: Bgly 3C 50
Oak Ri. BD19: Hun 5B 134
Oak Rd. HD2: Hud 6G 163
    LS7: Leeds 4B 78
    LS12: Leeds 4E 97
    LS15: Leeds 3B 100
    LS25: Gar 4E 103
    LS27: Morl 5H 137
Oak Royd LS25: Gar 4F 103
Oakroyd Av. LS26: Rothw 3B 142
Oakroyd Av. BD6: B'frd 4C 110
Oakroyd Cl. BD11: Birk 2E 135
    HD6: Brigh 4B 152
Oak Royd Cotts. HX3: Hal 1F 159
Oakroyd Dr. BD11: Birk 3E 135
    HD6: Brigh 4B 152
Oakroyd Fold LS27: Chur 5C 116
Oakroyd Mt. LS28: Stan 3A 94
Oakroyd Rd. BD6: B'frd 4B 110
Oakroyd Ter. BD8: B'frd 1D 90
    BD17: Bail 5D 52
    LS27: Chur 5C 116
    LS28: Stan 3A 94
Oakroyd Vs. BD8: B'frd 1D 90

Oaks, The BD15: Wils 3F 67
    LS10: Leeds 3C 140
    LS20: Guis 3C 40
    LS27: Chur 6B 116
Oaks Dr. BD15: All 3E 89
Oaksfield LS26: Meth 5D 144
Oaks Fold BD5: B'frd 2E 111
Oaks Grn. Mt. HD6: Ras 4H 161
Oakshaw Ct. BD4: B'frd 1G 111
Oaks La. BD8: B'frd 4F 89
    BD15: All, B'frd 3E 89
    BD23: B Spa 3A 30
Oak St. BD14: Clay 1D 108
    BD22: Haw 2D 64
    BD22: Oxen 6C 64
    HX5: Ell 5B 160
    HX6: Sow B 4H 147
    LS27: Chur 6B 116
    LS28: Pud 3G 93
    WF1: Out 5G 157
Oak Ter. HX1: Hal 2E 149
                              (off Battinson Rd.)
    HX6: Sow B 4H 147
                                      (off Oak Pl.)
    LS15: Leeds 6F 81
                                 (off Church La.)
Oak Tree Bus. Pk. LS14: Leeds 2C 80
Oak Tree Cl. LS9: Leeds 6G 79
Oak Tree Ct. BD20: Sils 1D 14
    LS9: Leeds 6G 79
                                (off Oak Tree Pl.)
    WF1: Out 5F 157
Oak Tree Cres. LS9: Leeds 6G 79
Oak Tree Dr. LS8: Leeds 6G 79
Oak Tree Gro. LS9: Leeds 6G 79
Oak Tree La. LS14: Leeds 1A 100
Oak Tree Mt. LS9: Leeds 6G 79
Oak Tree Pl. LS9: Leeds 6G 79
Oak Tree Wlk. LS9: Leeds 6G 79
Oak Vw. BD20: Sils 1E 15
    LS16: Leeds 2C 58
Oak Vs. BD8: B'frd 1D 90
Oakway BD11: Birk 3F 135
OAKWELL 4H 135
Oakwell Av. LS8: Leeds 3E 79
    LS12: Leeds 4D 96
Oakwell Cl. BD7: B'frd 2B 110
    BD11: Drig 2C 136
Oakwell Ct. LS13: Leeds 6D 74
    LS28: Fars 6H 73
                                     (off Water La.)
    WF17: Birs 4B 136
                                 (not continuous)
Oakwell Cres. LS8: Leeds 3E 79
Oakwell Dr. LS8: Leeds 3E 79
Oakwell Gdns. LS8: Leeds 3E 79
Oakwell Gro. LS13: Leeds 6E 75
Oakwell Hall 4H 135
Oakwell Hall Country Pk. 4G 135
Oakwell Ind. Est. WF17: Birs 4C 136
Oakwell Ind. Pk. WF17: Birs 4B 136
Oakwell Mt. LS8: Leeds 3E 79
Oakwell Oval LS8: Leeds 3E 79
Oakwell Rd. BD11: Drig 2C 136
Oakwell Ter. LS28: Fars 6H 73
Oakwell Way WF17: Birs 4C 136
OAKWOOD 3F 79
Oakwood HD6: Brigh 6H 151
Oakwood Av. BD2: B'frd 5D 70
    BD11: Birk 3E 135
    LS8: Leeds 3F 79
Oakwood Boundary Rd.
    LS8: Leeds 3F 79
Oakwood Cotts. LS16: Bgly 1C 50
Oakwood Ct. BD8: B'frd 3C 90
    LS8: Leeds 3G 79
Oakwood Dr. BD16: Bgly 2B 50
    LS8: Leeds 3F 79
    LS26: Rothw 6H 119
Oakwood Gdns. HX2: Hal 3D 128
    LS8: Leeds 3F 79
    LS28: Pud 5A 94
Oakwood Gth. LS8: Leeds 3G 79

Oakwood Grange LS8: Leeds 3G 79
Oakwood Grange La. LS8: Leeds . . .3G 79
Oakwood Grn. LS8: Leeds 3G 79
Oakwood Gro. BD8: B'frd 2A 90
    LS8: Leeds 3F 79
Oakwood Ho. LS13: Leeds 3H 73
                                  (off Rodley La.)
Oakwood La. LS8: Leeds 3F 79
    LS9: Leeds 6H 79
Oakwood Mt. LS8: Leeds 3F 79
Oakwood Nook LS8: Leeds 3F 79
Oakwood Pk. LS8: Leeds 4G 79
Oakwood Pl. LS8: Leeds 3F 79
Oakwood Ri. LS8: Leeds 3G 79
Oak Wood Rd. LS22: Weth 2D 12
Oakwood Ter. LS28: Pud 5A 94
Oakwood Vw. LS8: Leeds 3G 79
Oakwood Wlk. LS8: Leeds 3G 79
OAKWORTH 5C 46
Oakworth Crematorium
    BD22: Oak 4A 46
Oakworth Hall BD22: Oak 5C 46
Oakworth Rd. BD21: Keigh 2F 47
    BD22: Keigh 2F 47
Oakworth Station
    Keighley & Worth Valley Railway
    . . . . .6D 46
Oakworth Ter. BD22: Oak 5C 46
                                (off Dockroyd La.)
Oasby Cft. BD4: B'frd 4C 112
Oast Ho. Cft. WF3: Rob H 4F 141
Oastler Pl. BD12: Low M 1D 132
Oastler Rd. BD18: Ship 1H 69
    LS28: Cal 3F 73
Oastler Shop. Cen.
    BD1: B'frd 3C 6 (4E 91)
Oatland Cl. LS7: Leeds 1A 98
Oatland Ct. LS7: Leeds 1F 5 (1A 98)
                                 (not continuous)
Oatland Dr. LS7: Leeds 1A 98
Oatland Gdns. LS7: Leeds 1A 98
Oatland Grn. LS7: Leeds 1A 98
Oatland Hgts. LS7: Leeds 1G 5
Oatland La. LS7: Leeds 1A 98
Oatland Pl. LS7: Leeds 6A 78
Oatland Rd. LS7: Leeds 1A 98
Oatlands Dr. LS21: Otley 2E 23
Oatland Towers
    LS7: Leeds 1F 5 (1A 98)
Oats St. BD22: Keigh 3G 47
Oban Cl. WF3: Ting 6D 138
Oban Pl. LS12: Leeds 3A 96
Oban St. LS12: Leeds 3B 96
Oban Ter. LS12: Leeds 3B 96
    WF3: Ting 6D 138
Oberon Way BD16: Cot 3D 68
Occupation La. BD22: Oak 3D 46
    HX2: Illing 1C 128
    LS16: B'hpe 2D 42
    LS28: Pud 5G 93
Octagon Ter. HX2: Hal 5C 148
Octavia Ct. BD3: B'frd 2F 7 (3F 91)
Odda La. LS20: Hawk 4E 39
Oddfellows St. BD19: Scho 1F 153
    HD6: Brigh 5B 152
Oddfellow St. LS27: Morl 3A 138
Oddy Fold HX3: Hal 6F 129
Oddy Pl. BD6: B'frd 4B 110
    LS6: Leeds 3D 76
Oddy's Fold LS6: Leeds 1E 77
Oddy St. BD4: B'frd 4C 112
Odeon Cinema
    Bradford 3D 92
Odette Ct. BD16: Bgly 3E 51
Odile M. BD16: Bgly 3E 51
ODSAL 5D 110
Odsal Rd. BD6: B'frd 4C 110
                                 (not continuous)
Odsal Stadium 5E 111
ODSAL TOP 6E 111
Office Row BD22: Haw 1C 64
OGDEN .3B 106
Ogden Cres. BD13: Denh 1B 86

Ogden Ho. BD4: B'frd 1D 112
Ogden La. BD13: Denh 1B 86
   HD6: Ras 3H 161
   HX2: Ogd 3B 106
Ogden St. HX6: Sow B 6G 147
Ogden Vw. Cl. HX2: Illing 6B 106
Ogden Water Country Pk. 3A 106
Ogden Water Vis. Cen. 3A 106
Ogilby Ct. LS26: Wood 6D 120
Ogilby M. LS26: Wood 6D 120
O'Grady Sq. LS9: Leeds 4D 98
Old Allen Rd. BD13: Thorn, Wils . . .6E 67
   BD15: Wils 6E 67
Old Apple Tree La. BD15: All 2C 88
Old Arcade, The HX1: Hal 4C 164
Old Bank HX3: Hal 1H 149
                  (not continuous)
Old Barn Cl. LS17: Leeds 2G 59
Old Bell Ct. HX1: Hal 5B 164
Old Boston Rd. LS22: Weth 6F 13
OLD BRAMHOPE 2C 42
Old Brandon La. LS17: Shad 3A 62
Old Bridge Ri. LS29: I'ly 4C 10
Old Canal Rd. BD1: B'frd 1D 6 (3E 91)
Old Cawsey HX6: Sow B 5A 148
                  (not continuous)
Old Clock Mill Ct. BD13: Denh 3B 86
Old Cl. LS11: Leeds 5D 116
Old Cock Yd. HX1: Hal . . .4C 164 (2G 149)
Old Corn Mill La. BD7: B'frd 1A 110
Old Cottage Cl. HX3: Hip 2E 151
Old Dan La. HX4: Holy 6G 159
OLD DOLPHIN 3D 108
Old Earth HX5: Ell 4D 160
Old Farm App. LS16: Leeds 1H 75
Old Farm Cl. LS16: Leeds 1A 76
Old Farm Cres. BD4: B'frd 2H 111
Old Farm Cross LS16: Leeds 1A 76
Old Farm Dr. LS16: Leeds 1H 75
Old Farm Gth. LS16: Leeds 1A 76
Old Farm Pde. LS16: Leeds 1A 76
Old Farm Wlk. LS16: Leeds 1H 75
Old Farm Way HD6: Brigh 3A 152
Oldfield Av. LS12: Leeds 5C 96
Oldfield Cl. LS25: M'fld 4E 105
Oldfield Ct. LS17: Leeds 3C 78
Oldfield Ga. BD22: Haw 2A 64
Oldfield La. BD22: Haw 1A 64
   LS12: Leeds 5C 96
   LS22: Coll, Weth 2D 28
Oldfield St. HX3: Hal 3E 129
   LS12: Leeds 5C 96
Old Fold LS28: Fars 6H 73
Old Forge M. LS16: B'hpe 2F 43
Old Fort BD13: Denh 5C 86
Old Godley La. HX3: Hal 1A 150
Old Great Nth. La. LS25: M'fld 3D 104
Old Guy Rd. BD13: Que 3F 107
Old Hall Cl. BD22: Haw 3C 64
   WF1: Out 5E 157
Old Hall Rd. WF3: Ting 1F 155
Oldham St. HD6: Ras 2A 162
                  (off Bridge End)
Old Haworth La. LS19: Yead 6F 41
Old Heybeck La. WF3: W Ard 4D 154
Old Hollings Hill BD17: Esh 1A 54
   LS20: Guis 1A 54
Old La. BD11: Birk 1E 135
   BD11: Drig 6B 114
   BD13: Cull 3B 66
   HD2: Hud 6C 162
   HD6: Brigh 6B 152
   HX2: Lud 6D 126
   HX3: Hal 1A 164 (4E 129)
   LS11: Leeds 3F 117
   LS16: B'hpe, Yead 2C 42
   LS20: Hawk 5D 38
   LS21: Otley, Yead 1A 42
   LS29: Add 3G 9
   LS29: I'ly 6F 11
Old Lane Ct. HD6: Brigh 6B 152
                  (off Old La.)
Old Langley La. BD17: Bail 3D 52

Old Lee Bank HX3: Hal 6F 129
Old Lodge Hill LS29: I'ly 3B 10
Old Main St. BD16: Bgly 3B 50
Old Manse Cft. BD22: Oxen 1C 84
Old Market HX1: Hal 4C 164 (2G 149)
Old Marsh HX6: Sow B 4H 147
                  (off New Marsh)
Old Mill BD2: B'frd 4G 93
OLD MICKLEFIELD 3D 104
Old Mill BD2: B'frd 5A 72
   BD17: Ship 1B 70
Old Mill, The LS22: Weth 4E 13
Old Mill Bus. Pk. LS10: Leeds 1D 118
Old Mill Cl. LS29: Burl W 1F 21
Old Mill Gro. HX1: Hal 3C 148
Old Mill La. LS10: Leeds 1C 118
   LS23: Cliff 6C 30
Old Mill Yd. BD15: Wils 4H 67
Old Oak Cl. LS16: Leeds 2A 76
Old Oak Dr. LS16: Leeds 2A 76
Old Oak Gth. LS16: Leeds 2H 75
Old Oak Lawn LS16: Leeds 2A 76
Old Orchard, The LS13: Leeds 5D 74
   LS21: Pool 4E 25
   LS29: Men 1H 39
                  (off Station Rd.)
Old Oxenhope La. BD22: Oxen 4B 64
Old Park Ct. BD3: B'frd 4G 7 (4G 91)
Old Park Rd. BD10: B'frd 1A 72
   LS8: Leeds 5F 61
                  (not continuous)
Old Pool Bank LS21: Pool 1D 42
Old Popplewell La. BD19: Scho 1E 153
Old Power Way HX5: Ell 3C 160
Old Riding La. HX2: Lud 4F 127
Old Rd. BD7: B'frd 3G 109
   BD13: Denh 3B 86
   BD13: Thorn 5B 88
   LS27: Chur 5C 116
   LS28: Fars, Stan 2G 93
Oldroyd Cres. LS11: Leeds 3E 117
Old Run Rd. LS10: Leeds 3B 118
Old Run Vw. LS10: Leeds 5B 118
Old School, The LS29: Burl W 2E 21
                  (off Albert Simmons Way)
Old School Lofts LS12: Leeds 4A 96
Old School M. LS21: Otley 3F 23
   LS27: Chur 5C 116
Old Schools Gdns. HX3: Hal 6G 129
Old School Way BD17: Bail 4C 52
Oldside Ct. BD20: E Mor 4A 36
Old Smithy Ct. LS28: Cal 3F 73
                  (off Blackett St.)
Old Souls Mill BD16: Bgly 1A 50
                  (off Wood St.)
Old Souls Way BD16: Bgly 1A 50
Old Station Rd. HX2: Lud M 2D 146
Old Station Way LS29: Add 1D 8
Old Tannery BD16: Bgly 4B 50
                  (off Industrial St.)
Old Vicarage Cl. BD16: Cot 3D 68
Old Village School, The
   BD14: Clay 1D 108
                  (off Clayton La.)
Old Well Head
   HX1: Hal 6B 164 (4G 149)
Old Whack Ho. La. LS19: Yead 1D 54
Old Wood La. BD16: Bgly 4A 38
Olicana Cl. LS29: I'ly 4C 10
Olive Gro. BD8: B'frd 3G 89
Olive Lodge LS18: H'fth 6E 57
                  (off Broadgate La.)
Olive Pl. BD13: Que 4A 108
Oliver Cl. HX6: Sow B 5H 147
Oliver Ct. BD11: Drig 2H 135
Oliver Hill LS18: H'fth 4C 57
Oliver Mdws. HX5: Ell 4D 160
Oliver St. BD4: B'frd 6G 91
Olive Ter. BD16: Bgly 4C 50
                  (off Dubb La.)
Olive Yeates Way LS15: Leeds 1G 101
Olivia Ct. HX3: Hal 6F 129
                  (off Chester Rd.)

Olivia's Ct. BD9: B'frd 1G 89
Ollerdale Av. BD15: All 6C 68
                  (not continuous)
Ollerdale Cl. BD15: All 1C 88
Olrika Ct. LS7: Leeds 5B 78
Olympic Pk. BD12: Low M 2E 133
Olympic Way BD12: Low M 2E 133
One St. BD1: B'frd 4B 6
Onslow Cres. BD4: B'frd 3H 111
Ontario Pl. LS7: Leeds 3B 78
Opal One LS3: Leeds 3F 97
Opal St. BD22: Keigh 3G 47
Opal Three LS2: Leeds 2F 5
Open University
   Leeds 5E 5
Ophelia Cl. BD5: B'frd 1D 110
Orange St. BD3: B'frd 5A 92
   HX1: Hal 3B 164 (2G 149)
Orange Tree Gro. WF3: E Ard 2A 156
Orchard, The BD21: Keigh 6D 34
   LS23: B Spa 3B 30
   WF2: Wren 6D 156
Orchard Cl. HX2: Hal 3B 148
   WF2: Wren 6C 156
   WF3: E Ard 3B 156
Orchard Ct. LS16: Leeds 2D 76
                  (off St Chads Rd.)
   LS20: Guis 4C 40
                  (off Orchard La.)
Orchard Cft. LS15: Leeds 1D 100
   WF2: Wren 6C 156
Orchard Dr. LS22: Lin 6B 12
   LS28: Pud 3F 93
Orchard Ga. LS21: Otley 4E 23
                  (off Market St.)
Orchard Gro. BD10: B'frd 2B 72
   LS29: Men 1H 39
Orchard La. LS20: Guis 4C 40
   LS29: Add 1E 9
Orchard Mt. LS13: Leeds 4A 74
Orchard Mt. LS15: Leeds 1E 101
Orchard Pl. LS22: Weth 3D 12
Orchard Ri. HX6: Sow B 6F 147
Orchard Rd. LS15: Leeds 1D 100
Orchards, The BD16: Bgly 2C 50
   BD19: Gom 6G 135
   HD6: Ras 3H 161
   LS15: Leeds 1D 100
   LS26: Meth 5C 144
   WF3: W Ard 4D 154
Orchard Sq. LS15: Leeds 1D 100
Orchard St. LS21: Otley 4F 23
Orchard Vw. LS22: Weth 1E 13
Orchard Way HD6: Brigh 5A 152
   LS20: Guis 4C 40
   LS26: Rothw 1A 142
Orchid Cl. BD18: Ship 4D 70
Orchid Ct. WF3: Loft 5F 141
Orchid Way LS19: Raw 5E 55
Oriental St. LS12: Leeds 4C 96
Orion Cres. LS10: Leeds 6C 118
Orion Dr. LS10: Leeds 6C 118
Orion Gdns. LS10: Leeds 6D 118
Orion Pl. HX6: Sow B 5H 147
                  (off Greenups Ter.)
Orion Vw. LS10: Leeds 6D 118
Orion Wlk. LS10: Leeds 5D 118
Orleans St. BD6: B'frd 6H 109
Ormonde Dr. BD15: All 3C 88
Ormonde Pl. LS7: Leeds 6A 78
Ormond Rd. BD6: B'frd 4B 110
Ormondroyd Av. BD6: B'frd 1A 110
Ormond St. BD7: B'frd 1A 110
Orrell Gro. LS10: Leeds 3C 140
Orville Gdns. LS6: Leeds 5E 77
Osborne Gro. HX3: Hip 2F 151
Osborne St. BD5: B'frd 6D 90
   HX1: Hal 1D 148
Osborne Ter. LS13: Leeds 2F 95
Osbourne Dr. BD13: Que 4H 107
Osmond Ho. BD5: B'frd 6E 91
                  (off Croscombe Wlk.)
OSMONDTHORPE 3G 99

Osmondthorpe Cotts. LS9: Leeds 4G 99
Osmondthorpe La. LS9: Leeds 3G 99
Osmondthorpe Ter. LS9: Leeds 3F 99
Osprey Cl. LS17: Leeds 3D 60
   LS22: Coll 2B 28
Osprey Ct. BD8: B'frd 4E 89
Osprey Gro. LS17: Leeds 3D 60
Osprey Mdw. LS27: Morl 3D 138
Osterley Cres. BD10: B'frd 4C 72
Osterley Gro. BD10: B'frd 4C 72
Oswald Cl. LS20: Guis 4B 40
Oswald St. BD18: Ship 2D 70
Oswaldthorpe Av. BD3: B'frd 2B 92
Oswin Gdns. BD2: B'frd 5D 70
OTLEY 4E 23
Otley Golf Course 5A 22
Otley La. LS19: Yead 6F 41
Otley Mt. BD20: E Mor 4A 36
Otley Museum 4F 23
Otley Old Rd. LS16: Leeds 2G 57
   LS18: H'fth, Yead 1A 42
   LS19: Yead 1A 42
Otley Rd. BD2: B'frd 3G 91
   BD3: B'frd 1G 7 (4F 91)
   BD16: Bgly 5F 37
   BD17: Bail, Ship 6C 52
   BD18: Ship 3B 70
   BD20: E Mor 4A 36
   LS6: Leeds 2C 76
   LS16: Leeds 1B 58
   LS20: Guis 4A 40
   LS21: Burl W 3G 21
   LS29: Burl W 3G 21
   LS29: Men 6H 21
Otley RUFC 3F 23
Otley St. BD21: Keigh 1H 47
   HX1: Hal 2D 148
Ottawa Pl. LS7: Leeds 3B 78
Otterburn Cl. BD5: B'frd 1D 110
Otterburn Gdns. LS16: Leeds 4B 58
Otterburn St. BD21: Keigh 4A 34
Otterwood Bank LS22: Weth 2F 13
Ouchthorpe Fold WF1: Out 5G 157
Ouchthorpe La.
   WF1: Out, Wake 6G 157
Ouchthorpe M. WF1: Out 6G 157
OULTON 2E 143
Oulton Dr. LS26: Oul 4E 143
Oulton La. LS26: Oul 6E 121
   LS26: Rothw 2B 142
Oulton Park Golf Course 3D 142
Oulton Ter. BD7: B'frd 6C 90
Ounsworth St. BD4: B'frd 1H 111
Ouse Dr. LS22: Weth 1D 12
OUSEL HOLE 3A 36
Ouse St. BD22: Haw 2D 64
Outgang LS13: Leeds 6F 75
Outgang La. LS13: Leeds 6G 75
Outlands Ri. BD10: B'frd 1B 72
Outside La. BD22: Oxen 6A 64
OUTWOOD 5F 157
Outwood Av. LS18: H'fth 2F 75
Outwood Chase LS18: H'fth 1F 75
Outwood La. LS18: H'fth 2E 75
Outwood Pk. Ct. WF1: Out 5E 157
Outwood Station (Rail) 4E 157
Outwood Wlk. LS18: H'fth 2E 75
Ouzel Dr. BD6: B'frd 4E 109
OUZLEWELL GREEN 6H 141
Ouzlewell Grn. WF3: Loft 5H 141
OVAL, THE 1B 100
Oval, The BD8: B'frd 3G 89
   BD16: Bgly 5D 50
   BD17: Bail 5B 52
   LS10: Leeds 1B 118
   LS14: Leeds 1B 100
   LS20: Guis 5A 40
   LS21: Otley 2D 22
   LS25: Gar 4G 103
   LS26: Rothw 2B 142
   LS28: Fars 1A 94
Ovendale Hall HX3: Hal 5E 129
             (off Ovenden Rd.)

OVENDEN 5D 128
Ovenden Av. HX3: Hal 6E 129
Ovenden Cl. HX3: Hal 6E 129
Ovenden Cres. HX3: Hal 5E 129
Ovenden Grn. HX3: Hal 5E 129
Ovenden Rd. HX1: Hal 1A 164 (4E 129)
   HX3: Hal 1A 164 (4E 129)
Ovenden Rd. Ter. HX3: Hal 5E 129
Ovenden Ter. HX3: Hal 5E 129
Ovenden Way HX3: Hal 5D 128
OVENDEN WOOD 5A 128
Ovenden Wood Rd.
   HX2: Hal 5A 128
Overdale Av. LS17: Leeds 2E 61
Overdale Cl. LS22: Weth 3D 12
Overdale Dr. BD18: Ship 6F 53
Overdale Mt. HX6: Sow B 4A 148
Overdale Ter. BD22: Haw 2C 64
   LS15: Leeds 3C 100
Overend St. BD6: B'frd 4A 110
Evergreen Royd
   HX2: Mt T 3G 127
Overland Cres. BD10: B'frd 1B 72
Overland Pk. LS27: Gil 2E 137
Overland Trad. Est.
   LS27: Gil 2E 137
Over La. LS19: Raw 4G 55
Overmoor Fold BD10: B'frd 2G 71
Overton Dr. BD4: B'frd 3F 109
Over Wood HX2: Hal 3C 148
Ovington Dr. BD4: B'frd 4C 112
Owen Ct. BD16: Bgly 1C 50
Owens Quay BD16: Bgly 4B 50
Owlcotes Dr. LS28: Pud 3G 93
Owlcotes Gdns. LS28: Pud 3G 93
Owlcotes Gth. LS28: Pud 3F 93
Owlcotes La. LS28: Pud 3G 93
   LS28: Stan 2G 93
              (not continuous)
Owlcotes Rd. LS28: Pud 3F 93
Owlcotes Shop. Cen.
   LS28: Stan 2H 93
Owlcotes Ter. LS28: Pud 3G 93
Owler Ings Rd. HD6: Brigh 1A 162
Owler La. WF17: Birs 4A 136
Owler Pk. Rd. LS29: I'ly 2A 10
Owlers Cl. HD2: Hud 6F 163
OWLET 5D 70
Owlet Grange BD18: Ship 3C 70
Owlet Rd. BD18: Ship 2C 70
Owlett Mead WF3: Thpe H 6C 140
Owlett Mead Cl.
   WF3: Thpe H 6C 140
Owl La. WF12: Dew 6A 154
             (not continuous)
Owl Ridge LS27: Morl 4C 138
Owl St. BD21: Keigh 3H 33
             (off Parson St.)
Owlwood Cotts. WF10: All B 1G 145
Owlwood Ho's. WF10: All B 1G 145
Oxclose Rd. LS23: B Spa 3B 30
Oxclose Wlk. LS23: B Spa 2B 30
Oxendale Cl. LS26: Wood 1D 142
Oxenford Ct. LS16: Leeds 4A 58
OXENHOPE 1C 84
Oxenhope Station
   Keighley & Worth Valley Railway
   . . . . .6C 64
Oxford Av. LS20: Guis 3B 40
Oxford Cl. BD13: Que 5G 107
Oxford Cres. BD14: Clay 1D 108
   HX3: Hal 5H 149
Oxford Dr. LS25: Kip 4F 123
Oxford La. HX3: Hal 5H 149
Oxford Pl. BD3: B'frd 1F 7 (3F 91)
   BD17: Bail 5E 53
   LS1: Leeds 3C 4 (3H 97)
   LS28: Stan 2A 94
Oxford Rd. BD2: B'frd 1G 91
   BD13: Que 5G 107
   BD19: Gom 5F 135
   HX1: Hal 6B 164 (3G 149)
   LS7: Leeds 6A 78

Oxford Rd. LS20: Guis 4B 40
   WF17: Birs 6A 136
Oxford Row LS1: Leeds 3C 4 (3H 97)
             (not continuous)
Oxford St. BD14: Clay 1D 108
   BD21: Keigh 1G 47
   HX6: Sow B 4B 148
   LS20: Guis 4B 40
   LS27: Morl 5H 137
   WF3: E Ard 1C 156
Oxford Ter. BD17: Bail 5E 53
              (off Otley Rd.)
Oxford Vs. LS20: Guis 4C 40
Ox Heys Mdws. BD13: Thorn 5C 88
Oxley Gdns. BD12: Low M 6C 110
Oxley St. BD8: B'frd 3C 90
   BD12: Low M 1C 132
   LS9: Leeds 4D 98
Oxton Mt. LS9: Leeds 3D 98
Oxton Way LS9: Leeds 3D 98
Oyster Cl. LS27: Morl 4C 138

P

Pack Horse Yd. LS1: Leeds 4E 5
Packington St. BD13: Thorn 3G 87
Padan St. HX3: Hal 5H 149
Paddock BD9: B'frd 5C 70
   HX3: North 2A 130
Paddock, The BD4: B'frd 4C 112
             (off Tennis Av.)
   BD13: Cull 3B 66
   BD17: Bail 3F 53
   BD19: Scho 1F 153
   LS6: Leeds 2F 77
   LS14: T'ner 2H 63
   LS17: E Kes 5E 27
   LS26: Rothw 2A 142
Paddock Cl. BD11: Drig 2A 136
   BD12: Wyke 6C 132
   LS25: Gar 5G 103
Paddock Dr. BD11: Drig 2A 136
Paddock Grn. LS17: E Kes 6E 27
Paddock Ho. La.
   LS22: Sick 1D 26
Paddock La. BD16: Bgly 1F 51
   HX2: Hal 1A 148
Paddock Rd. HX3: North 2A 130
Paddock Vw. LS17: Bard 6F 27
Padgum BD17: Bail 3C 52
Padma Cl. BD7: B'frd 4B 90
Padmans La. LS23: B Spa 3B 30
Padstow Av. LS10: Leeds 2G 139
Padstow Gdns. LS10: Leeds 2G 139
Padstow Pl. LS10: Leeds 3G 139
Padstow Row LS10: Leeds 3G 139
Page Hill HX2: Illing 4C 128
Paget St. BD21: Keigh 6G 33
Pagewood Ct.
   BD10: B'frd 6G 53
Paignton Ct. LS13: Leeds 2F 95
Paisley Gro. LS12: Leeds 3A 96
Paisley Pl. LS12: Leeds 3A 96
Paisley Rd. LS12: Leeds 3A 96
Paisley St. LS12: Leeds 3A 96
Paisley Ter. LS12: Leeds 3A 96
Paisley Vw. LS12: Leeds 3A 96
Pakington St. BD5: B'frd 1D 110
Paley Rd. BD4: B'frd 1G 111
Paley Ter. BD4: B'frd 1G 111
Palin Av. BD3: B'frd 2B 92
Palm Cl. BD6: B'frd 5B 110
Palmer Rd. BD3: B'frd 3H 91
Palmerston Ho. BD4: B'frd 1C 112
             (off Tyersal La.)
Palmerston St. BD2: B'frd 1H 91
Palm St. HX3: Hal 5F 129
Pannal St. BD7: B'frd 2A 110
Pannell Hill WF10: All B 6B 124
Panorama Dr. LS29: I'ly 1A 18
Paper Hall, The 3F 7
Papyrus Vs. LS24: N Kym 5G 31

Parade, The BD4: B'frd 2C 112
  BD16: Cot 2C 68
  LS6: Leeds 4D 76
        (off North La.)
  LS16: B'hpe 2G 43
  LS19: Yead 1D 54
        (off Westfield Dr.)
  LS21: Otley 2C 22
Paradise HX2: Midg 1C 146
Paradise Fold BD7: B'frd 1G 109
PARADISE GREEN 1G 109
Paradise Gro. LS18: H'fth 1G 75
        (off Low La.)
Paradise La. HX2: Hal 3H 147
Paradise Pl. LS18: H'fth 1G 75
Paradise Rd. BD9: B'frd 5H 69
Paradise St. BD1: B'frd 3A 6 (4D 90)
        (not continuous)
  HX1: Hal 5A 164 (3F 149)
Paradise Vw. BD15: Wils 3F 67
Parc Mont LS8: Leeds 1G 79
Paris Gates HX3: Hal 4H 149
        (off Boys La.)
Parish Gate LS29: Burl W 2E 21
        (off Main St.)
Parish Ghyll Dr. LS29: I'ly 6B 10
Parish Ghyll La. LS29: I'ly 6B 10
Parish Ghyll Rd. LS29: I'ly 6C 10
Parish Ghyll Wlk. LS29: I'ly 6C 10
PARK 3F 53
Park, The HX3: Sou 5C 150
Park & Ride
  King Lane 4H 59
  Thornton Road 4A 6 (4D 90)
Park App. LS15: Leeds 3H 101
Park Av. BD10: B'frd 5H 53
  BD11: Drig 1A 136
  BD16: Bgly 5B 50
  BD18: Ship 1A 70
  BD21: Keigh 1H 47
  BD22: Oak 5D 46
  HX5: Ell 5A 160
  LS8: Leeds 1G 79
  LS12: Leeds 3B 96
  LS15: Leeds 1F 101
  LS19: Raw 3G 55
  LS19: Yead 6E 41
  LS25: Kip 4A 124
  LS26: Swil 4A 122
  LS27: Morl 4H 137
  LS28: Pud 4A 94
  WF1: Out 5E 157
  WF3: Loft 3G 157
Park Bottom BD12: Low M 2C 132
Park Bldgs. LS21: Pool 4F 25
Park Cir. LS10: Leeds 2H 139
Park Cliffe Rd. BD7: B'frd 1G 91
Park Cl. BD10: B'frd 4A 72
  BD11: Drig 1A 136
  BD13: Que 4H 107
  BD16: Bgly 3C 50
  BD21: Keigh 2A 48
  HX2: Hal 5H 127
  HX3: Hip 2G 151
  LS13: Leeds 6E 75
Park Copse LS18: H'fth 6C 56
Park Cotts. LS8: Leeds 6F 61
Park Ct. BD9: B'frd 1C 90
  LS21: Pool 5F 25
Park Cres. BD3: B'frd 1G 91
  HX3: Hal 6E 129
  HX6: Sow B 5B 148
        (off Grove St.)
  LS8: Leeds 5E 61
  LS12: Leeds 3B 96
  LS20: Guis 6A 40
  LS26: Rothw 1C 142
  LS27: Gil 1F 137
  LS29: Add 1E 9
Parkcroft LS28: Fars 1H 93
Park Cross St.
  LS1: Leeds 4C 4 (3H 97)
Park Dale LS29: Men 1G 39

Park Dr. BD9: B'frd 5A 70
  BD16: Bgly 2D 50
  HX1: Hal 3E 149
  HX2: Hal 4B 148
  LS12: N Far 2A 116
  LS18: H'fth 1B 74
  WF3: Loft 2G 157
Park Dr. Rd. BD21: Keigh 2A 48
Park Edge Cl. LS8: Leeds 2G 79
Parker's La. BD20: Keigh 2G 33
Parker St. WF3: E Ard 2A 156
Park Farm Ind. Est. LS11: Leeds . . .5H 117
Park Fld. LS29: Men 1G 39
Parkfield Av. HX5: Ell 5B 160
  LS11: Leeds 2G 117
Parkfield Cl. LS25: Kip 3H 123
  LS28: Pud 4H 93
Parkfield Ct. LS14: Leeds 6A 80
  LS27: Morl 4H 137
Parkfield Dr. BD13: Que 4H 107
  HX6: Tri 6G 147
  LS23: B Spa 3A 30
Parkfield Gro. LS11: Leeds 2G 117
Parkfield La. HX6: Norl 6B 148
Parkfield Mt. LS11: Leeds 2G 117
  LS28: Pud 4A 94
Parkfield Pl. LS11: Leeds 2G 117
Parkfield Rd. BD8: B'frd 1D 90
  BD18: Ship 1G 69
  LS11: Leeds 2G 117
Parkfield Row LS11: Leeds 2G 117
Park Flds. HX2: Hal 5H 127
Parkfield St. LS11: Leeds 6A 98
Parkfield Ter. LS28: Pud 4A 94
  LS28: Stan 2A 94
        (not continuous)
Parkfield Vw. LS11: Leeds 2G 117
Parkfield Way LS14: Leeds 6A 80
Park Gdns. HX2: Hal 4B 148
Park Gate BD1: B'frd 3F 7 (4H 91)
Park Gate Cl. LS18: H'fth 1D 74
Park Gate Cres. LS20: Guis 5B 40
Park Grn. BD20: Sils 2C 14
Park Gro. BD9: B'frd 5C 70
  BD13: Que 4H 107
  BD18: Ship 1H 69
  BD21: Keigh 5A 34
  HX3: North 6B 130
  LS6: Leeds 3D 76
  LS10: Leeds 3A 140
  LS18: H'fth 1B 74
  LS19: Yead 6E 41
  LS26: Swil 5A 122
  LS27: Gil 1F 137
Park Gro. Ct. BD9: B'frd 5C 70
Park Halt Station
  Middleton Railway 5B 118
Parkhead Cl. BD6: B'frd 1H 131
Park Hill HD2: Hud 5F 163
Park Hill Cl. BD8: B'frd 2F 89
Park Hill Dr. BD8: B'frd 2F 89
Park Hill Gro. BD16: Bgly 3C 50
        (off Staveley Rd.)
Park Holme LS7: Leeds 5C 78
Parkhome Est. LS26: Swil 4B 122
Park Ho. Cl. BD12: Low M 6E 111
Park Ho. Cres. BD12: Low M 6E 111
Park Ho. Gro. BD12: Low M 6E 111
Park Ho. Rd. BD12: Low M 1D 132
Park Ho. Wlk. BD12: Low M 6E 111
Parkin La. BD10: B'frd 1D 72
Parkinson App. LS25: Gar 3F 103
Parkinson Fold LS29: Add 1E 9
        (off Church St.)
Parkinson La. HX1: Hal 3C 148
Parkinson Rd. BD13: Denh 3C 86
Parkinson St. BD5: B'frd 1D 110
Parkinson Way LS20: Guis 3B 40
Parkland Av. LS27: Morl 4G 137
Parkland Bus. Cen. BD10: B'frd 2B 72
Parkland Cres. LS6: Leeds 6G 59
Parkland Dr. BD10: B'frd 2A 72
  LS6: Leeds 6G 59

Parkland Gdns. LS6: Leeds 1G 77
PARKLANDS 5C 80
Parklands BD16: Bgly 2D 50
  LS16: B'hpe 2F 43
  LS29: I'ly 5F 11
Parklands Cres. LS16: B'hpe 2G 43
Parklands Ga. LS16: B'hpe 2G 43
Parklands Wlk. LS16: B'hpe 3F 43
Parkland Ter. LS6: Leeds 1G 77
Parkland Vw. LS19: Yead 1F 55
        (not continuous)
Park La. BD5: B'frd 1D 110
  BD13: Que 4B 108
  BD14: Clay 1D 108
  BD17: Bail 3F 53
  BD21: Keigh 1A 48
  HX3: Hal 1H 159
  LS1: Leeds 3B 4 (3G 97)
  LS3: Leeds 3A 4 (3F 97)
  LS8: Leeds 5F 61
  LS20: Guis 6A 40
  LS25: Kip 5A 124
  LS25: Led 4G 125
        (not continuous)
  LS26: Meth 6A 144
  LS26: Rothw 2B 142
  WF10: All B 3H 145
Park La. Central LS6: Leeds 4D 76
        (off Bennett Rd.)
Park La. Ends HX2: Ogd 5B 106
Park La. M. LS17: Shad 3F 61
Park Lea HD2: Hud 5F 163
  LS10: Leeds 2A 140
Parklee Ct. BD21: Keigh 1B 48
Park Lodge BD15: Wils 4G 67
Park Mead BD10: B'frd 5H 53
Parkmere Cl. BD4: B'frd 6H 111
Park M. LS21: Pool 5F 25
Park Mt. LS5: Leeds 5A 76
  LS12: Leeds 3A 96
  LS21: Pool 6D 24
Park Mt. Av. BD17: Bail 4E 53
Park Nook HX3: Sou 1B 160
Park Pde. LS9: Leeds 5E 99
  LS27: Morl 4H 137
Park Pl. BD10: B'frd 5A 54
  HX1: Hal 3E 149
        (off Warley St.)
  LS1: Leeds 4C 4 (3H 97)
  LS8: Leeds 4H 79
Park Pl. E. HX3: Hip 2G 151
Park Pl. W. HX3: Hip 2G 151
Park Ri. LS13: Leeds 5E 75
Park Rd. BD5: B'frd 6E 91
  BD10: B'frd 5H 53
        (Ainsbury Av.)
  BD10: B'frd 4A 72
        (Victoria Rd.)
  BD12: Low M 6C 110
  BD16: Bgly 4B 50
  BD18: Ship 2C 70
  HX1: Hal 5A 164 (3F 149)
  HX5: Ell, Hal 3B 160
  HX6: Sow B 4A 148
  LS12: Leeds 3A 96
  LS13: Leeds 6E 75
  LS15: Leeds 5F 101
  LS19: Raw 3F 55
  LS19: Yead 6E 41
  LS20: Guis 6A 40
  LS23: B Spa 3A 30
  LS29: Men 1G 39
Park Row HD6: Brigh 1B 162
  LS1: Leeds 4D 4 (3H 97)
  LS21: Otley 3F 23
        (off Cross Grn.)
  LS28: Stan 2A 94
  LS29: Burl W 1F 21
Park Row Apartments LS1: Leeds . . .4D 4
Park School M. BD16: Bgly 4B 50
        (off Lime St.)
PARKSIDE 3F 111

Park Side BD14: Clay 1D 108
Parkside BD16: Bgly 3C 50
   HX3: Hal 5F 149
   LS18: H'fth 1C 74
Parkside Av. BD13: Que 4H 107
   LS6: Leeds 2F 77
Parkside Cl. LS4: Leeds 6B 76
   LS6: Leeds 1F 77
Parkside Ct. BD22: Cros R 1E 65
   LS14: Leeds 5C 80
Parkside Cres. LS6: Leeds 1F 77
   LS14: Leeds 5C 80
Parkside Dr. BD9: B'frd 6A 70
   LS14: Leeds 5C 80
Parkside Gdns. LS6: Leeds 2F 77
Parkside Grn. LS6: Leeds 2F 77
Parkside Gro. BD9: B'frd 6A 70
   LS11: Leeds 4G 117
Parkside Hgts. LS6: Leeds 6B 76
Parkside Ind. Est. LS11: Leeds 4A 118
Parkside La. LS11: Leeds 3A 118
Parkside Lawns LS6: Leeds 2F 77
Parkside Mt. LS11: Leeds 4G 117
Parkside Pde. LS11: Leeds 4G 117
Parkside Pl. LS6: Leeds 1F 77
Parkside Rd. BD5: B'frd 3D 110
   LS6: Leeds 2F 77
   LS16: Leeds 6D 58
   LS28: Fars 1H 93
Parkside Row LS11: Leeds 4G 117
Parkside Ter. BD13: Cull 3B 66
Parkside Vw. LS6: Leeds 1F 77
   LS14: Leeds 5C 80
Parkside Wlk. LS28: Fars 1A 94
Parks La. LS29: Midd 1C 10
PARK SPRING 4F 95
Park Spring Gdns. LS13: Leeds 2D 94
Park Spring Ri. LS13: Leeds 3D 94
Park Sq. BD6: B'frd 5H 109
   HX3: North 5C 130
     (off Hough)
   LS19: Raw 3G 55
     (off Batter La.)
   LS21: Pool 5F 25
   LS28: Pud 4A 94
   WF3: Loft 3G 157
Park Sq. E. LS1: Leeds 4C 4 (3H 97)
Park Sq. Nth. LS1: Leeds 4C 4 (3H 97)
Park Sq. Sth. LS1: Leeds 4C 4 (3H 97)
Park Sq. W. LS1: Leeds 4C 4 (3H 97)
Parkstone HD2: Hud 5F 163
Parkstone Av. LS16: Leeds 6A 58
Parkstone Dr. BD10: B'frd 4A 72
Parkstone Grn. LS16: Leeds 6A 58
Parkstone Gro. LS16: Leeds 6A 58
Parkstone Mt. LS16: Leeds 6A 58
Parkstone Pl. LS16: Leeds 6A 58
Park Stone Ri. HX3: She 1D 130
Park St. BD18: Ship 1A 70
   BD19: Cleck 3H 153
   BD22: Haw 2D 64
   HD6: Brigh 1B 162
   HX6: Sow B 5B 148
   LS1: Leeds 3C 4 (3H 97)
   LS12: Leeds 3A 96
   LS15: Leeds 3D 100
   LS19: Yead 6E 41
   LS27: Chur 5C 116
Park Ter. BD12: Low M 1C 132
     (off Fountain St.)
   BD18: Ship 1A 70
   BD21: Keigh 1D 48
     (off Bank Top Way)
   BD21: Keigh 6B 34
     (Frederick St.)
   HX1: Hal 3E 149
     (not continuous)
   HX3: Hal 6C 130
   HX3: Hip 2F 151
   LS6: Leeds 3D 76
   LS21: Otley 3F 23
     (off Cross Grn.)
   LS21: Pool 6C 24

Park Top LS28: Stan 2A 94
Park Top Cotts. BD16: Bgly 2D 50
Park Top Row BD22: Haw 2C 64
Park Vw. BD11: Birk 2E 135
   BD13: Que 3H 107
   BD19: Cleck 1H 153
   HX1: Hal 3E 149
   HX3: Hip 2G 151
   HX6: Sow B 4H 147
     (off Tuel La.)
   LS11: Leeds 2G 117
   LS13: Leeds 6E 75
     (not continuous)
   LS16: Leeds 3C 58
   LS19: Yead 6D 40
     (off South Vw.)
   LS25: Kip 4H 123
     (off Roger Fold)
   LS26: Swil 4A 122
   LS28: Pud 4A 94
   WF3: Loft 3G 157
Park Vw. Av. BD22: Cros R 1E 65
   HX3: North 6C 130
   LS4: Leeds 6D 76
   LS9: Raw 3G 55
Park Vw. Cres. LS8: Leeds 6F 61
Park Vw. Gro. LS4: Leeds 6D 76
Park Vw. Rd. BD9: B'frd 6B 70
   LS4: Leeds 1D 96
Park Vw. Ter. BD9: B'frd 6B 70
   BD16: Har 5F 49
   LS15: Leeds 3C 100
     (off Primrose La.)
   LS19: Raw 3F 55
Park Villa Ct. LS8: Leeds 6E 61
PARK VILLAS 5E 61
Park Vs. HX6: Sow B 5B 148
     (off Grove St.)
   LS8: Leeds 6E 61
Parkville Pl. LS13: Leeds 5E 75
Parkville Rd. LS13: Leeds 6E 75
Park Way BD21: Keigh 2A 48
   LS21: Pool 4F 25
   LS29: Men 1G 39
Parkway BD5: B'frd 3F 111
   BD13: Que 4H 107
   BD20: Stee 6B 14
     (Pot La.)
   BD20: Stee 5C 14
     (Stone Gro.)
   LS27: Gil 1E 137
Parkway Cl. LS14: Leeds 5A 80
Parkway Ct. LS14: Leeds 6A 80
Parkway Grange LS14: Leeds 6A 80
Parkways LS26: Oul 1D 142
Parkways Av. LS26: Oul 2D 142
Parkways Cl. LS26: Oul 1D 142
Parkways Ct. LS26: Oul 1D 142
Parkways Dr. LS26: Oul 1D 142
Parkways Gth. LS26: Oul 2D 142
Parkways Gro. LS26: Oul 1D 142
Parkway Towers LS14: Leeds 5A 80
Parkway Vw. LS14: Leeds 5D 80
     (Harewood La.)
   LS14: Leeds 6A 80
     (South Parkway)
Park W. LS26: Rothw 2A 142
PARKWOOD 1A 48
Park Wood Av. LS11: Leeds 6F 117
Parkwood Av. LS8: Leeds 2E 79
PARK WOOD BOTTOM 1B 48
Park Wood Cl. LS11: Leeds 6F 117
Parkwood Cl. LS8: Leeds 1E 79
Park Wood Crematorium
   HX5: Ell 2B 160
Park Wood Cres. LS11: Leeds 6F 117
Park Wood Dr. LS11: Leeds 5F 117
Parkwood Gdns. LS8: Leeds 2E 79
   LS28: Cal 3E 73
Parkwood M. LS8: Leeds 2E 79
Parkwood Ri. BD21: Keigh 1A 48

Parkwood Rd. BD18: Ship 2H 69
   LS11: Leeds 6F 117
   LS28: Cal 3F 73
Parkwood St. BD21: Keigh 1A 48
Park Wood Top BD21: Keigh 1B 48
Parkwood Vw. LS8: Leeds 1E 79
Parkwood Way LS8: Leeds 2E 79
Parkwy BD17: Bail 6H 51
Parliament Pl. LS12: Leeds 3D 96
Parliament Rd. LS12: Leeds 4D 96
Parlington Ct. LS15: Bar E 2E 83
Parlington La. LS25: Aber, Gar 6F 83
Parlington Mdw. LS15: Bar E 3E 83
Parma St. BD5: B'frd 6E 91
Parnaby Av. LS10: Leeds 4D 118
Parnaby Rd. LS10: Leeds 4D 118
Parnaby St. LS10: Leeds 4D 118
Parnaby Ter. LS10: Leeds 4D 118
Parratt Row BD3: B'frd 4B 92
Parrott St. BD4: B'frd 4B 112
Parry La. BD4: B'frd 6A 92
Parsley M. LS26: Meth 4C 144
Parsonage La. HD6: Brigh 6A 152
     (not continuous)
Parsonage Rd. BD4: B'frd 6B 92
   BD5: B'frd 2E 111
   LS26: Meth 4D 144
Parsonage St. HX3: Hal 6H 129
Parsons Grn. LS22: Weth 4F 13
Parson's La. LS29: Add 1A 8
     (not continuous)
Parsons Rd. BD9: B'frd 5A 70
Parson St. BD21: Keigh 5A 34
Partridge Cl. LS27: Morl 3D 138
Partridge Dr. BD6: B'frd 4E 109
Paslew Cl. BD20: E Mor 4F 35
Pasture Av. BD22: Oak 6C 46
   LS7: Leeds 2B 78
Pasture Cl. BD14: Clay 1F 109
Pasture Cres. LS7: Leeds 2B 78
Pasture Fold LS29: Burl W 1E 21
Pasture Gro. LS7: Leeds 2B 78
Pasture La. BD7: B'frd 1E 109
   BD14: Clay 1E 109
   LS7: Leeds 2B 78
   LS22: Kear 2A 26
Pasture Mt. LS12: Leeds 3B 96
Pasture Pde. LS7: Leeds 2B 78
Pasture Pl. LS7: Leeds 2B 78
Pasture Ri. BD14: Clay 1F 109
Pasture Rd. BD17: Bail 5D 52
   LS8: Leeds 5C 78
Pastureside Ter. E. BD14: Clay 1F 109
Pastureside Ter. W. BD14: Clay 1E 109
Pasture St. LS7: Leeds 2B 78
Pasture Ter. LS7: Leeds 2B 78
Pasture Vw. LS12: Leeds 3B 96
Pasture Vw. Rd. LS26: Rothw 2A 142
Pasture Wlk. BD14: Clay 1E 109
Patchett Sq. BD13: Que 4D 108
     (off Highgate Rd.)
Patent St. BD9: B'frd 1B 90
Paternoster La. BD7: B'frd 1A 110
Patricia Gdns. HX6: Sow B 4G 147
Patterdale App. LS22: Weth 4B 12
Patterson Ct. WF2: Wren 6D 156
Pattie St. BD20: Keigh 4H 33
Paulena Ter. LS27: Morl 5B 138
     (off Britannia Rd.)
Paul La. HD5: Hud 6H 163
Pavement La. HX2: Illing 5C 106
Pavilion Bus. Pk. LS12: Leeds 2C 116
Pavilion Cl. HX1: Hal 2D 148
   LS28: Stan 1A 94
Pavilion Ct. BD4: B'frd 5A 112
Pavilion Gdns. BD4: B'frd 2A 112
   LS26: Wood 1E 143
   LS28: Fars 1A 94
Pavilion Ho. LS14: Leeds 5D 80
     (off York Rd.)
Pavilion M. LS6: Leeds 6D 76

Pavilion Way—Pickerings, The

Pavilion Way LS28: Pud 4H **93**
Paw La. BD13: Que 6B **108**
Pawson St. BD4: B'frd 5B **92**
LS27: Morl 4H **137**
WF3: E Ard 1C **156**
WF3: Loft 5F **141**
Paxton Ct. LS12: Leeds 1H **95**
Peabody St. HX3: Hal 6E **129**
Peace Museum, The . . . . **.4D 6**
Peace St. BD4: B'frd 6A **92**
Peach Wlk. BD4: B'frd 1H **111**
Peacock Ct. LS19: Yead 1H **55**
Peacock Grn. LS27: Morl 4C **138**
Pearl St. BD22: Keigh 3G **47**
Pearson Av. LS6: Leeds 6E **77**
Pearson Fold BD12: O'haw 3F **133**
Pearson Gro. LS6: Leeds 6E **77**
Pearson La. BD9: B'frd 2F **89**
Pearson Rd. BD6: B'frd 5D **110**
Pearson Rd. W. BD6: B'frd 5D **110**
Pearson Row BD12: Wyke 4D **132**
Pearsons Bldgs. LS21: Otley 4F **23**
Pearsons Cl. LS14: Leeds 5C **80**
Pearsons Ct. LS14: Leeds 5C **80**
Pearsons Dr. LS14: Leeds 5C **80**
Pearsons Fold LS14: Leeds 5C **80**
Pearson St. BD3: B'frd 5A **92**
BD19: Cleck 3H **153**
LS10: Leeds 6B **98**
LS28: Cal 2F **73**
Pearsons Vw. LS14: Leeds 5C **80**
Pearsons Way LS14: Leeds 5C **80**
Pearson Ter. LS6: Leeds 6E **77**
Pear St. BD21: Keigh 4G **47**
BD22: Oxen 1C **84**
HX1: Hal 3D **148**
Peart Pl. LS10: Leeds 3B **140**
Pear Tree Acre LS23: T Arch 2C **30**
Pear Tree Cl. HX3: Hip 2H **151**
Pear Tree Ct. BD20: Sils 1E **15**
Pear Tree Gdns. LS15: Bar E 3E **83**
Peas Acre BD16: Bgly 5A **36**
Peasborough Vw. LS29: Burl W 3F **21**
Peasefold LS25: Kip 4H **123**
Peasehill Cl. LS19: Raw 3G **55**
Peasehill Pk. LS19: Raw 3G **55**
Peaselands BD18: Ship 2A **70**
Peckfield Bus. Pk.
LS25: M'fld 5C **104**
Peckfield Cotts. LS25: M'fld 1B **124**
Peckover Dr. LS28: Pud 2D **92**
Peckover St. BD1: B'frd 3F **7** (4F **91**)
Peel Cl. BD4: B'frd 5C **92**
Peel Ct. BD2: B'frd 1F **91**
Peel Ho. BD16: Bgly 5D **50**
Peel Mills *LS27: Morl 3B* ***138***
(off Commercial St.)
Peel Mills Bus. Cen. LS27: Morl . . .3B **138**
Peel Pk. Dr. BD2: B'frd 1H **91**
Peel Pk. Ter. BD2: B'frd 1H **91**
Peel Pk. Vw. BD3: B'frd 2G **91**
Peel Pl. LS29: Burl W 1E **21**
Peel Row BD7: B'frd 1A **110**
Peel Sq. BD8: B'frd 2B **6** (3D **90**)
LS5: Leeds 5A **76**
Peel St. BD13: Que 4B **108**
BD13: Thorn 5H **87**
BD15: Wils 5G **67**
BD16: Bgly 4D **50**
HX6: Sow B 5H **147**
LS27: Morl 3B **138**
Peel Vs. *LS27: Morl 3B* ***138***
(off Commercial St.)
Peep Grn. La. WF15: Liv 1H **163**
Pegholme Dr. LS21: Otley 5B **22**
Pelham Ct. BD2: B'frd 6H **71**
LS10: Leeds 4B **140**
Pelham Pl. LS7: Leeds 2A **78**
Pelham Rd. BD2: B'frd 6H **71**
Pelican Works LS26: Rothw 6F **119**
PELLON . . . . **.1C 148**
Pellon Ind. Est. *HX1: Hal 1D* ***148***
(off Queen's Rd.)
Pellon La. HX1: Hal 2A **164** (1D **148**)
Pellon La. Retail Pk. *HX1: Hal 1F* ***149***
(off Raglan St.)
Pellon New Rd. HX1: Hal 1D **148**
HX2: Hal 1C **148**
Pellon Ter. BD10: B'frd 6H **53**
Pellon Wlk. BD10: B'frd 6H **53**
Pemberton Dr.
BD7: B'frd 6A **6** (5D **90**)
Pembroke Cl. LS27: Morl 2H **137**
Pembroke Ct. *BD8: B'frd 3H* ***89***
(off St Leonard's Rd.)
Pembroke Dr. LS27: Morl 2H **137**
LS28: Pud 3A **94**
Pembroke Grange LS9: Leeds 1H **99**
Pembroke Ri. LS25: Kip 3A **124**
Pembroke Rd. LS28: Pud 3A **94**
Pembroke St. BD5: B'frd 1E **111**
Pembroke Towers
LS9: Leeds 6H **79**
Pembury Mt. LS15: Leeds 6H **81**
Penarth Rd. LS15: Leeds 1D **100**
Pendas Dr. LS15: Leeds 1F **101**
PENDAS FIELDS . . . . **.6H 81**
Pendas Gro. LS15: Leeds 6F **81**
Pendas Wlk. LS15: Leeds 1F **101**
Pendas Way LS15: Leeds 1F **101**
Pendil Cl. LS15: Leeds 3E **101**
Pendle Ct. BD13: Que 6A **108**
Pendle Rd. BD16: Bgly 4D **50**
Pendragon BD2: B'frd 6G **71**
Pendragon La. BD2: B'frd 6H **71**
Pendragon Ter. LS20: Guis 4B **40**
Penfield Gro. BD14: Clay 1E **109**
Penfield Rd. BD11: Drig 1B **136**
Pengarth BD16: Bgly 2D **50**
Penistone Hill Country Pk. . . . . **.3A 64**
Penistone M. BD22: Haw 2C **64**
Penlands Cres. LS15: Leeds 4F **101**
Penlands Lawn LS15: Leeds 4F **101**
Penlands Wlk. LS15: Leeds 4F **101**
Penn Cl. BD2: B'frd 5H **71**
Pennine Cl. BD13: Que 6H **107**
Pennine Ind. Est. LS12: Leeds 4B **96**
Pennine Vw. WF17: Birs 4C **136**
Pennington Ct. LS6: Leeds 6G **77**
Pennington Gro. LS6: Leeds 5G **77**
Pennington La. LS26: Oul 5D **142**
Pennington Pl. LS6: Leeds 6G **77**
Pennington St. LS6: Leeds 6G **77**
Pennington Ter. BD5: B'frd 1C **110**
LS6: Leeds 5G **77**
Pennithorne Av. BD17: Bail 3C **52**
Penn St. HX1: Hal 1E **149**
Pennwell Dean LS14: Leeds 4F **81**
Pennwell Gth. LS14: Leeds 4F **81**
Pennwell Ga. LS14: Leeds 4F **81**
Pennwell Grn. LS14: Leeds 4F **81**
Pennwell Lawn LS14: Leeds 4F **81**
Pennyfield Cl. LS6: Leeds 6F **59**
Pennygate BD16: Bgly 2F **51**
Penny Hill Centre, The
LS10: Leeds 1C **118**
Penny Hill Dr. BD14: Clay 1F **109**
Penny La. Way LS10: Leeds 1B **118**
Pennythorne Ct. LS19: Yead 2E **55**
Pennythorne Dr. LS19: Yead 2E **55**
Penraevon 1 Light Ind. Est.
LS7: Leeds 6A **78**
Penraevon Av. LS7: Leeds 6A **78**
Penraevon Ind. Est. *LS7: Leeds 6A* ***78***
(off Jackson Rd.)
Penraevon St. LS7: Leeds 6A **78**
Penrith Gro. LS12: Leeds 5C **96**
Penrose Dr. BD7: B'frd 2H **109**
Penrose Pl. HX3: North 5C **130**
Pentland Av. BD14: Clay 1E **109**
Pentland Cl. BD22: Keigh 1G **47**
Pentland Dr. LS25: Gar 6F **103**
Pentland Way LS27: Morl 4A **138**
Penuel Pl. HX3: Hal 6H **149**
Penzance Ct. *BD8: B'frd 3B* ***90***
(off Fearnsides St.)
Pepper Gdns. LS13: Leeds 5G **75**
PEPPER HILL
BD16 . . . . **.6D 48**
HX3 . . . . **.1C 130**
Pepper Hill Lea BD22: Keigh 5F **47**
Pepper Hills LS17: Leeds 3B **60**
Pepper La. LS10: Leeds 2D **118**
LS13: Leeds 5F **75**
Pepper Rd. LS10: Leeds 3D **118**
Percival St. BD3: B'frd 4H **7** (4G **91**)
LS2: Leeds 2D **4** (2H **97**)
Percy St. BD16: Bgly 4C **50**
BD21: Keigh 3H **47**
LS12: Leeds 5D **96**
Peregrine Av. LS27: Morl 3D **138**
Peregrine Way BD6: B'frd 4E **109**
Perkin La. *BD10: B'frd 6F* ***53***
(off W. Cote Dr.)
Per La. HX2: Illing 6B **106**
Perry Cl. BD22: Keigh 3G **47**
Perseverance La. BD7: B'frd 2A **110**
Perseverance Mill *LS6: Leeds 6H* ***77***
(off Cross Chancellor St.)
Perseverance Mills BD6: B'frd 4A **110**
Perseverance Rd. BD13: Que 2E **107**
HX2: Ogd 2E **107**
Perseverance St. BD12: Wyke 3C **132**
BD17: Bail 3D **52**
HX6: Sow B 4H **147**
LS28: Pud 4G **93**
Perseverance Ter. HX1: Hal 4E **149**
LS26: Rothw 3A **142**
Perth Av. BD2: B'frd 6E **71**
Perth Dr. WF3: Ting 1F **155**
Perth Ho. *BD4: B'frd 6B* ***92***
(off Parsonage Rd.)
Perth Mt. LS18: H'fth 3D **56**
Peterborough Pl. BD2: B'frd 6H **71**
Peterborough Rd. BD2: B'frd 1H **91**
Peterborough Ter. BD2: B'frd 6H **71**
Peterhouse Dr. LS21: Otley 4G **23**
Peter La. HX2: Hal 2H **147**
LS27: Morl 2D **138**
Peter Laylock Ind. Est.
LS7: Leeds 6A **78**
Petersfield Av. LS10: Leeds 6C **118**
Petersgarth BD18: Ship 1G **69**
Petrel Cl. BD6: B'frd 4E **109**
Petrel Way LS27: Morl 4C **138**
Petrie Cres. LS13: Leeds 4H **73**
Petrie Gro. BD3: B'frd 4C **92**
Petrie Rd. BD3: B'frd 4C **92**
Petrie St. LS13: Leeds 4H **73**
Pevensey Gth. *BD10: B'frd 3A* ***72***
(off Rowantree Dr.)
Peverell Cl. BD4: B'frd 2C **112**
Peveril Mt. BD2: B'frd 6A **72**
Pheasant Dr. WF17: Birs 4C **136**
Pheasant St. BD21: Keigh 5B **34**
Philip Gth. WF1: Out 4F **157**
Philippa Way LS12: Leeds 2C **116**
Philip's Gro. WF3: Loft 3G **157**
Phillips Cl. *LS18: H'fth 6E* ***57***
(off Broadgate La.)
Phil May Ct. *LS12: Leeds 5E* ***97***
(off Holdforth Grn.)
Phoebe La. HX3: Hal 5H **149**
Phoebe La. Ind. Est. HX3: Hal 5H **149**
Phoenix Av. LS25: M'fld 5C **104**
Phoenix Cl. LS14: Leeds 6C **80**
Phoenix Pastures
BD22: Keigh 4F **47**
Phoenix St. HD6: Brigh 1B **162**
Phoenix Way BD4: B'frd 5C **92**
Piccadilly BD1: B'frd 3C **6** (4E **91**)
Piccadilly Chambers
BD1: B'frd 3C **6**
Pickard Bank LS6: Leeds 4F **77**
Pickard Ct. LS15: Leeds 3E **101**
Pickard La. BD20: Sils 1E **15**
Pickering Av. LS25: Gar 3H **103**
Pickering Mt. LS12: Leeds 3D **96**
Pickerings, The BD13: Que 5A **108**

Pickering St. LS12: Leeds 3D 96
PICKLES HILL 3H 109
Pickles La. BD7: B'frd 3H 109
Pickles St. BD21: Keigh 2H 47
Pickpocket La.
 LS26: Rothw, Wood 6C 120
Pickup Bus. Pk. LS28: Stan 1B 94
Pickwood La. HX6: Norl 1C 158
PICKWOOD SCAR 1C 158
Picton Ho. BD8: B'frd 2C 90
 (off Green La.)
Picton St. BD8: B'frd 2D 90
Picture House, The 5A 34
 (off North St.)
Pictureville BD5: B'frd 5C 6 (5E 91)
Piece Hall, The 4D 164 (2H 149)
Piece Hall Art Gallery 4D 164
Piece Hall Yd. BD1: B'frd ..4D 6 (4E 91)
Piece Wood Rd. LS16: Leeds 4F 57
Pigeon Cote Cl. LS14: Leeds 3C 80
Pigeon Cote Rd. LS14: Leeds 3C 80
Piggott St. HD6: Brigh 6A 152
Pigman La. HX2: Hal 3G 147
Pilden La. WF3: E Ard 3A 156
Pilgrim Way LS28: Stan 1C 94
Pilot St. LS9: Leeds 1H 5 (2C 98)
Pinder Av. LS12: Leeds 1H 115
PINDER GREEN 6C 144
Pinder Gro. LS12: Leeds 1H 115
Pinders Grn. Ct. LS26: Meth 6C 144
Pinders Grn. Dr. LS26: Meth 6C 144
Pinders Grn. Fold LS26: Meth ...6C 144
Pinders Grn. Wlk. LS26: Meth ...6C 144
Pinder St. LS12: Leeds 1H 115
Pinder Vw. LS12: Leeds 1H 115
Pinebury Dr. BD13: Que 4G 107
Pine Cl. LS22: Weth 2E 13
Pine Ct. LS12: Leeds 5G 5 (4B 98)
Pine Cft. BD20: Keigh 4G 33
Pinedale BD16: Bgly 2B 50
Pines, The LS10: Leeds 3C 140
 LS17: Leeds 4F 61
Pines Gdns. LS29: I'ly 6B 10
Pine St. BD1: B'frd 3F 7 (4F 91)
 BD22: Haw 3C 64
 HX1: Hal 5B 164 (3G 149)
Pine Tree Av. LS23: B Spa 3C 30
Pinewood HD6: Brigh 6H 151
 (off Elmwood Dr.)
Pinewood Cl. LS29: I'ly 6C 10
Pinfold BD14: Clay 1E 109
Pinfold Cl. LS26: Meth 4D 144
Pinfold Ct. LS15: Leeds 3D 100
Pinfold Grn. HX6: Sow B 6E 147
Pinfold Gro. LS15: Leeds 3C 100
Pinfold Hill LS15: Leeds 3D 100
Pinfold La. HD2: Fix 5F 161
 HX6: Sow B 5D 146
 LS12: Leeds 4B 96
 LS15: Leeds 3C 100
 LS16: Leeds 1G 57
 LS25: Gar 4F 103
 LS26: Meth 4E 145
Pinfold Mt. LS15: Leeds 4D 100
Pinfold Rd. LS15: Leeds 4D 100
Pinfold Sq. LS15: Leeds 3C 100
Pin Hill La. HX2: Midg 6D 126
Pink St. BD22: Haw 4C 64
Pinnacle BD14: Clay 6E 89
 (off Bradford Rd.)
Pinnar Cft. HX3: Sou 5C 150
Pinnar La. HX3: Sou 4B 150
Pintail Av. BD6: B'frd 4E 109
Pipe & Nook La. LS12: Leeds 4H 95
Pipercroft BD6: B'frd 1G 131
Piper La. LS21: Otley 4D 22
Pipit Mdw. LS27: Morl 4C 138
Pippin Ct. HX2: Hal 4D 128
Pippins Grn. Av. WF2: Kirk 6H 155
Pirie Cl. BD2: B'frd 6F 71
Pitchstone Ct. LS12: Leeds 4F 95
Pitcliffe Way BD5: B'frd 1F 111
Pitfall St. LS1: Leeds 6F 5 (4A 98)

Pit Fld. Rd. WF3: Carl 5H 141
Pit Hill HX3: Hal 3H 149
Pit La. BD3: B'frd 3H 7 (4G 91)
 BD6: B'frd 6H 109
 BD13: Denh 3H 85
 BD13: Que, Thorn 2G 107
 BD19: Gom 5F 135
 LS25: M'fld 1C 124
 (not continuous)
 LS26: Meth 3D 144
Pits La. BD19: Scho 3E 153
Pitt Row LS1: Leeds 6E 5 (4A 98)
Pitts St. BD4: B'frd 1B 112
Pitt St. BD21: Keigh 6B 34
Pitt St. Bus. Cen. BD21: Keigh ...6B 34
Pitty Beck Vw. BD15: All 4D 88
Place, The LS17: Leeds 3B 60
Place's Rd. LS9: Leeds 4C 98
Plaid Row LS9: Leeds 3C 98
Plainfield HX6: Sow B 4B 148
Plains La. HX5: Ell 2B 160
Plane Tree Av. LS17: Leeds 3D 60
Plane Tree Cl. LS17: Leeds 3D 60
Plane Tree Cft. LS17: Leeds 3D 60
Plane Tree Gdns. LS17: Leeds ...3D 60
Plane Tree Gro. LS19: Yead 1H 55
Plane Tree Nest HX2: Hal 3C 148
Plane Tree Nest La. HX2: Hal ...3C 148
Plane Tree Ri. LS17: Leeds 3D 60
Plane Tree Rd. HX6: Sow B 4H 147
Plane Trees HX2: Hal 1B 148
Plane Trees Cl. BD19: Hun 4B 134
Planetrees Rd. BD4: B'frd 5A 92
Planetrees St. BD15: All 2C 88
Plane Tree Vw. LS17: Leeds 3D 60
Plantation Av. LS15: Leeds 4B 100
 LS17: Leeds 2E 61
Plantation Fold BD22: Keigh 3F 47
Plantation Gdns. LS17: Leeds ...2E 61
Plantation M. BD9: B'frd 4F 69
Plantation Pl. BD4: B'frd 1A 112
Plantations, The BD12: Low M ...1C 132
Plantation Way BD17: Bail 4D 52
Platform One LS5: Leeds 5B 76
 (off Station App.)
Platt Ct. BD18: Ship 1E 71
Playfair Rd. LS10: Leeds 3B 118
Playground LS12: N Far 2F 115
Playhouse Sq. LS2: Leeds ...4G 5 (3B 98)
Plaza, The LS2: Leeds 1E 5
Pleasance, The LS26: Swil 4A 122
Pleasant Ct. LS6: Leeds 6G 77
 (off Woodhouse St.)
Pleasant Mt. LS11: Leeds 6G 97
Pleasant Pl. BD15: All 2C 88
 LS11: Leeds 6G 97
Pleasant Row BD13: Que 5G 107
 (off Moor Cl. La.)
Pleasant St. BD7: B'frd 1A 110
 HX6: Sow B 5A 148
 LS11: Leeds 6G 97
Pleasant Ter. LS11: Leeds 6G 97
Pleasant Vw. HX2: Midg 6C 126
 WF3: Loft 2D 156
Pleasant Views BD13: Denh 2C 86
Pleasant Vw. Ter. WF3: Rob H ...3F 141
 (off Copley La.)
Plevna St. LS10: Leeds 3E 119
Plevna Ter. BD16: Bgly 3B 50
Plimsoll St. BD4: B'frd 1G 111
Plockwood Cotts. LS25: M'fld ...1A 124
Ploughcroft La. HX3: Hal 5F 129
Ploughman's Cft. BD2: B'frd 5E 71
Plover St. BD5: B'frd 2C 110
 BD21: Keigh 5A 34
Plover Way LS27: Morl 4C 138
Plowmans Wlk. LS19: Yead 1D 54
Plumpton Av. BD2: B'frd 3F 71
Plumpton Cl. BD2: B'frd 4G 71
Plumpton Dr. BD2: B'frd 3F 71
Plumpton End BD2: B'frd 3G 71
Plumpton Gdns. BD2: B'frd 3E 71
Plumpton Lea BD2: B'frd 3F 71

Plumpton Mead BD2: B'frd 3F 71
Plumpton Wlk. BD2: B'frd 3F 71
Plum St. BD21: Keigh 4G 47
 HX1: Hal 3D 148
Plumtree Hill LS29: Add 1D 8
 (off Main St.)
Plymouth Gro. HX1: Hal 1E 149
 (off Pellon La.)
Pochard Cl. BD6: B'frd 4E 109
Poets Pl. LS18: H'fth 5E 57
Pogson's Cotts. LS14: Leeds 4D 80
 (off York Rd.)
Point, The LS12: Leeds 5F 97
 (off Whitehall Pl.)
Pole Position Indoor Karting 6B 98
Pole Rd. BD22: Oak 5A 32
Pollard Av. BD16: Bgly 2D 50
 BD19: Gom 6F 135
Pollard Cl. BD19: Gom 6F 135
Pollard La. BD2: B'frd 2H 91
 LS13: Leeds 3D 74
POLLARD PARK 2H 7 (3G 91)
Pollard St. BD4: B'frd 6F 91
 BD16: Cot 3D 68
 WF3: Loft 3G 157
Pollard St. Nth.
 HX3: Hal 2C 164 (1H 149)
Pollard Way BD19: Gom 6F 135
Pollitt Av. HX6: Sow B 6E 147
Pomfret Pl. LS25: Gar 3H 103
Ponderosa Cl. LS8: Leeds 6D 78
Pond Farm Dr. HD6: Brigh 4G 151
Pondfields Cl. LS25: Kip 3H 123
Pondfields Crest LS25: Kip 3H 123
Pondfields Dr. LS25: Kip 3H 123
Pondfields Pl. LS25: Kip 3H 123
Pondfields Ri. LS25: Kip 3H 123
Pond St. BD21: Keigh 5A 34
Pond Ter. HD6: Brigh 4G 151
Pontefract Av. LS9: Leeds 4D 98
Pontefract La. LS9: Leeds, Swil ...3D 98
 (not continuous)
 LS15: Leeds 2C 120
Pontefract La. Cl. LS9: Leeds ...4D 98
Pontefract Rd. LS10: Leeds 3E 119
 LS26: Rothw 5H 119
Pontefract St. LS9: Leeds 4D 98
POOL 4E 25
Pool Bank Cl. LS21: Pool 4F 25
Pool Bank Ct. LS21: Pool 5F 25
Pool Bank New Rd.
 LS21: Pool 1D 42
Pool Bus. Pk. LS21: Otley 3B 24
Pool Ct. BD3: B'frd 3H 7 (4G 91)
Poole Cres. LS15: Leeds 1D 100
Poole Mt. LS15: Leeds 2D 100
Poole Rd. LS15: Leeds 1D 100
Poole Sq. LS15: Leeds 2D 100
Pool Rd. LS21: Otley, Pool 3G 23
Pool St. BD21: Keigh 4C 34
Pope St. BD21: Keigh 5B 34
Poplar Av. BD7: B'frd 3H 109
 BD18: Ship 4C 70
 HX6: Sow B 4A 148
 LS15: Leeds 1F 101
 LS22: Weth 2D 12
 LS25: Gar 4E 103
Poplar Cl. LS13: Leeds 3H 95
 LS29: Burl W 3F 21
Poplar Ct. BD7: B'frd 5B 90
 LS13: Leeds 3G 95
Poplar Cres. BD18: Ship 3C 70
 HX2: Illing 0D 106
 WF3: Ting 6C 138
Poplar Dr. BD18: Ship 4C 70
 BD20: Rid 6G 35
 LS18: H'fth 1B 74
Poplar Farm La. LS28: Fars 5A 74
Poplar Gdns. LS13: Leeds 3G 95
Poplar Gth. LS13: Leeds 3G 95
Poplar Ga. LS13: Leeds 3G 95

Poplar Grn. LS13: Leeds 3G 95
Poplar Gro. BD7: B'frd 3G 109
  BD16: Har 6E 49
  BD17: Bail 6G 51
  BD18: Ship 4C 70
  BD19: Cleck 3H 153
Poplar Mt. LS13: Leeds 3G 95
Poplar Pl. LS28: Pud 4F 93
Poplar Ri. LS13: Leeds 2G 95
Poplar Rd. BD7: B'frd 3A 110
  BD18: Ship 3C 70
Poplars, The HX3: Nor G 5A 132
  LS6: Leeds 5E 77
  LS16: B'hpe 3H 43
  LS20: Guis 3C 40
  WF3: Loft 1G 157
Poplars Pk. Rd. BD2: B'frd 5E 71
Poplar Sq. LS28: Fars 1H 93
Poplar St.
  HX3: Hal 1B 164 (1G 149)
  WF3: Loft 3G 157
Poplar Ter. BD16: Bgly 5C 50
  BD20: Rid 6H 35
  BD21: Keigh 6G 33
                        (off Lustre St.)
Poplar Vw. BD7: B'frd 3G 109
  HX3: Hal 3A 152
  LS12: N Far 2A 116
  LS13: Leeds 3G 95
  LS17: Shad 4B 62
Poplar Way LS13: Leeds 3G 95
Poplarwood Gdns. BD10: B'frd 4C 72
Popples HX2: Illing 6D 106
Popples Dr. HX2: Illing 6D 106
Poppleton Ct. WF3: Ting 6E 139
Poppleton Cft. WF3: Ting 1E 155
                        (off Lowry Rd.)
Poppleton Dr. WF3: Ting 6E 139
Poppleton Ri. WF3: Ting 1E 155
Poppleton Rd. WF3: Ting 6E 139
Poppleton Way WF3: Ting 6E 139
Popple Wells La. HX2: Hal 2F 147
Poppy Ct. BD6: B'frd 1H 131
Poppyfield Cl. LS22: Weth 3F 13
Poppy La. WF3: E Ard 1C 156
Porritt St. BD19: Cleck 6B 134
Portage Av. LS15: Leeds 4B 100
Portage Cres. LS11: Leeds 4A 100
Porter Wing HX1: Hal 4F 149
                        (off Haworth Cl.)
Portland Ct. BD21: Keigh 1H 47
Portland Cres. LS1: Leeds 2D 4 (2H 97)
Portland Gate LS1: Leeds 2D 4 (2H 97)
                        (not continuous)
  LS2: Leeds 2D 4 (2H 97)
Portland Ho. BD4: B'frd 5B 92
                        (off Fearnville Dr.)
  HX5: Ell 4B 160
                        (off Crown St.)
Portland Pl. BD16: Bgly 5C 50
  HX1: Hal 5C 164 (3G 149)
Portland Rd. HX3: Hal 1D 164 (1H 149)
  LS12: Leeds 5C 96
Portland St. BD5: B'frd 6D 6 (5E 91)
  BD22: Haw 2D 64
  HX1: Hal 3C 164 (2G 149)
  LS1: Leeds 3C 4 (3H 97)
  LS28: Pud 3C 94
Portland Way LS1: Leeds 2D 4 (2H 97)
Portman St. LS28: Cal 3F 73
Portree Dr. BD6: B'frd 4G 109
Portslade Ho. BD8: B'frd 2C 90
                        (off Green La.)
Portsmouth Av. BD3: B'frd 2G 91
Portwood St. BD9: B'frd 1F 89
Post Hill Ct. LS12: Leeds 4F 95
Post Hill Gdns. LS28: Pud 4C 94
Post Hill Vw. LS28: Pud 4C 94
Post Office Rd. BD2: B'frd 4A 72
Post Office Yd. LS29: Burl W 2G 21
Pot Ho. Rd. BD6: B'frd 5B 110
Pot La. BD20: Stee 5C 14
Potovens Ct. WF3: Loft 3G 157

Potovens La. WF1: Out 4F 157
  WF2: Carr G, Wren 6D 156
  WF3: Loft 4F 157
Potter Brow Rd. BD17: Bail 6C 38
Potter Cl. BD12: Low M 2E 133
POTTERNEWTON 5B 78
Potternewton Av. LS7: Leeds 3H 77
Potternewton Ct. LS7: Leeds 3A 78
Potternewton Cres. LS7: Leeds 4H 77
Potternewton Gdns. LS7: Leeds 3A 78
Potternewton Gro. LS7: Leeds 3H 77
Potternewton Hgts. LS7: Leeds 3A 78
Potternewton La. LS7: Leeds 3G 77
Potternewton Mt. LS7: Leeds 3A 78
Potternewton Vw. LS7: Leeds 3H 77
Potters Cft. WF3: Loft 3G 157
Potterton Cl. LS15: Bar E 1E 83
Potterton Ct. LS15: Bar E 1E 83
                        (off Potterton Cl.)
Potterton La. LS15: Bar E, Pott 2E 83
POTTERY FIELD 5B 98
Pottery La. LS26: Wood 6F 121
Pottery Rd. LS10: Leeds 1B 118
Pottery St. WF10: C'frd 6H 145
Poulton Pl. LS11: Leeds 2A 118
Powell Av. BD5: B'frd 1C 110
Powell Rd. BD16: Bgly 4D 50
  BD18: Ship 4D 70
Powell St. HX1: Hal 4B 164 (2G 149)
                        (not continuous)
Powerleague
  Leeds, Wellington Bri. St. 3F 97
Powerleague (North)
  Leeds, Limewood App. 2C 80
Pratt La. BD18: Ship 3C 70
Preachers M. BD16: Bgly 4C 50
                        (off Priestthorpe Rd.)
Premiere Pk. LS29: I'ly 6A 10
Premier Way HX5: Ell 3C 160
Prescott St. HX1: Hal 6B 164 (3G 149)
Prescott Ter. BD15: All 2D 88
Preston Bldgs. BD19: Scho 4F 7
                        (off Tabbs La.)
Preston La. HX2: Hal 5A 128
                        (not continuous)
  LS26: Gt P 6E 123
  WF10: All B 6E 123
Preston Pde. LS11: Leeds 3G 117
Preston Pl. HX1: Hal 2E 149
Preston St. BD7: B'frd 4C 90
Preston Ter. BD16: Bgly 2B 50
                        (off Sleningford Rd.)
Preston Vw. LS26: Swil 4B 122
Prestwick Cl. LS21: Otley 5B 22
Pretoria Rd. BD3: B'frd 4B 92
Pretoria Ter. HX2: Hal 1B 148
PRIEST HILL 1D 12
Priest Hill Gdns. LS22: Weth 2D 12
PRIESTHORPE 5F 73
Priesthorpe Av. LS28: Stan 1F 93
Priesthorpe Ct. LS28: Fars 5H 73
Priesthorpe La. LS28: Fars 6F 73
Priesthorpe Rd. LS28: Cal, Fars 5E 73
                        (not continuous)
Priestley Av. BD6: B'frd 5C 110
Priestley Centre for the Arts 4F 7
Priestley Cl. LS28: Pud 3B 94
Priestley Ct. LS18: H'fth 1G 75
  LS28: Pud 3B 94
Priestley Dr. LS28: Pud 2B 94
Priestley Gdns. LS28: Pud 3B 94
PRIESTLEY GREEN 6G 115
Priestley Hill BD13: Que 6G 107
Priestley Pl. HX6: Sow B 6G 147
Priestley Sq. WF17: Birs 5A 136
Priestley St. BD1: B'frd 2E 7 (3F 91)
  BD13: Thorn 5H 87
Priestley Ter. BD6: B'frd 4C 110
Priestley Vw. LS28: Pud 3B 94
Priestley Wlk. LS28: Pud 3B 94
Priestman Cl. BD8: B'frd 2C 90
Priestman St. BD8: B'frd 2C 90
PRIESTTHORPE 3C 50

Priestthorpe Cl. BD16: Bgly 3C 50
Priestthorpe La. BD16: Bgly 3C 50
Priestthorpe Rd. BD16: Bgly 4C 50
Primary Cl. HX2: Illing 1D 128
Primary Way BD2: B'frd 2H 91
Primitive St. WF3: Carl 4H 141
Primley Gdns. LS17: Leeds 3A 60
Primley Pk. Av. LS17: Leeds 3A 60
Primley Pk. Cl. LS17: Leeds 3B 60
Primley Pk. Ct. LS17: Leeds 2A 60
Primley Pk. Cres. LS17: Leeds 3A 60
Primley Pk. Dr. LS17: Leeds 3A 60
Primley Pk. Gth. LS17: Leeds 2B 60
Primley Pk. Grn. LS17: Leeds 2B 60
Primley Pk. Gro. LS17: Leeds 3A 60
Primley Pk. La. LS17: Leeds 3A 60
Primley Pk. Mt. LS17: Leeds 3B 60
Primley Pk. Ri. LS17: Leeds 3B 60
Primley Pk. Rd. LS17: Leeds 2A 60
Primley Pk. Vw. LS17: Leeds 2A 60
Primley Pk. Wlk. LS17: Leeds 2B 60
Primley Pk. Way LS17: Leeds 2A 60
Primrose Av. LS15: Leeds 3C 100
  LS26: Swil 4B 122
Primrose Bank BD16: Bgly 5D 50
Primrose Cl. LS17: Leeds 3C 100
Primrose Ct. LS17: Leeds 2B 60
  LS20: Guis 4C 40
                        (off Orchard Way)
Primrose Cres. LS15: Leeds 2C 100
Primrose Dr. BD16: Bgly 5D 50
  LS15: Leeds 3C 100
Primrose Gdns. LS15: Leeds 2C 100
Primrose Gth. LS15: Leeds 3B 100
Primrose Gro. BD21: Keigh 6C 34
  LS15: Leeds 2C 100
Primrose Hill BD7: B'frd 6C 90
                        (off Gt. Horton Rd.)
  BD16: Bgly 6E 51
  LS28: Stan 2A 94
Primrose Hill Cl. LS26: Swil 4B 122
Primrose Hill Dr. LS26: Swil 4B 122
Primrose Hill Gdns. LS26: Swil 4B 122
Primrose Hill Gth. LS26: Swil 5B 122
Primrose Hill Grn. LS26: Swil 5B 122
Primrose Hill Gro. LS26: Swil 4B 122
Primrose La. BD2: B'frd 5D 70
  BD16: Bgly 4E 51
  LS11: Leeds 2A 118
  LS15: Leeds 3B 100
                        (not continuous)
  LS23: B Spa 4A 30
Primrose Rd. LS15: Leeds 3C 100
Primrose Row BD17: Bail 3F 53
Primrose St. BD8: B'frd 1A 6 (3C 90)
  BD21: Keigh 6C 34
Primrose Wlk. LS27: Chur 5C 116
Primrose Way HX3: She 6F 109
Primrose Yd. LS26: Oul 2E 143
Prince Albert Sq. BD13: Que 3D 108
Prince Edward Gro. LS12: Leeds 1A 116
Prince Edward Rd. LS12: Leeds 1A 116
Prince Henry Rd. LS21: Otley 1E 23
Prince Henrys Ct. LS21: Otley 2E 23
Princeroyd Way BD7: B'frd 4A 90
Princes Av. LS8: Leeds 2F 79
Prince's Ct. BD18: Ship 3B 70
  LS17: Leeds 6A 60
Prince's Cres. BD2: B'frd 6E 71
Prince's Ga. HX3: Hal 5F 149
Prince's Gro. LS6: Leeds 4D 76
Princess Ct. LS15: Leeds 5F 101
Princess Flds. LS15: Leeds 5F 101
Princess Sq. LS1: Leeds 6C 4 (4H 97)
Princess Rd. LS29: I'ly 6C 10
Princess St. HD6: Brigh 1B 162
  HX1: Hal 3C 164 (2G 149)
  HX4: Gree 4H 159
  HX6: Sow B 5A 148
  LS19: Raw 3E 55
  WF1: Out 5F 157

Princess Ter. HX1: Hal 4F **149**
(off Charlotte Cl.)
Prince's St. BD6: B'frd 5B **110**
(Alexander St.)
BD6: B'frd 6G **109**
(School St.)
Prince St. BD4: B'frd 4A **112**
BD20: Sils 2D **14**
BD22: Haw 2D **64**
WF10: All B 6F **123**
Prince's Way BD1: B'frd 5C **6** (5E **91**)
Princeton Cl. HX2: Hal 6C **128**
PRINCEVILLE 4B **90**
Princeville Rd. BD7: B'frd 4A **90**
Princeville St. BD7: B'frd 4B **90**
(not continuous)
Prior St. BD21: Keigh 5C **34**
Priory Cl. BD16: Bgly 3C **50**
LS22: Weth 2F **13**
Priory Ct. BD8: B'frd 1A **6** (3D **90**)
BD16: Bgly 3C **50**
BD19: Gom 6E **135**
Priory Gro. BD16: Bgly 3C **50**
Priory Ho. BD10: B'frd 2A **72**
(off Cavendish St.)
Priory Pl. HD2: Hud 6F **163**
Priory Rd. HD6: Brigh 1C **162**
Privas Way LS22: Weth 5F **13**
Privet Dr. BD22: Oak 5D **46**
Privilege St. LS12: Leeds 4B **96**
Proctor St. BD4: B'frd 3B **112**
Prod La. BD17: Bail 5G **51**
Progress Av. BD16: Har 6E **49**
Prologis Pk. BD5: B'frd 4G **111**
Prospect Av. BD18: Ship 2C **70**
HX2: Hal 5C **148**
LS13: Leeds 6E **75**
LS28: Pud 3H **93**
Prospect Bldgs. WF3: E Ard 2A **156**
(off Bradford Rd.)
Prospect Bus. Pk. BD16: Bgly 5C **50**
(off Bradford Rd.)
Prospect Cl. BD18: Ship 2C **70**
HX2: Hal 5C **148**
Prospect Ct. HX2: Hal 1H **147**
LS14: T'ner 2H **63**
LS27: Morl 2A **138**
(off Prospect Pl.)
Prospect Cres. BD22: Keigh 2E **47**
LS10: Leeds 2B **118**
Prospect Dr. BD22: Keigh 2E **47**
Prospect Gdns. LS15: Leeds 3D **100**
Prospect Gro. BD18: Ship 2C **70**
LS28: Pud 3H **93**
Prospect La. BD11: Birk 2F **135**
Prospect M. LS27: Morl 2A **138**
(off Prospect Pl.)
Prospect Mt. BD18: Ship 2C **70**
BD22: Keigh 2E **47**
Prospect Pl. BD2: B'frd 1A **92**
BD9: B'frd 2H **89**
BD13: Que 4A **108**
HD6: Brigh 1A **162**
HX2: Hal 4D **128**
HX2: Mt T 4G **127**
HX3: Nor G 5A **132**
(off Village St.)
LS13: Leeds 6E **75**
LS18: H'fth 1D **74**
LS26: Rothw 3B **142**
LS27: Morl 2A **138**
WF3: Loft 5F **141**
Prospect Rd. BD3: B'frd 1F **7** (2F **91**)
(not continuous)
BD16: Bgly 2E **51**
LS29: Burl W 3E **21**
Prospect Row HX2: Hal 4D **128**
HX2: Mix 6A **106**
LS29: Burl W 5C **20**
Prospect Sq. LS28: Fars 1H **93**
Prospect St. BD4: B'frd 4F **91**
BD6: B'frd 6H **109**
BD10: B'frd 4A **72**

Prospect St. BD13: Thorn 5A **88**
BD18: Ship 2C **70**
BD22: Haw 3C **64**
BD22: Keigh 5B **34**
HX3: Hal 1D **164** (1H **149**)
LS19: Raw 4G **55**
LS28: Fars 6H **73**
LS28: Pud 3G **93**
Prospect Ter. BD15: All 2E **89**
BD20: Rid 3D **34**
HX2: Lud M 4E **147**
LS9: Leeds 4D **98**
(off Lavender Wlk.)
LS13: Leeds 4A **74**
(Airedale Mt.)
LS13: Leeds 6E **75**
(Prospect Vw.)
LS18: H'fth 6E **57**
LS25: M'fld 5E **105**
LS26: Rothw 3B **142**
LS28: Fars 6H **73**
LS13: Leeds 6E **75**
Prospect Vw. BD13: Que 6G **107**
LS13: Leeds 6E **75**
Prospect Vs. HX2: Illing 1D **128**
LS22: Weth 3E **13**
Prospect Wlk. BD18: Ship 2C **70**
Prospect Way HD6: B Bri 3B **152**
Prosper St. LS10: Leeds 1C **118**
Providence Av. BD17: Bail 3C **52**
LS6: Leeds 5G **77**
Providence Bldgs. HX3: Sou 5C **150**
(off New St.)
Providence Ct. BD22: Oak 5C **46**
LS27: Morl 2A **138**
(Bank St.)
LS27: Morl 2A **138**
(Wide La.)
Providence Cres. BD22: Oak 5C **46**
Providence La. BD22: Haw, Oak 5C **46**
Providence Mt. LS27: Morl 2A **138**
(off Bank St.)
Providence Pl. BD12: Wyke 3C **132**
HD6: Brigh 2C **162**
HX6: Sow B 4A **148**
LS2: Leeds 1E **5** (2A **98**)
LS15: Swil C 5A **102**
LS25: Gar 4E **103**
LS27: Morl 3G **137**
LS28: Stan 2A **94**
Providence Rd. LS6: Leeds 5G **77**
Providence Row BD2: B'frd 6H **71**
BD17: Bail 3C **52**
BD20: E Mor 3A **36**
HX2: Hal 4D **128**
HX2: Mix 6A **106**
Providence St. BD1: B'frd . . .4B **6** (4D **90**)
BD13: Que 6E **133**
HX5: Ell 4B **160**
LS28: Fars 1H **93**
(not continuous)
Providence Ter. BD13: Thorn 5H **87**
LS2: Leeds 6G **77**
Providence Vs. BD19: Scho 6E **133**
(off Providence Rd.)
LS23: Cliff 6B **30**
Providence Works LS27: Morl 3F **137**
(off Howden Clough Rd.)
Prune Pk. La. BD15: All 6A **68**
PUDSEY 3B **94**
Pudsey Bus. Cen. LS28: Pud 4B **94**
Pudsey Leisure Cen. 4A **94**
Pudsey Rd. LS12: Leeds 3F **95**
LS13: Leeds, Pud 4D **94**
Puffin Cl. BD6: B'frd 4E **109**
Pule Gth. La. HX3: Hal 4F **129**
PULE HILL 4F **129**
Pullan Av. BD2: B'frd 5H **71**
Pullan Dr. BD2: B'frd 5A **72**
Pullan Gro. BD2: B'frd 5A **72**
Pullan La. BD17: Esh 2A **54**
Pullan St. BD5: B'frd 6D **90**
Pullan Way LS27: Morl 6H **137**

Pullman Ct. LS11: Leeds 4E **117**
LS27: Morl 2B **138**
Pullman Ho. LS11: Leeds 4E **117**
Pulmans Pl. HX3: Hal 1G **159**
(off Skircoat Grn.)
Pulmans Yd. HX3: Hal 1G **159**
Pulse Sports & Fitness 5F **71**
Pump La. HX3: Hal 1B **150**
WF3: W Ard 4E **155**
Pundles HX2: Illing 5C **106**
Purbeck Ct. BD4: B'frd 3C **112**
Purbeck Gro. LS25: Gar 5F **103**
Purcell Dr. BD20: Sils 1D **14**
Purley Wlk. BD6: B'frd 5B **110**
Pyebank BD15: Wils 3F **67**
PYE NEST 4D **148**
Pye Nest Av. HX2: Hal 4B **148**
Pye Nest Dr. HX2: Hal 5C **148**
Pye Nest Gdns. HX2: Hal 4C **148**
Pye Nest Gro. HX2: Hal 4C **148**
Pye Nest Ri. HX2: Hal 5C **148**
Pye Nest Rd. HX2: Hal 5B **148**
HX6: Sow B 5B **148**
Pye Nook BD12: Low M 6D **110**
Pymont Ct. WF3: Loft 6G **141**
Pymont Dr. LS26: Wood 6C **120**
Pymont Gro. LS26: Wood 6D **120**
Pym St. LS10: Leeds 6B **98**
Pyrah Fold BD12: Wyke 3C **132**
Pyrah Rd. BD12: Low M 6D **110**
Pyrah St. BD12: Wyke 3D **132**

Q

QBM Bus. Pk. WF17: Birs 5B **136**
Q F Ind. Est. BD4: B'frd 1H **111**
Quail Av. BD6: B'frd 4E **109**
Quail St. BD21: Keigh 5B **34**
Quaker Ho. LS2: Leeds 1G **97**
Quaker La. BD5: B'frd 2B **110**
Quakers La. LS19: Raw 2F **55**
Quaker St. BD3: B'frd 2H **91**
Quarrie Dene Ct. LS7: Leeds 3A **78**
Quarry, The LS17: Leeds 1G **59**
LS22: Weth 3E **13**
Quarry Bank Ct. LS5: Leeds 3H **75**
Quarry Cotts. BD20: Stee 6D **14**
LS18: H'fth 6D **56**
Quarry Ct. HX3: Hal 2A **150**
Quarry Dene LS16: Leeds 1C **76**
Quarry Dene Pk. LS16: Leeds 6C **58**
Quarry Farm Rd. LS21: Pool 6C **24**
Quarryfield Ter. WF3: E Ard 2B **156**
Quarry Gap Row BD4: B'frd 5C **92**
Quarry Gdns. LS17: Leeds 1G **59**
QUARRY HILL 4H **5** (3B **98**)
Quarry Hill HX6: Sow B 6H **147**
LS26: Oul 2E **143**
LS28: Fars 6H **73**
(off Wesley St.)
Quarry Hill La. LS22: Weth 2D **12**
(not continuous)
Quarry Ho. LS2: Leeds 4H **5** (3C **98**)
Quarry La. LS27: Morl 5B **138**
WF12: Dew 3A **154**
WF12: Dew, Morl 2A **154**
Quarry Mt. LS6: Leeds 5G **77**
LS19: Yead 6G **41**
(off King St.)
Quarry Mt. Pl. LS6: Leeds 5G **77**
Quarry Mt. St. LS6: Leeds 5G **77**
Quarry Mt. Ter. LS6: Leeds 5G **77**
Quarry Pl. BD2: B'frd 1H **91**
LS6: Leeds 6G **77**
Quarry Rd. HD6: Ras 4A **162**
HX3: Hal 5C **128**
LS21: Pool 6C **24**
LS26: Wood 1F **143**
Quarry St. BD9: B'frd 5A **70**
BD21: Keigh 6B **34**
LS6: Leeds 6G **77**
Quarry Ter. LS18: H'fth 6D **56**

Quaver La. BD15: All 2D 88
Quay Cl. BD6: B'frd 5A 110
Quay One LS9: Leeds 6H 5
Quayside BD17: Ship 1B 70
Quayside, The BD10: B'frd 1C 72
Quayside Ho. LS11: Leeds 6D 4
Quba Ct. BD8: B'frd 1C 90
Quebec BD16: Cot 3D 68
Quebec Ho. BD21: Keigh 1H 47
                    (off Aireworth St.)
Quebec St. BD1: B'frd 5C 6 (5E 91)
    BD21: Keigh 1H 47
    HX5: Ell 4C 160
    LS1: Leeds 4D 4 (4H 97)
Queen Elizabeth St.
    WF1: Out 5F 157
Queen's Arc. LS1: Leeds 4E 5
Queen's Av. BD2: B'frd 6F 71
QUEENSBURY 4A 108
Queensbury Golf Course 5B 108
Queensbury Rd. HX3: Hal 3F 129
Queensbury Sq. BD13: Leeds 4A 108
Queensbury Swimming Pool 4A 108
Queens Cl. BD16: Bgly 4D 50
    LS7: Leeds 1A 78
    LS26: Wood 1E 145
Queens Ct. BD16: Bgly 4B 50
    BD18: Ship 1H 69
    BD19: Gom 5F 135
                       (off Queen St.)
    LS1: Leeds 5F 5
    LS17: Leeds 6A 60
    LS26: Wood 1E 145
    LS28: Pud 3A 94
Queenscourt LS27: Morl 3A 138
Queens Dr. HX3: Sou 5C 150
    LS28: Pud 3H 93
    LS29: I'ly .6B 10
    WF3: Carl 4H 141
Queen's Dr. La. LS29: I'ly 6B 10
Queensfield Dr. BD5: B'frd 1D 110
Queen's Gdns. LS29: I'ly 6C 10
Queen's Ga. HX3: Hal 5F 149
Queensgate BD1: B'frd 4D 6 (4E 91)
Queen's Gro. BD21: Keigh 2H 47
    LS27: Morl 4H 137
Queens Hall LS27: Morl 4H 137
Queenshill App. LS17: Leeds 5A 60
Queenshill Av. LS17: Leeds 5A 60
Queenshill Cl. LS17: Leeds 5A 60
Queenshill Cres.
    LS17: Leeds 4A 60
Queenshill Dr. LS17: Leeds 5H 59
Queenshill Gdns. LS17: Leeds 5H 59
Queenshill Gth. LS17: Leeds 5A 60
Queenshill Lawn LS17: Leeds 5A 60
                   (off Queenshill App.)
Queenshill Rd. LS17: Leeds 5A 60
Queenshill Vw. LS17: Leeds 5A 60
Queenshill Wlk. LS17: Leeds 5A 60
Queens Mead HX3: North 4C 130
Queen's Pl. BD18: Ship 1H 69
    LS21: Otley 4E 23
    LS27: Morl 3B 138
Queen Sports Club 4F 149
Queen's Prom. LS27: Morl 2A 138
Queen Sq. LS2: Leeds 2E 5 (2A 98)
Queen Sq. Ct.
    LS2: Leeds 2D 4 (2H 97)
Queen's Ri. BD2: B'frd 6F 71
Queen's Rd. BD2: B'frd 1D 90
    BD8: B'frd 1D 90
    BD16: Bgly 1A 50
    BD18: Ship 1H 69
    BD21: Keigh 3G 47
    HX1: Hal 2D 148
    HX3: Nor G 5H 131
    LS6: Leeds 1E 97
    LS23: B Spa 3A 30
    LS27: Morl 4H 137
    LS29: I'ly .6C 10
Queens St. BD13: Cull 3B 66

Queens Ter. LS20: Guis 4B 40
    LS21: Otley 4E 23
Queensthorpe Av. LS13: Leeds 3F 95
Queensthorpe Cl. LS13: Leeds 3G 95
Queensthorpe Ri. LS13: Leeds 3F 95
Queen St. BD6: B'frd 6G 109
    BD10: B'frd 2B 72
    BD15: Wils 5G 67
    BD16: Bgly 4B 50
    BD17: Bail 6C 52
    BD19: Gom 5F 135
    BD20: Sils 2E 15
    BD20: Stee 6C 14
    BD22: Haw 3C 64
    HX4: Gree 5G 159
    HX6: Sow B 6E 147
    LS1: Leeds 5B 4 (4G 97)
    LS10: Leeds 3E 119
    LS19: Raw 3F 55
    LS26: Wood 1E 145
    LS27: Morl 2A 138
                      (not continuous)
    WF1: Out 5F 157
    WF3: Carl 4H 141
    WF3: E Ard 1B 156
Queensview LS14: Leeds 4C 80
Queen's Wlk. LS6: Leeds 3A 76
Queensway BD16: Bgly 4D 50
    BD21: Keigh 6A 34
              (within Airedale Shop. Cen.)
    HX1: Hal 1D 148
    LS15: Leeds 3E 101
    LS19: Yead 4D 40
    LS20: Guis, Yead 4C 40
    LS25: Gar 4D 102
    LS26: Rothw 1A 142
    LS27: Morl 3A 138
Queenswood Cl. LS6: Leeds 3A 76
Queenswood Ct. LS6: Leeds 5C 76
Queenswood Dr. LS6: Leeds 2A 76
Queenswood Gdns. LS6: Leeds 5C 76
Queenswood Grn. LS6: Leeds 2A 76
Queenswood Hgts. LS6: Leeds 4C 76
Queenswood Mt. LS6: Leeds 4B 76
Queenswood Ri. LS6: Leeds 4B 76
Queenswood Rd. LS6: Leeds 4B 76
Queen Victoria Cres. HX3: North . . .4D 130
Queen Victoria St. LS1: Leeds 4F 5
Quincy Cl. BD2: B'frd 5A 72
Qureshi Vw. BD8: B'frd 2C 90

R

Raby Av. LS7: Leeds 6B 78
RABY PARK 3E 13
Raby Pk. LS22: Weth 3D 12
Raby St. LS7: Leeds 6B 78
Raby Ter. LS7: Leeds 6B 78
Racecourse App.
    LS22: Weth 1G 13
Race Moor La. BD22: Oak 4B 46
Racemoor La. BD22: Oak 4D 46
Rachel Ct. LS9: Leeds 1F 99
Radcliffe Av. BD2: B'frd 4G 71
Radcliffe Gdns. LS28: Pud 5A 94
Radcliffe Gro. LS28: Pud 5A 94
Radcliffe La. HX2: Midg 5C 126
    LS28: Pud 4A 94
Radcliffe Ter. LS28: Pud 5A 94
Radfield Dr. BD6: B'frd 4E 111
Radfield Rd. BD6: B'frd 4E 111
Radnor St. BD3: B'frd 4A 92
    LS12: Leeds 5E 97
Radwell Dr. BD5: B'frd 6C 6 (6E 91)
Raeburn Dr. BD6: B'frd 6A 110
Rae Ct. WF3: S'ley 4H 157
Rae Rd. BD18: Ship 3B 70
Raglan Av. BD22: Keigh 1F 47
Raglan Ct. HX1: Hal 2E 149
                   (off Crossley Gdns.)
Raglan Gdns. HX1: Hal 2E 149
                   (off Crossley Gdns.)

Raglan Rd. LS2: Leeds 6G 77
    LS6: Leeds 6G 77
Raglan St. BD3: B'frd 4B 92
    BD13: Que 4B 108
    BD22: Keigh 1F 47
    HX1: Hal 2E 149
Raglan Ter. BD3: B'frd 4C 92
Raikes Av. BD4: B'frd 2D 112
Raikes La. BD4: B'frd 3E 113
    BD4: E Bier 5C 112
    WF17: Birs 5A 136
Raikes Wood Dr. BD4: E Bier 6C 112
Rail Balk La. LS22: Weth 2D 12
                       (not continuous)
Railes Cl. HX2: Lud 6D 126
Railes Cotts. HX2: Lud 6D 126
Railsfield Cliff LS13: Leeds 1F 95
                       (off Bath La.)
Railsfield Mt. LS13: Leeds 2E 95
Railsfield Ri. LS13: Leeds 2E 95
Railsfield Way LS13: Leeds 1F 95
Railway Cotts. LS25: M'fld 5E 105
Railway Rd. BD10: B'frd 1H 71
    LS15: Leeds 1E 101
                      (not continuous)
    LS29: I'ly .5D 10
Railway St. BD4: B'frd 3A 112
    BD20: Keigh 4A 34
    HD6: Ras 2B 162
    LS9: Leeds 5H 5 (4C 98)
Railway Ter. BD12: Low M 2E 133
    HD6: Clift 1C 162
                      (off Clifton Comn.)
    HX3: Hal 1E 159
    LS29: I'ly .5E 11
    WF1: Out 4F 157
    WF3: E Ard 6A 140
Rainbow M. BD6: B'frd 1H 131
Raincliffe Gro. LS9: Leeds 3E 99
Raincliffe Mt. LS9: Leeds 4E 99
Raincliffe Rd. LS9: Leeds 3E 99
Raincliffe St. LS9: Leeds 3E 99
Raincliffe Ter. LS9: Leeds 4E 99
Raistrick Way BD18: Ship 1D 70
Rake Bank HX2: Mix 3B 128
Rakehill Rd. LS15: Bar E, Scho 2H 81
Raleigh St. HX1: Hal 4D 148
Rampart Rd. LS6: Leeds 6G 77
Ramsden Av. BD7: B'frd 6G 89
Ramsden Ct. BD7: B'frd 1A 110
Ramsden Pl. BD14: Clay 6D 88
Ramsden St. HX3: Hal 5C 128
    LS25: Kip 5F 123
Ramsey St. BD5: B'frd 2D 110
Ramsey Ter. LS21: Otley 3E 23
Ramsgate WF3: Loft 6F 141
Ramsgate Cres. WF3: Loft 6F 141
Ramsgate St. HX1: Hal 2D 148
Ramsgill Cl. BD6: B'frd 5G 109
Ramshead App.
    LS14: Leeds 3C 80
Ramshead Cl. LS14: Leeds 2C 80
Ramshead Cres. LS14: Leeds 2B 80
Ramshead Dr. LS14: Leeds 2B 80
Ramshead Gdns. LS14: Leeds 2B 80
Ramshead Gro. LS14: Leeds 3C 80
Ramshead Hgts. LS14: Leeds 4C 80
                        (Bailey's La.)
    LS14: Leeds 3C 80
                       (Eastdean Rd.)
Ramshead Hill LS14: Leeds 3C 80
Ramshead Pl. LS14: Leeds 3C 80
Ramshead Vw. LS14: Leeds 3C 80
Randall Pl. BD9: B'frd 6A 70
Randall Well St.
    BD7: B'frd 5B 6 (5D 90)
Randolph St. BD3: B'frd 3C 92
    HX3: Hal 1B 164 (6G 129)
    LS13: Leeds 1C 94
Random Cl. BD22: Keigh 2F 47
Rand Pl. BD7: B'frd 6C 90
Rand St. BD7: B'frd 6C 90
Ranelagh Av. BD10: B'frd 4C 72

Range Bank
HX3: Hal 1C **164** (6G **129**)
Range Bank Top HX3: Hal 6G **129**
(off Range La.)
Range Ct. HX3: Hal 1C **164**
Range Gdns. HX3: Hal 6G **129**
Range La. HX3: Hal 1C **164** (1G **149**)
Ranger's Wlk. LS25: Aber 1G **105**
Range St. HX3: Hal 6G **129**
Ransdale Dr. BD5: B'frd 2D **110**
Ransdale Gro. BD5: B'frd 2D **110**
Ransdale Rd. BD5: B'frd 2D **110**
RASTRICK 3H **161**
Rastrick Comn. HD6: Ras 3A **162**
Rathlin Rd. WF12: Dew 6A **154**
Rathmell Rd. LS15: Leeds 4A **100**
Rathmell St. BD5: B'frd 4D **110**
Raven Bank HX2: Lud M 3D **146**
Raven Rd. LS6: Leeds 5E **77**
Ravenscar Av. LS8: Leeds 3E **79**
Ravenscar Mt. LS8: Leeds 3E **79**
Ravenscar Ter. LS8: Leeds 3E **79**
Ravenscar Vw. LS8: Leeds 3E **79**
Ravenscar Wlk. LS8: Leeds 3E **79**
RAVENSCLIFFE 5C **72**
Ravenscliffe Av. BD10: B'frd 4B **72**
Ravenscliffe Cl. HX3: Hal 1F **159**
Ravenscliffe Rd. LS28: Cal 3D **72**
Ravenscroft Rd. HX3: Hal 6F **149**
Ravens Mt. LS28: Pud 4B **94**
Ravenstone Dr. HX4: Gree 5G **159**
Raven St. BD16: Bgly 4B **50**
BD21: Keigh 6H **33**
HX1: Hal 2D **148**
Ravensworth Cl. LS15: Leeds 6H **81**
Ravensworth Way LS15: Leeds . . .6H **81**
Raven Ter. BD8: B'frd 4E **89**
RAWDON .4H **55**
Rawdon Crematorium LS19: Raw . .6A **56**
Rawdon Dr. LS19: Raw 4F **55**
Rawdon Golf Course 4F **55**
Rawdon Hall Dr. LS19: Raw 4F **55**
Rawdon Pk. LS19: Raw 2F **55**
Rawdon Rd. BD22: Haw 2C **64**
LS18: H'fth, Yead 5A **56**
Rawdon St. BD22: Keigh 1G **47**
Raw End Rd. HX2: Hal 6F **127**
Rawfolds Av. WF17: Birs 5B **136**
Raw Hill HD6: Ras 3H **161**
Raw La. HX2: Illing 2B **128**
Raw La. Bottom HX2: Sow B 6D **146**
Rawling St. BD21: Keigh 2H **47**
Rawling Way LS6: Leeds 4G **77**
RAW NOOK 1E **133**
Rawnook BD12: Low M 2E **133**
Rawroyds HX4: Gree, Holy 6G **159**
Rawson Av. BD3: B'frd 3B **92**
HX3: Hal 6F **149**
Rawson Pl. BD1: B'frd 3C **6** (4E **91**)
HX6: Sow B 6G **147**
LS11: Leeds 2A **118**
Rawson Quarter Shop. Complex
BD1: B'frd 3C **6**
Rawson Rd. BD1: B'frd 3B **6** (4E **91**)
Rawson Sq. BD1: B'frd 3C **6** (4E **91**)
(not continuous)
BD10: B'frd 6H **53**
Rawson St. BD12: Wyke 3D **132**
HX1: Hal 4B **164** (2G **149**)
Rawson St. Nth. HX3: Hal 6F **129**
Rawson Ter. LS11: Leeds 2A **118**
Rawson Wing HX1: Hal 4G **149**
(off Charlotte Cl.)
Rawson Yard HX6: Sow B 6E **147**
Raygill Cl. LS17: Leeds 2F **61**
Raylands Cl. LS10: Leeds 1D **140**
Raylands Ct. LS10: Leeds 1D **140**
Raylands Fold LS10: Leeds 1D **140**
Raylands Gth. LS10: Leeds 1D **140**
Raylands La. LS10: Leeds 1D **140**
Raylands Pl. LS10: Leeds 1D **140**
Raylands Rd. LS10: Leeds 1D **140**
Raylands Way LS10: Leeds 2C **140**

Rayleigh St. BD4: B'frd 1G **111**
Raymond Dr. BD5: B'frd 3E **111**
Raymond St. BD5: B'frd 3E **111**
Raymond Dr. BD5: B'frd 3E **111**
Raynbron Cres. BD5: B'frd 3F **111**
Raynel App. LS16: Leeds 4A **58**
Raynel Cl. LS16: Leeds 3H **57**
Raynel Dr. LS16: Leeds 4A **58**
Raynel Gdns. LS16: Leeds 3A **58**
Raynel Gth. LS16: Leeds 4A **58**
Raynel Grn. LS16: Leeds 4A **58**
Raynel Mt. LS16: Leeds 3A **58**
Raynel Way LS16: Leeds 3H **57**
Rayner Av. BD8: B'frd 2H **89**
Rayner Dr. HD6: Brigh 5A **152**
Rayner Gdns. LS28: Fars 6A **74**
Rayner Mt. BD15: All 3D **88**
Rayner Rd. HD6: Brigh 5A **152**
Raynham Cres. BD21: Keigh 5E **33**
Raynor Ter. LS28: Pud 3B **94**
Raynville App. LS13: Leeds 1G **95**
Raynville Av. LS13: Leeds 6G **75**
Raynville Cl. LS13: Leeds 6G **75**
Raynville Ct. LS13: Leeds 1G **95**
Raynville Cres. LS12: Leeds 1H **95**
Raynville Dene LS12: Leeds 6H **75**
Raynville Dr. LS13: Leeds 6G **75**
Raynville Gdns. LS12: Leeds 1H **95**
Raynville Gth. LS12: Leeds 1H **95**
Raynville Grange *LS13: Leeds* 1G **95**
(off Raynville Rd.)
Raynville Grn. LS13: Leeds 1G **95**
Raynville Gro. LS13: Leeds 6G **75**
Raynville Mt. LS13: Leeds 6G **75**
Raynville Pl. LS13: Leeds 1G **95**
Raynville Ri. LS13: Leeds 1G **95**
Raynville Rd. LS12: Leeds 6G **75**
LS13: Leeds 6F **75**
Raynville St. LS13: Leeds 6G **75**
Raynville Ter. LS13: Leeds 6G **75**
Raynville Wlk. LS13: Leeds 1G **95**
Raynville Way LS12: Leeds 1H **95**
Raywood Cl. LS19: Yead 5E **41**
Reade St. *HX3: Hal* 1G **159**
(off St Anne's Rd.)
Rebecca St. BD1: B'frd 2A **6** (3D **90**)
Recreation Av. LS11: Leeds 1G **117**
Recreation Cres. LS11: Leeds 1F **117**
Recreation Gro. LS11: Leeds 1F **117**
Recreation La. HX5: Ell 5A **160**
Recreation Mt. LS11: Leeds 1F **117**
Recreation Pl. LS11: Leeds 1F **117**
Recreation Rd. HX6: Sow B 5A **148**
LS11: Leeds 3F **117**
Recreation Row LS11: Leeds 1F **117**
Recreation St. LS11: Leeds 1F **117**
Recreation Ter. LS11: Leeds 1F **117**
Recreation Vw. LS11: Leeds 1F **117**
Rectory Cl. LS25: Gar 4F **103**
Rectory Dr. WF17: Bat 6C **136**
Rectory Row BD21: Keigh 6H **33**
Rectory St. LS9: Leeds 2C **98**
Redbarn Cl. LS10: Leeds 5A **140**
Redbarn Ct. LS10: Leeds 5A **140**
Redbeck Cotts. LS18: H'fth 1A **74**
Red Beck Rd. HX3: Hal 6B **130**
Red Beck Va. BD18: Ship 4A **70**
Red Brick La. HX6: Sow B 6C **146**
Red Brink La. HX6: Sow B 6B **146**
Redbrook Way BD9: B'frd 4F **69**
Redburn Av. BD18: Ship 4A **70**
Redburn Dr. BD18: Ship 4A **70**
Redburn Rd. BD18: Ship 4B **70**
Redcar La. BD20: Keigh, Stee 2B **32**
Redcar Rd. BD10: B'frd 3C **72**
Redcar St. HX1: Hal 2D **148**
Redcliffe Av. BD21: Keigh 6G **33**
Redcliffe Gro. BD21: Keigh 6G **33**
Redcliffe St. BD21: Keigh 6G **33**
(not continuous)
Redcote La. LS4: Leeds 2B **96**
LS12: Leeds 3B **96**
Redcourt *LS12: Leeds* 4C **96**
(off Athone Gro.)

Red Delph Gdns. BD13: Que 4H **107**
Redding Mill BD20: Stee 6C **14**
Redding Wood La. BD20: Stee 6C **14**
Redesdale Gdns. LS16: Leeds 4A **58**
Red Hall App. LS14: Leeds 6C **62**
Red Hall Av. LS17: Leeds 6B **62**
Red Hall Chase LS14: Leeds 6C **62**
Redhall Cl. LS11: Leeds 4E **117**
Red Hall Ct. LS14: Leeds 6C **62**
Red Hall Cres. WF1: Wake 6F **157**
Redhall Cres. LS11: Leeds 4E **117**
Red Hall Cft. LS14: Leeds 6C **62**
Red Hall Dr. LS14: Leeds 6C **62**
Red Hall Gdns. LS17: Leeds 6B **62**
Red Hall Gth. LS14: Leeds 6C **62**
Redhall Ga. LS11: Leeds 4E **117**
Red Hall Grn. LS14: Leeds 6C **62**
Red Hall La. LS14: Leeds 6C **62**
LS17: Leeds 6B **62**
Red Hall Va. LS14: Leeds 1C **80**
Red Hall Vw. LS14: Leeds 6C **62**
Red Hall Wlk. LS14: Leeds 6C **62**
Red Hall Way LS14: Leeds 6C **62**
Redhill Av. WF3: W Ard 4E **155**
Redhill Cl. BD4: B'frd 3D **112**
WF3: W Ard 4E **155**
Redhill Cres. WF3: W Ard 4E **155**
Redhill Dr. WF3: W Ard 4E **155**
Red Holt Av. BD21: Keigh 3G **47**
Red Holt Cres. BD21: Keigh 3G **47**
Red Holt Dr. BD21: Keigh 3G **47**
Red Ho. Gdns. LS29: Men 2G **39**
Redhouse La. LS7: Leeds 2C **78**
Red House Mus. 6F **135**
Red La. LS28: Fars 6G **73**
Red Lodge Cl. LS8: Leeds 5H **79**
Redman Cl. BD22: Haw 2B **64**
Redman Gth. BD22: Haw 2B **64**
Redmire Cl. LS14: Leeds 5D **80**
Redmire Dr. LS14: Leeds 5C **80**
Redmire Gro. LS14: Leeds 5C **80**
Redmire St. BD3: B'frd 4C **92**
Redmire Vw. LS14: Leeds 5C **80**
Redpoll Dr. WF10: All B 3H **145**
Redpoll Way BD6: B'frd 4E **109**
Redshank Cl. BD6: B'frd 4E **109**
Redshaw Rd. LS12: Leeds 5D **96**
Red Va. BD19: Gom 5F **135**
Redvers Cl. LS16: Leeds 6A **58**
Redwald Dr. LS20: Guis 4B **40**
Redwing Dr. BD6: B'frd 4E **109**
Redwood Av. WF3: Ting 1G **155**
Redwood Cl. BD10: B'frd 2A **72**
BD21: Keigh 2C **48**
LS19: Yead 6D **40**
LS26: Wood 1G **143**
Redwood Cres. BD4: B'frd 5H **111**
Redwood Dr. HD2: Hud 6D **162**
Redwood Gro. LS19: Yead 6D **40**
Redwood Way LS19: Yead 6D **40**
Reedling Dr. LS27: Morl 4C **138**
Reed Rd. LS12: Leeds 5D **96**
Reedsdale Av. LS27: Gil 6E **115**
Reedsdale Dr. LS27: Gil 6E **115**
Reedsdale Gdns. LS27: Gil 6E **115**
Rees Way BD3: B'frd 1F **7** (3F **91**)
Reeth Rd. HD6: Ras 3G **161**
Reevy Av. BD6: B'frd 5H **109**
Reevy Cres. BD6: B'frd 6G **109**
Reevy Dr. BD6: B'frd 5A **110**
Reevylands Dr. BD6: B'frd 5A **110**
Reevy Pk. Ct. BD6: B'frd 5G **109**
Reevy Rd. BD6: B'frd 5H **109**
Reevy Rd. W. BD6: B'frd 5F **109**
Reevy St. BD6: B'frd 4A **110**
Reevy Yd. *BD6: B'frd* 5B **110**
(off Green End Rd.)
Reform St. BD19: Gom 6F **135**
Regal Pde. LS15: Leeds 1D **100**
Regency Ct. BD8: B'frd 3B **90**
LS6: Leeds 5E **77**
LS29: I'ly 6C **10**
Regency Gdns. WF3: W Ard 1G **155**

Regency Pk. Gro.—Ring Rd. Beeston

Regency Pk. Gro. LS28: Pud 6A **94**
Regency Pk. Rd. LS28: Pud 6A **94**
Regency Vw. BD3: B'frd 1G **91**
Regent Av. LS18: H'fth 2E **75**
Regent Cl. HD6: Ras 5G **161**
LS18: H'fth 2E **75**
Regent Ct. HX3: Hal 5E **149**
LS1: Leeds 5F **5**
LS18: H'fth 2E **75**
Regent Cres. LS18: H'fth 2D **74**
Regent Ho. HX5: Ell 4B **160**
Regent Pde. *HX6: Sow B 5A **148***
(off Wharf St.)
Regent Pk. Av. LS6: Leeds 5F **77**
Regent Pk. Ter. LS6: Leeds 5F **77**
Regent Pl. BD10: B'frd 6G **53**
HX6: Sow B 4H **147**
WF3: Thpe H 5D **140**
Regent Rd. LS18: H'fth 2D **74**
LS29: I'ly 5C **10**
Regent St. BD10: B'frd 2B **72**
(Haigh Hall Rd.)
BD10: B'frd 6G **53**
(Northlea Av.)
BD13: Que 4B **108**
BD22: Haw 2D **64**
HX1: Hal 5A **164** (3G **149**)
LS2: Leeds 3H **5** (3B **98**)
LS7: Leeds 3H **5** (3B **98**)
(New York Rd.)
LS7: Leeds 2B **78**
(Well La.)
Regent Ter. LS6: Leeds 1F **97**
LS7: Leeds 2B **78**
Regina Dr. LS7: Leeds 3B **78**
Regina Ho. LS13: Leeds 3F **95**
Reginald Mt. LS7: Leeds 5B **78**
Reginald Pl. LS7: Leeds 5B **78**
Reginald Row LS7: Leeds 5B **78**
Reginald St. BD5: B'frd 2D **110**
LS7: Leeds 5B **78**
Reginald Ter. LS7: Leeds 5B **78**
Reginald Vw. LS7: Leeds 5B **78**
Reighton Cft. BD10: B'frd 3C **72**
Rein, The LS14: Leeds 3B **80**
Rein Gdns. WF3: Ting 1C **154**
Rein M. WF3: Ting 1C **154**
Rein Rd. LS18: H'fth 2D **74**
LS27: Morl 6B **138**
WF3: Ting 6B **138**
Reins Av. BD17: Bail 6B **52**
Reins Rd. HD6: Ras 3G **161**
Rein St. LS27: Morl 6C **138**
Reinwood Av. LS8: Leeds 4H **79**
Rembrandt Av. WF3: Ting 1F **155**
Renaissance Ct. LS27: Chur 5C **116**
Renaissance Dr. LS27: Chur 5C **116**
Renee Cl. BD4: B'frd 5A **112**
Renshaw St. BD10: B'frd 6H **53**
Renton Av. LS20: Guis 4B **40**
Renton Dr. LS20: Guis 5B **40**
Renton Lea LS20: Guis 5B **40**
Reservoir Ct. LS28: Cal 3E **73**
Reservoir Pl. BD13: Que 3G **107**
Reservoir Rd. HX2: Hal 1C **148**
Reservoir Vw. BD13: Thorn 5G **87**
Restmore Av. LS20: Guis 3B **40**
Retford Pl. BD7: B'frd 6C **90**
Reva Cl. BD16: Bgly 3D **50**
Reva Syke Rd. BD14: Clay 2D **108**
Revie Rd. LS11: Leeds 2F **117**
Revie Rd. Ind. Est. LS11: Leeds ...2F **117**
Revis Barber Hall BD5: B'frd 6C **90**
Rex Cinema
Elland 4B **160**
Reyden M. LS12: Leeds 5C **96**
Reydon Wlk. BD6: B'frd 4H **109**
Reyhill Gro. BD5: B'frd 6D **6** (6E **91**)
Reynolds Av. BD7: B'frd 6G **89**
Rhine St. BD4: B'frd 6G **91**
Rhodes Ct. *LS27: Morl 4B **138***
(off High St.)
Rhodes Gdns. WF3: Loft 3G **157**
Rhodesia Av. BD15: All 3E **89**
HX3: Hal 6G **149**
Rhodes La. LS23: Cliff 5H **29**
Rhodes Pl. BD17: Ship 1B **70**
Rhodes St. BD18: Ship 1A **70**
HX1: Hal 4A **164** (2F **149**)
Rhodes Ter. BD2: B'frd 5H **71**
LS12: Leeds 5E **97**
Rhodesway BD8: B'frd 4F **89**
Rhondda Pl. HX1: Hal 3C **148**
Rhum Cl. BD6: B'frd 1H **131**
Rhyddings Gdns. LS29: I'ly 5F **11**
Rhylstone Mt. BD7: B'frd 5H **89**
Rialto Ct. LS13: Leeds 4A **74**
Ribble Ct. *BD20: Sils 2E **15***
(off Wharfe Ct.)
Ribblesdale Av. LS25: Gar 5H **103**
Ribble St. BD21: Keigh 5C **34**
Ribbleton Gro. BD3: B'frd 2H **7** (3G **91**)
Riccall Nook BD10: B'frd 3B **72**
Richard Dunn Sports Cen. 4D **110**
Richard Gossop Ct.
LS29: Burl W 2E **21**
Richard Pl. *HD6: Brigh 5A **152***
(off Richard St.)
Richardshaw Dr. LS28: Stan 2A **94**
Richardshaw La.
LS28: Pud, Stan 2A **94**
Richardshaw Rd. LS28: Stan 2A **94**
Richardson Av. BD6: B'frd 5C **110**
Richardson Cres. LS9: Leeds 4F **99**
Richardson Rd. LS9: Leeds 4F **99**
Richardson St. BD12: O'haw 3G **133**
Richard St. BD3: B'frd 4G **7** (4G **91**)
HD6: Brigh 5A **152**
Richmond Av. HX6: Sow B 6F **147**
LS6: Leeds 5E **77**
Richmond Cl. HX1: Hal ...2B **164** (1G **149**)
LS13: Leeds 1C **94**
LS26: Rothw 1B **142**
LS27: Morl 4A **138**
Richmond Ct. LS9: Leeds 4D **98**
LS13: Leeds 4A **74**
LS26: Rothw 1B **142**
*LS29: I'ly 6E **11***
(off Richmond Pl.)
Richmond Cft. LS9: Leeds 4D **98**
Richmondfield Av. LS15: Bar E 3E **83**
Richmondfield Cl. LS15: Bar E 3E **83**
Richmondfield Cres. LS15: Bar E 3E **83**
Richmondfield Cross LS15: Bar E ...3E **83**
Richmondfield Dr. LS15: Bar E 3E **83**
Richmondfield Gth. LS15: Bar E 2E **83**
Richmondfield Gro. LS15: Bar E 3E **83**
Richmondfield La. LS15: Bar E 3E **83**
Richmondfield Mt. LS15: Bar E 3E **83**
Richmondfield Wlk. LS15: Bar E 3E **83**
Richmondfield Way LS15: Bar E 3E **83**
Richmond Gdns. HX6: Sow B 6F **147**
LS28: Pud 4C **94**
Richmond Grn. St. *LS9: Leeds 4C **98***
(off Cross Catherine St.)
Richmond Gro. BD19: Gom 5F **135**
RICHMOND HILL 4D **98**
Richmond Hill App. LS9: Leeds 4C **98**
Richmond Hill Cl. LS9: Leeds 4C **98**
Richmond Ho. *HX1: Hal 4G **149***
(off Charlotte Cl.)
*LS8: Leeds 5F **61***
(off Street La.)
Richmond M. BD18: Ship 1H **69**
Richmond Mt. LS6: Leeds 5E **77**
Richmond Pl. BD18: Ship 1H **69**
LS29: I'ly 6E **11**
Richmond Rd. BD7: B'frd 4A **6** (4C **90**)
(not continuous)
BD18: Ship 1H **69**
HX1: Hal 2A **164** (1F **149**)
LS6: Leeds 5E **77**
LS28: Fars 1G **93**
Richmond St. BD21: Keigh 5H **33**
HX1: Hal 2A **164** (1F **149**)
LS9: Leeds 6H **5** (4C **98**)
Richmond Ter. *HX2: Lud 6E **127***
(off High St.)
LS20: Guis 4B **40**
LS21: Otley 4D **22**
LS28: Pud 4C **94**
Richmond Way LS25: Gar 6F **103**
Rickard St. LS12: Leeds 5F **97**
Ridding Ga. LS21: Otley 2C **22**
Riddings Rd. LS29: I'ly 6D **10**
RIDDLESDEN 4D **34**
Riddlesden Golf Course 1H **33**
Riddlesden St. BD20: Rid 4D **34**
Riddlesden Vw. BD21: Keigh 6D **34**
Rider Rd. LS6: Leeds 5H **77**
Rider St. LS9: Leeds 3C **98**
Ridge, The LS22: Lin 6C **12**
Ridge Cl. LS20: Guis 5A **40**
Ridge Gro. LS7: Leeds 4G **77**
Ridge Hill HD6: Ras 2G **161**
Ridge Lea HD6: Ras 2H **161**
Ridge Mt. LS6: Leeds 5G **77**
Ridgemount Rd. BD20: Rid 3C **34**
Ridge Rd. LS7: Leeds 5H **77**
LS25: Aber, Kip, Leeds 5B **124**
Ridge Ter. LS6: Leeds 4E **77**
Ridge Vw. LS13: Leeds 3E **95**
Ridgeview HX5: Ell 5E **161**
Ridge Vw. Gdns. BD10: B'frd 2A **72**
Ridge Vw. Rd. HD6: Ras 2A **162**
Ridgeway BD13: Que 5B **108**
BD15: All 3C **88**
BD18: Ship 3E **71**
LS8: Leeds 3D **78**
LS20: Guis 5H **39**
Ridgeway Cl. LS8: Leeds 3D **78**
Ridgeway Dr. WF17: Bat 6C **136**
Ridgeway Gdns. HD6: Brigh 4G **151**
Ridgeway Mt. BD22: Keigh 2F **47**
Ridgeway Ter. *LS6: Leeds 5G **77***
(off Delph La.)
Ridgewood Cl. BD17: Bail 4E **53**
Riding Head La. HX2: Lud 6E **127**
Riding Hill HX3: She 1G **131**
Riding La. HX2: Hal 4A **128**
Ridings, The BD20: Keigh 2H **33**
Ridings Bus. Pk. HX1: Hal 3D **148**
Ridings Cl. WF3: Loft 3F **157**
Ridings Ct. WF3: Loft 3F **157**
Ridings Cft. BD5: B'frd 4H **111**
Ridings Gdns. WF3: Loft 3F **157**
Ridings La. WF3: Loft 3F **157**
Ridings M. WF3: Loft 3F **157**
Ridings Sports Centre, The 4D **128**
Ridings Way BD6: B'frd 4G **109**
WF3: Loft 3F **157**
Ridleys Fold LS29: Add 1D **8**
Rievaulx Av. BD8: B'frd 3C **90**
Rievaulx Cl. LS23: B Spa 4A **30**
Riffa Bus. Pk. LS21: Cast 2H **25**
Rigton App. LS9: Leeds 3C **98**
Rigton Bank LS17: Bard 1F **45**
Rigton Cl. LS9: Leeds 3D **98**
Rigton Dr. LS9: Leeds 3C **98**
Rigton Grn. LS9: Leeds 3C **98**
LS17: Bard 1G **45**
RIGTON HILL 5G **27**
Rigton Lawn LS9: Leeds 3C **98**
Rigton M. LS9: Leeds 3C **98**
Rigton St. BD5: B'frd 2D **110**
Riley La. HX2: Illing 5D **106**
Rillbank La. LS3: Leeds 2F **97**
Rillbank St. *LS3: Leeds 2F **97***
(off Woodsley Rd.)
Rillington Mead BD10: B'frd 3B **72**
Rills Mead LS21: Otley 4E **23**
Rilston St. BD7: B'frd 5B **90**
Rimswell Holt BD10: B'frd 3C **72**
Ringby La. HX3: Hal 3F **129**
Ring Hay Rd. BD4: B'frd 4E **113**
Ring Rd. Adel LS16: Leeds 5D **58**
Ring Rd. Beeston
LS11: Leeds 4E **117**
LS12: Leeds 1C **116**

Ring Rd. Beeston Pk.
LS10: Leeds 5G 117
LS11: Leeds 5G 117
Ring Rd. Bramley LS13: Leeds 3F 95
Ring Rd. Cross Gates LS15: Leeds ..6E 81
Ring Rd. Farnley LS12: Leeds 3F 95
Ring Rd. Halton
LS13: Leeds, Pud 1F 93
LS28: Fars 1F 93
Ring Rd. Halton LS15: Leeds 2E 101
Ring Rd. Horsforth LS16: Leeds ...1G 75
LS18: H'fth, Leeds 1G 75
Ring Rd. Lwr. Wortley
LS12: Leeds 5H 95
Ring Rd. Meanwood LS6: Leeds ...5E 59
LS16: Leeds 5E 59
LS17: Leeds 5E 59
Ring Rd. Middleton LS10: Leeds ..5D 118
Ring Rd. Moortown LS6: Leeds ...5G 59
LS17: Leeds 5G 59
Ring Rd. Seacroft LS14: Leeds ...1B 80
Ring Rd. Shadwell LS17: Leeds ..4G 61
Ring Rd. Weetwood LS16: Leeds ..6B 58
Ring Rd. West Pk. LS16: Leeds ...6H 57
Ringshaw Dr. BD19: Gom 6E 135
Rington Rd. LS11: Leeds 2H 117
Ringway LS25: Gar 5D 102
Ringwood Av. LS14: Leeds 1B 80
Ringwood Ct. WF1: Out 4H 157
Ringwood Cres. LS14: Leeds 6C 62
Ringwood Dr. LS14: Leeds 1C 80
Ringwood Edge HX5: Ell 5H 159
Ringwood Gdns. LS14: Leeds 1C 80
Ringwood Mt. LS14: Leeds 1C 80
Ringwood Rd. BD5: B'frd 2B 110
Ripley Av. WF3: E Ard 6B 140
Ripley La. LS20: Guis 2C 40
Ripley Rd. BD4: B'frd 1F 111
(Bowling Pk. Dr.)
BD4: B'frd 1F 111
(St Dunstans Technology Pk.)
Ripley St. BD5: B'frd 1E 111
(not continuous)
BD15: All 1C 88
BD20: Rid 4D 34
HX3: Hip 2A 152
Ripley Ter. HX2: Lud M 2D 146
Ripon Av. HX5: Ell 4B 160
Ripon St. HX1: Hal 3C 148
Ripon Ter. HX3: Hal 6F 129
Rise, The HX3: North 5C 130
LS5: Leeds 4A 76
LS25: Kip 4G 123
Risedale Av. WF17: Birs 5D 136
Risedale Cl. WF17: Birs 5D 136
Rishworthian Ct. HX3: Hal 2E 159
Rishworth St. BD22: Keigh 1F 47
Rivadale Vw. LS29: I'ly 4D 10
Rivendale LS15: Leeds 3C 140
River Bank Way HX5: Ell 2D 160
Riverdale LS22: Weth 5F 13
Riverdale Cl. LS21: Otley 3E 23
Riverdale Gdns. LS21: Otley 3E 23
LS23: B Spa 4D 30
Riverdale Rd. LS21: Otley 3E 23
Riverine HX6: Sow B 5B 148
River Mt. BD21: Rid 4C 34
Riverside BD16: Bgly 2H 49
BD21: Keigh 6C 34
LS22: Weth 4D 12
Riverside Av. LS21: Otley 1F 23
Riverside Bus. Pk. LS29: I'ly 4E 11
Riverside Cl. LS21: Otley 2F 23
Riverside Ct. BD17: Ship 6A 52
HX3: Hal 6H 149
LS1: Leeds 6F 5 (4A 98)
Riverside Cres. LS21: Otley 1F 23
Riverside Dr. BD19: Cleck 6B 134
LS21: Otley 1F 23
Riverside Est. BD17: Ship 1A 70
Riverside Landings BD16: Bgly 4B 50
(off Ferrand La.)

Riverside Pk. LS21: Otley 2F 23
Riverside Wlk. LS23: B Spa 3B 30
LS29: I'ly 4B 10
Riverside Way LS1: Leeds ...6B 4 (4G 97)
Riverside W. LS1: Leeds 6A 4 (4G 97)
River St. BD21: Keigh 4C 34
BD22: Haw 2D 64
HD6: Brigh 2C 162
River Vw. LS18: H'fth 6D 56
LS23: B Spa 4D 30
LS29: I'ly 4G 11
WF10: C'frd 6H 145
River Wlk. BD16: Bgly 4B 50
HX6: Sow B 6H 147
Riverwood Dr. HX3: Hal 1F 159
Riviera Gdns. LS7: Leeds 3A 78
Rivock Av. BD20: Keigh 2F 33
BD20: Stee 5D 14
Rivock Gro. BD20: Keigh 2F 33
Roach Grange Av. LS25: Kip 2G 123
Road End HX4: Gree 4G 159
Roans Brae BD10: B'frd 3C 72
Robb Av. LS11: Leeds 4G 117
Robb St. LS11: Leeds 4G 117
Robert Ho. LS27: Morl 2B 138
(off Pullman Ct.)
Roberts Av. LS9: Leeds 1F 99
Roberts Bldgs. HX2: Hal 2B 148
(off Gibbet St.)
Roberts Ct. LS9: Leeds 1F 99
Robertsgate WF3: Loft 6F 141
Robertsgate Sq. WF3: Loft 6F 141
(off Robertsgate)
Robertshaw Pl. BD16: Bgly 5C 50
Robertson Av. HD6: Ras 3A 162
Roberts Pl. BD1: B'frd 2B 6 (3D 90)
LS9: Leeds 2F 99
Roberts St. BD22: Lay 1C 46
LS26: Wood 1E 143
Robert St. BD3: B'frd 5G 7 (5G 91)
BD22: Cros R 1F 65
HX3: Hal 5E 129
Robert St. Nth. HX3: Hal 5G 129
Roberts Wharf LS9: Leeds ...6H 5 (5C 98)
Robina Cl. LS23: B Spa 4A 30
Robin Chase LS28: Pud 4B 94
Robin Cl. BD2: B'frd 5A 72
Robin Dr. BD2: B'frd 5A 72
BD20: Stee 5B 14
Robin Hill WF17: Bat 6C 136
ROBIN HOOD 4F 141
Robin Hood Way HD6: Clift 1E 163
Robin La. LS28: Pud 4A 94
Robins, The LS29: Burl W 3E 21
Robins Ct. BD12: O'haw 3G 133
Robin's Gro. LS26: Rothw 2B 142
Robinson Ct. BD7: B'frd 5H 89
Robinson La. LS25: Kip 4H 123
Robinson St. WF10: All B 3H 145
Robin St. BD5: B'frd 1C 110
Robin Wlk. BD18: Ship 3D 70
Robinwood Ct. LS8: Leeds 6E 61
Roby Ho. BD1: B'frd 3A 6 (4D 90)
Rochdale Rd. HX2: Hal 4B 148
HX4: Gree 4B 158
HX6: Sow B, Tri 6G 147
Rocheford Cl. LS10: Leeds 2D 118
Rocheford Ct. LS10: Leeds 2D 118
Rocheford Gdns. LS10: Leeds 2D 118
Rocheford Gro. LS10: Leeds 2D 118
Rocheford Wlk. LS10: Leeds 2D 118
Rochester Gdns. LS13: Leeds 5B 74
Rochester Pl. HX5: Ell 5B 160
(off Savile Rd.)
Rochester St. BD3: B'frd 4A 92
BD18: Ship 3C 70
Rochester Ter. LS6: Leeds 5D 76
Rochester Wynd LS17: Leeds 3E 61
Rockcliffe Av. BD17: Bail 6C 52
Rock Cliffe Mt. HX2: Lud M 2D 146
Rock Ct. LS27: Morl 2B 138
Rockery Cft. LS18: H'fth 5E 57

Rockery Rd. LS18: H'fth 5E 57
Rockfield LS19: Yead 6G 41
(off Rockfield Ter.)
Rockfield Ter. LS19: Yead 6G 41
Rockhill Cl. WF17: Bat 6B 136
Rockhill La. BD4: B'frd 6G 111
(not continuous)
Rockingham Cl. LS15: Leeds 6H 81
Rockingham Rd. LS15: Leeds 6H 81
Rockingham Way LS15: Leeds 6H 81
Rockland Cres. BD7: B'frd 6G 89
Rocklands Av. BD17: Bail 3C 52
Rocklands Pl. BD17: Bail 3C 52
Rock La. BD13: Thorn 3G 87
LS13: Leeds 5D 74
Rock Lea BD13: Que 4B 108
Rockley Grange Gdns.
LS25: Gar 6D 102
Rockley Hall Yd. LS1: Leeds 4F 5
Rocks La. HX2: Ogd 5B 106
Rocks Rd. HX3: Hal 6E 149
Rock St. HD6: Brigh 6A 152
Rocks Vw. HX2: Hal 5E 149
Rock Ter. BD8: B'frd 2D 90
BD13: Thorn 5H 87
BD22: Oak 1B 46
HX3: Hip 1F 151
LS15: Leeds 3B 100
LS27: Morl 2B 138
WF12: Dew 3B 154
Rock Vw. HX4: Holy 6G 159
Rockville Ter. HX1: Hal 4E 149
LS19: Yead 1G 55
(off Rufford Ridge)
Rockwell La. BD10: B'frd 3A 72
Rockwood Cl. HD2: Hud 5E 163
Rockwood Cres. LS28: Cal 1E 93
Rockwood Gro. LS28: Cal 6F 73
Rockwood Hill Ct. LS28: Cal 1E 93
Rockwood Rd. LS28: Cal 1E 93
Roderick St. LS12: Leeds 4B 96
Rodin Av. BD8: B'frd 4F 89
RODLEY 4A 74
Rodley Hall LS13: Leeds 4B 74
(off Club La.)
Rodley La. LS13: Leeds 5C 74
(Airedale Quay)
LS13: Leeds 5G 73
(Calverley La.)
LS28: Cal 3G 73
Rodley Nature Reserve 4C 74
Rods Mills La. LS27: Morl 4B 138
Rods Vw. LS27: Morl 4B 138
Roebuck St. WF17: Birs 6B 136
Roeburn Cl. BD6: B'frd 4G 109
Roedhelm Rd. BD20: E Mor 4F 35
Roe Ho. BD17: Bail 6B 52
(off Greenwood Rd.)
Roger Ct. BD2: B'frd 1H 91
Roger Fold LS25: Kip 4H 123
Rogerson Sq. HD6: Brigh 6A 152
Rogers Pl. LS28: Pud 3B 94
Roils Head Rd. HX2: Hal 2H 147
Rokeby Gdns. BD10: B'frd 3C 72
LS6: Leeds 4C 76
Roker La. LS28: Pud 6B 94
ROKER LANE BOTTOM 1C 114
Roman Av. LS8: Leeds 5E 61
Romanby Shaw BD10: B'frd 3B 72
Roman Ct. LS8: Leeds 5F 61
Roman Cres. LS8: Leeds 5F 61
Roman Dr. LS8: Leeds 5F 61
Roman Gdns. LS8: Leeds 5E 61
Roman Gro. LS8: Leeds 5E 61
Roman Mt. LS8: Leeds 5F 61
Roman Pl. LS8: Leeds 5F 61
Roman Ter. LS8: Leeds 5E 61
Roman Vw. LS8: Leeds 5F 61
Rombald Grange LS29: I'ly 6E 11
Rombalds Av. LS12: Leeds 3C 96
Rombalds Cl. LS29: Men 1F 39
Rombalds Cres. BD20: Sils 3F 15
LS12: Leeds 2C 96

Rombalds Cft. LS19: Yead 6F **41**
Rombalds Dr. BD16: Bgly 4D **50**
Rombalds Gro. LS12: Leeds 3C **96**
Rombalds La. LS29: I'ly 6G **11**
Rombalds Pl. LS12: Leeds 2C **96**
Rombalds St. LS12: Leeds 2C **96**
Rombalds Ter. LS12: Leeds 3C **96**
Rombalds Vw. LS12: Leeds 2C **96**
   LS21: Otley 1B **22**
   LS29: I'ly 4F **11**
Romford Av. LS27: Morl 4A **138**
Romford Cl. BD6: B'frd 1H **131**
Romney Mt. LS28: Pud 6C **94**
Romsey Gdns. BD4: B'frd 2B **112**
Romsey M. BD4: B'frd 2B **112**
Rona Cft. LS26: Rothw 2C **142**
Ronald Dr. BD7: B'frd 5A **90**
Ron Lawton Cres. LS29: Burl W . . .3D **20**
Rookery HX3: Hal 6H **149**
Rookery, The LS29: Add 1D **8**
Rookery La. HX3: Hal 6H **149**
Rookery Pl. HD6: Brigh 6B **152**
Rookes Av. BD6: Gar 5C **110**
Rookes La. HX3: Hip, Nor G 6A **132**
Rookes La. Top HX3: Nor G 5A **132**
Rook La. BD4: B'frd 3H **111**
Rooks Av. BD19: Cleck 6A **134**
Rooks Cl. BD12: Wyke 6D **132**
Rook's Nest Rd. WF1: Out 5G **157**
   WF3: S'ley 5G **157**
Rook St. BD16: Bgly 4B **50**
Rookwith Pde. BD10: B'frd 3B **72**
Rookwood Av. LS9: Leeds 3G **99**
   LS25: Kip 5G **123**
Rookwood Cres. LS9: Leeds 3G **99**
Rookwood Cft. LS9: Leeds 4G **99**
Rookwood Gdns.
   LS9: Leeds 3G **99**
Rookwood Hill LS9: Leeds 3G **99**
Rookwood Mt. LS9: Leeds 3G **99**
Rookwood Pde. LS9: Leeds 3H **99**
Rookwood Pl. LS9: Leeds 3G **99**
Rookwood Rd. LS9: Leeds 3G **99**
Rookwood Sq. LS9: Leeds 3H **99**
Rookwood St. LS9: Leeds 4G **99**
Rookwood Ter. LS9: Leeds 3G **99**
Rookwood Va. LS9: Leeds 4G **99**
Rookwood Vw. LS9: Leeds 3G **99**
Rookwood Wlk. LS9: Leeds 3G **99**
Rooley Av. BD6: B'frd 5D **110**
Rooley Banks HX6: Sow B 6E **147**
Rooley Cl. BD5: B'frd 4E **111**
Rooley Cres. BD6: B'frd 4E **111**
Rooley Hgts. HX6: Sow B 6D **146**
ROOLEY HILL 6D **146**
Rooley La. BD4: B'frd 4F **111**
   BD5: B'frd 4D **110**
   HX6: Sow B 6D **146**
ROOMS 5H **115**
Rooms Fold LS27: Morl 1A **138**
Rooms La. LS27: Gil, Morl 5H **115**
Rooms Way LS27: Morl 6H **115**
Roper Av. LS8: Leeds 1D **78**
Roper Gdns. HX2: Mix 3B **128**
Roper Grn. HX2: Mix 3B **128**
Roper Gro. LS8: Leeds 1D **78**
Roper Ho. HX2: Mix 3B **128**
Roper La. BD13: Que 2F **107**
   HX2: Brad 5D **106**
Roper St. BD21: Keigh 6H **33**
Rope Wlk. HX2: Wain 1F **127**
Roscoe St. LS7: Leeds 1B **98**
Roscoe Ter. LS12: Leeds 4B **96**
Roseate Grn. LS27: Morl 4C **138**
Rose Av. LS18: H'fth 2D **74**
Rose Bank BD8: B'frd 2C **90**
    (off E. Squire La.)
   BD12: Wyke 3D **132**
   HX2: Hal 4D **148**
   LS29: Burl W 3E **21**
Rosebank Cl. LS17: Leeds 6B **62**

Rosebank Cres. LS3: Leeds 1F **97**
Rosebank Gdns. LS3: Leeds 2F **97**
Rosebank Ho. LS3: Leeds 1F **97**
Rose Bank Pl. BD8: B'frd 4G **89**
Rosebank Rd. LS3: Leeds 2F **97**
Rosebank Row LS3: Leeds 2F **97**
Roseberry St. BD22: Oak 5D **46**
Rosebery Av. BD18: Ship 2C **70**
   HX3: Hal 5H **149**
Rosebery Mt. BD18: Ship 2D **70**
Rosebery Rd. BD8: B'frd 1C **90**
Rosebery St. HX5: Ell 5B **160**
   LS28: Pud 3G **93**
Rosebery Ter. HX1: Hal 1E **149**
   LS28: Stan 1B **94**
Rose Bowl, The
   Leeds Metropolitan University
   . . . . .2D **4**
Rosebud Wlk. LS8: Leeds 1C **98**
Rosechapel Cl. BD6: B'frd 1H **131**
Rosecliffe Mt. LS13: Leeds 6D **74**
Rosecliffe Ter. LS13: Leeds 1E **95**
Rose Ct. LS25: Gar 4G **103**
Rose Cft. LS17: E Kes 5E **27**
Rosedale Av. BD15: All 1B **88**
Rosedale Bank LS10: Leeds 4B **118**
Rosedale Cl. BD17: Bail 5A **52**
Rosedale Ct. BD4: E Bier 6C **112**
   WF3: W Ard 3E **155**
Rosedale Dr. WF3: W Ard 3E **155**
Rosedale Fold BD10: B'frd 3A **72**
Rosedale Gdns. LS10: Leeds 4B **118**
    (not continuous)
   WF3: Ting 1H **155**
Rosedale Grn. LS10: Leeds 4B **118**
Rosedale Ri. LS23: B Spa 4A **30**
Rosedale Wlk. LS10: Leeds 4B **118**
Rose Gro. HX2: Lud 4E **127**
   HX6: Sow B 4G **147**
   LS26: Rothw 1H **141**
Rose Gro. La. HX6: Sow B 4F **147**
Rose Heath HX2: Illing 6B **106**
Rose Hill HX6: Sow B 5A **148**
    (off Tuel La.)
Rosehill Cres. BD12: Low M 2C **132**
Rosehip Ri. BD14: Clay 2D **108**
Roselee Cl. HX3: Hal 6A **150**
Rose Lynn Ter. BD6: B'frd 6H **109**
    (off Halifax Rd.)
Rosemary Av. LS12: Leeds 4D **96**
    (off Armley Gro. Pl.)
Rosemary Cl. HD6: Ras 2A **162**
Rosemary Gdns. BD15: All 2C **88**
Rosemary Gro. HX3: Hal 6A **150**
    (not continuous)
Rosemary Hill HX3: Hal 1A **160**
Rosemary La. HD6: Ras 2A **162**
   HX3: Hal 6A **150**
Rosemary Pl. HD6: Ras 2A **162**
    (off Rosemary La.)
Rosemary Ter. HX3: Hal 6A **150**
Rose Mdws. BD22: Keigh 2E **47**
Rosemont LS16: B'hpe 2F **43**
    (off Breary La.)
Rosemont Av. LS13: Leeds 1E **95**
   LS28: Pud 3B **94**
Rosemont Dr. LS28: Pud 3B **94**
Rosemont Gro. LS13: Leeds 1D **94**
Rosemont La. BD17: Bail 5E **53**
Rosemont Pl. LS13: Leeds 1E **95**
Rosemont Rd. LS13: Leeds 1E **95**
Rosemont St. LS13: Leeds 1E **95**
   LS28: Pud 3B **94**
Rosemont Ter. LS13: Leeds 1E **95**
   LS28: Pud 3B **94**
Rosemont Vw. LS13: Leeds 1D **94**
Rosemont Vs. LS28: Pud 3B **94**
Rosemont Wlk. LS13: Leeds 1E **95**
ROSEMOUNT 5C **160**
Rose Mt. BD2: B'frd 6G **71**
   BD4: B'frd 5E **113**
   HX2: Hal 5E **149**

Rosemount LS7: Leeds 3A **78**
    (off School La.)
Rosemount Av. HX5: Ell 5C **160**
Rosemount Cl. BD21: Keigh 6H **33**
    (off Well St.)
Rosemount Gdns. BD8: B'frd 1D **90**
Rose Mt. Pl. LS12: Leeds 5D **96**
Rosemount Ter. HX5: Ell 5C **160**
Rosemount Wlk. BD21: Keigh 6H **33**
    (off Well St.)
Roseneath Pl. LS12: Leeds 5D **96**
Roseneath St. LS12: Leeds 5D **96**
Roseneath Ter. LS12: Leeds 5D **96**
Rose Pl. HX2: Lud M 4E **147**
Rose St. BD8: B'frd 2B **90**
   BD21: Keigh 6D **34**
   BD22: Haw 3C **64**
   HX1: Hal 3D **148**
   LS18: H'fth 1D **74**
Rose Ter. HX1: Hal 2E **149**
    (off Battinson Rd.)
   HX2: Hal 5E **149**
   LS18: H'fth 1C **74**
   LS29: Add 1D **8**
Rosetta Dr. BD8: B'frd 3H **89**
Rosevale Vw. HX6: Sow B 4A **148**
Roseville Bus. Pk. LS8: Leeds 1C **98**
Roseville Rd. LS8: Leeds 1H **5** (1C **98**)
Roseville St. LS8: Leeds 1C **98**
Roseville Ter. LS15: Leeds 6F **81**
    (off Church La.)
Roseville Way LS8: Leeds 1C **98**
Rosewood Av. BD20: Rid 4D **34**
   LS25: Kip 2F **123**
Rosewood Ct. LS17: Leeds 4G **59**
    (off Cranmer Cl.)
   LS26: Rothw 6B **120**
Rosewood Gro. BD4: B'frd 6B **92**
Rosgill Dr. LS14: Leeds 4B **80**
Rosgill Grn. LS14: Leeds 4C **80**
Rosgill Wlk. LS14: Leeds 4B **80**
Rosley Mt. BD6: B'frd 1H **131**
Roslyn Pl. BD7: B'frd 5B **90**
Rossall Rd. LS8: Leeds 5D **78**
Rossefield App. LS13: Leeds 2F **95**
Rossefield Av. LS13: Leeds 1F **95**
Rossefield Chase LS13: Leeds 1F **95**
Rossefield Cl. LS13: Leeds 1F **95**
Rossefield Dr. LS13: Leeds 1F **95**
Rossefield Gdns. LS13: Leeds 1F **95**
Rossefield Gth. LS13: Leeds 1F **95**
Rossefield Grn. LS13: Leeds 1F **95**
    (off Rossefield Dr.)
Rossefield Gro. LS13: Leeds 1F **95**
Rossefield Lawn LS13: Leeds 1F **95**
Rossefield Pde. LS13: Leeds 1F **95**
    (off Rossefield Wlk.)
Rosse Fld. Pk. BD9: B'frd 5B **70**
Rossefield Pl. LS13: Leeds 1F **95**
Rossefield Rd. BD9: B'frd 5A **70**
Rossefield Ter. LS13: Leeds 1F **95**
Rossefield Vw. LS13: Leeds 1F **95**
Rossefield Wlk. LS13: Leeds 1F **95**
Rossefield Way LS13: Leeds 1F **95**
Rossendale Pl. BD18: Ship 2A **70**
Rosse St. BD8: B'frd 4A **90**
   BD18: Ship 1B **70**
Rossett Bus. Pk. LS13: Leeds 5D **74**
Rossett Ho. BD3: B'frd 2F **7**
Ross Gro. LS13: Leeds 5C **74**
Rossington Gro. LS8: Leeds 5C **78**
Rossington Pl. LS8: Leeds 5C **78**
Rossington Rd. LS8: Leeds 4E **79**
Rossington St.
   LS2: Leeds 3D **4** (3H **97**)
Rosslyn Gro. BD22: Haw 3C **64**
Rossmore Dr. BD15: All 2E **89**
Ross Ter. LS13: Leeds 5C **74**
Rothbart Gdns. BD16: Bgly 3E **51**
Rothbury Gdns. LS16: Leeds 4B **58**
Rothery Ct. HX1: Hal 1E **149**
    (off Crossley Gdns.)
Rothesay Ter. BD7: B'frd 5C **90**

ROTHWELL 2A **142**
Rothwell Country Pk. 5C **120**
Rothwell Dr. HX1: Hal 4F **149**
ROTHWELL HAIGH 1H **141**
Rothwell La. LS26: Rothw 1C **142**
Rothwell Mt. HX1: Hal 4F **149**
Rothwell Rd.
  HX1: Hal 6A **164** (4F **149**)
Rothwell Sports Cen. 3E **143**
Rough Hall La. HX2: Wain 2F **127**
Roundell Av. BD4: B'frd 5H **111**
Roundfield Pl. *BD13: Thorn* 4H **87**
                    (off West La.)
ROUNDHAY 6E **61**
Roundhay Av. LS8: Leeds 4D **78**
Roundhay Cl. LS8: Leeds 6E **61**
Roundhay Cres. LS8: Leeds 4D **78**
Roundhay Gdns. LS8: Leeds . . .4D **78**
Roundhay Golf Course 5G **61**
Roundhay Gro. LS8: Leeds 4D **78**
Roundhay Mt. LS8: Leeds 4D **78**
Roundhay Park 6F **61**
Roundhay Pk. La. LS17: Leeds . . .2F **61**
Roundhay Pl. LS8: Leeds 4D **78**
Roundhay Rd. LS7: Leeds 1B **98**
  LS8: Leeds 5E **79**
Roundhay Vw. LS8: Leeds 4D **78**
Roundhead Fold BD10: B'frd 1C **72**
Round Hill *BD13: Que* 5G **107**
                     (off Rope La.)
  HX2: Illing 1D **128**
Roundhill Av. BD16: Cot 1D **68**
Round Hill Cl. HX2: Illing 1D **128**
Roundhill Cl. BD13: Que 3D **108**
Roundhill Mt. BD16: Cot 2D **68**
Round Hill Pl. BD13: Que 3D **108**
Roundhill Pl. BD1: B'frd 4B **6** (4D **90**)
Round Hill Rd. LS28: Pud 4G **93**
Roundhill St. BD5: B'frd 1D **110**
Roundhouse Bus. Pk.
  LS12: Leeds 6A **4** (4F **97**)
Round St. BD5: B'frd 2E **111**
                (not continuous)
Round Thorn Pl. BD8: B'frd 3A **90**
Roundway, The LS27: Morl 3G **137**
Roundwood BD18: Ship 2G **69**
Roundwood Av. BD10: B'frd 4C **72**
  BD17: Bail 4F **53**
Roundwood Glen BD10: B'frd 2C **72**
Roundwood Rd. BD17: Bail 4E **53**
Roundwood Vw. BD10: B'frd 3C **72**
Rouse Fold BD4: B'frd 6F **7** (6F **91**)
Row, The *LS19: Raw* 3E **55**
               (off Apperley La.)
Rowan Av. BD3: B'frd 4C **92**
  LS16: Leeds 2C **58**
Rowanberries BD14: Clay 2D **108**
Rowanberry Cl. BD2: B'frd 5H **71**
Rowan Cl. LS21: Pool 5G **25**
  WF17: Birs 5C **136**
Rowan Ct. BD2: B'frd 2A **92**
  LS19: Raw 2F **55**
  LS26: Wood 1G **143**
Rowan Dr. HD6: Clift 6C **152**
Rowan M. WF3: Rob H 5E **141**
Rowan Pl. LS25: Gar 5H **103**
Rowans, The BD17: Bail 4H **51**
  LS13: Leeds 6B **74**
  LS16: B'hpe 3H **43**
  LS22: Weth 3G **13**
  WF3: Rob H 5E **141**
Rowan St. BD20: Keigh 3G **33**
Rowan Trade Pk. BD4: B'frd . . .1H **111**
Rowantree Av. BD17: Bail 3B **52**
Rowan Tree Ct. WF1: Out 4F **157**
Rowantree Dr. BD10: B'frd 3H **71**
Rowan Way HX3: North 3G **33**
Rowanwood Gdns. BD10: B'frd . . .4C **72**
Rowany Gdns. LS29: I'ly 6F **11**
Row Bottom Ter. HX6: Sow B 5D **146**
Rowland Meyrick Way
  LS22: Weth 3G **13**
Rowland Pl. LS11: Leeds 2H **117**

Rowland Rd. LS11: Leeds 2H **117**
Rowlands Cl. BD13: Thorn 5F **87**
Rowland Ter. LS11: Leeds 2H **117**
Row La. HX6: Sow B 6D **146**
Rowlestone Ri. BD10: B'frd 3C **72**
Rowley Dr. LS29: I'ly 6H **11**
Rowsley St. BD21: Keigh 6B **34**
Rowton Thorpe BD10: B'frd 3C **72**
Roxburgh Gro. BD15: All 3D **88**
Roxburgh M. LS12: Leeds 1H **95**
Roxby Cl. LS9: Leeds 2C **98**
Roxby St. BD5: B'frd 2D **110**
Roxholme Av. LS7: Leeds 4C **78**
Roxholme Gro. LS7: Leeds 4C **78**
Roxholme Pl. LS7: Leeds 4C **78**
Roxholme Rd. LS7: Leeds 4C **78**
Roxholme Ter. LS7: Leeds 4C **78**
Royal Arc. BD21: Keigh 6A **34**
Royal Armouries Museum, The
                     .6H **5** (5B **98**)
Royal Armouries Sq. *LS10: Leeds* . .5B **98**
                (off Armouries Dr.)
Royal Cl. BD7: B'frd 2H **109**
  LS10: Leeds 3B **118**
Royal Ct. LS10: Leeds 3B **118**
Royal Dr. LS10: Leeds 3B **118**
Royal Gdns. BD9: B'frd 6F **69**
  LS10: Leeds 3B **118**
Royal Gro. LS10: Leeds 3B **118**
Royal Ind. Pk. HX1: Hal . . .4A **164** (2F **149**)
Royal Lofts, The *HX6: Sow B* 6H **147**
                (off Sowerby St.)
Royal London Ind. Estate, The
  LS11: Leeds 4F **117**
Royal Pk. Av. LS6: Leeds 1F **97**
Royal Pk. Gro. LS6: Leeds 6F **77**
Royal Pk. Mt. LS6: Leeds 6F **77**
Royal Pk. Rd. LS6: Leeds 1E **97**
Royal Pk. Ter. LS6: Leeds 1F **97**
Royal Pk. Vw. LS6: Leeds 6F **77**
Royal Pl. LS10: Leeds 3B **118**
Royal Ter. LS23: B Spa 3B **30**
Royd HX6: Sow B 6E **147**
Royd Av. BD16: Bgly 4E **51**
Royds Cres. HX1: Hal 1C **148**
Royd End BD15: Wils 4G **67**
Royd Farm *HX2: Illing* 6C **106**
                (off Keighley Rd.)
Royd Ho. Gro. BD21: Keigh 2C **48**
Royd Ho. Rd. BD21: Keigh 2C **48**
Royd Ho. Wlk. BD21: Keigh 2C **48**
Royd Ho. Way BD21: Keigh 2C **48**
Royd Ings Av. BD21: Keigh 4A **34**
Roydlands St. HX3: Hip 1F **151**
Roydlands Ter. HX3: Hip 2F **151**
Royd La. BD20: Keigh 4H **33**
  HX2: Illing 6C **106**
  HX3: Hal 3E **129**
                (not continuous)
Royd Mill Bus. Pk. HD6: Brigh . . .2C **162**
Royd Moor Rd. BD4: B'frd 4D **112**
Royd Mt. HX3: Hal 5G **129**
Roydon Gro. BD9: B'frd 1A **90**
Royd Pl. HX3: Hal 5G **129**
Royds, The HX3: Hal 6F **149**
Royds Av. BD11: Birk 2F **135**
  HD6: B Bri 1B **152**
Roydscliffe Dr. BD9: B'frd 5H **69**
Roydscliffe Rd. BD9: B'frd 6H **69**
Royds Cl. LS12: Leeds 1C **116**
Royds Cl. *LS26: Rothw* 2B **142**
                 (off Royds La.)
Royds Cres. HD6: B Bri 2B **152**
Roydsdale Way BD4: B'frd 1G **133**
Royds Ent. Pk. BD6: B'frd 4G **109**
Royds Farm Rd. LS12: Leeds 3C **116**
ROYDS GREEN 5C **142**
Royds Gro. WF1: Out 4G **157**
Royds Hall Av. BD6: B'frd 5C **110**
Royds Hall La. BD6: B'frd 1A **132**
  BD6: B'frd, Low M 2A **132**
  BD12: Low M, Wyke 4A **132**
Royds Hall Rd. LS12: Leeds 1C **116**

Royds La. LS12: Leeds 1C **116**
  LS26: Oul, Rothw 3B **142**
Royds Pk. LS12: Leeds 1C **116**
Royds Pk. Cres. BD12: Wyke 3D **132**
Roydstone Rd. BD3: B'frd 3B **92**
Roydstone Ter. BD3: B'frd 3B **92**
Royd St. BD12: Wyke 3C **132**
  BD13: Thorn 5G **87**
  BD15: Wils 5G **67**
  BD20: Keigh 3H **33**
                (not continuous)
Royds Wood BD18: Ship 4A **70**
Royd Ter. HX3: Hal 5E **149**
Royd Vw. LS28: Pud 5G **93**
Royd Way BD21: Keigh 4A **34**
Royd Well BD11: Birk 2F **135**
Royd Wood BD22: Oxen 5D **64**
Roydwood Ter. BD13: Cull 3B **66**
Roy Rd. BD6: B'frd 4F **109**
Royston Cl. WF3: E Ard 3B **156**
Royston Hill WF3: E Ard 3B **156**
Ruby St. BD22: Keigh 3G **47**
  LS9: Leeds 1H **5** (2C **98**)
Rudding Av. BD15: All 2C **88**
Rudding Cres. BD15: All 2C **88**
Rudd St. BD7: B'frd 1A **110**
Rudgate LS23: T Arch 1G **31**
  LS24: N Kym, Tad 5H **31**
Rudgate Ct. LS23: T Arch 1G **31**
Ruffield Side BD12: Wyke 2C **132**
Rufford Av. LS19: Yead 1F **55**
Rufford Bank LS19: Yead 1G **55**
Rufford Cl. LS19: Yead 1G **55**
Rufford Cres. LS19: Yead 1G **55**
Rufford Dr. LS19: Yead 1G **55**
Rufford Gdns. LS19: Yead 1F **55**
RUFFORD PARK 1F **55**
Rufford Pl. HX3: Hal 5F **149**
Rufford Ridge LS19: Yead 1G **55**
Rufford Ri. LS19: Yead 1F **55**
Rufford Rd. HX3: Hal 5F **149**
  HX5: Ell 5B **160**
Rufford St. BD3: B'frd 4A **92**
Rufford Vs. HX3: Hal 5F **149**
Rufus St. BD5: B'frd 2B **110**
  BD21: Keigh 5A **34**
Rugby Av. HX3: Hal 4D **128**
Rugby Dr. HX3: Hal 4D **128**
Rugby Gdns. HX3: Hal 4D **128**
Rugby Mt. HX3: Hal 4D **128**
Rugby Pl. BD7: B'frd 5B **90**
Rugby Ter. HX3: Hal 4D **128**
Rumple Cft. LS21: Otley 1C **22**
Runnymede Ct. *BD10: B'frd* 2H **71**
                 (off Cobden St.)
Runswick Av. LS11: Leeds 6F **97**
Runswick Gro. BD5: B'frd 4D **110**
Runswick Pl. LS11: Leeds 6F **97**
Runswick St. BD5: B'frd 4D **110**
  LS11: Leeds 6F **97**
Runswick Ter. BD5: B'frd 4D **110**
  LS11: Leeds 6G **97**
Rupert Rd. LS29: I'ly 4C **10**
Rupert St. BD21: Keigh 5A **34**
  BD22: Cros R 1F **65**
Rush Cft. BD10: B'frd 6F **53**
Rushcroft Ter. BD17: Bail 4C **52**
Rushdene Ct. BD12: Wyke 6C **132**
Rushmoor Rd. BD4: B'frd 3B **112**
Rusholme Dr. LS28: Fars 6G **73**
Rushton Av. BD3: B'frd 3C **92**
Rushton Hill HX2: Hal 6A **128**
Rushton Hill Cl. HX2: Hal 6A **128**
Rushton Rd. BD3: B'frd 3B **92**
Rushton St. HX1: Hal 1D **148**
  LS28: Cal 3F **73**
Rushton Ter. BD3: B'frd 4C **92**
Rushworth St. HX3: Hal 6E **129**
Rushy Fall Mdw. BD22: Keigh 5G **47**
Ruskin Av. BD9: B'frd 6F **69**
  WF1: Wake 6D **156**
Ruskin Cres. LS20: Guis 5D **40**
Ruskin St. LS28: Stan 2G **93**

Ruskin Ter. HX3: Hal 6E 129
Russell Av. BD13: Que 5A 108
Russell Ct. LS17: Bard 2F 45
Russell Gro. BD11: Birk 2F 135
  LS8: Leeds 5D 78
Russell Hall La. BD13: Que 4A 108
Russell Rd. BD13: Que 5H 107
Russell Sq. BD21: Birk 2F 47
Russell St. BD5: B'frd 6B 6 (6D 90)
  BD13: Que 4A 108
  BD18: Ship 4C 70
  BD21: Keigh 6H 33
  HX1: Hal 4C 164 (2G 149)
  LS1: Leeds 4D 4 (3H 97)
Russell Way HD6: Brigh 5B 152
Russetts, The HX3: Hal 1A 150
Rustic Av. HX3: Sou 5C 150
Rustless Cl. BD19: Cleck 3G 153
Ruswarp Cres. BD10: B'frd 3B 72
Ruth Ho. BD3: B'frd 3F 7
Ruth St. BD22: Cros R 1E 65
Ruthven Vw. LS8: Leeds 6E 79
Rutland Ct. LS25: Kip 3H 123
  LS26: Wood 1F 143
Rutland Ct. LS28: Pud 3A 94
                                    (off Richardshaw La.)
Rutland Dr. LS25: Kip 3H 123
Rutland Ho. BD16: Bgly 4C 50
                                        (off Clyde St.)
Rutland Mt. LS3: Leeds 3A 4 (3F 97)
Rutland St. BD4: B'frd 1G 111
  BD21: Keigh 2H 47
  LS3: Leeds 3A 4 (3G 97)
Rutland Ter. LS3: Leeds 3A 4 (3F 97)
Ryan Gro. BD22: Keigh 5D 32
Ryan Pl. LS8: Leeds 5E 79
Ryan St. BD5: B'frd 2D 110
Ryburn Bldgs. HX6: Sow B 6H 147
                                    (off Town Hall St.)
Ryburn Ct. HX1: Hal 2D 148
                                      (off Hanson La.)
Ryburn Golf Course 2A 158
Ryburn Ho. HX1: Hal 2D 148
                                        (off Clay St.)
Ryburn St. HX6: Sow B 6H 147
Ryburn Ter. HX1: Hal 2D 148
Ryburn Vw. HX2: Hal 4C 148
Rycroft Bri. BD16: Cot 3C 68
  LS13: Leeds 2C 94
Rycroft Cl. LS13: Leeds 2D 94
Rycroft Ct. LS13: Leeds 2D 94
Rycroft Dr. LS13: Leeds 2D 94
Rycroft Gdns. LS13: Leeds 2C 94
Rycroft Pl. LS13: Leeds 2D 94
Rycroft Dr. BD18: Ship 4D 70
Rycroft Towers LS13: Leeds 2C 94
Rydal Av. BD9: B'frd 5C 70
  BD17: Bail 6G 51
  LS25: Gar 5F 103
Rydal Cres. LS27: Morl 2D 138
Rydal Dr. LS27: Morl 2D 138
Rydale Ho. HX6: Sow B 6H 147
Rydall Pl. LS11: Leeds 6F 97
Rydall St. LS11: Leeds 6F 97
Rydall Ter. LS11: Leeds 6F 97
Rydal St. BD21: Keigh 1G 47
Ryder Gdns. LS8: Leeds 2E 79
Rydings, The HD6: Brigh 6A 152
Rydings Av. HD6: Brigh 6A 152
Rydings Cl. HD6: Brigh 6H 151
Rydings Dr. HD6: Brigh 6H 151
Rydings Wlk. HD6: Brigh 6H 151
Rye Cl. HX2: Illing 1D 128
Ryecroft BD16: Har 6D 48
Ryecroft Cl. BD4: B'frd 3D 112
  HX3: Hip 2A 152
  WF1: Out 4G 157
Ryecroft Cres. HX2: Hal 6B 128
Ryecroft La. HD6: Ras 3C 162
  HX2: Hal 1B 148
Ryecroft Rd. BD16: Har 5B 48
Ryecroft Ter. HX2: Hal 6B 128

Ryedale Av. LS12: Leeds 1B 116
Ryedale Cl. LS14: Leeds 4B 80
Ryedale Holt LS12: Leeds 6C 96
Ryedale Pk. LS29: I'ly 6F 11
Ryedale Way BD15: All 1C 88
  WF3: W Ard 1D 154
Ryefield Av. BD14: Clay 6D 88
Ryefield Way BD20: Sils 3E 15
Ryelands Gro. BD9: B'frd 5F 69
Rye Gth. LS22: Weth 1D 12
Rye La. HX2: Hal 6H 127
Rye Pl. LS14: Leeds 2B 100
Rye St. BD21: Keigh 3H 47
Rylands Av. BD16: Bgly 4D 50
Rylands Mdw. BD22: Haw 1E 65
Rylstone Gdns. BD3: B'frd 1G 91
Rylstone Rd. BD17: Bail 5H 51
Rylstone St. BD21: Keigh 5B 34
Rylston Gdns. HX3: Hal 6F 149
Rysworth Av. BD16: Bgly 6H 35
Rysworth Bri. BD16: Bgly 1H 49
Rysworth Cres. BD16: Bgly 6H 35
Ryton Dale BD10: B'frd 3C 72

S

Sable Crest BD2: B'frd 5F 71
Sackville App. LS7: Leeds 6A 78
Sackville Rd. BD20: Sils 1E 15
Sackville St. BD1: B'frd 4C 6 (4E 91)
  LS7: Leeds 6A 78
Saddlers Cft. LS29: I'ly 5C 10
Saddler St. BD12: Wyke 3C 132
Saddleworth Rd.
  HX4: Bark, Gree 6A 158
  HX5: Ell 4H 159
Sadler Cl. LS16: Leeds 3C 58
Sadler Copse LS16: Leeds 3C 58
Sadler Way LS16: Leeds 3C 58
Sadlers Wlk. LS22: Weth 3F 13
Saffron Cl. HX6: Sow B 4A 148
Saffron Dr. BD15: All 2D 88
Sagar Pl. LS6: Leeds 5D 76
Sage Gro. HD6: Ras 4G 161
Sage St. BD5: B'frd 1C 110
Sahara St. BD8: B'frd 1D 90
St Abbs Cl. BD6: B'frd 6C 110
St Abbs Dr. BD6: B'frd 6C 110
St Abbs Fold BD6: B'frd 6C 110
St Abbs Ga. BD6: B'frd 6C 110
St Abbs Wlk. BD6: B'frd 6C 110
St Abbs Way BD6: B'frd 6C 110
St Aidans Rd. BD17: Bail 5D 52
  LS26: Gt P 5E 123
St Aidans Sq. BD16: Bgly 1A 50
                                  (off Old Souls Way)
St Alban App. LS9: Leeds 2G 99
St Alban Cl. LS9: Leeds 2G 99
St Alban Cres. LS9: Leeds 2G 99
St Alban Gro. LS9: Leeds 2G 99
St Alban Mt. LS9: Leeds 2G 99
St Alban Rd. LS9: Leeds 2G 99
St Albans Av. HX3: Hal 6G 149
                                      (not continuous)
St Albans Cft. HX3: Hal 5H 149
St Alban's Pl. LS2: Leeds 2F 5 (2A 98)
St Alban Rd. HX3: Hal 1E 149
St Andrew's Av. LS27: Morl 4G 137
St Andrews Cl. HX2: Hal 2E 129
  LS13: Leeds 4A 74
  LS19: Yead 5G 41
  LS27: Morl 4G 137
St Andrews Ct. HD6: Brigh 5A 152
                                        (off Mary St.)
  LS3: Leeds 3F 97
                                    (off St Andrew's St.)
  LS19: Yead 5F 41
                                        (off Haw La.)
St Andrews Cres. BD12: O'haw 3G 133
St Andrew's Cft. LS17: Leeds 3H 59

St Andrews Dr. HD6: Brigh 5A 152
  LS17: Leeds 3A 60
St Andrew's Gro. LS27: Morl 4H 137
St Andrews Pl. BD7: B'frd 5C 90
  LS3: Leeds 3F 97
St Andrew's Rd. LS19: Yead 6G 41
St Andrew's St. LS3: Leeds 3F 97
St Andrews Ter. LS27: Morl 5G 137
St Andrew's Vs. BD7: B'frd 4C 90
St Andrew's Wlk. LS17: Leeds 3A 60
St Annes Cl. LS5: Leeds 5C 76
St Annes Dr. LS4: Leeds 5C 76
St Annes Pl. LS5: Leeds 5B 76
St Anne's Rd. HX3: Hal 1G 159
  LS6: Leeds 5C 76
St Anne's Roman Catholic Cathedral
                                  . . . . . .3D 4 (3H 97)
St Anne's St. LS2: Leeds 3D 4 (3H 97)
St Annes Ter. BD17: Bail 5D 52
St Ann's Av. LS4: Leeds 1D 96
St Ann's Cl. LS4: Leeds 6C 76
St Ann's Gdns. LS4: Leeds 6C 76
St Ann's Grn. LS4: Leeds 5C 76
St Ann's La. LS4: Leeds 5C 76
St Ann's Mt. LS4: Leeds 6D 76
St Ann's Pl. HX1: Hal 1E 149
St Ann's Ri. LS4: Leeds 6B 76
St Anns Sq. HX6: Sow B 5A 148
  LS4: Leeds 6C 76
St Ann's Way LS4: Leeds 6C 76
St Anthony's Dr. LS11: Leeds 3F 117
St Anthonys Gdns. BD18: Ship 3D 70
                                      (off Wrose Rd.)
St Anthony's Rd. LS11: Leeds 3E 117
St Anthony's Ter.
  LS11: Leeds 4E 117
St Armands Ct. LS25: Gar 4F 103
St Augustines Ct. LS8: Leeds 6D 78
                                    (off Harehills Pl.)
St Augustine's Ter.
  BD3: B'frd 1G 7 (2G 91)
  HX1: Hal 2E 149
St Barnabas Rd. LS11: Leeds 5H 97
St Bartholomews Cl.
  LS12: Leeds 4C 96
St Benedicts Chase LS13: Leeds 4F 75
St Benedicts Dr. LS13: Leeds 4G 75
St Benedicts Gdns. LS13: Leeds 4G 75
St Bevan's Rd. HX3: Hal 1E 149
St Blaise Ct. BD5: B'frd 6D 6 (6E 91)
St Blaise Sq. BD1: B'frd 3D 6 (4E 91)
St Blaise Way BD1: B'frd 3D 6 (3D 91)
St Catherine's Bus. Complex
  LS13: Leeds 5F 75
                                        (off Broad La.)
St Catherines Cres. LS13: Leeds 5F 75
St Catherine's Dr. LS13: Leeds 5F 75
St Catherines Grn. LS13: Leeds 5F 75
St Catherine's Hill LS13: Leeds 5F 75
St Catherines Wlk.
  LS8: Leeds 3E 79
St Cecilia St. LS2: Leeds 4H 5 (3B 98)
St Chad's Av. HD6: Brigh 4G 151
  LS6: Leeds 3C 76
St Chad's Dr. LS6: Leeds 3C 76
St Chad's Gro. LS6: Leeds 3C 76
St Chads Pde. LS16: Leeds 3D 76
St Chad's Ri. LS6: Leeds 3C 76
St Chads Rd. BD8: B'frd 2B 90
  LS16: Leeds 3D 76
St Chad's Vw. LS6: Leeds 4C 76
St Christopher's Av.
  LS26: Rothw 2B 142
St Christophers Dr. LS29: Add 1D 8
St Clair Rd. LS21: Otley 3F 23
                                      (not continuous)
St Clair St. LS21: Otley 3F 23
St Clair Ter. LS21: Otley 3F 23
                                      (off St Clair St.)
St Clare's Av. BD2: B'frd 1B 92
St Clements Av. LS26: Rothw 2A 142
St Clements Cl. LS26: Rothw 3H 141
St Clements Ri. LS26: Rothw 2H 141

St Cyprian's Gdns. LS9: Leeds 1F 99
St Davids Cl. WF3: Rob H 5F 141
St Davids Ct. HX3: Hal 6F 129
   LS11: Leeds *5H 97*
   (off David St.)
St Davids Gth. WF3: Rob H 5F 141
St Davids Rd. LS21: Otley 1C 22
   WF3: Rob H 5F 141
St Dunstans Technology Pk.
   BD4: B'frd 1F 111
St Edmunds Ct. LS8: Leeds 5E 61
St Edward's Ter. *LS23: Cliff* *6B 30*
   (off High St.)
St Elmo BD13: Que 6G 107
St Elmo Gro. LS9: Leeds 3E 99
St Eloi Av. BD17: Bail 3C 52
St Enoch's Rd. BD6: B'frd 4B 110
St Francis Cl. LS11: Leeds 2H 117
St Francis Gdns. HD2: Fix 6A 162
St Francis Pl. LS11: Leeds 5H 97
St Gabriel Ct. LS14: Leeds 4F 81
St Gabriels Ct. LS18: H'fth 3D 56
St George Bldg. *LS1: Leeds* *2G 97*
   (off Gt. George St.)
St George's Av. LS26: Rothw 6G 119
St George's Concert Hall 5E 7
St Georges Cres. HX3: Hal 6F 129
   LS26: Rothw 6G 119
St George's Pl. BD4: B'frd 1H 111
   BD5: B'frd 6C 6 (6E 91)
St Georges Rd. HX3: Hal 6E 129
   LS1: Leeds 2C 4 (2H 97)
   LS10: Leeds 2B 140
St George's Sq. HX3: Hal 6F 129
St George's Sq.
   BD3: B'frd 5H 7 (5H 91)
St George's Ter. HX3: Hal 6F 129
St Giles Cl. HD6: Brigh 4G 151
St Giles Ct. HX3: Hip 2G 151
St Giles Gth. LS16: B'hpe 2F 43
St Giles Rd. HD6: Brigh 3G 151
   HX3: Hip 2G 151
St Helena BD13: Denh 2C 86
St Helena Rd. BD6: B'frd 4B 110
St Helenas Caravan Pk.
   LS18: H'fth 4E 43
St Helens Av. LS16: Leeds 4D 58
St Helens Cl. LS16: Leeds 4D 58
   (not continuous)
St Helens Cft. LS16: Leeds 4C 58
St Helen's Dr. LS25: M'fld 3D 104
St Helens Gdns. LS16: Leeds 4C 58
St Helens Gro. LS16: Leeds 4C 58
St Helens La. LS16: Leeds 4B 58
St Helens M. LS24: N Kym 5H 31
St Helen's St. LS10: Leeds 6B 98
St Helens Way LS16: Leeds 4D 58
   LS29: I'ly 5F 11
St Helier Gro. BD17: Bail 3D 52
St Hilaire Wlk. *LS10: Leeds* *3C 140*
   (off Topliss Way)
St Hilda's Av. LS9: Leeds 5D 98
St Hilda's Cres. LS9: Leeds 5D 98
St Hilda's Mt. LS9: Leeds 5D 98
St Hilda's Pl. LS9: Leeds 5D 98
St Hilda's Rd. LS9: Leeds 5D 98
St Hilda's Ter. BD3: B'frd 3C 92
St Hughes Lodge *LS12: Leeds* *3C 96*
   (off Armley Lodge Rd.)
St Ians Cft. LS29: Add 2D 8
St Ives Est. BD16: Har 5G 49
St Ives Gdns. HX3: Hal 6G 149
St Ives Gro. BD16: Har 5G 49
   LS12: Leeds 3A 96
St Ives Mt. LS12: Leeds 3A 96
St Ives Pl. BD16: Har 5G 49
St Ives Rd. BD16: Har 4H 49
   (Cross Gates La.)
   BD16: Har 6G 149
   (St Ives Pl.)
   HX3: Hal 6G 149
St James App. LS14: Leeds 5C 80
St James Av. LS18: H'fth 6E 57

St James Bus. Pk.
   BD1: B'frd 5F 7 (5F 91)
St James Cl. BD17: Bail 4E 53
   LS12: Leeds 3H 95
St James Ct. HD6: Brigh 6B 152
   HX1: Hal 3B 164
St James Cres. LS28: Pud 4F 93
St James Dr. LS18: H'fth 6E 57
St James M. LS12: Leeds 3H 95
   LS15: Leeds 6F 81
St James Pl. *BD17: Bail* *3F 53*
   (off Otley Rd.)
St James Rd. BD17: Bail 3F 53
   HX1: Hal 3B 164 (2G 149)
   LS29: I'ly 6C 10
St James's Ct. LS9: Leeds 1C 98
St James's Mkt.
   BD4: B'frd 6G 7 (5G 91)
St James Sq. HX3: North 5C 130
St James's Sq. BD5: B'frd 6E 91
St James's St. LS22: Weth 4E 13
St James St. HX1: Hal 3B 164 (2G 149)
St James Ter. LS18: H'fth 6F 57
St James Wlk. LS18: H'fth 6F 57
St Johns LS29: I'ly 6C 10
St Johns Av. LS6: Leeds 1F 97
   LS14: T'ner 2H 63
   LS28: Fars 1H 93
   LS29: Add 1D 8
St John's Cen. LS2: Leeds 3E 5 (3A 98)
St John's Church 3E 5 (3A 98)
St Johns Cl. BD4: B'frd 3A 112
   BD20: Sils 2E 15
   LS6: Leeds 1F 97
St John's Ct. BD17: Bail 5E 53
   BD20: Keigh *3G 33*
   (off St John's Rd.)
   LS7: Leeds 5B 78
   LS14: T'ner 2H 63
   LS19: Yead 1E 55
St Johns Cres. BD8: B'frd 3G 89
St John's Cross HX2: Brad 5E 107
St John's Dr. LS19: Yead 1E 55
St John's Gro. LS6: Leeds 1F 97
St John's La. HX1: Hal 6B 164 (3G 149)
St Johns M. *BD13: Cull* *3B 66*
   (off Station Rd.)
St John's Pk. LS29: Men 6F 21
St Johns Pl. BD11: Birk 1E 135
   HX1: Hal 6B 164
   LS5: Leeds *3H 75*
   (off Vicarage Ter.)
St John's Rd. BD20: Keigh 3G 33
   LS3: Leeds 2A 4 (2F 97)
   LS19: Yead 1E 55
   LS23: Cliff 4B 30
   LS29: I'ly 5G 11
St John's St. BD20: Sils 2E 15
   LS26: Oul 2E 143
St John's Ter. LS3: Leeds 1F 97
St John St. HD6: Bus 2A 162
St John's Vw. LS23: B Spa 4A 30
St Johns Wlk. LS26: Swil 4B 122
St Johns Way BD22: Keigh 1F 47
   LS19: Yead 1E 55
St John's Yd. LS26: Oul 2E 143
St Josephs Ct. LS19: Raw 5F 55
   LS25: Gar *4E 103*
St Jude's Pl. BD1: B'frd 1B 6 (3D 90)
St Jude's St. BD8: B'frd 1A 6 (3D 90)
   HX1: Hal 4F 149
St Laurence's Cl. BD2: B'frd 4D 70
St Lawrence Cl. LS28: Pud 4H 93
St Lawrence St. LS7: Leeds 2H 78
St Lawrence Ter. LS28: Pud 4A 94
St Leonards Cl. LS29: Add 2D 8
St Leonard's Ct. BD8: B'frd 2H 89
St Leonard's Farm Pk. 2A 54
St Leonard's Gro. BD8: B'frd 2H 89
St Leonard's Rd. BD8: B'frd 2H 89
St Lukes Cl. BD5: B'frd 6D 90
   BD19: Cleck 2H 153
   LS23: Cliff 6B 30

St Luke's Cres. LS11: Leeds 1G 117
St Luke's Grn. LS11: Leeds 1G 117
St Luke's Rd. LS11: Leeds 1G 117
St Luke's St. LS11: Leeds 1G 117
St Luke's Ter. BD19: Cleck 2H 153
   BD20: E Mor 5H 35
St Luke's Vw. LS11: Leeds 1G 117
St Margaret's Av. BD4: B'frd 3B 112
   LS8: Leeds 3E 79
   LS18: H'fth 6D 56
   LS26: Meth 4D 144
St Margaret's Cl. LS18: H'fth 5D 56
St Margaret's Dr. LS8: Leeds 3E 79
   LS18: H'fth 5D 56
St Margaret's Gro. LS8: Leeds 3E 79
St Margaret's Pl. BD7: B'frd 6B 90
St Margaret's Rd. BD7: B'frd 5B 90
   LS18: H'fth 5D 56
   LS26: Meth 4D 144
St Margaret's Ter. BD7: B'frd 6B 90
   LS29: I'ly 6D 10
St Margaret's Vw. LS8: Leeds 3E 79
St Mark's Av. BD12: Low M 2C 132
   LS2: Leeds 1G 97
St Mark's Ct. LS6: Leeds 6H 77
St Mark's Flats *LS2: Leeds* *6G 77*
   (off Providence Rd.)
St Mark's Ho. *LS2: Leeds* *6H 77*
   (off St Mark's Rd.)
St Mark's Pl. BD12: Low M 2C 132
St Mark's Rd. LS2: Leeds 1H 97
   LS6: Leeds 6G 77
   (not continuous)
St Mark's St. LS2: Leeds 1G 97
St Mark's Ter. BD12: Low M 2C 132
St Martins BD7: B'frd 4C 90
   LS7: Leeds 4A 78
   LS21: Otley 1D 22
St Martin's Cres. LS7: Leeds 4B 78
St Martin's Dr. LS7: Leeds 3B 78
St Martin's Fld. LS21: Otley 2D 22
St Martins Fold WF3: Rob H 5F 141
St Martin's Gdns. LS7: Leeds 4A 78
St Martin's Gro. LS7: Leeds 4B 78
St Martin's Rd. LS7: Leeds 4B 78
St Martin's Ter. LS7: Leeds 4B 78
St Martin's Vw. HD6: Brigh 6A 152
   LS7: Leeds 4B 78
St Mary Magdalenes Cl.
   BD8: B'frd 1A 6 (3D 90)
St Mary's Av. BD12: Wyke 5C 132
   LS26: Swil 4A 122
St Marys Cl. BD12: Wyke 5B 132
   LS7: Leeds 4B 78
   LS12: Leeds 5D 96
   LS25: Gar 5F 103
   LS29: I'ly 5E 11
   WF3: W Ard 2C 154
St Mary's Ct. LS7: Leeds 4B 78
   WF10: All B 3H 145
St Mary's Cres. BD12: Wyke 6B 132
St Mary's Dr. BD12: Wyke 5C 132
St Mary's Gdns. BD12: Wyke 5C 132
St Mary's Gth. LS17: E Kes 6D 26
St Mary's Ga. HX5: Ell 4B 160
St Mary's Hall LS9: Leeds 3H 5
St Mary's La. LS9: Leeds 3H 5 (3C 98)
St Mary's Mt. BD12: Wyke 5B 132
St Mary's Pk. App. LS12: Leeds ...3H 95
St Mary's Pk. Ct. LS12: Leeds 3H 95
St Mary's Pk. Cres. LS12: Leeds ..3H 95
St Mary's Pk. Grn. LS12: Leeds ...3H 95
St Mary's Rd. BD4: B'frd 6B 92
   BD8: B'frd 1C 90
   BD9: B'frd 1C 90
   BD20: Rid 3D 34
   LS7: Leeds 4B 78
St Mary's Sq. BD12: Wyke 5C 132
   LS27: Morl 3A 138
St Mary's St. LS9: Leeds 3H 5 (3B 98)
   LS23: B Spa 3B 30
St Mary St. HX1: Hal 5A 164 (3F 149)

St Mary's Wlk. LS25: M'fld 4D 104
St Mathew Way LS14: Leeds 4G 81
St Matthews Cl. BD15: Wils 5F 67
St Matthews Ct. HX3: North 5C 130
St Matthew's Dr. HX3: North 4C 130
St Matthews Gro. BD15: Wils 5G 67
St Matthews Rd. BD5: B'frd 4D 110
St Matthew's St.
    LS11: Leeds 6G 97
St Matthews Wlk. LS7: Leeds 1A 78
St Matthias Ct. LS4: Leeds 1D 96
St Matthias Gro. LS4: Leeds 1D 96
St Matthias Ter. LS4: Leeds 2D 96
    (not continuous)
St Matthias Ter. LS4: Leeds 1D 96
St Michael Ct. LS13: Leeds 6E 75
St Michaels Cl. BD16: Cot 3D 68
St Michael's Ct. LS6: Leeds 4D 76
St Michael's Cres.
    LS6: Leeds 5D 76
St Michael's Gro. LS6: Leeds 5D 76
St Michael's La. LS4: Leeds 6C 76
    LS6: Leeds 5D 76
St Michael's Rd. BD8: B'frd 3C 90
    LS6: Leeds 5D 76
St Michael's Ter. LS6: Leeds 5D 76
St Michael's Vs. LS6: Leeds 5D 76
    (off St Michael's Cres.)
St Michaels Way LS29: Add 2D 8
St Nicholas Rd. LS29: Burl W 3F 21
St Oswalds Cl. LS26: Meth 5C 144
St Oswald's Sth. LS20: Guis 4D 40
St Oswald's Ter. LS20: Guis 4C 40
St Paul's Av. BD6: B'frd 5B 110
    BD11: Birk 2F 135
St Pauls Bldgs. HX5: Ell 5B 160
    (off Langdale St.)
St Paul's Cl. BD8: B'frd 2C 90
    (off Church St.)
St Paul's Gro. BD6: B'frd 5B 110
    LS29: I'ly 5F 11
St Paul's Pl. LS1: Leeds 4C 4 (3H 97)
St Pauls Ri. LS29: Add 2D 8
St Paul's Rd. BD6: B'frd 5B 110
    BD8: B'frd 1C 90
    (not continuous)
    BD11: Birk 2F 135
    BD18: Ship 2A 70
    BD21: Keigh 1B 48
    HX1: Hal 4D 148
St Paul's St. LS1: Leeds 4B 4 (3G 97)
    LS27: Morl 4B 138
St Peter's Av. HX6: Sow B 6E 147
    LS26: Rothw 2B 142
St Peter's Bldgs. LS9: Leeds 4H 5
St Peters Cl. LS21: Otley 3F 23
    WF17: Birs 6H 135
St Peters Ct. LS11: Leeds 1A 118
    LS13: Leeds 6F 75
    LS29: Add 2D 8
St Peter's Cres. LS27: Morl 1A 138
St Peter's Gdns. LS13: Leeds 6E 75
St Peter's Gth. LS14: T'ner 1H 63
St Peter's Mt. LS14: Leeds 1F 95
St Peter's Pl. LS9: Leeds 4H 5 (3B 98)
    LS9: Leeds 4H 5 (3B 98)
St Peter's Sq. HX6: Sow B 6E 147
    LS9: Leeds 4H 5 (3B 98)
St Peter's St. LS2: Leeds 4G 5 (3B 98)
St Peters Vw. LS27: Morl 1A 138
    (off Rooms La.)
St Peter's Way LS29: Men 1F 39
St Philip's Av. LS10: Leeds 2H 139
St Philip's Cl. LS10: Leeds 2H 139
    LS29: Burl W 2F 21
St Philip's Dr. LS29: Burl W 3F 21
St Philip's Way LS29: Burl W 2F 21
St Phillips Ct. BD8: B'frd 2A 90
    (off Thorn St.)
St Richard's Rd. LS21: Otley 1C 22
St Stephen's Ct. BD20: Stee 5C 14
    HX3: Hal 1E 159
    LS9: Leeds 3D 98

St Stephen's Rd. BD5: B'frd 2D 110
    BD20: Stee 6C 14
    LS9: Leeds 3D 98
    LS28: Cal 2E 73
St Stephen's St. HX3: Hal 1E 159
St Stephen's Ter. BD5: B'frd 2E 111
    HX3: Hal 1F 159
Saint St. BD7: B'frd 1A 110
St Thomas Gdns. HD2: Hud 5F 163
St Thomas Row
    LS2: Leeds 2G 5 (2B 98)
St Thomas's Rd.
    BD1: B'frd 3B 6 (4D 90)
St Vincent Ct. LS28: Pud 5A 94
    (off Littlemoor Rd.)
St Vincent Rd. LS28: Pud 5A 94
St Wilfrid's Av. LS8: Leeds 5E 79
    (not continuous)
St Wilfrid's Cir. LS8: Leeds 6F 79
St Wilfrid's Cl. BD7: B'frd 6H 89
St Wilfrid's Cres. BD7: B'frd 6H 89
    LS8: Leeds 5F 79
St Wilfrid's Dr. LS8: Leeds 5E 79
St Wilfrid's Gth. LS8: Leeds 6F 79
St Wilfrid's Gro. LS8: Leeds 5E 79
St Wilfrid's Rd. BD7: B'frd 6H 89
St Wilfrid's St. LS28: Cal 2F 73
St Wilfrids Ter. LS21: Pool 4E 25
    (off Main St.)
St Winifred's Cl. HX2: Illing 2B 128
Salamanca Cres.
    LS10: Leeds 3C 140
Salcombe Pl. BD4: B'frd 3A 112
Salem Pl. LS10: Leeds 6F 5 (5A 98)
    LS25: Gar 4E 103
Salem St. BD1: B'frd 2C 6 (3E 91)
    BD13: Que 4H 107
Salisbury Av. BD17: Bail 4C 52
    LS12: Leeds 3C 96
Salisbury Ct. LS18: H'fth 6F 57
Salisbury Gro. LS12: Leeds 3C 96
Salisbury M. LS18: H'fth 6F 57
    WF3: Ting 6D 138
Salisbury Pl. HX3: Hal 6F 129
    HX3: Hip 1E 151
    LS28: Cal 3E 73
Salisbury Rd. BD9: B'frd 4C 70
    BD12: Low M 1C 132
    BD19: Scho 1F 153
    BD22: Keigh 1G 47
    LS12: Leeds 3C 96
Salisbury St. HX6: Sow B 6G 147
    LS19: Raw 3F 55
    LS28: Cal 3E 73
Salisbury Ter. HX3: Hal 6F 129
    LS12: Leeds 3C 96
Salisbury Vw. LS12: Leeds 3C 96
    LS18: H'fth 6F 57
Salmon Cres. LS18: H'fth 6E 57
Sal Nook Cl. BD12: Low M 6D 110
Sal Royd Rd. BD12: Low M 2E 133
SALTAIRE .1H 69
Saltaire BD22: Cros R 1F 65
Saltaire Brewery 6C 52
Saltaire Rd. BD16: Bgly 2F 51
    BD18: Ship 1H 69
Saltaire Station (Rail) 6H 51
Saltburn Pl. BD9: B'frd 1H 89
Saltburn St. HX1: Hal 2D 148
SALTERHEBBLE 6H 149
Salterhebble Hill HX3: Hal 1H 159
Salterhebble Ter. HX3: Hal 6H 149
    (off Huddersfield Rd.)
Salterlee HX3: North 5A 130
Salters Gdn. LS28: Pud 4A 94
    (off Crawshaw Rd.)
Salt Horn Cl. BD12: O'haw 2F 133
Saltonstall La. HX2: Wain 2D 126
Salts Mill BD18: Ship 6A 52
Salts Mill Rd. BD18: Ship 1A 70
Salt St. BD8: B'frd 2C 90
    HX1: Hal 1E 149
Samara West Mt. LS2: Leeds 2A 4

Sams Yd. LS15: Bar E 2D 82
    (off Elmwood La.)
Samuel St. BD21: Keigh 5H 33
Samuel Way BD18: Ship 1D 70
Sanctuary Way BD16: Bgly 6F 37
Sandacre Cl. BD10: B'frd 6C 72
Sandale Wlk. BD6: B'frd 6H 109
Sandall Cl. LS25: Kip 3H 123
Sandal Magna HX3: She 6G 109
Sandals Mt. BD17: Bail 4C 52
Sandals Rd. BD17: Bail 4C 52
Sandal Ter. HX6: Sow B 6A 148
Sandal Way WF17: Birs 6B 136
Sandalwood M. BD15: All 4C 88
Sandbeck App. LS22: Weth 1E 13
Sandbeck Ct. LS22: Weth 2F 13
Sandbeck Ind. Est. LS22: Weth 2F 13
Sandbeck La. LS22: Weth 2F 13
    (not continuous)
Sandbeck Pk. LS22: Weth 2F 13
Sandbeck Way LS22: Weth 2F 13
Sandbed Ct. LS15: Leeds 6F 81
Sandbed La. LS15: Leeds 6F 81
Sandbed Lawns LS15: Leeds 6F 81
Sandbeds BD13: Cull 4A 66
    BD13: Que 4A 108
Sandbeds Cres. HX2: Hal 6C 128
Sandbeds Rd. HX2: Hal 1B 148
Sandbeds Ter. HX2: Hal 6C 128
Sanderling Ct. BD8: B'frd 4E 89
Sanderling Gth. LS10: Leeds 2B 140
Sanderling Way LS10: Leeds 2B 140
Sanderson Av. BD6: B'frd 4C 110
Sanderson La. LS26: Oul 5C 142
    (not continuous)
Sandfield Av. LS6: Leeds 3E 77
Sandfield Gth. LS6: Leeds 3E 77
Sandfield Rd. BD10: B'frd 3H 71
Sandfield Vw. LS6: Leeds 3E 77
    (off Highbury Mt.)
SANDFORD .5G 75
Sandford Pl. LS5: Leeds 5A 76
Sandford Rd. BD3: B'frd 4A 92
    (not continuous)
    LS5: Leeds 6B 76
Sandforth Av. HX3: Hal 5G 129
Sandgate Dr. LS25: Kip 2H 123
Sandgate La. LS25: Gar, Kip 2A 124
    LS25: Kip 4A 124
    (not continuous)
Sandgate Ri. LS25: Kip 3A 124
Sandgate Ter. LS25: Kip 4A 124
Sandgate Wlk. BD4: B'frd 3D 112
Sandhall Av. HX2: Hal 2B 148
Sandhall Cres. HX2: Hal 2B 148
    (off Sandhall Grn.)
Sandhall Dr. HX2: Hal 2B 148
Sandhall Grn. HX2: Hal 2B 148
    (not continuous)
Sandhall La. HX2: Hal 2B 148
Sandhill Cl. BD8: B'frd 3F 89
Sandhill Ct. LS17: Leeds 4B 60
Sandhill Cres. LS17: Leeds 3C 60
Sandhill Dr. LS17: Leeds 3B 60
Sandhill Fold BD10: B'frd 2G 71
Sandhill Gro. LS17: Leeds 2C 60
Sandhill La. LS17: Leeds 4B 60
Sandhill Lawns LS17: Leeds 4B 60
Sandhill Mt. BD10: B'frd 3H 71
    LS17: Leeds 2C 60
Sandhill Oval LS17: Leeds 2C 60
SANDHILLS .4G 63
Sandholme Cres. HX3: Hip 2F 151
Sandholme Dr. BD10: B'frd 3H 71
    LS29: Burl W 3F 21
Sandholme Fold HX3: Hip 2F 151
Sandhurst Av. LS8: Leeds 6E 79
Sandhurst Gro. LS8: Leeds 6E 79
Sandhurst Mt. LS8: Leeds 5E 79
Sandhurst Pl. LS8: Leeds 6E 79
Sandhurst Rd. LS8: Leeds 6E 79
Sandhurst St. LS28: Cal 2E 73

Sandhurst Ter. LS8: Leeds 6E 79
Sandiford Cl. LS15: Leeds 6F 81
Sandiford Ter. LS15: Leeds 6F 81
Sandleas Way LS15: Leeds 1H 101
Sandlewood Cl. LS11: Leeds 6G 97
Sandlewood Ct. LS6: Leeds 6F 59
Sandlewood Cres. LS6: Leeds 6F 59
Sandlewood Grn. LS11: Leeds 6H 97
Sandmead Cl. BD4: B'frd 2C 112
  LS27: Morl 1A 138
Sandmead Cft. LS27: Morl 1A 138
Sandmead Way LS27: Morl 1A 138
Sandmoor Av. LS17: Leeds 1B 60
Sandmoor Chase LS17: Leeds 2B 60
Sandmoor Cl. BD13: Thorn 5A 88
  LS17: Leeds 2B 60
Sandmoor Ct. LS17: Leeds 2B 60
Sandmoor Dr. LS17: Leeds 1B 60
Sandmoor Gdns. HX3: She 2D 130
Sandmoor Gth. BD10: B'frd 6H 53
Sand Moor Golf Course 1A 60
Sandmoor Grn. LS17: Leeds 1A 60
Sandmoor La. LS17: Leeds 1B 60
Sandmoor M. LS17: Leeds 2B 60
Sandon Gro. LS10: Leeds 3C 118
Sandon Mt. LS10: Leeds 3C 118
Sandon Pl. LS10: Leeds 3C 118
Sandown Av. HX2: Illing 3C 128
Sandown Rd. HX2: Illing 3C 128
Sandpiper App. LS27: Morl 4C 138
Sandpiper M. BD8: B'frd 4E 89
Sandringham App. LS17: Leeds 4C 60
Sandringham Av. LS28: Pud 5A 94
Sandringham Cl. BD14: Clay 6F 89
  LS27: Morl 2C 138
Sandringham Ct. BD14: Clay 6F 89
  HD2: Hud 6D 162
  LS17: Leeds 3B 60
Sandringham Cres. LS17: Leeds 4B 60
Sandringham Dr. LS17: Leeds 4B 60
  WF3: W Ard 2F 155
Sandringham Fold LS27: Morl 2C 138
Sandringham Gdns. LS17: Leeds 4B 60
Sandringham Grn. LS17: Leeds 3C 60
Sandringham Ho. LS17: Leeds 2B 60
Sandringham Mt. LS17: Leeds 4C 60
Sandringham Rd. BD14: Clay 6F 89
  LS22: Weth 3E 13
Sandringham Way LS17: Leeds 4B 60
Sandsend Cl. BD9: B'frd 6F 69
Sandside Cl. BD5: B'frd 3F 111
Sandstone Dr. LS12: Leeds 4E 95
Sand St. BD21: Keigh 5A 34
  BD22: Haw 3C 64
Sandway LS15: Leeds 1D 100
Sandway Gdns. LS15: Leeds 1D 100
Sandway Gro. LS15: Leeds 1D 100
Sandyacres LS26: Rothw 1B 142
Sandyacres Cres. LS26: Rothw 1B 142
Sandyacres Dr. LS26: Rothw 1B 142
Sandy Bank Av. LS26: Rothw 1B 142
Sandy Banks BD16: Har 1F 67
Sandy Beck BD15: All 6B 68
Sandyfoot HX4: Bark 6A 158
Sandy Fore HX2: Mt T 3F 127
Sandy Ga. BD20: Keigh 5G 33
Sandygate Ter. BD4: B'frd 6B 92
Sandy Gro. LS26: Rothw 1B 142
SANDY LANE 5C 68
Sandy Lobby LS12: Pool 5E 25
Sandymoor BD15: All 5C 68
Sandy Wlk. LS16: B'hpe 3H 43
Sandy Way LS19: Yead 6F 41
Sandywood Cl. LS18: H'fth 2E 75
Sandywood St. BD21: Keigh 5A 34
Sangster Way BD5: B'frd 4G 111
Santa Monica Cres. BD10: B'frd 2G 71
Santa Monica Gro. BD10: B'frd 2G 71
Santa Monica Rd. BD10: B'frd 2G 71
Santorini LS12: Leeds 5A 4 (4G 97)
Sapgate La. BD13: Thorn 5A 88
Sapling Gro. Cotts. HX2: Hal 5D 148
Saplin St. BD8: B'frd 2B 90

Sarah St. WF3: E Ard 1B 156
Sardinia St. LS10: Leeds 6B 98
Savannah Way LS10: Leeds 5F 119
Savile Av. LS7: Leeds 6B 78
Savile Cl. HD6: Clift 6D 152
Savile Cres. HX1: Hal 6A 164 (3F 149)
Savile Dr. HX1: Hal 6A 164 (4F 149)
  LS7: Leeds 5B 78
Savile Glen HX1: Hal 6A 164 (3F 149)
Savile Grn. HX1: Hal 6B 164 (3G 149)
Savile La. HD6: Clift 6D 152
Savile Lea HX1: Hal 6A 164 (3F 149)
Savile M. HX1: Hal 4F 149
Savile Mt. HX1: Hal 6A 164 (4F 149)
  LS7: Leeds 6B 78
Savile Pde. HX1: Hal 4F 149
SAVILE PARK 4E 149
Savile Pk. HX1: Hal 4E 149
  HX3: Hal 5F 149
Savile Pk. Gdns. HX1: Hal 4F 149
Savile Pk. Mills HX1: Hal 4F 149
       (off Moorfield St.)
Savile Pk. Rd. BD19: Hun 4F 149
  HX1: Hal 6A 164 (4F 149)
Savile Pk. St. HX1: Hal 4E 149
Savile Pk. Ter. HX1: Hal 4E 149
       (off Moorfield St.)
Savile Pl. LS7: Leeds 6B 78
Savile Rd. HX1: Hal 6A 164 (3F 149)
  HX5: Ell 5B 160
  LS7: Leeds 6B 78
  LS26: Meth 4D 144
Savile Row HX1: Hal 5A 164 (3F 149)
Savile Royd HX1: Hal 6A 164 (4F 149)
Savile St. BD19: Cleck 6B 134
Savile Ter. HX1: Hal 4E 149
       (off Haugh Shaw Rd.)
Savile Way HX5: Ell 3C 160
Saville Cl. WF3: Loft 6G 141
Saville Ct. LS21: Otley 4D 22
Saville Grange HX3: Hal 5F 149
Saville Grn. LS9: Leeds 3D 98
Saville Pk. HX1: Hal 4D 148
Saville's Sq. LS27: Morl 3A 138
       (off Queen St.)
Savins Mill Way LS5: Leeds 5A 76
Savoy Ct. LS28: Stan 2H 93
Sawley St. BD21: Keigh 1H 47
Saw Mill La. LS29: Add 1E 9
Saw Mill St. LS11: Leeds 5H 97
Saw Mill Yd. LS11: Leeds 5H 97
SAWOOD 2F 85
Sawood La. BD22: Oxen 2F 85
Sawrey Pl. BD5: B'frd 6B 6 (5D 90)
Sawyers Gth. LS29: Add 1E 9
Saxilby Rd. BD20: E Mor, Rid 4F 35
Saxon Ct. BD12: Wyke 4B 132
  LS17: Leeds 4H 59
Saxon Ga. LS17: Leeds 5H 59
Saxon Grn. LS17: Leeds 5G 59
Saxon Gro. LS17: Leeds 4G 59
Saxon Mt. LS17: Leeds 4H 59
Saxon Rd. LS17: Leeds 5G 59
Saxon St. BD8: B'frd 3C 90
  HX1: Hal 2D 148
Saxstead Ri. LS12: Leeds 5C 96
Saxton LS9: Leeds 4C 98
Saxton Av. BD6: B'frd 4G 109
Saxton Ct. LS25: Gar 3F 103
Saxton Gdns. LS9: Leeds 4C 98
       (off The Avenue)
Saxton Ho. LS19: Yead 1F 55
Saxton La. LS9: Leeds 5H 5 (4C 98)
Sayers Cl. LS5: Leeds 5B 76
Sayle Av. BD4: B'frd 4H 111
Sayner La. LS10: Leeds 5B 98
Sayner Rd. LS10: Leeds 5B 98
Scala Ct. LS10: Leeds 6B 98
Scalebor Pk. Cl. LS29: Burl W 3E 21
Scalebor Sq. LS29: Burl W 3D 20
Scales La. BD4: B'frd 6A 112
Scaley St. BD3: B'frd 4B 92
Scampston Dr. WF3: E Ard 6B 140

Scandinavia Ter. BD19: Cleck 6B 134
Scarborough Gro. BD18: Ship 2A 70
Scarborough Junc. 2E 95
  LS13: Leeds 2E 95
Scarborough La. WF3: Ting 1D 154
Scarborough Rd. BD18: Ship 2A 70
  LS21: Otley 4D 22
Scarborough St. WF3: Ting 6D 138
Scarborough Ter. HX5: Ell 5B 160
SCAR BOTTOM 5E 45
Scar Bottom La. HX4: Gree 4D 158
SCARCROFT 5E 45
Scarcroft Ct. LS14: S'cft 5F 45
Scarcroft Golf Course 5D 44
Scarcroft Vw. LS17: Leeds 1B 62
SCARCROFT HILL 6G 45
Scargill Bldgs. LS27: Morl 3D 138
Scargill Cl. LS9: Leeds 2D 98
Scargill Grange LS9: Leeds 3D 98
Scar Head HX6: Sow B 6H 147
Scar Head Rd.
  HX6: Sow B 6H 147
SCARLET HEIGHTS 4B 108
Scarlet Hgts. BD13: Que 4B 108
Scarr & Long Wood Nature Reserve
  . . . . .6E 149
Scarr Bottom Rd. HX2: Hal 5D 148
Scarsdale La. LS17: Bard 5G 27
Scarsdale Ridge LS17: Bard 5G 27
Scarth Av. LS9: Leeds 1E 99
Scar Top HX4: Gree 4D 158
       (not continuous)
Scarwood Cl. BD16: Bgly 3C 50
Scatcherd Gro. LS27: Morl 3H 137
Scatcherd La. LS27: Morl 4H 137
Scatcherd Pk. Av. LS27: Morl 2A 138
Scatcherd's Bldgs. LS27: Morl 1A 138
Schofield Cl. LS27: Morl 3A 138
       (off Queenscourt)
Scholars Ga. LS25: Gar 6E 103
Scholars Wlk. BD2: B'frd 6H 71
Scholars Way BD20: Rid 3D 34
  LS15: Leeds 5G 101
Scholebroke La. LS28: Pud 2G 113
SCHOLEBROOK 2G 113
Scholebrook Ct. BD4: B'frd 4C 112
       (off Broadfield Cl.)
Scholebrook La. BD4: B'frd 2G 113
SCHOLEMOOR 6H 89
Scholemoor Av. BD7: B'frd 6G 89
Scholemoor Crematorium
  BD7: B'frd 5G 89
Scholemoor La. BD7: B'frd 6G 89
Scholemoor Rd. BD7: B'frd 6H 89
SCHOLES
  BD19 . . . . .1F 153
  BD22 . . . . .6A 46
  LS15 . . . . .3H 81
Scholes La. BD19: Scho 1F 153
  HX4: Gree 2E 159
  LS15: Leeds 1G 81
Scholes Lodge La.
  LS15: Scho 4A 82
Scholes St. BD5: B'frd 3D 110
Scholey Av. HD6: Ras 3A 162
SCHOLEY HILL 6A 144
Scholey Rd. HD6: Ras 3A 162
School Cl. HX2: Illing 6D 106
  LS12: N Far 2F 115
School Cote Brow HX3: Hal 1F 129
School Cote Ter. HX3: Hal 1F 129
School Cres. HX2: Illing 6D 106
School Cft. LS26: Rothw 1A 142
School Fold BD12: Low M 1B 132
Schoolgate LS15: Bar E 2E 83
SCHOOL GREEN 5C 88
School Grn. BD13: Thorn 5C 88
  HD6: Ras 3A 162
  LS16: B'hpe 3G 43
School Grn. Av.
  BD13: Thorn 5B 88
School Ho. HX3: North 4C 130
School Ho. Fold BD20: Rid 3D 34

School La. BD5: B'frd 3C 110
   BD6: B'frd 4B 110
   BD21: Keigh 6B 34
   HX2: Brad, Illing 1D 128
   HX3: Sou 6C 150
   (not continuous)
   LS6: Leeds 3E 77
   LS7: Leeds 2A 78
   LS15: Leeds 5G 101
   (Colton Rd. E.)
   LS15: Leeds 3C 100
   (Pinfold Gro.)
   LS17: E Kes 6E 27
   LS22: Coll 3B 28
   LS29: Add 1C 8
School M. LS12: Leeds 4C 96
School Pl. BD12: Wyke 3C 132
School Ridge BD13: Thorn 3G 87
School Rd. BD22: Keigh 6F 33
   LS22: Weth 3F 13
School Sq. BD3: B'frd 4B 92
School St. BD1: B'frd 3D 6 (4E 91)
   BD4: B'frd 2A 112
   (Cutler Hgts. La.)
   BD4: B'frd 6G 109
   (Shetcliffe Rd.)
   BD6: B'frd 6G 109
   BD12: Low M 1C 132
   BD12: O'haw 3G 133
   BD13: Cull 3B 66
   BD13: Denh 3C 86
   BD14: Clay 1D 108
   BD15: Wils 4G 67
   BD16: Cot 2D 68
   BD19: Cleck 3H 153
   BD20: Keigh 3G 33
   BD20: Stee 6C 14
   HX1: Hal 5D 164 (3H 149)
   HX4: Gree 3F 159
   LS27: Chur 5C 116
   LS27: Morl 3B 138
   LS28: Fars 6H 73
   LS28: Pud 5H 93
   (not continuous)
   WF3: W Ard 4D 154
   WF17: Birs 6B 136
School Ter. BD19: Scho 1F 153
   LS25: Gar 3G 103
School Vw. LS6: Leeds 6E 77
School Wlk. BD22: Keigh 6F 33
School Yd. Vw. HX3: Hal 6G 129
Sconce La. BD16: Bgly 5A 38
   BD17: Bail 5A 38
Score Hill HX3: North 3C 130
Scoresby St. BD1: B'frd . . .4F 7 (4F 91)
Scotchman Cl. LS27: Morl 5H 137
Scotchman La. LS27: Morl 6G 137
Scotchman Rd. BD9: B'frd 1H 89
Scotch Pk. Trad. Est. LS12: Leeds . . .3D 96
SCOTLAND 2D 56
Scotland HX2: Midg 5C 126
Scotland Cl. LS18: H'fth 4D 56
Scotland La. HX2: Midg 5B 126
   LS18: H'fth 5C 42
Scotland Mill La. LS6: Leeds 5F 59
   LS17: Leeds 5F 59
Scotland St. WF17: Birs 5G 135
Scotland Way LS18: H'fth 3C 56
Scotland Wood Rd. LS17: Leeds 5F 59
Scott Cl. LS26: Swil 4A 122
SCOTT GREEN 6D 114
Scott Grn. LS27: Gil 5D 114
Scott Grn. Cres. LS27: Gil 5D 114
Scott Grn. Dr. LS27: Gil 5D 114
Scott Grn. Gro. LS27: Gil 5E 115
Scott Grn. Mt. LS27: Gil 5D 114
Scott Grn. Vw. LS27: Gil 5E 115
SCOTT HALL 4A 78
Scott Hall Av. LS7: Leeds 4A 78
Scott Hall Cres. LS7: Leeds 3H 77
Scott Hall Dr. LS7: Leeds 5A 78
Scott Hall Grn. LS7: Leeds 4A 78
Scott Hall Gro. LS7: Leeds 4A 78

Scott Hall Pl. LS7: Leeds 4A 78
Scott Hall Rd. LS7: Leeds 6A 60
   LS17: Leeds 6A 60
Scott Hall Sports Cen. 3A 78
Scott Hall Sq. LS7: Leeds 4A 78
Scott Hall St. LS7: Leeds 5A 78
Scott Hall Ter. LS7: Leeds 5A 78
Scott Hall Wlk. LS7: Leeds 5A 78
Scott Hall Way LS7: Leeds 3A 78
Scott La. BD19: Gom 6F 135
   BD20: Rid 3C 34
   LS22: Weth 4E 13
   LS27: Morl 5F 137
Scott La. W. BD20: Rid 3B 34
Scott M. LS22: Weth 4E 13
Scotts Almshouse's
   LS10: Leeds 4C 118
Scotts Bldgs. LS6: Leeds 3D 76
   (off Mansfield Pl.)
Scotts Hill Cl. LS14: T'ner 2H 63
Scott St. BD6: B'frd 5D 110
   BD21: Keigh 6H 33
   LS28: Pud 5B 94
Scott Wood La. LS7: Leeds 4H 77
Scotty Bank HD6: Ras 1A 162
Scotty Cft. La. HD6: Ras 2A 162
   (off Bramston St.)
Scotty La. BD8: B'frd 2C 90
   (off Carlisle Rd.)
Scout Bottom La. HX7: Myth 1A 146
Scout Rd. HX2: Lud M 1A 146
   HX7: Myth 1A 146
Scriftain La. LS22: K Dei 1E 13
Sculptor Pl. HD6: Brigh 6A 152
   (off Waterloo Rd.)
SDH Ind. Est. HX6: Sow B 6H 147
SEACROFT .4C 80
Seacroft Av. LS14: Leeds 4D 80
Seacroft Cres. LS14: Leeds 4D 80
Seacroft Ga. LS14: Leeds 4D 80
   (not continuous)
Seacroft Ind. Est. LS14: Leeds 1D 80
   (not continuous)
Seaforth Av. LS9: Leeds 6E 79
Seaforth Gro. LS9: Leeds 6E 79
Seaforth Mt. LS9: Leeds 6E 79
Seaforth Pl. LS9: Leeds 6E 79
Seaforth Rd. LS9: Leeds 6E 79
Seaforth Ter. LS9: Leeds 6E 79
Seaton St. BD3: B'frd 4H 7 (4H 91)
Second Av. BD3: B'frd 2A 92
   BD21: Keigh 1H 47
   HX3: Hal 5F 149
   LS12: Leeds 4E 97
   LS17: Bard 6G 27
   LS19: Raw 2G 55
   LS22: Weth 4F 13
   LS26: Rothw 6B 120
   WF1: Wake 6F 157
   WF15: Liv 5H 153
Second St. BD12: Low M 1E 133
Sedan St. HX1: Hal 5B 164
Sedbergh Cl. BD10: B'frd 3B 72
   LS15: Leeds 4A 100
Sedbergh Dr. LS29: I'ly 6E 11
Sedbergh Pk. LS29: I'ly 6D 10
Sedbergh Rd. HX1: Hal 4H 149
   HX3: Hal 4H 149
Sedgegarth LS14: T'ner 1H 63
Sedge Gro. BD22: Haw 1C 64
Sedgewick St. WF17: Birs 6A 136
Sedgwick Cl. BD8: B'frd 2A 6 (3D 90)
Sedfield Ter. BD1: B'frd 3A 6 (4D 90)
Seed Hill Ter. BD20: Stee 6D 14
Seed Row BD4: B'frd 5H 111
Seed St. BD12: Low M 1D 132
See Mill La. HX3: Hal 5F 129
Sefton Av. HD6: Brigh 4H 151
   LS11: Leeds 2G 117
Sefton Ct. LS6: Leeds 3D 76
Sefton Cres. HD6: Brigh 4H 151

Sefton Dr. HD6: Brigh 4H 151
   LS29: I'ly 6D 10
Sefton Gro. BD2: B'frd 6H 71
Sefton Pl. BD2: B'frd 6H 71
   BD21: Keigh 5A 34
Sefton St. BD21: Keigh 5A 34
   HX1: Hal 1E 149
   LS11: Leeds 2H 117
Sefton Ter. HX1: Hal 1E 149
   LS11: Leeds 2G 117
Selborne Gro. BD9: B'frd 6B 70
   BD21: Keigh 2G 47
Selborne Mt. BD9: B'frd 1C 90
Selborne Ter. BD9: B'frd 1B 90
   BD18: Ship 3B 70
Selborne Vs. BD9: B'frd 1B 90
   (off Selborne Gro.)
   BD14: Clay 2E 109
Selby HX2: Illing 1B 128
Selby Av. LS9: Leeds 3A 100
Selby Rd. LS9: Leeds 3A 100
   LS15: Leeds, Swil C 3C 100
   LS25: Gar, M'fld 6D 102
Seldon St. BD5: B'frd 2B 110
Select Ct. LS28: Fars 5H 73
Selene Cl. BD19: Gom 5G 135
SELLARS FOLD 1A 110
Sellerdale Av. BD12: Wyke 6D 132
Sellerdale Dr. BD12: Wyke 5D 132
Sellerdale Ri. BD12: Wyke 6D 132
Sellerdale Way BD12: Wyke 6D 132
Sellers Fold BD7: B'frd 1A 110
Selside Ho. BD10: B'frd 1A 72
   (off Woodfield Cl.)
Seminary St. LS2: Leeds 1B 4 (2G 97)
Semon Av. BD2: B'frd 4F 71
Senior Way BD5: B'frd 6C 6 (5E 91)
   (not continuous)
Serin Wlk. BD6: B'frd 4F 109
Servia Dr. LS7: Leeds 6A 78
Servia Gdns. LS7: Leeds 6A 78
   LS7: Leeds 6H 77
Servia Hill LS6: Leeds 6H 77
   LS7: Leeds 6H 77
Servia Rd. LS7: Leeds 6H 77
Service Rd. LS9: Leeds 2G 119
Seven Acres BD13: Denh 3B 86
Seven Hills Point LS27: Morl 2B 138
Sevenoaks Mead BD15: All 2D 88
Seventh Av. LS26: Rothw 6C 120
   WF15: Liv 4H 153
Severn Dr. LS25: Gar 6H 103
Severn Rd. BD2: B'frd 6G 71
   LS10: Leeds 2D 118
Severn Way LS10: Leeds 1D 118
Sewage Works Rd.
   LS9: Leeds 2G 119
Sewell Rd. BD3: B'frd 5H 91
Seymour St. BD3: B'frd 5H 7 (5G 91)
Shackleton Ter. BD16: Har 6E 49
SHADWELL .3B 62
Shadwell La. LS17: Leeds 5B 60
Shadwell Pk. Av. LS17: Leeds 2G 61
Shadwell Pk. Cl. LS17: Shad 2G 61
Shadwell Pk. Ct. LS17: Shad 3G 61
Shadwell Pk. Dr. LS17: Shad 3G 61
Shadwell Pk. Gdns.
   LS17: Shad 2G 61
Shadwell Pk. Gro. LS17: Shad 3G 61
Shadwell Wlk. LS17: Leeds 4C 60
Shaftesbury Av. BD9: B'frd 1F 89
   BD18: Ship 2C 70
   HD6: Ras 4B 162
   LS8: Leeds 6E 61
Shaftesbury Ct. BD9: B'frd 2F 89
Shaftesbury Pde. LS9: Leeds 2G 99
Shaftesbury Rd. LS8: Leeds 5E 61
Shafton La. LS11: Leeds 6F 97
Shafton Pl. LS11: Leeds 6F 97
Shafton St. LS11: Leeds 6F 97
Shafton Vw. LS11: Leeds 6F 97
Shakespeare App.
   LS9: Leeds 2D 98
Shakespeare Av. LS9: Leeds 2D 98

Shakespeare Cl.—Sholebroke Mt.

Shakespeare Cl.
BD3: B'frd 2H **7** (3G **91**)
LS9: Leeds 2D **98**
LS20: Guis 5D **40**
Shakespeare Ct. *LS9: Leeds 2D 98*
(off Shakespeare App.)
Shakespeare Gdns. LS9: Leeds 2D **98**
Shakespeare Grange LS9: Leeds 2D **98**
Shakespeare Lawn LS9: Leeds 2D **98**
Shakespeare Rd. LS20: Guis 5C **40**
Shakespeare St.
HX1: Hal 4C **164** (3G **149**)
LS9: Leeds 1D **98**
Shakespeare Towers LS9: Leeds 1D **98**
Shakespeare Va. LS9: Leeds 2D **98**
Shakespeare Wlk. LS9: Leeds 2D **98**
Shalimar St. HX1: Hal 2D **148**
Shambles, The LS22: Weth 4E **13**
Shancara Ct. WF3: Ting 6E **139**
Shann Av. BD21: Keigh 5F **33**
Shann Cres. BD21: Keigh 5F **33**
Shann La. BD20: Keigh 5F **33**
Shannon Cl. HD6: Ras 4G **161**
LS29: I'ly 6B **10**
Shannon Rd. HD6: Ras 4G **161**
LS9: Leeds 3C **98**
Shannon St. LS9: Leeds 3C **98**
Shann St. BD2: B'frd 5D **70**
Shapla Cl. BD22: Keigh 1G **47**
Sharket Head Cl. BD13: Que 4A **108**
Sharp Av. BD6: B'frd 5C **110**
Sharpe St. BD5: B'frd 6C **6** (5E **91**)
Sharp Ho. Pl. LS10: Leeds 3D **140**
Sharp Ho. Rd. LS10: Leeds 3C **140**
Sharp La. LS10: Leeds 2C **140**
(Dolphin Rd.)
LS10: Leeds 2B **140**
(Dunlin Dr.)
WF3: Rob H, Thpe H 2C **140**
Sharp M. LS6: Leeds 4F **77**
Sharp Row LS28: Pud 5A **94**
Sharp St. BD6: B'frd 4C **110**
SHAW 1B **84**
Shaw Barn Cft. LS22: Weth 4C **12**
Shaw Barn La. LS22: Weth 4C **12**
Shaw Booth La. HX2: Wain 3F **127**
Shaw Cl. HX4: Holy 6G **159**
LS20: Guis 5D **40**
LS25: Gar 6G **103**
SHAW CROSS 6A **154**
Shaw Hill HX1: Hal 4G **149**
Shaw Hill La. HX3: Hal 4H **149**
SHAW LANE 5E **41**
Shaw La. BD13: North 1B **130**
BD21: Keigh 5B **48**
BD22: Oxen 1B **84**
HX3: Hal 4H **149**
HX5: Ell 3E **161**
HX6: Norl 2A **158**
LS6: Leeds 4D **76**
LS20: Guis 4D **40**
Shaw La. Gdns. LS20: Guis 4D **40**
Shaw Leys LS19: Yead 5E **41**
Shaw Lodge HX1: Hal 4H **149**
Shaw Mt. HX2: Lud M 1E **147**
Shaw Royd LS19: Yead 5E **41**
Shaw Royd Ct. *LS19: Yead 5E 41*
(off Shaw Royd)
Shaws La. LS15: Bar E 3C **82**
Shaw St. BD12: Low M 1B **132**
BD19: Cleck 2H **153**
HX4: Holy 6G **159**
Shaw Vs. *LS20: Guis 4D 40*
(off Queensway)
Shay, The 6C **164** (4G **149**)
SHAY BROW 6B **68**
Shay Cl. BD9: B'frd 5H **69**
Shay Ct. LS6: Leeds 6H **77**
Shay Cres. BD9: B'frd 5G **69**
Shay Dr. BD9: B'frd 5G **69**
Shayfield La. WF3: Carl, Loft 5G **141**
Shay Fold BD9: B'frd 5G **69**
Shay Gap Rd. BD22: Lay 1C **46**
Shay Ga. BD15: Wils 5A **68**
Shay Grange BD9: B'frd 4G **69**
Shay Grange Golf Course 5G **69**
Shay Gro. BD9: B'frd 5H **69**
Shay La. BD4: B'frd 2D **112**
BD9: B'frd 4G **69**
BD15: Wils 4H **67**
HX2: Hal 4E **129**
HX3: Hal 4E **129**
Shay St. LS6: Leeds 6H **77**
Shay Syke HX1: Hal 6D **164** (3H **149**)
Sheaf St. LS10: Leeds 5B **98**
SHEARBRIDGE 5B **90**
Shearbridge Pl. BD7: B'frd 5C **90**
Shearbridge Rd. BD7: B'frd 5C **90**
Shearbridge Ter. BD7: B'frd 6C **90**
Shearers Ho. LS9: Leeds 6H **5**
Shearing Path LS29: Add 1C **8**
Shear's Yd. LS2: Leeds 5G **5** (4B **98**)
Shed St. BD21: Keigh 6A **34**
Sheep Hill La. BD13: Que 3D **108**
SHEEPSCAR 6B **78**
Sheepscar Ct. LS7: Leeds 1B **98**
Sheepscar Gro. LS7: Leeds 1G **5** (2B **98**)
Sheepscar Row LS7: Leeds 1B **98**
Sheepscar St. Nth. LS7: Leeds 6A **78**
Sheepscar St. Sth.
LS7: Leeds 1H **5** (1B **98**)
Sheepscar Way LS7: Leeds 6B **78**
Sheila Henry Dr. BD6: B'frd 3E **109**
Shelby Grange BD10: B'frd 3A **72**
Sheldon Ridge BD4: B'frd 6H **111**
Sheldrake Av. BD8: B'frd 4E **89**
SHELF 2E **131**
Shelf Hall La. HX3: She 2D **130**
Shelf Moor HX3: She 6E **109**
Shelf Moor Rd. HX3: She 6E **109**
Shelldrake Dr. LS10: Leeds 2B **140**
Shelley Cl. LS26: Oul 4E **143**
Shelley Ct. BD16: Bgly 3C **50**
Shelley Cres. LS26: Oul 4E **143**
Shelley Gro. BD8: B'frd 3G **89**
Shell La. LS28: Cal 3F **73**
Shelton Ct. BD13: Denh 2C **86**
Shepcote Cl. LS16: Leeds 4H **57**
Shepcote Cres. LS16: Leeds 4H **57**
Shepherds Cft. BD22: Haw 2D **64**
Shepherds Fold HX3: North 4B **130**
Shepherd's Gro. LS7: Leeds 5C **78**
Shepherd's La. LS7: Leeds 5C **78**
LS8: Leeds 5C **78**
Shepherd's Pl. LS8: Leeds 5D **78**
Shepherds Thorn La.
HD2: Brigh, Hud 4B **162**
HD6: Ras 4B **162**
Shepherd St. BD7: B'frd 1A **110**
Shepton Apartments *BD5: B'frd 6E 91*
(off Park Rd.)
Sherborne Dr. BD22: Keigh 2E **47**
Sherborne Rd. BD7: B'frd 6A **6** (5D **90**)
BD10: B'frd 6H **53**
Sherbourne Dr. LS6: Leeds 6E **59**
Sherbrooke Av. LS15: Leeds 4B **100**
Sherburn App. LS14: Leeds 3E **81**
Sherburn Cl. BD11: Birk 1F **135**
LS14: Leeds 3E 81
(off Sherburn App.)
Sherburn Ct. *LS14: Leeds 3E 81*
(off Sherburn App.)
Sherburn Gro. BD11: Birk 1F **135**
Sherburn Pl. LS14: Leeds 3E **81**
Sherburn Rd. HD6: Ras 3F **161**
LS14: Leeds 3E **81**
Sherburn Rd. Nth. LS14: Leeds 1D **80**
Sherburn Row *LS14: Leeds 3E 81*
(off Sherburn App.)
Sherburn Sq. *LS14: Leeds 3E 81*
(off Sherburn Pl.)
Sherburn Wlk. *LS14: Leeds 3E 81*
(off Sherburn App.)
Sheridan Cl. LS28: Pud 5B **94**
Sheridan Ct. LS28: Pud 5B **94**
Sheridan Ho. LS27: Gil 1E **137**
Sheridan St. BD4: B'frd 1G **111**
WF1: Out 4G **157**
Sheridan Way LS28: Pud 5B **94**
Sheriff Ct. BD16: Bgly 2E **51**
Sheriff La. BD16: Bgly 2E **51**
Sherwell Gro. BD15: All 2E **89**
Sherwell Ri. BD15: All 2E **89**
Sherwood Av. HD2: Hud 6F **163**
Sherwood Cl. BD16: Bgly 2E **51**
Sherwood Gdns. WF3: Loft 5F **141**
Sherwood Grn. WF3: Rob H 4E **141**
Sherwood Gro. BD18: Ship 1G **69**
Sherwood Ind. Est. WF3: Rob H 4F **141**
Sherwood Pl. BD2: B'frd 1H **91**
Sherwood Rd. HD6: Brigh 1C **162**
Sherwood Wlk. LS10: Leeds 3C **140**
Sherwood Way LS26: Wood 6D **120**
Sherwood Works HD6: Brigh 2D **162**
Shetcliffe La. BD4: B'frd 5H **111**
Shetcliffe Rd. BD4: B'frd 5H **111**
Shetland Cl. BD2: B'frd 5F **71**
Shibden Fold HX3: Hal 6A **130**
Shibden Gth. HX3: Hip 2C **150**
Shibden Grange Dr. HX3: Hal 6B **130**
Shibden Hall 1B **150**
Shibden Hall Cft. HX3: Hal 1C **150**
Shibden Hall Folk Mus. 1B **150**
Shibden Hall Rd. HX3: Hal 1A **150**
SHIBDEN HEAD 6G **107**
Shibden Head Ct. BD13: Que 6G **107**
Shibden Head La. BD13: Que 6G **107**
Shibden Mill Fold HX3: North 4A **130**
Shibden Park 1B **150**
Shibden Park & Cunnery Wood Nature Reserve 1B **150**
Shibden Vw. BD13: Que 6H **107**
Shield Cl. LS15: Leeds 6G **81**
Shield Hall La. HX6: Sow B 5C **146**
SHIPLEY 2B **70**
Shipley Airedale Rd.
BD1: B'frd 5F **7** (5F **91**)
BD3: B'frd 2E **7** (3F **91**)
Shipley Flds. Rd. BD18: Ship 4B **70**
(not continuous)
Shipley Glen Cable Tramway 5H **51**
Shipley Golf Course 6B **50**
Shipley Lanes 2B **70**
Shipley Station (Rail) 2B **70**
Shipley Swimming Pool 2A **70**
Ship St. HD6: Brigh 1B **162**
Shipton M. LS27: Morl 4B **138**
Ship Yd. LS1: Leeds 4E **5**
Shire Cl. BD6: B'frd 6H **109**
LS27: Morl 5B **138**
Shire Ct. LS27: Morl 6B **138**
Shiredene LS6: Leeds 4E **77**
Shire Gro. LS27: Morl 6A **138**
Shire Oak Rd. LS6: Leeds 4E **77**
Shire Oak St. LS6: Leeds 4D **76**
Shire Rd. LS27: Morl 5B **138**
Shires Bus. Pk. BD7: B'frd 6A **90**
Shires Ct. LS23: B Spa 3C **30**
Shires Rd. LS20: Guis 5C **40**
Shirley Av. BD12: Wyke 6B **132**
WF17: Birs 5H **135**
Shirley Cl. LS21: Otley 4F **23**
Shirley Cres. BD12: Wyke 6B **132**
Shirley Dr. LS13: Leeds 5E **75**
Shirley Gro. BD19: Gom 6F **135**
HX3: Hip 2A **152**
Shirley Mnr. Gdns. BD12: Wyke 6B **132**
Shirley Pl. BD12: Wyke 6C **132**
Shirley Rd. BD4: B'frd 4B **112**
BD7: B'frd 5B **90**
BD19: Gom 6F **135**
Shirley St. BD13: Denh 2C **86**
BD18: Ship 1H **69**
BD22: Haw 2B **64**
Shoebridge Av. BD20: East 5A **14**
Sholebroke Av. LS7: Leeds 5B **78**
Sholebroke Ct. LS7: Leeds 5B **78**
Sholebroke Mt. LS7: Leeds 5A **78**

Sholebroke Pl. LS7: Leeds 5B 78
Sholebroke St. LS7: Leeds 5A 78
Sholebroke Ter. LS7: Leeds 4B 78
Sholebroke Vw. LS7: Leeds 5B 78
Shone Ct. LS27: Morl 5B 138
Shop La. WF3: Loft 1F 157
Shoreham Rd. LS12: Leeds 4C 96
Short Cl. BD12: Wyke 2B 132
Short La. LS7: Leeds 2A 78
Short Row BD12: Low M 1D 132
Shortway BD13: Thorn 5C 88
   LS28: Stan 2E 93
Showcase Cinema
   Birstall 3D 136
Shrike Cl. BD6: B'frd 4E 109
Shroggs, The BD20: Stee 6C 14
Shroggs Rd. HX3: Hal 1A 164 (5D 128)
Shroggs St. HX1: Hal 1E 149
Shroggs Vue Ter. HX1: Hal 1E 149
Shuttle Fold BD22: Haw 1D 64
Shuttleworth La. BD8: B'frd 3G 89
Shuttocks Cl. LS25: Kip 2G 123
Shuttocks Fold LS25: Kip 2H 123
Shutts, The LS26: Rothw 2G 141
Shutts La. HX3: Nor G 5G 131
Sickleholme Ct. HD2: Hud 6E 163
Sicklinghall Rd. LS22: Weth 4A 12
SIDDAL 6A 150
Siddal Gro. HX3: Hal 5H 149
Siddal La. HX3: Hal 5A 150
Siddall St. LS11: Leeds 5H 97
Siddal New Rd. HX3: Hal 4H 149
Siddal Pl. HX3: Hal 6A 150
Siddal St. HX3: Hal 6A 150
Siddal Top La. HX3: Hal 5A 150
Siddal Vw. HX3: Hal 5A 150
Side Copse LS21: Otley 3F 23
Sidings, The BD18: Ship 1C 70
   LS20: Guis .4B 40
Sidings Cl. BD2: B'frd 6D 70
Sidney St. LS1: Leeds 4F 5 (3A 98)
Siegen Cl. LS27: Morl 3A 138
Siegen Mnr. LS27: Morl 3A 138
   (off Wesley St.)
Siegfried Wlk. BD16: Bgly 3E 51
Silk Mill App. LS16: Leeds 5G 57
Silk Mill Av. LS16: Leeds 4F 57
Silk Mill Bank LS16: Leeds 5F 57
Silk Mill Cl. LS16: Leeds 4F 57
Silk Mill Dr. BD20: E Mor 4A 36
   LS16: Leeds 5F 57
Silk Mill Gdns. LS16: Leeds 5F 57
Silk Mill Grn. LS16: Leeds 5G 57
Silk Mill M. LS16: Leeds 5H 57
Silk Mill Rd. LS16: Leeds 5F 57
Silk Mill Way LS16: Leeds 5G 57
Silkstone Cl. LS25: Gar 2H 103
Silkstone Ct. LS15: Leeds 2E 101
Silkstone Rd. BD3: B'frd 4H 91
Silkstone Sq. WF10: All B 3H 145
Silkstone Way LS15: Leeds 2E 101
Silk St. BD9: B'frd 1A 90
Silk Warehouse BD9: B'frd 1B 90
Silsbridge St. BD1: B'frd 4A 6
SILSDEN 2E 15
Silsden Driving Range 4D 14
Silsden Golf Course 3G 15
Silsden Ho. Gdns. BD20: Sils 1C 14
Silsden Rd. BD20: Rid 1C 34
   LS29: Add 2A 8
Silson La. BD17: Bail 3E 53
Silver Birch Av. BD12: Wyke 5D 132
Silver Birch Cl. BD12: Wyke 5D 132
Silver Birch Dr. BD12: Wyke 5D 132
Silver Birch Gro. BD12: Wyke 5D 132
Silver Ct. LS13: Leeds 2B 94
Silver Cross Way LS20: Guis 4B 40
Silverdale Av. BD20: Rid 4C 34
   LS17: Leeds 2F 61
   LS20: Guis .5C 40
Silverdale Cl. LS20: Guis 6C 40
Silverdale Cres. LS20: Guis 5C 40
Silverdale Dr. LS20: Guis 6C 40

Silverdale Grange LS20: Guis 6C 40
Silverdale Gro. LS20: Guis 6B 40
Silverdale Mt. LS20: Guis 6C 40
Silverdale Rd. BD5: B'frd 3E 111
   LS20: Guis .6B 40
Silverdale Ter. HX4: Gree 5E 159
Silverhill Av. BD3: B'frd 2B 92
Silverhill Dr. BD3: B'frd 2B 92
Silverhill Rd. BD3: B'frd 2A 92
Silver Ho. LS2: Leeds 1E 5
Silver Royd Av. LS12: Leeds 5H 95
Silver Royd Cl. LS12: Leeds 5H 95
Silver Royd Dr. LS12: Leeds 5H 95
Silver Royd Gth. LS12: Leeds 5H 95
Silver Royd Gro. LS12: Leeds 5H 95
SILVER ROYD HILL 5H 95
Silver Royd Hill LS12: Leeds 5H 95
Silver Royd Pl. LS12: Leeds 5H 95
Silver Royd St. LS12: Leeds 5H 95
Silver Royd Ter. LS12: Leeds 5H 95
Silver Royd Way LS12: Leeds 5H 95
Silver St. BD8: B'frd 2B 90
   HX1: Hal 4B 164 (2G 149)
   LS11: Leeds 5G 97
   WF1: Wake .6F 157
Silvertrees LS8: B'hpe 2F 43
Silverwood Av. HX2: Hal 6A 128
   (not continuous)
Silverwood Wlk. HX2: Hal 6A 128
Silwood Dr. BD2: B'frd 6A 72
Simes St. BD1: B'frd 3B 6 (4D 90)
Simm Carr HX3: North 3H 129
Simm Carr La. HX3: North 3H 129
Simmonds La. HX1: Leeds 4H 149
Simmons Ct. LS9: Leeds 5D 98
Simmons Way LS8: Leeds 5F 79
Simms Dene BD15: All 5C 68
Simon Cl. BD4: B'frd 3D 112
Simon Fold BD12: Wyke 5C 132
Simon Marks Ct. LS12: Leeds 6C 96
   (off Lynwood Gth.)
SIMPSON GREEN 6A 54
Simpson Gro. BD10: B'frd 6A 54
   LS12: Leeds 4D 96
Simpsons Fold E.
   LS10: Leeds 6F 5 (4A 98)
Simpsons Fold W. LS10: Leeds 6F 5
Simpson St. BD21: Keigh 6G 33
   HX3: Hal 5F 129
   WF3: E Ard 1C 156
Simpson Ter. HX1: Hal 4F 149
   (off Haworth Cl.)
Sinclair Rd. BD2: B'frd 4F 71
Sinden M. BD10: B'frd 5H 53
Sinderhill Ct. HX3: North 3C 130
Singleton St. BD1: B'frd 1D 6 (3E 91)
Sion Hill HX3: Hal 6A 150
Sir Francis Crossley's Almshouses
   HX1: Hal .2F 149
   (off Lister La.)
Sir George Martin Dr.
   LS16: Leeds 3D 58
Sir Isaac Holden Pl. BD7: B'frd 4B 90
Sir Karl Cohen Sq. LS12: Leeds 4B 96
Sir Wilfred Pl. BD10: B'frd 1H 71
Siskin Cl. LS27: Morl 4B 138
Siskin Dr. BD6: B'frd 4E 109
Siskin Way WF10: All B 3H 145
Sissons Av. LS10: Leeds 3H 139
Sissons Cres. LS10: Leeds 3H 139
Sissons Dr. LS10: Leeds 3H 139
Sissons Grn. LS10: Leeds 3H 139
Sissons Gro. LS10: Leeds 3H 139
Sissons La. LS10: Leeds 3H 139
Sissons Mt. LS10: Leeds 4G 139
Sissons Pl. LS10: Leeds 3H 139
Sissons Rd. LS10: Leeds 3G 139
Sissons Row LS10: Leeds 3H 139
Sissons St. LS10: Leeds 3H 139

Sissons Ter. LS10: Leeds 3G 139
Sissons Vw. LS10: Leeds 4G 139
Sixth Av. BD3: B'frd 2A 92
   LS26: Rothw 6C 120
   WF15: Liv 4H 153
Sizers Ct. LS19: Yead 2E 55
Skelda Ri. LS29: I'ly 6D 10
Skellow Dr. BD4: B'frd 4E 113
Skelton Av. LS9: Leeds 3F 99
Skelton Cres. LS9: Leeds 3F 99
Skelton Grange Cotts.
   LS9: Leeds 2G 119
Skelton Grange Rd.
   LS10: Leeds 3F 119
Skelton Mt. LS9: Leeds 3F 99
Skelton Pl. LS9: Leeds 3F 99
   (off Ivy Av.)
Skelton Rd. LS9: Leeds 3F 99
Skeltons La. LS14: Leeds, T'ner 6D 62
Skelton St. LS9: Leeds 3F 99
Skelton Ter. LS9: Leeds 3F 99
Skelton Wlk. BD10: B'frd 2B 72
Skelwith App. LS14: Leeds 1C 100
Skelwith Wlk. LS14: Leeds 1C 100
Skinner La. BD8: B'frd 1G 5
   LS7: Leeds 1G 5 (2B 98)
Skinner St. LS1: Leeds 4A 4
Skippon Ter. LS14: T'ner 2H 63
Skipton Cl. WF3: E Ard 6B 140
Skipton Ri. LS25: Gar 4H 103
Skipton Rd. BD20: Keigh 2F 33
   BD20: Sils .2B 14
   BD20: Stee .6B 14
   BD21: Keigh 5A 34
   LS29: Add 1C 8
   LS29: I'ly 4G 9
SKIRCOAT GREEN 1F 159
Skircoat Grn. HX3: Hal 1G 159
Skircoat Grn. Rd. HX3: Hal 6G 149
Skircoat Lodge HX3: Hal 6F 149
Skircoat Moor Cl. HX3: Hal 5E 149
Skircoat Moor Rd. HX1: Hal 4D 148
   HX3: Hal 4D 148
Skircoat Rd.
   HX1: Hal 6C 164 (3G 149)
Skirdon Ct. HX2: Illing 6C 106
Skirrow St. BD16: Cot 3D 68
Skye Vw. LS26: Rothw 2B 142
Skylark Av. BD6: B'frd 4E 109
Skyline LS9: Leeds 4H 5 (3B 98)
Sky Plaza LS2: Leeds 1E 5
Slack Bottom Rd. BD6: B'frd 5A 110
Slack End BD6: B'frd 6H 109
Slack La. BD22: Oak 4A 46
   HX2: Midg .3B 126
SLACK SIDE 4H 109
Sladdin Row BD13: Que 5G 107
Slade Cl. LS23: B Spa 4B 30
Slade Ho. BD2: B'frd 1B 92
   (off St Clare's Av.)
Slade La. BD20: Rid 3C 34
   HD6: Ras 5G 143
Sladen Bri. BD22: S'bury 2A 64
Sladen St. BD21: Keigh 6G 33
SLAID HILL 3F 61
Slaid Hill Ct. LS17: Leeds 2F 61
Slate Quarry La. BD16: Bgly 3D 50
Slaters Rd. LS28: Stan 2A 94
Slates La. LS29: I'ly 2C 10
Slaymaker La. BD22: Oak 4B 46
Slead Av. HD6: Brigh 5H 151
Slead Ct. HD6: Brigh 5H 151
Slead Cres. HD6: Brigh 5H 151
Slead Gro. HD6: Brigh 5H 151
Slead Royd HD6: Brigh 5H 151
SLEAD SYKE .5G 151
Slead Syke Sports Cen. 4H 151
Slead Vw. HD6: Brigh 5H 151
Sledmere Cft. LS14: Leeds 3E 81
Sledmere Gdn. LS14: Leeds 3E 81
Sledmere Grn. LS14: Leeds 3E 81
   (off Sledmere Pl.)

Sledmere La. LS14: Leeds 3E **81**
(not continuous)
Sledmere Pl. LS14: Leeds 3E **81**
Sledmere Sq. *LS14: Leeds* *3E 81*
(off Sledmere Pl.)
Sleningford Gro. BD18: Ship 1G **69**
Sleningford Ri. BD16: Bgly 2B **50**
Sleningford Rd. BD16: Bgly 2A **50**
BD18: Ship 1G **69**
Sleningford Ter. *BD16: Bgly* *2B 50*
(off Sleningford Rd.)
Slicer's Yd. *BD16: Bgly* *4B 50*
(off Busfeild St.)
Slingsby Cl. BD10: B'frd 1B **72**
Slippy La. HX2: Mix 2A **128**
Smalewell Cl. LS28: Pud 5H **93**
Smalewell Dr. LS28: Pud 5G **93**
Smalewell Gdns. LS28: Pud 5G **93**
Smalewell Grn. LS28: Pud 5H **93**
Smalewell Rd. LS28: Pud 5G **93**
(Smalewell Dr.)
LS28: Pud 5F **93**
(Tyersal La.)
Smallpage *BD13: Que* *4A 108*
(off Albert Rd.)
Small Page Fold BD13: Que 4A **108**
Smallwood Gdns. WF12: Dew 6B **154**
Smallwood Rd. WF12: Dew 6A **154**
(not continuous)
Smeaton App. LS15: Leeds 6G **81**
Smeaton Ct. LS18: H'fth 1G **75**
Smeaton Gro. LS26: Swil 3A **122**
Smiddles La. BD5: B'frd 3D **110**
Smith Art Gallery 6A **152**
Smith Av. BD6: B'frd 4C **110**
Smith Cres. HD6: Ras 3G **161**
Smitherd's St. BD21: Keigh 1H **47**
Smithfield Av. HX3: Hip 1E **151**
Smith Ho. Av. HD6: Brigh 4A **152**
Smith Ho. Cl. HD6: Brigh 3A **152**
Smith Ho. Cres. HD6: Brigh 4A **152**
(not continuous)
Smith Ho. Dr. HD6: Brigh 3A **152**
Smith Ho. Gro. HD6: Brigh 4A **152**
Smith Ho. La. HD6: Brigh 4A **152**
HX3: Hip 4A **152**
Smithies La. WF17: Birs 6A **136**
Smith La. BD9: B'frd 1G **89**
Smith Rd. BD7: B'frd 2A **110**
Smiths Cotts. *LS6: Leeds* *3D 76*
(off Weetwood La.)
Smithson St. LS26: Rothw 3B **142**
Smith's Ter. HX3: Hal 4E **129**
Smith St. BD4: B'frd 5H **111**
BD7: B'frd 4A **6** (4D **90**)
BD16: Cot 3D **68**
BD21: Keigh 5G **33**
Smiths Yd. *HX6: Sow B* *5A 148*
(off Town Hall St.)
Smithville BD21: Rid 4D **34**
Smithy Carr La. HD6: Brigh 5A **152**
Smithy Ct. BD19: Scho 6F **133**
LS22: Coll 2B **28**
Smithy Fold BD13: Que 3E **109**
HX5: Ell 5E **161**
Smithy Greaves LS29: Add 2G **9**
Smithy Hill BD6: B'frd 4C **110**
BD13: Denh 4C **86**
BD22: Oak *3F 47*
(off Keighley Rd.)
Smithy La. BD15: Wils 3G **67**
LS16: Leeds 1G **57**
LS17: Bard 3E **45**
LS29: Burl W 3E **21**
WF3: Ting 1F **155**
Smithy Mills La. LS16: Leeds 5D **58**
Smithy St. HX1: Hal 3D **164** (2H **149**)
Smools La. LS27: Morl, Chur 6B **116**
Snaith Wood Dr. LS19: Raw 6G **55**
Snaith Wood M. LS19: Raw 6G **55**
Snake Hill BD12: O'haw 2G **133**
Snake La. LS9: Leeds 5E **99**
Snape Dr. BD7: B'frd 3F **109**

Snape St. BD21: Keigh 3A **48**
Snelsins La. BD19: Cleck 6A **134**
Snelsins Rd. BD19: Cleck 6A **134**
Snowden App. LS13: Leeds 6G **75**
Snowden Cl. LS13: Leeds 1F **95**
Snowden Cres. LS13: Leeds 1F **95**
Snowden Fold LS13: Leeds 1F **95**
Snowden Gdns. LS13: Leeds 1G **95**
Snowden Grn. *LS13: Leeds* *1F 95*
(off Snowden Cl.)
Snowden Gro. LS13: Leeds 1F **95**
Snowden Lawn LS13: Leeds 1F **95**
Snowden Rd. BD18: Ship 3D **70**
(not continuous)
Snowden Royd LS13: Leeds 1F **95**
Snowden St. BD1: B'frd 2C **6** (3E **91**)
Snowdens Wlk. BD14: Clay 1F **109**
Snowden Va. LS13: Leeds 1F **95**
Snowden Wlk. LS13: Leeds 1F **95**
Snowden Way LS13: Leeds 6F **75**
Snowdrop M. BD15: All 3D **88**
SNOW HILL 6E **157**
Soaper Ho. La. HX3: Hip 5E **131**
Soaper La. BD6: B'frd 6E **109**
HX3: She 6E **109**
Sod Ho. Grn. HX3: Hal 4E **129**
Sofia Cl. LS9: Leeds 1F **99**
Sofia Ct. *LS13: Leeds* *5F 75*
(off Wellington Gth.)
Soho St. BD1: B'frd 4B **6** (4D **90**)
HX1: Hal 2C **164**
SOIL HILL 2C **106**
Solomon Hill HX2: Lud 6D **126**
Solstice Way HX2: Illing 2B **128**
Somerdale Cl. LS13: Leeds 2F **95**
Somerdale Gdns. LS13: Leeds 2F **95**
Somerdale Gro. LS13: Leeds 2F **95**
Somerdale Wlk. LS13: Leeds 2F **95**
Somerset Av. BD17: Bail 3B **52**
HD6: Ras 4B **162**
Somerset Rd. LS28: Pud 3A **94**
Somers Pl. LS1: Leeds 4C **4**
Somers St. LS1: Leeds 4B **4** (3H **97**)
Somerton Dr. BD4: B'frd 3B **112**
Somerville Av. BD6: B'frd 6B **110**
LS14: Leeds 1B **100**
Somerville Dr. LS14: Leeds 1B **100**
Somerville Grn. LS14: Leeds 1B **100**
Somerville Gro. LS14: Leeds 1B **100**
Somerville Mt. LS14: Leeds 1B **100**
Somerville Pk. BD6: B'frd 5B **110**
Somerville Ter. LS21: Otley 3F **23**
Somerville Vw. LS14: Leeds 1B **100**
Sommerville M. LS28: Stan 2G **93**
Sonning Rd. BD15: All 3D **88**
Soothill La. WF17: Bat, Dew 4A **154**
Sorrel Way BD17: Bail 3F **53**
Sorrin Cl. BD10: B'frd 1G **71**
Soureby Cross Way BD4: E Bier . . .6D **112**
Sth. Accommodation Rd.
LS9: Leeds 6C **98**
LS10: Leeds 6B **98**
Southampton St.
BD3: B'frd 1F **7** (2F **91**)
LS17: E Kes 5E **27**
South Bank BD13: Que 4B **108**
South Bradford Golf Course 5E **111**
Southbrook Ter.
BD7: B'frd 5B **6** (5D **90**)
South Carr HX2: Lud 6D **126**
South Cliffe BD13: Thorn 5A **88**
HX2: Hal 2E **129**
Southcliffe *HX3: Sou* *4A 150*
(off Bank Top)
Southcliffe Dr. BD17: Bail 6B **52**
Southcliffe Way BD17: Bail 6C **52**
South Cl. LS20: Guis 5H **39**
Sth. Clough Head HX2: Hal 2G **147**
Southcote Pl. BD10: B'frd 1H **71**
Southcote St. *LS28: Fars* *1H 93*
(off Northcote St.)
South Cft. Av. BD11: Birk 1E **135**
Southcroft Dr. BD11: Birk 6E **113**

Southcroft Ga. BD11: Birk 1E **135**
Southdown Cl. BD9: B'frd 1G **89**
Southdown Ct. *BD9: B'frd* *1G 89*
(off Southdown Cl.)
Southdown Rd. BD17: Bail 6B **52**
South Dr. LS20: Guis 5H **39**
LS28: Fars 6H **73**
South Edge BD18: Ship 2G **69**
BD20: Keigh 5G **33**
HX3: Hip 2F **151**
Southedge Cl. HX3: Hip 2E **151**
Southedge Ter. HX3: Hip 2F **151**
South End Av. LS13: Leeds 2G **95**
South End Ct. LS13: Leeds 1G **95**
South End Gro. LS13: Leeds 2G **95**
South End Mt. LS13: Leeds 2G **95**
South End Ter. LS13: Leeds 2G **95**
Sth. Farm Cres. LS9: Leeds 1G **99**
Sth. Farm Rd. LS9: Leeds 1G **99**
Southfield LS16: B'hpe 3H **43**
Southfield Av. BD6: B'frd 5C **110**
BD20: Rid 3D **34**
LS17: Leeds 5C **60**
Southfield Dr. BD20: Rid 3E **35**
LS17: Leeds 5C **60**
Southfield Grange Sports Cen. 3B **110**
Southfield La. BD5: B'frd 2B **110**
BD7: B'frd 1A **110**
LS29: Add 1C **8**
Southfield Mt. BD20: Rid 3D **34**
LS10: Leeds *4C 118*
(off Woodville Mt.)
LS12: Leeds 4C **96**
Southfield Rd. BD5: B'frd 2C **110**
BD16: Bgly 6C **50**
LS29: Add 1D **8**
LS29: Burl W 2E **21**
Southfield Sq. BD8: B'frd 2C **90**
Southfield St. LS12: Leeds 4C **96**
Southfield Ter. BD11: Birk 1E **135**
HX3: Hip 6E **131**
LS12: Leeds *4C 96*
(off Southfield Mt.)
LS29: Add 1D **8**
Southfield Way BD20: Rid 3E **35**
Southgate BD1: B'frd 4C **6** (4E **91**)
HX1: Hal 4C **164** (2G **149**)
HX5: Ell 4B **160**
LS20: Guis 6H **39**
LS26: Oul 1E **143**
South Gro. BD18: Ship 2F **69**
HD6: Brigh 4G **151**
Sth. Hawksworth St. LS29: I'ly 5D **10**
South Hill LS10: Leeds 6D **118**
South Hill Cl. LS10: Leeds 6D **118**
South Hill Cft. LS10: Leeds 6D **118**
South Hill Dr. BD16: Bgly 5E **51**
South Hill Gdns. LS10: Leeds 6D **118**
South Hill Gro. LS10: Leeds 6D **118**
South Hill Ri. LS10: Leeds 6D **118**
South Hill Way LS10: Leeds 6D **118**
Sth. Holme La. HD6: Brigh 5G **151**
Southlands BD17: Bail 6B **52**
HX2: Brad 4D **106**
LS18: H'fth 6D **56**
Southlands Av. BD13: Thorn 5E **89**
BD16: Bgly 6C **50**
BD20: Rid 4E **35**
LS17: Leeds 1A **78**
LS19: Raw 5H **55**
Southlands Cl. LS17: Leeds 6A **60**
Southlands Cres. LS17: Leeds 1A **78**
Southlands Dr. BD20: Rid 4E **35**
LS17: Leeds 1A **78**
Southlands Gro. BD13: Thorn 5D **88**
BD16: Bgly 6B **50**
BD20: Rid 4E **35**
Southlands Gro. W. BD20: Rid 3E **35**
Southlands Mt. BD20: Rid 4E **35**
Southlands Rd. BD20: Rid 3E **35**
South La. HX3: She 6D **108**
South La. Gdns. HX5: Ell 6B **160**
South Lea WF3: Ting 6F **139**

Southlea Av. BD22: Oak 5E **47**
Southlea Cl. BD12: O'haw 2G **133**
South Lee LS18: H'fth 6D **56**
Sth. Leeds Bus. Cen.
  LS11: Leeds 6A **98**
South Leeds Golf Course 1G **139**
South Leeds Stadium 5A **118**
South Leeds Tennis Cen. 5A **118**
Southleigh Av. LS11: Leeds 5G **117**
Southleigh Cres. LS11: Leeds . . .5G **117**
Southleigh Cft. LS11: Leeds 5H **117**
Southleigh Dr. LS11: Leeds 5G **117**
Southleigh Gdns. LS11: Leeds . . .5G **117**
Southleigh Gth. LS11: Leeds . . .5H **117**
Southleigh Grange
  LS11: Leeds 5H **117**
Southleigh Gro. LS11: Leeds . . .5G **117**
Southleigh Rd. LS11: Leeds 5G **117**
Southleigh Vw. LS11: Leeds 5G **117**
South Mead LS16: B'hpe 3H **43**
Southmere Av. BD7: B'frd 2A **110**
Southmere Cres. BD7: B'frd 2H **110**
Southmere Dr. BD7: B'frd 2H **109**
    (Horton Ind. Est.)
  BD7: B'frd 2A **110**
    (Southmere Rd.)
Southmere Gro. BD7: B'frd 2A **110**
Southmere Oval BD7: B'frd 3H **109**
Southmere Rd. BD7: B'frd 2A **110**
Southmere Ter. BD7: B'frd 2A **110**
South Mt. LS17: E Kes 5D **26**
Sth. Nelson St. LS27: Morl 2A **138**
Southolme Cl. LS5: Leeds 3H **75**
SOUTHOWRAM 5C **150**
Southowram Bank HX3: Hal 2H **149**
South Pde. BD8: B'frd 2D **90**
  BD19: Cleck 1H **153**
  HX1: Hal 6D **164** (3H **149**)
  HX5: Ell 6B **160**
  LS1: Leeds 4D **4** (3H **97**)
  LS6: Leeds 4D **76**
  LS21: Otley 4F **23**
    (off Croft St.)
  LS27: Morl 3B **138**
  LS28: Pud 5H **93**
  LS29: I'ly 5C **10**
South Pde. Cl. LS28: Pud 5A **94**
South Pk. Ter. LS28: Pud 1B **114**
South Pk. Way WF2: Carr G 5D **156**
South Parkway LS14: Leeds 6A **80**
    (not continuous)
Sth. Parkway App.
  LS14: Leeds 6A **80**
South Pl. LS27: Morl 3B **138**
    (off South St.)
South Ridge LS25: Kip 4G **123**
South Rd. BD9: B'frd 5C **70**
  BD13: Cull 4B **66**
South Row LS18: H'fth 6E **57**
Sth. Royde Av. HX3: Hal 5G **149**
Southroyd Gdns. LS28: Pud 6B **94**
Southroyd Pde. LS28: Pud 6A **94**
    (off Fartown)
Southroyd Pk. LS28: Pud 6A **94**
    (not continuous)
Southroyd Ri. LS28: Pud 6A **94**
Southroyd Vs. LS28: Pud 6A **94**
South Selby HX2: Illing 1B **128**
South Sq. BD13: Thorn 5H **87**
South Sq. Cen. BD13: Thorn 5H **87**
    (off South Sq.)
South St. BD5: B'frd 2C **110**
  BD12: O'haw 3G **133**
  BD13: Denh 3B **86**
  BD13: Thorn 4H **87**
  BD20: E Mor 5H **35**
  BD21: Keigh 2H **47**
  HD6: Brigh 6A **152**
  HX1: Hal 5A **164** (3H **149**)
  HX4: Holy 6F **159**
  LS19: Raw 3F **55**
  LS27: Morl 3B **138**

South Ter. HX3: North 4C **130**
South Vw. BD6: B'frd 1G **131**
  BD9: B'frd 5C **70**
  BD10: B'frd 2B **72**
  BD13: Que 3G **107**
  BD15: Wils 4G **67**
  BD19: Scho 2F **153**
  BD20: E Mor 4F **35**
  BD22: Haw 2C **64**
  HX2: Hal 2E **129**
    (off Blackmires)
  HX3: Hal 5A **150**
  HX3: Sou 5C **150**
  HX4: Bark 4B **158**
    (off Barsey Grn. La.)
  HX6: Lud M 4F **147**
  LS15: Leeds 1E **101**
    (off Church La.)
  LS18: H'fth 2E **75**
  LS19: Yead 6D **40**
  LS20: Guis 4C **40**
  LS22: Coll 3H **27**
  LS22: Weth 1E **13**
  LS23: Cliff 6B **30**
  LS26: Rothw 1A **142**
  LS27: Chur 6B **116**
  LS28: Pud 4B **94**
  LS28: Stan 2G **93**
  LS29: Men 2G **39**
  WF3: W Ard 4D **154**
  WF17: Birs 6B **136**
Southview Bus. Pk.
  LS20: Guis 6C **40**
South Vw. Cl. BD4: E Bier 6C **112**
  LS19: Yead 6D **40**
South Vw. Cotts. LS17: Shad 4B **62**
South Vw. Ct. HX3: Hip 3F **151**
South Vw. Cres. LS19: Yead 6D **40**
South Vw. Dr. BD4: E Bier 6D **112**
South Vw. Rd. BD4: E Bier 6D **112**
  LS19: Yead 6F **41**
South Vw. Ter. BD16: Bgly 2E **51**
  BD17: Bail 4C **52**
  BD20: Sils 2D **14**
  HX1: Hal 1D **148**
    (off Kelsey St.)
  LS19: Yead 1G **55**
  LS21: Otley 4F **23**
    (off Crow La.)
Southwaite Cl. LS14: Leeds 5B **80**
Southwaite Gth. LS14: Leeds . . .5B **80**
Southwaite La. LS14: Leeds 5B **80**
Southwaite Lawn LS14: Leeds . . .5B **80**
Southwaite Pl. LS14: Leeds 5B **80**
South Way BD4: E Bier 6C **112**
  BD18: Ship 2F **69**
Southway BD16: Bgly 2D **50**
  LS18: H'fth 4C **56**
  LS20: Guis 5G **39**
  LS29: I'ly 6F **11**
Southwood Cl. LS14: Leeds 5E **81**
Southwood Cres. LS14: Leeds . . .5E **81**
Southwood Ga. LS14: Leeds 5E **81**
Southwood Rd. LS14: Leeds 5E **81**
Sovereign Bus. Pk. LS10: Leeds . .5B **98**
Sovereign Cl. WF17: Birs 6B **136**
Sovereign Ct. BD2: B'frd 5A **72**
  LS17: Leeds 1C **60**
Sovereign Mill LS27: Morl 4B **138**
    (off Sth. Queen St.)
Sovereign Pk. BD17: Bail 1H **91**
Sovereign Pl. LS1: Leeds . . .6D **4** (4H **97**)
Sovereign Quay LS1: Leeds 6E **5**
Sovereign Rd. WF1: Out 6F **157**
Sovereign Sq. HD6: B Bri 2B **152**
Sovereign St. HX1: Hal . . .4A **164** (2F **149**)
  LS1: Leeds 6D **4** (4A **98**)
Sowden Bldgs. BD2: B'frd 1H **91**
Sowden Grange BD13: Thorn 5H **87**
    (James St.)
  BD13: Thorn 5H **87**
    (Lane End)

Sowden La. BD12: Wyke 4A **132**
  HX3: Nor G 4H **131**
Sowden Rd. BD9: B'frd 1F **89**
Sowden St. BD7: B'frd 2B **110**
Sowden's Yd. LS16: Leeds 3D **76**
SOWERBY 6E **147**
SOWERBY BRIDGE 5A **148**
Sowerby Bridge Pool 6H **147**
Sowerby Bridge Station (Rail) . . .6A **148**
Sowerby Cft. HX6: Sow B 1A **158**
Sowerby Cft. La.
  HX6: Norl, Sow B 6H **147**
Sowerby Grn. HX6: Sow B 6D **146**
Sowerby La. HX2: Lud M 2B **146**
Sowerby New Rd.
  HX6: Sow B 6E **147**
Sowerby St. HX6: Sow B 6H **147**
Sowerby Town HX6: Sow B 6D **146**
Sowood Hill Vw. HX3: Hal 1D **164**
Sowood St. LS4: Leeds 1C **96**
Spa Bldgs. LS29: I'ly 5D **10**
    (off The Grove)
Spa Ind. Est. LS7: Leeds 5A **78**
Spa La. BD16: Bgly 2C **50**
  LS23: B Spa 4C **30**
Spalding Towers LS9: Leeds 2C **98**
    (off Lindsey Gdns.)
Spa M. LS23: B Spa 4C **30**
Spandola Ct. BD21: Keigh 5F **33**
Spanefield La. HX2: Wain 3F **127**
Sparable La. BD16: Bgly 4E **51**
Spark Ho. La. HX6: Sow B 6A **148**
Spartal La. WF10: Leeds 5C **124**
Spartan Rd. BD12: Low M 2D **132**
Spear Fir LS17: Bard 3C **44**
Spearhead Way BD21: Keigh 5A **34**
Speedwell Mt. LS6: Leeds 6H **77**
Speedwell St. LS6: Leeds 6H **77**
Speeton Av. BD7: B'frd 3G **109**
Speeton Gro. BD7: B'frd 3F **109**
Speights Pl. BD4: B'frd 3A **112**
    (off Dawson La.)
Spen App. LS16: Leeds 2H **75**
Spen Bank LS16: Leeds 2H **75**
Spence La. LS12: Leeds 5F **97**
Spenceley St. LS2: Leeds 6G **77**
    (not continuous)
Spencer Av. BD7: B'frd 6A **90**
  BD20: Sils 1E **15**
  LS27: Morl 5A **138**
Spencer Bus. Factory
  BD4: B'frd 3A **112**
Spencer Mt. LS8: Leeds 6C **78**
Spencer Pl. LS7: Leeds 6C **78**
Spencer Rd. BD7: B'frd 6H **89**
    (not continuous)
Spencers Ct. HX1: Hal 5C **164**
    (off Wellington Pl.)
Spencer St. BD21: Keigh 6G **33**
    (not continuous)
Spen Cl. BD4: B'frd 6H **111**
Spen Cres. LS16: Leeds 1A **76**
Spen Dr. LS16: Leeds 1B **76**
Spen Gdns. LS16: Leeds 2H **75**
Spen Grn. LS16: Leeds 2H **75**
Spen La. BD19: Cleck, Gom 6E **135**
  LS5: Leeds 4A **76**
  LS6: Leeds 3A **76**
  LS16: Leeds 6A **58**
    (not continuous)
Spen Lawn LS16: Leeds 2H **75**
Spen M. LS16: Leeds 2A **76**
Spennithorne Av. LS16: Leeds . . .5A **58**
Spennithorne Dr. LS16: Leeds . . .6A **58**
Spen Rd. LS16: Leeds 1A **76**
Spenser Ri. LS20: Guis 5D **40**
Spenser Rd. LS20: Guis 5D **40**
Spensers Ho. LS12: Leeds 1D **4**
Spenslea Gro. LS27: Morl 5A **138**
Spen Vw. La. BD4: B'frd 6H **111**
Spen Wlk. LS16: Leeds 2H **75**
Spen Way LS16: Leeds 3A **76**
Spibey Cres. LS26: Rothw 6H **119**

Spibey La. LS26: Rothw 6H **119**
Spicer St. BD5: B'frd 2C **110**
Spiers Gth. BD6: B'frd 4D **110**
Spiggs HX3: North 4B **130**
Spindle Point HX2: Hal 2E **129**
Spindles, The LS10: Leeds 5B **118**
Spindle St. HX2: Hal 2E **129**
Spink Pl. BD8: B'frd 2A **6** (3D **90**)
Spinks Gdns. LS14: Leeds 5D **80**
Spink St. BD8: B'frd 2A **6** (3D **90**)
Spinkwell Cl. BD3: B'frd 1E **7** (2F **91**)
Spinners Chase LS28: Pud 4A **94**
Spinners Cl. HX1: Hal 1D **148**
Spinners Ga. BD4: B'frd 5C **92**
Spinners Way BD19: Scho 1F **153**
  BD22: Haw 3C **64**
Spinney, The BD20: E Mor 5H **35**
  HD6: Brigh 4A **152**
  LS9: Leeds 4C **98**
  LS17: Leeds 5C **60**
  LS19: Raw 5E **55**
  LS22: Weth 3D **12**
Spinneyfield Ct. LS9: Leeds 4C **98**
Spinney Ri. BD4: B'frd 4D **112**
Spinning Mill, The BD22: Haw 1B **64**
Spinning Mill Ct. BD18: Ship 6G **51**
  (Hirst La.)
  BD18: Ship 1G **69**
  (Sherwood Gro.)
Spion Kop LS14: T'ner 2H **63**
Spire Hgts. BD16: Bgly 4F **51**
Spofforth Hill LS22: Weth 3C **12**
Spofforth Wlk. LS25: Gar 4H **103**
Spool Ct. HD6: B Bri 2C **152**
Spout Hill HD6: Ras 5G **161**
Spout Ho. La. HD6: Brigh 3G **151**
Spring Av. BD21: Keigh 1C **48**
  LS27: Gil 6E **115**
SPRING BANK 3A **48**
Spring Bank BD13: Cull 4A **66**
  HX2: Lud 6E **127**
  HX6: Sow B 4G **147**
  LS5: Leeds 5A **76**
Springbank LS19: Raw 4E **55**
  LS25: Gar 6C **102**
Springbank Av. LS27: Gil 6E **115**
  LS28: Fars 6A **74**
Springbank Cl. LS28: Fars 6H **73**
Spring Bank Cres. LS6: Leeds 5E **77**
Springbank Cres. LS25: Gar 5C **102**
  LS27: Gil 5E **115**
Springbank Dr. LS28: Fars 6A **74**
Springbank Gro. LS28: Fars 6A **74**
Spring Bank Ind. Est.
  HX6: Sow B 6H **147**
Springbank M. WF3: Loft 2D **156**
Spring Bank Ri. BD21: Keigh 3A **48**
Springbank Ri. LS28: Fars 6A **74**
Springbank Rd. LS27: Gil 5E **115**
  LS28: Fars 6H **73**
Spring Bank Ter. LS20: Guis 4C **40**
Springcliffe BD8: B'frd 2B **90**
Springcliffe St. BD8: B'frd 2B **90**
Spring Cl. BD16: Bgly 5D **50**
  BD21: Keigh 1C **48**
  LS25: Gar 5H **103**
  (Firtree Av.)
  LS25: Gar 3G **103**
  (Newhold Ind. Est.)
Spring Cl. Av. LS9: Leeds 5D **98**
Spring Cl. Gdns. LS9: Leeds 5D **98**
Spring Cl. St. LS9: Leeds 5D **98**
Spring Cl. Wlk. LS9: Leeds 5D **98**
Springdale Cres. BD10: B'frd 1A **72**
Spring Dr. BD21: Keigh 1C **48**
Spring Edge Nth. HX1: Hal 4E **149**
Spring Edge Sth. HX1: Hal 4E **149**
Spring Edge W. HX1: Hal 4D **148**
Spring Farm La. BD6: Har 6E **49**
Spring Farm M. BD15: Wils 4G **67**
SPRINGFIELD 3H **71**

Springfield BD13: Que 4H **107**
  HX2: Midg 6C **126**
  HX3: Hip 1E **151**
  HX3: North 4A **130**
  HX6: Sow B 6G **147**
  LS23: B Spa 3B **30**
  LS23: Cliff 6B **30**
Springfield Av. BD7: B'frd 6H **89**
  LS27: Morl 1H **137**
  LS29: I'ly 5E **11**
  WF3: Loft 2G **157**
Springfield Cl. LS18: H'fth 6G **57**
  WF3: Loft 2G **157**
Springfield Commercial Cen.
  LS28: Fars 5A **74**
Springfield Ct. BD20: Keigh 5G **33**
  LS17: Leeds 3E **61**
  LS19: Yead 5E **41**
  LS20: Guis 4C **40**
  (off West St.)
Springfield Cres. LS27: Morl 1A **138**
Springfield Dr. WF15: Liv 4H **153**
Springfield Gdns. BD20: Keigh 5G **33**
  LS18: H'fth 6F **57**
  LS28: Pud 5B **94**
Springfield Grn. LS10: Leeds 3C **118**
Springfield Gro. BD16: Bgly 3B **50**
  HD6: Brigh 4A **152**
Springfield La. BD4: B'frd 3A **114**
  LS27: Morl 1A **138**
Springfield M. LS20: Guis 4C **40**
  LS27: Morl 1A **138**
Springfield Mt.
  LS2: Leeds 1A **4** (2G **97**)
  LS12: Leeds 3A **96**
  LS18: H'fth 3F **57**
  LS29: Add 1D **8**
Springfield Pl. BD1: B'frd . . .1B **6** (3D **90**)
  BD10: B'frd 2H **71**
  LS10: Leeds 3C **118**
  (Leasowe Rd.)
  LS10: Leeds 3C **119**
  (Pontefract Rd.)
  LS20: Guis 4C **40**
  LS21: Otley 4D **22**
  LS25: Gar 5C **102**
Springfield Ri. LS18: H'fth 6F **57**
  LS26: Rothw 3B **142**
Springfield Rd. BD17: Bail 3B **52**
  BD20: Keigh 5G **33**
  HX5: Ell 4D **160**
  LS20: Guis 5C **40**
  LS27: Morl 1H **137**
  WF3: Loft 2G **157**
Springfield St. BD8: B'frd 3C **90**
  LS26: Rothw 3B **142**
Springfields Vw. HX4: Gree 4F **159**
Springfield Ter. BD8: B'frd 3C **90**
  BD13: Thorn 5A **88**
  BD19: Scho 6F **133**
  HX2: Midg 6C **126**
  HX3: Hip 1E **151**
  LS17: Leeds 3E **61**
  (off Springfield Ct.)
  LS28: Stan 2H **93**
Springfield Vw. LS25: Kip 4H **123**
  (off Hanover Pl.)
Springfield Vs. LS27: Gil 5D **114**
Springfield Wlk. LS18: H'fth 6F **57**
Spring Gdn. Cotts. BD20: Sils 2D **14**
  (off South Vw. Ter.)
SPRING GARDENS 1B **136**
Spring Gdns. BD1: B'frd 1B **6** (3E **91**)
  BD11: Drig 2A **136**
  BD20: Sils 2D **14**
  (off Elliott St.)
  HX2: Mix 4C **128**
  HX3: Nor G 5H **131**
  HX6: Sow B 4H **147**
  LS27: Chur 6C **116**
  LS29: Burl W 2F **21**

Spring Gdns. La. BD20: Keigh 3G **33**
Spring Gdns. Mt. BD20: Keigh 4H **33**
Spring Gdns. Rd. BD9: B'frd 6A **70**
Spring Gdn. St. BD13: Que 4A **108**
Spring Gro. BD10: B'frd 2H **71**
  HX1: Hal 2C **148**
Spring Gro. Av. LS6: Leeds 1E **97**
Spring Gro. Vw. LS6: Leeds 1E **97**
Spring Gro. Wlk. LS6: Leeds 1E **97**
Spring Hall Cl. HX3: She 2D **130**
Spring Hall Ct. HX1: Hal 1C **148**
Spring Hall Dr. HX2: Hal 3C **148**
Spring Hall Gdns. HX2: Hal 2C **148**
Spring Hall Gro. HX2: Hal 2C **148**
Spring Hall La. HX1: Hal 3C **148**
Spring Hall Pl. HX1: Hal 2C **148**
Spring Hall Sports Facility 4H **149**
Spring Head HX2: Hal 6C **128**
  HX3: She 2E **131**
Springhead BD22: Oak 1B **64**
Springhead Mills BD22: Haw 1C **64**
Spring Head Rd. BD13: Thorn 5A **88**
  BD22: Haw 1B **64**
Springhead Rd. LS26: Rothw 1C **142**
Spring Head Ter. BD13: Thorn 4G **87**
Spring Hill BD15: Wils 4G **67**
  BD17: Bail 4H **51**
  BD18: Ship 2E **71**
  LS7: Leeds 5A **78**
  LS16: Leeds 3E **59**
Springhill Cl. WF1: Out 4E **157**
Spring Hill Cotts. LS6: Leeds 3E **77**
  (off Monk Bri. Rd.)
Spring Hill Pl. BD15: Wils 4G **67**
Springhills WF1: Out 4E **157**
Spring Hill Ter. LS6: Leeds 3E **77**
  (off Monk Bri. Rd.)
Spring Holes La. BD13: Thorn 4G **87**
Springhurst Rd. BD18: Ship 2A **70**
Spring La. BD16: Bgly 1F **51**
  HX4: Gree 4E **159**
  LS22: Weth 4H **13**
Springlodge Pl. BD8: B'frd 2D **90**
Springmead Dr. LS25: Gar 5F **103**
Spring Mill St. BD5: B'frd 6E **91**
Spring Mt. BD21: Keigh 2C **48**
Spring Pk. Rd. BD15: Wils 3G **67**
Spring Pl. BD7: B'frd 6A **6** (6C **90**)
  BD21: Keigh 2C **48**
Spring Ri. BD21: Keigh 1C **48**
Spring Rd. LS6: Leeds 5E **77**
Springrove Ter. LS6: Leeds 1E **97**
Spring Row BD13: Que 4A **108**
  BD16: Har 6F **49**
  BD21: Keigh 1H **47**
  (not continuous)
  BD22: Cros R 1F **65**
  BD22: Oxen 2E **85**
  HX2: Mix 6A **106**
Spring Royd HX2: Lud M 1C **146**
Springroyd Ter. BD8: B'frd 3H **89**
Springs La. LS29: I'ly 5E **11**
Springs Rd. LS19: Yead 1C **54**
Springs Ter. LS29: I'ly 5E **11**
Spring St. BD10: B'frd 2H **71**
  BD15: All 6C **68**
  BD21: Keigh 5A **34**
  BD22: Cros R 1F **65**
  (off Bingley Rd.)
  HD6: Brigh 1A **162**
Springswood Av. BD18: Ship 2A **70**
Springswood Pl. BD18: Ship 2A **70**
Springswood Rd. BD18: Ship 2A **70**
Spring Ter. BD21: Keigh 1C **48**
  HX3: Hal 2D **164** (1H **149**)
  HX6: Sow B 1A **158**
Springvale Works HD6: Brigh 5G **151**
Spring Valley LS28: Stan 2A **94**
Spring Valley Av. LS13: Leeds 2E **95**
Spring Valley Cl. LS13: Leeds 2E **95**
Spring Valley Ct. LS13: Leeds 2E **95**
Spring Valley Cres. LS13: Leeds 2E **95**
Spring Valley Cft. LS13: Leeds 2E **95**

Spring Valley Dr. LS13: Leeds 2E **95**
Spring Valley Vw. LS13: Leeds 2E **95**
Spring Valley Wlk. LS13: Leeds 2E **95**
Spring Vw. BD13: Thorn 3G **87**
    (off Lower Hgts. Rd.)
  HX2: Lud M 3D **146**
  LS27: Gil 5F **115**
Spring Vw. Rd. HX2: Lud M 3D **146**
Spring Way BD21: Keigh 1C **48**
Springwell Av. LS26: Swil 4A **122**
Springwell Cl. LS19: Yead 1G **55**
Springwell Ct. LS12: Leeds 5F **97**
  WF3: Ting 6E **139**
Springwell Dr. BD5: B'frd 1E **111**
Springwell Rd. LS12: Leeds 5F **97**
  LS26: Swil 4A **122**
Spring Wells BD22: Oak 3C **46**
Springwell St. LS12: Leeds 5F **97**
Springwell Ter. BD6: B'frd 4A **110**
  LS19: Yead 1G **55**
Springwell Vw. LS12: Leeds 5G **97**
  WF17: Birs 6B **136**
    (off South Vw.)
Springwood Av. BD5: B'frd 2F **111**
  HX3: Hal 1F **159**
Springwood Bus. Pk.
  HX4: Holy 6G **159**
Springwood Cl. WF3: Thpe H 6C **140**
Springwood Ct. LS8: Leeds 3F **79**
    (off Bk. Wetherby Rd.)
  LS27: Morl 6B **138**
Springwood Dr. HX3: Hal 1F **159**
Spring Wood Gdns. BD5: B'frd 3F **111**
  HX3: Hal 2F **159**
Springwood Gdns. LS8: Leeds 3F **79**
Springwood Gro. LS8: Leeds 3G **79**
Springwood M. LS8: Leeds 3G **79**
Springwood Pl. BD2: B'frd 1E **91**
    (off Bolton Rd.)
Springwood Rd. LS8: Leeds 3F **79**
  LS19: Raw 4E **55**
Springwood Ter. BD2: B'frd 1E **91**
    (off Bolton La.)
Spruce Dr. HX3: North 3C **130**
Spruce Hgts. HD6: Brigh 3A **152**
Spruce St. BD21: Keigh 5B **34**
Spur Dr. LS15: Leeds 6D **81**
Square HX1: Hal 4C **164** (2G **149**)
  HX2: Wain 1F **127**
  HX3: North 4C **130**
Square, The BD8: B'frd 4E **89**
  BD20: E Mor 4H **35**
    (off Hartley's Sq.)
  HX3: Sou 4A **150**
  LS18: H'fth 1D **74**
  LS23: B Spa 4C **30**
  LS25: Kip 4G **123**
Square Chapel Centre for the Arts
  ....4D **164** (2H **149**)
Square Rd. HX1: Hal 4D **164** (2H **149**)
Square Grn. BD8: B'frd 2H **89**
Squire La. BD8: B'frd 2H **89**
  BD9: B'frd 2H **89**
Squirrel La. BD13: Thorn 6F **87**
Squirrel Way LS17: Leeds 3D **60**
Stable Ct. LS28: Cal 3F **73**
    (off Bk. Thornhill St.)
Stable Fold BD12: Wyke 5D **132**
Stable La. HX3: Hal 6F **129**
Stable M. BD16: Cot 2A **68**
Stables, The LS21: Otley 3E **23**
    (off Wesley St.)
  LS22: Weth 4E **13**
    (off High Cliffe Ter.)
Stables La. LS23: B Spa 4C **30**
Stackgarth HD6: Ras 3A **162**
Stadium Rd. BD6: B'frd 5E **111**
Stadium Way LS11: Leeds 2E **117**
Stafford Av. HX3: Hal 5G **149**
Stafford Grn. HX3: Hal 6G **149**
Stafford Pde. HX3: Hal 6G **149**

Stafford Pl. HX3: Hal 5G **149**
Stafford Rd. HX3: Hal 6G **149**
Stafford Sq. HX3: Hal 6H **149**
Stafford St. BD4: B'frd 1H **111**
  LS10: Leeds 1C **118**
  LS27: Morl 5H **137**
  WF10: C'frd 6H **145**
Stainbeck Av. LS7: Leeds 3F **77**
Stainbeck Cnr. LS7: Leeds 2A **78**
    (off Harrogate Rd.)
Stainbeck Gdns. BD6: B'frd 5F **109**
  LS7: Leeds 2H **77**
Stainbeck La. LS7: Leeds 2G **77**
Stainbeck Rd. LS7: Leeds 3F **77**
Stainbeck Wlk. LS7: Leeds 3H **77**
Stainburn Av. LS17: Leeds 6C **60**
Stainburn Cres. LS17: Leeds 6B **60**
Stainburn Dr. LS17: Leeds 6B **60**
Stainburn Gdns. LS17: Leeds 6C **60**
Stainburn Mt. LS17: Leeds 1C **78**
Stainburn Pde. LS17: Leeds 6B **60**
Stainburn Ter. LS17: Leeds 1B **78**
Stainburn Vw. LS17: Leeds 1B **78**
Stainburn Vw. LS17: Leeds 6C **60**
Staincliffe Ct. BD20: Sils 2D **14**
Stainland Rd. HX4: Bark 6A **158**
  HX4: Gree 2H **159**
  HX4: Holy, Stainl 6F **159**
Stainmore Cl. LS14: Leeds 6C **80**
Stainmore Pl. LS14: Leeds 6C **80**
Stainton Cl. BD6: B'frd 5G **109**
Stainton La. WF3: Carl 3H **141**
Staircase La. LS16: B'hpe 5F **25**
  LS21: Pool 5F **25**
Stairfoot Cl. LS16: Leeds 2D **58**
Stairfoot La. LS16: Leeds 2D **58**
  LS17: Leeds 2D **58**
Stairfoot Vw. LS16: Leeds 2D **58**
Stairfoot Wlk. LS16: Leeds 2D **58**
Staithe Av. LS10: Leeds 2B **140**
Staithe Cl. LS10: Leeds 2B **140**
Staithe Gdns. LS10: Leeds 2B **140**
Staithes, The BD17: Bail 4C **52**
    (off Baildon Rd.)
Staithgate La. BD4: B'frd 1G **133**
  BD6: B'frd 4F **111**
Stake La. HX7: Crag V 2A **146**
Stallabrass St. BD8: B'frd ...2A **6** (3C **90**)
Stamford St. BD4: B'frd 6H **91**
Stammergate La. LS22: Lin 2B **28**
Stamp Hill Cl. LS29: Add 1B **8**
Stanacre Pl. BD3: B'frd 1F **7** (3F **91**)
Stanage La. HX3: She 6E **109**
Stanbeck Ct. LS7: Leeds 1A **78**
Standale Av. LS28: Pud 3H **93**
Standale Cres. LS28: Pud 3H **93**
Standale Ri. LS28: Pud 3H **93**
Standard Vs. LS12: Leeds 1B **116**
Stanhall Av. LS28: Stan 2H **93**
Stanhall M. LS28: Stan 2H **93**
Stanhope Av. LS18: H'fth 5E **57**
Stanhope Cl. LS18: H'fth 5E **57**
Stanhope Cotts. LS21: Pool 4E **25**
    (off The Old Orchard)
Stanhope Dr. LS18: H'fth 4D **56**
Stanhope Dr. LS18: H'fth 1D **74**
Stanhope Gdns. WF3: Thpe H 6C **140**
Stanhope Gro. WF3: Thpe H 6C **140**
Stanhope Rd. WF3: Thpe H 6C **140**

STANKS 4F **81**
Stanks App. LS14: Leeds 5F **81**
Stanks Av. LS14: Leeds 5F **81**
Stanks Cl. LS14: Leeds 5G **81**
Stanks Cross LS14: Leeds 5G **81**
Stanks Dr. LS14: Leeds 3E **81**
Stanks Gdns. LS14: Leeds 4F **81**
Stanks Gth. LS14: Leeds 5G **81**
Stanks Grn. LS14: Leeds 5G **81**
Stanks Gro. LS14: Leeds 5F **81**
Stanks La. Nth. LS14: Leeds 3E **81**
Stanks La. Sth. LS14: Leeds 5F **81**
Stanks Pde. LS14: Leeds 5F **81**
Stanks Ri. LS14: Leeds 5G **81**

Stanks Rd. LS14: Leeds 5F **81**
Stanks Way LS14: Leeds 5F **81**
Stanley Av. LS9: Leeds 1D **98**
Stanley Ct. HX1: Hal 2D **148**
    (off Walsh St.)
Stanley Dr. LS14: Leeds 5F **61**
Stanley Gro. LS20: Guis 5C **40**
Stanley Ho. LS10: Leeds 5B **98**
Stanley La. WF1: Out 5H **157**
Stanley Pl. LS9: Leeds 1E **99**
Stanley Rd. BD2: B'frd 5D **70**
  BD22: Keigh 3G **47**
  HX1: Hal 3D **148**
  LS7: Leeds 6B **78**
  LS9: Leeds 1D **98**
Stanley St. BD10: B'frd 2B **72**
    (Fieldgate Rd.)
  BD10: B'frd 1H **71**
    (Moorfield Pl.)
  BD16: Bgly 4C **50**
  BD18: Ship 4C **70**
  BD21: Keigh 5H **33**
  BD22: Cros R 1E **65**
  HD6: Brigh 6B **152**
  HX6: Sow B 5A **148**
Stanley St. Nth. HX2: Hal 2E **129**
    (off Shay La.)
Stanley St. W. HX6: Sow B 6H **147**
    (off Salisbury St.)
Stanley Ter. LS9: Leeds 1E **99**
    (not continuous)
  LS12: Leeds 4C **96**
Stanley Vw. LS12: Leeds 4C **96**
Stanmore Av. LS4: Leeds 6C **76**
Stanmore Cres. LS4: Leeds 6C **76**
Stanmore Gro. LS4: Leeds 6C **76**
Stanmore Hill LS4: Leeds 6D **76**
Stanmore Mt. LS4: Leeds 6C **76**
Stanmore Pl. BD7: B'frd 6A **90**
  LS4: Leeds 6C **76**
Stanmore Rd. LS4: Leeds 6C **76**
Stanmore St. LS4: Leeds 6C **76**
Stanmore Ter. LS4: Leeds 6C **76**
Stanmore Vw. LS4: Leeds 6C **76**
Stannary Pl.
  HX1: Hal 2A **164** (1F **149**)
Stannery End La. HX7: Crag V 2A **146**
STANNINGLEY 1B **94**
Stanningley Av. HX2: Mix 2H **127**
Stanningley By-Pass
  LS13: Leeds 3A **94**
  LS28: Stan 2G **93**
Stanningley Ct. LS28: Stan 1B **94**
    (off Leeds & Bradford Rd.)
Stanningley Dr. HX2: Mix 2H **127**
Stanningley Fld. Cl. LS13: Leeds ..2C **94**
Stanningley Grn. HX2: Mix 1A **128**
Stanningley Ind. Est.
  LS28: Stan 2H **93**
Stanningley Loft LS28: Stan 2A **94**
    (off Town St.)
Stanningley Rd. HX2: Mix 2H **127**
  LS12: Leeds 2G **95**
  LS13: Leeds 1C **94**
  LS28: Stan 1B **94**
Stansfield Cl. HX1: Hal 2E **149**
Stansfield Ct. HX6: Sow B 6H **147**
Stansfield Fold LS18: H'fth 5E **57**
    (off Rockery Rd.)
Stansfield Pl. BD10: B'frd 6H **53**
Stanwick Ho. BD2: B'frd 5D **70**
Staples La. BD21: Keigh 2G **65**
Stapleton Ho. BD2: B'frd 5D **70**
Stapper Grn. BD15: Wils 3F **67**
Starkie St. BD21: Keigh 1H **47**
Starling M. BD15: All 4D **88**
    (off Greenway Dr.)
Star St. BD5: B'frd 2C **110**
Star Ter. HD6: Ras 4G **161**
Starting Post BD10: B'frd 2F **71**
Station Apartments
  LS15: Leeds 1E **101**
    (off Station Rd.)

Station App. HX1: Hal 5D **164** (3H **149**)
  LS5: Leeds 5B **76**
  LS29: Burl W 3E **21**
Station Av. LS13: Leeds 1D **94**
Station Bri. *BD21: Keigh* *6B **34***
  (off Bradford Rd.)
Station Cl. LS25: Gar 4F **103**
Station Cotts. LS14: T'ner 1H **63**
  LS24: N Kym 5G **31**
Station Ct. BD1: B'frd 4E **7** (4F **91**)
  LS15: Leeds 2E **101**
  LS25: Gar 3F **103**
Station Cres. LS12: Leeds 4B **96**
Station Flds. LS25: Gar 4F **103**
Station Gdns. LS15: Scho 2H **81**
  LS22: Weth 4D **12**
Station Ho. *LS25: M'fld* *5E **105***
  (off Old Great Nth. Rd.)
Station Ind. Pk. HX2: Lud M 2D **146**
Station La. BD11: Birk 1E **135**
  HX4: Gree 3H **159**
  LS14: T'ner 1H **63**
  LS22: Coll 2B **28**
  LS26: Wood 6F **121**
  WF3: E Ard 6B **140**
  WF3: Ting 5E **139**
  (not continuous)
Station Mt. LS13: Leeds 1D **94**
Station Pde. LS5: Leeds 5B **76**
Station Pl. LS13: Leeds 1E **95**
Station Plaza *LS29: I'ly* *5D **10***
  (off Railway Rd.)
Station Rd. BD1: B'frd 1E **91**
  BD11: Drig 2A **136**
  BD12: Low M 2E **133**
  BD12: Wyke 5A **132**
  BD13: Cull 3A **66**
  BD13: Denh 3B **86**
  BD13: Que 3B **108**
  BD14: Clay 1E **109**
  BD15: Wils 6D **66**
  BD17: Bail 4C **52**
  BD17: Esh 1H **53**
  BD18: Ship 1B **70**
  BD20: Stee 6D **14**
  BD22: Haw 2C **64**
  BD22: Oak 5D **46**
  BD22: Oxen 6C **64**
  HD2: Hud 6G **163**
  HD6: Clift 1C **162**
  HX2: Lud M 2D **146**
  HX3: Hal 2E **129**
  HX3: Hip 2E **151**
  HX3: Nor G 5A **132**
  HX6: Sow B 6H **147**
  LS12: Leeds 4B **96**
  LS15: Leeds 1E **101**
  LS15: Scho 2H **81**
  LS18: H'fth 5E **57**
  LS20: Guis 4B **40**
  LS21: Arth 5H **25**
  LS21: Otley 4E **23**
  LS25: Gar 4F **103**
  LS25: Kip 5F **123**
  LS26: Meth 4D **144**
  LS27: Morl 2A **138**
  LS29: Burl W 3E **21**
  LS29: I'ly 5D **10**
  LS29: Men 1H **39**
  WF10: All B 3H **145**
Station Rd. Ind. Est.
  LS25: Kip 6F **123**
Station Sq. LS28: Stan 2G **93**
Station St. LS28: Pud 5H **93**
Station Ter. LS13: Leeds 1E **95**
Station Vw. BD20: Stee 6D **14**
  BD22: Oxen 6C **64**
  LS15: Leeds 2E **101**
Station Wlk. LS27: Morl 2B **138**
Station Way LS12: Leeds 4B **96**
Station Works Ind. Pk.
  BD21: Keigh 6C **34**
Staups La. HX3: North 5B **130**

Staveley Ct. BD16: Bgly 3C **50**
  BD18: Ship 1F **69**
  BD22: Keigh 3G **47**
Staveley Dr. BD18: Ship 2F **69**
Staveley Gro. BD22: Keigh 4G **47**
Staveley M. BD16: Bgly 3C **50**
Staveley Rd. BD7: B'frd 5B **90**
  BD16: Bgly 3C **50**
  BD18: Ship 1F **69**
  BD22: Keigh 4G **47**
Staveley Way BD22: Keigh 3G **47**
Staverton Gro. BD13: Thorn 4A **88**
Staverton St. HX2: Hal 2C **148**
Stax Trade Cen. LS27: Morl 6A **138**
Staybrite Av. BD16: Cot 2C **68**
STAYGATE 3E **111**
Staygate Grn. BD6: B'frd 4E **111**
Staynton Cres. HD2: Hud 6F **163**
  (not continuous)
STEAD 2A **20**
Stead Hill Way BD10: B'frd 4A **72**
Steadings Way BD22: Keigh 2E **47**
Stead La. BD16: Bgly 1F **51**
  LS14: T'ner 2H **63**
  LS29: Burl W 3B **20**
Steadman Ter. BD3: B'frd 5H **91**
Steadman Ter. BD3: B'frd 5H **91**
Stead Rd. BD4: B'frd 5C **112**
Stead St. BD17: Ship 1B **70**
  HX1: Hal 4A **164** (2F **149**)
  (not continuous)
Steads Yd. LS18: H'fth 5E **57**
Steel Grn. LS12: N Far 2A **116**
Steel Ter. *LS26: Rothw* *2B **142***
  (off Bk. Gillett La.)
Steep Bank Side HX3: Hal 3A **150**
Steeplands HD2: Hud 5F **163**
STEEP LANE 5B **146**
Steep La. HD2: Hud 5F **163**
  HX6: Sow B 5A **146**
Steeple Cl. LS27: Morl 6B **138**
Steerforth Cl. *BD5: B'frd* *2E **111***
  (off Mumford St.)
STEETON 6C **14**
Steeton Gro. BD20: Stee 5C **14**
Steeton Hall Gdns. BD20: Stee 5C **14**
Steeton & Silsden Station (Rail) 5D **14**
Stell Hill BD22: Keigh 2D **46**
Stephen Cl. HX3: North 6C **130**
Stephen Cres. BD2: B'frd 6E **71**
Stephen Rd. BD6: B'frd 3H **109**
Stephen Row *HX3: North* *5C **130***
  (off Towngate)
Stephenson Dr. LS12: N Far 2F **115**
Stephenson Ho. *LS27: Morl* *2B **138***
  (off Pullman Ct.)
Stephenson Rd. BD15: All 1H **87**
Stephensons Way LS29: I'ly 5D **10**
Stephenson Way LS12: N Far 2F **115**
  WF2: Carr G 4D **156**
Stepping Stones BD20: E Mor 5A **36**
Steps, The LS6: Sow B 4A **148**
Steps La. HX6: Sow B 4A **148**
Sterling Ct. WF3: Ting 5E **139**
Sterling Way WF3: Ting 5D **138**
Stewart Cl. BD2: B'frd 4A **72**
  LS15: Leeds 4E **101**
Stewart St. BD22: Cros R 1E **65**
Sticker La. BD4: B'frd 2A **112**
Stile Hill Way LS15: Leeds 4H **101**
Stile Way BD9: B'frd 6B **70**
Stillington Ho. BD2: B'frd 5D **70**
Stirling Cres. BD4: B'frd 2C **112**
  LS18: H'fth 3C **56**
Stirling Rd. LS29: Burl W 2D **20**
Stirling St. BD20: Sils 1E **15**
  HX1: Hal 5A **164** (3F **149**)
Stirling Way LS25: Gar 4H **103**
Stirrup Gro. BD2: B'frd 5F **71**
Stirton St. BD5: B'frd 2D **110**
Stock A Ho's. BD16: Cot 3B **68**
STOCKBRIDGE 4C **34**

Stockbridge Wharf BD20: Rid 4D **34**
Stockeld Rd. LS29: I'ly 5C **10**
Stockeld Way LS29: I'ly 4C **10**
Stockheld La. LS15: Leeds, Scho . . .6H **63**
Stockhill Fold BD10: B'frd 1B **72**
  (not continuous)
Stockhill Rd. BD10: B'frd 2B **72**
Stockinger La. LS29: Add 1D **8**
Stock La. HX2: Hal 3H **147**
Stocks App. LS14: Leeds 5D **80**
Stocksfield Vw. BD13: Que 4D **108**
Stocks Hill LS11: Leeds 6G **97**
  LS12: Leeds 3C **96**
  LS26: Meth *4D **144***
  (off Hicks La.)
  LS29: Men 1F **39**
Stocks Hill Cl. BD20: E Mor 4H **35**
Stocks Hill Gth. *LS29: Men* *1F **39***
  (off Stocks Hill)
Stocks La. BD13: Que 3D **108**
  HX2: Lud, Mt T 6E **127**
  HX6: Sow B 6E **147**
Stocks Ri. LS14: Leeds 5D **80**
Stocks Rd. LS14: Leeds 5E **81**
Stocks St. LS7: Leeds 6A **78**
Stod Fold HX2: Ogd 5A **106**
Stogden Hill BD13: Que 4D **108**
Stone Acre Ct. BD5: B'frd 3E **111**
Stonebank Gdns. LS17: Bard 1F **45**
Stonebridge App. LS12: Leeds 5G **95**
Stonebridge Av. LS12: Leeds 5H **95**
Stone Bri. Ct. *LS12: Leeds* *5G **95***
  (off Farnley Cres.)
Stonebridge Gro. LS12: Leeds 5G **95**
Stonebridge Idlecroft Rd.
  BD10: B'frd *1H **71***
  (off Idlecroft Rd.)
Stonebridge La. LS12: Leeds 6G **95**
Stone Bri. Lea *LS12: Leeds* *5G **95***
  (off Farnley Cres.)
Stone Brig Grn. LS26: Rothw 3H **141**
Stone Brig La. LS26: Rothw 3H **141**
STONE CHAIR 3D **130**
Stonechat Ri. LS27: Morl 3C **138**
Stone Cliffe *HX3: Hal* *5E **149***
  (off Skircoat Moor Cl.)
Stonecliffe Bank LS12: Leeds 5G **95**
Stonecliffe Cl. LS12: Leeds 5G **95**
Stonecliffe Cres. LS12: Leeds 5G **95**
Stonecliffe Dr. LS12: Leeds 5G **95**
Stonecliffe Gdns. LS12: Leeds 5G **95**
Stonecliffe Gth. LS12: Leeds 5G **95**
Stonecliffe Grn. LS12: Leeds 5G **95**
Stonecliffe Gro. LS12: Leeds 5G **95**
Stonecliffe Lawn LS12: Leeds 5G **95**
Stonecliffe Mt. LS12: Leeds 5G **95**
Stonecliffe Pl. *LS12: Leeds* *5G **95***
  (off Stonebridge La.)
Stonecliffe Ter. LS12: Leeds 5G **95**
Stonecliffe Vw. LS12: Leeds 5G **95**
Stonecliffe Wlk. LS12: N Far 6G **95**
Stonecliffe Way LS12: Leeds 5G **95**
Stone Ct. BD20: E Mor 5H **35**
Stonecroft BD2: B'frd 5A **72**
Stone Cft. Ct. LS26: Oul 2E **143**
Stonecroft Fold HX2: Lud M 4D **146**
Stonecroft Mt. HX6: Sow B 3A **148**
Stonecross BD15: Wils 4G **67**
Stonedale Cl. LS21: Pool 5G **25**
Stonedene LS6: Leeds 1F **77**
Stonedene Pk. LS22: Weth 3F **13**
Stonefield Cl. LS14: S'cft 5F **45**
Stonefield Cl. BD2: B'frd 4H **71**
Stonefield Pl. WF17: Birs 6B **136**
Stonefield St. BD19: Cleck 3G **153**
Stonefield Ter. LS27: Chur 5C **116**
Stone Fold BD17: Bail 5A **52**
Stonegate BD16: Bgly 2C **50**
  LS7: Leeds 6A **78**
  (not continuous)
Stonegate App. LS7: Leeds 3F **77**
Stonegate Chase LS7: Leeds 2F **77**
Stonegate Cl. LS17: Leeds 4B **60**

Stonegate Cres. LS7: Leeds 2G 77
Stonegate Dr. LS7: Leeds 2G 77
Stonegate Edge LS7: Leeds 2G 77
Stonegate Farm Cl.
  LS7: Leeds 2F 77
Stonegate Gdns. LS7: Leeds 2F 77
Stonegate Grn. LS7: Leeds 3F 77
Stonegate Gro. LS7: Leeds 2G 77
Stone Ga. Ho. BD1: B'frd 2D 6
Stonegate La. LS7: Leeds 2F 77
Stonegate M. LS7: Leeds 3F 77
Stonegate Pl. LS7: Leeds 3F 77
Stonegate Rd. BD10: B'frd 3H 71
  LS6: Leeds 2F 77
  LS17: Leeds 2F 77
Stonegate Vw. LS7: Leeds 2F 77
Stonegate Wlk. LS7: Leeds 3G 77
Stonegate Way LS17: Leeds 5A 60
Stone Gro. BD20: Stee 6C 14
  (not continuous)
Stone Hall M. BD2: B'frd 5A 72
Stone Hall Rd. BD2: B'frd 5H 71
Stonehaven Ct. BD21: Keigh 2C 48
Stone Hill BD16: Bgly 3D 50
Stonehouse Dr. BD13: Que 5G 107
Stone Ho. Fold BD22: Oak 5B 46
Stonehurst LS14: Leeds 5F 81
Stone La. BD22: Oxen 1A 84
Stonelea BD4: B'frd 5E 113
Stonelea Ct. LS6: Leeds 4D 76
  LS7: Leeds 2G 77
Stonelea Dr. HD6: Ras 4H 161
Stoneleigh BD13: Que 4B 108
Stoneleigh Av. LS17: Leeds 3D 60
Stoneleigh Cl. LS17: Leeds 3D 60
Stoneleigh Ct. BD19: Scho 6E 133
  LS17: Leeds 3D 60
Stoneleigh Gth. LS17: Leeds 4D 60
Stoneleigh La. LS17: Leeds 4D 60
Stoneleigh Way
  LS17: Leeds 4D 60
Stone Mill App. LS6: Leeds 2E 77
Stone Mill Ct. LS6: Leeds 2E 77
Stone Mill Way LS6: Leeds 2E 77
Stone Pits La. LS27: Gil 1F 137
Stone Stay Fold LS29: Add 1C 8
Stone St. BD1: B'frd 3D 6 (4E 91)
  BD13: Que 3G 107
  (off Derwent Pl.)
  BD15: All 6C 68
  BD17: Bail 5E 53
  BD22: Haw 3C 64
  (off Jacky La.)
Stone Ter. BD16: Har 5F 49
Stone Vs. LS6: Leeds 3D 76
Stonewaite Ct. LS26: Wood 1D 142
Stoney Battery
  HX3: Hal 1C 164 (1G 149)
Stoney Brow HX3: Hal 5A 150
Stoneycroft LS18: H'fth 1D 74
  LS19: Raw 3G 55
  (off Batter La.)
Stoneycroft La. BD20: Keigh 3H 33
Stoney Hill HD6: Ras 1A 162
Stoneyhurst Sq. BD4: B'frd 2C 112
Stoneyhurst Way BD4: B'frd 2C 112
Stoney La. HX2: Hal 4D 148
  HX3: Hal 4E 129
  HX3: Hip 2A 152
  HX3: Sou 4E 151
  HX7: Myth 5A 126
  LS17: Shad 2C 62
  LS18: H'fth 1D 74
  LS29: Burl W 5C 20
  WF2: Kirk 4B 156
  WF3: E Ard 4A 156
Stoney Ridge Av. BD9: B'frd 5D 68
Stoney Ridge Rd. BD16: Cot 5D 68
Stoney Ri. LS18: H'fth 1D 74
Stoney Rock Ct. LS9: Leeds 2D 98
Stoney Rock Gro. LS9: Leeds 2D 98
Stoney Rock La. LS9: Leeds 2D 98
STONEY ROYD 4H 149

Stoney Royd LS29: Burl W 1E 21
  (off Main St.)
Stoney Royd Ter. HX3: Hal 5H 149
Stoneys Fold BD15: Wils 3F 67
Stoney Springs Ho.
  HX2: Lud M 1B 146
Stoney Springs Ind. Units
  HX2: Lud M 1B 146
Stoney St. BD20: Keigh 3H 33
Stoneythorpe LS18: H'fth 1D 74
Stony Cft. La. HX4: Bark 6A 158
Stony La. BD2: B'frd 4A 72
  BD15: All 1B 88
  BD22: Oak 1A 46
  HX4: Gree 3E 159
Stony Royd LS28: Fars 6G 73
Stoodley Ter. HX2: Hal 3C 148
Storey Pl. LS14: Leeds 2A 100
Storiths Ct. LS29: Add 2D 8
Stormer Hill HX6: Norl 1B 158
Stormer Hill La. HX6: Norl 1B 158
Storr Hill BD12: Wyke 3C 132
Storr Hill Ter. BD12: Wyke 3C 132
Storth Lea HX5: Ell 6D 160
Storth Vw. HX5: Ell 6D 160
Story Stones BD16: Bgly 2F 51
Stott Cl. HX1: Hal 1D 148
Stott Gap BD13: Thorn 4H 87
Stott Hill BD1: B'frd 3E 7 (4F 91)
Stott Rd. LS6: Leeds 6E 77
Stott St. LS12: Leeds 4D 96
Stott Ter. BD2: B'frd 5B 72
STOURTON 4F 119
Stourton Bus. Pk.
  LS10: Leeds 3E 119
Stourton Rd. LS29: I'ly 4B 10
Stowe Gro. LS9: Leeds 3G 99
Stowell Mill St. BD5: B'frd 1D 110
Stradbroke Ct. HX6: Sow B 3A 148
Stradbroke Way LS12: Leeds 5C 96
Strafford Way BD10: B'frd 1C 72
Straightacres La. BD10: B'frd 4B 72
Straight La. HX2: Mix 2B 128
  LS29: Add 4A 8
Straits BD17: Bail 3C 52
Strand BD16: Cot 3D 68
Strangford Ct. BD10: B'frd 1B 72
Stratford Av. LS11: Leeds 2G 117
Stratford Ct. LS7: Leeds 3A 78
Stratford Rd. BD7: B'frd 6B 90
Stratford St. LS11: Leeds 3H 117
Stratford Ter. LS11: Leeds 2H 117
Strathallan Dr. BD17: Bail 4D 52
Strathmore Av. LS9: Leeds 1E 99
Strathmore Cl. BD2: B'frd 6H 71
Strathmore Dr. BD17: Bail 3B 52
  LS9: Leeds 6E 79
Strathmore Rd. LS29: I'ly 5G 11
Strathmore St. LS9: Leeds 1F 99
Strathmore Ter. LS9: Leeds 6E 79
Strathmore Vw. LS9: Leeds 1E 99
Stratton Cl. HD6: Ras 2B 162
Stratton Pk. HD6: Ras 2B 162
Stratton Rd. HD6: Ras 2B 162
Stratton Vw. BD4: B'frd 1C 112
Stratton Wlk. BD15: All 3C 88
Strawberry Av. LS25: Gar 5E 103
Strawberry Flds. BD21: Keigh 5A 34
Strawberry La. LS12: Leeds 4C 96
  (not continuous)
Strawberry Rd. LS12: Leeds 4C 96
Strawberry St. BD20: Sils 2D 14
  BD21: Keigh 5A 34
Straw Vw. BD10: B'frd 1F 71
Stray, The BD10: B'frd 3G 71
Stream Head BD13: Thorn 2F 87
Stream Head Rd. BD13: Thorn 1F 87
Streamside LS6: Leeds 3E 77
Street, The LS29: Add 2C 8
  (Hart Rhydding La.)
  LS29: Add 1B 8
  (Stamp Hill Cl.)

Street 1 LS23: T Arch 3E 31
Street 2 LS23: T Arch 3F 31
Street 3 LS23: T Arch 2F 31
  (not continuous)
Street 4 LS23: T Arch 2F 31
Street 5 LS23: T Arch 1F 31
Street 6 LS23: T Arch 1F 31
  (not continuous)
Street 7 LS23: T Arch 1F 31
Street 8 LS23: T Arch 1G 31
  (not continuous)
Street La. BD20: E Mor, W Mor 2F 35
  LS8: Leeds 5E 61
  LS17: Leeds 5A 60
  LS27: Gil 2E 137
Strensall Grn. BD6: B'frd 5G 109
Stretchgate La. HX2: Hal 1C 148
Stretton Av. LS6: Leeds 6E 59
Strickland Av. LS17: Shad 3B 62
Strickland Cl. LS17: Shad 3B 62
Strickland Cres. LS17: Shad 3B 62
Stringer Cl. BD4: B'frd 5A 112
Strone, The BD10: B'frd 6D 54
STRONG CLOSE 6C 34
Strong Cl. Gro. BD21: Keigh 6C 34
Strong Cl. Rd. BD21: Keigh 6C 34
Strong Cl. Way BD21: Keigh 6C 34
  (off Strong Cl. Gro.)
Stuart Cl. BD5: B'frd 1E 111
  (off Swarland Gro.)
Stuart Pl. HD2: Hud 6F 163
Stubbing La. HX4: Gree, Holy 6C 158
Stubbings Farm (Caravan Site)
  LS21: Otley 5A 24
Stubbings Rd. BD17: Bail 5H 51
Stubbing Way BD18: Ship 3C 70
  (not continuous)
Stubbs La. WF3: E Ard 2C 156
Stubham Ri. LS29: I'ly 4C 10
Stubley Farm M. LS27: Morl 2A 138
Stubs Beck La. BD19: Cleck 5B 134
Stub Thorn La. HX3: Sou 3B 150
Studdards Fold BD7: B'frd 1A 110
Studdley Cres. BD16: Bgly 4D 50
Studfold Vw. LS14: Leeds 6C 80
Studio Rd. LS3: Leeds 2E 97
Studleigh Ter. HD6: Brigh 4G 151
  (off Brooklyn Ter.)
Studley Av. BD6: B'frd 6B 110
Studley Cl. BD20: E Mor 4H 35
Studley Rd. BD3: B'frd 1F 91
Studley Ter. LS28: Pud 3A 94
STUMP CROSS 6B 130
Stumps, The BD18: Ship 6E 53
Sturges Gro. BD2: B'frd 1H 91
Sturton Av. LS25: Gar 3G 103
Sturton Grange La.
  LS25: Gar 4H 103
Sturton Gro. HX2: Illing 6C 106
Sturton La. HX2: Illing 6C 106
  LS25: Gar 3G 103
Stutely Gro. HD2: Hud 6E 163
Styebank La. LS26: Rothw 1B 142
Styes La. HX6: Sow B 3D 146
Sty La. BD16: Bgly 1A 50
Styveton Way BD20: Stee 5B 14
Suffield Cl. LS27: Gil 5D 114
Suffield Cres. LS27: Gil 5D 114
Suffield Dr. LS27: Gil 5D 114
Suffield Rd. LS27: Gil 5D 114
Suffolk Ct. LS19: Yead 6F 41
Suffolk Pl. BD2: B'frd 5F 71
SUGAR HILL 6C 136
Sugar Hill LS29: Add 1D 8
Sugar Hill Cl. LS26: Oul 4E 143
Sugar Well App. LS7: Leeds 4G 77
Sugar Well Ct. LS7: Leeds 5H 77
Sugar Well Mt. LS7: Leeds 4G 77
Sugar Well Rd. LS7: Leeds 4G 77
Sugden Cl. HD6: Ras 3A 162
Sugden End BD22: Cros R 2F 65
Sugden Ho. Farm
  BD21: Keigh 2H 65

Sugden Pl. BD6: B'frd 6G **109**
(off Beck Hill)
Sugden's Almshouses
  BD22: Oak 4D **46**
Sugden St. BD1: B'frd 3A **6** (4C **90**)
  BD12: O'haw 3F **133**
Sulby Gro. BD10: B'frd 2C **72**
Summerbank Cl. BD11: Drig 6B **114**
Summerbridge Cres.
  BD10: B'frd 4B **72**
  BD19: Gom 5G **135**
Summerbridge Dr. BD10: B'frd 4B **72**
Summerdale BD19: Gom 5F **135**
Summerfield Av. HD6: B Bri 3B **152**
  LS13: Leeds 6C **74**
Summerfield Cl. BD17: Bail 4B **52**
Summerfield Ct. HX2: Har 2E **129**
Summerfield Dr. BD17: Bail 4B **52**
  LS13: Leeds 6C **74**
Summerfield Gdns.
  LS13: Leeds 6C **74**
Summerfield Grn. BD17: Bail 4B **52**
  LS13: Leeds 6C **74**
Summerfield Gro. BD17: Bail 4B **52**
Summerfield Pk. BD17: Bail 4B **52**
Summerfield Pl. LS13: Leeds 6C **74**
  LS28: Stan 3A **94**
(off Richardshaw La.)
Summerfield Rd. BD10: B'frd 3A **72**
  LS13: Leeds 6C **74**
Summerfield Wlk. LS13: Leeds . . .6C **74**
Summergate Pl. HX1: Hal 3D **148**
Summergate St. HX1: Hal 3D **148**
Summer Hall Ing BD12: Wyke 3B **132**
Summerhill Av. BD20: Stee 5D **14**
Summerhill Dr. BD20: Stee 5D **14**
Summerhill Gdns.
  LS6: Leeds 5F **61**
Summerhill Gro. LS25: Gar 4D **102**
Summerhill La. BD20: Stee 5D **14**
Summerhill Pl. LS8: Leeds 5F **61**
Summerhill Rd. LS25: Gar 4D **102**
  LS26: Meth 4D **144**
Summer Hill St. BD7: B'frd 6A **90**
Summerlands Gro. BD5: B'frd 3G **111**
Summerland Ter. HX6: Sow B 5B **148**
Summer Lea BD10: B'frd 1G **71**
Summerley Ct. BD10: B'frd 2H **71**
Summerscale St. HX1: Hal 1E **149**
Summerseat Pl. BD7: B'frd 6A **90**
Summerset Pl. BD2: B'frd 1H **91**
(off Green Pl.)
Summersgill Sq. LS18: H'fth 1D **74**
Summer St. HX1: Hal 4D **148**
Summerville Rd. BD7: B'frd 5C **90**
  LS28: Stan 2G **93**
Summit St. BD21: Keigh 5H **33**
Sunbeam Av. LS11: Leeds 2H **117**
Sunbeam Gro. LS11: Leeds 2H **117**
Sunbeam Pl. LS11: Leeds 2H **117**
Sunbeam Ter. LS11: Leeds 2H **117**
  WF3: Ting 6E **139**
Sunbridge Rd. BD1: B'frd 2A **6** (4D **90**)
Sun Bldgs. HX2: Wain 2E **127**
Sunderland Cl. HD6: Brigh 6A **152**
(off Thornhill Bri. La.)
Sunderland Rd. BD9: B'frd 1B **90**
Sunderland St. BD21: Keigh 1H **47**
  BD22: Cros R 1F **65**
  HX1: Hal 4A **164** (2F **149**)
Sundown Av. BD7: B'frd 1G **109**
Sun Field LS28: Stan 2H **93**
Sunfield Cl. LS28: Stan 1H **93**
Sunfield Dr. LS28: Stan 1H **93**
Sunfield Gdns. LS28: Stan 1H **93**
Sunfield Pl. LS28: Stan 2H **93**
Sun Fold HX1: Hal 6D **164** (3H **149**)
Sunhill Dr. BD17: Bail 5G **51**
Sunhurst Cl. BD22: Oak 5C **46**
Sunhurst Dr. BD22: Oak 5C **46**
Sun La. BD22: Haw, S'bury 2A **64**
  LS29: Burl W 1D **20**

Sunningdale BD8: B'frd 3F **89**
  LS25: M'fld 3D **104**
Sunningdale Av. LS17: Leeds 3G **59**
Sunningdale Cl. LS17: Leeds 3G **59**
Sunningdale Cres. BD13: Cull 4C **66**
Sunningdale Dr. LS17: Leeds 3G **59**
Sunningdale Grn. LS17: Leeds . . .3G **59**
Sunningdale Wlk. LS17: Leeds . . .3G **59**
Sunningdale Way LS17: Leeds . . .3G **59**
SUNNYBANK 4F **159**
Sunny Bank BD9: B'frd 1F **89**
  BD12: Wyke 3E **133**
  BD13: Que 4B **108**
  BD18: Ship 2B **70**
  HX3: Nor G 5H **131**
  LS8: Leeds 4D **78**
  LS27: Chur 5C **116**
(off Sunny Gro.)
Sunny Bank LS25: M'fld 5F **105**
Sunny Bank Av. BD5: B'frd 4D **110**
Sunnybank Av. BD3: B'frd 2D **92**
  LS18: H'fth 2D **74**
Sunnybank Cl. BD19: Scho 2F **153**
Sunny Bank Ct. LS19: Yead 6H **41**
Sunnybank Cres. HX4: Gree 4E **159**
  HX6: Sow B 5A **148**
(off Beech Rd.)
  LS19: Yead 6H **41**
Sunnybank Dr. HX4: Gree 4F **159**
  HX6: Sow B 5A **148**
Sunnybank Grange HD6: Brigh . .1H **161**
Sunny Bank Gro. LS8: Leeds 4D **78**
Sunnybank Gro. BD3: B'frd 2D **92**
Sunny Bank Ho. LS28: Fars 6H **73**
Sunny Bank La. HX3: Sou 4D **150**
(not continuous)
Sunnybank La. BD3: B'frd 2D **92**
  HX4: Gree 4F **159**
Sunny Bank Mills LS28: Fars 6H **73**
Sunny Bank Rd. BD5: B'frd 4D **110**
  HD6: Brigh 1A **162**
  HX2: Mix 2H **127**
Sunnybank Rd. HX4: Gree 4E **159**
  LS18: H'fth 2D **74**
Sunnybank St. HX6: Sow B 5A **148**
  LS18: H'fth 2D **74**
Sunny Bank Ter. HX3: Hal 6G **129**
Sunnybank Ter. HD6: Brigh 6A **152**
  LS18: H'fth 2D **74**
Sunny Bank Vw. LS8: Leeds 4D **78**
Sunny Brae Cres. BD16: Bgly 5D **50**
Sunny Brow La. BD9: B'frd 1F **89**
Sunnycliffe BD20: E Mor 5H **35**
  HX3: Hip 2G **151**
Sunny Dale BD13: Denh 1B **86**
Sunnydale Av. HD6: Ras 3A **162**
Sunnydale Cres. LS21: Otley 5B **22**
Sunnydale Gro. BD21: Keigh 1D **48**
Sunnydale Pk. BD20: E Mor 4A **36**
Sunnydale Ridge LS21: Otley 5B **22**
Sunnydene LS14: Leeds 2B **100**
Sunnyfield WF3: E Ard 2A **156**
Sunny Gro. LS27: Chur 5C **116**
Sunny Gym 4E **13**
Sunnyhill Av. BD21: Keigh 2F **47**
Sunnyhill Gro. BD21: Keigh 2F **47**
Sunny Lea Ter. BD6: B'frd 5D **110**
(off Scott St.)
Sunnylee Est. LS21: Otley 3E **23**
Sunny Mt. BD16: Har 6F **49**
  BD20: Rid 6G **35**
  BD21: Keigh 5H **33**
  BD22: Keigh 5E **33**
  HX3: Hip 2E **151**
Sunnymount Ter. WF17: Birs 6B **136**
(off South Vw.)
Sunnyridge Av. LS28: Pud 3F **93**
Sunnyside HD6: Brigh 3D **162**
  HX3: Hip 2F **151**
  WF3: Ting 1D **154**
(off Dewsbury Rd.)
Sunnyside Av. WF3: Ting 1D **154**
Sunnyside La. BD3: B'frd 2F **91**

Sunnyside Rd. LS13: Leeds 2D **94**
Sunny Side St.
  HX3: Hal 1C **164** (6G **129**)
Sunnyview WF3: E Ard 2A **156**
Sunnyview Av. LS11: Leeds 2F **117**
Sunnyview Gdns. LS11: Leeds . . .2F **117**
Sunnyview Ho. LS11: Leeds 2F **117**
(off Manorfield)
Sunnyview Ter. LS11: Leeds 2F **117**
Sunrise Cl. BD5: B'frd 6E **91**
Sunrise Ct. BD5: B'frd 6E **91**
  LS27: Gil 6E **115**
Sunset Av. LS6: Leeds 1E **77**
Sunset Cres. HX3: Sou 4A **150**
Sunset Dr. LS6: Leeds 2E **77**
  LS29: I'ly 4F **11**
Sunset Hill Top LS6: Leeds 1E **77**
Sunset Mt. LS6: Leeds 2E **77**
Sunset Ri. LS6: Leeds 1E **77**
Sunset Rd. LS6: Leeds 1E **77**
Sunset Ter. LS29: I'ly 4G **11**
Sunset Vw. LS6: Leeds 1E **77**
Sunshine Ct. BD6: B'frd 6H **109**
Sunshine Mills LS12: Leeds 4A **96**
Sun St. BD1: B'frd 2F **7** (3F **91**)
  BD20: East 6A **14**
  BD21: Keigh 1A **48**
  BD22: Haw 3C **64**
  LS19: Yead 6G **41**
  LS28: Stan 2A **94**
Sun Way HX3: Sou 4B **150**
Sun Wood Av. HX3: She 3D **130**
Sun Wood Ter. HX3: She 3D **130**
Suresnes Rd. BD21: Keigh 6H **33**
Surgery St. BD22: Haw 3D **64**
Surprise View 6E **23**
Surrey Gro. BD5: B'frd 1E **111**
  LS28: Pud 3A **94**
Surrey Rd. LS28: Pud 3A **94**
Surrey St. BD21: Keigh 5C **34**
  HX1: Hal 3C **148**
Sussex App. LS10: Leeds 2D **118**
Sussex Av. LS10: Leeds 2D **118**
  LS18: H'fth 4E **57**
Sussex Gdns. LS10: Leeds 2D **118**
Sussex Grn. LS10: Leeds 2D **118**
Sussex Pl. LS10: Leeds 2D **118**
Sussex St. BD21: Keigh 5C **34**
  LS9: Leeds 4C **98**
(not continuous)
Sutcliffe Ct. HX3: Sou 4A **150**
(off Bank Top)
Sutcliffe Fold BD13: Que 4C **108**
Sutcliffe Pl. BD6: B'frd 5D **110**
Sutcliffe Rd. HX3: Hip 2E **151**
Sutcliffe St. HX2: Hal 1C **148**
Sutcliffe Ter. HX3: Hal 6G **129**
(off Range Bank)
Sutcliffe Wood La. HX3: Hip 2E **151**
Sutherland Av. LS8: Leeds 6E **61**
Sutherland Cres. LS8: Leeds 5E **61**
Sutherland Mt. LS9: Leeds 1E **99**
Sutherland Rd. HX3: Hip 1G **151**
  LS9: Leeds 1E **99**
Sutherland St. LS12: Leeds 5E **97**
Sutherland Ter. LS9: Leeds 1E **99**
Sutton App. LS14: Leeds 2A **100**
Sutton Av. BD2: B'frd 4F **71**
Sutton Cl. BD16: Bgly 5B **50**
Sutton Cres. BD4: B'frd 1C **112**
  LS14: Leeds 2A **100**
Sutton Dr. BD13: Cull 4B **66**
Sutton Gro. BD4: B'frd 6C **92**
  LS27: Morl 4A **138**
Sutton Ho. BD4: B'frd 5C **92**
Sutton Pl. BD4: B'frd 6C **92**
Sutton St. LS12: Leeds 5F **97**
Swaine Hill Cres. LS19: Yead 6E **41**
Swaine Hill St. LS19: Yead 6E **41**
Swaine Hill Ter. LS19: Yead 6E **41**
SWAIN GREEN 6B **92**
SWAIN HOUSE 4F **71**

Swain Ho. Cres. BD2: B'frd 4G 71
Swain Ho. Rd. BD2: B'frd 4G 71
Swain Mt. BD2: B'frd 4G 71
SWAIN ROYD LANE BOTTOM 6B 68
Swale Ct. BD20: Sils 3E 15
(off Ings Way)
Swale Cres. LS25: Gar 5H 103
Swale Ri. LS22: Weth 1D 12
Swales Moor Rd. HX3: Hal 2F 129
Swallow Av. LS12: Leeds 5A 96
Swallow Cl. LS12: Leeds 3H 95
   LS17: Leeds 3D 60
   LS21: Pool 5F 25
Swallow Cres. LS12: Leeds 5H 95
Swallow Dr. LS17: Leeds 3D 60
   LS21: Pool 5F 25
SWALLOW HILL 4H 95
Swallow Hill WF17: Bat 6C 136
Swallow Mt. LS12: Leeds 5A 96
Swallow St. BD21: Keigh 5B 34
Swallow Va. LS27: Morl 3D 138
Swallow Vw. LS12: Leeds 3H 95
Swan Apartments LS1: Leeds 4E 5
Swan Av. BD16: Bgly 3D 50
Swan Bank La. HX3: Hal 4H 149
Swan Ct. LS20: Guis 3B 40
Swan Hill BD9: B'frd 5C 70
Swan St. BD5: B'frd 6C 6 (5E 91)
   LS1: Leeds 4E 5
SWARCLIFFE 5E 81
Swarcliffe App. LS14: Leeds 5E 81
Swarcliffe Av. LS14: Leeds 5E 81
Swarcliffe Bank LS14: Leeds 4E 81
Swarcliffe Dr. LS14: Leeds 5E 81
Swarcliffe Dr. E. LS14: Leeds 5F 81
Swarcliffe Grn. LS14: Leeds 5E 81
Swarcliffe Pde. LS14: Leeds 5E 81
Swarcliffe Rd. LS14: Leeds 4E 81
Swardale Grn. LS14: Leeds 5E 81
Swardale La. LS14: Leeds 5E 81
Swarland Gro. BD5: B'frd 6E 91
SWARTHA 1G 15
Swartha La. BD20: Sils 1G 15
Sweet St. LS11: Leeds 5H 97
Sweet St. W. LS11: Leeds 5G 97
(not continuous)
Swift Dr. BD6: B'frd 4E 109
SWILLINGTON 4A 122
SWILLINGTON COMMON 5A 102
Swillington La. LS15: Swil 3A 122
   LS26: Swil 4H 121
Swimrite Swimming Pool 4G 129
SWINCLIFFE 3E 135
Swincliffe Cl. BD19: Gom 3E 135
Swincliffe Cres. BD19: Gom 4E 135
Swincliffe Gdns. BD19: Gom 4E 135
Swinegate LS1: Leeds 6E 5 (4A 98)
Swine La. BD20: E Mor, Rid 5F 35
Swine Mkt. HX1: Hal 4B 164
SWINNOW 1C 94
Swinnow Av. LS13: Leeds 2C 94
Swinnow Cl. LS13: Leeds 2C 94
Swinnow Cres. LS28: Stan 1C 94
Swinnow Dr. LS13: Leeds 2C 94
Swinnow Gdns. LS13: Leeds 2C 94
Swinnow Gth. LS13: Leeds 2C 94
Swinnow Grn. LS28: Pud 2B 94
Swinnow Gro. LS13: Leeds 2C 94
Swinnow La. LS13: Leeds 1C 94
   LS28: Stan 1C 94
SWINNOW MOOR 3D 94
Swinnow Rd. LS13: Leeds 3B 94
   LS28: Leeds, Pud 3B 94
Swinnow Shop. Cen. LS13: Leeds . . .3C 94
Swinnow Vw. LS13: Leeds 2C 94
Swinnow Wlk. LS13: Leeds 2C 94
Swinroyd Cl. BD11: Birk 2F 135
Swinton Pl. BD7: B'frd 6B 90
Swinton Ter. HX1: Hal 4D 148
Swires Rd. BD2: B'frd 2A 92
   HX1: Hal 6A 164 (3F 149)

Swires Ter.
   HX1: Hal 6A 164 (3F 149)
Swithen's Ct. LS26: Rothw 3B 142
Swithen's Dr. LS26: Rothw 3A 142
Swithen's Gro. LS26: Rothw 3A 142
Swithen's La. LS26: Rothw 3B 142
Swithen's St. LS26: Rothw 3B 142
Sycamore Av. BD7: B'frd 4H 89
   BD16: Bgly 5B 50
   LS8: Leeds 4D 78
   LS15: Leeds 3C 100
   LS25: Kip 3F 123
   WF2: Wren 6D 156
Sycamore Chase LS28: Pud 4B 94
Sycamore Cl. BD3: B'frd 1G 7 (3G 91)
   LS6: Leeds 5G 77
   LS7: Leeds 2F 77
   LS15: Leeds 3A 100
   LS16: B'hpe 4H 43
Sycamore Ct.
   BD3: B'frd 1G 7 (3G 91)
   LS8: Leeds 3G 79
Sycamore Cft. LS11: Leeds 2H 117
Sycamore Dr. BD19: Cleck 2H 153
   HX3: Hip 3A 152
   HX5: Ell 5H 159
   LS29: Add 1E 9
Sycamore Fold LS11: Leeds 2H 117
   LS21: Pool 5F 25
Sycamore Gdns. LS14: Leeds 5E 81
Sycamore Gro. BD20: East 6A 14
Sycamore Row LS13: Leeds 5C 74
Sycamores, The HX2: Illing 1C 128
   LS15: Bar E 2D 82
   LS16: B'hpe 4H 43
   LS20: Guis 3C 40
Sycamore Vw. BD22: Keigh 1F 47
   HD6: Brigh 6H 151
Sycamore Wlk. LS28: Fars 1H 93
Sycamore Way WF17: Birs 6B 136
Sydenham Pl. BD3: B'frd 1G 91
Sydenham Rd. LS11: Leeds 5F 97
Sydenham St. LS11: Leeds 5F 97
Sydney St. BD16: Bgly 4C 50
   LS26: Wood 1F 143
   LS28: Fars 1H 93
Syedna Way BD8: B'frd 3A 90
Syke Av. WF3: W Ard 2D 154
Syke Cl. WF3: W Ard 2C 154
Syke Gdns. WF3: W Ard 2D 154
Syke Grn. LS14: S'cft 5E 45
Syke House La. HX4: Gree 5D 158
Syke La. BD13: Que 6B 108
   HX2: Ogd 3C 106
   HX3: Hip 6G 131
   HX6: Sow B 6H 147
   LS14: S'cft 5C 44
Syke Rd. BD9: B'frd 6A 70
   LS22: Weth 4G 13
   WF3: W Ard 2D 154
Sykes Bottom BD22: Oak 5D 46
Sykes Head BD22: Oak 4D 46
Syke Side BD20: Keigh 3H 33
Sykes La. BD12: O'haw 3G 133
   BD20: Sils 3D 14
   BD22: Oak 4D 46
   WF17: Bat, Dew 5A 154
Sykes Yd. HX1: Hal 4D 148
(off Haugh Shaw Rd. W.)
Syke Ter. WF3: W Ard 2C 154
Sylhet Cl. BD1: B'frd 2B 6 (3D 90)
Sylvan Av. BD13: Que 5H 107
Sylvan Vw. LS18: H'fth 6E 57
Syringa Av. BD15: All 5C 68

T

Tabbs Ct. BD19: Scho 6F 133
Tabbs La. BD19: Scho 6E 133
Tagore Ct. BD3: B'frd 3B 92
Tagore Ho. LS6: Leeds 6E 77
(off Brudenell Rd.)

Talbot Av. LS4: Leeds 6C 76
   LS8: Leeds 5C 60
   LS17: Leeds 5C 60
Talbot Ct. LS8: Leeds 6D 60
Talbot Cres. LS8: Leeds 5D 60
Talbot Fold LS8: Leeds 6D 60
Talbot Gdns. LS8: Leeds 5D 60
Talbot Gro. LS8: Leeds 5D 60
Talbot Ho. HX5: Ell 5B 160
Talbot Mt. LS4: Leeds 6C 76
Talbot Ri. LS17: Leeds 5D 60
Talbot Rd. LS8: Leeds 5D 60
Talbot St. BD7: B'frd 4B 90
   BD21: Keigh 6G 33
(off Bk. Sladen St.)
Talbot Ter. LS4: Leeds 6C 76
   LS26: Rothw 3A 142
Talbot Vw. LS4: Leeds 6C 76
Talbot Yd. LS26: Meth 4E 145
Tall Trees LS17: Leeds 4A 60
Tamar St. BD5: B'frd 1C 110
Tamworth St. BD4: B'frd 5C 92
Tandy Trad. Estate, The
   LS12: Leeds 2D 96
Tanfield Dr. LS29: Burl W 1E 21
Tanglewood LS11: Leeds 6G 117
Tanglewood Ct. BD6: B'frd 4A 110
Tan Ho. Ct. BD4: B'frd 6H 111
Tanhouse Hill HX3: Hip 2E 151
   LS18: H'fth 1G 75
(not continuous)
Tan Ho. La. BD15: Wils 3E 67
   HX3: North 3C 130
Tanhouse Pk. HX3: Hip 2E 151
Tan Ho. Yd. LS27: Chur 4C 116
Tan La. BD4: B'frd 1H 133
Tannerbrook Cl. BD14: Clay 1F 109
Tanner Hill Rd. BD7: B'frd 2G 109
Tanner St. WF15: Liv 4H 153
Tannery, The LS3: Leeds 3F 97
(off Cavendish St.)
Tannery Bus. Cen. HX3: North 4C 130
Tannery Ct. BD10: B'frd 1B 72
   LS28: Pud 3A 94
Tannery Sq. LS6: Leeds 2E 77
Tannery Yd. LS28: Pud 4B 94
Tannett Grn. BD5: B'frd 3F 111
Tansy End BD22: Oxen 1E 85
Tanton Cres. BD14: Clay 1F 109
Tanton Wlk. BD14: Clay 1F 109
Tarn Ct. BD20: Keigh 5F 33
   LS29: I'ly 6E 11
(off Moorside Ct.)
   WF1: Out 6F 157
Tarnhill M. BD5: B'frd 1E 111
Tarn La. BD22: Lay 5A 32
   LS17: Leeds, S'cft . . . . .1G 61 & 6A 44
Tarn M. LS29: I'ly 6E 11
(off Moorside Ct.)
Tarnside Dr. LS14: Leeds 6B 80
Tarn Vw. Rd. LS19: Yead 6H 41
Tarran Way WF3: Rob H 3E 141
Tatefield Gro. LS25: Kip 5G 123
Tatefield Pl. LS25: Kip 4G 123
Tatham's Ct. HX1: Hal 4D 148
(off High Shaw Rd. W.)
Tatham Way LS8: Leeds 3G 79
Tatton La. WF3: Thpe H 5D 140
Taunton Ho. BD5: B'frd 6E 91
(off Croscombe Wlk.)
Taunton St. BD18: Ship 1A 70
Taverngate BD20: Hawk 5E 39
Tavistock Cl. LS12: Leeds 5D 96
Tavistock M. LS12: Leeds 5D 96
Tavistock Pk. LS12: Leeds 5D 96
Tavistock Way
   LS12: Leeds 5D 96
Tawny Beck LS13: Leeds 3E 95
Tawny Cl. BD4: B'frd 4C 112
   LS27: Morl 3D 138
Tay Ct. BD2: B'frd 4B 72
Taylor Av. BD20: Sils 2D 14
Taylor Gro. LS26: Meth 4E 145

Taylor La. HX2: Brad 2D **106**
LS11: Bar E 3B **82**
Taylor Rd. BD6: B'frd 5D **110**
(not continuous)
Taylors Cl. LS14: Leeds 5D **80**
Tayson Ho. BD1: B'frd 4F **7**
(off Chapel St.)
Tealbeck App. LS21: Otley 4F **23**
Tealbeck Ho. LS21: Otley 4E **23**
Tealby Cl. LS16: Leeds 5G **57**
Teal Ct. BD20: Stee 5B **14**
Teal Dr. LS27: Morl 3D **138**
Teale Ct. LS7: Leeds 4C **78**
Teale Dr. LS7: Leeds 4C **78**
Teal Ho. BD20: East 5A **14**
Teal La. HX3: North 3B **130**
(not continuous)
Teal M. BD20: Stee 5A **14**
LS10: Leeds 2B **140**
Teasdale St. BD4: B'frd 2H **111**
(not continuous)
Teasel Bank LS28: Pud 4F **93**
Teasel Cl. BD20: O'haw 2G **133**
Teasel Row LS12: Leeds 3C **96**
(off Eyres Mill Side)
Teasel Vw. LS28: Pud 4F **93**
(off Bradley La.)
Techno Cen. LS18: H'fth 5E **57**
Tees St. BD5: B'frd 2C **110**
Telephone Pl. LS7: Leeds 1H **5** (2B **98**)
Telford Cl. BD20: Sils 3F **15**
LS10: Leeds 3C **118**
Telford Ct. BD7: B'frd 5B **90**
Telford Gdns. LS10: Leeds 3C **118**
Telford Pl. LS10: Leeds 3C **118**
Telford St. LS10: Leeds 3C **118**
Telford Ter. LS10: Leeds 3C **118**
Telford Wlk. LS10: Leeds 3C **118**
Telford Way WF2: Carr G 4C **156**
Telscombe Dr. BD4: B'frd 3B **112**
Temperance Ct. LS18: H'fth 1D **74**
Temperance Fld.
BD12: Wyke 4C **132**
BD19: Scho 1F **153**
Temperance St. LS28: Stan 2A **94**
Tempest Grn. BD6: B'frd 4C **110**
(off Chapel St.)
Tempest Pl. LS11: Leeds 2G **117**
Tempest Rd. LS11: Leeds 2G **117**
Templar Gdns. LS22: Weth 2F **13**
Templar La. LS2: Leeds 3G **5** (3B **98**)
LS15: Leeds 5F **81**
Templar Pl. LS2: Leeds 3G **5** (3B **98**)
Templars Cl. HX4: Gree 4E **159**
Templar St. LS2: Leeds 3F **5** (3A **98**)
Templars Way BD8: B'frd 3G **89**
LS25: Gar 5F **103**
Temple Av. LS15: Leeds 5C **100**
LS26: Rothw 6B **120**
Temple Bank Flats BD9: B'frd 2G **89**
Temple Cl. LS15: Leeds 5C **100**
Temple Ct. LS15: Leeds 4B **100**
LS26: Rothw 6B **120**
Temple Cres. LS11: Leeds 2G **117**
Temple Ga. LS15: Leeds 4D **100**
Templegate Av. LS15: Leeds 5C **100**
Templegate Cl. LS15: Leeds 4D **100**
Templegate Cres. LS15: Leeds 5D **100**
Templegate Dr. LS15: Leeds 4C **100**
Templegate Grn. LS15: Leeds 4D **100**
Templegate Ri. LS15: Leeds 5C **100**
Templegate Rd. LS15: Leeds 5C **100**
Templegate Vw. LS15: Leeds 5C **100**
Templegate Wlk. LS15: Leeds 4D **100**
Templegate Way LS15: Leeds 5D **100**
Temple Grn. LS26: Rothw 6C **120**
Temple Gro. LS15: Leeds 4C **100**
Temple La. LS15: Leeds 4D **100**
Temple Lawn LS26: Rothw 6C **120**
Temple Lea LS15: Leeds 4C **100**
Temple M. LS15: Leeds 4D **100**
(off Selby Rd.)
Temple Newsam Golf Course 5B **100**

Temple Newsam Home Farm
(Rare Breeds) 6D **100**
Temple Newsam House 6D **100**
Temple Newsam Pk. 1B **120**
Templenewsam Rd. LS15: Leeds . . .4B **100**
Templenewsam Vw.
LS15: Leeds 5B **100**
Temple Pk. Cl. LS15: Leeds 4C **100**
Temple Pk. Gdns. LS15: Leeds 4C **100**
Temple Pk. Grn. LS15: Leeds 4C **100**
Temple Rhydding BD17: Bail 5C **52**
Temple Rhydding Dr.
BD17: Bail 5C **52**
Temple Ri. LS15: Leeds 5C **100**
Temple Row BD21: Keigh 6H **33**
(off Russell St.)
LS15: Leeds 5G **101**
(off Colton Rd. E.)
Temple Row Cl. LS15: Leeds 5G **101**
Templers Ga. HX2: Hal 6B **128**
Templar Ter. LS27: Morl 5B **138**
Templestowe Cres. LS15: Leeds 2E **101**
Templestowe Dr. LS15: Leeds 3E **101**
Templestowe Gdns.
LS15: Leeds 3D **100**
Templestowe Hill LS15: Leeds 2D **100**
Temple St. BD9: B'frd 1B **90**
BD21: Keigh 6H **33**
Temple Vw. WF3: Loft 6G **141**
Temple Vw. Gro. LS9: Leeds 4E **99**
(not continuous)
Temple Vw. Pl. LS9: Leeds 4D **98**
Temple Vw. Rd. LS9: Leeds 3D **98**
Temple Vw. Ter. LS9: Leeds 4D **98**
Temple Vue LS6: Leeds 3D **76**
(off Mansfield Pl.)
Temple Wlk. LS15: Leeds 3D **100**
Tenbury Fold BD4: B'frd 2C **112**
Tenbury Rd. BD18: Ship 3E **71**
Tenby Ter. HX1: Hal 1D **148**
(off Osborne St.)
Tennis Av. BD4: B'frd 4C **112**
Tennis Way BD17: Bail 6A **52**
Tennyson Av. HX6: Sow B 6F **147**
WF3: S'ley 3H **157**
Tennyson Ct. LS28: Pud 5B **94**
Tennyson Ho. LS29: I'ly 4G **11**
(off Blackthorn La.)
Tennyson Pl. BD3: B'frd 3H **91**
HX3: Hip 1E **151**
Tennyson Rd. BD6: B'frd 5B **110**
Tennyson St. BD21: Keigh 2H **47**
HX3: Hal 6E **129**
LS20: Guis 5D **40**
LS27: Morl 3B **138**
LS28: Fars 1H **93**
LS28: Pud 5B **94**
Tennyson Ter. LS27: Morl 3B **138**
Tentercroft BD17: Bail 3C **52**
Tenterden Way LS15: Leeds 6H **81**
Tenterfield Ri. HX3: North 6C **130**
Tenterfields BD10: B'frd 1B **72**
HX2: Lud M 4E **147**
Tenterfields Bus. Pk.
HX2: Lud M 4E **147**
Tenterfields Ho. BD10: B'frd 1C **72**
Tenterfield Ter. HX3: North 6C **130**
Tenterfield Way BD14: Clay 1D **108**
Tenth Av. WF15: Liv 4H **153**
Ten Yards La. BD13: Thorn 2D **86**
Terminus Pde. LS15: Leeds 1E **101**
(off Farm Rd.)
Tern Pk. LS22: Coll 2B **28**
Tern St. BD5: B'frd 2B **110**
Terrace, The BD3: B'frd 1F **91**
LS23: B Spa 4C **30**
LS28: Pud 1A **114**
Terrace Gdns. HX3: Hal 6F **129**
Terracotta Dr. BD15: All 2C **88**
Terrington Crest BD14: Clay 1F **109**
Terry Rd. BD12: Low M 2E **133**
Tesla La. LS20: Guis 3B **40**
Tetley Dr. BD11: Birk 3E **135**

Tetley La. HX3: North 5C **130**
Tetley Pl. BD2: B'frd 6F **71**
Tetley St. BD1: B'frd 4B **6** (4D **90**)
Teville Cl. BD4: B'frd 1G **111**
Tewit Cl. HX2: Illing 6D **106**
Tewit Gdns. HX2: Illing 6D **106**
(not continuous)
Tewit Grn. HX2: Illing 6D **106**
Tewit Hall Gdns. HX2: Illing 1D **128**
Tewit Hall Rd. BD3: B'frd 3A **92**
Tewit La. HX2: Illing 6D **106**
Tewit Cl. BD20: Stee 5B **14**
Tewitt La. BD13: Thorn 1D **86**
BD16: Bgly 1D **50**
Texas St. LS27: Morl 5B **138**
Thackeray Rd. BD10: B'frd 5B **72**
Thacker Ga. Rd. HX2: Lud M 5B **146**
THACKLEY 5H **53**
Thackley Av. BD10: B'frd 5G **53**
Thackley Ct. BD18: Ship 1C **70**
THACKLEY END 6G **53**
Thackley Old Rd.
BD18: Ship 1C **70**
Thackley Rd. BD10: B'frd 5G **53**
Thackley Vw. BD10: B'frd 5G **53**
Thackray Ct. LS18: H'fth 1G **75**
Thackray Medical Mus. 1D **98**
Thackray St. HX2: Hal 2B **148**
LS27: Morl 4A **138**
Thames Dr. LS25: Gar 5G **103**
Thanet Gth. BD20: Sils 3E **15**
Thane Way LS15: Leeds 6G **81**
Thatchers Way BD19: Gom 6E **135**
Theaker La. LS12: Leeds 3B **96**
Theakston Mead BD14: Clay 1E **109**
Thealby Cl. LS9: Leeds 3C **98**
LS9: Leeds 2C **98**
Thealby Lawn LS9: Leeds 2C **98**
Thealby Pl. LS9: Leeds 3H **5** (3C **98**)
Thearne Grn. BD14: Clay 1F **109**
Theatre in the Mill, The 5C **90**
Theatre Wlk. LS1: Leeds 4E **5**
(within The Core Shop. Cen.)
Theodore St. LS11: Leeds 4G **117**
Third Av. BD3: B'frd 2A **92**
BD21: Keigh 1H **47**
HX3: Hal 5F **149**
LS12: Leeds 5D **96**
LS22: Weth 4F **13**
LS26: Rothw 6B **120**
WF1: Wake 6G **157**
WF15: Liv 5H **153**
Third St. BD12: Low M 1E **133**
Thirkhill Ct. BD5: B'frd 1E **111**
Thirkleby Royd BD14: Clay 1E **109**
Thirlmere Av. BD12: Wyke 6E **133**
HX5: Ell 4D **160**
Thirlmere Cl. LS11: Leeds 5E **117**
Thirlmere Dr. LS22: Weth 3B **12**
WF3: Ting 1G **155**
Thirlmere Gdns. BD2: B'frd 1H **91**
LS11: Leeds 5E **117**
Thirlmere Gro. BD17: Bail 6G **51**
(not continuous)
Thirsk Dr. LS25: Kip 3G **123**
Thirsk Grange BD14: Clay 6F **89**
Thirsk Gro. LS10: Leeds 4B **140**
Thirsk Row LS1: Leeds 5C **4** (4H **97**)
Thirteenth Av. WF15: Liv 4H **153**
Thistle Way LS27: Gil 2F **137**
Thistlewood Rd. WF1: Out 4H **157**
Thomas Ct. BD6: B'frd 4C **110**
Thomas Dr. LS20: Guis 3B **40**
Thomas Duggan Ho.
BD18: Ship 2B **70**
(off Manor La.)
Thomas Fold BD2: B'frd 1H **91**
(off Idle Rd.)
Thomas Pl. BD18: Ship 2C **70**

Thomas St.—Throstle La.

Thomas St. BD22: Haw 3D **64**
HD6: Ras 2A **162**
HX1: Hal 4C **164** (2G **149**)
HX4: Holy 6F **159**
HX5: Ell 5C **160**
LS6: Leeds 6G **77**
Thomas St. Sth. HX1: Hal 3D **148**
Thomas St. W. HX1: Hal 4E **149**
Thompson Av. BD2: B'frd 4F **71**
Thompson Cl. HX3: Hip 2E **151**
Thompson Dr. WF2: Wren 6D **156**
Thompson Grn. BD17: Bail 5A **52**
Thompson La. BD17: Bail 6A **52**
Thompson St. BD18: Ship 1A **70**
Thoresby Gro. BD7: B'frd 2G **109**
Thoresby Pl.
LS1: Leeds 3C **4** (2H **97**)
Thornaby Dr. BD14: Clay 1E **109**
Thornacre Cres. BD18: Ship 3E **71**
Thornacre Rd. BD18: Ship 2E **71**
Thorn Av. BD9: B'frd 5E **69**
Thorn Bank HX2: Lud 6D **126**
Thorn Bank Av. BD22: Oak 3F **47**
Thornber Bank *BD20: Sils 1E* ***15***
(off Thornber Gro.)
Thornber Gro. BD20: Sils 1E **15**
Thornberry Dr. WF15: Liv 4H **153**
Thornbridge M. BD2: B'frd 5H **71**
THORNBURY **4C 92**
Thornbury Av. BD3: B'frd 3B **92**
LS16: Leeds 2C **76**
Thornbury Cres. BD3: B'frd 3B **92**
Thornbury Dr. BD3: B'frd 3B **92**
Thornbury Gro. BD3: B'frd 3B **92**
Thornbury Rd. BD3: B'frd 4B **92**
Thornbury St. BD3: B'frd 4B **92**
Thorncliffe Rd. BD8: B'frd 2D **90**
BD22: Keigh 1F **47**
Thorn Cl. BD18: Ship 3E **71**
Thorn Cres. LS8: Leeds 6F **79**
Thorncrest BD17: Bail 4C **52**
Thorncroft Rd. BD6: B'frd 4H **109**
Thorn Cross LS8: Leeds 5G **79**
Thorndale Ri. BD2: B'frd 5E **71**
Thorndene Way BD4: B'frd 6E **113**
Thorn Dr. BD9: B'frd 5F **69**
BD13: Que 6G **107**
LS8: Leeds 6F **79**
Thorne Cl. LS28: Pud 3F **93**
Thornefield Cres. WF3: Ting 1D **154**
Thorne Gro. LS26: Rothw 1B **142**
THORNER **2H 63**
Thorner La. LS14: S'cft 5F **45**
LS14: T'ner 5G **63**
Thornes Farm App. LS9: Leeds 6H **99**
Thornes Farm Way LS9: Leeds 6H **99**
Thornes Pk. BD18: Ship 4D **70**
HD6: Ras 2A **162**
Thorneycroft Rd. BD20: E Mor 4F **35**
Thorney La. HX2: Midg 6C **126**
Thornfield BD16: Bgly 3A **50**
BD22: Haw 2D **64**
Thornfield Av. BD6: B'frd 5D **110**
LS28: Fars 6G **73**
Thornfield Ct. LS15: Leeds 1D **100**
Thornfield Dr. LS15: Leeds 1D **100**
Thornfield Hall *BD13: Thorn 5A* ***88***
(off Thornton Rd.)
Thornfield M. BD16: Bgly 6A **36**
LS15: Leeds 1D **100**
Thornfield Mt. WF17: Birs 6C **136**
Thornfield Pl. BD2: B'frd 6A **72**
Thornfield Ri. HX4: Gree 4F **159**
Thornfield Rd. LS16: Leeds 1B **76**
Thornfield Sq. BD2: B'frd 6A **72**
Thornfield St. HX4: Gree 4F **159**
Thornfield Ter. BD15: Wils 5F **67**
Thornfield Way LS15: Leeds 1D **100**
Thorn Gth. BD19: Cleck 3H **153**
BD20: Keigh 4G **33**
Thorngate BD13: Denh 1D **86**
Thorn Gro. BD9: B'frd 5F **69**
LS8: Leeds 6F **79**
Thornhill Av. BD18: Ship 4D **70**
BD22: Oak 4E **47**
Thornhill Beck La.
HD6: Brigh, Clift 5B **152**
Thornhill Bri. La. HD6: Brigh 6A **152**
Thornhill Cl. LS28: Cal 2F **73**
Thornhill Ct. LS12: Leeds 5C **96**
Thornhill Cft. LS12: Leeds 5B **96**
Thornhill Dr. BD10: Cal 1D **72**
BD18: Ship 4D **70**
LS28: Cal 1F **73**
Thornhill Gro. BD18: Ship 4D **70**
BD20: Stee 5B **14**
LS28: Cal 2F **73**
Thornhill Ho. *BD3: B'frd 3C* ***92***
(off Thornhill Pl.)
Thornhill Pl. BD3: B'frd 3C **92**
HD6: Ras 2A **162**
LS12: Leeds 5B **96**
Thornhill Rd. BD20: Stee 4B **14**
HD6: Ras 3H **161**
LS12: Leeds 5B **96**
THORNHILLS **5C 152**
Thornhills La. HD6: Clift 5C **152**
Thornhill St. LS12: Leeds 5B **96**
LS28: Cal 2F **73**
Thornhill Ter. BD3: B'frd 3B **92**
THORNHURST **6G 27**
Thorn La. BD9: B'frd 5F **69**
(not continuous)
LS8: Leeds 2D **78**
Thornlea Cl. LS19: Yead 2D **54**
Thorn Lee HX2: Lud 6E **127**
Thornleigh Gdns. LS9: Leeds 5D **98**
Thornleigh Gro. LS9: Leeds 5D **98**
Thornleigh Mt. LS9: Leeds 5D **98**
Thornleigh St. LS9: Leeds 5D **98**
Thornleigh Vw. LS9: Leeds 5D **98**
Thornmead Rd. BD17: Bail 5D **52**
Thorn Mt. LS8: Leeds 5G **79**
Thorn Royd Dr. BD4: B'frd 3D **112**
Thornsgill Av. BD4: B'frd 2A **112**
Thorn St. BD8: B'frd 2H **89**
BD22: Haw 1E **65**
WF17: Birs 6A **136**
Thorn Ter. HX2: Lud 6E **127**
LS8: Leeds 5F **79**
THORNTON **5H 87**
Thornton Av. LS12: Leeds 4A **96**
Thornton Cl. WF17: Birs 4B **136**
Thornton Ct. *BD8: B'frd 3H* ***89***
(off Lane Ends Cl.)
Thornton Gdns. LS12: Leeds 4A **96**
Thornton Gro. LS12: Leeds 4A **96**
Thornton La. BD5: B'frd 2C **110**
Thornton Moor Rd.
BD13: Denh 3G **85**
BD22: B'frd, Oxen 3G **85**
Thornton Old Rd. BD8: B'frd 4F **89**
Thornton Recreation Cen. **5D 88**
Thornton Rd. BD1: B'frd 3A **90**
BD7: B'frd 3A **90**
BD8: B'frd 3A **90**
BD13: Denh, Thorn 6C **86**
BD13: Que 3H **107**
HD6: Ras 3G **161**
Thornton Road (Park & Ride)
. . . .**4A 6 (4D 90)**
Thornton Rd. Ind. Est.
BD8: B'frd 3A **90**
Thornton's Arc.
LS1: Leeds 4E **5** (3A **98**)
Thorntons Dale LS18: H'fth 3D **74**
Thornton Sq. *HD6: Brigh 1A* ***162***
(off Briggate)
Thornton St. BD1: B'frd 3A **6** (4C **90**)
BD19: Cleck 3G **153**
HX1: Hal 4D **148**
LS29: Burl W 1E **21**
Thornton Ter. HX1: Hal 4D **148**
Thornton Vw. Rd. BD14: Clay 2E **109**
Thorn Tree Cotts. HX3: Sou 5F **151**
Thorn Tree St. HX1: Hal 4D **148**
Thorn Vw. HX2: Lud 6E **127**
HX3: Hal 5G **129**
HX5: Ell 5C **160**
LS8: Leeds 6G **79**
Thornville LS27: Chur 6B **116**
Thornville Av. LS6: Leeds 1E **97**
Thornville Ct. BD8: B'frd 1C **90**
LS6: Leeds 1E ***97***
(off Thornville Rd.)
Thornville Cres. LS6: Leeds 6E **77**
Thornville Gro. LS6: Leeds 1E **97**
Thornville Mt. LS6: Leeds 1E **97**
Thornville Pl. LS6: Leeds 1E **97**
Thornville Rd. LS6: Leeds 1E **97**
Thornville Row LS6: Leeds 1E **97**
Thornville St. LS6: Leeds 1E **97**
Thornville Ter. LS6: Leeds 1E **97**
Thornville Vw. LS6: Leeds 1E **97**
Thorn Wlk. LS8: Leeds 6G **79**
Thorny Bank HX6: Norl 1B **158**
Thorold Ho. *BD10: B'frd 2A* ***72***
(off Haigh Beck Vw.)
THORP ARCH **2C 30**
Thorp Arch Grange
LS23: T Arch 1D **30**
Thorp Arch Pk. LS23: T Arch 2C **30**
Thorp Arch Trad. Est.
LS23: T Arch 1F **31**
THORPE **2A 72**
Thorpe Av. BD13: Thorn 5C **88**
Thorpe Cl. LS20: Guis 5H **39**
Thorpe Ct. LS10: Leeds 4A **140**
Thorpe Cres. LS10: Leeds 3A **140**
Thorpe Dr. LS20: Guis 4A **40**
THORPE EDGE **2A 72**
Thorpe Gdns. LS10: Leeds 3A **140**
Thorpe Gth. LS10: Leeds 4H **139**
Thorpe Gro. BD13: Thorn 5D **88**
LS10: Leeds 3A **140**
Thorpe La. LS10: Leeds 6F **139**
LS20: Guis 5G **39**
WF3: Ting 6F **139**
Thorpe Lodge *WF3: Loft 6G* ***141***
(off Long Thorpe La.)
Thorpe Lwr. La.
WF3: Rothw, Thpe H 5D **140**
Thorpe Mt. LS10: Leeds 4H **139**
THORPE ON THE HILL **5B 140**
Thorpe Pk. LS15: Leeds 4H **101**
Thorpe Pl. HX6: Sow B 6C **146**
Thorpe Rd. BD13: Thorn 5C **88**
LS10: Leeds 2A **140**
LS28: Pud 3H **93**
WF3: E Ard 2A **156**
Thorpe Sq. LS10: Leeds 3B **140**
Thorpe St. BD21: Keigh 5A **34**
HX3: Hal 5F **129**
LS10: Leeds 3A **140**
LS15: Leeds 3C **100**
Thorpe Ter. HX2: Lud 6D **126**
(Solomon Hill)
HX2: Lud 6D **126**
(South Carr)
Thorpe Vw. LS10: Leeds 4A **140**
Thorp Gth. BD10: B'frd 2H **71**
Thorverton Dr. BD4: B'frd 5C **112**
Thorverton Gro. BD4: B'frd 5C **112**
Threadneedle St. *HX1: Hal 4D* ***148***
(off Thorn Tree St.)
Threap Cft. HX2: Illing 1D **128**
Threelands BD11: Birk 1E **135**
Three Nooked M. *BD10: B'frd 1B* ***72***
(off Albion Rd.)
Threshfield BD17: Bail 4C **52**
Threshfield Cres. BD11: Birk 1E **135**
Thrice Fold BD10: B'frd 1F **71**
Thrift Way BD16: Bgly 5B **50**
Throstle Av. LS10: Leeds 4H **139**
Throstle Bank *HX2: Hal 4D* ***148***
(off Gainest)
Throstle Dr. LS10: Leeds 4G **139**
Throstle Hill LS10: Leeds 4H **139**
Throstle La. LS10: Leeds 4H **139**

Throstle Mt. HX2: Lud M 4F 147
  LS10: Leeds 4H 139
Throstle Nest Cl. LS21: Otley 1B 22
Throstle Nest Rd. BD20: Sils 1D 14
Throstle Nest Vw. LS18: H'fth 2E 75
Throstle Pde. LS10: Leeds 4H 139
Throstle Pl. LS10: Leeds 4H 139
Throstle Rd. LS10: Leeds 4A 140
Throstle Rd. Nth. LS10: Leeds 2C 140
Throstle Sq. LS10: Leeds 4B 140
Throstle Row LS10: Leeds 4H 139
Throstle St. LS10: Leeds 4H 139
Throstle Ter. LS10: Leeds 4A 140
Throstle Vw. LS10: Leeds 4B 140
Throstle Wlk. LS10: Leeds 4H 139
Throxenby Way BD14: Clay 1E 109
Thrum Hall Cl. HX1: Hal 2D 148
Thrum Hall Dr. HX1: Hal 2D 148
Thrum Hall Ind. Pk. HX2: Hal 1C 148
Thrum Hall La. HX1: Hal 2D 148
Thrush St. BD21: Keigh 5B 34
Thryberg St. BD3: B'frd 5H 7 (4G 91)
Thurlestone Ct. BD20: E Mor 5F 35
Thurley Dr. BD4: B'frd 3H 111
Thurley Rd. BD4: B'frd 3H 111
Thurnscoe Rd. BD1: B'frd 1B 6 (3D 90)
  (not continuous)
Thursby St. BD3: B'frd 4H 7 (4H 91)
Thurston Gdns. BD15: All 3D 88
Thwaite Ct. LS18: H'fth 1G 75
THWAITE GATE 2D 118
Thwaite Ga. LS10: Leeds 2D 118
Thwaite La. LS10: Leeds 2E 119
Thwaite Mills Watermill Mus. 2F 119
THWAITES .6D 34
Thwaites Av. LS29: I'ly 5E 11
Thwaites Bank BD21: Keigh 6D 34
Thwaites Bri. BD21: Keigh 6C 34
THWAITES BROW 1D 48
Thwaites Brow Rd.
  BD21: Keigh 6D 34
Thwaites La. BD21: Keigh 6C 34
Tibgarth LS22: Lin 6B 12
Tichborne Rd. BD5: B'frd 2E 111
Tichborne Rd. W. BD5: B'frd 2E 111
Tickhill St. BD3: B'frd 5H 7 (5H 91)
Tilbury Av. LS11: Leeds 1F 117
Tilbury Gro. LS11: Leeds 1F 117
Tilbury Mt. LS11: Leeds 1F 117
Tilbury Pde. LS11: Leeds 1F 117
Tilbury Rd. LS11: Leeds 1F 117
Tilbury Row LS11: Leeds 1F 117
Tilbury Ter. LS11: Leeds 1F 117
Tilbury Vw. LS11: Leeds 1F 117
Tile La. LS16: Leeds 4D 58
  (not continuous)
Tile St. BD8: B'frd 2B 90
Tile Ter. HD6: Ras 2A 162
Tiley Sq. BD5: B'frd 1E 111
Till Carr La. HX3: Hip 2A 152
Tillotson Av. HX6: Sow B 6G 147
Tillotson's Bldgs. HX2: Lud M 2D 146
Tillotson St. BD20: Sils 1D 14
Timber St. BD21: Keigh 5C 34
  HX5: Ell 5B 160
Timble Dr. BD16: Bgly 3D 50
Tim La. BD22: Oak 5B 46
Timmey La. HX6: Sow B 4G 147
Timothy Taylor Brewery 2H 47
Tingle Vw. LS12: N Far 2A 116
TINGLEY 6E 139
Tingley Av. WF3: Ting 6E 139
Tingley Comn. LS27: Morl 5B 138
Tingley Cres. WF3: Ting 6C 138
Tingley Hall Ri. WF3: Ting 6E 139
Tinkler Stile BD10: B'frd 1F 71
TINSHILL 3F 57
Tinshill Av. LS16: Leeds 4G 57
Tinshill Cl. LS16: Leeds 4G 57
Tinshill Cres. LS16: Leeds 3G 57
Tinshill Dr. LS16: Leeds 2G 57
Tinshill Gth. LS16: Leeds 3G 57
Tinshill Gro. LS16: Leeds 3G 57

Tinshill La. LS16: Leeds 4F 57
TINSHILL MOOR 2G 57
Tinshill Mt. LS16: Leeds 3G 57
Tinshill Rd. LS16: Leeds 4F 57
Tinshill Vw. LS16: Leeds 3G 57
Tinshill Wlk. LS16: Leeds 2G 57
Tintern Av. BD8: B'frd 4F 89
Tisma Dr. BD4: B'frd 5A 112
Titan Cen. BD12: Wyke 5C 132
Titania Cl. BD16: Cot 3D 68
Tithe Barn Fold LS15: Bar E 2D 82
Tithe Barn La. LS17: Bard 3D 44
Tithe Barn Vw. HD6: Ras 3C 162
Tithe Ho. Way HD2: Hud 5E 163
Titus St. BD18: Ship 1H 69
Tiverton Wlk. BD4: B'frd 3C 112
Tivoli Pl. BD5: B'frd 2C 110
  LS29: I'ly 6E 11
Toby La. BD7: B'frd 6A 90
Todd Ter. BD7: B'frd 1B 110
Todley Hall Rd. BD22: Oak 1A 46
Todwell La. BD5: B'frd 2C 110
Tofts Av. BD12: Wyke 5C 132
Tofts Gro. HD6: Ras 4G 161
Tofts Gro. Fold HD6: Ras 4H 161
Tofts Gro. Gdns. HD6: Ras 4H 161
Tofts Gro. Pl. HD6: Ras 4H 161
  (off Tofts Gro.)
TOFTSHAW .5B 112
Toftshaw Fold BD4: B'frd 5B 112
Toftshaw La. BD4: B'frd 5C 112
Toftshaw New Rd. BD4: B'frd 5B 112
Tofts Ho. Cl. LS28: Pud 4A 94
Tofts Rd. LS28: Pud 4H 93
Toft St. LS12: Leeds 5D 96
Toller Dr. BD9: B'frd 6G 69
Toller Gro. BD9: B'frd 6H 69
Toller La. BD8: B'frd 6G 69
  BD9: B'frd 6G 69
Toller Pk. BD9: B'frd 6H 69
Tollgate Ct. BD8: B'frd 2A 90
Tolworth Fold BD15: All 3D 88
Tomling Cote La. BD20: Sils 3G 15
Tomlinson Bldgs. BD10: B'frd 6G 53
Tonbridge Cl. BD6: B'frd 5H 109
TONG 3H 113
Tong App. LS12: Leeds 5F 95
Tong Dr. LS12: Leeds 4F 95
Tong Ga. LS12: Leeds 4F 95
Tong Grn. LS12: Leeds 4F 95
Tong Hall Bus. Pk. BD4: B'frd 3H 113
Tong La. BD4: B'frd 5G 113
Tong Moor Side BD11: Birk 6E 113
TONG PARK 2F 53
Tong Pk. BD17: Bail 2F 53
Tong Rd. Bus. Pk.
  LS12: Leeds 4C 96
Tong Sports Centre & Pool 5D 112
TONG STREET 4C 112
Tong St. BD4: B'frd 3A 112
Tongue La. LS6: Leeds 1F 77
Tong Wlk. LS12: Leeds 4F 95
Tong Way LS12: Leeds 4F 95
Tonson Ct. BD21: Keigh 5A 34
Tony Miller App. BD17: Ship 1C 70
TOOTHILL 4A 162
Toothill Av. HD6: Ras 4A 162
Toothill Bank HD6: Ras 3A 162
Toothill La. HD6: Ras 5A 162
Toothill La. Sth. HD6: Ras 6H 161
TOPCLIFFE .5C 138
Topcliffe Av. LS27: Morl 3D 138
Topcliffe Cl. WF3: Ting 5D 138
Topcliffe Ct. LS27: Morl 3E 139
Topcliffe Fold LS27: Morl 5C 138
Topcliffe Grn. LS27: Morl 3D 138
Topcliffe Gro. LS27: Morl 5C 138
Topcliffe La. LS27: Morl 5C 138
  WF3: Ting 4D 138
Topcliffe Mead LS27: Morl 3D 138
Topcliffe M. LS27: Morl 3D 138
Top Fold LS12: Leeds 5B 96

Topliss Way LS10: Leeds 3C 140
Top Moor Side LS11: Leeds 6G 97
Tops Health Club 5F 157
  (off Cobham Pde.)
Tor Av. BD12: Wyke 6C 132
Torcote Cres. HD2: Hud 6C 162
Tordoff Av. BD7: B'frd 6G 89
Tordoff Grn. BD6: B'frd 5B 110
Tordoff Pl. LS5: Leeds 5A 76
Tordoff Rd. BD12: Low M 1E 133
Tordoff Ter. LS5: Leeds 5A 76
Tornwood Cl. BD22: Oak 5B 46
Toronto Pl. LS7: Leeds 3B 78
Toronto Sq. LS1: Leeds 4D 4
Toronto St. LS1: Leeds 4D 4 (3H 97)
  LS6: Leeds 1E 97
  (off Queen's Rd.)
Torre Cl. LS9: Leeds 3E 99
Torre Cres. BD6: B'frd 4F 109
  LS9: Leeds 3F 99
Torre Dr. LS9: Leeds 2E 99
Torre Gdns. LS9: Leeds 3D 98
Torre Grn. LS9: Leeds 3D 98
Torre Gro. BD6: B'frd 4F 109
  LS9: Leeds 2E 99
Torre Hill LS9: Leeds 3F 99
Torre La. LS9: Leeds 3F 99
Torre Mt. LS9: Leeds 2E 99
Torre Pl. LS9: Leeds 3E 99
Torre Rd. BD6: B'frd 4F 109
  LS9: Leeds 3D 98
Torre Sq. LS9: Leeds 2F 99
Torre Vw. LS9: Leeds 2F 99
Torre Wlk. LS9: Leeds 2F 99
Torridon Cres. BD6: B'frd 1G 131
TOULSTON .2F 29
Tourist Info. Cen.
  Bradford 5D 6 (5E 91)
  Halifax 4D 164 (2H 149)
  Haworth 2B 64
  Ilkley 5D 10
  Leeds Station 5D 4 (4H 97)
  Otley 4E 23
  Wetherby 4E 13
Tow Bank Cl. LS23: B Spa 3B 30
Towcester Av. LS10: Leeds 4B 140
Tower Ct. LS12: Leeds 3D 96
  LS29: I'ly 5D 10
  (off Wharfe Vw. Rd.)
Tower Drive, The LS21: Pool 5G 25
Tower Gdns. HX2: Hal 5D 148
Tower Gro. LS12: Leeds 3A 96
Tower Hill HX6: Sow B 1H 157
Tower Ho. St. LS2: Leeds 2F 5 (2A 98)
Tower La. LS12: Leeds 3H 95
  (not continuous)
Tower Pl. LS12: Leeds 3H 95
Tower Rd. BD18: Ship 1G 69
Towers, The LS12: Leeds 3H 95
Towers Sq. LS6: Leeds 1G 77
Tower St. BD2: B'frd 1H 91
Tower Vw. LS6: Leeds 1F 77
Tower Vw. HX2: Hal 4C 148
  (off Plane Tree Nest La.)
Tower Works
  LS11: Leeds 6C 4 (4H 97)
Towler Dr. LS13: Leeds 4A 74
Town Cl. LS18: H'fth 6D 56
Townclose Vw. LS25: Kip 5F 123
TOWN END
  BD14 .6D 88
  LS12 . . . . .6B 96
  LS13 . . . . .1G 95
  LS27 . . . . .3A 138
  WF3 . . . . .6G 141
Town End BD7: B'frd 1A 110
  LS25: Gar 3E 103
  LS27: Gil 6F 115
  LS27: Morl 3B 138
  (off Middleton Rd.)
Town End Cl. LS13: Leeds 2G 95
Townend Pl. LS28: Pud 3B 94
Town End Rd. BD14: Clay 6D 88

Townend Rd. LS12: Leeds 6B 96
Town End Yd. LS13: Leeds 1F 95
Townfield BD15: Wils 4G 67
Town Flds. Rd. HX5: Ell 5A 160
Town Ga. BD10: B'frd 1H 71
　　BD12: Wyke 5C 132
　　BD19: Scho 1F 153
　　LS20: Guis 4C 40
　　LS28: Cal 2F 73
Towngate BD17: Bail 3D 52
　　　　　(off Northgate)
　　BD18: Ship 2D 70
　　BD21: Keigh 6A 34
　　HD6: Clift 6D 152
　　HX2: Midg 6B 126
　　HX3: Hip 1E 151
　　HX3: North 5C 130
　　HX3: Sou 5C 150
　　HX6: Sow B 6D 146
Towngate Av. HD6: Clift 6D 152
Town Ga. Cl. LS20: Guis 4C 40
Towngate Ho. HX5: Ell 5B 160
Town Hall Bldgs. HX5: Ell 3D 52
　　　　　(off Southgate)
Town Hall Hd. HX6: Sow B 5H 147
Town Hall Sq. LS19: Yead 6F 41
Town Hall St. BD21: Keigh 6A 34
　　HX5: Ell 5B 160
　　HX6: Sow B 6H 147
Town Hall St. E.
　　HX1: Hal 3C 164 (2G 149)
TOWN HEAD 1F 15
Town Head Fold LS29: Add 1C 8
Town Hill St. BD16: Cot 3D 68
Town La. BD10: B'frd 6H 53
Townley Av. HX3: Sou 5C 150
Town Sq. LS18: H'fth 6D 56
　　　　　(off Kerry Gth.)
Town St. BD11: Birk 1E 135
　　LS7: Leeds 2B 78
　　LS10: Leeds 2H 139
　　LS11: Leeds 4E 117
　　LS12: Leeds 3A 96
　　LS13: Leeds 6E 75
　　　　　(Bell La.)
　　LS13: Leeds 4A 74
　　　　　(St Andrew's Cl.)
　　LS18: H'fth 1D 74
　　LS19: Raw 4H 55
　　LS19: Yead 6F 41
　　LS20: Guis 4C 40
　　LS27: Gil 6E 115
　　LS28: Fars 6H 73
　　LS28: Stan 2A 94
　　WF3: Carl 4H 141
Town St. Ct. LS18: H'fth 6D 56
Town St. M. LS7: Leeds 2B 78
Town St. Wlk. LS7: Leeds 2B 78
Town Wells Dr. LS28: Cal 3F 73
Trackside BD12: O'haw 2F 133
Trafalgar Gdns. LS27: Morl 4A 138
Trafalgar Rd. LS29: I'ly 5D 10
Trafalgar Sq. HX1: Hal 4E 149
Trafalgar St. BD1: B'frd 2C 6 (3E 91)
　　HX1: Hal 4E 149
　　LS2: Leeds 3G 5 (3B 98)
Trafford Av. LS9: Leeds 1F 99
Trafford Gro. LS9: Leeds 6E 79
Trafford Ter. LS9: Leeds 1F 99
Train Fix Health Club 2F 31
Tramways BD12: O'haw 2F 133
　　LS20: Guis 4A 40
Tranbeck Rd. LS20: Guis 4H 39
Tranfield Av. LS20: Guis 5A 40
Tranfield Cl. LS20: Guis 5A 40
Tranfield Ct. LS20: Guis 5A 40
Tranfield Gdns. LS20: Guis 4A 40
Tranmere Ct. LS20: Guis 4A 40
Tranmere Dr. LS20: Guis 4A 40
Tranmere Pde. LS20: Guis 4A 40
　　　　　(off Tranmere Ct.)
TRANMERE PARK 5H 39
Tranquility LS15: Leeds 1E 101

Tranquility Av. LS15: Leeds 1E 101
Tranquility Ct. LS15: Leeds 1H 27
　　　　　(off Tranquility Av.)
Tranquility Wlk. LS15: Leeds 1E 101
Tranter Gro. BD4: B'frd 6C 92
Tranter Pl. LS15: Leeds 3A 100
Tray Royd HX2: Midg 5C 126
Treadwells Mills BD1: B'frd 3F 7
Tredgold Av. LS16: B'hpe 3G 43
Tredgold Cl. LS16: B'hpe 3G 43
Tredgold Cres. LS16: B'hpe 3G 43
Tredgold Gth. LS16: B'hpe 3G 43
Treefield Ind. Est.
　　LS27: Gil 1F 137
Tree La. HX2: Wain 2F 127
Trees St. BD8: B'frd 2C 90
Tree Tops Ct. LS8: Leeds 2G 79
Tree Top Vw. BD13: Que 3G 107
Trelawn Av. LS6: Leeds 4D 76
Trelawn Cres. LS6: Leeds 4D 76
Trelawn Pl. LS6: Leeds 4D 76
Trelawn St. LS6: Leeds 4D 76
Trelawn Ter. LS6: Leeds 4D 76
Tremont Gdns. LS10: Leeds 3C 118
Trenam Pk. Dr. BD10: B'frd 5G 53
Trenance Dr. BD18: Ship 2H 69
Trenance Gdns. HX4: Gree 4D 158
Trenholme Av. BD6: B'frd 1B 132
Trenic Cres. LS6: Leeds 6D 76
Trenic Dr. LS6: Leeds 6D 76
Trent Av. LS25: Gar 5H 103
Trentham Av. LS11: Leeds 2H 117
Trentham Gro.
　　LS11: Leeds 2H 117
Trentham Pl. LS11: Leeds 2H 117
Trentham Row LS11: Leeds 2H 117
Trentham St. LS11: Leeds 3H 117
Trentham Ter. LS11: Leeds 2H 117
Trenton Dr. BD8: B'frd 2C 90
Trent Rd. LS9: Leeds 3D 98
Trent St. LS11: Leeds 6H 97
Trescoe Av. LS13: Leeds 2G 95
Trevelyan Sq. LS1: Leeds 5E 5 (4A 98)
Trevelyan St. HD6: Brigh 4A 152
Trevor Foster Way
　　BD5: B'frd 3F 111
Trevor Ter. WF2: Carr G 3C 156
Triangle BD6: B'frd 5D 110
　　　　　(off Odsal Rd.)
Triangle, The LS3: Leeds 2F 97
　　　　　(off Burley Rd.)
Triangle Bus. Pk. WF17: Birs 4C 136
Trimmingham La. HX2: Hal 3B 148
Trimmingham Rd. HX2: Hal 3B 148
Trimmingham Vs. HX2: Hal 3C 148
Trinity Bus. Cen. HX1: Hal 6C 164
Trinity Chapel LS28: Pud 3A 94
　　　　　(off Wesley Sq.)
Trinity Cl. HX2: Illing 1E 129
　　LS18: H'fth 4D 56
Trinity Ct. LS8: Leeds 2C 78
Trinity Fold HX1: Hal 5B 164
Trinity Leeds LS1: Leeds 5E 5 (4A 98)
Trinity One LS9: Leeds 6H 5 (4B 98)
Trinity Pl. BD16: Bgly 5C 50
　　HX1: Hal 5B 164 (3G 149)
　　HX3: Hip 2E 151
　　　　　(off Barfield Rd.)
Trinity Ri. LS21: Otley 4F 23
Trinity Rd. BD5: B'frd 6D 90
　　HX1: Hal 5B 164 (3G 149)
Trinity Row
　　HX1: Hal 5B 164 (3G 149)
Trinity St. BD21: Keigh 5A 34
　　　　　(off Spring St.)
　　HX1: Hal 5B 164
　　LS1: Leeds 4E 5 (3A 98)
Trinity Ter. WF17: Birs 6H 135
Trinity Vw. HD12: Low M 6E 111
　　HX3: Hal 3H 149
　　LS28: Fars 5H 73
　　　　　(off Bryan St.)
Trinity Wlk. BD12: Low M 6E 111

Trip Gth. LS22: Lin 1B 28
Trip La. LS22: Lin 1H 27
Tristram Av. BD5: B'frd 3G 111
Tristram Centre, The
　　LS12: Leeds 1E 117
Triumph Cl. LS11: Leeds 5G 97
Trojan Cl. LS27: Morl 2A 138
　　　　　(off Troy Hill)
Trooper La. HX3: Hal 4H 149
Trooper Ter. HX3: Hal 4H 149
Tropical World 6F 61
Trough La. BD13: Denh 2F 85
Troughton St. LS28: Pud 6B 94
Trough Well La. WF2: Wren 5C 156
Troutbeck Av. BD17: Bail 6G 51
　　　　　(not continuous)
TROY 5E 57
TROYDALE 5D 94
Troydale Gdns. LS28: Pud 6D 94
Troydale Gro. LS28: Pud 6D 94
Troydale La. LS12: Pud 5C 94
　　LS28: Pud 5C 94
Troydale Pk. LS28: Pud 6D 94
TROY HILL 2A 138
Troy Hill LS18: H'fth 5E 57
　　LS27: Morl 2A 138
Troy Mills LS18: H'fth 5E 57
Troy Ri. LS27: Morl 2B 138
Troy Rd. LS18: H'fth 5E 57
　　LS27: Morl 2A 138
Trueman Ct. BD12: Low M 1E 133
TRUNCLIFFE 4D 110
Truncliffe BD5: B'frd 4D 110
Truncliffe Ho. BD5: B'frd 4D 110
　　　　　(off Truncliffe)
Truro St. LS12: Leeds 3C 96
Tudor Barn Ct. BD18: Ship 2D 70
Tudor Cl. LS28: Fars 1G 93
Tudor Ct. BD5: B'frd 6E 91
　　　　　(off Swarland Gro.)
Tudor Cft. HD2: Hud 6F 163
Tudor Gdns. LS11: Leeds 3E 117
Tudor Lawns LS8: Leeds 2G 79
　　WF2: Carr G 4C 156
Tudor St. BD5: B'frd 1D 110
Tudor Way LS11: Leeds 4E 117
Tuel La. HX6: Sow B 4H 147
Tufters Fold HD6: B Bri 2B 152
Tufton St. BD20: Sils 2D 14
Tulip Retail Pk.
　　LS10: Leeds 2B 118
Tulip St. BD22: Haw 4C 64
　　LS10: Leeds 2B 118
Tulyar Ct. BD16: Bgly 4D 50
Tumbling Hill St.
　　BD7: B'frd 5A 6 (5D 90)
Tundra Gro. BD16: Bgly 3E 51
Tunnel St. BD13: Denh 3B 86
Tunnicliffe Pl. BD20: Sils 2D 14
Tunnicliffe Way BD3: B'frd 4D 92
Tunstall Grn. BD4: B'frd 2C 112
Tunstall Rd. LS11: Leeds 2A 118
Tunwell La. BD2: B'frd 5A 72
Tunwell St. BD2: B'frd 5A 72
Turbary Av. LS28: Fars 1A 94
Turbury La. HX4: Gree 3C 158
Turf Ct. BD13: Cull 4A 66
Turf La. BD13: Cull 3A 66
Turkey Hill LS28: Pud 5B 94
　　　　　(not continuous)
Turks Head Yd. LS1: Leeds 4E 5
Turlow Ct. LS9: Leeds 6H 5 (4B 98)
Turnberry Av. LS17: Leeds 3H 59
Turnberry Cl. LS17: Leeds 3H 59
　　WF3: Ting 1D 154
Turnberry Ct. BD20: Keigh 2G 33
Turnberry Dr. LS17: Leeds 3H 59
　　WF3: Ting 1D 154
Turnberry Fold LS17: Leeds 3H 59
Turnberry Gdns.
　　WF3: Ting 1D 154
Turnberry Gro. LS17: Leeds 3H 59
Turnberry Pk. Rd. LS27: Gil 3F 137

Turnberry Pl. LS17: Leeds 3H 59
Turnberry Ri. LS17: Leeds 3H 59
Turnberry Vw. LS17: Leeds 3H 59
Turnbull Ct. LS8: Leeds 4H 79
Turner Av. BD7: B'frd 6H 89
Turner Av. Sth. HX2: Illing 2B 128
Turner Av. Nth. HX2: Illing 2C 128
Turner Cl. WF3: Ting 1E 155
Turner Cres. LS21: Otley 2F 23
Turner Dr. WF3: Ting 1E 155
Turner Farm HX2: Illing 6C 106
(off Keighley Rd.)
Turner Ho. LS5: Leeds 5H 75
Turner La. HX3: Hal 1D 164 (6H 129)
(not continuous)
LS29: Add 1A 8
(Addingham Wharfedale Rd.)
LS29: Add 3A 8
(Straight La.)
Turner Pl. BD7: B'frd 6B 90
HX2: Illing 2C 128
Turners Ct. HX3: Hal 5F 129
Turner St. LS28: Fars 6H 73
Turner's Yd. LS13: Leeds 1F 95
LS28: Fars 6H 73
Turner Vw. HX2: Illing 3C 128
(off Bank Edge Rd.)
Turney St. HX3: Hal 5E 129
(not continuous)
Turn Lea HX2: Lud 6D 126
Turnpike Cl. BD11: Birk 3E 135
Turnpike St. HX5: Ell 4C 160
Turnshaw Rd. BD22: Oak 5A 46
Turnsteads Av. BD19: Cleck 1H 153
Turnsteads Dr. BD19: Cleck 6A 134
Turnstone Ct. LS10: Leeds 2B 140
Turnways, The LS6: Leeds 5C 76
Turton Grn. LS27: Gil 6F 115
Turton Va. LS27: Gil 1F 137
Tweed Ct. WF17: Birs 6C 136
Tweedy St. BD15: Wils 4G 67
Twelfth Av. WF15: Liv 4H 153
Twentyman Wlk. LS10: Leeds 3B 140
Twenty Twenty
LS2: Leeds 2H 5 (2B 98)
Twickenham Ct. BD8: B'frd 1D 90
Twine La. HX7: Myth 6A 126
Twine St. LS10: Leeds 6C 98
Twinge La. HX3: Sou 3B 150
Tyas Gro. LS9: Leeds 4F 99
TYERSAL 5C 92
Tyersal Av. BD4: B'frd 4D 92
Tyersal Cl. BD4: B'frd 5D 92
Tyersal Ct. BD4: B'frd 5C 92
Tyersal Cres. BD4: B'frd 5D 92
Tyersal Dr. BD4: B'frd 5D 92
Tyersal Gth. BD4: B'frd 5D 92
TYERSAL GATE 1C 112
Tyersal Grn. BD4: B'frd 5D 92
Tyersal Gro. BD4: B'frd 5D 92
Tyersal La. BD4: B'frd 1C 112
BD4: B'frd, Pud 1C 112
LS28: Pud 5F 93
Tyersal M. BD4: B'frd 5D 92
Tyersal Pk. BD4: B'frd 5C 92
Tyersal Rd. BD4: B'frd 5C 92
Tyersal Ter. BD4: B'frd 5C 92
Tyersal Vw. BD4: B'frd 5C 92
Tyersal Wlk. BD4: B'frd 5D 92
Tyler Ct. BD10: B'frd 1A 72
Tynedale Ct. LS7: Leeds 3G 77
Tyne St. BD3: B'frd 2F 7 (3F 91)
BD21: Keigh 6B 34
BD22: Haw 2D 64
Tynwald Cl. LS17: Leeds 5G 59
Tynwald Dr. LS17: Leeds 5G 59
Tynwald Gdns. LS17: Leeds 5G 59
Tynwald Grn. LS17: Leeds 4G 59
Tynwald Hill LS17: Leeds 5G 59
Tynwald Mt. LS17: Leeds 5G 59
Tynwald Rd. LS17: Leeds 5G 59
Tynwald Wlk. LS17: Leeds 4G 59
Tyrls, The BD1: B'frd 5D 6 (5E 91)

Tyrrel St. BD1: B'frd 4D 6 (4E 91)
Tyson St. BD1: B'frd 2B 6 (3D 90)
HX1: Hal 3C 149

U

Ullswater Cl. HX5: Ell 4D 160
Ullswater Cres. LS15: Leeds 4A 100
LS26: Wood 1E 143
Ullswater Dr. BD6: B'frd 1H 131
LS22: Weth 3C 12
Ullswater Ri. LS22: Weth 3C 12
UNDERCLIFFE 1G 91
Undercliffe La. BD3: B'frd 2G 91
Undercliffe Old Rd. BD2: B'frd 2H 91
Undercliffe Ri. LS29: I'ly 1G 19
Undercliffe Rd. BD2: B'frd 6H 71
Undercliffe St. BD3: B'frd 2H 91
Undercliffe Ter. HX2: Hal 5D 148
(off Scarr Bottom Rd.)
Underwood Dr. LS19: Raw 5F 55
Underwood Ho. BD3: B'frd 2F 7
Union Bri. Mill LS28: Pud 1D 114
Union Ct. LS21: Otley 4D 22
Union Cross Yd.
HX1: Hal 3C 164 (2G 149)
Union Ho. LS7: Leeds 3E 109
Union Ho. La. BD13: Que 3E 109
Union La. HX2: Ogd 5B 106
Union Pl. LS11: Leeds 5H 97
Union Rd. BD7: B'frd 6B 90
BD12: Low M 6C 110
Union St. BD13: Que 4A 108
BD16: Bgly 6A 36
BD17: Bail 5E 53
HX1: Hal 4C 164 (2G 149)
HX4: Gree 4H 159
HX6: Sow B 4A 148
LS2: Leeds 4F 5 (3B 98)
LS21: Otley 4D 22
LS27: Chur 5C 116
WF17: Birs 6A 136
Union St. Sth. HX1: Hal 3G 149
Union Ter. LS7: Leeds 3A 78
United Bus. Pk. LS12: Leeds 1E 117
Unity Cl. LS6: Leeds 5H 77
Unity Ct. HD6: Ras 3H 161
Unity Hall Ct. WF3: W Ard 2F 155
Unity St. BD20: Rid 3D 34
WF3: Carl 4H 141
Unity St. Nth. BD16: Bgly 5B 50
Unity St. Sth. BD16: Bgly 5B 50
Unity Ter. HX1: Hal 3C 148
University Academy Keighley
Athletics Track 4H 33
University of Bradford
Cobden & Forster Buildings . . .5C 90
(off Campus Rd.)
Laisteridge Lane Campus 6C 90
School of Health Studies 5B 70
School of Management 5B 70
Tumbling Hill St. 5A 6 (5C 90)
University of Bradford Sports Cen.
. . . . .6A 6 (5C 90)
University of Leeds
Woodhouse Lane . . .1B 4 (2G 97)
University Rd. LS2: Leeds 1G 97
Unwin Pl. BD9: B'frd 1G 89
Upcroft Ct. BD13: Que 3G 107
Upland Cres. LS8: Leeds 4E 79
Upland Gdns. LS8: Leeds 5E 79
Upland Gro. LS8: Leeds 4E 79
Upland Rd. LS8: Leeds 5E 79
Uplands BD20: Keigh 4G 33
Uplands Av. BD13: Que 3D 108
Uplands Cl. BD13: Que 3D 108
Uplands Cres. BD13: Que 3D 108
Uplands Gro. BD13: Que 3D 108
Up. Accommodation Rd.
LS9: Leeds 3C 98
Up. Ada St. BD18: Ship 1H 69

Up. Addison St. BD4: B'frd 6F 7 (6F 91)
Up. Allerton La. BD15: All 3A 88
UPPER ARMLEY 2H 95
Up. Ashley La. BD17: Ship 1B 70
Upper Bankhouse HX2: Mt T 3H 127
Up. Basinghall St.
LS1: Leeds 3D 4 (3H 97)
Up. Batley La. WF17: Bat 6B 136
Up. Batley Low La.
WF17: Bat 5D 136
Up. Bell Cft. HX3: Sou 5C 150
Up. Bell Hall HX1: Hal 4E 149
Up. Bentley Royd HX6: Sow B 6G 147
(not continuous)
Upper Bolton Brow HX6: Sow B . . .4B 148
Upper Bonegate HD6: Brigh 6B 152
UPPER BROCKHOLES 5B 106
Up. Calton St. BD21: Keigh 2H 47
Up. Carr La. LS28: Cal 3E 73
Up. Castle St. BD5: B'frd 6E 91
Up. Chelsea St. BD21: Keigh 2H 47
UPPER COMMON 3D 132
Upper Ellistones HX4: Gree 4E 159
(off Martin Grn. La.)
Up. Ellistones Ct. HX4: Gree 4E 159
UPPER EXLEY 2A 160
UPPER FAGLEY 1C 92
Up. Fawth Cl. BD13: Que 4C 108
Up. Ferndown Grn. BD15: All 2C 88
Upper Field Ho. La.
HX6: Sow B 6D 146
Up. Fountain St. HX6: Sow B 5H 147
Up. Fyfe La. BD17: Bail 4E 53
Upper Gaukroger HX6: Sow B 6F 147
Up. George St. BD6: B'frd 4B 110
HX1: Hal 4B 164
Up. Gilbert Flds. HX4: Bark 5A 158
Up. Grange Av. BD15: All 3D 88
UPPER GREEN
BD7 . . . . .1G 109
WF3 . . . . .2D 154
Upper Grn. BD7: B'frd 2H 109
BD17: Bail 5B 52
Up. Green Av. BD19: Scho 1F 153
WF3: W Ard 2D 154
Up. Green Cl. WF3: W Ard 2E 155
Up. Green Dr. WF3: W Ard 2E 155
Up. Green La. HD6: Brigh 4G 151
Up. Green Royd HX2: Mt T 3G 127
Up. Green Way WF3: W Ard 2D 154
Upper Haley BD22: Oxen 6D 64
Up. Hall Fold HX4: Bark 6A 158
Up. Hall Vw. HX3: North 4C 130
Upper Headley BD13: Thorn 6H 87
Up. Heights Rd. BD13: Thorn 3G 87
Up. High Lees HX2: Midg 5C 126
Up. Hird St. BD21: Keigh 2G 47
Up. House Cotts. BD13: Que 3C 108
Up. House St. BD4: B'frd 6H 91
Up. Hoyle Ing BD13: Thorn 4B 88
Upper Jackroyd HX3: Hal 6D 128
Up. Kell HX2: Wain 1F 127
Up. Kingston HX1: Hal 3C 148
Up. Kirkgate HX1: Hal 4D 164
Upper La. HX3: North 3B 130
Upper Langwith LS22: Coll 3G 27
Up. Lombard St. LS19: Raw 3E 55
UPPER MARSH 4A 64
Up. Marsh HX3: Sou 4B 150
Up. Marsh La. BD22: Oxen 4A 64
Up. Martin Grn. HX4: Gree 4E 159
Up. Mary St. BD18: Ship 1H 69
Upper Mdws. BD13: Que 5A 108
Up. Mill Cotts. BD17: Esh 2H 53
Upper Millergate BD1: B'frd 4C 6
Up. Mill Row BD20: E Mor 3A 36
Uppermoor LS28: Pud 4G 93
Uppermoor Cl. LS28: Pud 5H 93
UPPER MOOR SIDE 3E 115
Up. Mosscar St.
BD3: B'frd 4H 7 (4G 91)

Up. Nidd St. BD3: B'frd 5H 91
Up. Parish Ghyll La. LS29: I'ly 6B 10
Up. Park Ga. BD1: B'frd 3F 7 (4F 91)
Upper Piccadilly
   BD1: B'frd 3C 6 (4E 91)
Up. Pierce Cl. BD22: Cros R 6F 47
Upper Pikeley BD15: All 3H 87
Up. Quarry Rd. HD2: Hud 5G 163
Upper Range HX3: Hal 6G 129
   (off Woodlands Gro.)
Up. Reap Hurst HX2: Mt T 3G 127
Up. Rushton Rd. BD3: B'frd 2B 92
Up. School St. BD20: Stee 6C 14
Up. Seymour St.
   BD3: B'frd 5H 7 (4H 91)
Upper Slack HX2: Wain 1F 127
Upper St. WF3: Ting 6F 139
   (off Bradford Rd.)
Up. Sutherland Rd. HX3: Hip 1G 151
Upper Tewit HX2: Illing 6D 106
UPPER TOWN 1C 84
Upper Town BD22: Oxen 1C 84
Up. Town St. LS13: Leeds 6E 75
Up. Washer La. HX2: Hal 4D 148
Up. Well Royd HX2: Hal 2A 148
Up. Westlock Av. LS9: Leeds 2E 99
Up. West Scausby HX2: Illing 5D 106
Up. White Lees HX7: Myth 6A 126
Up. Willow Hall HX2: Hal 3B 148
Up. Woodlands Rd. BD8: B'frd 2A 90
Up. Woodview Pl.
   LS11: Leeds 3H 117
   (off Woodview St.)
UPPER WORTLEY 5B 96
Up. Wortley Cl. LS12: Leeds 4B 96
   (off Up. Wortley Dr.)
Up. Wortley Dr. LS12: Leeds 4B 96
Up. Wortley Rd. LS12: Leeds 4B 96
UPPER WYKE 4D 132
Upton's Yd. LS1: Leeds 4E 5
Upton Wlk. BD15: All 3D 88
Upwood BD20: W Mor 1G 35
Upwood Holiday Pk.
   BD22: Oxen 6E 65
Upwood La. BD20: E Mor 3H 35
Ure Cres. BD8: B'frd 1A 6 (3C 90)
Ure Gro. LS22: Weth 1D 12
Usher St. BD4: B'frd 6G 91
Uttley St. HX3: Hal 5F 129

V

Vale, The LS6: Leeds 4F 77
   LS22: Coll 3A 28
Vale Av. LS8: Leeds 5E 61
Vale Gro. BD13: Que 4B 108
   BD20: Sils 2D 14
Vale Mill La. BD22: Haw 6D 46
Valentine Ct. BD13: Thorn 4A 88
Valentine M. WF3: Loft 1G 157
Vales, The BD22: Oxen 1C 84
Vale St. BD21: Keigh 4C 34
   HD6: Brigh 6A 152
Vale Ter. BD22: Oak 6D 46
Vale Vw. BD20: Sils 2D 14
Valley, The LS17: Leeds 1G 59
Valley Av. HX3: Hip 1A 152
Valley Cl. LS17: Leeds 1G 59
Valley Cl. BD1: B'frd 2E 91
   BD11: Drig 5C 114
   LS6: Leeds 5D 76
   LS17: Leeds 1B 78
   (off Allerton Grange Gdns.)
Valley Dr. LS15: Leeds 2C 100
   LS26: Gt P 5E 123
   LS29: I'ly 5F 11
Valley Farm Rd. LS10: Leeds 4E 119
Valley Farm Way
   LS10: Leeds 4E 119
Valley Fold BD13: Que 3A 108
Valley Gdns. LS7: Leeds 1A 78
Valley Grn. LS28: Pud 5B 94

Valley Gro. HX2: Illing 6D 106
   LS28: Pud 5B 94
Valley Hgts. BD13: Denh 2B 86
Valley Mills LS27: Drig 5D 114
Valley Mt. LS13: Leeds 3C 94
   LS25: Kip 3F 123
Valley Pde. BD8: B'frd 2D 90
Valley Pl. BD1: B'frd 2E 91
Valley Ridge LS25: Kip 2F 123
   (not continuous)
Valley Ri. LS13: Leeds 4E 75
Valley Rd. BD1: B'frd 1C 6 (1D 90)
   BD18: Ship 2B 70
   BD21: Keigh 6D 34
   LS13: Leeds 4E 75
   LS25: Kip 2F 123
   LS27: Morl 2B 138
   LS28: Pud 5A 94
   LS29: I'ly 4F 11
Valley Rd. Retail Pk.
   BD1: B'frd 1D 6 (3E 91)
Valley Sq. LS28: Pud 5B 94
Valley Ter. LS17: Leeds 4D 60
Valley Vw. BD16: Har 6E 49
   BD17: Bail 6B 52
   HX2: Illing 6D 106
   HX3: Nor G 5H 131
   LS21: Arth 5H 25
   LS21: Pool 6D 24
   LS28: Pud 4C 94
Valley Vw. Cl. BD22: Oak 4E 47
Valley Vw. Gdns.
   BD22: Cros R 1E 65
Valley Vw. Gro. BD2: B'frd 6G 71
Valley Way HX2: Illing 6D 106
Vancouver Pl. LS7: Leeds 3C 78
Vantage Point LS27: Morl 6H 137
Varley St. LS28: Stan 2H 93
   (not continuous)
Varleys Yd. LS28: Pud 4C 94
Vaughan St. BD1: B'frd 3A 6 (4D 90)
   HX1: Hal 4D 148
Vegal Cres. HX3: Hal 5D 128
Venice M. BD17: Bail 5D 52
Ventnor Cl. BD19: Gom 5F 135
Ventnor St. BD3: B'frd 4H 7 (4G 91)
Ventnor Ter. HX3: Hal 5F 149
Vento Cl. BD6: B'frd 5B 110
Verdun Rd. BD6: B'frd 5A 110
Vere Sq. BD5: B'frd 1E 111
Veritys St. LS28: Pud 3B 94
Verity Spur LS9: Leeds 3A 100
Verity St. BD4: E Bier 6D 112
Verity Vw. LS9: Leeds 2A 100
Vermont St. LS13: Leeds 1C 94
Vernon Ct. BD20: Keigh 5H 33
Vernon Pl. BD2: B'frd 1H 91
   BD13: Que 6G 107
   LS28: Stan 2H 93
Vernon Rd. LS1: Leeds 1C 4 (2H 97)
Vernon St. BD22: Cros R 1F 65
   LS2: Leeds 2D 4 (2H 97)
Vesper Cl. LS5: Leeds 3H 75
Vesper Ct. LS5: Leeds 3G 75
Vesper Ct. Dr. LS5: Leeds 3G 75
Vesper Gdns. LS5: Leeds 4H 75
Vesper Ga. Cres. LS5: Leeds 4H 75
Vesper Ga. Dr. LS5: Leeds 3G 75
Vesper Ga. Mt. LS5: Leeds 3H 75
Vesper Gro. LS5: Leeds 5A 76
Vesper La. LS5: Leeds 4H 75
Vesper Mt. LS5: Leeds 5A 76
Vesper Pl. LS5: Leeds 5A 76
   LS27: Morl 5A 138
   (off High St.)
Vesper Ri. LS5: Leeds 3G 75
Vesper Rd. LS5: Leeds 3F 75
Vesper Ter. LS5: Leeds 5A 76
Vesper Wlk. LS5: Leeds 4G 75
Vesper Way LS5: Leeds 3G 75
Vestry Rd. BD4: B'frd 2H 111
Viaduct Rd. LS4: Leeds 2D 96
Viaduct St. LS28: Stan 2H 93

Viaduct Theatre 1B 164
   (in Dean Clough)
Vicarage Av. LS5: Leeds 5B 76
   LS27: Gil 1E 137
Vicarage Cl. BD12: Wyke 5C 132
   WF1: Out 4F 157
Vicarage Dr. LS28: Pud 4H 93
Vicarage Gdns. BD11: Birk 2E 135
   HD6: Ras 3H 161
   LS21: Otley 4E 23
Vicarage M. BD2: B'frd 6G 71
   LS5: Leeds 5B 76
   (off Vicarage Ter.)
Vicarage Pl. LS5: Leeds 5B 76
Vicarage Rd. BD18: Ship 1E 71
   LS6: Leeds 1F 97
Vicarage St. LS5: Leeds 5B 76
Vicarage Ter. LS5: Leeds 5B 76
Vicarage Vw. LS5: Leeds 5B 76
Vicar La. BD1: B'frd 4E 7 (4F 91)
   (not continuous)
   LS1: Leeds 4F 5 (3A 98)
   LS2: Leeds 4F 5 (3A 98)
Vicar Pk. Dr. HX2: Hal 1H 147
Vicar Pk. Rd. HX2: Hal 2H 147
Vicars Rd. LS8: Leeds 5D 78
Vicars Ter. LS8: Leeds 5D 78
   WF10: All B 3H 145
Vickerman St. HX1: Hal 3D 148
   (not continuous)
Vickers Av. LS5: Leeds 6H 75
Vickersdale LS28: Stan 1A 94
Vickersdale Ct. LS28: Stan 1A 94
Vickersdale Gro. LS28: Stan 1A 94
   (off Arthur St.)
Vickers Pl. LS28: Stan 1A 94
Vickers St. LS27: Morl 5H 137
Victor Dr. LS20: Guis 5C 40
Victoria Av. BD2: B'frd 5B 72
   BD18: Ship 1H 69
   BD21: Keigh 5A 34
   BD22: Haw 1C 64
   HD6: Clift 6C 152
   HX1: Hal 3D 148
   HX5: Ell 5A 160
   HX6: Sow B 5A 148
   LS9: Leeds 3E 99
   LS18: H'fth 2C 74
   LS19: Yead 1H 55
   LS26: Rothw 3A 142
   LS27: Morl 2A 138
   LS29: I'ly 5B 10
   LS29: Men 6F 21
   WF1: Out 6F 157
Victoria Chase HD6: B Bri 1B 152
Victoria Cl. LS18: H'fth 2C 74
   LS19: Yead 6H 41
   LS29: I'ly 5C 10
   WF10: All B 3H 145
Victoria Ct. BD18: Ship 1H 69
   (off Victoria Av.)
   BD21: Keigh 5H 33
   LS6: Leeds 5C 76
   LS15: Leeds 5F 81
   LS21: Otley 4E 23
   (off Station Rd.)
   LS22: Weth 4F 13
   (off Horsefair)
   LS27: Morl 2A 138
   (off Victoria M.)
   WF17: Birs 6B 136
Victoria Ct. M. LS6: Leeds 6E 77
Victoria Cres. HX5: Ell 5B 160
   LS18: H'fth 2C 74
   LS28: Pud 4G 93
Victoria Dr. BD2: B'frd 5B 72
   HX3: North 4D 130
   LS18: H'fth 2C 74
   LS27: Morl 1B 138
   LS29: I'ly 5B 10
Victoria Gdns. LS18: H'fth 2D 74
   LS28: Pud 4G 93
   LS29: I'ly 5B 10

Victoria Grange Dr. LS27: Morl 2A 138
Victoria Grange Way
  LS27: Morl 2A 138
Victoria Gro. LS9: Leeds 3F 99
  LS18: H'fth 3C 74
  LS28: Pud 4G 93
  LS29: I'ly 5B 10
Victoria Hall
  Keighley 5B 34
Victoria Ho's. LS5: Leeds 5A 76
  (off Church St.)
Victoria Ind. Est. BD2: B'frd 5A 72
Victoria Ind. Pk. LS14: Leeds 2D 80
Victoria La. LS18: H'fth 2C 74
Victoria M. BD21: Keigh 6H 33
  (off Cartmel Rd.)
HX5: Ell .5B 160
  (off John St.)
  LS18: H'fth 2C 74
  LS27: Morl 2A 138
Victoria Mills 1 BD17: Ship 6B 52
Victoria Mills 2 BD17: Ship 6B 52
Victoria Mt. LS18: H'fth 1C 74
Victorian Arc. LS29: I'ly 5D 10
  (off Church St.)
Victoria Pk. BD18: Ship 2H 69
  HX1: Hal 2E 149
Victoria Pk. Av.
  LS5: Leeds 6G 75
  LS13: Leeds 6G 75
Victoria Pk. Gro.
  LS5: Leeds 6H 75
  LS13: Leeds 6G 75
Victoria Pk. St. BD21: Keigh 5B 34
Victoria Pk. Vw. BD21: Keigh 5B 34
Victoria Pl. BD10: B'frd 4A 72
  HD6: Ras 2B 162
  HX2: Lud M 4E 147
  HX3: North 4D 130
  LS11: Leeds 5H 97
  LS19: Yead 6E 41
  LS23: Cliff 6B 30
  LS26: Meth 4C 144
Victoria Quarter LS1: Leeds . . .4F 5 (3A 98)
Victoria Ri. LS28: Pud 4G 93
Victoria Rd. BD2: B'frd 4A 72
  BD6: B'frd 5A 110
  BD10: B'frd 4A 72
  BD18: Ship 1H 69
  BD21: Keigh 1H 47
  BD22: Haw 2D 64
  BD22: Oak 5D 46
  HD6: B Bri 1B 152
  HX1: Hal 2E 149
  HX3: Hip 2F 151
  HX5: Ell 5H 159
  HX6: Sow B 6H 147
  LS5: Leeds 5A 76
  LS6: Leeds 6E 77
  LS11: Leeds 5H 97
  LS14: Leeds 2D 80
  LS20: Guis 5B 40
  LS26: Rothw 1H 141
  LS27: Chur, Morl 2A 138
  LS28: Fars 1H 93
  LS28: Pud 4G 93
  LS29: Burl W 2E 21
  LS29: I'ly 5B 10
Victoria Sq. LS1: Leeds 3C 4 (3H 97)
Victoria St. BD1: B'frd 1B 6 (3D 90)
  BD2: B'frd 1A 92
  BD10: B'frd 5H 53
  BD13: Cull 3C 66
  BD13: Que 4B 108
  BD14: Clay 1D 108
  BD15: All 6C 68
  BD15: Wils 5G 67
  BD16: Bgly 6A 36
  (New St.)
  BD16: Bgly 5B 50
  (York Cres.)
  BD17: Bail 6C 52
  BD17: Ship 1B 70

Victoria St. BD19: Cleck 6B 134
  BD22: Oak 5D 46
  (off Victoria Rd.)
  HD6: Clift 6C 152
  HD6: Ras 2B 162
  HX1: Hal 3B 164 (2G 149)
  HX4: Gree 4H 159
  HX6: Sow B 6H 147
  LS3: Leeds 2A 4 (2F 97)
  LS7: Leeds 2B 78
  LS22: Weth 4E 13
  LS27: Chur 6C 116
  LS27: Morl 2H 137
  LS28: Cal 3E 73
  WF1: Out 5F 157
  WF10: All B 3H 145
  WF17: Birs 6B 136
Victoria Ter. BD18: Ship 6H 51
  BD21: Keigh 5B 34
  (off Berry St.)
  HX1: Hal 3E 149
  (off Hopwood La.)
  HX2: Hal 5E 149
  HX2: Lud M 4E 147
  HX3: Hip 2F 151
  LS3: Leeds 2A 4 (2F 97)
  LS5: Leeds 5D 76
  LS6: Leeds 3D 76
  LS19: Yead 6G 41
  LS20: Guis 4C 40
  (off West Pde.)
  LS28: Stan 1B 94
  LS29: Add 1D 8
  (off Main St.)
Victoria Theatre, The 5B 164
Victoria Vs. LS28: Stan 2A 94
Victoria Wlk. LS1: Leeds 4E 5
  (within The Core Shop. Cen.)
  LS18: H'fth 2C 74
Victoria Way WF1: Out 6F 157
Victoria Works HX2: Hal 6E 107
Victor Rd. BD9: B'frd 1B 90
Victor St. BD3: B'frd 4C 92
  BD9: B'frd 1B 90
Victor Ter. BD9: B'frd 1B 90
  HX1: Hal 1E 149
Victory Rd. LS29: I'ly 5D 10
Vienna Ct. LS27: Chur 5C 116
View, The LS8: Leeds 1D 78
  LS17: Leeds 1F 59
View Cft. Rd. BD17: Ship 1C 70
Viewlands LS29: Midd 2E 11
Viewlands Cres. LS29: Men 6B 22
Viewlands Mt. LS29: Men 6B 22
Viewlands Ri. LS29: Men 1B 40
View Pl. BD13: Que 3G 107
View Rd. BD20: Keigh 5G 33
View Row BD15: All 3E 89
Vignola Ter. BD14: Clay 6E 89
Villa Gdns. HX3: She 1F 131
Village, The LS23: T Arch 2C 30
Village Av. LS4: Leeds 1D 96
Village Gdns. LS15: Leeds 5F 101
  (not continuous)
Village Golf Course, The 4A 44
Village Hotel & Leisure Club
  Leeds 1C 76
Village M. BD15: Wils 4G 67
Village Pl. LS4: Leeds 1D 96
Village St. HX3: Nor G 4H 131
Village Street, The
  LS4: Leeds 1D 96
Village Ter. LS4: Leeds 6D 76
Villa Gro. BD16: Bgly 3C 50
Villa Mt. BD12: Wyke 6C 132
Villa Rd. BD16: Bgly 3C 50
Villa St. HX6: Sow B 5A 148
Villier Ct. BD15: All 2D 88
Vincent Av. BD20: East 6A 14
Vincent St.
  BD1: B'frd 4B 6 (4D 90)
  HX1: Hal 3D 148
Vine Cl. HD6: Clift 1D 162

Vine Ct. HD6: Clift 1D 162
  LS20: Guis 5C 40
Vine Gth. HD6: Clift 6D 152
Vine Gro. HD6: Clift 1D 162
Vine Ind. Est. HD6: Brigh 6H 151
Viney Pl. BD2: B'frd 6H 71
Vinery Av. LS9: Leeds 3E 99
Vinery Gro. LS9: Leeds 3E 99
Vinery Mt. LS9: Leeds 4E 99
Vinery Pl. LS9: Leeds 4E 99
Vinery Rd. LS4: Leeds 1D 96
Vinery St. LS9: Leeds 3E 99
Vinery Ter. LS9: Leeds 4E 99
Vinery Vw. LS9: Leeds 4E 99
Vine St. BD7: B'frd 6B 90
  BD19: Cleck 6A 134
  HX1: Hal 6A 164 (3F 149)
Vine Ter. E. BD8: B'frd 3G 89
Vine Ter. W. BD8: B'frd 3G 89
Vintage Carriages Trust Museum of
  Rail Travel 3H 47
  (off Halifax Rd.)
Vint Ri. BD10: B'frd 2G 71
Violet Rd. WF3: E Ard 1D 156
Violet St. BD22: Haw 4C 64
  HX1: Hal 2E 149
Violet St. Nth. HX1: Hal 1E 149
Violet Ter. HX6: Sow B 5A 148
Virgin Active
  Bradford 3D 92
  Leeds, Cardigan Flds. Rd. . . .2C 96
  Leeds, Centaur Ho. 3B 4
  Leeds, The Light 3D 4
Virginia Cl. WF3: Loft 3E 157
Virginia Ct. WF3: Loft 3E 157
Virginia Dr. WF3: Loft 3E 157
Virginia Gdns. WF3: Loft 3E 157
Virginia St. BD14: Clay 2E 109
Virginia Ter. BD14: Clay 2E 109
  (off Virginia St.)
  LS14: T'ner 2H 63
Vivian Pl. BD7: B'frd 2A 110
Vivien Rd. BD8: B'frd 3E 89
Vollan's Ct. LS14: Leeds 4C 80
Vue Cinema
  Halifax 3C 164 (2G 149)
  Leeds, Cardigan Flds. Rd. 2D 96
  Leeds, The Headrow . . .3E 5 (3A 98)
Vulcan St. BD4: B'frd 4B 112
  HD6: Brigh 2C 162

Waddington St. BD21: Keigh 1A 48
Wade Ho. Av. HX3: She 1E 131
Wade Ho. Rd. HX3: She 2E 131
Wade La. LS2: Leeds 3E 5 (3A 98)
Wade St. HX1: Hal 3C 164 (2G 149)
  LS28: Fars 6H 73
Wadlands Cl. LS28: Fars 5H 73
Wadlands Dr. LS28: Fars 6G 73
Wadlands Gro. LS28: Fars 5G 73
Wadlands Ri. LS28: Fars 6G 73
Wadsworth BD22: Oxen 2C 84
Wadsworth Ct. BD19: Cleck 1H 153
  HX1: Hal 1E 149
Wadsworth St. HX1: Hal 1D 148
  (not continuous)
Waggon Rd. LS10: Leeds 3B 140
Wagon La. BD16: Bgly 6C 50
Wagtail Cl. BD6: B'frd 4E 109
Waides Bldgs. LS26: Meth 4E 145
Waincliffe Cres. LS11: Leeds 4F 117
Waincliffe Dr. LS11: Leeds 5F 117
Waincliffe Gth. LS11: Leeds 4F 117
Waincliffe Ho. BD4: B'frd 5B 92
  (off Fearnville Dr.)
Waincliffe Mt. LS11: Leeds 4F 117
Waincliffe Pl. LS11: Leeds 4F 117
Waincliffe Sq. LS11: Leeds 4F 117
Waincliffe Ter. LS11: Leeds 5F 117

Waindale Cl. HX2: Mt T 4G 127
Waindale Cres. HX2: Mt T 4G 127
Wainfleet Ho. BD3: B'frd 3C 92
(off Rushton Rd.)
Wainhouse Rd. HX1: Hal 4D 148
Wainhouse Ter. HX2: Hal 4D 148
(off Burnley Rd.)
Wainhouse Tower 4D 148
Wainman Sq. BD12: Wyke 4C 132
Wainman St. BD12: Wyke 4C 132
BD17: Bail 3D 52
BD17: Ship 1B 70
HX1: Hal 2D 148
WAINSTALLS 1F 127
Wainstalls La. HX2: Wain 2E 127
Wainstalls Lodge La.
HX2: Wain 2E 127
Wainstalls Rd. HX2: Wain 1F 127
Waites Ter. LS21: Otley 4F 23
Wakefield 41 Ind. Pk.
WF2: Carr G 4D 156
(Telford Way)
WF2: Carr G 3D 156
(Trevor Ter.)
Wakefield Av. LS14: Leeds 2B 100
Wakefield Ga. HX3: Hal 5D 148
Wakefield Rd.
BD4: B'frd 6F 7 (5F 91)
(not continuous)
BD11: Drig 1B 136
(not continuous)
HD6: B Bri 2F 151
HD6: Brigh, Hud 1B 162
(not continuous)
HX3: Hal 5B 148
HX3: Hip 2F 151
HX6: Sow B 5B 148
LS10: Leeds 3D 118
LS25: Gar 5C 102
LS26: Gar, Kip, Swil 5G 121
LS26: Leeds, Rothw 6F 119
LS26: Oul 6D 142
LS27: Gil, Morl 2E 137
WF14: Mir 2F 163
Walden Dr. BD9: B'frd 6E 69
Walesby Cl. LS16: Leeds 5G 57
Walford Av. LS9: Leeds 3E 99
Walford Gro. LS9: Leeds 3E 99
Walford Mt. LS9: Leeds 3E 99
Walford Rd. LS9: Leeds 3E 99
Walford Ter. LS9: Leeds 3E 99
Walk, The BD21: Keigh 1A 48
LS28: Fars 1G 93
Walker Av. BD7: B'frd 6G 89
(not continuous)
Walker Dr. BD8: B'frd 3B 90
Walkergate LS21: Otley 4E 23
Walker Ho. LS5: Leeds 5H 75
Walker La. HX6: Sow B 5B 148
Walker Pl. BD18: Ship 1D 70
LS27: Chur 6B 116
Walker Rd. BD12: O'haw 3F 133
LS18: H'fth 6D 56
LS29: Men 1F 39
Walkers Bldgs. LS28: Pud 3A 94
(off Clifton Hill)
Walker's Grn. LS12: Leeds 1C 116
Walker's La.
LS12: Leeds 1C 116
(not continuous)
Walkers Mt. LS6: Leeds 4F 77
Walker's Pl. BD20: Sils 3E 15
Walkers Row LS19: Yead 6E 41
Walker St. BD4: B'frd 5H 111
BD19: Scho 1F 153
Walker Ter. BD4: B'frd 1H 111
BD13: Cull 4B 66
Walker Vw. LS10: Leeds 3B 140
Walker Wood BD17: Bail 5H 51
Wallace Gdns. WF3: Loft 3F 157
Wallace St. HX1: Hal 3D 148
Wallbank Dr. BD18: Ship 3C 70
Wallingford Mt. BD15: All 4D 88

Wallis St. BD8: B'frd 4H 89
(Greenside La.)
BD8: B'frd 4A 90
(Waterside Rd.)
HX6: Sow B 5H 147
Wall St. BD22: Keigh 1F 47
Walmer Gro. LS28: Pud 6B 94
Walmer Vs. BD8: B'frd 2D 90
Walmsley Rd. LS6: Leeds 6E 77
Walnut Bus. Pk. HX1: Hal 2E 149
Walnut Cl. LS14: Leeds 1E 81
Walnut St. BD3: B'frd 5A 92
BD21: Keigh 3H 47
HX1: Hal 2E 149
Walshaw St. BD7: B'frd 1A 110
Walsh La. BD16: Bgly 1B 50
HX3: Hal 6F 129
LS12: N Far 3E 115
Walsh's Sq. HX1: Hal 4E 149
(off Moorfield St.)
Walsh St. HX1: Hal 2D 148
Walter Clough La.
HX3: Sou 4D 150
Walter Cres. LS9: Leeds 4D 98
Walter St. BD2: B'frd 5D 70
BD10: B'frd 1H 71
LS4: Leeds 2D 96
Walton Cft. LS28: Fars 6H 73
(off Water La.)
Walton Dr. BD11: Drig 1B 136
Walton Gdns. LS23: T Arch 1D 30
Walton Gth. BD11: Drig 2B 136
Walton La. BD19: Scho 4E 153
Walton Rd. LS22: Weth 4F 13
LS23: T Arch 2D 30
Waltons Bldgs. HX2: Hal 3D 128
Waltons Hgts. WF15: Liv 5H 153
Walton St. BD4: B'frd 6F 91
HX6: Sow B 5H 147
LS10: Leeds 1C 118
LS11: Leeds 5H 97
Walt Royd HX2: Mix 4B 128
Waltroyd Rd. BD19: Cleck 2H 153
Wand La. HX3: Hip 1E 151
Wansford Cl. BD4: B'frd 3C 112
Wanstead Cres. BD15: All 3D 88
WAPPING 2F 7 (3F 91)
Wapping Rd. BD3: B'frd 1E 7 (3F 91)
Warburton Pl. BD6: B'frd 4C 110
Ward Ct. HD6: Ras 4H 161
Ward La. LS10: Leeds 4B 118
Wardle Cres. BD21: Keigh 5F 33
Wardman St. BD21: Keigh 5C 34
Wards End BD13: Thorn 4H 87
HX1: Hal 4C 164 (3G 149)
Ward St. BD7: B'frd 2A 110
BD21: Keigh 1H 47
Wareham Cnr. BD4: B'frd 3C 112
Warehouse, The LS5: Leeds 5H 75
(off Broad La.)
Warhurst Rd. HX5: Ell 3C 160
WARING GREEN 6A 152
Warings Bldgs. WF3: W Ard 2D 154
Warlbeck LS29: I'ly 5B 10
Warley Av. BD3: B'frd 3B 92
Warley Dene HX2: Hal 3H 147
Warley Dr. BD3: B'frd 4B 92
Warley Edge HX2: Hal 2A 148
Warley Edge La. HX2: Hal 2H 147
Warley Gro. BD3: B'frd 3B 92
HX2: Hal 2B 148
Warley Rd. HX1: Hal 2B 148
HX2: Hal 2B 148
Warley St. HX1: Hal 3E 149
WARLEY TOWN 3H 147
Warley Town La. HX2: Hal 2G 147
Warley Vw. HX2: Hal 2B 148
LS13: Leeds 5D 74
Warley Wood HX2: Hal 4F 147
Warley Wood Av. HX2: Lud M 4F 147
Warley Wood La. HX2: Lud M 4E 147
Warm La. LS19: Yead 2E 55

Warmleigh Pk. BD13: Que 4F 107
Warneford Sq. HX1: Hal 4D 148
(off Haugh Shaw Rd. W.)
Warnford Gro. BD3: B'frd 2B 112
Warrel's Av. LS13: Leeds 6E 75
Warrel's Ct. LS13: Leeds 1E 95
Warrel's Gro. LS13: Leeds 1E 95
Warrel's Mt. LS13: Leeds 1E 95
Warrel's Pl. LS13: Leeds 6E 75
Warrel's Rd. LS13: Leeds 6E 75
Warrel's Row LS13: Leeds 1E 95
Warrel's St. LS13: Leeds 1E 95
Warrel's Ter. LS13: Leeds 1E 95
Warren Av. BD16: Bgly 2D 50
Warren Dr. BD16: Bgly 3D 50
Warren Farm Cotts.
LS25: M'fld 6D 104
Warren Ho. Cotts. LS25: M'fld 1D 124
Warren Ho. La. LS19: Yead 4H 41
Warren Ho. Rd. WF10: All B 3H 145
Warren La. BD16: Bgly 2D 50
LS21: Arth 5H 25
Warren Lodge Gdns.
HX3: Hal 6F 149
Warren Pk. HD6: Brigh 4G 151
Warren Pk. Cl. HD6: Brigh 4G 151
Warrenside HD2: Hud 6E 163
Warrens La. BD11: Drig 2H 135
WF17: Birs 3H 135
Warren Ter. BD16: Bgly 4E 51
Warrenton Pl. BD7: B'frd 6A 90
Warrior Factory Martial Arts & Fitness Cen.
. . . . .1E 151
Warton Av. BD4: B'frd 4H 111
Warwick Cl. BD4: B'frd 1H 111
HX1: Hal 5F 149
(off Free School La.)
Warwick Ct. LS18: H'fth 2E 75
Warwick Dr. BD4: B'frd 1H 111
Warwick Rd. BD4: B'frd 1H 111
Waryn Ho. BD10: B'frd 2A 72
(off Haigh Beck Vw.)
Washburn Ct. BD20: Sils 2E 15
(off Wharfe Ct.)
LS22: Weth 1D 12
Washer La. HX2: Hal 5C 148
Washer La. Ind. Est. HX2: Hal 5D 148
Washington Pl. LS13: Leeds 3C 94
Washington St. BD8: B'frd 2H 89
HX3: Hal 6E 129
LS3: Leeds 3E 97
LS13: Leeds 3C 94
Washington Ter. LS13: Leeds 3C 94
Wastwater Dr. BD6: B'frd 1H 131
Watercock St. BD4: B'frd 6G 91
Waterfront M. BD10: B'frd 1C 72
Water Gdns. LS26: Rothw 6H 119
Watergate HX3: Hip 2E 151
LS26: Meth 6A 144
Water Hill HX6: Sow B 4G 147
Water Hill La. HX2: Hal 4G 147
HX6: Sow B 4G 147
Water Ho. Ct. LS18: H'fth 2D 74
Waterhouse Ct. LS10: Leeds 1B 118
(off Joseph St.)
Waterhouse Dr. WF3: E Ard 2H 155
Waterhouse St. BD21: Keigh 6G 33
HX1: Hal 4B 164 (2G 149)
Watering La. LS27: Morl 4D 138
WF3: Ting 4D 138
Watering Mdw. LS27: Morl 3D 138
Water La. BD1: B'frd 3A 6 (4C 90)
(not continuous)
BD21: Keigh 1H 47
HX1: Hal 6D 164 (3H 149)
HX3: Hal 6D 164 (3H 149)
LS11: Leeds 6E 5 (4A 98)
(Bridge End)
LS11: Leeds 6C 4 (5G 97)
(Globe Rd.)
LS12: Leeds 4F 95
LS18: H'fth 6B 56
LS28: Fars 6H 73

Waterlily Rd.—Wellington Rd. Ind. Est.

Waterlily Rd. BD9: B'frd 1A **90**
Waterloo Apartments
  LS10: Leeds 6F **5**
Waterloo Cnr. LS26: Oul 4C **142**
Waterloo Cres. BD10: B'frd 1D **72**
  LS13: Leeds 6F **75**
Waterloo Fold BD12: Wyke 5D **132**
Waterloo Gro. LS28: Pud 3F **93**
Waterloo La. LS13: Leeds 6F **75**
Waterloo Mills BD20: Sils 2E **15**
Waterloo Mt. LS28: Pud 3F **93**
Waterloo Rd. BD16: Bgly 4B **50**
  HD6: Brigh 6A **152**
  LS10: Leeds 1C **118**
  LS28: Pud 3F **93**
Waterloo St. LS10: Leeds 6F **5** (4A **98**)
Waterloo Ter. HX6: Sow B 3A **148**
  LS13: Leeds 6F **75**
Waterloo Way LS13: Leeds 6F **75**
Watermans Pl. LS1: Leeds 6D **4**
Water Mill Ct. BD22: Oak 1B **46**
Waterside BD16: Bgly 2H **49**
  BD20: Sils 3F **15**
  BD22: Oxen 1C **84**
  HX3: Hal 3H **149**
Waterside La. LS13: Leeds 4B **74**
Waterside Ind. Pk.
  LS10: Leeds 2F **119**
Waterside Rd. BD8: B'frd 3A **90**
  LS10: Leeds 3F **119**
Watersole La. LS22: Weth 5G **13**
Water Stalls Rd. HX7: Crag V 6A **146**
Water St. HD6: Brigh 6B **152**
  HX6: Sow B 6H **147**
Waters Wlk. BD10: B'frd 1C **72**
Waterwheel La. BD22: Oak 5B **46**
Waterwood Cl. WF3: W Ard 2F **155**
Watery La. BD20: Sils 1F **15**
Watford Av. HX3: Nor G 4H **131**
Watkin Av. BD13: Thorn 5B **88**
Watkinson Av. HX2: Hal 2D **128**
Watkinson Bungs. HX2: Illing 3C **128**
        (off Cumberland Cl.)
Watkinson Dr. HX2: Hal 3D **128**
Watkinson Rd. HX2: Hal 3D **128**
Watmough St. BD7: B'frd 2A **110**
Watson Cl. BD22: Oxen 1C **84**
Watson Mill La. HX6: Sow B 6H **147**
Watson Rd. LS14: Leeds 2B **100**
Watson's La. LS24: N Kym 6G **31**
Watson St. LS27: Morl 4H **137**
Watt Av. WF10: All B 3H **145**
Wattlesyke LS22: Coll 2D **28**
Watts St. BD14: Clay 1D **108**
Watt St. BD4: B'frd 5B **92**
Watty Hall Av. BD6: B'frd 3A **110**
Watty Hall La. BD6: B'frd 3B **110**
Watty Hall Rd. BD6: B'frd 3A **110**
Wauds Gates BD17: Bail 6C **52**
        (off Rockcliffe Av.)
Waveney Rd. LS12: Leeds 5C **96**
Waver Grn. LS28: Pud 4A **94**
Waverley Av. BD7: B'frd 6B **90**
  BD20: Rid 5F **35**
Waverley Cres. HX3: Hip 2E **151**
Waverley Gth. LS11: Leeds 1H **117**
Waverley Pl. BD7: B'frd 6B **90**
Waverley Rd. BD7: B'frd 6B **90**
  HX5: Ell 6B **160**
Waverley Ter. BD7: B'frd 6B **90**
  HX3: Hip 2E **151**
        (off Barfield Rd.)
Waver Spring Barns
  LS22: Comp 5D **28**
Waverton Grn. BD6: B'frd 6H **109**
Wavertree Pk. Gdns.
  BD12: Low M 3C **132**
Wayland App. LS16: Leeds 3D **58**
Wayland Cl. LS16: Leeds 3D **58**
Wayland Ct. LS16: Leeds 3D **58**
Wayland Cft. LS16: Leeds 3D **58**
Wayland Dr. LS16: Leeds 3D **58**
Wayside Av. LS14: S'cft 4F **45**

Wayside Ct. BD20: Keigh 3G **33**
Wayside Cres. BD2: B'frd 4H **71**
  LS14: S'cft 3F **45**
WAYSIDE GARDENS 4F **45**
Wayside M. BD20: Sils 2F **15**
Wayside Mt. LS14: S'cft 3F **45**
Weardale Cl. BD4: B'frd 4A **112**
Weatherhead Pl. BD20: Sils 2F **15**
Weatherhouse Ter.
  HX2: Hal 6B **128**
Weaver Ct. BD10: B'frd 1H **71**
        (off Moorfield Pl.)
Weaver Gdns. LS27: Morl 4D **138**
Weavers Cotts. BD22: Oxen 1C **84**
        (off Station Rd.)
Weavers Ct. BD13: Que 3G **107**
  HX6: Sow B 3A **148**
  LS12: Leeds 4B **96**
  LS28: Pud 6B **94**
Weavers Cft. BD10: B'frd 5G **53**
  LS28: Pud 5B **94**
Weavers Fold LS19: Raw 3F **55**
        (off New Rd. Side)
Weavers Grange LS20: Guis 3C **40**
Weavers Hill BD22: Haw 3C **64**
Weavers Ho. LS9: Leeds 6H **5**
Weavers La. BD13: Cull 3B **66**
Weavers Row LS28: Pud 5B **94**
Weaver St. LS4: Leeds 2D **96**
Weavers Wlk. BD20: Sils 1E **15**
Weaverthorpe Pk. BD4: B'frd 4C **112**
Weaverthorpe Rd. BD4: B'frd 4C **112**
Weaving Shed, The
  HX6: Sow B 5A **148**
        (off Old Cawsey)
Webb Dr. BD2: B'frd 1G **91**
Webb's Ter. HX3: Hal 1H **149**
Weber Ct. BD3: B'frd 4A **92**
        (off Harewood St.)
Webster Pl. BD3: B'frd 3H **7** (4H **91**)
Webster Row LS12: Leeds 5B **96**
Webster St. BD3: B'frd 4H **91**
Webton Ct. LS7: Leeds 2B **78**
Wedgemoor Cl. BD12: Wyke 3C **132**
Wedgewood Ct. LS8: Leeds 6E **61**
Wedgewood Dr. LS8: Leeds 1E **79**
Wedgewood Gro. LS8: Leeds 1E **79**
Weetlands Cl. LS25: Kip 3H **123**
WEETWOOD 2D **76**
Weetwood Av. LS16: Leeds 2D **76**
Weetwood Cl. LS16: Leeds 1C **76**
Weetwood Cres. LS16: Leeds 1D **76**
Weetwood Grange Gro.
  LS16: Leeds 1B **76**
Weetwood Ho. Ct. LS16: Leeds . . .1B **76**
Weetwood La. LS16: Leeds 6C **58**
Weetwood Mnr. LS16: Leeds 1C **76**
Weetwood Mill La.
  LS16: Leeds 1C **76**
Weetwood Pk. Dr. LS16: Leeds . . .1B **76**
Weetwood Rd. BD8: B'frd 3A **90**
  LS16: Leeds 1B **76**
Weetwood Ter. LS16: Leeds 1D **76**
Weetwood Wlk. LS16: Leeds 1C **76**
Welbeck Dr. BD7: B'frd 1G **109**
Welbeck Ri. BD7: B'frd 1G **109**
Welbeck Rd. LS9: Leeds 4E **99**
  WF17: Birs 5B **136**
Welburn Av. HX3: Hip 2F **151**
Welburn Dr. LS16: Leeds 2B **76**
Welburn Gro. LS16: Leeds 2B **76**
Welburn Mt. BD6: B'frd 5G **109**
Welbury Dr. BD8: B'frd 1C **90**
Weldon Ct. BD4: B'frd 1C **112**
Welfare Av. LS15: Bar E 2B **82**
Welham Wlk. BD3: B'frd 1G **7** (3G **91**)
Welland Dr. LS25: Gar 5G **103**
Wellands Grn. BD19: Cleck 2H **153**
Wellands La.
  BD19: Cleck, Scho 1F **153**
Wellands Ter. BD3: B'frd 4A **92**
Well Bank Rd. BD4: B'frd 2B **112**

Well Cl. LS19: Raw 4G **55**
  LS26: Gt P 5E **123**
  LS29: Add 1C **8**
Well Cl. Pl. HD6: Brigh 6A **152**
  LS2: Leeds 1A **98**
Well Cl. Ri. LS7: Leeds 1A **98**
Well Cl. St. HD6: Brigh 6A **152**
Well Cft. BD18: Ship 2B **70**
Wellcroft LS21: Otley 4F **23**
Wellcroft Gdns. HX3: Hip 1E **151**
Wellcroft Gro. WF3: W Ard 2F **155**
Weller Cl. BD5: B'frd 2E **111**
        (off Boynton St.)
Wellesley Ho. BD4: B'frd 5B **92**
        (off Wellington St.)
Wellesley St. BD1: B'frd 3F **7** (4F **91**)
Wellfield Gdns. BD13: Que 2H **107**
Wellfield La. LS29: Burl W 1E **21**
Wellfield Pl. LS6: Leeds 4D **76**
        (off Chapel St.)
Wellfield Ter. LS27: Gil 6E **115**
Well Fold BD10: B'frd 1H **71**
Well Gth. LS15: Leeds 1E **101**
Wellgarth BD6: B'frd 6H **109**
  HX1: Hal 6A **164** (4G **149**)
Well Gth. Bank LS13: Leeds 5D **74**
Well Gth. Mt. LS15: Leeds 1E **101**
Well Gth. Vw. LS13: Leeds 5E **75**
Wellgate HX4: Gree 3G **159**
Well Grn. Ct. BD4: E Bier 6C **112**
Well Grn. La. HD6: Brigh 4H **151**
Well Gro. HD6: Brigh 4H **151**
Wellhead Cl. LS16: B'hpe 2G **43**
Well Head Dr.
  HX1: Hal 6B **164** (3G **149**)
Well Head Ho. HX1: Hal 6C **164**
Well Head La.
  HX1: Hal 6B **164** (3G **149**)
  HX6: Sow B 6C **146**
Well Head Ri. HX1: Hal 4G **149**
WELL HEADS 4E **87**
Well Heads BD13: Denh, Thorn . . .5D **86**
Well Hill LS19: Yead 6F **41**
  LS21: Otley 4D **22**
Well Hill Ct. LS19: Yead 1F **55**
        (off Well Hill)
Wellholme HD6: Brigh 6B **152**
Well Holme Mead LS12: N Far 2G **115**
Well Ho. Av. LS8: Leeds 4E **79**
Well Ho. Ct. LS8: Leeds 4E **79**
Well Ho. Cres. LS8: Leeds 4E **79**
Well Ho. Dr. LS8: Leeds 4E **79**
Well Ho. Gdns. LS8: Leeds 4E **79**
Well Ho. Rd. LS8: Leeds 4E **79**
Wellington Arc. HD6: Brigh 1B **162**
        (off Briggate)
Wellington Bri. St.
  LS1: Leeds 5A **4** (4F **97**)
  LS3: Leeds 4A **4** (3F **97**)
Wellington Bus. Cen.
  HX5: Ell 4C **160**
Wellington Ct. BD11: Birk 1E **135**
  HX2: Hal 1C **148**
Wellington Cres. BD18: Ship 2A **70**
Wellington Gdns. LS13: Leeds 6F **75**
Wellington Gth. LS13: Leeds 5F **75**
Wellington Gro. BD2: B'frd 1H **91**
  LS13: Leeds 5F **75**
  LS28: Pud 4G **93**
WELLINGTON HILL 1B **80**
Wellington Hill LS17: Leeds 4C **62**
Wellington Mt. LS13: Leeds 5F **75**
Wellington Pl. BD2: B'frd 6A **72**
  HX1: Hal 5D **164** (3G **149**)
  LS1: Leeds 5A **4** (4G **97**)
Wellington Rd. BD2: B'frd 6H **71**
  BD15: Wils 5F **67**
  BD21: Keigh 1A **48**
  LS1: Leeds 5A **4** (4F **97**)
  LS12: Leeds 5E **97**
  LS29: I'ly 5D **10**
Wellington Rd. Ind. Est.
  LS12: Leeds 4F **97**

Wellington St. BD1: B'frd 3E 7 (4F 91)
BD2: B'frd 6H 71
BD4: B'frd 5B 92
BD10: B'frd 2H 71
BD11: Birk 1E 135
(off Wellington Ct.)
BD13: Que 4B 108
BD15: All 2E 89
BD15: Wils 5G 67
BD16: Bgly 4B 50
LS1: Leeds 4A 4 (3F 97)
(not continuous)
LS27: Morl 3A 138
Wellington St. Sth.
HX1: Hal 5D 164 (3H 149)
Wellington St. W.
HX1: Hal 6A 164 (3F 149)
Wellington Ter. LS13: Leeds 5F 75
Well La. BD19: Scho 6F 133
HD6: Clift 1E 163
HD6: Ras 3H 161
HX1: Hal 3D 164 (2H 149)
LS7: Leeds 2B 78
LS19: Raw 4G 55
LS19: Yead 1F 55
LS20: Guis 4C 40
LS25: Kip 4G 123
Well Royd Av. HX2: Hal 2A 148
Well Royd Cl. HX2: Hal 2B 148
Wells, The HX2: Hal 4C 148
(Green La.)
HX2: Hal 2A 148
(Up. Well Royd)
Wells Ct. HX3: Hal 6F 129
LS19: Yead 6F 41
(off Well La.)
LS29: I'ly 6D 10
(off Wells Prom.)
Wells Cft. LS6: Leeds 2E 77
Wells Gro. LS20: Guis 4C 40
Wells Ho. HX6: Sow B 5A 148
(off Church Vw.)
Wells M. LS29: I'ly 6D 10
(off Wells Prom.)
Wells Mt. LS20: Guis 4C 40
Wells Prom. LS29: I'ly 5D 10
Wells Rd. LS20: Guis 4C 40
LS29: I'ly 1C 18
Wells Ter. BD22: Lay 6C 32
HX3: Nor G 5A 132
(off Rookes La.)
Wellstone Av. LS13: Leeds 2D 94
Wellstone Dr. LS13: Leeds 2D 94
Wellstone Gdns. LS13: Leeds 3D 94
Wellstone Gth. LS13: Leeds 3D 94
Wellstone Grn. LS13: Leeds 2D 94
Wellstone Ri. LS13: Leeds 3D 94
Wellstone Rd. LS13: Leeds 3D 94
Wellstone Way LS13: Leeds 3D 94
Well St. BD1: B'frd 4E 7 (4F 91)
BD13: Denh 3B 86
BD15: Wils 4G 67
BD21: Keigh 6H 33
HX4: Holy 6F 159
LS20: Guis 4C 40
(off Wells Rd.)
LS28: Fars 6H 73
Wells Wlk. LS29: I'ly 6D 10
Well Ter. LS20: Guis 4C 40
Well Vw. LS20: Guis 4C 40
Welton Gro. LS6: Leeds 6E 77
Welton Mt. LS6: Leeds 6E 77
Welton Pl. LS6: Leeds 6E 77
Welton Rd. LS6: Leeds 6E 77
Welwyn Av. BD18: Ship 2F 71
Welwyn Dr. BD17: Bail 5C 52
BD18: Ship 2F 71
Welwyn Rd. WF12: Dew 6A 154
Wembley Av. BD13: Thorn 5B 88
Wenborough La. BD4: B'frd 2D 112
Wendel Av. LS15: Bar E 2D 82
Wendover Ct. LS16: Leeds 4D 58
Wendron Way BD10: B'frd 2H 71

Wenlock St. BD3: B'frd 5G 7 (5G 91)
Wenning St. BD21: Keigh 5C 34
Wensley Av. BD18: Ship 2A 70
LS7: Leeds 2A 78
Wensley Bank BD13: Thorn 5G 87
Wensley Bank Ter.
BD13: Thorn 5G 87
Wensley Bank W. BD13: Thorn 5G 87
Wensley Cres. LS7: Leeds 2A 78
Wensleydale Av. LS12: Leeds 1H 95
Wensleydale Cl. LS12: Leeds 1H 95
Wensleydale Ct. LS7: Leeds 2A 78
(off Stainbeck La.)
Wensleydale Cres.
LS12: Leeds 1H 95
Wensleydale Dr. LS12: Leeds 1H 95
Wensleydale M. LS12: Leeds 1H 95
Wensleydale Pde. WF17: Bat 6A 136
Wensleydale Ri. BD17: Bail 3E 53
LS12: Leeds 1H 95
Wensleydale Rd. BD3: B'frd 4C 92
Wensleydale Way BD20: Rid 4F 35
Wensley Dr. LS7: Leeds 1H 77
Wensley Gdns. LS7: Leeds 1H 77
Wensley Grn. LS7: Leeds 2H 77
Wensley Gro. HD6: Ras 3G 161
LS7: Leeds 2A 78
Wensley Lawn LS10: Leeds 3A 140
Wensley Rd. LS7: Leeds 1H 77
Wensley Vw. LS7: Leeds 2A 78
Wentworth Av. LS17: Leeds 3H 59
Wentworth Cl. LS29: Men 1G 39
Wentworth Ct. HD6: Ras 4H 161
Wentworth Cres. BD4: B'frd 3D 112
LS17: Leeds 3A 60
Wentworth Dr. HX2: Illing 6D 106
Wentworth Farm Res. Pk.
LS12: N Far 3F 115
Wentworth Ga. LS22: Weth 3B 12
Wentworth Gro. HX2: Illing 6D 106
Wentworth Ter. LS19: Raw 4H 55
(off Town St.)
Wentworth Way LS17: Leeds 3A 60
Wepener Mt. LS9: Leeds 2F 99
Wepener Pl. LS9: Leeds 2F 99
Wesleyan St. BD4: B'frd 2A 112
Wesley App. LS11: Leeds 3F 117
Wesley Av. BD12: Low M 6E 111
LS12: Leeds 4C 96
Wesley Av. Sth. BD12: Low M 1E 133
Wesley Cl. LS11: Leeds 2F 117
WF17: Birs 6A 136
Wesley Ct. HX1: Hal 3C 164 (2G 149)
LS6: Leeds 6G 77
(off Woodhouse St.)
LS11: Leeds 3F 117
LS19: Yead 6D 40
(off South Vw.)
Wesley Cft. LS11: Leeds 2F 117
Wesley Dr. BD12: Low M 6E 111
Wesley Gth. LS11: Leeds 2F 117
Wesley Grn. LS11: Leeds 3F 117
Wesley Gro. BD10: B'frd 6A 54
Wesley Ho. LS11: Leeds 3E 117
WESLEY PLACE 1D 132
Wesley Pl. BD12: Low M 1E 133
(off Breaks Rd.)
BD20: Sils 2E 15
BD21: Keigh 4G 47
HX6: Sow B 6D 146
LS9: Leeds 4C 98
LS12: Leeds 4C 96
LS29: Add 1D 8
Wesley Rd. LS12: Leeds 4C 96
LS28: Stan 2G 93
Wesley Row LS28: Pud 3A 94
Wesley Sq. LS28: Pud 4A 94
Wesley St. LS11: Leeds 2F 117
LS13: Leeds 4B 74
LS21: Otley 3E 23
LS27: Morl 3A 138
LS28: Fars 6H 73
LS28: Stan 1H 93

Wesley Ter. LS9: Leeds 4C 98
(off Up. Accomodation St.)
LS13: Leeds 6F 75
(Bellmount Vw.)
LS13: Leeds 4B 74
(Wesley St.)
LS25: Gar 4F 103
LS28: Pud 3A 94
Wesley Vw. LS13: Leeds 4B 74
LS28: Pud 4A 94
Wesley Way BD16: Bgly 5F 37
West 26 Ind. Est. BD19: Cleck 5A 134
Westacres HD6: Ras 3B 162
WEST ARDSLEY 1E 155
West Av. BD15: All 6B 68
BD17: Bail 4C 52
HX3: Hal 5F 149
HX3: Hip 2A 152
LS8: Leeds 1G 79
LS23: B Spa 2A 30
West Bank BD9: B'frd 5H 69
BD20: Sils 1D 14
BD22: Keigh 5F 33
(off W. Bank Ri.)
HX2: Illing 3B 128
(not continuous)
W. Bank Cl. BD22: Keigh 5F 33
W. Bank Gro. BD20: Rid 3C 34
W. Bank Ri. BD22: Keigh 5F 33
W. Bank Rd. BD20: Rid 3B 34
Westborough Dr. HX2: Hal 2B 148
West Bottom HX6: Norl 1A 158
Westbourne Av. LS11: Leeds 2H 117
LS25: Gar 5D 102
(not continuous)
Westbourne Cl. LS21: Otley 5C 22
Westbourne Cres. HX3: Hal 6H 149
LS25: Gar 5D 102
Westbourne Dr. LS20: Guis 4A 40
LS25: Gar 5D 102
LS29: Men 6F 21
Westbourne Gdns. LS25: Gar 5D 102
Westbourne Gro. HX3: Hal 6H 149
LS21: Otley 5C 22
LS25: Gar 5D 102
Westbourne Mt. LS11: Leeds 2H 117
Westbourne Pl. LS11: Leeds 2H 117
LS28: Stan 2H 93
Westbourne Rd. BD8: B'frd 1B 90
Westbourne St. LS11: Leeds 2H 117
Westbourne Ter. BD13: Que 4A 108
(off Albert Rd.)
HX3: Hal 6H 149
LS25: Gar 5D 102
Westbourne Vs. LS21: Otley 4C 22
WEST BOWLING 2E 111
West Bradford Golf Course 6E 69
WEST BREARY 2H 43
Westbrook Cl. LS18: H'fth 5D 56
Westbrook Ct. HX1: Hal 2A 164
Westbrook La. LS18: H'fth 5D 56
Westburn Av. BD22: Keigh 1F 47
Westburn Cres. BD22: Keigh 2F 47
Westburn Gro. BD22: Keigh 2F 47
Westburn Pl. BD19: Cleck 2H 153
Westburn Way BD22: Keigh 2F 47
Westbury Cl. BD4: B'frd 6B 92
Westbury Ct. HX1: Hal 3C 148
Westbury Gdns. LS16: Leeds 2A 76
Westbury Gro. LS10: Leeds 3D 118
Westbury Mt. LS10: Leeds 4D 118
Westbury Pl. HX1: Hal 3C 148
Westbury Pl. Nth. LS10: Leeds 3D 118
Westbury Pl. Sth.
LS10: Leeds 4D 118
Westbury Rd. BD6: B'frd 4F 109
Westbury St. BD4: B'frd 6B 92
HX5: Ell 4C 160
LS10: Leeds 3D 118
Westbury Ter. HX1: Hal 3C 148
LS10: Leeds 4D 118
W. Busk La. LS21: Otley 5A 22
West Byland HX2: Illing 6C 106

WEST CARLTON 2F 41
W. Chevin Rd. LS21: Otley 1B 40
 LS29: Men 1B 40
Westcliffe Av. BD17: Bail 3B 52
Westcliffe Dr. HX2: Hal 2B 148
Westcliffe M. BD18: Ship 2B 70
 (off Westcliffe Rd.)
Westcliffe Rd. BD18: Ship 2A 70
Westcombe Av. LS8: Leeds 5E 61
Westcombe Ct. BD12: Wyke 3C 132
W. Cote Dr. BD10: B'frd 6F 53
Westcott Ho. BD8: B'frd 2C 90
 (off Green La.)
West Ct. LS8: Leeds 1G 79
 LS13: Leeds 2E 95
West Cft. BD12: Wyke 5C 132
 LS29: Add 1D 8
Westcroft Av. HX3: She 3D 130
Westcroft Rd. BD7: B'frd 1A 110
West Dale LS23: B Spa 2A 30
Westdale Dr. LS28: Pud 3H 93
Westdale Gdns. LS28: Pud 3H 93
Westdale Gro. LS28: Pud 3H 93
Westdale M. LS28: Pud 3H 93
 (off Westdale Gro.)
Westdale Ri. LS28: Pud 3H 93
Westdale Rd. LS28: Pud 3H 93
W. Dean Cl. BD13: Que 5A 108
West Dene BD20: Sils 1E 15
 LS17: Leeds 1D 60
West Dr. BD22: Oxen 6C 64
WEST END
 BD13 .5H 107
 BD19 .1H 153
 LS18 .6B 56
West End BD13: Que 5H 107
 BD19: Cleck 1H 153
 HX1: Hal 3C 148
 LS12: N Far 2F 115
 LS23: B Spa 2A 30
 LS27: Gil 6E 115
West End App. LS27: Morl 4F 137
West End Cl. LS18: H'fth 6B 56
West End Dr. BD19: Cleck 3H 153
 LS18: H'fth 6B 56
West End Golf Course 1A 148
West End Gro. LS18: H'fth 6B 56
West End La. LS18: H'fth 6B 56
Westend La. BD1: B'frd 3B 6
West End Ri. LS18: H'fth 6B 56
West End Rd. HX1: Hal 3C 148
 LS28: Cal 3F 73
Westend St. BD1: B'frd 3B 6 (4D 90)
West End Ter. BD2: B'frd 4H 71
 BD18: Ship 1A 70
 LS20: Guis 4A 40
Westercroft HX3: North 4D 130
Westercroft Gth. BD13: Que 5G 107
 (off Moor Cl. La.)
Westercroft La. HX3: North 4D 130
Westercroft Vw. HX3: North 4D 130
Westerley Cres. BD20: Sils 2C 14
Westerly Cft. LS12: Leeds 3C 96
Westerly Ri. LS12: Leeds 3C 96
 (off Mistresses La.)
Western Av. BD20: Rid 2A 34
 WF17: Birs 6C 136
Western Cl. BD6: B'frd 6H 109
Western Fold BD6: B'frd 6H 109
Western Gro. LS12: Leeds 6B 96
Western Mt. LS12: Leeds 6B 96
Western Pl. BD13: Que 4D 108
Western Rd. LS12: Leeds 6B 96
Western St. LS12: Leeds 6B 96
Western Way BD6: B'frd 6H 109
WESTERTON 2F 155
Westerton Cl. WF3: W Ard 1H 155
Westerton Ct. BD12: O'haw 2H 133
Westerton Rd. WF3: W Ard 2D 154
Westerton Wlk.
 WF3: W Ard 1H 155
W. Farm Av. LS10: Leeds 2H 139
Westfell Cl. BD22: Keigh 1F 47

Westfell Rd. BD22: Keigh 1F 47
Westfell Way BD22: Keigh 1F 47
WESTFIELD 1D 54
West Fld. HX6: Norl 1A 158
Westfield BD13: Thorn 5C 88
 HX3: Sou 6B 150
 LS7: Leeds 2A 78
 LS28: Stan 2H 93
Westfield Av. HX3: Hip 2F 151
 LS12: Leeds 3H 95
 LS19: Yead 1D 54
 LS25: Kip 4G 123
 WF10: All B 2G 145
Westfield Bldgs. LS27: Morl 6C 138
 (off Tingley Comn.)
Westfield Bungs.
 WF10: All B 2G 145
Westfield Cl. LS19: Yead 1D 54
 LS26: Rothw 3G 141
Westfield Cotts. LS25: Kip 4H 123
 (off High St.)
Westfield Ct. LS3: Leeds 2F 97
 (off Westfield Ter.)
 LS26: Rothw 3G 141
Westfield Cres. BD2: B'frd 2H 91
 BD18: Ship 3E 71
 BD20: Rid 3D 34
 LS3: Leeds 1F 97
 (Bk. Rosebank Cres.)
 LS3: Leeds 2F 97
 (Westfield Rd.)
 WF2: Kirk 6H 155
Westfield Dr. BD20: Rid 4D 34
 HX3: Hip 2F 151
 LS19: Yead 1C 54
Westfield Gdns. HX3: Hip 2F 151
 LS25: Kip 3F 123
Westfield Gro. BD10: B'frd 1G 71
 BD18: Ship 3E 71
 LS19: Yead 1D 54
 WF10: All B 2G 145
Westfield Ho. BD10: B'frd 1F 71
 (off Garsdale Av.)
Westfield Ind. Est. LS19: Yead 1E 55
Westfield La. BD10: B'frd 1F 71
 BD12: Wyke 5C 132
 BD18: Ship 3E 71
 BD19: Scho 5C 132
 LS14: T'ner 3G 63
 LS23: Cliff 6B 30
 LS25: Kip 3F 123
Westfield M. BD13: Thorn 5C 88
Westfield Mills LS12: Leeds 3A 96
 (off Greenock Rd.)
Westfield Mt. LS19: Yead 1D 54
Westfield Oval LS19: Yead 1C 54
Westfield Pl. BD19: Scho 6E 133
 HX1: Hal 3E 149
 LS27: Morl 3A 138
 WF2: Kirk 6H 155
Westfield Rd. BD9: B'frd 1A 90
 BD14: Clay 1D 108
 BD20: Rid 4D 34
 LS3: Leeds 2F 97
 LS26: Rothw 4G 141
 LS27: Morl 3A 138
 WF3: Carl 4G 141
Westfield St.
 HX1: Hal 5A 164 (3F 149)
Westfield Ter. BD2: B'frd 2H 91
 BD14: Clay 1D 108
 BD17: Bail 3C 52
 HX1: Hal 1E 149
 LS3: Leeds 2F 97
 LS7: Leeds 2A 78
 WF10: All B 2G 145
Westfield Yd. LS12: Leeds 6B 96
West Fold BD17: Bail 3C 52
WEST GARFORTH 6D 102
Westgarth LS22: Lin 6B 12
West Gth. M. BD17: Bail 5B 52
WESTGATE 1G 157
West Gate BD21: Keigh 6H 33

Westgate BD1: B'frd 2A 6 (4D 90)
 BD2: B'frd 5A 72
 BD17: Bail 3C 52
 BD18: Ship 1B 70
 HD6: Clift 1E 163
 HX1: Hal 4C 164 (2G 149)
 HX5: Ell 4B 160
 LS1: Leeds 4A 4 (3G 97)
 (not continuous)
 LS20: Guis 5G 39
 LS21: Otley 4D 22
 LS22: Weth 4E 13
Westgate Cl. WF3: Loft 1G 157
Westgate Ct. LS22: Weth 4E 13
 (off Westgate)
 WF3: Loft 1G 157
Westgate Gdns. BD21: Keigh 1H 47
 (off Aireworth St.)
Westgate Gro. WF3: Loft 1G 157
WESTGATE HILL 5E 113
Westgate Hill St. BD4: B'frd 5D 112
Westgate Ho. LS28: Pud 3G 93
Westgate La. WF3: Loft 1F 157
 (not continuous)
Westgate Mall BD1: B'frd 4C 6
Westgate Mkt.
 HX1: Hal 4C 164 (2G 149)
Westgate Pl. BD4: B'frd 5E 113
Westgate Ter. BD4: B'frd 5E 113
W. Grange Cl. LS10: Leeds 4B 118
W. Grange Dr. LS10: Leeds 4B 118
W. Grange Fold LS10: Leeds 4B 118
W. Grange Gdns. LS10: Leeds 4B 118
W. Grange Gth. LS10: Leeds 4B 118
W. Grange Grn. LS10: Leeds 4B 118
W. Grange Rd. LS10: Leeds 5B 118
W. Grange Wlk. LS10: Leeds 4B 118
West Gro. BD17: Bail 3C 52
West Gro. St. LS28: Stan 2H 93
West Gro. Ter.
 HX1: Hal 4A 164 (2F 149)
West Hall LS19: Yead 1G 55
West Hall Ct. LS16: B'hpe 2G 43
West Hall La. LS29: Nes 1F 9
West Hill Av. LS7: Leeds 2A 78
Westhill Av. BD13: Cull 4C 66
West Hill St. HX1: Hal 2E 149
West Hill Ter. LS7: Leeds 2A 78
Westholme Rd. HX1: Hal 2D 148
Westholme St. BD1: B'frd 4B 6 (5D 90)
Westland Ct. LS11: Leeds 5H 117
Westland Rd. LS11: Leeds 4H 117
Westlands Dr. BD15: All 2D 88
Westlands Gro. BD15: All 2E 89
Westland Sq. LS11: Leeds 5H 117
West La. BD13: Thorn 4H 87
 BD17: Bail 4H 51
 BD19: Gom 6F 135
 BD21: Keigh 5F 33
 BD22: Haw 2B 64
 HX3: Sou 6B 150
 LS23: B Spa 2A 30
Westlea Av. BD20: Rid 4D 34
W. Lea Cl. LS17: Leeds 6H 59
W. Lea Cres. LS19: Yead 1D 54
 WF3: W Ard 2D 154
W. Lea Dr. LS17: Leeds 6H 59
 WF3: W Ard 2D 154
W. Lea Gdns. LS17: Leeds 6H 59
W. Lea Gth. LS17: Leeds 6H 59
W. Lea Gro. LS19: Yead 1D 54
W. Leeds St. BD21: Keigh 6G 33
Westleigh BD16: Bgly 3C 50
Westleigh Cl. BD17: Bail 5A 52
Westleigh Dr. BD17: Bail 5A 52
Westleigh Rd. BD17: Bail 4A 52
Westleigh Way BD17: Bail 4A 52
Westlock Av. LS9: Leeds 2E 99
West Lodge LS29: Burl W 3E 21
W. Lodge Gdns. LS7: Leeds 3A 78
Westmead LS28: Stan 2E 93
Westminster Av. BD14: Clay 1C 108
Westminster Cl. LS13: Leeds 5B 74

Westminster Cres. BD14: Clay 1C 108
  LS15: Leeds 4A 100
Westminster Cft. LS13: Leeds 5B 74
Westminster Dr. BD14: Clay 1C 108
  LS13: Leeds 5B 74
Westminster Gdns. BD14: Clay ...1C 108
Westminster Pl. BD3: B'frd ..1F 7 (2F 91)
Westminster Rd.
  BD3: B'frd 1F 7 (2F 91)
  HX3: Hip 3F 151
Westminster Ter.
  BD3: B'frd 1F 7 (2F 91)
Westmoor Av. BD17: Bail 3B 52
Westmoor Cl. BD17: Bail 3B 52
Westmoor Pl. LS13: Leeds 6D 74
Westmoor Ri. LS13: Leeds 6D 74
Westmoor Rd. LS13: Leeds 6D 74
Westmoor St. LS13: Leeds 6D 74
Westmoreland Mt.
  LS13: Leeds 5F 75
WEST MORTON 3G 35
West Mt. Pl. HX1: Hal 1E 149
  (off West Mt. St.)
West Mt. St. LS11: Leeds 2G 117
WESTON 1H 21
Weston Av. BD13: Que 4H 107
Weston Cres. LS21: Otley 2C 22
Weston Dr. LS21: Otley 1B 22
Weston La. LS21: Otley 2B 22
Weston Pk. Vw. LS21: Otley 1B 22
Weston Ridge LS21: Otley 1C 22
Weston Rd. LS29: I'ly 5D 10
Weston St. BD22: Keigh 2F 47
Weston Va. Rd. BD13: Que 5H 107
Westover Av. LS13: Leeds 6E 75
Westover Cl. LS13: Leeds 6F 75
Westover Dr. LS28: Pud 4G 93
Westover Gdns. LS28: Pud 4G 93
Westover Grn. LS13: Leeds 6E 75
Westover Gro. LS13: Leeds 6E 75
Westover Mt. LS13: Leeds 6E 75
Westover Rd. LS13: Leeds 6E 75
Westover St. LS13: Leeds 6E 75
Westover Ter. LS13: Leeds 6E 75
Westover Vw. LS13: Leeds 6E 75
West Pde. HX1: Hal 5A 164 (3F 149)
  HX6: Sow B 5B 148
  LS16: Leeds 1A 76
  LS20: Guis 4C 40
  LS26: Rothw 2B 142
  LS29: I'ly 5E 11
West Pde. Flats HX1: Hal 5A 164
WEST PARK
  LS16 ....1A 76
  LS23 ....2A 30
West Pk. LS20: Guis 3A 40
  LS28: Pud 4H 93
West Pk. Av. LS8: Leeds 4F 61
West Pk. Chase LS8: Leeds 4E 61
West Pk. Cl. LS8: Leeds 4E 61
West Pk. Ct. LS8: Leeds 4F 61
West Pk. Cres. LS8: Leeds 5F 61
West Pk. Dr. LS16: Leeds 1A 76
West Pk. Dr. E. LS8: Leeds 4E 61
West Pk. Dr. W. LS8: Leeds 4D 60
West Pk. Gdns. LS8: Leeds 5F 61
West Pk. Gro. LS8: Leeds 4E 61
West Pk. Ind. Est. BD7: B'frd ...1H 109
West Pk. Pl. LS8: Leeds 5F 61
West Pk. Rd. BD8: B'frd 3H 89
  LS8: Leeds 5F 61
West Pk. St. HD6: Brigh 1B 162
West Pk. Ter. BD8: B'frd 3H 89
West Pk. Vs. LS8: Leeds 4F 61
West Pk. Wlk. LS16: Leeds 2A 76
  (off Old Oak Dr.)
W. Pasture Cl. LS18: H'fth 6B 56
West Point
  LS1: Leeds 5B 4 (4H 97)
Westray LS12: Leeds 5A 4 (4F 97)
West Rd. LS9: Leeds 2G 119
West Rd. Nth. LS9: Leeds 2G 119
WEST ROYD 1E 71

West Royd BD15: Wils 4G 67
  HX3: Hip 1E 151
Westroyd BD13: Que 2G 107
  (off Brighouse & Denholme Rd.)
  LS28: Pud 5G 93
W. Royd Av. BD2: B'frd 5H 71
  BD18: Ship 1D 70
  HX1: Hal 3E 149
Westroyd Av. BD19: Hun 4B 134
  LS28: Pud 5G 93
W. Royd Cl. BD18: Ship 1D 70
  HX1: Hal 4E 149
W. Royd Cres. BD18: Ship 1E 71
Westroyd Cres.
  LS28: Pud 6G 93
  (not continuous)
W. Royd Dr. BD18: Ship 1E 71
Westroyd Gdns. LS28: Pud 5G 93
W. Royd Gro. BD18: Ship 1E 71
WESTROYD HILL 5H 93
W. Royd Ho. LS28: Fars 1H 93
W. Royd Mt. BD18: Ship 1E 71
W. Royd Rd. BD18: Ship 1E 71
W. Royd Ter. BD18: Ship 1E 71
W. Royd Vs. HX1: Hal 4E 149
  (off Kings Cross Rd.)
W. Royd Wlk. BD18: Ship 1E 71
W. Scausby Pk. HX2: Illing 6C 106
WEST SCHOLES 2H 107
West Shaw BD22: Oxen 6B 64
W. Shaw La. BD22: Oxen 6A 64
Westside Ct. BD8: B'frd 3A 90
  (off Washington St.)
West Side Retail Pk.
  LS20: Guis 6D 40
Westside Vw. BD11: Drig 1A 136
  (off West St.)
West St. BD1: B'frd 5F 7 (5F 91)
  BD2: B'frd 6H 71
  BD11: Drig 2A 136
  BD17: Bail 3C 52
  BD19: Gom 6F 135
  HD6: B Bri 2B 152
  HD6: Brigh 6A 152
  HX1: Hal 2E 149
  HX3: She 3D 130
  HX4: Holy 6F 159
  HX6: Sow B 6H 147
  LS1: Leeds 4A 4 (3F 97)
  LS20: Guis 4C 40
  LS27: Morl 4B 138
  LS28: Stan 3A 94
  LS29: I'ly 5D 10
West Ter. LS29: Burl W 1E 21
West Ter. St. LS28: Stan 2H 93
  (off West Gro. St.)
WEST VALE 4H 159
West Vale LS12: Leeds 6E 97
Westvale M. LS13: Leeds 2G 95
West Vw. BD4: B'frd 1G 111
  BD11: Birk 3F 135
  BD16: Bgly 2E 51
  BD17: Bail 3C 52
  (off Newton Way)
  BD19: Scho 6F 133
  BD20: Sils 1E 15
  HX1: Hal 3D 148
  (off Vickerman St.)
  HX3: Hal 5F 129
  HX3: Hip 1F 151
  HX4: Holy 6E 159
  HX6: Sow B 5A 148
  LS11: Leeds 1G 117
  LS19: Yead 3F 55
  LS21: Arth 5H 25
  LS21: Otley 4F 23
  LS25: Kip 3H 123
  LS25: M'fld 5F 105
  LS26: Oul 2E 143
  LS28: Fars 1H 93
  (off New St.)
  LS29: I'ly 6D 10
  WF2: Kirk 6H 155

West Vw. Av. BD18: Ship 2E 71
  HX2: Hal 2C 148
  LS29: Burl W 2E 21
Westview Av. BD20: Keigh 5G 33
West Vw. Cl. BD18: Ship 2E 71
West Vw. Ct. LS19: Yead 6D 40
Westview Cl. BD20: Keigh 5G 33
West Vw. Cres. HX2: Hal 2C 148
Westview Gro. BD20: Keigh 5G 33
West Vw. Dr. HX2: Hal 2B 148
West Vw. Rd. HX3: Hal 5F 129
  LS29: Burl W 2E 21
West Vw. St. BD22: Cros R 1C 46
West Vw. Ter. HX2: Brad 4D 106
  HX2: Hal 1C 148
Westview Way BD20: Keigh 5H 33
W. Villa Rd. LS20: Guis 4C 40
Westville LS29: I'ly 5C 10
Westville Av. LS29: I'ly 5C 10
Westville Cl. LS29: I'ly 5C 10
Westville Rd. LS29: I'ly 5C 10
Westville Way BD13: Thorn 5H 87
Westward Ho. HX3: Hal 3E 129
West Way BD18: Ship 2E 71
  LS1: Leeds 4A 4 (3G 97)
Westway BD9: B'frd 1E 89
  BD16: Bgly 2D 50
  BD20: Keigh 5F 33
  LS20: Guis 5H 39
  LS25: Gar 5D 102
  LS28: Pud 6G 73
Westways Cl. WF2: Wren 6D 156
Westways Dr. LS8: Leeds 2G 79
West Winds LS29: Men 6E 21
Westwinn Gth. LS14: Leeds 1E 81
Westwinn Vw. LS14: Leeds 6E 63
Westwood BD9: B'frd 5H 69
Westwood Av. BD2: B'frd 4H 71
Westwood Cl. LS27: Morl 1B 138
Westwood Cotts. LS23: Cliff 6C 30
Westwood Cl. LS10: Leeds 2G 139
Westwood Cres. BD16: Cot 1C 68
Westwood Dr. LS29: I'ly 1B 18
Westwood Gro. BD2: B'frd 4H 71
Westwood Hall BD6: B'frd 4E 109
Westwood Ho. BD13: Que 4A 108
Westwood Ri. LS27: Morl 1B 138
  LS29: I'ly 1B 18
West Wood Rd. LS10: Leeds 3F 139
  LS27: Chur 3F 139
Westwood Side LS27: Morl 6A 116
W. Woods Rd. LS22: Coll 3F 29
  LS23: B Spa, B'ham, Cliff 3F 29
Westwood St. HD5: Hud 5G 163
Westwood Way LS23: B Spa 4B 30
Westy Bank Cft. BD20: Stee 3C 32
W. Yorkshire Ind. Est.
  BD4: B'frd 5B 112
West Yorkshire Playhouse, The
  ....4H 5 (3B 98)
W. Yorkshire Retail Pk.
  WF17: Birs 3C 136
WETHERBY 4E 13
Wetherby Bus. Pk.
  LS22: Weth 3F 13
Wetherby Golf Course 5C 12
Wetherby Grange LS22: Weth 1G 29
Wetherby Gro. LS4: Leeds 1C 96
Wetherby Leisure Cen. 5E 13
Wetherby Pl. LS4: Leeds 1D 96
Wetherby Racecourse 3H 13
Wetherby Rd. LS8: Leeds 3F 79
  LS14: Bard, Leeds, S'cft 2A 80
  LS14: S'cft 6B 62
  LS17: Bard 6G 27
  LS17: Leeds 6B 62
  LS22: K Dei 1E 13
  LS24: N Kym 5F 31
WETHERBY SERVICE AREA 1G 13
Wetherby Ter. LS4: Leeds 1C 96
Wet Shod La. HD6: Brigh 5G 151

Wetton Ct. BD3: B'frd 4B 92
Wetville BD22: Oxen 6C 64
Weybridge Ho. BD8: B'frd 2C 90
(off Trenton Dr.)
Weyhill Dr. BD15: All 3D 88
Weymouth Av. BD15: All 3C 88
Weymouth St.
HX1: Hal 3B 164 (2G 149)
Whack Ho. LS19: Yead 1D 54
(off Westfield Av.)
Whack Ho. Cl. LS19: Yead 1E 55
Whack Ho. La. LS19: Yead 1E 55
Whalley La. BD13: Denh 1B 86
Wharf App. LS1: Leeds 6C 4
LS11: Leeds 6C 4 (4H 97)
Wharfdale Av. LS29: Men 3H 39
Wharfdale Ct. LS29: Men 3G 39
Wharfdale Cft. LS29: Men 3G 39
Wharfdale Fold LS29: Men 3G 39
Wharfe Bank LS22: Coll 3G 27
Wharfebank Bus. Cen.
LS21: Otley 4C 22
Wharfe Cl. LS16: Leeds 3D 58
LS29: Burl W 2F 21
Wharfe Cres. LS21: Pool 4F 25
Wharfedale Av. LS7: Leeds 5H 77
Wharfedale Bus. Pk.
BD4: B'frd 4B 112
Wharfedale Cl. LS12: Leeds 1H 95
Wharfedale Ct. LS14: Leeds 4B 80
LS21: Otley 3E 23
LS21: Pool 4F 25
(off Main St.)
Wharfedale Cres. LS25: Gar 6F 103
Wharfedale Dr. LS29: I'ly 5E 11
Wharfedale Gdns. BD17: Bail 3E 53
Wharfedale Gro. LS7: Leeds 5H 77
Wharfedale Lawns LS22: Weth 4E 13
Wharfedale M. LS29: I'ly 3F 23
Wharfedale Mt. HX3: She 2D 130
LS7: Leeds 5H 77
Wharfedale Pl. LS7: Leeds 5H 77
Wharfedale Ri. BD9: B'frd 1E 89
WF3: W Ard 2D 154
Wharfedale Rd. BD4: B'frd 6G 111
Wharfedale St. LS7: Leeds 5H 77
Wharfedale Ter. LS22: Coll 2A 28
Wharfedale Vw. LS7: Leeds 5H 77
LS29: Add 1C 8
LS29: Men 1G 39
Wharfe Grange LS22: Weth 4D 12
Wharfe Gro. LS22: Weth 4D 12
Wharfe M. LS29: Men 1H 39
Wharfe Pk. LS29: Add 1E 9
Wharfe Rein LS22: Coll 3G 27
Wharfeside La. LS29: I'ly 4E 11
Wharfeside LS23: B Spa 4D 30
Wharfe St. LS21: Otley 3F 23
Wharfe Vw. LS21: Pool 4E 25
LS22: Weth 4D 12
Wharfe Vw. Rd. LS29: I'ly 5D 10
Wharf St. BD3: B'frd 2E 7 (3F 91)
BD17: Ship 1B 70
HD6: Brigh 1B 162
HX6: Sow B 5A 148
LS2: Leeds 5G 5 (4B 98)
Wharncliffe Cres. BD2: B'frd 5B 72
Wharncliffe Dr. BD2: B'frd 5B 72
Wharncliffe Gro. BD2: B'frd 5B 72
BD18: Ship 3B 70
Wharncliffe Rd. BD18: Ship 4B 70
Whartons, The LS21: Otley 1E 23
Wharton Sq. BD13: Que 4D 108
(off Highgate Rd.)
Wheater Rd. BD7: B'frd 6A 90
Wheaters Fold LS28: Stan 2A 94
(off Woods Row)
Wheatfield Cl. LS28: Fars 5A 74
Wheatfield Ct. LS28: Pud 5H 93
Wheathead Dr. BD22: Keigh 2E 47
Wheathead Dr. BD22: Keigh 2F 47
Wheathead La. BD22: Keigh 2E 47

Wheatlands LS28: Fars 6G 73
LS29: I'ly 5E 11
Wheatlands Av. BD9: B'frd 1G 89
Wheatlands Cres. BD9: B'frd 1G 89
Wheatlands Dr. BD9: B'frd 1G 89
Wheatlands Gro. BD9: B'frd 1G 89
Wheatlands Sq. BD9: B'frd 1G 89
WHEATLEY 5C 128
Wheatley Av. LS29: I'ly 6G 11
Wheatley City HX3: Hal 5C 128
(off City La.)
Wheatley Cl. HX3: Hal 6E 129
LS29: I'ly 5G 11
Wheatley Dr. HX2: Mix 3B 128
Wheatley Gdns. LS29: I'ly 6G 11
Wheatley Gro. LS29: I'ly 6G 11
Wheatley La. HX3: Hal 6E 129
LS29: I'ly 6G 11
Wheatley Lane Ends HX3: Hal 5C 128
(off Wuheatley Rd.)
Wheatley Ri. LS29: I'ly 6G 11
Wheatley Rd. HX3: Hal 5C 128
(Denfield La.)
HX3: Hal 6D 128
(Greenwood's Ter.)
LS29: I'ly 6E 11
Wheaton Av. LS15: Leeds 3C 100
Wheaton Ct. LS15: Leeds 3C 100
(off Wheaton Av.)
Wheat St. BD22: Keigh 3G 47
Wheelwright Av. LS12: Leeds 6A 96
Wheelwright Cl. LS12: Leeds 6A 96
(not continuous)
Whernside Ct. LS29: Men 2H 39
(off Jackson Wlk.)
Whernside Mt. BD7: B'frd 3G 109
Whernside Way HX2: Mt T 4G 127
Wherwell Rd. HD6: Ras 2B 162
Whetley Cl. BD8: B'frd 3C 90
Whetley Gro. BD8: B'frd 2A 90
Whetley Hill BD8: B'frd 2B 90
Whetley La. BD8: B'frd 3A 90
Whetley St. BD8: B'frd 3C 90
(off Denby St.)
Whetley Ter. BD8: B'frd 3C 90
Whewell St. WF17: Birs 6A 136
Whiddon Cft. LS29: Men 6F 21
Whimbrel Cl. BD8: B'frd 4E 89
Whimbrel M. LS27: Morl 4C 138
Whinberry Pl. WF17: Birs 4B 136
Whinbrook Ct. LS17: Leeds 6A 60
Whinbrook Cres. LS17: Leeds 6A 60
Whinbrook Gdns. LS17: Leeds 6A 60
Whinbrook Gro. LS17: Leeds 6A 60
Whincover Bank LS12: Leeds 6H 95
Whincover Cl. LS12: Leeds 6H 95
Whincover Cross LS12: Leeds 6H 95
Whincover Dr. LS12: Leeds 6G 95
Whincover Gdns. LS12: Leeds 6H 95
Whincover Grange LS12: Leeds 6H 95
Whincover Gro. LS12: Leeds 6H 95
Whincover Hill LS12: Leeds 6H 95
Whincover Mt. LS12: Leeds 6H 95
Whincover Rd. LS12: Leeds 6G 95
Whincover Vw. LS12: Leeds 6H 95
Whincup Gdns. LS10: Leeds 3C 118
(off Telford Pl.)
Whinfield LS16: Leeds 3B 58
Whinfield Av. BD22: Keigh 5E 33
Whinfield Cl. BD22: Keigh 5F 33
Whinfield Dr. BD22: Keigh 5E 33
Whingate LS12: Leeds 3A 96
Whingate Av. LS12: Leeds 4A 96
Whingate Bus. Pk. LS12: Leeds 4B 96
Whingate Cl. LS12: Leeds 4A 96
Whingate Ct. LS12: Leeds 4B 96
Whingate Grn. LS12: Leeds 4A 96
Whingate Gro. LS12: Leeds 4A 96
Whingate Rd. LS12: Leeds 4A 96
Whin Knoll Av. BD21: Keigh 5F 33
WHINMOOR 1D 80
Whinmoor Ct. LS14: Leeds 6C 62
Whinmoor Cres. LS14: Leeds 6C 62

Whinmoor Gdns. LS14: Leeds 6B 62
Whinmoor Way LS14: Leeds 2E 81
(not continuous)
Whinney Brow BD10: B'frd 1F 71
Whinney Fld. HX3: Hal 5G 149
Whinney Hill Rd. BD4: B'frd 6C 92
BD13: Que 4B 108
(off Sandbeds)
Whinney Hill Pk. HD6: Brigh 4A 152
Whinney Royd La. HX3: North 2C 130
Whinn Moor La.
LS17: Leeds, Shad 4A 62
LS23: T Arch 2D 30
Whins La. BD31: Keigh 6G 33
Whin St. BD21: Keigh 6G 33
Whin Wood Grange
LS14: Leeds 1D 80
Whiskers La. HX3: North 4A 130
Whisperwood Cl. WF1: Out 4H 157
Whisperwood Rd. WF1: Out 4H 157
Whitaker Av. BD2: B'frd 6A 72
Whitaker Cl. BD2: B'frd 6A 72
Whitaker Ho. HX1: Hal 4G 149
(off Charlotte Cl.)
Whitaker St. LS28: Fars 2H 93
Whitaker Wlk. BD22: Oxen 1C 84
Whitburn Way BD15: All 3D 88
Whitby Rd. BD8: B'frd 2A 90
(not continuous)
Whitby Ter. BD8: B'frd 2A 90
Whitcliffe Mount Sports Cen. 1H 153
Whitcliffe Rd. BD19: Cleck 1H 153
White Abbey Rd.
BD8: B'frd 1A 6 (3C 90)
Whitebeam La. LS10: Leeds 5B 118
Whitebeam Wlk. BD2: B'frd 4H 71
White Birch Ter. HX3: Hal 5C 128
Whitebridge Av. LS9: Leeds 3A 100
Whitebridge Cres. LS9: Leeds 2A 100
Whitebridge Spur
LS9: Leeds 2A 100
Whitebridge Vw. LS9: Leeds 2A 100
White Castle Ct. BD13: Que 3F 107
Whitechapel Cl. LS8: Leeds 3F 79
Whitechapel Gro. BD19: Scho 6G 133
Whitechapel Rd.
BD19: Cleck, Scho 6F 133
Whitechapel Way LS8: Leeds 3F 79
Whitecliffe Cres. LS26: Swil 3A 122
Whitecliffe Dr. LS26: Swil 3A 122
Whitecliffe La. LS26: Swil 3A 122
Whitecliffe Ri. LS26: Swil 3A 122
WHITECOTE 5E 75
Whitecote Gdns. LS13: Leeds 5D 74
Whitecote Hill LS13: Leeds 5D 74
Whitecote Ho. LS13: Leeds 4D 74
Whitecote La. LS13: Leeds 5D 74
Whitecote Ri. LS13: Leeds 5D 74
WHITE CROSS 3A 40
White Cross HD2: Hud 6E 163
Whitefield Pl. BD8: B'frd 3A 90
Whitegate HX2: Ogd 6B 106
HX3: Hal 5H 149
LS17: E Kes 5E 27
Whitegate Dr. HX3: Hal 5H 149
Whitegate Rd. HX3: Hal 4H 149
Whitegate Ter. HX3: Hal 5H 149
Whitegate Top HX3: Hal 5A 150
White Gro. LS8: Leeds 1E 79
Whitehall LS12: Leeds 6A 4 (4G 97)
Whitehall Av. BD12: Wyke 6C 132
Whitehall Ct. LS12: N Far 1A 116
Whitehall Cft. LS12: Leeds 1B 116
(off Whitehall Dr.)
LS26: Rothw 2B 142
Whitehall Cross LS12: N Far 1H 115
Whitehall Dr. LS12: Leeds 1B 116
Whitehall Grn. LS12: Leeds 1A 116
Whitehall Gro. BD11: Birk 2F 135
BD11: Drig 1H 135
Whitehall Ind. Est. LS12: N Far 1H 115
White Hall La. HX2: Wain 1G 127
Whitehall Pk. LS12: N Far 1H 115
Whitehall Pl. LS12: Leeds 5F 97

Whitehall Quay
LS1: Leeds 5C **4** (4H **97**)
Whitehall Rd. BD11: Drig, N Far . .1H **135**
(not continuous)
BD12: Scho, Wyke 6E **133**
BD19: B'frd, Cleck 5A **134**
HX3: Hip 6G **131**
LS1: Leeds 6A **4** (5F **97**)
LS12: Leeds, N Far 6A **4** (4D **114**)
Whitehall Rd. E. BD11: Birk 3E **135**
Whitehall Rd. W. BD11: Birk 5C **134**
BD19: Hun 5B **134**
Whitehall St. HX3: Hip 2F **151**
Whitehall Vs. HX3: Hip 1G **151**
Whitehall Waterfront
LS1: Leeds 6B **4** (4D **97**)
Whitehaven Cl. BD6: B'frd 6H **109**
Whitehead Cl. BD4: B'frd 5B **92**
Whitehead Gro. BD2: B'frd 2A **92**
Whitehead Pl. BD2: B'frd 1A **92**
Whitehead's Ter. HX1: Hal 2D **148**
Whitehead St. BD3: B'frd 5H **91**
Whitehill Cotts. HX2: Illing 2C **128**
Whitehill Cres. HX2: Illing 1C **128**
Whitehill Dr. HX2: Illing 1C **128**
Whitehill Grn. HX2: Illing 1D **128**
Whitehill Rd. HX2: Illing 2C **128**
White Holme Dr. LS21: Pool 5G **25**
White Horse Cl. WF17: Birs 5D **136**
Whitehouse Av. LS26: Gt P 5D **122**
Whitehouse Cres. LS26: Gt P 5E **123**
Whitehouse Dr. LS26: Gt P 5D **122**
Whitehouse La. LS19: Yead 5A **42**
LS26: Swil, Kip 2C **122**
Whitehouse St. LS10: Leeds 6B **98**
White Laithe App. LS14: Leeds 1D **80**
White Laithe Av. LS14: Leeds 1D **80**
White Laithe Cl. LS14: Leeds 1D **80**
White Laithe Ct. LS14: Leeds 1D **80**
White Laithe Cft. LS14: Leeds 1D **80**
White Laithe Gdns.
LS14: Leeds 1D **80**
White Laithe Gth. LS14: Leeds 6D **62**
White Laithe Grn. LS14: Leeds 1E **81**
White Laithe Gro. LS14: Leeds 1E **81**
White Laithe Rd. LS14: Leeds 1D **80**
White Laithe Wlk. LS14: Leeds 1E **81**
Whitelands LS19: Raw 3E **55**
LS28: Pud 3B **94**
Whitelands Cres. BD17: Bail 4D **52**
Whitelands Rd. BD17: Bail 4D **52**
White La. BD6: B'frd 4D **110**
BD22: Oak 5A **46**
White La. Top *BD6: B'frd* *5D 110*
(off White La.)
White Lee Cft. HX7: Myth 6A **126**
Whiteley Av. HX6: Sow B 6F **147**
Whiteley Cft. LS21: Otley 4E **23**
Whiteley Cft. Cl. LS21: Otley 4E **23**
Whiteley Cft. Gth. LS21: Otley 4D **22**
Whiteley Cft. Ri. LS21: Otley 4E **23**
Whiteley Cft. Rd. LS21: Otley 4D **22**
Whiteley St.
HX1: Hal 5A **164** (3F **149**)
Whitelock St.
LS7: Leeds 1G **5** (2B **98**)
White Moor La. BD22: Oxen 4C **84**
Whitemoor Way BD13: Denh 5C **86**
White Rose Av. LS25: Gar 4F **103**
White Rose Mead LS25: Gar 4G **103**
White Rose Shop. Centre, The
LS11: Leeds 6E **117**
White Rose Way LS25: Gar 4G **103**
Whites Cl. BD9: B'frd 6F **69**
White's Ter. BD8: B'frd 2B **90**
Whitestone Cres. LS19: Yead 6F **41**
Whitestone Dr. BD20: E Mor 4H **35**
White St. LS26: Wood 1F **143**
White's Vw. BD8: B'frd 3B **90**
Whiteways BD2: B'frd 6E **71**
White Wells Spa Cottage 1D **18**
White Windows Cotts.
HX6: Sow B 6G **147**

Whitfield Av. LS10: Leeds 1C **118**
Whitfield Gdns. LS10: Leeds 1C **118**
Whitfield Mill BD10: B'frd 1C **72**
Whitfield Pl. LS10: Leeds 1C **118**
Whitfield Sq. LS10: Leeds 1C **118**
Whitfield St. LS8: Leeds 6D **78**
Whitfield Way LS10: Leeds 1C **118**
Witham Cl. LS23: B Spa 3B **30**
Witham Rd. BD18: Ship 1G **69**
WHITKIRK 2E **101**
Whitkirk Cl. LS15: Leeds 3G **101**
Whitkirk La. LS15: Leeds 3F **101**
WHITKIRK LANE END 3F **101**
Whitlam St. BD18: Ship 1H **69**
Whitley Dr. HX2: Illing 1D **128**
Whitley Gdns. *LS8: Leeds* *6C 78*
(off Gledhow Rd.)
WHITLEY HEAD 1C **32**
Whitley La. HX3: Sou 4C **150**
Whitley Pl. WF10: All B 3H **145**
Whitley Rd. BD21: Keigh 2G **47**
Whitley St. BD3: B'frd 4G **7** (4G **91**)
BD16: Bgly 4B **50**
Whittle Cres. BD14: Clay 6D **88**
Whitton Cft. Rd. LS29: I'ly 5D **10**
Whitty La. HX2: Hal 3H **147**
Whitwell Av. HX5: Ell 4D **160**
Whitwell Dr. HX5: Ell 4D **160**
Whitwell Grn. La. HX5: Ell 5D **160**
Whitwell Gro. HX5: Ell 4D **160**
Whitwell St. BD4: B'frd 6G **91**
Whitwood La. HD6: B Bri 2C **152**
(not continuous)
Whitworth Ter. *HX1: Hal* *4G 149*
(off Emily Way)
Whyment Cl. LS27: Chur 4C **116**
Whytecote End BD12: Wyke 3C **132**
WIBSEY .4B **110**
Wibsey Bank BD6: B'frd 4D **110**
Wibsey Pk. Av. BD6: B'frd 5H **109**
Wicken Cl. BD10: B'frd 3A **72**
Wicken La. BD13: Thorn 4H **87**
Wicket, The LS28: Cal 2F **73**
Wickets, The BD2: B'frd 1A **92**
LS6: Leeds 2F **77**
LS15: Leeds 4G **101**
Wickets Cl. BD6: B'frd 5D **110**
Wickham Av. BD6: B'frd 5C **110**
LS23: B Spa 4A **30**
Wickham Cl. LS23: B Spa 3A **30**
Wickham St. BD19: Scho 1F **153**
LS11: Leeds 2G **117**
Widdop Cl. BD6: B'frd 3E **109**
Wide La. BD22: Oak 4A **46**
LS27: Morl 3A **138**
Wigan St. BD1: B'frd 4A **6** (4D **90**)
Wigeon App. LS27: Morl 3C **138**
Wighill La.
LS23: T Arch, W'ton 1G **31**
LS24: Tad 1G **31**
Wightman St. BD3: B'frd 2G **91**
Wignall St. BD20: Keigh 3H **33**
Wigton Chase LS17: Leeds 2E **61**
Wigton Ga. LS17: Leeds 1C **60**
Wigton Grn. LS17: Leeds 1C **60**
Wigton Gro. LS17: Leeds 1C **60**
Wigton La. LS17: Leeds 1C **60**
Wigton Pk. Cl. LS17: Leeds 1D **60**
WIKE 4A **44**
Wike La. LS17: Bard, E Kes 3B **44**
Wike Ridge Av. LS17: Leeds 2E **61**
Wike Ridge Cl. LS17: Leeds 1F **61**
Wike Ridge Ct. LS17: Leeds 1F **61**
Wike Ridge Fold LS17: Leeds 1E **61**
Wike Ridge Gdns. LS17: Leeds 2F **61**
Wike Ridge Gro. LS17: Leeds 2F **61**
Wike Ridge La.
LS17: Leeds, Wike 2F **61**
Wike Ridge M. LS17: Leeds 2F **61**
Wike Ridge Mt. LS17: Leeds 2F **61**
Wike Ridge Vw. LS17: Leeds 2F **61**
Wilday Cl. BD16: Bgly 1A **50**
Wilderness Rd. HX5: Ell 5E **161**

Wild Flower Way
LS10: Leeds 3B **140**
Wild Gro. LS28: Pud 4E **93**
Wild Heather Cl. BD13: Cull 4A **66**
Wilfred Av. LS15: Leeds 3D **100**
Wilfred St. BD14: Clay 1F **109**
LS15: Leeds 3D **100**
Wilfred Ter. LS12: Leeds 1A **116**
Wilkinson Fold BD12: Wyke 4C **132**
Wilkinson Ter. BD7: B'frd 5H **89**
Wilkinson Way LS21: Otley 2C **22**
Wilkin St. BD21: Keigh 6H **33**
Willans Av. LS26: Rothw 6A **120**
Willerton Cl. WF12: Dew 6B **154**
William Av. LS15: Leeds 3A **100**
LS26: Wood 1E **145**
William Fison Ride
LS29: Burl W 3D **20**
William Foster Way
LS29: Burl W 3D **20**
William Henry St. BD18: Ship 6H **51**
HD6: Brigh 6A **152**
William Hey Ct. LS9: Leeds 1F **99**
William La. LS28: Pud 4H **93**
William Ri. LS15: Leeds 3A **100**
Williams Ct. LS28: Fars 6H **73**
Williamson St. HX1: Hal 1E **149**
Williamson Rd. BD20: Stee 6B **14**
Williamson St. HX1: Hal 1E **149**
Williams Rd. BD20: Stee 6B **14**
William St. BD4: B'frd 4B **112**
BD5: B'frd 6C **6** (5E **91**)
BD6: B'frd 6H **109**
BD13: Denh 2B **86**
HD6: Ras 2A **162**
HX4: Gree 5H **159**
LS6: Leeds 6E **77**
LS27: Chur 5C **116**
LS28: Stan 1B **94**
(Milestone Ct.)
LS28: Stan 2H **93**
(Sun Field)
William Vw. LS15: Leeds 3A **100**
Willis Cl. LS9: Leeds 4C **98**
Willoughby Ter. LS11: Leeds 6F **97**
Willow App. LS4: Leeds 2E **97**
Willow Av. BD2: B'frd 3G **71**
LS4: Leeds 2E **97**
LS23: Cliff 5B **30**
Willow Bank BD20: Rid 3B **34**
HX1: Hal 4E **149**
HX2: Lud M 3D **146**
Willow Bank Cl. BD15: All 4D **88**
Willow Cl. BD6: B'frd 6C **110**
HX2: Hal 3B **148**
LS4: Leeds 2E **97**
LS20: Guis 4C **40**
LS29: Burl W 2E **21**
Willow Cit. HX5: Ell 5A **160**
LS21: Pool 5F **25**
Willow Cres. BD2: B'frd 3G **71**
HX6: Sow B 4A **148**
LS15: Leeds 4B **100**
LS23: Cliff 5B **30**
Willow Cft. LS29: Men 1G **39**
Willowcroft BD19: Cleck 2H **153**
Willowdale LS10: Leeds 3C **140**
Willow Dene Av. HX2: Hal 4B **148**
HX2: Hal 6C **110**
HX2: Hal 3B **148**
WILLOW FIELD 4A **148**
Willowfield Av. HX2: Hal 4B **148**
Willowfield Cl. HX2: Hal 3B **148**
Willowfield Cres. BD2: B'frd 3G **71**
HX2: Hal 3B **148**
Willowfield Dr. HX2: Hal 4B **148**
Willowfield Lodge HD6: Ras 4G **161**
Willowfield Rd. HX2: Hal 3B **148**
Willowfield St. BD7: B'frd 5B **90**
Willowfield Ter. HX2: Hal 4C **148**
Willowfield Vw. HX2: Hal 3B **148**
Willow Gdns. BD2: B'frd 3G **71**
HX2: Hal 4C **148**
LS20: Guis 4C **40**

Willow Gth. LS4: Leeds 2E 97
Willow Gth. Av. LS14: Leeds 1D 80
Willow Gth. Cl. LS14: Leeds 1D 80
Willow Glade LS23: Cliff 6B 30
Willow Grn. WF1: Wake 6F 157
Willow Gro. BD2: B'frd 3G 71
   BD21: Keigh 4G 47
   (off Halifax Rd.)
   LS23: Cliff 5B 30
   LS25: Kip 2F 123
Willow Hall Dr. HX6: Sow B 4B 148
Willow Hall Fold HX6: Sow B 4B 148
   (off Willow Hall La.)
Willow Hall La. HX6: Sow B 4B 148
Willow Ho. LS7: Leeds 2B 78
Willow Ho's. HX6: Sow B 4B 148
   (off Rochdale Rd.)
Willow Ind. Complex
   HX6: Sow B 6G 147
Willow La. LS20: Bail, Guis 1F 53
   LS23: Cliff 5B 30
Willow Mt. HX3: She 1F 131
   (off Witchfield Hill)
Willow Pk. WF1: Wake 6F 157
Willow Pk. Dr. HX3: She 1F 131
Willow Ri. HX2: Hal 3B 148
Willow Rd. LS4: Leeds 2E 97
   LS28: Fars 1G 93
Willows, The BD16: Har 6F 49
   BD17: Bail 5G 51
   HX2: Illing 6C 106
   LS10: Leeds 3C 140
   LS17: Leeds 5A 60
   LS26: Wood 1F 143
   (off Aberford Rd.)
Willow Sq. LS26: Oul 2E 143
Willow St. BD8: B'frd 3H 89
   BD19: Cleck 6B 134
   HX1: Hal 3E 149
   HX6: Sow B 5B 148
Willow Ter. HX6: Sow B 4A 148
   LS1: Leeds 1B 4 (2G 97)
Willow Tree Cl. BD21: Keigh 2B 48
Willow Tree Gdns.
   LS29: Burl W 1F 21
Willowtree Gdns. BD16: Bgly 2E 51
Willow Va. LS22: Weth 2D 12
Willow Valley Golf Course 4F 153
Willow Vw. HX6: Sow B 4B 148
   (off Bairstow Mt.)
Willow Vs. BD2: B'frd 3G 71
Willow Well Rd. LS15: Leeds 3B 100
Wills Gill LS20: Guis 4D 40
Will St. BD4: B'frd 1B 112
Wilman Hill BD6: B'frd 4B 110
   (not continuous)
Wilmer Dr. BD9: B'frd 5A 70
   BD18: Ship 4A 70
Wilmer Rd. BD9: B'frd 6A 70
Wilmington Gro. LS7: Leeds 6A 78
Wilmington St. LS7: Leeds 1A 98
   (off Wilmington Gro.)
Wilmot Rd. LS29: I'ly 5E 11
Wilmur Mt. HX2: Lud M 3E 147
WILSDEN 4G 67
WILSDEN HILL 3F 67
Wilsden Hill Rd. BD15: Wils 4F 67
Wilsden Old Rd. BD16: Har 6F 49
Wilsden Rd. BD15: All 5A 68
   BD16: Har 6F 49
Wilson Av. BD20: Stee 5B 14
Wilson Ct. WF1: Out 5G 157
Wilson Dr. WF1: Out 5F 157
Wilson Fold BD12: Low M 2D 132
Wilson Rd. BD12: Wyke 3D 132
   BD16: Bgly 3B 50
   HX1: Hal 4D 148
Wilson's Row LS26: Meth 4F 145
Wilson St. BD8: B'frd 2C 90
Wilsons Yd. LS28: Stan 2H 93
Wilton Av. HD2: Hud 5E 163
Wilton Gro. LS6: Leeds 3E 77

Wilton Rd. LS29: I'ly 6C 10
Wilton St. BD5: B'frd 6B 6 (5D 90)
   HD6: Brigh 6H 151
Wimborne Dr. BD15: All 2E 89
   BD21: Keigh 5F 33
Winbrooke Ter. BD8: B'frd 4A 110
Winburg Rd. BD7: B'frd 6A 90
Winburn Ter. HX2: Hal 3H 147
Winchester Gdns. BD4: B'frd 6B 92
Winchester Ho. HX6: Sow B 5A 148
   (off Church Vw.)
Winchester St. LS12: Leeds 4D 96
Winden Cl. WF3: Loft 4G 157
Winden Gro. WF3: Loft 4F 157
Windermere Av. LS29: Men 5G 21
Windermere Dr. LS17: Leeds 1F 59
   LS25: Gar 5F 103
Windermere Ri. HD6: B Bri 3B 152
Windermere Rd. BD7: B'frd 2G 109
   BD17: Bail 6H 51
   (not continuous)
Windermere Ter. BD7: B'frd 2G 109
Winders Dale LS27: Morl 1H 137
Windgate BD20: Sils 3F 15
WINDHILL 2C 70
Windhill Old Rd. BD10: B'frd 6F 53
   BD18: Ship 6F 53
Winding Ri. HD6: B Bri 2B 152
Winding Rd.
   HX1: Hal 3C 164 (2G 149)
Winding Way LS17: Leeds 2H 59
Windle Royd La. HX2: Hal 2A 148
Windmill App. LS10: Leeds 5C 118
Windmill Chase LS26: Rothw 3A 142
Windmill Cl. LS10: Leeds 6C 118
Windmill Cotts. LS15: Leeds 5H 101
Windmill Ct. LS12: Leeds 5A 96
   LS14: Leeds 3D 80
Windmill Cres. HX3: North 5C 130
Windmill Dr. HX3: North 5C 130
Windmill Fld. Rd. LS26: Rothw 3A 142
Windmill Fold LS19: Yead 1G 55
   (off Windmill La.)
Windmill Gdns. LS15: Leeds 4F 101
Windmill Ga. LS12: Leeds 4A 96
Windmill Grn. LS26: Rothw 3A 142
Windmill Health & Strength Club
   . . . . .1B 110
   (off Ebenezer Pl.)
WINDMILL HILL 5G 93
Windmill Hill BD6: B'frd 4A 110
   HX3: North 6C 130
   LS28: Pud 5G 93
Windmill La. BD6: B'frd 4C 110
   HX3: North 5C 130
   LS19: Yead 1G 55
   LS26: Rothw 3A 142
   LS27: Gil 1F 137
   LS29: Men 1B 40
   WF17: Bat 6C 136
Windmill Pl. LS19: Yead 1G 55
   (off Windmill La.)
Windmill Ri. LS12: Leeds 5A 96
Windmill Rd. LS10: Leeds 5C 118
   LS23: B'ham 6C 30
Windrush Ct. LS7: Leeds 5B 78
   (off Chapeltown Rd.)
Windsor Av. BD20: Sils 1D 14
   LS15: Leeds 3D 100
Windsor Cl. LS25: Kip 3G 123
   WF12: Dew 6B 154
Windsor Ct. BD5: B'frd 6E 91
   (off Swarland Gro.)
   BD18: Ship 2B 70
   (off Manor La.)
   LS13: Leeds 1F 95
   LS17: Leeds 5C 60
   LS27: Morl 3A 138
   WF12: Dew 6A 154
Windsor Cres. BD22: Oak 5B 46
   HX2: Hal 6C 128
   LS26: Rothw 1A 142
Windsor Gdns. WF12: Dew 6B 154

Windsor Grn. LS25: Gar 4H 103
Windsor Gro. BD13: Thorn 5H 87
   BD22: Oak 5B 46
Windsor Mt. LS15: Leeds 3D 100
Windsor Oval WF3: W Ard 4D 154
Windsor Pl. HD2: Hud 6E 163
Windsor Rd. BD18: Ship 2B 70
   BD22: Oak 5B 46
   WF12: Dew 6A 154
   WF17: Bat 6C 136
Windsor St. BD4: B'frd 6G 91
   HX1: Hal 6B 164 (3G 149)
Windsor Ter. HX6: Sow B 6H 147
   LS27: Gil 6F 115
Windsor Vw. WF12: Dew 6B 154
Windsor Vs. HX3: Nor G 5H 131
Windsor Wlk. HX3: Hip 3A 152
   WF17: Bat 5D 136
Windy Bank La. BD13: Que 1F 129
   HX3: Que 1F 129
   WF15: Liv 4H 153
Windy Gro. BD15: Wils 5H 67
   (not continuous)
Wine Tavern La. HX6: Sow B 6B 146
Wine Tavern Rd. HX6: Sow B 6B 146
Winfield Dr. BD4: E Bier 1C 134
Winfield Gro. LS2: Leeds 1H 97
   (off Devon Rd.)
Winfield Pl. LS2: Leeds 1H 97
Winfield Ter. LS2: Leeds 1H 97
   (off Devon Rd.)
Wingate Av. BD22: Keigh 1F 47
Wingate Way BD22: Keigh 1F 47
Wingfield Ct. BD16: Bgly 3C 50
Wingfield Mt. BD3: B'frd 3H 91
Wingfield St. BD3: B'frd 3H 91
Winker Grn. Lodge
   LS12: Leeds 3C 96
   (off Eyres Mill Side)
Winker Grn. Mills LS12: Leeds 3B 96
   (off Eyres Mill Side)
Winnard Row BD5: B'frd 3F 111
Winnipeg Pl. LS7: Leeds 3B 78
Winn Mt. LS13: Leeds 3D 74
Winnow La. LS23: B Spa 4G 29
Winrose App. LS10: Leeds 6C 118
Winrose Av. LS10: Leeds 5B 118
Winrose Cl. BD12: Wyke 3C 132
Winrose Cres. LS10: Leeds 5B 118
Winrose Dr. LS10: Leeds 5B 118
Winrose Gth. LS10: Leeds 5C 118
Winrose Gro. LS10: Leeds 5C 118
Winrose Hill LS10: Leeds 4C 118
Winscar Av. BD6: B'frd 4E 109
Winslow Rd. BD10: B'frd 5C 72
Winstanley Ter. LS6: Leeds 6E 77
   (off Victoria Rd.)
Winston Gdns. LS6: Leeds 4C 76
Winston Mt. LS6: Leeds 4C 76
Winston Ter. BD7: B'frd 6A 90
Winterbourne Av. LS27: Morl 1B 138
Winterburn Hill HX2: Hal 3G 147
Winterburn La. HX2: Hal 2G 147
Winterburn St. BD21: Keigh 5A 34
Winter Ct. BD15: All 6C 68
Winter Hill HX3: Sou 6C 150
Winterneb HX2: Lud M 4E 147
Winter St. HX1: Hal 4D 148
Winterton Dr. BD12: Low M 2C 132
Winthorpe Av. WF3: Thpe H 5B 140
Winthorpe Cres.
   WF3: Thpe H 5B 140
Winthorpe St. LS6: Leeds 3F 77
Winthorpe Vw. WF3: Thpe H 5C 140
Winton Grn. BD6: B'frd 1B 132
Winton Mill HX6: Sow B 5A 148
Wintoun St. LS7: Leeds 1G 5 (2B 98)
Wira Ho. LS16: Leeds 6H 57
Wirefield Rd. BD22: Keigh 3G 47
WIRING FIELD 4C 96
Wistons La. HX5: Ell 4C 160
   (not continuous)
WITCHFIELD 1F 131

Witchfield Ct. HX3: She 1F **131**
(off Burned Rd.)
Witchfield Grange HX3: She 1E **131**
Witchfield Hill HX3: She 1F **131**
Witham Way LS25: Gar 5G **103**
Withens Hill Cft. HX2: Illing 6B **106**
Withens New Rd.
HX2: Ogd, Wain 3A **106**
Withens Rd. HX2: Wain 1F **127**
WF17: Birs 5A **136**
Withinfield Ct. HX3: Sou 5C **150**
Within Flds. HX3: Sou 5C **150**
Withins Cl. BD5: B'frd 3B **110**
Woburn Ter. BD14: Clay 1D **108**
Wold Cl. BD13: Thorn 5H **87**
Wolley Av. LS12: N Far 2F **115**
Wolley Ct. LS12: N Far 2F **115**
Wolley Dr. LS12: N Far 2F **115**
Wolley Gdns. LS12: N Far 2F **115**
Wolseley Rd. LS4: Leeds 2D **96**
(not continuous)
Wolseley Ter. BD14: Clay 6E **89**
Wolseley Ter. HX1: Hal 2D **148**
(off Battinson Rd.)
Wolston Cl. BD4: B'frd 3C **112**
Womersley Ct. LS28: Pud 5H **93**
(off Womersley Pl.)
Womersley Pl. LS28: Pud 5H **93**
LS28: Stan 2F **93**
Womersley St. HX1: Hal 2D **148**
Woodacre Cres. LS17: Bard 2E **45**
Woodacre Grn. LS17: Bard 1E **45**
Woodacre La. LS17: Bard 1E **45**
Woodale Av. BD9: B'frd 6F **69**
Woodbine Gro. BD10: B'frd 2H **71**
Woodbine St. BD3: B'frd 3G **7** (4G **91**)
HX1: Hal 4E **149**
Woodbine Ter. BD10: B'frd 2H **71**
HX1: Hal 4E **149**
(off Woodbine St.)
LS6: Leeds 3E **77**
LS13: Leeds 6E **75**
LS18: H'fth 2E **75**
(off Wood La.)
WOODBOTTOM 1H **73**
Wood Bottom LS19: Raw 1H **73**
Woodbottom Cl. BD17: Bail 5D **52**
Wood Bottom La. HD6: Brigh 4F **151**
Woodbourne LS8: Leeds 2G **79**
Woodbourne Av. LS17: Leeds 6A **60**
Woodbridge Av. LS25: Gar 2A **104**
Woodbridge Cl. LS6: Leeds 4B **76**
Woodbridge Cres. LS6: Leeds 3A **76**
Woodbridge Fold LS6: Leeds 4A **76**
Woodbridge Gdns.
LS6: Leeds 4A **76**
Woodbridge Gth. LS6: Leeds 4B **76**
Woodbridge Grn. LS6: Leeds 4B **76**
Woodbridge Lawn LS6: Leeds 4A **76**
Woodbridge Pl. LS6: Leeds 4A **76**
Woodbridge Rd. LS6: Leeds 4A **76**
Woodbridge Va. LS6: Leeds 4A **76**
Woodbrook Av. HX2: Mix 2A **128**
Woodbrook Cl. HX2: Mix 2A **128**
Woodbrook Pl. HX2: Mix 2A **128**
Woodbrook Rd. HX2: Mix 2A **128**
Wood Cl. BD17: Bail 5B **52**
LS7: Leeds 2A **78**
LS26: Rothw 1H **141**
Woodcot Av. BD17: Bail 5D **52**
Wood Cote Fold BD22: Oak 1B **66**
Wood Cres. LS26: Rothw 1H **141**
Wood Cft. HD6: Ras 2H **161**
HX6: Sow B 6E **147**
Woodcroft Grange HX2: Hal 3B **148**
Woodcross BD17: Morl 1A **138**
Woodcross Ct. BD5: B'frd 1D **110**
Woodcross End LS27: Morl 6A **116**
Woodcross Fold LS27: Morl 1A **138**
Woodcross Gdns.
LS27: Morl 1A **138**
Woodcross Gth. LS27: Morl 6A **116**
Wood Dr. LS26: Rothw 1G **141**

WOODEND
BD18 . . . . .2D **70**
WF10 . . . . .2F **145**
Woodend WF10: All B 1F **145**
Wood End Cl. HX3: Hal 6F **149**
Wood End Cl. BD5: B'frd 3F **111**
Wood End Cres. BD18: Ship 1D **70**
Woodend Cres. WF10: All B 2F **145**
Wood End La. HX4: Bark 5B **158**
Woodeson Ct. LS13: Leeds 4B **74**
Woodeson Lea LS13: Leeds 4B **74**
Woodfield Av. HX4: Gree 4F **159**
Woodfield Cl. BD10: B'frd 1A **72**
Woodfield Ct. LS8: Leeds 5H **79**
Woodfield Dr. HX4: Gree 5F **159**
Woodfield Rd. BD13: Cull 2C **66**
Woodfield Ter. LS28: Pud 5B **94**
Woodford Av. HX3: Hal 5H **149**
Woodford Cl. BD15: All 3C **88**
Woodgarth Gdns. BD4: B'frd 2D **112**
Wood Gro. LS12: Leeds 4F **95**
WOODHALL 1E **93**
Woodhall Av. BD3: B'frd 2C **92**
LS5: Leeds 3G **75**
Woodhall Cl. LS28: Stan 1E **93**
Woodhall Ct. LS15: Leeds 5F **101**
LS28: Cal 4E **73**
Woodhall Cres. HX3: Hal 6E **149**
Woodhall Cft. LS28: Stan 1E **93**
Woodhall Dr. LS5: Leeds 3G **75**
Woodhall Gro. LS26: Meth 4D **144**
(not continuous)
WOODHALL HILLS 6E **73**
Woodhall Hills LS28: Cal 6D **72**
Woodhall Hills Golf Course 5D **72**
Woodhall La. LS28: Cal, Stan 6E **73**
WOODHALL PARK 1F **93**
Woodhall Pk. HX3: North 4C **130**
Woodhall Pk. Av. LS28: Stan 1E **93**
Woodhall Pk. Cres. E.
LS28: Stan 2F **93**
Woodhall Pk. Cres. W. LS28: Stan . .2E **93**
Woodhall Pk. Dr. LS28: Stan 2E **93**
Woodhall Pk. Gdns. LS28: Stan 2F **93**
Woodhall Pk. Gro. LS28: Stan 2E **93**
Woodhall Pk. Mt. LS28: Stan 1E **93**
Woodhall Pl. BD3: B'frd 2C **92**
Woodhall Retail Pk.
BD3: B'frd 2C **92**
Woodhall Rd. BD3: B'frd 3C **92**
BD3: B'frd, Cal 2C **92**
LS28: Cal 6C **72**
Woodhall Ter. BD3: B'frd 2C **92**
Woodhall Vw. BD3: B'frd 2D **92**
Woodhead La. HD6: Clift 2E **163**
LS27: Gil 6E **115**
Woodhead Rd. BD7: B'frd 5B **90**
WF17: Birs 4D **136**
Woodhead St. HX2: Hal 1C **148**
Wood Hill LS26: Rothw 1H **141**
Wood Hill Ct. LS16: Leeds 3F **57**
Wood Hill Cres. LS16: Leeds 4E **57**
Wood Hill Gdns. LS16: Leeds 3F **57**
Wood Hill Gro. LS16: Leeds 4E **57**
Wood Hill Ri. LS16: Leeds 3F **57**
Woodhill Ri. BD10: B'frd 1C **72**
Wood Hill Rd. LS16: Leeds 4F **57**
Woodhill Vw. LS22: Weth 3E **13**
WOODHOUSE
BD21 . . . . .2A **48**
HD6 . . . . .3C **162**
LS2 . . . . .1H **97**
Woodhouse BD16: Bgly 5C **50**
Woodhouse Av. BD21: Keigh 2A **48**
WOODHOUSE CARR 6H **77**
WOODHOUSE CLIFF 5G **77**
Woodhouse Cliff LS6: Leeds 5G **77**
Woodhouse Cl. BD21: Keigh 2A **48**
WF3: E Ard 3H **155**
Woodhouse Dr. BD21: Keigh 2A **48**
Woodhouse Flats LS2: Leeds 6G **77**
(off St Mark's St.)

Woodhouse Gdns. HD6: Ras 3C **162**
Woodhouse Gro. BD15: All 5C **68**
BD21: Keigh 2A **48**
WOODHOUSE HILL 3C **118**
Woodhouse Hill Av. LS10: Leeds . .3C **118**
Woodhouse Hill Gro.
LS10: Leeds 3C **118**
Woodhouse Hill Pl.
LS10: Leeds 3C **118**
Woodhouse Hill Rd. LS10: Leeds . .3C **118**
(not continuous)
Woodhouse La. HD6: Ras 4B **162**
HX3: Hal 6E **149**
LS1: Leeds 1D **4** (1G **97**)
LS2: Leeds 1C **4** (6G **77**)
WF2: Kirk 6G **155**
WF3: E Ard, Kirk 6G **155**
Woodhouse Rd. BD21: Keigh 2A **48**
Woodhouse Sq.
LS3: Leeds 2B **4** (3G **97**)
Woodhouse St. LS6: Leeds 6G **77**
Woodhouse Ter. BD6: B'frd 5E **111**
Woodhouse Wlk. BD21: Keigh 2A **48**
Woodhouse Way BD21: Keigh 2B **48**
WOODKIRK 2D **154**
Woodkirk Av. WF3: Ting 1C **154**
Woodkirk Gdns. WF12: Dew 3B **154**
Woodkirk Gro. BD12: Wyke 6C **132**
WF3: Ting 1D **154**
Woodland Av. LS26: Swil 4A **122**
Woodland Cl. BD9: B'frd 5E **69**
LS15: Leeds 3E **101**
Woodland Ct. LS8: Leeds 4E **79**
Woodland Cres. BD9: B'frd 5D **68**
LS26: Rothw 1H **141**
LS26: Swil 4A **122**
Woodland Dr. LS18: H'fth 5E **57**
Woodland Dr. HD6: Brigh 6H **151**
HX2: Hal 4B **148**
LS7: Leeds 2B **78**
LS10: Leeds 3D **140**
LS26: Swil 4H **121**
Woodland Glade Sports & Leisure Cen.
. . . . .6D **162**
Woodland Gro. BD9: B'frd 4E **69**
LS7: Leeds 5C **78**
LS26: Swil 4A **122**
Woodland Hill LS15: Leeds 3D **100**
Woodland Ho. BD10: B'frd 2A **72**
(off Fairhaven Grn.)
Woodland La. LS7: Leeds 2B **78**
Woodland Mt. LS7: Leeds 5C **78**
Woodland Pk. LS26: Oul 2E **143**
Woodland Pk. Rd.
LS6: Leeds 4E **77**
Woodland Ri. LS15: Leeds 3E **101**
Woodland Rd. LS15: Leeds 3D **100**
WOODLANDS 5G **129**
Woodlands BD12: O'haw 2G **133**
BD17: Bail 3E **53**
LS17: Leeds 5C **60**
LS29: I'ly 5F **11**
WF3: E Ard 2A **156**
Woodlands, The LS21: Pool 5G **25**
LS26: Oul 2E **143**
(off Farrer La.)
Woodlands Av. BD13: Que 4D **108**
BD19: Gom 6E **135**
HX3: Hal 6G **129**
LS28: Stan 2G **93**
Woodlands Cl. BD10: B'frd 6D **54**
BD13: Thorn 5H **87**
HD2: Hud 5G **163**
LS14: S'cft 5E **45**
LS29: I'ly 5B **10**
WF3: E Ard 2A **156**
Woodlands Ct. BD8: B'frd 2A **6**
BD16: Bgly 2A **50**
LS16: Leeds 6B **58**
LS25: Kip 5H **123**
LS28: Pud 6H **93**
Woodlands Cres. BD19: Gom 6E **135**
Woodlands Cft. LS25: Kip 5H **123**

Woodlands Dr. BD10: B'frd 6D **54**
  BD19: Gom 6E **135**
  LS19: Raw 5E **55**
  LS25: Gar 5H **103**
  LS27: Morl 1H **137**
  WF3: E Ard 2H **155**
Woodlands Fold BD11: Birk 2F **135**
Woodlands Gdns. LS14: S'cft 1E **63**
Woodlands Gro. BD13: Que 4C **108**
  BD16: Cot 2D **68**
  BD17: Bail 5H **51**
  HX3: Hal 6G **129**
  LS25: Kip 5A **124**
  LS28: Stan 2G **93**
  LS29: I'ly 5B **10**
Woodlands Mill BD20: Stee 6C **14**
  (off Mulberry La.)
Woodlands Mt. HX3: Hal 5G **129**
  (not continuous)
Woodlands Pk. BD19: Cleck 4H **133**
  LS14: S'cft 5E **45**
Woodlands Pk. Gro.
  LS28: Pud 6H **93**
Woodlands Pk. Rd. LS28: Pud 6H **93**
Woodland Sq. HD6: Brigh 2C **162**
  LS12: Leeds 3H **95**
Woodlands Ri. BD22: Haw 3C **64**
  LS29: I'ly 5A **10**
Woodlands Rd. BD8: B'frd 3A **90**
  BD13: Que 4C **108**
  BD16: Bgly 3E **51**
  BD19: Gom 6E **135**
  HX3: Hal 6G **129**
  HX5: Ell 3B **160**
  WF17: Bat 6C **136**
Woodlands St. BD8: B'frd 3C **90**
Woodlands Ter. BD8: B'frd 2A **90**
  BD12: O'haw 2H **133**
  LS28: Stan 2G **93**
Woodlands Vw. BD19: Gom 6E **135**
  BD22: Oak 5C **46**
  HX3: Hal 6G **129**
  (off Range St.)
  LS14: S'cft 6E **45**
  LS25: Kip 5A **124**
Woodland Ter. HX3: Hal 6G **129**
  LS7: Leeds 2G **77**
Woodland Vw. LS7: Leeds 2B **78**
  LS28: Cal 2E **73**
  WF3: W Ard 4D **154**
Woodland Vs. LS14: Leeds 5F **81**
Wood La. BD2: B'frd 5E **71**
  BD16: Bgly 6B **36**
  HD6: Brigh 1F **161**
  HX2: Hal 1B **128**
  HX2: Midg 1B **126**
  HX3: Hip 6D **130**
  HX3: Sou 6D **150**
  HX6: Sow B 6E **147**
  LS6: Leeds 4D **76**
  LS7: Leeds 2A **78**
  (not continuous)
  LS12: Leeds 3F **95**
  LS12: N Far 3F **115**
  LS13: Leeds 5E **75**
  (Bellmount Pl.)
  LS13: Leeds 3F **95**
  (Ring Rd. Farnley)
  LS15: Leeds, Scho 4G **81**
  LS17: Bard 2F **45**
  LS18: H'fth 2E **75**
  LS23: T Arch 1C **30**
  LS26: Gt P, Swil 1E **145**
  LS26: Rothw 6F **119**
  LS28: Cal 2F **73**
Wood La. Ct. LS6: Leeds 4E **77**
Woodlark Cl. BD6: B'frd 4F **109**
Woodlea LS23: B Spa 3B **30**
Woodlea App. LS6: Leeds 6F **59**
  LS19: Yead 1D **54**
Woodlea Av. LS6: Leeds 6F **59**
Woodlea Chase LS6: Leeds 1F **77**
Woodlea Cl. LS19: Yead 2D **54**

Woodlea Ct. LS6: Leeds 1F **77**
  LS17: Leeds 3F **61**
Woodlea Cft. LS6: Leeds 6F **59**
Woodlea Dr. LS6: Leeds 6F **59**
  LS19: Yead 2D **54**
Woodlea Fold LS6: Leeds 6F **59**
Woodlea Gdns. LS6: Leeds 6F **59**
Woodlea Gth. LS6: Leeds 6F **59**
Woodlea Ga. LS6: Leeds 1F **77**
Woodlea Grn. LS6: Leeds 6F **59**
Woodlea Gro. LS6: Leeds 1F **77**
  LS11: Leeds 2F **117**
  (off Woodlea Mt.)
  LS19: Yead 1D **54**
Woodlea Hall LS6: Leeds 6F **59**
Woodlea Holt LS6: Leeds 6F **59**
Woodlea La. LS6: Leeds 6F **59**
Woodlea Lawn LS6: Leeds 6F **59**
Woodlea Mt. LS11: Leeds 2F **117**
  LS19: Yead 1D **54**
Woodlea Pk. LS6: Leeds 1F **77**
Woodlea Pl. LS6: Leeds 6F **59**
  LS11: Leeds 2G **117**
Woodlea Rd. LS19: Yead 1D **54**
Woodlea Sq. LS6: Leeds 1F **77**
Woodlea St. LS11: Leeds 2F **117**
Woodlea Vw. LS6: Leeds 1F **77**
  LS19: Yead 2D **54**
Woodleigh Av. BD5: B'frd 4E **111**
  LS25: Gar 4C **103**
  (off Providence Pl.)
Woodleigh Hall M. LS19: Raw 6H **55**
Woodleigh Hall Vw.
  LS19: Raw 6A **56**
WOODLESFORD 6E **121**
Woodlesford HX2: Hal 5A **128**
Woodlesford Cres. HX2: Hal 5H **127**
Woodlesford Station (Rail) 6F **121**
Woodliffe Ct. LS7: Leeds 2A **78**
Woodliffe Cres. LS7: Leeds 2A **78**
Woodliffe Dr. LS7: Leeds 2A **78**
Woodman Av. HD2: Hud 6F **163**
  HX5: Ell 6B **160**
Woodman Ct. BD6: B'frd 1G **131**
Woodman St. LS15: Leeds 3C **100**
Woodman Works HX5: Ell 6B **160**
Woodman Yd. LS16: Leeds 3D **76**
  (off Otley Rd.)
Wood Moor Ct. LS17: Leeds 1C **60**
Wood Mt. HX2: Hal 5D **148**
  LS26: Rothw 1G **141**
Wood Nook BD13: Denh 6D **66**
Woodnook Cl. LS16: Leeds 5F **57**
Woodnook Dr. LS16: Leeds 5F **57**
Woodnook Gdns. LS16: Leeds 5F **57**
Wood Nook La. HX6: Sow B 4A **148**
Woodnook Rd. LS16: Leeds 4F **57**
Wood Nook Ter. LS28: Stan 2G **93**
Woodpecker Cl. BD15: All 4D **88**
Woodpecker Rd.
  LS29: Burl W 1E **21**
Wood Pl. BD8: B'frd 1A **6** (3C **90**)
  BD9: B'frd 5C **70**
Wood Rd. BD5: B'frd 1E **111**
  BD9: B'frd 5C **70**
WOOD ROW 4B **144**
Wood Row LS26: Meth 4B **144**
Woodrow Cres. LS26: Meth 4A **144**
Woodrow Dr. BD12: Low M 1E **133**
Woodroyd HX2: Lud M 4F **147**
Woodroyd Av. BD5: B'frd 3F **111**
Woodroyd Cres. HX6: Lud M 4G **147**
Woodroyd Dr. HX3: Hal 5D **128**
Woodroyd Gdns.
  HX2: Lud M 4F **147**
  LS29: I'ly 6H **11**
Woodroyd Ter. BD5: B'frd 3F **111**
  (not continuous)
WOODSIDE
  BD6 .6A **110**
  HX3 . . . . .1B **164** (1G **149**)
Wood Side HX4: Bark 6B **158**

Woodside BD18: Ship 1D **70**
  BD20: Keigh 4G **33**
  HX4: Gree 5H **159**
  LS26: Meth 4A **144**
  WF2: Wren 6C **156**
Woodside Av. BD16: Cot 2B **68**
  BD18: Ship 1G **69**
  LS4: Leeds 1C **96**
  LS7: Leeds 2F **77**
  WF2: Wren 6C **156**
Woodside Cl. LS27: Morl 1A **138**
Woodside Ct. BD13: Cull 3B **66**
  LS16: Leeds 6H **57**
  LS18: H'fth 1G **75**
  (off Broadgate La.)
  LS18: H'fth 1G **75**
  (Tanhouse Hill)
  LS29: I'ly 3C **10**
Woodside Cres. BD16: Cot 2B **68**
  HX3: Hal 1A **164** (6F **129**)
Woodside Dr. BD16: Cot 2B **68**
  LS27: Morl 6A **116**
  WF2: Wren 6C **156**
Woodside Gdns. LS27: Morl 6A **116**
Woodside Gro. HX3: Hal 6G **129**
  HX4: Gree 5G **159**
Woodside Hill Cl. LS18: H'fth 1G **75**
Woodside Lawn LS12: Leeds 4F **95**
Woodside M. LS7: Leeds 2F **77**
Woodside Mt.
  HX3: Hal 1A **164** (1F **149**)
Woodside Pk. Av. LS18: H'fth 1F **75**
Woodside Pk. Dr. LS18: H'fth 1F **75**
Woodside Pl.
  HX3: Hal 1A **164** (6F **129**)
  LS4: Leeds 1C **96**
Woodside Rd.
  BD12: Low M, Wyke 4C **132**
  BD20: Sils 2C **14**
  HX3: Hal 1A **164** (1F **149**)
  LS23: B Spa 4H **29**
Woodside St. WF10: All B 1F **145**
Woodside Ter. HX3: Hal 6G **129**
  HX4: Gree 5H **159**
  LS4: Leeds 1C **96**
Woodside Vw. BD16: Cot 2B **68**
  HX3: Hal 1A **164** (6F **129**)
  HX4: Gree 5G **159**
  (off Workhouse La.)
  LS4: Leeds 1C **96**
  LS10: Leeds 3C **140**
  WF3: Loft 1F **157**
Woodsley Fold BD13: Thorn 5F **87**
Woodsley Grn. LS6: Leeds 1F **97**
Woodsley Rd. BD10: B'frd 3G **71**
  LS2: Leeds 2E **97**
  LS3: Leeds 2E **97**
  LS6: Leeds 2E **97**
Woodsley Ter. LS2: Leeds 1A **4** (2G **97**)
Woods M. LS29: I'ly 5E **11**
Wood Sq. HX3: Hal 5F **129**
Woods Row LS28: Stan 2A **94**
Woodstock Cl. LS16: Leeds 4D **58**
Woodstock Wlk. BD5: B'frd 6E **91**
  (off Park Rd., not continuous)
Wood St. BD8: B'frd 1A **6** (3C **90**)
  BD12: Low M 1D **132**
  BD15: All 2E **89**
  BD16: Bgly 1A **50**
  BD17: Bail 6C **52**
  BD20: Stee 6C **14**
  BD21: Keigh 1A **48**
  BD22: Haw 3C **64**
  HD6: Brigh 1B **162**
  HX5: Ell 5C **160**
  LS18: H'fth 5E **57**
  LS27: Morl 2H **137**
  WF3: E Ard 1B **156**
Woodthorne Cft. LS17: Leeds 3E **61**
Woodthorpe BD13: Denh 3B **86**

Wood Top BD18: Ship 1D **70**
  HD6: Brigh 4G **151**
Woodvale Cl. BD4: B'frd 6C **92**
Woodvale Cres. BD16: Bgly 2C **50**
Woodvale Gro. BD7: B'frd 6G **89**
Woodvale Office Pk.
  HD6: Brigh 5B **152**
Woodvale Rd. HD6: Brigh 6B **152**
Woodvale Ter. LS18: H'fth 2F **75**
Woodvale Way BD7: B'frd 6G **89**
Wood Vw. BD12: O'haw 3G **133**
  BD13: Cull 3C **66**
  BD13: Denh 5C **86**
  BD17: Bail 6A **52**
  HX3: Hal 5E **149**
  LS27: Chur 5D **116**
  LS29: I'ly 4F **11**
Woodview BD8: B'frd 6D **70**
  BD11: Drig 6H **113**
  BD13: Denh 6A **66**
  BD22: Oak 3E **47**
Woodview Av. BD17: Bail 3F **53**
Woodview Cl. LS18: H'fth 5E **57**
Woodview Ct. LS14: Leeds 5F **81**
Wood Vw. Dr. BD2: B'frd 1A **92**
Woodview Gro. LS11: Leeds 3H **117**
Woodview M. LS14: Leeds 4F **81**
Woodview Mt. LS11: Leeds 3H **117**
Woodview Pl. LS11: Leeds 3H **117**
Woodview Rd. BD22: Oak 3F **47**
  LS11: Leeds 3H **117**
Woodview St. LS11: Leeds 3H **117**
Wood Vw. Ter. LS27: Chur 5D **116**
  WF12: Dew 3B **154**
Woodview Ter. BD8: B'frd 6D **70**
  BD21: Keigh *3H 47*
     (off Hainworth La.)
  LS11: Leeds 3H **117**
Woodville Av. LS18: H'fth 6F **57**
Woodville Ct. LS8: Leeds 6F **61**
Woodville Cres. LS18: H'fth 6G **57**
Woodville Gro. BD22: Cros R 1F **65**
  LS10: Leeds 4C **118**
  LS18: H'fth 1F **75**
Woodville Mt. LS10: Leeds 4C **118**
Woodville Pl. BD9: B'frd 5H **69**
  HD2: Hud 5E **163**
  LS18: H'fth 6G **57**
Woodville Rd. BD20: Keigh 5H **33**
Woodville Sq. LS10: Leeds 4C **118**
Woodville St. BD18: Ship 1D **70**
  HX3: Hal 6E **129**
  LS18: H'fth 1G **75**
Woodville Ter. BD5: B'frd 6D **90**
  BD18: Ship 1D **70**
  BD22: Cros R *1F 65*
     (off Gott St.)
  LS18: H'fth 6F **57**
Wood Vine St. LS28: Stan 2G **93**
Woodway BD16: Cot 2B **68**
  LS18: H'fth 2E **75**
Woodway Dr. LS18: H'fth 2E **75**
Woodworth Gro. BD21: Keigh 4H **47**
Woolcomb Ct. BD9: B'frd 1B **90**
Woolcombers Way BD4: B'frd 6B **92**
Wooler Av. LS11: Leeds 3G **117**
Wooler Dr. LS11: Leeds 3G **117**
Wooler Gro. LS11: Leeds 3G **117**
Wooler Pl. LS11: Leeds 3F **117**
Wooler Rd. LS11: Leeds 3F **117**
Wooler St. LS11: Leeds 3F **117**
Wool Exchange, The 4D **6**
Woolford Way WF3: Loft 3H **157**
Wool Ga. BD16: Cot 2D **68**
Wooller Rd. BD12: Low M 2D **132**
Woollin Av. WF3: W Ard 4E **155**
Woollin Cres. WF3: W Ard 3E **155**
Woolpack HX1: Hal 3C **164** (2G **149**)
     (not continuous)
Woolrow La. HD6: B Bri 3C **152**
Woolshops HX1: Hal 4C **164** (2G **149**)
Wootton St. BD5: B'frd 1E **111**

Worcester Av. LS10: Leeds 3D **140**
Worcester Cl. WF3: E Ard 6A **140**
Worcester Dr. LS10: Leeds 3D **140**
Worcester Pl. BD4: B'frd 1G **111**
Worden Gro. BD7: B'frd 1G **109**
Wordsworth Ct. LS26: Oul 4E **143**
Wordsworth Dr. LS26: Oul 4E **143**
Wordsworth Ho. *LS29: I'ly* *4G 11*
     (off Blackthorn Rd.)
Wordsworth Way BD16: Bgly 2C **50**
Workhouse La. HX2: Hal 2G **147**
  HX2: Midg 5B **126**
  HX4: Gree 5H **159**
Workouts Health & Fitness Cen. . . .*1G 47*
     (off Oakworth Rd.)
Workout Warehouse Health & Fitness Cen.
  . . . . .4D **164**
Works Skatepark, The 6B **98**
World's End LS19: Yead 1C **47**
Wormald Lea BD4: B'frd 2C **112**
     (off Kirkwall Dr.)
Wormald Row
  LS2: Leeds 3E **5** (3A **98**)
Worrall St. LS27: Morl 4H **137**
Worsnop Bldgs. BD12: Wyke 3C **132**
Worsnop St. BD12: Low M 1D **132**
Worstead Rd. BD22: Cros R 6F **47**
Worsted Cl. HX1: Hal 1D **148**
Worsted Ho. LS6: Leeds 6H **5**
Worth Av. BD21: Keigh 4C **34**
Worth Bri. Rd. BD21: Keigh 5C **34**
Worthing Head Cl.
  BD12: Wyke 4D **132**
Worthing Head Rd.
  BD12: Wyke 4C **132**
Worthing St. BD12: Wyke 4D **132**
Worthington Ct. BD8: B'frd 2A **6**
Worthington St.
  BD8: B'frd 2A **6** (3C **90**)
Worth Valley Vw. BD22: Oak 5D **46**
WORTH VILLAGE 5C **34**
Worthville Cl. BD21: Keigh 2A **48**
Worth Way BD21: Keigh 1A **48**
WORTLEY 5C **96**
Wortley Hgts. LS12: Leeds 5D **96**
Wortley La. LS11: Leeds 5F **97**
  LS12: Leeds 5F **97**
Wortley Moor La. LS12: Leeds 5B **96**
Wortley Moor La. Trad. Est.
  LS12: Leeds 5B **96**
Wortley Moor Pde.
  LS12: Leeds 4A **96**
Wortley Moor Rd. LS12: Leeds 4A **96**
Wortley Pk. LS12: Leeds 5D **96**
Wortley Rd. LS12: Leeds 4A **96**
Wortley St. BD16: Bgly 4D **50**
Wortley Towers LS12: Leeds 5E **97**
Wrangharm Av. LS6: Leeds 6F **77**
Wrangharm Pl. LS6: Leeds 6F **77**
Wrangharm Ter. LS6: Leeds 6F **77**
Wren Av. BD7: B'frd 6G **89**
Wrenbeck Av. LS21: Otley 1E **23**
Wrenbeck Cl. LS21: Otley 1E **23**
Wrenbeck Dr. LS21: Otley 1E **23**
Wrenbury Av. LS16: Leeds 2F **57**
Wrenbury Cres. LS16: Leeds 2F **57**
Wrenbury Gro. LS16: Leeds 2G **57**
Wren Dr. LS27: Morl 4D **138**
Wren Hill WF17: Bat 6C **136**
Wren St. BD21: Keigh 5A **34**
  BD22: Haw 2D **64**
Wrenthorpe Rd. WF2: Wren 6D **156**
Wrexham Rd. LS29: Burl W 2D **20**
Wright Av. BD22: Oak 4D **46**
Wright St. BD22: Oak 5D **46**
Wrigley HX2: Illing 1C **128**
Wrigley Av. BD4: B'frd 4H **111**
Wrigley Hill HX2: Illing 2C **128**
Wroe Cres. BD12: Wyke 4C **132**
Wroe Pl. BD12: Wyke 4C **132**
Wroe Ter. BD12: Wyke 4C **132**
WROSE 3D **70**

Wrose Av. BD2: B'frd 4G **71**
  BD18: Ship 3D **70**
Wrose Brow Rd. BD18: Ship 1D **70**
Wrosecliffe Gro.
  BD10: B'frd 1F **71**
Wrose Dr. BD18: Ship 3D **70**
Wrose Gro. BD2: B'frd 3F **71**
  BD18: Ship 3D **70**
Wrose Hill Pl. BD2: B'frd 4D **70**
Wrose Mt. BD18: Ship 3E **71**
Wrose Rd. BD2: B'frd 3F **71**
  BD18: Ship 3D **70**
Wrose St. BD22: Bail 3C **52**
  BD18: Ship 3D **70**
Wrose Vw. BD17: Ship 3E **53**
Wycliffe Cl. LS13: Leeds 4H **73**
Wycliffe Dr. LS17: Leeds 5B **60**
Wycliffe Gdns. BD18: Ship 1A **70**
Wycliffe Rd. BD18: Ship 1A **70**
  LS13: Leeds 4H **73**
Wycoller Rd. BD12: Wyke 3C **132**
Wycombe Grn. BD4: B'frd 2C **112**
WYKE 4C **132**
Wykebeck Av. LS9: Leeds 4H **99**
Wykebeck Cres. LS9: Leeds 3H **99**
Wykebeck Gdns. LS9: Leeds 3H **99**
Wykebeck Gro. LS9: Leeds 3H **99**
Wykebeck Mt. LS9: Leeds 4H **99**
Wykebeck Pl. LS9: Leeds 3A **100**
Wykebeck Rd. LS9: Leeds 3H **99**
Wykebeck Sq. LS9: Leeds 3H **99**
Wykebeck St. LS9: Leeds 3H **99**
Wykebeck Ter. LS9: Leeds 3H **99**
Wykebeck Valley Rd.
  LS9: Leeds 1H **99**
Wykebeck Vw. LS9: Leeds 3H **99**
Wyke Bottoms BD12: O'haw 3F **133**
WYKE COMMON 5D **132**
Wyke Cres. BD12: Leeds 5D **132**
Wyke La.
  BD12: O'haw, Wyke 5C **132**
Wykelea Cl. BD12: Wyke 4D **132**
Wyke Old La. HD6: B Bri 2B **152**
Wyncliffe Ct. LS17: Leeds 5A **60**
Wyncliffe Gdns. LS17: Leeds 5B **60**
Wyncroft Gro. LS16: B'hpe 3H **43**
Wyncroft Ri. BD18: Ship 4D **70**
Wyndham Av. BD2: B'frd 6F **71**
Wyndy Ridge BD13: Thorn 4G **87**
Wynford Av. LS16: Leeds 6B **58**
Wynford Gro. LS16: Leeds 6B **58**
Wynford Mt. LS16: Leeds 6A **58**
Wynford Ri. LS16: Leeds 6A **58**
Wynford Ter. LS16: Leeds 6A **58**
Wynford Way BD12: Low M 5E **111**
Wynmore Av. LS16: B'hpe 3G **43**
Wynmore Cres. LS16: B'hpe 3H **43**
Wynmore Dr. LS16: B'hpe 3H **43**
Wynne St.
  BD1: B'frd 2A **6** (3D **90**)
Wynyard Dr. LS27: Morl 3H **137**
Wyre Cl. BD6: B'frd 4G **109**
Wytehill Chase HX3: North 3C **130**
Wyther Av. LS5: Leeds 6H **75**
Wyther Dr. LS5: Leeds 6A **76**
Wyther Grn. LS5: Leeds 6A **76**
Wyther La. LS5: Leeds 6H **75**
Wyther La. Ind. Est.
  LS5: Leeds 6A **76**
Wyther Pk. Av. LS12: Leeds 2H **95**
Wyther Pk. Cl. LS12: Leeds 2H **95**
Wyther Pk. Cres. LS12: Leeds 2H **95**
Wyther Pk. Gro. LS12: Leeds 1H **95**
Wyther Pk. Hill LS12: Leeds 1H **95**
     (not continuous)
Wyther Pk. Mt. LS12: Leeds 2H **95**
     (not continuous)
Wyther Pk. Pl. LS12: Leeds 1H **95**
Wyther Pk. Rd. LS12: Leeds 2G **95**
Wyther Pk. Sq. LS12: Leeds 1G **95**
Wyther Pk. St. LS12: Leeds 2H **95**
Wyther Pk. Ter. LS12: Leeds 2H **95**
Wyther Pk. Vw. LS12: Leeds 1H **95**

Wyvern Cl. BD7: B'frd 6H 89
Wyvern Pl. HX2: Hal 1C 148
Wyvern Ter.
  HX2: Hal 1C 148
Wyvil Cres. LS29: I'ly 5G 11
Wyvil Rd. LS29: I'ly 4G 11

Y

Yarborough Cft. HX3: North 3C 130
Yardley Way
  BD12: Low M 1E 133
Yard No. 4 WF17: Bat 6B 136
Yarn Cl. HX1: Hal 1D 148
Yarn Ct. HD6: B Bri 2C 152
Yarn St. LS10: Leeds 6C 98
Yarra Ct. LS27: Gil 6F 115
Yarwood Gro. BD7: B'frd 2G 109
Yateholm Dr. BD6: B'frd 4E 109
Yate La. BD22: Oxen 1C 84
Yates Flat BD18: Ship 3D 70
YEADON .6G 41
Yeadon Airport Ind. Est.
  LS19: Yead 4A 42
Yeadon Dr. HX3: Sou 5C 150
Yeadon Moor Rd. LS19: Yead 1A 56
              (Bayton La.)
  LS19: Yead 5C 42
              (Scotland La.)
Yeadon Row LS18: H'fth 2E 75
              (off Regent Av.)
Yeadon Stoops LS19: Yead 1H 55
              (off Bayton La.)
Ye Farre Cl. HD6: Brigh 5A 152
Yeoman Ct. BD6: B'frd 3E 109
Yewbank Cl. LS29: I'ly 5C 10
Yewbank Ter. LS29: I'ly 5C 10

Yew Cft. LS29: I'ly 5C 10
              (off Westville Rd.)
Yewdall Rd. LS13: Leeds 4H 73
Yewdall Way BD10: B'frd 3A 72
Yew La. LS25: Gar 5H 103
Yew Pk. HD6: Brigh 4G 151
YEWS GREEN 2A 108
Yew Tree Av. BD8: B'frd 2F 89
Yew Tree Cl. BD18: Ship 3D 70
Yew Tree Cotts.
  HX2: Midg 6C 126
Yew Tree Ct. LS17: Leeds 4G 59
Yew Tree Cres. BD8: B'frd 2G 89
Yew Tree Cft. HX2: Midg 6C 126
Yew Tree Dr. LS26: Wood 1G 143
Yew Tree Gro. BD8: B'frd 2G 89
Yew Tree La. BD15: All 3H 87
  LS15: Leeds 4G 101
Yew Trees HX3: Sou 5C 150
Yew Trees Av. HX3: North 4C 130
York Cres. BD16: Bgly 5C 50
York Ga. LS21: Otley 6C 22
York Gate Garden 2D 58
York Ho. BD10: B'frd 2A 72
  HX5: Ell 4B 160
              (off Westgate)
  HX6: Sow B 5A 148
              (off Beech Rd.)
  LS28: Fars 1H 93
              (off Cotefields Av.)
York Pl. LS1: Leeds 4C 4 (3H 97)
  LS22: Weth 3E 13
York Rd. LS9: Leeds 3C 98
              (not continuous)
  LS14: Leeds 2A 100
  LS15: Leeds, T'ner 3E 81
  LS22: Weth 3F 13
  LS29: Burl W 2F 21

York Rd. Ind. Est.
  LS22: Weth 3F 13
Yorkshire County Cricket Club 5D 76
Yorkshire Dr. BD5: B'frd 4G 111
Yorkshire Indoor Cricket Centre, The
              . . . . .5D 76
Yorkshire Way BD7: B'frd 2B 110
York St. BD8: B'frd 4G 89
  BD13: Que 4H 107
  BD16: Bgly 5C 50
  HD6: Ras 2A 162
              (Capel St.)
  HD6: Ras 2A 162
              (off Thomas St.)
  HX1: Hal 5A 164 (3F 149)
  LS2: Leeds 5G 5 (4B 98)
  LS9: Leeds 5G 5 (4B 98)
York Ter. HX3: Hal 6F 129
  LS29: Burl W 2F 21
York Towers LS9: Leeds 3E 99
York Towers Pde.
  LS9: Leeds 3E 99
              (off York Towers)
Young St. BD8: B'frd 3H 89
Young St. Ind. Est. BD8: B'frd 3H 89

Z

Zara Sports Centre, The 5F 69
Zealand St. BD4: B'frd 1B 112
Zermatt Gro. LS7: Leeds 3A 78
Zermatt Mt. LS7: Leeds 3A 78
Zermatt St.
  LS7: Leeds 3B 78
Zermatt Ter. LS7: Leeds 3B 78
Zetland Pl. LS8: Leeds 6D 78
Zoar St. LS27: Morl 3A 138

MIX
From responsible sources
FSC® C015185
www.fsc.org

The representation on the maps of a road, track or footpath is no evidence of the existence of a right of way.

The Grid on this map is the National Grid taken from Ordnance Survey® mapping with the permission of the Controller of Her Majesty's Stationery Office.

Copyright of Geographers' A-Z Map Company Ltd.

No reproduction by any method whatsoever of any part of this publication is permitted without the prior consent of the copyright owners.

SAFETY CAMERA INFORMATION

PocketGPSWorld.com's CamerAlert is a self-contained speed and red light camera warning system for SatNavs and Android or Apple iOS smartphones/tablets. Visit www.cameralert.co.uk to download.

Safety camera locations are publicised by the Safer Roads Partnership which operates them in order to encourage drivers to comply with speed limits at these sites. It is the driver's absolute responsibility to be aware of and to adhere to speed limits at all times.

By showing this safety camera information it is the intention of Geographers' A-Z Map Company Ltd., to encourage safe driving and greater awareness of speed limits and vehicle speed. Data accurate at time of printing.

HOSPITALS, HOSPICES and selected HEALTHCARE FACILITIES covered by this atlas.

N.B. Where it is not possible to name these facilities on the map, the reference given is for the road in which they are situated.

AIREDALE GENERAL HOSPITAL 5B **14**
  Skipton Road
  Steeton
  KEIGHLEY
  BD20 6TD
  Tel: 01535 652511

BIERLEY CYGNET HOSPITAL 4H **111**
  Bierley Lane
  BRADFORD
  BD4 6AD
  Tel: 01274 686767

BRADFORD ROYAL INFIRMARY 2G **89**
  Duckworth Lane
  BRADFORD
  BD9 6RJ
  Tel: 01274 542200

CALDERDALE ROYAL HOSPITAL .6H **149**
  Huddersfield Road
  Salterhebble
  HALIFAX
  HX3 0PW
  Tel: 01422 357171

CHAPEL ALLERTON HOSPITAL 4C **78**
  Chapeltown Road
  LEEDS
  LS7 4SA
  Tel: 0113 2623404

CORONATION HOSPITAL (ILKLEY) 6E **11**
  Springs Lane
  ILKLEY
  LS29 8TG
  Tel: 01943 609666

ECCLESHILL COMMUNITY HOSPITAL 4B **72**
  Harrogate Road
  BRADFORD
  BD10 0JE
  Tel: 01274 323200

ECCLESHILL NHS TREATMENT CENTRE 4C **72**
  Harrogate Road
  BRADFORD
  BD10 0EP
  Tel: 01274 623 000

ELLAND SPIRE HOSPITAL 4C **160**
  Elland Lane
  ELLAND
  HX5 9EB
  Tel: 01422 324000

LEEDS CHILDREN'S HOSPITAL 2B **4**
  Leeds General Infirmary
  Clarendon Wing
  LEEDS
  LS1 3EX
  Tel: 0113 2432799

LEEDS DENTAL INSTITUTE .2B **4** (2G **97**)
  Clarendon Way
  LEEDS
  LS2 9LU
  Tel: 0113 2440111

LEEDS GENERAL INFIRMARY 2C **4** (2H **97**)
  Great George Street
  LEEDS
  LS1 3EX
  Tel: 0113 243 2799

LEEDS NUFFIELD HEALTH HOSPITAL 3B **4** (3G **97**)
  2 Leighton Street
  LEEDS
  LS1 3EB
  Tel: 01133 507543

LEEDS SPIRE HOSPITAL 2E **79**
  Jackson Avenue
  LEEDS
  LS8 1NT
  Tel: 0113 2693939

LYNFIELD MOUNT HOSPITAL 1F **89**
  Heights Lane
  BRADFORD
  BD9 6DP
  Tel: 01274 494194

MALHAM HOUSE DAY HOSPITAL 2A **4** (2G **97**)
  25 Hyde Terrace
  LEEDS
  LS2 9LN
  Tel: 0113 3055000

MANORLANDS (SUE RYDER) HOSPICE 6C **64**
  Hebden Road
  Oxenhope
  KEIGHLEY
  BD22 9HJ
  Tel: 01535 642308

MARIE CURIE HOSPICE (BRADFORD) 4H **91**
  Maudsley Street
  BRADFORD
  BD3 9LE
  Tel: 01274 337000

MARTIN HOUSE CHILDREN'S HOSPICE 4C **30**
Grove Road
Boston Spa
WETHERBY
LS23 6TX
Tel: 01937 845045

METHLEY PARK SPIRE HOSPITAL 4A **144**
Methley Lane
Methley
LEEDS
LS26 9HG
Tel: 01977 518518

NHS WALK-IN CENTRE (HALIFAX) 2F **149**
within Horne Street Health Centre
Horne St.
HALIFAX
HX1 5UA
Tel: 01422 399858

NHS WALK-IN CENTRE (LEEDS GENERAL INFIRMARY) 2C **4**
Leeds General Infirmary
Great George Street
LEEDS
LS1 3EX
Tel: 0113 243 2799

OVERGATE HOSPICE 5H **159**
30 Hullenedge Road
ELLAND
HX5 0QY
Tel: 01422 379151

ST GEMMA'S HOSPICE 6B **60**
329 Harrogate Road
LEEDS
LS17 6QD
Tel: 0113 2185500

ST JAMES'S UNIVERSITY HOSPITAL 1D **98**
Beckett Street
LEEDS
LS9 7TF
Tel: 0113 2433144

ST LUKE'S HOSPITAL (BRADFORD) 1D **110**
Little Horton Lane
BRADFORD
BD5 0NA
Tel: 01274 734744

ST MARY'S HOSPITAL 3H **95**
Green Hill Road
LEEDS
LS12 3QE
Tel: 0113 2790121

SEACROFT HOSPITAL 2C **100**
York Road
LEEDS
LS14 6UH
Tel: 0113 2648164

SHIPLEY HOSPITAL 2A **70**
98 Kirkgate
SHIPLEY
BD18 3LT
Tel: 01274 773390

WESTBOURNE GREEN COMMUNITY HEALTH CARE CENTRE
. . . . 1B **90**
50 Heaton Road
BRADFORD
BD8 8RA
Tel: 01274 202485

WESTWOOD PARK DIAGNOSTIC TREATMENT CENTRE 4E **109**
Swift Drive
Cooper Lane
BRADFORD
BD6 3NL
Tel: 01274 425990

WHARFEDALE HOSPITAL 1D **22**
Newall Carr Road
OTLEY
LS21 2LY
Tel: 01943 465522

WHEATFIELDS SUE RYDER HOSPICE 4E **77**
Grove Road
Headingley
LEEDS
LS6 2AE
Tel: 0113 2787249

WYKE CYGNET HOSPITAL 1B **152**
Huddersfield Road
Wyke
BRADFORD
BD12 8LR
Tel: 01274 605500

YORKSHIRE CLINIC, THE 2E **69**
Bradford Road
BINGLEY
BD16 1TW
Tel: 01274 550600

YORKSHIRE EYE HOSPITAL 2C **72**
937 Harrogate Road
Apperley Bridge
BRADFORD
BD10 0RD
Tel: 0800 358 0825